The
Encyclopedia
of the South

The Encyclopedia of the South

edited by Robert O'Brien
with
Harold H. Martin

Facts On File Publications
New York, New York • Oxford, England

The Encyclopedia of the South

Library of Congress Cataloging in Publication Data

O'Brien, Robert, 1932–
    The encyclopedia of the South.

    Includes index.
    1. Southern States—Dictionaries and encyclopedias.
I. Title.
F207.7.027   1984   975′.003′21   82-12098
ISBN 0-87196-728-6

Printed in the USA

9 8 7 6 5 4 3 2 1

CONTENTS

ACKNOWLEDGMENTS

Alabama *Journal,* page 222

Birmingham Convention & Visitors Bureau, page 43

Burt Photo Collection, page 226

Collection of Carolina Art Association, Gibbes Art Gallery, Charleston, S.C., pages 72, 391

Courtesy of the Archives: The Coca-Cola Company, page 26

Division of Archives & History, Raleigh, N.C., page 225

Florida Dept. of Commerce—Division of Tourism, pages 65, 365

Florida Dept. of State, Florida Photographic Collection, pages 129, 153, 221, 271, 392

Georgia Dept. of Archives and History, page 27

Governor's Office, State of Alabama, page 438

Harry Ransom Humanities Research Center, The University of Texas at Austin, pages 69, 79, 385, 408, 410

Henry Morrison Flagler Museum, Palm Beach, Fla., page 138

Historic New Orleans, 533 Royal
1974.25.1514, page 24
1974.25.27.262, page 240

Kentucky Dept. of Public Information, pages 148, 219

Library of Congress, pages 2, 9, 51, 55, 115, 119, 201, 376, 452
Photo by Wm. A. Barnhill, page 15

Louisiana Office of Tourism, pages 17, 246, 255 (left)

Memphis Chamber of Commerce, page 180

Metro-Dade Dept. of Tourism, page 270

Missouri Historical Society, pages 88, 279, 360

National Archives, pages 28, 63, 234, 314, 349, 350

New York Public Library Picture Collection, pages 14, 30, 31, 32, 48 (right), 105, 111, 181, 198, 206, 247, 255 (right), 262, 329, 431

Opryland U.S.A., page 170

Photo by Ralph R. Thompson, page 133

St. Louis Regional Commerce & Growth Association, page 361

St. Mary's City Commission, page 362

State Photographic Archives, Strozier Library, F.S.U., page 144

Tennessee State Library and Archives, page 104

Tennessee Tourist Development, page 334

Tennessee Valley Authority Information Center, page 404

Texas Dept. of Highways & Public Transportation, page 193

Tuskegee Institute, page 439
Photo by P. H. Polk, page 68

UPI-Bettmann, page 239

U.S. Dept. of Agriculture, page 48 (left)

The Valentine Museum, Richmond, Va., page 99

Virginia Division of Tourism, page 204

Virginia State Library, pages 16, 287, 290, 461

Virginia State Travel Service, pages 77, 301, 442, 454

West Virginia Governor's Office of Economic & Community Development, page 184
Photo by Gerald S. Ratliff, pages 90, 450

Woolaroc Museum, Bartlesville, Oklahoma, page 355

INTRODUCTION

History

The term encyclopedia (fr. Gk *enkyklios,* circular, and *paideia,* education) traditionally refers to a reference work with entries on various subjects generally arranged alphabetically. *The Encyclopedia of the South* follows this convention and focuses on a "circle of knowledge" framed by geography. This volume comprises Alabama, Arkansas, Florida, Georgia, Kentucky, Louisiana, Maryland, Mississippi, Missouri, North Carolina, South Carolina, Tennessee, Texas, Virginia, and West Virginia.

All but West Virginia constitute the region known as "Dixie," a characterization acquired from a song of the same name written in 1859 by Daniel D. Emmett. The song, in turn, is a back-reference to the demarcation laid (1763–67) by English surveyors Charles Mason and Jeremiah Dixon indicating the boundary between Pennsylvania and Maryland. The Mason-Dixon Line was extended in 1779 to mark the boundary between Pennsylvania and Virginia (present-day West Virginia). The line was employed before the Civil War to separate free states from slave states, and remains in current use as the popular divider between North and South.

All states south of the Mason-Dixon Line, with the exceptions of the border slave states of Maryland and Kentucky which were held for the Union, belonged to the pro-slavery Confederate States.

Highlights

The iconography of this region, supplemented by modern and period illustrations, is outlined in this volume by several broad categories:

Cultural
Biographies
Academic institutions
Social, political and religious movements
Historical events
Folk culture terms and expressions
Historical documents

Geographic
Urban, suburban and rural profiles
Topography
Place names
Climate
State maps

Statistical
Education and transportation data
Labor force and employment rates
Land use, ownership, and land areas
Corporate tax rates
Population density
Individual tax rates
Per-capita income

Political
Counties and county seats
Governors and state executive branch staffs
State fact sheets

Thematic
Tourism, railroads, tobacco, architecture, ragtime, etc.

These categories and levels of ordering are intended to be representative in scope rather than comprehensive—designed for the reader who wants a ready overview of a multitude of regional subjects in a one-volume encyclopedia. Additionally, *The Encyclopedia of the South* is a useful supplement to atlases, gazetteers, almanacs and condensed biorgraphies— reference works which, because of space limitations, cannot devote broad attention to a particular subject within a specialized field, such as the South.

From A (Hank Aaron, 1934–) to Z (John Joachim Zubly, 1724–81), biographies also play an important role in understanding an area. Beginning with Virginia Dare, the first Anglo-Saxon child born in America (1578), and extending through the lives of early colonists, explorers, settlers and modern figures, we learn that the South was as much shaped by its native daughters and sons as their surroundings shaped them. While William

Faulkner, Marianne Moore and Ty Cobb are prominent Southern figures, in this volume some of Southern history's lesser-known feminist lights emerge as well: Capt. Sally Tompkins, who was the only woman commissioned as officer in the Confederate army; Anna Carroll, military strategist responsible for planning Gen. Ulysses S. Grant's Tennessee Campaign; and the unique life of Amy Marcy Cheney Beach (popularly known as Mrs. H. H. A. Beach), whose *Eilende Wolken* was the first composition written by a woman to be performed by the New York Symphony (1892).

How This Book Is Organized

Article headings are in **boldface** type and they are alphabetized to the comma. Thus **ARKANSAS, University of** precedes **ARKANSAS INDIANS**. Bioghraphical articles are alphabetized by the subject's inverted name, **WASHINGTON, Booker T.** An important feature within many articles is the use of SMALL CAPITAL LETTERS to indicate cross-referencing and which will direct the reader to a related article.

Indian place names often display a variety of spellings and consistent rules of romanization have been used to accord with standard philological methodology.

Lastly, as an additional aid, an extensive Bibliography (page 521) has been appended for the reader who is interested in pursuing regional subjects more deeply.

A

AARON, Henry Louis "Hank" (Mobile, Ala., Feb. 5, 1934 —). Baseball player. A slugger with the Braves, who came with them to Atlanta in 1966, he passed Babe Ruth as No. 1 on the all-time home run list to earn a lifetime record of 755 home runs. The National League's Most Valuable Player in 1957 and an all-star six times, he became director of player personnel for the Atlanta Braves in 1977. Aaron was inducted into the Baseball Hall of Fame in 1982.

ABERDEEN PROVING GROUNDS, Md. Oldest U.S. Army testing ground, established in 1917, near Aberdeen, Md., on the Chesapeake Bay. Ballistic research and development and testing of bombs, guns, and special vehicles are conducted at this facility. Part of the complex, which covers 79,369 acres, is the Army Ordnance School and Army Test and Evaluation Committee.

ABILENE, Tex. City (pop. 98,315), seat of Taylor Co., in northwest central Texas. It was settled in 1881 as a railhead for the Texas and Pacific Railway to accommodate overland cattle drives. Abilene's economy is now based on agriculture, livestock, and industry, with some manufacturing related to agriculture, including light machinery. It is the home of Abilene Christian University, Hardin-Simmons College, McMurry College, and the West Texas Medical Center. The annual West Texas Fair and various rodeos and stock shows are held in Abilene. Dyess Air Force Base is located six miles to the southwest.

ABOLITION MOVEMENT. Organized attempt to outlaw institutionalized slavery that relied on means ranging from philosophical debate to outright and illegal violence. The movement's greatest influence was in the United States, England, and the West Indies.

Institutionalized slavery had declined in Europe during the Middle Ages, when serfs began taking the place of slaves as feudalism spread. With the colonization of the New World, however, came a sudden demand for labor that led to the capture of some nine million West Africans by 1800 and exportation of them as slaves to British colonies in America and the West Indies. Quaker sects in both England and New England were the first to protest this slave trade in 1671. Only after the French Revolution, however, did the worldwide political climate become receptive to the idea of abolition. England's Abolition Society, founded in 1787,

1

was enabled by this general change in attitudes to end the British slave trade in 1807.

Slavery in America was a thornier issue than in England because it had strong economic foundations. George Washington and Thomas Jefferson condemned slavery, but they both owned slaves, and the 13 original colonies were only held together at the Constitutional Convention of 1787 when James Madison succeeded in drafting a document that did not use the word "slave." Eli Whitney's cotton gin, invented in 1793, made the South economically reliant on cotton crops and therefore on slave labor.

In the early 1800s Southern insistence on the right to own slaves brought increasingly hostile Northern responses. In 1831 William Lloyd Garrison began publication of the *Liberator*, which helped draw many famous names to the cause, including the poet John Greenleaf Whittier, clergyman Theodore Weld, and free black Americans such as Frederick DOUGLASS. In 1833 Garrison founded the American Anti-Slavery Society in Philadelphia.

Although a strongly moral movement, abolitionism was legally and politically problematic, and Abraham Lincoln in fact opposed abolitionist measures during his term in Congress from 1847 to 1849. The movement exacerbated antagonism between North and South on peripheral issues such as the admission of new states and it encouraged acts of violence such as John BROWN's famous raid on the U.S. Armory at HARPERS FERRY in 1859.

In 1854 the abolition movement was a factor in the founding of the Republican Party, which opposed slavery, and in 1860 Republican Abraham Lincoln was elected president. Lincoln's Emancipation Proclamation of 1863 and the Thirteenth Amendment of 1865 abolished slavery, but they also revealed the woefully inadequate preparation of the country for such a change. The FREEDMEN'S BUREAU, in opera-

A slave sale in the Old South

tion from 1865 to 1872, offered erratic assistance to former slaves and none to former owners. Although blacks were given the right to vote, the laws were largely ignored or avoided for many years. The lack of enforcement of these laws resulted in the eruption of civil rights battles in the South in the 1940s and 1950s.

ACADIANS. Original French settlers of Nova Scotia in the early 1600s. They were driven from their lands by the English in the 1760s and 1770s, and approximately 4,000 settled in the bayou country of Louisiana parishes along the Gulf of Mexico. Nicknamed "Cajuns," they were an agricultural people who spoke a "patois," that combined archaic French with inflections and words taken from the English, Negro, Spanish, and German. The Cajuns still maintain a separate folk culture and have deep-rooted feelings for family. It is not unusual to find families with over 20 children. They are often confused with the CREOLES, another large French-speaking group, who are descendants of the original French settlers.

ACOLAPISSA INDIANS ("those who listen and see"). Tribe of Muskogean linguistic stock located slightly north of the mouth of the Pearl River in Louisiana. They were generally noted for their good relationship with settlers, but in 1714 they massacred a number of NATCHITOCHES INDIANS whom they had previously welcomed as their neighbors when the Natchitoches suffered a crop failure. The Acolapissa later merged with the HOUMA INDIANS.

ACUERA INDIANS. Tribe of Muskogean linguistic stock that lived inland in Florida around the headwaters of the Ocklawaha River and was allied with the UTINA INDIANS. There are reports of great hostilities when they were first encountered by NARVAEZ and DE SOTO in the early 1500s.

ADAI INDIANS. Tribe located in what is now Natchitoches Parish, Louisiana. Originally thought to have an independent status because their dialect was so diverse, they are now placed in the Caddoan linguistic group.

ADAIR, James (County Antrim, Ireland, c. 1709 — N.C., c. 1783). Indian trader and author. Coming to America in 1735, he developed trade with the Indians of South Carolina and was known among them as a diplomat and peace envoy. Adair wrote a history of the Indians in which he theorized that the natives were actually descendants of an ancient tribe of Jews.

ADAIR, John (Chester Co., S.C., Jan. 9, 1757 — Harrodsburg, Ky., May 19, 1840). Pioneer and governor. He became well known as a political leader and Indian fighter after moving to Kentucky in 1786. Adair served as U.S. senator from Kentucky in 1805-06. He led a group of Kentucky volunteers during the War of 1812 at the Battle of NEW ORLEANS. While governor of Kentucky (1820-24) he improved the state government to stave off economic depression. Adair served in the U.S. House of Representatives from 1831 to 1833.

ADLER, Cyrus (Van Buren, Ark., Sept. 13, 1863 — Philadelphia, Pa., Apr. 7, 1940). Scholar and educator. He graduated from the University of Pennsylvania (1883) and Johns Hopkins University (1887), where he was an instructor and associate professor of Semitic languages (1884-93). Adler worked for the Smithsonian Institute in Washington, D.C. (1892-1908) as librarian and assistant secretary. He also served as curator of historic archaeology and religions at the U.S. National Museum in Washington (1889-1908). In 1908 Adler transferred to Philadelphia where he assumed the presidency of Dropsie College of Hebrew and Cognate Learning. He then moved to New York City to become acting president (1916) and president (1924) of the Jewish Theological Seminary of America. The founder of the American Jewish Historical Society in 1892, he edited the *Jewish Encyclopedia* and the *American-Jewish Year Book.*

AGNEW, Spiro Theodore (Baltimore, Md., Nov. 9, 1918 —). Vice president of the United States. After serving in the army during World War II, Agnew studied law at the University of Baltimore. He became interested in politics, and after holding several municipal offices he was elected governor of Maryland in 1967. In 1968 he was elected vice-president of the U.S. as President Richard Nixon's running mate. While vice-president, Agnew was known for his singular speaking style and his often fiery attacks upon the press. During his second term as vice-president, Agnew was charged with contract payoffs and income tax violations. On October 10, 1973, Spiro Agnew resigned from office and pleaded "nolo contendere" (no contest) to his charges. He received three years' probation and a $10,000 fine.

AGRICULTURAL WHEEL PARTY. A political party of the late 19th century that rose out of the growing popularity of regional farm organizations. The National Farmers Alliance and Agricultural Wheel merged their one million members into the Southern Alliance. It supported such Populist candidates as William Jennings Bryan.

AIKEN, Conrad (Savannah, Ga., Aug. 5, 1889 — Savannah, Ga., Aug. 17, 1973). Poet and critic. Aiken was traumatized as a youth by the scene of his father killing his mother and then committing suicide, leaving the boy to be brought up by an aunt in Massachusetts. She sent him to Harvard, where he became close friends with T.S. ELIOT before graduation in 1912. In 1914 he began to write poetry under the influence of Eliot and of the French symbolists. His verse was known for its musical qualities, and *Selected Poems* (1929) was awarded the Pulitzer Prize. Also a critic and novelist, Aiken held the poetry chair at the Library of Congress from 1950-52. In 1969 he was awarded the National Medal for literature.

AIKEN, S.C. City (pop. 14,978), seat of Aiken Co., in western South Carolina. A winter resort, especially popular with horse enthusiasts for its thoroughbred breeding and polo matches, it is also a retirement community. Settled during the Revolutionary War, Aiken provided equipment to Confederate troops during the Civil War and was the scene of violent racial riots after that war. It was here that the Democrats launched their 1876 campaign to reestablish white political supremacy. Aiken produces fertilizer, fiberglass, and ice cream. It is the home of the Thoroughbred Hall of Fame, Hopeland Gardens, and Aiken State Park.

AIS INDIANS. Tribe that lived along Indian River on the southeastern coast of Florida, thought to have been of Muskogean linguistic stock. Governor Mendez de Canco, who traveled the entire east coast of Florida in 1597, reported great numbers of them but they disappear from historical records in the early 1700s.

AKOKISA INDIANS. Name given by the Spaniards to ATAKAPA INDIANS living in southeastern Texas.

ALABAMA. State in the center of the lower tier of southern states extending from the Mis-

Alabama

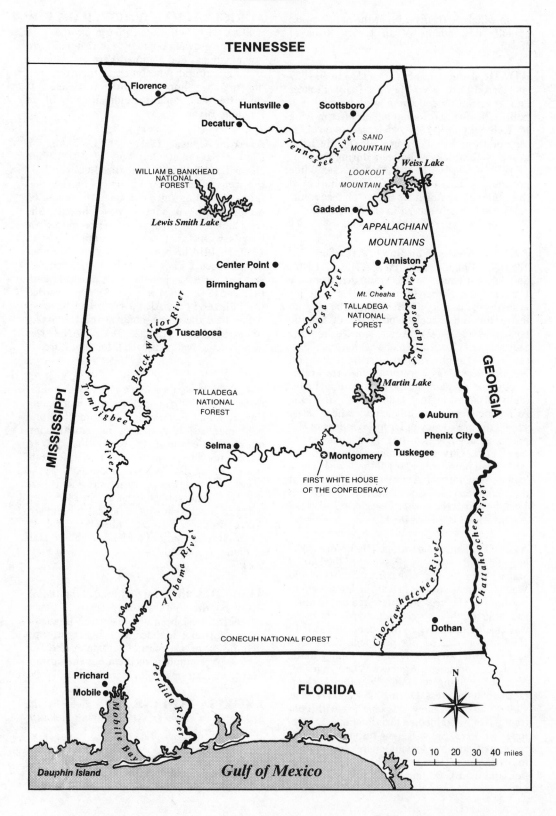

TENNESSEE

Florence

Huntsville ● Scottsboro ●

Decatur ●

Tennessee River

SAND MOUNTAIN

Weiss Lake

LOOKOUT MOUNTAIN

WILLIAM B. BANKHEAD NATIONAL FOREST

Gadsden ●

APPALACHIAN MOUNTAINS

Lewis Smith Lake

Center Point ● Anniston ●

Birmingham ● + *Mt. Cheaha*

TALLADEGA NATIONAL FOREST

Coosa River

Tallapoosa River

Black Warrior River

Tuscaloosa ●

Tombigbee River

TALLADEGA NATIONAL FOREST

Martin Lake

Auburn ●

Phenix City ●

Selma ● ⊕ Montgomery

Tuskegee ●

FIRST WHITE HOUSE OF THE CONFEDERACY

GEORGIA

MISSISSIPPI

Alabama River

Choctawhatchee River

Chattahoochee River

CONECUH NATIONAL FOREST

Dothan ●

Prichard ●

Mobile ●

Perdido River

Mobile Bay

FLORIDA

N

Dauphin Island

Gulf of Mexico

0 10 20 30 40 miles

STATE OF ALABAMA

Name: For the Alabama tribe that derived its name from the Choctaw *alba* ("plant") and *amo* ("reapers"): "plant reapers." The river was named for the tribe; the territory and state for the river.

Nickname: Cotton State, Heart of Dixie, Cotton Plantation State, Lizard State, Yellowhammer State.

Motto: We Dare Defend Our Rights.

Capital: Montgomery.

Counties: 67. **Places over 10,000 population (1980)**: 44.

Symbols & Emblems: *Flower*: Camelia. *Bird*: Yellowhammer. *Fish*: Tarpon. *Tree*: Southern (Longleaf) Pine. *Song*: "Alabama."

Population (1980): 3,893,888. **Rank**: 25th.

Population Density (1980): 76.7 people per sq. mi. **Rank**: 26th.

Racial Make-up (1980): *White*: 2,869,688 (73.8%). *Black*: 995,623 (25.6%). *American Indian*: 7,561 (0.2%). *Asian & Pacific Islander*: 9,695 (0.3%). *Other*: 7,494 (0.2%). *Spanish Origin*: 33,100 (0.9%).

Largest City (pop. 1980): Birmingham (284,413). *Others*: Mobile (200,452), Montgomery (178,157), Huntsville (142,513), Tuscaloosa (75,143), Dothan (48,750), Gadsden (47,565), Decatur (42,002).

Area: 50,767 sq. mi. **Rank**: 29th.

Highest Point: Cheaha Mountain (2,407 ft.), Cleburne Co.

Lowest Point: sea level, Gulf of Mexico.

State Government:
ELECTED OFFICIALS (4-year terms expiring Jan. 1987, etc.): *Governor* ($63,839); *Lt. Governor* ($35,985); *Sec. of State* ($32,940); *Attorney General* ($58,000); *Treasurer* ($45,000).

GENERAL ASSEMBLY (Salary: $4,800 plus $65 per diem living expense allowance.): *Senate* (55 members), *House of Representatives* (105 members).

CONGRESSIONAL REPRESENTATIVES: *Senate* (terms expire 1985, 1987, etc.). *House of Representatives* (7 members).

Admitted to the Union: Dec. 14, 1819 (22nd state).

Alabama

sissippi River to the Atlantic Ocean. To the west Alabama has a land border with the state of Mississippi that represents its greatest north-south extent of 340 miles. To the east it has a slightly shorter border with Georgia that is formed by a land boundary in the upper half and the CHATTAHOOCHEE RIVER in the lower half. The difference in length is caused by the western panhandle of Florida, which forms the southern border of Alabama except for a 53-mile coastline on the Gulf of Mexico in the southwest corner of the state. To the north Alabama has a 190-mile land border with Tennessee.

Alabama was originally called "the heart of Dixie" because of its central location in the Confederate States, but this nickname is also appropriate because of its central role in the history of the south. The BLACK BELT of rich farmlands in the center of the state was once typical of the old agrarian South, when the cash crop of cotton and the plantation society that it supported formed the basis of the character of the South. Alabama was also a key member of the Confederacy, which had its first capital at MONTGOMERY. In the RECONSTRUCTION era the struggle between "radical" Republicans and Democrats in Alabama was emblematic of the worst fortunes of the post-Civil War South. In modern times Alabama remained one of the last strongholds of resistance to social change in the South, and its insistence on states' rights over federal government was indicated by its display of the Confederate flag above the American flag outside the state capitol well into the 20th century. For this reason the state became a key battleground in the struggle for civil rights in the 1960s, when Martin Luther KING, Jr. and his supporters drew national attention to the state with their march from SELMA to Montgomery in 1965.

Changes in voting rights laws and a shift from an agricultural to an industrial economy have since significantly altered the character of Alabama. Political reform, however slow, has improved relations between the racial populations in the state and ended a traditional flight of young black citizens to northern states. Although Alabama dropped from 21st to 22nd in U.S. population rank in the 1970s, its growth rate in that decade was in fact slightly above the national average, and the local population recorded a significant gain from net migration movements in the same years. The key factor in this shift of population patterns has been increased industrialization, which is based in population centers such as BIRMINGHAM in the

north and MOBILE on the Gulf Coast. A corollary shift in the past decades has been one toward increased urbanization: urban residents outnumbered rural ones in Alabama for the first time in 1960, and in 1980 urban residents outnumbered rural ones by a proportion of three to two. These changes have made Alabama a contributing member, if not a leader, in the creation of a "new South" based on modern industrialization and Sun Belt living conditions attractive to residents of the Northeast and Great Lakes states.

Topographically, Alabama is the single state link between the APPALACHIAN and Gulf Coast regions of the South. The Appalachians run southwest into the state to a point near Birmingham that is the southernmost extent of the range. This highland region of northeast Alabama includes SAND MOUNTAIN and the Cumberland Plateau; the high point in the state is CHEAHA MOUNTAIN (elev. 2,407 feet) located between Birmingham and the Georgia border. Northwest and central Alabama lies within the province of the Interior Low Plateau that covers much of the eastern portion of the Mississippi basin. It is here that the Black Belt of dark, loamy soils that supported Alabama's cotton crop are found. In the extreme south, surrounding MOBILE BAY on the Gulf Coast, Alabama lands lie within the Gulf coastal plain, a low-lying and swampy region that broadens as it extends west into the state of Mississippi. The Appalachian region of the state isolates the TENNESSEE RIVER, which runs a course from east to west across northern Alabama. The other principal rivers of the state, the TOMBIGBEE, the ALABAMA, and the CHATTAHOOCHEE, run south to the Gulf of Mexico. The northern location of its highlands gives most of the state a climate influenced by the Gulf; one of ample precipitation, long and hot summers, and short, mild winters.

Before its European exploration, Alabama was the home of Indian tribes that left relics at Russell Cave, in the northeastern corner of the state, that may date as far back as 6,000-10,000 B.C. Although little is known about these people, the European discovery of southern Alabama was well documented by the Spanish, who sent expeditions to Alabama led by Alonso de Pineda (1519) and Panfilo de NARVAEZ (1528). Inland exploration of Alabama was first accomplished by Hernando DE SOTO, who met and defeated the CHOCTAW Indian chief TUSCALOOSA in 1540. Although Spanish sailors such as Tristan De Luna continued to explore Alabama, particularly around Mobile Bay, storms and Indian attacks encouraged settlement activities in more favorable places, such as the Florida coast.

Consequently, Alabama waited more than another century for its first permanent settlement, which was made on DAUPHIN ISLAND at the mouth of Mobile Bay by the French in 1701. The French settlement of the region was effected from Louisiana, and by 1736 they had extended their settlements 120 miles upstream on the Tombigbee River to a point near today's city of DEMOPOLIS. Their local settlements were so extensive that for a time Mobile served as the French capital of the LOUISIANA TERRITORY.

As in the neighboring states, however, the English were a third party to the settlement of Alabama. The English claim to the region dated from the 1663 grant of Carolina to the "Eight Lords Proprietors" of that coastal colony, and in 1732 parts of Alabama were also included in the patent for Georgia issued to James Oglethorpe. The English came into full control in 1763, when the Treaty of Paris ceded them French claims east of the Mississippi River. At the end of the American Revolution in 1783, most of Alabama came into U.S. possession, although the southern part of the state remained within the West Florida colony ceded instead to Spain. The division between these two territories was settled by the Treaty of San Lorenzo in 1795. From 1780 the Mobile area was in Spanish hands until the War of 1812, when it was captured for the U.S. by Gen. James WILKINSON.

The earliest years of American Alabama were scarred by Indian wars. In 1813 a federation of Indian tribes led by TECUMSEH, who had been driven out of the more northern states, raided Fort Mims and massacred the settlers there. This brought the U.S. army under Andrew JACKSON into the region, and his defeat of the CREEK Nation at HORSESHOE BEND on the TALLAPOOSA RIVER near Montgomery in 1814 cleared the way for settlement by American farmers. In 1817 what had been the Mississippi Territory was divided into the state of Mississippi and the Alabama Territory. On December 14, 1819, Alabama was admitted to the Union as the 22nd state.

By that time the COTTON crop had already emerged as the economic foundation of Alabama. Principally located in the central Black Belt region, this one-crop economy spawned an elegant plantation society of architectural and cultural distinction, but it also insured the inevitability of secession from the Union in the pre-Civil War battle over state sovereignty. The election of Abraham Lincoln in 1860 eliminated the possibility of compromise on the issue for Alabama, which passed an ordinance of secession on January 7, 1861, and hosted the convention of southern states at Montgomery that formed the CONFEDERATE STATES OF AMERICA on February 4, 1861. Montgomery remained the capital of the Confederacy until later in that year, when it moved to RICHMOND, Va. The most important engagement in the state was the naval BATTLE OF MOBILE BAY on August 5, 1864, when Union Admiral David FARRAGUT managed to establish a successful blockade of Alabama's most important port. This led to the occupation of the state by the Union army in the spring of 1865 and eventual surrender with the rest of the Confederacy.

Alabama was not a passive participant in RECONSTRUCTION. The state was given a provisional government in May of 1865 by President Andrew JOHNSON, but the legislature's refusal to ratify the 14th Amendment on citizenship rights brought about the imposition of military rule in 1867. This was ended by approval of the 14th Amendment in 1868, but resistance to voting rights, in particular, remained a cause of domestic hostility and outright violence. The election of Democrat George S. HOUSTON as governor in 1874 brought a formal close to Reconstruction, but refusal to recognize the voting rights of black citizens continued until the poll tax was abolished by the 24th Amendment in 1964 and the Voting Rights Act of 1965 enforced local acceptance of universal suffrage. It was in this same modern era that black civil rights groups organized the "Freedom Riders" campaign to integrate public transportation in Montgomery in 1956 and King led his nonviolent marchers from Selma to Montgomery in 1965. Social reforms in the years since then culminated in the 1982 election of Governor George WALLACE for an unprecedented third time; once an ardent segregationist, Wallace was elected in 1982 with a sizable proportion of black votes.

The 20th century has seen the emergence of an urban, as distinct from rural, Alabama. The roots of this change extend back to 1880, when the first blast furnace opened in Birmingham. Since then increasing industrialization, notably since World War II, has caused a population movement toward the employment possibilities in the cities. Birmingham, called the "Pittsburgh of the South" for its iron and steel industries, remains the largest urban center in the state, with a metropolitan area population of almost 850,000. Mobile, the state's great port and center of its petroleum industry, is the second largest, with a metropolitan area population of more than 440,000 and a growth rate in the 1970s of 18%. The other large urban centers in the state are the northern city of HUNTSVILLE, home of The GEORGE C. MARSHALL SPACE FLIGHT CENTER, and the central city of Montgomery, a diversified manufacturing center and the state capital.

The statewide population of Alabama is 26% black and less than 1% Hispanic. Almost 70% of the population are life-long residents, a proportion that ranks among the highest in the South. Alabama ranked 17th among the U.S. states in population in 1940 and only 22nd in 1980, but this has been caused by sudden growth in other states rather than lack of local population growth.

Alabama's manufactures now generate some $9.7 billion per year, or more than five times the amount of any other single sector of the economy. Steel in Birmingham and oil refining in Mobile are the most important industrial activities, but chemicals, paper and pulp products, and food processing are key manufactures distributed evenly across the state. Mining and farming are the other principal businesses of the state, generating approximately the same income per year. Alabama's mineral yield is taken from the Appalachian region, where coal and iron are important, and from the Gulf Coast, where offshore rigs drill oil and natural gas. The state farmlands are principally located in central Alabama, with poultry and eggs generating the greatest portion of the state farm income, and livestock including dairy cows occupying the greatest number of state farms. TOURISM, to natural preserves and Civil War monuments alike, is also an important industry in Alabama. Timber from the Appalachian region and commercial fishing out of Mobile on the Gulf Coast are industries with a long history in the state that continue to make a limited but significant contribution to the Alabama economy.

ALABAMA. Best-known Confederate cruiser of the Civil War. Built in England in 1862 the vessel was credited with crippling or sinking 66 Union vessels before the Union warship *Kearsarge* sank it in the English Channel off Cherbourg (June 19, 1864).

ALABAMA, University of. State-supported coed institution, part of the University of Alabama system. (Other campuses are in BIRMINGHAM and HUNTSVILLE). Founded in 1831, this historic school is located in University, Ala., near Tuscaloosa and 50 miles from Birmingham. The University of Alabama is the state's first institution of higher learning. It is most famous for its collegiate sports program, particularly football in which it is a perennial national contender. Until recently Alabama football was under the leadership of the legendary coach, Paul "Bear" Bryant. This school has the nation's largest Army ROTC program, and an exceptionally advanced Computer Center. The Amelia G. Gorgas Library has an extensive collection of microfilms, maps, and manuscripts and is a regional depository for U.S. government publications. The 720-acre campus has 120 other buildings.

Academically, the University offers over 300 majors and degrees. Major university divisions are the Colleges of Arts and Sciences, Commerce and Business Administration, Community Health Sciences, Education, Engineering, and Nursing; and the Schools of Communication, Home Economics, Law, Social Work; New College; Graduate School and Graduate School of Library Service. Some 93% of the students are from the South, 80% from Alabama. The university does seek a national student body. Full-time graduate or professional study is pursued by 40% of the university's students immediately after graduation.

Library: 1,200,000 volumes, 12,511 journal subscriptions, 12,000 records/tapes. Faculty: 994. Enrollment: 17,918 total graduate and undergraduate; 6,794 men, 6,497 women (full-time). Degrees: Certificate or Diploma, Bachelor's, Master's, Doctorate.

ALABAMA INDIANS ("to camp" or "weed gatherers"). Tribe of Muskogean linguistic stock, that was located on the upper portion of the ALABAMA RIVER. Generally a peaceful tribe, they established a friendship with the French settlers. A part of the tribe moved westward in the 1760s, settling in Mississippi, with some going as far as Texas. Those who remained joined in the CREEK War and lost their lands as a result of the Treaty of Fort Jackson in 1814. They gave their name not only to the Alabama River but to the state itself.

ALABAMA RIVER, Ala. A navigable river that rises in central Alabama and stretches 315 miles south to the Gulf of Mexico at MOBILE. Formed by the confluence of the COOSA and the TALLAPOOSA, it is one of the state's five major rivers and is a source of hydroelectric power.

Painting of the Alamo by Theodore Gentilz

ALAMO, The. Spanish mission in SAN AN-TONIO, Tex., most famous as the site of a massacre of Texan defenders during a battle in the War of Texas Independence. Named for a Spanish word meaning "cottonwood," it was built as a mission in 1744 and converted into a fort by the Spanish colonizers of Mexico in 1793.

The Alamo was captured by rebels for the cause of Texan independence from Mexico in December of 1835. Mexican troops under Gen. Antonio Lopez De SANTA ANNA arrived in February 1836 and demanded surrender of the fort; the rebels fired a cannon to signal their defiance, and Santa Anna raised a red flag to indicate that no quarter would be given.

Santa Anna's siege of the Alamo began on February 24, 1836 when his 6,000 Mexican troops surrounded 184 defenders. Col. William Barret TRAVIS commanded the Texans during the illness of commander James BOWIE. The defenders included frontiersman Davy CROCKETT and James Butler BONHAM of South Carolina. They held the fort against overwhelming odds until March 6, 1836, when the Mexicans mounted the walls in fierce hand-to-hand combat.

Virtually all the Texan defenders of the Alamo were killed, although some accounts differ about the number of non-combatants and defenders of Mexican origin spared by Santa Anna. Davy Crockett is said by some to have surrendered and then been executed, and Jim Bowie is said to have been shot in his sickbed. Because of this massacre, "Remember the Alamo" became the rallying cry for the subsequent Battle of SAN JACINTO, at which Texas won its independence.

ALAPAHA RIVER. River originating in the south central part of Georgia, flowing south-southeast into northern Florida's Hamilton Co.

for 190 miles. There it merges with the SU-WANEE RIVER ten miles south of Jasper.

ALBANY, Ga. City (pop. 73,934), seat of Dougherty Co., located in southwestern Georgia east of Atlanta. Founded in 1836 by Nelson Tift, who laid the streets out checkerboard fashion, it grew as a water transportation center at the navigable head of the Flint River, later as a focus for wagon trade with neighboring plantations, and then after 1857 as a regional rail hub of Southwestern Rail. Present-day businesses in Albany include textile, farm equipment, and pharmaceutical manufacturing, and pecan and peanut farming.

ALBEMARLE, N.C. Town (pop. 15,110), seat of Stanly Co., southern North Carolina. An industrial community, incorporated in 1857, which serves as the marketing center for the region. Manufacturing includes carpets, hosiery, yarn, flour, and lumber. Corn, cotton, and wheat are raised, and there are numerous dairy farms.

ALBEMARLE POINT, S.C. Charleston Co. Site of historical importance on the west bank of the ASHLEY RIVER. It was there in March 1670 that an English colony of 148 people established the state's first settlement, then called Charles Town.

ALBEMARLE SOUND, N.C. Arm of the Atlantic Ocean situated in northeastern North Carolina. Fed by the ROANOKE and CHOWAN Rivers, the sound stretches inland for about 60 miles.

ALCORN, James L. (Golconda, Ill., Nov. 4, 1816 — Coahoma Co., Miss., Dec. 20, 1894). Politician. After teaching in Arkansas, he was appointed deputy sheriff of Livingston County, Ky. Alcorn then was admitted to the bar and set up practice in Mississippi. A supporter of Henry Clay, he was elected to the state senate (1848-56). In 1865 he won a seat to the U.S. Senate but was not allowed to take it because the federal government refused to recognize the government of Mississippi until it signed the 13th Amendment. In 1869 he became governor, resigning two years later to enter the U.S. Senate (1871-77). Alcorn advocated racial separatism.

ALEXANDRIA, La. City (pop. 51,565), seat of Rapides Parish, on the RED RIVER, in central

Louisiana. A commercial and industrial center of rich farmland and forest regions, it produces lumber, cotton, and sugar cane for processing plants. Industries include oil refineries and manufacturing plants for brick, road machinery, turpentine, tar, valves and pipe fittings, and concrete products. It is called "Convention City" because of the facilities it provides in its city hall and coliseum. A U.S. Air Force base is located six miles northwest of the city. Alexandria was laid out in 1810 on the site of a French fort built in 1720 to protect portage around rapids which at that time obstructed navigation on the river. It was incorporated as a city in 1832 with a commission council government. During the CIVIL WAR Union forces captured and burned the city. It was rebuilt after the war and the rapids eliminated.

ALEXANDRIA, Va. City (pop. 103,217), located south of Washington, D.C., in northern Virginia. Alexandria has no county affiliation, a rare situation made possible by an act of Congress in 1852. The city was once an important river port, but is now primarily residential with some industries which produce cinder blocks, fertilizers, machinery, chemicals, lumber products, shirts, refrigerator cars, and furniture. Rich in history, Alexandria was first settled in 1695, and was originally known as Belhaven before being named after John ALEXANDER, who held the original land grant to the area. In 1789 Congress included Alexandria as a part of the District of Columbia. It wasn't until 1847 that the city once again became part of Virginia. During the Civil War it was the capital of the "restored government of Virginia." There are many historic buildings in Alexandria, including the Carlyle House, Gadsby's Tavern, and the home of Robert E. Lee's father, Henry "Light-Horse Harry" LEE. *The Alexandria Gazette* is one of the oldest newspapers in the country, publishing regularly since 1784.

ALIEN AND SEDITION LAWS. Government security acts against internal foes. Up to 1798 the greater part of the immigrants to the United States had been either Frenchmen driven into exile because of political troubles at home, or the English, Scotch, and Irish who had espoused ultra-republican principles and had fled from the severe measures of repression adopted against them at home. It is estimated that by 1798 there were 30,000 Frenchmen and 50,000 former subjects of Great Britain living in this country. Among them were some with noble aims, but others were political intriguers,

regarded as dangerous. In 1798, Congress passed acts for the security of the government against internal foes. By the first Act (June 18) naturalization laws were made more stringent, and alien enemies could not become citizens at all. By the second Act (June 25), which was limited to two years, the president was authorized to order out of the country all aliens he might judge to be dangerous to the peace and safety of the United States. By the third Act (July 6), in case of war declared against the U.S., or an actual invasion, all resident aliens, natives or citizens of the hostile nation, might, upon proclamation of the president, issued according to his discretion, be apprehended and secured or removed. Although the President never had occasion to put these Alien Laws into force, many who felt the laws had been aimed at them quickly left the country.

On July 14, 1798, an act was passed by Congress for the punishment of sedition. It made it a high misdemeanor, punishable by a fine and imprisonment, for any person to unlawfully combine in opposing measures of the government properly directed by authority, or attempting to prevent government officers executing their trusts, or inciting to riot and insurrection. The act also extended to any person found guilty of printing or publishing "false, scandalous, and malicious writing" against the government, either House of Congress or the president, with intent to defame them or bring them into dispute or contempt. The laws were vigorously opposed by many in the administration and these extreme measures were probably the reason for the Federalist defeat two years later.

ALLATOONA LAKE, Ga. Bartow Co. Artificial lake created by the U.S. Army Corps of Engineers as a hydroelectric power source. Kennesaw Mountain to the north overlooks the lake, which is situated in a mineral belt (limestone, iron, bauxite) where gold was once mined.

ALLEGHENY MOUNTAINS. Part of the APPALACHIAN MOUNTAIN range, beginning in northern Pennsylvania and extending southwestward through Maryland, West Virginia, and Virginia. The Alleghenies are commercially important for their coal and natural gas deposits. Heights in the southern portion of the range exceed 4,000 ft. while the northern portion rarely exceeds 2,000 ft. The Allegheny Front is a rugged western plateau that extends into Kentucky and eastern Ohio.

ALLEY SPRINGS, Mo. Shannon Co. Spring rising in a 200-ft.-diameter circular basin and generating an average 78 million gallons daily. It is located on an offshoot of the CURRENT RIVER in south central Missouri and is surrounded by a 407-acre state park.

ALLIGATOR. Reptile of the order Crocodilia which inhabits the swamps, lakes, and rivers of the southeastern U.S. Often confused with crocodiles, which are far less common, alligators frequent inland waters and rarely venture into salt water. Despite their reputation as being extremely dangerous, an unmolested alligator will seldom attack a person. The species found in the Southern states, *Alligator mississipiensis*, averages ten feet in length and is black with a yellowish belly; there are raised articulations along its spine. The presence of alligators is sometimes considered desirable because their diet of turtles protects game fish. Alligator farms are common tourist attractions, particularly in Florida.

ALLSTON, Robert Francis (All Saints' Parish, S.C., Apr. 21, 1801 — near Georgetown, S.C., Apr. 7, 1864). Planter, politician, and author. Allston attended West Point and graduated in 1821. After serving one year as a harbor surveyor, he resigned his commission to take up farming. Applying his knowledge of engineering and science, he was able to turn vast acres of lowland swamps into one of the state's last great rice plantations. He served as surveyor general of South Carolina for two terms, as a state assemblyman for many years, and as president of the state senate from 1847-56. Allston was active in the secession movement of 1847-52. He was elected governor by the legislature for the term 1856-58, during which time he advanced agriculture in the state and improved the public schools. His writings on agriculture greatly influenced planters of the time. His works include: *South Carolina Rice Plantation, A Memoir of the Introduction and Planting of Rice in South Carolina*, and *An Essay on Sea Coast Crops.*

ALLSTON, Washington (Plantation on Waccamaw River, S.C., Nov. 5, 1779 — Cambridge, Mass., July 9, 1843). Artist and author. The first U.S. romantic painter of note and a popular author of the day, Allston graduated from Harvard in 1801 and then studied abroad where he crossed paths with European romantic painters and acquainted himself with the Venetian and Roman masters. As with many artists of the period, Allston became fascinated with dramatic subject matter and with dramatic use of light. Early works such as 'Dead Man Revived by Touching the Bones of the Prophet Elisha" (1811-13) were large scale and bold. Later works such as "Moonlight Landscape" (1819) and "The Flight of Florimell" (1819) were quieter but no less striking. Allston spent 20 years reworking his allegorical work, "Belshazzar's Feast," with which he was evidently never truly satisfied. Samuel F.B. Morse was one of his many pupils. Allston was the author of *The Sylphs of the Seasons with Other Poems* (1813) and the novel *Monaldi* (1841).

ALLUVIAL LANDS. A term that refers to the territory along the lower Mississippi River. In Louisiana, this land extends from the border with Arkansas to the Gulf of Mexico, covering about one-third of the state. The alluvials are characterized by broad ridges and hollows which parallel the Mississippi. The ridges are divided into two classifications, the frontlands, which are fields atop the ridges, and backlands, long stretches of clay and silt which begin where the frontlands slope away from the river.

ALSTON, Joseph (All Saints' Parish, S.C., c. 1779 — Charleston, S.C., Sept. 10, 1816). Planter and politician. He studied law but abandoned a legal career to start his own plantation. Entering politics, he was elected to the South Carolina legislature (1802-12) and was governor (1812-14). He was the son-in-law of Aaron Burr.

ALTAMAHA RIVER, Ga. River rising in south central Georgia, traveling east-southeast for more than 150 miles to empty into the Atlantic Ocean. Its name is a corruption of the Indian word meaning "way to Tama Country." Formed by the OCONEE and OCMULGEE Rivers, it is highly developed for hydroelectricity. Hatch Nuclear Plant Visitors Center is found on the river near Baxley.

AMADAS (Amidas), Philip (Hull, England, 1550 — c. 1618). British navigator. Sent by Sir Walter RALEIGH, he and Arthur BARLOWE explored the North American coast (1584). Their positive report led to the colonization of ROANOKE ISLAND.

AMARILLO, Tex. City (pop. 149,230), seat of Potter Co., but partially located in Randall Co. in southwest Texas. The major city of the

Texas panhandle, Amarillo originated in 1887 as a railroad construction camp, and was incorporated in 1892. The city grew after 1900 due to the importance of local wheat cultivation and cattle ranching. It grew again in the 1920s with the discovery of gas and oil. After the Depression, extensive irrigation improvements increased agricultural production. In more recent years Amarillo developed zinc smelters and helicopter factories and it is now the site of a major government helium plant and atomic research project.

AMERICUS, Ga. City (pop. 16,120), seat of Sumter Co., southwestern Georgia. An industrial center, settled in 1832 and chartered as a city in 1855, it is located in a farming and timber area. Charles LINDBERGH made his first solo flight from an airfield here.

AMES, Adelbert (Rockland, Maine, Oct. 31, 1835 — Ormond, Fla., April 13, 1933). Military officer and politician. A graduate of West Point Military Academy (1861), he fought on the Union side in the Civil War. Ames was awarded the Congressional Medal of Honor for his gallantry at the Battle of BULL RUN. He moved south and during RECONSTRUCTION was appointed provisional governor of Mississippi on March 15, 1868. His governorship was troubled by the Vicksburg riot in 1874. He later served in the U.S. Senate (1870-74) and as governor (1874-76). Ames also fought in the Spanish-American War.

AMICALOLA FALLS, Ga. Lumpkin Co. The highest waterfalls in the state (729 ft.), which are created by a mountain stream plunging down the western side of the Amicalola Ridge, near the APPALACHIAN TRAIL.

AMITE RIVER, La. River beginning in southern Mississippi that crosses the Louisiana border, traveling southwest to meet the Comite River at Baton Rouge. From there it takes a southeast swing and eventually empties into Lake MAUREPAS.

ANDERSON, Richard Heron (Statesburg, S.C., Oct. 7, 1821 — Beaufort, S.C., June 26, 1879). Confederate general. He took command of the 1st corps when Longstreet was wounded during the WILDERNESS Campaign (1864) and defended SPOTSYLVANIA by executing an unexpected midnight march. Serving the U.S. as a cavalry officer (1842), he fought well during the

Mexican War. After secession he resigned his commission and joined the Confederates, fighting with the Army of Northern Virginia through the Battle of GETTYSBURG. Appointed major general in 1862 and lieutenant general after Spotsylvania, he led the defense of PETERSBURG and RICHMOND.

ANDERSON, Robert (Near Louisville, Ky., June 14, 1805 — Nice, France, Oct. 26, 1871). Army officer. He defended Fort SUMTER in the first battle of the Civil War (April 12, 1861). When South Carolina seceded, Anderson was given command of Charleston Harbor and moved his troops to the most defensible post, Fort Sumter. After a 34-hour bombardment he surrendered the Fort but he himself escaped. He was made a brigadier in the regular army in May 1861 and headed the Department of Kentucky from June to October. He retired in 1863.

ANDERSON, S.C. City (pop. 27,313), seat of Anderson Co., located in the northwestern part of the state, in the Blue Ridge foothills near the east shore of the Savannah River. Named for Gen. Robert ANDERSON, a Civil War hero, the city was settled in 1826 in Cherokee Indian territory by Scotch-Irish migrants from Virginia and Pennsylvania. Because of its early use of electric power, Anderson, now near the Hartwell Hydroelectric Dam, has been called "electric city." It is the home of Anderson Junior College (1848).

ANDERSONVILLE, Ga. Village (pop. 267), Sumter Co., in the southeastern quarter of the state, 60 miles southwest of Macon. Andersonville was the site of the Confederacy's Andersonville Prison, which has been preserved as a Federal Park. By 1863, the number of prisoners of war being held by the South at Richmond threatened public security. Hasty arrangements were made to transfer the unfortunate captives to a stockade then being constructed at Andersonville. Inadequate housing, drainage, water, and staff led to rampant disease. Nearly 13,000 prisoners died there between 1864 and 1865, increasing bitterness in the North. After the war the prison was used as a hospital.

ANDREWS, Eliza Frances (Washington, Ga., Aug. 10, 1840 — Rome, Ga., Jan. 21, 1931). Author, educator. and botanist. Andrews earned a B.A. in the first graduating class at Georgia's La Grange Female College (1857). A school principal (1873-81) and faculty member at Wesleyan Female College at Macon, Ga. (1885-96), she then taught high-school botany (1898-1903). The Civil War and Reconstruction are the central themes of her novels and of her most famous book, *The War-Time Journal of a Georgia Girl* (1908). A committed Marxist, she contributed work to the *International Socialist Review*. Her books include *Botany All the Year Round* (1903) and *A Practical Course in Botany* (1911).

ANDREWS, Frank Maxwell (Nashville, Tenn., Feb. 3, 1884 — Iceland, May 4, 1944). Air Force officer. Appointed the first commander of the U.S. Army Air Force (1936-39), he succeeded Gen. Dwight D. EISENHOWER as commanding general of the U.S. Armed Forces in Europe (1943). A graduate of West Point (1906), Andrews began his career with the cavalry in the Philippines and Hawaii, transferring to the newly formed aviation section of the Signal Corps in 1917. An early advocate of strategic air power and a promoter of bombardment tactics, he was instrumental in developing the B-17 aircraft. During his early years of command he shaped the air force of the World War II era. Andrews died in a plane accident.

ANDREWS, Mary Raymond Shipman (Mobile, Ala., Apr. 2, 1860 — Syracuse, N.Y., Aug. 2, 1936). Author. Andrews wrote highly-acclaimed short stories: romantic adventures and moral tales set against the Canadian wilderness, the horrors of World War I, and the worlds of lawyers and clergy. Her stories appeared in *Scribner's Magazine*, *Harper's Monthly*, *Ladies Home Journal*, and other periodicals. Her most famous tale, "The Perfect Tribute" (1906), recounts Lincoln's professed disappointment at the reception given his *Gettysburg Address*.

ANDROS, Sir Edmund (London, England, Dec. 6, 1637 — London, England, Feb. 27, 1714). Colonial governor. The son of a loyalist supporter of Charles I, Andros rose in military rank in the English campaign against the Dutch in the late 1660s and early 1670s. He was appointed governor of New York and "the Jerseys," a disputed territory, in 1674, and recalled to London amid charges of corruption in 1681. It was during this term as governor, nevertheless, that he was knighted in 1678. Because England feared loss of economic control over its American colonies due to French interference, the Dominion of New England was chartered in 1686 with Boston as its capital and

Andros as its governor. The boundaries of this consolidated territory were extended in 1688 to include New York and New Jersey. Andros' authoritarian approach to colonial politics and his harsh taxation demands on the fledgling local economy made him extremely unpopular with the American colonists. When word of the arrival of William, Prince of Orange, in England reached America in 1689, the colonists deposed Andros and sent him to England for trial in 1690. In London, however, he was given an immediate reprieve, and in 1692 he returned to America as governor of Virginia (1692-1697). He again encountered hostility from colonists and charges of corruption from London. He was finally recalled to England for financial improprieties in 1698. At home he served as governor of Guernsey for a two-year term beginning in 1704. Andros lies buried in St. Anne's church in the Soho section of London.

ANNAPOLIS, Md. City (pop. 31,740), seat of Anne Arundel Co. and state capital, located on the west shore of Chesapeake Bay at the mouth of the SEVERN RIVER 25 miles south of Baltimore. The site of the present city was settled in 1649 by Puritans who fled from Virginia. The town was first called Providence, then Town of Proctor's and finally, in 1694, Annapolis after the heir to the British throne, Princess Anne. The city was incorporated in 1708 and was the principal harbor for the colony until commerce shifted to Baltimore during the American Revolution. Following the war, the U.S. Congress met in Annapolis and accepted the resignation of George Washington as commander in chief of the Continental Army on December 23, 1783. The city was also the site of the Annapolis Convention of 1786, a forum for constitutional discussion in advance of the Philadelphia convention that formally approved the U.S. Constitution. The U.S. NAVAL ACADEMY was located in Annapolis in 1845 by George Bancroft, the secretary of the Navy to President James Polk.

The city is an especially scenic one because of the presence of dignified naval academy and state government buildings. Its colonial character is preserved by the state house (1772), St. Anne's Church (late 17th century), and numerous 18th century homes. Annapolis is also the location of St. John's College (1696).

ANNISTON, Ala. City (pop. 29,534), seat of Calhoun Co., located 61 miles northwest of Birmingham in the foothills of the Appalachian

Mountains. It was settled in 1872 as a private village by the Woodstock Iron Company and named Woodstock. It was later renamed for Annie Taylor, the wife of one of the founders. Anniston was incorporated as a town in 1873 and as a city in 1879. Rich in iron ore, Anniston became one of the world's largest producers of cast-iron soil pipe. Other industry includes the manufacture of textiles and electrochemical products. The Regar Museum of Natural History (1930) is located here, as is Camp McClellan, a U.S. army post.

ANTIETAM, Battle of. Principal battle of a campaign by the Confederate army to invade the North in the wake of its qualified victory at the second battle of BULL RUN. The Battle of Antietam was fought on September 17, 1862, in Maryland, near the Potomac River. In it Gen. Robert E. LEE's forces were defeated by the Union army under Gen. George B. McCLELLAN. The North named the battle after a local creek, but the Confederacy called it the battle of Sharpsburg, after the nearest village.

The Antietam campaign began on September 9, 1862. On that date Lee issued orders to move northward. By "Special Order 191," which was intercepted by the Union army, he sent six divisions under Gen. Stonewall JACKSON to take HARPERS FERRY and three divisions under Gen. James LONGSTREET to take Hagerstown. On September 13 Longstreet was recalled because the order had been intercepted, but on September 15 Harpers Ferry was taken. Although completely outnumbered, Lee decided to make a stand along Antietam Creek near Sharpsburg because he thought McClellan too cautious to attack. However, McClellan did seize the opportunity of a split in Confederate ranks and attacked Lee on September 17.

The Union army decimated the Confederate army on what has been called "the bloodiest single day in the war." Forces sent by Jackson

Drawing of Union Gen. Ambrose Burnside's division at the bridge during the Battle of Antietam

from Harpers Ferry arrived by night, however, thus preventing a complete rout. On the night of September 18 Lee retreated back into Virginia. McClellan, who still held some 35,000 fresh troops, failed to pursue the Confederate troops and so, in the opinion of some, squandered an opportunity to end the war in 1862. Nevertheless, it was this Union victory that encouraged President Abraham Lincoln to issue the Emancipation Proclamation.

ANTIN, Mary (Plotzk, Russia, June 13, 1881 — Suffern, N.Y., May 15, 1949). Author. Immigrating to the United States from Poland in 1894, she settled with her family in Boston's South End. She attended Boston public schools, Girls' Latin School, and came to the attention of EDWARD EVERETT HALE and HATTIE HECHT, who arranged for the publication of her *From Plotzk to Boston* (1899), recounting her voyage to America. This is also the theme of her most famous work, *The Promised Land* (1912). Her *They Who Knock* (1914) countered the rising prejudice against immigrants.

APACHE INDIANS ("enemy"). Tribe of Athabascan linguistic stock that roamed over portions of western Texas, New Mexico, and Arizona. As wanderers, they did not cultivate the soil and had only temporary chiefs to lead them. A warlike tribe, they resisted all attempts, especially by the Spanish, to civilize and Christianize them, and because of their constant raiding gave the United States government more trouble than any of the other southwestern Indian tribes.

APALACHEE BAY, Fla. A 30-mile-wide portion of the Gulf of Mexico in the north central part of the state, bounded by the coasts of Wakulla County, Jefferson County, and part of Taylor County. Located 25 miles south of Tallahassee, its marshy shore, which receives the AUCILLA, OCHLOCKONEE, and SAINT MARKS rivers, is a federal wildlife refuge.

APALACHEE INDIANS ("people of the other side"). Tribe of Muskogean linguistic stock, located in the vicinity of St. Mark's River, Fla., with branches of the tribe extending northward into the Appalachian range. They were first noted by the NARVAEZ expedition (1528). Warlike and hostile toward the colonists for nearly a century, in the early 1600s they requested missionaries and were Christianized. Trouble broke out again in 1702, the result of Apalachee complaints that they were being forced to work on fortifications at St. Augustine. The uprising was defeated by colonists who were joined by CREEK Indians, and the Apalachee were nearly destroyed, with more than 1,000 sold into slavery.

APALACHICOLA INDIANS ("people of the other side"). Tribe of Muskogean linguistic stock that lived in the region of the Apalachicola River in Georgia, to which they gave their name. Being generally friendly with the early Spanish caused them at times to be attacked by Indian tribes allied to the English. Legends say that an early treaty between the Apalachicola and MUSKOGEE INDIANS resulted in the formation of the CREEK Confederacy.

APALACHICOLA RIVER, Fla. River formed by the merging of the FLINT and CHATTAHOOCHEE rivers in the southwest corner of Georgia at Chattahoochee, just above the state line. The Apalachicola flows south for 112 miles to empty into Apalachicola Bay, a protected part of the ATLANTIC INTRACOASTAL WATERWAY, in the Gulf of Mexico. Its dredged channel runs some six miles up the river.

Primitive textile industry in the Appalachian Mountains of Arkansas

APPALACHIAN MOUNTAINS. Mountain system running from New Brunswick, Canada, southward into central Alabama, it is a general term applied to a group of ranges including the ALLEGHENY, BLUE RIDGE, BLACK, GREAT SMOKY, and CUMBERLAND. Formed of sedimentary rock, the system has a longitudinal valley that in its southern region divides the mountains into two parts (The Great Appalachian Valley). The system's highest point is Mount MITCHELL in the Black Mountains (6,684 ft.). Rivers in the central part of the system, the Potomac and Susquehanna, drain into the Atlantic. In the southern region the Cumberland and Tennessee Rivers drain westward. The mountains were a deterrent to early westward expansion and consequently played an important role in the development of colonies concentrated along the seacoast. Coal, iron, gas, and petroleum deposits, along with valuable lumber, have given the mountains a commercial importance in addition to recreational and tourist opportunities.

APPALACHIAN PLATEAU, Va. One of the five physiographical areas in the state, located near the Kentucky line. Dotted with streams, the region is covered with deep ravines cut through limestone outcroppings. The name comes from that of a near destitute Indian village, "Apalchen," discovered by early Spanish explorers.

APPALACHIAN TRAIL. A 2,050-mile hiking path that extends from Springer Mountain, Ga., to Mount Katahdin, Maine, passing through 14 states and numerous state parks and forests. The trail has primitive campsites every seven to eight miles, which are maintained by numerous private clubs and government agencies working together under the Appalachian Trail Conference.

APPLEGATE, Jesse (Kentucky, July 5, 1811 — Oregon, Apr. 2, 1888). Surveyor and rancher. He pioneered the settlement of Oregon. Applegate's *Day with the Cow Column in 1843* (1844), relating his trek to Oregon with 1,800 cattle and 900 people, attracted attention to the region. He served in the provisional government until Oregon joined the Union (1849), opened a southern route to the region, and promoted the Oregon-California rail line.

APPOMATTOX, Surrender at. The symbolic end of the Civil War, delivered by Gen. Robert E. LEE to Union Gen. Ulysses S. GRANT

Appomattox Courthouse where Gen. Robert E. Lee surrendered to Gen. Ulysses S. Grant

on April 9, 1865, at Appomattox Courthouse in central Virginia. It was followed by the later surrender of other Confederate leaders. The surrender at Appomattox marked the failure of Lee's final attempt to join his forces with those of Gen. Joseph E. JOHNSTON in North Carolina. For this purpose Lee began to move west from Petersburg on April 2. Grant dispatched the Union cavalry under Gen. Philip H. Sheridan in pursuit south of the Appomattox River, thus cutting off Lee's route to the Carolinas. The Union forces encircled Lee's troops and trapped them at Appomattox Station on April 8 and at Clover Hill near the courthouse on the morning of April 9.

APPOMATTOX, Va. Town (pop. 1,345), seat of Appomattox Co., located 20 miles southeast of Lynchburg where a major military conflict led to Gen. Robert E. LEE's surrender to Gen. Ulysses S. GRANT on April 9, 1865 at Appomattox Courthouse. Incorporated in 1926, Appomattox was named a national historical monument in 1940. Industry includes canneries and sawmills. Tobacco is grown in the area and there is dairy farming.

APPOMATTOX RIVER, Va. River rising in Appomattox Co., eventually becoming a tributary of the JAMES. The name comes from the Algonquin Indian word, apamutiky, meaning "a sinuous tidal estuary."

ARANSAS, Tex. City (pop. 7,173), located in Aransas, San Patricio, and Nueces counties. This deepwater port on the Corpus Christi channel and the GULF INTRACOASTAL WATERWAY is in an important oil producing and refining area. Commercial and sport fishing bring in additional revenue. The city was settled in 1890 and incorporated in 1910.

ARCHITECTURE. Among American regions the South is unique in its complex blend of architectural influences. There is no single architectural mode in the South; rather, there are five distinct styles found in its landmark buildings.

The first is the Spanish style, associated most closely with the Catholic missions that spread northward from Mexico into Texas. This style is noted for its ornately tiled facades, barrel vaults, thick adobe walls, and twin frontal towers. The purest examples of this style were built

Oak Alley Plantation near St. James, La., built 1830-39 by Jacques Roman III

in the early 1700s around San Antonio, where the most famous is the mission of San Jose. In comparison with this period, the missions that later extended northward along the California coast were poorly constructed and only sparsely decorated. Throughout the South, especially in Texas, there are many residences that incorporate both the material and the style of Spanish architecture.

The second important early influence on Southern architecture was the Gothic style imported from England. These buildings were of necessity constructed of wood, usually by a method called half-timber in which gaps between wall beams are sheathed with clapboard. Most 17th century homes in Virginia were built in the Gothic style: they can be identified by their central chimneys, overhanging second story, and small casement windows. The first churches were built in the Gothic style. One of these is St. Luke's in Smithfield, Va., built in 1632; its buttresses, pointed arches, and tracery are all based on English models.

In the South in the 18th century the Gothic style was supplanted by the Georgian style. It featured peripheral chimneys which permitted central hallways, numerous vertical sash windows, and details, or "orders," such as corner columns and decorative enframements on centered, ground-level entranceways. Many of the buildings preserved at colonial Williamsburg in Virginia are Georgian in style.

The single most famous architect in the old South was Thomas Jefferson, and he found his inspiration in Roman rather than English architecture. His design for the State Capitol in Richmond, Va., was modeled on a Roman structure called the Maison Carree in Nimes, France. For the library at the University of Virginia in Charlottesville, Jefferson looked to the Pantheon in Rome. In both cases, and in a number of smaller buildings at the university, Jefferson was forced to adapt his model to new functional purposes and this was in keeping with his goal of providing students with examples of successful modifications of classical forms to modern purposes.

It was a different classical model that provided the inspiration for the most famous form of architecture associated with the South. This was the Greek revival style incorporated into most of the famous mansions of the Southern plantations. One distinctive feature of these homes was the porch, which sprawled in large proportions to encourage outdoor life in the warm climate. George Washington's Greek revival home at Mount Vernon, Va., was the first plantation mansion with a two-story front porch. Columns were used to delineate the extent of these porches, and in this feature plantation mansions adapted the frontal lines of Greek temples. Construction was still of necessity in wood rather than marble but some homes, such as the Lee mansion in Arlington, Va., frankly modeled themselves on the temples of ancient Greece. It was from this model that Southern architecture adopted the frontal portico rising to roof height, such as that on the White House in Washington, D.C., designed by James Hoban. A final influence of the Doric Greek temple on this design was peripheral wings, such as those attached to the Capitol building in Washington by Thomas Walter during the Greek Revival. The purest examples of Greek revival plantation architecture are the D'Evereaux, Linden, and Dunleith mansions in Natchez, Miss.

ARKABUTLA RESERVOIR, Miss. A 75-mile long artificial lake, in DeSoto and Tate counties, northwestern Mississippi, that is part of the YAZOO BASIN. Created by the U.S. Army Corps of Engineers as a flood control and recreation project, it was formed by damming the COLDWATER RIVER.

ARKANSAS. State located in the central region of the south on the west bank of the Mississippi River. The river forms its boundary to the east with Tennessee, on the upper third, and Mississippi on the lower two-thirds. To the north Arkansas has a straight land boundary with Missouri that is broken near the Mississippi River by the "boot heel" of Missouri, that extends southward into Arkansas. Arkansas's principal western boundary is with Oklahoma and its principal southern one with Louisiana, but the southwestern corner of the state is broken by a rectangular extension of Texas south of the Red River.

In Arkansas there is an even balance between the two principal landscapes of the American South: hill country and bottomland. A diagonal drawn across the state through the central capital city of LITTLE ROCK separates the rugged highland country of northwestern Arkansas from the fertile farmlands of the southeastern part of the state. Little Rock remains the only large metropolitan area in the state, and the populations of both regions have until recently lived predominantly in small towns.

Economically and demographically, Arkansas has developed at a different pace than the rest of the South. A sudden drop in cotton prices and the effects of mismanagement of public works projects such as roads in the 1920s brought the state to the brink of bankruptcy in the 1930s. These "dust bowl" years in neighboring states did not have an immediate impact on Arkansas, largely because of federal intervention to manage the state debt. However, in the 1940s, when the rest of the South was recovering from the Great Depression, Arkansas fell into a period of economic recession and population emigration. Between 1940 and 1960 the state recorded a net population loss of more the 160,000, or more than 8% of the total population. In the same period Little Rock suffered from the struggle to integrate its schools, a long impasse that tarnished the state image in the minds of many. Industrial development programs instituted at that time, however, have since restored the economy. Defense industries, rising prices for the state oil deposits and local reserves of specialized ores such as bauxite and bromide have all combined to create an industrial center in Arkansas that is the basis of a new state economy. As a result, the state virtually regained its 1940 population level by 1970, and the 1970s brought a population increase of 19%, or half again the national average.

The highland and lowland topographical areas of Arkansas are nearly equal in size. The highland region consists of the OZARK PLATEAU along the Missouri border, the BOSTON MOUNTAINS just south of it, and, across the Arkansas River valley, the OUACHITA MOUNTAINS. The river valley itself is perhaps the most dramatic topographical area in the state, a 35-mile wide belt of deep canyons and steep peaks that include the highest point in the state at Mount MAGAZINE (2,753 ft.). The lowlands of the south and east of the state all fall within the Gulf Coastal Plain, a formation that includes all of the Arkansas-Louisiana border region and tapers toward the Mississippi River in the south. Most of the region consists of prairie lands of rolling hills, but the southeastern corner of the state is a swampier region of delta bottomlands built up by the serpentine course of the MISSISSIPPI RIVER. The principal rivers of the state, the OUACHITA, ARKANSAS, and WHITE, all flow toward this low-lying southeastern corner of the state.

The earliest residents of what is now Arkansas were the Indians known as Mound Builders who once populated the entire lower Mississippi valley. Remnants of this native society are still visible in the HOT SPRINGS area. By the time of the European exploration of Arkansas, the most populous Indians were the OSAGE, a tribe that resisted the inroads of the Europeans into the region. Arkansas, like the neighboring Mississippi states, was first explored by the Spaniard Hernando DE SOTO in 1541 and then by the Frenchmen Jacques MARQUETTE and Louis JOLLIET in 1673. In 1682, LA SALLE, on his way to the mouth of the Mississippi, claimed the river basin for France and named it Louisiana after Louis XIV.

It was La Salle's lieutenant, Henri de Tonti, who established the first permanent settlement in Arkansas in 1686. This was ARKANSAS POST, at the mouth of the Arkansas River, and it remained the principal city of the region until the 1800s. The primary French interest in Arkansas was based on fur trapping, but Arkansas Post had additional importance as a stopover port on the Mississippi between the French settlements to the north in Canada and to the south in Louisiana. Settlement of this isolated interior territory lagged behind that of the Gulf Coast region, especially after the land speculation on the Mississippi basin by the Scottish businessman John Law was exposed as a fraud in 1720. Lacking even a minimal population, Arkansas became a pawn in the diplomatic negotiations of the time. France ceded the region to Spain in 1762, and then regained possession in 1800. Under the Spanish agreements with the United States after the Revolution, however, American settlement was encouraged. This was one of the factors that brought about the LOUISIANA PURCHASE from France by the U.S. in 1803. What is now Arkansas was included in the purchase; it was set off from the Louisiana District as part of the Missouri Territory and became the distinct Arkansas Territory in 1819.

As a territory, Arkansas was a frontier of violence, land battles, and rustlers, all unchecked by effective law enforcement. The ordinary settler's sense of unjust treatment by the federal government was deepened in the 1820s when the U.S. flooded Arkansas with Indian groups displaced from east of the Mississippi River. Later agreements moved the Indians farther west to Oklahoma, but the local sense of unfair treatment by Washington, D.C., would remain an influence on the political events surrounding the civil rights struggles of the 1950s.

By 1835 the Arkansas population had reached the 50,000 requirement for statehood, and it was admitted to the Union on June 15, 1836, as the 25th state. It was admitted as a slave state, and its fortunes at this time were entangled with the issues of slavery and states' rights. Cotton became the basis of the economy after statehood, and the wealth and political power this crop brought with it were concentrated in the lowland plantation regions of southeastern Arkansas. A cotton boom in the 1850s added to this imbalance of wealth and power in a single region of the state. By 1860 one-quarter of the state population of more than 430,000 consisted of slaves, and the cotton interests in the state were sufficiently powerful to carry Arkansas to secession. This move was resisted by the small farmers of the northwestern highlands, however, and Arkansas did not officially secede until May 6, 1861, a month after the beginning of the Civil War. The Union army took effective control of the state after the Battle of PEA RIDGE in 1862, although pockets of Confederate resistance held out until the end of the war in 1865.

In the years following the war Arkansas suffered from Washington's RECONSTRUCTION policies and from corrupt CARPETBAGGERS and SCALAWAGS. The legislature refused to ratify the 13th Amendment against slavery, and for this Arkansas was placed under military rule in 1867. It was readmitted to the Union in 1868, but only over the veto of President Andrew Johnson. Political corruption and insurrectionary groups such as the KU KLUX KLAN continued to hinder economic recovery, however. It was only the spread of the railroads at the end of the 19th century and the influx of new farmers they brought that permitted diversification of the cotton crop economy. This period of consistent growth, limited to some extent by the sharecropping system that restricted farm yield, continued until the 1930s, the advent of the period of economic decline and population loss.

The post-World War II economic recovery programs of Arkansas have returned the state to a period of population growth. Since economic recovery was tied to industrialization, this period has seen a movement of the population from the farmlands to the cities of the state. The largest population center in the state is LITTLE ROCK, which is also its leading manufacturing city. Located in the center of the state on the Arkansas River, Little Rock, originally created from scratch to serve as the capital of Arkansas Territory in 1821, is now a city of more than 150,000 residents and the heart of a metropolitan area of nearly 400,000 residents that grew at a rate of 22% in the 1970s. FORT SMITH, on the Arkansas River at the Oklahoma border, is also a manufacturing center and the

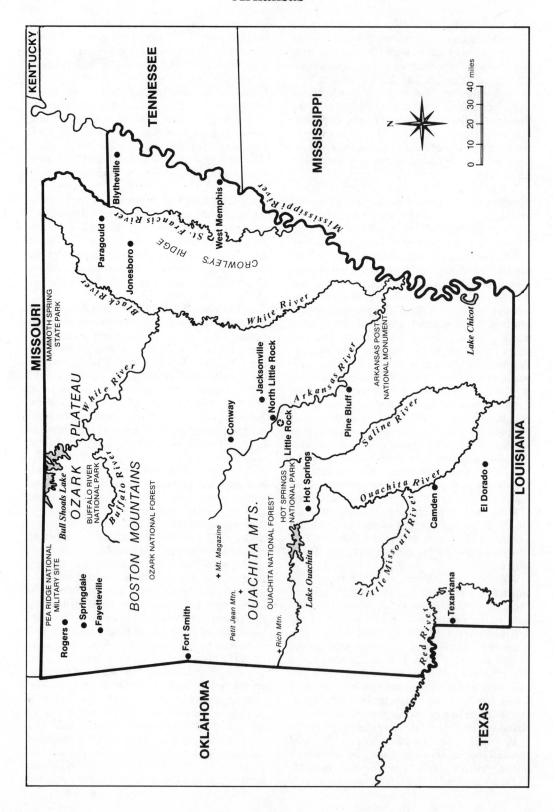

STATE OF ARKANSAS

Name: From *Ugakhpah* ("downstream people"), the self-designation of the Siouan tribe better known as the Quapaw.

Nickname: Land of Opportunity, Bear State, Bowie State, Hot Water State, Guinea Pig State, Toothpick State, Wonder State, Razorback State.

Motto: *Regnat Populus* (The People Rule).

Capital: Little Rock.

Counties: 75. **Places over 10,000 population (1980)**: 29.

Symbols & Emblems: *Flower*: Apple Blossom. *Bird*: Mockingbird. *Tree*: Pine. *Song*: "Arkansas."

Population (1980): 2,285,513. **Rank**: 33rd.

Population Density (1980): 43.9 people per sq. mi. **Rank**: 35th.

Racial Make-up (1980): *White*: 1,810,002 (82.7%). *Black*: 373,192 (16.3%). *American Indian*: 9,411 (0.6%). *Asian & Pacific Islander*: 6,732 (0.3%). *Other*: 6,176 (0.3%). *Spanish Origin*: 17,873 (0.7%).

Largest City (pop. 1980): Little Rock (158,461). *Others*: Fort Smith (71,384), North Little Rock (64,149), Pine Bluff (56,576), Fayetteville (36,604), Hot Springs (35,166), Jonesboro (31,530), West Memphis (28,138), Jacksonville (27,589), El Dorado (26,685).

Area: 52,078 sq. mi. **Rank**: 27th.

Highest Point: Magazine Mountain (2,753 ft.), Logan Co.

Lowest Point: Ouachita River (55 ft.), Ashley/Union Cos.

State Government:
ELECTED OFFICIALS (2-year terms expiring Jan. 1985, etc.): *Governor* ($35,000); *Lt. Governor* ($14,000); *Sec. of State* ($22,500); *Attorney General* ($26,500); *Treasurer* ($22,500).

GENERAL ASSEMBLY (Salary: $7,500 plus $20 per legislative day and up to $308 weekly expenses.): *Senate* (35 members), *House of Representatives* (100 members).

CONGRESSIONAL REPRESENTATIVES: *Senate* (terms expire 1985, 1987, etc.). *House of Representatives* (4 members).

Admitted to the Union: June 15, 1836 (25th state).

hub of a metropolitan area of more than 200,000 residents of both states. FAYETTEVILLE, in the northwestern corner of the state, is a metropolitan area of 178,000 residents, and Texarkana on the Texas border in the southwest of the state is the home of 127,000 residents of both states. The towns surrounding WEST MEMPHIS, Arkansas, on the Mississippi River are part of the metropolitan area of Memphis, Tennessee.

The total population decline of the 1940s and 1950s has since been reversed by growth throughout the state. Of the net population growth of more than 360,000 in the 1970s, well over one-third was attributed to immigration to Arkansas by residents of other states. Most of this immigration was of white residents, but the same decade saw a long tradition of black emigration from Arkansas brought to a virtual end. The statewide population is now 20% black. One result of the shift in population patterns is the fact that only slightly more than one-half of Arkansas residents were born in the state. Although the economy has been revived to significant degrees, Arkansas remains the third-lowest state in the U.S. in per capita income.

The principal industries of Arkansas, ranked in importance to the state economy, are manufacturing, agriculture, and mining. The manufacturing sector of the economy is extremely diversified, with leading products as various as processed foods, electronic equipment, wood and wood pulp goods, and refined ores. The greatest number of state farms are devoted to cattle, but most of Arkansas's farm income is produced by feed grains and poultry. Arkansas leads all states in poultry hatcheries and production of broilers. Most of the state's mine income is derived from petroleum and natural gas, which are drilled in the southern regions of Arkansas and processed in the cities of EL DORADO and TEXARKANA. However, Arkansas leads all states in yield of the metal ore bauxite and the non-metallic ore bromide, both of which are mined in the northern highlands of the state. In recent years tourism has also become a leading industry; visitors to the state now spend more than $1 billion per year, most of it in the scenic Ozark and Ouachita highland regions of Arkansas.

ARKANSAS, University of. State-supported coed, land-grant college located in Fayetteville, Ark., in the northwest part of the state. The University of Arkansas at Fayetteville is the oldest and largest of the state's four university campuses. The other three are located in Monticello, Little Rock, and Pine Bluff. Founded as the Arkansas Industrial University in 1871, the present-day university has evolved as one of the state's best schools, offering graduate, undergraduate, and professional degrees in many areas. Undergraduates take courses in the colleges of Business Administration, Engineering, Agriculture and Home Economics, Arts and Sciences, and Education, and in the schools of Pharmacy and Nursing.

In addition to its 329-acre campus, the university maintains 9,546 acres of experiment stations. The school does not seek a national student body: 80% are from the South.

Library: 918,000 volumes, 9,300 journal subscriptions. Faculty: 750. Enrollment: 15,604 total graduate and undergraduate; 7,479 men, 5,467 women (full-time). Degrees: Associate's, Bachelor's, Master's, Doctorate.

ARKANSAS INDIANS. Another name for the QUAPAW INDIANS who lived near the mouth of the ARKANSAS RIVER.

ARKANSAS POST, Ark. Community, Arkansas Co., at the mouth of the Arkansas River. Founded by French settlers as a trading post in 1686, it was the first white settlement and the first territorial capital. The post was an important river port for many years.

ARKANSAS POST, Battle of. Civil War engagement fought January 11, 1863 in southeast Arkansas. It was the end of a successful campaign by Union Gen. John A. McClernand to capture the Confederate gunboat installation on the Arkansas River at Fort Hindman, for which the battle is sometimes named.

McClernand had been given orders by President Abraham Lincoln to assist in the assault of VICKSBURG. He raised an army in the west and moved against Vicksburg without consulting Gen. Ulysses S. Grant, commander of that operation. McClernand reached the area in December, 1862, just as Gen. William Tecumseh Sherman was abandoning his attack on CHICKASAW BLUFFS. He then decided independently to move up the Arkansas River against Fort Hindman. After a day of confusion caused by a lack of communication between land and river forces, he launched a coordinated attack on the morning of January 11 that brought the surrender of the fort by 3:00 P.M. McClernand was then ordered back down the Arkansas River to assist in the campaign against Vicksburg.

ARKANSAS RIVER, Ark. River which rises in the Rocky Mountains, central Colorado, and travels approximately 1,460 miles southeast to join the MISSISSIPPI RIVER, north of Greenville, Miss. It is Arkansas's largest river and principal waterway. It has a drainage basin of some 185,000 square miles. Dams along the river within this state include the Blue Mountain on the PETIT JEAN and the Nimrod Dam on the FOURCHE LA FAVE. *The Eagle*, the first U.S. steamboat, journeyed up the Arkansas River here in 1822.

ARKANSAS RIVER VALLEY, Ark. Broad valley region which is situated between the OZARK PLATEAU and the OUACHITA MOUNTAINS. The ARKANSAS RIVER flows through the center southeast to the Mississippi border. While it is lower than the land regions to the north and south of it, this valley has the highest peaks in the state, including the MAGAZINE, the NEBO, and the Petit Jean. The valley is rich in coal and natural gas deposits.

ARKANSAS STATE UNIVERSITY. State-supported university located in Jonesboro, Ark., 120 miles northeast of Little Rock. Founded in 1909, this multipurpose institution has 800 acres of land, numerous buildings, agricultural research plots, and farms for agricultural programs. The school's original purpose was to give northeast Arkansas residents the opportunity to learn advanced mechanical and agricultural methods. The school became a junior college in 1918, a senior college in 1925, and in 1967 a university. The university also maintains a branch campus in Beebe, Ark. The South provides 90% of the school's students. Undergraduates are offered courses in the University's colleges of Technology and Management, Nursing, Education, Agriculture, Business, Communication, Liberal Arts and Fine Arts. For recreation, off-campus opportunities abound. The Jonesboro area offers theaters, parks, shopping, boating, and fishing.

Library: 310,656 volumes, 1,823 journal subscriptions, 8,308 records/tapes. Faculty: 339. Enrollment: 2,853 men, 2,976 women (full-time). Degrees: Certificate or Diploma, Associate's, Bachelor's, Master's.

ARLINGTON, Tex. City (pop. 160,123), Tarrant Co., northern Texas. Orignially settled in 1843 on Indian land as Bird's Fort, it was renamed after Gen. Robert E. Lee's ancestral home. The city was incorporated in 1896. Rapid development of aerospace and automobile industries in the 1950s doubled the population and made the city an industrial and commercial center. Arlington features the University of Texas at Arlington, Bible Baptist Seminary, Six Flags Over Texas (a large amusement park), and Turnpike Stadium, the home of the Dallas-Fort Worth ball teams.

ARLINGTON, Va. City (pop. 152,599), seat of Arlington Co., northern Va. on the Potomac River. The city has long been a heavily populated suburb of Washington, D.C. which is located across the river. The area was ceded by Virginia to the U.S. government (1789) as a part of the District of Columbia, but it was returned to the state in 1846. The area west of the city is farmland and noted for the breeding of horses. Arlington is the site of the Pentagon, ARLINGTON NATIONAL CEMETERY and Arlington House.

ARLINGTON NATIONAL CEMETERY, Arlington, Va. A national cemetery located across the POTOMAC RIVER from Washington, D.C. The Department of the Army maintains this federal burial ground, which covers some 420 acres with more than 90,000 grave sites. The majority of those buried there are U.S. soldiers killed in the line of duty. Other graves found there include those of President John F. Kennedy, generals George Marshall, John Pershing, and Phillip Sheridan, and Admiral Robert Peary. The Tomb of the Unknown Soldier is located here. The land was originally part of the Arlington House estate, built by playwright George Custis, the adopted son of George Washington, whose daughter married Confederate general Robert E. Lee. During the Civil War, Union troops seized Arlington House, turning it into a hospital and in 1864 into a military cemetery. The house became the property of the federal government in 1883. Arlington House, also know as the Custis-Lee Mansion, is open to visitors. Thousands come to the cemetery each year for the annual Memorial Day observance.

ARMISTEAD, Lewis Addison (New Bern, N.C., Feb. 18, 1817 — Gettysburg, Pa., July 3, 1863). Confederate general. At Gettysburg he commanded a brigade in the famous charge of GEN. GEORGE PICKETT, which gravely penetrated the Union lines. He was mortally wounded and where he fell a monument stands indicating "the high tide" of the Confederacy.

Louis and Lil Armstrong with the King Oliver Band

ARMSTRONG, Louis Daniel "Satchmo" (New Orleans, La., July 4, 1900 — New York, N.Y., July 6, 1971). Black jazz musician. Though his musical education was mostly self-taught, he took trumpet lessons from noted jazz artist Joe "King" Oliver, and became an accomplished player of that instrument, as well as the bugle, clarinet, and cornet. He made his professional debut in 1917 as a trumpeter with the "Kid" Ory band in New Orleans and, in 1922, joined the Creole Jazz Band in Chicago. Organizing his own band in 1925, he soon earned a reputation as one of the foremost jazz trumpeters of all time as well as an outstanding jazz vocalist. He made several successful international tours and recorded some 1,500 pieces, including *Ain't Misbehavin'* and *Tiger Rag,* as well as appearing in several motion pictures, including *High Society* (1956). He published his autobiography, *Satchmo, My Life in New Orleans* (1954).

ARMSTRONG, Samuel Chapman (Maui, Haw., Jan. 30, 1839 — Hampton, Va., May 11, 1893). Educator. The son of missionaries, he graduated from Williams College. During the Civil War he commanded black troops and in 1868 was instrumental in persuading the American Missionary Association to set up Hampton Normal and Agricultural Institute. Established as a school to provide vocational training for emancipated slaves, it later admitted American Indians. Armstrong was head of the institute until his death.

ARNALL, Ellis Gibbs (Newnan, Ga., March 20, 1907 —). Politician. A graduate of the University of Georgia Law School (1931), he served in the state legislature of Georgia (1933-37) and was assistant attorney general and then attorney general (1939-43) before his election as governor (1943-47). A liberal, he wrote *The Shore Dimly Seen* (1946) and *What the People Want* (1948).

ASHEBORO, N.C. City (pop. 15,252), seat of Randolph Co., central North Carolina. Founded in 1779 and chartered in 1796, it developed industrially because of the waterpower furnished by the DEEP and UHARIE rivers. There is diversified farming with such major products as corn, tobacco, and wheat. Manufactures include chairs, hosiery, and shoes.

ASHEVILLE, N.C. City (pop. 53,281), seat of Buncombe Co., west central North Carolina, in the Appalachian Mountains at the junction of the FRENCH BROAD and SWANNANOA rivers. It is the eastern gateway to the Great Smoky Mountains National Park and the Cherokee Indian Reservation. The area was settled in 1794 by John Burton, who originally named it Morristown. It was later renamed for Gov. Samuel Ashe. With the arrival of the Western North Carolina Railroad in 1880, the city became a market for livestock and tobacco goods. Asheville was incorporated as a town (1797) and a city (1883). Manufactures include textiles, paper products, and furniture. The city is the birthplace of author Thomas WOLFE, whose home is preserved as a memorial, and is the site of the Biltmore estate, the home of George W. Vanderbilt, which has grounds designed by the famous landscape architect, Frederick Law Olmsted.

ASHLAND, Ky. City (pop. 27,064), Boyd Co., in the northeastern corner of the state, close to the tri-state border with Ohio and West Virginia. Settled in 1786 and once the main route to the isolated parts of several nearby states, Ashland later became the heart of early Kentucky iron production. Incorporated in 1870, it was linked by the Chesapeake and Ohio railroads to other major cities and became important to the statewide industrial economy. It was the home of Henry CLAY, whose plantation gives the town its name.

ASHLEY, William Henry (Powhatan County, Va., c. 1778 — Cooper City, Mo., Mar. 26, 1838). Fur trader, explorer, and Congressman. He gained financially from the War of 1812 by his manufacture of gunpowder and mining of lead. He was elected lieutenant governor of Missouri in 1820, and in 1822 entered into a fur-trading business that expanded and prospered despite sharp opposition from Indians. He developed a flexible method of gathering furs at rendezvous points, rather than at fixed trading posts, extending trapping south, north, and into the Rockies. An intrepid adventurer, he was the first to travel the Green River of Wyoming, considered today practically unnavigable, doing so in buffalo skin boats loaded with hides and supplies for his trappers. Defeated for governor (1824) and senator (1829), he was elected to Congress in 1831 on an anti-Jackson ticket. In Congress (1831-37) he promoted expansion west and opposed compromise on Indian issues.

ASHLEY RIVER, S.C. River originating in Berkeley Co., with a length of some 60 miles. It runs generally south to the coast, where it joins the COOPER RIVER at CHARLESTON to drain into the Atlantic Ocean.

ASSATEAGUE ISLAND, Md. Worcester Co. A 22-mile island along the coasts of Maryland and Virginia, in southeastern Maryland, situated between CHINCOTEAGUE BAY and the Atlantic Ocean. Largely undeveloped, the island has been preserved in its natural coastal wilderness state and offers a national seashore and state park, and a refuge for wild ponies.

ATAKAPA INDIANS ("man eaters"). Tribe of Tunican linguistic stock that lived along the coast of Louisiana and in Texas up to Trinity Bay. Although generally friendly with settlers, they gained a sinister reputation because they at times ate the flesh of their enemies.

ATCHAFALAYA Bay, La. Inlet of the Gulf of Mexico, in southern Louisiana. It is the terminus of the ATCHAFALAYA RIVER.

ATCHAFALAYA RIVER, La. River rising in eastern Louisiana, where it branches from the RED RIVER. One of the MISSISSIPPI RIVER's primary branches in Louisiana, it is a navigable waterway that flows generally southward approximately 170 miles to empty into ATCHAFALAYA BAY. The river passes through several lakes, and many flood control projects have been constructed along its course.

ATHENS, Ala. City (pop. 14,558), seat of Limestone Co., northern Alabama, near the Tennessee border. Settled in 1814 and incorporated in 1818, it is situated in a farming region. During the Civil War, Union troops sacked and occupied the city in 1862, holding it until Gen. N. B. Forrest recaptured it for the Confederacy in 1864. Present industries include sawmills, gristmills, and cotton gins.

ATHENS, Ga. City (pop. 49,549), seat of Clarke Co., in northeastern Georgia, 70 miles east of Atlanta. Athens was created in 1801 as the seat of the University of Georgia and incorporated in 1872. The Navy Supply School was later moved to Athens. Located in rich farmland, it is the hub of regional trade and local manufacturing. Athens contains many homes dating from the early 1800s, including the

Henry Grady Residence, the Benjamin Hill Home, now housing the president of the University, and the Joseph H. Lumpkin House, where the first garden club in the United States was organized.

ATLANTA, Ga. City (pop. 425,022), state capital and seat of Fulton Co., in north central Georgia. Sometimes referred to as the "Dogwood City" because of the thousands of beautiful dogwoods that bloom here every spring, Atlanta is most important as the communications and transportation capital of the southeastern U.S. Major employers in Atlanta are the government, transportation, communications, banking, insurance, and retailing sectors as well as many manufacturers of pulp and paper products, automobiles, textiles, chemicals, steel, candy, and fertilizers. The city has a business population of over 1,000 companies and is the headquarters for many major corporations, including Coca-Cola. It is known as a tourist and convention capital because its many hotels and meeting and entertainment facilities attract people from all over the world.

The Creek Indians originally occupied the present site of Atlanta, which was founded in 1837 as the southern terminus of a railroad being built northward to Chattanooga, Tenn. Originally known as Terminus, and then as Marthasville (after the daughter of a railroad official), Atlanta was given its present name in 1845 and incorporated as a city in 1847.

It was the railroad that put Atlanta on the map, even in its early years. By the outbreak of the Civil War, Atlanta had developed into a major rail center. The city was burned by Union Gen. William Tecumseh SHERMAN (1864) on his famous "march to the sea." He destroyed Atlanta because it was the central point from which goods and troops could be shipped to all parts of the South. By razing this strategic rail center, Sherman believed he could bring the South to its knees. The destruction of Atlanta did indeed contribute to the ultimate victory of northern forces, but it also gave Atlanta a new start in life. After the Civil War, many Southern cities returned to business as usual, processing and exporting cotton and other crops. Few of them experienced any measure of prosperity. Atlanta, instead, rebuilt its transportation facilities completely for new growth in a modern era. As the headquarters for federal government activities during RECONSTRUCTION, new blood and considerable money

A 1909 delivery truck for the Coca-Cola Company, which was founded in Atlanta, Ga. in 1886

was brought into Atlanta. Both newcomers from the North and native Atlantans labored to rebuild the city. In 1877 Atlanta became the permanent state capital. In the years to come it remained a city constantly on the move, thanks to its extensive rail lines.

These rail lines still play an important role in Atlanta's economy, but a modern-day highway system and one of the world's largest, most up-to-date airports also move a great deal of freight and a great number of passengers in and out of the city on a daily basis. Three daily newspapers are published here, and there are a large number of radio stations as well as commercial and educational television stations.

In 1973 Atlanta became the first major Southern city to elect a black mayor. Blacks account for two-thirds of the population, and the city is known for its long history of good relations between blacks and whites.

Atlanta is home to both the Atlanta Braves major league baseball team and the Atlanta Falcons football team. Visitors can enjoy the Atlanta Memorial Cultural Center and the High Museum of Art. Fort McPherson and Dobbins Air Force Base are located here, as is the Communicable Disease Center and the headquarters for the Sixth Federal Reserve District. Martin Luther King, Jr. is buried in Atlanta. Although few Civil War era buildings survive, visitors can see the State Capitol building, the Memorial Arts Center, and Wren's Nest, home of Uncle Remus creator Joel Chandler HARRIS. An educational center as well, Atlanta has more than twenty institutions of higher education, including AGNES SCOTT COLLEGE, EMORY UNIVERSITY, the GEORGIA INSTITUTE OF TECHNOLOGY, Oglethorpe College, Georgia State College, Atlanta University, MOREHOUSE COLLEGE, CLARK COLLEGE, Morris Brown College, and the Interdenominational Theological Center.

Rebuilding of railroad tracks amid the ruins of a locomotive roundhouse, Atlanta, Ga., 1865

ATLANTA, Siege of. Civil War action by the Union army that led to the fall of the Georgia capital on September 1, 1864. The Union force was commanded by Gen. William Tecumseh SHERMAN, who after taking and occupying the city ordered it burned in November, 1864.

Following the Confederate defeat at PEACHTREE CREEK on July 20, Sherman took up positions north and east of Atlanta by July 25. The Confederate troops in the city, under the command of Gen. John Bell HOOD, numbered 37,000, less than half of the Union strength. Throughout August, Sherman attempted to extend his lines around the city and cut off Hood's supply and escape routes. On August 31, Hood sent a force south of Atlanta to protect a rail link at Jonesboro. When this action failed, he prepared to evacuate Atlanta, which he did at 5:00 P.M. on September 1. Sherman pursued him south, but returned to Atlanta on September 4 because of the danger of overextending his own lines.

Hood later returned north and ineffectually attempted to harrass Sherman's occupation of Atlanta. Sherman's position, however, was indeed tenuous. He chose to advance rather than to retreat, evacuated the civilian population of Atlanta, and burned the city to protect his rear forces. Thus freed from the need to defend Atlanta, Sherman began his "MARCH TO THE SEA" across Georgia toward Savannah.

ATLANTIC INTRACOASTAL WATERWAY. Paralleling the Atlantic coast, it extends from Key West, Fla., to Massachusetts Bay. It is a toll-free route and utilizes sounds, bays, rivers, and canals. From Norfolk, Va., southward (1,134 mi.) it has relatively little commercial traffic and is used primarily by pleasure crafts. Deep-draft ocean-going vessels use only the northern route. Completely protected from the sea, it was important during World War II as a means to avoid coastal submarines. There is a controlled depth of 6.1 feet in the Dismal Swamp Canal (from Deep Creek, Va., to South Mills, N.C.) which has a lock lift of 12 feet at each end.

AUBURN UNIVERSITY. State-supported coed university located 116 miles southwest of Atlanta, Ga., in Auburn, Ala. The University also maintains a commuter campus at Montgomery, Ala., for the benefit of area residents.

The Auburn University at Auburn was founded in 1856, and was originally called the East Alabama Male College. In 1872 it was renamed the Alabama Polytechnic Institute and turned over to the state. The school became Auburn University in 1960 and its Montgomery campus was added in 1967. The main campus now has 1,871 acres and over 90 buildings.

Admission to the University is selective. Of freshmen admitted, 94% graduated in the top two-fifths of their high school class. A good selection of academic programs and courses is offered in the schools of Arts and Sciences, Agriculture, Architecture and Fine Arts, Business, Education, Engineering, Home Economics, Nursing, Pharmacy, and Veterinary Medicine.

While most of the undergraduates are from the South, 20% are from the North Central U.S., and 2% are from the Middle Atlantic states. Some 30% of Auburn graduates go on to full-time graduate study: 2% business school, 1% law, 2% medical, 1% dental. The University is among the nation's top 120 institutions producing dental school entrants. Fully 50% to 60% of all Auburn graduates pursue careers in business and industry.

Library: 1,085,000 volumes, 16,000 journal subscriptions, 7,500 records/tapes. Faculty: 1,076. Enrollment: 18,329 total graduate and undergraduate; 9,227 men, 6,671 women (full-time). Degrees: Bachelor's, Master's, Doctorate.

AUGUSTA, Ga. City (pop. 47,532), seat of Richmond Co., a port on the SAVANNAH RIVER, on the fall line where the Piedmont Plateau meets the coastal plain. James OGLETHORPE, who founded the state as a penal colony to rehabilitate debtors, settled the area in 1735 when he established a frontier trading post. It was incorporated as a town in 1789, and as a city in 1798. The city was the scene of many battles during the American Revolution, twice serving as the state capital during the war and again in 1786-98. The Georgia state convention ratified the U.S. Constitution there on January 2, 1798. Later the Confederacy operated its largest gunpowder factory in Augusta during the Civil War. (The 176-foot chimney still stands on the original site.) Augusta served as one of the South's earliest milling towns and still acts as an important center for cotton trading and textile manufacturing. Also important are local deposits of such minerals as kaolin and firebrick. Many of the city's offices, public buildings, and homes, reflecting Georgian and Classical Revival architecture, have been restored and are now open to the public. Clark Hill Dam, one of a series of 11 located above

Augusta for flood control and energy production, helps maintain water levels in the developing river port located below the city. Augusta State College, the University of Georgia School of Medicine, and Paine College are located here, and the Masters Invitational Golf Tournament is played here each April.

AUSTIN, Stephen Fuller (Austinville, Va., Nov 3, 1793 — Columbia, Tex., Dec. 27, 1836). Colonizer of Texas. The son of the prominent American businessman Moses Austin, Stephen Austin was raised in Missouri and in 1821 inherited a Texas land grant on the death of his father. With the consent of the Spanish governor of Mexico, he then settled 300 original families at San Felipe de Austin on the Gulf Coast. By 1834 his successful commercial and social planning had attracted another 750 American families to the settlement, and tensions between Mexicans and Americans threatened to erupt into outright war. A known spokesman for amicable relations with Mexico, Austin presented the settlers' grievances to the government in Mexico City in 1833, but he was then arrested in Santillo on his return trip. Released in 1835 without a trial, he returned to

Stephen Fuller Austin

Texas having given up hope for continuing relations with Mexico and joined in the military actions for independence. His change of heart came too late to please most Texans, and in 1836 they elected Sam Houston president of their independent republic over Austin, who died within the year while serving as secretary of state.

AUSTIN, Tex. City (pop. 345,496), state capital and seat of Travis Co., in central Texas on the Colorado River. An important educational, industrial, agricultural, and research center, Austin also has a great deal of manufacturing, producing such products as boats, defense items, candy, furniture, structural steel, brick and tile, and electronics equipment. Austin is also a convention city.

Austin was named for Stephen F. AUSTIN, the "Father of Texas." The city originally consisted of three Spanish missions, built near the present site of the city in 1730. Actual settlement of the site, called Waterloo, began in 1838. The town was incorporated in 1839, renamed Austin, and was selected to be the capital of the newly formed Republic of Texas. For two years the capital was moved to Houston because of Indian attacks and the threat of a Mexican invasion, but Austin citizens were successful in having the capital returned to their city in 1870.

Industry and commerce came to Austin after the Civil War, thanks to the arrival of the railroad and the city's proximity to the famous CHISHOLM TRAIL. A dam built across the Colorado River in 1893 made the city one of the first in the state to have its own electric plant.

Historical attractions include the granite state capitol and Austin's famous mercury vapor lamps, installed on 27 high towers in 1896. The O. Henry Museum, Texas Memorial Museum, and Elisabeth Ney Museum are here, as is the famous French Legation building (1841). Bergstrom Air Force Base is seven miles to the south. Nearby recreational areas include Lake Austin, Town Lake, and Barton Springs. Austin boasts its own orchestra and ballet society.

A major educational center, Austin is home to the University of TEXAS, the Texas state schools for the blind and deaf, the Episcopal Theological Seminary of the Southwest, Concordia Lutheran College, Huston-Tillotson College, and St. Edwards University.

AVERY ISLAND, La. Iberia Parish, southern Louisiana. A round island, approximately two miles in diameter, surrounded by swamps and sea marshes. Rock salt has been mined here since its discovery by white settlers in the late 18th century. Tabasco is also manufactured. Tourists flock to the island to visit Jungle Gardens, a collection of exotic flora, created by Edward Avery McIlhenny. There is also a sanctuary for water birds.

AVOYEL INDIANS ("people of the rocks," referring to their trading of flint with other tribes). Small Indian tribe of Muskogean linguistic stock. They lived in the area of Marksville, Louisiana.

AYLLON, Lucas Vasquez de (c. 1475, prob. Toledo, Spain — San Miguel de Guadalupe, Va.? N.C.? S.C.?, Oct. 18, 1526). Spanish explorer. In 1522 he explored the region of what is now CAPE FEAR, S.C. A year later he obtained a charter from Emperor Charles V of Spain to find a strait to the Spice Islands and permission to colonize. Ayllon examined the coast north of Florida prior to settling a colony (1526) that he named San Miguel de Guadalupe, which was disbanded after the founder's death in a fever epidemic. Its site was on a large river variously identified as the PEE DEE (S.C.), the SANTEE (S.C.), the CAPE FEAR (N.C.) and the JAMES (Va.). This settlement marked probably the first importation of slaves into the U.S.

B

BACON, Nathaniel (Suffolk, Eng., Jan. 2, 1647 — Gloucester Co., Va., Oct. 1676). Rebel leader. Bacon arrived in Virginia in the early 1670s after being discovered to be part of a plot to defraud a neighbor of a rightful inheritance. In Virginia, Bacon became a planter, dividing his time between two estates given him by his father. In 1676 he disagreed with his cousin Gov. William Berkeley's refusal to move against the Indians who were attacking the colony. Bacon set off against the Indians despite Berkeley's order to abandon the expedition. Instead, Bacon turned his forces against the governor in what became known as BACON'S REBELLION. Bacon died shortly afterwards of malaria and his rebellion fell apart.

BACON'S REBELLION. Popular rebellion led by Nathaniel BACON, which took place in Virginia in 1676. Following the failure of Governor Sir William BERKELEY to protect the Virginia frontier from Indian invasion, and angered at Berkeley's arbitrary rule, the people formed a force under Bacon's leadership. After two successful but unauthorized attacks against the Pamunkey, Susquehannah, and Occaneechie Indians, Bacon and his followers forced the Virginia Council to adopt reform measures, but Berkeley declared Bacon's group rebels and

Nathaniel Bacon confronts Governor William Berkeley

30

traitors. The rebels captured Jamestown, burned it, and forced Berkeley to flee. The rebellion collapsed after Bacon's untimely death from malaria and Berkeley returned to power.

BAGNELL DAM, Mo. Dam constructed by the U.S. Army Corps of Engineers on the Osage River in central Missouri, southwest of Jefferson City. One of the state's largest hydroelectric power sources (148 feet high, spanning 2,543 feet), it provides most of the electricity for the St. Louis region. Completed in 1931, it forms the Lake of the OZARKS.

BAILEY, Ann (Liverpool, Eng., 1742 — Gallia Co., Ohio, Nov. 22, 1825). Colonial heroine. She came to Virginia in the 1760s and, following the death of her first husband at the Battle of Point Pleasant, donned male clothing and became a scout. When Fort Lee was attacked by Indians in 1791, she rode, according to legend, 100 miles through remote, uninhabited territory to Fort Savannah and returned with needed ammunition.

BAKER, Howard Henry, Jr. (Huntsville, Tenn., Nov. 15, 1925 —). Politician. A graduate of the University of Tennessee College of Law in 1948, he set up practice in Knoxville (1949-66). He was elected as the first Republican senator from the state of Tennessee. An unsuccessful presidential candidate in 1980, Baker was appointed majority leader of the U.S. Senate in 1981, where he had previously served as Senate minority leader (1977-81). His role as vice chairman of the committee investigating the Watergate scandal during 1973 brought him national attention. Baker is the son-in-law of the late Sen. Everett Dirksen.

BALTIMORE, Lord (George Calvert) (Yorkshire, England, 1580 — London, England, Apr. 15, 1632). Proprietor of the Maryland colony. The first Lord Baltimore, George Calvert, was a 1597 graduate of Oxford who became a member of Parliament in 1609, was knighted in 1617, and became secretary of state to James I in 1619. In 1625 he converted to Catholicism in allegiance to the king, for which he was awarded the barony of Baltimore in Ireland. Long a member of both the New England and Virginia Companies, he had founded a colony in Newfoundland that failed in 1629 because of the severe climate there. Having petitioned for lands further south, he was awarded a grant north of the Potomac River in 1632, but died before the grant was finally approved.

His grant then passed to his son, the second Lord Baltimore, Cecilius Calvert (1605-1675). Beset by political difficulties stemming from his father's conversion to Catholicism, Cecilius Calvert never visited the grant. He assigned administrative responsibility to deputies, one his younger brother Leonard Calvert (1606-1647). It was under the authority of Cecilius Calvert that Maryland, named for the English queen, passed the first Act of Toleration (1649) to protect religious freedoms in the New World.

The third Lord Baltimore, Charles Calvert (1637-1715), was sent to Maryland as deputy governor in 1661 before succeeding to the title on the death of his father in 1675. After traveling to England in regard to border disputes, he ruled as resident governor from 1679-1684. During a second trip to England to resolve a bitter boundary dispute with William Penn, however, his provincial government was overthrown by a Protestant rebellion (1689), and because he was a Catholic the Anglican English authorities refused to recognize his rights to Maryland.

The fourth Lord Baltimore, Benedict Leonard Calvert (1679-1715), converted to Anglicanism in 1713 to restore the family's political fortunes, but he died only one month after his

George Calvert, the first Lord Baltimore and Proprietor of the Maryland Colony

father. In that month he did, however, regain the title to Maryland.

The fifth Lord Baltimore, Charles Calvert (1699-1751), went to Maryland in 1732. During his governorship he managed to settle the northern boundary dispute with William Penn by ceding 2.5 million acres to Pennsylvania.

The sixth Lord Baltimore, Frederick Calvert (1731-1771), was indifferent to Maryland affairs. He died without heirs in Naples, Italy, and the title passed to Henry Harford, thus ending 139 years of proprietorship by the Calvert family.

BALTIMORE, Md. City (pop. 786,775), 40 miles northeast of Washington, D.C., on the Patapsco River near Chesapeake Bay. The area was first settled in the 1660s and because of its natural deep harbor, soon became a tobacco port. The city, named for Charles Calvert, fifth Lord BALTIMORE, was chartered in 1729 and incorporated in 1796. It separated from Baltimore county in 1851 and became an independent governmental unit. Economic growth first occurred in the 1730s when there was a great demand for flour in Europe; the cultivation of tobacco was all but abandoned and grist mills began to spring up in the area.

During the Revolutionary War Baltimore was a shipbuilding center; this industry continued through the War of 1812 and World Wars I and II and still exists today. A unique sailing vessel, the Baltimore Clipper, was developed during the Revolution and was a favorite of privateers who preyed on British ships. The city was the site of Fort McHenry, which withstood a 30-hour English attack during the War of 1812, and was the inspiration for Francis Scott Key's "Star Spangled Banner."

Economic growth experienced in the early 1800s suffered a setback when the Erie Canal was completed in 1825. To offset the competition, a group of Baltimore businessmen organized the BALTIMORE & OHIO RAILROAD and the area's importance as a shipping center was gradually regained. The outbreak of the Civil War, during which the city remained with the Union, resulted in military occupation and numerous pro-South demonstrations because of its geographic location. The economic disruption caused by the war had not yet been overcome when, in 1904, a fire almost completely destroyed Baltimore's business district.

Modern development of the city dates from the "great fire." Along with rebuilding, a sewage system was established, streets were improved, and a water purification system was im-

plemented. World War I brought about increased demands on the city; exports of wheat and coal were expanded, and refineries were constructed to handle the importation of oil. The economic surge also brought about social changes—the sudden influx of industrial workers, both white and black, resulted in massive slum areas. This problem was not seriously attacked until the late 1940s, however, because of renewed demands made on the city during World War II. The area became involved in steel production; shipbuilding was accelerated; and Baltimore's harbor facilities were enlarged, making it a world-famous import-export center.

At the close of the war the city embarked on an urban renewal program to abolish its slums. In 1967 it was chosen as one of 63 U.S. cities to participate in a Model City Development program. Although ideally this program of coordinated civic, educational, and physical development was impressive, the late 1960s brought about racial demonstrations, and federal troops were needed to restore order. Despite the racial conflicts Baltimore continued to modernize and grow and it is now the 10th-largest city in the nation. Bethlehem Steel has become a major industrial establishment, and there has been an increase in the manufacture of copper and fertilizer, the refinement of sugar, and the production of highly technical commodities.

The city has long been an educational and cultural center in the U.S. Numerous institutions of higher learning are located here, principally JOHNS HOPKINS UNIVERSITY, Goucher College, Morgan State College, the Maryland Institute, the Peabody Institute, and several Catholic institutions.

Among Baltimore's numerous museums are the Baltimore Museum of Art, the Peale Museum (1814), the Walters Art Gallery, the Davis Planetarium, the B & O Transportation Museum, the home of Edgar Allan Poe, and the

Laying out the town of Baltimore, Md., in 1730

home of Babe Ruth. The Baltimore Symphony Orchestra is the oldest municipal orchestra in the country and the Baltimore Civic Opera was founded in 1932.

The city is the home of the Baltimore Orioles professional baseball team and the Baltimore Colts professional football team. The Preakness horse race, first run in 1873, is held annually at the city's nationally known Pimlico Racetrack.

BALTIMORE AND OHIO RAILROAD. The first public railroad in the United States, developed as a means of competing with the Erie Canal. The B&O was chartered in 1827 and the first 14 miles of track, running from Baltimore to Ellicott's Mills, were opened on May 22, 1830, using horses to pull the cars. Within a year the company switched to steam power when Peter Cooper produced the *Tom Thumb*, a one-ton steam locomotive that traveled 80 miles on a ton of coal. The *Tom Thumb* was pitted against a horsedrawn car in a famous contest and although the horsecar came in first the B&O company was sufficiently impressed to switch to steam. By 1833 special baggage cars and eight-wheeled passenger cars carrying 60 people had been added to the line. The B&O was extended to West Virginia in 1852, to Cincinnati and St. Louis in 1857, to Chicago in 1874, to Philadelphia in 1886, and to New York City in 1887.

BANANA RIVER, Fla. A 30-mile shallow lagoon located in Brevard Co., on the east central coast of the state. It separates Merritt Island and Cape Canaveral, and is connected on the north and south to the Indian River lagoon.

BANKHEAD, Tallulah Brockman (Huntsville, Ala., Jan. 31, 1903 — New York, N.Y., Dec. 12, 1968). Actress. Her flamboyant style and husky voice held wide audience appeal on stage and in the media of the mid-century. Her better known roles included plays *Dark Victory* (1934), *Rain* (1935), *The Little Foxes* (1939), and the film *Lifeboat* (1944). She was the daughter of William Brockman BANKHEAD.

BANKHEAD, William Brockman (Moscow, Ala., Apr. 12, 1874 — Washington, D.C., Sept. 15, 1940). Politician. Serving as a U.S. Representative from Alabama (1917-40), he became prominent under President Franklin D. Roosevelt. He was elected chairman of the House rules committee in 1934, Democratic floor leader in 1935, and speaker of the House

of Representatives in 1936. He was the father of Tallulah BANKHEAD.

BARATARIA BAY, La. Inlet of the Gulf of Mexico, in southeastern Louisiana, between the Mississippi River and LAFOURCHE BAYOU. It measures 12 by six miles and is the center of the state's shrimp industry. Barataria was a notorious shelter for pirates and smugglers under Jean Laffitte. PORT SULPHUR is on the bay.

BARBOURSVILLE, W.Va. Town (pop. 2,871), Cabell Co., in western West Virginia. It is a residential suburb of Huntington at the confluence of the Mud and Guyandot Rivers. The town was chartered in 1813.

BARDSTOWN, Ky. City (pop. 6,155), seat of Nelson Co., central Kentucky. It was here reportedly that Stephen Foster wrote "My Old Kentucky Home." Manufactures include bourbon, paper and plastic products as well as apparel.

BARKER, Mary Cornelia (Atlanta, Ga., Jan. 20, 1879 — Atlanta, Ga., Sept. 15, 1963). Educator, labor activist. A graduate of Agnes Scott College (1900), she taught (1904-22) and served as principal (1922-44) in the Atlanta public schools. A progressive educator and administrator, she was a firm supporter of teachers' rights and in 1905 helped found and lead the Atlanta Public School Teachers' Association. In 1919 Barker brought the APSTA into the American Federation of Teachers and served as national president of the AFT (1923, 1925).

BARKLEY, Alben William (Graves Co., Ky., Nov. 24, 1877 — Lexington, Va., Apr. 30, 1956). Vice President of the U.S. He began his career as a lawyer in Paducah, Ky.(1898), becoming prosecuting attorney of McCracken County in 1905, and county judge in 1909. A Democrat, he served seven successive terms in the U.S. House of Representatives (1913-27), and was elected to the U.S. Senate in 1926, where he served for 23 years, including a stint as the Senate majority leader (1937-46). Barkley was an influential supporter of Social Security measures, the Agricultural Adjustment Administration, the Rural Electrification Administration, and the Farm Security Administration. He served as Vice-President under Harry S. TRUMAN (1949-53), bringing to the post a reputation as one of the major planners of the Democratic New Deal of the 1930s. In 1952 he was nominated as a presidential candidate but withdrew because of concern about his age. He served in the Senate again from 1954 until his death.

BARKLEY, Lake, Ky. State's second-largest lake, covering 57,920 acres, in several counties in Kentucky's western lakes region, dipping into northern Tennessee. It is the primary feature of a 3,600-acre state resort park which is part of a Tennessee Valley Authority project, and is separated from its sister lake, the KENTUCKY, by the Land Between the Lakes.

BARNARD, Edward Emerson (Nashville, Tenn., Dec. 16, 1857 — Williams Bay, Wis., Feb. 6, 1923). Astronomer. He was astronomer at the Lick Observatory in California from 1887 to 1895, and then became professor of practical astronomy at the Yerkes Observatory at the University of Chicago. He won recognition from the Academy of Sciences of France and the Royal Astronomical Society of Great Britain for his discovery of 16 comets and Jupiter's fifth satellite (1892) and numerous other contributions to astronomy.

BARNES SOUND, Fla. Body of water in Dade Co., at the southeast tip of the state. Protected from the Atlantic by the island of Key Largo, it is connected to the north with Biscayne Bay and to the south with Florida Bay.

BARNETT, Ross Robert (Carthage, Miss., 1898 —). Politician. Governor of Mississippi from 1960 to 1964, Barnett, a segregationist, became nationally known when he refused to allow James Meredith, a black, admission to the all-white University of Mississippi. This refusal in 1962 violated a federal court order, and federal troops were sent in to quell the ensuing riots.

BARNEY, Joshua (Baltimore, Md., July 6, 1759 — Pittsburgh, Pa., Dec. 1, 1818). Naval officer. Barney served with distinction during the American Revolution. Captured three times by the British, his accomplishments included the capture of the British warship *General Monk* in Delaware Bay in 1782. He also served heroically during the War of 1812, when he was responsible for hindering the British advance on Washington.

BARRETT, Janie Porter (Athens, Ga., Aug. 9, 1865 — Hampton, Va., Aug. 27, 1948). Social reformer. The daughter of black slaves, she graduated from Hampton Institute (1884), decided on a life of social service, and began teaching (1884-89). In 1890 she founded the Locust Street Social Settlement, a vocational center for black girls. In 1908 she was elected president of the Virginia State Federation of Colored Women's Clubs. Barrett served as resident superintendent of the Virginia Industrial School for Colored Girls in Richmond (1914-40). In 1930 she participated in the White House Conference on Child Health and Protection.

BARRETT, Kate Harwood Waller (Falmouth, Va., Jan. 24, 1857 — Alexandria, Va., Feb. 23, 1925). Social reformer. Earning an M.D. at Women's Medical College of Georgia (1892), in 1893 she established a home for unwed mothers in Atlanta, which became the fifth Florence Crittenton Home. She then served as vice-president and general superintendent (1895-1909) and then president (1909-25) of the National Florence Crittenton Mission. Barrett redirected the organization from its evangelical attempts to convert prostitutes to providing pre-natal care and vocational counseling.

BARRON, James (Hampton, Va., 1769 — Norfolk, Va., Apr. 21, 1851). Naval officer. After serving in the Virginia Navy he became a lieutenant in the U.S. Navy in 1798. He attained the rank of commodore in 1807, and his flagship, the *Chesapeake*, was involved in a confrontation with the British *Leopard*. The incident resulted in Barron's court-martial and, though later reinstated, his remaining years in the military were served under a cloud of doubt and suspicion. Believing that Stephen DECATUR was responsible for his troubles, Barron challenged him to a duel in 1820, which ended with Decatur's death.

BARROWS, Katherine Isabel Hayes Chapin (Irasburg, Vt., Apr. 17, 1845 — Croton-on-Hudson, N.Y., Oct. 25, 1913). Ophthalmologist, social reformer. Widowed, she returned from missionary work in India for medical studies. Then, with an agreement with her second husband, she went on to complete medical education in New York City and in Vienna, returning as an eye surgeon. The couple moved to Cambridge, Mass. in 1871. In 1880 she gave up medical practice to aid her husband in his many prison-reform and editorial activities and continued these after his death, in 1909 serving as a delegate to the International Prison Congress in Paris.

BARTHOLOMEW BAYOU, La. River originating in Pine Bluff, Ark., that runs through the southern half of that state to enter northern Louisiana, passing Bastrop. There it merges with the OUACHITA RIVER. Total length is 140 miles.

BARTON, Clara (Oxford, Mass., Dec. 25, 1821 — Glen Echo, Md., Apr. 12, 1912). Founder of the American Red Cross. She created the "American Amendment" to the constitution of the Red Cross, providing aid in all severe crises, not just in war. Initially a teacher, after 18 years she went to Washington, D.C., to work in the Patent Office. During the Civil War she voluntarily acquired and distributed supplies for the wounded. After the war she organized a bureau of records in Washington to locate missing soldiers. During the Franco-Prussian war she helped victims of the war as a member of the International Red Cross. Returning to the United States in 1873, she worked to organize the American National Red Cross, becoming its first president (1881-1904). Author of several histories of the Red Cross, she also worked to bring the U.S. into the Geneva Convention.

BARTRAM, William (Kingsessing, now Philadelphia, Pa., Feb. 9, 1739 — Kingsessing, Pa., July 22, 1823). Naturalist. The son of John Bartram, a distinguished botanist, he joined his father in a botanical excursion and exploration of eastern Florida in 1765. He was later employed in botanical exploration and collections in Georgia and the Carolinas. In 1791, Bartram published an account of his travels, including descriptions of the CREEK, CHOCTAW, and CHEROKEE Indians and vivid accounts of the American wilderness, which influenced writers such as Samuel Taylor Coleridge and William Wordsworth. He made one of the first complete tables of American ornithology.

BARUCH, Bernard Mannes (Camden, S.C., Aug. 19, 1870 — New York, N.Y., June 20, 1965). Financier and presidential adviser. Beginning as an office boy at 19, he accumulated a fortune through his speculations on Wall Street. Baruch was appointed by President Woodrow Wilson to the advisory commis-

sion of the Council of National Defense in 1916. He was chairman of the War Industries Board during World War I, and a member of the Economic Council at Versailles. Baruch was adviser to President Franklin Roosevelt on wartime economic mobilization during World War II, and after the war helped formulate United Nations policies, particularly concerning the use of atomic energy.

BARUCH, Simon (Schwersen, now in Poland, July 29, 1840 — June 3, 1921). Physician. A Confederate army surgeon (1862-65), he practiced in South Carolina and later in New York City following the war's end. Baruch established the first U.S. municipal bathhouses in Chicago and New York City.

BASS, Mary Elizabeth (Carley, Miss., April 5, 1876 — New Orleans, La., Jan. 26, 1956). Physician, feminist. A graduate of Woman's Medical College of Pennsylvania (1900), in 1908 she helped found the New Orleans Hospital and Dispensary for Women and Children and became one of the first two women on Tulane's medical school faculty (1911-41). She served as first vice-president (1919-25) and president (1925-27) of the Women Physicians of the Southern Medical Association and as president of the American Medical Women's Association (1921-22). She wrote widely about women in medicine, including a column in the *Journal of the American Medical Women's Association* (1946-56).

BASS, Sam (Mitchell, Ind., July 21, 1851 — Round Rock, Tex., July 21, 1878). Bandit and folklore figure. He moved to Texas about 1870 and pursued various jobs, including deputy sheriff, until 1875, when he became a "Robin Hood" type stage and train robber. On September 19, 1877, his gang allegedly made away with $65,000 in the Big Spring Union Pacific train robbery. He was sought by Texas Rangers and later fatally shot by them.

BASSETT, John Spencer (Tarboro, N.C., Sept. 10, 1867 — Washington, D.C., Jan. 27, 1928). Historian. He founded and edited the *South Atlantic Quarterly* (1902), a Southern critical magazine. A history professor at Trinity College (now Duke University) from 1893 to 1906, he then went to Smith College, Northampton, Mass. Bassett published many works of history and biography, including *The Federalist System, 1789-1801* (1906), *The Life* *of Andrew Jackson* (1911), *The Middle Group of American Historians* (1917), and *Expansion and Reform, 1889-1926* (1926).

BASSETT, Richard (Bohemia Manor, Delaware, Apr. 2, 1745 — Bohemia Manor, Delaware, Sept. 15, 1815). Politician. He signed the federal constitution and backed its ratification in Delaware. Elected to the Delaware legislature, he served as U.S. senator (1789-93), governor (1799-1801), and was later appointed by President John Adams as "midnight judge" with the U.S. circuit court.

BATE, William Brimage (Castalian Springs, Tenn., Oct. 7, 1826 — Washington, D.C., Mar. 9, 1905). Army officer and politician. He served in both the Mexican War and the Confederate army, starting as a private and working his way up to major general. Bate was governor of Tennessee (1882-86) and served in the U.S. Senate (1887-1905).

BATES, Edward (Belmont, Va., Sept. 4, 1793 — St. Louis, Mo., Mar. 25, 1869). Lawyer and attorney general. From a Quaker family, he was a Southerner who freed his own slaves. Beginning practice in law (1821), he was elected in Missouri to the House of Representatives for one term (1826-28). Proposed as an antislavery candidate for President by the Republicans (1860), he gained 48 votes, but withdrew in favor of Abraham Lincoln, who appointed him attorney general in 1861.

BATON ROUGE, La. City (pop. 219,486), state capital (1849) and seat of East Baton Rouge Parish, southeast central Louisiana. A port at the head of deepwater navigation on the Mississippi River, set on high bluffs, the area was settled in 1719 by the French. They built and garrisoned a fort there, naming the site for a red cypress tree that marked a boundary set between Indian tribes. The area was ceded to Britain in 1763 at the end of the French and Indian Wars, but was taken over by the Spanish during the American Revolution when they overpowered a British garrison there in the First Battle of Baton Rouge in September, 1779. In 1800 the Spanish ceded the land to France and Napoleon sold the territory to the U.S. in 1813. However, the Spanish continued to claim the land along with western Florida. Area citizens rebelled against the Spanish control in the Second Battle of Baton Rouge on September 23, 1810 and established the West-

ern Florida Republic, which was annexed to the U.S. three months later. The city was incorporated in 1817. During the Civil War it was captured and almost continuously held by Union troops.

The construction of Standard Oil's major refinery in 1909 played a key role in the city's industrial development, leading the way for many other businesses to transfer there. It is attractive economically because of its abundant natural resources and proximity to the ocean and river; industrial plants now line both sides of the Mississippi all the way down to New Orleans. The city still has much of its old Spanish charm, and there are a number of antebellum plantations nearby. The main campus of Louisiana State University is here, and Southern University is located five miles north of the city.

BAXTER, Elisha (Rutherford, Co., N.C., Sept. 1, 1827 — Batesville, Ark., May 31, 1899). Politician and jurist. Major figure in Arkansas government during the RECONSTRUCTION era. His career was tied closely to that of Joseph Brooks, whom he defeated in his run for the governorship in 1872. Baxter fought for an amendment to restore Southern white privileges.

BAY SAINT LOUIS, Miss. Town (pop. 7,891), seat of Hancock Co., western Mississippi. A winter resort popular because of its location on the bay of the Gulf of Mexico. The land for the settlement was granted by the Spanish government in 1789 and the town was founded as Shieldsborough. It developed first as a summer retreat for wealthy Natchez farmers. It now manufactures electric appliances, and plastic and metal products. There is also logging and seafood packing.

BAYLOR, Robert Emmet Bledsoe (Lincoln or Bourbon Co., Ky., May 10, 1791 — Washington Co., Tex., Dec. 30, 1873). Judge and Baptist leader. Baylor was a member of the Kentucky and Alabama legislatures before becoming a Supreme Court judge in Texas. In that capacity, he helped draft the state constitution. He was co-founder of the first Baptist College in Texas, later named BAYLOR UNIVERSITY. An associate justice of the Texas supreme court, Baylor helped draft the state constitution.

BAYLOR UNIVERSITY Independent Baptist coed institution located on a 300-acre campus in the central Texas city of Waco. Founded in 1845, Baylor is the oldest Texas university in continuous operation and it is regarded as one of the nation's most important church-related institutions. It is named after Texas jurist Robert E. B. BAYLOR. This strongly Baptist, somewhat conservative university was originally located in Independence, Tex., but moved to Waco in 1886. The Waco campus is the site of the Colleges of Arts and Sciences, the Graduate School, and the Schools of Nursing, Law, Music, Business, and Education. The Medical and Dental Schools are based in Dallas and Houston. There is also a school of Nursing in Dallas.

Academic emphasis is on liberal arts and sciences, religion, education, law, nursing, business, computer and engineering science, predentistry and premedicine. There are over 100 major areas of study and 35 degree programs. The South provides 80% of the student and over 30% of graduates pursue full-time graduate study.

Library: 961,567 volumes, 89,000 microform titles, 7,756 journal subscriptions, 13,500 records/tapes. Faculty: 485. Enrollment: 10,067 total graduate and undergraduate: 3,875 men, 4,549 women (full-time). Degrees: Bachelor's, Master's, Doctorate.

BAYOGOULA INDIANS ("bayou people"). Tribe of Muskogean linguistic stock that lived in the area of Iberville Parish, Louisiana, used the alligator as their tribal emblem, and were the first Indians encountered by IBERVILLE in 1699.

BAYOU BOEUF RIVER, La. Broad tributary of the ATCHAFALAYA RIVER, which runs near Morgan City. Its name is said to have originated when a cattleboat sunk (boeuf is the French word for cattle). In 1869 the skeletal remains of an ancient mastodon were discovered in the river valley.

BAYOU PIERRE RIVER, Miss. Branch of the Mississippi River, originating near Port Gibson at the Louisiana border. It arcs 70 miles first east then south, and terminates north of Brookhaven.

BAYOU TECHE RIVER, La. Waterway in south central Louisiana. New Iberia is one of the chief communities on the banks of this bayou, which runs through the sugar cane belt and is noted for its fish and wildlife. Once lined with large plantations, Bayou Teche was the setting for Longfellow's *Evangeline*, with a commemorative area in St. Martinsville.

BAYOUS. Creeks, minor rivers, and secondary water courses that have little or no current and are usually marshy and sluggish. The term is primarily used in the Gulf Coast and lower Mississippi and Louisiana regions. The word is an adaptation of the Choctaw Indian word "bayuk." Without inlets and outlets they tend to turn into a marshy swamp and eventually disappear.

BAYTOWN, Tex. City (pop. 43,980), Harris Co., southeastern Texas on Galveston Bay. It is an industrial center with oil refineries, petroleum, and synthetic rubber plants, and steel plate mills. Originally settled in 1822, the unincorporated community became part of adjoining Pelling in 1845. Pelly and Goose Creek were later consolidated to form the present city of Baytown, which was incorporated in 1948. Oil was discovered here in 1916 and is still shipped from the Houston Ship Channel at Baytown. Lee College was founded here in 1934.

BEACH, Amy Marcy Cheney (Henniker, N.H., Sept. 5, 1867 — New York, N.Y., Dec. 27, 1944). Composer and concert pianist. A child prodigy, in 1883 she premiered as a concert pianist in Boston to critical praise. In 1892 her *Mass* in E flat major became the first woman's composition performed by the prestigious Handel and Haydn Society of Boston, as was her *Eilende Wolken* (Opus 18) for the New York Symphony. Her reputation was solidified with a commission to write the *Festival Jubilate* for the 1892 World Columbian Exposition in Chicago. Beach toured Europe to critical and popular acclaim (1911-14). Her 150 works have generally been discussed with those of the Boston classicists, well constructed, late romantic with broad melodies and beautiful harmonies. Her *Gaelic Symphony* (Opus 32) and Browning songs are still popular.

BEAN, Roy (Mason Co., Ky., 1825 — Langtry, Tex., Mar. 16, 1903). Frontier lawman. A justice of the peace, he was known as "the law west of the Pecos," having set up a court in his saloon, with a lawbook and a six-shooter. In 1896 he staged the Fitzsimmons-Maher heavyweight boxing championship fight on a sandbar in the Rio Grande after Texas refused to permit the licensing of the contest.

BEAUMONT, Tex. City (pop. 118,102), seat of Jefferson Co., 28 miles from the Gulf of Mexico at the head of navigation of the NECHES RIVER, 16 miles from Port Arthur, and 70 miles from Galveston. The second-largest port in Texas and a prime location of the oil industry, Beaumont's industries include petrochemicals, shipping, ship and barge construction, manufacture of drill and pipeline equipment, and the milling of rice products. The railroad expansion of the 1890s, which brought five lines to the area, and the discovery of the SPINDLETOP oil well nearby in 1901, brought prosperity to the city. A shipping depot for timber and African slaves before the Civil War, little growth occurred in Beaumont until the turn of the century, when the population went from less than 10,000 in 1900 to more than 50,000 in 1925. Chartered in 1881, Beaumont houses its own art museum and symphony orchestra as well as Lamar State College (1923).

BEAUREGARD, Pierre Gustave Toutant (St. Bernard Parish, La., May 28, 1815 — New Orleans, La., Feb. 20, 1893). Confederate general. He graduated from West Point Military Academy in 1838, served in the Mexican War (1846-48), and became superintendent of West Point in 1861. After serving only five days he was removed because of his declaration of loyalty to Louisiana if the state seceded from the Union. He resigned from the United States Army and was appointed brigadier general in the Confederate army, directing the attack on FORT SUMTER that began the Civil War. Under Gen. Joseph E. JOHNSTON he was responsible for the Confederate victory at the first battle of BULL RUN in 1861. The following year he succeeded to the command of Gen. Albert Sydney Johnston (who was killed at Shiloh) and retreated to Corinth, Miss. Later Beauregard defended Charleston against the siege by Union forces, blocked Gen. Benjamin F. Butler's move up the James River to Richmond, Va., and held Petersburg, Va., against Ulysses S. Grant. When the war ended, he was with Gen. Joseph E. Johnston in North Carolina. After the war he became president of the Jackson and Mississippi Railroad and director of the Louisiana State Lottery, refusing offers to command the armies of Roumania and the Khedive of Egypt. He wrote several books, including *Principles and Maxims of the Art of War* (1863) and

A Commentary on the Campaign of Manassas (1891).

BEAVER DAM, Ark. Dam on the WHITE RIVER of northwest Arkansas, in the Ozark region, creating the 30,000-acre Beaver Lake. The dam was constructed by the U.S. Army Corps of Engineers as a hydroelectric power project.

BEAVER RESERVOIR, Ark. This 30,000-acre reservoir, designed and constructed by the U.S. Army Corps of Engineers, is located near Rogers. With a shoreline measuring 483 miles, it offers a variety of water sports and camping facilities.

BECKLEY, W.Va. City (pop. 20,492), and seat of Raleigh Co. in southern West Virginia. This coal mining center is nicknamed the "smokeless coal capital of the world." Local factories produce electronic devices, mining machinery and supplies, as well as dairy and food products. Lumber is another important industry.

BEECH FORK RIVER, Ky. Offshoot of the Rolling Fork River. It begins at Boston in central Kentucky, travels in an east-southeast direction for more than 50 miles, and terminates near Lincoln Homestead Park.

BELL, John (Nashville, Tenn., Feb. 15, 1797 — Dover, Tenn., Sept. 10, 1869). Senator, Secretary of War, and presidential candidate. He favored slavery but opposed secession, and supported President Abraham Lincoln until the firing on FORT SUMTER. He began law practice in 1814, was elected to the state senate (1817), and to the House of Representatives (1827-41), where he was speaker (1834-35). A Democrat in 1827, Bell broke with the party's leader, Andrew Jackson, in 1834 and became a Whig in 1836. Due to his work for the party, President William H. Harrison appointed him secretary of War (1841), but after Harrison's death he returned to private life. Bell was again elected to the Senate (1847), where he, although a slaveholder, opposed the expansion of slavery and supported the Compromise of 1850. Because of his vigorous Unionism he was nominated by the Constitutional Union Party for President (1860). He took no part in the Civil War.

BELLE GLADE, Fla. Town (pop. 15,535), Palm Beach Co., southeastern Florida, near the southern tip of Lake Okeechobee. Settled in 1925 and incorporated in 1928, it was almost completely destroyed by a 1928 hurricane that killed hundreds. Today Belle Glade is a center for the surrounding truck farming region. Cattle are also raised here.

BELLE GROVE, Battle of. See CEDAR CREEK, Battle of.

BELMONT, Battle of. The second engagement in the western theater of the Civil War, fought November 7, 1861, on the west bank of the Mississippi in the southeast corner of Missouri.

On November 1, Gen. Ulysses S. GRANT was ordered to move his 3,000 Union troops south from their camp in Cairo, Illinois, to threaten a Confederate camp of 4,000 troops in Columbus, Kentucky. On November 6, Grant received an erroneous report that the Confederates planned to cross the river and amass at Belmont. On the basis of this information Grant attacked Belmont on November 7, when he routed the Confederates from their camp. The Confederates fell back to the river, where they were protected by artillery fire across the Mississippi from Columbus, where the main body of the Confederate force had remained the entire time. Although victorious, Grant, in his first Civil War battle, is thought by some to have needlessly endangered his troops in an attack on an unimportant position, motivated by misinformation.

BELTON, Mo. City (pop. 12,708), Cass Co., south of Kansas City. Founded in 1871, it is best known as the home and burial place of temperance leader Carrie NATION. There is a garment factory, and local farms produce corn, oats, and wheat. A U.S. Air Force base is nearby.

BENJAMIN, Judah Philip (St. Croix, Virgin Islands, Aug. 6, 1811 — Paris, France, May 6, 1884). Lawyer and statesman. Brought to Charleston, S.C., as a child, he was educated at Yale College and practiced law in New Orleans, La. He became prominent in politics, first as a member of the Whig Party and then as a Democrat. He served as Louisiana's U.S. Senator from 1852 until 1861, when that state seceded from the Union, and he became Confederate attorney general, secretary of war, and secretary of state during the Civil War years. When Confederate President Jefferson Davis

was captured (1865), Benjamin fled to Great Britain, where he resumed his law practice and was appointed a queen's counsel in 1872. He was regarded as one of the most learned members of the British bar and his *Treatise on the Law of Sale of Personal Property* (1868) was considered a legal classic there.

BENNETT, Belle Harris (Whitehall, Ky., Dec. 3, 1852 — Richmond, Ky., July 20, 1922). Social reformer. In 1892 she became head of the Woman's Parsonage and Hope Mission Society, in 1896 was elected president of the Home Mission Society, and in 1898 president of the Women's Board of Home Missions. She soon extended the Mission's work to social justice for the urban poor, recent immigrants, blacks, and workers. She campaigned vigorously against racial prejudice, for women's suffrage, child labor reform, and lay rights within the Southern Methodist Church. Bennett was the first woman delegate to the Southern Methodist General Conference (1922) and served as president of the Women's Missionary Council for foreign missions (1910-22).

BENNETT SPRINGS, Mo. Dallas and LaClede Co. Vacation spot on the NIANGUA RIVER in central Missouri. The sixth-largest spring in the state, it has a flow of approximately 95,000,000 gallons a day over a six-foot dam. It is part of a 574-acre state park, which includes a fish hatchery. An annual hillbilly festival is held here each June.

BENT, Charles (Charleston, W.Va., Nov. 11, 1799 — Taos, N.M., Jan. 19, 1847). Pioneer and fur trader. From 1828-1832, with his brother William, he built and operated Bent's Fort, a famous trading post on the banks of the Arkansas River near what is now La Junta, Colorado. He was appointed civil governor of New Mexico in 1846, and a year later he was assassinated during a Mexican and Pueblo Indian uprising.

BENT, William (St. Louis, Mo., May 23, 1809 — Boggsville, N.M., May 19, 1869). Frontiersman. A younger brother of noted trader Charles BENT, he managed Bent's Fort, sometimes called Fort William in his honor, for many years. He was a well-known and respected trader in the West. He has been called the first resident of Colorado.

BENTON, Thomas Hart "Old Bullion" (Hillsboro, N.C., Mar. 14, 1782 — Washington, D.C., Apr. 10, 1858). Democratic Party leader and writer. He spent his early years in Tennessee as a lawyer. After serving in the War of 1812, however, Benton moved to St. Louis, Mo. where for two years (1818-20) he was the editor of the *Missouri Enquirer*. He was elected to the U.S. Senate in 1821 and served for 30 years, becoming the chief spokesman for the Jacksonians in the upper house. He crusaded for the distribution of public lands to settlers and westward expansion. In the 1830s he led a successful fight to dissolve the Bank of the United States, supported hard money (as opposed to uncertain specie) and advocated a federal independent treasury. He believed in the abolition of slavery, and this unpopular stance cost him political support in Missouri.

BENTONVILLE, Ark. City (pop. 8,756), seat of Benton Co., extreme northwest Arkansas, on the Ozark Plateau. Settled in 1837, it is a prime shipping point for poultry, and its manufactures include clothing, electronic controls, cheese and canned goods. The area also boasts mineral springs and a resort, Bella Vista.

BENTONVILLE, Battle of. Civil War engagement fought March 19, 1865, in North Carolina near Raleigh. It was the last important engagement in the area, and it led directly to Confederate Gen. Joseph E. JOHNSTON's surrender to Union Gen. William Tecumseh Sherman.

Having reached Savannah, S.C., at the end of his MARCH TO THE SEA on December 10, 1864, Sherman turned north in early 1865 to join Gen. Ulysses S. Grant in Virginia. The Battle of Bentonville was the only significant resistance he encountered. The shattered Confederate army in the region had been reorganized under Johnston, who mustered 21,000 troops for a stand at Bentonville. On March 19 he successfully attacked the leading wing of Sherman's force under Gen. Henry Slocum. However, by March 21 Sherman had arrived with the main body of his force, nearly 80,000 troops, and Johnston withdrew to Smithfield.

Johnston asked for surrender terms on April 14, 1865, and the surrender was accepted by Sherman on April 26. Robert E. Lee had already surrendered at Appomattox on April 9.

BERKELEY, Lady Frances (Hollingbourne, Kent, Eng., 1634 — Green Spring, Va., c. 1695). Colonial aristocrat. Arriving in Vriginia in 1650, she married SAMUEL STEPHENS, later governor of the Albemarle colony. Widowed in 1669, she married Sir WILLIAM BERKELEY, governor of Virginia, and with him became known for her opposition to NATHANIEL BACON. During the latter's rebellion Lady Frances served as her husband's agent in London (1676-77) and returned with a royal agent and 1,000 troops. With her husband's removal to England in 1677 and death there later that year, Lady Berkeley organized the "Green Spring Faction" in opposition to the new royal governor. In 1680 she married THOMAS LUDWELL.

BERKELEY, Sir William (Bruton, Somersetshire, Eng., 1606 — Twickenham, Middlesex, Eng., July 9, 1677). Colonial governor. After graduating from Oxford (1629), he was named a commissioner of Canada in 1632 and served successfully for nine years. In 1641 he was appointed governor of Virginia. During his first term of office, he established diverse manufacturing and agricultural projects, quelled the Indian attacks by capturing Indian Chief Openchancanough and persecuted dissenters. After the English Revolution, he was forced from the governorship in 1652 because of his Royalist leanings and expulsion of the Puritans from the colony. In 1660, with Charles II's rise to power, Berkeley was reinstated as governor. However, his second tenure was disastrous. He indulged in religious persecution and excessive taxation and refused to mount an attack against marauding Indians, which precipitated BACON'S REBELLION. Because of his harsh treatment of the rebels he was recalled to England and died shortly thereafter.

BERRY, Harriet Morehead (Hillsborough, N.C., July 22, 1877 — Chapel Hill, N.C., Mar. 24, 1940). Public offocial. A graduate of the later University of North Carolina at Greensboro (1897), she did graduate work at U.N.C., Chapel Hill (1905). She was secretary (1904) and director (1917-18) of the State Geological and Economic Survey. A strong proponent of a state road system, in 1921 she framed the bill authorizing its construction. She returned to public service in North Carolina's Department of Agriculture (1925-37), organizing and supervising the state's savings and loan associations. Berry served as chairman of the Chapel Hill Equal Suffrage League and as vice-president of the state League.

BERRY, Martha McChesney (Rome, Ga., Oct. 7, 1866 — Atlanta, Ga., Feb. 27, 1942).

Educator. In 1902 she opened the Boy's Industrial School (Mount Berry School for Boys) with her own inheritance to instruct the local mountain children. In 1909 she followed this with the Martha Berry School for Girls. In both she provided vocational and academic instruction in exchange for manual labor. In 1926 she founded Berry College. By 1960 there were 16,000 Berry school graduates. Theodore Roosevelt said of the Berry Schools, "This is the real thing."

BERRY, Raymond (Corpus Christi, Tex., Feb. 27, 1933 —). Football player. He graduated from Southern Methodist University and played with the Baltimore Colts (1955-67) where he was the favorite target of Johnny Unitas's passes. He was inducted into the Pro Football Hall of Fame in 1973.

BESSEMER, Ala. City (pop. 31,729), Jefferson Co., north central Alabama. Henry De Bardeleben, the coal and iron magnate who also developed nearby Birmingham, founded the area in 1887. The town's economy is still based on industries producing iron and steel.

BETHESDA, Md. Unincorporated city (pop. 56,527), Montgomery Co., west central Maryland. A prosperous residential suburb of Washington, D.C., it developed around and was named for Bethesda Presbyterian Church. It is a noted headquarters for research centers for many health institutions, including the National Cancer Institute. A naval medical center is also found here.

BETHUNE, Mary McLeod (Mayesville, S.C., July 10, 1875 — Daytona Beach, Fla., May 18, 1955). Educator. She was special adviser to President Franklin Roosevelt on the problems of minorities in the U.S. A teacher in Southern schools (1895-1904), she later founded the Institute for Girls in Daytona (1904), which became the Bethune-Cookman College in 1923. During World War II she assisted the secretary of war in selecting officer candidates for the WACs and was an observer for the department of state at the U.N. in 1945. From 1936 to 1944, she was director of the division of Negro affairs of the National Youth Administration.

BIBB, William Wyatt (Amelia Co., Va., Oct. 3, 1781 — Autauga Co., Ala., July 10, 1820). Doctor and politician. After receiving his degree in medicine from the University of Pennsylvania (1801), he was a practicing doctor in Georgia until his election as a state legislator. He went on to serve as U.S. representative (1807-13), and U.S. senator (1813-16). In 1817 President James Monroe appointed him governor of the territory of Alabama, a post he held until his death.

BIDAI INDIANS ("brushwood"). Tribe of Atakapan linguistic stock inhabiting the Big Thicket region of Texas. They are reported to have been intermediaries between the Spanish and APACHE INDIANS in the sale of firearms.

BIENVILLE, Jean Baptiste le Moyne, Sieur de (Montreal, Canada, Feb. 23, 1680 — Paris, France, Mar. 7, 1766). Explorer and governor. He helped found a French colony at the mouth of the Mississippi (1698). The first settlement was on the Gulf Coast at Old Biloxi, La., (1699). When Bienville assumed command in 1701, he moved the headquarters, Fort Louis, to Mobile Bay (1702), later (1710) to the present-day site of Mobile. Bienville served as governor of the Louisiana colony from 1706 to 1712, and again from 1717 to 1724. During his second tenure he moved the colony's base to the Mississippi and had the city of New Orleans laid out in 1718. He promulgated the Code Noir, which regulated slavery in 1824. His code, considered humane, remained in effect until Louisiana achieved statehood. In 1725 he was recalled to France, where he remained until he resumed governorship of the colony in 1733. His stewardship, plagued by problems from the previous administration and by Indian wars, was a difficult one, and in 1743 he asked to be relieved. He returned to Paris, where he lived quietly until his death.

BIG BEND NATIONAL PARK. A 1,080-square mile national park in western Texas on the Mexican border. Considered the last great wilderness region in the state, it is named for the Big Bend of the Rio Grande, which forms its southern border. The park has dramatic contrasts of scenery and geological features. Also found there are fossil trees, millions of years old. The Chisos Mountains, which are surrounded by desert, as well as the Boquillas, Mariscal, and Santa Elena canyons, are located within the park. The state donated the land to the federal government in 1935 and the park was established in 1944.

BIG BLACK MOUNTAIN, Ky. Harlan Co., eastern Kentucky, near Lynch, in the CUMBERLAND MOUNTAINS. The highest peak in the state (4,145 feet), this mountain is a vacation and hiking spot.

BIG BLACK RIVER, Miss. Navigable river, one of two major tributaries of the Mississippi River in this state, draining the west central basin. The river rises in north central Mississippi and flows 330 miles southwest to join the Mississippi south of Vicksburg. It traverses almost the entire width of the state.

BIG CYPRESS SWAMP, Fla. Collier Co., southwestern Florida. It is a large forest morass (2,400 square miles) at the western border of the EVERGLADES, containing the SEMINOLE Indian Reservation. Big Cypress is also a center for lumbering and oil production.

BIG RIVER, Mo. Branch of the MERAMEC RIVER. From its source east of St. Louis, it runs 100 miles southeast, through east central Missouri, to drain into CLEARWATER LAKE. It flows through a valley boasting the largest lead production in the world and passes the Salem Plateau.

BIG SANDY RIVER, Ky./W.Va. Waterway that heads north to create part of the Kentucky-West Virginia border before entering the Ohio River at Catlettsburg, Ohio. The source of this 85-mile-long river is at Louisa, Ky., at the junction of the Tug Fork and Levisa rivers.

BIG SPRING, Tex. Town (pop. 28,804), seat of Howard Co., western Texas. The site of Howard County Junior College, Big Spring's economy is based primarily on the petroleum industry, farming (mostly cotton), and cattle. Big Spring State Park is its leading tourist attraction.

BIG SPRINGS, Mo. Carter Co., south central Missouri. It is one of the largest springs in the U.S. with an average daily flow of 600,000,000 gallons. The spring begins beneath a 250-foot limestone cliff, topples over a ledge, then rebounds in a massive spray before coursing to the CURRENT RIVER. It is found at the center of a 4,416-acre state park. The city of Van Buren is nearby.

BILBO, Theodore Gilmore (Poplarville, Miss., Oct. 13, 1877 — New Orleans, La., Aug.

21, 1947). Politician. After earning his law degree from Vanderbilt University, Bilbo, an ultraconservative, white supremacist, was elected governor of Mississippi (1916-20 and 1928-32). In 1935 he was elected to the U.S. Senate, and at the time of his death, he was under congressional investigation for bribery and for intimidating black voters.

BILOXI, Miss. City (pop. 49,311), on a peninsula between inland BILOXI BAY and the Mississippi Sound area of the Gulf of Mexico. Settled in 1699, it was originally part of Old Biloxi, now Ocean Springs across the bay, and as such the French capital of the Louisiana Colony until 1722. The location of Jefferson DAVIS's last home "Beauvoir," it was incorporated in 1838 and its present economy is based on tourism, fishing and processing of fish products and light manufacturing.

BILOXI BAY, Miss. Body of water seventeen miles long and one mile to three miles wide, situated on the Mississippi Sound, southeastern Mississippi. Considered the state's major bay, it is a resort area with important shrimp and oyster processing. The Biloxi River enters here. The bay is crossed by a bridge joining Biloxi and Ocean Springs.

BILOXI INDIANS ("first people"). Tribe of the Siouan linguistic group that spoke a dialect unlike most of their neighbors. First encountered by IBERVILLE in 1699, they lived along the lower course of the Pascagoula River in Mississippi and gave their name to the present city of Biloxi, as well as the first two capitals of Louisiana, Old and New Biloxi.

BINGHAM, George Caleb (Augusta Co., Va., Mar. 20, 1811 — Kansas City, Mo., July 7, 1879). Politician and artist. Bingham and his family moved to Franklin, Mo. when he was a boy. It was here that Bingham developed into a portrait painter. Although he held a variety of political offices, including a term in the Missouri legislature and as state treasurer (1862-65), he is known first as a painter. His works reflect the rough-and-tumble, colorful side of frontier politics and life on the river. Some of his most famous paintings are *Stump Speaking, Jolly Flatboatmen in Port* (1857), *County Election* (1851-52), *Raftsmen Playing Cards* (1847), and *Fur Traders Descending the Missouri* (1845). He had a talent for skillfully packing his canvases with characters and action. Later in life he became more absorbed with landscape, concentrating on light and space. In 1875 he served as adjutant general of Missouri. The last years of his life were spent teaching at the University of Missouri.

BIRMINGHAM, Ala. City (pop. 284,413), seat of Jefferson Co., in Jones Valley, north-central Alabama. Birmingham is the largest city in Alabama and the center of an expanding metropolitan area of more than 830,000 residents. Prior to the 1870s cotton fields covered the present site of the city, but since those years Birmingham has risen to prominence as the steel and iron capital of the South. This was due to nearby deposits of coal, iron ore, limestone, and special minerals including quartz, marble, clay, sand, gravel, bauxite, pyrite, dolomite, millstone, and barites. Minerals are not the only reason for the city's impressive manufacturing reputation. Transportation facilities, including a major barge channel that leads to the Gulf of Mexico, help move Birmingham's goods all over the world. Energy is also abundant, supplied by local steam, electric, and hydroelectric plants. Manufactured products include steel, mining and milling products, heavy machinery, pipe, wire castings, bolts, steel

tanks and freight cars. In addition, textiles, acetylene, waxes, shellac, lumber products, electronic equipment, feed, food products, and aircraft are produced here.

The city was founded in 1871 by the Elyton Land Company and the Louisville and Nashville Railroad. They named the city after Birmingham, England. Industrialization soon followed despite a cholera epidemic in 1873 that killed most of the community's inhabitants. Major population and industrial growth took place after 1910. Although urban problems that brought Martin Luther KING's civil rights protests in the 1960s have plagued Birmingham, it remains the population, industrial, and cultural center of the state.

The city's many points of interest include restored colonial and Victorian homes, and the Birmingham Museum of Art. A famous 50-foot statue of Vulcan, god of metalworking and blacksmithing, dominates the top of nearby Red Mountain. The statue is reputed to be the second-largest cast-iron statue. The arts are well represented in Birmingham. The city has its own opera company and symphony orchestra along with ballet and theater groups. Area colleges and universities include Miles College, Daniel Payne College, BIRMINGHAM-SOUTHERN

U.S. Steel plant in Birmingham, Ala.

COLLEGE, Samford University, and the medical and dental colleges of both the Southern Research Institute and the University of Alabama.

BIRNEY, James Gillespie (Danville, Ky., Feb. 4, 1792 — Perth Amboy, N.J., Nov. 25, 1857). Politician and author. A lawyer, he started his practice in Danville and in 1816 was elected to the Kentucky legislature and, after he moved to Alabama, to the legislature there, where he introduced provisions on slavery reform. In 1833, he returned to Kentucky, freed his slaves, and helped found the Kentucky Anti-Slavery Society. Editor of the *Philanthropist*, he became the executive secretary of the American Anti-Slavery Society (1837) and joined its offshoot, the Liberty Party. In 1840 and 1844, he was the party's unsuccessful candidate for the presidency. He wrote *American Churches, The Bulwarks of American Slavery* (1840).

BISCAYNE NATIONAL PARK, Fla. A 175,000-acre national park found near HOMESTEAD, in Dade Co., which offers prime marine habitat as well as coral keys and reefs. A favorite tourist spot, it is 96% covered by water.

BISSELL, Emily Perkins (Wilmington, Del., May 31, 1861 — Wilmington, Del., Mar. 8, 1948). Social activist, antisuffragist. By 1889 she had founded the West End Reading Room in Wilmington, which pioneered public kindergarten, boy's clubs, and public playgrounds in the state. In 1904 she helped organize the Delaware branch of the American Red Cross, and in 1907 originated the American Christmas Seal stamp and helped popularize it. Bissell also headed the Delaware Anti-Tuberculosis Society (1908-48). While active in child-labor, maximum-hour, public-health, and educational reform movements, she opposed womens' suffrage, fearing it would add to women's burdens and to the black and immigrant vote.

BISTENEAU, Lake, La. Lake between Bossier, Webster and Bienville Parishes in northwestern Louisiana. It is part of a 750-acre state park in the Red River valley and was formed by the damming of the Red by the Great Raft.

BLACK, Hugo Lafayette (Harlan, Ala., Feb. 27, 1886 — Bethesda, Md., Sept. 25, 1971). Senator and U.S. Supreme Court Justice. A Democrat, Black was U.S. senator from Alabama from 1925 to 1937. Appointed to the U.S. Supreme Court by President Franklin D. Roosevelt in 1937, he was a leading liberal activist during his 34 years on the bench. Black staunchly defended those freedoms granted in the Bill of Rights and was noted for vigorous dissents from majority opinion.

BLACK BELT, Ala. Black clay soil prairie located between the northern and southern ends of the East Gulf Coastal Plain. Large plantations producing cotton were developed here, employing a large slave labor force. In 1915 a boll weevil outbreak wiped out cotton production and farmers turned to livestock raising.

BLACK MOUNTAINS, N.C.. Chain of peaks in western North Carolina, part of the Blue Ridge Mountains in the Appalachian system. Mount MITCHELL (6,684 feet) is the highest point. Several resort centers are found on the chain.

BLACK RIVER, Ark. Partly navigable river with source in southeast Missouri. It flows 200 miles southeast, then southwest, to meet the WHITE RIVER near Newport, Arkansas. It was once a heavily traveled tributary of the White.

BLACK RIVER, Mo. Major river of southeastern Missouri, with source in Reynolds Co. It runs through CLEARWATER LAKE, coursing generally southeast for 200 miles into central Arkansas to eventually become the WHITE RIVER.

BLACK WARRIOR RIVER, Ala. Navigable river beginning in north central Alabama. It is a principal tributary of the TOMBIGBEE RIVER and flows almost 200 miles southwest to the Tombigbee at Demopolis. The Black Warrior is an important commercial transportation route and hydroelectric power source.

BLACKSBURG, Va. Town (pop. 30,638), Montgomery Co., in the Appalachian Mountains in southwestern Virginia. Settled in 1745, it is the site of Virginia Polytechnic Institute (founded 1872). Clayton Lake and Hungry Mother state parks are nearby, as is the scenic resort, Mountain Lake. It is a residential suburb of Roanoke.

BLACKSHEAR, Lake, Ga. Shared by four counties in southwestern Georgia. It is found at the northern end of the FLINT RIVER in a coastal plain and timber area.

BLACKSTOCKS, Battle of. Revolutionary War engagement fought 40 miles north of Columbia, South Carolina, on November 20, 1780. It was an unsuccessful attempt by the British to disperse the Revolutionary militia under Gen. Thomas Sumter. The British force sent northwest from Camden was commanded by Lt. Col. Banastre Tarleton in pursuit of a retreating Sumter. Sumter made a stand at Blackstocks Plantation, where he managed to repell Tarleton's fatigued cavalry but was himself seriously wounded.

BLACKSTONE, Va. Town (pop. 3,624), Nottoway Co., in south central Virginia. The town is a trading center and tobacco market in an agricultural area. The town was once called Black's and White's, named for two taverns that stood opposite each other on the state route.

BLACKWATER RIVER, Va. River that flows through numerous counties before becoming a tributary of the Nottoway. It was first called Indian River, but juniper trees which caused a blackening of the water influenced the name change.

BLACKWATER RIVER, Fla. River rising in southern Alabama, southwest of Andalusia, flows about 55 miles southwest through Okaloosa and Santa Rosa counties in northwestern Florida. Near Bagdad, the Blackwater empties into Blackwater Bay, the northeastern arm of Pensacola Bay.

BLADENSBURG, Md. Town (pop. 7,691), Prince George's Co., in western Maryland, six miles northeast of Washington, D.C., and a residential suburb of that city. In the War of 1812 it was the scene of a battle between U.S. militia under Brigadier Gen. William H. Winder and British regulars. The militia lost and the British advanced and burned Washington.

BLAIR, Francis Preston (Abingdon, Va., Apr. 12, 1791 — Silver Spring, Md., Oct. 18, 1876). Politician and journalist. After graduating from Transylvania University (1811), he was admitted to the bar (1817). He entered politics, supporting Andrew Jackson, and writing articles supporting Congress's power to levy tariffs and other issues. From 1830 to 1841 he edited *The Globe*, the journal of the Jacksonian party. A member of the Kitchen Cabinet, he exerted great power during the Jackson Administration. Because of his antislavery leanings, he helped found the Republican Party and presided over its national convention in 1856. Blair returned to the Democratic Party after Lincoln's death because of his opposition to Radical Republicanism.

BLAIR, Francis Preston, Jr. (Lexington, Ky., Feb. 19, 1821 — St. Louis, Mo., July 9, 1875). Union general and statesman. Following his admission to the bar, he opened up a law office in St. Louis, Missouri, where he also founded the Free Soil paper, *The Barnburner*. Blair was an organizer and leader of the FREE SOIL MOVEMENT in Missouri. Although a slave owner himself, he denounced the open practice of slavery and its expansion. In 1856, he became the sole Free Soil candidate to win election to Congress (1857-59, 1861-62) from a slave state. Blair led the forces that kept Missouri in the Union prior to the Civil War and, during the War, he served under Grant and Sherman. In 1868, he was the Democratic Party's candidate for vice president. Blair again served in Congress (1870) and was a U.S. Senator (1871-73). He was the son of Francis Preston BLAIR.

BLAIR, James (Edinburgh, Scotland, 1656 — Virginia, Apr. 18, 1743). Clergyman and founder of William and Mary College. Ordained in the Church of England (1679), Blair refused to take an oath supporting the legitimate claim to the English throne of the Roman Catholic Duke of York (James II) and lost his Edinburgh parish. In 1685, on his arrival in America, he became the rector of Varina parish, Henrico Co., Virginia. In 1689, on his appointment as the bishop's representative in Virginia, he advocated the establishment of a college in the colony. King William III and Queen Mary granted him a charter and financial backing for the project. When the college was founded in Williamsburg in 1693 it was named the College of WILLIAM AND MARY. It is the second-oldest institution of higher learning in the U.S. Blair served as the first president of the college and as rector of Bruton parish in Williamsburg (1710-43).

BLAIR, Montgomery (Franklin Co., Ky., May 10, 1813 — Silver Spring, Md., July 27, 1883). Lawyer, statesman, counsel for Dred

SCOTT. The son of Francis Preston BLAIR, he was Postmaster General during President Abraham Lincoln's first term, and was noted for his reforms of the postal system and for his battles within the cabinet. After the assassination, he defended Lincoln's plan for RECONSTRUCTION, seeking moderate treatment for the South. He later supported Samuel Tilden's claims to the presidency (1876) by proposing a resolution, unpopular with the Republicans, which would have denied the office to Rutherford Hayes.

BLAND, Richard Parks (Hartford, Ky., Aug. 19, 1835 — Lebanon, Mo., June 15, 1899). Politician. He taught school in Kentucky before settling in Missouri (1855), where he became a lawyer. A promoter of western interests, in 1872 he won election to Congress and became known as "Silver Dick," because he championed unlimited minting of silver money. He proposed the bill that was modified, to his dismay, to become the Bland-Allison Act (1878), promoting silver mintage. He was a leader of the western radicals during the Democratic convention of 1896.

BLEASE, Coleman, L. (Newberry, S.C., Oct. 8, 1868 — Columbia, S.C., Jan. 19, 1942). Politician. A practicing lawyer in South Carolina, he was elected to the state house of representatives (1890-94, 1899-1900). Blease was a powerful figure in the state Democratic party, being elected to the state senate (1904-08), as governor (1911-15) and U.S. Senator (1925-31).

BLOUNT, James Henderson (Jones Co., Ga., Sept. 12, 1837 — Macon, Ga., Mar. 8, 1903). Statesman. He was a major factor in President Grover Cleveland's decision not to annex Hawaii. Appointed special commissioner to the islands (1893), where U.S. interests had deposed Queen Liliuokalani, he was given authority as U.S. minister there by Cleveland, ending the protectorate.

BLOW, Susan Elizabeth (St. Louis, Mo., June 7, 1843 — New York, N.Y., Mar. 26, 1916). Educator. Educated in New York City, she was a student of Friedrich Froebel's philosophy. She opened the first successful public kindergarten in a suburb of St. Louis, Mo., in 1873. The following year she opened a school to train kindergarten teachers.

BLUE MOUNTAIN DAM, Ark. In the Ozark National Forest, near Paris, Arkansas, built by the U.S. Army Corps of Engineers. The impounding of the river brought about an artificial lake of the same name, with a 315-mile shoreline, in a highly popular summer recreation region.

BLUE RIDGE LAKE, Ga. Lake in Fannin Co., northern Georgia, part of Chattahoochee National Forest. It was impounded in 1930 with a dam (167 feet high), on the Toccoa River. Twelve miles long with a 102-mile shoreline, it is in an outdoor and water recreation area in a summer resort region.

BLUE RIDGE MOUNTAINS. Range in the southern portion of the APPALACHIAN system, it runs for 615 miles from Carlisle, Pa. to Mount Oglethorpe, Ga., and is from 10 to 65 miles wide. The highest peaks in several states are included in the range: Mount ROGERS, Va. (5,720 feet), SASSAFRAS MOUNTAIN,, S.C. (3,560 feet), BRASSTOWN BALD, Ga. (4,784 feet). Also included in the Blue Ridge range is the highest peak east of the Mississippi, Mount Mitchell, N.C. (6,684 feet). The mountains are commercially important for their hardwood forests, and the system is well known for its breathtaking scenery along the SKYLINE DRIVE and the Blue Ridge Parkway. The Appalachian Trail runs along the system's crest. Due to its rough terrain, small, isolated communities still remain in the mountains.

BLUE RIDGE PROVINCE, Va. One of the five physiographical areas in the state, it begins at the western end of the PIEDMONT PROVINCE and extends from the POTOMAC RIVER to the southern boundary of Virginia. The highest peaks in the state, Mount ROGERS and WHITETOP, are in the southwestern part of the province. The mountains have a violet tint when the atmosphere is clear, hence the name Blue Ridge.

BLUE SPRINGS, Mo. City (pop. 25,927), Jackson Co., southeast of Independence. A major trade center and residential community in a farm and fruit region, it was incorporated in 1904. Manufactures include metal and plastic products. Local agriculture includes dairying and many orchards. *Press Woman* (1937), a journalism magazine, is published here monthly.

BLUEFIELD, W.Va. City (pop. 16,060), in the Appalachian coalfields of Mercer Co. It is the southernmost city in West Virginia and also the highest city (elev. 2,558 feet) in the U. S. east of Denver, Col. It was incorporated in 1889, and in 1924 the town of Graham, Va., a Bluefield suburb, changed its name to Bluefield, thus creating a sister city just over the state line. Both are named after their fields of blue wildflowers. In spring, Bluefield hosts the Annual Southern Appalachian Industrial Exhibit.

BLUEGRASS. Popular name given to the plants from the grass genus *Poa*, both wild and cultivated. The most common type in the U.S. is that found in Kentucky. This grass flourishes in the heavy limestone soil around Lexington, where it serves as grazing fodder for thoroughbred racehorses. It is also used as a covering for lawns and golf courses.

BLUEGRASS MUSIC. Often considered a forerunner of the later jazz and country and western forms of music, bluegrass is a type of folk music developed in the southern U.S. and named for Kentucky's BLUEGRASS region. Like jazz, it is often improvised and its composition is marked by rapid tempos. It is usually played on the guitar and banjo.

BLUEGRASS REGION, Ky. Division of the state covering the north central area, from Kentucky to southern Ohio, named for the grass which is predominant there. To the north and west flows the Ohio River. It is a fertile area, with heavy corn and tobacco production. Racehorse breeding is a major industry. The region offers the state's largest cities and a good portion of its manufacturing.

BLUES. An improvisatory, black American musical form of the 20th century related to, but developing separately, from JAZZ. Its precise origins are unknown, but blues is thought to have developed from a combination of British ballads and plantation work calls or "hollers." The term "blues" and its music and lyrics express a state of mind—melancholy or depression—the singer expressing his or her hopes, fears or frustrations. Developing in the South, probably in Mississippi, its popularity eventually spread, traveling to Chicago, where it eventually became electrified, and Memphis, whose Beale Street became the "home of the blues." Although in its earliest forms, blues was mostly improvised by singers and instrumentalists, by 1912 blues songs began to be written and published. W.C. HANDY's "Memphis Blues" (1912), "St. Louis Blues" (1914) and "Beale Street Blues" (1917) brought the music to a much wider audience. By the 1920s, when blues began to be recorded, the form had evolved into a popularized version usually accompanied by jazz bands. Some of the popular blues singers from that era were Lottie Beamon from Kansas City, Ma Rainey from Georgia and, the most popular of all, Bessie Smith (1894-1937), from Tennessee. Later blues artists included Sam "Lightning" Hopkins from Texas (1912-82), B. B. King (1925–) from Mississippi and Muddy Waters (1925-83) also from Mississippi, who greatly influenced many ROCK stars, both American and British.

BLUESTONE RESERVOIR, W.Va. Largely in Summers Co., it is a U-shaped artificial lake, measuring 28 miles long, formed by damming the BLUESTONE River in southern West Virginia. One end of the reservoir extends south into Virginia. The reservoir is a recreational and water supply source.

BLUESTONE RIVER, W.Va. River rising in Virginia's Tazewell Co. It flows northeast 30 miles through West Virginia's south end to terminate at the BLUESTONE RESERVOIR at Pipestem.

BLUFF HILLS, Miss. (Also known as Loess Hills.) Chain of upland region hills, east of the Mississippi Delta. These easily eroded bluffs extend from Tennessee, through Mississippi, and into Louisiana.

BLYTHEVILLE, Ark. Town (pop. 24,314), Mississippi Co., in northeastern Arkansas near the Missouri border. Settled in the 1850s, its early economy was based on cotton and it became an important market center and shipping point. Present manufactures include, along with cotton and agricultural produce, shoes, chemicals, dog food, mobile homes, and textiles.

BOCA RATON, Fla. City (pop. 49,505), Palm Beach Co., southeastern Florida. Its name is Spanish for "rat's mouth." Established in 1924 and incorporated in 1950, it is a noted resort and retirement community and is the site of Florida Atlantic University.

BODCAU BAYOU RIVER, Ark. Large man-made reservoir on the lower part of the Red River. It serves as a flood control unit for the region.

BODENHEIM, Maxwell (Hermanville, Miss., May 23, 1893 — New York, N.Y., Feb. 6, 1954). Author and poet. Bodenheim's poetry includes *Selected Poems* (1946). His prose includes *Blackguard* (1923), *Replenishing Jessica* (1925), *Georgia Man* (1927), and *My Life and Loves in Greenwich Village* (1954).

BOEUF RIVER, La. River originating in Arkansas, and flowing generally southwest into northern Louisiana, eventually meeting the OUACHITA RIVER, north of Harrisonburg. It is 140 miles long.

BOGUE CHITTO RIVER, Miss. River rising in the Pine Hills of southwestern Mississippi. From there, it flows 100 miles southeast, crossing the Louisiana border. It arcs over to join the PEARL RIVER at the west central boundary of the two states.

BOLL WEEVIL. Beetle (*Anthonomous grandis*) that lays its eggs and feeds on the young bolls of cotton plants. It is a snout beetle, and the snout with which it bores into bolls represents half its body length of about one-quarter inch. Females lay up to 300 eggs that hatch in three days as grubs that immediately begin to feed. They exist as larvae for two weeks, and are ready to reproduce four days after reaching adulthood. The adult goes into a dormant stage during the winter. The insects first migrated to the U.S. from warmer Mexican climates and caused the most serious crop damage previous to 1922, when modern chemical spraying techniques became available. They remain a threat today, however, sometimes requiring sprayings

each week to check successive generations of the insect.

BOONE, Daniel (near Reading, Pa., Nov. 2, 1734 — Charette, Mo., Sept. 26, 1820). Frontiersman and explorer. Before he was 20 years old, Boone's Quaker parents moved south from Pennsylvania to the Yadkin River Valley in North Carolina. Following service under Braddock in Pennsylvania in the French and Indian War, Boone returned to the South and began his explorations through the Appalachian ridges. For two years beginning in 1767 Boone and companions, including John Finley, traveled through the Cumberland Gap and explored the lands of present-day Kentucky. In 1775 he founded the Kentucky settlement of Boonesboro.

The Daniel Boone of legend first caught the popular imagination during the Revolution, when he was captured by the British, escaped by pretending to cooperate with them, and then rode 160 miles in four days to alert fellow patriots about an imminent attack. True to the image of the uneducated woodsman, he he was careless about legal title to lands, and this cost him his own cleared lands in the new territory.

Daniel Boone, the legendary Kentucky pioneer

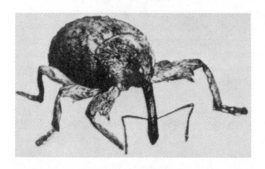

The Boll Weevil, a threat to cotton crops

Disgusted by this introduction of imperfect law into the wilderness, he moved to the Spanish territory of Missouri, where he was again deprived of land for failing to register his claim. In deference to his service to the country, however, Congress granted him 850 acres in Missouri in 1814.

Boone has been a popular figure in American folklore ever since the publication in 1784 of his spectacular autobiography, in fact a romantic version of his experiences written by John Filson. His fame had spread to Europe by the time Byron portrayed him as the great natural man in *Don Juan* (1823), and it was increased at home after James Fennimore Cooper made him the prototype of Natty Bumpo in *The Leatherstocking Tales.*

BOONE, N.C. Town (pop 10,191), seat of Watauga Co., northwestern North Carolina. Named for Daniel Boone, who lived in the area, it is a mountain resort surrounded by oak, pine, and spruce timber. Products include sauerkraut and shoes. Appalachian State University is here.

BOONVILLE, Mo. City (pop. 7,090), seat of Cooper Co., located in mid-state on the south bank of the Missouri River. Settled in 1810, incorporated in 1839, and chartered a city in 1896, it was named for Daniel BOONE. An important trading post on the Missouri and on the Santa Fe Trail, it was a center of conflict during the Civil War. Industries include stone quarrying, shoe and veneer manufacture, and bottling. In an area of chicken and dairy farms, Boonville is the location of Missouri Training School (1899) and Kemper Academy (1884).

BOOTH, Edwin (Bel Air, Md., Nov. 13, 1833 — New York, N.Y., June 7, 1893). Actor. The son of actor Junius Brutus Booth, Edwin Booth made his debut in Boston (1849) as Tressel in Shakespeare's Richard III in that Shakespeare play, and became famous when he performed the title role in New York City (1857). Producer and actor in many Shakespearean performances notable for their scholarly grounding, he saw his career ruined by the assassination of Abraham Lincoln in 1865 by his brother John Wilkes BOOTH. In his later years Edwin Booth did reestablish his reputation. He built the Booth Theatre in New York City in 1869 and presented Shakespeare's plays with international stars until 1873. He toured England with Henry Irving from 1880-82. He later formed the Players Club.

BOOTH, John Wilkes (Bel Air, Md., Aug. 26, 1838 — Bowling Green, Va., Apr. 26, 1865). Actor and assassin of Abraham Lincoln. The son of actor Junius Brutus Booth and brother of actor Edwin BOOTH, John Wilkes Booth was a popular performer in Shakespearean roles in a company that traveled throughout Virginia. In 1859 he was a member of the Virginia regiment that captured and executed John Brown. Booth initially planned the abduction of President Abraham Lincoln, but when this failed, he turned to the idea of assassination, which he carried out at Ford's Theater in Washington, D.C., on April 14, 1865. Having fatally shot the President, he leapt to the stage and shouted "*Sic semper tyrannis!* The South is avenged." After two weeks he was traced to the barn in Virginia where he was either shot attempting to escape or shot himself.

BOQUILLAS CANYON, Tex. Extremely narrow pass created by a great opening in a mountain of rock through which the RIO GRANDE RIVER flows. Average depth of the canyon wall is 1,600 feet. Its name is Spanish for "little mouths."

BORBUESE RIVER, Mo. Branch of the MERAMEC RIVER, rising in central Missouri. The river begins east of the city of Union and runs southwest approximately 50 miles.

BORDEN, Gail, Jr. (Norwich, N.Y., Nov. 9, 1801 — Borden, Tex., Jan. 11, 1874). Inventor, surveyor, newspaper publisher, and western pioneer. He established *The Telegraph and Texas Register* in San Felipe, Texas, in 1835. An advocate of the Republic of Texas, the *Telegraph* ultimately became the first permanent state newspaper and the first newspaper in Houston. Borden helped write the first state constitution and laid out the city of Galveston. In the 1850s he returned to New York and was an early inventor of evaporated milk, coffee, tea, cocoa, and beef extract products, and he founded the dairy company now known as Borden Inc.

BOREMAN, Arthur Ingram (Waynesburg, Pa., July 24, 1823 — Apr. 19, 1896). Politician. A member of the Virginia House of Delegates (1855-61) he opposed secession and was instrumental in the Wheeling Convention that led to the establishment of West Virginia as a separate state, which stayed loyal to the Union. In 1863 Boreman became governor of the new state and served until 1869. From 1869-75 he was a Republican U.S. Senator.

BOSTON MOUNTAINS, Ark. Chain of ridges, averaging 1,000-2,000 feet high, in northern Arkansas, north of the Arkansas River. This chain is part of the OZARK PLATEAU. The highest peak is 2,400 feet. The Boston peaks are considered to be the most rugged mountains of this plateau and they are popular with vacationers for their forest, trails, and hunting and fishing areas. The WHITE RIVER originates in these mountains.

BOUDINOT, Elias Cornelius (nr. Rome, Ga., Aug. 1, 1835 — Fort Smith, Ark., Sept. 27, 1890). Attorney and crusader for Indian rights. After settling in Fayetteville, Ark., he studied law and was admitted to the bar in 1856. He was chairman of the Democratic state central committee and was a delegate to the Confederate Congress in 1863. In later years, he worked in the U.S. government, specializing in Indian welfare and citizen rights.

BOWIE, James (Burke Co., Ga., 1796 — San Antonio, Tex., Mar. 6, 1836). Adventurer and pioneer. In his youth a reputed slave trader who dealt with pirate Jean LAFFITE, he moved to Louisiana and bought a sugar plantation where he introduced steam power for grinding cane. A member of the state legislature, he allegedly killed a man in a duel. Having gone to Texas about 1828, he befriended Mexican Vice-Governor Juan Martin de Veramendi, whose daughter he married, and he assumed Mexican citizenship. Bowie became interested in the Texas revolutionary movement and became a colonel in the Texas Army. He joined Col. William B. TRAVIS to defend the ALAMO, an abandoned mission in San Antonio. There he was killed by Santa Anna's troops. He popularized the Bowie knife, a large single-edged steel hunting knife thought to be designed by his brother Rezin.

BOWIE, Md. Town (pop. 33,695), Prince George's Co., west central Maryland. The town, incorporated in 1874, has experienced much growth recently, owing to its proximity to Washington, D.C., which makes it a popular residential suburb. The area also offers various recreational facilities including the Bowie Racetrack. It is the site of Bowie State College.

BOWIE, William (Annapolis Junction, Md., May 6, 1872 — Washington, D.C., Aug. 28, 1940). Geodesist. After graduating from Trinity College, he served for the next 42 years on the U.S. Coast and Geodetic Survey, 27 of those years as director. Bowie helped to develop the theory of isostasy, concerning the equilibrium of the earth's crust.

BOWLING GREEN, Ky. City (pop. 40,450), seat of Warren Co., on the Barren River. It is a shipping and marketing center for tobacco. Meat and poultry are processed here. Manufacturing includes clothing and car parts. Founded in 1780, it was occupied by the Confederates during the Civil War until Union troops took over in 1862. Western Kentucky State College is found here as are the remains of the South Union Shaker Colony, which was active in the 1800s. Lost River Cave is nearby.

BOWMAN, Isaiah (Waterloo, Ont., Canada, Dec. 26, 1878 — Baltimore, Md., Jan. 6, 1950). Geographer, educator, and author. Producer of the first comprehensive study of physiographic divisions of the U.S. (1911), he led major field studies of the Andes (1905-09) and directed the American Geographical Society (1915-35), which he enlarged to international stature. As president of Johns Hopkins (1935-48), he established several departments in physical sciences. An adviser to President Woodrow Wilson, he served the U.S. at the Paris Peace Conference (1918-19). An advisor to President Franklin D. Roosevelt, Bowman was a delegate to the Dumbarton Oaks Conference (1944) and the U.N. conference in San Francisco (1945).

BOYD, Belle (Martinsburg, W.Va., May 9, 1844 — Kilbourne, Wis., June 11, 1900). Actress, lecturer, Confederate spy. With her town's occupation by Union forces in 1861, Boyd began spying, circulating freely in the society of Union officers. Her most important service came in 1862 during Jackson's march on Harper's Ferry, which made her famous in both South and North. Arrested and imprisoned several times, she was banished to Canada (1864) and sailed to England, where she wrote her memoires, *Belle Boyd, in Camp and Prison* (1865). Returning to the U.S., she acted (1866-69) and in 1886 began touring as a dramatic lecturer on her war experiences, stressing the need for national unity.

BOZEMAN, John M. (Georgia, 1835 — Yellowstone, Mont., Apr. 20, 1867). Pioneer. He established the Bozeman Trail, a shorter route to the goldfields of Montana. Opposed by the Sioux for his attitude toward their land rights, he was killed in an unexpected Indian attack on his Yellowstone camp.

BRADENTON, Fla. City (pop. 30,170), seat of Manatee Co., in southwestern Florida, on Tampa Bay at the mouths of the Braden and Manatee rivers. Founded in 1878 and incorporated in 1903, Bradenton was named for the builder of the Braden Castle (1854), Dr. Joseph Braden. It is a shipping point for citrus fruit and truck parts. A junior college and a memorial marking the spot where DE SOTO landed in 1539 are found here.

BRADFORD, Augustus Williamson (Bel Air, Md., Jan. 9, 1806 — Baltimore, Md., Mar. 1, 1881). Politician. A graduate of St. Mary's College (1824), Bradford served as a delegate to the Washington peace conference before serving as governor of Maryland from 1862 to 1866. His aid and support for the Union during the Civil War was important to the Union cause.

BRADFORD, John (Prince William Co., Va., June 6, 1749 — Fayette Co., Ky., Mar. 20, 1830). Printer and publisher. He was the founder of the first newspaper in Kentucky, the *Kentucky Gazette* (1787), and the following year he published the *Kentucke Almanac*. Bradford was made Printer of the Territory and, in 1792, printed the first book to be published in the state, a book which contained the acts of the state legislature. When Transylvania University was founded in 1799, he became the first chairman of the board (1799-1811).

BRADFORD, Roark Whitney (Lauderdale Co., Tenn., Aug. 21, 1896 — New Orleans, La., Nov. 13, 1948). Author. He wrote stories about blacks and their lives in the South. His works include *Ol' Man Adam an' His Chillun* (1928), which Marc Connelly used as a basis for the play *The Green Pastures* (1930). The production earned Bradford and Connelly a Pulitzer prize.

BRADLEY, Joseph Philo (Berne, N.Y., Mar. 14, 1813 — Washington, D.C., Jan. 22, 1892). Supreme Court justice. He helped establish the guidelines that draw the line between Constitutional "exclusive" power of Congress over interstate commerce and the taxing powers of the states. A master lawyer, particularly concerned with complex projects such as railroad litigation, he was appointed to the court in 1870. Considered one of the most intelligent thinkers in the court, he was an important factor in the period of RECONSTRUCTION. His votes were decisive in making Rutherford B. Hayes president (1877), helping retain postwar legal tender legislation, and invalidating the congressional statute forbidding race discrimination in public places (1883). Bradley was also instrumental in causing the court to support government regulation of railway and grain elevator prices.

BRADY, Mathew B. (Lake George, N.Y., c. 1823 — New York, N.Y., Jan. 15, 1896). Photographer. Trained to do daguerreotypes by Samuel F. B. Morse, he was noted for his portraits of famous people of his time, including almost every President from John Quincy Adams to William McKinley. He began capturing Abraham Lincoln on film in 1860 and was soon winning prizes for his work. Earning a small fortune as a photographer, almost $100,000, he

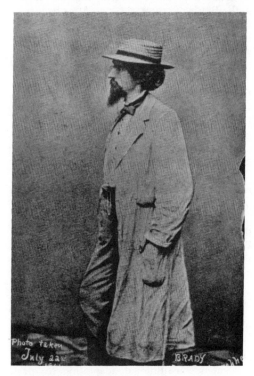

Mathew B. Brady, July 22, 1861, following his return from the Battle of Bull Run

spent it to finance his extensive photographic coverage of the Civil War, not only supervising the work of his photo teams, but personally covering Bull Run, Antietam, Gettysburg, Fredericksburg, and Petersburg. He produced memorable photographic portraits of Lincoln and of Robert E. Lee after the war. Financially wiped out, he sold plates and equipment and, though aided by Congress, died a pauper in a charity ward.

BRAGG, Braxton (Warrenton, N.C., Mar. 22, 1817 — Galveston, Tex., Sept. 27, 1876). Confederate general. A West Point graduate, Bragg fought in the Seminole Wars (1837-41), and served in the Mexican War under Zachary Taylor. Joining the Confederates during the Civil War, he led a strong assault across Tennessee to invade Louisville, Ky. (1862), but was held to a standstill at Perryville and retreated to Tennessee. Criticized by many in the Confederacy, he retained his position as commander of the Army of Tennessee principally because of the friendship of Jefferson Davis. However in 1863 he was repeatedly outmaneuvered by Gen. William Rosecrans, at MURFREESBORO and elsewhere, until his victory in the Battle of CHICKAMAUGA. After he lost at Chattanooga he was made military adviser to Davis. In 1865 he surrendered with Gen. Joseph Johnston to Union Gen. William T. Sherman, after opposing Sherman's March.

BRANDEIS, Louis (Louisville, Ky., Nov. 13, 1856 — Washington, D.C., Oct. 5, 1941). U.S. Supreme Court Justice. The son of immigrants from Austria-Hungary, Brandeis graduated from Harvard Law School at the age of 21 without having attended college. He first practiced law in St. Louis, but by 1879 he had returned to Boston to specialize in corporate law during the boom years of the American free-enterprise economy. He was appointed to the Supreme Court by President Woodrow Wilson in 1916, and when he took his seat after stormy ratification hearings in Congress he became the first Jewish justice.

During his 23 years on the court Brandeis became famous for dissenting opinions, often with Oliver Wendell Holmes, in opposition to the majority led by Chief Justice William Howard Taft. He was a proponent of regulations on big business and the "living law" position that advocated constitutional adaptation to meet new social needs. He remained, however, an activist for uncurbed freedoms of speech and the press. Following retirement in 1939, he devoted himself to Zionist causes.

BRASSTOWN BALD, Ga. Peak in Towns Co., northeast Georgia. Found in the Blue Ridge of the Appalachian Mountains, Brasstown Bald is also known as Mount Enotah and is the highest peak (4,784 feet) in the state. Its observation deck affords a view of four states. The Enotah Trail is here.

BRAZOS RIVER, Tex. River originating in the Llano Estacado in eastern New Mexico and northwest Texas. It flows more than 870 miles generally southeast to enter the Gulf of Mexico at Freeport, Tex. One of the state's major waterways, it is important because of its many irrigation, flood control and hydroelectric projects. The main river is formed by the Double Mountain Fork, which runs to meet the Salt Fork. Rich soil surrounding the river was crucial for the development of the large plantations during Texas settlement time. Large boats can travel from the Gulf for about 40 miles upstream. POSSUM KINGDOM LAKE is found on the river.

BRAZOSPORT, Tex. Community made up of ten cities, including Clute, Brazoria, Oyster Creek, Quintana, Surfside, Freeport, Jones Creek, Lake Barbara, Lake Jackson, and Richwood. Businesses include fishing and tourism.

BRECKINRIDGE, John (Staunton, Va., Dec. 2, 1760 — Lexington, Ky., Dec. 14, 1806). Lawyer and politician. Educated at William and Mary College, he practiced law before moving to Kentucky. He was attorney general in that state (1795-97), and was elected to the state legislature (1798-1800). From 1801 to 1805 he served as a Democratic U.S. senator and was an advocate of western expansion and development. President Thomas Jefferson appointed him U.S. attorney general (1805) and he died while in office. He was the grandfather of John Cabell BRECKINRIDGE.

BRECKINRIDGE, John Cabell (near Lexington, Ky., Jan. 15, 1821 — Lexington, Ky., May 17, 1875). Vice president and Confederate officer. Born into a family of politicians and lawyers, the grandson of John BRECKINRIDGE, he began as a lawyer and in 1849 won election to the Kentucky legislature. Elected as a Democrat to the House of Representatives

(1851-55), he was later nominated and elected vice president serving under James Buchanan for one term (1857-61). When the Democratic Party divided in 1860, Breckinridge was chosen presidential candidate by the Southern faction. He was defeated by Abraham Lincoln. In March, 1861, he succeeded John CRITTENDEN as U.S. senator but resigned later that year to become a Confederate brigadier general. In the last few months of the war, Breckinridge served as the Confederate secretary of war, fleeing to Europe after the war's end. He returned in 1869 and resumed his law career.

BRECKINRIDGE, Sophonisba Preston (Lexington, Ky., Apr. 1, 1866 — Chicago, Ill., July 30, 1948). Educator and social reformer. She was the first woman to be admitted to the bar in Kentucky (1897), and was the first woman to represent the U.S. at an international conference when she was a delegate to the Pan-American Conference in Uruguay (1933). A professor at the University of Chicago (1925-33), Breckinridge was president of the American Association of Schools of Social Work (1934).

BRENT, Margaret (Gloucester (?), England, c. 1601 — Peace Plantation, Va., c. 1671). Colonial aristocrat. Arriving in Maryland in 1638 with recommendations from Lord Baltimore, she quickly accumulated large land holdings and influence. She served as Governor Calvert's executor during the 1647 Ingle Rebellion and helped restore order to the colony. Brent then demanded the full voting rights of a man in the colonial assembly. Her actions alienated Lord Baltimore, however, and by 1651 she had moved to the Northern Neck of Virginia.

BREVARD, N.C. Town (pop. 5,323), seat of Transylvania Co., in western North Carolina. Incorporated in 1867 with seven voters, all of whom held local office, this is a mountain vacation area with the Pesgah National Forest nearby. Brevard is a music center, as well, with the Transylvania Music Camp and Festival. Paper and film products are made here and it is the home of Brevard College.

BRICKELL, Henry Herschel (Senatobia, Miss., Sept. 13, 1889 — Branchville, Conn., May 29, 1952). Editor, writer, and translator. He wrote for *The New York Evening Post* (1919), was an editor for Henry Holt, Inc.

(1928-33), and in 1934 began writing literary reviews for the *Post* that gained national attention. A contributor to many magazines, including *The Saturday Review*, he was a friend of major writers of the 1930s and 1940s. He judged the O. Henry awards (1940), and wrote *Writers on Writing* and *Our Living Novelists* (1949).

BRIDGER, James (Richmond, Va., Mar. 17, 1804 — Kansas City, Mo., July 17, 1881). Fur trader and guide. His first expedition was into the Missouri River area with William Ashley (1822). He was the first white man to visit the Great Salt Lake in 1824. After years of fur trapping in that region he served as a guide and in 1843 established a fort on the Oregon Trail. In 1857 he led an expedition to the region now known as Yellowstone Park.

BRIDGETON, Mo. City (pop. 18,445), St. Louis Co., northwest of St. Louis, Mo. The community was settled in 1765 and incorporated in 1843. In 1852 the land around Bridgeton Commons was leased to individuals for a term of 999 years at an annual rent of between 10 and 75 cents per acre. Today it is largely residential, with some farming and industry. A monthy table tennis magazine has been published here since 1933.

BRINKLEY, David McClure (Wilmington, N.C., July 10, 1920 —). News commentator. He helped develop documentary television techniques for NBC with the *Huntley-Brinkley Report* (1956-71), which won the Peabody, Sylvania, and Emmy awards. Brinkley is noted for his terse, dry sense of humor.

BRISTOE STATION, Battle of. Civil War engagement on October 14, 1863, in northeast Virginia near Culpeper. It was won by the North, but Gen. Robert E. LEE's Bristoe campaign to reconsolidate his forces after the defeat at GETTYSBURG was generally successful.

After Gettysburg both Lee and Union Gen. George G. Meade moved south into Virginia and maneuvered for position east of the Blue Ridge Mountains. On October 14, at Bristoe Station, Confederate troops under Gen. A. P. Hill attacked what they thought to be a small Union force. They found themselves under heavy fire from three divisions and from artillery from the southeast. The Confederate troops were decimated, with nearly two thousand casualties, and the Northern troops, veterans who had repelled Pickett's Charge at Gettysburg, obtained a second boost in morale.

The month-long Bristoe campaign, however, ended with the cautious Meade retreating 40 miles to a safe position. Although the distance was insignificant, this enabled Lee to destroy railroad links that took the Union weeks to repair.

BRISTOL, Tenn. City (pop. 23,986), Sullivan Co., in northeastern Tennessee. Built around a fort constructed here in 1771 by Col. Issac Shelby, ore mines were once important to the local economy. Manufacturing now includes paper and pulp products, textiles, office machines, and electronic equipment as well as tobacco processing. King College (1867) is here and the Spring National Drag Race is held each June. There are actually two municipalities within this one city: the one in Tennessee and BRISTOL, Va.

BRISTOL, Va. City (pop. 19,042), Bristol Co., on the Virginia-Tennessee border. The city is separated from BRISTOL, Tenn. by the state line which runs through its center. Each municipality has its own government, but economically it is a single unit. A market center for tobacco, its other manufactures include paper and pulp products, textiles, office machines, and electronic equipment. Bristol in the site of King College (1867).

BRISTOW, Benjamin Helm (Elkton, Ky., June 20, 1832 — New York, N.Y., June 22, 1896). Lawyer and politician. Admitted to the Kentucky bar in 1853, he was a Union officer in the Civil War and fought at the battles of Fort Donelson and Shiloh. He was a state senator (1863-65), U.S. attorney for the Kentucky District (1866-70), and the first U.S. solicitor general (1870-72). President Ulysses S. Grant appointed him secretary of the Treasury in 1874, and in that capacity he reorganized the department and broke up the powerful "Whiskey Ring," which involved tax fraud on whiskey distilling. He was forced to resign two years later after a falling out with Grant. He was a contender for the Republican nomination for President in 1876 but lost to Rutherford B. Hayes. In 1878 he moved to New York City, where he became a corporate lawyer and a founder of the American Bar Association.

BROCK, William Emerson (Mocksville, S.C., March 14, 1872 — Chattanooga, Tenn.,

Aug. 5, 1950). Politician. He first worked as a salesman but an interest in banking led him to serve as chairman of the Liberty loan drives during World War I. He was later a trustee of the University of Chattanooga, of Emory and Henry College, and of Martha Washington College for Girls. He was elected as a Democrat to fill the U.S. Senate vacancy for the state of Tennessee left by the death of Lawrence Tyson (1929-31).

BROOKE, John Mercer (Tampa, Fla., Dec. 18, 1826 — Lexington, Va., Dec. 14, 1906). Naval officer and scientist. He designed the Confederate ironclad, *Virginia* (which had been converted from the steam frigate *Merrimack*), and the "Brooke Gun," the most powerful cannon produced in the South. He invented a deep-sea sounding device while teaching at the Virginia Institute of Technology.

BROOKGREEN GARDENS, S.C. Georgetown Co., located north of Georgetown, South Carolina. Popular tourist attraction covering part of Brookgreen as well as three other former rice plantations. Brookgreen offers a wide variety of plants and trees native to the state, as well as a sculpture collection and a zoo featuring U.S. animals.

BROOKHAVEN, Miss. Town (pop. 10,800), seat of Lincoln Co., southern Mississippi. The town is situated in an area of diversified farming and livestock raising. There are lumber mills, creamery facilities, and cotton ginning factories. Manufactures include thermometers, bricks, electronic equipment, and wire.

BROOKINGS, Robert Somers (Cecil Co., Md., Jan. 22, 1850 — Washington, D.C., Nov. 15, 1932). Businessman and philanthropist. He founded the Brookings Institution, Washington, D.C., as a study center for economics and government. Employed at 17 in a woodenware company, he owned the company at 22, which he expanded to include real estate, lumber, and transportation. He retired at 46 (1896) to become a philanthropist. He helped relocate and enlarge WASHINGTON UNIVERSITY in St. Louis, Mo., was an original trustee of the Carnegie Endowment for International Peace, and served as chairman of the price fixing committee during World War I.

BROOKS, Preston Smith (Edgefield District, S.C., Aug. 6, 1819 — Washington, D.C., Jan. 27, 1857). Politician. A Democratic congressman from South Carolina (1852-57), he publicly attacked Massachusetts Senator Charles Sumner in 1856 for Sumner's slanderous speech against Brooks' uncle, senator Andrew Butler one of the authors of the Kansas-Nebraska Act. The attack was considered an indication of how the relationship between the North and South was deteriorating. He resigned from Congress but was immediately reelected and served from 1856 until his death.

BROWN, Benjamin Gratz (Lexington, Ky., May 28, 1826 — St. Louis, Mo., Dec. 13, 1885). Politician. A Yale graduate (1847), he was admitted to the Kentucky bar before he moved to Missouri. There he entered politics as a Thomas Hart BENTON supporter. While in the state legislature (1852-58), he spoke out against slavery and later affiliated with the Free Soil movement. In 1857, Brown was an unsuccessful candidate for governor, but later did hold that office (1871-73). During the Civil War he enlisted in the Union Army. As U.S. senator (1863-67) he was a principal in the move to replace President Abraham Lincoln with Fremont in 1864, and promoted immediate emancipation and firm treatment of recessionists. In 1872 he was the unsuccessful vice-presidential candidate on the Democratic ticket headed by Horace Greeley.

BROWN, Charlotte Eugenia Hawkins (Henderson, N.C., June 11, 1883 (?) — Greensboro, N.C., Jan. 11, 1961). Educator. After attending State Normal School in Salem, Mass., she returned south to teach for the American Missionary Association (1900-01) and then at Bethany Institute for black children (1901), of which she became head (1902-52). By the 1940s this renamed Palmer Memorial Institute enjoyed a widespread reputation for academic and social excellence. Brown was the first black woman admitted to Boston's Twentieth Century Club (1928).

BROWN, John (Torrington, Conn., May 9, 1800 — Charlestown, Va., Dec. 2, 1859). Abolitionist. A descendant of Peter Brown of the *Mayflower*, he moved with his family at an early age to Ohio, where he worked as a tanner. He became a dealer in wool and visited Europe on business, but was unsuccessful in all his business ventures.

In 1855 he moved to Kansas, where, as an anti-slavery champion, he played an active role in the conflicts of the Civil War in that territory. An intensely earnest man, he had early on conceived the idea that he might become a liberator of slaves, and in May, 1859, he began the action which ended so disastrously for him at HARPERS FERRY.

Brown spent the summer of 1859 in preparation. He hired a farm a few miles from Harpers Ferry and his followers joined him there one by one. Their plan was to seize the government armory and railroad bridge for the purpose of arming insurgent slaves in Virginia. They attacked the night of October 16 (Brown, 17 white men, and five negroes) and took possession of the government buildings. News of the attack spread and by the next night the militia had arrived, including Robert E. Lee with a troop of 90. Brown and his followers were captured and two of Brown's sons who had accompanied him were killed. The bold leader was speedily tried for murder and treason, was found guilty on October 29, and on December 2, 1859 was hanged. Although Brown's attempt to free the slaves was a total failure, it proved to be an important event which drew national at-

Abolitionist John Brown, who led the raid on Harpers Ferry

August 29-30, 1862, on the same field in Virginia about 30 miles southwest of Washington, D.C. They were named by the Union army for the creek that crosses the battlefield. However, the Confederate army, which won both battles, called them Manassas after the nearest Virginian town.

The first Battle of Bull Run was the first major battle of the Civil War. The Confederate army under Gen. Pierre BEAUREGARD gathered in the middle of July, 1861, at the railroad junction in Manassas for an assault on Washington. Union Brig. Gen. Irvin McDowell was ordered to clear the junction and reached nearby Centreville, Va., on July 18. He hesitated to attack, allowing the Confederate forces of Gen. Joseph E. JOHNSTON to travel from Winchester to Manassas and join Beauregard's army on July 20 via an undefended rail line. The first Battle of Bull Run commenced on Sunday, July 21, when McDowell attacked and apparently penetrated Confederate lines. Gen. Thomas JACKSON's regiment, however, held "like a stone wall" and so earned him his nickname. The inexperienced Union forces then began a retreat that degenerated into disorganized flight from the field. The Confederate army, however, failed to pursue and take full advantage of the rout.

In the second Battle of Bull Run, a year later, 62,000 Union troops under Major Gen. John Pope attacked Stonewall Jackson's 20,000 troops, not knowing that Confederate reinforcements under Gen. James LONGSTREET were hidden behind the lines. The Union army pushed forward until it came to Longstreet's position, where it was repelled by artillery fire on the second day of the fighting. Pope supervised an orderly retreat back across Bull Run, but he was relieved of his command on September 2.

BULL SHOALS DAM, Ark. Flood control and hydroelectric power facility constructed on the WHITE RIVER in northern Arkansas in 1951. The 258-foot dam created BULL SHOALS LAKE. The electricity generated here is transferred to the entire region.

BULL SHOALS LAKE, Ark. Lake created by the U.S. Army Corps of Engineers in northern Arkansas, on the WHITE RIVER. It was formed by the construction of BULL SHOALS DAM, near Mountain Home, Ark. The lake, which is 87 miles long with a 1,000-mile shoreline, is one of the largest Ozark lakes and serves as a flood control unit and hydroelectric power source. Twenty-one recreation areas provide facilities for water sports and camping.

BUNDICK CREEK, La. Waterway rising in western Louisiana. It travels generally south for 45 miles to empty into Bundick Lake, a recreation spot.

BURGESSES, House of. The name of the General Assembly of the Colony of Virginia. It was the first representative assembly in the new world. It first met on July 30, 1619 in Jamestown and heard sessions there until 1699, when it moved to Williamsburg. It consisted of a governor's council of six members chosen by the Virginia Company in London and 22 Burgesses, who were elected by the freemen of the Virginia Colony. Despite the opposition of King James I who was unsympathetic to popular representation, the group met sporadically, unauthorized by the crown until 1639. In that year James' successor, Charles I, granted the permanent establishment of the body. The House of Burgesses made Virginia the first example of a partly self-administrating colony in the new world. It administrated the colony until 1775, often in opposition to the Royal Governor and the interests of the crown. It was in the House of Burgesses that Patrick HENRY denounced the STAMP ACT in 1765, leading the group to pass resolutions against the act. On June 20, 1775, shortly after the outbreak of the Revolutionary War, the House adjourned for the last time.

BURGESS, John William (Giles Co., Tenn., Aug. 26, 1844 — Brookline, Mass., Jan. 13, 1931). Educator. A post-Civil War graduate of Amherst College, he won admission to the Massachusetts bar in 1869 but never practiced. He began a long and successful career in 1871, teaching at Columbia University, the University of Berlin, and many other institutions. Burgess was considered influential in helping Columbia make the transition from a college to a university.

BURKBURNETT, Tex. Town (pop. 10,668), Wichita Co., in north central Texas. Settled in 1907, Burkburnett became a boomtown in 1918 when a 3,000-barrel oil gusher came in, causing the so-called "Burk Boom." Today its industrial plants produce such items as chemicals, plastics, and rodeo equipment.

BURLESON, Albert Sidney (San Marcos, Tex., June 7, 1863 — Austin, Tex., Nov. 24, 1937). Postmaster General. The grandson of Edward BURLESON, he graduated from Baylor University and the University of Texas law school. He was a Democratic U.S. Congressman from 1899 to 1913. Appointed Postmaster General (1913-21) by President Woodrow Wilson, he advocated government ownership of communications and prevented the mailings of publications he considered defamatory to the government. He established the airmail service in 1918.

BURLESON, Edward (Buncombe Co., N.C., Dec. 15, 1798 — Austin, Tex., Dec. 26, 1851). Pioneer and politician. He fought in the Texas revolution and in 1840 successfully commanded forces against the Cherokee Indians in east Texas. He was a senator and then vice president of the Texas Republic, but in 1844 was defeated in a bid for the Texas presidency.

BURLINGTON, N.C. City (pop. 37,266), Alamance Co., in the north central part of the state, between Greensboro and Durham. The Battle of Alamance, a pre-Revolutionary conflict with the British, is memorialized as a state park in Burlington. Elon College (1889) is located nearby. The city's economy is based on textiles, electronic equipment, and metallurgy.

BURNET, David Gouverneur (Newark, N.J., April 4, 1788 — Galveston, Tex., Dec. 5, 1870). Politician. The grandson of William Burnet, governor of New York and New Jersey (1720-28), he went to Texas about 1817, where his legal training established him as a spokesman for American settlers during the problems with the Mexican government. He promoted independence from Mexico, drew up a declaration of independence, and was made president ad interim of the Republic and served eight months in 1836.

BURNET, Tex. Town (pop. 3,850), seat of Burnet Co., 45 miles northwest of Austin. It is often called "Versatile County," because of its wealth of natural resources and potential products. Burnet's economy is today dependent on stone quarrying, graphite products, farming, ranching, and tourism.

BURNETT, Frances Eliza Hodgson (Manchester, England, Nov. 24, 1849 — Plandome, N.Y., Oct. 29, 1924). Author. In 1865 she moved to Knoxville, Tenn., with her family. She began writing for periodicals and in 1872 one of her earliest stories was published in *Scribner's Magazine.* Burnett was noted for her children's novels that include *Little Lord Fauntleroy* (1886) and *Sara Crewe* (1888).

BURNS, Otway (Onslow Co., N.C., 1775 — Portsmouth, N.C., Oct. 25, 1850). Privateer. Commanding the Baltimore clipper, *Snap Dragon,* he captured millions of dollars worth of British shipping during the War of 1812 and had a $50,000 reward posted for his capture by the British. After the war he became a shipbuilder and served in the North Carolina legislature (1821-35).

BURNSIDE, Ambrose Everett (Liberty, Ind., May 23, 1824 — Bristol, R.I., Sept. 13, 1881). Military officer and politician. A graduate of West Point (1847), he accompanied Gen. Patterson to Mexico that same year as a member of a corps of artillery. He was quartermaster of the Mexican Boundary Commission (1850-51) before resigning to establish a factory in Rhode Island that manufactured breech-loading rifles (his own invention). At the outbreak of the Civil War he joined the 1st Rhode Island Volunteers as a colonel. He attained the rank of major general for his exemplary service at the Battle of BULL RUN (August 6, 1861). Gen. Burnside commanded the expedition that captured Roanoke Island, served in the Maryland Campaign under Gen. George McClellen, and was in the battles of South Mountain and ANTIETAM. After failing in an attack on Lee at FREDERICKSBURG, he resigned. Assigned to the command of the Dept. of the Ohio, he was active in suppressing disloyal elements in that region. In 1866 he was elected governor of Rhode Island and served three terms. He was elected to the U.S. Senate in 1875 and reelected in 1880, serving until his death. Burnside was the originator of the fashion of long side-whiskers or sideburns.

BURTON LAKE, Ga. Lake in Rabun Co., northeastern Georgia. It is one of a chain of lakes formed by the construction of hydroelectric dams. The Georgia Power Company built this lake, which impounds the Tallulah River at the base of Snake Mountain. Burton has a 65-mile shoreline.

BUSCH GARDENS, Fla. Adventure park in Hillsborough Co., located on the Gulf Coast of Florida at Tampa. Trains and monorails transport visitors through a 300-acre complex of tropical plants, African animals, and exotic birds. It is also called the Dark Continent.

BUSH CREEK, Md. Offshoot of the Monocacy River, branching at Lime Kiln in northern Maryland. From that point it moves east-southeast about 30 miles to drain into Triadelphia Lake at the border of Howard and Montgomery Counties.

BUTLER, Ala. Town (pop. 1,882), seat of Choctaw Co., southwestern Alabama, near the Mississippi border. Lumber, oil, and minerals are located in this area. Manufactures include paper and plywood and agriculture includes peanut farming and cotton.

BUTLER, Selena Sloan (Thomasville, Ga., Jan. 4, 1872 (?) — Los Angeles, Ca., Oct. 7, 1964). Educator. A school teacher around Atlanta (1888-93), she studied at Emerson School of Oratory in Cambridge, Mass. (1894) before returning to Atlanta in 1895. A founder of the Georgia Colored Parent-Teacher Association (1920) and the National Congress of Colored Parents (1926), she fought against racial discrimination, for the improvement of black education, and helped promote integration in the National Parent-Teacher Association (PTA). In 1970 she was honored as a founder by the then-integrated National PTA.

BUTLER, William Orlando (Jessamine Co., Ky., Apr. 19, 1791 — Carrollton, Ky., Aug. 6, 1880). Military officer. He was the Democratic candidate for vice president (1848) on the Lewis Cass ticket which was defeated by Zachary Taylor. Butler fought in the War of 1812, under Andrew Jackson at Pensacola, in the Battle of New Orleans, and later fought in the Mexican War. He was a Democrat U.S. Congressman from 1839 to 1843. During the Civil War he opposed secession and supported the Union cause.

BYRD, Harry Flood Jr. (Martinsburg, W.Va., June 10, 1887 — Berryville, Va., Oct. 20, 1966). Politician. The brother of Richard E. BYRD, he served in the Virginia state senate (1915-25) and was elected governor of Virginia (1926-30). In 1933 he became U.S. senator from that state and was continuously reelected until his death. A conservative Democrat and advocate of government economy, Byrd was

chairman of the Senate Finance Committee for 10 years.

BYRD, Richard Evelyn (Winchester, Va., Oct. 25, 1888 — Boston, Mass., Mar. 11, 1957). Pilot, military officer, and explorer. A member of Virginia's famous Byrd family, and brother of Harry Flood BYRD, Richard Byrd graduated from the U.S. Naval Academy in 1912 and served in World War I. Along with Floyd Bennett, he was the first man to fly to the North Pole and back (1926). In the three following decades he explored and gathered scientific information on Antarctica. In those years he established the base Little America on the Ross Ice Shelf (1928-30) and from there flew to the South Pole. In the years that followed, Byrd directed many Antarctic expeditions and in 1933-35 conducted many studies of the earth and outer space from his base. After World War II he headed the massive Operation Highjump, when a great deal of mapping and exploration of unknown Antarctic areas was undertaken. He flew over the South Pole again in 1956. His book *Alone* was written in 1938.

BYRD, William I (England, 1652 — Westover, Va., Dec. 4, 1704). Colonial planter. Arriving in America as a youth, he settled on land (later the site of Richmond) on the James River in Virginia. An aristocrat, his fortune was built on trade and speculation in frontier land. In 1703 he was president of the Virginia Council.

BYRD, William II (Westover, Va., Mar. 28, 1674 — Westover, Va., Aug. 26, 1744). Colonial planter, politician, and writer. Educated in England, he inherited a large estate from his father, William BYRD I, and increased it to 179,000 acres. A member of the House of Burgesses and a Virginia Council member, he also headed a commission that surveyed the Virginia-North Carolina boundary from the ocean westwards for 240 miles. An important colonial author, his works include *A History of the Dividing Line, A Journey to the Land of Eden* and *A Progress to the Mines.* At his death his library contained nearly 4,000 volumes and was probably one of the largest libraries in America at that time.

BYRNE, Andrew (Navan, Ireland, Dec. 5, 1802 — Little Rock, Ark., June 10, 1862). Roman Catholic bishop. He volunteered to come to America for his church and served the Charleston, S.C., diocese. In 1844 he was appointed first bishop of the diocese of Little Rock, Ark., where he promoted Catholic immigration to the southwest.

BYRNES, James Francis (Charleston, S.C., May 2, 1879 — Columbia, S.C., Apr. 9, 1972). Politician. While working as a reporter and editor for his own Aiken, S.C., newspaper, he studied law. Elected to the U.S. Congress (1911-25), he then moved on to the U.S. Senate (1931-41) and served as a budgetary expert for the New Deal administration. Appointed Secretary of State by President Harry Truman (1945-47), he worked to end post-war differences with Russia. He later became governor of South Carolina (1951-55).

C

CABELL, James Branch (Richmond, Va., Apr. 14, 1879 — Richmond, Va., May 5, 1958). Novelist and essayist. He often explained that his name, properly pronounced, rhymed with "rabble." Cabell attended the College of William and Mary and taught Greek and French there for one year (1896-97). This was followed by newspaper work in Virginia, New York, and West Virginia. His principal work was a series of novels begun with *Jurgen* (1919), set in a mythical French province called "Poictesme," concerning the history of the descendents of one Dom Manuel from 1234 to 1750. All of these novels, among them *The Cream of the Jest* (1917), were brought together in an eighteen-volume *Storiesende Edition* (1927-30). These were considered important and sexually controversial works in Cabell's day, but their reputation has declined since his death. His non-fictional works include *Beyond Life* and *Some of Us.*

CABEZA, De Vaca Alvar Nunez (Jerez de la Frontera, Spain, c. 1490 — Seville, Spain, 1557). Spanish explorer. Cabeza was one of four survivors of an ill-fated expedition to the New World led by Panfilo de NARVAEZ (1527). Shipwrecked off the Texas coast, the four endured much suffering as Indian prisoners before their escape. Together they traveled through Texas, New Mexico, Arizona, and into Mexico, where their tales of riches encouraged new expeditions north. Cabeza later served as Governor of Paraguay (1540) but a revolt forced him to return to Spain, where he was sentenced to exile in North Africa. He was then pardoned by the King.

CADDO INDIANS. The ADAI and NATCH-ITOCHES Confederacies in Louisiana and the EYEISH, HASINAI, and KADOHADACHO Confederacies in Texas were referred to as Caddo Indians. They were generally agricultural and lived in thatched huts.

CADDO LAKE, La./Tex. Lake largely in Caddo Parish, northwestern Louisiana, extending into eastern Texas. The lake was created by the damming of the RED RIVER by the Great Raft. It is in a recreation area north of Shreveport, La.

CAESAR'S HEAD MOUNTAIN, S.C. Vertical cliff of metamorphic rock made up of bands that differ in color and composition, located in Greenville Co. in northwestern South Carolina's SALUDA RIVER Valley. It is surrounded by a resort community famous since the Civil War. The area is noted for having the lowest annual mean temperature of any spot in the state. Several different accounts have been given for the naming of the peak, including one alleging the mountain bears a likeness to the profile of Julius Caesar.

CAHABA RIVER, Ala. River rising northeast of Birmingham. It courses 200 miles generally southwest to the ALABAMA RIVER at Selma.

CAIRO, Ga. City (pop. 8,777), seat of Grady Co., southwestern Georgia, near the Florida border. In one of the most fertile agricultural areas in the state, Cairo was settled in 1866. Area crops include pecans, tobacco, and sugar cane.

CAJUNS. See ACADIANS.

CALCASIEU LAKE, La. Cameron Parish, southwestern Louisiana. A large resort lake found on the CALCASIEU RIVER, north of the Gulf of Mexico.

CALCASIEU RIVER, La. River rising in western Louisiana, coursing first southeast, then southwest for approximately 120 miles through a valley rich in natural gas, oil, and rice. Partly navigable and one of the state's major rivers, it passes through Lake Charles and CALCASIEU LAKE before it empties into the Gulf of Mexico. The waterway connects Lake Charles with the Intracoastal Waterway.

CALDWELL, Erskine (Coweta Co., Ga., Dec. 17, 1903 —). Short story writer, novelist, and journalist. Although his early short stories had already gained some attention, Caldwell did not become well known until the successful staging of his novel *Tobacco Road* (1932) two years after its first publication. He followed this with many stories and novels about the lives of poor black and white farmers in the deep South, such as *God's Little Acre* (1933) and *The Sure Hand of God* (1947).

CALHOUN, Ga. City (pop. 5,335), seat of Gordon Co., northwestern Georgia, on the Oostanaula River. It is an agricultural and light industrial community, which was once the headquarters of the Cherokee Indians. Gen. Sherman virtually destroyed the town during the Civil War.

CALHOUN, John Caldwell (Calhoun Mills, S.C., Mar. 18, 1782 — Washington, D.C., Mar. 31, 1850). Statesman and political philosopher. He spent a lifetime advocating states' rights and espousing the NULLIFICATION doctrine. Calhoun was largely self-taught until at the age of 18 he attended the "log college" of his brother-in-law, the Rev. Moses Waddel. Later he graduated from Yale and studied at the law school in Litchfield, Conn. He was admitted to the bar in South Carolina in 1807 and served as a state legislator for two sessions. In 1811 he married a cousin, Floride Bonneau Calhoun, whose family was wealthy and belonged to the Southern planter aristocracy. In the same year he was elected to Congress and continued to serve as legislator or cabinet member for the next 40 years of his life. He was secretary of War under President James Monroe, Vice-President under John Quincy Adams and Andrew Jackson, and secretary of State under President John Tyler. In his early years in Congress, Calhoun along with Henry Clay became spokesman for a nationalistic group of young leaders known as the "War Hawks." The group played an important role in stirring up sentiments for the war against England in 1812. Later Calhoun became the chief spokesman for

South Carolina statesman John C. Calhoun

states' rights. He was author of *Exposition and Protest*, a paper that declared the "tariff of abominations" unconstitutional. Calhoun opposed the MISSOURI COMPROMISE (1820) and supported measures to extend the slave-holding territory. In two books written during the 1840s Calhoun spelled out his political philosophy: *A Diquisition of Government* and *A Discourse on the Constitution and Government of the United States.*

CALL, Richard Keith (near Petersburg, Va., 1791 — Sept. 14, 1862). Lawyer and politician. After serving in the War of 1812 he studied law and set up a practice in Pensacola, Fla. A territorial delegate to Congress in 1823, he became the territory governor and led the fight against the Indians in the SEMINOLE WARS. A controversy with the War Department caused him to lose the governorship but he regained it after joining the Whig party. An advocate of statehood, he was defeated in 1845 for another term as governor. Although a slaveholder, he strongly opposed secession.

CALOOSAHATCHEE RIVER, Fla. River originating in Glades Co., Florida. Joined to Lake Okeechobee by the Caloosahatchee Canal, it flows generally west past Fort Meyers and empties into San Carlos Bay, a protected inlet of the Gulf of Mexico. A mile-wide tidal basin follows the Caloosahatchee for 19 miles inland.

CALUSA INDIANS ("fierce people"). Tribe thought to have been of Muskogean linguistic stock, that inhabited the west coast of Florida south of Tampa Bay on down through the Florida Keys. They were noted for the large amounts of gold and treasure they acquired from shipwrecked Spanish vessels. PONCE DE LEON encountered them in 1513, and in a subsequent visit in 1521 he was mortally wounded by them. During Spanish control, missionary efforts among the Calusa failed and they continued their practice of human sacrifice. Also known as the Muspa, they eventually crossed to Cuba or were incorporated into the SEMINOLE INDIANS who moved into their territory when pressed by American forces.

CALVERTT FAMILY See BALTIMORE, Lord.

CAMBRIDGE, Md. Town (pop. 11,703), seat of Dorchester Co., Eastern Shore, on the Choptank River. Situated in a good farming area, it was founded in 1684 as a plantation community with tobacco raising bringing prosperity to the area. Now it is known as a port of entry, and a commercial fishing and yacht center. Manufactures include electronics, cloth, and boats.

CAMDEN, Battles of. Revolutionary War victory by the British over the Continental Army on August 16, 1780, near CAMDEN in north central South Carolina on the Wateree River. Following the capture of Charleston, S.C., on May 12, 1780, the British extended their control by enforcing loyalty oaths and marshalling loyalists into their troops. On July 13 Gen. Horatio Gates was named by Congress to replace Gen. Benjamin Lincoln as commander of the Revolutionary forces in the southern theater of the war. The principal British force in the region was 8,000 men under Gen. Charles CORNWALLIS in Charleston. Although his own force of 3,000 was suffering from disease and lack of supplies, Gates chose to attack a British outpost at Camden commanded by Lord Francis Rawdon. When this became clear, Cornwallis, although under orders to act cautiously in the region, rushed to Rawdon's defense. The two forces met each other at Camden, and Gates, in a move that would draw severe criticism, decided to engage the far superior British force.

In the battle on August 16 the Revolutionary left flank panicked and fled, beginning a general retreat. Revolutionary losses were 750 dead and wounded, while British losses were less than 250 dead and wounded.

After the battle Gates fled into North Carolina, where he regrouped with a force numbering only 700 men. Cornwallis pursued, and it appeared that North Carolina would fall to the British. However, hearing of the British defeat at KING'S MOUNTAIN, an outpost near the North Carolina border, Cornwallis gave up the pursuit and made Camden his base of operations until 1781.

CAMPBELL, William Bowen (Sumner Co., Tenn., Feb. 1, 1807 — Lebanon, Tenn., Aug. 19, 1867). Politician. First a lawyer, he then served with distinction in the SEMINOLE and Mexican Wars. He was a Whig Congressman from Tennessee (1837-43), fought in the Mexican War, and in 1851 he became the last Whig governor of Tennessee. At the time of secession he was regarded as the most distinguished of the Tennessee politicians to maintain allegiance to the Union. Following the war he again served in Congress (1866-67).

CAMPBELL'S STATION, Battle of. See KNOXVILLE, Siege of.

CANAVERAL, Cape, Fla. Cape located in Brevard Co. on the east central coast of the state. It is the extremity of a system of barrier islands projecting into the Atlantic, 15 miles northeast of Cocoa. Long the site of a lighthouse, Canaveral became site of the Kennedy Space Center, a U.S. Air Force installation for launching missiles. It had been briefly called Cape KENNEDY, after the assassination of President John F. Kennedy. The first missile launch from here was in 1950, and in 1969 this was the launching site of the first spacecraft to send men to the moon.

CANBY, Edward Richard Sprigg (Kentucky, Aug., 1817 — Lava Beds, California, Apr. 11, 1873). Military officer. He graduated from West Point in 1839, and served in the Seminole and Maxican Wars. He was a Union brigadier general during the Civil War and stopped the Confederate invasion of the South-

Lift-off of the space shuttle *Columbia* at the Kennedy Space Center, Cape Canaveral, Fla.

west, leading volunteer troops. Canby took MOBILE, Ala. (1865), and was killed in a Modoc Indian raid in California.

CANDLER, Asa Griggs (Villa Rica, Ga., Dec. 30. 1851 — Atlanta, Ga., Mar. 12, 1929). Pharmacist and soft drink manufacturer. A student of medicine and a successful wholesale drug manufacturer, he bought the formula for Coca-Cola in 1887, developed a method of manufacture, and engineered its worldwide success. In 1919 he received $25 million for the rights to the industry he had created. Much of his fortune was given to develop the medical school of Emory University, Atlanta.

CANEY FORK RIVER, Tenn. Branch of the CUMBERLAND RIVER rising in central Tennessee and coursing west and northwest 145 miles to empty into the Cumberland near Carthage. CENTER HILL and GREAT FALLS Lakes are on it. Rock Island, a fishing resort, is found on the river's bank.

CANNON, James Jr. (Salisbury, Md., Nov. 13, 1864 — Chicago, Ill., Sept. 6, 1944). Clergyman and prohibitionist. He entered the ministry as a Methodist Episcopalian in 1888, was elected bishop in 1918, and retired in 1938. A leading Anti-Saloon Leaguer and head of the World League Against Alcoholism, his influence was extensive until the repeal of Prohibition in 1933. Vehemently opposed to the presidential candidacy of Alfred E. Smith (1928), he was called before a Senate lobby committee to answer charges concerning his use of funds in Virginia during the campaign. He defied the committee and was later acquitted in federal court.

CANTON, Miss. City (pop. 11,116), seat of Madison Co., in central Mississippi. With a number of fine old antebellum houses, it is a manufacturing and agricultural center for the county. Lumber, furniture, and fertilizer are made here. There are also poultry and livestock farms, and cotton is produced.

CANYON, Tex. City (pop. 10,724), seat of Randall Co., located in the Panhandle of Texas. Settled in 1892 and named for Palo Duro Canyon, the town's present economy is largely dependent upon WEST TEXAS STATE UNIVERSITY. Ranching and farming are also important. The Panhandle-Plains Historical Museum is located in Canyon.

CAPE CORAL, Fla. City (pop. 32,103), on the southwestern coast of Florida at the mouth of the Caloosa Natchee River. The first family settled here in 1958 and in 1970 the city was incorporated. It is the second-largest city in Florida in area, extending 11 miles along the river, and is basically residential with some light industry.

CAPE FEAR INDIANS. Small tribe thought to have been of Siouan linguistic stock. They inhabited the region of the CAPE FEAR RIVER, North Carolina.

CAPE FEAR RIVER, N.C. River formed by the junction of the DEEP and HAW Rivers, southwest of Raleigh. From there it courses 200 miles southeast through the piedmont and coastal plains. Partially navigable, it enters the Atlantic Ocean north of Cape Fear.

CAPE GIRARDEAU, Mo. City (pop. 34,361), Cape Girardeau Co., in southeastern Missouri on the Mississippi River. Its manufactures include clothing, shoes, and electrical appliances. Founded as a trading post in 1793 and incorporated in 1892, Cape Girardeau was a successful river port until the Civil War. Its manufacturing era began after the Mississippi System linked the city with the West and the South. It is the home of Southeast State University.

CARAWAY, Hattie Ophelia (Bakerville, Tenn., Feb. 1, 1878 — Falls Church, Va., Dec. 21, 1950). Politician. When her attorney husband Thaddeus, a U.S. senator, died in 1931, the governor of Arkansas appointed her to fill his spot, making her the second woman to sit in the U.S. Senate. Her election in 1932 made her the first woman elected to the Senate. She later became the first woman to head a Senate committee and the first to preside over a Senate session (1943).

CARPETBAGGER. Term used for Northerners who came to the South during the RECONSTRUCTION period after the Civil War. Although some went with honorable intentions, many went for political advancement and personal financial gain which resulted in widespread corruption. Some came as individuals, others as agents of reconstruction organizations such as the FREEDMEN'S BUREAU. By controlling the Negro vote, they formed political coalitions, often working with Southern SCALA-

WAGS, and dominated the Republican governments. The name carpetbagger came from the valise (carpetbag) in which they carried their possessions, that was symbolic of their unstable future.

CARROLL, Anna Ella (Kingston Hall, Md., Aug. 29, 1815 — Washington, D.C., Feb. 19, 1893). Military strategist and pamphleteer. She was planner of the Tennessee Campaign executed by Gen. Ulysses S. Grant (1862). Influential in national politics and involved with the Know-Nothing movement, Carroll served President Abraham Lincoln as a pamphleteer, publicizing his wartime policies.

CARROLL, Charles (Annapolis, Md., Sept. 19, 1737 — Baltimore, Md., Nov. 14, 1832). Political leader and last living signer of the Declaration of Independence. He was a leading patriot before and during the Revolution, serving on committees of correspondence, observation, and safety (1744-76). A member of the board of war of the Continental Congress (1776-79), he, Samuel CHASE, Benjamin Franklin, and cousin John CARROLL went to Canada to try to convince the settlers there to side with the colonies or stay neutral (1776). A member of the Maryland senate (1777-1800) and the U.S. Senate (1789-92), Carroll became an active Federalist. As a prominent Roman Catholic his influence on the Catholic post-colonial population was important to the organization of an effective central government in the new nation.

CARROLL, John (Upper Marlborough, Md., Jan. 8, 1735 — Baltimore, Md., Dec. 3, 1815). First U.S. Roman Catholic bishop. At St. John's Chapel, Forest Glen, Md., he organized the Select Body of Clergy and began the Catholic Academy (1786), which became Georgetown University. Consecrated bishop in 1790, he held his first synod in Baltimore in 1791. His administration, backed by President George Washington and Benjamin Franklin, expanded to include Indian missions, the Danish West Indies, and the Diocese of New Orleans. Continued growth of American Catholicism saw Carroll elected the first U.S. Archbishop in 1808. A patriot priest, he was sent by the Continental Congress in 1776, with cousin Charles CARROLL, Benjamin Franklin, and Samuel CHASE, to convince Canada to aid the colonies or to stay neutral.

CARROLLTON, Ga. City (pop. 14,078), seat of Carroll Co., western Georgia, on the Little Tallapoosa River. An enterprising commercial center that processes the products of this fertile farm area, Carrollton has textile mills and manufactures numerous items of apparel. It is the home of West Georgia College.

CARROLLTON, Tex. City (pop. 40,591), located in Dallas and Denton Co., northeastern Texas. Carrollton was established in 1872 as a railroad station for the Missouri, Kansas and Texas, and the St. Louis and Southwestern Railroads. Now a residential area, it is one of the fastest-growing communities in Texas.

CARSON, Christopher "Kit" (Madison Co., Ky., Dec. 24, 1809 — Fort Lyon, Colo., May 23, 1868). Scout and frontiersman. After leaving home at age 17 to join a band of traders, he explored the Far West. Carson guided John C. Fremont's first government-funded expeditions to California (1842-46). He served as guide to the force under Gen. Stephen Kearney that captured California for the U.S. during the Mexican War. Famous as an Indian fighter and Indian expert, Carson became the Indian agent at Taos, New Mexico, in 1853, leaving the post to join the Union army during the Civil War, where he was promoted to the rank of colonel. In January, 1868, he was appointed superintendent of Indian affairs for the Colorado Territory.

CARSON, Rachel Louise (Springdale, Pa., May 27, 1907 — Silver Spring, Md., Apr. 14, 1964). Environmentalist and author. After receiving her Master's degree at Johns Hopkins University (1932), she went on to work for the U.S. Fish and Wildlife Service. Carson wrote several books stressing the dependence of human welfare on nature. Her best-known work is *Silent Spring* (1962), in which she exposed the dangers of DDT and other pesticide use.

CARTER, William Hodding, Jr. (Hammond, La., Feb. 3, 1907 — Greenville, Miss., Apr. 4, 1972). Journalist. In 1938 he became editor and publisher of *Delta Democratic-Times*, Greenville, Miss. Carter won the 1945 Pulitzer Prize for his editorials against racial segregation in the South and was called "the spokesman for the New South." He wrote *The Winds of Fear* (1944) and other books.

CARTER, James Earl "Jimmy" (Plains, Ga., Oct. 1, 1924 —). Georgia governor and 39th President of the U.S. Carter was born on a peanut farm to which he returned after his presidency. He attended Georgia Tech before attending the U.S. Naval Academy at Annapolis, graduating in 1946. He then served in the Navy's nuclear submarine program and did graduate work in nuclear physics at Union College in New York. When his father died in 1953, Jimmy Carter returned home to run the family farm. He had by that time married Rosalynn Smith. They have three sons and a daughter.

Carter's political career was notable for his successful challenges to the authority of established party politicians. After an unsuccessful run for the governorship of Georgia in 1966, he devoted himself full-time to a campaign for the next election and became governor in 1970 without previous political experience. Georgia law limited him to a single term, so in 1974 he launched a marathon bid for the U.S. presidency that had permanent effects on presidential primary politics. In the 1976 election he succeeded in unseating the incumbent President, Gerald R. Ford.

Carter's presidency was considered a great victory for the deep South, and he attempted to reform Washington politics by replacing lifelong bureaucrats. Among his principal foreign policy achievements were the Camp David summit meetings between Israel and Egypt and the ratification of treaties to surrender the Panama Canal to that country's own government by the year 2000. The end of his term was marred by the seizure of the American Embassy in Iran by militant followers of the Ayatollah Khomeini, however, and a worsening economic situation at home further contributed to his defeat in the 1980 presidential election.

CARTER, Samuel Powhatan (Elizabethton, Tenn., Aug. 6, 1819 — Washington, D.C., May 26, 1891). Naval officer and Civil War general. An 1846 graduate of Annapolis, he was transferred from the Navy to the war department during the Civil War to organize Union troops in eastern Tennessee. He became a major general before he went back to the Navy, retiring as a rear admiral.

CARTHAGE, Mo. City (pop. 11,104), seat of Jasper Co., in southwestern Missouri on the Spring River. Named for the ancient North African city that once rivaled Rome, it was settled in 1842 and incorporated in 1873. Carthage is noted for its gray marble quarries. During the Civil War it was destroyed by Confederate soldiers (1863), but it was rebuilt three years later. The city is an agricultural trade center (dairy products, grains, and fruits) with diversified manufactures (clothing, concrete, and explosives). Outlaw Belle STARR was born here. George Washington CARVER's birthsite is nearby.

CARVER, George Washington (Carthage, Mo., 1864 — Tuskegee, Ala., Jan. 5, 1943). Black agriculturalist and experimenter. He became a free man early in his life after being born into slavery on the Moses Carver estate. Educated at Simpson College and the State Agricultural College, both in Iowa, Carver earned his Master's degree in science in 1896. Immediately thereafter, he was named chairman of the department of agriculture at Tuskegee Institute in Alabama, where he devoted the remainder of his life to agricultural research. Carver developed products derived from peanuts, sweet potatoes, and soybeans, as well as from cotton wastes, and extracted blue, purple, and red pigments from clay for use in

George Washington Carver at work in his lab

dying. He was noted for his achievements in improving the Southern economy through agriculture, striving particularly to elevate the position of fellow Blacks. Among his many honors, he was named a fellow of The Royal Society, London. Carver's home was made into a national monument in 1953.

CARY, N.C. City (pop. 21,612), Wake Co., in north central North Carolina. A suburb west of Raleigh, it was founded around 1852. Farming is still important here, with cotton and tobacco the chief products. Manufactures include chemicals, electric signs, food products, and machinery. It is the birthplace of author, educator, and ambassador Walter Hines PAGE.

CASTOR RIVER, Mo. River rising in Genevieve Co., Missouri, winding first south, then east for about 75 miles. It passes the Whitewater River before going on to drain into the Mississippi River at CAPE GIRARDEAU.

CATAHOULA LAKE, La. Lake principally in LaSalle Parish, central Louisiana. One of the largest fresh-water lakes in its part of the state, it is a favorite for spring fishing and duck hunting.

CATAWBA INDIANS. Tribe of Siouan linguistic stock that occupied the region between the Yadkin and Catawba Rivers on each side of the boundary line between North and South Carolina. The Catawbas assisted the Carolinians against the TUSCARORA INDIANS in 1711 but four years later they joined a powerful league of southern Indians to rid their country of settlers. In 1751 the English endeavored to bring peace between the Catawba and Iroquois, who had carried on a violent war for many years. The attempt succeeded when the commissioner for South Carolina, William BULL, took the chief sachem of the Catawbas with him to a convention in Albany, N.Y. The Catawbas were again active allies of the Carolinians in 1760 when the CHEROKEES made war upon them. Though few in number at the time of the Revolution, they joined the Americans against the English. Their name has been given to a variety of grape, and numerous places in the South have taken that name either from the tribe directly or from the name of the grape.

CATAWBA RIVER, S.C. Another name for the northern end of the waterway known as the WATEREE. It rises in the mountains of western North Carolina and runs south-southeast.

The stretch known as the Catawba is about 250 miles long, but the river has a total length of about 400 miles. It is an important hydroelectric source.

CATOCHIN MOUNTAINS, Md. Mountain range that runs from south of the Potomac River in Virginia, through Maryland, and into Pennsylvania, paralleling the Monocacy River. High Knob is the tallest peak. The Catochins attract many summer tourists.

CATONSVILLE, Md. Unincorporated city (pop. 33,208), Baltimore Co., in northern Maryland. It is a quiet, residential community that serves as a suburb for Baltimore to the east. First called Johnnycake for an inn established here, much of its early growth was linked to the presence of Roman Catholic schools. Today it primarily offers comfortable housing and large stores.

CATTLE. A major agricultural resource of the South, which each year accounts for one-quarter of the entire U.S. total sales of cattle. There are more than 380,000 farms in the South raising cattle, and their combined sales totaled $7.1 billion in 1980.

Texas leads all states in cattle production with sales of $4.4 billion per year; this is 50% more than any other state in the country. In the region, Kentucky ranks second with sales of $404 million per year, Florida third with sales of $307 million per year, Tennessee fourth with sales of $302 million per year, and Arkansas fifth with sales of $244 million per year.

Cattle is the leading farm commodity in Texas. Although total sales are far lower, cattle is also the leading farm commodity in Virginia and West Virginia.

CAWEIN, Madison Julius (Louisville, Ky., Mar. 23, 1865 — Louisville, Ky., Dec. 8, 1914). Poet. His themes deal largely with the spiritual and supernatural. After receiving encouragement from William Dean Howells, Cawein became nationally recognized and published more than 2,700 poems.

CEDAR CREEK, Battle of. Civil War engagement, part of the Shenandoah campaign, fought on October 19, 1864, near Strasburg in northern Virginia. Sometimes called Belle Grove or Middletown, the battle is usually

Cattle herd on the West Texas Plain

named after a tributary of the North Fork of the Shenandoah River that crossed the field. Although this was the most fiercely contested of the battles, Cedar Creek ended as the third consecutive victory of the Union army's Shenandoah campaign under Gen. Philip H. Sheridan.

The Confederate forces under Gen. Jubal EARLY were reeling from defeats at the third Battle of WINCHESTER and at FISHERS HILL. Regrouped on the south bank of the North Fork of the Shenandoah, however, Early believed his troops capable of defending Cedar Creek and so halting the Union advance. On October 19 he advanced northward across the river to the creek, forcing the Union troops to fall back one mile. Sheridan himself had remained in Winchester, but on the morning of the 19th he made a dramatic ride to Cedar Creek. After arriving in the late morning he ordered the Union advance that broke the Confederate line and sent Early into full retreat the next day. Although most believe the Union would have been victorious even in Sheridan's absence, his dramatic appearance on the field became legendary because of a popular poem called "Sheridan's Ride" by T. Buchannan Read.

CEDAR CREEK, Va. Tributary of the North Fork of the Shenandoah, with its source in Frederick Co., north of Strasburg. The name comes from a heavily cedared area near its lower end. In October, 1864, Gen. P. H. Sheridan defeated Gen. Jubal A. EARLY in the Civil War battle of CEDAR CREEK.

CEDAR KEY, Fla. Small island off the west central coast of the state, in Levy Co., connected to the mainland by a causeway. A busy port and rail station in the mid-1800s, the city (pop. 900) of Cedar Key is noted for fishing and manufacture of palmetto brushes.

CEDARTOWN, Ga. City (pop. 8,619), seat of Polk Co., in northwestern Georgia, near the Alabama border, in the piedmont region. Once a Cherokee settlement, it was incorporated in 1854. Today it is a residential community with some light industry including the production of textiles, which began in the 1920s.

CEMENT. Building material produced from limestone, mixed with water and sand to form concrete, and a major non-fuel mineral resource of the South. The simplest variety, called natural cement, has been produced for

centuries by baking and grinding limestone. Today, however, 96% of the cement produced is the special, stronger variety called Portland cement. It is produced by baking a manufactured carbonate of lime mixed with clay. This elimination of impurities found in natural limestone gives Portland cement greater adhesive properties.

Today the U.S. produces 77 million short tons of cement per year, creating an industry that employs 28,000 people at more than 200 establishments. California is the leading state in cement production, with Texas ranking second in the nation and first in the South. The south Atlantic states produce a far smaller volume of cement, but it is of greater proportionate importance to their mineral industries. Cement is the leading mineral product of South Carolina and an important mining yield in Virginia, Maryland, North Carolina, and Georgia.

CENTER HILL LAKE, Tenn. Artificial reservoir created by impounding the CANEY FORK River for purposes of flood control and hydroelectric power generation in DeKalb Co., Tenn. Its shoreline measures 415 miles and its dam is 2,160 feet long.

CENTRAL BASIN, Tenn. An elliptical-shaped basin covering 6,450 square miles located within the HIGHLAND RIM. It is considered one of the best agricultural regions in the state.

CHADWICK, French Ensor (Morgantown, W.Va., Feb. 29, 1844 — New York, N.Y., Jan. 27, 1919). Naval officer and historian. He was the first U.S. naval attache to London, a member of the *Maine* court of inquiry (1898), and commander of the *U.S.S. New York* as well as chief of staff at the Battle of Santiago (1898) during the Spanish American War. Promoted to rear admiral while president of the Naval War College (1900-03), he later commanded the South Atlantic Squadron. Chadwick authored many books on military strategy.

CHAFFEE, Camp, Ark. Actually part of FORT SMITH, it is located on the Arkansas River. During World War II, it served as an important army development training center.

CHAKCHIUMA INDIANS ("red crawfish"). Tribe whose linguistic stock is uncertain. They inhabited the Yalobusha River region in Mississippi. A warlike tribe, their friendly associations with the French led to their destruction by the CHOCTAW and CHICKASAW Indians.

CHAMBERLAIN, Daniel Henry (West Brookfield, Mass., June 23, 1835 — Charlottesville, Va., Apr. 13, 1907). Politician. A Yale graduate (1862), Chamberlain served in the Massachusetts militia before setting up a law practice in Charleston, S.C. In 1868 and 1872 he was elected South Carolina attorney general, and was governor from 1874 to 1876. During his administration he encouraged higher education for blacks, which led to his defeat in his second run for governorship. Chamberlain later set up a law practice in New York City.

CHAMPION'S HILL, Battle of. Civil War engagement fought May 16, 1863, midway between Vicksburg and Jackson in east central Mississippi. In his campaign to take Vicksburg, Union Gen. Ulysses S. Grant captured JACKSON on May 14, 1863, before turning east toward his goal. Confederate Gen. John C. Pemberton, in command of VICKSBURG, sent a force to meet the Union Army at Champion's Hill. Pemberton had ordered Gen. W. W. Loring to attack first, but he failed to do so. In the subsequent Confederate retreat from Champion's Hill, Loring also failed to return to Vicksburg in time to assist in its defense against the Union siege. Champion's Hill was one of the bloodiest battles in the Vicksburg campaign: counting those wounded, killed, and missing, the Union side lost almost 2,500 men and the Confederate side lost more than 3,500.

CHANCELLORSVILLE, Battle of. Civil War engagement fought May 2-4, 1863, in northeast Virginia. A victory at great cost for the South, it is known as "Lee's masterpiece" because the Confederate leader brilliantly outmaneuvered far superior Union forces.

After the defeat of the Union army at FREDERICKSBURG in 1862, Gen. Joseph Hooker succeeded Gen. Ambrose Burnside as leader of the Army of the Potomac. Gen. Robert E. LEE, meanwhile, had strengthened his position in northeast Virginia preparatory to a second attempt to invade the North. To counteract this threat of invasion, Hooker led his army of 130,000 to the Rappahannock River near Chancellorsville to attack Lee's army of 60,000. Hooker successfully crossed the river and entered the forestland on its south bank on May 1.

Lee's great tactical maneuver consisted principally in sending almost half of his troops, under Gen. Stonewall JACKSON, around Hooker's right flank. This was possible because of the density of the forest, which provided cover for Jackson and slowed Hooker's advance. It was accomplished on May 2, but in the course of the operation Jackson was mistakenly shot and mortally wounded by his own men. He died eight days later.

Jackson was succeeded in the field by Gen. J.E.B. STUART, who launched the main attack against Hooker on May 3. Lee also moved north against Hooker on May 3, causing the Union Army to overestimate the Confederate strength. Hooker, who still maintained numerical superiority, retreated back across the Rappahannock on May 6.

In addition to the loss of Jackson, the victory was costly for the Confederacy because its casualties of 13,000 represented more than 20% of Lee's Army of Northern Virginia. Union casualties numbered 17,000.

CHANCELLORSVILLE, Va. Town (pop. 10,979), located in Spotsylvania Co., between Richmond, Va., and Washington, D.C. Chancellorsville is famous as the site of one of the major conflicts of the Civil War, the Battle of CHANCELLORSVILLE, in which almost 30,000 soldiers died, including Gen. "Stonewall" JACKSON in May, 1863. The Union army was led by Gen. Joseph Hooker, the Confederate army by Gen. Robert E. LEE.

CHANDLER, Albert Benjamin "Happy" (Corydon, Ky., July 14, 1898 —). Politician and baseball commissioner. He was governor of Kentucky (1935-39, 1955-59), as well as U.S. senator from the state (1939-45). He resigned as senator to become commissioner of organized baseball and served until 1951.

CHAPEL HILL, N.C. City (pop. 32,421), Orange Co., northern North Carolina. This residential community is best known as the home of the University of NORTH CAROLINA (1795). The first student to this institution walked 170 miles to attend and was the only student for two weeks. The Carolina Playmakers, affiliated with the university, began here in 1918. The Moorehead Planetarium is also located here. The city was founded in 1792 at the edge of the Piedmont Plateau. Corn, tobacco, and wheat are raised.

CHAPIN, Sarah Flournoy Moore (Sallie) (Charleston, S.C., Mar. 14, 1830 (?) — Charleston, S.C., Apr. 19, 1896). Prohibitionist, author. She converted to the temperance movement in 1879, organized the Charleston Women's Christian Temperance Union (1880), served as a delegate to the National W.C.T.U. convention in Washington, D.C. (1881), as president of the South Carolina W.C.T.U. (1883), and as national superintendent of the Southern Department of the W.C.T.U. (1883-89). Her efforts were rewarded in 1893 with the closing of all bars in South Carolina and the state monopolization over liquor sales. She wrote *FitzHugh St. Clair* (1872), a romantic novel of the Civil War.

CHARITON RIVER, Mo. River rising in southern Iowa, flowing south through the middle of Missouri to join the Missouri River near Glasgow. Partially navigable, the total length of the Chariton is 120 miles.

CHARLESS, Joseph (Westmeath, Ireland, July 16, 1772 — St. Louis, Mo., July 28, 1834). Printer and publisher. After immigrating to New York in 1796, he went to Philadelphia and finally Kentucky in search of work. In 1800, Charless joined the staff of *The Gazette*, in Lexington. Finally settling in Missouri, he began publishing the *Missouri Gazette* in 1808. Charless was noted for his support of Henry Clay and his strong political commentary.

CHARLESTON, S.C. City (pop. 69,510), seat of Charleston Co. and the oldest, second-largest city in South Carolina. An historic seaport, Charleston is situated on the peninsula between the Cooper and Ashley rivers, in southeastern South Carolina. It is famous for its many well-preserved colonial and antebellum homes and other buildings. Charleston was settled in 1670 and named Charles Town, after King Charles II. The name was changed to Charleston in 1783 following the Revolutionary War and the withdrawal of British troops that occupied the city from 1780-82. Charleston was involved in armed conflict with the colonies of Louisiana and Florida during Queen Anne's War (1702-13) and soon afterwards with a local Indian league led by Chief Yamasee. The seat of South Carolina's Provincial Congress in 1775, Charleston acted as the state capital until 1788. Incorporated in 1794, it was an important cotton and rice exporter in the early 1800s, but protective tariffs imposed by the European markets effectively ended this

An early painting of Charleston, S.C. in the 1850s, by John William Hill

trade. Instead, Charleston became a pioneer in railroad building. In 1830 the first American steam engine to go into regular service, *The Best Friend of Charleston*, began operating out of the city. In 1860 the South Carolina Ordinance of Secession was passed in Charleston, and the Civil War officially began here with the capture of nearby Fort SUMTER by Confederate forces on April 14, 1861. After the Civil War, Charleston's economy diversified. Fertilizer became a major industry, based on nearby phosphate deposits. A severe earthquake in 1886 caused extensive damage and an economic slowdown, but still left many historic buildings standing.

With the dredging of the harbor to allow entrance of large ocean-going vessels, port activity increased dramatically. Military installations were built and manned during the early 1900s, helping the area's economy. Later, the completion of the enormous SANTEE-COOPER hydroelectric project in 1942 further spurred industry. Products now being made in Charleston include paper and pulp, asbestos materials, clothing, cigars, rubber products, fertilizer, petroleum, forest products, and iron and scrap steel goods.

A very cosmopolitan city, Charleston has attracted many different peoples in its 300-year history. The first settlers were English, followed by French Huguenots, Irish, German, and Swiss newcomers. The largest 18th century colonial American Jewish settlement was here. Charleston also has a large black population. Points of interest include White Point Gardens, Cypress Gardens, The Dock Street Theatre, Heward-Washington House (1770) and the Joseph Manigualt House (1803). Charleston is home to the College of South Carolina, Baptist College, The Citadel military college, South Carolina Medical University, and U.S. Naval and Air Force bases.

CHARLESTON, Siege of. Revolutionary War action by the British army against the coastal South Carolina city that began on April 1, 1780 and ended with the fall of the city on May 12, 1780. The maneuvers at Charleston were an attempt by the British to extend their control of the Southern colonies following their capture of Savannah, Ga., in 1778 and successful defense of the city in the fall of 1779. Following his defeat at Savannah, Gen. Benjamin Lincoln consolidated a force of 5,000 Continental militiamen in Charleston. Encouraged by the news from Savannah, British Gen. Henry Clinton sailed south from Rhode Island with 8,000 troops to take Charleston. By the time the siege began, Clinton's superior forces had been reinforced by the British fleet of Admiral Marriot Arbuthnot.

Lincoln's position was hopeless, but he agreed to defend the city at the urgings of South Carolina's colonial authorities. He managed to hold the city for six weeks, although by the end of April his only escape route had been cut off. On May 12, having had 250 killed and wounded during the siege, Lincoln was forced to surrender the entire remaining Revolutionary force and its munitions to the British.

Having captured Lincoln's force and gained effective control of South Carolina, Gen. Clinton returned to New York. In command of the British army in South Carolina he left Lord Charles Cornwallis, who soon after initiated the Battle of Camden.

CHARLESTON, W.Va. City (pop. 63,968), seat of Kanawha Co. and state capital of West Virginia in the Allegheny Mountains at the confluence of the Elk and Kanawha Rivers. The city is considered the hub of the Kanawha Valley industry and produces chemicals, coal, glass, steel, and timber.

The original site was purchased (reportedly for less than $1) in 1788 by Col. George Clendenin, who named the settlement Charles Town and built Fort Lee. The city soon became an important shipping and transportation point because of its location on the route to the Ohio Valley. Frontiersmen like Simon Kenton and Daniel BOONE were attracted to the area, the latter representing the settlement in the Virginia Assembly (1790-91). Charleston was incorporated in 1794. Local brine wells were discovered and worked as early as 1795, and the city developed into an important salt center by 1823. During the Civil War, residents were divided in allegiance. Union troops seized the city after the Battle of CHARLESTON on September 13, 1862. The city challenged Wheeling for the designation as state capital and after an 1877 election, it became the permanent capital in 1885. The State Capitol, completed in 1932 by Cass Gilbert, houses a museum of art and natural history. Three colleges, including West Virginia State College, are based in or near the city.

CHARLOTTE, N.C. City (pop. 314,447), seat of Mecklenburg Co., in the Piedmont region near the Catawba River, south central North Carolina. Originally settled in 1750 and incorporated in 1768, it was the center of the nation's major gold production until the California Gold Rush (1849), and a U.S. mint was established here. During the Civil War Charlotte served as a Confederate naval yard and, in 1865, Confederate President Jefferson Davis convened his last full cabinet meeting here. As a major distribution point, its diversified manufacturing includes machinery, textiles, metal, and food products. The first North Carolina college was chartered here in 1771 but was disallowed by English officials. Presidents Andrew JACKSON and James POLK were born nearby and attended city schools. The city's official emblem is a hornet's nest, which was the nickname given Charleston by Lord Cornwallis during his occupation of the city in 1780. It is the home of the University of North Carolina at Charlotte, Queens College, Central Piedmont Community College, Johnson C. Smith University, and Kings College.

CHARLOTTESVILLE, Va. City (pop. 45,010), seat of Albemarle Co., in central Virginia. Charlottesville is an important educational center. It has some manufacturing along with publishing, cattle and horse raising, and is where many research firms have offices. Named for Queen Charlotte, consort of England's George III, it was settled in the 1730s. Charlottesville is home to the University of VIRGINIA, founded in 1819 by Thomas Jefferson. One of the nation's historic shrines, MONTICELLO, the home of Jefferson is here. Other famous residents of Charlottesville include George Rogers CLARK, Meriwether LEWIS, William CLARK, and Presidents James MADISON and James MONROE.

CHASE, Samuel (Somerset Co., Md., Apr. 17, 1741 — Baltimore, Md., June 19, 1811). Legislator, Supreme Court justice, and signer of the Declaration of Independence. An active opponent of the Stamp Act and a member of the Continental Congress, he helped convince Maryland to support colonial withdrawal from England. Twenty years a member of the Maryland legislature, he became chief judge of the state general court in 1788. President George Washington appointed Chase to the Supreme Court in 1796, where he served as an outspoken member for fifteen years, strengthening dueprocess clauses relative to government power over liberty and property (*Calder* vs. *Bull*, 1798). Chase, a Federalist, used his court as a political weapon against the Jeffersonian Republicans. As a result, the House voted impeachment (1805) for arbitrary rulings in trials for treason and sedition (*Fries* vs. *Callendar*,

1800). His acquittal by the Senate (1805) increased judicial independence.

CHATTAHOOCHEE NATIONAL FOREST, Ga. A 745,614-acre national forest covering the state's BLUE RIDGE MOUNTAINS and extending north, with elevations of 1,000 to 5,000 feet. It is a highly popular tourist and nature attraction with sites for camping.

CHATTAHOOCHEE RIVER, Ala./ Fla./Ga. River rising in northeast Georgia. It flows 435 miles southwest then south to join the FLINT River at the Florida border, emptying into Lake SEMINOLE. The Chattahoochee forms a section of the Georgia boundary with Alabama and Florida. Colored red from Georgia clay, the river is an important trade and commercial route. Dams constructed since 1950, including the Walter F. George Lock and Dam, have made the river navigable to Columbus, Ga.

CHATTANOOGA, Tenn. City (pop. 169,565), seat of Hamilton Co., located on Moccasin Bend of the Tennessee River near the Georgia border. An important industrial city as well as a favorite destination of tourists, Chattanooga has many transportation lines (the river, railroads, and highways) for shipping. The city's many industries produce such products as farm implements, chemicals, clay products, clothing, iron and steel products, machinery, furniture, nuclear reactors, and steam boilers. There are also large insurance and warehousing concerns. Chattanooga is headquarters for the powerful Tennessee Valley Authority (TVA), which, with its nearby hydroelectric plants, as well as administrative offices, contributes significantly to the city's economic lifeblood.

An historic city, Chattanooga's original inhabitants were CHICKAMAUGA INDIANS, a branch of the Cherokee tribe. Named Ross's Landing afer John Ross, who established a trading center here in 1815 to do business with the Indians, the community was renamed in 1837 and incorporated in 1851. The railroad came through in the 1840s, augmenting river travel, which had previously been the chief way to move people and goods in and out of the city. During the Civil War, Chattanooga was an important Confederate communications point. A major object of capture by Union forces, the city finally fell in 1863 after the battles of CHICKAMAUGA and CHATTANOOGA. The city continued to grow after the war but its most significant growth was experienced in the 1930s with the coming of the TVA.

The many historic points of interest include the enormous Chickamauga and Chattanooga Military Park, which takes in nearby Lookout Mountain, Signal Mountain, and other peaks. Nearby Lake Chickamauga provides watersports and recreational opportunities. Chattanooga has a symphony, opera, and the well-known Hunter Gallery of Art. Institutions of higher education include the University of Tennessee at Chattanooga, Covenant College, Tennessee Temple College, and the Seventh Day Adventist Southern Missionary College.

CHAWASH INDIANS ("raccoon place [people]"). Tribe of Tunican linguistic stock located on Bayou La Fourche, east of the Gulf of Mexico, and across the Mississippi River. Generally friendly with the French, they were nearly destroyed in 1729 when Governor Perrier, following an attack by the Natchez Indians on New Orleans, allowed a band of Negro slaves to attack the Chawash. Little is known of them after this period and it is supposed that they joined the WASHA tribe with whom they had been closely associated.

CHEAHA, Mount, Ala. Cleburne Co. The state's highest peak (2,407 feet), found in the Talladega Mountains on the northwest edge of the Piedmont, in the Appalachian Trail area. It is part of a state park.

CHEAT RIVER, W.Va. Waterway created by the merging of the Shavers and Black Rivers in northern West Virginia. A branch of the MONONGAHELA RIVER, it then runs 78 miles north, through the Laurel Mountains and Cheat Lake, to drain into the Monongahela at Point Marion, Pa.

CHENNAULT, Claire Lee (Commerce, Tex., Sept. 6, 1893 — New Orleans, La., July 27, 1958). Military aviator. A former high school principal in Texas, Chennault joined the U.S. Army Air Service in World War I. Retired from the army, in 1937 he became air adviser to Generalissimo Chiang Kai-shek of China, and in 1941 he organized the Flying Tigers, volunteer American fliers who fought with China against Japan. He was recalled to the army in 1942, and in 1943, Chennault became commander of the U.S. 14th Air Force in China. He retired as a major general in 1945.

CHERAW INDIANS. Tribe thought to have been of Siouan linguistic stock, mentioned by DE SOTO chronicles in 1540. In the 1600s they moved from South Carolina to Henderson, Polk, and Rutherford counties in North Carolina. The Cheraw incorporated with the CATAWBA in the early 1700s after suffering attacks from the Iroquois and engaging in constant hostilities against North Carolina settlers.

CHEROKEE INDIANS. Tribe of Hokan-Siouan linguistic stock that inhabited the hilly regions of Tennessee, North Carolina, South Carolina, Georgia, and northern Alabama. They have been called the "mountaineers of the South" and were one of the most important tribes in North America. When DESOTO first saw them in the 16th century they already had an advanced culture based on agriculture. In 1711 they united with the Carolina settlers and CATAWBAS against the TUSCARORA tribe, but they joined the great Indian league against the Carolinians in 1715. The British government sent Sir Alexander Cumming (1730) to conclude a treaty of peace with the Cherokee, and after meeting with them Cumming took seven members of the tribe with him to England. In 1750 the Cherokee suffered from a severe smallpox epidemic which destroyed half their population.

Their relationship with the settlers remained friendly until a confrontation in 1759 when two Cherokee chiefs were accused of killing a white man. Two years of war followed until their defeat in 1761 by Colonel James Grant. During the Revolution they sided with the British. In 1796, President Washington announced that the Cherokee tribe would be used in an educational experiment and Dartmouth College set up grants to educate them. The Cherokees adopted a form of government modeled after that of the United States (1820), including a written constitution, and established themselves as the Cherokee Nation (1827). They published the first Indian newspaper in 1828.

Pressure brought about by settlers advancing on their lands in Georgia caused the Cherokee living in that region to sign the Treaty of New Echota (1835), which bound the entire tribe to move west of the Mississippi and in 1838 the tribe was deported, by military force, to the Indian territory in Oklahoma. Their chief during this period was John ROSS. During the Civil War they divided their allegiance between the North and the South. In 1906 their tribal government came to an end and they became U.S. citizens.

CHEROKEE NATIONAL FOREST. A 624,000-acre forest found in two separate strips along the Tennessee-North Carolina border. It boasts more than 500 trails, including the Appalachian. Named for the Indian tribe that once inhabited the land, the forest includes river gorges, rocky mountains, streams, large forest areas, and waterfalls. It lies northeast and southwest of the GREAT SMOKY MOUNTAINS NATIONAL PARK.

CHERRY POINT MARINE CORPS AIR STATION, N.C. The largest U.S. Marine Corps air base, it serves as the headquarters for the Marine Corps Air Bases, Eastern Area, and features a marine aircraft wing. The station was built in 1942 and covers 12,000 acres of land that was formerly forest and swamps, in Cracen Co., N.C. It was named for a former post office that served regional lumber camps until 1935. Facilities for major aircraft overhaul are found here.

CHESAPEAKE, Va. City (pop. 114,226), located in southeastern Virginia on the Elizabeth River. A merger of Norfolk Co. and the city of South Norfolk formed the city of Chesapeake in 1963, making it the largest city in Virginia in area (over 340 square miles). Settled in the mid-1600s, extensive development did not begin until the 1900s. The economy of Chesapeake includes farming and the manufacture of lumber, fertilizer, and cement, and it is a storage site for grain and petroleum products. The city adopted a council-manager form of government.

CHESAPEAKE **AFFAIR, The.** Naval encounter off the coast of Virginia on June 22, 1807, that was a contributing cause of the War of 1812. Commanded by Commodore James Barron, the *Chesapeake* left Norfolk, Va., and was confronted by the British frigate *Leopard*, which demanded rights to inspect the American ship for deserters from the British Napoleonic War. The demand was refused, and the *Chesapeake* fired a shot across the bow of the British vessel. The *Leopard* then captured the *Chesapeake*, and the British removed four deserters, two of them American by birth. The British refused reparations for the event until 1811, when the two Americans were returned. Despite this, the *Chesapeake* affair remained a rallying cry against British intervention in American waters at the opening of the War of 1812.

CHESAPEAKE AND OHIO CANAL, Md. An abandoned project originally planned to connect the Potomac River with the Ohio River. Funds were raised for the waterway in 1828, through generous contributions from landowners along the Potomac and Chesapeake Bay, in an effort to establish an artificial water channel as a trade route to the Ohio River Valley. In 1837, with about 100 miles finished, the project was slowed down until construction ended completely in 1850. At a total cost of $11 million, the waterway extends approximately 185 miles westward. Active use of the canal stopped in the early 1920s.

CHESAPEAKE BAY, Va./Md. Separating the eastern shore of Maryland from Virginia, the bay was once called the Gateway to the New World, referring to the three shiploads of colonists who arrived on April 26, 1607. Its Indian name means "Mother of Waters" or "Great Salt Bay." Two capes mark the 15-mile stretch of water where it meets the Atlantic, Charles on the north and Henry on the south (named for the two oldest sons of James I). Numerous military confrontations occurred in and around the Bay during the Revolution, the War of 1812, and the Civil War.

The inlet is 200 miles long and varies in width from four to 40 miles. One of the most important ports of entry on the eastern seacoast, the area is dotted with deep tidal rivers and bays that form a system of natural harbors. BALTIMORE and NORFOLK are the most important ports. The largest rivers emptying into the Bay are the JAMES, PATUXENT, POTOMAC, RAPPAHANNOCK, SUSQUEHANNA, and YORK. Along with the area's commercial importance, it is also a popular recreational spot and a fisherman's paradise, noted for its oysters and crabs, which are also sold commercially. There is a U.S. naval base at Hampton Roads.

In 1964 the CHESAPEAKE BAY BRIDGE-TUNNEL was opened to connect Virginia Beach/Norfolk with the Eastern Shore (peninsula) of Virginia, eliminating the long inland route around the Bay.

CHESAPEAKE BAY BRIDGE-TUNNEL, Va. Often referred to as one of the Seven Wonders of the Modern World, the complex system consists of two tunnels (totaling two miles), two bridges (totaling 3.6 miles), and 12 miles of trestles for a total length of 17.6 miles. Opened in 1964 after three and a half years of construction time, it connects Virginia Beach/Norfolk with the Eastern Shore (penin-

A portion of the 17.5-mile Chesapeake Bay Bridge-Tunnel complex

sula) of Virginia, and provides a short, easy route to avoid the long inland detour via Baltimore, Washington, and Richmond. The cost, privately financed by revenue bonds, was $20 million. Upon payment of the bonds through toll monies, the facility will pass gratis to the state (it is scheduled to be paid off in the year 2000).

CHESAPEAKE CAPES, Battle of. Revolutionary War naval battle fought off the mouth of the Chesapeake Bay in Virginia on September 5, 1781. British commander Lord Charles Cornwallis had chosen to defend Yorktown, Va., although his superiors feared he would be cut off from the sea. He was cut off on August 30, when the French fleet under Admiral Francois De Grasse entered the bay. On August 31 the British fleet under Admiral Thomas Graves and Rear Admiral Samuel Hood sailed from New York to assist Cornwallis. De Grasse sailed out of the bay to meet them on September 5. The naval battle was indecisive, but following it the British ships returned to New York and the French returned to the bay. Cornwallis remained cut off from the sea, and this was one of the direct causes of his surrender to Commander-in-chief George Washington at Yorktown on October 19.

CHESDIN LAKE, Va. Reservoir on the Appomattox River covering 3,500 acres in Chesterfield, Amelia, and Dinwiddie Counties. Constructed for recreational use and as a water supply to nearby cities, its name is a combination of *Ches*terfield and *Din*widdie.

CHESNUT, Mary Boykin Miller (Camden, S.C., Mar. 31, 1823 — Camden, S.C., Nov. 22, 1886). Author. Born and married into families of prominence, she knew most of the South's civilian and military elite. With the on-

set of the Civil War she kept a detailed diary of events, attitudes, and high society that has become a valued historical source. Her diary is also a witness to the strong abolitionist feeling current in the South even during the war. Never wholly published, it was edited in 1905 as *A Diary from Dixie.*

CHESTERTOWN, Md. Town (pop. 3,300), seat of Kent Co., Eastern Shore, on the Chester River across from Kent Island, where one end of the Chesapeake Bay Bridge is located. The first Maryland settlement was made here and it is the home of Washington College (1782), and Emmanuel Church, a Protestant Episcopal Church that declared its independence from the Church of England.

CHEVES, Langdon (Rocky River, S.C., Sept. 17, 1776 — Columbia, S.C., June 26, 1857). Lawyer and politician. He became one of Charleston's leading lawyers after his admission to the bar in 1797. He was a member of the South Carolina legislature (1802-10), and during his term in the U.S. House of Representatives (1811-15), he was one of the "war hawks," who advocated financial preparedness, and a House speaker. Although he opposed the formation of the Second Bank of the U.S., he became its director and president in 1819, helping it out of financial trouble.

CHIAHA INDIANS. Tribe of Muskogean linguistic stock, that lived first in eastern Georgia and Burns Island, Tenn., later moving to the middle course of the Chattahoochee River. Encountered by DESOTO in 1540, they were part of the Upper Creek Confederacy and following the CREEK WAR some moved on to the Indian Territory in Oklahoma and others to Florida.

CHICKAHOMINY INDIANS. Tribe of Algonquian linguistic stock residing in the area of the CHICKAHOMINY River (to which they gave their name) in Virginia. They were members of the POWHATAN Confederacy.

CHICKAHOMINY RIVER, Va. A 90-mile river rising in eastern Virginia and flowing southeast to join the JAMES. Its name is Indian in origin, coming from the word "checahamined" (land of much grain), referring to the fertile, productive area through which it flows. The Chickahominy was the scene of heavy fighting during the Peninsula Campaign of the Civil War.

CHICKAMAUGA, Battle of. Civil War engagement fought September 19-20, 1863, in northwest Georgia. A victory for the Confederate army under Gen. Braxton BRAGG, it provided a glimmer of hope for the Confederacy between the losses of VICKSBURG and Chattanooga.

The Battle of Chickamauga was a tactically complex one marked by poor communications and general confusion on both sides. The Union army under Gen. William Starke Rosecrans moved south into Georgia and occupied high ground west of Chickamauga Creek in the mistaken belief that Bragg was evacuating Chattanooga, just across the Tennessee border. Bragg wasted good opportunities to attack groups of the Union force isolated by hills such as Lookout Mountain and Missionary Ridge. The battle commenced on September 19 after a chance encounter between the sides, and it turned in the Confederacy's favor on September 20 when Gen. James LONGSTREET happened by chance upon a break in the Union line. Late on the second day of fighting Rosecrans left the field in the belief that the battle was lost, but Union Gen. George Henry Thomas ("The Rock of Chickamauga") held his position and prevented Confederate pursuit.

Rosecrans, who was relieved of his command because of Chickamauga, lost 16,000 of his 58,000 troops. Bragg, whose reputation rose with the victory, lost 18,000 of his 66,000 troops.

CHICKAMAUGA LAKE, Tenn. Body of water on the Tennessee River, in Hamilton Co., formed by a Tennessee Valley Authority dam northeast of Chattanooga in 1936. It serves as a navigation and hydroelectric power source. The lake has an 810-mile shoreline and covers 35,400 acres.

CHICKASAW BLUFFS, Battle of. Civil War engagement fought December 29, 1862, on the outskirts of Vicksburg, Miss., on the east bank of the Mississippi River. It was one of the earliest maneuvers by Union Gen. Ulysses S. Grant to capture VICKSBURG amd so to split the Confederacy along the Mississippi River. The Union assault on the Chickasaw Bluffs was commanded by Gen. William Tecumseh Sherman, who brought his troops down the Mississippi and landed at the YAZOO RIVER north of Vicksburg on December 26. This force of 32,000 then required two days to move through the river swamps to the foot of the bluffs. When

they attacked on December 29, the Confederate defenders numbering only 6,000 were able to inflict heavy casualties by firing down from protected positions at the top of the bluffs. By the time Sherman abandoned his attack, the Union had lost nearly 2,000 men while the Confederate defenders had lost scarcely 200. "I reached Vicksburg at the time appointed," Sherman later wrote, "landed, assaulted, and failed."

CHICKASAW INDIANS. Tribe of Muskogean linguistic stock that inhabited northern Mississippi and extended into Alabama, South Carolina, Georgia, Arkansas, Kentucky, Oklahoma, and Tennessee. One of the most warlike tribes of the Gulf area, they were early friends of the English and inveterate foes of the French, who twice (1736 and 1740) invaded their country under BIENVILLE and De NOAILLES. Legends say the Chickasaw came from west of the Mississippi River under the guardianship of a great dog, and with a pole for a guide. At night they stuck the pole in the ground, and went in the direction it leaned every morning. Their dog drowned while crossing the Mississippi, and after a while their pole, in the interior of Alabama, remained upright, and there they settled. Though constantly at war with the CHOCTAW and other CREEK Indians, they were closely related to the Choctaw in language and culture.

The Chickasaw favored the English in the Revolution but in 1795 joined the settlers in the CREEK WAR. In 1834 they ceded all their lands to the U.S. (6.5 million acres for which they received $3.5 million), and joined the Choctaw in Oklahoma. During their migration a smallpox epidemic destroyed a large number of their tribe. In 1855 they were politically separated from the Choctaws and set up an independent government modeled after that of the United States. This government lasted until it merged with the state of Oklahoma.

CHICKASAWHAY RIVER, Miss. River rising in eastern Mississippi's Red Hills, at the Okatibbee Reservoir. It travels south southwest to join the PASCAGOULA River and enter the Mississippi Sound, with a length of about 150 miles.

CHICOT LAKE, Ark. The state's largest natural lake, found in the southeastern tip of Arkansas alongside the Mississippi River, near the Louisiana border. It is actually a riverbed lagoon and an abandoned channel of the Mississippi now separated from it by high levees. The lake is oxbow or crescent shaped, 15 miles long, and about a half-mile wide. A state park offering camping, fishing, and swimming surrounds Chicot Lake. At the upper end of the lake is Stuart's Island, which once held an outlaw stronghold before it was burned in the early 19th century.

CHINCOTEAGUE BAY, Md. Long, narrow inlet along the southeastern Maryland and northeastern Virginia Atlantic coasts, extending for more than 50 miles. It separates AS-SATEAGUE, CHINCOTEAGUE, and other islands from the mainland coast. The area is a favorite vacation spot.

CHIPOLA RIVER, Fla. River originating in several branches near Dorthan in southern Alabama, it flows south through northwest Florida's Jackson, Calhoun, and Gulf counties to join the APALACHICOLA RIVER above Wehwahitchka. The Chipola is navigable for 40 miles.

CHISHOLM TRAIL. Cattle trail that ran from San Antonio, Tex., to Abilene, Kan. The trail was named for Indian trader Jesse Chisholm, who drove a wagon loaded with buffalo hides down it in 1866. It played a major role in the development of the cattle industry in the southwest. In 1867 a cattle shipping depot serving the Kansas Pacific Railroad was opened in Abilene. Between that time and 1871, a reported 1.5 million head of cattle were brought along the trail for shipment to the East Coast. The trail went practically unused after 1871, except for a brief hiatus during the 1880s when the Santa Fe Railroad moved into Kansas.

CHITIMACHA INDIANS ("those who have pots"). Tribe of Tunican linguistic stock that inhabited Louisiana on the lower course of Bayou La Teche, on Grand River, and on Grand Lake. Noted for their excellent basket making, they were once the most powerful tribe of the northern Gulf Coast west of Florida. Years of war with the French in the early 1700s resulted in many Chitimacha being turned into slaves. Peace was concluded in 1718 and they were given a reservation, but their numbers rapidly declined. In 1881 considerable linguistic material was collected from the few survivors.

Chuck wagon at mealtime during a cattle drive

CHOCTAW INDIANS. The largest Indian tribe belonging to the southern Muskogean linguistic group, found in the southern part of Mississippi and western Alabama. A peaceful, agricultural people, they became allies of the early French settlers. In the Revolutionary War they joined with the English but afterward were granted peaceable possession of their lands by the United States government. In the War of 1812 and the CREEK WAR they served with U.S. troops, and in 1820 ceded a part of their lands for a domain later to be called the IN-DIAN TERRITORY in Oklahoma. Emigration west of the Mississippi began as early as 1800 and in 1830, after the Treaty of Dancing Rabbit, the remaining Choctaws ceded their lands and moved west. They joined in an alliance with the Confederates during the Civil War and lost a large number of their tribe.

CHOCTAWHATCHEE BAY, Fla. Okaloosa and Walton Counties. This bay leads into the northwest portion of Florida from the Gulf of Mexico, and is connected to PENSACOLA BAY, 35 miles to the west, by the SANTA ROSA SOUND. It is part of the Intracoastal Waterway.

CHOCTAWHATCHEE RIVER, Ala./ Fla. River rising in central Barbour Co., Ala., and flowing southwest to Florida's Choctawhatchee Bay, where it produces a major delta sheltering the bay. About 174 miles long, it is navigable in the lower portion. Once its banks were heavily populated with Creek Indians.

CHOPIN, Kate O'Flaherty (St. Louis, Mo., Feb. 8, 1851 — St. Louis, Mo., Aug. 22, 1904). Author. Of Irish-Creole descent, she married a Louisiana businessman in 1870 and moved to New Orleans. She returned to St. Louis after his death and began to write, drawing largely on the life of the bayou. Her work, which includes *The Awakening* (1899) and *Bayou Folk* (1894), was considered controversial because of her treatment of American mores.

CHOPTANK RIVER, Md. Major waterway beginning in central Delaware and coursing southwest through eastern Maryland for 80 miles to drain into the CHESAPEAKE BAY at Hudson. It is one of the seven large rivers that cross the eastern shore of Maryland.

CHOUTEAU, Auguste Pierre (St. Louis, Mo., May 9, 1786 — Fort Gibson, Mo., Dec. 25, 1838). Fur trader. An 1806 graduate of the U.S. Military Academy at West Point, N.Y., he resigned his army post in 1807 and two years later became a member of his family's St. Louis Missouri Fur Company. In 1817 he was captured by the Spanish while on a trading expedition to the upper Arkansas River. He later settled in Oklahoma where he traded with the Osage Indians. Washington Irving was a member of one of Chouteau's expeditions, which is described in Irving's *Tour of the Prairies* (1835). He was the son of Rene Auguste CHOUTEAU.

CHOUTEAU, Jean Pierre (New Orleans, La., Oct. 10, 1758 — St. Louis, Mo., July 10, 1849). American Indian agent and fur trader. He moved to St. Louis in 1764 to join his brother Rene Auguste CHOUTEAU and help organize the family fur trading company. Granted exclusive rights with his brother to trade with the Osage Indians, he is credited with founding the first permanent settlement at Salina in what is now the state of Oklahoma. He served as the U.S. agent for all Indian tribes west of the Mississippi River (1804-07) and of the Osage tribe after 1807. He also served on the board of trustees of the city of St. Louis.

CHOUTEAU, Rene Auguste (New Orleans, La., 1749 — St. Louis, Mo., Feb. 24, 1829). American merchant. At age 14, he accompanied French merchant Pierre LACLEDE on an expedition authorized by the French government of Louisiana to trade west of the Mississippi River. In 1764 they established a post that would later become the city of St. Louis. The two men founded a major fur trading business, which Chouteau assumed with his brother Jean Pierre CHOUTEAU, after Laclede's death. When St. Louis became part of the U.S. in 1803, he became a court of common pleas justice in the territory and became president of the first board of trustees of St. Louis in 1809. He also represented the U.S. government in the negotiation of Indian treaties.

CHOWAN RIVER, N.C. Forty-five-mile-long river beginning at the confluence of two rivers north of Winston, North Carolina. It flows southeast into Albemarle Sound.

CHOWANOC INDIANS ("people of the south"). Tribe of Algonquian linguistic stock that inhabited the area at the junction of the Meherrin, Blackwater, and Chowan Rivers in North Carolina. A powerful Algonquian tribe, they made a treaty with the English Crown

(1663) that they soon broke, and they were placed on a reservation. Though they sided with the colonists in the TUSCARORA War, they were eventually placed on another reservation, with the Tuscarora, and were incorporated with that tribe in 1733.

CHRISTIANSBURG, Va. City (pop. 10,345), seat of Montgomery Co., in southwestern Virginia. It was founded in 1792 and first called Hans Meadow. It was later named for Col. William Christian, brother-in-law of Patrick Henry. Its economy is a blend of diversified farming and industry. Manufactures include textiles, canned goods, beverages, and lumber products.

CIVIL WAR, The. The war between Southern states attempting secession from the United States and the Northern ones battling to preserve the federal union; the most important internal conflict in American history and the great cataclysm in the history of the South. It lasted almost exactly four years, from the firing on the federal arsenal at Fort Sumter, South Carolina, on April 12, 1861, to the Southern surrender at APPOMATTOX COURT HOUSE, Virginia, on April 9 1865. This was not a true "civil war" because the intent was not to replace the federal government with another. Rather, it was a rebellion to achieve independence for the region to be known as the Confederate States of America. Hence other names have been proposed: the WAR BETWEEN THE STATES, the War of the Rebellion, the War of Secession, and the War for Southern Independence.

The Civil War is interpreted by most historians as the inevitable outcome of rifts between the Northern and Southern states present even in the days of the American Revolution. The two regions were polarized even then by different economic organizations and fundamentally divergent political interests. The South revolved around a "monoculture" of King Cotton, a labor intensive economy epitomized by large plantations worked by slave labor. This was a "low capital" economy that permitted wealth to be amassed by hard work, given the opportunity of free trade unimpeded by tariffs. In contrast, the energies of the North were focused on industry, a "high capital" economy based on investment in equipment intensive manufacturing plants worked by an immigrant labor force and kept competitive by protective tariffs. This economic contrast oversimplifies the actual demography of the two regions,

which were scarcely all plantations or all industrial plants; but it does precisely identify the political power within each, which was vested, respectively, in a minority of prosperous slave owners or of manufacturers.

The provocation for war originally focused on tariff issues and only later shifted to the constitutional issues of secession and the abolition of slavery. In the forty years before the war, the rift between the regions widened and evolved into an intense political struggle for control of the opening American West. Congressional opponents struggled to bolster the political strength of either North or South by admitting territories to the Union as either "free" or "slave" states. Beginning with the MISSOURI COMPROMISE of 1820, which brought Missouri into the union as a "slave" state and Maine into the Union as a "free" state, compromise solutions predominated, with Kentuckian Henry CLAY serving as "the great compromiser." The final such compromise was negotiated in 1850, after which admission status was dependent on "popular sovereignty," the right of internal self-determination institutionalized by the Kansas-Nebraska Act of 1854.

In effect, popular sovereignty invited outside agitation, notably the violent clashes between the New England abolitionists and proslavery Missouri antagonists who vied for control of the Kansas Territory in the late 1850's. At the same time, Northern abolitionists enraged the South with subversions such as the "underground railroad" which smuggled slaves to freedom, while the North was itself outraged by the 1857 DRED SCOTT DECISION of the Supreme Court that blocked prohibition of slavery in the territories. Harriet Beecher Stowe's rather sentimental version of slave existence in *Uncle Tom's Cabin*, published in 1852, fueled Northern bias against all Southerners, while John BROWN's irrational 1859 raid on HARPER'S FERRY to foment a slave rebellion intensified Southern anger at encroachment by outside abolitionists.

While secessionist sentiment spread through the South, President James Buchanan pursued a course of appeasement that amounted to inaction. The only possible course of reconciliation was election of a Democratic President acceptable to North and South in 1860. But the Democrats split, with the North supporting Stephen A. Douglas of Illinois and the South supporting John C. Breckinridge of Kentucky. This gave the victory, with 40% of the popular vote, to Abraham LINCOLN of the new Republican party, formed six years earlier on the platform of excluding slavery from the territories.

The 1860 election of this "Black Republican" was the final straw for secessionists, particularly in South Carolina, where ordinances of secession were passed even before Lincoln was inaugurated. As the inauguration drew near, desperate compromises were proposed, notably the Crittenden Plan, proposed by John J. CRITTENDEN of Kentucky, to modify popular sovereignty and protect existing slavery. But his bill failed in Congress and by February, 1861, secession changed from threat to fact with the formation of the Confederate States of America by South Carolina, Alabama, Mississippi, Florida, Georgia, Louisiana, and Texas. Their constitutional justification was the concept of state's rights, the argument that the Union was a federal league of sovereign states, each of which retained the legal right to withdraw. On these grounds the seven states seceded under the Presidency of Jefferson DAVIS and appropriated federal outposts within their borders. On his inauguration in March, 1861, Lincoln threatened no immediate emancipation of slaves, but he did vow to hold all federal outposts, one of which was Fort Sumter in the Charleston, South Carolina harbor. When Lincoln ordered the provisioning of Sumter, hoping to embarass the South should it "fire on bread," Jefferson Davis ordered an artillery bombardment, which captured the fort without any loss of life. Lincoln responded with a demand for volunteers to end the "insurrection." The Confederacy viewed this as a declaration of war, and the seven original seceeding states were joined by Arkansas, North Carolina, Tennessee, and, most important, Virginia, which lost its West Virginia counties to the Union in 1863. By May, the South had a new national capital at Richmond, Virginia, and the U.S. had become, in Lincoln's words, "a house divided."

At the moment of that division, the United States Army was a small force devoted to westward conquests and the Navy had been relatively inactive since the War of 1812. Both were as deeply split over the issue of secession as the nation as a whole, and both faced massive resignations by Confederate sympathizers. Hence the contending sides were forced to mobilize for war virtually from scratch. Shifting allegiances led to a traumatic "war between brothers" unparalleled in American history. In this effort the North possessed seemingly overwhelming advantages, with 23 states, 7 territories, and a population of 22 million constantly growing from immigration. In addition, the North held virtually all available munitions factories and railroad equipment, 80% of American bank deposits, including most of the South's, and a working government streamlined to delegate responsibility and to muster resources.

The South included but 11 states with a population of 9 million, more than one-third of which consisted of slaves. Its single valuable economic resource was cotton, a potential attraction to allies, especially Britain and France, whose textile industries relied on Southern cotton. The South found some early support from Europe, notably in shipbuilding, but as the Union's military supremacy became apparent European countries became more wary of aiding a losing cause, and "cotton diplomacy" proved a misplaced hope.

However, the South did possess less tangible assets. It had a great military tradition, and for its leaders could draw upon some of the most brilliant graduates of West Point, the U.S. Military Academy. It was also fighting for a treasured local heritage and against palpable oppressors. The North, in contrast, had to fight against a distant evil, and its internal unrest was apparent in persistent draft riots, especially those in New York City in 1863. Finally, the South could succeed by fighting to a stalemate; the North could succeed in restoring the Union only by the complete conquest of an enormous quadrant of continental North America.

The military campaigns of the war matched dissimilar tactical geniuses. Robert E. LEE, formal in demeanor and traditionalist in strategy, resigned his U.S. commission "to return to my native state and share the miseries of my people." Frustrated for much of the war by meddlesome intrusions from Jefferson Davis, also a West Point graduate, Lee based his campaign on the traditional strategy of limited objectives. His opponent, Ulysses S. GRANT, was a gruff, slovenly, and frequently despondent leader who rejoined the army for the war and rose to Union commander-in-chief only after three predecessors had failed to gain Lincoln's respect. To many, Grant is the first modern general because he was the first to fight a "total war," one aimed at the complete economic destruction of the enemy rather than at the limited objective of conquest of its troops.

The armies matched forces in two principal theaters, to the east and the west of the Appalachian Mountains. The land campaigns began where they would end, in the Eastern theater, at the first Battle of Manassas, or BULL RUN, on July 21, 1861. The blue-coated "Billy Yanks" advancing on Richmond for a quick victory were driven from the field by the gray-coated "Johnny Rebs," fueling Confederate optimism and shattering any Union hope of speedy conquest.

The Union responded with the Peninsular Campaign of Gen. George B. McCLELLAN's Army of the Potomac. Landing near Yorktown in March of 1862, McClellan planned to advance up the peninsula between the York and James Rivers to capture Richmond. Deprived of a James River route by the inconclusive meeting of the ironclads *Monitor* and *Virginia* (*Merrimack*), and frustrated by the month-long resistances of beseiged YORKTOWN, McClellan advanced only with counter-productive caution. As he drew near Richmond, Lee's Army of Northern Virginia, protected by a diversionary inland attack by Thomas J. (Stonewall) JACKSON in his brilliant Shenandoah Valley campaign, met the Union Army in several related battles and finally drove it into retreat in the SEVEN DAYS' BATTLE of June 25-July 1, 1862.

Lee followed up this victory by driving northward toward the Second Battle of Manassas, or Bull Run, at the end of August, 1862, when a foolhardy Union frontal attack was driven into disorderly retreat all the way to Washington, D.C. For military reasons and in hope of attracting foreign allies, Lee then pressed his advantage in the ANTIETAM campaign into Maryland. At the Battle of Antietam in Sharpsburg, on the Potomac River, his advance was halted on September 17, 1862. Lee was forced into retreat after 26,000 troops on both sides were killed or wounded in the single bloodiest day of the Civil War. When the Union attempted to press its own momentary advantage at the end of the year, however, it was defeated by Lee at FREDERICKBURG, Virginia, on December 13, 1862.

In 1863 the fighting in the east was renewed at CHANCELLORSVILLE, Virginia, near the Rappahannock River. There in early May Lee defeated a superior Union force, but at the cost of the death of Stonewall Jackson. Then Lee took advantage of Union hesitation and launched his boldest invasion. He marched into Pennsylvania, where the pivotal battle of the war was fought at GETTYSBURG on July 1-3, 1863. After three days of harrowing fighting for the advantages of meager ridges, the Confederate Army was driven from the field, with losses of more than 20,000 troops.

In the Western theater, the Union's strategy was to split the Confederacy along the Mississippi River. It was here that Grant first established his reputation with the capture of Forts Henry and Donelson in western Tennessee in February, 1862. From there he proceeded down the Tennessee River to Pittsburg Landing, where he defeated the south in the April Battle of SHILOH, a grim two-day struggle that is said to have formed Grant's resolve for a war of complete conquest. Over the subsequent year Union forces made inexorable gains along both the upper and lower Mississippi. Moving down the river, Grant isolated VICKSBURG, Mississippi, as the last important stronghold of southern resistance. After a second six-week siege, he captured Vicksburg on July 4, 1863, a blow that fell on the Confederacy a day after the retreat from Gettysburg.

In the fall of 1863 the war moved into the interior of the South and entered its final phases. An important confederate victory at CHICKAMAUGA, Tennessee, in September was followed by the devastating loss of the important railroad center of CHATTANOOGA in a series of battles in November. In 1864 Grant, installed as commander-in-chief, chose a two-pronged campaign against Richmond and Atlanta. He personally led the Virginia campaign against Lee, a brutal, year-long struggle between Grant's superior numbers and Lee's brilliant defensive tactics. Grant pressed on despite nearly catastrophic losses at SPOTSYLVANIA (May 8-12, 1864) and COLD HARBOR (June 3, 1864), and then found himself mired in a nine-month siege of PETERSBURG. Meanwhile, the Atlanta campaign of 90,000 troops under Union Gen. William Tecumseh SHERMAN moved south from Tennessee the summer of 1864, always slowed, but never halted by the defensive tactics of Confederate Gen. Joseph E. JOHNSTON. Sherman captured Atlanta on September 2, began his famous 'MARCH TO THE SEA" on November 15, and arrived in Savannah on December 21, having left a 200-mile long and 60-mile wide path of destruction in his wake.

Sherman moved northward in the spring of 1865 while Grant closed off Lee's final avenues of excape. Completely outnumbered, Lee found himself outflanked and ultimately cut off from railroad support of Petersburg and Richmond. He abandoned both cities on the night of April 2-3, 1865, and began a final 80-mile flight westward along the Appomattox River. Trapped and horrified at the mounting casualties of these final battles, Lee surrendered to Grant at the house of Wilber McLean at the crossroads of Appomattox Court House on April 9, 1865. This was the symbolic end of the Confederacy, although it was followed by several later surrenders by Southern troops in other regions.

Abraham Lincoln, assassinated on April 14, 1865, never witnessed the fruits of the struggle he had overseen. The two primary goals of the war had been fully realized: centralized federal government had been preserved, and institutionalized slavery had been abolished. The costs of these accomplishments, however, defy accurate assessment. By most estimates, more than 600,000 troops died and another 500,000 were wounded. The toll wholly borne by the South of the RECONSTRUCTION era that followed the war is even harder to gauge. Reconstruction encouraged economic mismanagement and political corruption, forced humiliating oaths of allegiance on occupied states with no alternative to rejoining the Union, and drove some embittered Southerners into covert and violent white supremacy organizations, such as the KU KLUX KLAN. Far from settling the rifts that underlay it, the Civil War left the South with a permanent sense of itself as a noble and embattled entity within the United States.

CLAIBORNE, William (Westmoreland Co., England, c. 1587 — c. 1677). Colonist. After arriving in Virginia (1621) he served as secretary of State and headed exploratory expeditions. Claiborne took up armed resistance to Lord Baltimore's settlement of Maryland in the 1630s and was sent to England to answer charges. Although Parliament decided in favor of Lord Baltimore, Claiborne returned to Virginia, and subsequently drove Governor Leonard Calvert out of Maryland, taking control of that state for several years.

CLAIBORNE, William Charles Coles (Sussex Co., Va., 1775 — Nov. 23, 1817). After following a law career in Tennessee he was appointed a state supreme court judge (1796). He was a member of Congress from Tennessee (1797-1801), and was elected governor of the Mississippi Territory in 1801. Claiborne became governor of the new territory of Orleans (1803-12) after the acquisition of the Louisiana Purchase. When Louisiana was admitted to the Union (1812) he was elected governor of the new state and served until 1816.

CLARK, Alvan Graham (Fall River, Mass., July 10, 1832 — Cambridge, Mass., June 9, 1897). Astronomer and manufacturer of astronomical lenses. He became a partner with his father, Alvan Clark (1804-1887), in Alvan Clark & Sons and directed the production of as-

tronomical lenses at the Naval Observatory, Washington, D.C., the Lick Observatory, Calif. He produced the 40-inch lens for what was then the world's largest refracting telescope at Yerkes Observatory, Wisc. He also discovered 16 double stars as well as the companion star to Sirius.

CLARK, Charles (Cincinnati, Ohio, 1810 — Mississippi, Dec. 18, 1877). Military officer and politician. He taught school before being elected as a Whig to represent Jefferson Co., Miss. in the state legislature (1838-44). Later he advocated the immediate secession of the state and became one of the first four-star brigadier generals of Mississippi, a rank he maintained when the state militia was absorbed into the Confederate Army. He served as governor from 1863 to 1865.

CLARK, George Rodgers (Charlottesville, Va., Nov. 19, 1752 — Locust Grove, Va., Feb. 13, 1818). Frontiersman and military officer. He conducted a successful military campaign against the British and their Indian allies in the area that is now southern and central Illinois (1778-81). Some historians claim that it was these victories (Kaskaskia, Cahokia, and Vincennes) that enabled the U.S. to obtain the land northwest of the Ohio in the Treaty of Paris at the end of the war. However, Clark and his men never received payment for their years of service to Virginia, despite many promises. Before the war, Clark had been a surveyor and a scout in Lord Dunmore's 1774 campaign to halt Indian raids on Kentucky settlers and surveyors. Soon afterwards, he helped settle Transylvania (what is now parts of Kentucky and Tennessee) and led a successful rebellion against the unscrupulous proprietors, asking Virginia to take over the territory, which it did. After the Revolutionary War, Clark fought a campaign against the Wabash Indians, that was unsuccessful because of the mutiny of most of his men. He was subsequently stripped of his military rank through the questionable methods of former general James WILKINSON.

CLARK, James Beauchamp "Champ" (Lawrenceburg, Ky., Mar. 7, 1850 — Washington, D.C., Mar. 2, 1921). Politician. Clark settled in Bowling Green, Mo., in 1876 where he began a career as a newspaper editor, city and county prosecuting attorney, Missouri state legislator, and member of the U.S. House (1893-95, 1897-1921). A disciple of Democrat and Populist leader William Jennings Bryan, his philosophy was progressive, representing the Western and Southern opinion on national matters. He revolted against House speaker Joseph G. Cannon's dictatorial control in 1910. At the 1912 Democratic national convention, he narrrowly lost the presidential nomination to Woodrow Wilson.

CLARK, John (Edgecomb Co., N.C., Feb. 28, 1766 — St. Andrews Bay, Fla., Oct. 12, 1832). Georgia political leader. He started his career as a soldier in the Revolutionary War while still a boy, went on to fight during the Indian conflicts, and eventually became a Georgia frontier leader and state legislator. He was governor of Georgia from 1819 to 1825.

CLARK, Tom Campbell (Dallas, Tex., Sept. 3, 1899 — New York, N.Y., June 13, 1977). Supreme Court associate justice. After serving as attorney general (1945-49), Clark was appointed to the Supreme Court by President Harry S. Truman. Primarily a conservative, Clark retired fom the bench in 1967, when his son Ramsey Clark (1927—) became U.S. attorney general.

CLARK, Walter (Halifax, N.C., Aug. 19, 1846 — May 19, 1924). Judge of supreme court of North Carolina (1899-1924). He became known nationally for original and independent judicial decisions. Commended for gallantry in service to the Confederate army, Clark wrote and spoke in favor of progressive trends while a judge.

CLARK, William (Caroline Co., Va., Aug. 1, 1770 — St. Louis, Mo., Sept. 1, 1838). Military officer, explorer, and public official. After joining the army in 1789, he served under Gen. Anthony Wayne against the Maumee Indians. In 1803, Clark was asked to join Meriwether Lewis in a trek to the Pacific Ocean to explore the Northwest Territory, which became known as the Lewis and Clark Expedition. Clark's written account of the three-year trip contributed tremendously to the country's understanding of that wilderness. His journals were published as *Original Journals of the Lewis and Clark Expedition, 1804-1806.* In 1807, Clark was appointed superintendent of Indian Affairs, and he was governor of the Missouri Territory from 1813 to 1821.

CLARK COLLEGE. Independent, coed college, affiliated with the United Methodist Chruch. Clark is located in the city of Atlanta, in the northwest section of Georgia. Founded in 1889 as a liberal arts college for Negroes, Clark today is open to students of all races, but the large majority are still black. Religious requirements are minimal.

The college offers degrees in business and management, education, communication, or social sciences. Some 30% pursue graduate or professional studies immediately after graduation. Clark does seek a national student body: 77% are from the South, 6% Northwest, 1% New England.

Library: 67,565 volumes, 429 journal subscriptions, 4,585 records/tapes. Faculty: 145. Enrollment: 660 men, 1,337 women (full-time). Degrees: Bachelor's.

CLARK HILL RESERVOIR, Ga. One of the state's largest lakes, in eastern Georgia on the Savannah River north of Augusta, created as a hydroelectric power project. It forms part of a natural boundary for this state and South Carolina.

CLARKE, Edith (Howard Co., Md., Feb. 10, 1883 — Olney, Md., Oct. 29, 1959). Electrical engineer. A graduate of Vassar (B.A., 1908) and member of Phi Beta Kappa, she did graduate work at the University of Wisconsin (1911-12) and MIT (M.S., 1919). She worked as a mathematical computer for American Telephone & Telegraph in New York City (1912-18), taught at Constantinople Woman's College in Turkey (1921), and returned as an engineer for General Electric (1922-45), where she pioneered systems analysis for large power networks. Clarke then taught electrical engineering at the University of Texas, Austin (1947-56). Her *Circuit Analysis of A-C Power Sysytems* (2 vols., 1943—50) is a standard. She was the first woman elected to membership in the American Institute of Electrical Engineers (1948).

CLARKSBURG, W.Va. City (pop. 22,371), seat of Harrison Co. This industrial and shipping center is situated on the west fork of the MONONGAHELA RIVER. It was the birthplace of Gen. "Stonewall" Jackson. During the Civil War, the city served as a major federal supply base. Oil, gas, and coal are the chief products here and factories manufacture glassware, caskets, cement, and zinc.

CLARKSDALE, Miss. City (pop. 21,137), seat of Coahoma Co., in northwest Mississippi. Settled in 1848 and incorporated in 1882, it is now a center for a large cotton market, in a timber and agricultural region. Cottonseed, soybeans, oil, furniture, and rubber items are produced.

CLARKSVILLE, Tenn. City (pop. 54,777), seat of Montgomery Co., in northern Tennessee on a peninsula at the confluence of the Cumberland and Red Rivers. Settled in 1784, the cultivation of tobacco began here almost immediately. Today it is a large leaf-tobacco market and trading center, which produces shoes, clothing, and air conditioners. There are limestone quarries and zinc is mined. It is the site of Austin Peay State University (1927) and Fort Campbell Army Base, it is the birthplace of black composer Clarence Cameron WHITE.

CLAXTON, Philander Priestly (Bedford, Co., Tenn., 1862 — Knoxville, Tenn., Jan. 12, 1957). Educator. He worked in several school posts in North Carolina before his appointment as professor of education at the University of Tennessee (1902-11). As the U.S. commissioner of education (1911-21), Clark helped expand the activities of the Bureau of Education.

CLAY, Cassius See ALI, Muhammad.

CLAY, Cassius Marcellus (Madison Co., Ky., Oct. 19, 1810 — Madison Co., Ky., July 22, 1903). Abolitionist and diplomat. Born on a slave-holding plantation called White Hall, Clay was educated at Yale and then served in the Kentucky state legislature (1835-51). Already known for anti-slavery positions, he joined the emancipationist Republican party soon after its formation in 1854. Following the election of Republican Abraham Lincoln, Clay was appointed U.S. ambassador to Russia (1861-62, 1863-69), and he helped to negotiate the U.S. purchase of Alaska from that country in 1867.

CLAY, Clement Claiborne (Madison County, Ala., Dec. 13, 1816 — Gurley, Ala., Jan. 3, 1882). Lawyer, senator, Confederate diplomat. Clay's political career began when he was elected to the U.S. Senate from Alabama (1853-61). He served in Canada during the American Civil War as a Southern agent to arrange peace negotiations with Washington, but he was denied Federal authorization to discuss the issues. Returning south near the end of the War, he was accused of inciting President Abraham Lincoln's assassination and imprisoned. Clay was released by President Andrew Johnson in 1866 without opportunity to defend his case.

CLAY, Green (Powhatan Co., Va., Aug. 14, 1757 — Madison Co., Ky., Oct. 31, 1826). Politician. Attracted by tales of Daniel Boone, he moved to Kentucky in 1777 where he worked as a surveyor. After amassing a fortune in land, he turned to politics, representing Madison County in the state legislature (1793-94), and as state senator (1795-98). In 1807 he was elected again to the senate, where he served as speaker. Clay County is named for him.

CLAY, Henry (Hanover Co., Va., Apr. 12, 1777 — Washington, D.C., June 19, 1852). Statesman, orator, speaker of the House of Representatives, secretary of War. Lawyer and Whig Party leader, his important contributions to his country number him among this country's greatest political leaders. Clay is perhaps best remembered for his famous quote, "I'd rather be right than President." In his nearly 40 years as an American political figure, Clay three times failed in his bid for the presidency (in 1824 when the House gave John Adams a majority vote; in 1832 to Andrew Jackson; and in 1844 to James K. Polk), largely because of his comments which lost him key supporters.

A man of little formal education, Clay nevertheless gained admittance to the Virginia bar in 1797 and became a vastly successful lawyer. He entered politics for the first time in 1801, as a member of the Kentucky constitutional convention. His first experience as U.S. senator came in 1806 when he filled an unexpired term, and in 1811 when he did so again. In 1811 he entered the House of Representatives and became speaker on his first day. In the years to follow he was to assume the speakership five more times and institute or take part in many major political events. He was a part of the famous "Great Triumvirate" along with John C. Calhoun and Daniel Webster. He was one of the proponents of War with Britain (the War of 1812) and was one of the commissioners appointed to make peace in 1815. One of his most notable contributions to his country was repeated success in keeping North and South from going to war. Hence he was known as the "Great Pacificator." Clay's most famous contributions were the Missouri Compromise of

1820 and the Compromise of 1850, which owed much to his eloquence as a speaker and his powerful political influence. Indeed, he worked all his life to keep his country together. Alongside his grave in Lexington, Ky., is a plaque with a quotation from one of his many famous speeches: "I know no North—no South—no East—no West."

CLAY, Laura (Lexington, Ky., Feb. 9, 1849 — Lexington, Ky., June 29, 1941). Suffragist. President of the Kentucky Woman Suffrage Association (1881-88), of its successor, the Kentucky Equal Rights Association (1888-1912), and first auditor of the National American Woman Suffrage Association (1895), she was also a staunch white supremacist and used states' rights and the women's movement as bulwarks to this racism. She therefore opposed the Federal Nineteenth Amendment and in 1919 broke with both the national and state suffrage movements to fight Kentucky's ratification.

CLAY, Lucius DuBignon (Marietta, Ga., April 23, 1897 — Chatham, Mass., April 16, 1978). General, diplomat, commander of the U.S. forces in Europe (1947-49), and military governor of the U.S. zone in Germany during the Berlin Airlift. A West Point graduate (1918), he was an army engineer until 1942, when he was put in charge of procurement in Washington (1942-44). He served briefly in active combat at Normandy as base section commander, prior to assignment to German reconstruction. Retiring in 1949, he was active in support of Dwight D. Eisenhower's candidacy for President in 1952; nearly a decade later President John F. Kennedy appointed Clay ambassador to Berlin to deal with the crisis there in 1961.

CLAYTON, Henry De Lamar (Barbour Co., Ala., Feb. 10, 1857 — Montgomery, Ala., Dec. 21, 1929). Politician. He was the prime author of the Clayton Amendment to the Sherman Antitrust Act in 1914. Elected to the House of Representatives from Alabama (1897-1915), he chaired the Democratic National Convention (1908) and the House Caucus of the 60th Congress (1907-09).

CLAYTON, Henry Helm (Murfreesboro, Tenn., 1861 — 1946). Meteorologist. He invented a box kite for use in sounding the atmosphere and is a developer of the science of aerology. He was on the staff of the Blue Hill Observatory and was a meteorologist in Argentina from 1913 to 1922. He is the author of several books on meteorology.

CLAYTON, Mo. City (pop. 14,219), seat of St. Louis Co., in northeastern Missouri. A residential suburb of St. Louis incorporated in 1919, it also serves as an educational hub of the area, offering many fine educational institutions including the Concordia Seminary.

CLAYTON, Powell (Bethel Co., Penn., Aug. 7, 1833 — Washington, D.C., Aug. 25, 1914). Politician. A Republican, he was best known as the "carpetbag" governor of Arkansas (1868-78). He also served Arkansas in the U.S. Senate (1871-77) and went on to become the U.S. ambassador to Mexico (1897-1905).

CLEAR LAKE, La. Lake in Natchitoches Parish, in northwest central Louisiana. Located between the Red River and Black Lake Bayou, it is part of a lake chain, with the Black on one side and the Saline on the other.

CLEARWATER, Fla. City (pop. 85,450), Pinellas Co., in western Florida on the Pinellas peninsula. It is linked to Tampa by a causeway, and another causeway connects the city proper with a four-mile-long island of white sandy Gulf beaches. The area has been noted as a winter resort since 1896. It is a major producer and shipper of fish, flowers, cigars, and citrus fruit. Cultural and educational facilities include the Clearwater Christian College and a junior college, as well as an art center, a theater, and a variety of recreational facilities. The population has grown from 52,074 in 1970.

CLEARWATER DAM, Mo. Reynolds Co. A hydroelectric dam facility on the Black River in southeastern Missouri that forms Clearwater Lake.

CLEARWATER LAKE, Mo. Large recreational reservoir created by a U.S. Army Corps of Engineers project that impounded the Black River, in Reynolds Co. The Ozark National Scenic Riverways are nearby.

CLEBURNE, Patrick Ronayne (Cork Co., Ireland, Mar. 17, 1828 — Franklin, Tenn., Nov. 30, 1864). Military officer. He came to the United States and settled in Helena, Ark., where he practiced law. At the outbreak of the

Civil War he entered the Confederate army and in March of 1861 planned the capture of the U.S. arsenal in Arkansas. In 1862 he was promoted to brigadier-general. Cleburne originated the Order of the Southern Cross and was known as "the Stonewall of the West." He was killed in the battle of Franklin, Tenn.

CLEMENS, Samuel Langhorn "Mark Twain" (Florida, Mo., Nov. 30, 1835 — Redding, Ct., Apr. 21, 1910). Novelist, short story writer, and humorist. When he was four years old, Clemens moved with his family to Hannibal, Mo., where he experienced a childhood of harmless adventures recalled in romantic fashion in *The Adventures of Tom Sawyer* (1876) and its more sophisticated sequel *The Adventures of Huckleberry Finn* (1884). His father died when he was young, and Clemens was employed in a variety of professions from the age of twelve, when he was apprenticed to a printer. The most important of these to his work was his experience as a pilot on Mississippi River steamers in his twenties; his pen name, Mark Twain, was taken from the riverboat term meaning safe water of two fathoms.

When the Civil War disrupted river traffic, Clemens traveled west to Nevada and California, where he was a stringer for several newspapers and established a reputation as a humorist of the rugged lifestyles there. He also became a popular lecturer, a trade that he would later pursue on European tours. It was as a journalist that he was sent on a tour of the Holy Land. The result was his first important work, *Innocents Abroad* (1869), a satire of Old World pretensions from the perspective of a commonsense American. This brought him the financial stability required for his marriage to the relatively aristocratic Olivia Langdon.

Clemens reached his literary peak with *Huck Finn*, the story of a boy and an escaped slave in flight down the Mississippi River in the pre-

"Huck Finn and Jim" in a painting by Thomas Hart Benton

Civil War South. It is a touchstone in American literature in both its address to the national trauma surrounding the slavery issue and its essential hostility to social organizations of all sorts and desire for the freedom of the frontier. Clemens' important other works include *A Connecticut Yankee in King Arthur's Court* (1889) and *Pudd'nhead Wilson* (1894). In these later years Clemens squandered a fortune on an ill-advised publishing scheme, regained it with an enormously popular European lecture tour, and oversaw construction of the elaborate Connecticut home, how a museum in Redding, Ct. His later works, such as *The Man That Corrupted Hadleyburg* (1899), reflect the embitterment and pain that Clemens felt on the deaths of two of his daughters and the long illness and death of his wife.

CLEMSON UNIVERSITY. State-supported, land-grant coed institution, located 30 miles southwest of Greenville in Clemson, S.C. Founded in 1839, the University was designed by its founder, Thomas G. Clemson, to be an agricultural college. The school was called Clemson College until 1964 when it attained its present name. Undergraduate study is offered by the colleges of Nursing, Sciences, Textile Science, Liberal Arts, Agricultural Sciences, Architecture, Education, Engineering, Forest and Recreation Resources, and Industrial Management. In a recent year, one third of all undergraduate degrees were conferred in Engineering. Some 78% of Clemson students are state residents. The school does seek a national student body.

The 600-acre campus is augmented by nearly 26,000 acres of university-owned land, some of which is used for forest and experimental agricultural purposes. In sports, the school has strong intramural and intercollegiate programs.

Library: 801,023 volumes, 102,028 microfilm titles, 13,390 journal subscriptions. Faculty: 1,005. Enrollment: 11,579 total graduate and undergraduate. Degrees: Bachelor's, Master's, Doctorate.

CLEVELAND, Tenn. City (pop. 26,415), seat of Bradley Co., in southeastern Tennessee. An industrial community settled in 1807, it is situated in the last area evacuated by the CHEROKEE INDIANS, who left in 1838. Ranges, furniture, chemicals, peaches, potatoes, and tomatoes are among its products. Lee College was founded here in 1968.

CLIBURN, Van [Harvey Lavan, Jr.] (Shreveport, La., July 12, 1934 —). Concert pianist. He was taught the piano by his mother before attending the Julliard School in N.Y., and graduating in 1954. Van Cliburn became internationally famous four years later when he won the International Tchaikovsky Piano Competition in Moscow.

CLIFTON, Chalmers (Jackson, Miss., 1889 —). Musical conductor. Clifton was named director of the American Orchestral Society in New York, in 1922, after studying music at Harvard and in Europe. He later established and directed the Federal Music Project in New York City.

CLIFTON FORGE, Va. Independent city (pop. 5,046) in western Virginia. Located 40 miles northeast of Roanoke, it was settled in 1880 and developed when a rail line came through the town. Along with agricultural produce and cattle, the town's manufactures include bottling, dental and medical supplies, knitwear, and pulp and lumber products.

CLINCH RIVER, Tenn. River rising from two forks in western Virginia, flowing 300 miles generally southwest through eastern Tennessee to empty into the Tennessee River at Kingsport. With the Powell River, it forms Norris Lake, and Watts Bar Lake is found at its mouth. The Clinch River once served as a principal route for settlers going to Tennessee. Today the river is the site of the controversial Clinch River Nuclear Breeder Reactor Plant.

CLINGMAN'S DOME, Tenn. The state's highest peak (6,642 feet) and the highest peak of the GREAT SMOKY MOUNTAINS, positioned along the Appalachian Trail in the southeastern corner of Tennessee, in Sevier Co. Its top is often shrouded in a blue haze.

CLINTON, Ky. Town (pop. 1,720), seat of Hickman Co., in southwestern Kentucky, near the Mississippi River. It was a Confederate stronghold at the beginning of the Civil War and is now a shipping point for corn, cotton, and tobacco. Manufactures include TV antennas, concrete, and apparel. The Columbus-Belmont Battlefield State Park is found here.

COAHUILTECAN INDIANS. Group of Indian tribes located in Mexico and most of Texas west of the San Antonio River and Cibolo Creek, of Coahuiltecan linguistic stock. In the early 1700s great numbers of them were gathered into missions but their numbers rapidly declined and they were all but extinct by the late 1800s.

COAL. Fossil fuel, mined from the earth, mostly composed of carbon, with varying amounts of mineral matter. In 1960 the South produced more than 50% of the country's coal; in 1980, after a renewed search for mineral fuels in other regions, it still produced 40% of the country's coal. Kentucky and West Virginia continued throughout this period to produce more bituminous coal than any other states. In 1980 Kentucky mined 150 million short tons of coal and West Virginia mined 122 million short tons. The other major coal-producing states in the South are Virginia, which mined 41 million short tons of coal in 1980, and Alabama, which mined 26 million short tons in 1980.

COASTAL MARSHES, La. Predominantly salt marshes extending along 1,500 miles of Louisiana's coastline. The land is characterized by flat, treeless plateaus and lowlands covered with multitudes of small, shallow lakes and lagoons, creating vast wetlands. Sloughs and bayous drain the marshes. Sand and shell ridges are found throughout the area. These lands have preserved many forest remains and archaeological artifacts.

COASTAL PLAIN, Va. One of the five physiographical areas in Virginia, it is usually referred to as the Tidewater region. Running along the eastern seaboard, it ranges in width from 35 miles near Richmond to 80 miles near Norfolk. The area is dotted with tidal rivers and bays, including the Chesapeake, forming many natural harbors. Much of the state's commercial and recreational interests are a result of this region.

COBB, Irwin S. (Paducah, Ky., June 23, 1876 — New York, N.Y., Mar. 10, 1944). Journalist and humorist. Although descended from a Virginia governor, Cobb was unable to afford a college education and so served his literary apprenticeship on newspapers such as the Paducah *News* before traveling to New York City in 1904. There he quickly acquired a reputation as a humorist in the tradition of Mark Twain and Bret Harte. He is best remembered for the long series of Judge Priest stories begun in 1915 and the autobiography *Exit Laughing* (1941).

Miner at work in a West Virginia coal mine

COBB, Thomas Reade Rootes (Jefferson Co., Ga., Apr. 10, 1823 — Fredericksburg, Va., Dec. 13, 1862). Confederate lawyer and general. An ardent secessionist, he helped write the confederate Constitution. Cobb edited 20 volumes of Georgian supreme court reports (1849-57) and wrote *A Digest of the Statute Laws of Georgia* (1851), and a state criminal code (1858-61). Organizer of Cobb's Legion, he was killed at the Battle of Fredericksburg.

COBB, Tyrus Raymond "Ty" (Narrows, Ga., Dec. 18, 1886 — Atlanta, Ga., July 17, 1961). Baseball outfielder. In 22 seasons with the Detroit Tigers he had the highest lifetime batting average (.367), the most hits (4,191), and, until recent years, the most stolen bases (892). Manager of the Tigers from 1921 to 1926, he was inducted into the Baseball Hall of Fame in 1936.

COCKE, William (Amelia Co., Va., 1748 — Miss., Aug. 22, 1828). Politician and military officer. He studied law before moving to a valley located between Virginia and Tennessee. Cocke fought in the Revolutionary War but was charged with cowardice. In 1775 he followed Daniel Boone into Kentucky. A onetime leader of the short-lived State of FRANKLIN in Eastern Tennessee, he helped create what is now the University of Tennessee while serving in the North Carolina legislature. In 1796 Cocke helped Tennessee achieve statehood.

COCKRELL, Francis Marion (Columbus, Mo., Oct. 1, 1834 — Washington, D.C., Dec. 13, 1915). Military officer and politician. He left a law practice to enlist as a Confederate private in the Civil War. He became a brigadier general in 1863 and fought in the battles of Carthage, Vicksburg, and Mobile. He entered Democratic politics in Missouri, served in the state legislature, and was elected to the U.S. Senate in 1874, serving until 1905.

COCOA BEACH, Fla. Town (pop. 10,926), Brevard Co., eastern Florida, on a barrier beach between the Banana River and the Atlantic Ocean. An ocean resort built on a dune ridge, Cocoa Beach is near Patrick Air Force Base. Manufactures include missile control systems, apparel, and optical instruments.

COCONUT GROVE, Fla. Part of the city of Miami, (pop. 23,000), in Dade Co., in southern Florida. It was originally an incorporated town but is now part of the city of Miami. Referred to locally as "the Grove," it is one of the oldest cultural centers in southern Florida. The community is noted for its natural beauty and exotic plant life, and it is a haven for aspiring artists.

COFFIN, Levi (New Garden, N.C., Oct. 28, 1789 — Cincinnati, Ohio, Sept. 16, 1877). Abolitionist. Born of Quaker parents, he operated a store in the Quaker settlement of Newport (now Fountain City), Ind., His home was a principal station for the UNDERGROUND RAILROAD, of which Coffin was an organizer and described as "president." He was also an agent for the Western Freedman's Aid Association.

COLD HARBOR, Battle of. Civil War engagement fought May 31-June 12, 1864, at New Cold Harbor, Virginia, ten miles northeast of Richmond. This was the final battle in the campaign of Gen. Ulysses S. GRANT, begun at Wilderness, to defeat and to destroy Gen. Robert E. LEE's army of Virginia. As he had before, at Spotsylvania and North Anna, Lee, although outnumbered, used defensive strategy to great effect.

At Cold Harbor Lee deployed 60,000 men under Gens. Richard ANDERSON, Jubal EARLY, and A. P. HILL. Grant's Union force, at 118,000, was nearly twice the Confederate strength. Grant prepared his forces for a frontal assault on the Confederate line on June 2, but it was delayed by heavy rains. The attack was launched on June 3, and the Union soldiers were repeatedly turned back by the entrenched Confederates. Grant, who lost 15,000 men, called a truce on June 7 to retrieve the dead in advance of his position. Lee, who lost only 2,000 men, enjoyed his last great victory of the war. After Cold Harbor Grant's tactics shifted to siege at Petersburg.

COLD HARBOR, Va. Town (pop. 8,966), in Hanover Co., located ten miles northeast of Richmond. Cold Harbor was the site of two battles of the Civil War, the second of which was one of the North's major defeats. The first (June 27, 1862) was between Union Gen. George McClellan and Confederate Gen. Robert E. Lee; the second Battle of COLD HARBOR was fought in 1864 between Union Gen. U. S. Grant and Gen. Lee.

COLDWATER RIVER, Miss. River rising in northern Mississippi. It flows west, through the ARKABUTLA Reservoir, then south to meet the Tallahatchie River.

COLLEGE PARK, Ga. City (pop. 24,632), Fulton Co., in northwestern Georgia. A suburb of Atlanta, it is primarily residential but has some light industry. Originally called Manchester, the name was changed in 1895 with the opening of Cox College. Georgia Military Academy (1900) is here.

COLLEGE PARK, Md. City (pop. 23,611), Prince George's Co., northwest of Washington, D.C. A residential suburb of Washington, it was incorporated in 1947. Much of the town is devoted to its position as seat of the principal schools of the University of Maryland, which has brought significant growth to the community. The university has a large stadium and an agricultural experiment station, which in the past has carried out noted research, especially in the field of tobacco yield increases and plant culture.

COLLEGE STATION, Tex. City (pop. 37,272), Brazos Co., in south central Texas. With adjoining Bryan, College Station forms the urban center of Brazos County. Site of TEXAS A&M UNIVERSITY (originally called the Agricultural and Mechanical College of Texas), College Station's economy revolves around its educational community.

COLLINS, Joseph Lawton (New Orleans, La., May 1, 1896 —). Military officer. He served as commander of the Army 7th Corps in Europe, which captured Cherbourg during World War II. His troops also led the breakout from Normandy, pierced the Siegfried Line, captured Aachen and Cologne, enveloped Ruher from the east and the south, then drove eastward to a meeting with the Russians on the Elbe River at Dessau.

COLONIAL HEIGHTS, Va. City (pop. 16,509), and county in southeastern Virginia. A residential suburb of Richmond, in 1781 Colonial Heights was the headquarters of Gen. LaFayette and from June to September, 1864, it was the headquarters of Gen. Robert E. Lee.

COLORADO RIVER, Tex. River providing the primary drainage system for the entire central section of the state, draining an area as large as Tennessee. The Llano Estacado is the origin for the waterway which proceeds southeast about 840 miles to empty into the Gulf of Mexico at Matagorda Bay. Austin is on its banks and six artificial lakes, including the BU-CHANAN and TRAVIS, are found on it, providing irrigation and hydroelectric power.

COLTER, John Staunton, Va., c. 1775 — Dundee, Mo., Nov., 1813). Guide. A member of the Lewis and Clark expedition (1803) he left the party to become a trapper. In 1807 he joined Manuel Lisa in an expedition to the area of the mouth of the Big Horn River, and later led an expedition to the Three Forks of the Missouri River. Information gathered by Colter was used in the compilation of the Lewis and Clark maps.

COLUMBIA, Mo. City (pop. 58,804), seat of Boone Co. on the Missouri River in central Missouri. The original settlement in 1819 was named Smithton. Growth was stimulated in 1822 with the rerouting through Columbia of Boone's Lick Trail. Incorporated in 1826, the city pledged $117,900 in 1839 to construct the first state university west of the Mississippi, now the University of MISSOURI. The economy is based on education, professional organizations, insurance companies, and some light industry. The state cancer hospital and mental health clinic are located in Columbia.

COLUMBIA, S.C. City (pop. 99,269), seat of Richland Co., capital of the state and its largest city, located in the center of South Carolina on the east bank of the CONGAREE RIVER. The site of a trading post in the early 1700s, the city was founded in 1786 to replace Charleston as the state capital. Agriculture, government, and industry are the major employers. Almost a third of all Columbians are employed by the county, state, or federal government. Industry plays an important role with over 300 factories producing lumber, electronic equipment, structural steel, synthetic fibers, chemicals, processed food, textiles, and aerospace products. Columbia is the marketing and distribution center of a large farming area.

Originally occupied by CONGAREE INDIANS, Columbia was later farmed and taken over by cotton plantations. Cotton milling was a major industry in the early 1800s. Columbia was incorporated as a city in 1854, and during the Civil War it was the location of many Confederate agencies as well as being an important transportation center. Much of the city was burned in 1865 when Union Gen. William T. Sherman's troops captured and occupied it. In the 1880s the city experienced substantial industrial growth with the influx of textile producers and other manufacturing concerns. Among the many points of interest are Ainsley Hall Mansion, President Woodrow Wilson's boyhood home (now a museum), the State House and Governor's Mansion, Riverbanks Park Zoo, Columbian Museum of Art, and the Town Theater (1919), one of the oldest little theaters in the nation. Colleges and universities include the University of South Carolina, Benedict College, Allen University, COLUMBIA College, Lutheran Theological Seminary, and Columbia Bible College.

COLUMBIA, Tenn. City (pop. 25,767), seat of Maury Co., in southwest central Tennessee. It was built on the low limestone bluffs of the Duck River in 1807, and during its early years was beset by earthquakes and floods. Columbia was the home of President James Polk and the seat of Columbia Military Academy. Products include hosiery, hospital supplies, and carbon and graphite electrodes. There is diversified farming in the area.

COLUMBIA COLLEGE. Church-related, liberal arts institution for women, located in the central South Carolina city of Columbia. This United Methodist-affiliated college was founded in 1854 and is known for its liberal arts programs, which place strong emphasis on career preparation. Situated on 32 acres, the school has an attractive blend of old and new buildings. Almost all students are from the South, with 90% of these being South Carolina residents. Most undergraduate degrees are conferred in education, interdisciplinary studies, fine and applied arts, business and management, and letters. Some 20% of students immediately pursue full-time graduate or professional study after graduating.

Library: 145,000 volumes, 850 journal subscriptions. Faculty: 77. Enrollment: 908 women (full-time), 195 women (part-time). Degrees: Bachelor's, Master's.

COLUMBUS, Ga. City (pop. 169,441), seat of Muscogee Co., in western Georgia at the head of navigation on the CHATTAHOOCHEE RIVER, on the fall line. Founded in 1828, it was a major river port until the coming of the railway in the 1840s, at which time the first textile mill was constructed. Columbus was well known as a supply post during the Indian wars, the Mexican War, and the Civil War, when it was occupied by Union troops. Industrial growth in the 20th century was aided by the development of hydroelectric power, which turned the city into a major industrial and shipping center. Today it is a major producer of textiles in the state, along with bottling works, meat packing, and iron works. The U.S. Infantry School is nearby.

COLUMBUS, Miss. City (pop. 27,383), seat of Lowndes Co., located nine miles from the Alabama border, on the TOMBIGBEE RIVER, west of Birmingham and southeast of Memphis, Tenn. It is an agricultural, educational, and industrial center. Manufactures include men's clothing, electrical equipment, bricks, ornamental stone, automobile plates, furniture, and lumber. A port of entry in the 1800s and a landing for the steamship *Cottonplant* (1822), it has many antebellum houses. Franklin Academy (1821) the oldest free public school in Mississippi is here, as is Mississippi State College for Women (1884) the first state-supported school for women in the United States, and a U.S. Air Force Base.

COMANCHE INDIANS. Tribe of the Shoshonean linguistic group inhabiting northwestern Texas and beyond as far as the Arkansas River. A roving and warlike tribe, they called themselves "live people," believing in one supreme Father and claiming to have come from the setting sun. The TEXAS RANGERS were organized as protection against their raids. Noted as expert horsemen, they are credited with introducing horses to the Indians of the northern plains. In 1865 a reservation was set up for them which consisted of the Texas Panhandle and part of Oklahoma. They surrendered all of this land except for a tract in southwest Oklahoma in 1867, although they did not settle on the remaining tract until after their last uprisings in the 1870s.

COMBAHEE RIVER, S.C. Southern expanse of the stream known as the Salkehatchie River. After coursing about 40 miles, it drains into St. Helena's Sound on the southeast coast of South Carolina.

COMMITTEES OF CORRESPONDENCE. The colonial assemblies that ordered the convocation of the First Continental Congress on September 5, 1774. Such colonial committees were assembled to organize a common

core of resistance to the oppression of Great Britain by way of correspondence, prior to the start of the Revolutionary War. Virtually every colony had created such a committee by 1774, fighting such regulations as the Sugar Act and the STAMP ACT. The Virginia House of Burgesses formed its committee in 1773 and James MADISON was elected to serve as its representative from Orange County in 1774.

COMPROMISE OF 1850. Compromise on the question of slavery, which postponed disunion. In 1849, after the annexation of Texas when there were 15 free states and 15 slave states providing a numerical balance in the U.S., California requested admission to the Union as a free state, setting in motion a crisis on the problem of slavery. Antislavery groups in the North supported California as its constitution excluded slavery. Southern states feared to see the balance upset. To avert the threat of disunion, Senator Henry CLAY of Kentucky proposed a compromise consisting of five separate measures. Passed by Congress in September, 1850, after long debate, they provided for the admission of California with its antislavery constitution, the prohibition of slavery in the District of Columbia, the organization of New Mexico and Utah with no prohibition against slavery, a rigid provision concerning the mandatory return of fugitive slaves, and a settlement in which New Mexico was to receive disputed Texas territory, which cost the federal government $10 million. The Compromise was, however, only a temporary salve for the feelings of discord and in a decade the Civil War began.

CONECUH RIVER, Ala. Largest tributary of the Escambia River, rising in Peachburg, Ala. It flows southwest for more than 130 miles to just north of the Florida border where it joins Escambia Creek to create the river. The Conecuh was once popular for hook-and-jam flatboats.

CONFEDERATE STATES OF AMERICA. The government of the 11 Southern states that seceded from the Federal U.S. government in Washington, D.C., and existed as a separate republic from 1861 to 1865. The Union, or North, fought the Confederacy, or South, in the Civil War to challenge its right to secede. When the Union prevailed over the Confederacy, the secessionist government was dissolved and the states readmitted to the Union.

A confederated republic differs from a federated republic in that the states rather than the central government are sovereign. The original 13 states in fact existed as a "confederation" until 1789, when the word 'federation" was introduced to strengthen the powers of the central government. The Confederated States of America, therefore, was a government organized to protect states' rights over federal rights. What provoked this movement was the issue of whether the Federal government could abolish slavery throughout the nation without regard for the wishes of individual states.

South Carolina became the first state to ratify articles of secession, an action it believed to be entirely within its legal powers, on December 20, 1860. Representatives from South Carolina met with those of Georgia, Mississippi, Florida, Alabama, and Louisiana on February 4, 1861, in Montgomery, Ala., and ratified a provisional constitution for their Confederacy. They were later joined in secession by Texas, Arkansas, North Carolina, Virginia, and Tennessee. Of these states, Virginia was the most torn by the issue, and its northwestern counties eventually separated themselves from the state for this reason and were admitted to the Union as the state of West Virginia in 1863. After reaching provisional agreements, the seceding states ratified a permanent constitution on March 11, 1861, and on May 29 of that year they declared Richmond, Va., the capital of the Confederate States of America.

Some central government was a necessity, even if its powers were to be curbed, and after a provisional appointment on February 18, 1861, the states elected Jefferson DAVIS of Mississippi their president for a six-year term beginning on February 22, 1862. A U.S. senator, Mexican War hero, and wealthy plantation owner, Davis was a soft-spoken and meticulous politician who dutifully managed the affairs of the new republic without flamboyance or apparent alarm despite the immense problems immediately confronting the Confederacy. His chief rival for the position was Alexander H. STEVENS of Georgia, a more ambitious and charismatic politician who became so disenchanted with Davis's policies that he eventually urged his own state's secession from the Confederacy. The most important members of Davis's cabinet were: Judah P. BENJAMIN of Louisiana, first attorney general and then Secretary of War; James A. Seddon of Virginia, also Secretary of War for a time; Christopher G. Memminger of South Carolina, Secretary of the Treasury; Stephen R. Mallory of Florida, Secretary of the Navy; and John H. Regan of Texas, postmaster general.

As the organization of this cabinet suggests, the Confederacy for the most part duplicated the constitutional government of the Union. Despite these titular similarities, however, the Confederacy altered the balance of power in keeping with its goal of sovereign states' rights, and for this reason it must be considered the most important and most premeditated attempt to revise the Constitution in U.S. history. The sovereignty of states over central government included the power of states to impeach Confederate officials operating within their borders. Government officials were not required to pledge an oath of allegiance to the confederated government in Richmond. Futhermore, the Richmond government was prohibited from organizing any internal improvements, with the exception of navigational ones, and its powers of taxation were relatively limited. The most significant Confederate addition to the constitution was that it admitted the word "slavery": while the Confederacy outlawed international slave trading, it legalized domestic slavery and prohibited the Richmond government from legislating controls on slavery as an infringement of property rights.

All of these alterations concerned only peacetime operations of government, and the Confederate constitution in fact left the wartime powers of government unchanged. It was the continuance of the centralized powers in times of war that compromised the secessionist states' experiment in confederation and sowed the seeds of their own internal dissent. Had they been allowed to secede without military intervention from the Union—as some states fully expected they would be—the Confederacy would in all likelihood have been a success. The requirements of war, however, necessitated legislation from Richmond that destroyed the unity of the Southern states. In April of 1862 Richmond passed the first draft law in America, and in 1863 it permitted government impressment of goods for the war effort. These acts, along with inevitable taxes to fund the central government, led many Southerners to believe that their own Confederacy had countermanded the very freedoms for which they had seceded from the Union.

These developments were examples of the damage done to a well-planned constitutional government by the overwhelming demands of a grim war effort. At the time of secession, the population of the South was about half that of the North, or about nine million. Of this population, however, 3.5 million were slaves who could scarcely be expected to contribute to the success of the Confederacy. The remaining population was perhaps richer in educated citizens and politicians than that of the North, but the South's most patriotic and intellectually vigorous citizens were quickly sent off for military service. The South also remained inferior to the North in transportation facilities: of the mere 9,000 miles of railroad track in the Confederacy, most was rendered useless by a profusion of multiple gauges and a hopelessly uneven system of distribution. The Southern states with the exception of Virginia were also virtually without industries that could be adapted for wartime production. Powder factories were eventually established, but rifles remained scarce throughout the war. These conditions worsened year by year, for despite the historical prominence given to field battles, the great blow to the South delivered by the North was a successful blockade of port facilities from 1861 until the end of the war.

The greatest deficiencies of the South, however, were economic. At the time of secession only some $27 million in gold was located within the Confederacy, including the Northern deposits it appropriated. Of this, $15 million was in 1861 loaned to the government in Richmond, which spent it on European military supplies rendered undeliverable by the North's naval blockade. Lacking gold, the Confederacy was forced to begin issue of paper notes in 1861 and to follow this with increasingly large issues in every year through 1865. This paper currency was at first welcomed with patriotic fervor, but soon individual states and even cities began to issue their own promissory notes and the result was a chaos of redundant and progressively inflated currencies. In 1861 a Confederate paper dollar was worth 90 cents of gold, by 1862 it fell to 40 cents, and after the military defeat at Gettysburg in 1863 it fell to 6 cents. By the end of the war the government itself acknowledged its own monetary bankruptcy.

The great hope of the South at the time of secession was based on cotton crops, the "white gold" that would enable the republic to establish itself as a world economic power. At that time the South produced two-thirds of the world cotton supply. The Union blockade destroyed its ability to export the product, however, and an agricultural shift to foodstuffs proved unsuccessful, ensuing cotton surpluses did further damage to Confederate unity by encouraging trade with the enemy. What food crops were produced were commonly impressed by the military at minimal prices, further discouraging growers, and the Confederacy's dream of victory based on agricultural self-sufficiency was proved an illusion.

At the time of secession the hopes of the Confederacy were also to some extent based on expectations of immediate diplomatic recognition by other countries hungry for its cotton exports and in many cases unsympathetic with the trade policies of the Union. This was especially true of England, with its extensive midlands textile industries, and France, with its continuing cultural as well as economic ties with regions sold in the Louisiana Purchase of 1803. In both cases, however, fear of reprisals from the Union outweighed desires for trade with the Confederacy. In 1863 the South did nevertheless succeed in negotiating a $15-million loan in the form of bonds redeemable in cotton at a fixed price after the war from the French banking house of Erlanger and Company. The optimism this loan encouraged was shattered when untrained Confederate representatives in Europe mismanaged the sale of the bonds there, leaving the South with a minuscule immediate gain and an enormous future debt. Similar changes of mood accompanied Confederate diplomatic negotiations with Mexico and Canada, countries often but inaccurately rumored to be about to enter the war on the side of the South.

Because the Confederacy was from the moment of its birth confronted with all of these difficulties, most historians consider its simple survival for even four years to have been a triumph of sorts. A well-formulated legal and political entity, the Confederacy was effectively isolated by the North and inevitably succumbed to practical deficiencies in a war of attrition. Despite enormous sacrifice and some military and political brilliance, the secessionist states were at the end of the war an economic and political wasteland further abused by the RECONSTRUCTION policies of the victors.

DATES OF CONFEDERATE STATES'
SECESSION FROM THE UNION

South Carolina	Dec. 24, 1860
Mississippi	Jan. 9, 1861
Florida	Jan. 10, 1861
Alabama	Jan. 11, 1861
Georgia	Jan. 19, 1861
Louisiana	Jan. 26, 1861
Texas	Feb. 23, 1861

Arkansas	May 6, 1861
North Carolina	May 21, 1861
Virginia	May 23, 1861
Tennessee	June 8, 1861

CONGAREE INDIANS. Small tribe of Siouan linguistic stock that resided on the CONGAREE RIVER (to which they gave their name) in South Carolina. They fought the colonists in the Yamasee War (1715) and at its close many were shipped to the West Indies as slaves.

CONGAREE RIVER, S.C. The BROAD and SALUDA Rivers meet to form this waterway near Columbia, S.C. At the northwest tip of Lake Marion, it joins the WATEREE to become the SANTEE RIVER.

CONNALLY, John Bowden (Floresville, Tex., Feb. 27, 1917 —). Politician. Connally was twice elected governor of Texas (1963-69), and was Secretary of the Navy under President John Kennedy (1961-62). He was seriously wounded in Dallas during the incident that claimed President Kennedy's life on November 22, 1963. Originally a conservative Democrat, Connally joined the Republican party in 1975 and was Secretary of the Treasury under President Richard Nixon.

CONNALLY, Thomas Terry (McLennan Co., Tex., Aug. 19, 1877 — Washington, D.C., Oct. 28, 1963). Politician. He began his political career in Texas as a state legislator before becoming a U.S. representative (1917-29) and a U.S. senator (1929-53). Connally, a Democrat, often supported the administration on foreign matters, but not domestic issues and was chairman of the Senate Foreign Committee (1941-46, 1949-53). *My Name is Tom Connally* (1954) is his autobiography.

CONWAY, Ark. City (pop. 20,375), seat of Faulkner Co., in central Arkansas. Originally the site of a French trading post, Conway was settled in the 1860s. The town is situated in a farming area that produces cotton and dairy products. Manufactures include shoes, lumber, and truck bodies. Hendrix College (1876) is located here, as is the University of Central Arkansas and Conway Lake.

CONWAY, Moncure Daniel (Stafford County, Va., Mar. 17, 1832 — Paris, France, Nov. 15, 1907). Abolitionist, clergyman, and author. After graduation from Dickinson Col-

lege, Conway became a Methodist minister but soon left that church to join the Unitarians. However, his fervent anti-slavery views were not tolerated by the Unitarians. Dismissed from his pastorate, he devoted his energies to the abolitionist cause, setting up a colony for fugitive slaves in Yellow Springs, Ohio, and then becoming co-editor of Boston's antislavery paper, the *Commonwealth*, in 1862. During the Civil War he traveled to England to deliver anti-slavery lectures. Conway wrote over 70 books and pamphlets, which include *The Life of Thomas Paine*, 2 vols. (1892), *Collected Works of Thomas Paine*, 4 vols. (1894-96), and *Autobiography* (1904).

CONWAY, S.C. Town (pop. 10,240), seat of Horry Co., eastern South Carolina. Once a major stop on the chief north-south stagecoach line, it is now a tobacco shipping point on the Waccamaw River. Crops include corn, melons, potatoes, and strawberries. Manufactures include bricks, lumber, veneer, and plywood. The town offers the Traveler's Chapel, a meditation building, and the Horry County Museum.

COOKEVILLE, Tenn. City (pop. 20,350), seat of Putnam Co., in northeast Tennessee. Lots for the town were sold in 1854. Today it is a trade center for an agricultural region which also makes tools and dies, athletic equipment, candy, and flour. There are also bottling, granite, and marble works. Tennessee Technical University (1915) is here.

COOPER, Anna Julia Haywood (Raleigh. N.C., Aug. 10, 1859 (?) — Washington, D.C., Feb. 27, 1964). Educator, historian. A graduate of Oberlin College (B.A., 1884; M.A., 1888), she taught Latin at Washington (M Street, later Dunbar) High School in the District of Columbia (1887). As principal there (1901-06) she drew sharp criticism and was ousted for her advocacy of higher education for blacks and women. In 1914 she began doctoral studies at Columbia University, publishing her dissertation, *Le Pèlerinage de Charlemagne*, in Paris in 1925 but won her doctorate at the Sorbonne after publishing *L'Attitude de la France à l'Égard de l'Esclavage pendant la Révolution* that year. She returned to Dunbar High School (1925-30) and later published *The Grimke Family* (1951).

COOPER, John Montgomery (Rockville, Md., Oct. 28, 1881 — Washington, D.C., May

22, 1949). Anthropologist, priest, and author. In 1935 he became head of the department of anthropology at Catholic University, Washington, D.C., the first such department in a Catholic university. His work dealt with the "marginal peoples" of the Americas, the Algonquian tribes of northern Canada, the Gros Ventre Indians of Montana, and the natives of Tierra del Fuego, whom he believed had been driven with their aboriginal cultures to less desirable habitats by later migrations. He was president of the American Anthropological Association (1940), and founded the quarterly *Primitive Man.*

COOPER RIVER, S.C. River that joins with the ASHLEY in Charleston to drain into the Atlantic Ocean. Its source is in Berkeley Co., and it is some 50 miles long.

COOSA RIVER, Ala. Partially navigable river which originates in northwest Georgia and travels south for 286 miles to central Alabama to join the TALLAPOOSA and form the ALABAMA RIVER. One of the state's five chief rivers, it is an important hydroelectric power source. The Jordan, Lay, and Mitchell Dams are found along the river.

COOSAWATTEE RIVER, Ga. River created by the confluence of the Ellijay and Cartecay Rivers in northern Georgia. It travels southwest for 30 miles to become the OOSTANAULA RIVER.

COOSAWHATCHIE RIVER, S.C. Sixty-mile-long stream which rises in Allendale Co., and runs through southern South Carolina. The river flows generally southeast to empty into Port Royal Sound.

COPPERAS COVE, Tex. Town (pop. 19,469), Coryell Co., in central Texas. It was supposedly named for a copper spring in the cove of a nearby mountain. A former farming and ranching center, Copperas Cove today is primarily a business center servicing the military community of nearby Fort Hood.

CORAL GABLES, Fla. City (pop. 43,241), Dade Co., near Miami in southern Florida. It was founded in 1925 by George E. Merrick and named for the gable-roofed house on his family citrus farm. A planned community, it was built in just a few years and incorporated in 1925. Its navigable waterways and facilities for recreation include access to Biscayne Bay and the Atlantic. Coral Gables is the home of the University of MIAMI.

CORAL SPRINGS, Fla. City (pop. 37,349), Broward Co., covering over 20 square miles, midway between Miami and Palm Beach in southern Florida. A residential community with some light industry, it has experienced rapid growth since its development began in 1966.

CORBIN, Ky. City (pop. 8,075), Whitley Co., in southeastern Kentucky. Incorporated in 1894, it did not really generate major industry until the advent of the railroad. It is now a major railroad center, with repair shops. Coal is also shipped from here. Manufactures include textiles, auto parts, and insulation products. The Levi Jackson Wilderness Road and Cumberland Falls State Parks are found here.

COREE INDIANS. Small tribe of Algonquian linguistic stock that inhabited the coast of upper North Carolina. Along with other small tribes they occupied lands once owned by the powerful HATTERAS INDIANS. They were allies of the TUSCARORA INDIANS in an attack upon the English in 1711 and were defeated. The remaining Coree were given a reservation in 1715 where they remained until they became extinct.

CORINTH, Battles of. Two battles in the western theater of the Civil War were fought in Corinth, Miss., in the northeast corner of the state. In the first, fought April 29-June 10, 1862, the Confederate army was forced to surrender its base of operations in the town. In the second, fought October 3-4, 1862, it failed to retake the town from the Union army.

The first battle of Corinth was a Union victory in pursuit of the Confederate army defeated at Shiloh in April of 1862. The Confederates under Gen. Pierre BEAUREGARD fell back from Shiloh to Corinth, where they were reinforced to a strength of 66,000 for a defense of the town. The Union army reached Corinth with 110,000 troops; they were nominally under the command of Gen. Henry Halleck, with Gen. Ulysses S. Grant second-in-command. This force first met resistance at Seven Mile Creek, and it then took a month to advance from there 20 miles to the outskirts of Corinth. As the Union forces prepared to bombard the town, Beauregard conceded to their superior numbers and retreated south on May 30. He was pursued by Union Gen. John Pope until June 10, when Halleck decided against invading inland Mississippi.

The second battle of Corinth was an attempt to recapture the city by Confederate Gen. Earl Van Dorn. Van Dorn believed the Union garrison was inferior to his own army of 22,000, but in fact the Union troops under Gen. William Starke Rosecrans numbered 23,000. Van Dorn attacked on October 3, 1862, forcing the Union army back within its own lines. His own troops were dispersed, however, and he began to pull back under heavy fire on October 4. For this ill-advised attack and subsequent retreat Van Dorn was investigated; although cleared of charges, he was transferred to another command.

CORINTH, Miss. City (pop. 13,389), seat of Alcorn Co., in northeastern Mississippi. Founded c. 1855, it served as a strategic railroad post during the Civil War, and two battles were fought here. Telephone equipment, organs, clothing, and furniture are manufactured. Agricultural products include soybeans, cotton, corn, and poultry.

CORN. Generic name used throughout the world for grain crops, and used in the United States for the grain more precisely called maize, or Indian corn. This crop was cultivated by North American Indians long before European exploration of the continent, and it is now so domesticated that it never reverts to the wild state. U.S. corn is a popular seasonal food and canned vegetable, but the bulk of the U.S. harvest is used for animal feed. The great "corn belt" of the U.S. lies across the Plains states, but the South accounts for more than 10% of the harvest per year of corn for grain.

In 1980 Texas led all Southern states in corn, with a harvest of 117 million bushels worth $410 million. It was followed, among states in the region, by Missouri with 110 million bushels, and by Kentucky and North Carolina with 104 million bushels each. The only state in the South without a significant corn harvest is West Virginia.

CORNWALLIS, Lord Charles (London, England, Dec. 31, 1738 — Ghazipur, India, Oct. 5, 1805). British general. He opposed British measures that led to the Revolutionary War, but accepted the commission of major general and the command of an expedition under Sir Peter Parker in 1776. Cornwallis commanded British reserves at the battle of Long Island, lost the battle of Princeton to Gen. George Washington, and later aided in the capture of Philadelphia. After a brief trip to England, Cornwallis returned to America and began his Carolina campaign. In May, 1780, he was involved in the capture of Charleston, S.C., defeated Gen. Horatio Gates near Camden, S.C., in August of that year, and on March 15, 1781 he fought Gen. Nathanael Greene at the battle of GUILFORD COURT HOUSE. Driven from the Carolinas, Cornwallis invaded Virginia, fortified YORKTOWN, and there surrendered his army of 7,000 men to American and French forces on October 19, 1781. Upon his return to England he was offered and accepted the post of governor general in India.

CORONADO, Francisco Vasquez de (Salamanca, Spain, Feb. 25, 1510 — Mexico, c. Nov. 12, 1554). Spanish explorer. He was particularly noted for his finds on expeditions from Mexico in what is now the American Southwest. Coronado was the first to record such sights as the Grand Canyon. While he was unsuccessful in his hunts for treasure, he did bring back invaluable information on this region, and opened up the Southwest to the Spanish.

CORPUS CHRISTI, Lake, Tex. Artificial lake in Live Oak, Jim Wells, and San Patricio Counties, in southern Texas on the Nueces River. It was one of the first completed projects of its kind and supplies water to the city of Corpus Christi. Its 1,200-acre state park was opened to the public in 1936.

CORPUS CHRISTI, Tex. City (pop. 231,999), Nueces Co., on the southeastern coast of Texas on the Gulf Intracoastal Waterway. Discovered by the Spanish on Corpus Christi Day in 1519, Corpus Christi is a major American seaport and resort area. Settled around 1839, the area was a center for the wool market between 1870 and 1880. After 1880, cattle packing houses and stockyards flourished. In 1923 Corpus Christi developed its first natural gas well, and in 1926, opened its port, two events that caused its population to start mushrooming. Today Corpus Christi serves the large petrochemical and agricultural area surrounding it. Chemicals, petroleum, coal products, and processed foods are its main manufactures. The Corpus Christi Naval Air Station (1941) is a leading employer in the city. The Art Museum of South Texas, the Corpus Christi Museum, and the Museum of Science and History are located here.

CORSICANA, Tex. City (pop. 19,972), seat of Navarro Co., in northeast central Texas. Settled in 1848, Jose Antonio Navarro named it for the French island where his father was born. The city gained notoriety in 1894 when oil was struck, the first time such a discovery was made west of the Mississippi. The state's first oil refinery was constructed here two years later. Besides oil production and refinement, the local economy depends largely on agricultural produce, including cotton, grain, and cattle. Navarro Junior College is located here.

COSSATOT RIVER, Ark. Long, narrow river with its source in western Arkansas. It parallels the Oklahoma border on its journey south to drain into Millwood Lake.

COTTON. The pliable white seed hairs produced by the pod, or boll, of plants of the genus *Gossypium*, cultivated around the world as a source of textile fibers. The name is of uncertain Arabic etymological origin, transferred into Old French *coton* and Middle English *cotoun*.

Although closely associated with the American "cotton belt" extending from Virginia west to Texas, the cotton plant has prehistoric and international origins. The plant may have been cultivated in Mexico as long ago as 5000 B.C. and in India as long ago as 3000 B.C. On his first expedition to the New World in 1492, Columbus found a widespread growth of indigenous cotton on the Bahama Islands. The plant, then, has a long history in most tropical and subtropical lattitudes around the globe.

Although long used for cloth, cotton did not become an important commercial crop until an efficient means of removing the fibers from the bolls and spinning them into yarn had been devised. The first spinning inventions were devised in England, where John Kay invented the fly shuttle (1733), James Hargreaves invented the spinning jenny (1764), and Edmund Cartwright invented the power loom (1785). Harvesting of the raw material lagged behind spinning techniques, however, until Eli Whitney invented the cotton gin (1793). This made adequate fiber supplies available for cotton mills, the first American one having been built in Pawtucket, R.I., by Samuel Slater in 1790. By 1800 cotton had become one of the most important American industries. Textile manufacture was at that time principally located in New England, while field crops were as a matter of climatic necessity located in the Southern

Laborers picking cotton in Surrey County, Va. in the 1890s

states, where they were the basis of plantation society reliant on slave labor. By 1900, however, the textile industry began to relocate closer to the source of its raw material, with major mill towns springing up in North Carolina and South Carolina. These states continue to be leaders in textile production, but in a modern development the crop has moved out of the old South, being replaced by soybeans, toward the irrigated farmlands of Texas and California.

There are four principal varieties of *Gossypium* cultivated for cotton fiber. *G. arboreum* originated in India, and *G. herbaceum* is associated with Arab countries. In the United States cultivation is based on *G. barbadense*, known as Egyptian cotton, and *G. hirsutum*, called American upland cotton and the source of most of the world's cotton fiber. These varieties grow as shrubby plants anywhere from three to six feet in height. They are thickest at the bottom and combine leaf foliage with boll growth. The boll itself forms at the base of a blossom. It remains closed for a period of about six weeks, during which the fiber growth of the seeds fills the cavity of the boll. When ready for harvest, the boll opens and exposes its white raw cotton.

Cultivation of cotton begins with dense sowing of seeds and subsequent thinning of the young sprouts. Cotton plants are delicate and extremely susceptible to both vegetable and insect pests. Weeds are generally controled by mechanical cultivation of furrows or by flame cultivation, accomplished with jets of gas flame. Insects, the most famous being the boll weevil, are controlled by spraying. Harvesting, once the back-breaking hand labor that spawned the slave trade, is now entirely mechanized. The plants are first chemically defoliated to expose the bolls and to prevent rot. The crop is then gathered by mechanical "pickers," when dense, or "strippers," when sparse. Before shipment to textile markets, the cotton is processed by being cleaned of remaining sticks and stems, sent through a cotton gin to separate the seeds from the fiber, and bundled into compressed 480-pound bales.

The quality of the cotton fiber yielded by any crop is graded for apparel use when satisfactory and household use in upholstery and rugs when not. The seeds are also of value, their hulls being used for animal feed and fertilizer and their kernels as a source of cottonseed oil.

LEADING U.S. COTTON STATES

State	Harvest in Bales
Texas	3,305,000
California	3,150,000
Arizona	1,413,000
Mississippi	1,150,000
Louisiana	455,000
Arkansas	450,000
Alabama	275,000

COULTER, Ellis Merton (Hickory, N.C., 1890 —). Historian. He received his Ph.D. at the University of Wisconsin (1917) and taught there until going to the University of Georgia where he became a professor of history (1923). A noted historian, he wrote numerous volumes about the South, particularly about the Civil War and Reconstruction periods, including *The Confederate States of America, 1861-1865* (a "History of the South" series, vol. 7, 1950).

COUNTRY AND WESTERN MUSIC. Popular American musical form that originated in the South among rural whites. In the 19th century the folk music tradition derived from British roots combined with Afro-American and other ethnic music began to be transformed into a truly American idiom, particularly in the mountainous Appalachian regions of the South, where it came to be known as "hillbilly" music. At first the music was usually performed at county fairs, churches and other local occasions. The growth of the form was given a great boost during the 1920s with the arrival of radio and the emergence of such groups as the Carter Family, led by Alvin Pleasant "A. P." Carter (1891-1960), his wife Sara (1898–), and his sister-in-law Maybelle (1909–). At the same time, there appeared a former railroad brakeman, Jimmie Rodgers (1897-1933), known for his yodeling (best represented in "Blue Yodel"), who went on to be dubbed "the father of country music." The birth date of modern country music is often given as Aug. 4, 1927, when both the Carters and Rodgers made their first recordings in Bristol, Tennessee.

A variation on the country theme appeared in the 1930s with the rise of western music, popularized by "the singing cowboy," Gene Autry (1907–) who extended its influence through films, as did Tex Ritter (1905-73) and Roy Rogers (1911–), "the king of the cowboys," who emerged from the successful Western group Sons of the Pioneers. Western was but one of a variety of allied forms ranging from the folk tradition of Woodie Guthrie (1912-67) to the big-band western swing of Bob Wills (1905-75) to the banjo instrumentals of bluegrass music, as exemplified by Bill Monroe

(1911–), Lester Flatt (1914–) and Earl Scruggs (1924–).

The mainstream of country music received a major boost in 1927 with the establishment to the GRAND OLE OPRY by George Hay (1895-1968), which made Nashville, Tennessee the Mecca for country music, and served as a showcase for a generation of talent, including Roy Acuff (1903–), Ernest Tubb (1914-84), "Tennessee Ernie" Ford (1919–), Hank Williams (1923-53) and Webb Pierce (1926–).

The postwar tradition has seen a widespread growth in the popularity of country and western, although it is strongest in the South and Southwest, which still supply the majority of the performers. While it has been influenced by other forms, notably ROCK MUSIC, the tradition has been maintained by such artists as Johnny Cash (1932–), Willie Nelson (1933–), Loretta Lynn (1935–), Merle Haggard (1937–), and Waylon Jennings (1937–). Other stars have modified the country approach to reach a wider audience through television and film. These include Glenn Campbell (1936–), Kenny Rogers (1941–), Dolly Parton (1946–) and Barbara Mandrell (1948–). See also GOSPEL MUSIC.

COVINGTON, Ga. City (pop. 10,856), seat of Newton Co., in north central Georgia. The city was incorporated in 1854 and named for Revolutionary War Gen. Leonard Covington. There is diversified farming, and manufactures include fertilizer, surgical supplies, and foam products.

COVINGTON, Ky. City (pop. 49,013), seat of Kenton Co., in north central Kentucky on the Ohio River. Six bridges connect the city to Cincinnati, Ohio. Manufactures include electrical equipment, machine tools, paper, sheet metal, freight cars, petroleum, and candied fruits. A ferry and tavern were first established here in 1801 and the city was incorporated in 1834.

COWPENS, Battle of. Revolutionary War victory by patriots over the British fought on January 17, 1781, at "the Cowpens" on the Broad River in the northern part of South Carolina. It followed the defeat of the British at King's Mountain in the fall of 1780, and so solidified support in the region for the patriotic cause and forced the British into desperate countermaneuvers.

After his defeat at Camden, Gen. Horatio Gates was replaced as commander of the Revolutionary forces in the south by Gen. Nathaniel Greene. Greene, George Washington's own choice for the command, fought a masterful campaign of controlled retreats and diversionary tactics. The battle of Cowpens took shape when Greene divided his force and sent 1,000 troops under Gen. Daniel Morgan southwest of the main body of the Continental army. The British commander Lord Charles Cornwallis sent a force of similar strength under Col. Banastre Tarleton to contain this movement south.

At the Battle of Cowpens on January 17, Morgan had his troops sham retreat, and the tactic effectively lured the British into a devastating cross fire. British losses were more than 100 killed, more than 200 wounded, and more than 600 captured. Casualties for the Continental militia totaled 12 killed and 60 wounded.

Following the Battle of Cowpens, Morgan retreated back north and rejoined the main body of Greene's force. Tarleton's force was almost completely lost to Cornwallis, who, now forced into a defensive posture, moved to confront the Revolutionary side at Guilford Courthouse in North Carolina.

COXETTER, Louis Mitchell (Nova Scotia, Dec. 10, 1818 — Charleston, S.C., July 10, 1873). Privateer and blockade runner. After settling in Charleston, S.C., as a youth, he captained transport ships during the Mexican War. At the outbreak of the Civil War he worked with the Confederacy. Coxetter captured ten ships (1861) as captain of the *Jefferson Davis*. He turned to blockade running because of the increasingly effective Union blockade.

CRABS. Shellfish of commercial importance along the Chesapeake Bay and Atlantic waters of the South. The most important variety for human consumption is the blue-claw crab. The crab catch in Chesapeake Bay averages about 65 million pounds per year, and that in the Atlantic waters of the South averages 55 million pounds per year. In both cases the crab catch is the most important shellfish resource. In the Gulf of Mexico the crab catch averages about 45 million pounds per year, but there it is far exceeded by the catch of shrimp. See also FISHING, Commercial.

CRAFT, Ellen (Clinton, Ga., c.1826 — Charleston, S.C., c.1897). Fugitive slave and abolitionist. At Christmas 1848 Craft assumed the disguise of a deaf white master, whose injured arm made it impossible for him to sign hotel registers, and her husband William that of his slave. Fleeing north on savings from William's cabinetmaking, they evetually reached Boston. Here they became well-known figures, but discovery by Georgia slave hunters spurred their flight to Nova Scotia and thence to England. Here they gained great fame, attended school, and joined British abolitionist circles. They returned to the U.S. in 1867, where they bought a plantation near their old home in South Carolina and founded an industrial school for blacks.

CRAIGHEAD, Edwin Boone (Ham's Prairie, Mo., Mar. 3, 1861 — Oct. 22, 1920). Educator. A graduate of Central College, Mo., (1883), he became a professor of Greek at Wofford College (1890). Craighead served as president of numerous colleges, including Clemson Agricultural College (1893-97), Central College (1897-1901), Missouri State Normal School (1901-04), Tulane University (1904-12), and Montana State University (1912-15). In his later years, Craighead established and edited the newspaper *New Northwest* in Missoula, Mo.

CRAVEN, Avery Odelle (Randolph Co., N.C., Aug. 12, 1886 — Chesterton, Ind., Jan. 21, 1980). Historian and educator. He was a leader of the historical school which contends that the Civil War might have been avoided. His many works include *Soil Exhaustion as a Factor in the Agricultural History of Virginia and Maryland 1606-1860* (1925), *The Repressible Conflict, 1830-1861* (1939), and *An Historian and the Civil War* (1964).

CRAWFORD, William Harris (Amherst Co., Va., Feb. 24, 1772 — Elberton, Ga., Sept. 15, 1834). Lawyer and politician. Crawford is best remembered for being one of four presidential candidates in the election of 1824. Although Crawford received more electoral votes than his three fellow candidates—Henry Clay, Andrew Jackson and John Quincy Adams, he did not have enough to command a majority. The House of Representatives selected Adams to be President. As a young man Crawford taught school and practiced law before entering politics. A member of the U.S. Senate from Georgia (1807-13), President James Madison appointed him minister to France (1813-15). In 1815 he was named Secretary of War and in 1816 became Secretary of the Treasury, a post he held until 1825. From 1827 until his death he served as a circuit judge in Georgia.

CREEK INDIANS. The name given to a powerful but loosely organized confederacy of Indian tribes, the most dominant of which were the MUSKOGEE. The domain of the Confederacy extended from the Atlantic westward, including a great portion of Alabama and Georgia and the whole of Florida. It was geographically divided between the Upper and Lower Creeks. When the Carolinas and Louisiana began to be settled by the English and French, they all courted the Creek Nation. The English won the allegiance of Lower Creeks and the French the Upper Creeks. When the French power in America was overthrown, the entire Creek Nation became subject to English influence, and the Creeks allied themselves with the British during the Revolution. A peace was concluded by Washington in 1790 but when the War of 1812 broke out they again joined the British.

The Confederacy was at this time under the control of Alexander MCGILLIVRAY, son of a Scotch trader. After his death, friction developed in the Creek nation between those opposed and those in favor of the whites. Led by the Shawnee chief TECUMSEH, many Upper Creeks broke into open hostilities against the whites, and aroused the vengeance of the U.S. government by the massacre at Fort Mims (1813), beginning the Creek War. Troops led by Gen. Andrew Jackson entered Creek country, destroying their towns and killing or capturing 2,000 Creeks. The Creeks made their last stand at the Battle of Horseshoe Bend in March, 1814.

Strained relations continued between the Upper and Lower Creeks despite the government's attempts to reunite them in the Indian Territory in Oklahoma. Leaders of the Creek Confederacy finally came to terms, and between 1836 and 1840 they emigrated and settled in the new territory. Relations between the two factions were still strained for some time and they were slow to accept missionary attempts and schools. An elective government of the Upper and Lower Creeks was finally established with both groups having representation. This government continued until the Confederacy was incorporated into the state of Oklahoma.

CREEL, George Edward (Lafayette Co., Mo., Dec. 1, 1876 — San Francisco, Calif., Oct. 2, 1953). Journalist. Beginning his career as a news reporter for the *Kansas City World* (1894), and then on his own newspaper *The Kansas City Independence* (1899), Creel established a reputation as a dedicated investigative reporter. In 1917, President Woodrow Wilson appointed him head of the U.S. Committee on Public Information. Creel ran unsuccessfully against novelist Upton Sinclair for the Democratic nomination for governor of California in 1934. He published 13 books including *War Criminals and Punishment* (1944).

CREOLE. A large French-speaking group of Louisianans living in urban areas, the Creoles are descendants of French (and occasionally Spanish) early settlers who arrived in the 1700s. Not to be confused with the Cajuns or ACADIANS who live in rural Louisiana and are descendants of the Nova Scotia exiles who immigrated here in the 1760s and 1770s, the Creoles are said to speak a "cultured" French with little influence of Negro, English, or German. The term Creole has since been extended to include a type of cooking. The Creoles are a clannish group with a very regimented society of their own; their loyalties often excluding those of "Louisiana society" because they are not Creole. Generally Roman Catholic, they celebrate holidays with gusto and frequently have ceremonial blessings of sugar cane crops, shrimp harvests, etc. Creole cooking is directly related to the urban, luxury ways of the early settlers and specializes in subtle flavors and sauces that require expensive ingredients.

CRESAP, Michael (Allegheny Co., Md., June 29, 1742 — New York, Oct. 18, 1775). Indian fighter and Revolutionary War soldier. Cresap was accused of war atrocities while fighting the Indians and possibly starting Lord Dunmore's War (1774), but was later exonerated of those charges. He became a captain in the American Revolution but died early in the war.

CRESCENT LAKE, Fla. Lake between Flagler and Putnam Counties, in northeastern Florida. It runs south to north for about 14 miles with a breadth of one to three miles and empties into the St. Johns River. Crescent City (pop. 1,393) is located midway on the western shore.

CRESWELL, John Andrew Jackson (Port Deposit, Md., Nov. 18, 1828 — Elkton, Md., Dec. 23, 1891). Politician and postmaster general of the U.S. A graduate of Dickinson College, Creswell served both as U.S. congressman (1863-65) and U.S. senator (1865-67) from Maryland before being appointed postmaster

general by President Ulysses S. Grant (1869-74). As postmaster general, he was credited with far-reaching reforms in the postal system.

CRITTENDEN, John Jordan (Versailles, Ky., Sept. 10, 1787 — Woodford County, Ky., July 26, 1863). Politician. Beginning his public career as the territorial attorney general in Illinois in 1809, he returned to his native Kentucky, was elected to the state legislature, and won election to the U.S. Senate in 1817, serving intermittently until 1861. An opponent of the financial policies of Andrew Jackson and Martin Van Buren, he became the U.S. attorney general under President William Henry Harrison's Whig administration in 1840. His resignation came after Harrison's death, when successor John Tyler vetoed a Whig-supported national banking act. After another Senate term, he served as governor of Kentucky (1848-50), and following the demise of the Whig party in 1854, he first joined the Know Nothing party and then the Constitutional Union party, which worked to unite the divided states by ignoring the question of slavery. After the election of Abraham Lincoln, he proposed the Crittenden Compromise, a measure seeking to forestall the Civil War by restoring and extending the Missouri Compromise Line, to grant slavery rights in the District of Columbia, and to reimburse slaveholders for runaway slaves. Following the defeat of his proposal and the onset of the Civil War, two of his sons fought on opposing sides as major generals.

CRITTENDEN, Thomas Leonidas (Russellville, Ky., May 15, 1819 — Annadale, N.Y., Oct. 23, 1893). Union general. He served in the Mexican War, was U.S. consul to Liverpool (1849-53), and practiced law in Frankfort, Conn. A Unionist, he joined the Union Army at the outbreak of the Civil War and was promoted to major general (1862) for his service at Shiloh. Crittenden's troops deserted him at the battle of Chickamauga, but a court of inquiry exonerated him for his defeat and he served later in the Army of the Potomac. He was the son of John J. CRITTENDEN.

CRITTENDEN, Thomas Theodore (Shelbyville, Ky., Jan. 1, 1832 — Kansas City, Mo., May 29, 1909). Politician. After fighting in the Civil War with the Union Army, he served as state attorney general and then in the U.S. House of Representatives (1873-75, 1877-79) for Missouri. During his time as governor

(1881-85), he worked to bring civil order to the state and broke up the Jesse James gang. He was the nephew of John J. CRITTENDEN.

CROCKETT, David (Limestone, Tenn., Aug. 17, 1786 — San Antonio, Tex., Mar. 6, 1836). Legendary frontiersman, soldier, humorist, and politician. Crockett first made a name for himself as a scout for Gen. Andrew Jackson during the Creek War (1813-15). He later joined the Tennessee militia and attained the rank of colonel. In 1821 he won election to the Tennessee legislature, chiefly on the strength of his humor and storytelling abilities. His subsequent election to the U.S. Congress in 1827 (he failed to win in his first attempt in 1825) was marked by independent voting and stringent opposition to the policies of Jackson. He was relected in 1833 and defeated once more in 1835 owing to a great deal of opposition organized by supporters of Jackson. Later in 1835 Crockett joined the Americans in Texas and died there at the ALAMO (1836) when the Mexican army, under the command of Gen. Santa Anna, overran the fort, killing all 184 defenders.

Crockett's expert marksmanship, witty stories and anecdotes, and his valiant death at the

Legendary frontiersman and soldier Davy Crockett

Alamo contributed greatly to making him a legend. He was presented as the author of several books (possibly dictated), including *A Narrative of the Life of David Crockett* (1834).

CROOKED RUN RIVER, Va. Tributary of the Rapidan, with source in Madison Co., Va. It was named because of its crooked flowing pattern along the boundary of Culpeper Co.

CROSS, Hardy (Nansemond, Co., Va., Feb. 10, 1885 — Virginia Beach, Va., Feb. 11, 1959). Engineer. He made outstanding contributions to the field of structural engineering. Cross discovered a new method of calculating "moments" in the framework of a structure that eliminated the ponderous amounts of calculations which had previously been necessary. His discovery became known as the Moment Distribution Method or the Hardy Cross Method. After the publication of his Method in 1930, Cross was named professor of structural engineering at the University of Illinois, and in 1937 he became a professor at Yale. He retired from Yale in 1951 as professor emeritus, and in 1958, the British Institution of Structural Engineers gave Cross its gold medal.

CROSS LAKE, La. Lake in Caddo Parish, in northwestern Louisiana. Cross Lake sits at the western edge of Shreveport and plays a large part in the city's recreational life.

CROWDER, Enoch Herbert (Edinburg, Mo., Apr. 11, 1859 — Washington, D.C., May 7, 1932). Army officer and administrator of the Selective Service Act. An 1881 graduate of the U.S. Military Academy at West Point, N.Y., Crowder fought in the cavalry against the Indians in the West and served as judge advocate to U.S. troops in the Philippines in the Spanish-American War (1898). He was sent to Cuba where he served as secretary of state and justice (1906-08). In 1911, Crowder was appointed judge advocate general of the U.S. Army and became the provost marshal to administer the Selective Service Act when the law was enacted in May, 1921. He also served four years as the first U.S. ambassador to Cuba, beginning in 1923.

CROWLEY, La. City (pop. 16,036), seat of Acadia Parish, in southwestern Louisiana. One of the nation's largest rice producers, Crowley serves as a shipping, and storing center for this product. Soybeans and cotton are also raised and there is some light manufacturing along with oil and gas wells. There is a rice experimental station, a rice museum, and the International Rice Festival, featuring a frog derby, is held here every October.

CROWLEY'S RIDGE, Ark. Long, narrow strip of hills beginning at the Missouri border and running 150 miles to Helena, Ark. Its peaks reach 550 feet. Situated on an alluvial plain, it is best known for its yellow topsoil. The area is named for Benjamin Crowley, whose homestead and tomb remain on the ridge. A 271-acre state park is found here.

CRUMP, Edward Hull (near Holly Springs, Miss., Oct. 2, 1876 — Memphis, Tenn., Oct. 16, 1954). Politician. Crump held numerous political offices in Memphis, Tenn., before he was elected mayor (1909-16, 1939-41), and U.S. congressman (1931-33). He became known as "Boss" Crump because of his strong hold on the state political machinery. However, the failure of his candidates in the 1948 Democratic primaries upset his position and power.

CULPEPER, Va. Town (pop. 6,621), seat of Culpeper Co., in west central Virginia. Located in a rich agricultural region, Culpeper was founded in 1759. The town was the place of muster for the Culpeper Minute Men in 1775. Along with agricultural produce, dairying, and livestock, present manufactures include wire rope, bottling, steel tanks, and lumber.

CULPEPER'S REBELLION. Colonial revolt in South Carolina in 1677. Colonists of Albemarle Co., led by John Culpeper, charged English proprietors and governors with malfeasance and treason, stating they were more interested in becoming wealthy than governing properly. They seized the proprietors and thus the government and sent charges against them to England. The colonists ran the county for one year, appointing Culpeper as their governor. The proprietors eventually restored their power, ending the rebellion.

CUMBERLAND, Lake, Ky. A 50,250-acre lake extending into several counties in south central Kentucky, about 20 miles from the Tennessee border. Located on the Cumberland River, it is one of the state's major water recreational sites with a 3,000-acre state park on its shores. A two-story fishery is also found here.

CUMBERLAND, Md. City (pop. 25,933), seat of Allegany Co., in the western panhandle of Maryland on the Potomac River, surrounded by the Allegheny Mountains. The third-largest city in the state, Cumberland is an industrial center in a region of farms, forests, and coal deposits. The city ships coal, limestone, and manufactured products including sheet metal, missile components, plate glass, bricks, tires, and beer. Originally the site of an Indian village, the town became successively a trading post, pioneer settlement, and, in 1755, Fort Cumberland, built as an outpost against the French and Indians. George Washington was among the commanders of Fort Cumberland.

CUMBERLAND FALLS, Ky. Falls in Whiteley and McCreary Co., in southern Kentucky. Nicknamed the "Niagara of the South" because it is the largest waterfall east of the Rockies and south of Niagara Falls, the 150-foot wide falls drop 68 feet into the Cumberland River, near Corbin, Ky. During a full moon, the falls offer the only moonbow in the Western Hemisphere.

CUMBERLAND GAP. At the boundary of Virginia, Kentucky, and Tennessee, it is a natural pass through the Cumberland Mountains at an elevation of 1,650 ft. In 1750 it was discovered and named by Dr. Thomas Walker. The Gap was a strategic military point during the Civil War and was alternately held by Confederate and Union troops. In 1955 the Cumberland Gap National Historical Park was established.

CUMBERLAND ISLAND, Ga. Island in Camden Co., and part of the Sea Island chain in southeastern Georgia along the Atlantic coast. It is the largest island, measuring 22 miles long

The Cumberland Gap

and one to five miles wide and is largely privately owned. Forts were built here for protection during the early settlement years but were later taken over as outlaw hideouts. A resort area, Cumberland Island has some agriculture.

CUMBERLAND MOUNTAINS.

Also referred to as the Cumberland Plateau, an area over 400 miles long and 50 miles wide in the southwestern APPALACHIAN MOUNTAINS system. It reaches from northern Alabama to West Virginia. The highest elevation is Big Black Mountain (4,145 feet) in Kentucky. Rivers having their source in the plateau are the Tennessee, Kentucky, and Cumberland. A heavily forested area, it is also rich in deposits of coal, sandstone, and limestone.

CUMBERLAND RIVER.

River nearly 700 miles long rising in eastern Kentucky, and flowing a winding course through Tennessee before becoming a tributary of the Ohio at Smithland, Ky. Numerous dams dot the river and its tributaries both for power and navigation. A natural drop in the river, CUMBERLAND FALLS (63 feet) is in Whitley Co., Ky. Most of the Cumberland's tributaries are downstream of the falls. The largest city on the river is Nashville, Tenn.

CUMBERLAND VALLEY, Md.

A division of the great Appalachian Valley situated to the north of the Shenandoah Valley. The region begins at the Potomac River at the Maryland border and extends northward to meet the Susquehanna River in Pennsylvania.

CUMMING, Kate

(Edinburgh, Scotland, 1828 (?) — Rosedale, Ala., June 5, 1909). Hospital administrator and Civil War diarist. She volunteered for nursing work in 1862 just in time for the battle of Shiloh and was appointed a hospital administrator by the end of that year. She served at Chattanooga (1862-63) and throughout Georgia during Sherman's March (1864). Her diary, which she published as *A Journal of Hospital Life in the Confederate Army of Tennessee* (1866), is of great historical interest and has been reissued several times.

CURRENCY, Colonial.

From the days of the early settlers, a shortage of hard money (specie) plagued the New World. It was a major problem, and one that Britain never confronted. To mint coins for colonial use would have been expensive and difficult—a heavy drain on England's supply of gold, silver and copper. The problem, moreover, was compounded by the attitude of the mercantilist Board of Trade, which believed that money should flow into England but not out—consequently, even the exportation of coins for colonial use was expressly forbidden. The colonists, of course, found substitutes. WAMPUM (Indian money consisting of shell beads strung on a strand of hemp or the tendon of an animal) was widely used. Barter was used as a medium of exchange, as was commodity money—better known as country pay. Examples of country pay include tobacco in Virginia, Maryland, and North Carolina; and rice in South Carolina and Georgia—the value was fixed in English shillings. Foreign coins from Spain, France, Portugal, and Holland were also used as legal tender, with the colonies setting their own rates of exchange. In Virginia, for example, the legislature in 1645 forbade dealing by barter, abolished the use of tobacco as currency and established the Spanish dollar—the "piece of eight" valued at six shillings—as the only legal tender. Ten years later (1655) it was revalued at five shillings. But the desperate need for hard money remained. By the 1690s the colonies began to print their own paper money, but with little attempt to secure the issues. The Board of Trade recognized the problem, but did not try to solve it, only to regulate it. Royal proclamations in 1704 and 1707 established rates of exchange for the shilling but they could not be enforced and were ignored. Throughout the colonies, inflation was rampant. In 1734 Virginia again resorted to the use of country pay. Planters deposited their tobacco in public warehouses and received certificates ("crops notes") in the amount deposited. As these were transferable, they were, in effect, as good as money. Unfortunately, during the 1750s, droughts resulted in crop losses and the price of tobacco rose precipitously. The Virginia Assembly passed the Two Penny Acts (1755 and 1758), which effectively set the price of tobacco at two cents a pound—far below the free market price. The Anglican clergy, which in the colonies collected their salaries in tobacco, objected to the devaluation and brought suit against the 1758 act. Rev. James Maury presented the suit (1763) at Hanover Court, Va., and thus the case is known as the Parson's Cause. The clergy had the backing of the Privy Council in England and the act was declared null and void. A jury was then called to determine how much the parson would collect for the tobacco. However, a brilliant defense plea by young Patrick HENRY, resulted in the tobacco being valued at one cent per pound. The following year (1764) the Currency Act—one of the hated Grenville Acts, which included the STAMP ACT and the American Revenue Act (or Sugar Act)—was passed. The act sought to prevent the colonies from paying debts in England with depreciated currency. It was aimed principally at Virginia, which had issued £250,000 of legal tender paper money during the Pontiac (Indian) Wars. The act galvanized the colonies into action, uniting them in a common cause and paving the way to the REVOLUTIONARY WAR.

CURRENT RIVER, Mo. River rising in Texas Co., in southern Missouri south of the Ozarks, flowing first southeast, then southwest, past the Arkansas border for 125 miles to join the BLACK River. The Current's name is drawn from the swiftness of its flow, which daily amounts to about 40 million gallons.

CURRITUCK SOUND, Va. Body of water beginning at the mouth of Albemarle Sound. It extends 35 miles to the north into North Carolina. An area of barrier beaches, it is also noted for its duck and goose hunting.

CURRY, Jabez Lamar Monroe (Lincoln Co., Ga., June 5, 1825 — Richmond, Va., Feb. 12, 1903). Educator and politician. Curry established state normal schools, was president of Howard College (1865), was agent of the Peabody and State Funds (1881-1903), and fostered rural education in the South. A member of Congress from Alabama (1857-61) and of the Confederate Congress (1861-64), Curry served as U.S. minister to Spain (1885-88).

CUSABO INDIANS ("Coosawhatchie River people"). Tribe of Muskogean linguistic stock that lived in southern South Carolina. The Cusabo were first encountered by the Spanish in 1521 and 70 of them were taken as slaves. Repeated attempts by Europeans to colonize the area failed until the English arrived in 1670. They founded Charleston on Cusabo land and from that time on relationships were generally friendly. The Cusabo joined the colonists against the TUSCARORA INDIANS (1711-12) and were shortly thereafter granted Palawana Island, probably as a result of their assistance.

CYPRESS. Collective name for several genera of resinous evergreens. The Cypress genus native to the South is *Taxodium*, often called the bald cypress. It is distinct from other varieties for thriving in swamps and river bottoms as well as on dry land. The bald cypress has only limited commercial value, although it is used to some extent for shingles and interior furnishings.

CYTHIANA, Ky. City (pop. 5,881), seat of Harrison Co., in northern Kentucky on the southern fork of the Licking River. Cythiana is in a farm area producing tobacco, cotton and nuts. There are tobacco warehouses and redrying plants, along with diversified light manufacturing.

D

DABNEY, Charles William (Hampden Sidney, Va., June 19, 1855 — Asheville, N.C., June 15, 1945). Educator. From 1880 to 1887 he was director of the North Carolina Agricultural Experiment Station. He then became president of the University of Tennessee (1887-1904). He was president of the University of Cincinnati (1904-20) and throughout his career was noted as a promoter of public education.

DADEVILLE, Ala. Town (pop. 3,263), seat of Tallapoosa Co., in east central Alabama near Lake Martin. Founded in 1832 and incorporated in 1837, Dadeville is in a rich timber and mineral area. Its principal product is textiles. North of town on the Tallapoosa River at Horseshoe Bend is the site where Andrew Jackson defeated the Creek Indians in 1814.

DAINGERFIELD, Elliot (Harpers Ferry, Va., Mar. 26, 1859 — Oct. 22, 1932). Painter. Daingerfield is best known for religious pictures and landscapes. Moving to New York City to study art (1880), he first exhibited at the National Academy in 1880. His better-known works include "Christ Stilling the Tempest," "Storm Breaking Up," "The Child Mary," and the mural at the Lady Chapel of St. Mary the Virgin, New York. He wrote monographs on George Innes (1911) and R. A. Blakelock (1914).

DAIRY PRODUCTS. A major farm resource in the South, which accounts for nearly one-fifth of the total sales of dairy products in the U.S. Wisconsin leads all states in dairy products, with sales of $1.89 billion per year. By comparison, in the South, Texas ranks first with sales of $356 million per year, Florida ranks second with sales of $226 million per year, Kentucky ranks third with sales of $202 per year, and Virginia ranks fourth with sales of $194 million per year. Dairy products are the second-most valuable farm commodity in three of the states of the South: Maryland, Virginia, and West Virginia. In sales of whole milk, Texas leads the Southern states with sales of $492 million per year and Florida ranks second with sales of $317 million per year.

DALE, Richard (Norfolk Co., Va., Nov. 6, 1756 — Philadelphia, Pa., Feb. 26, 1826). Naval officer. Dale joined the American Revolutionary War as a lieutenant in the Virginia Navy. Captured by the British, he was made a mate on an English ship. Dale was recaptured in July, 1776, by the Revolutionary navy and made a master's mate on the *Lexington* under John Barry. However, in September, 1777, he was again captured by the British and imprisoned in England. He escaped a year later and became 1st lieutenant under Capt. John Paul Jones on the *Bon Homme Richard* where he took part in the victory over the *Serapis.* After the war, Dale was appointed a captain of the navy. He resigned from the navy in 1802 because of a dispute.

DALE, Sir Thomas (England, c. 1590 — Masulipatam, India, Aug. 9, 1619). Colonial governor. After an early career as a soldier in Scotland Dale was sent to Virginia to help restore order in the colony. He was acting governor of Virginia from May to August, 1611, and again served from 1614-16. Though Dale was a severe administrator, he helped bring the colony through its early years and was instrumental in the establishment of tobacco cultivation.

DALE HOLLOW RESERVOIR, Tenn. Shared by Clay and Pickett Counties, in northern Tennessee, it is a man-made lake extending into southern Kentucky. The U.S. Army Corps of Engineers developed this project on the OBET RIVER by building a 200-foot dam. The reservoir is 61 miles long with a 620-mile shoreline. A national fish hatchery is here.

DALLAS, Tex. City (pop. 904,078), seat of Dallas Co., in central Texas. Dallas is a major industrial, financial, educational, and cultural center of the American Southwest. The second-largest city in Texas it is the center of an enormous urban area comprising several counties and many communities. A city of millionaires, the name Dallas has become a cliche for wealth and power.

Economically, Dallas is highly diversified. Oil has been the leading industry since the early part of the 20th century, and today many major oil companies are headquartered in Dallas and have producing wells in the immediate vicinity. Natural gas production is also of great importance. Big business has spawned a major financial community of banks, insurance companies, and real estate concerns. But the financial community of Dallas depends upon more than the oil business for its existence. Dallas has always been a major center of trade: primarily cotton, livestock, and other agricultural products. Two area aircraft firms supply an enormous number of jobs to area residents. Other major employers are geophysical companies whose opera-

tions extend throughout the world. On the retail level, almost 17% of the city's work force is employed in retail-related industry. Manufacturing is a big business whose products include machinery, non-durable goods, cotton ginning equipment, and electronic equipment.

The settlement of Dallas began in 1841 when John Neely Bryan built his cabin on the shore of the Trinity River. The community was named for the Vice President of the United States, George Mifflin Dallas. When the nearby Fourierist utopian colony at La Reunion failed, many of its French and Swiss inhabitants came to Bryan's fledgling settlement. Dallas continued to expand, experiencing its first significant growth in the 1870s as a cotton center when the railroad came to town. Incorporated as a city in 1871, cattle also figured prominently in the city's economy at that time. By 1920 almost 40% of the nation's cotton came from the Dallas area. The discovery of the vast East Texas oil field in 1930 spurred the city's already active oil and gas industry. Since then the city has grown phenomenally, with business and employment opportunities attracting thousands of workers and scores of major corporations.

As in Houston, employment opportunities have attracted a wide variety of people to Dallas. There are many Mexicans, Blacks, and Indians, and white groups are represented by a cross section of ethnic backgrounds. A city of both slums and sprawling middle-class neighborhoods, Dallas is most famous for the extravagant mansions of its very rich. A communications center, Dallas has two newspapers, seven television stations, and 35 radio stations, which are shared with the nearby FORT WORTH area. The city is also served by a variety of transportation facilities: major truck and bus lines, railroads, and two sizable airports (Love Field and the Dallas-Fort Worth Airport, the largest in the Southwest).

There is a great deal to see and do in Dallas and the immediate area, which overlaps into Fort Worth. The downtown section of Dallas contains many interesting buildings, such as the world-famous Neiman-Marcus Company clothing store. The State Fair Park hosts the state's largest annual exposition. The city's Museum of Natural History and The Dallas Museum of Fine Arts are of special interest. The city has many municipal parks. A center of culture, Dallas has its own ballet and opera companies as well as a nationally famous symphony orchestra. The city has professional baseball, football, hockey, and soccer teams.

Many colleges and universities are located in Dallas. They include SOUTHERN METHODIST UNIVERSITY, the University of TEXAS at Arlington, TEXAS WOMAN'S UNIVERSITY in Denton, Bishop College, Dallas Baptist College, the University of DALLAS, and BAYLOR UNIVERSITY's College of Dentistry. A leading medical and scientific center, Dallas institutions provide research and development programs and studies in such fields as molecular sciences, geophysics, and solar physics. Two nationally known private secondary schools, the St. Mark's School for Boys and the Hockaday School for Girls, are located here.

DALLAS, University of. Roman Catholic coed institution located in Dallas, Tex. The University was founded in 1955 when the Roman Catholic Diocese of Dallas/Fort Worth bought 1,000 acres northwest of the city for the purpose of creating a university that would be open to students of all faiths.

Undergraduates take courses in the Constantin College of Liberal Arts. Graduate programs abound and include a five-year M.B.A., the Graduate School of Management (largest in the the Southwest), plus programs in art, theology, literature, philosophy, psychology, and politics. The largest number of students, 55%, are from the South, 19% from the North Central region, and 12% from the Middle Atlantic states. Full-time graduate study is immediately pursued by 21% of graduates: 7% attend medical school, 2% business school, 6% law school. Fully 51% of the University's students choose careers in business and industry.

Library: 143,000 volumes, 70,000 microform titles, 810 journal subscriptions, 2,075 records/tapes. Faculty: 181. Enrollment: 2,766 total graduate and undergraduate. Degrees: Bachelor's, Master's, Doctorate.

DALTON, Ga. City (pop. 20,743), seat of Whitfield Co., in extreme northwest Georgia in the Appalachian Valley. Situated in a farming region, Dalton is an industrial community incorporated in 1847. Important tufted-textile production began in the late 19th century. A junior college and the Chickamauga and Chattanooga National Military Park are found in the area.

DALY, Augustin (Plymouth, N.C., July 20, 1838 — Paris, France, June 7, 1899). Theatrical manager and drama critic. Daly's Theatre on Broadway, headlining such stars as John Drew and Ada Rehan, was famous for its magnificent Shakespearean productions. Daly also established a theater in London where his company performed annually (1893).

DAN RIVER, Va. River rising in Patrick Co., Va., and flowing through North Carolina before reentering Virginia and joining the Roanoke. William BYRD named this river in 1728 while surveying the Virginia-North Carolina border.

DANIELS, Jonathan Worth (Raleigh, N.C., Apr. 26, 1902 —). Newspaper editor and author. Daniels served as administrative assistant to President Franklin Roosevelt (1943-45), and edited the Raleigh *News and Observer* while his father, Josephus DANIELS, served as ambassador to Mexico (1933-42). On the death of his father (1948), Daniels became editor and the paper reflected his views as a Southern liberal. Daniels has published novels and histories about the past and recent South.

DANIELS, Josephus (Washington, N.C., May 18, 1862 — Raleigh, N.C., Jan. 15, 1948). Publisher, Secretary of the Navy, and diplomat. The publisher and occasional editor of the *State Chronicle* (1885-1904) and the *News and Observer* (1904-48), both of Raleigh, Daniels led movements for utility regulation, prohibition, suffrage, and labor reform. He was an early supporter of populist William Jennings Bryan (1896), and aided Bryan in his presidential campaigns, later shifting to Woodrow Wilson in 1913. As Secretary of the Navy under Wilson, Daniels improved departmental efficiency and selected Franklin Roosevelt as assistant secretary. As President, F.D.R. later appointed Daniels ambassador to Mexico (1933-41).

DANVILLE, Ky. City (pop. 12,942), seat of Boyle Co., in central Kentucky. One of the oldest communities in the state, Danville was first settled in 1775 and incorporated in 1836. Transylvania University, originally a seminary, opened here in 1780 before it was moved to Lexington. Centre College of Kentucky and a state-operated school for the deaf are located here. The site of the state constitutional conventions, Danville is now a manufacturing center located in an agricultural region.

DANVILLE, Va. City (pop. 45,642), Pittsylvania Co., located on the Dan River in the Piedmont section of southern Virginia near the North Carolina border. It was discovered and settled by William Byrd II in 1728. By the early 1800s, the Dan River and the Richmond-Danville Railroad had made Danville an important transportation center. Its economy includes the production of tobacco (Danville's is one of the world's largest bright-leaf tobacco markets), and the manufacture of textiles, paint, castings, millwork, and sausages. Educational facilities include Stratford and Averett junior colleges, and Danville Technical and Virginia Polytechnical Institutes. When Jefferson DAVIS and his cabinet fled here from Richmond in April, 1865, Danville became the "last capital of the Confederacy."

D'ARBONNE LAKE, La. Lake in Union and Lincoln Parishes, in northern Louisiana. Sixteen miles long and covering 13,000 acres, D'Arbonne Lake is the largest body of water in this part of the state and is the principal recreation spot for these two parishes. Part of a state park, the lake is fed by the Comey Bayou with the Bayou D'Arbonne its outlet.

DARDENELLE DAM, Ark. Largest dam in the Arkansas River Navigation System, it is found on the Arkansas River in central Arkansas. This U.S. Army Corps of Engineers project was built to create Dardanelle Lake.

DARE, Virginia (Roanoke Island, N.C., Aug. 18, 1587 — ?). First white child born in America of European ancestry. Her parents, Ananias and Eleanor Dare, were members of the second expedition sent to America by Sir Walter Raleigh. Under the command of John White, Virginia Dare's maternal grandfather, this expedition landed on Roanoke Island in July, 1587, and joined an earlier party that had suffered from vicious Indian attacks. Nine days after Virginia's birth, John White sailed for England to procure needed supplies. He was unable to return immediately because of the English war with Spain. When relief arrived on Roanoke Island in 1591, they found no trace of the settlers, who were presumably massacred by Indians. Virginia, named for the colony of which Roanoke Island was then a part, has since become the subject of many legends about her life with the Indians or supernatural reappearance.

DARLINGTON, S.C. Town (pop. 7,989), seat of Darlington Co., in northeast South Carolina. Settled in 1798, it was the site of the Darlington War (1894), where three people

An artist's rendering of Virginia Dare, the first white child born in America

were killed and several more injured in an outbreak aroused by a new law permitting private homes to be searched without warrant for concealed alcohol. Electrical parts, car gears, and paper cups are currently manufactured. Darlington is noted as the home of the Stock Car Hall of Fame and the Southern 500 stock car race held each Labor Day.

DAUPHIN ISLAND, Ala. Island off the southwest coast of Alabama, in Mobile Co., and adjacent to the Mississippi Sound. A seaside resort and the state's largest coastal island, Dauphin is known for its beaches and Fort Gaines State Park. Each summer a Deep Sea Fishing Rodeo is held here. Dauphin was originally called Massacre Island when first settled as part of Louisiana in 1699 because of the large number of human bones found scattered about the island.

DAVID, Camp, Md. Official retreat of the U.S. President and his family located in the Catoctin Mountains about 70 miles from Washington, D.C. This 200-acre complex was acquired by President Franklin Roosevelt in 1942 and originally named "Shangri-La" after the fictional paradise in the then-popular film, *Lost Horizon.* In 1953 President Dwight D. Eisenhower renamed the retreat Camp David after his grandson. The complex features both entertainment and meeting areas, is under the jurisdiction of the office of military assistant to the President, and is patrolled by the U.S. Marine Corps. Several important international meetings have been held here including the Camp David Peace Accords between Israel and Egypt in 1979.

DAVIDSON COLLEGE. Independent, church-related coed liberal arts college, located 20 miles north of Charlotte in Davidson, N.C. Founded in 1836, this Presbyterian-controlled former men's college was named for Gen. William Lee Davidson. Students are required to take two terms of religious studies.

Most undergraduate degrees are conferred in social sciences, interdisciplinary studies, letters, and biological science. Some 26% of all students pursue graduate study immediately upon graduation, with 13% entering medical school, 1% dental school, 15% law school, 15% business school. Careers in business are chosen by 30% of Davidson students and the school is ranked among the nation's top 50 producers of business executives. Some 60% of students are from the South, 22% are from Middle Atlantic states, and 8% are from the North Central region.

Library: 260,000 volumes, 12,000 microform titles, 1,600 journal subscriptions. Faculty: 115. Enrollment: 900 men, 450 women (full-time). Degrees: Bachelor's.

DAVIE, William Richardson (Egremont, England, 1756 — Lancaster Co., N.C., Nov. 29, 1820). Revolutionary officer and politician. Davie served under Casimir Pulaski and Nathanael Greene in the Carolinas. Having established a law practice in Halifax, N.C., Davie was a state legislator (1786-98), governor of North Carolina (1798-99), and peace commissioner to France for President John Adams in connection with the XYZ Affair (1799).

DAVIS, Benjamin Oliver (Washington, D.C., July 1, 1877 — N. Chicago, Ill., Nov. 26, 1970). Military officer. After studying at How-ard University Davis became a lieutenant of volunteers in the Spanish-American War. In 1899 he enlisted in the Army as a private. He was military attache in Liberia (1911-12) and in 1940 became the first Negro general in the U.S. army. Davis became assistant to the inspector general of the army in 1941 and retired in 1948. He is the father of Benjamin Oliver DAVIS, Jr.

DAVIS, Benjamin Oliver, Jr. (Washington, D.C., Dec. 18, 1912 —). Military officer. The first Negro graduate of West Point (1936), Davis served as an infantry officer before joining the U.S. air force. He was a distinguished combat pilot during World War II and in 1954 became the first Negro general in the U.S. air force. (In 1940 his father, Benjamin Oliver DAVIS, had become the first Negro general in the U.S. army.) In 1961 he was appointed director of airpower and organization in the USAF.

DAVIS, Dwight Filley (St. Louis, Mo., July 5, 1879 — Washington, D.C., Nov. 28, 1945). Politician and tennis player. Davis graduated from both Harvard and Washington University Law School. From 1925 to 1929 he was Secretary of War, but he is best remembered for the tennis trophy he donated in 1900 and which is named after him: the Davis Cup.

DAVIS, Henry Winter (Annapolis, Md., Aug. 16, 1817 — Baltimore, Md., Dec. 30, 1865). Politician. Davis became interested in politics some time after graduating from Kenyon College in 1837. He represented Maryland for four terms in the U.S. House of Representatives, 1855 to 1861 and 1863 to 1865 (originally as a member of the Know-Nothings) where he actively supported the Union cause but also fought many of President Abraham Lincoln's programs, including RECONSTRUCTION.

DAVIS, Jeff (Little River Co., Ark., May 6, 1862 — Little Rock, Ark., Jan. 3, 1913). Politician. Admitted to the state bar at age 19, Davis opened up practice in Russelville, Ark. He became attorney general of Arkansas (1898-1900), was elected governor (1901-06), and U.S. senator (1907-13). Davis was important in antitrust politics.

DAVIS, Jefferson (Fairview, Ky., June 3, 1808 — New Orleans, La., Dec. 6, 1889). President of the Confederate States of America. He was the son of Samuel Emory Davis, a Georgia-born planter who fought in the Revolution.

Davis grew up in Mississippi and was educated at Transylvania University, Ky., and at West Point, graduating in 1828. He married Zachary Taylor's daughter, who died after three months of marriage (1835). Davis spent the next seven years in seclusion on his Mississippi plantation, where, as on other Davis plantations, the slaves were by all accounts treated extremely well and were allowed to hold their own trials.

In 1845 Davis married Varina Howell and entered politics. Elected to Congress, he resigned in 1846 to command a Mississippi regiment in the Mexican War. He was appointed U.S. senator in 1847, but resigned to run for governor in 1851 as a proponent of Southern rights and expansion of slave territory. In his only defeat he lost by a narrow margin. In 1853 he was appointed Secretary of War by President Franklin Pierce. He served the interests of the South, pressing for the acquisition of Cuba and engineering the Gadsden Purchase of land along the Mexican border for use as a southern railroad route to the Pacific. In 1857 he reentered the Senate and proved extremely influential as a spokesman for the South. He fought for accommodation for the South's views and saw withdrawal from the Union as a last resort.

When Mississippi seceded on January 9, 1861, Davis resigned from the Senate 12 days later, still pleading for reconciliation. He was commissioned major general of Mississippi's forces, but two weeks later was unanimously chosen provisional president of the Confederacy at the Confederate convention in Montgomery, Ala. and inaugurated February 18, 1861. He was offically elected President of the Confederate States in Richmond on February 22, 1862. Davis hoped to negotiate a peaceful withdrawal, but President Abraham Lincoln, despite urging from Secretary of State William H. Seward and head of the Army Gen. Winfield Scott, and a lack of popular support, refused all overtures. With the firing on Fort Sumter, April 12, the war officially began.

Davis was President of a new nation that found itself at war with a country that had four times its white population, an infinitely superior manufacturing capacity, and a well-equipped army and navy. The South seemed beaten at the beginning. But Davis created factories, sent abroad to purchase arms and supplies, and tried to gain European recognition for his fledgling nation. The Union was victorious in the first months of the war but then in July and August, 1862, Gen. Robert E. LEE won victories in the Seven Days Battle and the second Battle of Bull Run. Davis finally pushed

through conscription in late 1862, rousing an enmity against him that continued until war's end. Davis, of necessity, gradually assumed more and more power as the war went on in direct contradiction to the philosophy of states' rights on which the Confederacy was based.

With the defeat at GETTYSBURG (July, 1863), the tide turned against the Confederacy. From then on it was a struggle of attrition. Lee surrendered on April 9, 1865, at Appomattox, and Davis was captured in Georgia, on May 10, 1865.

He was imprisoned for two years at Fort Monroe, Va., and released two years later on bail. Davis never regained U.S. citizenship and never again served in office. Made a scapegoat for the humiliations of the South, he is now generally seen as a man who served his cause honorably and to the best of his abilities.

DAVIS, John Lee (Carlisle, Ind., Sept. 3, 1825 — Washington, D.C., Mar. 12, 1889). Naval officer. One of the youngest ship commanders of the Civil War, Davis' naval exploits, largely in southern U.S. waters, led to his involvement in several major sea battles and his rise to the rank of rear admiral (1885).

DAVIS, John William (Clarksburg, W.Va., Apr. 13, 1873 — Charleston, S.C., Mar. 24, 1955). Lawyer and politician. Davis received both his bachelor's (1892) and law (1895) degrees from Washington and Lee University. After election to Congress from West Virginia in 1910, he resigned to become solicitor general of the U.S. (1913), simultaneously serving as counselor for the Red Cross. In 1918, Davis served at a conference in Switzerland concerned with the treatment of World War I prisoners of war, and then served as ambassador to Great Britain (1918-21). After election to the presidency of the American Bar Association (1922), he won the Democratic presidential nomination (1924) but was soundly defeated in the election by Calvin Coolidge. Davis then returned to private practice, and took 140 cases to the Supreme Court, often without a fee.

DAVIS, Mollie Evelyn Moore (Ladiga (?), Ala., Apr. 12, 1844 — New Orleans, La., Jan. 1, 1909). Author. Aside from regular contributions to the *Houston Telegraph* (1875-79) and the *New Orleans Picayune* (1879-1914), Davis also wrote many romantic novels. These fall into a Texas group, including *Under the Man-Fig* (1895) and *The Wire Cutters* (1899), and a Louisiana group, including *The Queen's Gar-*

den (1900) and her most famous book, *The Price of Silence* (1907). She wrote several works for children, including *Under Six Flags* (1897), a history of Texas, and plays, including *A Bunch of Roses* (1903). Volumes of her poetry appeared in 1867, 1869, 1872, and 1927.

DAVIS, Norman Hezekiah (Normandy, Tenn., Aug. 9, 1878 — Hot Springs, Va., July 2, 1944). Banker and diplomat. Having begun his career in Cuban sugar enterprises, Davis moved into banking, before he became the first U.S. finance commissioner in Europe in World War I. He also served in many official positions under President Woodrow Wilson and was president of the American Red Cross (1938-44).

DAVIS MOUNTAINS, Tex. Mountain range found in the region of the upper Limpia Canyon of western Texas, primarily in Jeff Davis Co. A popular summer recreation area, the Davis's highest peak is Mt. LIVERMORE, also known as Old Baldy.

DAYTONA BEACH, Fla. City (pop. 54,176), Volusia Co., on the northern portion of the state's Atlantic coast, 45 miles northeast of Orlando. Daytona was named for its earliest large landowner Mathias Day. Settled in 1870 and incorporated in 1876, the city has been a popular resort throughout its history. Because its 25 miles of sand beaches are unusually hard-packed, Daytona Beach has been the site of automobile races since 1903. In addition to the Daytona International Speedway, its present attractions include the Oceanfront Amusement Park and City Island Park for greyhound racing. It is the home of Bethune Cookman College and Embry-Riddle Aeronautical University.

DE BOW, James Dunwoody Brownson (Charleston, S.C., July 10, 1820 — Elizabeth, N.J., Feb. 27, 1867). Editor and statistician. De Bow was editor of the *Southern Quarterly Review* and won attention for his article "The Oregon Question." In 1846, he began publishing a New Orleans political magazine which espoused his ardent secessionist beliefs. He was appointed chairman of political economy at the University of Louisiana and served as superintendent of the 1850 U.S. Census. During the Civil War he was the Confederacy's agent for the purchase of cotton.

DE FUNIAK SPRINGS, Fla. Town (pop. 5,563), seat of Walton Co., in northwestern Florida. Built around a large spring in the center of town, it is located in an agricultural and timbering area. De Funiak is the site of Florida's first Confederate monument.

DE LA WARR, Thomas West, Baron (Hampshire, England, July 9, 1577 — at sea near the Azores, June 7, 1618). Colonial governor. Appointed first governor of Virginia in 1609, on his arrival in Jamestown he found the colonists discouraged and in need of food and ready to abandon the colony. After constructing forts and sending for supplies, he himself went to England to plead the cause of the colonists, but died on his return trip to America. Delaware Bay was named for him.

DE MEZIERES Y CLUGNY, Athanase (Paris, France, c. 1715 — San Antonio, Tex., Nov. 2, 1779). French explorer and Indian agent in Spanish Louisiana. De Mezieres arrived in Louisiana in the 1730s, and stayed on in Louisiana after France had ceded the territory to Spain. He was made lieutenant governor of the Natchitoches district (1769), and was responsible for concluding many treaties with hostile Indian tribes.

DE RIDDER, La. City (pop. 11,057), seat of Beauregard Parish, in southwestern Louisiana. Incorporated in 1907, today De Ridder produces citrus fruit, as well as corn, oats, rye, sorghum, and sweet potatoes. Beauregard Museum is located here.

DE SOTO, Hernando [Fernando] (Jerez de los Caballeros, Estremadura, Spain, 1496? — near modern Ferriday, La., May 21, 1542). Spanish explorer. In 1539 he set out with a large expedition of over 500 men from Havana, Cuba, to explore and conquer Florida and points north. Landing probably at Tampa Bay, he marched north into the Carolinas and then into what is now Georgia and Alabama. On Oct. 18. 1540, he fought and won a major victory over the Mobile Indians under Chief TUSCALOOSA at Mabila in present-day Clarke Co., Alabama. Continuing west, he discovered the Mississippi River, possibly on May, 21, 1541. He continued on into Arkansas, east Texas, and back into Louisiana where he was taken ill and died. In order to conceal his mortality from Indians who believed him a god, he was secretly buried in the Mississippi River. After his death,

Spanish explorer Hernando De Soto landing in Florida in 1539

the expedition was led by Luis de Moscoso who reached Tampico, Mexico by sea in 1543.

DEAD LAKE, Fla. Lake in Calhoun and Gulf Counties, in northwestern Florida. A widening (one mile by ten miles) of the dredged portion of the Chipola River, it empties via a cut-off into the Apalachicola River near Wewahitchka.

DECATUR, Ala. City (pop. 42,002), seat of Morgan Co., located in northern Alabama on the south shore of the Tennessee River. It was named in 1826 for Stephen DECATUR. In 1832 the city became the terminal for Alabama's first railroad from Tuscumbia. Occupied by North and South during the Civil War, Decatur was not completely destroyed, and its antebellum architecture remains an attraction to visitors. Decatur's fine recreational facilities and diversified industry derive from its fortunate location on a navigable portion of the Tennessee River. It manufactures air-conditioning equipment and secondary metal materials.

DECATUR, Ga. City (pop. 18,404), seat of DeKalb Co., and suburb of Atlanta located in

northwestern Georgia. Originally a trade center for small farmers in the area, Decatur's growth resulted from the transportation advantages of Atlanta. Named for Stephen DECATUR, it was incorporated as a town in 1823 and chartered as a city in 1922. Now an attractively landscaped residential suburb, Decatur is also an industrial center whose industries include foods, cameras, paints, and warehousing. It is the home of AGNES SCOTT COLLEGE FOR WOMEN (1889) and Columbia Theological Seminary, both administered by the Presbyterian Church.

DECATUR, Stephen (Sinepuxent, Md., Jan. 5, 1779 — Bladensburg, Md., Mar. 22, 1820). Naval officer. Decatur aided in the destruction of the captured American frigate *Philadelphia*, in Tripoli Harbor in 1804, during the Tripolitan War, forr which he was promoted to captain. He served with distinction in the War of 1812 and ended his career as a naval commissioner. Decatur is known for his statement "our country, right or wrong." The cities of DECATUR in Alabama and Georgia are named for him. He was mortally wounded in a duel with James BARRON.

DEEP CREEK LAKE, Md. Lake in Garrett Co., in northwestern Maryland. This is the largest lake in the state, covering 4,000 acres. Deep Creek Lake was created as a hydroelectric power source by the damming of a tributary of the Youghiogheny River. It is part of a state forest in the Allegheny Mountains.

DEER PARK, Tex. Town (pop. 22,648), Harris Co., in southeast Texas. An industrial suburb of Houston, Deer Park's manufactures include plastics, paper products, carbon, petroleum products, and chemicals. San Jacinto Junior College (1961) is nearby.

DEERFIELD BEACH, Fla. Town (pop. 39,193), Broward Co., in southern Florida. It was named because of the once numerous deer in the area. Its development began after World War II when it became popular with tourists. Deerfield is noted for its one-mile beach and 722-foot fishing pier. The community has some light industry, particularly in the field of electronics.

DEL RIO, Tex. City (pop. 30,034), seat of Val Verde Co., in extreme south central Texas near the border of Mexico. Founded in 1868 and incorporated in 1911, Del Rio's economy revolves around sheep and goat ranching, and Laughlin Air Force Base. Tourist attractions include the Val Verde Winery and the Whitehead Memorial Museum, the site of which was once the largest trading center between San Antonio and El Paso.

DELAND, Fla. City (pop. 15,354), seat of Volusia Co., in west central Florida. The center of a fertile citrus area, DeLand manufactures apparel and medical supplies. Founded in 1876, it is known as a resort and is the home of Stetson University (1886).

DELANY, Martin Robinson (Charles Town, Va., May 6, 1812 — Xenia, Ohio, Jan. 24, 1885). Negro leader. Born the son of free Negroes, Delany studied medicine at Harvard. He was an advocate of the return of slaves to Africa and was instrumental in the formation of the National Emigration Convention (1854). A member of the FREEDMEN'S BUREAU, Delany was defeated in his run for lieutenant governor of South Carolina (1874).

DELAWARE CREEK, Tex. Stream rising in Culberson Co., in the Delaware Mountains of western Texas. It flows northeast past the Guadelupe Mountain National Park and crosses the border of New Mexico to empty into Red Bluff Lake at the northwest corner of Texas.

DELAWARE INDIANS ("men"). Tribe of Algonquian linguistic stock. Though their dominant region was further north, they are thought to have lived, or at least hunted, in the northeastern part of Maryland.

DELMARVA PENINSULA. Part of the Eastern Shore, this peninsula is situated between the Chesapeake Bay and the Atlantic Ocean. It is primarily in Delaware but extends into Maryland and Virginia. The name is derived from syllables of the states' names. It is a highly popular duck hunting and deep-sea fishing area.

DELRAY BEACH, Fla. City (pop. 34,325), Palm Beach Co., southeastern Florida on the Atlantic coast. Settled in 1901, Delray Beach is a tourist resort in the center of an agricultural area. It is noted for its flower production.

DEMOPOLIS, Ala. City (pop. 7,678), Hale Co., in west central Alabama. Demopolis is

found at the confluence of the Black Warrior and the Tombigbee Rivers. Bonapartists in exile founded the original settlement in 1818 and it was incorporated in 1821. Cotton, soybeans, and sorghum are raised and there is some light manufacturing.

DEMOPOLIS DAM, Ala. Dam in Marengo Co., in western Alabama. Demopolis is one of the largest dams in the state, impounding the Black Warrior River. Demopolis Lake is created by this dam.

DENISON, Tex. Town (pop. 23,884), Grayson Co., located in northeastern Texas on Lake TEXOMA on the Oklahoma border. Denison was founded in 1858 as a stop on the Butterfield Overland Mail Route. The birthplace of Dwight D. EISENHOWER (1890-1969), Denison is currently a manufacturing, transportation, and tourism center.

DENISON DAM, Tex. Dam on the Red River which created Lake TEXOMA in northeastern Texas and southern Oklahoma. In 1944 the main dam was constructed (165 feet high, 17,200 feet long) and waters flooded the community of Preston, Tex. The dam's primary purpose is flood control and hydroelectric power generation.

DENTON, Tex. Town (pop. 48,063), seat of Denton Co., in central Texas. Founded in 1855, Denton is best known as a college town today. North Texas State University and TEXAS WOMAN'S UNIVERSITY are located here. Denton's present manufactures include food products, clothing, trucks, and brick.

DENVER, James William (Winchester, Va., Oct. 23, 1817 — Washington, D.C., Aug. 9, 1892). Army officer and politician. After serving in the Mexican War Denver went to California where he served as a state senator, secretary of State, and U.S. representative. In 1857 President James Buchanan appointed him commissioner of Indian affairs and the next year he was appointed territorial governor of Kansas. He was instrumental in bringing about the separation of Colorado and Kansas, and Denver, Colo., is named for him.

DES MOINES RIVER, Mo. River rising in southwestern Minnesota, and traveling 535 miles generally southeast to meet the Mississippi River in Iowa. It forms the northeastern border of Missouri. Several flood control projects are found along the Des Moines.

DEVIL'S RIVER, Tex. River rising in Crockett Co., at the Edwards Plateau. It flows south to Juno where it meets the Johnson Draw to drain into the RIO GRANDE at the Armistad Reservoir. Its total length is 125 miles.

DICKEY, Sarah Ann (Dayton, Ohio, Apr. 25, 1838 — Clinton, Mass., Jan. 23, 1904). Educator. A country school teacher around Dayton (1857-63), she moved south as a missionary and taught in Vicksburg, Miss. during the Civil War. After graduating from Mount Holyoke Seminary in Massachusetts (1869), she returned to Mississippi. By 1873 she had gained enough support from both blacks and whites to found a school for black freedwomen, which opened in 1875 as the Mount Hermon Female Seminary. The school survived poverty, threats from the KU KLUX KLAN, and the murder of its black chairman of the board, CHARLES CALDWELL. The school also supported a land-reform program for neighboring black families.

DICKINSON, Tex. Town (pop. 7,505), Galveston Co., in southeastern Texas. Dickinson is named for one of Stephen F. Austin's Old Three Hundred Colonists. Once called the "Strawberry Capital of the World," Dickinson has changed from a farming to a residential suburb of Galveston.

DIDRICKSON, Mildred "Babe" (Port Arthur, Tex., June 26, 1913 — Galveston, Tex., Sept. 27, 1956). Athlete. Didrickson became a pro athlete after the 1932 Olympic Games in Los Angeles, at which she set two world records. She excelled in a variety of sports, including basketball, baseball, billiards, and swimming. In 1947 she began her career as a pro golfer, winning every possible women's title at least once during the next decade. Named outstanding woman athlete of the first half of the 20th century by an Associated Press poll, Didrickson was married to George Zaharias, a pro wrestler. Her autobiography *This Life I've Led* was published in 1955, a year before her death from cancer.

DILLARD, James Hardy (Nansemond Co., Va., Oct. 24, 1856 — Charlottesville, Va., Aug. 2, 1940). Educator. A professor and later dean at Tulane University, Dillard became president of the Jeanes Foundation for Negro rural schools (1907-31) and was an advocate of Negro education and civil rights.

DIMOCK, Susan (Washington, N.C., Apr. 24, 1847 — At sea, off the Scilly Islands, England, May 7, 1875). Physician and surgeon. In 1864 she became a student at New England Hospital for Women and Children under Drs. MARIE ZAKRZEWSKA and LUCY E. SEWALL. In 1867 she was denied admission to Harvard Medical School as a woman. She traveled to Europe and graduated from the University of Zurich Medical School (1871), did graduate work in Vienna and Paris, and returned to Boston in 1872. As resident physician and chief surgeon at New England Hospital (1872-75), she reorganized its training programs and administration.

DISMAL SWAMP. Area in southwest Virginia and northeast North Carolina. Dismal Swamp is a hunter's paradise. Over the centuries fallen trees and other vegetation have formed an organic mass of peat. It was explored by Col. William Byrd in 1728, who could find little good to say about the area. In 1828 a 22-mile canal was constructed through the swamp to connect the Chesapeake Bay with Albemarle Sound. A dense forest of juniper and cypress, the water is an amber color because of the fallen trees, but despite the color the water was valued during early years because it remained fresh for so long a time when taken aboard ships. The area covers approximately 600 square miles.

DISTRICT OF COLUMBIA See Washington, D.C.

DIVINE, Father George Baker (Savannah, Ga., c. 1882 — Lower Merion Township, Pa., Sept. 10, 1965). Preacher and founder of the Peace Mission movement that emphasized equality among races. Born George Baker, he established a small church and began his work in Georgia, moving north in 1914 after his arrest as a public nuisance. Settling in the New York City area, he called himself Reverend Major J. Divine, and in 1930, following a self-proclaimed rebirth, he adopted the name Father Divine. A Black whose movement was based in Harlem, his mission was interracial and spread quickly through New York City and elsewhere. Divine was thought by many to be the earthly manifestation of God and although he never claimed to be, he never disavowed the statement.

DIXON, Thomas (Shelby, N.C., Jan. 11, 1864 — Raleigh, N.C., Apr. 3, 1946). Novelist. Dixon studied history, practiced law, and had short careers on the stage and in politics before becoming a minister. In 1899 he turned to writing, particularly about the Reconstruction era. Dixon's pro-Southern *The Clansmen* (1905) was his best-known work and served as the basis for the film *The Birth of a Nation* (1915).

DOBBS, Arthur (Co. Antrim, Ireland, Apr. 2, 1689 — Brunswick, England, Mar. 28, 1765). Colonial governor. Surveyor general of Ireland (1730), Dobbs was an important backer of the expedition under Christopher Middleton to locate a Northwest Passage (1741-42), and an advocate of land reforms in Ireland. His governorship of North Carolina (1754-65) was noted for conflict growing out of Dobbs' arbitrary decisions while attempting to serve the best interests of both citizenry and Empire.

DODD, William Edward (Clayton, N.C., Oct. 21, 1869 — Round Hill, Va., Feb. 9, 1940). Historian and statesman. Dodd published many books and articles on history and national trends, including popular essays warning post-World War I Americans of the dangers of isolationism. Appointed professor of history at Randolph-Macon College (1900), he was designated as the first American professor of Southern history at the University of Chicago (1908-33). Alarmed at the turn of events in the 1920s and 30s, he took on the German ambassadorship (1933-37) only to return to his Virginia farm, dismayed and ill.

DODDS, Warren "Baby Dodds" (New Orleans, La., Dec. 28, 1898 — Chicago, Ill., Feb. 14, 1959). Jazz musician. Renowned as one of the greatest jazzmen, Dodds started out playing drums in New Orleans and on the Mississippi riverboats. He joined Joe "King" Oliver (1921) and during his career worked with many noted musicians, among them Sidney Bechet, Jelly Roll Morton, and Louis Armstrong.

DONALD, David (Goodman, Miss., Oct. 1, 1920 —). Historian and educator. After earning his Ph.D. at the University of Illinois (1946), Donald taught successively at Columbia, Smith, Princeton, and Johns Hopkins. Winner of the 1961 Pulitzer prize for biography for *Charles Sumner and the Coming of the Civil War* (1960), Donald's published works include *Lincoln's Herndon* (1948) and *Lincoln Reconsidered* (1956).

DONELSON, Andrew Jackson (Nashville, Tenn., Aug. 25, 1800 — Memphis, Tenn., June 26, 1871). Diplomat, lawyer, and politician. Named for his uncle, Andrew Jackson, Donelson served as Jackson's aide-de-camp during the Seminole campaign and as his private secretary during Jackson's voter campaigns and his presidency. In 1844 Donelson was appointed charge d'affaires to the Texas Republic where he successfully conducted negotiations for annexation. He also served as minister to Prussia (1846-49) and in 1856 ran as the Know-Nothing Party's vice presidential candidate.

DONIPHAN, Alexander William (Mason Co., Ky., July 9, 1808 — Richmond, Va., Aug. 8, 1887). Lawyer and army officer. A 3,600-mile march which Doniphan led (1846-47) under hostile conditions during the Mexican War, subduing opposing Mexican and Indian forces en route, is one of the great expeditions in American history. He served three terms in the Missouri state legislature (1836, 1840, 1854), and in 1838 Doniphan, then brigadier general of the state militia, was in charge of driving the Mormons out of Missouri. However, he refused orders to execute Joseph Smith and other Mormon leaders. Although opposed to secession, Doniphan turned down offers of high command in the Union Army.

DORCHEAT BAYOU, Ark./La. Bayou with its source in Arkansas. It runs south-southeast into northern Louisiana for 50 miles to terminate in Lake BISTENEAU.

DORSEY, James Owen (Baltimore, Md., Oct. 31, 1848 — Washington, D.C., Feb. 4, 1895). Ethnologist. After being ordained a Protestant deacon in 1871, Dorsey became a missionary to the Pawnee Indians in the Dakota Territory. He was named to the Bureau of American Ethnology in 1879 and, because of his linguistic abilities, he was sent by the bureau to study such Indian tribes as the Sioux, Osage, Kansa, and Yakoman. Dorsey's published works include *Omaha Sociology* (1884), *Osage Traditions* (1888), and he edited *Dakota Grammar, Texts, and Ethnography* by Stephen Return Riggs (1893).

DORSEY, Sarah Anne Ellis (Natchez, Miss., Feb. 16, 1829 — New Orleans, La., July 4, 1879). Author. She wrote under the penname "Filia Ecclesiae," which she shortened to "Filia." A girlhood friend of Mrs. Varina Howell Davis, she invited ex-Confederate President JEFFERSON DAVIS to Beauvoir, her plantation, to write his memoires. Dorsey acted as his amanuensis, eventually selling her estate to the statesman and willing all her possessions to him. Her literary output includes *Recollections of Henry Watkins Allen* (1866) and the romantic adventures *Agnes Graham* (1869), *Athalie* (1872), and *Panola, A Tale of Louisiana* (1877).

DOTHAN, Ala. City (pop. 31,440), seat of Houston Co., located in southeastern Alabama 95 miles below Montgomery. Settled as Poplar Head in the mid-1800s by lumbermen interested in its long-leaf pine timber, Dothan was renamed for a community mentioned in Genesis upon the recommendation of J.Z.S. Connelly, a Methodist preacher. Incorporated in 1885, it developed as a manufacturing center after completion of the railroad to the area in 1889. Today it produces farm equipment, cottonseed products, and fertilizers.

DOUGLAS, Ga. City (pop. 10,980), seat of Coffee Co., in south central Georgia. Incorporated in 1895, today's manufacturing includes garments and mobile homes. Livestock, tobacco, and foodstuffs are raised and processed. It is the home of South Georgia College.

DOUGLASS, Frederick [Frederick Augustus Washington Bailey] (Tuckahoe, Md., Feb., 1817 — Washington, D.C., Feb. 20, 1895). Journalist, orator, and antislavery activist. Son of a brilliant black woman slave and a white father, Douglass was taught to read at the home of his second master, where, though well treated, he made his first attempt to escape. After training as a ship's caulker, he successfully escaped to New York (1838), and then to New Bedford, Mass., where he took work as a laborer. At an antislavery rally in Nantucket in 1841, he spoke so effectively that he was given a position with the Massachusetts Anti-Slavery Society, for which he lectured in the northern and middle states and in Europe. His work in England was so well received that a fund was raised for his release from slavery. Douglass went on to publish an antislavery weekly, *The North Star*, later named *Frederick Douglass's Paper*, in Rochester, N.Y. A conservative constitutional abolitionist, Douglass rejected John Brown's attack at Harpers Ferry (1859) but was among the first to promote enlistment of Negro soldiers in the Civil War. After the war, Douglass continued to serve the U.S. in several federal posts as diplomat to Santo Domingo and Haiti and marshall of Washington, D.C.

DRED SCOTT DECISION. Decision by the U.S. Supreme Court written in 1857 by Roger TANEY, a member of the Court's Southern majority. It stated that (1) moving a slave to "free" territory did not result in freedom for that slave; (2) Congress had no power to exclude slaves from territories; and (3) Negroes could not be citizens. This ruling added much fuel to the growing antagonism between supporters of the slavery system and abolitionists just prior to the outbreak of the Civil War. The decision involved Dred Scott, a Missouri slave who was taken to reside in Illinois, a free state, by his master. From Illinois he was taken to the free territory of Wisconsin before returning to Missouri. The Dred Scott Decision, in which Scott was declared still a slave, was one of the numerous events leading to the Civil War.

Dred Scott

DREWRY'S BLUFF, Battle of. Civil War engagement on May 16, 1864, in Chesterfield Co., Virginia, just south of Richmond. In it the Confederate forces of Gen. Pierre BEAUREGARD defeated the Union forces of Gen. Ben Butler. Butler, in command of the Army of the James, had been ordered by the new Union commander Gen. Ulysses S. GRANT to operate south of the James in advance of an attempt to attack Richmond. Beauregard had replaced Gen. George E. Pickett as the Confederate leader in the area in April, 1864. Butler's base of operations was an earthworks at Bermuda Hundred, and when he advanced out of these defenses to Drewry's Bluff on May 12 Beauregard took the opportunity for attack. In the battle on May 16, Beauregard failed to deploy his forces effectively. Despite legend, they were not inferior to Butler's. As a result, Butler was enabled to flee back to his Bermuda Hundred defenses. He remained there, in the words of his commander, Gen. Grant, "bottled up in Bermuda Hundred."

DRISCOLL, Clara (St. Mary's, Texas, Apr. 2, 1881 — Corpus Christi, Texas, July 17, 1945). Philanthropist, politician. The heiress of the vast Driscoll oil fortune, she returned from France in 1899 and immediately enlisted in the campaign to save the ruins of the Alamo Mission in San Antonio. She contributed most of the funds needed to restore it and in 1925 became president of the Daughters of the Republic of Texas, which administered the memorial. In 1939 Texas set aside a public holiday to honor this "Saviour of the Alamo." In the 1920s and 1930s Driscoll was actively engaged in Democratic national politics, supporting Al Smith and then F.D.R.

DRISKILL, Mount, La. Peak in Bienville Parish, in northwestern Louisiana near Bryceland. Mount Driskill is the highest peak in the state (535 feet).

DRUMMOND LAKE, Va. Body of water in Nansemond Co., surrounded by DISMAL SWAMP and the city of Chesapeake. The state's largest natural lake (some three miles in diameter), Drummond Lake is thought to have been named for William Drummond, a governor of North Carolina.

DRY TORTUGAS ISLANDS, Fla. Small island group extending into the Gulf of Mexico 65 miles east of Key West in southern Florida. Discovered and named by Ponce de Leon in 1513, the islands later gained notoriety as a pirate base. Today they are best known as a bird and marine life area. Loggerhead Key, largest of the group, contains a lighthouse, while Bush Key houses extensive rookeries. Garden Key, also known as Shark Island, is the site of Fort Jefferson National Monument, which contains the largest masonry fortification in the Americas.

DUCK RIVER, Tenn. River rising in central Tennessee. It winds through a fertile farm region for 250 miles to drain into the Tennessee River southwest of Waverly. Flooding of this river in 1811 severely damaged the new communities in its valley. Duck River is noted for its abundance of catfish, buffalo fish, drum fish, and bass.

DUDLEY, William "Bullet Bill" (Bluefield, Va., Dec. 24, 1921 —). Football player. A graduate of the University of Virginia, he spent ten years with a variety of pro teams. Playing for the Pittsburgh Steelers in 1946, he led the National Football League in rushing, receptions, and punt returns. He was inducted into the Pro Football Hall of Fame in 1966.

DUKE, James Buchanan Durham, N.C., Dec. 23, 1856 — New York, N.Y., Oct. 10, 1925). Tobacco merchant and philanthropist. With his brother, Benjamin, Duke entered his father's tobacco business at an early age and rose to president (1890) of the American Tobacco Company, a combination of cigarette manufacturers. He also led several other tobacco combinations. Ordered by the Supreme Court in 1911 to dissolve the trust, Duke was principally responsible for the arrangements. In 1905 he formed the Southern Power Company which began development of the Southern Piedmont River. He established a trust fund with his holdings in the company which contributed to charitable institutions, including Trinity College in Durham which was expanded to form Duke University.

DUKE UNIVERSITY. Independent coed university affiliated with the Methodist Church, located in Durham, N.C., a city 250 miles southwest of Washington, D.C. Founded in 1838, the school was organized as Trinity College in 1852. It was moved to Durham in 1892 and in 1924 changed its name to Duke University when James B. DUKE's substantial trust fund allowed for expansion. Trinity College was retained as the name of the men's undergraduate school. The Woman's College was added in 1925, followed by the School of Engineering (1939) and the School of Nursing (1953). In 1972 Trinity College and the Woman's College were merged to form the coed Trinity College of Arts and Sciences.

The university comprises three campuses: the 8,000-acre West Campus; the 110-acre East Campus, which is one and a half miles from the center of Durham; and the North campus, near the hospital. Undergraduate divisions of Duke include Trinity College and the Schools of Engineering and Nursing. Other divisions include the Graduate School of Arts and Sciences, and the Schools of Medicine, Business, Divinity, Law, and Forestry. Duke students come from all 50 states and almost 50 foreign countries; 35% are from the Middle Atlantic states, 6% North Central, 40% South. Full-time graduate study is pursued by 20% of all students immediately upon graduating, with 18% entering law school, 10% medical school, 2% dental school. Duke is ranked as one of the country's top 120 producers of dental school entrants, and as one of the top 100 producers of successful medical school applicants. It is also highly ranked as an educator of future business executives.

Library: 3,000,000 volumes, 5,000,000 manuscripts, 32,000 journal subscriptions. Faculty: 1,256. Enrollment: 8,821 total graduate and undergraduate; 3,093 men, 2,670 women (full-time). Degrees: Bachelor's, Master's, Doctorate.

DULANY, Daniel (Ireland, 1685 — Annapolis, Md., Dec. 5, 1753). Colonial politician. After arriving in America in 1703, Dulany joined the Maryland assembly in 1722, opposing the governor on many occasions. He later served as receiver general (1733) and commissary general (1736). In 1734 he was a founder of the Baltimore Iron Works.

DULANY, Daniel Annapolis, Md., June 28, 1722 — Baltimore, Md., Mar. 17, 1797). Colonial politician. The son of Daniel DULANY, and a prominent Maryland lawyer, Dulany denounced the Stamp Act in his dissertation *Considerations on the Propriety of Imposing Taxes in the British Colonies.*

DULLES, John Foster (Washington, D.C., Feb. 25, 1888 — Washington, D.C., May 24, 1959). Secretary of State and doplomat. He was a leading influence in the United Nations and on U.S. policies toward Communism. The brilliant product of a family of diplomats, Dulles attended the second Hague Conference with his grandfather while enrolled at Princeton. After World War I, he was legal counsel to the Versailles Conference and served on the reparations committee; after World War II he helped create the U.N. by working on the charter at Dumbarton Oaks and acted as senior adviser to the U.S. delegation at San Francisco (1945). Through extensive personal diplomacy he negotiated the peace treaty with Japan (1950) and a treaty with Austria. As Secretary of State, (1953-59) Dulles stood against Red China in Quemoy-Matsu, worked for French cooperation in European defense, and applied the principle that if ". . . you are scared to go to the brink, you are lost" to Communism.

DUNBAR, William (Morayshire, Scotland, 1749 — Natchez, Tenn., Oct. 1810). Planter and scientist. Dunbar was appointed surveyor general of the District of Natchez (1798), working as an agent of the Spanish in defining the boundary between U.S. and Spanish holdings east of the Mississippi. He then became a U.S. citizen, and under commission from President Jefferson investigated the Arkansas area. His studies included meteorology, astronomy, and biology.

DUNCANVILLE, Tex. Town (pop. 27,781), Dallas Co., in central Texas. Named for politician John Duncan (1851-90), the town was founded in 1882. A residential area today, Duncanville's population has jumped from 14,105 in 1970.

DUNDALK, Md. Unincorporated city (pop. 85,377), Baltimore Co., in northeastern Maryland. A large industrial community which is a suburb southeast of Baltimore, Dundalk produces auto bodies, ships, and other steel manufactures. It is home to Dundalk Community College and the historic site, Fort McHenry. Fort Holabird is nearby.

DUNEDIN, Fla. City (pop. 30,203), Pinellas Co., in western Florida on the Gulf of Mexico. A residential and resort community which merges with Clearwater, Dunedin extends more than three miles along St. Joseph's Sound. Settled around 1865 and incorporated in 1899, it was once one of the chief Gulf ports between Cedar Key and Key West. Dunedin now processes citrus fruit.

DUNMORE, John Murray, Earl of (Scotland, 1732 — Ramsgate, England, May 5, 1809). Colonial governor. A Scottish peer, Dunmore served as governor of New York for 11 months before being transferred to Virginia in 1771. In 1774 he led the successful campaign against Indians known as Lord Dunmore's War. At the outbreak of the Revolution Dunmore, who had twice dissolved the procolonist House of Burgesses, removed Virginia's powder supplies to a ship and declared martial law. Forced to return to England (1776), Dunmore later became governor of the Bahamas.

DUPUY, Eliza Ann (Petersburg, Va., 1814 — New Orleans, La., Dec. 29, 1880). Author. She wrote her first novel, *Merton: A Tale of the Revolution*, about 1835 and in 1843 published her most famous, *The Conspirator*, the story of Aaron Burr's failed attempt to found a western empire. Other historical adventures followed: *The Country Neighborhood* (1855), *The Huguenot Exiles* (1856), and *The Planter's Daughter: A Tale of Louisiana* (1857). From about 1860 until her death Dupuy wrote almost exclusively for the *New York Ledger*, providing it with pulp adventures and romances that did not match her earlier work.

DURHAM, N.C. City (pop. 95,438), seat of Durham Co., in east central North Carolina. The community was first settled around 1750 and called Prattsburg for William Pratt, a major landowner. However, when Pratt refused to donate land for a railroad station, the land was contributed by another landowner, Bartlett Durham. The new site was located approximately two miles west of Prattsburg and was named Durham Station. The new town was incorporated in 1867 and then again in 1869 because the first Constitution was invalid due to the fact that North Carolina was not then a part of the Union. An educational center, the philanthropy of the Duke family played a key role in educational and cultural development. James Buchanan DUKE endowed DUKE UNIVERSITY in 1924. Robert F. MORRIS led the major growth of the tobacco industry which turned Durham into an important manufacturing center by 1900. Another key factor in its development is also credited to the Duke family, who opened a textile factory there in 1974. Tobacco and textiles are still a major part of the economy. The Bennett Place Street Historical Site commemorates the surrender of Confederate Gen. Joseph Johnston to Gen. William Sherman on April 26, 1865.

DUVAL, William Pope (Richmond, Va., 1784 — Washington, D.C., Mar. 19, 1854). Lawyer and politician. Appointed the first territorial governor of Florida (1822-34), Duval helped select Tallahassee as the site of the state capital and was responsible for the diplomatic aspects of the peaceful removal of the Seminole Indians to south Florida.

DUVENECK, Frank (Covington, Ky., Oct. 9, 1848 — Cincinnati, Ohio, Jan. 3, 1919). Portrait artist and teacher. Duveneck's "Whistling Boy" in the Cincinnati Art Museum and "Old Woman" in the Metropolitan Museum characterize his work. He is known for bold brush strokes, strong color, and dynamic presentation of character.

E

EADS, James Buchanan (Lawrenceburg, Ind., May 23, 1820 — Nassau, Bahama Islands, Mar. 8, 1887). Engineer and inventor. Self-educated, Eads invented a diving bell which he used to successfully salvage sunken steamboats from rivers. In 1861, he was commissioned by the North to build a fleet of 14 steam-powered, armor-plated gunboats to guard the western rivers during the Civil War, and completed the contract in 100 days. His best-known achievement is the Eads Bridge, constructed of steel and masonry (1867-74), across the Mississippi River at St. Louis, Mo. He also deepened the mouth of the river by means of huge jetties which directed the water so that the river dredged its own channel. Eads' later years were spent working at major engineering projects around the world, including the construction of a ship railway across the Isthmus of Tehuantepec in Mexico.

EAGLE PASS, Tex. City (pop. 21,407), seat of Maverick Co., in southern Texas on the border of Mexico. Named for the frequency of Mexican eagles that once flew over the land, Eagle Pass was settled in 1850. It is a gateway to Mexico and a tourism center. Other industries include oil production and agribusiness.

EAKER, Ira Clarence (Field Creek, Tex., Apr. 13, 1896 —). Pioneer aviator and military commander. During World War II, Eaker served as head of the 8th Army Air Force (1943) and the Allied air forces in the Mediterranean (1944). He was deputy commanding general, USAF, from 1945 to 1947.

EARLY, Jubal Anderson (Franklin Co., Va., Nov. 3, 1816 — Lynchburg, Va., Mar. 2, 1894). Confederate soldier. Early rose from brigade to corps commander during the Civil War. He was at his best against superior forces, particularly in the 1864 Shenandoah Valley campaign, highlighted by the advance on Washington, D.C. Originally an opponent of secession, Early rallied to his native Virginia, fought valiantly throughout the war, and refused to swear allegiance to the Union after the South had been defeated.

A determined, stubborn, and caustic leader, who spared neither himself nor his subordinates, Early distinguished himself often during the war. From the First Battle of BULL RUN (1861) to the end of the war, his timely arrival often meant the difference between victory and defeat. In 1864, during the final months of the war, he consistently tied up Union forces in the Shenandoah and to the east, winning victories at CHAMBERSBURG and CEDAR CREEK and threatening Washington, D.C. (July). But on October 19, Sheridan defeated Early at Cedar Creek, and at Waynesboro in March, he lost to Gen. George Custer. Public opinion turned against him and Lee reluctantly removed him in March, 1865, a month before Appomattox.

EASLEY, S.C. City (pop. 14,264), Pickens Co., in northwest South Carolina. Established and developed as a railroad station in 1874, Easley today is a trading center in a cotton region. There is diversified farming and industry, including textiles, textile machinery, and clothing.

EAST BAY, La. Inlet of the Gulf of Mexico at the Southwest Pass, situated at the southeastern tip of Louisiana. Nearby Burrwood is the site of the headquarters of the U.S. Army Corps of Engineers.

EAST FORK CLARKS RIVER, Ky. River originating in western Kentucky's McCraken Co., winding southeasterly for 50 miles to end just past the Tennessee border. Its course takes it very close to the Kentucky Lake shore.

EAST POINT, Ga. City (pop. 35,633), Fulton Co., in northern Georgia near Atlanta. A junction of the West Point and Central Georgia Railroads, during the Civil War it was a major supply depot for the Confederacy. Today it is an industrial enclave of textile, paper, machinery, and concrete manufacturers.

EAST RIDGE, Tenn. City (pop. 21,236), Hamilton Co., in southeastern Tennessee on the border of Georgia. Incorporated in 1921, East Ridge is primarily a residential suburb of Chattanooga.

EAST TOHOPEKALIGA LAKE, Fla. Lake located at the northern border of Osceola Co., in central Florida. About five miles in diameter, it is connected by a canal to Tohopekaliga Lake to the southwest.

EASTERN PANHANDLE, W.Va. Name commonly given to that portion of the state stretching northward and eastward, wedging itself between Maryland and Virginia. The Blue Ridge Mountains touch its easternmost tip and the Allegheny and Appalachian Mountains, including Spruce Knob Mountain, are also in this

area. Sand used in glass manufacturing is mined in its valley.

EASTERN SHORE, Md. Name given to the eastern half of the state divided from the Maryland mainland (or Western Shore) by the Chesapeake Bay. It is part of the Atlantic coastal plain and offers very fertile farmland. It is also a key resort region. The land is basically flat with some marsh areas, including Pocomoke Swamp, which extends from Pocomoke Sound to the Delaware line. The state's second-largest deepwater port, Cambridge, is on the Eastern Shore.

EASTON, Md. Town (pop. 7,536), seat of Talbot Co., on the Chesapeake Bay. Settled in 1710, a Quaker meetinghouse built here dates back to 1683. An agricultural trade center, processing and canning of farm products, along with seafood packing is done here.

EATON, John Henry (Halifax, N.C., June 18, 1790 — Washington, D.C., Nov. 17, 1856). Politician. First a lawyer and writer, Eaton was appointed, then elected, U.S. senator from Tennessee (1818-29) before becoming Secretary of War under President Andrew Jackson (1829-31). First married to Myra Lewis, a ward of Andrew Jackson, Eaton's second marriage to Margaret O'Neill caused such consternation in Washington society that it disrupted the Jackson cabinet and led to Eaton's resignation. Defeated for reelection to the Senate, Jackson appointed him governor of Florida (1834-36) and minister to Spain (1836-40).

EATON, Margaret O'Neale (Washington, D.C, 1796 — Washington, D.C., Nov. 8, 1879). Wife of John EATON, secretary of War under President Andrew Jackson. She had met then-Senator Eaton in her father's inn and married him in January, 1829, prior to his appointment by President Jackson as Secretary of War. Floride Calhoun, wife of the Vice President, with other cabinet wives, snubbed "Peggy," causing a break in the cabinet and between Jackson and Calhoun. Though Jackson stood by his friend and his friend's wife, Eaton resigned in 1831, was made minister to Spain in 1836, and died in 1856, after which Peggy married an Italian dancing master who later defrauded her of her property and eloped with her granddaughter.

EDEN, Charles (England, 1673 — Edenton, N.C., Mar. 26, 1722). North Carolina governor. Eden became governor of the colony under the Lords Proprietors (1714-22). He worked for religious development in the region and established a social system based on various grades of society, in which he was in the highest level. Eden was linked unfavorably to pirate Edward Teach, better known as Blackbeard, but was exonerated of any wrongdoing. The town of Queen Anne's Creek was renamed Edenton in his honor.

EDEN, N.C. City (pop. 15,672), Rockingham Co., in northern North Carolina. A farming and industrial town near the Virginia border, Eden's manufactures include beverages, bedding, and bricks. Local farms produce corn, tobacco, and wheat.

EDINBURG, Tex. City (pop. 18,706), seat of Hidalgo Co., located near the southernmost tip of Texas 50 miles from Brownsville. Originally the site of Hidalgo Village, Eden changed its name when it became the county seat. Oil, natural gas, and citrus fruits are produced and there are creameries, ironworks, planing mills, and cotton gin industries in the area. Edinburg houses Moore Air Force Base, Pan American College, and the most diffused school system in the U.S., spread over 945 square miles.

EDISTO RIVER, S.C. Tidal stream originating in north and south forks in west central South Carolina. Marshes dot its course as it travels southeast and south to drain into the Atlantic Ocean. Just before its end, the Edisto separates into two channels rounding Edisto Island. It is a good oyster source.

EDMONDS, Sarah Emma Evelyn (New Brunswick, Canada, Dec. 1841 — La Porte, Texas, Sept. 5, 1898). Civil War soldier. She escaped from an overbearing father and, disguised as a man, took the name Frank Thompson and began a career as a traveling Bible salesman. With the start of the Civil War "Frank" enlisted in the Union army and served in the battles of First Bull Run and Fredericksburg and the first Peninsula campaign. She also served as a spy behind Confederate lines "disguised" as a woman. In 1863 she deserted, probably to avoid army hospital treatment. In 1865 she published a fictionalized best-selling account of her adventures, *Nurse and Spy in the Union Army*. Deciding to seek an Army pension in 1884, Edmonds revealed her secret to enlist the support of former comrades and re-

ceived her benefits from Congress later that year.

EDWARDS PLATEAU, Tex. This landmass rises from the COASTAL PLAIN on the south and takes up much of the south central portion of Texas forming the southern end of the GREAT PLAINS. Its subhumid climate produces mesquite shrubs and grasses fed upon by cattle, goats, and sheep. Many rivers flow through the plateau including the Medina, Frio, Concho, and San Saba.

EGG PRODUCTION. Each year the Southern states produce approximately 40% of the U.S. egg supply. The leader of the region is Georgia, which in 1981 produced 5.5 million eggs. Other important egg producers in the South (ranked by 1981 production): Arkansas (3.9 million), Texas (3.2 million), Alabama (3.0 million), North Carolina (3.0 million), and Florida (2.8 million).

EISENHOWER, Dwight David "Ike" (Denison, Tex., Oct. 14, 1890 — Washington, D.C., Mar. 28, 1969). Soldier and 34th President of the United States. Two years after Eisenhower's birth, his family moved from Texas to Abilene, Kansas, where the future President was raised. He began his career in the military with study at the U.S. Military Academy at West Point, graduating in 1915. One year later he married Mamie Geneva Doud, who would prove to be one of the most popular presidential first ladies.

After serving the army in various areas of the world, Eisenhower was stationed in the Philippines and spent four years on the staff of Gen. Douglas MacArthur. His march to high command began with his appointment as commander of the Allied Forces landing in North Africa in 1942 and award of the rank of full general in 1943. In 1944, as Supreme Commander of the Allied Expeditionary Forces in Europe, he directed the D-Day invasion of Occupied France at Normandy Beach. After accepting the surrender of the German Army at Rheims on May 7, 1945, Eisenhower remained in Europe to oversee the U.S. Occupation Forces in Germany. He then returned to the U.S. as Army Chief of Staff (1945-48). He described the course of the war in *Crusade in Europe*, which was published in 1948 and became a best-seller.

Eisenhower's first non-military position was as president of Columbia University in New York City, a post he occupied from 1948 to

1953 with a leave of absence in 1950 taken to command the forces of the new North Atlantic Treaty Organization alliance. Having resigned from the army in 1952, he was considered for a presidential nomination by both the Republican and the Democratic parties. He accepted the Republican nomination, and in the 1952 presidential election he defeated Adlai E. Stevenson, the Democratic candidate whom he would defeat again in 1956.

As President, Eisenhower espoused moderately conservative policies. He hastened the end of the Korean War, but defended other American involvements in southeast Asia. He sent troops to enforce school desegregation in Little Rock, Arkansas, but refused to oppose the anti-Communist agitation of Senator Joseph McCarthy. Known as a grandfatherly figure with a great love of golf, Eisenhower retired in 1960 to a farm near Gettysburg, Pa.

EL DORADO, Ark. City (pop. 26,685), seat of Union Co., located 15 miles north of the Louisiana border near the Ouachita River. The area was explored by De Soto in 1541. El Dorado was founded in the 1840s by a commission instructed to locate a central county seat. Served by railroads since 1889, its economy has been based on cotton and oil, which was discovered in 1921. El Dorado is now the location of the Arkansas State Commission for Oil and Gas.

ELECTRIC AND ELECTRONIC EQUIPMENT. A major U.S. industry and one of the principal sectors of manufacturing in the South. Electric equipment, which includes household appliances, industrial apparatus, radio and TV equipment, communications equipment such as telephones, and electronic equipment such as computer accessories and hardware, is the second leading manufacture of Maryland, Florida, and Arkansas. It ranks third among manufactures in Mississippi and Kentucky.

ELEVEN POINT RIVER, Mo. Beginning south of the Salem Plateau, then flowing 80 miles south southeast through Oregon Co. It crosses the Arkansas border to meet the Current River.

ELIZABETH CITY, N.C. City (pop. 13,784), seat of Pasquotank Co., in northeastern North Carolina on the Pasquotank River. The river serves as a link on the Intracoastal

Waterway making Elizabeth City a shipping point. Founded in 1793, it is also a retail trade center and tourist resort. During the Civil War, the arrival of Federal troops in 1862 caused such fear and anger that citizens set fire to their own homes and the courthouse. A state university is here and the International Cup Regatta is held each September.

ELIZABETHTON, Tenn. Town (pop. 12,431), seat of Carter Co., in northeastern Tennessee. One of the earliest settlements in the state, the town was incorporated in 1799. Elizabethton is an industrial town in the Happy Valley at the confluence of the Watauga and Dee Rivers. Chairs, rayon products, and concrete are produced here and agriculture includes corn, tobacco, and wheat. A soldier's monument honors Mary Patton, who made the gunpowder for Tennesseans at the Battle of King's Mountain.

ELIZABETHTOWN, Ky. Town (pop. 15,380), seat of Hardin Co., in central Kentucky. Settled in 1780, it was the home of Abraham Lincoln's father, Thomas, who built Heritage House. The local museum offers a Lincoln collection. Manufacturing includes automobile hoses, men's slacks, and steel magnets. Fort Knox is located nearby.

ELKHORN TAVERN, Battle of. See PEA RIDGE, Battle of.

ELKINS, W.Va. City (pop. 8,536), seat of Randolph Co. Elkins is a railroad terminus which also serves as the entrance to the Monongahela National Forest. Products manufactured here include scientific lab furniture and supplies, clothing, beverages, and lumber. It is the home of Davis and Elkins College.

ELLINGTON, Edward Kennedy "Duke" (Washington, D.C., Apr. 29, 1899 — New York, N.Y., May 24, 1974). Composer and musician. One of the most famous jazz musicians of this century, Ellington made his first professional appearance at the age of 17. He formed his own band, played in Washington, D.C., and New York City, and wrote his first show *The Chocolate Kiddies* (1924), which ran in Berlin, Germany, for two years. Influenced by Stravinsky, Debussy, Respighi, and Gershwin, Ellington's music was for decades the sole popular jazz expression controlled by classical form. Often referred to as the "father of American jazz" some of his most noted works include *Mood Indigo, Sophisticated Lady,* and *Solitude.* His more complex orchestrations include *Creole Rhapsody* (1932), *Black, Brown and Beige* (1943), *Harlem* (1951), and *Night Creatures* (1955). Internationally important by 1934, he and his orchestra made numerous trips abroad. By the 1940s they were being heard on the hit parade, in Broadway shows, at Carnegie Hall, and at the New York Metropolitan Opera House. Ellington also made hundreds of recordings and appeared in numerous motion pictures.

ELLIOTT, Jesse Duncan (Hagerstown, Md., July 14, 1782 — Philadelphia, Pa., Dec. 10, 1845). Naval officer. Because of his service during the War of 1812, Elliott was appointed commander of Lake Erie. Events during the battle of Lake Erie (1813) led to an ongoing disagreement between Elliott and his successor O. H. Perry.

ELLIOTT, Sarah Barnwell (Savannah, Ga., Aug. 29, 1848 — Sewanee, Tenn., Aug. 30, 1928). Author and suffragist. She published her first novel in 1879 and in the 1880s began writing fiction that contrasted the talented and vituous poor against the indolent rich. In 1891 she published her best-known work, *Jerry,* which ranks among America's best naturalist novels, and followed this with many short stories and the novels *The Durket Sperret* (1898) and *The Making of Jane* (1901). Moving to New York City in 1895, she entered its literary and feminist circles. Returning to her life-long home in Sewanee, Tenn. in 1902, she devoted herself to the suffrage movement and served as president of the Tennessee Equal Suffrage Movement (1912-13).

EL PASO, Tex. City (pop. 425,259), seat of El Paso Co., located in extreme western Texas on the Rio Grande River. An industrial and agricultural center, the city is also a port of entry, situated directly across from the Mexican city of Juarez. Together, both cities are known as the "International City."

Mineral production (mining, smelting, refining) is an important industry, with copper, gold, silver, lead, petroleum, and zinc all found nearby. Other industries include the manufacture of apparel and cement and building materials, and tourism. An important agricultural and livestock center, El Paso annually handles a great deal of beef, peppers, long staple cotton, pears, onions, alfalfa, pecans, sugar beets, and tomatoes.

Although the present-day site of El Paso did not experience settlement until 1827, the area was first visited by the Spaniard CABEZA DE VACA in 1536 and officially claimed for Spain in 1598. The first permanent European settlement was founded nearby in 1659. El Paso became a part of Texas in 1846, was named Franklin for a short while, and was incorporated in 1873. With the coming of the railroad in 1881 the city experienced rapid growth.

Points of interest include the El Paso Museum of Art and the El Paso Centennial Museum. The city has its own symphony orchestra and is the home of the annual Sun Bowl football game. Area attractions include nearby Fort Bliss (1849), the nation's largest guided missile center. Biggs Field Air Force Base and William Beaumont Hospital are part of the fort. The city's major educational institution is the University of TEXAS at El Paso.

EMMITSBURG, Md. Town (pop. 1,552), Frederick Co., in northern Maryland near the Pennsylvania border. The town was originally founded around a convent established by Elizabeth Ann Seton, the first American-born saint (1809). Mother Seton is buried in the chapel at St. Joseph College here. A largely Catholic residential community, Emmitsburg is also the home of the Grotto of Lourdes Replica.

EMORY UNIVERSITY. Independent, coed university located in Georgia's capital city of Atlanta. Founded as a college by the Methodist Church (1836), the school today puts no religious demands upon its students. For many years, Emory has been regarded as one of the South's most prestigious and academically sound universities. The school became a university in 1915 when it moved to its present 550-acre location in Atlanta. The original campus, Oxford College, in Oxford, Ga., is still operated by the University as a two-year college.

Admission to Emory is very selective: 75% of the freshmen admitted were in the top 10% of their high school class. The University seeks a national student body, and 53% are from the South, 32% Middle Atlantic, and 7% North Central. At Emory, these students are confronted by a vast array of academic offerings, many available through the University's well-known Emory College, the undergraduate arts and sciences school. The other major academic divisions at Emory are the professional schools of law, medicine, dentistry, nursing, business administration, and theology; the division of Allied Health Professions; a graduate school of arts and sciences; and the two-year undergraduate Oxford College. After graduation, 25% of Emory's students pursue full-time graduate or professional studies, with 13% entering law school and 8% each into medical and business schools. Emory is ranked one of the nation's top 14 producers of successful dental school applicants, in the top 100 for medical school entrants, with 30% of all Emory graduates choosing careers in business and industry.

The school's academic facilities are diverse and impressive. The Yerkes Regional Primate Research Center is one of the country's largest and most famous. The Woodruff Library houses millions of manuscripts, volumes, journals, and a large special collection and rare book section. Other facilities include a 62-foot research vessel, based off the Georgia coast, and the 40-acre Lullwater Biological Field Laboratory. Recreationally, Emory students are offered a great deal by the cultural and historic richness of Atlanta. The beaches of Florida and Georgia are within driving distance as are the mountains of north Georgia and the Carolinas.

Library: 1,600,000 volumes, 811,000 microforms, 1,180,000 manuscripts, 14,500 journal subscriptions, 2,491 records/tapes. Faculty: 1,305. Enrollment: 7,977 total graduate and undergraduate; 2,052 men, 1,991 women (full-time). Degrees: Diploma or Certificate, Bachelor's, Master's, Doctorate.

EMORY, William Hemsley (Queen Annes Co., Md., Sept. 7, 1811 — Washington, D.C., Dec. 1, 1887). Army general. After graduating from West Point in 1831, Emory served as a topographer under Gen. S. W. Kearny in the Mexican War. During the Civil War, he was promoted to brigadier general, fighting in the Peninsular and Shenandoah campaigns. He retired from the army in 1876.

ENID LAKE, Miss. Lake in Panola, Lafayette, and Yalobusha Counties, in north central Mississippi. This man-made reservoir is situated on a branch of the Little Tallahatchie River. It is a flood control project designed by the U.S. Army Corps of Engineers.

ENO INDIANS ("mean" or "people disliked").Tribe thought to have been of Siouan linguistic stock, that resided on the Eno River (to which they gave their name) in Orange and Durham Co., N.C. They later moved to South Carolina.

ENOTAH, Mount. See BRASSTOWN BALD.

ENTERPRISE, Ala. City (pop. 18,033), Coffee Co., in southeastern Alabama. Enterprise was founded in 1884 and incorporated in 1896. Once a cotton area, a boll weevil infestation killed off this crop from 1910 to 1915, forcing residents to begin diversified farming. The new approach was so prosperous that a monument to the boll weevil was erected in Enterprise (1919). Today textile, apparel, aluminum, peanut, lumber, and concrete products are manufactured.

ESCAMBIA RIVER, Ala./Fla. River beginning in southeastern Alabama at the junction of Escambia Creek and the CONECUH RIVER. It courses through northwest Florida to Escambia Bay, an arm of Pensacola Bay, with a total length of 230 miles.

ESCATAWPA RIVER, Ala./Miss. River that begins north of Yellow Pine in southwestern Alabama and crosses the Mississippi line. It flows south for about 85 miles to Pascagoula.

ETOWAH RIVER, Ga. River beginning in northern Georgia's Blue Ridge, coursing about 150 miles southwest to Rome. It then joins the OOSTANAULA River to form the Coosa. Hydroelectric power projects include the Allatoona Dam (184 feet) near Cartersville.

EULESS, Tex. City (pop. 24,002), Tarrant Co., in east central Texas. Euless experienced a revival with the growth of the Dallas-Fort Worth metropolitan area in the late 1940s and early 1950s.

EUREKA SPRINGS, Ark. City (pop. 1,989), seat of Carroll Co., in northwestern Arkansas in the heart of the Ozark Mountains. Its 63 springs, open for public use, include the therapeutic Basin Spring discovered by physician-pioneer Alvah Jackson in 1854. Located in scenic splendor, blessed by a mild climate, and containing fine recreational facilities, Eureka Springs is called "the little Switzerland of America." It is home, in October, of the Ozark Folk Festival. It was incorporated as a city in 1880.

EUSTIS LAKE, Fla. Lake in Lake Co., in central Florida. About five miles long by three miles wide, Eustis is part of a system of lakes including lakes Griffin, Harris, Dora, and

Apopka, which are connected and drained to the north by the Oklawaha River.

EUTAW SPRINGS, Battle of. Revolutionary War engagement, part of the Carolina Campaign, fought September 8, 1781, on the Santee River 50 miles north of Charleston, S.C. It was the last in a series of British defeats of the Revolutionary Army during the southern campaign of American Gen. Nathanael Greene. However, the damage done to the British force was so severe that it was unable to mount another offensive in the war.

The British forces in the South had been in a controlled retreat toward Charleston marked by defensive actions at Hobkirk's Hill and Fort Ninety-Six. Unable to gain a clear victory in these battles, Greene moved on Charleston itself. Col. Alexander Stuart had recently replaced Lord Francis Rawdon as British commander. He moved north from Charleston to confront Greene on September 8 at Eutaw Springs near Nelson's Ferry. Both forces had equal strengths of approximately 2,300 troops.

In one of the bloodiest battles in the war, the Continental militia first drove the British back from their line and captured their camp. The American troops stopped there, however, to loot the camp and to drink the British supply of rum. While the Revolutionary troops were in disorder, Stuart regrouped and counterattacked his own camp. This charge routed the patriots in the camp and forced Greene into general retreat.

The British sustained some 700 casualties, or approximately one-third of their force killed or wounded. The American side suffered 500 casualties. The decimated British forces withdrew to Charleston and Savannah, which they held until 1782. Without winning a battle, Greene had won his campaign to drive the British from the South. It was the seriousness of his own losses during the campaign that prevented him from taking Charleston and Savannah.

EVANS, Luther Harris (Sayersville, Tex., Oct. 13, 1902 —). Librarian. Evans was director of the Historical Records Survey under the Works Progress Administration (1935). He was appointed librarian of Congress in 1945. From 1962 to 1967, he served as director of International and Legal Collections, Columbia University Libraries.

EVERGLADES, Fla. Swampy, subtropical region extending for about 100 miles, beginning south and east of Lake Okeechobee, to the

The Everglades, a swampy, subtropical region in southern Florida

southern tip of the Florida peninsula. Ranging from 50 to 75 miles in width, it contains mostly sedge, or saw grass, and hammocks, which are island clumps of vegetation. The Everglades are edged to the east by higher ground, which contains several of the major resort cities, West Palm Beach, Miami, and Coral Gables. Big Cypress Swamp is at the western extreme of the Everglades as is the Seminole Indian Reservation. Average rainfall is over 60 inches a year. Reclamation efforts by state and federal agencies to produce land for farming began in 1905, including diking the south shore of Lake Okeechobee and constructing extensive canals and ditches which help drain over four million acres of the land in the area. The EVERGLADES NATIONAL PARK (1947), established in Dade and Monroe Counties, includes portions considered not suitable for cultivation.

EVERGLADES NATIONAL PARK, Fla. A 1,400,333-acre park found in southwestern Florida, it forms the largest subtropical wilderness in the U.S. The area (half land, half water) which once covered nearly all of the southern third of the state, includes saw grass and swamp, mangrove forests, long sandy beaches, and a vast array of subtropical flora and fauna. Lake OKEECHOBEE is found at its northern end. One of the most popular natural attractions in the country, much of it can only be explored with the help of trained guides.

EWELL, Benjamin Stoddert (Washington, D.C., June 10, 1810 — James City, Va., June 19, 1894). Educator. A graduate of West Point in 1832 and brother of Gen. Richard S. EWELL, Ewell was professor of mathematics at Hampden-Sidney College from 1840-46. He went to William and Mary College (1848) as mathematics professor and became president in 1854. He opposed secession until the Civil War, when he became a colonel in the Confederate army. Most of his military career was spent as chief of staff to Gen. J. E. JOHNSTON. After the war he used his influence to promote RECONSTRUCTION. Ewell succeeded in obtaining federal funds to reopen William and Mary, which had suffered extensive damage during the war, and was successful in his attempt. When it closed again in 1881 for financial reasons, he spent his own funds to maintain it until federal funding again became available in 1888. Until his death Ewell was president emeritus of that college.

EWELL, Richard Stoddert (Washington, D.C., Feb. 8, 1817 — Spring Hill, Tenn., Jan. 25, 1872). Military officer. A graduate of West Point in 1840 and brother of Benjamin S. EWELL, Ewell served in the Mexican War and attained the rank of captain. In 1861 he joined the Confederate army and was promoted to major general that same year. Ewell was conspicuous in the Shenandoah Valley campaign of Virginia, in the battles of Richmond, Malvern Hill, and Cedar Mountain, and during the siege of Petersburg. In the battle of Bull Run (August, 1862), he lost a leg. Upon his return to duty in May, 1863, he was made lieutenant general and he led Gen. Lee's advance at Gettysburg. In 1865 he was captured by Gen. Sheridan at Sailor's Creek and was held prisoner for four months. After the war he engaged in stock raising in Tennessee.

EWING, John (East Nottingham, Md., July 22, 1732 — Norristown, Pa., Sept. 8, 1802). Educator and minister. After graduating from Princeton (then called the College of New Jersey), Ewing was named pastor of the First Presbyterian Church in Philadelphia (1759), a lifetime position, and during his later years served as professor of philosophy and provost of the University of Pennsylvania.

EXCELSIOR SPRINGS, Mo. City (pop. 10,424), Clay Co., in western Missouri. Early travelers to the area claimed the springs here had medicinal powers. Because of this, the city developed in 1880, seven years before the arrival of the railroad. Today Excelsior Springs is a popular health resort on the Fishing River. Plastics are manufactured here.

EYEISH INDIANS. Tribe of Caddoan linguistic stock. They lived in northeastern Texas on Ayish Creek, between the Sabine and Neches Rivers.

EZEKIEL, Mordecai Joseph Brill (Richmond, Va., May 10, 1899 —). Agricultural economist. After working with the Dept. of Agriculture as a statistical analyst he became assistant chief economist to the Federal Farm Board (1930). Ezekiel worked as director of the economic division of the Food and Agriculture Organization of the United Nations (1947-50), and wrote several books on agricultural economic development.

F

FABIUS RIVER, Mo. Originating just south of the Iowa-Missouri border. It runs 100 miles southeast through the northeastern corner of Missouri to enter the Mississippi River.

FAIR OAKS, Battle of. Civil War engagement in the PENINSULAR CAMPAIGN fought at a railroad junction eight miles east of Richmond, Va., on May 31-June 1, 1862. Sometimes called Fair Oaks and Seven Pines, the battle was one of a series of actions by which the Confederate army hoped to slow the advance of the Union army toward Richmond.

The battle followed several days of rain, and it took place along the banks of a swollen CHICKAHOMINY RIVER. The Union army was divided between the north and south banks of the river. On May 31 Confederate Gen. Joseph E. JOHNSTON ordered an attack along the south bank, but this was delayed when Gen. James LONGSTREET's southern army took the wrong route along the south bank. This and other miscalculations have given the engagement the name "Battle of Strange Errors."

By late on May 31 Longstreet had pushed back the Union army, but Confederate confidence that the swollen river was impassable was proven misplaced when Union reinforcements forded it. Gen. Johnston was severely wounded on May 31 and replaced by Gen. G. W. Smith. When the battle was resumed on June 1, the Union army recovered the ground it had lost, although Gen. McClellan proved too cautious to take advantage of this situation. On June 1, Gen. Robert E. LEE arrived to take full command of the army and to reorganize it for the SEVEN DAYS' BATTLES later in the month.

FAIRFAX, Thomas, Baron (Kent, England, Oct. 22, 1693 — near Winchester, Va., Dec. 9, 1781). Colonial proprietor. He came to Virginia (1735) to settle the disputed land boundaries of the Northern Neck (land located between the Rappahannock and Potomac Rivers) which he had inherited from his grandfather, the 2nd Baron Culpepper, governor of Virginia. His claim of some 5 million acres was confirmed and he settled in Virginia, at Belvoir on the Potomac, where he became a friend of George Washington. He later built Greenway Court near Winchester. After the Revolution, in 1785, the proprietorship was canceled.

FAIRFAX, Va. City (pop. 19,930), seat of Fairfax Co., in northeastern Virginia. A city of many colonial homes, including MOUNT VERNON, it is close to the Washington, D.C., metropolitan area. Its courthouse, built in 1800, contains the wills of George and Martha Washington.

FAIRMONT, W.Va. City (pop. 23,863), seat of Marion Co., in east central West Virginia at the junction of the West Fork and Tygart Valley Rivers. Settled after the American Revolution, it was incorporated as Middletown (1820) and renamed in 1843. In 1852, with the arrival of the Baltimore and Ohio Railroad, it became a political and industrial power. Present industries include mining and manufacture of mining equipment and glass containers.

FALL, Albert Bacon (Frankfort, Ky., Nov. 26, 1861 — El Paso, Tex., Nov. 30, 1944). Politician. After earning his law degree (1891), Fall settled in the New Mexico Territory, and in 1912 he was elected to the U.S. Senate. President Warren Harding appointed him Secretary of the Interior in 1921 and he served until 1923. In 1931, a Senate investigation found him guilty of bribery in the Teapot Dome scandal, and he served nine months in prison.

FALL CREEK FALLS, Tenn. Van Buren Co. Popular vacation site in the Cumberland Plateau, it is part of a park on the Caney Fork River, near the confluence of the Collins and Rocky Rivers. The waterfall drops 256 feet and the entire area covers 16,800 acres. Much of the power generated here is used by Nashville.

FALLS CHURCH, Va. Independent city (pop. 9,515) located ten miles from Washington, D.C. It is the site of Falls Church built in 1767. The church was used as a military recruiting station during the Revolutionary War and as a hospital during the Civil War, after which Congress appropriated funds for its restoration. Today the city is a residential suburb of Washington, D.C., with some light business.

FANNIN, James Walker (Georgia, c. Jan. 1, 1804 – Goliad, Tex., Mar. 27, 1836). Supporter of the Texas Revolution. Admitted to West Point Military Academy in 1819, Fannin left school after a fight with another student. In 1834, he moved to Texas and became active in the revolutionary movement. He led a small force into Mexico, without the support of Gen. Sam HOUSTON, but they were caught in retreat and executed under the direct orders of Gen. Santa Anna.

FANNING, Edmund (Suffolk Co., N.Y., Apr. 24, 1739 — London, England, Feb. 28, 1818). Loyalist during the American Revolution. Fanning established a law practice in North Carolina and became a supporter of colonial governor William Tryon. He served as Tryon's secretary in New York where he raised a regiment of Loyalists (1777) who fought in area skirmishes throughout the Revolution.

FARMERS ALLIANCE. A grass roots political movement that developed in the 1870s and 1880s, which served as the basis for the Populist movement in this country. Thousands of farmers from the South, West, and Midwest banded together to protest declining crop prices and rising farm costs. The alliance took on a political structure and began working within the federal government to increase the world money supply and institute federal regulation of the railroads. The alliance gave way to the Populist movement of the 1890s.

FARMERS BRANCH, Tex. Town (pop. 24,863), Dallas Co., in central northern Texas. Farmers Branch once served as the site for meetings between Sam HOUSTON and Indian tribal representatives. Today it is a residential area with varied manufacturing concerns.

FARMVILLE, Va. Town (pop. 5,679), seat of Prince Edward Co., in south central Virginia on the Appomattox River. Located in an agricultural region, it is a processing point and market center for tobacco. Other manufactures include electronics, shoes, and lumber products. Farmville is the site of Longwood College, and Hampden Sydney College (established 1776) is nearby.

FARRAGUT, David Glasgow (Knoxville, Tenn., July 5, 1801 — Portsmouth, N.H., Aug. 14, 1870). Union Naval officer. Farragut's Civil War command "Damn the torpedoes. Full steam ahead!" (given during the 1864 Civil War battle of Mobile Bay) earned him a place in history. An orphan, Farragut was adopted in 1810 by the American naval commander David Porter. Farragut began his long naval career by serving with Porter during the War of 1812 as a midshipman. Ten years later he led a squadron to the West Indies to combat pirates. Farragut then commanded the U.S.S. *Ferret* for many years.

At the start of the Civil War, Farragut gave up his home in Virginia and sided with the

Union. During the war he served valiantly, first as commander of the squadron assigned to blockade the mouth of the Mississippi River and to capture New Orleans. It was a mission Farragut accomplished with brilliance. He and his ship were later instrumental in the capture of Vicksburg (1863), greatly assisting the land forces of Gen. Ulysses S. Grant. Farragut added to his considerable naval reputation during the Battle of Mobile Bay (1864) when he ordered his fleet, under attack from Confederate ship and fort artillery, to "damn the torpedoes" and proceed through a minefield. The ships followed his lead and the Confederates surrendered their two forts shortly afterwards. Farragut retired from active duty in 1866 and a grateful Congress appointed him admiral.

FARRAR, Edgar Howard (Concordia, La., June 20, 1849 — Biloxi, Miss., Jan. 6, 1922). Lawyer. Farrar practiced corporation law in New Orleans and was active in municipal reform. He helped found Tulane University and was the author of *Legal Remedy for Plutocracy* (1902) and *State and Federal Quarantine Powers* (1905).

FAUBUS, Orval Eugene (Combs, Ark., Jan. 7, 1910 —). Politician. As governor of Arkansas (1956-67), he summoned the National Guard (1957) to block federally directed integration at Little Rock Central High School. His stand, which forced the use of federal troops to carry out integration, gained Faubus the popularity that won him his many terms as governor.

FAULKNER, William (New Albany, Miss., Sept. 25, 1897 — Oxford, Miss., July 6, 1962). Novelist and short-story writer. The son of a prominent family in the Oxford area, always described as "Jefferson" in his novels, Faulkner was steeped in local history from an early age. Unsuccessful as a student, he worked in menial positions at the University of Mississippi both before and after his service in the Canadian Royal Air Force in World War I. In 1924 he became a journalist in New Orleans, where he encountered a thriving literary scene and was befriended by the short-story writer Sherwood Anderson. It was through Anderson's efforts that Faulkner's first novel, *Soldier's Pay*, was published in 1926.

Following travel in Europe, Faulkner returned to Oxford, married his childhood sweetheart Estelle Franklin and set up housekeeping in a mansion called Rowan Oak. It was then that he began the period of his greatest literary productivity in a series of novels set in the fictional Yoknapatawpha County. Among these were *Sartoris* (1929), *The Sound and the Fury* (1929), *As I Lay Dying* (1930), *Sanctuary* (1931), *Light in August* (1932), and *Absalom, Absalom!* (1936). All of these novels explore the experiences of different generations of an extended family negotiating the transition from the traditional agrarian South to more modern times. They are complex in style and structure, relating events from the perspective of individual characters for psychological depth, and out of chronological order to suggest the influence of the past on the present.

Faulkner's work had attracted surprisingly little critical attention until Malcolm Cowley edited *The Portable William Faulkner* in 1946. This led to the first important critical assessments of his literary importance and to the Nobel Prize for literature in 1950. Later an occasional teacher at universities, Faulkner continued to write until the end of his life, but his later work is generally considered to be of less interest. He also spent time as a scriptwriter in Hollywood, and among his screen credits is *The Big Sleep* (1946) directed by Howard Hawks.

William Faulkner in a photograph taken at the University of Virginia

FAY, Sidney Bradshaw (Washington, D.C., Apr. 13, 1876 — Lexington, Mass., Aug. 29, 1967). Historian. Fay received his Ph.D. from Harvard in 1900 and was a professor of history at Dartmouth, Smith, and Harvard. An authority on European diplomatic history, he is most noted for his work, *The Origins of the World War* (1928).

FAYETTEVILLE, Ark. City (pop. 36,604), seat of Washington Co., in northwestern Arkansas near the Oklahoma and Missouri borders. The home of 13 Arkansas governors and the first congressman from Arkansas, Fayetteville was originally called Washington Courthouse, but it was renamed for Fayetteville, Tenn., in 1929. Its historic growth dates from the days when it was a stop on the overland mail route. Incorporated in 1836, during the Civil War the town was occupied by Federal troops who destroyed Arkansas College, and it is the site of both Union and Confederate cemeteries. Among its most important present industries is education: Fayetteville is the home of the University of ARKANSAS, Arkansas College, and several other institutions.

FAYETTEVILLE, N.C. City (pop. 47,106), seat of Cumberland Co., in the south central portion of North Carolina at the navigable head of the Cape Fear River. One of the oldest cities in the state (1739), it was first settled by Highlanders and called Campbelltown after the town of that name in Scotland. Combined with nearby Cross Creek, it incorporated as Fayetteville in 1783, and became the first community named for the Marquis de Lafayette. It was the first state capital (1789-93). Fayetteville was the center of the state's "wagon trade" in the 1850s and the easternmost point on the nation's longest wood-plank road that ran 129 miles northwest to Bethania. A tobacco and cotton growing region today, Fayetteville is the home of the State Teachers College, Fort Bragg, and Pope Air Force Base.

FEAR, Cape, N.C. Brunswick Co. Promontory located near the southernmost point of the North Carolina coastline, extending into the Atlantic Ocean. Its name comes from the fact that numerous heavy storms occur here, creating hazardous conditions for ships passing close by. In 1903 a lighthouse was constructed and a lightship was stationed off Frying-Pan Shoals (which jut out 20 miles into the Atlan-

tic) to warn vessels. It is now a popular vacation area.

FEE, John Gregg (Bracken Co., Ky., Sept. 9, 1816 — Berea, Ky., Jan. 11, 1901). Clergyman and abolitionist. Fee's dedication to the abolitionist cause in Kentucky resulted in his disinheritance by slaveholding parents and his founding of the school that became Berea College (1857). Forced to leave Kentucky in 1859, Fee returned in 1863 to spend the rest of his life as pastor of the church in Berea and trustee of the college.

FELTON, Rebecca Ann Latimer (DeKalb Co., Ga., June 10, 1835 — Atlanta, Ga., Jan. 24, 1930). First woman U.S. senator. After managing several of her husband's Congressional campaigns (1874-80, 1890, 1894), she became well-known in state circles and campaigned for prison and educational reform, temperance, and women's rights. Nevertheless, Felton was an avid racist, called for mass lynchings to subjugate blacks, and inveighed against Catholics, Jews, Darwin, and child-labor laws in her *Atlanta Journal* column. A political ally of THOMAS E. WATSON, in 1920 she was named to fill out his term in the U.S. Senate, which she did for one day, before relinquishing her seat to Georgia's next senator-elect.

FELTON, William Harrell (Oglethorpe Co., Ga., June 19, 1823 — Cartersville, Ga., Sept. 24, 1909). Surgeon and congressman. Felton was a leading independent Democrat in Georgia and an opponent of machine politics. An ordained Methodist minister and a practicing physician, Felton fought corruption, promoted education, advanced penal reform, and improved institutions of charity. He served three terms in Congress (1875-81).

FENHOLLOWAY RIVER, Fla. River in the northwestern corner of the Florida peninsula, in Taylor Co. Rising east of Foley and it runs generally southwest to empty into the Gulf of Mexico south of Apalachee Bay.

FENWICK, Benedict Joseph (Leonardtown, Md., Sept. 3, 1782 — Boston, Mass., Aug. 11, 1846). Roman Clergyman. Fenwick was educated at Georgetown and ordained a Roman Catholic priest in 1808. In 1825 he became bishop of Boston, and helped to found Holy Cross College, in Worcester, Mass.

FENWICK, Edward Dominic (St. Marys Co., Md., Aug. 19, 1768 — Wooster, Ohio, Sept. 26, 1832). Clergyman. Fenwick joined the Dominican order in 1790 after being educated in Belgium and was ordained a Roman Catholic priest in 1793. In 1805 he founded the mother-house of the Dominican Order in the United States near Springfield, Kentucky. He was made bishop of Cincinnati in 1822, and in 1831 he established the Athenaeum, now Xavier University and founded *The Catholic Telegraph*, a weekly newspaper.

FERGUSON, James Edward (Bell County, Tex., Aug. 31, 1871 — Austin, Tex., Sept. 21, 1944). Politician. A champion of the small farmer, Ferguson became governor of Texas in 1915. Accused of corruption, he was impeached during his second term in 1917, but resurfaced as "the man behind the governor" when his wife, Miriam A. Wallace FERGUSON, served Texas as governor in 1924 and again in 1932.

FERGUSON, Miriam A. (Bell Co., Tex., June 13, 1875 — Austin, Tex., June 25, 1961). Texas governor. Mrs. Ferguson was the wife of state governor James Edward FERGUSON. When he was not allowed to run for reelection in 1924, she ran in his place, winning the vote of small farmers. Although she held the office, it was generally known that James was the one who ran the state. She was reelected in 1932 with a policy of government retrenchment.

FERGUSON, Patrick (Pitfour, Scotland, 1744 — Kings Mtn., S.C., Oct. 7, 1780). British military officer. He entered the British army at the age of 18 and came to America in 1777, serving under Lord Charles Cornwallis first in the North and then in the South. After the siege of Charleston in 1780 he was promoted to major and was detached by Cornwallis to organize and train the Tory Militia in South Carolina. He was killed in the Battle of KINGS MOUNTAIN. Ferguson was the inventor of an early model of the breech-loading rifle in 1776.

FERRIS, Warren Angus (Glen Falls, N.Y., Dec. 26, 1810 — Rinehardt, Tex., Feb. 8, 1873). Fur trader and surveyor. A former fur trader in the Rockies, Ferris went to Texas in 1836, where he surveyed a large part of northern Texas. His *Life in the Rocky Mountains*, published serially in 1842-43 in the *Western Literary Messenger*, and in 1940 in book form, is considered an important document in early Western history.

FEW, William (near Baltimore, Md., June 8, 1748 — Fishkill-on-Hudson, N.Y., July 16, 1828). Politician and statesman. Active throughout the American Revolution, Few served in the Continental Congress from 1780 to 1788 and was one of the signers of the Constitution. He served as U.S. senator from Georgia from 1789-1793.

FIELD, Charles William (Woodford Co., Ky., Apr. 6, 1828 — Washington, D.C., Apr. 9, 1892). Confederate general and engineer. He resigned from the Army to become an officer in the Confederate Army. After commanding an infantry brigade at Mechanicsville (1862) he was severely wounded in the Second Battle of BULL RUN. Field continued as an important Southern commander to the end of the Civil War and later served in the Egyptian army.

FILSON, John (Chester County, Pa., c. 1753 — Cincinnati, Ohio, Oct., 1788). Kentucky pioneer. Filson wrote *Discovery, Settlement, and Present State of Kentucke* (1784), the appendix of which contained "The Adventures of Col. Daniel Boon," reported to be Boone's autobiography, and became the instrument for spreading Boone's fame.

FINLEY, James Bradley (N.C., July 1, 1781 — Cincinnati, Ohio, Sept. 6, 1856). Methodist missionary and author. Raised on the Ohio frontier, he became a Methodist preacher in 1810 and for 21 years was district superintendent of a wilderness circuit for the Western Conference of the Methodist Church. A noted evangelical pioneer, he co-founded the Wyandott Indian Mission. His books and journals provide valuable insights about the Ohio frontier settlement.

FIRST CONTINENTAL CONGRESS. The Virginia House of Burgesses is credited with initiating this American colonial government. It was created in response to the passing of the so-called Intolerable Acts by the British Parliament (1774), which had been enacted to penalize the colonists for their growing rebellious behavior, most notably for the Boston Tea Party. The first session of the congress was held in Carpenter's Hall, Philadelphia, on September 5, 1774, and was soon to be charged with formulating the methods and means of the

Revolutionary War and its fight for colonial independence. Fifty delegates from 12 colonies sat in the first session. Georgia sent no representatives and Canada declined the invitation to join the American rebellion. Peyton Randolph of Virginia was unanimously elected president of the assembly. Its first important step was the issuance of the Declaration of Rights and Grievances, a petition outlining colonial complaints to King George III of Great Britain. The congress also called for a boycott of British goods, and non-compliance and armed force, if necessary, against British taxation measures. The First Continental Congress adjourned on October 26, 1774, with a recommendation to convene a second session in 1775.

FISHDAM FORD, Battle of. Revolutionary War engagement fought near the Broad River northwest of Camden, S.C., on November 9, 1780. Following the loss of his force at Fishing Creek in August of 1780, Revolutionary army Gen. Thomas SUMTER assembled another group of recruits and operated north of the British stronghold in Camden. At Fishdam Ford on November 9, a British force sent north by Commander Lord Charles Cornwallis in Camden suprised, but failed to disperse, Sumter's troops. This led to a similar action later in November at Blackstocks.

FISHERS HILL, Battle of. Civil War engagement fought on September 22, 1864, near Strasburg on the Shenandoah River in northern Virginia. It was a victory for the Union army, and after the third battle of Winchester, the second consecutive victory for Union Gen. Philip H. Sheridan's Shenandoah Valley campaign. After Confederate Gen. Jubal EARLY's Washington Raid, he was chased southward by Sheridan. Following the Confederate defeat at WINCHESTER, Early took up a position on the heights outside Strasburg called Fishers Hill. Sheridan overcame this Confederate advantage by ordering forces under Gen. George Crook on a flanking maneuver that brought them behind Early's line, which was thin and defended by dismounted cavalry. As Crook attacked from the rear on September 22, Sheridan also launched a frontal assault that managed, against all odds, to climb the heights of Fishers Hill. Among the cost to the Confederacy of the battle were more than 1,000 men taken prisoner and valuable artillery pieces abandoned.

FISHING, Commercial. An important industry in the Gulf of Mexico, the Atlantic, and Chesapeake waters surrounding the Southern states. In all these areas the bulk of the commercial catch consists of herring, particularly a variety called menhaden, known by a number of local names and used, according to grade, as food, pet food, and fertilizer. The value of the catch, however, is more dependent on shellfish, especially shrimp in the Gulf, crabs in the Atlantic, and clams in the Chesapeake. In addition, catches of other well-known food fish, such as cod, flounder, and haddock, are taken far offshore, and not classified by region.

The most valuable commercial fishing industries in the South are in the Gulf states. Texas, with a yearly catch worth $174 million, and Louisiana, with a yearly catch worth $153 million, lead all states in the region in commercial fishing. The catch along the Gulf Coast of Florida is worth $86 million per year, and that of Alabama and Mississippi is worth $25 million per state. In the Atlantic, North Carolina has a catch worth $70 million per year and the east coast of Florida has one worth $40 million per year. Virginia dominates Chesapeake fishing with a catch worth $85 million per year, while the commercial catch in Maryland is worth $45 million per year. There is some limited commercial fishing in the Mississippi River and its tributaries, but all Southern states along these waters have a combined catch worth less than $20 million per year.

FISHING CREEK, Battle of. Revolutionary War engagement fought August 18, 1780, on the Wateree River 40 miles north of Camden, S.C. A Revolutionary force under Gen. Thomas SUMTER, in flight from the British victory at Camden, was surprised by the British pursuit force of Lt. Col. Banastre Tarleton. Sumter's men were cooking and bathing, and he himself was sleeping, when they were surprised by Tarleton. The British suffered only about 15 casualties while killing 150 Americans, capturing another 300, and commandeering valuable munitions. Sumter managed to escape on bareback.

FISK UNIVERSITY. Independent coed university, located in the Tennessee state capital of Nashville. Founded in 1865, the University began as a school for Negroes, located in an army barracks. Gen. Clinton B. Fisk helped start the school along with members of the American Missionary Society. College-level instruction began in 1871. While Fisk is open to all races, the student body of this 40-acre school is presently 99% black. The majority of undergraduate degrees are conferred in Business and Management, Social Sciences, Biological Sciences, Education, Letters and Psychology. Full-time graduate or professional study is pursued by 51% of the student body soon after graduating. Geographically, the student body is a varied one: 33% are from the South, 14% Middle Atlantic, 29% North Central, and 13% West/Northwest.

Library: 186,174 volumes, 596 journal subscriptions. Faculty: 92. Enrollment: 331 men, 694 women (full-time). Degrees: Bachelor's, Master's.

FITZHUGH, George (Prince William Co., Va., Nov. 4, 1806 — Huntsville, Tex., July 30, 1881). Editor and author. A leading advocate of slavery and Negro inferiority, Fitzhugh was a contributing editor of the Richmond *Examiner* (1854) and encouraged action against abolitionists. He wrote *Sociology for the South* (1854), *Cannibals All! or, Slaves Without Masters* (1856) and with George R. Gleddon *Types of Mankind* (1856).

FITZPATRICK, Benjamin (Greene Co., Ga., June 30, 1802 — Wetumpka, Ala., Nov. 25, 1869). Politician. A lawyer and land developer, Fitzpatrick moved to Alabama when it was still part of the Mississippi Territory. He served two terms as governor (1841-45) before his election to the U.S. Senate (1848-49, 1853-61). He opposed secession but supported the Confederacy in the Civil War, and was important in the early phase of Reconstruction. In 1860 the Democratic National Convention nominated him for Vice President but he declined.

FITZPATRICK, Thomas (County Cavan, Ireland, c. 1799 — Washington, D.C., Feb. 7, 1854). Mountain man and guide. Except for a period when he was part owner of the Rocky Mountain Fur Company, Fitzpatrick spent most of his career as a guide. He led such expeditions as the Ashley expedition up the Missouri River and John C. Fremont's expedition to California.

FIVE FORKS, Battle of. Civil War engagement fought March 30-April 1, 1865, just southwest of Petersburg, Va. It was an attempt by the Confederate army to protect an escape route for Lee from PETERSBURG, and the Union victory at Five Forks insured both the fall of Petersburg on April 2 and Gen. Robert E. Lee's surrender at APPOMATTOX COURTHOUSE on April 19. On March 29 Lee sent a Confederate force under Gen. George E. PICKETT to Five Forks to defend a railroad link by which he hoped to regroup with Gen. Joseph E. JOHNSTON's Confederate force in North Carolina. Over three days the Confederate troops attempted the impossible task of both holding Five Forks and protecting their rear-guard link to Petersburg. Pickett made his stand at Five Forks as ordered, although he has been criticized for not protecting his troops despite those orders. He was forced to abandon Five Forks on April 1.

FLAGET, Benedict Joseph (Contournat, France, Nov. 7, 1763 — Nazareth, Ky., Feb. 11, 1850). Clergyman. Ordained a Roman Catholic priest in 1786, Flaget taught theology before sailing to America in 1792. In 1810 he was consecrated a Catholic bishop. Besides teaching at Georgetown College, he, with a faithful following, was responsible for the expansion of the Roman Catholic Church into Tennessee, Ohio, and several other states. Flaget is responsible for the establishment of many schools including St. Thomas Seminary, St. Joseph College and St. Mary's College. He died in Kentucky after more than 60 years of service to the Church.

FLAGLER, Henry Morrison (Hopewell, N.Y., Jan. 2, 1830 — West Palm Beach, Fla., May 20, 1913). Businessman. A financier, he helped J. D. Rockefeller found Standard Oil. After securing his family fortune, Flagler became interested in the development of the luxury tourist industry in Florida during a visit there for his wife's health (1884). He purchased and improved the railroad from Jacksonville to St. Augustine and built the FLORIDA EAST COAST RAILROAD, running from Jacksonville to Key West. Flagler also constructed luxury hotels in St. Augustine and Miami.

FLEMING, Walter Lynwood (Brundidge, Ala., April 8, 1874 — Nashville, Tenn., Aug. 3, 1932). Historian, educator, and author. Fleming is best known as a scholar for his studies of the Southern RECONSTRUCTION period. Fleming served as dean of Arts and Sciences and director of graduate study at Vanderbilt University (1923-28).

FLETCHER, Alice Cunningham (Cuba, Mar. 15, 1838 — Washington, D.C., Apr. 6,

Henry Morrison Flagler, financier and developer of the Florida East Coast Railroad

1923). Ethnologist. A student of the American Indian, she pioneered the study of Indian music and contributed to the welfare of plains and prairie Indians, with whom she lived for several years. She adopted a son from the Omaha tribe, Francis La Flesche, and with him she wrote *The Omaha Tribe* (1911), a well-regarded anthropological report on Indians. A special agent for Indians (1883-93), she was also with the Peabody Museum (1882-1923).

FLETCHER, John Gould (Little Rock, Ark., Jan. 3, 1886 — Little Rock, Ark., May 10, 1950). Author and poet. Fletcher won the 1939 Pulitzer Prize for his *Selected Poems* (1938). Other collections include *South Star* (1941) and *The Burning Mountain* (1946).

FLETCHER, Thomas Clement (Herculaneum, Mo., Jan. 22, 1827 — Washington, D.C., Mar. 25, 1899). Governor of Missouri. During the Civil War, Fletcher led Union troops at Vicksburg and Atlanta, attaining the rank of brigadier general of volunteer forces. He was governor of Missouri from 1865 to 1869.

FLINT RIDGE CAVE SYSTEM, Ky. Cave system in west central Kentucky that includes MAMMOTH CAVE National Park. A connection between the Mammoth and Flint River systems was first discovered in 1972. The exact dimensions of this system are unknown, with less than 40 miles of caverns having been explored. Popular for its archaeological artifacts and unique formations, these caverns were formed by underground river erosion of the limestone.

FLINT RIVER, Ga. Rises in west central Georgia, running south southwest for 330 miles to the southwestern corner of the state, where it merges with the Chattahoochee River to form the Apalachicola, finally emptying into Lake Seminole. It is navigable to Bainbridge and was once a steamship route. Macon is among the major communities lining its banks. Today it is a major hydroelectric energy source.

FLORENCE, Ala. City (pop. 37,029), seat of Lauderdale Co., in northwestern Alabama on the Tennessee River. Founded in 1818 and incorporated in 1826, the area became attractive to industry due to the waterpower available from Muscle Schoals Dam, which was constructed during World War I. Besides cotton and mining, electrometallurgical, rubber, steel, and chemical industries are found here. Florence is the birthplace of songwriter William C. HANDY, and is home to the University of North Alabama.

FLORENCE, Ky. City (pop. 15,586), Boone Co., in north central Kentucky. Situated in a bluegrass farm region, Florence was incorporated in 1830. It is noted for its racetrack.

FLORENCE, S.C. City (pop. 30,062), seat of Florence Co., in eastern South Carolina. Florence began as a railroad town in the 1850s and grew during the Civil War as a shipping center for troop equipment. About 8,000 Federal soldiers were held prisoner near here. Today it is a popular transportation, distribution, and marketing center. Products include furniture, garments, and mobile radio systems, and nearby farms raise tobacco and cotton. Francis Marion College was founded here in 1970. Highlights include the Florence Air Missile Museum and a memorial park and shrine for Civil War poet laureate Henry TIMROD, who taught here in 1859.

FLORIDA. State in the extreme southeast of the South and the continental U.S. Its dominant feature is a 450-mile peninsula extending southeast from the mainland between the Atlantic Ocean and the Gulf of Mexico, a configuration that gives Florida a longer coastline than any U.S. state with the exception of Alaska and California. On the mainland Florida includes a 375-mile east-west panhandle that narrows in places to a north-south width of about 40 miles. North of this panhandle the state borders Alabama and Georgia. South of the peninsula Florida also includes an arc of coral islets known as the Florida Keys that reach southward to Key West, which is less than 100 miles from the Caribbean nation of Cuba.

Historically and socially, Florida is unique among the Southern states. It was the site of the earliest European settlement in the U.S., the Spanish city of St. Augustine, founded in 1565. For much of its early history Florida was dominated by Spanish and French influences, rather than the British influence that predominated in the more northern American colonies. Even after the formation of the United States, Florida remained a Spanish territory, and it was not annexed to the U.S. until 1821.

Although its history thus antedates that of many other Southern states, the social character of Florida is almost entirely a creation of the 20th century. In 1900 there were barely 500,000 people living in the state; today there are nearly ten million, and Florida is the most populous state in the South after Texas. This population growth has been especially phenomenal in the decades since 1950, when the state population passed the two million mark for the first time. The attractive climate of the state has made it famous as a haven for retired persons, and much of its modern population growth comes from immigration from other states, especially those in the Northeast U.S. The warm climate combined with the miles of sandy beaches found along both its Atlantic Ocean and Gulf of Mexico coastlines has also made tourism the most important industry in Florida.

The northern panhandle and the southern peninsula of Florida are distinct topographical areas. The entire state consists of low-lying lands, but the panhandle is hilly in comparison with the peninsula. The western panhandle includes the state's highest point (elev. 345 feet) in Walton County on the Alabama border, and the eastern panhandle is notable for the Tallahassee Hills. The topography most characteristic of the state, however, is the sandy lowlands and beaches that cover most of the peninsula. The Atlantic coast is fringed with barrier islands separated from the mainland by tidal lagoons, and the Gulf Coast is notable for deep harbors at Tampa, on the peninsula, and Pensacola, at the western extreme of the panhandle. The interior of the peninsula is characterized by a ridge of low hills that supports most of the state's famous citrus crops. Even this ridge, however, is broken by lowlands, and from the OKEFENOKEE SWAMP on its Georgia border to the EVERGLADES at the southern tip of the peninsula the land mass of Florida is always low-lying enough to trap and hold large inland bodies of water.

The first European explorer to land on the Florida peninsula was PONCE DE LEON whose Spanish expedition landed near what is now St. Augustine in 1513. He was most likely in search of gold rather than the legendary "Fountain of Youth," and he also became the first European to discover the resolute hostility of the local Indians when he was killed by an arrow wound in 1521. The Spanish continued their explorations of Florida from outposts in the West Indies. Panfilo de NARVAEZ landed in Tampa Bay in 1528, Hernando DE SOTO arrived at the same bay in 1539, and Tristan de LUNA sailed into Pensacola Bay in 1559. It was in this era that the Spanish discovered Florida's suitability for citrus fruit; they brought oranges, not native to the New World, with them as seed from North Africa.

The first French expeditions to Florida arrived at the mouth of the St. John's River in 1562. Their construction of a fort there brought a quick response from Philip II of Spain, who dispatched Pedro MENENDEZ DE AVILES to defend the Spanish claims. In 1565 Menendez destroyed the French garrison, called Fort Caroline and commanded by Rene de LAUDONNIERE, and in the same year he established the settlement at St. Augustine. From this point the Spanish sent missionaries north and south along the coast, and for two hundred years Florida remained a disputed possession of Spain, France, and England, with dominance over the territory often being influenced by conflicts in Europe. In the seesaw struggles of this era, the Spanish established Pensacola in 1698, saw it fall to the French in 1719, and upon regaining it made the city the capital of Spanish West Florida. Contemporary events along the Atlantic coast included an attack on St. Augustine by James Oglethorpe of Georgia in 1740, and a mass emigration of SEMINOLE INDIANS

GEORGIA

Tallahassee

Apalachicola R.

APALICHICOLA

NATIONAL

FOREST

Gulf of Mexico

Suwannee R.

Jacksonville

OSCEOLA NATIONAL
FOREST

Atlantic Ocean

St. Augustine

Gainesville

OCALA
NATIONAL
FOREST

St. Johns R.

Ocala

SILVER
SPRINGS

Lake George

Daytona Beach

DeLand

Lake Monroe

Sanford

Apopka Lake

Orlando

WALT
DISNEY
WORLD

CAPE CANAVERAL

N

Dade City

Dunedin

Clearwater

Tampa

Lakeland

CYPRESS
GARDENS

Lake Kissimmee

Melbourne

Kissimmee R.

St. Petersburg

Bradenton

Sarasota

Istokpoga Lake

Fort
Pierce

Intracoastal Waterway

Lake Okeechobee

West Palm
Beach

Fort Myers

BIG CYPRESS
SEMINOLE INDIAN
RESERVATION

Boca Raton

Delray
Beach

Pompano
Beach

Naples

EVERGLADES

ALLIGATOR ALLEY

Fort Lauderdale

*Big Cypress
Swamp*

BIG CYPRESS
NATIONAL
PRESERVE

Hollywood

North Miami

Hialeah

Miami Beach

Coral
Gables

Key Biscayne

*Ten Thousand
Islands*

NATIONAL

Miami

Kendall

PARK

Key Largo

Plantation

Florida Keys

Key West

Straits of Florida

0 10 20 30 40 50 miles

ALABAMA

Perdido R.

Escambia R.

Choctawhatchee R.

CHOCTAWHATCHEE
NATIONAL FOREST

Pensacola

Panama City

STATE OF FLORIDA

Name: Spanish ("flowering").

Nickname: Sunshine State, Alligator State, Everglade State, Flower State, Peninsular State, Orange State, Gulf State.

Motto: In God We Trust.

Capital: Tallahassee.

Counties: 67. **Places over 10,000 population (1980):** 169.

Symbols & Emblems: *Flower:* Orange Blossom. *Bird:* Mockingbird. *Tree:* Sabal Palmetto Palm. *Song:* "Swanee River."

Population (1980): 9,739,992. **Rank:** 7th.

Population Density (1980): 180.0 people per sq. mi. **Rank:** 11th.

Racial Make-up (1980): *White:* 8,178,387 (84.0%). *Black:* 1,342,478 (13.8%). *American Indian:* 19,316 (0.3%). *Asian & Pacific Islander:* 56,756 (0.6%). *Other:* 143,055 (1.5%). *Spanish Origin:* 857,898 (8.8%).

Largest City (pop. 1980): Jacksonville (540,896). *Others:* Miami (346,931), Tampa (271,523), St. Petersburg (236,893), Fort Lauderdale (153,256), Hialeah (145,254), Orlando (128,394), Hollywood (117,188).

Area: 54,153 sq. mi. **Rank:** 22nd.

Highest Point: (345 ft.), Walton Co.

Lowest Point: sea level, Atlantic Ocean.

State Government:
ELECTED OFFICIALS (4-year terms expiring Jan. 1987, etc.): *Governor* ($69,550); *Lt. Governor* ($60,455); *Sec. of State* ($59,385); *Attorney General* ($59,385); *Treasurer* ($59,385).

GENERAL ASSEMBLY (Salary: $12,000 plus $50 per diem.): *Senate* (40 members), *House of Representatives* (120 members).

CONGRESSIONAL REPRESENTATIVES: Senate (terms expire 1985, 1987, etc.). *House of Representatives* (19 members).

Admitted to the Union: Mar. 3, 1845 (27th state).

from southern Georgia to fill a void left by the massacre of local tribes by the Spanish.

England came into full possession of Florida at the close of the Seven Year's War in 1763. It established twin colonies based on the Spanish model: West Florida had its capital at Pensacola, and East Florida had its capital at St. Augustine. Both colonies remained loyalist through the American Revolution, and they returned to Spanish control after the failure of the British to retain control of the 13 American colonies. The 31st parallel, still the border of much of the panhandle, was recognized as a boundary by the Spanish and American governments in 1795, but in the years that followed, the U.S. made unsuccessful overtures to purchase Florida, as well as encouraging rebellion by the English-speaking population against the Spanish governors. In 1814 the U.S. army under the command of Andrew Jackson entered Pensacola on its way to New Orleans to end the War of 1812, and in 1817 Jackson brought his troops back to Florida to quell the First Seminole War. These encroachments and the influx of American settlers into the territory made U.S. possession inevitable, and on February 22, 1819, the American and Spanish governments signed the Florida Purchase Treaty. Jackson returned to Pensacola as military governor of Florida in 1821, and it was organized as a U.S. territory in 1822. Tallahassee was designated the new capital in 1824.

The great trauma of the young territory was the Second Seminole War, which lasted from 1835 until 1842 and was ignited by the Seminole refusal to relocate to the U.S. Indian Territory in what is now Oklahoma. The Indian resistance to the U.S. plans was led by OSCEOLA, whose guerrilla tactics effectively thwarted the maneuvers of the U.S. cavalry in Florida. Osceola was eventually captured through a breech of peace talk agreements by the military, and he died a prisoner in a military garrison in South Carolina. By the conclusion of the war there were too few Seminoles to offer resistance to the U.S. or to make relocation of the tribe a serious issue. Once this threat had been eliminated, Florida, as a slave state, became the 27th state in the Union on March 3, 1845.

Although Florida had an extensive plantation society in the years before the Civil War, the majority of the population consisted of small farmers who were not reliant on institutionalized slavery. The secession of Georgia and Alabama and Florida's isolation from the North made Unionism impractical, however, and Florida seceded to join the Confederacy on January 10, 1861. The state's role in the Civil War effort consisted largely of supplying food for Confederate troops and coastal havens for vessels running the Union blockade of Southern ports. Too distant and sparsely populated to suffer seriously from Reconstruction policies, Florida redrafted its constitution in 1865 and was readmitted to the Union in 1868.

Modern Florida began to evolve in the 1890s with the introduction of railroads across what had been impassable swamplands. Henry Morrison FLAGLER was the principal developer of the Atlantic coast, and Henry B. PLANT served a similar role on the Gulf Coast. Both encouraged or actually built railroad links, and both invested heavily in the construction of large luxury hotels to attract wealthy tourists from the Northern states in winter. Much of this construction, as in the case of West Palm Beach on the Atlantic and Tampa on the Gulf, was done virtually from scratch. Miami, for example, was incorporated in 1896 because the railroad had reached it and despite the fact that it included only a handful of homes. With transportation links complete by the 1920s, an era of wild land speculation and get-rich-quick schemes began. It slowed when the land speculation market collapsed in 1926 and 1928, but it has scarcely ended even today. One conspicuous factor other than tourism in the continuing prosperity of Florida was the decision by the U.S. military to locate installations in the state for year-round training. Begun in World War II, this federal investment in the state is epitomized by the John F. Kennedy Space Center at Cape Canaveral.

As a result of this modern-day boom, Florida is now the most densely populated state in the South except for Maryland, the fastest-growing state in the region in population, and also the most urban state in the region. The largest metropolitan areas in the state are Miami on the Atlantic coast and Tampa on the Gulf Coast, both of which account for more than 1.5 million people and are among the 25 largest metropolitan areas in the country. The largest city population in the state is in Jacksonville, which expanded its boundaries in 1968 to include most of Duval County. Florida's remarkable population growth of more than seven million people in 30 years between 1950 and 1980 is accounted for mainly by its attractiveness to retired persons from other states. As a result of this, more than 20% of the state population is over the age of 65 years, by far the highest proportion of senior citizens in the U.S. Because of this influx, Florida's population also includes a greater proportion of persons of foreign birth or foreign stock than any other Southern state. The population is 14% black and 9% Hispanic, groups that are the most urban component of the population. The Spanish-speaking population is especially visible in the greater Miami area, and it was noticeably swollen by the "boat lift" of Cuban refugees in 1980.

As it has been since the foundation of modern Florida in the 1890s, tourism is the most important single industry in the state economy. Florida now attracts more than 35 million tourists per year to its beaches, resorts, and amusement areas such as Disney World, and tourist businesses generate $16.5 billion per year. Manufacturing is the second-most important business, with the leading manufactured goods being food products including citrus juices, electrical equipment, chemicals, and paper and wood pulp goods. In agriculture, crops are of more importance than livestock, largely because Florida grows 70% of the U.S. citrus fruit harvest, most of it on the ridge that runs down the interior of the peninsula. Livestock, especially dairy animals, are the principal farm business on the northern panhandle, and truck farming of vegetables such as tomatoes is common throughout the state. Mining is also an important business, because Florida accounts for 80% of the phosphate rock yield in the U.S. These categories of industry are comparable to those found in other Southern states, but Florida is also notably diverse, with economic activities such as finance, international commerce, and aerospace programs that are far more extensive than those found in other states.

FLORIDA, University of. Coed university, part of the State University System of Florida located in the city of Gainesville in central Florida. Founded in 1853, this is a combination land grant college and state university. The 2,000-acre campus has over 500 buildings. The school also owns and maintains an additional 14,000 acres throughout the state.

Admission to the university is highly selective for out-of-state students, many of whom are from the Middle Atlantic states. The South provides 93% of the students. Academic offerings are myriad. Undergraduate studies are available through the colleges of Liberal Arts and Sciences, Agriculture, Architecture, Fine Arts, Business Administration, Education, Engineering, Health Related Professions, Journalism and Communications, Nursing, Pharmacy, Physical Education, Health and Recreation; and the schools of Forest Resources and Con-

servation, Accounting, and Building Construction. After graduation 20% of the students pursue full-time graduate study. The university is one of the nation's top producers of medical school entrants, and among the top 120 schools producing dental school entrants, with 45% of its graduates choosing careers in business and industry.

Library: 2,200,000 volumes, 23,000 journal subscriptions, 3,532 records/tapes. Faculty: 2,802. Enrollment: 33,242 total graduate and undergraduate; 13,518 men, 9,986 women (full-time). Degrees: Bachelor's, Master's, Doctorate.

FLORIDA AGRICULTURAL AND MECHANICAL UNIVERSITY. Coed university and land-grant college that is part of the State University system. The 418-acre campus is located in the western Florida city of Tallahassee, the state capital. The school also maintains a residence in Jacksonville affiliated with the Duval County Medical Center for its nursing students. Founded in 1887, the school was chartered as the Florida State Normal and Industrial School for the education of Negro youths. The University still serves a mostly black student body. A large number of majors are available to students. Studies are offered through the colleges of Science and Technology, Humanities, Social and Behavioral Sciences, and Education; and the schools of Nursing, Pharmacy, and Business Administration. The South supplies 95% of the University's students; 88% are black; 88% are state residents.

Library: 300,000 volumes, 3,000 journal subscriptions. Faculty: 327. Enrollment: 2,302 men, 2,212 women (full-time); 358 men, 428 women (part-time). Degrees: Associate's, Bachelor's, Master's.

FLORIDA BAY, Fla. Shallow, semi-protected stretch of water to the south of Florida between the peninsula and the Florida Keys. It is connected by Barnes Sound to Biscayne Bay to the northeast and opens to the Gulf of Mexico on the west. The bay, which with its many islands is part of the EVERGLADES National Park, has several channels dredged for navigation.

FLORIDA EAST COAST RAILROAD. Railway from Jacksonville to Key West. Built (1885-1912) by Henry Morrison FLAGLER in stages, the railroad (198 miles) opened up the entire east coast of Florida to agriculture, set-

A section of the Florida East Coast Railroad, the "railroad that went to sea"

tlement, and tourism. The cities of PALM BEACH and MIAMI owe their origins to it. After a hurricane (1935) destroyed the stretch across the FLORIDA KEYS, it was replaced by a highway.

FLORIDA INSTITUTE OF TECHNOLOGY. Independent, coed institution located 17 miles south of the Kennedy Space Center in Melbourne, Fla. Founded in 1958 by its current president, Dr. Jerome P. Keuper, the school specializes in engineering and science programs. The original purpose of the institute was to provide specialized courses to specialists who worked at Cape Canaveral. For the past 25 years, the school has continued to offer advanced science and engineering curricula to both undergraduate and graduate students alike.

Admission to the institute is selective. The school attracts students from all over the country, (New England represents 40% of the student body), the Kennedy Space Center, and the armed forces. There are many major academic divisions including the schools of Science and Engineering, Aeronautics, Management and Humanities, Professional Psychology, Applied Technology, Medical Research Institute, and the graduate school. After graduation 20% of the students pursue full-time graduate study, 2% enter business school, 1% medical school.

Academic facilities at both the 146-acre main campus and the 85-acre Jensen Beach campus abound. They include the Science and Research Center, the Medical Research Institute, a 15-acre botanical garden, extremely sophisticated telescopes, 40 aircraft, and three seagoing research vessels. The immediate area is rich in recreational diversions. The subtropical climate and close proximity to the water insures a wealth of water sports.

Library: 95,000 volumes, 760 journal subscriptions. Faculty: 332. Enrollment: 5,784 total graduate and undergraduate. Degrees: Associate's, Bachelor's, Master's, Doctorate.

FLORIDA KEYS, Fla., Monroe and Dade Co. A 150-mile chain of coral and limestone islands stretching southwest from Virginia Key, just below Miami, around the southern tip of the peninsula to Key West, which is about 100 miles north northeast of Cuba. Sometimes considered to include the Dry Tortugas Islands, 65 miles farther out, the Keys are narrow islands containing dense shrubbery and mangrove swamps, similar to the West Indies. Key Largo

(28 miles long) is the largest of the Keys. Key West contains the southernmost city in the United States. Most of the Keys are linked by a highway constructed during the 1930s.

FLORIDA STATE UNIVERSITY. Coed university, part of the State University System of Florida located in Tallahassee, Fla. Founded in 1857, the university was originally known as the Seminary West of Suwannee. The school was for women only, and did not become coeducational until 1947. Since then the university's academic reputation and size have grown dramatically. Physically, the 344-acre campus has a large variety of academic and residential buildings and facilities, ranging in architectural style from Gothic to futuristic. Academically, the school awards more than 100 Ph.D.s per year, one of only two dozen American institutions to do so. The university has maintained its leadership in nuclear research. It also has a sophisticated Computer Center and the Edward Ball Marine Laboratory on the Gulf Coast. Major university academic divisions are the Colleges of Social Sciences, Arts and Sciences, Law, Business, Home Economics, Communication, and Nursing; and the Schools of Library Science, Music, Theater, Criminology, Social Work, and Visual Arts. There is also the Department of Dance and the Division of Continuing Education. Students at the university are mostly from the South, with 4% Middle Atlantic. Admission is very selective for out-of-state students.

Library: 1,253,427 volumes, 13,543 journal subscriptions. Faculty: 1,275. Enrollment: 22,424 total graduate and undergraduate; 6,885 men, 8,285 women (full-time). Degrees: Associate's, Bachelor's, Master's, Doctorate.

FLORISSANT, Mo. City (pop. 55,372), St. Louis Co., in central western Missouri. The name is French for "flowering" and Florissant still shows a strong French and Spanish influence. Traders passed through the area many times before the French finally developed it into a settlement in 1785. Spaniards changed the city's name to St. Ferdinand, after the church built there (1821) but the name reverted to its original in 1939. Today it is a residential city outside of St. Louis. Each May, the Valley of Flowers Festival is held here.

FLOYD, John Buchanan (Smithfield, Va., June 1, 1806 — Abingdon, Va., Aug. 26, 1863). Secretary of War, governor of Virginia, and Confederate general. Floyd was a states' rights advocate but originally opposed secession. Elected a member of the Virginia assembly and governor (1849-52), he was appointed to James Buchanan's cabinet (1857-60), where he opposed reinforcing Charleston Harbor, began to advocate secession, and finally resigned under charges of financial cheating and transferring arms to the South. Appointed brigadier general in the Confederate Army by Jefferson Davis, Floyd held command in western Virginia, at the defeat of FORT DONELSON, and as major general of the army of Virginia.

FOOTE, Henry Stuart (Fauquier Co., Va., Feb. 28, 1804 — Nashville, Tenn., May 19, 1880). Politician. After practicing law for several years, Foote was elected to the U.S. Senate from Mississippi (1847-52). From 1852 to 1854, he was governor of Mississippi having defeated Jefferson DAVIS. His published works include *The Bench and Bar of the South and Southwest* (1876).

FORCE, Peter. (Passaic Falls, N.J., Nov. 26, 1790 — Washington, D.C., Jan. 23, 1868). Editor and historian. Force learned the printing trade in New York City and was president of the New York Typographical Society in 1812. In 1815 he settled in Washington, D.C., became a newspaper editor and publisher and served as mayor (1836-40). He was major general of the militia of the District of Columbia in 1860. In 1833 Force negotiated a contract with the U.S. government for the preparation and publication of a documentary history of the American colonies covering the entire period of the Revolution. He prepared and published nine volumes of the *American Archives* covering the years 1774-76 and had the tenth prepared when Congress refused to make further appropriations for the work. Force had gathered an immense collection of books, manuscripts, maps, and plans and in 1867 his entire collection was purchased by the government for $100,000 and was transferred to the Library of Congress. Force's first publication in Washington was the *National Calendar*, an annual volume of national statistics, which was published from 1820-36.

FORKED DEER RIVER, Tenn. River in western Tennessee formed at the juncture of three sprawling forks. It travels west to drain into the Mississippi River at Hales Point. Jackson sits at the center of its valley and numerous swamplands are found along its banks.

FORREST CITY, Ark. City (pop. 13,803), seat of St. Francis Co., situated at the foot of Crowley's Ridge in east central Arkansas. Settled in 1868 and incorporated in 1871, Forrest City today is an industrial city with diversified manufactures. Peaches are raised in the area.

FORREST, French (St. Mary's Co., Md., Oct. 4, 1796 — Washington, D.C., Nov. 22, 1866). Naval officer. Forrest served meritoriously in battle in the Mexican War and was commander of the navy shipyard in Washington. In 1861 he resigned to join the Confederate navy, and he was responsible for readying the *Merrimack* for battle.

FORREST, Nathan Bedford (Bedford Co., Tenn., July 13, 1821 — Memphis, Tenn., Oct. 29, 1877). Planter, slave trader, and Confederate general. Forrest was famous for his tactical genius, which enabled him to win many Civil War victories. He had little formal education, but had amassed a small fortune from his various activities at the outbreak of the Civil War. Forrest joined the Confederate forces in 1861 as a private and then led a cavalry unit of which he became lieutenant colonel. Although he had no prior military training he earned a reputation as a brilliant strategist and commander. His famous phrase "Get there first with the most men" aptly illustrates the tactic he used repeatedly to win military engagements, or forestall Union troop advances. During the Civil War Forrest took part in many engagements including SHILOH (1862), Nashville (1864), and Brices Cross Road (1864), where he soundly defeated a larger and stronger Union force. Beaten in a battle at Selma, Ala. (1865), Forrest surrendered his forces a month afterwards.

Although he achieved military fame, Forrest severely blotted his brilliant record by allowing his troops to massacre 300 black Union soldiers after the capture of Fort Pillow in April of 1864. After the war Forrest became deeply involved in the Ku Klux Klan.

FORSYTH, John (Fredericksburg, Va., Oct. 22, 1780 — Washington, D.C., Oct. 21, 1841). Statesman. A graduate of Princeton, he practiced law in Virginia until his election to the House of Representatives (1813-18, 1823-27) and to the Senate (1818-19). After he served as governor of Georgia (1827-29) and another term as U.S. senator (1829-34), President Andrew Jackson appointed him Secretary of State, a position he also held under President Martin Van Buren.

FORT BEND, Tex. This frontier outpost on the site of present-day Richmond was first settled in 1822. In 1838, when Richmond became the county seat of the newly formed Fort Bend County, the Fort Bend settlement was absorbed into it.

FORT BENNING, Ga. The largest infantry post in the U.S. It is the site of the U.S. Army Infantry Center that includes an infantry school and board which conducts airborne and ranger training programs. The post, established in 1918 near Columbus, covers 182,000 acres.

FORT BLISS, Tex. Located near El Paso, Fort Bliss was founded in 1848. During the Civil War it was headquarters for the Confederate Army in the Southwest and during the 1800s it became a "service station" for troops seeking Geronimo, the plundering Apache chief. In 1944 the U.S. Army set up an Air Defense Center for guided missiles at Fort Bliss. The fort today houses one of the major tourist attractions in Texas—a replica of the original post, given by the citizens of El Paso to Fort Bliss on its 100th anniversary.

FORT BRAGG, N.C. Cumberland Co. Army installation established in 1918. Fort Bragg covers 132,000 acres in central North Carolina. It was named for Confederate Army general Braxton Bragg and is now the home base of the U.S. Army airborne combat units. Also found here is the Special Warfare Center, which prepares soldiers in both guerrilla and psychological warfare. During World War II, the army trained its first two airborne divisions at Fort Bragg and it has since become the official headquarters of the 82nd Airborne Division and the XVIII Air Corps.

FORT CAROLINE, Fla. Duval Co. Site on the ST. JOHN'S RIVER of a French Huguenot settlement, headed by Rene de LAUDONNIERE, in June, 1554. The Spanish overcame the colony, slaughtering all but a few settlers and were overcome in their turn when the French destroyed the Spanish garrison in 1568. Gun batteries were established here during the Civil and Spanish-American Wars, and a national monument, with a replica of the Fort, now stands here.

FORT DONELSON, Battle of. Civil War engagement fought February 14-16, 1862, on the Cumberland River in eastern Tennessee near the Kentucky border. It was the second

The 82nd Airborne Division training at Fort Bragg, N.C.

surrendered unconditionally, bringing Grant fame for his message and ceding their own hopes to occupy parts of neutral Kentucky.

FORT HENRY, Ky. A military post located on the Tennessee River near the Tennessee border. It was important during the Civil War because, along with FORT DONELSON, it made up the center of the Confederate military base in Kentucky and Tennessee. Union forces moved on Fort Henry in February, 1862, capturing both forts by the end of the month, greatly reducing the Confederate position in these two states.

FORT HENRY, Battle of. Revolutionary War engagement in what is now Wheeling, W.Va., fought September 11-13, 1782, and considered by many to be the last battle in the war. The battle took place at Fort Patrick Henry, the former Fort Crawford renamed in 1776. In it a small band of patriots survived attack by approximately 250 Indians and 40 Tory soldiers. The famous legend associated with the battle is that Elizabeth Zane managed to retrieve a keg of powder from an outbuilding because the attackers were so surprised to see a woman cross the open ground.

FORT HENRY, Battle of. Civil War engagement fought on February 6, 1862, in eastern Tennessee where the Tennessee River enters Kentucky. It was the opening of the Fort Henry and FORT DONELSON campaign, the first Union penetration of Confederate territory from the west. The Union army approached Fort Henry, an incomplete earthworks fortification, with riverboats under Adm. Andrew Hull Foote and support forces on foot under Gen. Ulysses S. Grant. As they approached, the Confederate force was reduced to 100 troops, the rest being sent back to man nearby Fort Donelson. Fort Henry surrendered after a single bombardment from Foote's boats.

After taking Fort Henry, Foote's boats went back down the Tennessee to approach Fort Donelson along the Cumberland River. Grant, after a late arrival at Fort Henry because of flooded roads, proceeded overland to Fort Donelson after cutting his own telegraph lines so that his plan could not be countermanded.

FORT HINDMAN, Battle of. See ARKANSAS POST, Battle of.

Confederate defeat in the FORT HENRY and Fort Donelson campaign of the Union army under Gen. Ulysses S. Grant. Following their successful bombardment of Fort Henry, the Union riverboats under Adm. Andrew Hull Foote arrived at Fort Donelson via the Cumberland River on February 14. Here, however, they were themselves bombarded by the Confederate garrison under Gen. John Buchanan FLOYD. By the night of February 14 this Confederate edge had been offset by the arrival of Grant's army on the land side of the fort.

On February 15 the outnumbered Confederate forces had managed to clear a route for their inevitable retreat toward Nashville. At that moment Floyd proved tragically indecisive, and the Confederate forces neither retreated nor held their original positions. With his troops in imminent danger, Floyd surrendered his command to Gen. Simon BUCKNER and escaped from the fort with 3,000 of his own Virginia troops.

On February 16, Buckner requested terms for the surrender of the fort from Grant. Grant responded with the famous message: "No terms except unconditional and immediate surrender can be accepted." The Confederate force then

FORT HOOD, Tex. U.S. Army post located between Killeen and Gatesville in south central Texas. Founded in 1942, Fort Hood has more concentrated armored power than anywhere else in the U.S., and the largest population (combined military and civilian) of any post in the Western world.

FORT KNOX, Ky. A 110,000-acre U.S. military reservation, in Hardin and Meade Counties, in northern Kentucky. First established in 1917 as a World War I training post and named for the first Secretary of War Henry Knox, it did not become a permanent post until 1932. In 1936 the major part of the nation's gold bullion was stored here. An extension of the University of Kentucky and the Patton Museum, a collection of calvary and armor, are here.

FORT LAUDERDALE, Fla. City (pop. 153,256), seat of Broward Co., located on the southeast coast of Florida at the mouth of New River, part of the Intracoastal Waterway. Named for Maj. William Lauderdale, who used the fort as a base from which to scour the Everglades for Seminole Indians, it is known for its 160 miles of ocean, river, bay, and canal frontage and its fine resort facilities. Over 1,000 boats a year use its Bahia Mar Yacht Basin. Port Everglades to the south is the deepest harbour on the Atlantic south of Norfolk, Va., and ranks third in the state for cargo handling. An isolated, lonely region until the 20th century, it had 52 residents in 1900, 175 when incorporated in 1911, and less than 9,000 in 1930. Its growth since is testimony to the phenomenal development of Florida as a resort center during the past 50 years.

FORT LOUDON LAKE, Tenn. Lake primarily located between Knox Co. and Blout Co. in northeastern Tennessee. A dam built by

The Gold Depository of the U.S. Treasury at Fort Knox, Ky.

the Tennessee Valley Authority transformed a wild 55-mile expanse of the Tennessee River into this lake, spanning 14,600 acres, extending to Knoxville.

FORT LOUDON MASSACRE. Frontier Indian attack. In 1760, Oconastoto, chief of the CHEROKEE INDIANS, made a general attack on the frontier settlements of the Carolinas in consequence of a dispute between the Indians and English settlers. On August 9 of that year, at the head of 10,000 CREEK INDIANS and Cherokees, he forced the garrison of Fort Loudon to surrender. In violation of the surrender terms, he treacherously killed all his prisoners (over 200). As a result of the massacre the colonists burned Cherokee towns and forced Oconastoto into an alliance that lasted until the Revolutionary War, when he was induced by a British Indian agent to again attack the colonists.

FORT McHENRY, Bombardment of. War of 1812 action by the British against the installation in the harbor of Baltimore, Md., September 13-14, 1814. The British had advanced along the Potomac River, defeated a superior American force at the Battle of BLADENSBURG on August 24 and then burned Washington, D.C. In 15 hours of intermittent bombardment of Fort McHenry in Baltimore, however, they failed to obtain the surrender of its defenders. The sight of the flag flying through the night over the fort inspired Francis Scott KEY to write "The Star-spangled Banner." Soon afterwards his poem became a popular song set to the melody of the English song "To Anacreon in Heaven." It was declared the national anthem in 1916.

FORT MYERS, Fla. City (pop. 36,638), seat of Lee Co., located on Florida's Gulf Coast. The city is on the southern bank of the Calosahatchee River, the western part of the Okeechobee Waterway that joins the Gulf of Mexico with the Atlantic Ocean. Built as a military outpost during the SEMINOLE INDIAN WARS (1841) and incorporated in 1905, Fort Myers has prospered as a shipping point for farm produce, a winter resort, and a retirement community. It is the heart of the Fort Myers-Cape Coral metropolitan area with a population of more than 200,000 and a growth rate during the 1970s in excess of 30%.

FORT NINETY-SIX, Siege of. Revolutionary War action lasting from May 22 to June

19, 1781, in which the Continental militia unsuccessfully attempted to subdue a British outpost in central South Carolina. After the siege was abandoned, the British evacuated the outpost as part of a general retreat toward Charleston.

The Revolutionary army of Gen. Nathaniel Greene had failed to defeat the British army at Guilford Courthouse and at Hobkirk's Hill, but it was nevertheless steadily advancing southward. Fort Ninety-Six, named for the distance from Fort Prince George, then became the principal immediate objective in this advance. It was defended by 550 troops under the command of Col. John Cruger. His commanding officer Lord Francis Rawdon had issued orders to abandon the fort, but they were intercepted and never reached Cruger.

Greene surrounded the fort on May 22 with scarcely 1,000 troops, the rest of his force having been sent elsewhere in South Carolina. The British withstood his efforts to breech the fortifications over the next month, during which Greene employed a variety of tactics including a Maham Tower and flaming African arrows. On June 12, one of a series of parties of reinforcements succeeded in reaching the fort to assist the defenders. Rawdon himself was known to be nearing the fort, and so on June 18 Greene ordered a direct assault. When this failed he began a retreat toward Charlotte on June 19. Rawdon arrived to relive the defenders on June 21.

The fort was abandoned by the British soon after Rawdon's arrival. During the siege the Recolutionary Army had lost 57 killed and 70 wounded; the British had lost 27 killed and 58 wounded.

FORT PICKENS, Fla. Santa Rosa Co. A former United States military post on Santa Rosa Island, built in 1834. At the beginning of the Civil War, it was occupied by Southern forces and considered a basically neutral installation with an agreement by the Union interests that the fort would not be attacked. But following the secession of Florida (1861), the Union Army rushed in to seize the fort which remained in their control from the first battle at Fort Sumter until the end of the war.

FORT PIERCE, Fla. City (pop. 33,802), seat of St. Lucie Co., in southeastern Florida on the Indian River. Fort Pierce was developed from three separate towns surrounding a U.S. Army garrison established in 1838 during the SEMINOLE INDIAN WARS. Incorporated in 1901,

it is a resort area and processing center for fruit and vegetables. There are commercial fisheries and lumber is manufactured.

FORT PULASKY, Ga. U.S. Army fort on Cocksput Island, at the mouth of the Savannah River, constructed in the 1930s and 1840s. During the Civil War it was taken by the Confederate Army in January, 1861, but Union forces retook the fort in April, 1862. Fort Pulasky became a national monument in 1924.

FORT SMITH, Ark. City (pop. 71,384), seat of Sebastian Co., located at the Oklahoma border south of the junction of the Arkansas and Poteau Rivers. It was originally an army post (1817) named for Gen. Thomas A. Smith, but the army turned the installation over to the U.S. district court in 1871. The courtroom and gallows used by Judge Issac C. PARKER, who was known as the "Hanging Judge," have been reconstructed. It is the location of one of the nation's largest horse and mule markets, and Fort Chafee Army Base, several lakes, and facilities for mountain recreation are found here. Fort Smith is a major industrial center with diversified manufacturing and coal mines.

FORT STOCKTON, Tex. Town (pop. 8,688), seat of Pecos Co., located on the Old San Antonio Road, once a mail route connected to San Diego. Today, its livelihood comes mainly from the petroleum industry, farming, and tourism. The site of Old Fort Stockton (opened in 1869 and abandoned in 1886) is a main attraction.

FORT WALTON BEACH, Fla. City (pop. 20,829), Okaloosa Co., in northwestern Florida on the Gulf of Mexico. It was the site of a fort of the same name built during the SEMINOLE INDIAN WARS. Incorporated in 1941, it is a large summer resort popular because of its location and proximity to Choctawhatchee National Forest.

FORT WORTH, Tex. City (pop. 385,141), seat of Tarrant Co., located in the rolling range country of north central Texas. Surrounded by ranches and farms, Fort Worth is an industrial center for over 20 suburbs. Fort Worth was a jumping-off point for settlers heading westward during the 1840s and 1850s, and in 1847 a cavalry outpost was established on the city's present site to protect settlers on their way west. In 1853 the outpost was named Fort Worth in memory of Gen. William J. Worth, a former commander of the U.S. Army's Texas Department. Fort Worth developed into a cattle town in the 1870s because of the nearby CHISHOLM TRAIL, along which cowboys drove vast herds of longhorn cattle to Kansas, and the city became known as "Cowtown." With the coming of the railroad, Fort Worth was transformed into an important cattle shipping center. Grain milling became an important industry a few years later. In the early 1900s economic bounty again struck Fort Worth with the discovery of oil. While oil, grain, and beef are still important to the city's economy, the present-day major employers are Bell Helicopter Company and the Fort Worth General Dynamics division and there is extensive manufacturing.

Fort Worth's many points of interest include the Fort Worth Zoo, Six Flags Over Texas amusement park, several famous art museums, Trinity Park, and Fort Worth Botanical Gardens. An educational center, Fort Worth is home to Texas Christian University, Fort Worth Christian College, Southwestern Baptist Theological Seminary, Texas Wesleyan College, and Tarrant County Junior College.

FORTIER, Alcee (St. James Parish, La., June 5, 1856 — St. James Parish, La., Feb. 14, 1914). Educator, historian, and author. A professor at the University of Louisiana (now Tulane University), Fortier's most important works include the *History of Louisiana* (1904), along with studies of Louisiana folklore and Creole history and customs. A civic leader, he was director of the Louisiana Historical Society for 18 years, and was a president of the American Folklore Society.

FORTUNE, Timothy Thomas (Marianna, Fla., Oct. 3, 1856 — Philadelphia, Pa., June 2, 1928). Journalist. After completing his education at Howard University, Fortune became the influential editor of the *Globe* (1882), a Negro daily. He remained in this position until his death, devoting his career to the campaign for equal rights. His works include *Black and White: Land, Labor, and Politics in the South* (1884) and *The Negro in Politics* (1885).

FOUNTAIN OF YOUTH. Located in Fountain of Youth Park, St. Augustine, Fla. It is a popular tourist attraction advertised as having been visited by PONCE DE LEON in 1513 during his search for a Fountain of Youth. The fountain itself is a well in a missionlike rock

grotto. The park also includes an Indian burial ground and a planetarium.

FOURCHE LA FAVE RIVER, Ark. A navigable waterway begining in western Arkansas north of Blue Mountain, traveling some 120 miles east to meet the Arkansas River. Its course takes it near the Ouachita National Forest. Named for an early French settler, it is also known as Lefevre's Fork. It is noted for bass, bream, and crappie fishing.

FOXX, James Emory "Jimmy" (Sudlersville, Md., Oct. 22, 1907 — Miami, Fla., July 21, 1967). Baseball infielder with the American League Philadelphia and Boston clubs who hit 30 or more home runs for 12 consecutive seasons (1929-1940). He was inducted into the Baseball Hall of Fame in 1951.

FRANCIS, David Rowland (Richmond, Ky., Oct. 1, 1850 — London, England, Jan. 15, 1927). Statesman. A grain merchant, Francis was mayor of St. Louis, Mo., (1885-89), before becoming Democratic governor of the state (1889-93). Secretary of the Interior (1896-97) under President Glover Cleveland, he gained a presidential proclamation that set aside millions of acres of forest reserves. In 1916 he was appointed ambassador to Russia, and remained in the post through the Russian Revolution to try to keep Russia in the war against Germany.

FRANKFORT, Ky. City (pop. 21,907), state capital and seat of Franklin Co., located in north central Kentucky. Gen. James WILKINSON founded the community in 1786 on the Kentucky River. The city was originally known as Frank's Ford, after Stephen Frank, a frontiersman killed in an Indian skirmish at a local fording place on the river in 1780. Frankfort became the capital of the state in 1792 and was incorporated as a city in 1839. During the Civil War, the city was occupied by Confederate Gen. Braxton Bragg, who was later driven out by Gen. D. C. Buell. In 1937, the city sustained widespread property damage due to a major flood of the Ohio River Valley. A trading center for the bluegrass region's tobacco, corn, and thoroughbred horses, the city offers diversified industry and limestone quarries. Manufactures include furniture, candy, bourbon, textiles, electronic and metal products. The graves of frontier pioneer Daniel Boone and his wife, Rebecca, are in the city cemetery and the Experimental Game Farm is located nearby.

FRANKLIN, Battle of. Civil War engagement fought November 30, 1864, in central Tennessee south of Nashville. In this battle the Union army, in retreat from Gen. John Bell HOOD'S campaign toward Nashville, successfully executed a defensive maneuver to protect itself while fleeing across the Harpeth River. Having lost ATLANTA to the Union army of Gen. William Tecumseh Sherman, Hood moved north to invade Tennessee while Sherman moved south on the 'MARCH TO THE SEA. The first resistance Hood encountered in Tennessee was the Union force of Gen. John M. Schofield, which, being outnumbered, began a withdrawal north from Pulaski, Tenn., toward Nashville along the Nashville and Decatur railroad line. Schofield reached Franklin on the morning of November 30, where his retreat was slowed by poor fords across the Harpeth River. He had moved most of his heavy equipment across the river by 3:00 P.M., but the Confederates attacked his defensive line less than an hour later. The subsequent battle was a bloody one of brave Confederate charges and hand-to-hand combat. Unable to break the Union line, Hood ceased the attack at 11:00 P.M., allowing Schofield to withdraw toward Nashville during the night. Nearly equal forces were actually engaged in the battle, with the Union side losing more than 2,000 and the Confederate side more than 6,000 men.

Franklin was also the scene of an earlier, less important skirmish on April 10, 1863. In it the Confederate army of Gen. Earl VAN DORN attacked, without success, the Union force of Gen. Gordon Granger.

FRANKLIN, La. City (pop. 9,584), seat of St. Marys Parish, in south central Louisiana. Named for Ben Franklin, the city was founded in 1800. It is historically known for opposing secession from the Union and for the Battle of Irish Bend (1863) during the Civil War. Several antebellum plantations and old manor houses remain in this area, which is rich in wildlife and fish. There are oil wells nearby, and rice and sugarcane are grown here.

FRANKLIN, State of. An independent political state that incorporated what is now Greene, Sullivan, and Washington counties in eastern Tennessee. The state was founded in 1784 when North Carolina, which then held jurisdiction over those lands, ceded this area to the Continental Congress (June, 1784). The residents came together and set up their own government, electing John SEVIER governor for three years and establishing a taxation system, laws, and magistrates. After drawing up a constitution they requested admission to the Union as a state but were refused Congressional recognition. The state existed for four years, although North Carolina repealed its action in December, 1784.

FRANKLIN, Tenn. Town (pop. 12,407), seat of Williamson Co., located in central Tennessee on the Harpeth River. The first home foundation in Franklin was laid in 1780 and the town was incorporated in 1815. One of the bloodiest battles of the Civil War was fought here on Nov. 30, 1864 when about 8,500 men were felled within one hour. More ranking officers were killed or injured here than in any other major battle of the war. Franklin's manufactures include boots, gift wrap, and bedding. Local farms produce corn, hay, mixed grains, tobacco, and livestock.

FREDERICK, Md. City (27,557), seat of Frederick Co., located in northwestern Maryland. Frederick's major source of employment is Fort Detrick, a U.S. Army biological research center. Major industries are canning, electronics, eyeglass frames, and clothing. The city features annual tours of its many historic sites. In 1765 judges of the circuit court here repudiated the British Stamp Act. In 1864 Confederate Gen. Jubal A. EARLY collected $200,000 from local banks for sparing the city. Tradition has it that Confederate Gen. Thomas J. (Stonewall) Jackson attended services at a local church the Sunday before the battle of Antietam and slept through a strong pro-Union sermon. The city was incorporated in 1817.

FREDERICKSBURG, Battle of. A major Civil War battle and a victory for the South fought on December 13, 1862. In it Gen. Robert E. LEE and the Confederate army prevented the Union army under Gen. Ambrose E. Burnside from crossing the Rappahannock River near the northeast Virginia city for which the battle is named. Burnside had replaced Gen. George B. McClellan as commander of the army of the Potomac on November 7, 1862. He shifted the line of attack east in order to approach Richmond through Fredericksburg. His advance troops arrived at the Rappahannock opposite Fredericksburg on November 17, when the Confederate forces in the city were unprepared for an attack. Burnside, however, decided to await pontoon equipment rather than to force a crossing. The delay enabled Lee, in Fredericksburg, to gather his forces and position them on the strategically important hills on the south side of the river.

Having bridged the river, Burnside attempted to advance from the north to the south bank on December 13. Successive waves of Union soldiers were sent across the river, and were destroyed at the foot of the hills of the south bank by Confederate troops under Gen. James LONGSTREET. Union dead on December 13 alone were 12,000, but Burnside was only disuaded from renewing the attack on the following day by the opposition of his junior officers. The Union army withdrew from its position on December 15. The defeat ended Burnside's first campaign south and caused widespread discouragement among Union politicians and citizenry.

FREDERICKSBURG, Va. Independent city (pop. 15,222), within Spotsylvania Co., in northeastern Virginia north of Richmond. Lying at the navigable head of the Rappahannock River, the city was settled in 1671, incorporated as a town in 1781 and developed as a port. It remains today a marketing center for the surrounding agricultural region which specializes in dairy and beef cattle. Fredericksburg also has some light manufacturing industry, two institutions of higher learning including Mary Washington College of the University of VIRGINIA, and many tourist attractions. Among Fredericksburg's historic sites are Spotsylvania National Military Park, the scene of several Civil War battles, the homes of George Washington's mother and sister, and the law office of James Monroe. Across the Rappahannock River is "Ferry Farm," the family estate on which Washington spent part of his boyhood. The Civil War Battle of FREDERICKSBURG was fought here on December 13, 1862.

FREE SOIL PARTY. Political party founded in 1848 upon the principle that the slave system should not be extended into the territories recently acquired from Mexico. Organized after the War with Mexico when Texas was about to become a state, the Free-Soil Party was founded by dissident members of the Democratic and Whig parties, later joined by members of the Liberty party, who held their first convention in Buffalo, N.Y., August 9, 1848. Represented were all the non-slave states, along with delegates from Delaware, Maryland, Virginia, and the District of Columbia. Their platform called for "Free Soil, Free Speech, Free Labor, and Free Man," and the confinement of slavery to the slave states. Their ticket, which ran Martin Van Buren for President of the U.S. and Charles Francis Adams for Vice President, received a popular vote of 291,000 but no electoral votes. In 1852 candidates John P. Hale for President and George W. Julian for Vice President received a popular vote of 157,000. Although the party virtually disappeared in 1856 it formed the nucleus of the historical Republican Party.

FREEDMEN'S BUREAU. Government agency established by an act of Congress on March 3, 1865, after the Civil War for the purpose of protecting the rights of recently freed slaves. The Bureau of Freedmen, Refugees, and Abandoned Lands was attached to the War Department and Gen. Oliver O. Howard was appointed commissioner, with military powers. The jurisdiction of the bureau, which was divided into ten districts each with an assistant commissioner, covered both the slave states that had seceded and the border slave states that stayed loyal to the Union. It engaged in relief work and educational activities, and was criticized for both, amid charges of corruption and abuse, some of which were justified. The year after its establishment, an act was passed enlarging the bureau's powers but the bureau was discontinued on July 1, 1868, in the middle of RECONSTRUCTION, with the exception of educational supervision which continued in force by an act of Congress until 1870.

FREEMAN, Douglas Southall (Lynchburg, Va., May 16, 1886 — Richmond, Va., June 13, 1953). Editor and historian. He received his Ph.D. from Johns Hopkins and later became editor of the *News Leader* (1915-49), the evening paper in Richmond, Va. A noted biographer and authority on military strategy, among his works is *R. E. Lee* (4 vols. 1934-35), which won the Pulitzer prize in 1935. His seven volume biography of George Washington (1949-57) won the Pulitzer prize in 1958.

FREEPORT, Tex. Town (pop. 13,444), Brazoria Co., in southeast Texas on the Gulf of Mexico. One of the nine cities comprising Brazosport, Freeport was founded in 1912 by New York businessmen hoping to cultivate the town's rich sulfur deposits. Today, Freeport's industries include petrochemical plants, marine repairs, and shrimp processing.

FREMONT, Jessie Benton (near Lexington, Va., May 31, 1824 — Los Angeles, Calif., Dec. 27, 1902). Author. The daughter of Thomas Hart BENTON, she married John Charles FREMONT. A firm supporter of her husband's varied exploits, she was also a noted author. Along with numerous periodicals, her works include *A Year of American Travel* (1878), *Far West Sketches* (1890) and *The Will and the Way Stories* (1891).

FREMONT, John Charles (Savannah, Ga., Jan. 21, 1813 — New York, N.Y., July 13, 1890). Surveyor, military and political leader. Noted for opening and exploring California, Fremont began his career as a lieutenant of topography for the army corps of engineers (1838-41) under Jean Nicollet, with whom he helped map the Mississippi, Missouri, and Des Moines Rivers. He married Sen. Thomas Hart BENTON'S daughter, Jessie, in 1841 and began mapping for the war department from the Mississippi to the Pacific, touring through Wyoming (1842) and again through the Columbia, Truckee, Carson, and Snake River valleys (1843). A second trip, during the Mexican War, resulted in his planting a U.S. flag on the peak of Gavilan Mountain, supporting the Bear Flag Rebellion, and haphazardly conducting the conquest of the "state." A third excursion coincided with the discovery of gold; Fremont became a millionaire. Elected U.S. senator from California (1850-51), he was defeated for reelection by pro-slavers, and defeated for President by James Buchanan (1856). In 1878, penniless, and living on his wife's earnings from writing, he was appointed governor of the Arizona Territory.

FRENCH BROAD RIVER, N.C./Tenn. River with a source in the Blue Ridge Mountains in western North Carolina. It flows some 204 miles north then west northwest into Tennessee. Near Knoxville, the French Broad joins the Holston to become the Tennessee River. The river is impounded by Douglas Dam near Seviersville, and forms Lake Douglas.

FRIO RIVER, Tex. Waterway rising in the Edwards Plateau, running 160 miles southeast to meet the Nueces River to form Lake Corpus Christi. Its name is Spanish for "cold."

FRISCH, Frank Francis "Fordham Flash" (New York, N.Y., Sept. 9, 1898 — Wilmington, Del., March 12, 1973). Baseball in-fielder with the St. Louis Cardinals from 1927 to 1937 who managed the team from 1933 to 1938. He held several fielding records and and was the National League's Most Valuable Player in 1931. He was inducted into the Baseball Hall of Fame in 1947.

FRONT ROYAL, Va. Town (pop. 11,126), seat of Warren Co., in north central Virginia on the Shenandoah River. Incorporated in 1788, it was originally called "Hill Town." During the Civil War the Confederate spy, Belle BOYD, was instrumental in Gen. Andrew Jackson's capture of Union troops in the town. Textiles are the base of the town's economy, along with tourism because of Front Royal's location at the beginning of the SKYLINE DRIVE. Shenandoah National Park and the Skyline Caverns are nearby. Randolph-Macon Academy, a military preparatory school for boys, was established here in 1892.

FRONT ROYAL, Battle of. Civil War battle in northern Virginia on May 23, 1862, and a victory for the Confederate army under Gen. Stonewall JACKSON. In the midst of his Shenandoah Valley campaign, Jackson amassed his forces at Strasburg on the north fork of the Shenandoah River. By March 23, the Confederate troops numbered 16,000, and on that day they marched against 1,000 Union troops in nearby Front Royal. The Union forces managed to withstand the attack until evening, but soon after darkness virtually all of them were captured, wounded, or killed. The Confederate army lost a mere 50 men. It captured a large cache of supplies, but these were lost when the Union army returned to the site on May 30.

FRUIT. A major agricultural resource of the South, one that supports canning, freezing, juice, and other food processing industries. The

Aerial view of orange groves in central Florida

single most important fruit crops in the South are citrus: Florida leads the nation in harvest of oranges and tangerines, and Florida and Texas lead the nation in harvest of grapefruit. Peaches are also an important crop in South Carolina and Georgia, which rank second and third in the nation, respectively, in annual peach harvest.

FUGITIVE SLAVE ACT. A law passed September 18, 1850, as part of the COMPROMISE OF 1850 resolutions of Henry Clay. Intended to strengthen the previous 1793 fugitive slave act, the law attempted to appease the South and provided for the return without trial of runaway slaves to their owners and stiff penalties to anyone aiding their escape. The law so favored the slaveowners that it caused a backlash of sentiment in the North.

FULBRIGHT, James William (Sumner, Mo., Apr. 9, 1905 —). U.S. senator. A Rhodes scholar who earned his law degree at George Washington University, Fulbright rose to prominence in Arkansas politics. He became president of the University of ARKANSAS (1939-41), and was elected as a Democrat to the U.S. House of Representatives (1943-45) and to the U.S. Senate (1945-75). He was author of the Fulbright Act (1946) which established an international, educational exchange program. In 1959 he became chairman of the Senate Foreign Relations Committee.

FURMAN UNIVERSITY. Independent, church-related coed liberal arts college located in the northwestern South Carolina city of Greenville. Furman University is the South's oldest Baptist institution of higher learning. Founded in 1826 as a college for men, a merger with a women's college took place in 1933. The present campus was opened in 1958.

Admission to Furman is very selective. Twenty-five percent of students go on to graduate study, with 3% entering medical school, 5% law school, and 5% business school. Furman is ranked among the nation's top 200 developers of business executives. The South provides 86% of Furman's students, and 10% are from the Middle Atlantic states, 3% are from New England.

The school offers a wide variety of intramural and intercollegiate sports. The 750-acre campus also includes a 30-acre lake and an 18-hole golf course. The nearby city of Greenville has shops, restaurants, and additional social and recreational diversions for Furman students.

Library: 285,000 volumes, 1,600 journal subscriptions, 1,400 records/tapes. Faculty: 157. Enrollment: 3,450 total graduate and undergraduate. Degrees: Bachelor's, Master's.

G

GADSDEN, Ala. City (pop. 47,565), seat of Etowah Co., located in northeastern Alabama on the west bank of the Coosa River and in the foothills of the Appalachian Mountains. Settled in 1840 and named for James GADSDEN, the railroad man who later negotiated the Gadsden Purchase of New Mexico from Mexico in 1853, the city is favored by rich supplies of coal, hydroelectric energy, and fertile farmland. Emma Sansom guided Confederate Gen. Nathan Bedford Forrest through the flooded Gadsden area in 1863, allowing him to defeat and capture Union Col. Abel D. Streight and his troops. Gadsden was incorporated as a city in 1871.

GADSDEN, Christopher (Charleston, S.C., Feb. 16, 1724 — Charleston, S.C., Aug. 28, 1805). Revolutionary leader. After his education in England, Gadsden returned to Charleston where he became a wealthy merchant and supported the opposition against British taxation. He served in the Continental Congress (1774-76), advocating independence. In 1788 he helped ratify the U.S. constitution at the South Carolina convention.

GADSDEN, James (Charleston, S.C., May 15, 1788 — Charleston, S.C., Dec. 26, 1858). Diplomat, soldier, and rail executive. A Yale graduate (1806), Gadsden became a lieutenant of army corps of engineers in 1812. He supervised the transfer of the SEMINOLE INDIANS, first to south Florida (1823), then to the far West (1832). He became president of a South Carolina railroad (1840) and U.S. minister to Mexico (1853), in which capacity he negotiated a route for a southern railway, which he had long promoted, known as the Gadsden Purchase. He exceeded his instructions, and the purchase was ratified by only a narrow margin in the Senate.

GAINES, Edmund Pendleton (Culpeper Co., Va., Mar. 20, 1777 — New Orleans, La., June 6, 1849). Military officer. Gaines joined the U.S. Army at the age of 22 and was responsible for the arrest of Aaron Burr (1807). After serving in the War of 1812 he became an Indian commissioner and led campaigns against the Creeks and Seminoles. He also took aprt in the Black Hawk War. At the beginning of the Mexican War he faced a court of inquiry for using his own authority to call volunteers but the charges were dismissed. He was the brother of George Strother GAINES.

GAINES, George Strother (Stokes Co., N.C., c. 1784 — State Line, Miss., Jan. 21,

1873). Pioneer and Indian agent. Gaines was influential in keeping the CHOCTAW INDIANS out of Tecumseh's confederation against the American settlers. Gaines opened the Alabama territory to settlement with the founding of Gaines' Trace. When the Choctaws were removed to western lands, he aided their chiefs in selecting sites and accompanied their migration. He was the brother of Edmund Pendleton GAINES.

GAINES' MILL, Battle of. See SEVEN DAYS' BATTLE.

GAINESVILLE, Fla. City (pop. 81,371), seat of Alachua Co., in north central Florida. The area is part of a tract originally granted to Don Fernando de la Mata Arredondo in 1817. Today Gainesville has businesses involved in the processing of citrus fruit, poultry farming, and forestry products. It is the heart of a metropolitan area of nearly 150,000, and its own population increased more than 15% during the 1970s. Gainesville is the home of the University of FLORIDA.

GAINESVILLE, Ga. City (pop. 15,280), seat of Hall Co., in north central Georgia on Lake Lanier. Situated in the foothills of the Blue Ridge mountains, Gainesville was incorporated in 1821. Today it is a trade center for this part of the state and boasts a busy textile industry. It is near Riverside Military Academy, the Chattahoochee National Forest, Brenau College (1878), and a junior college.

GAINESVILLE, Tex. Town (pop. 14,081), seat of Cooke Co., in northeastern Texas. Settled in the 1850s, and a way station on the CHISOLM TRAIL, Gainesville began as a prosperous cattle and cotton farming area. Pipes, clothing, and artificial lures are among its current manufactures.

GAINETT'S AND GOULDING'S FARMS, Battle of. See SEVEN DAYS' BATTLE.

GAITHERSBURG, Md. Town (pop. 26,424), Montgomery Co., in west central Maryland northwest of Washington, D.C. Incorporated in 1878, it is a trade center for a large livestock region. Gaithersburg's industry and proximity to the nation's capital has played a major role in its growth (1960 pop. 3,847). It is the home of the U.S. Coast and Geodetic Observatory.

GALLATIN, Tenn. City (pop. 17,191), seat of Sumner Co., in northern Tennessee on the Cumberland River. Established in 1802, it is known for its breeding of Tennessee walking horses and is the site of a large number of antebellum homes. Today it is the farming and livestock market of the county, producing tobacco, corn, furniture, locks, keys, and tools.

GALLOWAY, Charles Betts (Kosciusko, Miss., Sept. 1, 1849 — Jackson, Miss., May 12, 1909). Methodist bishop. After graduating from the University of Mississippi, Galloway began a career in the ministry. Noted for his oratory he became a bishop in 1886. Galloway was known for his missionary zeal, his support of education and his advocacy of better race relations.

GALLOWAY, Joseph (near West River, Md., c. 1731 — Watford, England, Aug. 19, 1803). Colonial statesman and loyalist. Galloway believed the conflict with Britain could be solved by creating a constitution for the empire, which he presented to the first Continental Congress in 1776 in his "A Plan of a Proposed Union between Great Britain and the Colonies." The plan, providing for a president-general appointed by the king and a legislature selected by the colonial assemblies with the rights and powers of the House of Commons, was defeated by one vote and later erased from the records. Elected to the Pennsylvania assembly in 1756 and its speaker from 1766 to 1775, Galloway fought for the Loyalist cause under Gen. William Howe and was Britain's wartime civil administrator of Philadelphia until it was taken by the patriots in 1778. Thought by many to be the finest of the American Tories, Galloway exiled himself to England (1778), leaving wife and lands behind.

GALVESTON, Tex. City (pop. 61,902), seat of Galveston Co., located at the northeast end of Galveston Island, which extends 32 miles along the Gulf of Mexico in southeast Texas. The city was settled in the 1830s and named for Don Bernardo de Galvez, viceroy of Mexico. The city's commercial power was dampened in the late 1800s by competition from other ports and the hurricane of 1900, which killed over 5,000. As a result, when the worst hurricane in Texas history hit there in 1961, the 17-foot, 8-mile-long wall that had been erected did much to prevent damage and kept the death toll under 50. Known as a resort and shipping center, Galveston's industries include oil, insurance, banking, and education; it is the home of the University of TEXAS School of Medicine.

GALVESTON BAY, Tex. An inlet of the Gulf of Mexico in southeastern Texas. Galveston Bay serves as the key water connection point between Galveston and Houston. The Spanish were known to have explored the bay by the early 16th century but major exploration of the area as a port of entry did not come until the 18th century. Pirates, including those under Jean LAFFITE, are known to have frequented the region. In 1896 the port was expanded to accept larger vessels by construction of a $3 million jetty system. Today it is a major shrimping and fishing area.

GAMBLE, Hamilton Rowan (Winchester, Va., Nov. 29, 1798 — Jefferson City, Mo., Jan. 31, 1864). Politician. After serving as presiding justice of the State Supreme Court in Missouri (1851-55), Gamble was appointed provisional governor (1861-64). He opposed the Confederacy and devised a system to gradually free the slaves. Unionists who sought immediate emancipation tried unsuccessfully to force Gamble's resignation.

GARDEN, Alexander (Scotland, c. 1730 — London, England, Apr. 15, 1791). Scottish-American naturalist. Garden came to the U.S., settling in Charleston, S.C., where he collected flora and fauna and corresponded with European colleagues. He is noted for his discovery of new species including the congo snake and mud eel, and the gardenia is named for him.

GARLAND, Augustus Hill (Tipton Co., Tenn., June 11, 1832 — Washington, D.C., Jan. 26, 1899). Politician. Garland was an important Arkansas lawyer who practiced at the U.S. Supreme Court level until elected to serve in the Confederate House of Representatives during the Civil War. Despite a presidential pardon after the war, his application to resume his practice was denied, which led to his successful landmark lawsuit in 1867. He was then refused his seat when elected to the U.S. Senate later that same year. He was ultimately elected governor of Arkansas (1874-76) and U.S. senator (1877-85). He served as attorney general under President Glover Cleveland (1885-89).

GARLAND, Tex. City (pop. 138,857), Dallas Co., in northeast central Texas. Garland is an industrial center (manufactures include scientific instruments, electrical equipment, and chemicals), with a strong agricultural base in the nearby blacklands, irrigated in the 1950s. The city was founded (1887) when Embree and Duck Creek, two rival railroad station communities, were amalgamated by an act of Congress. It was named for Attorney General Augustus H. Garland.

GARNER, John Nance "Cactus Jack" (Red River Co., Tex., Nov. 22, 1868 — Uvalde, Tex., Nov. 7, 1967). Vice President (1933-41) under Franklin D. Roosevelt. Admitted to the Texas bar in 1890, Garner served two terms in the state legislature (1898-1902) before being elected to the U.S. House of Representatives, where he remained for 30 years (1903-33). He supported the graduated income tax and the Federal Reserve system. In 1917, he was called one of the most influential politicians in Congress. He was named Speaker of the House in 1931, after serving as Democratic whip and floor leader. Garner was a candidate for the presidency at the 1932 Democratic National Convention but released his delegates to ensure Roosevelt's nomination, and became Vice President. He retired to his Texas ranch after finishing his second term as Roosevelt's Vice President

GARNET, Henry Highland (Kent County, Md., Dec. 23, 1815 — Monrovia, Liberia, Feb. 13, 1882). Clergyman and reformer. After escaping from slavery in 1824, Garnet moved to the North and was educated in New York State schools. A Presbyterian minister, Garnet became a popular abolitionist speaker. He lost his popularity, however, when he began advocating violence.

GARRETTSON, Freeborn (Maryland, Aug. 15, 1752 — Rhinebeck, N.Y., Sept. 26, 1827). Clergyman. After being ordained a Methodist minister in 1784 and having freed his slaves, Garrettson traveled through New England and parts of Canada organizing new churches. He was considered an important force in spreading the Methodist faith in America. He wrote *The Experience and Travels of Mr. Freeborn Garrettson* (1791).

GARY, Martin Witherspoon (Cokesbury, S.C., Mar. 25, 1831 — Edgefield, S.C., Apr. 9, 1881). Military officer. A Harvard graduate (1854), Gary won admission to the bar (1855), became a successful criminal lawyer, and was elected to the South Carolina legislature (1860), where he was a leader in the secession movement. During the Civil War, Gary fought in the Confederate Army. State senator from Edgefield Co. from 1876 to 1880, he was an unsuccessful candidate for U.S. senator.

GARZA-LITTLE ELM RESERVOIR, Tex. Man-made lake situated northwest of Dallas, Denton Co., in central Texas. Created by the construction of a dam to impound the Trinity River, it provides Dallas with much of its water supply and serves as a recreation area.

GASCONADE RIVER, Mo. Major waterway having its source in southern Missouri in the Ozark Mountains. The river passes east of Springfield and travels 265 miles northeast to the Missouri River. During early settlement days, lumber camps were established along the river to take advantage of the dense pine woods. The Gasconade is noted for its fishing.

GASTON, Lake, N.C./Va. Lake in Warren and Halifax Co., in northern North Carolina extending into Virginia . A 34-mile-long lake on the Roanoke River covering 20,300 acres, it is a major recreation spot for the city of Roanoke Rapids.

GASTON, William (New Bern, N.C., Sept. 19, 1778 — Raleigh, N.C., Jan. 23, 1844). Legislator and judge. Gaston was critical of U.S. military policies during the War of 1812 while in Congress (1813-17) and declined further national service. He was a justice of the North Carolina Supreme Court (1833-44) and was noted for his clear, liberal judgements.

GASTONIA, N.C. City (pop. 47,333), seat of Gaston Co., located in the southwestern corner of North Carolina, twenty miles west of Charlotte and eight miles north of the South Carolina border. Incorporated in 1877, Gastonia is a large cotton-milling center. Named for William Gaston, judge and congressman, it was the site of an important textile strike (1929) that resulted in the killing of a police chief and sentencing of seven union leaders for murder.

GATES, Horatio (Maldon, Essex, England, c. 1728 — New York, N.Y., Apr. 10, 1806). Revolutionary War general. Although he served with British forces in New York and Virginia in the 1750s, his interests were allied with the colonists. He returned to England, but upon hearing from George Washington that land was available in the Virginia colony, he set sail for America and arrived in 1772. Gates became a successful Virginia planter and, sympathetic to the patriots' cause, joined the Continental Army in 1775. In 1776 he was promoted to major general, and in 1777 he replaced Philip J. Schuyler as commander of the Northern Department. He gained a decisive victory over Britsh forces at the battle of Saratoga, but confusion arose over the time lapse involved in Gates' notification of the Saratoga victory, and he was accused of attempting to secure command of the entire Continental Army, a position held by Washington. Gates was relieved of his command until 1780 when he was put in charge of the Southern Department. He subsequently suffered a devastating defeat by Lord Charles Cornwallis at the battle of CAMDEN, S.C., on August 16, 1780. A proposed investigation of the defeat by Congress never took place. However, except for serving briefly in the army in 1782, Gates' military career was finished. Later, after freeing his slaves and selling his plantation, Gates settled in New York City and was a member of the New York State legislature.

GATES, John Warne (near Turner Junction, Ill., May 8, 1855 — Paris, France, Aug. 9, 1911). Speculator and industrialist. "Bet a million" Gates, as he was called, rose from a traveling salesman to become founder of the American Steel and Wire Company of New Jersey (1898), one of the leading trusts of his day. He was prominent in developing the area of Port Arthur, Texas.

GATES, Sir Thomas (Colyford, England, c. 1550 — East Indies, 1621). Colonial governor. A member of Sir Fancis Drake's expedition (1585-86), Gates became an investor in the Virginia Company and returned to Jamestown with new settlers in 1610. Finding the colonists in a deplorable state after the "starving time," he attempted to return them to England but was stopped by Lord de la Warr who arrived with fresh provisions. Gates continued back to England and, with his wife and daughters, returned to Jamestown in 1611 with new colonists and supplies. He remained and served as governor until 1614 and was largely responsible for the early success of the colony.

GATEWAY ARCH, Mo. A 630-foot stainless-steel arch which dominates the Jefferson National Expansion Memorial in St. Louis,

Mo. The arch was created by Eero Saarinen to commemorate the city's role as the "Gateway to the West."

GATLING, Richard Jordan (Hertford County, N.C., Sept. 12, 1818 — New York, N.Y., Feb. 26, 1903). Inventor and developer of the rapid-fire gun given his name. Gatling began working with his father devising machines for sowing and thinning cotton. He was a few months behind John Ericsson in patenting a screw propeller for steamboats (1838), but successfully adapted the cotton-sowing machine to planting other grains, revolutionizing the industry. Earning an M.D. (1850), he continued to invent inventions such as a hemp-breaking machine (1847) and a steam plow (1857). Federal acceptance of Gatling's 250-shot-per-minute gun came in 1866, just after the end of the Civil War. He later improved the gun to fire 1,200 shots a minute.

GAULEY RIVER, W.Va. A 75-mile waterway originating in Pocahontas Co. in east central West Virginia. The river flows southeast to drain into the Kanawha River at Gauley Bridge. Summerville Lake is found along the river.

GAYARRE, Charles Etienne Arthur (New Orleans, La., Jan. 9, 1805 — New Orleans, La., Feb. 11, 1895). Politician and historian. Gayarre experienced a successful political career, although beset by ill health, that included his election to the U.S. Senate (1835) but immediate resignation because of health, and his appointment as Louisiana Secretary of State (1846-53). His chief literary work was his four-volume *History of Louisiana* (1851-66).

GAYOSO DE LEMOS, Manuel (Spain, c. 1752 – Louisiana, July 18, 1799). Colonial official. Gayoso was a Spanish official in Louisiana who was appointed governor of the newly organized District of Natchez (1787). He was an advocate of separating the American West from the United States. Later, obeying secret orders from Spain, he managed to delay relinquishing the Natchez Region until 1798 despite U.S. possession in 1795.

GEORGE, James Zachariah (Monroe Co., Ga., Oct. 20, 1826 — Mississippi, Aug. 14, 1897). Confederate general, senator, and judge. He was a Democratic senator from Mississippi (1881-97), and as a member of the State Consti-

tutional Convention, George wrote the "grandfather clause" of the Mississippi constitution of 1890, which halted black suffrage. He helped draft the Sherman Antitrust Act (1890), and was a leader in the white supremacy movement after the Civil War.

GEORGE, Lake, Fla. Lake in Volusia and Putnam counties, in the northeastern part of the state. It is formed by a widening of the St. Johns River, running south to north for about 11 miles with a width of five to seven miles.

GEORGE C. MARSHALL SPACE FLIGHT CENTER, Ala. The National Aeronautics and Space Administration created this facility in HUNTSVILLE, Ala., in 1960. In 1982, it reported an annual payroll of $112 million, employing almost 4,000 persons. Its plants developed the rocketry which helped land the first manned ship on the moon.

GEORGE P. COLEMAN MEMORIAL BRIDGE, Va. Extending from Yorktown to Gloucester Point, it is the world's largest double-swing span bridge with two 500-foot swinging spans. It was named for George P. Coleman, the state's second highway commissioner.

GEORGETOWN, Ky. City (pop. 10,972), seat of Scott Co., in north central Kentucky. The community was first settled in 1776 as a pioneer station around Royal Spring, which still supplies water at a rate of about 1,000 gallons an hour. Royal Bridge was built in 1796 by the Reverand Elijah Craig and is believed to be the site where the first bourbon whiskey was produced in 1789. Georgetown is a processing center for this bluegrass farm region and is the site of Georgetown College (1787).

GEORGETOWN, Washington, D.C. Residential section at the junction of the Potomac River and Rock Creek. It was settled in the late 1600s, and incorporated as a city in 1789. The town had been part of the District of Columbia since 1871, but in 1878, with the revocation of its charter, it became a part of the city of Washington. Today, Georgetown is primarily a residential suburb of Washington. A section of Georgetown called the "Heights," known for its beautiful old homes and cobblestone streets, was preserved by an act of Congress in 1950. The city is the seat of both Georgetown University (1789) and the Georgetown Visitation Junior College (1799).

Georgia

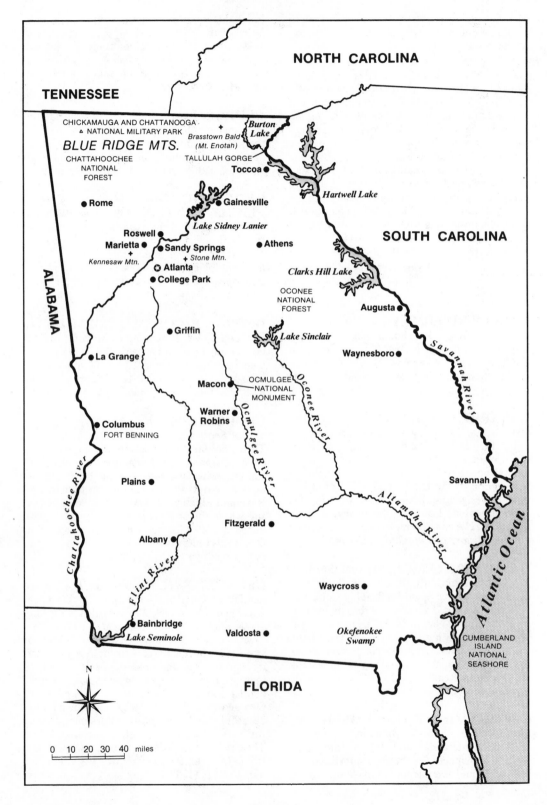

NORTH CAROLINA

TENNESSEE

CHICKAMAUGA AND CHATTANOOGA
△ NATIONAL MILITARY PARK

BLUE RIDGE MTS.

CHATTAHOOCHEE
NATIONAL
FOREST

Brasstown Bald
(Mt. Enotah)

Burton
Lake

TALLULAH GORGE

● Toccoa

Hartwell Lake

● Rome

● Gainesville

Lake Sidney Lanier

SOUTH CAROLINA

● Roswell
Marietta ●
+ Kennesaw Mtn.

● Sandy Springs
+ *Stone Mtn.*

● Athens

⊙ Atlanta
● College Park

Clarks Hill Lake

OCONEE
NATIONAL
FOREST

● Augusta

ALABAMA

● Griffin

Lake Sinclair

● Waynesboro

Savannah River

● La Grange

● Columbus
FORT BENNING

Macon ●

OCMULGEE
NATIONAL
MONUMENT

Warner ●
Robins

Ocmulgee River

Oconee River

Chattahoochee River

● Plains

Altamaha River

Savannah ●

● Fitzgerald

Albany ●

Flint River

Waycross ●

Atlantic Ocean

● Bainbridge
Lake Seminole

Valdosta ●

Okefenokee
Swamp

CUMBERLAND
ISLAND
NATIONAL
SEASHORE

N

FLORIDA

0 10 20 30 40 miles

STATE OF GEORGIA

Name: For George I (1683-1760), King of England (1727-1760).

Nickname: Peach State, Empire State of the South, Cracker State, Goober State, Buzzard State.

Motto: Wisdom, Justice and Moderation.

Capital: Atlanta.

Counties: 159. **Places over 10,000 population (1980):** 56.

Symbols & Emblems: *Flower:* Cherokee Rose. *Bird:* Brown Thrasher. *Tree:* Live Oak. *Song:* "Georgia On My Mind."

Population (1980): 5,464,265. **Rank:** 12th.

Population Density (1980): 94.1 people per sq. mi. **Rank** 22nd.

Racial Make-up (1980): *White:* 3,948,007 (72.3%). *Black:* 1,465,457 (26.8%). *American Indian:* 7,619 (0.2%). *Asian & Pacific Islander:* 24,461 (0.5%). *Other:* 18,721 (0.3%). *Spanish Origin:* 61,261 (1.1%).

Largest City (pop. 1980): Atlanta (425,022). *Others:* Columbus (169,441), Savannah (141,634), Macon (116,860), Albany (73,934), South Augusta (51,072), Augusta (47,532), Sandy Springs (46,877), Athens (42,549).

Area: 58,056 sq. mi. **Rank:** 21st.

Highest Point: Brasstown Bald Mountain (4,784 ft.), Towns/Union Cos.

Lowest Point: sea level, Atlantic Ocean.

State Government:
ELECTED OFFICIALS (4-year terms expiring Jan. 1987, etc.): *Governor* ($71,314); *Lt. Governor* ($41,496); *Sec. of State* ($51,896); *Attorney General* ($57,672); *Treasurer* ($41,310).

GENERAL ASSEMBLY (Salary: $7,200 plus $50 per diem for 40 regular session and 40 special session legislative days.): *Senate* (56 members), *House of Representatives* (180 members).

CONGRESSIONAL REPRESENTATIVES: *Senate* (terms expire 1985, 1987, etc.). *House of Representatives* (10 members).

Admitted to the Union: Jan. 2, 1788 (4th state to ratify the Constitution). One of the original 13 colonies.

GEORGIA. State on the lower Atlantic seaboard of the South. Its entire southern border is a slightly irregular land border with Florida. To the west Georgia has a border with Alabama that is formed by a surveyed line in the northern half and the Chattahoochee River in the southern half. Its short northern land borders are with Tennessee, to the northwest, and North Carolina, to the northeast. To the east Georgia has a border of almost 150 miles with South Carolina across the Savannah River and a coastline of approximately 100 miles on the Atlantic Ocean.

Georgia was the youngest and the most sparsely settled of the original 13 colonies that rebelled against the English in the Revolutionary War. It was also one of the crucial Southern states in the struggle of the American Civil War. Georgia, the largest state east of the Mississippi River, was also typical of the Southern states at the close of the Civil War: its economy was excessively reliant on one crop, cotton, and its political mechanisms were slow to adjust to the sudden suffrage of its substantial black population.

However, in the 20th century Georgia has emerged as a symbol of the "New South." It began the transition from an agricultural economy to an industrial one before any other state in the region. With the exception of Florida and Texas, which are special cases on the periphery of the region, Georgia has emerged as the most populous state in the deep South, except for North Carolina, and the fastest-growing state in population, with the exception of South Carolina. Atlanta has basically become the capital of the New South because of its contemporary financial importance, its role as a hub of air transportation routes within the region, and its great population and commercial growth in the 1970s. In that same decade Georgia, once considered a backwater preserve of field crops and magnolia-lined plantations, emerged as a force in U.S. national politics with the election of President Jimmy CARTER, the first President from the deep South since before the Civil War.

The lands of Georgia decline in elevation from its northern precincts toward its southern border with Florida. The extreme northern fringe of the state lies within the Blue Ridge Mountain region of the South. This is a sparsely populated and extremely scenic forested region of the state, one that includes the highest point in Georgia at BRASSTOWN BALD (4,784 feet) and numerous other points over 4,000 feet in elevation. From this region the state lands fall off to the Piedmont Plateau, 18,000 square miles of Georgia lands surrounding the north central city of Atlanta. The Piedmont, declining in elevation from an average of 2,000 feet in the north to an average of 1,000 feet in the south, includes most of the population centers and most of the manufacturing industries of the state. The southern half of Georgia consists of Atlantic Coastal Plain. The border between this region and the Piedmont is marked by the fall line hills, a band of river rapids and waterfalls flowing south that extends across the state on an east-northeast line from Columbus on the Alabama border, through the cental city of Macon and toward Augusta on the South Carolina border. South of this fall line, half of the Georgia state area consists of flatlands that once supported the vast cotton crop. Along the Atlantic coast, the lands of Georgia fall to elevations that permit flooding by the sea, resulting in a series of inland waterways and a belt of barrier islands like those found in South Carolina and North Carolina. In the extreme southeast of the state, along the Florida border, the lands of Georgia lie so low that the great OKEFENOKEE SWAMP of cyprus forests has spread over nearly 7,000 square miles.

The earliest known inhabitants of what is now Georgia were the mysterious Indian "mound builders" who created earthern lodges that are now preserved in Ocmulgee National Mounument near Macon. By the time of the European discovery and exploration of North America, Georgia's lands were controlled by the CHEROKEE INDIANS in the hilly northern regions and by the CREEK INDIANS in the flat southern regions. The first European to visit inland Georgia was Hernando DE SOTO of Spain, who traveled through a point near Macon in his journey to the Mississippi from Tampa Bay, Florida, in the early 1540s. By the late 1500s the Spanish, who founded St. Augustine, Fla., in 1565, had established missionary outposts on the Georgia coast, notably a Jesuit one at St. Catherine's Island. At first, their only competition for these lands came from the French, but it was the English who would successfully "plant" farmers in what is now Georgia.

The only British right to these lands was a dubious one established by the explorations of the Cabots in 1497-98. By the time of Charles II, however, British strongholds in Virginia were extending their control southward. In 1663, Charles II granted the lands south of Virginia to the "Eight Lords Proprietors" of Carolina, thus deliberately infringing on the claims of the Spanish in Florida. By 1700 the

British had effective, if not legal, control over the Georgia coast. In 1717 a utopian idealist named Sir Robert Montgomery proposed an asylum for debtors and religious dissenters to be located in the remote areas west of the Savannah River, and this proposal marks the beginnings of modern Georgia. In 1732 George II granted a charter for such an asylum to a group of concerned social reformers headed by James Edward OGLETHORPE, who named the region Georgia in honor of the monarch. A party of colonists was dispatched to the region to establish this settlement, and in 1733 they founded the city of Savannah. They fought with the Spanish for clear title to the lands until 1742, when the British victory at the Battle of Bloody Marsh pushed the Spanish south of the St. Mary's River on the present Florida border. Oglethorpe's dream of a haven for imprisoned debtors' and dissenters' was never realized, however, largely because of the failure of such commercial schemes as cultivating mulberry trees to create a silk trade, and he and his fellow philanthropists surrendered their charter in 1752.

As a royal colony subsequent to that date, Georgia entered the Revolutionary era predominantly loyalist but outraged by the 1763 proclamation that limited its western claims. It was only at the Continental Congress of 1776 that the colony finally espoused rebellion, and as the southernmost colony in the rebellion it soon became a crucial battleground. The British took SAVANNAH in December of 1778, repelled an atttack of patriots aided by the French navy in 1779, and held the city until the late months of 1782. Following the conclusion of the war in 1783, Georgia became the fourth state to ratify the constitution, which it did on January 2, 1788.

In the early years of statehood Georgia became economically prosperous because of the invention near Savannah of the cotton gin by Eli WHITNEY in 1793, which insured the efficient processing of its expanding cotton crop. Georgia also became an ardent proponent of states' rights over federal government in the same era. First the "Yazoo Fraud" beginning in 1795 led to the loss of land claims west of the Chattahoochee River, the present Alabama border, and then the failure of the federal government to honor an 1802 agreement to relocate Georgia's Indians to Oklahoma further alienated the state from the national government. While still prosperous because of the cotton crop, which required slave labor to harvest, Georgia had already become an antagonist of the politicians in Washington, D.C.

In the years before the Civil War, Georgia secessionists were kept in check by powerful Unionists such as Alexander H. STEPHENS, who would later become Vice President of the Confederacy and a critic of Confederate President Jefferson DAVIS. Radical abolitionist movements and the eventual election of Abraham Lincoln finally forced the cotton interest in the state to act on its own behalf, however, and on January 19, 1861, Georgia became the fifth state to secede from the Union. Coastal Georgia was soon effectively blockaded by the Union navy, and in 1862 Fort Pulaski fell to the Union forces. Although Georgia was the site of one of the great Confederate victories in 1863, at CHICAMAUGA, the state was devastated in 1864 by Union Gen. William Tecumseh Sherman's MARCH TO THE SEA. He laid seige to Atlanta in the summer of that year and the city fell on September 2. Sherman then marched southeast, destroying everything in his path, and captured Savannah in December, 1864.

Following the end of the war in April of 1865, Georgia effectively evaded the intervention of the CARPETBAGGERS from the North who manipulated and plundered some neighboring Confederate states. This enabled slavery factions to maintain their foothold in state politics, however, and their regressionist policies failed to offset the state war debt, encouraged inefficient sharecropping, abetted the insurrectionary activities of the KU KLUX KLAN, and left the state under military governorship until 1870. The subsequent failure to move out of a cotton crop economy and to guarantee legal voting rights to black citizens left Georgia for many decades in the throes of economic depression and social malaise. Northern interests had begun to construct factories on the Piedmont Plateau by the end of the 19th century, however, and these industries provided a base for economic recovery after the Great Depression of the 1930s. In 1946 the lowering of the voting age to 18 years and the abolition of the relic poll tax provided the political impetus for reform. The civil rights march to Albany, Ga., by Martin Luther KING, Jr., in 1962 and the segregationist governorship of Lester MADDOX begun in 1967 again threatened to make Georgia a symbol of entrenched conservatism, but the election as governor of future President Jimmy Carter in 1970 epitomized a new wave of progressivism that encouraged economic investment in the state.

Today maufacturing interests have made Georgia an increasingly urban state. Atlanta, in the center of its industrial Piedmont region, is a rapidly growing metropolitan area that includes more than one-third of the state's residents. The second-largest population seat is the textile center of MACON, also in central Georgia. Both COLUMBIA, on the Alabama border, and AUGUSTA, on the South Carolina border, are large metropolitan areas that include residents of neighboring states. Savannah, a city of historic landmarks, is the largest metropolitan area in coastal Georgia. The statewide population passed the 50% urban mark in 1960 and the 60% urban mark in 1970. In the 1970s a long tradition of emigration from Georgia, especially by black residents, was reversed by a net gain from immigration to Georgia of some 128,000 residents from other states. In 1980 Georgia's population was 27% black and 1% Hispanic.

Today the most important component of the Georgia state economy is the manufacture of metal and paper goods, chemicals, and textile products. Transportation equipment including aircraft is among the important heavy industries in the state, and naval stores such as resin, turpentine, and pine oil are among the leading traditional manufactures. The agricultural interests in the state have been tranformed since the increase in manufacturing and simultaneous BOLL WEEVIL blights of the 1920s. Once devoted to a vast crop of cotton, Georgia's farms now produce large amounts of poultry and eggs and harvest large crops of peanuts, corn, tobacco, and peaches. Finance, symbolized by the large number of corporate headquarters in Atlanta, is now an important sector of the state economy, and tourism in Georgia, especially to its coastal resorts and urban convention centers, is now a business that accounts for more than $2 billion per year.

GEORGIA, University of. Coed state institution, part of the university system of Georgia. The University of Georgia is located in Athens, a small city 65 miles east of Atlanta. Founded in 1785, the school is America's first state chartered university. The 350-acre campus had experienced restrained growth since its founding, but since 1950 academic offerings and facilities have multiplied dramatically.

Admission to the school is selective, even more so for out-of-state applicants, which the university does not actively seek. Academically, the University of Georgia consists of 13 undergraduate and graduate schools: Franklin College of Arts and Sciences; colleges of Agriculture, Business and Administration, Education; schools of Home Economics, Forest Resources, and the Henry W. Grady School of Journalism. Also offered are five-year degree programs in the schools of Pharmacy and Environmental Design. The South provides 93% of the students, Middle Atlantic 3%, North Central 2%, and 25% go on to further study.

Notable university facilities include many new buildings for science, ecology research, fine arts, and pharmacy. Recreationally, the school has a solid intramural and intercollegiate sports program. The cultural attractions of Atlanta are little more than an hour away.

Library: 1,985,646 volumes, 1,859,981 titles on microform, 12,500 journal subscriptions, 30,200 records/tapes. Faculty: 1,918. Enrollment: 23,462 total. Degrees: Bachelor's, Master's, Doctorate.

GEORGIA INSTITUTE OF TECHNOLOGY. Coed, land grant engineering school, part of the university system of Georgia. Located in Georgia's capital city of Atlanta, the institute has earned the reputation as one of the nation's finest engineering schools, and the South's most respected. Founded in 1885, this rapidly growing institution is noted not only for the quality of education it offers, but its unusually high percentage of black engineering students.

Admission to the school is very selective, and 98% of the institute's freshmen graduated in the top fifth of their high school class. The South provides 76% of the students, New England 11%, North Central 5%. A national student body is being sought. Academically, students may declare majors in 12 different engineering fields, textiles, mathematics, sciences, industrial management, and architecture, and 62% of degrees granted undergraduates are in engineering. Full-time graduate study is pursued by 25% of the institute's graduates. The institute is among the nation's top 100 producers of medical school entrants, and in developing business executives. Of the school's entire undergraduate body, 75% choose careers in business and industry. Academic facilities include the AC Network Calculator Laboratory Computing Center, the Architecture Building, and the 7,000-seat Alexander Memorial Coliseum, which boasts an unsupported dome cover. Recreationally and culturally, the school supports a strong sports program, and is famous for its football team. Campus activities and events are amply supplemented by those of Atlanta, a city of theaters, fine shops and restaurants, parks, music, and professional sports teams.

Library: 1,000,000 volumes, 1,365,000 microform titles, 6,200 journal subscriptions. Faculty: 662. Enrollment: 11,261 total. Degrees: Bachelor's, Master's, Doctorate.

GETTYSBURG, Battle of. Civil War engagement fought on July 1-3, 1863, in southern Pennsylvania ten miles north of the Maryland border. It was a fiercely contested battle, ultimately won by the North. The defeat ended Gen. Robert E. LEE'S second attempt to invade the North, and for this reason it is considered by many modern historians to have been the turning point in the Civil War. Lee's Gettysburg campaign was an attempt to move the eastern theater of war from Virginia to the Cumberland Valley of Pennsylvania. He started north from Fredericksburg on June 3, leaving Gen. J.E.B. STUART's troops south of the Potomac River in Maryland to occupy the Union army under Gen. George Meade. On June 24 Stuart attempted to move around Meade toward the east to rejoin Lee in Pennsylvania. In doing so he managed to capture Union supplies, but he also lost contact with Lee and so arrived in Gettysburg too late to influence the outcome of the battle.

On July 1 the battle commenced with the Confederate army northwest of Gettysburg and the Union army southeast of it. In the first cavalry engagements the Union army was driven back, but in retreat it occupied the strategic high ground of Cemetery Ridge. On July 2 the Confederate attack was delayed until 4:00 P.M., allowing the North to regroup. On this second day of battle, the Union army successfully defended Cemetery Ridge and also occupied high ground at Round Top and Little Round Top, farther south. On July 3 Meade counterattacked, shrewdly anticipating Lee's full assault on Cemetery Ridge. Lee's attack finally took the form of "Pickett's charge," although Gen. George E. PICKETT did not, in fact, lead it. This cavalry assault broke the Union line on Cemetery Ridge, but it was soon driven back with heavy casualties because of a lack of support troops.

Heavy rain on the next day, the Fourth of July, allowed Lee to retreat with his demoralized troops and prevented effective pursuit by Meade. Although victorious, the Union army had lost more men, some 14,500, than the Confederate army. Four months later, on November 19, 1863, Abraham Lincoln dedicated the national cemetery on the battlefield with his "Gettysburg Address."

GIBBONS, James (Baltimore, Md., July 23, 1834 — Baltimore, Md., Mar. 24, 1921). Clergyman and author. He was ordained a Roman Catholic priest in 1861, consecrated bishop of Richmond, Va., in 1872, and appointed the second American cardinal by Pope Leo XIII in 1886. He wrote *The Faith of Our Fathers* (1876), still one of the most popular apologetics published in the U.S. A regular contributor to national magazines, author of five theological books, and first Chancellor of the Catholic University of American (1889), Cardinal Gibbons was praised by President Theodore Roosevelt as one of the most respected and valuable Americans of his time.

GIBSON, Randall Lee (Woodford Co., Ky., Sept 10, 1832 — Hot Springs, Ark., Dec. 15, 1892). Confederate general, congressman, and educator. A lawyer and sugar planter in Louisiana, Gibson served as an officer in the Civil War, mostly in the western campaigns. He was a Democratic member of the House of Representatives (1873-85) and the U.S. Senate (1883-92) from Louisiana. Gibson was involved in promoting navigation improvements of the Mississippi River and helped create the Mississippi River Commission in 1879. He helped reorganize the University of Louisiana as TULANE UNIVERSITY and was the first president of its board of administrators.

GILDERSLEEVE, Basil Lanneau (Charleston, S.C., Oct. 12, 1831 — Baltimore, Md., Jan. 9, 1924). Philologist. After studying at Princeton, Berlin, Bonn, and Gottingen, Gildersleeve began a career at the University of Virginia (1856-76), later becoming professor of Greek at the new Johns Hopkins University (1876-1915). His *Latin Grammar* (1867) provides a clear, thorough coverage of grammatical theory and his mastery of the patterns of Greek language was demonstrated in *Syntax of Classical Greek from Homer to Demosthenes* (2 vols. 1900, 1911). He was considered the finest classical scholar of his time in America.

GILES, William Branch (Amelia Co., Va., Aug. 12, 1762 — Amelia Co., Va., Dec. 4, 1830). Politician. A lawyer, Giles was U.S. representative (1790-1798) as an anti-Federalist, as a Democrat (1801-03), and U.S. senator (1804-15). He was an opponent of Alexander

Hamilton's proposal for the Bank of the United States and unsuccessfully brought charges of corruption against Hamilton. He was governor of Virginia (1827-30), and was reelected in 1830 but declined to serve.

GILLEM, Alvan Cullem (Jackson Co., Tenn., July 29, 1830 — Nashville, Tenn., Dec. 2, 1875). Military officer. Gillem saw service in the Union Army in Tennessee during the Civil War and advanced to the rank of major general. After the war, he played an important role in the reorganization of the Tennessee state government and during RECONSTRUCTION he was in command of the military in Arkansas and Mississippi.

GILLESPIE, John Birks "Dizzy" (Cheraw, S.C., Oct. 21, 1917 —). Jazz musician. Gillespie began playing the trumpet as a teenager and went on to study at the Laurinburg Institute, N.C. He played with jazz greats Earl Hines and Billy Eckstein, among others, before forming his own band in 1946. Considered one of the leaders of the bebop movement in jazz, he has made U.S. State Department cultural tours and is well known abroad. He currently has his own quintet and is featured on many records. He is the author of *To Be Or Not. . . To Bop* (1979).

GILMER, Elizabeth Meriwether (Dorothy Dix) (Montgomery Co., Tenn., Nov. 18, 1861 — New Orleans, La., Dec. 16, 1951). Journalist. In 1894 she began writing for the New Orleans *Daily Picayune* and in 1895 started her own weekly column of social satire under the pen name "Dorothy Dix." In 1901 she won national attention for her reporting on CARY NATION for William Randolf Hearst and began covering crime news for his *New York Journal* (1901-17). She then returned to New Orleans to devote full time to her "Dorothy Dix" advice column (1917-49) drawing up to 60 million readers. Gilmer also wrote several books.

GILMER, Thomas Walker (Albemarle Co., Va., Apr. 6, 1802 — aboard the *Princeton*, Feb. 28, 1844). Statesman. A practicing lawyer until his election to the Virginia legislature, Gilmer was later elected governor of the state (1840). After a term in Congress (1841-44) he was appointed secretary of the Navy in 1844. His death, along with the deaths of other public officials, as the result of a gun explosion aboard the *Princeton* (1844), brought about the question of succession to the presidency in case of a common disaster.

GILMOR, Harry (Baltimore, Md., Jan. 24, 1838 — Mar. 4, 1883). Military officer. During the Civil War Gilmor effectively led a small Confederate cavalry unit against Union forces in the Shenandoah Valley, and was responsible, against his wishes, for the burning of Chambersburg, Pa. He wrote *Four Years in the Saddle* (1866).

GILMORE, Patrick Sarsfield (County Galway, Ireland, Dec. 25, 1829 — St. Louis, Mo., Sept. 24, 1892). Bandleader and composer. Immigrating to the U.S. in 1849, Gilmore led several bands before he took over the Boston Brigade Band in 1859. His entire band enlisted in the Union Army during the Civil War. A virtuoso cornet player, he was noted for his 1869 and 1872 performances in which he led 10,000 performers with church bells, cannon fire, and a 100-piece Anvil Chorus. Considered the leading U.S. bandmaster of the 19th century, Gilmore is credited with composing "When Johnny Comes Marching Home" (1863).

GIST, Christopher (Maryland, c. 1706 — S.C.?, Ga.?, 1759). Explorer and frontiersman. As an agent for the Ohio Company, Gist explored the Kentucky and Virginia territories, including much of the Ohio River Valley. He served as a guide to both George Washington and Gen. Edward Braddock in later trips.

GIST, William Henry (Charleston, S.C., Aug. 22, 1807 — Union District, S.C., Sept. 30, 1874). Politician. A wealthy plantation owner, Gist was elected to the lower house of the state legislature (1840-44). He became a member of the state senate (1844-56) and then was elected governor (1858-60), advocating state secession.

GLASGOW, Ellen Anderson Gholon (Richmond, Va., Apr. 22, 1873 — Richmond, Va., Nov. 21, 1945). Novelist. Glasgow was instrumental in moving Southern regional fiction away from romantic stereotypes toward a more realistic treatment of social predicaments specific to the modern South. She achieved her first critical success with *The Battle-Ground* (1902), a novel that challenged the notion that the Confederate Army consisted entirely of gentlemen. Other novels satirical of Southern chivalric pretensions include *Barren Ground* (1925) and *The Romantic Comedians* (1926). She is now appreciated for her insight into the social status of women, notably in the novel *The Sheltered Life* (1932) and the posthumously published *The Woman Within* (1954). Her novel *In This Our Life* (1941) won the Pulitzer Prize in 1942.

GLASS, Carter (Lynchburg, Va., Jan. 4, 1858 — Washington, D.C., May 28, 1946). Politician. After a long career in journalism, Glass entered Washington politics and stayed until his death at age 88. As a member of the U.S. House of Representatives from Virginia (1902-18) he was responsible for framing and sponsoring the Federal Reserve Act of 1913. In 1918 he was appointed Secretary of the Treasury by President Woodrow Wilson. In 1920 he filled a U.S. Senate seat and retained that position until 1946. In the Senate, Glass supported Franklin Roosevelt for election in 1932 and continued to support him in foreign policy decisions. However, Glass objected strongly to the New Deal, and many other of Roosevelt's domestic policies. The Glass-Steagall Act (1933) was an important piece of legislation that established the now-familiar Federal Deposit Insurance Corporation, separated commercial banks from investment banking, and put restraints on bank speculation.

GLENBURNIE, Md. Unincorporated town (pop. 37,263), Anne Arundel Co., in west central Maryland. A residential suburb south of Baltimore, Glenburnie was named for a major landholder in the 1880s. It is located on the Patapsco River.

GOLDSBORO, N.C. City (pop. 31,871), seat of Wayne Co., located in east central North Carolina 50 miles southeast of Raleigh on the north bank of the Neuse River. Primarily a railway shipping depot and market for the coastal plain area, it was named for a prominent railway engineer, M. C. Goldsborough. Though the city contains diverse manufacturing plants, its primary industry is bright leaf tobacco. Near the end of the Civil War Goldsboro was the point at which the armies of Union Gens. Herman and Scholfield united prior to their march on Durham in 1865.

GOLDSBOROUGH, Louis Malesherbes (Washington, D.C., Feb. 18, 1805 — Washington, D.C., Feb. 20, 1877). Admiral. He commanded the North Atlantic Blockading Squadron that harried the Virginia and North Carolina coasts (1861-62). Promoted to rear admiral for capturing Roanoke Island in February, 1862, Goldsborough resigned command due to a dispute over the Battle of Richmond. He earlier served as a commissioner to explore California and Oregon (1849-50) and as superintendent of the U.S. Naval Academy at Annapolis, Md. (1853-57).

GOLIAD, Massacre of. Slaughter of Texans fighting for independence from Mexico. During the War of Texas Independence, Goliad, on the San Antonio River in southeast Texas was taken by Texas rebels on October 12, 1835. It was then evacuated after the fall of the Alamo on March 6, 1836. Later in the same month a force of Texans under James W. FANNIN was captured near Goliad while attempting to invade Mexico. More than 300 of them, including Fannin, were shot by Mexican troops on orders from Mexican Gen. Jose Urrea on March 27, 1836.

GOOCH, Sir William (Yarmouth, England, Oct. 21, 1681 — Bath, England, Dec. 17, 1751). Colonial governor. Although appointed lieutenant governor, Gooch was actually the chief executive of the Virginia colony during his term (1727-49). He ruled with equity and was instrumental in promoting the production of tobacco. In 1746 he was knighted and in 1747 was made a major general. His return to England was due to ill health.

GOODNIGHT, Charles (Macoupin Co., Ill., Mar. 5, 1836 — Tucson, Ariz., Dec. 12, 1929). Texas cattleman and Indian scout. After a distinguished career as a Texas Ranger and trailblazer, Goodnight became one of the first cattle ranchers in New Mexico and Colorado. In 1877 he and John Adair set up a 1-million-acre ranch with 100,000 head of cattle in the Texas Panhandle, and three years later he organized the Panhandle Stockmen's Association to curb rustling and promote purebred cattle. He was also involved in breeding experiments with beef cattle and buffalo.

GORDON, John Brown (Upson Co., Ga., Feb. 6, 1832 — Miami, Fla., Jan. 9, 1904). Military officer and politician. Gordon's leadership during the Civil War in the Confederate WILDERNESS CAMPAIGN and Shenandoah Valley Campaign (1864) was outstanding and contributed to his rise from captain to lieutenant general. Gordon returned to his law practice in Georgia following the war and soon became an influential Democrat in state politics. He was U.S. senator from Georgia (1873-80; 1891-97) and governor (1886-90). In 1890 he organized the United Confederate Veterans and served as its commander-in-chief until his death.

GORGAS, William Crawford (Mobile, Ala., Oct. 3, 1854 — London, England, July 3, 1920). Physician. A sanitary expert, Gorgas' programs for mosquito control reduced yellow fever and malaria in Havana (1898-1902) and Panama (1904), facilitating the construction of the Panama Canal. In 1914 he was appointed surgeon general of the U.S. Army, and two years later became an adviser to the International Health Board.

GORMAN, Arthur Pue (Woodstock, Md., Mar. 11, 1839 — Washington, D.C., June 4, 1906). Politician. Gorman held various state offices before his election in 1880 to the U.S. Senate. He was minority leader of the Senate (1889-93, 1895-98, 1903-06), and majority leader (1893-95). A Democratic leader, Gorman ran Grover Cleveland's presidential campaign. He co-authored the Wilson-Gorman Tariff Act of 1894.

GOSPEL MUSIC. An American musical form derived from traditional English hymns blended with 19th century popular music. In the 19th and early 20th centuries, many of the gospel singers, such as Homer Rodeheaver (1880-1955), were associated with the touring entourages of such prominent evangelists as Billy Sunday (1862-1935). Black gospel music evolved from white gospel traditions combined with spirituals and Afro-American rhythms. The black gospel tradition became firmly rooted in Southern church services and revival meetings during the early 20th century and developed concurrently with the other black musical forms—JAZZ, RAGTIME and BLUES. As the music became more sophisticated, and as professional composers and performers began to replace the folk traditions and amateurs who preceded them, both white and black gospel began to evolve into the more popular forms known today. Increased publication of gospel songs, recordings and local concerts further increased the popularity of the forms but this enthusiasm reached much larger proportions with the arrival of radio in the 1920s. These years saw the rise of many who retain their fame in

gospel circles: the Speer Family, particularly Tom "Dad" (1891-1966) and Lena Brock "Mom" (1900-67); the Stamps, Frank (1898-1965) and Virgil (V.O.) (1892-1940); George Bennard (1873-1958), composer of "Old Rugged Cross"; and the publishing Vaughan family of James D. (1864-1941) and Glenn Kieffer (1893-1969).

After World War II, the popularity of gospel music continued unabated, covering a wide range from the black, bluesy music of Mahalia Jackson (1911-72) to the pop music style of Pat Boone (1934–). Among the many others who have set their stamp on the form are the Blackwood Brothers, the Florida Boys, Evie Tornquist, the Bill Gaither Trio and the members of The Happy Goodman Family.

GOTTSCHALK, Louis Moreau (New Orleans, La., May 8, 1929 — Tijuca, Brazil, Dec. 18, 1869). Pianist and composer. One of the first U.S. pianists to achieve international recognition, and the first U.S. composer to utilize Latin-American and Creole folk themes and rhythms. His compositions include "Gran Tarantella," and "La Bamboula."

GOUCHER COLLEGE. Independent, liberal arts college for women located eight miles north of downtown Baltimore, Md. Founded in 1885, Goucher moved from its original Baltimore site to its present 330-acre location in 1950. Goucher is one of the few prestigious women's colleges that did not become coeducational during the 1960s and 1970s. This decision has not hurt the college's excellent reputation and the school continues to attract high-caliber female applicants from all over the country, and from many foreign countries.

Admission is very selective, with 69% of those enrolling from the Middle Atlantic states, 10% New England, 8% South, and 4% North Central. The school offers students a well-balanced selection of majors, including the usual arts and sciences, performing arts, education, international relations, premedical studies, and dance therapy. In addition to undergraduate programs, a Master of Arts program is offered in art therapy and dance movement therapy. All Goucher students are eligible, at no extra cost, to take courses at such area colleges as Johns Hopkins (a school with which Goucher enjoys extensive academic and social exchanges), Loyola College, Maryland Institute College of Art, Towson State University, Morgan State University, the College of Notre Dame of Maryland, Baltimore Hebrew College, and Essex Community College. After graduation 16% of Goucher students pursue full-time graduate study, 4% enter law school, 4% medical school, 1% dental school, 5% business school.

Library: 219,085 volumes, 6,662 microfilm titles, 875 journal subscriptions, 5,171 records/tapes. Faculty: 133. Enrollment: 900 (full-time); 120 (part-time). Degrees: Bachelor's, Master's.

GOURGUES, Dominique de (Mont-de-Marsan, Landes, France, c. 1530 — Tours, France, 1593). French soldier. To revenge the 1565 Spanish massacre of the Florida Huguenot colony of Jean RIBAUT, Gorgues, in charge of three ships, and with Indian support, captured Spanish forts along the Florida coast, putting hundreds to death.

GRADY, Henry Woodfin (Athens, Ga., May 24, 1850 — Atlanta, Ga., Dec. 23, 1889). Journalist and orator. Grady's speeches, notably "The New South" (1886), attempted to lessen tension between the states after the Civil War. Beginning his career in journalism after writing, as a student, a letter to the *Atlanta Constitution* that revealed his considerable talent, he edited several small papers and then took an assignment as Georgia correspondent for the *New York Herald*. He later bought an interest in and edited the *Atlanta Constitution* (1879-89).

GRAFTON, W.Va. Town (pop. 6,845), seat of Taylor Co., in northern West Virginia. The town was settled in 1852 and incorporated in 1856. An important rail center during the Civil War, the first land soldier to be killed in that war was shot here. The celebration of Mother's Day began here in 1908 when a local woman observed the anniversary of her mother's death. There are coal mines, diversified agriculture, and many factories producing prefabricated homes, boxes, and plastic goods.

GRAHAM, William Franklin "Billy" (Charlotte, N.C., Nov. 7, 1918 —). Evangelist and author. Called the most widely-known evangelist of the 20th century, Graham was ordained by the Southern Baptist Church (1939), prior to receiving his undergraduate degree from Wheaton College, Ill. (1943). He soon turned to the wider ministry of evangelism, more fully using his dynamic style of preaching. Beginning with an eight-week revival in Los Angeles, Cal., (1949), his audiences numbered in the hundreds of thousands and sometimes millions. Graham extended his ministry to Europe and England (1954) and has preached in Australia, Africa, the Middle East, and Russia. A personal counselor to Presidents, Grahams's mass appeal has helped to unify Protestants of many denominations.

GRAMBLING STATE UNIVERSITY. State-supported coed institution located in the village of Grambling, La., 60 miles east of Shreveport. Founded as a college for Negroes in 1901, Grambling still has a predominantly black student population. The University is probably most famous for its sports programs, particularly intercollegiate football. For years, Grambling has supplied U.S. professional football teams with an unusually high percentage of young players.

Academically, Grambling confers most of its degrees in Education, Business and Management, Public Affairs and Services, Social Sciences, and Engineering. After graduation 4% of Grambling students go on to further study. The vast majority, 79%, of undergraduates are Louisiana residents.

The 340-acre campus is a spacious one, dotted with playing fields, over fifty buildings, a large farm, and a stadium.

Library: 177,962 volumes, 1,217 journal subscriptions. Faculty: 200. Enrollment: 1,580 men, 1,630 women (full-time). Degrees: Associate's, Bachelor's, Master's.

GRAND OLE OPRY. A country and western music show that originates from Nashville, Tenn. The weekly performances are held at the Grand Ole Opry House. Its music center at Opryland is part of an entertainment park. Regular radio broadcasts of the show began in 1925.

GRAND PRAIRIE, Tex. City (pop. 71,462), Dallas, Ellis, and Tarrant Counties, located in northeast Texas. Part of the Dallas-Fort Worth metropolitan area, Grand Prairie was founded at the end of the Civil War. Home of the Texas Sports Hall of Fame, its manufactures today include industrial supplies, tanks, pipes, bottling, trailers, and aerospace equipment.

GRAND RIVER, Mo. River beginning in southwest central Iowa, near Creston. It travels southeast 215 miles through Missouri's northwest corner to meet the Missouri River, south of Brunswick.

The 4,400-seat Grand Ole Opry House in Nashville, Tenn.

GRANDVIEW, Mo. City (pop. 24,502), Jackson Co., in western Missouri south of Kansas City. A residential suburb of Kansas City, Grandview also lies in a farm region, producing corn and wheat. Incorporated in 1929, Richards-Gebaur Air Force Base is nearby.

GRANT, Ulysses Simpson (Point Pleasant, Ohio, Apr. 27, 1822 — Mt. McGregor, N.Y., July 23, 1885). Union general in the Civil War and 18th President of the United States. The son of a tanner, Grant was named Hiram Ulysses at birth but dropped the first name upon muster at West Point in 1839. Graduated from the U.S. Military Academy in 1843, he served with Zachary Taylor in the Mexican War but was forced to resign from the armed forces in 1854 because of his drinking. At the outbreak of the Civil War he was a failed businessman of no immediate interest to the draft boards formed by President Abraham Lincoln, but was finally enlisted in 1861 in the 21st Illinois Volunteers by a Union Army desperate for trained officers.

Grant was an untutored and relatively inarticulate tactician whose uncanny brilliance at SHILOH, VICKSBURG, and CHATTANOOGA brought him the appointment of Supreme Commander of the Union army in October of 1863. A shabby man in personal appearance, he presided with systematic authority and unflinching calculation over a Union campaign that brought him the surrender of Gen. Robert E. Lee at Appomattox Court House on Apr. 9, 1865.

Nominated for Secretary of State by President Andrew Johnson after the war, Grant was never approved by Congress for that office. He later parted ways with Johnson but was nevertheless elected President on the Republican ticket of 1868 and then reelected in 1872. Both administrations were marred by the ravages of RECONSTRUCTION and by corruption, although Grant himself never benefited by any of the graft that was rampant during his tenure in office. At the end of his life he was financially ruined, writing his memoirs for the future benefit of his family and petitioning the military for a resumption of his resigned commission for the pension it would bring his heirs.

GRASTY, Charles Henry (Fincastle, Va., Mar. 3, 1863 — London, England, Jan. 14,

1924). Editor and publisher. He was editor and publisher of the Baltimore *News* (1892-1908) and the Baltimore *Sun* (1910-14), where he warned against municipal corruption. During World War I Grasty was an important foreign correspondent for the Associated Press and the New York *Times*.

GRAVES, Dixie Bibb (Montgomery, Ala., July 26, 1882 — Montgomery, Ala., Jan. 21, 1965). Politician. Active in civic affairs, she was appointed as a Democrat in 1937 to fill a U.S. Senate vacancy brought about by the resignation of Hugo Black to serve on the Supreme Court.

GRAYSON, Cary Travers (Culpepper Co., Va., Oct. 11, 1878 — Washington, D.C., Feb. 15, 1938). Naval officer and surgeon. A graduate of the Navy medical school, he attained the rank of rear admiral and was personal physician to three Presidents, Theodore Roosevelt, William Taft, and Woodrow Wilson. In 1935 he was chairman of the American Red Cross.

GREAT APPALACHIAN VALLEY REGION. A chain of lowlands of the Appalachian Mountains that extends from Canada to Alabama ranging in width from eight to 53 miles, with an average elevation of 600 to 800 feet. Also know as the Great Valley, much of this area in the South was held by the Cherokee Indian Nation until 1838. The Georgia section is drained by the Etowah and Oostanaula Rivers. It features Amicolala Falls and Mount Oglethorpe.

GREAT BRIDGE, Battle of. Revolutionary War action fought nine miles from Norfolk, Va., on December 9, 1775. It was the first engagement of the war after Bunker Hill in Boston and the first Revolutionary War battle in the South. The patriot forces near Norfolk were commanded by Col. William Woodford, and the royal governor of Virginia, John Murray Dunmore, attempted to quell their resistance at Great Bridge. According to legend, Dunmore was tempted from an impregnable position by misleading information delivered by a servant of Maj. Thomas Marshall. Marshall's son, John, later Chief Justice, was also present at the battle. When Dunmore's Tory soldiers attempted to advance, they were repelled in an action lasting less than 25 minutes. The patriots killed 13 of the Tories and captured munitions without losing a man.

GREAT FALLS LAKE, Tenn. A 22-mile-long artificial reservoir near Kingsport in extreme northeastern Tennessee near the Virginia border. Constructed by the Tennessee Valley Authority, it impounds the Caney Fork of the Cumberland River.

GREAT PLAINS, Tex. A vast region stretching from the north central plains into New Mexico with the Llano Estacado forming the border between Texas and New Mexico and the Edward Plateau bordering its south. This semi-arid, treeless expanse is largely on a high plateau, with elevations ranging from 2,000 to 6,000 feet. The Texas Panhandle, which occupies a large section of the Great Plains is mostly used as a grazing area. Several rivers including the Canadian run through this area.

GREAT SMOKY MOUNTAINS. The western portion of the Appalachian Mountains, they extend from Ashville, N.C., to Knoxville, Tenn. The highest point is CLINGMAN'S DOME (6,642 feet), named for Thomas Lanier Clingman, a geologist who explored the area in the mid-1800s. Once a headaquarters of the CHEROKEE INDIANS, the mountains are named for the blue haze covering their upper regions.

GREAT SMOKY MOUNTAINS NATIONAL PARK. Located in eastern Tennessee and northern North Carolina, the park covers 273,000 acres in North Carolina and 236,000 acres in Tennessee. Established in 1930, this is a popular tourist area that occupies the area between the Little Tennessee and Pigeon Rivers. Originally established to preserve its hardwood forest, it covers the highest elevation area of the Great Smoky Mountains.

GREAT VALLEY PROVINCE, Va. One of the five physiographical areas of the state. Often referred to as the Valley of Virginia, it lies west of the Blue Ridge and varies in width from 35 miles in the north (to the West Virginia line) to 100 miles in the south (near the Tennessee border). It is a series of valleys, probably the best known of which is the Shenandoah in the north.

GREEN, Duff (Woodford, Co., Ky., Aug. 15, 1791 — Dalton, Ga., June 10, 1875). Political journalist and member of President Andrew Jackson's advisory circle, known as the "kitchen cabinet." A veteran of the War of 1812, Green moved to Missouri where he became a government surveyor and mail contractor and served in the state legislature. When he became the owner of the St. Louis *Enquirer*, he supported Jackson for the 1824 run for the presidency and in 1825 purchased the *United States Telegraph*, a Washington, D.C.-based periodical which became the chief organ of the Jacksonian Democrats. Jackson appointed him congressional printer in 1828 but Green left Jackson's circle in 1831 to support John C. Calhoun. In April, 1842, John Tyler, successor to the presidency after the death of William Henry Harrison, appointed him the unofficial representative to England, where his political articles were widely read. Green established *The Republic* in New York upon his return from abroad (1844), editorially supporting the South and slavery, free trade, railroad construction, and the U.S. acquisition of California, Oregon, and Texas.

GREEN, Paul Eliot (Lillington, N.C., Mar. 17, 1894 — Chapel Hill, N.C., May 4, 1981). Playwright. Green is noted for realistic dramas portraying the life of blacks and white tenant farmers in the South. He won the 1927 Pulitzer prize for best American play for *In Abraham's Bosom* (1926), but is best remembered for *Johnny Johnson*, with music by Kurt Weill (1936) and *Native Son*, in collaboration with Richard Wright (1941).

GREEN COVE SPRINGS, Fla. Town (pop. 4,154), seat of Clay Co., in northeast Florida on the west bank of the St. John's River. A small resort community popular because of its mineral springs, it was a fashionable spa in the late 19th century. Settled in 1830, its developers included condensed-milk manufacturer Gail Borden and chain store magnate J. C. Penney. There is also some farming, commercial fishing, and lumbering here.

GREEN RIVER, Ky. Rising in central Kentucky, travels west-northwest to meet the Ohio River near Evansville, Ind. The longest river in the state (770 miles), the Green is an important trade and transportation route. Much of Kentucky's coal barge traffic traverses the river, which runs through several large commercial and industrial communities.

GREEN SPRING, Battle of. Revolutionary War engagement fought near Williamsburg, Va., on July 6, 1781. In it British Commander Lord Charles Cornwallis repelled, but failed to defeat decisively, the Revolutionary forces of Marquis de LAFAYETTE and Anthony WAYNE. In the events leading to the seige of YORKTOWN, Cornwallis was preparing to abandon WILLIAMSBURG and move south across the James River. Knowing he was pursued by Lafayette, Cornwallis shammed operations to ford the river while preparing to defend Green Spring on the north bank. By the time Lafayette discovered this, an advance guard under Wayne had entered the trap. Lafayette rescued Wayne at some cost, and Cornwallis was denied a more decisive victory only by the fall of darkness, which protected the American forces.

GREENBELT, Md. City (pop. 16,000), Prince George's Co., in west central Maryland. A suburb of Washington, D.C., chartered in 1937, it is a modern community that was planned and built by the U.S. Government as a model experimental city. Completed in 1938, early residents were mostly federal employees attracted by the low-priced housing. Goddard Space Flight Center is located here.

GREENBRIAR RIVER, W.Va. Source in eastern West Virginia, coursing 175 miles southwest, paralleling the Virginia border. Near Hinton it meets the New River to enter the Bluestone Reservoir.

GREENEVILLE, Tenn. Town (pop. 14,097), seat of Greene Co., in eastern Tennessee. Founded in 1783, Greeneville was the capital of the short-lived Free State of FRANKLIN during its last two years. It was also the home of President Andrew JOHNSON, from which he began his political career. There are large tobacco warehouses and factories produce radios, televisions, and electronic equipment. Tusculum College (1794), the Davy Crockett Tavern, and Pioneer Museum are found here.

GREENSBORO, N.C. City (pop. 155,642), seat of Guilford Co., located in north central North Carolina 75 miles northwest of Raleigh. Experiencing great growth in population during the past few decades, Greensboro has over 250 industrial plants producing more than 130 products. Incorporated in 1837, the city is named for Gen. Nathaniel Greene, who led the Revolutionary troops in the Battle of Guilford Court House (1781), now the site of a national military park. Greensboro is the home of several colleges: Agricultural and Technical College of North Carolina (1891), Bennett College (1873), Greensboro College (1838), Guilford College (1834), Immanuel Lutheran College (1903), and the Greensboro branch of the University of NORTH CAROLINA (1891). Greensboro is also the birth place of O. HENRY (William S. Porter) (1862-1910).

GREENVILLE, Miss. City (pop. 40,613), seat of Washington Co., located on the east shore of the Mississippi River opposite Arkansas. Site of a $6-million bridge, protected by levees, and surrounded by rich delta land, Greenville produces the major portion of the state's cotton. Built on low-lying land, parts of the original settlement eroded into the river, other sections were burned by Union soldiers during the Civil War. A break in the delta north of Greenville flooded a 7,500-square-mile area in 1927, which resulted in extensive federal flood control projects. Hodding CARTER, winner of the Pulitzer Prize (1946), edited the *Greenville Delta Democrat-Times* here. In addition to cotton, present industries include livestock, chemicals, and rug manufacture.

GREENVILLE, S.C. City (pop. 58,242), seat of Greenville Co., located in northwest South Carolina in the foothills of the Blue Ridge Mountains. It was originally founded as the village of Pleasantburg (1786) and renamed Greenville in 1831. Power from the Reedy River changed it to an industrial city. It is near Paris Mountain State Park, and is the home of Furman University (1827) and Bob Jones University (1927). The present economy is based on retail outlets and manufacture of textiles and chemicals.

GREENVILLE, Tex. Town (pop. 22,161), seat of Hunt Co., in northeastern Texas. Located in a cotton-producing area, Greenville was once the location of one of the world's largest inland compressses for making cotton bales. Food processing and the manufacture of electronic parts are important to Greenville's present economy.

GREENWOOD, Lake, S.C. Artificial lake touching several counties in western South Carolina. This 25-mile-long lake was formed by impounding the Reedy River; it empties into the Saluda River in the southeast.

GREENWOOD, Miss. City (pop. 20,115), seat of Leflore Co., located in northwest Mississippi at the junction of the Tallachatchie and Yalobusha Rivers. Settled by John Williams in 1834 and incorporated 1844, Greenwood was an important shipping station for cotton bound for New Orleans. It was named for Greenwood Leflore, a Choctaw chief, plantation owner, and slave holder. Today it is an important grain storage center.

GREENWOOD, S.C. City (pop. 21,613), seat of Greenwood Co., in western South Carolina between the Saluda and Savannah Rivers. Settled by the Irish in 1824, Greenwood developed as a textile, manufacturing, and railroad center. Manufactures include cotton goods and surgical dressings; corn, cotton, and peaches are grown. Greenwood is the home of Lander College (1872), Greenwood Museum, and a state park.

GREERS FERRY DAM, Ark. A dam impounding the Little Red River in north central Arkansas, creating Greers Ferry Lake.

GREGG, Forrest (Sulphur Springs, Tex., Oct. 18, 1933 —). Football player. A graduate of Southern Methodist University, he played with the Green Bay Packers (1956-71), establishing himself as the premier offensive lineman in the game. He was inducted into the Pro Football Hall of Fame in 1977.

GREGG, Josiah (Overton Co., Tenn., July 19, 1806 — Calif., Feb. 25, 1850). Trader and author. His many journeys, especially along the Santa Fe Trail, led to the publication of his *Commerce of The Prairies* (1844). He was killed while leading a prospecting group in an expedition over the Coast Range.

GREGG, William (Carmichaels, W.Va., Feb. 2, 1800 — Edgefield District, S.C., Sept. 13, 1867). Cotton manufacturer. A successful silversmith and watchmaker who retired in 1838, Gregg turned to the development of cotton manufacturing. He established Graniteville, S.C. (1846), the first mill town in the South, by using native labor and materials. He believed that the South's agricultural economy could be changed to an industrial one. Graniteville, with its mill and houses for 300 employees was financially successful even with the outbreak of the Civil War and after. Gregg introduced factory-welfare programs, and his efforts to prove the South comparable to the North in industrial resources earned him the title "father of Southern cotton manufacture."

GRENADA, Miss. City (pop. 12,641), seat of Grenada Co., in north central Mississippi on the Yalobusha River. Settled in the early 1830s, Grenada today is a marketing and processing center for cotton, and timber. There is diversified light manufacturing. Grenada Lake and Hugh White State Park are nearby.

GRENADA LAKE, Miss. Reservoir in north central Mississippi touching several counties. Grenada Lake covers 64,600 acres and has a 282-mile shoreline. The U.S. Army Corps of Engineers formed this artificial lake by damming the Yalobusha River. Hugh White State Park is here.

GRENVILLE, Sir Richard (England, June 15, 1542 — Azores, Sept., 1591). British naval commander. Grenville was the commander of the fleet which carried 100 English colonists to Roanoke Island in 1585. He is famous for his battle against the Spanish fleet in the face of tremendous odds off Flores Island in the Azores (1591).

GRETNA, La. City (pop. 20,615), seat of Jefferson Parish, in southeastern Louisiana on the Mississippi River. German immigrants settled here early in the 19th century, calling the community Mechanicsham. In 1913, it merged with McDonoghville to form the present city, which serves as a residential suburb of New Orleans with some light industry.

GRIFFIN, Ga. City (pop. 20,728), seat of Spaulding Co., in west central Georgia. Griffin, incorporated in 1843, is the center of a large garment and textile industry. Food processing is also of importance in this farming and cotton region. A state-operated experimental agricultural station is near here.

GRIFFITH, D(avid) W(ark) (Crestwood, Ky., Jan 22, 1875 — Los Angeles, Cal., July 23, 1948). Film director. Born into a poor family, Griffith aspired to be a playwright, but lacking sufficient money to devote himself to literature he took a job in the theater's then-disreputable cousin, film. With the Biograph Company through 1913, Griffith produced as many as 100 short films in a single year, and in the process he began to discover the innovations in camera position that would be the basis of his artistic reputation. He introduced such innovations as the long shot, the close up and the moving shot. His first great film using these techniques was *The Birth of a Nation* (1915), a commercial and artistic landmark in the history of the industry. It was followed by *Intolerance* (1916), which was a financial failure but is now considered one of his major works. In 1920 Griffith formed the United Artists Corporation with Charlie Chaplin, Douglas Fairbanks, Sr., and Mary Pickford.

GRIMKE, Angelina Emily (Charleston, S.C., Feb. 20, 1805 — Hyde Park, Mass., Oct. 26, 1879). Abolitionist and women's rights advocate. Angelina Grimke followed her sister, Sarah Moore GRIMKE, in fighting slavery in America. Daughter of a slaveholding judge, she traveled throughout the North supporting the abolitionist movement and women's rights and eventually married fellow abolitionist, Theodore Dwight Weld. She was the author of many abolitionist pamphlets and so enraged Southerners that she was threatened with imprisonment if she returned to her native South Carolina.

GRIMKE, Archibald Henry (near Charleston, S.C., Aug. 17, 1849 — Washington, D.C, Feb. 25, 1930). Black rights advocate and author. Grimke's father was white and his mother a slave. He was educated at Lincoln University (1872) and received his law degree from Harvard (1874) before practicing law in Boston. He wrote numerous articles on black race advancement. He served as American consul to Santo Domingo (1894-98) and as president of the American Negro Academy (1903-16). His work won him the 1919 Springarn award from the National Association for the Advancement of Colored People (NAACP).

GRIMKE, Sarah Moore (Charleston, S.C., Nov. 26, 1792 — Hyde Park, Mass., Dec. 23, 1873). Ardent abolitionist and women's rights advocate. With her younger sister, Angelina GRIMKE, she took her impassioned antislavery crusade to large mixed audiences in the North. Such behavior outraged conservatives who believed women had no place in the public eye. Partly because of fierce reactions against her and her sister, Grimke took up the cause of women in America and was largely responsible for linking it to the antislavery crusade. She was the daughter of an aristocratic slaveholding judge and in her early childhood developed an aversion to slavery. As a young woman she moved to Philadelphia to become active in the antislavery movement. In her pamphlet, *An Epistle to the Clergy of the Southern States*, (1836), she called for the overthrow of slavery. Copies of this and pamphlets written by Angelina were burned in South Carolina and the two sisters were threatened with imprisonment should they return to the state.

GRITS. Ground hominy of a coarse or gritty texture and a traditional Southern breakfast accompaniment to ham (or bacon) and eggs as far north as Virginia. They are served boiled or, sometimes, fried.

GRUEN, Victor (Vienna, Austria, July 18, 1903 — Vienna, Austria, Feb. 16, 1980). Austrian-American architect. Best known for his innovative design of suburban shopping centers and for his solutions to problems in city planning, Gruen's projects for Fort Worth, Tex., were particularly noteworthy. He retired in 1968.

GRUNDY, Felix (Berkeley Co., Va., Sept. 11, 1777 — Nashville, Tenn., Dec. 19, 1840). Lawyer and statesman. After a successful law career in Kentucky Grundy moved to Tennessee and was elected to Congress (1811-14) where he was an advocate of the War of 1812. He was a U.S. senator from that state (1829-38, 1839-40). Appointed attorney general by President Martin Van Buren (1838), he resigned to return to the Senate.

GUADALUPE PEAK, Tex. (8,751 ft.) Mountain peak in the Guadalupe Mountain Range, Culberson Co., in western Texas. The highest peak in the state, it is located within a national park on the New Mexico border with salt lakes and salt flats to the west. Its crest is rounded and topped with pine trees.

GUADALUPE RIVER, Tex. A river formed in southeast Texas flowing 300 miles southeast to meet the San Antonio River. It is the largest of the spring-fed rivers and because of its steady, heavy flow is an important hydroelectric energy source.

GUALE INDIANS. Tribe of Muskogean linguistic stock that lived between St. Andrews Sound and the Savannah River on the coast of Georgia. One of the first regions where regular mission work was undertaken, missionary ef-forts among the Guale began in 1569 when Domingo Augustin wrote a grammar of their language.

GUERIN, Jules (St. Louis, Mo., Nov. 18, 1866 – Neptune, N.J., June 13, 1946) Painter and illustrator. Guerin painted murals for such important public and federal buildings as the Lincoln Memorial, Washington, D.C., the Federal Reserve Bank, San Francisco, Illinois Merchant's Bank in Chicago, and Louisiana's capitol in Baton Rouge.

GUILFORD COURTHOUSE, Battle of. Revolutionary War engagement fought March 15, 1781, in north central North Carolina. Although the British forced the Continental militia into retreat, the victory was so costly that it began the erosion of British control of the Carolinas. Having reached out and defeated the British at the Battle of COWPENS in January of 1781, the Revolutionary army in the South under Gen. Nathaniel GREENE fell back into Virginia. The British army of Lord Charles Cornwallis moved north in pursuit and then regrouped in Hillsboro, N.C. The march had exhausted Cornwallis's men and moved the force far from its base of supplies in South Carolina.

The battle on March 15 took place in heavily wooded land surrounding a farm clearing beside Guilford Courthouse. Greene attempted to repeat the tactic that succeeded at Cowpens, a sham retreat to lure the British into a cross fire. However, at Guilford Courthouse the controlled retreat quickly degenerated into disorderly flight, and the Revolutionary army was never able to seize the offensive. Although victorious, the British lost nearly 100 killed and more than 400 wounded to American casualties of less than 80 killed and less than 200 wounded.

After the Battle of Guilford Courthouse Cornwallis fell back to Wilmington on the coast of North Carolina, effectively ceding the state to Greene. The battle provoked the famous statement of Charles Fox in the House of Commons that "another such victory would destroy the British army."

GULF INTRACOASTAL WATERWAY. A sea-level, 1,100-mile waterway that extends from Apalachee Bay, Fla., to Brownsville, Tex., on the Mexican border. Natural portions have been linked by a series of canals and channels to provide an extremely important commercial route for ocean-going vessels. The waterway connects with the Mississippi River system so that barge travel can continue to such points as Chicago and Pittsburgh. Petroleum and petroleum products are among the principal items shipped through the route.

GULF STREAM. An ocean current that extends from the Gulf of Mexico to Newfoundland where it merges with the North Atlantic Drift. A deep blue in color, it is deep and narrow and flows at an average of four miles an hour. A result of ocean circulation, the stream flows over the northern colder waters. As it passes the Straits of Florida it is reinforced by the Trade Wind current.

GULFPORT, Miss. City (pop. (39,676), Harrison Co., located in southeastern Mississippi on the Gulf Coast, midway between New Orleans, La., and Mobile, Ala. It was founded in 1891 as the southern terminal of the Gulf and Ship Island Railroad by Col. William H. Hardy and developed by resident Joseph Jones, who built its deepwater harbor in 1902. On one of the world's longest man-made beaches, industries include timber, shipping, textiles, and tourism.

GUNTERSVILLE LAKE, Ala. The state's largest artificial lake, covering about 110 square miles, located in northeast Alabama and formed by a dam on the Tennessee River. The dam was built by the Tennessee Valley Authority and is a major hydroelectric power source and recreation area.

GUTHRIE, James (Bardstown, Ky., Dec. 5, 1792 — Louisville, Ky., Mar. 13, 1869). Statesman and soldier. He was active in the militia before going on to represent his county in the state legislature (1827-29). He was elected to the state senate (1831-41) and was Secretary of the Treasury under President Franklin Pierce (1853-57). He was a member of the U.S. Senate from 1865 to 1868. Guthrie was also a railroad promoter.

GUYANDOTTE RIVER, W.Va. A tributary of the Ohio River rising in the southern end of West Virginia and winding northwest 100 miles. It meets the Mud River and empties into the Ohio River near the border of Ohio.

GWIN, William McKendree (Sumter Co., Tenn., Oct. 9, 1805 — New York, N.Y., Sept. 3, 1885). Politician. A physician, Gwin entered politics in Mississippi and served as a U.S. congressman (1841-43) before moving to California where he was one of the first U.S. senators (1850-55, 1857-61) and a chief spokesman for slavery.

GWINNETT, Button (Gloucestershire, England, 1732 — near Savannah, Ga., May 19, 1777). Planter and politician. Gwinnett was a delegate from Georgia to the Continental Congress (1776-77), and a signer of the Declaration of Independence. He was acting president and commander in chief of Georgia (1777), and helped draft its first constitution. He was killed in a duel with his political rival Lachlan McINTOSH.

H

HABERSHAM, James (Beverley, Yorkshire, England, Jan., 1713 — New Brunswick, N.J., Aug. 28, 1775). Colonial governor. Acting governor of Georgia from 1771 to 1773, he was a Loyalist who dissolved the Assembly due to its radical activity prior to the Revolutionary War (1773). Habersham raised the first cotton in Georgia and promoted the introduction of slavery.

HADAS, Moses (Atlanta, Ga., June 25, 1900 — Aspen, Colo., Aug. 17, 1966). Classical scholar. A graduate of Emory University and long associated with Columbia University, Hadas edited and translated many Latin, Greek, Hebrew, and German classics into English. His works include *A History of Greek Literature* (1950) and *Humanism: The Greek Ideal and Its Survival* (1960).

HAGERSTOWN, Md. City (pop. 34,132), seat of Washington Co., in northwestern Maryland, 70 miles from Baltimore on Antietam Creek. Settled in the 1730s by Germans and Scotch-Irish, it was named Elizabethtown by Jonathan Hager, after his wife. Neighbors chose to call it Hagerstown and it was incorporated as such in 1814. Germanic in architecture and craftsmanship, it still contains Hager's original stone house, the only fort standing from the French and Indian Wars, and "Little Heiskell" a weathervane that has stood on all its town halls. Located near Harpers Ferry and Gettysburg, Hagerstown was a Civil War battlefield and is the burial ground of 5,000 Confederate soldiers. Present industries include the manufacture of aircraft and appliance parts and textiles.

HALES BAR LAKE, Tenn. The first major hydroelectric power development on the Tennessee River. It was constructed by private concerns in 1913 and sold to the Tennessee Valley Authority in 1939. Its dam measures 1,200 feet, and the power created here is distributed to Chattanooga and Nashville.

HALIFAX RESOLUTIONS. Also known as the "Halifax Resolves," it was the first formal sanction of American independence from British rule, and was adopted by the Fourth Provincial Congress in Halifax, N.C., on April 12, 1776.

HALLANDALE, Fla. City (pop. 36,517), Broward Co., in southeastern Florida on the Atlantic Coast. Horse and greyhound racetracks are the major sources of employment in

Hallandale. Its industries include vegetable packing, and the resort community of Golden Isles is located within the city limits.

HALTOM CITY, Tex. City (pop. 29,014), Tarrant Co., located in east central Texas northeast of Fort Worth. Primarily a residential suburb of Fort Worth, Haltom City's population rose dramatically after World War II, from 200 in 1940 to 23,133 in 1960.

HAMILTON, Andrew Jackson (Huntsville, Ala., Jan. 28, 1815 — Austin, Tex., Apr. 11, 1875). Politician. Hamilton commanded Texas volunteers during the Civil War, and was a member of Congress from Texas (1859-61). He was military governor of Texas by appointment of President Abraham Lincoln (1862), and provisional governor under President Andrew Johnson (1865-66). He was a justice of the state supreme court in 1866 and was opposed to Negro suffrage.

HAMILTON, James (Charleston, S.C., May 8, 1786 — Gulf of Mexico, Nov. 15, 1857). Politician. A lawyer, Hamilton won election to the U.S. House of Representatives from South Carolina (1822-29) where he was an advocate of states' rights. He was governor of South Carolina from 1830 to 1832. Hamilton worked as a diplomatic agent for Texas and Texas independence. He drowned in the Gulf of Mexico.

HAMMOND, James Henry (Newberry District, S.C., Nov. 15, 1807 — Beech Island, S.C., Nov. 13, 1864). Politician. Hammond became prominent as an attorney and plantation owner who supported secession and slavery in speeches as a congressman from South Carolina (1835-36). From 1842 to 1844 he was governor of South Carolina. While a U.S. senator (1857-60), he made his famous "Cotton is King" speech.

HAMPTON, S.C. Town (pop. 3,143), seat of Hampton Co., in southern South Carolina. Named for Civil War leader and state governor Wade HAMPTON (1818-1902), and incorporated in 1879, its present manufactures include elevators, plastics, and doors. Farms produce corn, cotton, and potatoes.

HAMPTON, Va. Independent city (pop. 122,617), at the mouth of the James River in southeastern Virginia. Hampton was settled in 1610 by Jamestown residents and given the Indian name Kecoughtan. It was given its present name in 1680, incorporated as a town in 1849, and incorporated as a city in 1908. It suffered the ravages of two wars first looted by the British in the War of 1812, and then during the Civil War it was burned by Confederate forces to avoid Union occupation. In 1952 Hampton merged with Elizabeth City County. Present industries include the packing of fish and the manufacture of building materials and fertilizer. The Syms-Eaton Academy, the HAMPTON INSTITUTE, and historic Fort Monroe are located here.

HAMPTON, Wade (Halifax Co., Va., 1752 — Columbia, S.C., Feb. 4, 1835). Military officer and politician. An extensive land and slave owner, he developed a large cotton plantation in South Carolina before joining the Revolutionary army and attaining the rank of major general. Distinguished as a partisan officer under Gen. SUMTER, Hampton was twice a member of Congress from South Carolina (1795-97, 1803-05). Imperious and overbearing in his nature and deportment, he was constantly quarreling with his subordinates. He was superseded by Gen. James Wilkinson in his command at New Orleans when the War of 1812 broke out, and was put in command of the army of the North with headquarters on Lake Champlain. In that post he gained no honors, and his career there was chiefly marked by disobedience to the orders of his superiors. In April, 1814, he resigned his commission and left the army. He later developed sugar plantations in South Carolina. In 1830 he was believed to have owned 3,000 slaves. He was the grandfather of Wade HAMPTON (1818-1902).

HAMPTON, Wade (Charleston, S.C., Mar. 28, 1818 — Columbia, S.C., Apr. 11, 1902). Military officer and politican. Although he opposed secession he organized "Hampton's Legion" for the Confederacy. A colonel at Bull Run, he attained the rank of brigadier general before the Battle of Seven Pines. Assigned to J.E.B. STUART's army of Northern Virginia, he fought heroically and was wounded five times. A lieutenant general, he served Gen. Robert E. Lee as chief of cavalry, defended Petersburg, opposed Sherman's march, and attempted to prevent President Jefferson Davis's capture after surrender. A conciliator after the war, he was governor of South Carolina (1876-79) and a Democratic U.S. senator (1879-91). He is the grandson of Wade HAMPTON (1752-1835).

HAMPTON INSTITUTE. Independent coed institution, located on a 201-acre campus in the Virginia peninsula city of Hampton. Hampton Institute was founded in 1868 by Gen. Samuel Chapman ARMSTRONG as a college for Negroes. The school today is still primarily black but has an interracial faculty and student body.

The school has experienced enormous growth in the last 100 years, and today academic emphasis is concentrated on the liberal arts, sciences, engineering, humanities, teacher education, architecture, and nursing. Major school divisions are the Schools of Arts and Letters, Pure and Applied Sciences, Business, Education, Nursing, and Graduate Studies. Middle Atlantic states provide 51% of students, 40% are from the South, and 5% are from New England. Graduate or professional studies are pursued by 22% of students.

Library: 180,000 volumes, 1,050 journal subscriptions; 28,000 microform titles. Faculty: 238. Enrollment: 3,230 total graduate and undergraduate: 1,189 men, 1,693 women (fulltime). Degrees: Bachelor's, Master's.

HAMPTON ROADS, Va. Harbor in southeastern Virginia, with the cities of Norfolk and Portsmouth on its south and Newport News on its north. Hampton Roads is one of the most important ports of entry on the eastern seaboard because of its connection with the Chesapeake Bay. It takes its name from the Earl of Southampton and the word "roads" refers to an area of water where ships are able to ride at anchor. The James, Nansemond, Elizabeth, and Lafayette Rivers empty into the harbor which has a water frontage of some 50 miles, is four miles long, and 40 feet deep.

HAMPTON ROADS PEACE CON-FERENCE. An unsuccessful attempt by Confederate and Union representatives on February 3, 1865, to end the Civil War. In January of that year, Francis P. Blair, Sr., a native Virginian who had long held federal posts, visited Confederate President Jefferson Davis in Richmond. A Confederate delegation consisting of Vice President Alexander H. Stephens, Assistant Secretary of War John A. Campbell, and Senator Robert M. T. Hunter then crossed the battle lines to Gen. Ulysses Grant's headquarters. In response to a request from Grant, President Abraham Lincoln agreed to come with Secretary of State William Seward to confer with the Confederates.

Although both parties met in good faith, negotiations aboard the *River Queen* in Hampton Roads Harbor, Va., actually had little chance of success since the Union and Confederate approaches to the conference differed radically. Although the South faced a desperate military and economic situation by this time, the Confederates expected to be treated as delegates from an independent country, while Lincoln offered rigid terms to the men he considered defeated insurgents. Responding to a suggestion by Blair, who also attended the four-hour meeting, Stephens proposed that an armistice be declared and that, while final peace terms were being negotiated, a joint military expedition to Mexico be undertaken to enforce the Monroe Doctrine against the French invaders there.

Lincoln rejected the Confederate proposal and offered peace on the basis of emancipation of the slaves, reunion of the North and South, and the unconditional disbanding of the Southern forces, while at the same time promising sympathetic treatment for the South. Since President Davis had not empowered his representatives to accept any terms except independence, the conference ended amicably but without agreement.

HANDY, William Christopher (Florence, Ala., Nov. 6, 1873 — New York, N.Y., Mar. 28, 1958). Black composer and musicologist. The son of a black minister, Handy worked as a schoolteacher and then became a bandmaster. He formed his own orchestra in 1903 and began composing and writing down the music of poor blacks. This music became popularly known as "the blues." His orchestra was noted for songs such as "St. Louis Blues" (1914) and "Beale Street Blues" (1917). The use of the "blue" lowered seventh note became characteristic of Handy's sound. The composer anthologized Negro spirituals and published studies of black musicians in the U.S.

HANGING ROCK, Battle of. Revolutionary War engagement fought north of Camden, S.C., on August 6, 1780. A victory for the Revolutionary militia, it helped set the stage for the major Battle of CAMDEN on August 16. Following his failure to capture a British outpost at Rocky Mountain, Gen. Thomas SUMTER moved with his volunteers to Hanging Rock, named for a local boulder. In a fiercely contested battle fought for four hours on August 6, his men and those of Col. W. R. Davis captured the British camp and its munitions, and inflicted losses of

Statue of composer W. C. Handy in Handy Park, Memphis, Tenn.

nearly 200 British killed and wounded to only 50 Revolutionary casualties.

HANNIBAL, Mo. City (pop. 18,811), Marion and Rolls Counties, in northeastern Missouri on the Mississippi River. As the boyhood home of Mark Twain (Samuel CLEMENS), many of the local attractions celebrate the writer. Twain's name appears on a bridge, lighthouse, museum, and statue. Each July, there is a Mark Twain fence painting contest. It was also the birthplace of Admiral Robert E. Coontz and portrait painter Carroll Beckwith. The site for this industrial city was granted in 1818. Present industries include the manufacture of shoes, steel, cement, and lumber products. There are also grain and dairy farms. Hannibal-LaGrange College is found here.

HANOVER, Va. Unincorporated town in Hanover Co. in east central Virginia. Nearby Hanovertown was nearly selected as the state capital in 1751, missing by only a few votes. Patrick Henry was a resident for many years and pleaded his first important case in the courthouse.

HANOVER JUNCTION, Battle of. See NORTH ANNA RIVER, Battle of.

HANSON, John (Charles Co., Md., Apr. 3, 1715 — Prince George Co., Md., Nov. 15, 1783). Politician. Hanson was a member of the Maryland senate (1757-73) and delegate to the Continental Congress (1780-83). Elected "President of the United States in Congress Assembled" (1781), under the Articles of Confederation, he served as presiding officer, with none of the constitutional powers of the national presidency, for one year.

HARDEE, William Joseph (Savannah, Ga., Oct. 12, 1815 — Wytheville, Va., Nov. 6, 1873). Military officer. A 1838 graduate of the U.S. Military Academy at West Point, N.Y., Hardee taught there and wrote a popular infantry manual in 1855. When Georgia seceded from the Union in January of 1861, he resigned his command and assumed command of the Confederate forces in northeast Arkansas. Promoted first to major general and then to lieutenant general, he saw action in many battles. In 1864 he took command of the military departments of South Carolina, Virginia, and Florida, and defended Savannah, Ga., against Gen. William Sherman's troops. After the war, he retired to his Alabama plantation.

HARDIN, John (Fauquier Co., Va., Oct. 1, 1753 — Shawneetown, now Hardin, Ohio, May, 1792). Military officer. Hardin served in Lord Dunmore's War (1774) and was a lieutenant during the Revolution. In 1786 he moved to Kentucky and took part in various expeditions against the Indians. He was killed while bearing a flag of truce in an attempt to negotiate a treaty with the Miami Indians.

HARDIN, John Wesley (Bonham, Tex., May 26, 1853 — El Paso, Tex., Aug. 9, 1895). Outlaw. Subject of a recent folk song by Bob Dylan, Hardin was a gambler and gunman who managed to avoid jail until 1877 when he was sentenced to 25 years for shooting a sheriff. He studied law in prison, and once pardoned, set up a practice in El Paso (1894). A year later, however, he was shot by a local constable.

HARDWOODS. See LUMBER.

HARLAN, John Marshall (Boyle Co., Ky., June 1, 1833 — Washington, D.C., Oct. 14, 1911). Military officer and jurist. A pre-Civil

War supporter of slavery, Harlan nevertheless joined the Union Army in 1861 and served until 1863. He campaigned against Abraham Lincoln and the Emancipation Proclamation in 1864, but while practicing law in subsequent years he became disillusioned by widespread violence against blacks that was tacitly condoned by Democratic politicians in Kentucky. He was instrumental in providing Kentucky support for the election of Rutherford B. Hayes in 1876, and for this he was awarded an appointment to the U.S. Supreme Court in 1877. A street constructionist, he became famous for dissenting from decisions that weakened civil rights laws. He supported the strengthening of civil liberties and backed the police power of the states.

HARLINGEN, Tex. City (pop. 43,543), Cameron Co., in southern Texas, 28 miles northwest of Brownsville. The city was founded in 1904, incorporated in 1910, and named after Harlingen, Netherlands. Harlingen began to develop when it became a station on the St. Louis, Brownsville, and Mexico (now Missouri Pacific) Railroad. The city is an agricultural center and a major distribution point for vegetables and citrus fruits from the lower Rio Grande Valley. Located on the Gulf Intracoastal Waterway, Port Harlingen has oil terminals, chemical plants, grain operations, and other industries.

HARNEY, William Selby (Haysboro, Tenn., Aug. 22, 1800 — Orlando, Fla., May 9, 1889). Military officer. In 1818 Harney entered the army and advanced to colonel's rank (1846), becoming the ranking cavalry officer under Gen. Winfield Scott in the Mexican War. A personal dispute with Scott led to his court-martial but he appealed and was eventually reinstated. In 1859 he ordered the occupation of San Juan Island, which led to a major boundary dispute with Britain, and for which he was recalled.

HARPERS FERRY, W.Va. Town (pop. 361), Jefferson Co., in extreme northwestern West Virginia about 55 miles northwest of Washington, D.C. Located in the Blue Ridge Mountains where West Virginia meets Maryland and Virginia, Harpers Ferry was settled in 1733 and incorporated in 1763. It is famous as the site of the HARPERS FERRY RAID (1859) led by John BROWN. Part of Virginia before the Civil War, it was a commercial and industrial center, a vital railroad link between the Ohio

Harpers Ferry, W. Va. in the 1800s, the site of abolitionist John Brown's raid in 1859

Valley and the East, and the site of an arsenal. Because of its strategic location, nine major engagements of the Civil War were fought in the vicinity. By war's end it was in ruins, and never regained its importance. It was established as a National Historic Park in 1944.

HARPERS FERRY RAID. Civil War raid. As the antislavery furor began to mount in the 1850s many abolitionists began to call for military action. One in particular was John BROWN, a Connecticut fanatic obsessed with the idea of freeing the slaves by force, who planned a raid on Harpers Ferry, Va. (now W.Va.)—a key rail junction and site of a military arsenal. On the night of October 16, 1859, Brown and 21 followers made a surprise attack on the town. Ironically, the first man they killed was a free Negro. By morning, they held the arsenal, the town, and the townspeople as hostages. At this point Brown and his men could easily have escaped, but he insisted upon attempting to hold their position. On October 18, the arsenal was retaken by a group of U.S. Marines led by Robert E. LEE. Brown was captured, tried, and executed.

HARPETH RIVER, Tenn. An important branch of the Cumberland River in Tennessee, running southeast approximately 90 miles. The Harpeth was once used as a route by flatboats carrying farm goods to market. Ironworks built along the river's banks at the beginning of the 19th century were among the first attempts at industrialization in the state. A major feature of the river is the narrows of Harpeth where the river takes a hairpin curve over a ridge eight-tenths of a mile long and 300 feet high.

HARRIS, George Washington (Allegheny City, Pa., Mar. 20, 1814 — Knoxville, Tenn., Dec. 11, 1869). Humorist. While living in the

Knoxville area, Harris worked in various capacities, including steamboat captain and metal worker. He wrote anti-Lincoln satires during the Civil War and was the author of one book, the humorous dialect story *Sut Lovingood Yarns Spun by a "Nat'ral Durn'd Fool"* (1867).

HARRIS, Isham Green (Franklin Co., Tenn., Feb. 10, 1818 — Washington, D.C., July 8, 1897). Politician. Following his admission to the bar (1841), Harris won election as a Democrat to the Tennessee senate in 1847, to the U.S. House of Representatives (1849-53), and was governor of the state (1857-61). A staunch Confederate, and one of the major forces behind Tennessee's secession, he left the state after several Union victories but returned to Memphis in 1867 and was elected to the U.S. Senate (1877-97). He was president pro tempore of the Senate from 1893 to 1895.

HARRIS, Joel Chandler (Eatonton, Ga., Dec. 9, 1848 — Atlanta, Ga., July 3, 1908). Author, journalist, and humorist. One of America's most celebrated regional authors, Harris is best known for his Uncle Remus stories, beginning with *Uncle Remus, His Songs and His Sayings* (1881) which included much contemporary black custom and love, interlaced with such anthropomorphic figures as Br'er Rabbit and the Tar Baby. However, keen as many of his insights are, they reflect a view of the Southern black as a happy, childlike "darky." Harris also provided some valuable portraits of poor Southern whites in such works as *Free Joe and Other Georgian Sketches* (1887).

HARRIS LAKE, Fla. Body of water in Lake Co., in central Florida. About 11 miles long by six miles wide, it is connected by canal with Lake Eustis, and is part of the chain of lakes along the route of the Oklawaha River.

HARRISON, Ark. City (pop. 9,567), seat of Boone Co., located in northwest Arkansas in the Ozark Mountains. Settled c. 1820 and incorporated in 1876, Harrison is today the commercial center of a manufacturing and agricultural region. Dairy cattle are raised and manufactures include church furniture, die castings and apparel. Lumbering is also a major industry. Mystic Cavern is nearby.

HARRISON, Byron Patton "Pat" (Crystal Springs, Miss., Aug. 29, 1881 — Washington, D.C., June 22, 1941). Politician. After several years of practicing law, Harrison was elected as a Democrat to the U.S. House of Representatives (1911-19) from Mississippi. In 1918 he was elected to the U.S. Senate where he served as chairman of the Senate Finance Committee and was president pro tempore for five months before his death.

HARRISON, William Henry (Berkeley, Charles City County, Va., Feb. 9, 1773 — Washington, D.C., Apr. 4, 1841). Soldier, congressman, and 9th President of the United States. Harrison was the third son of Benjamin Harrison, signer of the Declaration of Independence. Enrolled at Hampden-Sydney College in Virginia from 1787 to 1790, he entered the army in 1791 and fought in campaigns against the Indians in the Northwest Territory (now part of the midwestern states).

Harrison's rise to national prominence began when he was made secretary of the Northwest Territory in 1798 and served as its delegate to Congress in 1799. In 1800 he became the first governor of the Indiana Territory on the basis of his military rather than political abilities. After more than a decade in this office he captured the national imagination by defeating TECUMSEH'S Indian army at Tippecanoe, a tributary of the Wabash in Indiana. Harrison further distinguished himself against the British at the Battle of the Thames in 1813. He was elected to Congress as a Whig representative from Ohio (1816-19) and as a senator from that state (1825-28).

The Indian Wars remained his great claim to fame, however, and after an unsuccessful run for the presidency in 1836, he and vice presidential candidate John Tyler were victorious in 1840 with the slogan "Tippecanoe and Tyler too." After Harrison was inaugurated on the east portico of the Capitol building on March 4, 1841, he contracted pneumonia, and died one month later. His grandson Benjamin Harrison became the 23rd president of the U.S. in 1889.

HARRISONBURG, Va. Independent city (pop. 19,617) in northwestern Virginia. Settled in 1739 by Thomas Harrison, its early growth was rapid and its economy was based on agriculture. Now an industrial center, its manufactures include auto parts, furniture, bricks, and fertilizer, along with agricultural products. The city also has fish hatcheries and limestone quarries. Harrisonburg is the site of James Madison University, established in 1908.

HARROD, James (Big Cove, Pa., 1742 — 1793). Kentucky pioneer. While exploring the Kentucky River (1774), Harrod established the first permanent settlement in the state, named HARRODSBURG. Active in the pioneer fight against the Indians, he was elected to the Virginia legislature in 1779. He mysteriously disappeared in 1793 while on a trapping expedition and was never seen again.

HARRODSBURG, Ky. City (pop. 7,265), seat of Mercer Co., in central Kentucky. Founded in 1774 by James HARROD, Harrodsburg is the oldest settlement in the state. Kentucky's first school, which was operated here at Fort Harrod, is now preserved in a replica at Pioneer Memorial Park. A trade center, Harrodsburg's manufactures include clothing, dairy products, and optical glass. Grain, livestock, and tobacco are also produced. Harrodsburg is also a resort community noted for its mineral springs.

HART, Joel Tanner (Winchester, Ky., Feb. 10, 1810 — Florence, Italy, Mar. 1, 1877). Sculptor. Hart established himself with portrait busts of major figures including Henry Clay and President Andrew Jackson. He spent most of his productive years in Italy, working on a series of sculptural groups.

HARTWELL, Ga. City (pop. 4,855), seat of Hart Co., in extreme northeastern Georgia. Hartwell is a textile producing community also noted as a local market and shipping point for agricultural produce, particularly cotton and corn. The city was incorporated in 1856.

HARTWELL LAKE, Ga. Body of water in Hart Co., in northeastern Georgia near the South Carolina border. It is a major waterpower source created by the construction of a dam on the Savannah River.

HARVEY, William Hope (Buffalo, W.Va., Aug. 16, 1851 — Monte Ne, Ark., Feb. 11, 1936). Economist and writer. A practicing lawyer, Harvey advocated the free coinage of silver. His writings earned him the name "Coin Harvey." His most noted work was *Coin's Financial School* (1894) and it was referred to in William Jennings Bryan's "cross of gold" speech when he ran for the presidency in 1896.

HARVIE, John (Albemarle Co., Va., 1742 — near Richmond, Va., Feb. 6, 1807). Statesman and Revolutionary patriot. Harvie began his career as a Virginia lawyer before his involvement in the American Revolution, in which he served as colonel of the state's militia. The Continental Congress appointed him one of the commissioners of Indian affairs in 1776, and the following year he was named delegate to the Congress (1777-79). Harvie later served as mayor of Richmond (1785-86).

HASINAI CONFEDERACY ("our own folk"). Group of Indian tribes, all of Caddoan linguistic stock, that lived between the headwaters of the Neches and Trinity Rivers in northeast Texas. They were placed on a reservation with the Louisiana CADDO INDIANS in the early 19th century, but continued threats from nearby settlers forced them to move and seek safety in Oklahoma. They were noted as excellent pottery makers.

HATCH, William Henry (near Georgetown, Ky., Sept. 11, 1833 — Hannibal, Mo., Dec. 23, 1896). Politician. A lawyer and later an assistant adjutant general in he Confederate Army, Hatch was elected a Democratic U.S. Congressman from Missouri (1879-95). As chairman of the House Committee on Agriculture, Hatch was responsible for creating the Bureau of Animal Industry (1884) and gained the passage of the Hatch Act, which provided federal aid for research on scientific agriculture (1887). It was through his efforts that the Department of Agriculture rose to cabinet level (1889).

HATCHIE RIVER, Tenn. Tributary of the Mississippi River rising in western Tennessee and traveling approximately 150 miles east and southeast into central Mississippi. The city of Memphis was developed at the mouth of this waterway with land acquired by Andrew Jackson. It once served as a primary route between western Tennessee and New Orleans.

HATFIELDS AND THE MCCOYS, The. Most well-known of the infamous family feuds which plagued the southern Appalachians during the late 19th century. The feud began in 1873 when Randolf McCoy accused Floyd Hatfield of stealing a hog. It escalated on election day 1882 when Johnse Hatfield attempted to elope with Rosanna McCoy and a quarrel broke out during which Ellison Hatfield was killed. The Hatfields, led by Capt. Andersen "Devil Anse" Hatfield (1839-1921),

The West Virginia Hatfield clan in the 1880s. The family patriarch, "Devil Anse," is seated in the center

intercepted the killers as they were being taken to jail, carried them off to West Virginia and shot them. Law enforcement broke down as the killing went back and forth. Juries refused to convict and the governors of the two states refused to extradite the killers. The feud continued until 1896 when the various communities tired of the killing and the reputation they had acquired. Moreover, the coal fields and timber lands were being developed and such lawlessness interferred with business.

HATTERA INDIANS. Tribe of Algonquian linguistic stock. They lived in North Carolina in the area of Cape Hatteras to which they gave their name.

HATTERAS, Cape, N.C. Dare Co. Eastern North Carolina coastal promontory found at the tip of Hatteras Island across the Pamlico Sound. Hazardous conditions for ships led to the construction of lighthouses as early as 1798 and earned Hatteras the nickname "Graveyard of the Atlantic." The promontory is part of the Cape Hatteras National Seashore, which extends for more than 70 miles along the Outer Banks. This seashore is considered one of the most extensive undeveloped shore areas on the Atlantic coast.

HATTIESBURG, Miss. City (pop. 40,829), seat of Forest Co., in southeastern Mississippi on the west bank of the Leaf River, 65 miles from the Gulf of Mexico. Called the "Hub of South Mississippi," the town was founded by Col. William Hardy in 1881 and named for his wife. Located in a vast area of virgin pine, the early wealth of the community derived from lumbering. Incorporated as a city in 1884, it is the home of Mississippi Southern College, William Carey College, and Camp Shelby, an army training center.

HAW RIVER, N.C. River rising in Rockingham Co., in northern North Carolina. The river flows southeast approximately 75 miles and meets the Deep River near Haywood to form the Cape Fear River.

HAWKSBILL MOUNTAIN, Va. Highest point in the Shenandoah National Park (4,049 feet), in Page and Madison Counties. Its outline resembles the head of a hawk when viewed from the east.

HAY. Wild and cultivated grasses and other plants mown and dried for use as animal fodder. In the South, where hay is an important support of the cattle industry, most hay consists of timothy, alfalfa, or clover crops. In 1981 the Southern states produced nearly 30 million tons of hay, about one-fifth of the total U.S. production. The leading hay producers in the South in that year were Texas, with 6.9 million tons, and Missouri, with 6.7 million tons; these two states accounted for 46% of the South's hay crop. Other Southern states with large hay crops (ranked by 1981 harvest) are Kentucky (3.3 million tons), Tennessee (2.0 million tons), Arkansas (1.8 million tons), Mississippi (1.2 million tons), Alabama (1.1 million tons), and Georgia (1.0 million tons).

HAYES, Roland (Curryville, Ga., June 3, 1887 — Boston, Mass., Dec. 31, 1976). International tenor. Son of a former slave, Hayes was the first black singer to get worldwide recognition in classical music as well as in the black folk idiom.

HAYNE, Isaac (Charleston, S.C., Sept. 23, 1745 — Charleston, S.C., Aug. 4, 1781). Revolutionary War soldier. Hayne was an arms manufacturer for the colonial forces whose forge was destroyed by the British. He then joined the Continental Army serving until after the fall of Charleston. Family illness forced him to take an oath of allegiance to the British with the stipulation that he would not fight. When they forced him into military action, he rejoined the Continental Army. Captured by the British, and without benefit of trial, he was hung as a spy, which caused outrage in the Colonies.

HAYNE, Paul Hamilton (Charleston, S.C., Jan. 1, 1830 — Augusta, Ga., July 6, 1886). Poet. Unable to serve actively during the Civil War, he wrote patriotic poetry for the *Southern Illustrated News* of Richmond. His first collection, called *Poems*, was published in 1855. Hayne was the influential editor of *Russell's Magazine* (1857-60). His home and finances destroyed by the war, he moved his family to a shanty near Augusta, Ga., where he earned a small living writing. His works include *Avolio: A Legend of the Island of Cos* (1860) and *The Broken Battalions* (1885).

HAYNE, Robert Young (St. Paul's Parish, S.C., Nov. 10, 1791 — Asheville, N.C., Sept. 24, 1839). Politician. After receiving his law degree, he served in the War of 1812 as a captain and was a member of the South Carolina legislature (1814-18). He served in the U.S. Senate (1823-32) and became a spokesman for states' rights, opposing protective tariffs and defending slavery. Opposing the Foote Resolution (1830), Hayne contended, in a famous debate with Daniel Webster, that the Constitution was an agreement between states that retained the power to nullify any federal law to which they were opposed. He resigned his post in 1832 to give John C. CALHOUN a seat. As a member of the South Carolina nullification convention (1832), he announced their ruling that federal tariff laws were null and void in that state. He took the governorship (1832-34) in order to prepare the state to resist Andrew Jackson's anticipated attempts to enforce the tariff laws through the use of military force. Hayne was mayor of Charleston from 1835 to 1837.

HEFLIN, James Thomas (Randolph County, Ala., Apr. 9, 1869 — LaFayette Ala., Apr. 22, 1951). Politician. He was a member of the Alabama legislature (1896-1900) and secretary of the state (1902-04) before his election as a Democratic U.S. congressman (1904-20). He was a U.S. senator from 1920 to 1931 and a leader in the movement for white supremacy. Heflin was known as "Cotton Tom" for his theatricality in speeches that were delivered in support of the Southern farmer.

HELENA, Ark. City (pop. 9,598), seat of Phillips Co., on the eastern border of the state on the bank of the Mississippi River. Settled in the early 1800s, Helena was named for a settler's daughter and was incorporated in 1856. The location of a Civil War battle fought on the July 4th, 1863, which resulted in a Union victory, Helena provided seven generals for the Confederate Army. A port of entry and shipping center for cotton and lumber the city also manufactures tires, luggage, clothing, and cottonseed and bean oil. Rice, wheat, and soybeans are grown in the area.

HELPER, Hinton Rowan (Rowan Co., N.C., Dec. 27, 1829 — Washington, D.C., Mar. 8, 1909). Author. Although a believer in white supremacy and black inferiority, Helper wrote an antislavery book, *The Impending Crisis of the South: How to Meet It*, (1857) that had wide influence, demonstrating the disadvantage of slave holding to the Southern white economy. Limited in his education and background, his ideas were simplistic but they aided the antislavery forces. After serving President Abraham Lincoln as consul to Buenos Aires (1861), he wrote bitter separatist papers promoting deportation of blacks to Africa and South American.

HENDERSON, Ky. City (pop. 24,834), seat of Henderson Co., in northwest Kentucky on the Ohio River. Founded in 1797, Henderson is a prosperous community situated in a region that produces coal, corn, livestock, oil, and tobacco. Present manufactures include clothing, furniture, plastics, and truck axles. Audubon Memorial State Park is located here.

HENDERSON, Richard (Hanover Co., Va., Apr. 20, 1735 — Nutbush Creek, N.C., Jan. 30, 1785). Lawyer and land speculator. Henderson worked with Daniel Boone and set up the Transylvania Company (1774) to promote settlement in Kentucky, where Boonesboro was his first settlement. The company went bankrupt when he could not get recognition or financial support for his project from England, and much of the vast amount of land claimed by the company was voided by Virginia and North Carolina. He later colonized western Tennessee, establishing a settlement at French Lick (now Nashville), and helped survey the boundary between Virginia and North Carolina.

HENDERSONVILLE, Tenn. City (pop. 26,561), Sumner Co., in northern Tennessee 18 miles northeast of Nashville. Its phenomenal development from a 1970 population of 262 is almost completely a result of its popularity as a suburb of Nashville. Electric motor boats, glass windows, and office furniture are manufactured here.

HENRY, Cape, Va. Point of land in southeastern Virginia at the entrance to Chesapeake Bay. It is the site of the landing of the first Jamestown colonists on April 26, 1607.

HENRY, O. See O. HENRY.

HENRY, Patrick (Hanover Co., Va., May 29, 1736 — Charlotte Co., Va., June 6, 1799). Revolutionary leader and politician. Self-educated, Henry as a young man was a failed storekeeper and an indifferent farmer. As a lawyer, however, he gained fame soon after passing an oral bar examination. His most important early legal victory was the "Parson's Case" of 1763. Church of England ministers had sued for back pay and won their case, but Henry took over the defense on the question of damages and so succeeded in defending the colonists over the Anglican clergy that the award granted was one penny. On the basis of this performance he was elected to the Virginia House of Burgesses in 1765.

Once there Henry began the series of great oratorical performances that enshrined him in American history. His speeches were generally extemporary and recorded only by witnesses, but phrases such as "if this be treason, make the most of it" and "give me liberty or give me death" brought him a fame in excess of his actual influence on contemporary issues. A member of the Continental Congress (1774-76), he was, in fact, an opponent of the Declaration of Independence as harmful to states' rights, and worked to have the Bill of Rights added in 1776. He was elected governor of the Commonwealth of Virginia (1776-79) and served again as governor from 1784 to 1786. He later declined the appointment of U.S. senator and the offer of the position of Secretary of State under President George Washington.

HENSON, Josiah (Port Tobacco, Md., June 15, 1789 — Dresden, Ont, Canada, May 5, 1883). Clergyman. He was ordained a Methodist Episcopal minister in 1828 while a slave in Kentucky. After an unsuccessful attempt to buy his freedom, Henson escaped from slavery with his family (1830), and settled in Canada where he became a leader of former slaves. His autobiography *The Life of Josiah Henson* was published in 1849. He is said to have been the model for Uncle Tom in Harriet Beecher Stowe's UNCLE TOM'S CABIN.

HERMITAGE, The. The residence of President Andrew JACKSON, in central Tennessee east of Nashville. Constructed between 1819 and 1831 of bricks made on the estate, the house is a fine example of the plantation style of the time. A fire destroyed much of the first structure but the home was rebuilt in 1835. Jackson and his wife, Rachel, are buried there.

HEYWARD, DuBose (Charleston, S.C., Aug. 31, 1885 — Tryon, N.C., June 16, 1940). Author. Heyward's first novel, *Porgy* (1925), was based on his observations of Southern Negro life while a 17-year-old working on the Charleston waterfront. With his wife, Dorothy (1890-1961), he turned it into a play (1927) and, in collaboration with Ira and George Gershwin, a musical, *Porgy and Bess*, of operatic proportions. Other plays include *Mamba's Daughters* (1939) and *Brass Ankle* (1931). His novels all deal with unique cultural isolates such as the Carolina mountaineers in *Angel* (1926) and the Virgin Islanders under the New Deal in *Star Spangled Virgin* (1939). Heyward also wrote a collection of poetry *Carolina Chansons* (1922), with Hervey Allen.

HEYWARD, Thomas (near Charleston, S.C., July 28, 1746 — St. Luke's Parish, S.C., Mar. 6, 1809). Military officer and politician. He served as a delegate to the Continental Congress (1776-78), and was a signer of the Declaration of Independence. He fought in the Revolutionary War and was captured during the defense of Charleston. From 1782 to 1784 he was a member of the South Carolina legislature.

HIALEAH, Fla. City (pop. 145,254), Dade Co., in southeast Florida, five miles northwest of Miami. Hialeah was settled in 1921 as a residential suburb of Miami, and was incorporated in 1925. Manufactures include candy, concrete, and furniture, but the city is best known for the Hialeah Park Race Track.

HICKORY, N.C. City (pop. 20,757), Catawba Co., in western North Carolina, in the foothills of the Blue Ridge Mountains. Named for the hickory wagons once produced here, the town was founded in 1874 and incorporated in 1884. Today Hickory produces cotton and furniture, as well as cotton yarn, telephone cables, and transformers. It is the home of Lenoir Rhyne College, founded in 1891.

HICKS, Thomas Holliday (Dorchester Co., Md., Sept. 2, 1798 — Washington, D.C., Feb. 13, 1865). Politician. A member of the Maryland legislature, Hicks was governor (1857-62) at the start of the Civil War and was a major reason Maryland remained with the North during the conflict. Divided on secession, southern and eastern Maryland were pro-Confederate while the north and west wished to remain with the Union. Hicks was strongly pressured to call a special session of the legislature (1860-61), which he avoided, postponing official consideration of secession until the federal government could get military control of the state. He was a Republican U.S. senator from 1862 until his death.

HIGH POINT, N.C. City (pop. 62,806), Guilford Co., in northwestern North Carolina. Settled by Quakers in 1750 and incorporated in 1859, High Point is the highest ground on the rail line between Goldsboro and Charlotte. An industrial city, manufactures include furniture, hoisery, auto parts, and electronics. There are also cotton mills. It is the site of High Point College (1920).

HIGHLAND RIM, Tenn. Geographical land division that covers 9,300 square miles of central Tennessee. It merges with the Cumberland Plateau in the west and includes the Central Basin. In the eastern sector, underground waterways have hollowed out caverns in the rock.

HILL, Ambrose Powell (Culpeper Co., Va., Nov. 9, 1825 — Petersburg, Va., Apr. 2, 1865). Military officer. A graduate of West Point (1847), Hill entered the 1st Artillery and served in the war with Mexico and against the Seminoles Indians in Florida (1849-50). Resigning in 1861, he joined the Confederate Army and was made colonel of the 13th Virginia Infantry. He soon rose to major general, and was one of the most efficient officers in the campaigns in Virginia and Maryland (1862-63). A leading officer under Gen. Robert E. Lee in the defense of PETERSBURG and Richmond (1864-65), he was killed in the final struggle at Petersburg.

HILL, Benjamin Harvey (Jasper County, Ga., Sept. 14, 1823 — Atlanta, Ga., Aug. 16, 1882). Politician. He was a member of the Georgia legislature before becoming a senator in the Confederate Congress (1861-65). Although Hill opposed secession, he bowed to his state's decision. After the war Hill helped lead Georgia through reconstruction and became a major speaker for Southern causes in the U.S. Congress (1875-77) and the U.S. Senate (1877-82).

HILL, Daniel Harvey (York District, S.C., July 12, 1821 — Charlotte, N.C., Sept. 24, 1889). Military officer and educator. An 1842 West Point graduate who fought in the Mexican War, Hill resigned his commission to become professor of mathematics at Washington College (1849-54) and Davidson College (1854-59). During the Civil War, he served the Confederate Army in several major conflicts, including the Peninsula and Antietam campaigns. He was president of the University of

Arkansas (1877-84) and president of middle Georgia Military and Agricultural College (1886-89).

HILLIARD, Henry Washington (Fayetteville, N.C., Aug. 4, 1808 — Atlanta, Ga., Dec. 17, 1892). Politician. A lawyer and member of the Alabama legislature, Hilliard was charge d'affaires for the U.S. in Belgium (1842-44) and U.S. Congressman from Alabama (1845-51). He fought against the secession of Alabama but also opposed President Abraham Lincoln's call for volunteer troops and sided briefly with the South, serving as a brigadier general in the Confederate Army. He was U.S. minister to Brazil from 1877 to 1881.

HILLSBOROUGH, N.C. Town (pop. 3,019), seat of Orange Co., in northern North Carolina. Settled around 1700, Hillsborough was an early capital of the province of North Carolina. It was the birthplace of artist Thomas Hart BENTON, and site of Bingham School, one of the state's earliest military academies (1793). Manufactures include textiles, furniture, mobile homes, and electronics.

HILLSBOROUGH RIVER, Fla. Volusia Co. Actually a narrow lagoon in northeastern Florida, it is separated from the Atlantic Ocean by a narrow barrier island. It runs about 18 miles from Ponce de Leon Inlet in the north to Mosquito Lagoon in the south and is part of the Intracoastal Waterway.

HILTON HEAD ISLAND, S.C. Island in Beaufort Co., off South Carolina's southern Atlantic coast. Today one of the South's most popular year-round resorts, the island's development as such began in 1953. The biggest sea island between Florida and New Jersey, it has 12 miles of beaches, six marinas, and an airstrip, and plays host to many major golf and tennis events. A subspecies of raccoon discovered on the island is found nowhere else in the world.

HINDMAN, Thomas Carmichael (Knoxville, Tenn., Jan. 28, 1828 — Helena, Ark., Sept. 28, 1868). Politician. Elected to Congress from Arkansas in 1858, Hindman declined his seat in 1860 as a suppporter of secession. He fought in the Civil War as a Confederate major general, and lived for a time in Mexico. When he returned to Arkansas in 1868, he opposed

the reconstruction movement and this brought about his assassination.

HINES, Walker Downer (Russellville, Ky., Feb. 2, 1870 — Merano, Italy, Jan. 14, 1934). Lawyer and statesman. Educated at Ogden College and the University of Virginia, Hines became an official with the Louisville and Nashville Railroad. He was appointed director general of the U.S. Railroad Administration in 1919. Between 1920 and 1925, he served on special assignments for both President Woodrow Wilson and the League of Nations. He wrote *The War History of the American Railroads* (1928).

HINESVILLE, Ga. City (pop. 11,309), seat of Liberty Co., in southeastern Georgia. Located in a rich farm and timbering region, the town almost tripled in size between 1970 and 1980. Present industries include the manufacture of paper. U.S Fort Stewart is nearby.

HINTON, W.Va. Town (pop. 4,622), seat of Summers Co., in the southern part of the state. Settled in 1831 and incorporated in 1880, this resort community is situated on the New River near its junction with the Greenbrier River. Bluestone and Pipestem State Parks are nearby.

HITCHCOCK, Ethan Allen (Mobile, Ala., Sept. 19, 1835 — Washington, D.C., Apr. 9, 1909). Businessman and statesman. Hitchcock founded a plate glass manufacturing company in 1874. As Secretary of the Interior under Presidents William McKinley and Theodore Roosevelt (1898-1907), he prosecuted public land fraud and defended Indian rights.

HITCHITI INDIANS. Small tribe of the Muskogean linguistic group that first lived along the lower course of the Ocmulgee River and then moved into Chattahoochee County, Ga. They were members of the Lower CREEK Confederacy.

HIWASSEE RIVER, N.C./Tenn./Ga. An 80-mile waterway rising in southeastern Tennessee. It runs east into western North Carolina forming Lake Hiwassee, turns south through Catuga Lake, and terminates in northern Georgia. It is situated in what was once the heart of the Cherokee Indian territory.

HOBAN, James (Callan, Ireland, c. 1762 — Washington, D.C., Dec. 8, 1831). Architect.

Hoban arrived in this country in the late 1780s and his first major architectural design was the South Carolina statehouse (1790-91), which later burned (1865). He moved to Washington, D.C., in 1792 and entered competitions for the proposed federal buildings. His design for the president's mansion, later to be called the White House, was accepted and he supervised its construction. After it was burned by the British in 1814 he supervised its reconstruction. He continued to work on federal buildings for numerous years, particularly the War and State offices, which were begun in 1818.

HOBBY, Oveta Culp (Killeen, Tex., Jan. 19, 1905 —). Newspaper publisher and politician. The first woman parliamentarian for the Texas House of Representatives (1925-31, 1939-41), she went to work for the Houston *Post* after marrying its publisher William Pettus Hobby. In 1938 she became the paper's executive vice president and editor. Mrs. Hobby served as a colonel and director of the WACs in World War II, and became the first secretary of Health, Education and Welfare in 1953 under President Dwight Eisenhower. After her resignation (1955) she returned to the *Post*, and became chairman of the board in 1965.

HOBKIRK'S HILL, Battle of. Revolutionary War engagement fought April 25, 1781, ten miles north of Camden, S.C. The British were victorious, but this was a mere holding operation within their general retreat south whereby they surrendered the Carolinas to the Continental militia. Following his costly victory at Guilford Courthouse, N.C., British commander Lord Charles Cornwallis fell back to the coast, leaving Lord Francis Rawdon in Camden in defense of the Carolinas. This enabled the Revolutionary army under Gen. Nathanael Greene to seize the offensive and move south. Rawdon moved north to confront the patriots at Hobkirk's Hill on April 25, 1781. As they had at Guilford Courthouse, the Revolutionary militiamen panicked under the fire of the trained British troops. Greene was forced to withdraw entirely to avoid heavier losses. Both sides suffered casualties of approximately 250 killed and wounded out of equal forces of 1,500 troops. Having gained only time by the victory, Rawdon then began to fall back toward his base of supplies in Charleston, S.C.

HODGENVILLE, Ky. Town (pop. 2,459), seat of Larue Co., in south central Kentucky. Hodgenville was the birthplace of Abraham Lincoln and the log cabin where he was supposedly born is part of the National Historical Park. Settled in 1789, the town is a farming community with sawmills and limestone quarries.

HODGES, Luther Hartwell (Pittsylvania Co., Va., Mar. 9, 1898 — Chapel Hill, N.C., Oct. 6, 1974). Politician. After a successful career in textiles, Hodges was elected lieutenant governor of North Carolina (1952) and succeeded to the governorship in 1954. Reelected in 1956, his administration was instrumental in promoting the state as a site for new industry. He was U.S. Secretary of Commerce (1961-65).

HOGG, James Stephen (Cherokee County, Tex., Mar. 24, 1851 — Houston, Tex., Mar. 3, 1906). Politician. Hogg was Democratic governor of Texas from 1891 to 1895 and successfully established major economic reforms. He retired from politics in 1895 to resume his law practice.

HOGS. The Southern states account for 15% of the total U.S. sales of hogs each year. Iowa leads all states with sales of more than $2 billion per year. By comparison, the leading states in the South in sales of hogs in 1980 were North Carolina, with $282 million; Georgia, with $214 million; Kentucky, with $143 million; and Tennessee, with $127 million.

HOLDEN, William Woods (Orange Co., N.C., Nov. 24, 1818 — Raleigh, N.C., Mar. 1, 1892). Political journalist and politician. Holden was a reporter for the Raleigh *Star*, the state's leading Whig newpaper, while studying law. In 1843 he switched to the Democratic party as a condition of becoming editor of the North Carolina *Standard*. He was governor from 1868 to 1870 but his administration was marred by charges of corruption and incompetence. He was impeached for protecting corrupt elements and arbitrary action.

HOLIDAY, Eleanora "Billie," "Lady Day" (Baltimore, Md., Apr. 7, 1915 — New York, N.Y., July 17, 1959). Jazz singer. From the beginning of her professional career in 1930 through 1940, she performed with the most popular bands of the day including those of Benny Goodman, Count Basie, and Artie Shaw. She earned considerable fame as a solo performer until drug addiction ended her career and her life.

HOLLINS, George Nichols (Baltimore, Md., Sept. 20, 1799 — Baltimore, Md., Jan. 18, 1878). Naval officer. Hollins served with Commander Stephen Decatur during the War of 1812. During the Civil War, he joined the Confederate Navy and commanded ships fighting the Union vessels blockading the Mississippi River.

HOLLINS COLLEGE. Independent liberal arts college for women located in the town of Hollins College in southwestern Virginia, seven miles north of Roanoke. Founded as an academy in 1842, the college offers a variety of majors, including American studies, Russian studies, statistics, and theater arts. Most undergraduate degrees are conferred in social science, fine and applied arts, letters, foreign languages, psychology, and biological studies. Master of Arts degrees are offered in English and creative writing (the writing program is the country's second-oldest), psychology, liberal studies, and theater arts. The South provides 67% of students, 14% are from Middle Atlantic states, and 7% are from the North Central region. After graduation, 30% of students immediately pursue graduate study, many attending medical and law schools.

Library: 200,000 volumes, 1,250 journal subscriptions, 1,500 records/tapes. Faculty: 87. Enrollment: 914 total graduate and undergraduate: 805 women (full-time). Degrees: Bachelor's, Master's.

HOLLY SPRINGS, Battle of. Successful Civil War surprise attack by Confederate troops against a Union Army base in northern Mississippi on December 20, 1862. Confederate Gen. Earl Van Dorn commanded the operation, which began and ended in Granada, 75 miles south, and traveled the route of the Mississippi Central Railroad. The night attack on Holly Springs caught most of the Union garrison asleep and enabled Van Dorn to release Confederate prisoners and to destroy Union munitions. Because of this successful raid, Gen. Ulysses S. Grant was forced to withdraw his base of operations from Oxford, Miss., to Grand Junction, Tenn., from which point he launched his campaign against VICKSBURG.

HOLLYWOOD, Fla. City (pop. 117,188), Broward Co., on the southeast coast of Florida, 20 miles north of Miami. A jungle until 1921, the city was planned and developed by Joseph Young of California, who built the city around a broad avenue he called Hollywood Boule-vard. Hollywood has grown rapidly as a resort town and in real population since the 1950s. Other than tourism, its industries include the manufacture of electronic equipment, furniture, and surgical equipment.

HOLMES, David (York Co., Pa., Mar. 10, 1769 — Winchester, Va., Aug. 20, 1832). Politician. He was a practicing lawyer in Harrisonburg, Va., before becoming a U.S. congressman from that state (1797-1809). He became governor of the Territory of Mississippi (1809-17), and when Mississippi was admitted to the Union, Holmes was elected the state's first governor (1817-20). He was a U.S. senator from Mississippi from 1820 to 1825.

HOLMES CREEK, Ala./Fla. Waterway originating near Geneva in southern Alabama, flowing south through Holmes County for about 60 miles to join the Choctawhatchee River southeast of De Funiak Springs. The Holmes is navigable below Vernon, Fla.

HOLSTON RIVER, Tenn. River originating in northeastern Tennessee. It flows southwest approximately 115 miles to meet the French Broad River and form the Tennessee River. Settlement along the river began prior to the American Revolution and one of the the state's first water-powered mills was built on its banks. The Holston is the source of both Cherokee and Great Falls Lakes.

HOLT, Joseph (Breckenridge Co., Ky., Jan. 6, 1807 — Washington, D.C., Aug. 1, 1894). Lawyer and statesman. He was Secretary of War from January to March 1861. Holt's loyalty to the U.S. during the Civil War, despite personal sympathy for the cause of the South, influenced Kentucky to remain in the Union. He supported Lincoln's extension of military authority over areas of civilian concern during the war and was judge advocate general of the U.S. Army (1862-75). His responsibility for the prosecution of some of John Wilkes Booth's alleged accomplices darkened Holt's reputation.

HOMESTEAD, Fla. City (pop. 20,668), Dade Co., in southeastern Florida. Incorporated in 1913, Homestead is the trading center of a fruit and vegetable farming area on the border of the Everglades. It is the home of Everglades National Park and Homestead Air Force Base.

HOMEWOOD, Ala. City (pop. 21,271), Jefferson Co., in north central Alabama. Homewood is primarily a residential suburb of Birmingham. It was incorporated in 1921. Shades Mountain and Oak Mountain State Parks are nearby.

HOMOCHITTO RIVER, Miss. River rising in the Pine Hills. It flows approximately 70 miles southwest to reach the Mississippi River. It passes through Lake Mary. A national forest is on its banks.

HOOD, John Bell (Owingsville, Ky., June 1, 1831 — New Orleans, La., Aug. 30, 1879). Military officer. Hood served in the U.S. Cavalry following his graduation from West Point until the outbreak of the Civil War, when he joined the Confederacy and won quick promotion to colonel. He became lieutenant general in the spring of 1864 under Gen. Joseph E. Johnston, who was defending ATLANTA against oncoming Federal forces. In July, Confederate President Jefferson Davis transferred the command to Hood, who promptly attacked the Union Army but was forced back into the city. He then marched his troops out north and west but was met by the army of the Cumberland, under the command of Gen. George Thomas, which virtually destroyed his troops. Wounded many times and having lost his leg in battle, he resigned and moved to New Orleans.

HOOPER, Johnson Jones (Wilmington, N.C., June 9, 1815 — Richmond, Va., June 7, 1862). Author and journalist. Hooper became editor of the *East Alabamian* (1842), for which he wrote humorous tales of a tricky backwoodsman named Simon Suggs. His early works were published in book form as *Some Adventures of Captain Simon Suggs* (1846), and were followed by *A Ride with Old Kit Kuncker* (1849). A devoted secessionist and fearless editor, Hooper was elected secretary of the provisional congress of the Confederacy (1861), an office he filled until his death.

HOOVER, John Edgar Washington, D.C., Jan. 1, 1895 — Washington, D.C., May 2, 1972). Public official. A 1916 graduate of George Washington University Law School, Hoover was admitted to the bar and joined the U.S. Department of Justice in 1917. He served first as a file reviewer, then was promoted to the post of special assistant to Attorney General A. Mitchell Palmer. In May, 1924, he was named acting director of the FBI, was confirmed as head of the agency seven months later, and held the post for 48 years. At the time of his takeover, the agency was considered corrupted and disorganized by the Harding administration. In order to salvage its reputation, Hoover instituted a stronger, more selective policy regarding the choosing and training of FBI personnel; developed what was to become the world's largest fingerprint file; established a scientific crime lab and the FBI National Academy; and designated for training selected law enforcement officers from around the country. Concerned over the media attention devoted to gangsters and spies in the 1930s, Hoover successfully promoted an image of the FBI as a fair but firm intelligence organization devoid of political control. But by the 1970s Hoover's indiscretions and excessive powers had become a matter of national concern. In 1975 congressional investigators disclosed that he had abused his power, allegedly violating civil rights, and had conducted covert investigations for private gain. Despite the charges, he remained in power until his death.

HOPE, Ark. City (pop. 10,290), seat of Hempstead Co., in southwestern Arkansas. Located in a diversified agricultural region noted for its watermelons, Hope is a commercial shipping point. Industries today include timbering, brickwork, and egg processing. Settled in 1874 and incorporated in 1875, it is the site of a state university agricultural experiment station.

HOPE, John (Augusta, Ga., June 2, 1868 — Atlanta, Ga., Feb. 22, 1936). Educator and black leader. Dedicated to the intellectual and cultural preparation of Negro youth, Hope vowed publicly that he would demand complete Negro equality. He attended the Harpers Ferry Conference (1906) the only college president to do so, which led to the founding of the National Association for the Advancement of Colored People (N.A.A.C.P.). Son of a successful Scottish businessman in Augusta and the mulatto daughter of a freed slave, he sided early with the world of the oppressed black. After graduating from Brown University (1894) he taught at Negro colleges and became the first black president of Morehouse College (1906-29). He later helped found and presided over Atlanta University, the first black graduate school in the U.S. Hope also helped organize the Commission of Interracial Cooperation and advised the N.A.A.C.P. and Urban League in their early stages.

HOPEWELL, Va. Independent city (pop. 23,397), in southeast Virginia at the confluence of the James and Appomattox Rivers. A port of entry, Hopewell's harbor on the James is accessible to ocean-going vessels, and smaller vessels can reach Petersburg by traveling up the Appomattox. Settled in 1619 and incorporated in 1916, rapid growth did not occur until a munitions center was established here in 1913. Present manufactures include chemicals, textiles, paper box board, and synthetic tire cord, along with diversified farming and tobacco products.

HOPKINS, Johns (Anne Arundel Co., Md., May 19, 1795 — Baltimore, Md., Dec. 24, 1873). Businessman and philanthropist. With little formal education, Hopkins founded the trading firm of Hopkins Brothers in 1819 and later lent his business expertise to the banking and railroad industries. He left over $7 million for the establishment of JOHNS HOPKINS UNIVERSITY and Johns Hopkins Hospital. His first name comes from the surname of a maternal ancestor, Richard Johns.

HOPKINSVILLE, Ky. City (pop. 27,318), seat of Christian Co., in southwestern Kentucky. Tobacco is grown in the rich farm lands that surround this industrial city. Industries are varied and include the manufacture of bowling balls, clothing, and hardware material. A branch of the University of Kentucky system is located here and Jefferson Davis Memorial Park is nearby. The city was incorporated in 1804.

HORSESHOE BEND, Ala. Tallapoosa Co. in eastern Alabama on a turn of the Tallapoosa River. Andrew Jackson and his militia defeated the Creek Confederacy here on March 27, 1814. The 2,040-acre National Military Park established here in 1959 marks the site of the battle.

HOT SPRINGS, Ark. City (pop. 35,166), seat of Garland Co., in west central Arkansas. The city is a resort center within Hot Springs National Park, and there is also some light industry, timbering, and stock farms. Hot Springs was settled in 1807 and incorporated in 1876.

HOUMA, La. City (pop. 36,602), seat of Terrebonne Parish, in southern Louisiana. Houma has earned the title of "Venice of America" because it has a large number of bayous and canals including the Gulf Intracoastal Waterway Canal and Bayou Terrebonne. It is a major center for the oil industry and shrimp fleets, and has many seafood processing plants. Southdown Plantation and the Terrebonne Museum are here.

HOUMA INDIANS ("red"). Tribe of Muskogean linguistic stock that first inhabited the region on the east side of the Mississippi River close to the Mississippi-Louisiana boundary line. The Houma gave their name to Houma, La., the capital of Terrebonne Parish. When IBERVILLE visited them in 1700 he left a missionary among them and a church was constructed. Generally a peaceful tribe, they were nearly destroyed by TUNICA INDIANS that they had previously allowed to settle among them when the Tunicans had been driven from their home territory.

HOUSE, Edward Mandell (Houston, Tex., June 261, 1858 — New York, N.Y., Mar. 28, 1938). Diplomat. He was a political adviser to several Democratic governors between 1892 and 1904. Governor James Hogg gave House the honorary title of "colonel." He assumed a major role in Woodrow Wilson's 1912 presidential campaign, and refused a cabinet post, choosing instead to help Wilson in a variety of political and administrative functions. He became recognized as Wilson's chief agent in foreign affairs and helped explore mediation alternatives with European countries in World War I. He headed a U.S. mission to the Inter-Allied Conferences in London and Paris that led to the coordination of the Allied effort, and was one of the signers of the Treaty of Versailles in June 1917. After he advised Wilson to consider compromise for the ratification of the treaty and the entry of the U.S. into the League of Nations, the two men separated, never seeing each other again. House, along with Charles Seymour, edited a collection of essays by American delegates to the peace conference called *What Really Happened at Paris* (1921).

HOUSTON, David Franklin (Monroe, N.C., Feb. 17, 1866 — Cold Spring Harbor, N.Y., Sept. 2, 1940). Educator and statesman. Houston was president of the University of Texas (1905-08) and chancellor of Washington University in St. Louis, Mo., (1908-16) before becoming Secretary of Agriculture (1913-20) and Secretary of the Treasury (1920-21), both under President Woodrow Wilson.

HOUSTON, George Smith (Franklin, Tenn., Jan. 17, 1811 — Athens, Ala., Dec. 31, 1879). Politician. Admitted to the bar in 1831, Houston was Democratic U.S. congressman from Alabama (1841-49, 1851-61) and served almost continuously until the state's secession when he took the Union side. He became the first Democratic governor of Alabama after the Civil War (1874-78) and was a U.S. senator for ten months prior to his death.

HOUSTON, Samuel (Rockbridge Co., Va., Mar. 2, 1793 — Huntsville, Tex., July 26, 1863). Politician. As a child, Houston was brought to Tennessee where he spent whole years with the Cherokee Indians who named him "the Raven." In 1814 he distinguished himself at the Battle of Horseshoe Bend against the Creek tribes, leading to a close friendship with his commander, Andrew Jackson. After a brief study of the law, he entered Tennessee politics as a Jacksonian Democrat, serving in Congress from 1823 to 1827 and being elected

Sam Houston, promoter of Texas Independence and first president of the Republic of Texas

governor of Tennessee in 1827. He resigned his governorship two years later in the wake of a highly publicized separation from his wife of three months, and went to live with the Cherokees in what is now Oklahoma, taking an Indian wife there.

It was in 1833 that Houston first went to Texas, where he gained immediate fame as a hard-line proponent of the region's independence from Mexico. Named commander-in-chief of the Texas revolutionary troops in 1836, he responded to the massacre at the ALAMO in that year by capturing Mexican Gen. Santa Anna and his army of 1,500 at SAN JACINTO with almost no casualties to his own army of only 800. For this he was overwhelmingly elected president of independent Texas, serving from 1836 to 1838 and again from 1841 to 1844. Texas was admitted to the Union in 1845, and Houston served as both U.S. senator (1846-59) and governor (1859-61). An eloquent orator on the need to preserve the Union, he was forced to resign as governor in March of 1861 because the secessionist movement prevailed in the state and Houston refused to take the oath of allegiance to the Confederate States.

HOUSTON, Tex. City (pop. 1,594,086), seat of Harris Co., in southeastern Texas. Houston is the fifth-largest city in the U.S. and the third-largest port, owing to its direct linkage to the Gulf of Mexico, 50 miles away, via the Houston Ship Channel and the Gulf Intracoastal Waterway. Houston has had a steady population and commercial growth, which began here with the discovery of oil in the early 1900s. The Houston metropolitan area covers 6,931 square miles containing several counties and a multitude of communities, many of them annexed to the city in recent years.

The city is a major petrochemical and petroleum refining center. Besides oil and gas and shipping concerns, other significant industries in Houston include the manufacture of chemical and electrical equipment, government, medical, professional services, aerospace research, and agricultural activities. Thousands of people are employed in the city's enormous retail industry.

Houston was settled soon after the Mexicans were defeated by the troops of Sam HOUSTON at nearby San Jacinto and named in Houston's honor. From 1837 to 1839 and from 1842 to 1845 Houston was the capital of Texas. In spite of its humid, somewhat swampy location Houston grew steadily, becoming a major cotton shipping port by the middle of the 19th century, the result of successful efforts to link Houston with the Gulf of Mexico. As the waterway to the Gulf was improved, and with the coming of the railroad, Houston began to mushroom in population and land area. Cotton was king until 1901 when oil was discovered and since then, Houston's economy and history have been dominated by oil. Skilled and unskilled labor have been pouring into the city for years, supplying an almost ceaseless need for workers. This great growth has brought a diverse group of people to the semitropical climate of Houston. There are large minority populations of blacks, Mexicans, and others. In order to absorb the steady increases in population, the city has been forced to repeatedly expand. Because its low-density population is a deterrent to mass transportation, most residents rely on cars, which means that Houston, like many other major cities, has major traffic problems.

Houston has a wide variety of sports, cultural, and recreational offerings. Three professional sports teams are based here: the Houston Oilers football team, the Houston Rockets basketball team, and the Houston Astros baseball team. The Oilers and the Astros both play their home games in the famous Houston Astrodome, the world's first fully enclosed football and baseball stadium. Houston has its own ballet and opera companies, as well as the Houston Symphony Orchestra. There are professional theater groups, and the Museum of Natural Science and the Museum of Fine Arts. Houston's points of interest include the award-winning architecture of much of the ultramodern downtown area. Outside the city are the San Jacinto Monument and the Lyndon B. Johnson Space Center.

Transportation and communications have grown along with the city. The William P. Hobby Airport handles a great deal of private air traffic, and the Houston Intercontinental Airport is one of the world's largest. Many interstate trucking companies are based in the city as are bus and railroad lines. There are several television stations, over 30 radio stations, two large circulation newspapers, and many smaller publications.

A major educational center, Houston is home to 23 colleges and universities. Among them are Rice University, Texas Southern University, the University of Houston, Baylor University College of Medicine, many law schools, and the Texas Woman's University College of Nursing. The city is also the home of the American Society of Oceanography.

HOWELL, Clark (Barnwell Co., S.C., Sept. 21, 1863 — Atlanta, Ga., Nov. 14, 1936). Journalist. Successor of his father as editor-in-chief of the Atlanta *Constitution* (1897), Howell campaigned against municipal corruption in Atlanta. His series won the paper the 1929 Pulitzer Prize. He was a member of the Georgia House of Representatives (1886-91), and a state senator (1900-06). In 1906 he was an unsuccessful candidate for governor.

HOWELL, William Henry (Baltimore, Md., Feb. 20, 1860 — Baltimore, Md., Feb. 6, 1945). Physiologist. Howell graduated from Johns Hopkins University in 1881 and earned his Ph.D. there in 1884. Returning to Johns Hopkins in 1888, he taught until 1931. His research on blood, with L. E. Holt, yielded the discovery of heparin, the anticoagulant.

HUGHES, Howard Robard (Lancaster, Mo., Sept. 9, 1869 — Houston, Tex., Jan. 14, 1924). Inventor and industrialist. After working in the oil drilling business, Hughes invented a revolutionary cone-shaped drill bit (1908). He later founded the very successful Hughes Tool Company, which manufactured his bits and other related tools. He was the father of millionaire recluse Howard Hughes.

HUGHES, Langston (Joplin, Mo., Feb. 1, 1902 — New York, N.Y., May 22, 1967). Author. The product of a broken home, Hughes had already dropped out of Columbia University, shipped out on a vessel for Africa, and traveled in Europe by the time his verse was discovered by Vachel Lindsay in 1925. Hughes was then working as a busboy in Washington, D.C., but the subsequent praise for his work enabled him to graduate from Lincoln University in Pennsylvania in 1929 and to work in New York City as a prominent member of the Harlem literary revival. His free-verse poetry is especially noted for its colloquial rhythms, as in "The Negro Speaks of Rivers" (1926) and "Weary Blues" (1926). His writings include novels and autobiographical works.

HUGHES, Rupert (Lancaster, Mo., Jan. 31, 1872 — Los Angeles, Cal., Sept. 9, 1956). Author. After graduating from what is now Western Reserve University, he earned his Ph.D. from Yale in 1899. His published works include a three-volume biography of George Washington (1926-30) and the novel *What Will People Say?* (1914).

HULL, Cordell (Overton Co., Tenn., Oct. 2, 1871 – Bethesda, Md., July 23, 1955). Statesman. A captain in the Spanish-American War, Hull was elected as a Democrat from Tennessee to the U.S. House (1907-21, 1923-31) and the U.S. Senate (1931-33). He was author of the bill establishing the income tax system of 1913, the inheritance tax, the League of Nations, and the lowering of tariffs for world peace. Appointed Secretary of State by President Franklin D. Roosevelt (1933-44), Hull sponsored the reciprocal Agreements Act (1934), developed the "good neighbor policy" with Latin American, stood strongly against the expansion of Germany and Japan in the 1930s, and fostered plans for the U.N. during World War II. Retiring due to poor health in 1944, he had served longer than any prior Secretary of State and was awarded the Nobel Peace Prize in 1945.

HUMPHREYS, Benjamin Grubb (Claiborne Co., Miss., Aug. 24, 1808 — Leflore Co., Miss., Dec. 20 1882). Military officer and politician. In 1825 Humphreys entered West Point but was dismissed because of his involvement in a student riot. He returned to Mississippi where he studied law and became an attorney. He was a member of the state legislature (1838-40) and the state senate (1840-44) as an antebellum Whig. He fought in the major battles of the Civil War and attained the rank of brigadier general in the Confederate Army. Humphreys was elected the state's first governor after the war (1865-68).

HUMPHREYS, William Jackson (Gap Mills, W.Va., Feb. 3, 1862 — Washington, D.C, Nov. 10, 1949). Physicist. After receiving his Ph.D. from Johns Hopkins (1897), Humphreys taught at the University of Virginia before he joined the U.S. Weather Bureau (1905-35). He wrote numerous books on weather research, including *Weather, Proverbs and Paradoxes* (1923) and *Ways of the Weather* (1942). He is chiefly known for explaining the existence of the isothermal stratosphere.

HUNT, Gaillard (New Orleans, La., Sept. 8, 1862 — Washington, D.C., Mar. 20, 1924). Historian and editor. Hunt served in the Department of State as chief of the division of publications and chief of the division of manuscripts of the Library of Congress (1909-17). A noted historian, his works include *The Life of James Madison* (1902) and *Life in America One Hundred Years Ago* (1914).

HUNTER, David (Washington, D.C., July 21, 1802 — Washington, D.C., Feb. 2, 1886). Military officer. A graduate of West Point (1822), he was appointed colonel of the 6th Cavalry in 1861 and commanded the main column of Union troops as brigadier general in the first battle of Bull Run (July 1861) where he was severely wounded. In the spring of 1862 he was put in command of the Department of the South. He declared martial law and, giving a free interpretation to his instructions from the War Department, took measures for organizing regiments of Negro troops. To facilitate the business of recruiting, he issued a general order on May 9, 1862, which proclaimed the absolute freedom of all slaves within his department, declaring that "slavery and martial law, in a free country, are incompatible." This was a step too far in advance of public sentiment and the government policy of that period. President Abraham Lincoln annulled the order and Hunter then commanded the Department of West Virginia (1864) until succeeded by Gen. Philip Sheridan.

HUNTER, Robert Mercer Taliaferro (Essex County, Va., Apr. 21, 1809 — Lloyds, Va., July 18, 1887). Statesman. After graduating from the University of Virginia in 1828, Hunter was admitted to the bar (1830). He represented Virginia in the U.S. House of Representatives (1837-43) and was speaker from 1839 to 1841. He served again from 1845 to 1847 when he was elected to the U.S. Senate (1847-61). He played an active role in writing the Tariff Act, and in 1861 he lobbied strenuously for Virginia's secession from the Union. When Virginia did secede, Hunter served as Secretary of State of the Confederacy (1861-62), and from 1862 to 1865 he served as a Confederate senator. After the War, he served as treasurer of Virginia.

HUNTING ISLAND, S.C. One of the SEA ISLANDS located in Beaufort Co., off the southeastern coast of South Carolina, east of St. Helena's Island. A 5,000-acre state park here offers a wide variety of land and water recreation. A wildlife sanctuary as well as several pre-Revolutionary buildings are also found here.

HUNTINGTON, W.Va. City (pop. 63,684), seat of Cabell Co., in the westernmost part of West Virginia on the Ohio River. Huntington is situated near the intersection of the Kentucky, Ohio, and West Virginia state lines. It was named after Collis P. Huntington, president of the Chesapeake and Ohio Railroad, who founded it (1871) to serve as the company's western terminus. Huntington purchased approximately 5,000 acres of farmland along the Ohio River and hired Rufus Cook, a Boston architect, to plan the town. After suffering from periodic flooding for over 50 years an eleven-mile long protective wall was built. Present industries include coal processing and the manufacture of electrical equipment, glass products, and secondary metals. Marshall University was founded here in 1837.

HUNTSVILLE, Ala. City (pop. 142,513), seat of Madison Co., in northeastern Alabama. It was settled in 1807 and called Twickenham, but later incorporated (1811) and renamed for its founder, John Hunt. The state constitution was framed in Huntsville in 1819. It remained a center for hay, cotton, corn, and tobacco throughout its early history. Today its most important businesses are the manufacturing of sheet metals, textiles, and farm equipment. It is the home of the U.S. Redstone Arsenal, a rocket and guided-missile research center, and the George C. Marshall Space Flight Center.

HUNTSVILLE, Tex. Town (pop. 23,936), seat of Walker Co., in southeast Texas north of Houston. Settled in 1836, Huntsville was the home of many famous early Texans, including Sam HOUSTON. Today it is the site of the Texas State Penitentiary, created in 1847. From 1960 to 1970, Huntsville's population rose 47%, in part due to labor opportunities provided by extensive improvements to the penitentiary. Sam Houston State University is here.

HURST, John Fletcher (near Salem, Md., Aug. 17, 1834 — Washington, D.C., May 4, 1903). Educator and clergyman. After graduating from Dickinson College in 1854, Hurst went to Europe to study theology. He was consecrated a bishop of the Methodist Church in 1880, and later founded the American University in Washington, D.C. He wrote *A History of the Christian Church* (1900).

HURSTON, Zora Neale (Eatonville, Fla., Jan. 7, 1901 (?) — Ft. Pierce, Fla., Jan. 28, 1960). Author. She began publishing short stories and essays while studying anthropology at Barnard College, in 1928 becoming that school's first black graduate. She then returned south to research folk traditions (1927-32), publishing ethnographic studies that include *Mules and Men* (1935) and *Tell My Horse* (1938). Turning from academia, she won Rosenwald (1934) and Guggenheim (1936-37) fellowships and became the most prolific black writer of the 1930s. Her novels include *Jonah's Gourd Vine* (1934), *Their Eyes Were Watching God* (1937), and *Seraph and the Suwanee* (1948).

HUTCHINSON'S ISLAND, Battle of. Revolutionary War action in the harbor of Savannah, Ga., fought March 7, 1776. The events preceding the battle included the capture of the Royal Governor of Georgia, James Wright, on January 18 and his escape from the patriots on February 11. Wright took refuge aboard a ship in the harbor. When their demands were refused, the British took Hutchinson's Island in the harbor. The patriots defended Savannah by drifting burning ships in the direction of the British troop ships. Failing to take the city, the British abandoned it on March 7 and Governor Wright left Georgia.

I

IBERVILLE, Pierre Le Moyne, Sieur d'
(Montreal, Canada, July 16, 1661 — Havana, Cuba, July 9, 1706). Soldier and explorer. Iberville was the founder of the first permanent settlement in the French territory of Louisiana. From 1686 to 1697, during the war between Britain and France, he distinguished himself by leading a series of raids against British forts in the Hudson Bay area and by saving Acadia (Nova Scotia) for New France. After peace was declared, Louis XIV commanded Iberville to found a colony in Louisiana at the mouth of the Mississippi (1698). Accompanied by his brother BIENVILLE, he succeeded where LA SALLE had failed 13 years earlier. When war again broke out between Britain and France (1702), Iberville was given command of the West Indian fleet. He captured the islands of Nevis and St. Kitts (1706), and was preparing to launch an expedition against the British in the Carolinas, Boston, and New York when he died of yellow fever.

IBITOUPA INDIANS (people "at the source" of a river or stream). Small tribe thought to have been of Muskogean linguistic stock that lived on the Yazoo River in Holmes County, Mississippi.

ILLINOIS INDIANS ("men" or "people"). Tribe of Algonquian linguistic stock. They lived along the Illinois and Mississippi Rivers, some of them extending down into northeastern Arkansas and eastern Missouri.

INDEPENDENCE, Mo. City (pop. 111,806), seat of Jackson Co., in western Missouri just east of Kansas City. The area was settled in 1827, with the county named for Andrew Jackson and the city for his love of independence. Incorporated in 1849, the city was a starting point for the Santa Fe, Oregon, and California trails, and later became a rendezvous point for wagon trains heading for the California gold mines. President Harry S TRUMAN was born here and a library and museum bearing his name house his private papers and momentoes. Outlaws such as Frank James were once held in the county jail, built in 1859 and now restored as a museum. The world headquarters of the Reorganized Church of Jesus Christ of Latter Day Saints (Mormon) is located here. The city has a balanced manufacturing and agricultural economy. Present manufactures include farm machinery, cement, plastics, stoves, and furnaces.

197

INDIAN CORN. Indigenous American crop. When English settlers first arrived in Virginia, they found the Indians cultivating maize, and so the Europeans called it "Indian corn." It proved to be a blessing to the immigrants, and Indian corn appears among the earliest exports from America. In 1748 the two Carolinas exported 100,000 bushels a year. For several years before the Revolution, Virginia exported 600,000 bushels annually, and by the beginning of the 19th century the annual export was two million bushels. See also CORN.

INDIAN RIVER, Fla. River that is actually a lagoon located off the eastern coast of Florida running parallel to the shore from Brevard County in the north to St. Lucie Inlet 120 miles to the south. Ranging from two to five miles wide, it is protected from the Atlantic Ocean by extensive barrier islands. It is a region of extensive citrus growth and several resort cities.

INDIAN TERRITORY. Area in the eastern part of Oklahoma, which was called by this name although it was never regularly organized. As a result of treaties made between 1820 and 1845, most Southern Indian tribes were removed to this region by the United States government. Each tribe maintained its own government while in the territory, but when Oklahoma entered the union (1907) any Indians still living there became citizens of that state.

INDIGO. A blue dye made by fermenting the transparent sap of the *Indigofera* plant, and so by extension any deep blue color. Manufacture of indigo, although most extensive in India, was practiced in the American South long before the exploration of the region by Europeans. Some species of the genus *Indigofera* are native to states such as South Carolina, Georgia, and Florida, and in the 19th century the indigo

Slaves harvesting an indigo crop and processing it into blue dye

trade was an important part of the economy of these states. In 1897 a synthetic blue dye, aniline, was first manufactured as a by-product of coal tar; it has since completely replaced vegetable indigo in commercial use.

INGRAHAM, Duncan Nathaniel (Charleston, S.C., Dec. 6, 1802 — Charleston, S.C., Oct. 16, 1891). Naval officer. He fought in the War of 1812 and the Mexican War. In 1861 he resigned from the U.S. Navy to command Confederate ships along the South Carolina coast.

INGRAHAM, Prentiss (Adams County, Miss., Dec. 22, 1843 — Beauvoir, Miss., Aug. 16, 1904). Military officer and novelist. The son of novelist Joseph Holt Ingraham, he produced prodigious numbers of "dime novels." A soldier of fortune, he served in the Civil War and was later involved in the Cuban war for independence.

INNES, James (Caroline Co., Va., 1754 — Philadelphia, Pa., Aug. 2, 1798). Lawyer and orator. A commander during the Revolution, Innes served as a member of the Virginia legislature (1780-82, 1785-87). An advocate of the adoption of the U.S. Constitution in Virginia, his oratorical skill was considered almost equal to Patrick Henry's. In 1786 he was elected attorney general of the state.

IREDELL, James (Lewes, England, Oct. 5, 1751 — Edenton, N.C., Oct. 20, 1799). Jurist. Iredell helped organize the North Carolina legal system and supported the adoption of the U.S. Constitution. As associate justice of the U.S. Supreme Court (1790-99) Iredell was known for his dissenting opinion in *Chisholm vs Georgia* (1793) that a state could not be sued in Federal Court without its consent, which became the Eleventh Amendment to the U.S. Constitution in 1798.

IRON MOUNTAIN, Fla. Polk Co. Mountain located in central Florida in the midst of the lake region. About 325 feet high, it is the site of a 71-bell carillon, as well as a bird sanctuary and park established by editor and writer Edward W. Bok in 1929.

IROQUOIS INDIANS ("real adders"). Tribe of Iroquoian linguistic stock that originally lived in central New York state. After obtaining guns from the Dutch their dominating influence was felt all the way to the Gulf of Mexico. An aggressive, warlike people, the Iroquois formed a confederacy that is said to have had the most extensive governmental organization of any Indian group. The Iroquois Confederacy was formed c. 1570 in an effort to unite the Iroquois and other neighboring tribes who had been constantly hostile to each other. In 1655 the confederacy penetrated the land of the CATAWBA and CHEROKEE. A French invasion in 1693, and again in 1696, was disastrous to the confederacy, which lost half its warriors, but it recovered and swept victoriously southward early in the 18th century. In 1701 it made excursions as far as the Roanoke and Cape Fear Rivers, to the land of the kindred TUSCARORAS. So determined were the Iroquois to subdue the Southern tribes that when, in 1744, they ceded a part of their lands to Virginia, they reserved a perpetual privilege of a warpath through the territory. Under the influence of an English Indian Agent, William Johnson, the Iroquois sided with the English during the Revolution. At the close of the war the hostile Iroquois, dreading the vengeance of the Americans, took refuge in Canada (with the exception of the Oneida and Tuscarora tribes). At the height of their empire they are said to have numbered about 15,000.

IRVING, Tex. Town (pop. 109,943), Dallas Co., in northeast central Texas. Irving is a residential suburb of Dallas that has experienced rapid growth in recent years. Present manufactures include aircraft parts, machinery, and metal and paving products. It is the site of the University of Dallas, and the official home of the Dallas Cowboys football team.

ISLAND NO. 10, Tenn. An island in the Mississippi River, no longer in existence but important for its role in the Civil War. Confederate forces occupied much of this Tennessee-Missouri region until Gen. Ulysses S. Grant's advance along the Tennessee River persuaded them to give up all stations but those on this island and at New Madrid, Mo. On Mar. 14, 1862, even the Missouri post was deserted, leaving the Confederates with the island as its one remaining stronghold. Union forces were blocked because travel on the Mississippi meant passing the shoreline guns on Island No. 10. Finally Union troops bypassed the post by building a channel below it and, on April 8, sailed up the river, seized the island, and captured the 7,000 Confederate soldiers stationed there.

ISTOKPOGA, Lake, Fla. Lake, Highlands Co., in south central Florida, 25 miles northwest of Lake Okeechobee. About ten miles long and five miles wide, Lake Istokpoga is connected by a channel to Lakes Weohyakpka and Kissimmee to the north.

IUKA, Miss. Town (pop. 2,846), seat of Tishomingo Co., in the northeastern tip of Mississippi. The Civil War Battle of Iuka, in which 1,200 soldiers were killed and 1,500 were wounded, took place here on September 19, 1862. At the time almost all the homes and buildings were converted into emergency hospitals to care for the victims. Today Iuka is a popular resort because of the area's mineral springs. Gravel mining is important to the town's economy, as is the production of corn and cotton.

IZARD, Ralph (near Charleston, S.C., Jan. 23, 1741 — Charleston, S.C., May 30, 1804). Politician. Izard settled in England but his support of the Revolution forced him to move to Paris where he was appointed commissioner to Tuscany in 1777. He returned to America in 1779 and became a delegate to the Continental Congress from South Carolina (1782-83). He was U.S. senator from that state (1789-95), and was a founder of the College of Charleston.

J

JACKSON, Andrew (Waxhaw, S.C., Mar. 15, 1767 — The Hermitage, near Nashville, Tenn., June 8, 1845). Soldier and 7th President of the United States. Jackson was the son of Irish immigrants, and spent his youth roaming at will around the South Carolina and North Carolina border region, free from formal schooling. At the age of 13 he enlisted in the local militia to fight in the Revolutionary War, took part in the battle of HANGING ROCK, and was captured and imprisoned there by the British.

After the war Jackson began to study law on his own. Although it is doubtful that he did in fact master much law, he was admitted to the bar in 1787 and became a public prosecutor in Nashville, Tenn., while it was still a rowdy frontier outpost. In 1791 Jackson married Mrs. Rachel Donelson Robards and subsequently found that her divorce from her first husband was not yet final. Although they were legally married in a second ceremony in 1793, Jackson and his wife remained ripe for scandalous accusations from political opponents. Mrs. Jackson died in 1828, leaving Andrew Jackson to run a bachelor White House.

Jackson's political career began in 1796 as a delegate to the convention convened to draft Tennessee's constitution, and in the same year he was elected to Congress. In 1797 he resigned his congressional seat to occupy a vacant seat in the Senate, and in 1798 he resigned that seat, too, in order to return to Nashville as a judge of the Supreme Court. After he resigned the court position in 1804 he began construction on The Hermitage, his plantation near Nashville and lifelong home.

Jackson had during these years been promoted through the ranks of the Tennessee militia as a matter of course in peacetime. By the outbreak of the War of 1812 he had become a major general of Volunteers, and was ordered out to confront the CREEK INDIANS, then rising against the U.S. as allies of the British. Jackson defeated the Creeks at the Battle of HORSESHOE BEND in Alabama in 1814, and for this he was awarded the rank of major general in the U.S. Army. He was then sent to New Orleans and defended the city with 6,000 local militiamen against 12,000 veteran British troops. The battle was in fact fought after a peace treaty had been signed, but Jackson's victory made him a national hero nevertheless, and he added to this reputation in the SEMINOLE WARS in 1818.

For his success against the Seminole Indians Jackson was made territorial governor of Florida in 1821, but he returned to Tennessee and successfully campaigned for the U.S. Senate in 1823 as a war hero. Such was his appeal that in 1824 he garnered more popular and electoral

200

Cartoon of Andrew Jackson depicting his supposed autocratic ways

votes than John Quincy Adams in that year's presidential election, but because he lacked a clear majority, the choice fell to the House of Representatives and they chose Adams. In the presidential election of 1828 he trounced New England's Adams with support from the West and South, and he was reelected in 1832 after substituting open party conventions for congressional caucuses on party nominees.

To many, Jackson represented the voice of the common people and was regarded with some suspicion by landed and wealthy interests. He instituted the "spoils system" of party patronage jobs and the "kitchen cabinet" to keep himself informed. The first president from west of the Appalachians, he gained a reputation as a rowdy debater, friend of the common man, and enemy of privilege and pretension.

JACKSON, Battle of. Civil War engagement fought May 14, 1863, in the capital city of Mississippi. The principal battle of Jackson was an important victory for the Union army maneuvering to besiege VICKSBURG, 45 miles to the east. In his Vicksburg campaign, Gen. Ulysses S. Grant moved north from his Mississippi

River crossing at Bruinsburg. Instead of advancing directly on Vicksburg, he moved against Jackson, where the Confederate forces of Gen. Joseph E. JOHNSTON were gathering to reinforce Vicksburg. The Union army took Jackson on May 14, sending Johnston's force in retreat northward and preventing them from assisting the garrison in Vicksburg.

Jackson was also the scene of later fighting in the war. Johnston reoccupied the city when the Union forces turned to Vicksburg, and after the fall of Vicksburg the Union army returned to besiege Johnston in Jackson from July 9 to July 16, 1864, when Johnston evacuated. Less important skirmishes also occurred around Jackson on February 5, 1864 and July 3-9, 1864.

JACKSON, Claiborne Fox (Fleming Co., Ky., Apr. 4, 1806 — Little Rock, Ark., Dec. 6, 1862). Politician. He was a member of the Missouri legislature before being elected governor (1860-62). Jackson called for a state convention which voted against secession but also voted against the restraint of the South by the Federal government (1861). Refusing to grant troops to President Abraham Lincoln, his attempt to arm the state militia against Union incursion was frustrated.

JACKSON, Henry Rootes (Athens, Ga., June 24, 1820 — Savannah, Ga., May 23, 1898). Lawyer, diplomat, and military officer. A judge of the superior court in Georgia (1849-53), he was appointed minister to Austria in 1853 and served there until 1858. At the outbreak of the Civil War he was a major general of Georgia troops before attaining the rank of brigadier general. At the battle of Nashville (1864) he was captured and remained a prisoner until the end of the war. From 1885 to 1886 he served as minister to Mexico.

JACKSON, Mahalia (New Orleans, La., Oct. 26, 1911 — Evergreen Park, Ill., Jan. 27, 1972). Gospel singer. Jackson's career began as leader of a quartet who sang in churches. She began making records in 1934, and went on many concert tours in Europe and the U.S., including Carnegie Hall and Newport Jazz Festivals. She sang for President Dwight Eisenhower on his birthday in 1959 and at John F. Kennedy's inauguration. During the 1960s she became associated with the civil rights movement and became a symbol of black protest.

JACKSON, Miss. City (pop. 202,895), seat of Hinds Co. and state capital, on the west bank of the Pearl River 35 miles southwest of the geographical center of Mississippi. Originally a trading post called Le Fleur's Bluff, it was renamed for Andrew Jackson, who negotiated with the Choctaw Indians for the land in 1821. The city was incorporated in 1833. A plan of Thomas Jefferson's was used to lay out Jackson, and today modern skyscrapers stand beside old landmarks such as the governor's mansion; the old state capitol, which is now a museum; and the city hall, with its Ionic facade.

Burned during the Civil War by Gen. Ulysses S. Grant, Jackson recovered slowly. By the 20th century, however, it was the state's leading city because of rail lines, oil, and natural gas resources. The growth of Jackson's population has been rapid in the past few decades, and the city supports several theatrical and musical organizations. It is the site of several colleges, including Jackson State University, Millsaps College, Mississippi College, two branches of the University of Mississippi, Belhaven College, Jackson School of Law, and Campbell Junior College. Jackson is an important cottonseed oil manufacturing and distribution center. There are also fertilizer and bottling works, lumber, and meat-packing plants.

JACKSON, Tenn. City (pop. 49,131), seat of Madison Co., in western Tennessee on the South Fork of the Forked Deer River. Settled in 1819 as Alexandria, it was renamed for Andrew Jackson by his nephew. It was incorporated as a town in 1823 and as a city in 1845. A railroad center, it has been the home of several railroad presidents including Adam Huntsman, who so badly beat Davy Crockett in politics that Crockett left for Texas, and John Luther "Casey" JONES. It is the home of Union University (1825), Lambuth College (1843), and Lane College (1882). Jackson has varied industries, including the manufacture of textiles and wood and paper products.

JACKSON, Thomas Jonathan "Stonewall" (Clarksburg, Va., now W.Va., Jan. 21, 1824 — Guiney's Station, Va., May 10, 1863). Military officer. A self-educated son of itinerant farmers, Jackson won admission to the U.S. Military Academy at West Point. He graduated from there in 1846, served under Zachary Taylor in the Mexican War and in the Seminole Indian wars in Florida, and accepted a teaching position at Virginia Military Institute (VMI) in Lexington, Va. (1851-61).

When Virginia seceded from the Union in 1861, Jackson was ordered to go to the aid of his state with a detachment of VMI cadets and was awarded a commission in the Confederate army. It was at the victorious Battle of BULL RUN (Manassas) in the same year that Jackson's troops were described by Confederate Gen. Bernard Bee as standing "like a stone wall," the phrase that gave the nickname to this disciplined but popular commander. Jackson later distinguished himself in campaigns in the Shenandoah Valley, in defense of RICHMOND, at ANTIETAM, and finally at CHANCELLORSVILLE. It was in this last battle that Jackson, after a brilliant and victorious march to assist Gen. Robert E. Lee., was shot in the left arm by one of his own men in the confusion of the battle. He died a week later, the greatest tactical collaborator to Lee and one of the most popular of the Confederate generals.

JACKSON LAKE, Ga. Lake on the Ocmulgee River in Butts Co., formed by the Lloyds Shoals Dam as a hydroelectric source. The lake, like the town, was named for James Jackson, governor of the state from 1798 to 1801.

JACKSONVILLE, Ark. City (pop. 27,589), Pulaski Co., in central Arkansas. The city is a residential suburb of Little Rock, which is five miles southeast of Jacksonville. There is diversified light manufacturing.

JACKSONVILLE, Fla. City (pop. 570,400), seat of Duval Co., in northeast Florida near the mouth of the St. John's River. The site was laid out in 1822, following the U.S. acquisition of the land from Spain, was named for Andrew Jackson, and was incorporated in 1832. The outbreak of the SEMINOLE WAR limited growth in the area, as did the Civil War and the occupation of the city by Union troops. After the Reconstruction Era, the city began to develop as a winter resort, and as an industrial hub after harbor improvements increased shipping and transportation. The area continued to develop in spite of the yellow fever epidemic of 1888 and a major fire that caused widespread destruction in 1901.

With its present status as a deepwater port of entry, the city has become the major commercial, financial, industrial, and transportation center in the area. Four major beaches enhance the city's tourist and convention businesses: Atlantic Beach, Jacksonville Beach, Neptune

Beach, and Ponte Verda Beach. Other major attractions include the Civic Auditorium, the Municipal Zoo, Dallas Thomas Park, and a sports complex that includes the Gator Bowl. The economic base is additionally broadened by extensive U.S. naval facilities, and three major shipyards are located in the city. Education facilities include Jacksonville University, the University of North Florida, Jones College, Edward Waters College, and Florida Junior College. Also in the city are the Armmer Gallery of Art, the Jacksonville Art Museum and the Hayden Burns Library. Following a 1968 referendum, Jacksonville was consolidated with most of Duval County, making it the nation's largest city in area (827 square miles).

JACKSONVILLE, N.C. City (pop. 17,056), seat of Onslow Co., in southeast North Carolina on the New River. Founded in 1734 by English and German settlers, Jacksonville was attacked by Spanish buccaneers and pirates in the 1740s. Today Jacksonville is a summer resort with diversified farming and manufacturing. Its products include tobacco, plywood, boats, textiles, lumber, and oysters. The U.S. Marine Corps Camp Lejeune is nearby.

JACKSONVILLE, Tex. City (pop. 12,264), Cherokee Co., in east central Texas. Jacksonville's current manufactures include wood, plastic products, and baskets. Lon Morris College (1854) and Jacksonville College (1899) are located here. The city was founded in 1847 and incorporated in 1916.

JAMES, Jesse Woodson (Kearney, Mo., Sept. 5, 1847 — St. Joseph, Mo., Apr. 3, 1882). Outlaw. As a teenager, James fought unofficially with "Bloody" Bill Anderson's Confederate guerrilla band during the Civil War, and later with his brother, Frank James, he fought with Col. W. C. Quantrill's band. Badly injured by Union troops at the end of the war he turned to crime. He was declared an outlaw in 1866, and remained a fugitive for 15 years. An expert marksman, he organized the James gang (1867) which committed murders and robberies, most notably, train robberies. In 1876 all but the two James brothers in the gang were dead and, in 1881, Missouri Governor Thoms T. Crittenden offered a $410,000 reward for their capture, dead or alive. Jesse was fatally shot one year later by a former member of his gang.

JAMES, Lake, N.C. Resort lake situated on the Nolichucky River in western North Carolina in McDowell and Burke Counties. Mount Mitchell and the Black Mountains are just to the north.

JAMES RIVER, Mo. Waterway in the Ozark Mountains which begins in south central Missouri and flows 40 miles southwest to drain into a stream that connects with the White River.

JAMES RIVER, Va. River formed at the confluence of the Cowpasture and the Jackson Rivers in western Virginia. The James travels 340 miles across the state to enter Chesapeake Bay. One of the state's main rivers, it was of strategic importance during the Civil War and numerous battles took place along its shores. The largest river entirely in Virginia, it was named for the English king. The James has a drainage area of 9,700 miles and forms the boundaries of 18 counties and five cities along its course. Jamestown was founded on an island near the mouth of the river in 1607.

JAMES, Thomas (Maryland, 1782 — Monroe City, Ill., Dec., 1847). Pioneer. James served as a member of the 1809 expedition up the Missouri River, and the 1821 expedition over the Santa Fe Trail. He served in the Illinois state legislature (1825-28) and wrote *Three Years Among the Indians and Mexicans* (1846).

JAMESTOWN, Va. Site of the first permanent British settlement in America located on an island in the James River in central eastern Virginia, 15 miles inland from Chesapeake Bay. An organized community until the time of the American Revolution, Jamestown now exists only as an archeological excavation site of uncovered streets and foundations with displays of artifacts and a visitor's center where tourists may receive information and tours of the site. Founded on May 14, 1607, and named after King James I, Jamestown almost failed as a colony in its first three years because of its marshy location (which brought on disease and a high infant mortality rate), low morale, and Indian attacks. In 1610 the settlers, after going through a winter of extreme hardship called "the starving time," were ready to abandon the colony, despite the capable leadership of Captain John SMITH. The arrival of Lord DE LA WARR in the spring of 1610 with fresh supplies

Reproductions of the three ships that brought 105 English settlers to Jamestown, Va. in 1607

came as some of the colonists were actually preparing to leave.

The first capital of the Virginia colony, Jamestown was the original home of the House of Burgesses (1619), the continent's first representative legislative assembly. The cultivation of tobacco as a cash crop started here, and the community received the first African slaves to be brought to the American colonies. However, Jamestown's location on marshy land, and its susceptibility to fire (the statehouse burned down four times) resulted in the capital being moved to Williamsburg in 1699. After six or seven more decades, Jamestown was a town in name only. At present, the only structure still standing from the colony's first 90 years of existence is an old church tower (c. 1639).

JARRELL, Randall (Nashville, Tenn., May 6, 1914 — Chapel Hill, N.C., Oct. 14, 1965). Poet, author, and critic. A 1935 graduate of Vanderbilt University, Jarrell was a prolific poet whose work represented a sensitive and tragic view of life. His volumes include *Blood for a Stranger* (1942) and *The Woman at the Washington Zoo* (1960).

JASPER, William (near Georgetown, S.C., c. 1750 — Savannah, Ga., Oct. 9, 1779). Military officer. Jasper joined J. William Moultrie's troops (1775) and was ordered to Fort Sullivan during the Revolutionary War. Noted for raising the colonial flag over the fort while the British were firing (1776), he was later killed in action in Savannah.

JAZZ. Although the precise origins and overall definition of jazz have eluded musicologists, it is generally thought that jazz developed from the fusion of elements present in the musical heritage of 19th century Southern culture, specifically along the Mississippi River and most importantly in New Orleans. European musical tradition and Franco-Spanish Creole musical culture blended with the tradition African rhythms of the black community. This black tradition drew upon the "holler," or field work song, the spiritual and the special funeral music played by the marching bands of the black fraternal organizations. Another influence was the BLUES, its vocal traditions translated into instrumental terms and fused with another major element, RAGTIME. There are no recordings of the earliest jazz bands at the turn of the century. The first jazz records were made in 1917 by a white group, Nick La Rocca's (1889-1961) Original Dixieland Jazz Band, and were in the style that became known as New Orleans Jazz or Dixieland, an improvisatory style that emphasized separate, independent instrumental lines. Concerts given by the Original Dixieland Jazz Band in 1917 in New York led to the first official, critical acknowledgment of jazz. This group also became the first jazz ensemble to perform outside the United States, when it played in England in 1919. The popularity of this group led to widespread imitation, often leading to the erroneous assumption that Dixieland was the earliest jazz form. Another contemporary was Joseph "King" Oliver (1885-1938), a black cornetist and bandleader who formed a number of groups starting in the late teens, notably King Oliver's Creole Band. The music of the Creole Band, although using the New Orleans' style as a jumping-off point, exhibits a more expressive and disciplined style of individual and ensemble playing. Among the finest musicians who played with Oliver were pianist Ferdinand Joseph "Jelly Roll" Morton (1885-1941), saxaphonist Sidney Bechet (1897-1959), trombonist Weldon Leo "Jack" Teagarden (1905-64) and cornetist Louis ARMSTRONG, perhaps the greatest, and certainly the most famous, jazz soloist of all time. Jazz spread to other Southern cities like Memphis, St. Louis and Kansas City, as well as to Chicago, New York and the West Coast, and a number of styles emerged, often associated with a particular city or area. Other styles included the individual jazz of Duke (Edward Kennedy) Ellington and the big bands of Fletcher Henderson, Benny Goodman, Count (William) Basie and others in the 1930s and 1940s to progressive jazz after World War II. But long before this, jazz had ceased to be strictly a Southern phenomenon and had become a long-established national and international tradition.

JEFFERSON, Thomas (Old Shadwell, Va., Apr. 13, 1743 — Charlottesville, Va., July 4, 1826). Governor of Virginia, envoy to Europe, Secretary of State to George Washington, educator, architect, and 3rd President of the United States. Jefferson was the son of Peter Jefferson, a tobacco grower of Welsh descent, and Jane Randolph Jefferson. His father died when he was only 14 years of age, making him the owner of a substantial plantation and controller of a considerable financial estate. The boy proved well able to handle these respon-

sibilities, and his intellectual ambitions led him to enroll in the College of WILLIAM AND MARY. He graduated in 1762 after studying classics and music, interests he would retain throughout his political career. Even more important, however, was the college training in science and philosophy that would make Jefferson perhaps the most intellectual of the founding fathers of the country.

Jefferson was admitted to the bar in 1767 and practiced law for a time, but in 1769 he was elected to the Virginia House of Burgesses and began his career in public service. He remained a member of that legislature until 1774, framing state documents with enlightened philosophical underpinnings and legal exactitude, a combination that was later to benefit the nation as a whole. He married the widowed Martha Wayles Skelton in 1772; of their six daughters, four would die in early childhood. At the same time he was pursuing his other interests by designing his plantation home MONTICELLO, contruction of which began in 1770.

Jefferson's rise to national office began inauspiciously when he became ill and was unable to attend a state convention in 1774. In his place he sent a paper on colonial rights that was deemed too complex for the state's purposes. The document was so well received that it led to his appointment in 1776 to write a national declaration of rights for consideration in Philadelphia. He fulfilled this obligation by writing the basic draft of the Declaration of Independence. Notable for its insistence on "inalienable" rights over politically condoned ones, it stands as one of the most important literary as well as political documents of early American history.

Elected to the Virginia House of Delegates in 1776, Jefferson then succeeded Patrick Henry as governor in 1779. He resigned from this office in 1781, bowing to outraged charges of ineffectuality after a British invasion of Virginia, and during this restorative voluntary retirement he completed a history of the state. He was elected to the Continental Congress in 1783 and then became ambassador to France in 1785, serving for four years during the crucial period in which the new American republic began to formalize relations with Europe. He returned to America as Secretary of State to President George Washington in 1789, but conflicts with Secretary of the Treasury Alexander Hamilton caused Jefferson to retire from this office in 1793 for another fruitful period of writing at Monticello. In response to pleas from supporters he ran for president in 1796, finishing second to John Adams and under the electoral law of the time therefore became vice president. Under the same electoral law he became president in 1801 after a tie with Aaron Burr of New York and the decision in his favor by the House of Representatives.

As President, Jefferson strove to return federal government to the letter of constitutional law. His efforts in this direction included removing officers appointed by flagrant influence-peddling and preserving the Supreme Court's right to declare an act of Congress unconstitutional. His most popular achievement was the purchase of the Louisiana Territory from France in 1803 and commission of the Lewis and Clark expedition to explore the new lands. His least popular act, after reelection in 1805, was the Embargo Act of 1807, which closed American ports during war between England and France.

In 1809 Jefferson was finally able to retire permanently to Monicello, where he wrote and devoted himself to the design and construction of the University of Virginia in Charlottesville. The university opened in 1825, a year before his death, on the 50th anniversary of the Declaration of Independence.

Thomas Jefferson, third President of the United States

JEFFERSON CITY, Mo. City (pop. 33,619), seat of Cole Co. and the state capital, on the Missouri River near the center of the state. The land for a state capital was donated by an Act of Congress in 1821 with the stipulation that it be located within forty miles of the mouth of the Osage River. The city was named for President Thomas Jefferson, designed by Daniel M. Boone, son of the Kentucky pioneer, and incorporated in 1825. During the Civil War the city chose to remain a part of the Union, although loyalties were divided between the Union and Confederate sides. The Missouri state prison was constructed here in 1833, and public works allocation led state officials to place the state university elsewhere. Surrounded by farmlands, the city serves as an agricultural trading center. Diversified industries include the manufacture of shoes, cosmetics, small electrical appliances, and printing materials. The capitol, constructed of Carthage marble during 1911-18, features murals by the American artist Thomas Hart BENTON. Lincoln University, founded here in 1866 by black federal army veterans, is now integrated.

JENKINS, Albert Gallatin (Cabell Co., Va., now W.Va., Nov. 10, 1830 — Cloyd's Mountain, Va., May 21, 1864). Military officer. A lawyer with a degree from Harvard Law School, Jenkins was a Democratic Congressman from Virginia (1857-61) before resigning to join the Confederate cavalry. Attaining the rank of brigadier general, he led mountain raids in West Virginia and Ohio, and was involved in the campaign at Gettysburg. He died after surgery for a wound inflicted in a West Virginia battle.

JENKINS, Charles Jones (Beaufort District, S.C., Jan. 6, 1805 — Summerville, Ga., June 14, 1883). Politician. During his service as justice of the state supreme court (1860-65), Jenkins supported the concept of secession but felt the time was not right. He was Democratic governor of Georgia (1865-68) but lost his governor's seat when he refused to order the state treasury to pay for the expenses of a Reconstruction order. As a member of the Georgia Constitution Covention (1877), he took part in framing the state constitution.

JENKINS, Thornton Alexander (Orange Co., Va., Dec. 11, 1811 — Washington, D.C., Aug. 9, 1893). Naval officer. He was sent to England (1845) to study lighthouse systems, and upon his return he was instrumental in the establishment of the American Lighthouse Board. He stayed with the Union during the Civil War and as fleet captain, he commanded the *Hartford* when Gen. David Farragut passed by Confederate-held Forts Jackson and St. Philip below New Orleans (1862). He commanded the *Richmond* when Farragut captured Mobile in 1864. From 1865 to 1869 he was chief of the Bureau of Navigation, and in 1870 he was made a rear admiral.

JERICHO MILLS, Battle of. See NORTH ANNA RIVER, BATTLE OF.

JOHN PENNEKAMP CORAL REEF STATE PARK, Fla. The only undersea park in the continental U.S., it is located near Key Largo in extreme southern Florida. Marine and plant life cover the 55,011-acre state park where tourists can view living reef formations by diving underwater or from glass-bottom boats.

JOHNS ISLAND, Crossing to. Revolutionary War action south of Charleston, S.C., on December 28-29, 1781. A small band of British infantry had remained on Johns Island after the surrender at Yorktown (October, 1781). On December 28-29 a Revolutionary force under Col. John Laurens crossed the Wapoo River and landed on the island. They were immediately recalled, and no battle occurred, but the action is usually cited as the last in the Revolutionary War.

JOHNSON, Andrew (Raleigh, N.C., Dec. 29, 1808 — Carter's Station, Tenn., July 31, 1875). Senator, governor of Tennessee, and 17th President of the United States. Johnson came from a poor family and was apprenticed to a local tailor at age ten, and settled in Greenville, Tenn., in 1826. Uneducated, he only learned to read and write at the age of 17. His instructor was Eliza McCardle, whom he married in 1827; they eventually had three sons and two daughters.

Johnson's first political office was as alderman in 1828. He then became mayor of Greenville and served in the state legislature from 1835 to 1837 and 1839 to 1841. In 1843 he was elected to Congress, leaving in 1853 to become governor of Tennessee. A U.S. senator from 1857 to 1862, he was the only senator from the eleven secessionist states to remain loyal to the Union. Appointed military governor of Tennessee by President Abraham Lincoln in 1862, he

became Lincoln's choice for vice president in 1864 in order to help mend the breach between North and South after the expected Union victory in the Civil War. After the assassination of Lincoln, Johnson became president on April 15, 1865.

The aftermath of the war presented immense problems for Johnson, and he responded with a mixture of necessary action and outright belligerence that hastened his own fall from power. After offering an unpopular amnesty to Confederate states that ratified the abolition of slavery, he removed Secretary of War Edwin M. Stanton without the constitutionally required agreement of the Senate. For this he was impeached by the House of Representatives, but he remained in office when the Senate failed by a single vote to impeach him on the same charge. Abandoned by the Republican party at the end of his term, he was elected to the Senate seven years later in 1875, but died soon after.

JOHNSON, Cave (Springfield, Tenn., Jan. 11, 1793 — Clarksville, Tenn., Nov. 23, 1866). Politician. A lawyer, he was a Democratic congressman from Tennessee (1829-37, 1839-45). He supported James Polk for President, and Polk appointed him U.S. postmaster general (1845-49) when he was elected President. Johnson first introduced postage stamps to the U.S. postal system. Against secession, he nevertheless gave his support to the Confederacy.

JOHNSON, Herschel Vespasian (Burke Co., Ga., Sept. 18, 1812 — Louisville, Ga., Aug. 16, 1880). Politician. Johnson was a Democratic U.S. senator from Georgia (1848-49), state superior court judge (1849-53), Georgia governor (1853-57), and senator in the Confederate Congress (1862-65). He opposed secession but fought for both states' rights and unionism. Johnson ran unsuccessfully for the Vice Presidency with Stephen A. Douglas against Abraham Lincoln in 1860. Under the Confederacy he rejected conscription and the suspension of the writ of habeas corpus. Although elected to the U.S. Senate in 1866 after the close of the Civil War, Johnson was denied his seat.

JOHNSON, James (Orange Co., Va., Jan. 1, 1774 — Washington, D.C., Aug. 14, 1826). Military officer and politician. After settling in Kentucky, Johnson served as a lieutenant colonel under his brother Richard Mentor JOHNSON, in the battle of the Thames on October 5, 1813.

In 1824 he was elected a Democratic congressman from Kentucky and died in office.

JOHNSON, James Weldon (Jacksonville, Fla., June 17, 1871 — Wicasset, Maine, June 26, 1938). Author, diplomat, and promoter of black culture and civil rights. Graduated from Atlanta University (1894), Johnson became the first black admitted to the bar in Florida (1897). He served under President Theodore Roosevelt and President William Taft as consul to Venezuela (1906-08) and Nicaragua (1909-12). He worked with the National Association for the Advancement of Colored People as field secretary (1916-20) and executive secretary (1920-30). In 1901 Johnson moved to New York to collaborate with his brother, John Rosamond Johnson, on the lyrics for light operas and for popular songs such as "Under the Bamboo Tree" and "Congo Love Song." Their "Lift Every Voice and Sing" was considered virtually a black national anthem. Johnson also translated the Spanish opera *Goyescas* by Enriques Granados into English for production by the Metropolitan Opera (1916). He was professor of creative literature at Fisk University from 1930 to 1938.

JOHNSON, John Arthur "Jack" "Li'l Arthur" (Galveston, Tex., Mar. 31, 1878 — Raleigh, N.C., June 11, 1946). Boxer. The first black to hold the heavyweight boxing championship of the world, he gained the title by knocking out champion Tommy Burns in Sydney, Australia, on December 12, 1908. He was considered a controversial figure because of his two marriages to white women and his victory over popular white champion James J. Jefferies. In 1912 he was convicted under the Mann Act for transporting his wife over a state line before their marriage. Sentenced to a year in prison, he escaped to Canada, then Europe. He lost the title to Jess Willard in Havana, Cuba, on April 5, 1915 and surrendered himself to U.S. marshals in 1920.

JOHNSON, Lyndon Baines (Stonewall, Tex., Aug. 27, 1908 — Johnson City, Tex., Jan. 22, 1973). U.S. congressman, U.S. senator, and 36th President of the United States. All of Johnson's youth was spent in Texas, and he graduated with a B.S. from Southwest Texas State Teacher's College in 1930. While teaching public speaking in Houston, he served an apprenticeship in politics as an assistant to Congressman Richard M. Kleberg from 1931 to 1935. During this period he married Claudia

Alta Taylor, known as "Lady Bird" Johnson, and attended Georgetown University law school in Washington, D.C.

Johnson's first political office was as U.S. representative from Texas in 1937 to fill an office vacated by death. He was returned to Congress for a full term in 1938 and served until his election as U.S. senator from Texas in 1948. He became leader of the Senate Democrats in 1953 and was reelected in 1954. Having established himself as the primary stategist of the Democrats, he campaigned for the presidency in 1960 but agreed at the Democratic National Convention to run as vice president on a ticket with the more charismatic John F. Kennedy. Johnson became president when Kennedy was assassinated on November 22, 1963.

As president, Johnson launched a "Great Society" program of domestic reforms in the areas of civil rights, welfare, education, and taxation. After his reelection to a full term in 1964, however, his administration was troubled by an unpopular foreign policy commitment to the war in Vietnam. This single issue so severely eroded his national support that he declined to campaign in 1968 although eligible for a second full term in office.

JOHNSON, Reverdy (Annapolis, Md., May 21, 1796 — Annapolis, Md., Feb. 10, 1876). Politician and lawyer. A graduate of St. John's College (1811), Johnson was elected to the Maryland senate (1821-29). He served in the U.S. Senate first as a Whig and later as a Democrat (1845-49, 1863-68), where he was influential in turning the Senate vote to acquittal in President Andrew Johnson's impeachment trial. He was attorney general under President Zachary Taylor (1849-50), and served as a lawyer in many important court cases including the DRED SCOTT case. He was U.S. minister to England from 1868 to 1869.

JOHNSON, Richard Mentor (Beargrass, Ky., Oct. 17, 1780 — Frankfort, Ky., Nov. 19, 1850). U.S. Vice President. Johnson was educated at Transylvania University and admitted to the Kentucky bar in 1802. He was a member of the Kentucky legislature (1804-07), then served as a Democrat in the U.S. Congress (1807-19) and the U.S. Senate (1819-29). During the War of 1812, he led a group of Kentucky riflemen. He was again a U.S. congressman (1829-37) and was chosen vice president by the Senate because no candidate had received an electoral majority. He served under President Martin Van Buren for one term

(1837-41) and was an unsuccessful candidate for vice president in 1840.

JOHNSON, Richard W. (Livingston Co., Ky., Feb. 7, 1827 — St. Paul, Minn., Apr. 21, 1897). Union general. Johnson was division commander of volunteers in the Tennessee and Georgia campaigns. After the Battle of Nashville he was promoted to major general (1864) and later taught at the University of Missouri.

JOHNSON, Thomas (Calvert Co., Md., Nov. 4, 1732 — Frederick, Md., Oct. 26, 1819). Politician. As a member of Maryland's colonial assembly (1762-73), Johnson was an active opponent of the Stamp Act. He was a delegate to the Continental Congress from 1774 to 1777, and from 1777 to 1779 was governor of Maryland. He was appointed to the U.S. Supreme Court in 1791 and served until 1793.

JOHNSON, William (Charleston, S.C., Dec. 27, 1771 — Brooklyn, N.Y., Aug. 4, 1834). Jurist. A graduate of Princeton (1790), he was admitted to the South Carolina bar in 1793. He served in the South Carolina legislature (1794-98) and on the state's highest court (1798-1804) before becoming an associate justice of the U.S. Supreme Court. Johnson served with distinction on the court for 30 years (1804-34), when the court was under the domination of Chief Justice John Marshall, a Federalist. A President Thomas Jefferson appointee and a Jeffersonian Republican, Johnson was put on the court to counteract the heavy Federalist preponderance. He established himself as a man of independence on the court, rendering numerous separate opinions throughout his long career. Because of this practice, he is credited with firmly establishing the principle of dissent in the U.S. court.

JOHNSON CITY, Tenn. City (pop. 44,500), Washington Co., in northeastern Tennessee. Settled in the late 18th century by farmers and iron miners, it was first called Blue Plum and later Haynesville. It was renamed Johnson City after Henry Johnson, a prominent businessman and its first mayor. Industries include chemicals, plastics, and foundries. It is one of the largest producers of hardwood flooring in the nation. East Tennessee State College was established here in 1909.

JOHNSTON, Albert Sidney (Washington, Ky., Feb. 2, 1803 — Shiloh, Tenn., Apr. 6, 1862). Military officer. A graduate of the U.S. Military Academy at West Point (1826), Johnston served in the Black Hawk War (1832), the Mexican War (1846-48), and in a bloodless expedition against the Mormons in Utah (1857). He settled in Texas and, when that state seceded from the Union in 1861, he resigned his command of the Department of the Pacific to join the Confederate army where he was appointed the second ranking general by President Jefferson Davis. Named commander of the Confederate Western Department, he raised and organized the troops to guard a long and weak line from the Mississippi River to the Allegheny Mountains. His struggles with Federal troops led indirectly to the fall of Nashville, Tenn., in February, 1862, and he met bitter criticism for his actions. Johnston concentrated his troops at Corinth, Miss., determined to triumph over Gen. Ulysses S. Grant's troops at Pittsburgh Landing. He led a suprise assault on the Union Army at the Battle of SHILOH (April 6-7, 1862) but was himself fatally wounded on the first day of battle.

JOHNSTON, Annie Fellows (Evansville, Ind., May 15, 1863 — Pewee County, Ky., Oct. 5, 1931). Author. An author of children's books, after visiting the Pewee Valley near Louisville, Ky., Mrs. Johnston chose this area as the setting for several of her books, including *The Little Colonel* (1895).

JOHNSTON, Frances Benjamin (Grafton, W.Va., Jan. 15, 1864 — New Orleans, La., May 16, 1952). Photographer. She began taking photos in 1887 as illustrations for her magazine articles. In 1893 she won a commission for a book of photographs, *The White House*, and by 1904 joined Alfred Steiglitz's Photo-Secession. Her main focus lay with documentary style, however, and she won national fame with her pictures of Admiral Dewey's fleet in the Bay of Naples (1899), studies of industrial and mine workers (1891-1910), and black schools (1900). She balanced these with portraits of such national figures as Mark Twain, Theodore Roosevelt, and Susan B. Anthony. Johnston became a pioneer in historical documentation, recording the quickly disappearing colonial architecture of the South.

JOHNSTON, Gabriel (Scotland, 1699 — Chowon Co., N.C., July 17, 1752). Colonial governor. He was royal governor of North Carolina from 1734 until his death. Though popular, Johnston on a number of occasions dissolved the colonial assembly over financial disagreements. He was responsible for establishing free public education, land grants to immigrants, and the development of Wilmington. Johnston County is named for him.

JOHNSTON, Joseph Eggleston (Prince Edward Co., Va., Feb. 3, 1807 — Washington, D.C., Mar. 21, 1891). Military officer. Johnston graduated from West Point in 1829 and entered a long period of military service that included the Black Hawk and Seminole Wars and the Mexican War, where he distinguished himself for bravery. When the Civil War broke out he resigned his post as quartermaster general of the army and offered his services to the Confederate cause. One of the Confederacy's most important generals, Johnston led Confederate troops at the first battle of Bull Run. He was placed in command of the Army of Northern Virginia and unsuccessfully opposed Gen. George B. McClellan's drive in the Peninsular campaign. In 1862 he took command of the Department of the West where he led the defense of Vicksburg. He is best remembered for his masterful retreat in the spring of 1864 from Gen. William T. Sherman's vastly larger Union army. It is also said he was the only important Confederate general never to suffer a direct military defeat during the war. Johnston finally surrendered to Union forces on Apr. 26, 1865 at Durnham Station, N.C.

After the war he represented Virginia in the U.S. Congress (1879-81) and was U.S. commissioner of railroads (1885-91). Johnston was a pallbearer at the funerals of both Sherman and Gen. Ulysses S. Grant.

JOHNSTON, Olin DeWitt Talmadge (Honea Path, S.C., Nov. 18, 1896 — Columbia, S.C., April 18, 1965). Politician. Following his graduation from the University of South Carolina law school, he was admitted to the state bar (1924). He was elected to the state legislature (1923-24, 1927-30) and was governor of South Carolina (1935-39, 1943-45). He resigned to become a Democratic U.S. senator (1945-65).

JOHNSTON, Richard Malcolm (Powelton, Ga., Mar. 8, 1822 — Baltimore, Md., Sept. 23, 1898). Educator and author. Admitted to the bar (1844), he became professor of rhetoric at the University of Georgia (1857-61). He wrote many tales and sketches of rural life, including *Dukesborough Tales* (1871).

JOHNSTON, Samuel (Dundee, Scotland, Dec. 15, 1733 — near Edenton, N.C., Aug. 17, 1816). Politician. After serving in the North Carolina legislature he was a delegate to the Continental Congress (1781-82). He was governor from 1787 to 1789, and a Federalist U.S. senator from 1789 to 1793. He was the nephew of Gabriel JOHNSTON.

JOLLIET, Louis (Quebec City, Canada, Sept. 21, 1645 — Quebec, Canada, May/Oct., 1700). French-Canadian explorer and mapmaker. After studying for the priesthood, Jolliet left the seminary in 1667 to study hydrography in France. He returned to Canada in 1668 and became a fur trader. Because of his knowledge of the Great Lakes region and his studies in hydrography, Jolliet was chosen by New France intendant Jean Talon to explore and map the then-unknown Mississippi River. His group of seven, including Jesuit missionary Father Jacques MARQUETTE, set out from Lake Michigan on May 17, 1673. They traveled by canoe and on foot to the mouth of the Mississippi River, which they reached on June 17, 1673, and returned, covering 3,000 miles. He later explored Hudson's Bay and charted the Labrador coast. Jolliet was honored by the French government, given the island of Anticosti in the Gulf of St. Lawrence, and was appointed royal hydrographer of New France (1697).

JONES, Anson (Great Barrington, Mass., Jan. 20, 1798 — Houston, Tex., Jan. 9, 1858). Last president of the Republic of Texas. A doctor, he was an early supporter of Texas independence and was Secretary of State for Texas from 1841 to 1844, when he was elected president of Texas. In 1846, when Texas became the 28th state in the Union, Jones resigned his position to the new governor of the state, James Pickney Henderson.

JONES, Hilary Pollard (Hanover Co., Va., Nov. 14, 1863 — Washington, D.C., Jan. 1, 1938). Naval officer. A Naval Academy graduate (1884), Jones served in the Spanish-American War (1898) and commanded a cruiser division of the Atlantic Fleet during World War I. From 1922 to 1923 he was commander-in-chief of the U.S. fleet. He was a member of the U.S. delegation to the arms limitations talks in Geneva (1926-27), and attended the London Naval Conference in 1930.

JONES, Jesse Holman (Robertson Co., Tenn., Apr. 5, 1874 — Houston, Tex., June 1, 1956). Financier and politician. Based in Houston, Jones became a millionaire lumber magnate and land developer. President Herbert Hoover appointed him to the Reconstruction Finance Corporation in 1929 and the following year he became its chairman. When President Franklin D. Roosevelt merged the RFC with other agencies in 1939 he became head of the Federal Loan Administration. The following year he was appointed Secretary of Commerce, serving in that post until 1945. His close ties to business made him a vital member of the wartime cabinet.

JONES, John Luther "Casey" (Cayce, Ky., Mar. 14, 1864 — Vaughan, Miss., Apr. 30, 1900). Locomotive engineer. The subject of songs and poetry, Jones was famous for always bringing his train in on schedule and for unique signals with the engine whistle. Nicknamed for operating the telegraph at age 17 out of Cayce, Ky., he was running late with the dangerous Cannon Ball Express when he came upon a standing freight train. Ordering his fireman to jump, Jones applied the brakes and saved the passengers at the expense of his own life.

JONES, Thomas ap Catesby (Westmoreland Co., Va., Apr. 24, 1790 — Sharon, Va., May. 30, 1858). Naval officer. In 1805 he entered the Navy and from 1808 to 1812 he was engaged in the Gulf of Mexico in the suppression of piracy, smuggling, and the slave trade. Jones fought the British flotilla on Lake Borgne late in 1814, when he was wounded and captured. In 1842 he commanded the Pacific squadron and traveled to Hawaii.

JONESBORO, Ark. City (pop. 31,530), seat of Craighead Co., in northeastern Arkansas. Settled in 1859 and incorporated in 1883, Jonesboro is the distribution center for a major agricultural region that produces cotton, corn, and rice. Manufactures include shoes, lumber, and bricks. It is the home of Arkansas State University and a state park.

JONESBORO, Ga. City (pop. 4,132), seat of Clayton Co., in central Georgia. This is the site of the Battle of Jonesboro, which took place in 1864 when Union Gen. William T. Sherman tried to cut off the railroad to Macon. Union forces moved in and forced the Confederates out of the Atlanta area. Settled in 1823 and incorporated in 1859, Jonesboro is well known because many of the scenes in Margaret Mitchell's novel *Gone With the Wind* were placed here. The city is a residential suburb of Atlanta that produces wood products, machinery, and cotton.

JONESBORO, Tenn. Town (pop. 2,829), seat of Washington Co., in eastern Tennessee. Established in 1779, the first legislative sessions of the Free State of FRANKLIN were held here until 1785. It was a planned city with the town fathers not permitting any makeshift cabins. Today farms produce dairy products, hay, livestock, and poultry. The National Storytelling Festival is held here each October.

JOPLIN, Mo. City (pop. 38,893), Jasper and Newton Counties, in southwestern Missouri. The leading city of the Ozark region, Joplin was first settled in 1838 and incorporated as a city in 1873. It is most noted as a mining community, which produces lead and zinc. Manufactures include chemicals, missiles, leather goods, alcohol, insulation, and furniture. It is the home of Missouri Southern State College and *The Globe*, a daily newspaper published since 1896.

JOUETT, James Edward (near Lexington, Ky., Feb. 7, 1826 — Sandy Spring, Md., Sept. 30, 1902). Naval officer. Jouett was a blockade officer for the Union army during the Civil War. Commended for heroism at Mobile Bay (1864), Jouett was later commander of the North Atlantic Squadron (1884), and retired a rear admiral in 1890.

JUDSON, Edward. See BUNTLINE, Ned.

K

KADOHADACHO CONFEDERACY ("real chiefs"). Group of Indian tribes of Caddoan linguistic stock that lived in northeast Texas. One of the most dominant tribes of this Confederacy was the CADDO, who gave their name to the linguistic group of which they were a part.

KALB, Johann (Huttendorf, Germany, June 29, 1721 — Camden, S.C., Aug. 19, 1780). Military officer. Serving under Gen. Horatio Gates, Kalb defended CAMDEN against a superior British force. The British quickly drove the untrained militia, with Gates, from the field. Kalb remained, surrounded and unhorsed, fighting until he was captured. Wounded 11 times, he died three days later. Kalb began his military career as an officer in the French infantry in 1743. As a French agent in America (1768), he was impressed by Gen. George Washington, and later was granted a commission as major general by Congress (1778).

KANAWHA RIVER, W.Va. Tributary of the Ohio River, created by the confluence of the Gauley and New Rivers in south central West Virginia. It then runs approximately 98 miles northwest to enter the Ohio at Point Pleasant, draining a large portion of West Virginia. Brine and rock salt are mined in its valley.

KANNAPOLIS, N.C. Town (pop. 29,628), Cabarrus Co., in southwest central North Carolina in the Piedmont section. Purchased by James William Cannon in 1906 for a textile village, Kannapolis is noted for its colonial architecture and system of planned growth. Present manufactures include towels and sheets.

KANSAS CITY, Mo. City (pop. 448,159), Clay, Cass, Jackson, and Platte Counties, at the confluence of the Missouri and Kansas Rivers in central western Missouri. Today the second-largest city in Missouri, Kansas City was first settled in 1821 by French fur traders and served as a supply depot. The town grew rapidly as an outfitting point for expeditions, because the Santa Fe and Oregon Trails ran through the town. Trade for the year 1848 to 1849 was estimated at $5 million for the outfitting of 900 wagons and 2,000 travelers. Kansas City's commercial success suffered from a cholera epidemic in the mid-1800s that halved its population, and from the Civil War, which brought conflict within the town and disrupted its trade. In 1864 Union and Confederate troops engaged in the Battle of Westport (called the "Gettysburg of the West") on the outskirts of the town. In the midst of these problems, the town was incorporated as the City of Kansas on Feb. 22, 1853.

The arrival of the railroad in 1865 and a bridge constructed across the Missouri River in 1869 assured the commercial future of the city. Stockyards were built and packing houses were opened in the 1870s. By 1884 overhead trolley cars appeared, having been invented by John C. Henry of Kansas City. Influential in the development of the city was the editor and founder of the Kansas City *Star*, William Rockhill Nelson. He absorbed other local newspapers and began a crusade for civic improvement to make Kansas City as attractive as it was prosperous. Much of the community planning and culture evident today is the result of his interest.

In the early 1900s auto assembly plants opened and during World War II business in cattle and horses reached new heights. Often called the world's food captial, Kansas City today is first in the nation in farm equipment and the distribution and marketing of winter wheat. It is also a leader in production of automobiles and greeting cards, and is a center of frozen food storage and distribution.

Along with the University of Missouri at Kansas City, it is the site of 19 other colleges and universities. The city's hilly terrain contains over 100 parks, one of which is the 1,300-acre Swope Park. Numerous historical and cultural sites dot the city including the Nelson Gallery and Atkins Museum. There is a citizen-supported Philharmonic Orchestra and a Civic Orchestra that is an affiliate of the Conservatory of Music at the state university. Kansas City is also the site of the American Royal Livestock and Horse Show and the annual convention of the Future Farmers of America. The metropolitan area includes Kansas City, Kansas; the two cities are separated only by the state line.

KARANKAWAN INDIAN TRIBES.
Tribes of an independent linguistic stock that lived in Texas between Aransas and Trinity Bays on the Gulf of Mexico. CABEZA DE VACA lived among them after being shipwrecked in 1528. Fort St. Louis was built in their country by La Salle (1685) when he thought he was near the mouth of the Mississippi River. Because of their constant raiding, they were finally destroyed by the settlers by the mid-1800s.

KASKINAMPO INDIANS. Tribe of Muskogean linguistic stock that lived on an island

in the Tennessee River (thought to be the present Pine Island). They were frequently mentioned in De Soto's narratives, but after the early 18th century little is known of them and it is believed they joined the KOSATI INDIANS.

KEFAUVER, Carey Estes (Madisonville, Tenn., July 26, 1903 — Bethesda, Md., Aug. 10, 1963). Politician. A Democratic U.S. congressman from Tennessee (1939-49), Kefauver's election to the U.S. Senate in 1948 ended the political reign of Edward "Boss" Crump in that state. Kefauver gained national fame with his Kefauver Crime Committee (1950-51). The 1956 unsuccessful Democratic vice-presidential candidate (with Adlai Stevenson), he served in the Senate until his death in 1963. He was the author of *Crime in America* (1951).

KELLER, Helen Adams (Tuscumbia, Ala., June 27, 1880 — Westport, Conn., June 1, 1968). Author and lecturer. Keller lost her hearing and sight during an illness at 19 months of age. Under the tutelage of Anne Sullivan, she learned to speak, to use sign language and read braille, and to type. She graduated with honors from Radcliffe College in 1904. After college she made lecture tours and wrote books to promote interest in the handicapped and in the process became a world-famous inspiration for others. Her works include *The Story of My Life* (1903) and *Out of the Dark* (1913).

KELLY'S FORD, Va. Ford in the Rappahannock River that was the site of a Civil War battle on March 17, 1863. Cavalry troops clashed, with Gen. William Averell commanding the Union forces and Gen. Fitzhugh Lee commanding the Confederate forces. The outcome is disputed as both sides claimed a victory.

KEMPER, James Lawson (Madison Co., Va., June 11, 1823 — Gordonsville, Va., Apr. 7, 1895). Military officer and politician. A Confederate major general, Kemper was wounded and captured during Pickett's charge at Gettysburg (1863). In 1874, he was elected Democratic governor of Virginia and his administration (1874-78) was noted for its integrity and support of civil rights for blacks.

KEMPER, Reuben (Fauquier Co., Va., 1770 — Natchez, Miss., Jan. 28, 1827). Frontiersman. Kemper started the movement from the Mississippi Territory to free West Florida from Spanish control. His capture by the Spanish in 1805 created an international incident. He also fought Spanish rule in Mexico and defended New Orleans with Andrew Jackson.

KENDALL, Fla. Unincorporated town (pop. 73,758), Dade Co., in southern Florida. A suburban residential community with numerous subdivisions, this rapidly expanding area has no offical boundaries but covers approximately 80 square miles. It is the home of Miami-Dade Community College.

KENNEDY, Cape, Fla. Government space center, in Brevard Co. Cape Kennedy is the term used to refer to the Kennedy Space Center located on the part of Cape Canaveral that has been used for launching U.S. research missiles. For a time the entire cape was named for the late President John F. Kennedy but the local name Cape Canaveral has prevailed.

KENNESAW MOUNTAIN, Ga. Peak in Cobb Co., northwest central Georgia. It was the scene of the Civil War Battle of KENNESAW MOUNTAIN on June 27, 1864. That engagement has been memorialized in the Kennesaw Mountain National Battlefield Park, established in 1947, which spans 2,883 acres.

KENNESAW MOUNTAIN, Battle of. Civil War engagement fought June 27, 1864, northwest of Atlanta, Ga., near the town of Marietta. It was an uncharacteristic but ultimately successful direct assault on Confederate troops by Union Gen. William Tecumseh Sherman in his march across Georgia. Sherman's strategy of slowly pressuring the Confederate force of Gen. Joseph E. JOHNSTON back toward Atlanta was slowed in early June, 1864, by heavy rain. In his skillful withdrawal movement, Johnston had occupied Kennesaw Mountain by June 18. Sherman decided to attack this position in the interests of troop morale, which had declined after weeks of maneuvering for position in muddy hills. The principal Union assault on the mountain on June 27 was led by Gen. Jefferson Columbus Davis. Finding the Confederate position virtually impregnable, he dug in his own line a few yards away and refused to retreat. As Sherman moved to reinforce Davis, Johnston withdrew on July 2 to the Chattahoochee River.

KENT ISLAND, Md. Queen Annes Co., Chesapeake Bay in central Maryland. A year-round resort island, Eastern Bay is on its south shore and Chester is its major community.

KENTUCKY. State on the north central limit of the South. Its northern border is an irregular one formed by the east-to-west flow of the Ohio River, the traditional division in the area between Northern and Southern states. Across the Ohio to the north, Kentucky faces three Great Lakes states: Ohio in the east, Indiana and Illinois in the west. The entire southern border of Kentucky is a regular one with the state of Tennessee. To the east Kentucky faces West Virginia, across the Big Sandy River and its east fork the Tug, and Virginia, across the ridge line of the Pine Mountains. In the west Kentucky narrows to a 40-mile border with Missouri formed by the Mississippi River.

Kentucky was originally the first frontier of America, one isolated from the British colony in Virginia by mountains, and not opened to settlers until the time of the American Revolution. In the years since it became the 15th state in the Union in 1792, Kentucky has prospered quietly. Its population has increased at a steady but controlled rate since statehood. A border state, but west of the central battlefields of the Civil War, Kentucky was spared the devastation of that war even though it was the birthplace of the President of the Union, Abraham Lincoln and the President of the Confederacy, Jefferson Davis. In modern times Kentucky has also been spared the traumas of sudden urbanization and industrialization. Today it is principally a state of small towns evenly dispersed over its land area. Nearly 60% of its land area remains devoted to farming, and a great deal of this is given over to BLUEGRASS pastureland for thoroughbred horses. For these reasons much of Kentucky remains among the most scenic and best-preserved areas in the South. The state has been able to retain the character suggested by Stephen Foster's "My Old Kentucky Home," which was declared the state song in 1928.

The lands of Kentucky decline in elevation from the mountains along the eastern border with Virginia, and the entire state lies within the Ohio and Mississippi River basins. The highest point in the state is BIG BLACK MOUNTAIN (4,145 feet) on the Virginia border. Except for the range of Pine Mountains that includes this peak, most of eastern Kentucky is part of the Cumberland Plateau, a broken highland of streams and lakes that includes Kentucky's valuable eastern coal fields. From this plateau elevations decline toward the Interior Lowland Plateau that covers most of the central part of western Kentucky. One-half of the state area falls within a semicircular arc extending south from the Ohio River and surrounding the capital city of LEXINGTON. This arc is called the Highland Rim, and the area within it is the lush bluegrass region of the state, where meadows are tinted blue in June by the seed blossoms of the indigenous grass. South of the bluegrass region, and separated from it by distinctive "knobs" of low hills, most of central Kentucky falls within the Pennyroyal Plateau, a rugged region of hills and lakes. The Pennyroyal is notable for places where groundwater has dissolved the underlying limestone, creating huge caverns such as those at MAMMOTH CAVE National Park. South of Indiana, this west central region of Kentucky also includes the state's western coal fields. The narrowest part of far western Kentucky falls within the northernmost reach of the Gulf Coastal Plain, a vast triangular wedge covering much of the American South and reaching its apex at the meeting of the Ohio and Mississippi Rivers. This portion of Kentucky is isolated from the rest of the state by the Kentucky Dam on the Tennessee River that created Kentucky Lake, the largest artificial lake in the Tennessee Valley Authority system. This lake and Lake Barkley, formed by the Barkley Dam, surround a national recreational preserve called the Land Between the Lakes. Along its western border with Missouri, Kentucky includes a small portion of the Mississippi Alluvial Plain.

Before it was settled by colonists, Kentucky was known as the "Dark and Bloody Ground" because it was a battlefield for territorial conflicts between the Cherokee and Iroquois Indian tribes. Because these tribes remained stalemated during the era of European exploration of the North American interior, the early British and French explorers encountered little resistance. The first to view Kentucky was the Frenchman LA SALLE, who came down the Ohio River to the falls at what is now LOUISVILLE in 1669. Two years later an expedition sponsored by Sir William Berkeley and led by Thomas Batts traveled the same Ohio River route in search of a waterway to the Pacific Ocean. For more than 70 years after this trip, however, exploration of the area ceased, and the only white men to view what would become Kentucky were captives of the Indians or illicit traders with them.

The settlement of Kentucky from Virginia formally began with the formation of the Loyal and Ohio companies under British license in 1749. In 1750 an agent of the Loyal Company, Thomas WALKER, entered Kentucky through the CUMBERLAND GAP, which would become the main land route west from Virginia in the next few decades. Walker reached a point near what is now Barbourville in southeast Kentucky, but he was forced to turn back without exploring any further than the mountains. In the same year Christopher GIST of the rival Ohio Company came inland via the Potomac River and then crossed overland to the Ohio River. He, too, was soon forced to return, but in 1752 John Finley took this more northern route and came down the Ohio River to the falls at Louisville. It was Finley's account of the interior that provoked the interest of the frontiersman Daniel BOONE.

Further exploration was delayed by the French and Indian Wars, although Kentucky was visited by Daniel Boone in 1767. The first permanent settlement was not made until 1774, a year that saw a British treaty with the Ohio Indians and the establishment of Harrodsburg by James HARROD in central Kentucky. In 1775 the Transylvania Company purchased from the Cherokee Indians the land south of the Ohio River and between the Kentucky and Cumberland Rivers. Within a year the company had begun construction of the Wilderness Trail though the Cumberland Gap and had retained Daniel Boone to lead settlers to the claim. Boone succeeded in establishing settlements throughout the tract, beginning with Boonesboro in 1775. In 1778 Virginia declared the Transylvania Company claim illegal, but Virginia compensated the company and honored the claims of the settlers. In the same year the new settlement at the falls on the Ohio was named Louisville after Louis XVI of France, an ally of the Revolutionary cause.

During the Revolutionary War the settlers in Kentucky were spared British attack by their remote location, but this same circumstance left them to defend themselves from Indian attack without aid from Virginia. After the Revolution, continued migration to Kentucky brought the population to approximately 30,000 in 1784, and their distance from the seat of government in Virginia motivated the first debates about statehood. Virginia encouraged moves toward statehood, but it withheld its formal approval until after the Federal government agreed to accept Kentucky as a new state. The Kentuckians, however, thought the young

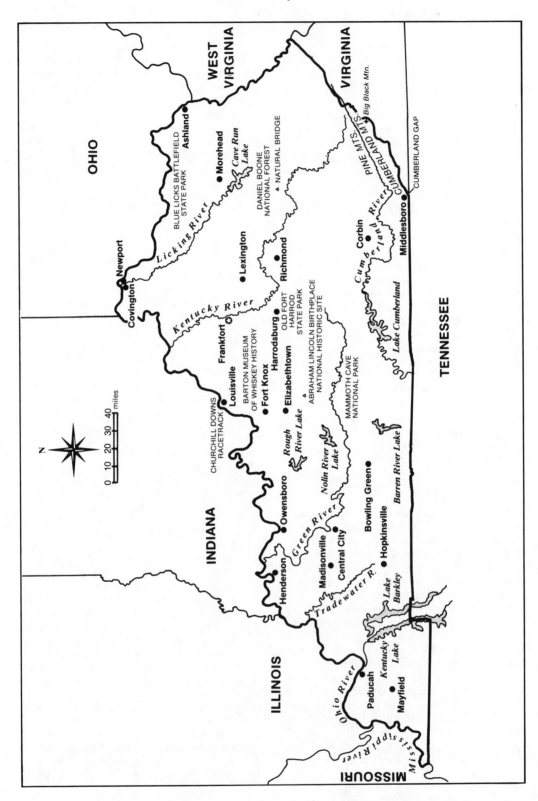

STATE OF KENTUCKY

Name: From the Wyandot Indian word *kem-tah-teh* ("land of tomorrow").

Nickname: Blue Grass State, Tobacco State, Hemp State, Corn-cracker State, Dark and Bloody Ground.

Motto: United We Stand, Divided We Fall.

Capital: Frankfort.

Counties: 120. **Places over 10,000 population (1980):** 31.

Symbols & Emblems: *Flower:* Goldenrod. *Bird:* Cardinal. *Tree:* Kentucky Coffee Tree. *Song:* "My Old Kentucky Home."

Population (1980): 3,661,433. **Rank:** 23rd.

Population Density (1980): 92.3 people per sq. mi. **Rank:** 23rd.

Racial Make-up (1980): *White:* 3,379,648 (92.3%). *Black:* 259,490 (7.1%). *American Indian:* 3,610 (0.1%). *Asian & Pacific Islander:* 9,971 (0.3%). *Other:* 8,714 (0.2%). *Spanish Origin:* 27,403 (0.7%).

Largest City (pop. 1980): Louisville (298,451). *Others:* Lexington-Fayette (204,165), Owensboro (54,450), Covington (49,013), Bowl-ing Green (40,450), Fort Knox (31,035), Paducah (29,315), Pleasure Ridge Park (27,332), Hopkinsville (27,318), Ashland (27,064), Frankfort (25,975).

Area: 39,669 sq. mi. **Rank:** 37th.

Highest Point: Black Mountain (4,145 ft.), Harlan Co.

Lowest Point: Mississippi River (257 ft.), Fulton Co.

State Government:

ELECTED OFFICIALS (4-year terms expiring Dec. 1987, etc.): *Governor* ($60,000); *Lt. Governor* ($51,010); *Sec. of State* ($51,010); *Attorney General* ($51,010); *Treasurer* ($51,010).

GENERAL ASSEMBLY (Salary: $100 per diem plus $75 per diem living expense.): *Senate* (38 members), *House of Representatives* (100 members).

CONGRESSIONAL REPRESENTATIVES: Senate (terms expire 1985, 1987, etc.). *House of Representatives* (7 members).

Admitted to the Union: June 1, 1792 (15th state).

Federal government was weak and ineffectual, and for this reason they briefly contemplated union with the Spanish colonies at the mouth of the Mississippi. Congress passed a preliminary act of admission to the Union in February, 1792, and Kentucky was admitted formally on June 1, 1792. The original state constitution was the first in the U.S. to provide full male white suffrage and election of governors and senators by electoral college.

Two enduring problems were cleared away in the early years of statehood. The threat of Indian attack was ended by Gen. Anthony Wayne's victory at the battle of Fallen Timbers in Ohio in 1794, and navigational rights on the Mississippi were granted by a treaty with Spain in 1795. These resolutions spurred a movement toward prosperity and consolidation that had already begun. In 1780 Kentuckians had established the first college west of the Alleghenies at Lexington, and in 1787 the *Kentucky Gazette* became the first newspaper west of the mountains.

Kentucky had become increasingly prosperous in the years preceding the Civil War, especially after the opening of the Kentucky and Ohio Railroad in 1832. The war, however, divided the state politically. There was a strong abolitionist movement in the state after 1850, but by that time slavery had become an entrenched institution in Kentucky. For a time state politicians, notably Henry CLAY, devoted all of their energies to compromise. In 1860 Kentuckians voted for the Federal constitution as endorsed by John Bell, but they did not vote for abolition as endorsed by President Abraham Lincoln. Following the outbreak of the war, Kentucky attempted to remain neutral by refusing Lincoln's call for Union volunteers and also banning Confederate troops from its soil. Neutrality proved impossible and Kentucky sided with the Union after state elections in August, 1861, gave Unionists their first sizable majority in the legislature. The state's wartime experience consisted for the most part of military occupation by both sides, spectacular raids by Confederate Gen. John H. Morgan, and the collapse of a limited secessionist coalition after the withdrawal of Confederate troops under Gen. Albert S. Johnson.

Post-Civil War Kentucky suffered from economic recession centered on the tobacco trade. By 1900 strife between growers and processors of tobacco had erupted into violence and led to the assassination of a Democratic candidate for governor. Farmers at this time formed "pools" to boost prices, and "nightriders" roamed the countryside to destroy the crops of those who refused to join these "pools." Armed forces were called out to control what had become virtual civil war by 1906, and the strife was ended only by an agreement between growers and buyers negotiated in 1908. In the 1930s similar, but less protracted, difficulties erupted in the coal industry in the form of coal strikes and investigations of union leaders on corruption charges.

Today Kentucky is a state of growing population and industry. In the 1970s the total population growth rate was above the national average, and totaled a net increase of 442,122. Of that increase a full one-quarter represents residents of other states who have moved to Kentucky, thus ending a long period of steady population loss to the industrial centers of the Great Lakes states. Some 7% of the population is black, a proportion that was unchanged between 1970 and 1980.

The largest city and metropolitan area in the state is the manufacturing center of Louisville on the Ohio River. The other large metropolitan areas including parts of Kentucky combined with other states. Evansville, Indiana-Kentucky; Cincinnati, Ohio-Kentucky; and Ashland, Kentucky-Ohio-West Virginia are the largest. Lexington, in the central bluegrass region of the state, is the center of a metropolitan area of 318,136 residents.

The greatest part of the Kentucky economy is manufacturing. Ashland in the east of the state is a center of heavy industry including steel, coke and fuel refining, while Louisville and Lexington are centers for the state's traditional manufactures of whiskey and tobacco products. Until 1970 Kentucky was the leading coal producer in the U.S., and western and eastern coal fields of Kentucky now generate $3.5 billion per year. Agriculture is also an important business, chiefly because Kentucky harvests a larger cash crop of tobacco than any state except North Carolina. Cattle, horses, and feed grain are among the other important agricultural products. Tourism, another important part of the economy, generates $1.2 billion per year.

KENTUCKY, University of. Coed land grant institution located in the central Kentucky city of Lexington. Founded in 1865, the school comprises 13 two-year community colleges scattered throughout the state, three professional colleges, 13 undergraduate colleges, and the graduate school.

Undergraduate studies are offered through the colleges of Arts and Sciences, Agriculture, Allied Health Professions, Business and Economics, Communications, Education, Engineering, Fine Arts, Home Economics, Nursing, Social Professions, Architecture, and Pharmacy. Kentucky provides 87% of the students, and 45% of graduates go on to further study.

The main campus covers 350 acres and the University also has 24,000 acres of farms and experimental stations throughout the state.

Library: 1,750,000 volumes, 1,860,000 microform titles, 25,000 journal subscriptions, 10,000 records/tapes. Faculty: 1,900. Enrollment: 21,944 total. Degrees: Bachelor's, Master's, Doctorate.

KENTUCKY DAM, Ky. The largest dam in the Tennessee Valley Authority system, in northern Kentucky, forming KENTUCKY LAKE. Completed in 1944, it harnesses water power from the Tennessee River. The dam stands 206 feet high, spans 8,422 feet, and features a lock system to allow vessels movement up and down the river.

KENTUCKY DERBY. Internationally renowned horse racing event held annually at Louisville's Churchill Downs. The derby began in 1875, making it America's longest-running annual horse race. The original purse of $2,850 has grown to almost a half million dollars. The course is 1 1/2 miles and is open only to three-year-old colts (carrying 126 pounds) and fillies (carrying 121 pounds). The Derby is part of the Triple Crown series (with the Preakness and the Belmont), and draws annual crowds of about 100,000. The event is held the first Saturday of May each year. Aristedes was the first winner.

KENTUCKY LAKE, Ky./Tenn. Artificial lake created by the U.S. Army Corps of Engineers, largely within Kentucky, with its south end dipping into northern Tennessee. With a length of 185 miles and a 2,380-mile shoreline, it is the largest artificial lake in the U.S. It is divided from Lake Barkley by a long, narrow land mass called the "Land Between the Lakes."

KENTUCKY RIVER, Ky. Waterway rising in Lee Co. It flows 260 miles southwest to the

Churchill Downs in Louisville, Ky., home of the Kentucky Derby since 1896

Ohio River. One of the state's major rivers, it is an important source of hydroelectric power.

KENTUCKY STATE UNIVERSITY.

State-supported coed liberal arts university, located on a 344-acre campus in the Kentucky state capital of Frankfort. Founded in 1886 as a college for Negroes, Kentucky State is now fully integrated, with blacks making up 48% of the student population. The South provides 90% of the students, 2% are from Middle Atlantic states, 3% are from North Central states; 15% of Kentucky State graduates go on to further study.

The university offers a moderate amount of majors. Of degrees conferred in a recent year 24% were in education, 22% business and management, 22% public affairs and services, and 14% social sciences.

Library: 137,739 volumes, 38,889 microform titles, 869 journal subscriptions, 9,582 records/tapes. Faculty: 172. Enrollment: 2,336 total graduate and undergraduate: 618 men, 518 women (full-time). Degrees: Certificate or Diploma, Associate's, Bachelor's, Master's.

KEOWEE RIVER, N.C/S.C. Waterway originating in the Blue Ridge Mountains of North Carolina near Lake Toxaway. The river runs south across the border to drain into Lake Keowee in northwestern South Carolina.

KEPPLER, Joseph (Vienna, Austria, Feb. 1, 1838 — New York, N.Y., Feb. 19, 1894). Political cartoonist and magazine publisher. After coming to St. Louis, Mo., from Austria, Keppler co-founded *Puck*, a German-language magazine (1871). The magazine failed but a later English version (1877) was successful, gaining Keppler recognition for his political cartoons.

KERNERSVILLE, N.C. Town (pop. 6,802), Forsyth Co., in northern North Carolina. Settled c. 1770 by German families, legend has it that one man bought the 400-acre town site at a cost of one gallon of rum for every 100 acres. Located in an agriculture and timber region, today Kernersville produces flour, hosiery, lumber, porcelain, and silk and rayon products.

KERNSTOWN, Battle of. Civil War engagement in northern Virginia fought on March 23, 1862. In it Gen. Stonewall JACKSON'S Confederate Army was repulsed by the superior Union forces under Gen. James Shields. Jackson was commanding the principal Confederate army in the Shenandoah Valley, and among his orders was the instruction to prevent Union troops in the area from leaving to join Gen. George B. McClellan's forces to the east. By March 22, Jackson was convinced that Shields had evacuated the valley, leaving behind a small rear guard. He then resolved to rout the rear guard, and attacked it near Kernstown on March 23, despite his professed opposition to fighting on Sundays. The Union army, however, was concealed north of Kernstown, and it outnumbered Jackson's forces two to one. The Confederate army, low on ammunition, was itself routed when Shields, who was wounded in the battle, came south to meet Jackson. Jackson withdrew further south, and the Union army held its position in the valley.

Kernstown was the site of a second battle on July 23-24, 1864. The second engagement was part of the retreat of Gen. Jubal EARLY following his successful diversionary Washington Raid. In this second Battle of Kernstown, Early defeated the Union forces of Gen. George Crook on their way south from the Potomac.

KERRVILLE, Tex. Town (pop. 15,276), seat of Kerr Co., on the banks of the Guadalupe River in central southern Texas. Kerrville was founded in the late 1840s and soon became a center for cattle, sheep, and goat raising. Called the "Mohair Center of the World," its present economy is based on tourism.

KEY, David McKendree (Greeneville, Tenn., Jan. 27, 1824 — Chattanooga, Tenn., Feb. 3, 1900). Politician. Key fought in the Confederate Army during the Civil War, and was promoted to lieutenant colonel. He was appointed to the U.S. Senate to fill a vacancy (1875-77), and in 1877 President Rutherford B. Hayes appointed him postmaster general of the U.S. despite his service to the Confederacy.

KEY, Francis Scott (Carroll Co., Md., Aug. 1, 1779 — Baltimore, Md., Jan. 11, 1843). Lawyer and author of U.S. national anthem. A graduate of St. John's College in Annapolis, Key began a law practice in Frederick, Md. Most of his verse was written early in his career as a pastime and he refused to consider it serious literary composition. During the War of 1812, Key was detained by British authorities prepared to attack Baltimore. On the night of September 13-14, 1814, he wrote "The Star-Spangled Banner" while watching the British shell one of the city's defenses, FORT MC HENRY. The poem was first published in the Baltimore *American* in 1814, and soon afterward it was joined with the music of "To Anacreon in Heaven" by the English composer John Stafford Smith. It was adopted as the national anthem in 1931. Key himself later became U.S. attorney for the District of Columbia (1833-41).

KEY LARGO, Fla. Narrow island in extreme southern Florida, which is part of a chain of limestone and coral islands that extend to Key West more than 100 miles out into the Gulf of Mexico. JOHN PENNEDAMP CORAL REEF STATE PARK, the only U.S. underseas park, is nearby.

KEY WEST, Fla. City (pop. 24,292), seat of Monroe Co., 60 miles southwest of the Florida mainland in the Gulf of Mexico. The southernmost point in the contiguous 48 states, this coral island is tropical in climate and vegetation, and is a year-round tourist resort. One of the oldest cities in modern Florida (1822), it is the site of Fort Taylor, built to protect the harbor in 1846 and a point of strategic importance in the Civil War and the Spanish-American War of 1898. A highway constructed in the 1930s connects Key West to the mainland. The island has since become famous as a vacation retreat for several U.S. Presidents. In 1980 it was the principal receiving point for thousands of Cuban refugees released in Havanna.

KEYAUWEE INDIANS. Small tribe of Siouan linguistic stock that lived in Guilford, Davidson, and Randolph Counties in North Carolina. In the early 1700s they settled on the Peedee River, S.C., and it is thought that they joined with the CATAWBA INDIANS for better protection from the settlers and hostile Indian tribes.

Key West, Fla., c. 1915—the southernmost point in the contiguous 48 states

KEYSER, W.Va. Town (pop. 6,569), seat of Mineral Co., in northeast West Virginia. Settled in 1802, this industrial center changed hands 14 times during the Civil War. Today it produces electronic devices, dresses, sheet metal, sand, and limestone. Corn, oats, and wheat are raised and there are numerous apple and cherry orchards. Potomac State College is here.

KICHAI INDIANS ("going in wet sand" or "water turtle"). Tribe of Caddoan linguistic stock that lived along the upper course of the Trinity River in Texas. They were assigned to a reservation on the Brazos River in 1855, but continued threats by settlers drove them to seek safety in Oklahoma with the Wichita Indians.

KICKAPOO INDIANS ("he stands about" or "he moves about"). Tribe of Algonquian linguistic stock that moved about the Midwest and for a time settled in Missouri, some of the tribe going on to Texas. They fought the colonists in the War of 1812 but assisted the U.S. government in the SEMINOLE WARS.

KILGORE, Tex. Town (pop. 10,968), Gregg and Rusk Counties, in northeast Texas. Founded in 1872, Kilgore was at one time known as the "Oil City of the World" because it had over 1,000 producing oil wells within its city limits. Still an oil center, other manufactures include clothing, bath fixtures, and metal products.

KILLEEN, Tex. Town (pop. 46,296), Bell Co., in central east Texas. Settled in 1882 and called Palo Alto, the town was named Killeen in honor of a railroad official. Located in one of the fastest-growing areas of the nation, Killeen is near Fort Hood, and military payrolls account for much of the town's economy.

KING, Martin Luther, Jr. (Atlanta, Ga., Jan. 15, 1929 — Memphis, Tenn., Apr. 4, 1968). Civil rights leader. The son of two generations of black Baptist ministers in the deep South, King graduated from Morehouse College in 1948. He received a divinity degree from Crozer Theological Seminary in 1951 and a doctorate in 1955 from Boston University, where he met Coretta Scott, who became his wife and who would carry on his work after his assassination.

In 1954 King accepted a ministry at the Dexter Avenue Baptist Church in Montgomery,

Ala. By December, 1955, racial tensions there focused on segregated bus seating led him to form the Montgomery Improvement Association, the first of many organizations he formed to pursue nonviolent resistance modeled on that led by Mahatma Gandhi in India. His leadership and nonviolent resistance brought about integration of the Montgomery buses in 1956, and to broaden his civil rights activities King formed the Southern Christian Leadership Conference in 1957. In 1959 moved to Atlanta, where he became assistant pastor to his father at the Ebenezer Baptist Church.

King first gained national fame for his civil rights demonstrations in Birmingham, Ala., in 1963. There his followers were abused by police and King was arrested, leading to the release of his famous *Letter from Birmingham Jail.* His most important demonstration was the March to Washington by 250,000 Americans on August 28, 1963, when he delivered the great "I Have a Dream" speech. For these and other accomplishments he was awarded the Nobel Peace Prize in 1964. In 1965 he led the Freedom March to Selma, Ala., for the cause of voter rights. The following year he brought his campaign to the North. During the later stages of his struggle, King opposed the Vietnam War, arguing that it drained resources from the war on hunger and poverty.

King was assassinated in Memphis, Tenn., in 1968 where he had gone to lead a strike of sanitation workers. James Earl Ray, a white man, was arrested and found guilty of the crime, but he has since claimed that a wider conspiracy was involved in the shooting.

KING, William Rufus de Vane (Sampson Co., N.C., Apr. 7, 1786 — Cahaba, Ala., Apr. 18, 1853). Congressman, diplomat, Vice President elect. King served in the North Carolina legislature (1807-09), was elected to the U.S. House of Representatives (1811-16), and was appointed to the legations at Naples and Russia (1816-18) under William Pinkney. Returning to Alabama (1818), he served in the U.S. Senate from that state (1819-44, 48-52). From 1844 to 1846 he served as Minister to France representing the U.S. case against foreign intervention in the annexation of Texas. In 1852 King was elected Vice President under Franklin Pierce. By a special act of Congress he was allowed to take the oath of office in Havana, Cuba, where he had gone for his health. He returned to his

The Freedom March from Selma to Montgomery, Ala. led by Martin Luther King in 1956

plantation in Alabama, where he died the following year.

KING RANCH, Tex. Massive ranch headquarters in Kingsville, Kleberg Co., in southeastern Texas. A ranching complex of nearly one million acres, the King Ranch has ranches in Texas, Kentucky, Pennsylvania, Australia, Argentina, and Brazil. There are several divisions of the main ranch, with the best known being Santa Gertrudis, which serves as the central base. Various breeds of beef cattle and thoroughbred racehorses are developed there. Many of these horses have become national and international champions, including Kentucky Derby winners in 1936, 1946, and 1950. Former steamboat captain Richard King founded the original ranch in 1853 and developed it into one of the largest cattle spreads in the world. Farming also became important after the advent of the artesian well in 1900. The complex stayed within the family until 1935, when it was divided. Since that time, oil production has been added to the central enterprise.

KING'S MOUNTAIN, Battle of. Revolutionary War engagement fought October 7, 1780, in north central South Carolina near the North Carolina border. A victory for the Revolutionary army over loyalist forces, it was the turning point in the southern theater of the Revolutionary War. After his victory at Camden in August, 1780, British Commander Lord Charles Cornwallis planned an invasion of North Carolina. It was his auxilary force, consisting primarily of American loyalists rather than trained British troops, that was surrounded and defeated by frontiersmen from North Carolina and Virginia at King's Mountain.

The British auxiliary force was commanded by Maj. Patrick Ferguson, who died in the battle and in the opinion of most should have fallen back to the main force. Instead he chose to make a stand with his force of 1,100, and in a single hour on October 7 more than 250 of these loyalists were killed. The patriots had surrounded Ferguson's party, and they were able to fire on his formation from behind protective ground cover. The massacre continued beyond ethical limits because of a lack of leadership on the Revolutionary side, and because of rumors that the British had accepted no quarter at earlier battles. The Revolutionary side lost less than 30 men. The surviving loyalist force was captured entirely, and nine prisoners were hanged as traitors.

King's Mountain demonstrated the capability of patriots in the South to contain the British with guerrilla tactics and loose amalgamations of frontier militia. It also turned popular sentiment in the South away from loyalist allegiances toward Revolutionary ones. King's Mountain forced Cornwallis to fall back to Camden and to abandon immediate plans for the invasion of North Carolina.

KING'S MOUNTAIN, N.C. Town (pop. 8,430), Cleveland Co., in southwest North Carolina near the South Carolina border. The town is near the site of an important Revolutionary battle where the scattered bones of the dead were not properly interred until 34 years later during a memorial service by survivors and relatives. The site is marked by a 4,000-acre national military park. Limestone, spodumene, and mica mines are found here, and manufactures include lumber, yarn and upholstery. There is also diversified farming.

KINGSPORT, Tenn. City (pop. 32,027), Sullivan Co., on the Holston River in northeast Tennessee near Johnson City. The settlement began as a docking point for ships on the Holston River, but it became firmly established when Col. James King (its namesake) built mills and factories. Incorporated in 1822, it is now an industrial center and one of the largest manufacturers of books in the U.S.

KINGSVILLE, Tex. City (28,808), seat of Kleberg Co., at the head of Baffin Bay on the Gulf coast of southern Texas near Corpus Christi. Founded on a 41,820-acre tract purchased by the KING RANCH enterprises (1903), it is the home of Texas College of Arts and Industries (1917) and headquarters of the King Ranch. Kingsville is a center for cattle and horse breeding, as well as oil and natural gas.

KINSTON, N.C. City (pop. 25,234), seat of Lenoir Co., on the northern bank of the Neuse River in southeast North Carolina. Kinston is a tobacco center whose first recorded home was built in 1740, 22 years before the town was incorporated. It is the birthplace of James Augustus Washington, one of the first men to administer medicine by hypodermic needle (1839). Fertilizer, lumber, and monuments are among Kinston's manufactures.

KIOWA INDIANS ("principal people"). Tribe of Tanoan linguistic stock that originally lived at the head of the Missouri River near Virginia City, Kan. Always bitter enemies of the settlers, they roamed parts of Texas allying themselves with other warlike tribes.

KIRBY-SMITH, Edmund (St. Augustine, Fla., May 16, 1824 — Sewanee, Tenn., Mar. 28, 1893). Military office and educator. After graduating from West Point (1845), Kirby-Smith fought with distinction in the Mexican War at Cerro Gordo and Contreras, and in Indian conflicts in Texas, where he was promoted to major (1860). When Florida seceded he took a commission with the South, and was promoted to brigadier general in 1861. Wounded at Bull Run, he led the advance troops in Gen. Braxton Bragg's Kentucky campaign; won at Richmond, Ky.; fought at Perryville and Murfeesboro, Tenn.; and took command of the Trans-Mississippi Department (1863) after being promoted to lieutenant general in 1862. Cut off from the east after Vicksburg, Kirby-Smith kept his section of the Confederacy self-supporting in the interim. He was the last Confederate general to surrender his troops on June 2, 1865. After the war, he served as president of the University of Nashville (1870-75).

KIRK, Alan Goodrich (Philadelphia, Pa., Oct. 30, 1888 — New York, N.Y., Sept. 15, 1963). Naval officer and diplomat. Graduated from the Naval Academy at Annapolis, he was stationed at the Naval Proving Ground, Indian Head, Md., during World War I. Kirk served in the bureau of ordnance and as gunnery officer aboard several ships, and was promoted to chief of staff for the commander of naval forces in Europe early in World War II. During the war Kirk led the task force that landed troops on Sicily, and he commanded 1,000 ships in the invasion of Normandy. Admiral Kirk retired from the navy (1946) and served as U.S. ambassador to Belgium (1946-49), the U.S.S.R. (1949-52), and the Republic of China (1963), until ill health forced his return to New York.

KIRKWOOD, Mo. City (pop. 27,987), St. Louis Co., in east central Missouri. It was settled with the development of the railroad in 1852, incorporated in 1865, and named for the railroad's chief engineer, James P. Kirkwood. Today it is an industrial and residential suburb of St. Louis.

KISSIMMEE LAKE, Fla. Osceola Co., in central Florida about 40 miles south of Or-

lando. The lake flows north to south as part of the route of the Kissimmee River. About 15 miles long by five miles wide, it contains several small islands.

KISSIMMEE PRAIRIES, Fla. River valley ranging from Osceola County south for about 140 miles to Lake Okeechobee. The region is noted for its large cattle ranges and citrus growing and its wilderness tracts are trapping areas.

KISSIMMEE RIVER, Fla. River in central Florida which begins its north-south course at Lake Tohopekaliga. It winds a crooked course through several lakes to enter Lake Okeechobee near Okeechobee City. It is 140 miles long.

KITTY HAWK, N.C. Site of the first sustained flight of a powered aircraft. On a narrow strip of sand known as Kill Devil Hill, the Wright brothers, Wilbur (1867-1912) and Orville (1871-1948), bicycle mechanics from Dayton, Ohio, made their first successful flight about 10:30 A. M. on Dec. 17, 1903. During the day thay made three more flights, the final one lasting 59 seconds over a distance of 852 feet.

KNIGHTS OF THE GOLDEN CIRCLE. Secret order organized in 1854 in Cincinnati, Ohio for Southern supporters in the North. Organized by Dr. George W. L. Bickley, it promoted the colonization of northern Mexico to extend proslavery interests. It became particularly popular in Texas and later spread to Kentucky, Indiana, Ohio, and Missouri. During the Civil War it sympathized with the Southern government but did not engage in treasonable activities. Reorganized in 1863 as the Order of American Knights and as the Sons of Liberty in 1864, the group reached a strength of between 200,000 and 300,000 members at its peak. It dissolved in 1865 at the same time as the Confederacy.

KNOTT, James Proctor (Raywick, Ky., Aug. 29, 1830 — Lebanon, Ky., June 18, 1911). Politician. While serving as a Democratic U.S. congressman (1867-71, 1875-83), Knott was chairman of the House committee on the judiciary. He was imprisoned for a short time at the onset of the Civil War for refusing to sign an oath of allegiance. He was governor of Kentucky from 1883 to 1887, and a delegate to the state constitutional convention in 1891.

The "Kitty Hawk," built by Orville and Wilbur Wright

KNOXVILLE, Siege of. Civil War engagement, November 17 – December 5, 1863, in which the Union army held the eastern Tennessee city despite siege and assault by Confederate troops. The events in Knoxville coincided with the Union's successful defense of Chattanooga, further south in Tennessee, and contributed to the serious erosion of Confederate hopes in late 1863. The Union force of Gen. Ambrose E. Burnside occupied Knoxville on September 2, 1863. In November the Confederate force of Gen. James LONGSTREET was sent against this position, in part for tactical reasons, and in part because of Longstreet's temperamental problems with the volatile Gen. Braxton BRAGG in Chattanooga. Longstreet approached from the south, through Loudon, Tenn., and in a brief clash with Union troops at Campbell's Station on November 16 he failed to prevent Burnside's withdrawal of all Union troops within the garrison at Knoxville. The siege commenced on the next day. Longstreet launched a single direct assault on the peripheral fortification of Fort Sanders on November 29, but this was turned back by the Union forces. After the Union victory at MISSIONARY RIDGE on November 25, Gen. Ulysses S. Grant sent a force under Gen. William Tecumseh Sherman to assist Burnside, who reported his position to be in serious danger. When Sherman reached Knoxville on December 5 after a forced march, he found Longstreet in withdrawal. Burnside had failed to pursue this Confederate withdrawal, and on December 9 he requested to be relieved of his command.

KNOXVILLE, Tenn. City (pop. 183,139), seat of Knox Co., in eastern Tennessee on the Tennessee River. Knoxville serves as the center of a metropolitan area that includes the cities of Maryville, Alcoa, and Oak Ridge, in Anderson, Blount, and Knox Counties. The diversified economy is based on agriculture (livestock and tobacco), manufacturing (chemicals, clothing, and textiles), and mining (marble and zinc ore). Tourism, because of the GREAT SMOKY MOUNTAINS NATIONAL PARK and the CUMBERLAND MOUNTAINS, also contributes significantly to the economy.

The area was first settled by Capt. James White, who established a pioneer outpost called White's Fort in 1785. A treaty with the Cherokee Indians opened the area to settlers. Renamed Knoxville in 1791 after Secretary of

War Henry Knox, and incorporated in 1812, it served as capital of the territory south of the River Ohio (1792-96) and state capital (1796-1812, 1817-19). The city was under Confederate control during the early years of the Civil War, but it was seized and defended by Federal troops in September, 1863, in the Siege of Knoxville.

The growth of the TENNESSEE VALLEY AUTHORITY (TVA) in the 1930s and the Oak Ridge atomic research facilities in the 1940s contributed to the growth of Knoxville. The TVA, in particular, brought cheap electric power and opened up new channels of transportation for industry. The University of Tennessee, Knoxville College, and the Tennessee School for the Deaf are located here. Historical sites include the Blount Mansion and the Confederate Memorial Hall. The Dogwood Arts Festival is held in Knoxville each April. In 1982 it was the site of the World's Fair.

KOCH, Frederick Henry (Covington, Ky., Sept. 12, 1877 — Miami Beach, Fla., Aug. 16, 1944). Dramatist and educator. A graduate of Ohio Wesleyan and Harvard University, Koch joined the staff of the University of North Carolina in 1918. Called the father of American folk drama, he introduced his course in playwriting at the university and founded the Carolina Playmakers. This group's playhouse became the first state-subsidized theater in America. His students included Thomas Wolfe and Maxwell Anderson. Eleven volumes of folk plays appeared under his editorship.

KORA INDIANS. Tribe of Tunican linguistic stock that lived on the lower course of the Yazoo River in Mississippi, but may have originally lived in the interior of Louisiana. They suffered defeats at the hands of Indians allied with the French, and eventually joined the CHOCTAW INDIANS.

KOSATI INDIANS. Tribe of Muskogean linguistic stock that lived in Alabama near the junction of the Coosa and Tallapoosa Rivers. Members of the Upper CREEK Confederacy, the tribe appears to have split in the late 1700s, some going to Texas, some to Florida. The ones remaining in Alabama eventually joined the Creek Confederacy's move to INDIAN TERRITORY in Oklahoma.

KOSCIUSKO, Miss. City (pop. 7,415), seat of Attala Co., in central Mississippi. Settled in the early 1830s on the old Natchez Trace, it was first called Peking then Paris because it was thought a foreign name might attract settlers. In 1934, the Kosciusko mound was built by 3,000 local children each bringing a cup of earth from their homes to duplicate a mound near Krakow, Poland, in memory of Thaddeus Kosciusko, a Polish hero of the Revolutionary War. Today it is a processing center for local agricultural products including corn, cotton, and hay. Motor homes, textiles, electric motors and wood and plastic produce are manufactured here.

KRUTCH, Joseph Wood (Knoxville, Tenn., Nov. 25, 1893 — Tucson, Ariz., May 22, 1970). Author and editor. After receiving his Ph.D. from Columbia (1923), Krutch became an editor of *The Nation* (1924-52). A noted literary critic, he taught at Columbia (1937-52), and among his most popular works are *Comedy and Conscience After the Restoration* (1924), *Edgar Allan Poe — A Study in Genius* (1926), and *The American Drama Since 1918* (1939). Beginning in the late 1940s he wrote numerous volumes on nature in the Southwest, among them *The Desert Year* (1952) and *The Voice of the Desert* (1955). In 1954 he published *The Measure of Man*, which won the National Book Award.

KU KLUX KLAN. Secret organization based on the idea of white supremacy. Organized in Pulaski, Tenn., in 1866 by Confederate veterans, the purpose of this secret, masked organization was to oppose the former slave and CARPETBAG governments set up during the Civil War Reconstruction period. Clad in long, white hooded robes, partly for disguise and partly to inspire terror, Ku Klux Klan members rode the countryside and employed violent measures in their suppression of blacks, with whippings and murders not uncommon. The organization spread throughout the South and similar socie-

Ku Klux Klan members display the American flag at a parade

ties such as the Knights of the White Camellia (founded in Louisiana in 1867) soon began appearing. The KKK became so violent and over-zealous in its activities that the first Grand Wizard of the Empire (the title given to the group's leader), Gen. Nathan B. FORREST, a former Confederate cavalry leader, called for its disbandment in 1869. Local organizations continued, particularly in rural regions, and in 1870 and 1871 Congress passed legislation to combat the KKK.

During World War I, William J. Simmons, an ex-minister, founded a new organization that assumed the Ku Klux Klan name. He dedicated the new Klan at Stone Mountain, Ga., on Thanksgiving eve, 1915. The new movement, largely anti-Catholic and anti-Semitic, believed in white Protestant supremacy, and even though it professed to be nonpolitical it was instrumental in controlling elections in some states. The movement was active in the North as well as the South and estimates of its membership in the 1920s were between two million and three million. Professional promoters Edward Y. Clarke and Mrs. Elizabeth Tyler were largely responsible for the Klan's popularity, and millions of dollars were collected in dues from members. The newly organized Klan used as its symbol a burning cross and these fiery crosses were seen across the country. When Alfred E. Smith, a Catholic, was nominated by the Democrats as the presidential candidate in 1928, the KKK became actively involved in the campaign. Their activity was short-lived, however, and during the depression of the 1930s they lost most of their dues-paying members; their membership sank to 30,000. In 1944 the government tried to collect nearly $700,000 owed in back taxes and what was left of the organization quickly disbanded.

In 1964, as a result of the Civil Rights Act, there was a resurgence of the Klan. Crosses were again burned and there was some public picketing. When four Klan members were arrested in connection with the murder of a white female civil rights worker in Alabama, Klan activities again began to dwindle. There have been, since then, sporadic KKK rallies in both the North and South but their support is minimal.

L

LA SALLE, Robert Cavelier, Sieur de
(Rouen, France, baptized Nov. 22, 1643 —
Texas, Mar. 19, 1687). French explorer. Arriving in Montreal in 1666, La Salle explored
Canada and the Great Lakes (1669-79) before
setting out with Henri de Tonti to find the
mouth of the Mississippi River. They descended the Mississippi to its mouth, the first
Europeans to do so, arriving in 1682. La Salle
claimed the territory for Louis XIV of France,
naming it Louisiana. La Salle returned from
France in 1684 to establish a settlement but
disembarked in Texas instead of Louisiana. La
Salle and a party of men tried unsuccessfully to
find the Mississippi, and in early 1687, at the
Brazos River, his men mutinied and killed him.

LACLEDE, Pierre Ligueste (Bedous,
France, c. 1724 — near the mouth of the Arkansas River, Ark., June 20, 1778). French fur
trader and frontiersman. Working in the fur
trade in New Orleans during the 1750s, Laclede
allied himself with his stepson Rene Auguste
CHOUTEAU and co-founded the trading post that
later became St. Louis, Mo. (1764).

LAFAYETTE, La. City (pop. 81,961), seat of
Lafayette Parish, in south central Louisiana.
Salvator and Anne Mouton, Acadian refugees
from Nova Scotia in the 1770s, are said to have
been the earliest settlers. Prominent descendants included Gen. Jean Jacques Mouton who
led vigilantes against cattle rustlers in 1859. It
was incorporated as a town in 1836, and as a
city in 1914. Today Lafayette is an important
oil shipping center on Vermillion Bayou.
Farms produce sugarcane, rice, cotton, corn,
and sweet potatoes. Industries include railroad
repair shops, cotton gins, cottonseed presses,
sugar refineries, creameries, and packing
plants. Natural gas and oil fields as well as salt
and sulfur mines are nearby. It is the home of
the University of Southwestern Louisiana.

LAFFITE, Jean (France, c. 1780 — unknown). Adventurer and privateer. Little is
known of his early life, but he was a partner in a
blacksmith business in New Orleans, La., in
1809. By 1810 Laffite had become the acknowledged leader of a band of outlaws operating out
of Barataria Bay, La., plundering Spanish
ships. Because the War of 1812 was keeping the
federal government occupied, Laffite and his
group were able to openly prey upon commerce
in the Gulf region. The English, in fact, offered
Laffite large rewards if he would aid in their attack on New Orleans. In a patriotic gesture,
Laffite informed Louisiana officials of the offer;

228

the government's response, however, was to imprison Laffite and his band. After promising to serve in the battle of New Orleans, they were released and pardoned, only to return to privateering. Texas, then under Spanish rule, became Laffite's new headquarters. He operated out of Galveston until several attacks on American vessels prompted the U.S. government in 1821 to send troops to curtail his activities. Laffite responded by burning the town and then disappeared. There were reports of Laffite operating in the Spanish Main, but by 1825 he was no longer heard of. It was variously reported that he died at sea during a battle, or died of a fever in a Central American village.

LAFOURCHE BAYOU, La. Bayou rising in southeastern Louisiana and running south to the Gulf of Mexico. Originally a Mississippi River outlet until it was cut off by the construction of a dam at Donaldsonville, it serves as a major tradeway, with Raceland as its shipping center.

LAKE CHARLES, La. City (pop. 75,051), seat of Calcasieu Parish, on the Calcasieu River in southwestern Louisiana. The city is the port of entry for the 21st U.S. Customs District, with the river and Calcasieu Lake providing a channel to the Gulf of Mexico. The first permanent settlement was in 1852; it was incorporated as a town in 1867, chartered as a city in 1886, and a commission form of government was established in 1913. The principal industry in early years was lumbering, and a pine and hardwood timber industry remains. A rich agricultural area surrounding the city produces rice and cattle. Plants now manufacture petroleum products and equipment, chemicals, concrete pipe, and synthetic rubber.

LAKE CITY, Fla. City (pop. 9,257), seat of Columbia Co., in northern Florida near the Suwannee River. Before 1859, it was called Alligator after a Seminole Indian chief. Today's industries include bottling works, mobile homes, cotton ginning and lumbering.

LAKE JACKSON, Tex. City (pop. 19,102), Brazoria Co., in southeastern Texas near the Gulf of Mexico. The largest community in BRAZOSPORT's nine-city complex, Lake Jackson was founded and developed by the Dow Chemical Company during 1941-42 to house its employees. Its name originates from a small lake nearby.

LAKE MURRAY DAM, S.C. Hydroelectric dam, largely in Saluda Co., located at the confluence of the Little and Bush Rivers in central South Carolina. It is east of the Saluda Dam.

LAKE WORTH, Fla. City (pop. 27,048), Palm Beach Co., in southeastern Florida on Lake Worth. It is a tourist resort that adjoins West Palm Beach on the north. Manufactures include sports equipment, storage batteries, chemicals, and paint. It was incorporated as a city in 1925.

LAKELAND, Fla. City (pop. 52,500), Polk Co., central Florida, east of Tampa in the heart of Florida's hill and lake country. The citrus headquarters for the west, it is the home of the Florida Citrus Commission and the Citrus Mutual. It is also the home of Florida Southern College, which has one of the largest displays of buildings by Frank Lloyd Wright in the U.S. It was settled in the 1870s and incorporated in 1885.

LAMAR, Joseph Rucker (Elbert Co., Ga., Oct. 14, 1857 — Washington, D.C., Jan. 2, 1916). Jurist. He served in the Georgia state legislature (1886-89) and on the state supreme court (1904-06) before being appointed associate justice of the U.S. Supreme Court (1911-16). Lamar compiled *The Code of the State of Georgia* (2 vols. 1896).

LAMAR, Lucius Quintus Cincinnatus (Putnam Co., Ga., Sept. 17, 1825 — Macon, Ga., Jan. 23, 1893). Military officer and politician. Admitted to the bar (1847), he became involved with politics when he entered the Georgia House of Representatives (1853). Moving to Mississippi in 1855, he was elected as a Democrat to the U.S. Congress (1857-60). He resigned to become a member of the Secession Convention and drafted the Mississippi ordinance of secession, afterward enlisting in the Confederate Army as lieutenant colonel (1861), later becoming colonel (1862). He resigned his commission to be appointed envoy to Russia by Confederate President Jefferson Davis, only to have authority denied by the Confederate senate. After the war, Lamar returned to Washington as a congressman (1873-77), senator (1877-85), and Secretary of the Interior (1885-88) under President Grover Cleveland. Conciliator of opposing factions in Congress and prominent in his efforts to reconcile the

North and the South after the war, he was appointed to the U.S. Supreme Court in 1887, where he remained for the rest of his life.

LAMAR, Mirabeau Buonaparte (Louisville Co., Ga., Aug. 16, 1798 — Richmond, Tex., Dec. 19, 1859). Second president of the Republic of Texas, diplomat, and poet. While president of the new republic (1838-41), Lamar opposed annexation to the U.S. He founded a new capital at Austin in 1840. Lamar served in the Mexican War and as U.S. minister to Nicaragua and Costa Rica (1857-59). He published romantic poetry in *Verse Memorials* (1857).

LAMINE RIVER, Mo. An offshoot of the Missouri River in central Missouri. It rises in Cooper County and moves south into Morgan County.

LANCASTER, S.C. Town (pop. 9,603), seat of Lancaster Co., in northern South Carolina. Lancaster, settled in the 1790s and incorporated in 1830, is in a farming area where cotton and corn are raised. Its diversified manufactures include garments, soybean oil, steel towers, brick and tiles.

LANE, Sir Ralph (Northamptonshire, England, c. 1530 — Dublin, Ireland, Oct., 1603). Colonist. He was the leader of the expedition sent by Sir Walter Raleigh in 1585, which was the first attempted English colony in America at Roanoke Island, N.C. Lane was left in command at Roanoke when Sir Richard GRENVILLE returned to England. He supervised the more than 100 colonists who landed on the continent in 1585, but they all withdrew to England with Sir Francis Drake after a year in the New World.

LANIER, Sidney (Macon, Ga., Feb. 3, 1842 — Lynn, N.C., Sept. 7, 1881). Poet and musician. Educated at Oglethorpe University, Lanier was a private in the Confederate Army who was captured near the end of the war and suffered for the remainder of his life from tuberculosis contracted in the garrison at Point Lookout, Md. In 1867 he published a Civil War novel called *Tiger-Lilies*, but his reputation is based primarily upon his poetry. Lanier's poems reveal two particular preoccupations, music and the South. He was a flutist who appeared with the Peabody Orchestra in Baltimore and in his poems, many of which were intended to be set to music, Lanier experi-

mented with special rhythms and meters in order to give his verse, such as "The Symphony," a marked melodic quality. He is perhaps best remembered for regional poems such as "Song of the Chattahoochee" and "The Marshes of Glynn."

LAREDO, Tex. City (pop. 91,449), seat of Webb Co., on the Rio Grande River in southwest Texas. A border city with major railroad and highway connections with Mexico, it was settled by Spanish families in the 1750s. Under Mexican jurisdiction after the Texas Revolution, it was ceded to the United States in 1848 after the Mexican War. An international commerce and tourist center because of its position on the border, its early economy was based on cattle raising and agriculture. Today its industries have expanded to include meatpacking and manufactures such as bricks, shoes, clothing and electronics. Fort McIntosh, established as Camp Crawford (1849) during the Mexican War, is in Laredo and is now the site of Laredo Junior College. Laredo State University (1969), a part of the University of South Texas, is also in the city. Across the Rio Grande in Mexico is Nuevo Laredo, a typical Mexican market town with curio shops and sidewalk stands.

LARGO, Fla. City (pop. 58,977), Pinellas Co., in western Florida on the Pinellas peninsula along the Gulf of Mexico. Situated in an area largely settled after the Civil War, today it is a resort city and a major processing and shipping point for area citrus and truck farm growers.

LASHLEY, Karl (Davis, W. Va., June 7, 1890 — Poitiers, France, Aug. 7, 1958). Neuropsychologist. He is best known for his research into the relationship between the brain's mass and its ability to learn. Lashley earned degrees from West Virginia University, the University of Pittsburgh, and Johns Hopkins. He taught at several universities between 1917 and 1955 including Harvard, and directed the Yerkes Laboratory of Primate Biology in Orange Park, Fla. He studied the relationship between behavior and brain damage in rats, and wrote *Brain Mechanisms and Intelligence* (1929).

LATANE, John Holladay (Staunton, Va., Apr. 1, 1869 — New Orleans, La., Jan. 1, 1932). Educator. An expert on diplomatic history, he was a professor at Washington and Lee

University (1902-13) and at Johns Hopkins (1913-30). An advocate of President Woodrow Wilson's political views, he was instrumental in the establishment of the Walter Hines Page School of International Relations at Johns Hopkins (1930). The author of several textbooks, his most noted work was *America as a World Power: 1897-1907* (1907).

LATROBE, Benjamin Henry (Fulneck, England, May 1, 1764 — New Orleans, La., Sept. 3, 1820). Architectural engineer. Considered to be the first U.S. architect of international stature, after a European education and apprenticeship, Latrobe immigrated to Virginia where his initial commission was the penitentiary in Richmond (1797). He introduced the Greek Revival style to the U.S. with the Bank of Pennsylvania in Philadelphia (1798-1800), which contained the first stone vault. Latrobe was appointed surveyor of public buildings in Washington by President Thomas Jefferson (1803) and he took charge of the completion of the Capitol. In 1814 he was recalled to Washington to rebuild the Capitol, which had been burned by the British.

LATTIMORE, Owen (Washington, D.C., July 29, 1900 —). Author and educator. After receiving his education in England and doing graduate work at Harvard, he traveled extensively in China and neighboring countries. An expert on Asian affairs he wrote numerous books before editing the *Journal of Pacific Affairs* (1934-41). During World War II he was adviser to Generalissimo Chiang Kai-shek, deputy director of the Pacific Bureau of the Office of War Information, and economic advisor to the Japanese Reparations Committee. In 1950 Senator Joseph McCarthy accused him of being an espionage agent for the Russians, and in 1952 he was accused of perjury on charges that he had lied about promoting communism. Lattimore was cleared both times and all government charges were dropped in 1955. He wrote of the experience in his book *Ordeal by Slander* (1950).

LAUDERHILL, Fla. Town (pop. 37,271), Broward Co., in southwestern Florida. A residential suburb of Fort Lauderdale with some light industry, Lauderhill is a newly developed area that was formerly pastureland. When it was incorporated in 1959, there were only eight families in the area.

LAUDONNIERE, Rene Goulaine de (France, fl. 1562-1582). French colonizer. He accompanied Jean RIBAUT on the first French expedition to Florida in 1562. In 1564 he helped establish Fort Caroline and was one of the few who escaped the slaughter there by Spanish attackers.

LAUREL, Md. Town (pop. 8,503), Prince George's Co., in west central Maryland. Laurel is an industrial and resort community founded in the late 17th century in a farm area. Manufactures include paint and electrical appliances. It is the home of the Laurel Racetrack and the Patuxent Wildlife Research Refuge. Fort George G. Meade is nearby.

LAUREL, Miss. City (pop. 21,897), seat of Jones Co., in southeast Mississippi north of Hattiesburg and near Tallahala Creek. Founded in 1882 in the midst of the largest yellow pine forest in the U.S., it was incorporated as a town in 1890 and by 1920 was the leading producer of yellow pine lumber in the world. The depletion of timber would have pauperized the city had not William Mason invented Masonite. The city's economy continues to be based on wood products and naval stores.

LAURENS, Henry (Charleston, S.C., Mar. 6, 1724 — Charleston, S.C., Dec. 8, 1792). Statesman, export merchant, and planter. Of French Huguenot descent, Laurens amassed great wealth as an exporter and planter before turning his attentions to affairs of state. He served as president of the first provincial congress in South Carolina and of the South Carolina Council of Safety (1775). He was a delegate to the Continental Congress (1777-80), serving as its president from November 1777 to December 1778. During the Revolutionary War, he was sent by Congress to Holland (1780) to negotiate a loan of $10 million. En route he was captured by the British and imprisoned in the Tower of London. The discovery from his papers that the Dutch were contemplating signing a pact with the colonists angered the British and led to a war between Holland and Great Britain. Laurens was held by the British until December 31, 1781 when he was exchanged for Lord Charles Cornwallis. In 1782 Laurens sailed to Paris to participate with Benjamin Franklin and John Jay in the preliminary peace negotiations to end the war with Great Britain. Ill health prevented him from being on hand to sign the final document. He was the father of John LAURENS.

LAURENS, John (Charleston, S.C., Oct. 28, 1754 — S.C., Aug. 27, 1782). Military officer. During the Revolution he was a member of Gen. George Washington's staff, and fought at Brandywine and other major battles. He was captured by the British in 1780 but exchanged. As special envoy to France in 1781 he secured arms and money for the Revolutionists. Returning to America, he helped draw up surrender terms for Lord Charles Cornwallis, including the exchange of Lord Cornwallis for his father, diplomat Henry LAURENS, who was a prisoner in the Tower of London.

LAURENS, S.C. Town (pop. 10,587), seat of Laurens Co., in western South Carolina. Laurens was a pre-Revolutionary Scotch and Irish settlement that was once the scene of race riots and Ku Klux Klan activities following the Civil War. President Andrew Johnson operated a tailor shop here. Today its chief manufactures include containers, carpets, and rayon. Agricultural products include cotton, peaches, and grain.

LAURINBURG, N.C. City (pop. 11,480), seat of Scotland Co., in southern North Carolina. Founded in the 1870s, today's manufactures include clocks, watches, and furniture. Diversified farming includes cotton, corn, and tomatoes. It is the home of St. Andrews Presbyterian College.

LAWSON, John (England, late 1600s — North Carolina, 1711). Explorer. Lawson arrived in Charleston, S.C., in 1700 and traveled through unexplored portions of North Carolina, reporting on the plant and animal life as well as the native population of the region. He wrote of his expeditions in *History of Carolina* (1709). He secured incorporation of Bath, N.C. (1705), and was founder of New Bern, N.C. (1708). Lawson was killed by the Tuscarora Indians.

LAZEAR, Jesse William (Baltimore Co., Md., May 2, 1866 — Cuba, Sept. 25, 1900). Physician and epidemiologist. A graduate of Johns Hopkins and Columbia, he did furthur study in Paris at Pasteur Institute. Practicing in Baltimore, he was affiliated with Johns Hopkins, where he began research work on malaria. Transferring to Cuba as assistant surgeon with the army (1900), he continued his laboratory work. There he joined the yellow fever team headed by Maj. Walter Reed, tending the mosquitoes under study and supervising their application to volunteers for experimentation. Though he could have avoided it, he was bitten "accidentally" and contracted yellow fever. A week later he died, proving that the disease was transmitted by mosquitoes. Reed rated Lazear's contribution to yellow fever control, and that of the other members of the commission, James Carroll and Aristides Agramonte, as equal to his own work in Cuba.

LE CONTE, Joseph (Liberty Co., Ga., Feb. 26, 1823 — Yosemite Valley, Calif., July 6, 1901). Geologist, author, and educator. A professor at the University of South Carolina (1857-69) and at the University of California at Berkeley (1869-96), Le Conte was a friend of naturalist James Audubon. He wrote prolifically on a broad range of scientific subjects, including coal, petroleum, and the action of the Gulf Stream.

LEDBETTER, Huddie "Leadbelly" (Mooringsport, La., 1888 — New York, N.Y., Dec. 6, 1949). Blues singer and composer. Ledbetter started his career by playing a guitar at dances in Texas and Louisiana. He became associated with blues singer "Blind Lemon" Jefferson for a time and became known as "Leadbelly." He was jailed for murder in 1918, put on a chain gang, and pardoned in 1925. Rearrested in 1930 for attempted murder, he was released in 1934; and was again arrested, for assault, in 1939. Writer John A. Lomax met him in prison and assembled his songs into a book, *Negro Folk Songs as Sung by Lead Belly* (1936). After his release from prison, Ledbetter toured France in 1949.

LEE, Arthur (Westmoreland Co., Va., Dec. 21, 1740 — Middlesex Co., Va., Dec. 12, 1792). Diplomat. A physician by training, Lee was a leader in the struggle with Greaat Britain. In 1770, while in England studying law, he was made colonial agent of Massachusetts. He became active in British political circles and continued to champion the American position to the British public. The Continental Congress appointed him agent in 1775 and the following year he joined Benjamin Franklin and Silas Deane in their efforts to negotiate alliances and win aid for the Revolutionary struggle from European powers. Despite quarrels among themselves, they were able to secure an alliance with France in 1778. Lee was a member of the Continental Congress (1781-84) and the Treasury Board (1785-89). He opposed the ratification of the Constitution on grounds that it would create a powerful central government. Lee was the brother of Francis Lightford Lee, William Lee and Richard Henry Lee.

LEE, Fitzhugh (Fairfax Co., Va., Nov. 19, 1835 — Washington, D.C., Apr. 28, 1905). Military officer and politician. He was nephew of Robert E. LEE. Known for his reconnaissance and tactical abilities, Lee was of great value to the Confederate cause as an expert cavalry leader against the Union forces. He was governor of Virginia (1886-90) and an unsuccessful candidate for the U.S. Senate (1893). During the Spanish American War he was given the rank of major general and has the distinction, along with Joseph Wheeler, of being one of only three former Confederate generals to serve in a similar rank in that later conflict.

LEE, Francis Lightfoot (Stratford, Va., Oct. 14, 1734 — Richmond Co., Va., Apr. 3, 1797). Politician. The brother of Richard Henry LEE, William LEE, and Arthur LEE, he became a member of the Virgina House of Burgesses (1758-76), and was a member of the Continental Congress (1775-79). Lee was active in framing the Articles of Confederation, and was a signer of the Declaration of Independence. He served in the Virginia state senate from 1780 to 1782.

LEE, George Washington Custis (Fortress Monroe, Va., Sept. 16, 1832 — Fairfax Co., Va., Feb. 18, 1913). Military officer and educator. The son of Robert E. LEE, he graduated from West Point (1854) and served in the Confederate Army (1861-65), attaining the rank of major general and acting as aide-de-camp to Confederate President Jefferson Davis. A professor at the Virginia Military Institute (1865-71), he went on to succeed his father as president of Washington and Lee University (1871-1897).

LEE, Henry (Prince William, Va., Jan. 29, 1756 — Cumberland Island, Ga., Mar. 25, 1818). Revolutionary War hero. Known as "Lighthorse Harry" for his daring cavalry exploits, Lee joined the Revolution in 1776, in the army of Gen. George Washington. He later commanded a combined infantry and cavalry command called "Lee's Legion" that saw action in many of the war's major engagements. Lee's best known military encounters were his defeat and capture of the British at Paulus

Hook, N.J., and his key role in Gen. Nathanael Greene's brilliant southern campaign (1780-81). After the war, Lee served in the Continental Congress (1785-88) and the Virginia legislature (1789-91). He was governor of Virginia (1792-95) and, as a major general, put down the WHISKEY REBELLION in 1794. He was elected as a Federalist to the U.S. Congress, and served from 1799 to 1801. His youngest son from his second marriage was Robert E. LEE, and he was the grandfather of William Henry Fitzhugh LEE.

LEE, Jesse (Prince George Co., Va., Mar. 12, 1758 — Hillsborough, Md., Sept. 12, 1816). Clergyman. Often referred to as the "Apostle of Methodism," he was an influential itinerant preacher in Virginia, Maryland, and North Carolina from 1783 to 1789. He was appointed presiding elder of the South District of Virginia (1801-15) and also served as chaplain in the U.S. House (1809-13) and Senate (1814). In 1810 he wrote *A Short History of Methodism in America.*

LEE, Richard (England, c. 1613 — Northumberland Co., Va., 1664). Colonist. He arrived in America in the early 1640s, eventually settling in Northumberland Co., Virginia, and was the ancestor of the Lee family in that state. He became a wealthy tobacco planter and was an influential political figure in the early colony as a member of the Virginia House of Burgesses.

LEE, Richard Henry (Westmoreland Co., Va., Jan. 20, 1732 — Westmoreland Co., Va., June 19, 1794). As a member of the Virginia House of Burgesses (1758-75), Lee joined Patrick Henry in strenuous objection to British colonial policy. He was a member of the Continental Congress (1774-80, 1784-87) and introduced a resolution leading to the Declaration of Independence. He served in the Continental Congress from 1784 to 1787, the first year as president. Lee opposed the ratification of the Constitution, as did Thomas Jefferson, on the grounds that it contained no bill of rights and created a powerful central government. He served in the U.S. Senate from 1789 to 1792, where he offered proposals leading to the acceptance of the Bill of Rights. He was the brother of Arthur LEE and Francis Lightfoot LEE.

LEE, Robert Edward (Westmoreland Co., Va., Jan. 19, 1807 — Lexington, Va., Oct. 12, 1870). Commander-in-chief of the Confederate

Army. He was the son of Col. Henry (Light-Horse Harry) LEE and Ann Hill Carter, both members of prominent Virginia families, which were active in colonial government and in the Revolution. After his graduation from West Point (1829), Lee was commissioned in the Corps of Engineers and began a brilliant military career. In 1831 he married May Custis, a great-grandaughter of Martha Washington. They lived at her father's residence, Arlington House (which became a National Memorial in 1925), until the Civil War.

Lee saw his first war service in the Mexican War (1846-48) under Gen. Winfield Scott. He won special praise for reconnaissance in the campaign leading to the capture of Mexico City, and advanced from captain to colonel. He was appointed superintendent of West Point (1852-55) and then spent several years in Texas containing the Indians. While on extended leave to settle his father-in-law's estate, he was ordered to HARPERS FERRY where he led a group of Marines and captured John BROWN.

In February 1861, after the secession of seven Southern states, Lee was recalled to Washington. While personally against slavery and secession, Lee decided that if it came to war, honor required him to side with Virginia and the South. Virginia seceded April 17 and the next day Lee refused Lincoln's offer of field command of the Union armies. On April 20, he resigned and assumed command of Virginia's forces, which later were absorbed into the Confederate Army. A failure in his first campaign to save Western Virginia, he went on to successfully fortify Charleston, Port Royal, and Savannah. In March 1862, Confederate President Jefferson Davis called Lee to Richmond as his adviser. Following Lee's plan, Gen. T. J. (Stonewall) JACKSON kept reinforcements from Union Gen. G. B. McClellan, who was threatening Richmond. After Gen. J. D. JOHNSTON was wounded, Davis placed Lee in command of the Army of Northern Virginia. Outnumbered, Lee went on to outmaneuver McClellan in the SEVEN DAYS battle (June 25-July 1, 1862). By unorthodox planning he and Jackson decisively defeated Maj. Gen. John Pope at the second Battle of BULL RUN (August 29-30, 1862).

His defensive skills were shown in the AN-TIETAM campaign in Maryland. After his orders fell into Union hands, Lee was caught by surprise, but skillfully withdrew his forces across the Potomac. His decision to fight the battle of FREDERICKSBURG (December 1862) defensively has been criticized. The Union forces fell back but casualties were high, and at CHANCELLORS-

VILLE (May 2-4, 1863) the battle was soured by the death of Gen. Stonewall Jackson. A bold assault into Pennsylvania failed badly, and the blame for the GETTYSBURG defeat (June-July, 1863) was accepted by Lee, although subordinates may have been mainly at fault.

Lee once again showed his brilliant defensive abilities in the Wilderness Campaign (May-June, 1864). Although he lost many fewer men than Gen. Ulysses S. Grant, they could not be replaced. Grant began the siege of Petersburg (the winter of 1864-65), and when Lee became general-in-chief of the Confederate armies in February 1865, there was little left to command. Lee surrendered to Grant at Appomattox Courthouse April 9, 1865.

Lee became president of Washington College (now Washington and Lee University), in 1866 and spent the rest of his life there. One of the

Gen. Robert E. Lee

greatest generals in U.S. history, he is widely acknowledged as a man of principle and integrity, and honored as a gentleman.

LEE, Stephen Dill (Charleston, S.C., Sept. 22, 1833 — Vicksburg, Miss., May 28, 1908). Military officer. Lee resigned as a U.S. frontier officer to take a Confederate commission when South Carolina seceded. An aide-de-camp to Gen. Pierre Beauregard at Fort Sumter (1861), he later commanded at the second Battle of Manassas, at Antietam, and was brigadier general at Vicksburg (1863). Promoted to lieutenant general, he fought at Atlanta and surrendered with Gen. Joseph Johnston in 1865. A gentleman planter and state senator during Reconstruction (1878), he was the first president of Mississippi Agricultural and Mechanical College (1880-89) and was commander-in-chief of the United Confederate Veterans.

LEE, William (Westmoreland Co., Va., Aug. 31, 1739 — Green Spring, Va., June 27, 1795). Diplomat. The brother of Richard Henry, Francis Lightfoot, and Arthur LEE, he was agent for Virginia in London, and became a merchant there. At the outbreak of the Revolution, Lee moved to France and the Continental Congress appointed him commercial agent at Nantes in 1777. He later became American minister at the Hague. He was dismissed from service after attempting to negotiate an unauthorized loan with Holland, and returned to Virginia.

LEE, William Henry Fitzhugh (Arlington, Va., May 31, 1837 — Alexandria, Va., Oct. 15, 1891). Military officer and politician. Also known as Rooney Lee, he was the second son of Robert E. LEE and the grandson of Henry LEE. He attained the rank of major general in the Confederate Cavalry and was wounded and captured at the Battle of Brandy Station (1863). Lee was a member of the state senate from 1875 to 1879, and was a Democratic Representative to Congress from Virginia from 1887 until his death.

LEE'S SUMMIT, Mo. City (pop. 28,741), Jackson Co., in western Missouri, southeast of Kansas City. Laid out in 1865, the city is one of the highest points between Kansas City and St. Louis. It was named for Dr. Pleasant Lea, an early resident. Present manufactures include electronic equipment, machinery, and leather goods. There is diversified farming and a large dairy industry in the area.

LEESBURG, Va. Town (pop. 8,357), seat of Loudon Co., in northern Virginia, 36 miles northwest of Washington, D.C. Settled in 1749, the town is located in an area of rich farmland and has long been noted for the breeding of horses and cattle. Present manufactures center around the aircraft and aerospace industries.

LEGARE, Hugh Swinton (Charleston, S.C., Jan. 2, 1797 — Boston, Mass., June 20, 1843). Politician. After an intense study of law and languages, he began his political career in the South Carolina legislature. He was co-founder and editor of the literary journal *Southern Review* (1828-32), and was elected to Congress as a Union Democrat (1837-39). President John Tyler appointed him attorney general (1841) in a cabinet where his unique understanding of national and international law made him a particularly valuable member. Upon the resignation of Daniel Webster as Secretary of State in May 1843, Legare filled the interim post until his sudden death a month later.

LeJEUNE, Camp, N.C. U.S. Naval Hospital and a U.S. Marine Corps training camp in eastern North Carolina near Jacksonville. Founded in 1941 and named for Lt. Gen. John Lejeune who was a Marine Corps commandant, it covers roughly 83,000 acres.

LEMOYNE, Pierre. See IBERVILLE, Pierre LeMoyne.

LENOIR, N.C. City (pop. 13,748), seat of Caldwell Co., in western North Carolina. Lenoir is an industrial and lumber center in an area of mountain resorts. Its manufactures include furniture, yarn, mirrors, and hosiery. Diversified farming includes cotton, tobacco, and corn.

LENOIR CITY, Tenn. City (pop. 5,446), Loudon Co., in eastern Tennessee, 24 miles southwest of Knoxville. Founded in 1840 on the Tennessee River, today there is diversified farming and industry. Manufactures include hosiery, canned goods, and foundry products.

LENUD'S FERRY, Battle of. Revolutionary War engagement on the Santee River near Charleston, S.C., fought May 6, 1780. In it the British routed a force of American cavalry hoping to reinforce Charleston against the British siege of that city.

The Revolutionay force under Col. Anthony White included survivors of the Battle of Monck's corner on April 14. By early May, White was maneuvering near Charleston in an attempt to join up with the larger Revolutionary force under Col. Abraham Buford, who would finally be isolated from Charleston by his defeat at Waxhaw Creek. On May 6 the British force in the area, commanded by Lt. Col Banastre Tarleton, victor in both of those battles, attacked White as he was attempting to cross Lenud's Ferry on the Santee to join Buford. In the surprise attack, the British killed 40 of the Americans and captured another 60 without losing a single man.

LESLIE, Miriam Florence Folline (New Orleans, La., June 5, 1836 — Sept. 18, 1914). Editor and publisher. Editor of the fashion and literary magazine *Frank Leslie's Lady's Journal* (1871), she subsequently became Leslie's wife and successor, and after his death legally took the name Frank Leslie (1882). Legendary among publishers, she was dubbed "The Empress of Journalism." An ardent feminist, she bequeathed much of her fortune to that cause. Her works include *Rents in Our Robes* (1888) and *Are Men Gay Deceivers?* (1893).

LETCHER, John (Lexington, Va., Mar. 29, 1813 — Lexington, Va., Jan. 26, 1884). Politician. A graduate of Washington Academy (now Washington and Lee University), Letcher was admitted to the bar and practiced law in Lexington. He was a Democratic member of Congress (1851-59) and governor of Virginia (1860-64). While he was governor, the state legislature passed its secession ordinance and, without waiting for it to be voted on by the people, Letcher turned over the entire forces of Virginia to the Confederacy. After the war he was a member of the state legislature (1875-77), and president of the Virginia Military Institute.

LEUTZE, Emanuel (Gmund, Wurttemberg, May 24, 1816 — Washington, D.C., July 18, 1868). Painter. Immigrating as a child with his family to Fredericksburg, Va., Leutze returned to Europe to train at the Royal Academy in Dusseldorf where he remained and worked until 1859. Returning to the U.S., he was commissioned to decorate the stair of the Capitol for which he produced "Westward the Course of Empire Takes its Way," often called "Westward Ho." Best known for "Washington Crossing the Delaware," a canvas of life-sized figures owned by the Metropolitan Museum of Art in New York City, he also did "Washington at Monmouth," and "Cromwell and Milton."

LEWIS, Meriwether (Albemarle Co., Va., Aug. 18, 1774 — Nashville, Tenn., Oct. 11, 1809). Military officer and explorer. An army captain in 1801, he was invited by President Thomas Jefferson to become his private secretary. Two years later Jefferson asked Lewis to undertake the exploration of much of the territory recently obtained in the Louisiana Purchase. Lewis and William CLARK, his former army superior, traveled thousands of miles, returning in 1806 with priceless diaries and maps that cleared up many misconceptions about the Northwest Territory and bolstered American claims to the region. The Lewis and Clark expedition also returned with animals, plants, and minerals, which yielded valuable scientific information. Jefferson appointed him governor of the Louisiana Territory in 1806. In 1809, on his way to Washington, he was murdered in a tavern outside of what is now Nashville, Tenn. Some historians say he took his own life, which was beset by personal problems and the strains of his governorship.

LEWISBURG, W.Va. Town (pop. 3,065), seat of Greenbrier Co., in southeast West Virginia. This mountain resort community is the home of Organ Cave and Lost World Caverns. Dairy, fruit, poultry, and stock farms, as well as a stone quarry, are in operation here and it is the home of Greenbrier College. The town was settled in 1769 and incorporated in 1782.

LEWISVILLE, Tex. Town (pop. 24,273), Denton Co., in northeast Texas. Founded in 1844, Lewisville was first called Holford Prairie Settlement. Today it is located near the Dallas-Fort Worth Airport and Lewisville Lake, which is a resort area for residents of the Dallas-Fort Worth metropolitan area. There is diversified farming and present manufactures include boats, clothing, and aluminum products.

LEXINGTON, Ky. City (pop. 204,165), seat of Fayette Co., in the heart of BLUEGRASS country, in north central Kentucky. A major horse-breeding center, it is the site of Keenland Race Track and the famous Red Mile Track, where many trotting records have been set. The city was named in response to the news of the Battle of Lexington, Mass., in 1775. It became the location of the first state legislature in 1792. Lexington has been called "the Athens of the West" because of its reputation as a local seat of culture. It is the home of the University of Kentucky, Transylvania University, College of the Bible, and Lexington Baptist College. A U.S. Public Health Hospital, Veterans' Hospital, and Eastern Kentucky State Hospital for the Mentally Ill are also located here. There are diversified industries including the manufacture of typewriters and electrical equipment, and the distillation of bourbon whiskey.

LEXINGTON, N.C. City (pop. 15,711), seat of Davidson Co., in west central North Carolina. Founded in 1775, it became the county seat in 1824. Today its manufactures include textiles, fiber glass, machinery, batteries, and plastics.

LEXINGTON, Va. City (pop. 7,292), seat of Rockbridge Co., on the Maury River in west central Virginia, 30 miles northwest of Lynchburg. Settled in 1777 by Presbyterians, it was named after the Revolutionary War battle at Lexington, Mass. Lexington was almost totally destroyed by fire in 1779, and rebuilt with funds raised through a lottery. Primarily an agricultural region, there is also mining of sulfur and limestone. The city is the home of Virginia Military Institute and Washington and Lee University. Lexington was incorporated as a town in 1841 and as a city in 1874.

LIBBY PRISON. Military prison camp in Richmond, Va., which was run by the Confederacy to house captured Union army officers in what was formerly a tobacco warehouse. It was notorious for its lack of food and sanitation facilities. It was a Union prison for Confederate prisoners following the fall of Richmond.

LICKING RIVER, Ky. River originating in eastern Kentucky, and flowing northwest for 230 miles to meet the Ohio River opposite Cincinnati, Ohio. The Licking has long been a trade and transportation route and is one of Kentucky's major rivers. George Rogers CLARK assembled his men at the river's mouth in 1780 to march up the Little Miami River. It was also the site of the Battle of Blue Licks in 1782.

LILLY, Bob (Olney, Tex., July 24, 1939 —). Football player. A graduate of Texas Christian, he was the first college player drafted by the Dallas Cowboys (1961-74). Lilly was a star defensive tackle for 14 seasons and a player in the Pro Bowl for 11 seasons. He was inducted into the Pro Football Hall of Fame in 1980.

LINCOLN, Abraham (Hardin, now Larue, Co., Ky., Feb. 12, 1809 — Washington, D.C., Apr. 14, 1865). Lawyer, orator, and 16th President of the United States. Lincoln was, in fact as well as fiction, born in a Kentucky log cabin, and at age seven he moved with his family to Indiana. There his mother Nancy Hanks Lincoln died, and his father Thomas remarried Mrs. Sarah Bush Johnston one year later in 1819. These events are known to have troubled Lincoln throughout his life, but his relationship with his step-mother was a rewarding one, although that with his father was not. Lincoln worked on Mississippi River flatboats, which brought him into contact with New Orleans slave markets. He settled in Salem, Ill., in 1831 where he found work as a surveyor and postmaster. He was at this time the tall and muscular wrestler and rail-splitter of legend, and he was also slowly mastering a range of literature unusually broad for a man without a formal education. The effect on Lincoln of the death of Ann Rutledge in 1835 soon after the two had become engaged, is one widely disputed, some claiming it to be mostly legend.

After serving in the militia during the Black Hawk War of 1832, Lincoln campaigned for the state legislature in that year and lost. In his second attempt in 1834 he was elected to the Illinois General Assembly, where he served four terms as a Whig supporter of Henry Clay. After years of private study of the law he was admitted to the bar in 1836 and began practice in Springfield, Ill. In 1842 he married Mary Todd Lincoln after a long and problematic courtship; they would have four sons.

Lincoln was elected to Congress as a Whig in 1846, but, after a single term in which he opposed both slavery and abolition as alternative evils as politically presented, he declined renomination. With the founding of the Republican party in 1854, however, Lincoln was drawn back into politics and away from compromise on slavery issues as espoused by the Whigs under Henry Clay. In 1858 he unsuccessfully challenged Democrat Stephen A. Douglas for a Senate seat, but his speeches during the famous Lincoln-Douglas debates established him as a national political figure. Nominated for the presidency in 1860 as an antislavery candidate, he ran a restrained campaign in hope of minimizing Southern hostility. The Southern states began to secede soon after his victory in the election even though his eloquent

"Farewell Address" to Illinois and his first inaugural address expressed hope that the Union could be preserved without war.

War became a fact when the Confederacy fired on Fort Sumter, S.C., on April 12, 1861. Granted sweeping war-time powers and faced with a crisis without parallel in American history, Lincoln handled both the military and political demands of the times with great authority. He elevated Ulysses S. Grant over ranking generals, a gamble soon vindicated on the field; he unified the North with moving oratorical performances such as the Gettysburg Address; and his Emancipation Proclamation of January 1, 1863, freed the slaves of the Southern states. It was followed by national abolition of slavery in the Thirteenth Amendment. Reelected in 1864, Lincoln was fatally shot at Ford's Theatre in Washington, D.C., by John Wilkes BOOTH, only five days after the surrender of the Confederate forces under Gen. Robert E. Lee.

LINCOLN UNIVERSITY. State-supported, comprehensive coed institution located in the Missouri state capital of Jefferson City. Lincoln University was founded in 1866 as a college for Negroes, but over the years the student body has become a predominantly white one, with blacks currently making up 39% of the school's population.

The school offers liberal arts, teacher education, and professional training programs. Most students graduate with degrees in either Business and Management, Education, Social Sciences, Public Affairs and Services, or Engineering. Missouri provides 69% of the students, and 18% pursue full-time graduate or professional study immediately after graduating.

Library: 35,000 volumes. Faculty: 189. Enrollment: 2,657 total graduate and undergraduate: 948 men, 731 women (full-time). Degrees: Certificate or Diploma, Associate's, Bachelor's, Master's.

LINDSAY, Robert Burns (Dumfrieshire, Scotland, July 4, 1824 — Tuscumbia, Ala., 1902). Politician. He emigrated to the U.S. at age 20, finally settling in Alabama, where he was admitted to the bar. In 1853 he was elected to the state legislature and in 1857 he became a member of the state senate. He was governor of Alabama from 1870 to 1872.

LIPAN INDIANS ("people"). Tribe of Athapascan linguistic stock that roamed the territory of West Texas southeast to the Gulf of Mexico. They made war on the Spanish frontier and desolated mission stations. Having learned the Spanish language, they advanced somewhat in civilization and became allies of the Mexican partisans in the revolution of that country. At the close of the war between Mexico and the United States (1848), they began raiding frontier settlements in Texas. They eventually retired to Mexico.

LISA, Manuel (New Orleans, La., Sept. 8, 1772 — St. Louis, Mo., Aug. 12, 1820). Fur trader and pioneer. Born of Spanish descent, he became an American citizen when Louisiana was purchased in 1803. He was one of the leading fur traders on the upper Mississippi River, and although he was granted the monopoly of trade with the Osage Indians in 1802, he lost it with the transfer of national domination in 1804. He led a number of expeditions and was considered a major factor in opening the Missouri River area to white traders and settlers. He established two forts: Fort Raymond, later Manuel's Fort, at the mouth of the Bighorn River; and Fort Lisa, near Omaha, Nebraska. He was a U.S. Indian subagent for tribes in the Missouri River region from 1814 to 1820.

LITTLE MISSOURI RIVER, Ark. River in southwestern Arkansas that rises in the Ouachita Mountains and flows 145 miles southeast to meet the Ouachita River. North of Murfreeesboro, it is dammed to create Lake Greeson.

LITTLE PEE DEE RIVER, S.C. Waterway rising in North Carolina and flowing 120 miles southeast, then south to meet the Pee Dee River near Bucksport, S.C.

LITTLE RED RIVER, Ark. River originating in north central Arkansas, and flowing southeast for 105 miles to the White River. A dam is found on the river east of Heber Springs.

LITTLE RIVER, Ala. River rising in northeast Alabama and flowing 30 miles from the Georgia line southwest to Weiss Reservoir. Noted for its rapids and waterfalls, it is located just east of LOOKOUT MOUNTAIN, and is also called the DeSoto River.

LITTLE ROCK, Ark. City (pop. 158,461), state capital and seat of Pulaski Co., on the Arkansas River in central Arkansas. Located in

U.S. paratroopers maintain order during the integration of Little Rock Central High School in 1957

the foothills of the Ouachita Mountains, the area was explored by Bernard de la Harpe in 1722, who noted two conspicuous rocks formations on the river bank and called them La Petit Roche and La Grande Roche. La Harpe set up a trading post near the Indian settlement at La Petit Roche. William Lewis, a trapper, built his home there in 1812, and after Arkansas became a U.S. territory in 1819, the site of Little Rock was surveyed and the territory's capital was transferred there from the Arkansas Post in 1821. Little Rock was incorporated as a town in 1831 and as a city in 1836.

The city became a major commercial center in the 1880s with the expansion of the railroads. Area industry went through diversified growth in the 1940s due to the proximity of important natural resources such as lumber, gas, coal, and oil. The city is also an agricultural market center for the region. A river port was established there in 1969 when a system of locks and dams was constructed on the Arkansas River.

In 1957 the city board of education adopted a graduated desegregation plan following a ruling by the U.S. Supreme Court that racial segregation was unconstitutional. The action by the school board, which allowed the registration of nine black children at Little Rock Central High School, caused racial uprising. Governor Orval FAUBUS ordered the state National Guard to prevent the children from entering the school but President Dwight D. Eisenhower sent in federal troops to maintain order.

Four colleges and universities as well as schools for the deaf and blind are located in the city. It was the birthplace of Gen. Douglas MacArthur, and MacArthur Park is named for him.

LITTLEFIELD, George Washington (Panola Co., Miss., June 21, 1842 — Nov. 10, 1920). Cattle baron and philanthropist. After serving in the Civil War Littlefield began a cat-

tle-driving business between Texas and the mid-West. He also established large cattle ranches throughout the state, and used his wealth to advance various institutions, particularly the University of Texas.

LIVERMORE, Mount, Tex. Jeff Davis Co., in western Texas. The highest peak in the Davis Mountains (8,382 feet), it is also known as Baldy Peak or Old Baldy. Today one of the world's largest observatories is situated on the mountain.

LLANO RIVER, Tex. River originating in the Edwards Plateau in southwest Texas, and flowing generally northeast for 150 miles to empty into the COLORADO River.

LLOYD, Alice Spencer Geddes (Athol, Mass., Nov. 13, 1876 — Caney Creek, Ky., Sept. 4, 1962). Educator, journalist. After publishing newspapers in Massachusetts, in 1916 she moved to Kentucky to establish a school for mountain children. Over the next five years she opened seven high schools in the back woods, attracting money and teachers from New England. In 1922 she founded tuition-free Caney Junior (now Alice Lloyd) College. Lloyd educated over 1,200 teachers for the mountain country.

LOCHLOOSA LAKE, Fla. Lake located at the southern line of Alachua Co., in north central Florida. It is part of a small chain of lakes and is connected to Orange Lake on the south.

LOCKWOOD, James Booth (Annapolis, Md., Oct. 9, 1852 — Cape Sabine, Arctic, Apr. 9, 1884). Explorer. In 1881 Lockwood joined the Arctic expedition under Adolphus W. Greely. During the expedition, Lockwood attained the northernmost point ever explored, Lockwood Island, which is named for him. In a later expedition in 1883, he discovered Grant Land. While on a trip to Cape Sabine he died two months before survivors of the party were rescued after a winter of starvation.

LOCUST CREEK, Mo. A 90-mile waterway which stretches from the Grand River in north central Missouri through Pershing Memorial Park to cross the Iowa state line.

LOCUST FORK RIVER, Ala. Waterway originating in north central Alabama near

Boaz. It runs a winding southwest course for 70 miles, ending just north of Birmingham.

LOGAN, Joshua (Texarkana, Tex., Oct. 5, 1908 —). Playwright, director, and producer. Winner of a Pulitzer Prize in 1950 for co-authoring *South Pacific* with Oscar Hammerstein, Logan is best known as the director of such plays as *Charley's Aunt* (1940), *Annie Get Your Gun* (1946), *Mr. Roberts* (1948), *South Pacific* (1949), *Picnic* (1953), and *Fanny* (1954). As a film director, his credits include *South Pacific* (1958), *Fanny* (1961), and *Camelot* (1967).

LOMAX, John Avery (Goodman, Miss., Sept. 23, 1867 — Greenville, Miss., Jan. 26, 1948). Author. A collector of folk songs, after earning his master's degree from Harvard University in 1907, Lomax taught English at numerous universities. His best known collection of songs was a collaboration with Huddie LEDBETTER called *Negro Folk Songs as Sung by Leadbelly* (1936).

"LONE STAR STATE." See TEXAS.

LONG BAY, N.C. Inlet of the Atlantic Ocean, which extends southwest from Cape FEAR in southern North Carolina and northeastern South Carolina. Myrtle Beach, S.C. is on the bay.

LONG, Crawford Williamson (Danielsville, Ga., Nov. 1, 1815 — Athens, Ga., June 16, 1878). Physician. After gaining his degree in medicine at the University of Pennsylvania (1839) he began an extensive practice in Jefferson, Ga. Observing the effects of ether as a source of entertainment, in 1842 he used it while removing a tumor from the neck of a patient, and succeeded in performing the surgery with relatively little discomfort. He continued to use the gas in surgical procedures and in 1849 published his findings in the *Southern Medical and Surgical Journal*. Although three others also claimed to be the first to use the gas, requesting Congressional rewards, Long asked for no monetary reward, only desiring the recognition of his discovery.

LONG, Huey Pierce (Winnfield, La., Aug. 30, 1893 — Baton Rouge, La., Sept. 10, 1935). Politician. The son of a farmer, Long was expelled from high school and traveled as a salesman before choosing law as a career. He was admitted to the Louisiana Bar in 1915 after only seven months of study at Tulane University. By that time he had already told Rose McConnell, whom he married in 1913, that he would eventually become President of the U.S.

His first political victory was his 1918 campaign for the state railroad commission, a body whose powers had been radically expanded by the time it was renamed the Public Service Commission in 1921. In these years Long attracted great popular loyalties by celebrated court battles to maintain low streetcar fares in Shreveport and low telephone rates throughout Louisiana. An unsuccessful candidate for governor in 1924, he won election to that office in 1928 as a progressive Democrat and maverick opponent of a powerful and wealthy New Orleans organization of Republican business interests.

Impeachment proceedings on the grounds of bribery were brought against Long after only one year in office, and he survived them by political maneuvering rather than proof of his own innocence. After this attempt to control his powers, he launched a sweeping campaign to solidify his political strength by legislative programs popular with rural voters and, some claim, outright graft and devious tampering

Huey Long doing a radio broadcast

with the electoral process. When his authority was challenged, he would reply with charismatic bravado, "I am the constitution of Louisiana."

Elected to the U.S. Senate in 1930, while retaining his governor's seat until he could turn it over to a loyal supporter, Long engaged in a fierce political battle to prevent Lieutenant Governor Paul Cyr from succeeding him as governor, which included calling out the National Guard to prevent the constitutional transfer of power. Cyr never became governor, and Long claimed his Senate seat in 1932. A proponent of depression-era economic grants that exceeded in scope President Franklin D. Roosevelt's New Deal. He formulated a "Share the Wealth" program. In 1934 he returned to Louisiana to consolidate his power in the state. He abolished local government and gained total control of the legislature and effectively acted as dictator. His intentions to launch a campaign for the presidency were known by the time he was assassinated by a political opponent in the Louisiana State Capitol.

LONGHORN CAVERN, Tex. Limestone cave complex in Burnet Co., in central Texas at the northern edge of the Edwards Plateau. It is noted for its unusual limestone and crystal formations. In past centuries, it served as a hiding place for Indians and outlaws, most notably the Sam Bass gang for which its main entrance is named. It was also a gun powder manufacturing station during the Civil War. The cavern has been only partially explored.

LONGSTREET, Augustus Baldwin (Augusta, Ga., Sept. 22, 1790 — Oxford, Miss., July 9, 1870). Author and educator. A lawyer and member of the Georgia legislature, Longstreet also wrote crudely realistic, humorous sketches which led to the works of such writers as Mark Twain. His works include *Georgia Scenes* (1835) and *Master William Mitten* (1864). Longstreet was president of Emory College (1839-48), Centenary College (1849), the University of Mississippi (1849-56), and the University of South Carolina (1857).

LONGSTREET, James (Edgefield Dist., S.C., Jan. 8, 1821 — Gainesville, Ga., Jan. 2, 1904). Military officer. A graduate of West Point, Longstreet resigned his commission in the U.S. Army to become a brigadier general in the Confederate Army (1861). He was an outstanding battle leader winning from Robert E.

LEE the nickname "Old War Horse." He fought skillfully at the first and second battles of BULL RUN (1862), CHATTANOOGA (1863), and in the Wilderness Campaign (1864). He commanded the right wing of Lee's army at ANTIETAM (1862) and the left wing of the Confederate Army at CHICKAMAUGA (1863). He was blamed by some for Lee's defeat at GETTYSBURG (July 1863) but Lee never directly criticized him. He was with Lee at the surrender at Appomattox Court House (April 9, 1865). After the war Longstreet became a businessman but, when he joined the Republican Party in a move to display his belief in peace, he was ostracized by his fellow Southerners. He held several federal posts in the latter part of his life.

LONGVIEW, Tex. City (62,762), seat of Gregg Co., in northeastern Texas, on the north bank of the Sabine River. Located in a rapidly growing urban region, Longview is in the heart of the east Texas oil fields with over 20,000 producing wells. Its manufactures include oil and oil-field machinery, steel, natural gas, chemicals, plastics, paper, building materials and agricultural equipment. The city was settled in 1865 and incorporated in 1872.

LOOKOUT, Cape, N.C. Caderet Co., at the southwest end of Cape Lookout National Seashore. The cape has 60 miles of undeveloped barrier islands and serves as a port of entry to Beaufort and Morehead City. A lighthouse constructed here in 1859 is still functional.

LOOKOUT MOUNTAIN, Ala. Large, elevated plateau (2,126 feet), near the Coosa and Little Rivers, in the Appalachian Mountain range in northeast Alabama and southeast Tennessee.

LOOKOUT MOUNTAIN, Battle of. Civil War engagement fought November 24, 1863, outside Chattanooga in southeast Tennessee. The Union army occupied Chattanooga after its defeat at CHICKAMAUGA just across the Georgia border, and it successfully defended the city against Confederate attacks at Lookout Mountain and MISSIONARY RIDGE on successive days.

Lookout Mountain lies south of Chattanooga and the battle there on November 24 was a flanking operation south of the main battle line at Missionary Ridge. Actually an elevated plateau, Lookout Mountain was occupied by Confederate forces under the command of Gen. Braxton BRAGG. It was stormed by the Union troops of Gen. Joseph Hooker, on orders from Gen. Ulysses S. Grant, on the morning of the 24th. The outnumbered Confederate forces held their position until midnight, when they withdrew under orders from Bragg to prepare for the next day's fighting at Missionary Ridge.

Lookout Mountain has been called "The Battle Above the Clouds" because of the elevation and because it was fought in heavy fog. On November 25, Union troops planted a U.S. flag atop it that was visible to the troops fighting for Missionary Ridge.

LOOKOUT MOUNTAIN, Tenn. Town (pop. 1,886), Hamilton Co., in southeastern Tennessee just south of Chattanooga at the Georgia border. A residential community situated near the mountain of the same name, it was incorporated in 1890. Today it is the home of Covenant College, established in 1955.

LORIMER, George Horace (Louisville, Ky., Oct. 6, 1867 — Wyncote, Pa., Oct. 22, 1937). Editor and author. After an education at Colby College and Yale University, and an unsuccessful business venture, he was hired as literary editor for the *Saturday Evening Post* in 1898. He became editor-in-chief (1899) and later president of Curtis Publishing Co. (1932). He is credited with salvaging the *Post* from near financial disaster, and making it one of the most successful magazines in the U.S.

LORING, William Wing (Wilmington, N.C., Dec. 4, 1818 — New York, N.Y., Dec. 30, 1886). Military officer. He served in the Seminole War and the Mexican War before becoming commander of the Oregon Military Department (1849-51). He joined the Confederate Army in 1861, attained the rank of major general, and headed campaigns in Georgia, Mississippi and Tennessee. In 1869 he joined the army of Khedive in Egypt where he served for ten years. Upon his return to the U.S. he wrote *A Confederate Soldier in Egypt* (1884).

LOUISA, Ky. Town (pop. 1,832), seat of Lawrence Co., in northeastern Kentucky at the border of West Virginia. Settled in 1790, the town is located at the junction where the Louisa and Tug Forks Rivers form the Big Sandy River. Big Sandy Dam was constructed here in 1896. There are oil and gas wells and coal mines

in the area, and tobacco, sorghum, and corn are raised.

LOUISIANA. State on the Gulf of Mexico that is the only one in the country crossed by the Mississippi River. It is irregular in shape, due to its numerous water boundaries, and it has a far larger area west of the river than east of it. The western portion is bounded inland by Texas to the west, a border largely formed by the SABINE River, Arkansas to the north, a land border drawn at the 33rd parallel, and Mississippi to the east across the river. The eastern portion is surrounded inland by Mississippi, with a northern land boundary at the 31st parallel, and an eastern border formed by the Pearl River. Louisiana has a 400-mile coastline to the south on the Gulf of Mexico, which is so indented by waterways and extended by the 85-mile delta at the mouth of the Mississippi River that it represents well over 7,000 miles of mapped shoreline.

Louisiana is a unique state because it has preserved a remarkable diversity of historical European influences. The population includes two unusual ethnic groups: the CREOLES, who are descendants of Spanish and French settlers, and the Cajuns, who are the descendants of French ACADIANS. Each group preserves a distinct linguistic dialect as well as cultural and ethnic heritages such as cooking. The legal code of Louisiana is also unique in the U.S. for its blend of Spanish and Napoleonic codes as distinct from English common law; these influences are also apparent in the political organization of the state, which is divided into county-like units called parishes. The special character of Louisiana is most apparent in the city of NEW ORLEANS, noted for its outstanding examples of Spanish and French architecture within the unusually cosmopolitan Latin Quarter. Topographically, Louisiana is also unique, and this is apparent in the special vocabulary of bayous and oxbow lakes used to describe the inland waters of its low-lying and swampy Gulf coast.

There is a marked distinction in modern Louisiana between the rural, agricultural, and largely Protestant northern portions of the state and the urban, industrial, and largely Catholic southern areas near the coast. The character of northern Louisiana resembles that of the neighboring states of Mississippi, Arkansas, and Texas. Southern Louisana is distinct within the region for its widespread use of the French language and for its cash crop of rice. For the past few decades the population of Louisiana has been growing at a rate in excess of the national average, and most of this growth is concentrated in the south of the state. Most of the state's large cities are located in the south, and they have made Louisiana the most urban state in the South after Maryland and Texas. The modern economic growth of the state is a product of shipping and heavy industry, and these activities are also located in southern Louisiana, where the 100-mile stretch of the Mississippi River between Baton Rouge and New Orleans has emerged as one of the principal industrial centers of the South.

All of Louisiana lies within the topographical area called the GULF COASTAL PLAIN, which reaches inland along the Mississippi River to the southern-most point of Illinois. This formation gives all of Louisiana extremely low elevations, and the high point in the state, located at Driskill Mountain in the north central region, has an elevation of only 535 feet. The main features within this general expanse of gently rolling hills are the ALLUVIAL lands of the Mississippi River and the swamplands of the Gulf coast. The Mississippi takes an extremely meandering course across the plain of Louisiana between banks of silt the river itself has built up. Beyond these banks lies the fertile bottomland, which is subject to flooding when the river rises. The small streams called BAYOUS are slacker waters flowing between similar banks of silt. The delta extension of the state created by silt carried down the Mississippi is crossed by small waterways so numerous they are termed "distributaries." Coastal Louisiana is largely swampland relieved by basins deep enough to collect Gulf waters in brackish lakes or river waters in fresh water lakes. The entire state has a warm and humid climate of hot summers and very mild winters, with heavy rainfall throughout the year.

Spanish sailors on the Gulf of Mexico began to record sightings of Louisiana in about 1500, and in 1519 Alonso de Pineda became the first to land and explore the region. Spanish exploration continued in the travels of Alvar Nunez CABEZA in 1530, and in the voyage down the Mississippi by members of the Hernanado DE SOTO expedition in 1543 after their journey overland from Florida. These explorers left no trace upon the land, however, and Sieur de LA SALLE (Rene Robert Cavelier) came down the Mississippi in 1682, claimed it for France, and named it Louisiana after King Louis XIV. The only outpost left by this exploration, however, was destroyed by Indians in 1689.

The first permanent settlement in Louisiana was established in 1714 by the French at NATCHITOCHES on the Red River in the northwest of the state. This trading post was financed by the French company already established in what is now Alabama and Mississippi, with the local interests being managed by Jean Baptiste Le Moyne, the "Father of Louisiana." He founded New Orleans in 1718 and named it after Philippe, Duc d'Orlenas. The city became the capital of the royal French colony of Louisiana in 1723.

Like other plantation colonies in the region, Louisiana became a negotiable property in the diplomatic relations of the time between France, Spain, and England. It came into Spanish possession with the Treaty of Fontainebleau in 1762, was divided and ceded in part to England with the Treaty of Paris in 1763, and was regained entirely by the Spanish with the second Treaty of Paris in 1783. The population became a strange mixture of frequently warring factions in this era: the French Acadians arrived in the 1750s after expulsion by the British from Nova Scotia, the French rebelled against the Spanish in 1768, and the Spanish revolted against the British in Baton Rouge in 1779. By the late 18th century the Spanish and the French had intermarried enough to form the distinct Creole portion of the population.

The young United States government came into possession of Louisiana through a series of events beginning in 1800. In that year the region was returned to French control by the Spanish, an exchange that took effect on December 1, 1803. Before it took effect, however, Napoleon Bonaparte had already decided against challenging Britain for possession of the region, and for this reason he opened negotiations with the U.S. to end his own claim to the region and simultaneously to deprive Britain of its claim to Louisiana. The U.S. agreed to buy the Louisiana Territory from France for $15 million. The sale took effect on December 20, 1803, just after the official exchange between Spain and France, and the U.S. thus doubled the area of its continental holdings. British objections to these proceedings were effectively thwarted by the admission to the Union of Louisiana as the 18th state on April 30, 1812, and the capture of New Orleans from the British by Andrew JACKSON on January 8, 1815.

Because of its advantageous location in an age of water transportation, Louisiana experienced an economic boom in the early years of statehood. Steamboat traffic on the Mississippi began in the year of statehood, and by

Louisiana

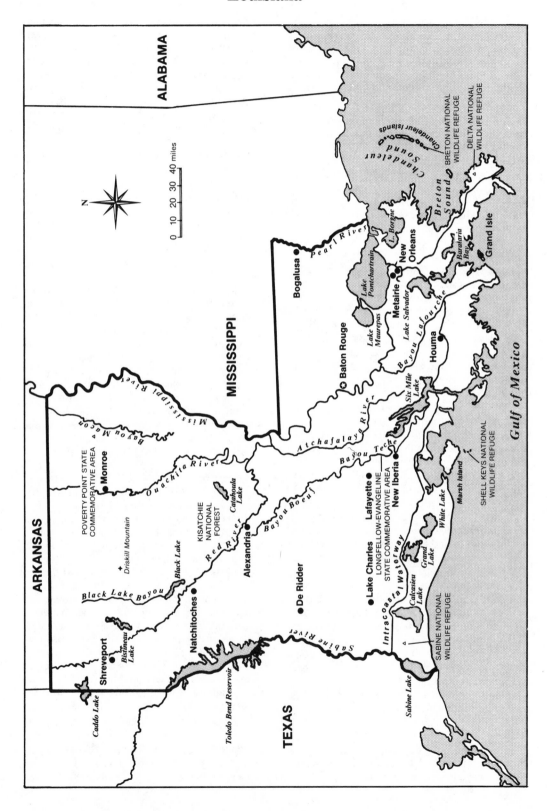

STATE OF LOUISIANA

Name: For Louis XIV (1638-1715), King of France (1643-1715).

Nickname: Pelican State, Creole State, Sugar State, Bayou State, Holland of America, Child of the Mississippi River.

Motto: Union, Justice and Confidence.

Capital: Baton Rouge.

Parishes: 64. **Places over 10,000 population (1980):** 49.

Symbols & Emblems: *Flower:* Magnolia. *Bird:* Eastern Brown Pelican. *Tree:* Cypress. *Song:* "Give Me Louisiana."

Population (1980): 4,203,972. **Rank:** 18th.

Population Density (1980): 94.5 people per sq. mi. **Rank:** 21st.

Racial Make-up (1980): *White:* 2,911,243 (69.3%). *Black:* 1,237,263 (30.0%). *American Indian:* 12,064 (0.3%). *Asian & Pacific Islander:* 23,771 (0.6%). *Other:* 19,631 (0.5%). *Spanish Origin:* 99,105 (2.4%).

Largest City (pop. 1980): New Orleans (557,482). *Others:* Baton Rouge (219,486), Shreveport (205,815), Metairie (164,160), Lafayette (81,961), Lake Charles (75,051), Kenner (66,382), Monroe (57,597), Alexandria (51,565).

Area: 44,521 sq. mi. **Rank:** 31st.

Highest Point: Driskill Mountain (535 ft.), Bienville Parish.

Lowest Point: New Orleans (-5 ft.), Orleans Parish.

State Government:

ELECTED OFFICIALS (4-year terms expiring Mar. 1988, etc.): *Governor* ($73,400); *Lt. Governor* ($63,367); *Sec. of State* ($60,169); *Attorney General* ($60,168); *Treasurer* ($60,168).

GENERAL ASSEMBLY (Salary: $75 per diem plus monthly living expense allowance totaling $16,800 per year.): *Senate* (39 members), *House of Representatives* (105 members).

CONGRESSIONAL REPRESENTATIVES: *Senate* (terms expire 1985, 1987, etc.). *House of Representatives* (8 members).

Admitted to the Union: Apr. 30, 1812 (18th state).

Madewood Plantation in Napoleonville, La., constructed in the 1840s

1840 cargo shipments down the river had made New Orleans the principal American port after New York City. The invention of the cotton gin in 1793 and a process for crystallizing sugar from cane in 1795 encouraged the spread of two valuable cash crops across the state in the early 1800s. In the years before the Civil War the agricultural interests of the state predominated over the shipping ones; in effect, plantation interests dependent on slavery predominated over commercial ones dependent on trade with the northern states. As a result Louisiana backed the secessionist John C. Breckinridge in the 1860 Presidential election, and it seceded from the Union on January 26, 1861. The Union Navy captured New Orleans in 1862, and Union control over the river became complete with its army victory at Vicksburg, Miss., in 1863. Confederate interests in Shreveport controlled western Louisiana for the duration of the war, but the state was forced to surrender to the Union on May 26, 1865.

After the war there were outbreaks of segregationist violence throughout Louisiana, particularly a 1866 race riot in New Orleans, and the state was placed under military government in 1867. In 1868 the state ratified the 13th Amendment against slavery and so gained readmission to the Union, but the subsequent activities of the KU KLUX KLAN and the local Knights of the White Camellia kept race relations in a state of tension well into the 20th century. This problem, along with the supremacy of political machines, caused postponement of necessary flood control, educational and agricultural improvements, and other public works projects, all of which became rallying cries in the rise to power of Huey P. LONG in the 1920s. A machine politician in his own right, Long was assassinated in 1935, but by that time he had succeeded in revitalizing the Louisiana economy.

Twentieth century industrialization has created a modern Louisiana that is more urban than surrounding states with the exception of Texas. The largest population center is New Orleans, which remains the second-leading port in the U.S. and a tourist capital because of its old-world ambience. Metropolitan New Orleans now includes nearly 1.2 million residents, or more than one-quarter of the total state population. It is linked to the north by a river corridor of heavy industry with the second-largest population center in the state, the capital city of BATON ROUGE. The other large metropolitan areas of Louisiana include SHREVEPORT, an oil city in the northwest corner of the state, LAKE CHARLES, an agricultural port in the southwest of the state, and ALEXANDRIA, a distinctly modern city near the geographical center of the state.

Louisiana's total population has consistently grown at a rate above the national average by natural increase rather than significant immigration by residents of other states. Some 70% of the state population are life-long residents, a proportion as high as that in less industrial states of the South. In composition the population is 29% black and more than 2% Hispanic.

The leading industries in Louisiana are mining and manufacturing, each of which generate several times the income from agriculture. The state is the U.S leader in production of natural gas, and it ranks third in oil production behind Alaska and Texas. The major manufactures of the state are refined fuels and petrochemicals derived from this mineral yield, but processed foods, transportation equipment, electronic goods, and apparel are also leading manufactures. Most of Louisiana's farm income is derived from soybeans, rice, cotton lint, and sugar cane. Commercial fishing is also a significant industry, with Louisiana leading all Gulf states in the value of its catch. Tourism, princi-

Artist's rendering of the levee at New Orleans, La. during the mid-1800s

pally to New Orleans, contributes an additional $2 billion per year to the Louisiana economy.

LOUISIANA PURCHASE. The largest and most important annexation to the original 13 states and purchased from France in 1803. The vaguely-defined area, which had been known as Louisiana, was first claimed by France when La Salle reached the mouth of the Mississippi River in 1682. He claimed all the land around the river and its tributaries, and named the area after Louis XIV. In 1762 the area was ceded to Spain in exchange for territory in Italy. Despite foreign sovereignty, the territory was settled by American colonists, particularly the Ohio River valley. The Mississippi River as a means of shipping goods was vital to the economy of the new settlements.

Although the Spanish were still in control in Louisiana, it became known in 1801 that they had secretly ceded the territory back to France. In 1795 Spain had granted the United States the right to use the river and to ship goods from the mouth of the river without paying duty. This right was revoked by Spain in 1802, and the port of New Orleans was closed to Americans. Although the port was soon reopened, the need to acquire New Orleans became apparent to President Thomas JEFFERSON who began negotiations the following year.

Because of the impending war with Britain, France was more interested in her international situation than she was interested in retaining Louisiana. Jefferson, who still considered Britain an enemy, saw the necessity of obtaining the territory so that it wouldn't fall into British hands.

Robert Livingston, the U.S. minister to France, and James Monroe, who had previous diplomatic dealings with France, were instructed by Jefferson to purchase New Orleans and Florida for $2 million. Negotiations opened in France in April, 1803. Charles Tal-

leyrand, Napoleon's representative, surprised Livingston and Monroe by asking what the United States would pay for all of Louisiana, not just the intended American purchase. Talleyrand's proposal to sell all of Louisiana was probably a result of Napoleon's concern that an Anglo-American alliance might take place because of French possession of the Mississippi, and because France needed funds for its impending war with England.

Bargaining began and by April 29 terms were agreed upon. The United States would pay France $15 million and the treaty, dated April 30, 1803, was signed several days later. Congress ratified the treaty on October 21, 1803. Although the boundaries for the new territory were controversial and not settled for several years, the United States had doubled its area.

LOUISIANA STATE UNIVERSITY AND AGRICULTURAL AND MECHANICAL COLLEGE. Coed university, part of the Louisiana State University system, located in the state's capital, Baton Rouge, on a 1,995-acre campus. Founded in 1860, LSU is the largest and oldest of all the Louisiana State University campuses.

Academic offerings are many and varied, and majors are offered in 128 fields, via the colleges of Arts and Sciences (including the schools of Geoscience and Journalism), Business Administration, Chemistry and Physics, Agriculture (including the schools of Forestry and Wildlife Management, Vocational Education, and Home Economics), Engineering, Education, and the schools of design and music. The South provides 92% of the students.

Library: 1,822,626 volumes, 1,073,997 microform titles, 18,578 journal subscriptions, 7,825 records/tapes. Faculty: 1,369. Enrollment: 27,236 total graduate and undergraduate: 10,893 men, 9,270 women (full-time). Degrees: Bachelor's, Master's, Doctorate.

LOUISVILLE, Ky. City (pop. 298,451), seat of Jefferson Co., in northern Kentucky. The largest city in the state, Louisville is the metropolitan center for the surrounding countryside which includes adjacent Kentucky counties and two Indiana counties across the Ohio River. Long an industrial city, Louisville's products include paints and varnishes, baseball bats, aluminum products, automobiles, bathtubs, tractors, cigarettes, and bonded bourbon whiskey. There are significant insurance, grain millage, meat, and poultry businesses in the city. Louisville is also a major publishing center, turning out books, magazines and other printed materials, including the American Printing House for the Blind.

The area was first settled in 1778 by George Rogers CLARK and his group of Scottish, Irish, and English settlers and soldiers. It was the time of the American Revolution, and Clark planned to use this small community as a military base for expeditions against nearby British strongholds. Louisville was originally named Fort-on-Shore, but in 1780 the Virginia legislature (Kentucky had not yet become a separate state) renamed the community in honor of King Louis XVI of France for his aid to the colonies during their fight with the British. In the years that followed, Louisville's location on the Ohio River made it an important trading center. Trade flourished, increasing dramatically after completion of a canal that circumnavigated the falls of the Ohio, which had previously interrupted travel up and down the river. The coming of the railroad, and additional river traffic, made Louisville "The Gateway to the South." It was incorporated in 1828. During the Civil War the city was the North's major supply depot for its armies operating in the western theatre. After the war, the city grew even more, reasserting itself rapidly as a major trade center in the recovering South. This economic progress, despite a disastrous river flood in 1937, has continued to the present day.

Socially, the city has always been progressive, ranking near the top of Southern cities which, in the last several decades, have worked hard to break down racial barriers by introducing innovative programs that aid the poor, assist depressed neighborhoods, and improve educational systems. In 1967 Louisville was a pioneer in adopting an ordinance that prohibited discrimination in the sale or rental of housing.

Culturally, Louisville offers opera, theatre, music, and other art forms. The city has a long and glorious horse racing heritage, and is home of the KENTUCKY DERBY. Two daily newspapers, a host of network and educational television stations, and several radio stations make up the city's communications network. Points of interest include the home of Zachary Taylor, the mansion of George Rogers Clark, the Churchill Downs Museum, the Filson Club, the J. B. Speed Art Museum, the Louisville Zoological Gardens, and the Rauch Memorial Planetarium. Louisville is the home of the Kentucky State Fair, one of the oldest agricultural fairs in the country. Louisville is also the home of many institutions of higher learning, including the University of Louisville (the nation's oldest municipal university), Spalding College, Bellarmine College, Jefferson Community College, Louisville Presbyterian Theological Seminary, and the Southern Baptist Theological Seminary.

LOUISVILLE, University of. State-supported university located in Louisville, Ky. Founded in 1798, it was the country's first municipal university, and became a Kentucky state institution in 1970. Undergraduate studies are offered through the College of Arts and Sciences, the School of Music, Speed Scientific School, and the schools of Business, Education, Medicine, Dentistry, Law, and Police Administration. The university has two campuses: 110 acres near downtown Louisville; and 238 acres in nearby Jefferson County. The South provides most of the students, 3% are from North Central states, and 10% are black; 42% go on to further study.

Library: 875,920 volumes, 366,890 microform titles, 6,629 journal subscriptions. Faculty: 1,692. Enrollment: 19,155 total. Degrees: Certificate or Diploma, Associate's, Bachelor's, Master's, Doctorate.

LOWNDES, Rawlins (St. Kitts, British West Indies, Jan., 1721 — Charleston, S.C., Aug. 24, 1800). Politician. Lowndes moved to Charleston, S.C., in 1730 where he became a noted lawyer and opponent of British rule, but was against armed rebellion. He was a member of the state legislature and was president of South Carolina (1778-79). He was a member of the state senate (1882-87) and helped draft the state constitution.

LOYOLA UNIVERSITY. Church-related, coed liberal arts institution in New Orleans, La., on a 19-acre campus. The school was founded in 1912 and is administered by the Society of Jesus.

Undergraduate studies are offered through the colleges of Arts and Science, Music, and Business Administration. Arts and Science majors include medical technology, computer science, drama, education, and communication. The South provides 83% of the students, 5% are from New England, 4% are from Middle Atlantic states, and 20% of all students pursue full-time graduate study immediately upon graduation: 18% enter law school, 1% medical school, 1% dental school.

Library: 280,000 volumes, 22,000 microform titles, 1,200 journal subscriptions. Faculty: 303. Enrollment: 4,616 total graduate and undergraduate. Degrees: Associate's, Bachelor's, Master's.

LUBBOCK, Tex. Town (pop. 173,979), seat of Lubbock Co., in northwest Texas. Lubbock was set up by two rival town builders who consolidated their townsites of Monterey and Old Lubbock in 1891. Today it is the center of the wealthiest agricultural region of Texas, and is the home of Texas Tech University and Lubbock Christian College.

LUDWELL, Philip (Bruton, Somerset, England, c. 1660 — England, c. 1704). Colonial governor. Brought to Virginia as an infant, he was later a member of the Virginia Governor's Council and the House of Burgesses. He was also governor of the northern part of Carolina from 1689-1691 and of Carolina province from 1691-1694.

LUFKIN, Tex. City (pop. 28,562), seat of Angelina Co., in eastern Texas, 117 miles north of Houston. Founded in 1882 and incorporated as a city in 1890, Lufkin is in the heart of lumbering country on the south bank of the Sam Rayburn Reservoir. The city's manufactures include newsprint, woodworking products, trailers, and oil field equipment. It is the site of Angelina Junior College and a state-run school for the mentally retarded.

LUKEMAN, Henry Augustus (Richmond, Va., Jan. 28, 1871 — New York, N.Y., Apr. 3, 1935). Sculptor. After studying at the National Academy of Design in New York, and additional study abroad, he worked under Launt Thompson and Daniel Chester French. Among his most famous works is the statue of Manu on the Appellate Court House in New York City, and the relief of Gen. Robert E. Lee on Stone Mountain in Georgia.

LUMBER. The South produces 30% of the U.S. lumber supply each year. The region includes more than 200 million acres of commercial timberland, or about 43% of the U.S. total. The leading states within the region are: Georgia, with 24 million acres; Alabama, with 21 million acres; North Carolina, with 19 million acres; and Arkansas, with 18 million acres. From these timberlands, the South annually harvests nearly 650 million board-feet of sawtimber, or about one-quarter of the U.S. total. The leaders in the region in sawtimber, ranked by production per year are: Georgia, North Carolina, Alabama, Louisiana, and Mississippi.

The Southern states also hold more than 30% of the U.S. growing stock of sawtimber. The leaders in the region in growing stock, measured in volume by millions of cubic feet, are: Georgia, North Carolina, Alabama, Virginia, and Mississippi.

Of the timber harvested each year in the South, two-thirds is softwood, such as Douglas fir and Southern pine, and one-third is hardwood, such as oak, cottonwood, walnut and poplar. Cypress is harvested in the Mississippi Valley.

LUMBERTON, N.C. City (pop. 18,340), seat of Robeson Co., in southern North Carolina on the Lumber River. Incorporated in 1787, Robeson became the first county in the state to prohibit the sale of alcoholic beverages in 1886. Today it is a known for its trade in tobacco and farm goods, and its marble works. Manufactures include cotton goods and prefabricated houses.

LUMPKIN, Joseph Henry (Oglethorpe Co., Ga., Dec. 23, 1799 — Athens, Ga., June 4, 1867). Jurist. Lumpkin was a member of the Georgia legislature and assisted in writing the state penal code. He was a leader in social and economic reform in his state and in the South, and was the first chief justice of the Georgia Supreme Court (1845-67).

LUNA Y ARELLANO, Tristan de (fl. 1530-1561). Spanish explorer. After serving under Francisco Coronado in a New Mexico expedition, Luna was named governor and captain general of Florida and sailed from Vera Cruz (June 11, 1559) with 1,500 colonists. They arrived at Pensacola Bay (August 14), but a violent storm (August 19) destroyed nearly all the ships and provisions. Luna pushed northward into Alabama, where his officers mutinied and removed him from command. Luna, who had invested all his money in the expedition, returned to Spain in 1561 and petitioned for reimbursement. His request denied, he died in poverty.

LURAY CAVERNS, Va. Page Co., in northern Virginia. The largest limestone cave system in the state, it was discovered in 1878 and is known worldwide for its stalactite and stalagmite formations. It is one of Virginia's most popular tourist attractions.

LYNCH, Charles (Lynchburg, Va., 1736 — Bedford Co., Va., Oct. 29, 1796). Military officer and politician. A Revolutionary patriot who served with Nathanael Greene at Guilford Court House, he gave his name to the term "lynch law" when he presided over an extralegal court (1780), in which convictions were followed by quick punishment. As a justice of the peace, he exceeded his authority, but his actions were later cleared by the state legislature.

LYNCH, Thomas Jr. (Winyaw, S.C., Aug. 5, 1749 — at sea, 1779). Patriot and politician. After receiving an education in England, Lynch served in the South Carolina legislature and was a captain in the Continental Army. He was a delegate to the Continental Congress (1776-77), and was a signer of the Declaration of Independence. He resigned due to poor health, and his ship was lost while sailing to France.

LYNCHBURG, Battle of. Civil War engagement fought on June 18, 1864, on the James River just east of the Blue Ridge Mountains. It was a victory for the South and a successful defense of the rail center in Lynchburg.
On June 5, Gen. Robert E. Lee named Gen. J. C. Breckenridge commander of Confederate troops in western Virginia. On June 12 Breckenridge requested reinforcements, and Lee ordered Gen. Jubal Early's men to join Breckenridge in Lynchburg. The battle commenced on June 18 when Breckenridge's Lynchburg positon was attacked by a Union advance party commanded by Gen. David Hunter. Recognizing the superiority of the Confederate forces, especially after Early's men began to arrive at noon on June 18, Hunter soon retreated to the west, surrendering control of the rail center to the South.

LYNCHBURG, Va. Independent city (pop. 66,743), in the central Piedmont section of Virginia on the James River. Settled in 1757 and incorporated in 1805, it is named for John Lynch, the son of an Irish immigrant who was the city's founder. The principal industries are drugs, cosmetics, nuclear reactors, and foundry products. It is the home of six colleges, including Lynchburg College, Randolph-Macon Woman's College, and a branch of the University of Virginia.

LYNCHES RIVER, N.C./S.C. River rising in southern North Carolina, and traveling 150 miles southeast, crossing the border of South Carolina, to empty into the Pee Dee River.

LYNDON B. JOHNSON SPACE CENTER. Formerly called the Manned Spacecraft Center, in Houston, Tex. The complex was begun in 1962 and became the headquarters of all manned space flight in January, 1964. It was re-named in 1973 after the death of former President, and native Texan, Lyndon Baines JOHNSON. It covers 1,600 acres and is the headquarters for training U.S. astronauts. It houses the National Aeronautics and Space Administration's Mission Control Center, which monitors the system functions of U.S. spacecraft after lift-off from Cape Canaveral, Fla. While the actual parts of the spacecraft are manufactured at various factories around the country, scientists and engineers here are responsible for the design and development of all parts and equipment. Soil and rock samples taken during the first manned moon landing in 1969 were analyzed in laboratories at the center.

M

MacARTHUR, Douglas (Little Rock, Ark., Jan. 26, 1880 — Washington, D.C., Apr. 5, 1964). Military leader. The son of professional soldier Arthur MacArthur and Virginian Mary Pinkney Hardy, Douglas MacArthur was born on a military base and had an erratic education because his father was transferred so often. He gained acceptance to West Point in 1899, however, and graduated first in his class in 1903 with the highest award of first captain.

His first assignments were in the Far East, including the Philippines, as an aide to his father. He first won recognition of his own tactical skills in World War I as commander of the 84th Infantry Brigade. This led to his appointment as Superintendent of West Point (1919-22). After serving in various posts in the U.S. and the Philippines he retired from the army in 1937.

As an expert on the Pacific, MacArthur was recalled to active duty in 1941 and sent by President Franklin Roosevelt to the Philippines. The islands fell to the Japanese, as expected, and it was on the occasion of that defeat that MacArthur issued his famous "I shall return" statement. After engineering important victories in New Guinea and elsewhere, he did indeed return to the recaptured Philippines on October 20, 1944. It was MacArthur who accepted the surrender of the Japanese army aboard the USS *Missouri* on September 2, 1945. Among his greatest accomplishments was the restoration of that country as Commander of Occupied Japan (1945-51).

Appointed commander of the UN forces in Korea in 1950, MacArthur drove communist forces back north of the 38th parallel, as required. He insisted, however, on continuing the invasion into the Chinese mainland, and for this he was dismissed by President Harry Truman, who feared provocation of another world war. He nevertheless returned a national hero, and in an address to Congress quoted to great effect the army ballad refrain "old soldiers never die; they just fade away." His popularity with the American public was long-lived, and MacArthur was twice considered a serious Republican candidate for U.S. President, in 1948 and 1952.

MACHAPUNGA INDIANS ("bad dust" or "much dirt"). Tribe of Algonquian linguistic stock that lived in North Carolina. They were a small tribe, but even with only one village existing in 1701, they joined in the TUSCARORA Indian war against the settlers.

MACHEN, John Gresham (Baltimore, Md., July 28, 1881 — Bismark, N.D., Jan. 1, 1937).

251

Theologian and author. He taught at Princeton Seminary (1906) and helped found Westminster Theological Seminary in Philadelphia (1929). He was an author of popular as well as theological literature, and was the leading spokesman for the conservative view of Presbyterian theology, stating in *Christianity and Liberalism* (1923) that liberal theology was untrue to Christianity, biblically and historically. In 1935 he was suspended from his ministry and in 1936 he established the Orthodox Presbyterian Church.

MACON, Ga. City (pop. 116,860), seat of Bibb Co., in the central part of the state, on the Ocmulgee River. Settled in 1806, it had become a major trade center by the 1860s. It became a Confederate gold repository during the Civil War because of its railroads, and its factories provided supplies for the South until the Union Army took the city in 1856. Reconstruction was slow, but by the beginning of the 20th century, with the introduction of flood control to stabilize the area, Macon became economically stable.

World War I increased employment and brought thousands of men to Camps Harris and Wheeler. After World War II, the U.S. Naval Ordnance Plant and Robins Air Base became permanent aspects of the local economy. Originally called Newtown, the city was renamed in 1823 after Nathaniel MACON and was incorporated in 1832. Macon is the home of Wesleyan College, Mercer University, and Georgia Academy for the Blind. It was the birthplace of poet Sidney Lanier. Present industries include transportation equipment, textiles and chemicals.

MACON, Nathaniel (Warren County, N.C. Dec. 17, 1757 — Macon, N.C., June 29, 1837). Politician. Interrupted in his studies at the College of New Jersey (now Princeton) by the Revolution, he studied law at Bute, now Warren County Courthouse, and served in the North Carolina senate (1780-82, 1784-85). He was elected as a Democrat to congress (1791-1815) and to the Senate (1815-28). A supporter of local rather than national sovereignty, Macon first aligned with Thomas Jefferson but later backed the "Quids" in criticizing Jefferson's loss of Republican principles and the choice of James Madison for the presidency. Voting for the War of 1812, he was unwilling to back conscription of the taxes needed for support. Macon was a strong states' rights advocate, was against improving roads, and

was opposed to the Bank of the U.S. He was also an outspoken defender of slavery. In 1825 he received 24 electoral votes for Vice President.

MADISON, Dorothea "Dolley" (Guilford Co., N.C., May 20, 1768 — Washington, D.C., July 12, 1849). First lady. Born Dolley Payne of Quaker parentage, she was first married to John Todd (1790-93), who died of yellow fever. She married James MADISON in 1794 and was White House hostess for President Thomas Jefferson, who was a widower, while her husband was Secretary of State. She was First Lady during her husband's presidency (1809-17), and was noted for her strong and entertaining personality and contributed significantly to the prestige of White House entertainment.

MADISON, James (Port Conway, Va., Mar. 16, 1751 — Montpelier, Va., June 28, 1836). Contributor to the U.S. Constitution, Secretary of State to Thomas Jefferson, and 4th President of the United States. Madison was the son of James Madison and Eleanor Rose Conway, for whose family the river port in King George County had been named. He attended the College of New Jersey (now Princeton), and by the time he graduated in 1771 he had been converted to the democratic ideals of the Enlightenment in England and to the cause of American independence.

When the Revolutionary War broke out, Madison was made the chairman of the Virginia Committee of Safety (1774), his reponsibility being to write pamphlets and resolutions attacking British attempts to preserve colonialism in America. It was in this office that he first demonstrated his great talent for such work, and on the basis of his accomplishments on that committee he was elected a member of the Virginia Constitutional Convention in 1776. In the service of his state he prepared its original Bill of Rights, was a member of the first Virginia Assembly, and sat on its Governor's Council.

Because of his special abilities in the drafting of legal documents acceptable to a variety of contentious parties, Madison was quickly drawn into national service by his close friend Thomas Jefferson. A member of the Continental Congress from 1780 to 1783 and from 1786 to 1788, Madison established his national fame as Chief Recorder at the Federal Constitutional Convention in 1787. More than any other participant in the events of that convention, Madison is credited with designing the constitution, providing a finished draft, and having it ratified, despite the opposition of iconoclast politicians such as Patrick HENRY, when the document was presented for ratification in his home state. In promoting his own constitutional ideals, Madison also became one of the principal contributors to *The Federalist.*

Madison was a U.S. Representative from Virginia between 1789 and 1797, and was President Thomas Jefferson's Secretary of State from 1801 to 1809. He was then elected President over C. C. Pickney of South Carolina, inaugurated on March 4, 1809, and served until 1817. He was re-elected in 1812 over De Witt Clinton of New York, his support in both cases being staunch adherence to Jeffersonian policies and opposition to free interpretations of the Constitution he had himself framed. Among the Jeffersonian policies his own administration preserved was the unpopular trade embargo on British goods, and when this brought about the War of 1812, which would end in stalemate in 1815, that conflict was referred to by critics as "Mr. Madison's War."

Madison married the very popular Dolly Payne Todd, a widow, in 1794. He enjoyed a long retirement writing on political topics from the his estate in Montpelier, Va., where he died.

MAGAZINE, Mount, Ark. Logan Co., part of the OUACHITA Mountain chain, in the Arkansas River Valley in west central Arkansas. The highest peak in the state (2,823 feet), it was once alleged to be the site of Confederate ammunition stores.

MAGOFFIN, Beriah (Harrodsburg, Ky., Apr.18, 1815 — Harrodsburg, Ky., Feb. 28, 1885). Politician. A lawyer, he was active in Kentucky politics and was elected to the state senate in 1850. He became governor in 1859 and served until his resignation in 1862. During his administration the state attempted to remain neutral and Magoffin refused a call for troops from both President Abraham Lincoln and Confederate President Jefferson Davis.

MAGRUDER, John Bankhead (Winchester, Va., Aug. 15, 1810 — Houston, Tex., Feb. 18, 1871). Military officer. A graduate of West Point (1830), he served in the war against Mexico and joined the Confederates in 1861. He commanded the defense of Richmond in 1862 and that same year commanded Confederate forces in Texas, New Mexico, and Arizona, and headed the expedition against the Nationals at Galveston, Tex.

MAHONE, William (Southampton County, Va., Dec. 1, 1826 — Washington, D.C., Oct. 8, 1895). Military officer, railroad president, and politician. After graduating from the Virginia Military Institute in 1847, he became a civil engineer. In 1860, he became president of the Norfolk and Petersburg Railroad, and in 1861 he joined the Confederate Army where he fought in many battles including Malvern Hill and Second Manassas. By 1864 he had been promoted to major general. After the war, Mahone became president of the Virginia and Tennessee Railroad. When his proposal for Virginia's financial recovery was opposed by the Democrats, he formed the Readjuster Party, which supported partial repudiation of the state debt. He was elected to the U.S. Senate in 1880 where he allied himself with the Republicans. His actions neutralized the Democrats' power, and their ire led to Mahone's defeat in 1887.

MAKEMIE, Francis (near Ramelton, Ireland, c. 1658 — New York, N.Y., 1708). Clergyman. He is best known for forming the first American presbytery (1706) which brought together the scattered Presbyterian churches in New Jersey, Pennsylvania, and Maryland. Makemie arrived in America in 1683 and for many years was an evangelist preacher in several of the colonies, including Virginia, Maryland, North Carolina, and Pennsylvania. Along with Increase Mather, he also helped defeat the efforts of the Church of England which wished to repress dissident churches in the colonies.

MALVERN, Ark. City (pop. 10,163), seat of Hot Spring Co., southwest central Arkansas, near the Ouachita River. Founded in 1873 and incorporated in 1876, Malvern is a residential and industrial community that manufactures bricks, lumber, aluminum products, and electrical cable.

MALVERN HILL, Battle of. See SEVEN DAYS', BATTLE OF.

MAMMOTH CAVE, Ky. Cave system in Hart Co., in central Kentucky. It is the longest of the known cave systems in the world, and has 200 charted miles of limestone caverns on five separate levels. Mammoth Cave is part of a 79-square-mile national park covering 51,000 surface acres, and about 30 miles of the Orson and Nolin Rivers. Echo River, which drains into the Green River, flows through the lowest level. White men first discovered the cave system in 1799, but Indians were believed to have lived here for centuries before. The mummified body of what was probably a pre-Columbian Indian was discovered here, and saltpetre was mined for gunpowder in the caves during the War of 1812.

MANAHOAC INDIANS. Tribe of Siouan linguistic stock that lived in northern Virginia. They vanished after being at war with the PO-WHATTAN and IROQUOIS Indians.

MANASSAS, Battles of. See BULL RUN, Battle of.

MANASSAS, Va. Town (pop. 15,438), seat of Prince William Co., located 25 miles southwest of Washington. D.C. The town was settled in 1853 and incorporated in 1873. During the Civil War it was the site of the battles of Manassas (see BULL RUN, Battle of). The battleground sites are now national parks. Along with farming and timbering, manufactures include electronic equipment and steel products.

MANATEE RIVER, Fla. River originating in the southwest part of the state near Manatee City, and flowing generally west for about 50 miles to enter the southern arm of Tampa Bay. Below Ellenton it is navigable.

MANCHESTER, Ga. City (pop. 4,796), Meriwether Co., in western Georgia. A highly industrial area, the town grew up around railroad machine shops and textile mills that opened here in the early 1900s. Located in an agricultural region, today's industries include lumbering and cotton ginning.

MANNING, Richard Irvine (Camden District, S.C., May 1, 1789 — Philadelphia, Pa., May 1, 1836). Politician. He was a captain of the state volunteers during the War of 1812 before launching his political career. He was a member of the state House of Representatives (1820-22), the state Senate (1822-24), and was governor of South Carolina from 1824 to 1826. He was elected as a Democrat to the U.S. Congress in 1834 and served until his death.

MANNS HARBOR, N.C. Dare Co., in northeast North Carolina. The harbor is located on the Alligator River in ALBEMARLE SOUND.

MANSFIELD, La. City (pop. 6,485), seat of De Soto Parish, in western Louisiana. The largest town in the parish, it serves as a shipping center for a farming, lumbering, and oil region. It is the site of the Battle of Sabine Crossroads (April 8, 1864), considered the most important battle fought west of the Mississippi River and the final great Confederate victory of the Civil War.

MANTEO BAY, N.C. Narrow bay near ROANOKE ISLAND that is a fishing harbor for the settlement of Manteo. Cape Hatteras National Seashore is across the bay.

MARCH TO THE SEA. Civil War campaign in which Union Gen. William Tecumseh Sherman marched from Atlanta to Savannah, Ga., in 24 days, meeting little resistance but nevertheless devastating a 50-mile-wide band of land in his path.

Sherman had taken ATLANTA on September 2, 1864, and burned the city in November of that year. On November 16 he started toward Savannah with 60,000 troops and 20 days' rations in a bold move to break the Confederacy despite the dangers of operating far behind enemy lines without communication with his own high command. He proceeded in a formation of two wings that left the limited Confederate defense in Georgia uncertain about his destination. He reached Savannah on December 10 and captured its principal fortification at Fort McAllister on December 13. When he threatened to bombard Savannah, the small Confederate force in the city under Gen. William Hardee withdrew on December 21.

When he entered Savannah, Sherman had justified his own disregard for textbook military tactics by reaching his destination, penetrating the heart of the Confederacy, and gaining a position from which he could move up the coast and rejoin the Union army in Virginia. The great significance of his "March to the Sea," however, lies in the ethical debate surrounding his decision to devastate the land in his path. Sherman's defenders argue that by burning farmland he deprived the Confederacy of needed food supplies and so shortened the war. Critics describe his actions as pure terrorism and argue that his lack of control over his own troops encouraged widespread murder, rape, and looting far beyond the limits of military ethics.

MARDI GRAS. A major cultural celebration which officially begins on January 6 and culmi-

The Mardi Gras parade, an annual event in New Orleans, La. since 1766

nates on Shrove Tuesday, the day before the Lenten season begins. The custom was brought to the U.S. in 1766 and flourishes in NEW ORLEANS, La. The event is organized months in advance and funded by special societies, called Krewes (there are over 200 Krewes in New Orleans), which hold costume balls and private parties throughout the Mardi Gras festival. Street parades begin the day before Mardi Gras Day. Everyone participating must wear a mask or costume except Rex, the King of the Carnival, who reigns on Mardi Gras Day. There is a special theme to the celebration each year. The custom dates back to an ancient Roman festival marking a period just before a fast. Mardi Gras is recognized as a legal holiday in eight parishes of Louisiana, as well as in Alabama and Florida, and festivities are found throughout the Southern United States.

MARGATE, Fla. City (pop. 36,044), Broward Co., in southeastern Florida, just west of POMPANO BEACH. Margate was incorporated as a town in 1955 and as a city in 1961. A tourist town, it is largely residential with some agriculture and light industry.

MARIAN, Lake, Fla. Lake in Osceola Co., in the east central part of the state. About five miles long and one to two miles wide, it is located west of Kenansville and about three miles east of Lake Kissimmee.

MARIANNA, Ark. City (pop. 6,220), seat of Lee Co., in eastern Arkansas, near the Mississippi River. Marianna was incorporated in 1877. It is the location of a University of Arkansas cotton experimental station and a U.S. soil conservation project. Clothing, auto seat frames, and lumber products are among today's industries, and cotton, rice, and soybeans are grown in the area.

MARIETTA, Ga. City (pop. 30,805), seat of Cobb Co., in the northwest part of the state, in the foothills of the Blue Ridge Mountains. Marietta was settled in 1833 and incorporated in 1834. An airplane factory was established here during World War II, and in 1951 it was reopened and manufactures jet aircraft. The Kenneshaw Mountain National Battlefield, a Civil War burial site for 10,000 Union soldiers, is nearby. It is also the site of Southern Technical Institute.

MARION, Francis (near Georgetown, S.C. 1732 — Berkeley Co., S.C., Feb. 27, 1795). Revolutionary War hero known as the "Swamp Fox." Of French Huguenot descent, Marion was a member of the first provincial Congress when it adopted the bill of rights in 1775, and subsequently rose in the ranks of the Continental Army. He fought against the British at Fort Johnson in 1775 and at Charleston in 1776, but it was following the defeat of Gen. Horatio GATES at Camden in 1780 that he began the activities that have made him a figure of legend. Driven into the swamps, the survivors of Savannah who formed "Marion's Brigade" launched an ultimately successful guerilla war

Revolutionary War hero Francis Marion, also known as the "Swamp Fox"

against the British. They would make a suprise attack, retreat into the swamps with captured supplies, and reappear far away for another attack. Marion himself constantly flirted with capture, and his strategy was singular for forbidding attacks on Tory homesteads and farms. His gallantry made him a popular figure in many early American novels and in William Cullen Bryant's poem "Song of Marion's Men" (1831).

MARION, Lake, S.C. Lake wedged between several counties in central South Carolina. This artificial body of water is the largest in the state, and was created in 1941 by impounding the SANTES River.

MARISCAL CANYON, Tex. Canyon in Brewster Co., at the point where the Rio Grande River winds around the BIG BEND. Its walls tower 1,950 feet over the river bed. It is noted as one of the largest and most hazardous canyons in the region.

MARMADUKE, John Sappington (Arrow Rock, Mo., Mar. 14, 1833 — Jefferson City, Mo., Dec. 28, 1887). Military officer. Marmaduke resigned from the federal army to join the Confederate army at the beginning of the Civil War. He was promoted to brigadier general after meritorious duty at the battle of Shiloh, and was captured in 1864. In 1884 he was elected governor of Missouri and served unti 1887.

MARQUETTE, Jacques (Laon, France, June 1, 1637 — near Ludington, Mich., May 18, 1675). Explorer and missionary. A Jesuit priest, Marquette went to Quebec, Canada, in 1666 to study Indian languages, and was appointed to work with the Ottawa Indians on the shore of Lake Huron. He established missions at Sault Ste. Marie and later at what is now St. Ignace, Mich. In 1672-73, with Louis JOLLIET, he set forth to explore what the Indians referred to as the "great river" — the Mississippi. They worked their way southward, reaching the mouth of the Arkansas River, and named it Rivière de la Conception. Here they were informed that the Mississippi extended to the Gulf of Mexico, and that the lower portion of the river was under Spanish rule. They returned north and while recovering his health Marquette wrote a journal of his trip that was published in 1681. In 1674 Marquette again set forth with the intention of doing missionary work among the Illinois Indians. His health

failed, however, and he died during the journey. The first to follow the course of the Mississippi, Marquette's journal and maps were instrumental in later explorations and settlements in the area.

MARSH ISLAND, La. Island in Iberia Parish, southwestern Louisiana, between Vermilion and West Blanch Bays and the Gulf of Mexico. The Russell Sage Game Refuge is found on this 79,300-acre island.

MARSHALL, John (near Germantown, Va., Sept. 24, 1755 — Philadelphia, Pa., July 6, 1835). Jurist. After obtaining a limited classical education, he joined the military service as a lieutenant at the outbreak of the Revolutionary War and was in the Battles of Brandywine, Germantown and Monmouth. He left the military service in 1781 and began the practice of law. He was a member of the Virginia convention that ratified the national Constitution, where he distinguished himself by his eloquence and logic, and was a member of the House of Burgesses (1780, 1782-88). President George Washington offered Marshall the post of Attorney General, but he declined. Washington also offered him the position of U.S. Minister to France, but it, too, was declined. He later accepted the post of special envoy to France from President John Adams. A recognized Federalist leader in Virginia, he was elected to Congress (1799-1800) and was appointed Secretary of State by Adams (1800-01). On the resignation of Chief Justice Ellsworth he was appointed his successor (1801) and held the office for 34 years until his death. As Chief Justice of the U.S. Supreme Court he was the principal founder of judicial review and the American system of constitutional law.

MARSHALL, Tex. Town (pop. 24,921), seat of Harrison Co., in northeast Texas. Settled in 1838, Marshall was the site of the first Western Union telegraph office in Texas (1854). Its primary industries today include petroleum, forestry products, chemicals, steel and tile. It is the home of East Baptist College (1917), and Wiley College (1873).

MARSHALL, Thurgood (Baltimore, Md., July 2, 1908–). Jurist. He became interested in civil rights while at Howard University and joined the National Association for the Advancement of Colored People (NAACP) on graduating (1933). In charge of legal services division for the NAACP (1940-61), he argued 32 cases before the Supreme Court, winning 29, and culminating with *Brown* vs *Board of Education*, (1954) which produced the decision that segregation in schools is unconstitutional. President John F. Kennedy appointed him to the Court of Appeals (1961) and President Lyndon B. Johnson appointed him as the first black Solicitor General (1965) and the first black Supreme Court Justice (1967). His judicial work is characterized by his statement (June, 1982) for the majority reversing a lower court mandate requiring plaintiffs to "exhaust state administrative remedies." He explained that the Civil Rights Act of 1971 allows "immediate access" to those whose rights are breached by the states, which are historically unwilling to protect individual rights.

MARSHALL UNIVERSITY. State-supported coed institution on a 60-acre campus in Huntington, W.Va., in the western part of the state. Founded in 1837 as Marshall Academy, the school was granted its university status in 1961. Marshall offers undergraduate studies in the College of Arts, Business and Education. The M.D. and Ph.D. degrees in biomedical sciences are offered at the graduate level. Most of the university's students are from the north central states.

Library: 334,780 volumes, 2,760 journal subscriptions, 10,092 records/tapes. Faculty: 514. Enrollment: 3,081 men, 3,402 women (total graduate and undergraduate). Degrees: Certificate or Diploma, Associate's, Bachelor's, Master's, Doctorate.

MARTIN, Francois Xavier (Marseilles, France, Mar. 17, 1762 — New Orleans, La., Dec. 10, 1846). Jurist. Upon immigrating to America (1780), he was admitted to the bar in North Carolina. Serving as U.S. judge in the Mississippi and Louisiana territories, his wide international background contributed greatly to the wedding of English, Spanish, and French law in Louisiana. He became a justice of the Louisiana supreme court in 1815 and chief justice in 1836.

MARTIN, Josiah (Antigua, British West Indies, Apr. 23, 1737 — London, England, July, 1786). Colonial governor. Commissioned royal governor of North Carolina in 1771, Martin's administration was the subject of much controversy with the legislature. He was finally forced to flee the colony in 1775 and was later involved in an unsuccessful plan to recapture the colony.

From 1779 to 1781 he served under Lord Charles Cornwallis in the Carolina campaigns.

MARTIN, Lake, Ala. Body of water in Tallapoosa Co. Located on the Tallapoosa River, it is the state's fourth-largest artificial lake, with a shoreline of about 750 miles. It was formed by Martin Dam, a hydroelectric development.

MARTIN DAM, Ala. Dam located between Elmore and Tallapoosa Counties, that is also known as the Logan Martin Dam. It was built to harness the hydroelectric potential of the Tallapoosa River in east central Alabama. It forms Lake MARTIN.

MARTINSBURG, W.Va. City (pop. 13,063), seat of Berkely Co., in the northeast part of the state, in the Shenandoah Valley, Martinsburg is the industrial and commercial focus of the Eastern Panhandle. Bunker Hill, the oldest known setlement in the state, was founded nearby c. 1729. Apples, wheat, and corn are the primary agricultural products, and manufactures include dynamite and car parts.

MARTINSVILLE, Va. Independent city (pop. 18,149), in the south part of the state. Located in the foothills of the Blue Ridge Mountains near the North Carolina border, it was first settled in 1793. An industrial town and tobacco market center, its present manufactures include furniture, nylon and cotton goods, containers, and lumber products.

MARY WASHINGTON COLLEGE. State-supported coed institution in Fredericksburg, Va., 50 miles from Washington, D.C. The college was founded in 1908 as a part of the University of Virginia, but in 1972 the state legislature separated it from the university. This primarily women's college offers a variety of liberal arts and sciences programs. Middle Atlantic states provide 85% of the students, and 10% of the students pursue graduate study immediately after graduation; 5% enter medical school, 2% go to business chool, and 30% of all graduates choose careers in business and industry. Library: 260,436 volumes, 1,145 journal subscriptions, 1,467 records/tapes. Faculty: 149. Enrollment: 382 men, 1,769 women (full-time), Degrees: Bachelor's, Master's.

MARYLAND. State located in the extreme northeast of the Southern region. Its northern border with Pennsylvania is the Mason-Dixon

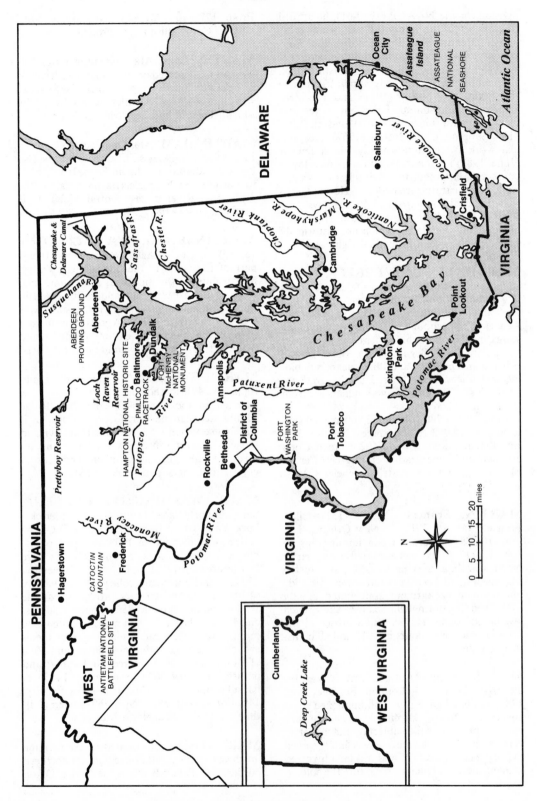

STATE OF MARYLAND

Name: For Henrietta Maria (1609-1699), wife of Charles I (1600-1649), King of England (1625-1649).

Nickname: Old Line State, Free State, Cockade State, Oyster State, Queen State, Monumental State.

Motto: *Fatti Maschli, Parole Femine* (Manly Deeds, Womanly Words).

Capital: Annapolis.

Counties: 23. **Places over 10,000 population (1980):** 82.

Symbols & Emblems: *Flower:* Black-Eyed Susan. *Bird:* Baltimore Oriole. *Tree:* White Oak. *Song:* "Maryland, My Maryland."

Population (1980): 4,216,446. **Rank:** 19th.

Population Density (1980): 428.7 people per sq. mi. **Rank:** 5th.

Racial Make-up (1980): *White:* 3,158,412 (75.1%). *Black:* 958,050 (22.7%). *American Indian:* 8,021 (0.2%). *Asian & Pacific Islander:* 64,276 (1.6%). *Other:* 27,687 (0.7%). *Spanish Origin:* 64,740 (1.6%).

Largest City (pop. 1980): Baltimore (786,755). *Others:* Silver Spring (72,893), Dundal (71,293), Bethesda (63,022), Columbia (52,518), Towson (51,083), Wheaton Glenmont (48,598), Aspen Hill (47,455), Rockville (43,411), Potomac (40,402).

Area: 9,837 sq. mi. **Rank:** 42nd.

Highest Point: Backbone Mountain (3,360 ft.), Garrett Co.

Lowest Point: sea level, Atlantic Ocean.

State Government:
ELECTED OFFICIALS (4-year terms expiring Jan. 1987, etc.): *Governor* ($75,000); *Lt. Governor* ($62,500); *Sec. of State* ($45,000); *Attorney General* ($62,500); *Treasurer* ($62,500).

GENERAL ASSEMBLY (Salary: $21,000 plus $60 per diem living expense allowance.): *Senate* (47 members). *House of Representatives* (101 members).

CONGRESSIONAL REPRESENTATIVES: *Senate* (terms expire 1985, 1987, etc.). *House of Representatives* (8 members).

Admitted to the Union: Apr. 28, 1788 (7th state to ratify the Constitution). One of the original 13 colonies.

line, a traditional boundary between the North and the South. Maryland is nearly bisected by the Chesapeake Bay. To the east of the bay one-third of the state land area lies on Delmarva Peninsula, which Maryland shares with Delaware and two counties of Virginia. To the west of the bay, Maryland occupies the land north of the extremely irregular course of the Potomac River. At its narrowest along the southern border with West Virginia, Maryland has a north-south extent of only 1.9 miles. The Potomac then turns southeast, giving Maryland a maximum north-south extent of approximately 100 miles along its principal inland border with Virginia.

The extremely irregular shape of Maryland brings together three regions distinct in topography, economy, and way of life. Western Maryland, the portion of the state north of West Virginia, is an Appalachian region of coal fields and rural mountain towns. Central Maryland, the portion of the state surrounding BALTIMORE and Washington, D.C., is a plateau that includes major industrial centers and densely populated metropolitan areas. This part of Maryland falls within the transportation corridor of highway and rail links that extends north from Washington to Boston, Mass. Eastern Maryland, the section isolated by the Chesapeake Bay, is a sandy plain of tobacco, dairy, and poultry farms noted for the scenic beauties of its beaches along the "eastern shore," as the whole region is called, of the bay. This unusual combination of landscapes and lifestyles, along with the proximity of Washington, D.C., has made tourism one of modern Maryland's most important industries.

The distinct topographical regions of the state are, from west to east, the Appalachian Mountains, the Piedmont Plateau, and the Atlantic Coastal Plain. The narrow western neck of the state lies within the Great Appalachian Valley, and it is surrounded by individual ranges extending southwest-northeast from West Virginia to Pennsylvania. The high point in the state (3,360 feet) lies in the Backbone Mountains at the conjunction of the state's southern and western borders with West Virginia; the other important ranges in the area include branches of the Blue Ridge Mountains and the Allegheny Mountains. The Piedmont Plateau of rolling hills extends from these mountains to a line running southwest-northeast through Washington and Baltimore. This limit is a portion of the "fall line" running from the Southern states to New England; along it the rivers of the plateau fall in rapids to

the coastal plain, thus marking the navigable head of the rivers and the historical site of industries driven by water power. The Atlantic Coastal Plain east of this line surrounds the Chesapeake Bay. It is a low-lying region of scrub vegetation notable for the large estuaries of its tidewater river mouths. Due to the moderating influence of the bay, with more than 2,400-square-miles of water area, the climate in eastern Maryland is far milder than in the inland mountains.

The first European exploration of Maryland was made by Captain John SMITH and other colonists from Jamestown in Virginia in 1608. They discovered an unusually agricultural society of Algonquin Indian tribes who maintained friendly relations with successive groups of English settlers. In 1631 Virginian William Claiborne established a trading post on Kent Island in Chesapeake Bay. However, in 1632 an official patent to the Chesapeake lands was granted to George Calvert, the first Lord BALTIMORE, by Charles I. He died in the same year, leaving the patent to his son Cecilius Calvert, whose brother, Leonard, led 200 colonists aboard the *Ark* and the *Dove* to Blakistone Island in the bay on March 25, 1634, the date now commemorated as Maryland Day. They later settled St. Mary's in the southern portion of the state, which remained the colonial capital until 1694.

The charter held by the Calverts granted unlimited governmental authority, thus establishing the colony as an independent palatinate with only ceremonial ties to the British crown. The Calverts were Catholics, and the goal of their state was religious toleration, which they made law with the 1649 "Acts concerning Religion." This encouraged Puritans from Virginia to relocate along the Chesapeake in the same year, when they founded the settlement of Providence, now Annapolis.

Early Maryland was embattled on two fronts: on the question of religious toleration and on the question of territorial possessions. William Claiborne remained a leader of Protestant opposition to the Catholic Calverts. Encouraged by the Cromwellian rule in England, he succeeded in seizing control of the colony from the Calverts in 1654. The so-called Toleration Act of 1649 was then repealed, and Catholics and other sects were persecuted by Protestants until the Calverts regained control in 1657. A similar rebellion occurred in 1689, when the Chesapeake lands were returned to British monarchial rule and the capital was moved from St. Mary's to Annapolis in 1694.

The Calverts were once again restored as proprietors in 1715, by which time their colony, by expansion westward and formation of a General Assembly, had been completely altered. At the same time the northern border of Maryland had become a matter of dispute with William Penn, who inherited the Pennsylvania and Delaware areas in 1682. This was settled in theory by an agreement of 1732, but the border line was only precisely fixed when it was surveyed by Charles Mason and Jeremiah Dixon between 1763 and 1767. In 1771 the final Calvert, Frederick, died, and the attempted transfer of the patent to his illegitimate son Henry Harford was undermined by the coming American Revolution.

With its unusual history of palatinate autonomy, Maryland was reluctant to tie its fortunes to that of the other colonies and to cede some of its own self-rule to a Continental Congress. The Maryland Convention voted for compromise rather than rebellion in May, 1776, and it was only two months later that its delegates were freed to vote for the Declaration of Independence. Isolated from the actual combat in the Revolution, Maryland supported the Continental Army principally with troops and provisions. On November 8, 1776, a state constitution was proclaimed without a popular vote, and in 1777 Thomas Johnson took office as the first state governor. Without far western land claims of its own, Maryland would not sign the Articles of Confederation until the other states had relinquished their own in 1781. However, its troops had proven heroic enough in the Revolution to earn Maryland the nickname the "Old Line State," and the Continental Congress came to Annapolis for its convention in 1783. It was there that George Washington resigned his military commission on December 23, 1783, and the treaty to end the Revolution was ratified on January 15, 1784. Maryland's central role in early American history was later solidified by the Annapolis Convention of 1786, which prepared the way for the constitution, and its agreement in 1791 to cede lands on the Potomac for a national capital to be called the District of Columbia.

Although it had been spared combat in the Revolution, Maryland became the central battleground of the War of 1812. There were several British landings along the Chesapeake, all of which were contested. The most important came in August of 1814, when British troops successfully landed at the mouth of the Patuxent River and began a march toward Washington. American troops met the British at Bladensburg, outside the capital, but they were defeated and the British burned Washington. The British then moved northeast to Baltimore, but they were unable to subdue the city. It was during the night-long and unsuccessful bombardment of Fort McHenry in this attack that Francis Scott Key wrote "The Star-Spangled Banner."

In the years preceding the Civil War Maryland, and Baltimore in particular, became an economic power. This was largely the result of a 1828 improvement program that initiated construction of the Baltimore and Ohio railroad and the Chesapeake and Ohio River Canal. This caused the labor force to grow considerably, and ultimately to rely on the labor of freed slaves, who represented half the black population before the war. These and other factors left the state in a difficult position at the outbreak of the war. The general Maryland sentiment was for gradual phasing-out of the slavery system, but over-zealous Abolitionists from the north had also alienated the population from the Union cause. As a result Maryland did not secede from the Union, but the entrance of the first Federal troops into Baltimore in 1861 caused a riot indicative of deep Southern sympathies. As a result of its ambiguous sympathies and location between the warring sides, Maryland contributed troops to both the Union and Confederate armies and was crossed by both several times in the course of the war. The only important battle fought within the state boundaries was the indecisive Battle of AN-TIETAM in September of 1862.

In the years following the war, Baltimore began its growth into a center for heavy industry. Principally due to improved rail and water transportation links, matters which often dominated state politics, this process continued into the present century. The 1950s saw a number of modern transportation links completed that insured Baltimore's central economic role in the state. These included Friendship International Airport, the Chesapeake Bay Bridge linking the eastern and western shores of the Chesapeake, the Baltimore-Washington Expressway, and the Baltimore Harbor Tunnel. Today Baltimore is the only large city in the state and the center of the country's 14th-largest metropolitan area. Half of Maryland's population lives within the Baltimore metropolitan area.

Maryland's total population, the 19th-largest in the country, grew by more than 1 million between 1960 and 1980. It has in this period become increasingly urban, based principally around Baltimore and in the suburbs of

Washington, D.C. In addition to natural increase, the state population gained some 48,000 new residents from net migration movements to and from other states. Much of this population growth consisted of minority groups: the black percentage of the population rose from 18% in 1970 to 23% in 1980, and in the same decade the proportions of Hispanic and Asian residents both reached 2% for the first time.

The greatest source of employment within the state economy is the manufacturing sector. Maryland's manufacturers employ 40% of the state work force, and they are diversified enough to have become important processors of raw material from other states. Heavy industry remains concentrated in Baltimore, where ships, aircraft, and machinery are produced from iron and other primary metals brought from states further inland. There are also diversified light manufacturers dispersed across the state that produce processed foods, chemical products, and electronic equipment. The greatest source of income within the state economy, however, is tourism, which generates $13 billion per year in comparison with $8 billion per year in value added by manufacture. The tourist industry benefits from visitors to Washington and to the Naval academy at Annapolis, but the natural beauties of both the inland mountains and the eastern shore of the Chesapeake make tourism a statewide business in Maryland. Agriculture is also an important industry to the state, which has 41% of its land area devoted to farming. Most of this business is conducted on the eastern shore, where poultry, tobacco, grains, and vegetables and fruit for canning are leading products. The economy inland is based principally on dairy farming, wood products harvested in the western mountains, and mining of stone and gravel. Commercial fishing is of less importance to the economy as a whole, but it is a visible industry and a matter of local pride in the eastern shore region.

MARYLAND, University of. University and land-grant college with five major 4-year campuses: the main campus—the Baltimore County campus—in Catonsville, the Baltimore campus, the Eastern Shore campus in Princess Anne, and two campuses in College Park.

The University of Maryland was founded in 1807, and total enrollment for all campuses is now over 65,000. In addition to the School of Architecture, the School of Library and Information Services, and the Graduate School, there are seven undergraduate colleges, and an extensive selection of majors including radio and television, microbiology, dramatic art, speech and hearing, and Russian. Middle Atlantic states provide 90% of the students.

Library: 1,335,018 volumes, 16,161 journal subscriptions, 35,113 records/tapes. Faculty: 2,299. Degrees: Certificate or Diploma, Bachelor's, Master's, Doctorate.

MARYVILLE, Tenn. City (pop. 17,480), seat of Blount Co., in southeastern Tennessee. Maryville is a suburb south of KNOXVILLE that has one of the world's largest aluminum plants. The city was built around Fort Craig (1785). Nearby is Oak Ridge, the original home of atomic power. Maryville College was established here in 1819.

MASON, George (Fairfax Co., Va., 1725 — Fairfax Co., Va., Oct. 7, 1792). Public official. One of the most important shapers of American government both during and after the Revolutionary War, Mason was a close friend of Thomas Jefferson and his opinions influenced Jefferson when he drafted the Declaration of Independence. Although Mason did not hold a higher public office than a seat in the Virginia House of Burgesses (1758-61), and served

Arrival of the Catholics in Maryland in 1634

as a member of the Constitutional Congress in Philadelphia, he did serve on the Committee of Safety during the Revolution and drafted Virginia's state constitution, which included clauses insuring men's inalienable rights, a thought which was to have far-reaching effects. He opposed the Constitution on the grounds that it created a powerful government with no gurantee of an individual's rights. Mason's objections, and those of others like him led to the adoption of the Bill of Rights in 1791. Before the Revolution Mason was a co-founder of the town of Alexandria, Va., and was actively involved in western expansion via his involvement in the Ohio Company.

MASON, James Murray (Analostan, Va., Nov. 3, 1798 — Alexandria, Va., Apr. 28, 1871). Politician. A practicing lawyer, Mason began his political career in the Virginia legislature. A Democrat, he was a member of the U.S. House of Representatives from 1837 to 1839, and was appointed to the Senate in 1847, serving there until the outbreak of the Civil War in 1861. While a senator, Mason drafted the Fugitive Slave law (1850), and favored secession of the South from the Union when Abraham Lincoln was elected president. During the Civil War he was involved in the Trent Affair when, as a commissioner of the Confederacy to Great Britain and France, he was taken from the British ship *Trent* and imprisoned in Boston. After his release he proceeded to London and spent the war years there as a representative of the Confederacy.

MASON, John Young (Greenville Co., Va., Apr. 18, 1799 — Paris, France, Oct. 3, 1859). Politician. A practicing lawyer, he was elected as a Democrat to Congress from Virginia (1831-37) and introduced a bill recognizing the independence of Texas. Mason became a judge of the U.S. district court of Virginia and subsequently of the general court of the state. He was Secretary of the Navy under President John Tyler, and attorney general and Secretary of the Navy under President James Polk. In 1853 President Franklin Pierce appointed him U.S. Minister to France.

MASON, Lucy Randolph (Alexandria, Va., July 26, 1882 — Atlanta Ga., May 6, 1959). Labor activist. While industrial secretary (1914-18) and general secretary (1923-32) of Richmond's YWCA, she pressed for child-labor and worker's compensation laws and for outreach to the black community. She became

executive secretary of the National Consumers' League and moved to New York City (1932-37), then joined the CIO Textile Workers Organizing Committee, touring the South to raise support (1937-53). Mason published her landmark *Standards for Workers in Southern Industry* (1931) and an autobiography, *To Win These Rights* (1952).

MASON, Tex. City (pop. 2,153), seat of Mason Co., in west central Texas. Named for the pre-Civil War army post Fort Mason, out of which settlement the town grew, Mason's economy today prospers from ranching and tourism.

MASON—DIXON LINE. The boundary line between the states of Pennsylvania and Maryland. It was popularly known as the dividing line between the free and slave states. In the debates on slavery before the admission of Missouri, John RANDOLPH used the words "Mason and Dixon's Line" as figurative of the division between the two systems of labor. The press and politicians echoed it, and in that connection it was used until the abolition of slavery by the Civil War. Surveyed in 1763-68 by the English surveyors Jeremiah Dixon and Charles Mason, it was the result of a lengthy dispute between the Penns of Pennsylvania and The Batlimores of Maryland. The 233-mile line, which does not extend west of the Ohio River, was completed at a cost of $75,000. Milestones brought from England were set along the line. Referred to as "crown stones," every fifth stone bore the arms of the Baltimore family on one side and the Penn family on the other.

MASON'S DECLARATION OF RIGHTS. Document authored by Virginia statesman George MASON, who served as a member of the Virginia Convention of May, 1776. This outline of colonial rights is said to have inspired Thomas Jefferson in his drafting of the Declaration of Independence as well as forming the basis for the Bill of Rights, the first ten amendments to the U.S. Constitution.

MASSANUTTEN MOUNTAINS, Va. Range of mountains, fifty miles in length, that extends from Strasburg to Harrisonburg. The range separates the Shenandoah Valley.

MATAGORDA BAY, Tex. Inlet of the Gulf of Mexico, on the southern Texas coast. This bay, along with its sister, Lavaca Bay, were explored as early as 1685. The bay is protected by the Matagorda Peninsula. Matagorda was once a major access point until the hurricanes of 1874 and 1886 so severely crippled its ports that its trade was shifted to Corpus Christi Bay.

MATAGORDA BAY CITY, Tex. Town (pop. 17,837), seat of Matagorda Co., on the southern coast of Texas. A tourist center, with fishing and hunting areas, its main industries today include petrochemical, plastics, fertilizer, and nuclear power plants.

MATAGORDA ISLAND, Tex. Island in Calhoun Co., in the Gulf of Mexico. Actually just a long sandbar located south of MATA-GORDA BAY, at the entrance of San Antonio Bay, it is important for fish and oyster production. A bombing and gunnery range is located here.

MATTAMUSKETT, Lake, N.C. Body of water in Hyde Co., in eastern North Carolina. It is the state's largest natural lake, and measures 15 miles long and about six miles wide.

MATTAPONI RIVER, Va. A tributary of the York River, it flows through central Caroline County and is the boundary between William and Queen Counties. The river drainage area covers 931 square miles.

MATTHEWS, James Brander (New Orleans, La., Feb. 2l, 1852 — New York, N.Y., Mar. 31, 1929). American essayist, drama critic, novelist, and educator. Educated at Columbia University, he was admitted to the bar but never practiced law. He became a professor of literature, then the first professor of dramatic literature in the U.S. at Columbia (1892-1924). He was a major figure in the New York literary world, served as regular critic for the *New York Times*, and published more than 40 books, including *A Confident Tomorrow* (1899).

MAUREPAS, Lake, La. Lake in the center of Livingston, St. John the Baptist, and Tangipahoa Parishes, in southeastern Louisiana, near Lake Pontchartrain.

MAURY, Dabney Herndon (Fredericksburg, Va., May 2l, 1822 — Peoria, Ill., Jan. 11, 1900). Military officer. A graduate of the U.S. Military Academy, he served with distinction in the Mexican War. He was an instructor at West Point from 1847 to 1852 and served in Texas and New Mexico until the outbreak of the Civil War when he joined the Confederate Army as a colonel. For his gallantry in the battle of Pea Ridge (1862), he was promoted to brigadier general.

MAURY, Matthew Fontaine (near Fredericksburg, Va., Jan. 14, 1806 — Lexington, Va., Feb. 1, 1873). Naval officer. Maury contributed greatly to the advancement of the oceanographic sciences, and was responsible for the development of the U.S. Naval Observatory and Hydrographic Office as well as the International Hydrographic Bureau. In 1855 he published the first oceanographic text, *The Physical Geography of the Sea and Its Meteorology*. His papers on ocean traffic led to the development of separate east-west shipping lanes across the Atlantic Ocean. His profile of the Atlantic floor helped make the laying of a transatlantic telegraph cable possible. During the Civil War, Maury joined the Confederate Navy and served as head of coast, harbor, and river defenses. In 1868 he accepted the professorship of meteorology at the Virginia Military Institute in Lexington, Va.

MAXEY, Samuel Bell (Tomkinsville, Ky., Mar. 30, 1825 — Eureka Springs, Ark., Aug. 16, 1895). Military officer and politician. He organized the 9th Texas Infantry during the Civil War, In 1864 he was promoted to major general and was given command of Indian Territory in the West by the Confederacy. There he convinced the tribes to back the anti-Union cause. He was elected as a Democrat from Texas to the U.S. Senate (1875-87).

MAYFIELD, Ky. City (pop. 10,705), seat of Graves Co., in southwestern Kentucky. Founded in 1823, it is a trade center situated in an agricultural area with clay deposits. There is a large tobacco market here, and other manufactures include shoes, furniture, and bricks.

MAYFIELD CREEK, Ky. Tributary of the Mississippi River, which rises at the Missouri border in western Kentucky. It flows east and south approximately 65 miles to Lynn Grove, just north of the Tennessee line. Mayfield and Wickliffe are two of the communities on its banks.

MAYNARD, George Willoughby (Washington, D.C. Mar. 5, 1843 — New York, N.Y., Apr. 5, 1923). Painter. He studied at the National Academy of Design and went on to further study abroad. Maynard painted portraits and figures, along with marine studies, but he is best remembered for his murals. He painted the Pompeian panels in the Library of Congress and in 1893 he did the exterior decoration of the agricultural building at the World's Fair in Chicago.

MAYSVILLE, Ky. City (pop. 7,983), seat of Mason Co., in northern Kentucky, on the Ohio River. A pioneer river gateway established in 1787, today it is the world's second-largest loose-leaf tobacco market. It is also a trade, transportation, and industrial center that produces shoes, condensed milk, gasoline, and textiles. Daniel Boone and his wife ran a tavern here in the late 18th century.

McADOO, William Gibbs (near Marietta, Ga., Oct. 31, 1863 — Washington, D.C., Feb. 1, 1941). Politician. Dissatisfied with his law practice in Tennessee, he moved to New York in 1892 and became involved with organizing the Hudson and Manhattan Railways, which built tunnels under the Hudson River. His coincidental meeting with Woodrow Wilson led to early and energetic support of Wilson's presidential campaign and ultimate appointment to the Wilson cabinet as Secretary of the Treasury (1913-18). Married to Wilson's daughter Eleanor in 1914, McAdoo came close to the Democratic nomination for the presidency in 1920 and caused the famous deadlock of 1924. He was also chairman of the Federal Reserve Board, and director general of U.S. railroads (1917-19). During World War I he managed four successful Liberty Bond campaigns. McAdoo was elected Senator from California and served in that capacity from 1933 to 1938.

McALLEN, Tex. City (pop. 67,042) Hidalgo Co., in southern Texas. Incorporated in 1911, McAllen is a port of entry and winter resort. Industries include packing and shipping of citrus fruits and vegetables, clothing, food processing, and petroleum products. McAllen is located seven miles from the International Bridge over the Rio Grande River to Reynosa, Mex. It was named for John McAllen whose ranch provided the site for the town, and it is the oil center for the lower Rio Grande Valley.

McCLELLAN, George Brinton (Philadelphia, Pa., Dec. 3, 1826 — Orange, N.J., Oct. 29, 1885). Military officer. After graduating from West Point in 1846, McClellan saw action in the Mexican War where he served with distinction. He later led expeditions West, instructed at West Point, and in 1857 resigned from the army. He rejoined in 1861 and was placed in command of volunteer forces. In July of 1861, he was promoted to major general and put in charge of the army of the Potomac in Washington, D.C., where he proved himself adept at organizing and motivating his troops. In November, 1861, McClellan replaced Gen. Scott as general-in-chief of the army. He led Union forces in the campaign against Richmond where his errors in judgement led to a Union retreat and McClellan's relief from command. He was again in command at ANTIETAM where he defeated Gen. Robert E. Lee but did not pursue the enemy. McClellan's continued poor judgement in battle led to his loss of command in 1862. In 1864 he was the Democratic candidate for the presidency but lost to incumbent Abraham Lincoln.

McCLERNAND, John Alexander (near Hardinsburg, Ky., May 30, 1812 — Springfield, Ill., Sept. 20, 1900). Politician and military officer. Admitted to the Illinois bar in 1832, he served in the Black Hawk War, was active in military affairs, and became a newspaper editor. A Democrat, he was elected to the U.S. House of Representatives (1843-51, 1859-61). He resigned from Congress after the outbreak of the Civil War and helped assemble troops in Illinois. He was commissioned brigadier general of volunteers in October, 1861. Promoted major general a year later, his independent behavior drew reprimands and, after his unauthorized capture of the Arkansas Post on January 11, 1863, Gen. Ulysses S. Grant recalled him and later relieved him of his command. Although President Abraham Lincoln reinstated him in February, 1864, he resigned ten months later.

McCOMB, Miss. City (pop. 12,331), Pike Co., in southwestern Mississippi. Founded c. 1857 in what is now a dairy and truck farming region near the Louisiana line, McComb was named for the president of the New Orleans, Jackson and Northern Railroad whose decision to establish railroad shops here was responsible for the town's rapid growth. Manufactures include quilts, lingerie, mattress pads, and aluminum windows.

McCORMICK, Cyrus Hall (Rockbridge Co., Va., Feb. 15, 1809 — Chicago, Ill., May 13, 1884). Inventor and philanthropist. He developed the first successful reaper (1831), which became the basis of all grain harvesting machines that followed. He set up his first factory in Chicago in 1847 under the management of his brothers. McCormick also established McCormick Theological Seminary, and engaged in real estate, mining, and railroading. The McCormick Company and the Deering Company combined in 1902 to form International Harvester, under McCormick's son, Cyrus, Jr.

McCORMICK, Robert Sanderson (Rockbridge Co., Va., July 26, 1849 — Chicago, Ill., April 16, 1919). Diplomat. He was secretary of legation in London (1889-92) and went on to become minister to Austria-Hungary in 1901 and the first ambassador there in 1902. He was ambassador to Russia (1902-05) and to France (1905-07).

McCULLERS, Carson (Columbus, Ga., Feb. 19, 1917 — Nyack, N.Y., Sept. 29, 1967). Novelist. She authored *The Heart is a Lonely Hunter* (1940) and *The Member of the Wedding* (1946). Partially paralyzed by a series of strokes while in her 20s, McCullers was bound to a wheelchair during her last years. She is also known for *Reflections in a Golden Eye* (1941), *Clock Without Hands* (1961) and *The Ballad of the Sad Cafe* (1951).

McCULLOCH, Ben (Rutherford, Co., Tenn., Nov. 11, 1811 — Pea Ridge, Ark., March 7, 1862). Military officer. After accompanying Davy CROCKETT to Texas, he distinguished himself as a soldier in the Texas Revolution (1836). In 1861 he was made a Confederate brigadier general and commanded forces in Arkansas, where he was killed in action at Pea Ridge.

McDONOGH, John (Baltimore, Md. Dec. 29, 1779 — Harrodsburg, Ky., Oct. 26, 1850). Merchant and philanthropist. Employed by a consignment agency, he was assigned to New Orleans, where he became quite successful, purchasing a large quantity of land both in Louisiana and western Florida. In 1806 he was elected director of the Louisiana State Bank, and in 1818 was an unsuccessful candidate for the U.S. Senate. He was the founder of a boys

school that still exists today; the McDonogh School in McDonogh, Md.

McDOWELL, Ephraim (Rockbridge Co., Va., Nov. 11, 1771 — Danville, Ky., June 25, 1830). Surgeon. After studying medicine in Staunton, Va., and in Edinburgh, Scotland, he returned to Danville to begin practice (1795). He performed the first successful ovarian surgery for the removal of a tumor in 1809, proving that abdominal operations were practical. McDowell performed two similar operations before reporting them in 1817 to a disbelieving profession.

McDUFFIE, George (near Augusta, Ga., Aug. 10, 1790 — Cherry Hill, S.C., Mar. 11, 1851). Politician. An advocate of nullification, McDuffie was a Democratic U.S. congressman from South Carolina (1821-34). He was governor of South Carolina from 1834 to 1836, and from 1842 to 1846 was a U.S. senator.

McGILLIVRAY, Alexander (Alabama, c. 1759 — Pensacola, Fla., Feb. 17, 1793). Indian chief. His father was a Scottish trader and his mother was a French-Creek. After a classical education he returned to his mother's people when Georgia confiscated his father's property during the American Revolution. He became a Creek chief and allied the Creeks to the British during the war. As his power grew he arranged a treaty with the Spanish (1784) and, with arms that they provided, he attacked colonial settlements in Virginia and Georgia. In 1790 he arranged a peace treaty with the United States. Still loyal to Spain he continued attacking frontier settlements.

McGREADY, James (Pennsylvania, c. 1758 — Henderson Co., Ky., Feb., 1817). Clergyman. A Presbyterian minister, his evangelistic work in Logan City, Ky. (1797-99) began the great religious revival which swept the South and West by 1800. McGready's encampments were the forerunners of the Camp Meeting movement. Disputes over his evangelical methods led to a splintering with the mother church which resulted in the formation of the Cumberland Presbyterian Church.

McINTOSH, Lachlan (Badenoch, Scotland, Mar. 17, 1725 — Savannah, Ga., Feb. 20, 1806). Military leader and politician. Brought to America as a child, he lived in the Scottish settlement which is now Darien, Ga. After serving with the Continental Army as a brigadier general, he was commissioned (1778) to bring rest among the hostile Indians in Pennsylvania and Virginia. Though unsuccessful in this task, he was a Georgia delegate to the Continental Congress (1784) and was a commissioner to the Creek and Cherokee Indians (1785).

McINTOSH, William (Creek Country: Carroll Co., Ga., 1775 — Carroll Co., May 1, 1825). Indian Chief. He was the son of a British officer and a Creek Indian woman. McIntosh was an American general during the War of 1812 and fought in the Seminole and Indian Wars. He was slain by Creek Indians for signing a treaty ceding their lands along the Chattahoochee River.

McLEAN, Va. Town (pop. 50,000), Fairfax Co., in the northeast part of the state. Located eight miles northwest of Washington, D.C., McLean has developed as a residential suburb in the Washington metropolitan area.

McPHERSON, James Birdseye (near Clyde, Ohio, Nov. 14, 1828 — near Atlanta, Ga., July 22, 1864). Military officer. After graduating from West Point in 1853, he was commissioned a second lieutenant in the army corps of engineers. At the outbreak of the Civil War, McPherson served Gen. Henry Halleck and Gen. Ulysses S. Grant under whom he performed meritoriously at Corinth and Shiloh. He was promoted to brigadier general in 1863. In 1864, in charge of the Tennessee army, McPherson was killed in his army's march to Atlanta under Gen. William Tecumseh Sherman.

McREYNOLDS, James Clark (Elkton, Ky., Feb. 3, 1862 — Washington, D.C., Aug. 24, 1946). Jurist. He was attorney general from 1913 to 1914, and was appointed a Supreme Court Justice (1914-41) by President Woodrow Wilson. As a "strict constructionist" he wrote more opinions declaring acts of Congress unconstitutional than any justice prior to him. He was also noted for antitrust litigation in connection with the office of attorney general. McReynolds' opposition to New Deal legislation led to his being a prime target of President Franklin Roosevelt's unsuccessful attempt to reconstruct the Court.

MECHANICSVILLE, Battle of. See SEVEN DAYS' BATTLE.

MECKLENBERG DECLARATION OF INDEPENDENCE. A declaration reportedly drawn up by the citizens of Mecklenberg County, N.C., on May 20, 1775, to break its ties with the English rule. While the legend of the declaration is still maintained in North Carolina, there is no documentation to prove its existence. What is known, is that the community drew up a set of anti-British resolutions on May 31, 1775, calling for the nullification of the authority of all Crown officials. Those resolutions were published in 1819, with embellishments from the Declaration of Independence.

MEDINA RIVER, Tex. River originating in the Edwards Plateau in south central Texas. It flows east-southeast approximately 170 miles to join the Guadelupe River at Gonzales. Lake Medina is on its course. The river valley was the site of the Battle of Medina in 1813, when the Mexican army sought and captured a band of revolutionaries trying to seize power. Of the 1,700 revolutionary soldiers captured only about 90 escaped. The government soldiers ordered those remaining to dig their own mass grave before they were lined up and shot. The corpses were left in the makeshift shallow graves for more than nine years before the Mexican government dug up the remains and buried them properly with military honors.

MEHERRIN INDIANS. Tribe of Iroquoian linguistic stock that lived along the Meherrin River (to which they gave their name) on the Virginia-North Carolina border. Allies of the TUSCARORA INDIANS, they are thought to have gone north with them in 1802.

MEHERRIN RIVER, Va. River rising in Mecklenberg Co., and flowing through Virginia before becoming a tributary of the Chowan River in North Carolina. The river takes its name from the MEHERRIN INDIANS who lived in the region.

MELBOURNE, Fla. City (pop. 46,536), Brevard Co., in eastern Florida, on the Indian River. Recreation spot and popular point of departure for hunters going inland to the headwaters of the St. John's River. It also processes and ships citrus fruit. Manufactures include electronic equipment and pleasure crafts. The

Florida Institute of Technology and Patrick Air Force Base are located nearby.

MEMMINGER, Christopher Gustavus (Wurttemberg, Germany, Jan. 9, 1803 — Charleston, S.C. Mar. 7, 1888). Politician. Following his family's move to the U.S., he became a prominent attorney in Charleston, S.C., a state legislator (1836), and education commissioner. He served in the state convention secession proceedings and was Confederate treasurer (1861-64).

MEMPHIS, Tenn. City (pop. 646,356), seat of Shelby Co., in southwestern Tennessee on the Mississippi River. Settled in 1797 and incorporated in 1826, the city is a major distributor of cotton and hardwood lumber, mixed feed, chemicals, and drugs. Agricultural produce includes cotton, livestock, poultry, soybeans, and vegetables. Several major educational and medical institutions are located in Memphis, including several divisions of the University of Tennessee, Southwestern University at Memphis, LeMoyne-Owen College, and Christian Brothers College. The city has gained fame as the home of the "blues," the jazz form first introduced by artists such as William C. HANDY, a black composer who performed almost exclusively in Memphis.

Founded in the late 1700s on the site of a Chickasaw Indian village, Memphis drew its name from an ancient Egyptian city because of its similar situation on a major river. Andrew JACKSON was among the founders of the city. Its early development depended largely on cotton, which was becoming the major commodity of the south. Development was encouraged by the transportation assets of position on both the river and on railroad networks. The city served as a Confederate military post in the Civil War until Union forces seized it in 1862 and occupied it for the remainder of the war.

Memphis was devastated in the 1870s by an epidemic of yellow fever that killed approximately 8,000 residents. The city soon went bankrupt because those who survived the epidemic often chose to flee the city and newcomers were dissuaded from settling there, and in 1876 the city was forced to give up its charter. City planners eventually improved public sanitation to prevent further epidemics. There was a gradual economic recovery, and in 1893 a new city charter was granted. By 1900 the population had grown to 100,000, making Memphis the state's largest city. During the 1920s the city gained an infamous reputation

for a high murder rate and alleged criminal traffic. Nevertheless, economic growth continued through World War II. Large U.S. Navy installations are located to the north of the city in the suburb of Millington. Chuckalissa, a prehistoric Indian town, is located to the south.

MENCKEN, H(enry) L(ouis) (Baltimore, Md., Sept. 12, 1880 — Baltimore, Md., Jan. 29, 1956). Philologist, author, and editor. He began his varied literary career as a reporter for Baltimore's *Morning Herald, Evening Herald* and *Sun.* Later a co-editor of *Smart Set* (1914-23), he founded the *American Mercury* with fellow critic George Jean Nathan in 1924 and served as its editor through 1933. His early books included *Ventures into Verse* (1908), *George Bernard Shaw: His Plays* (1905), *The Philosophy of Friedrich Nietzche* (1908) and the series of six collections of satirical essays called *Prejudices* (1919-27).

After visiting England, Mencken became interested in American linguistics, and the result of his research became the authoritative *The American Language* (1919), which was revised in 1921, 1923, and 1936, and followed by *Supplement One* (1946) and *Supplement Two* (1948). Like George Bernard Shaw, Mencken was known for his insistence on correct usage of language, his ability to deflate pretentious spokesmen on issues of his day, and his satirical essays on virtually any topic whatsoever. It was Mencken who invented the term "Bible-belt," and his facetious theory on the American invention of the bathtub was once naively quoted by President Harry Truman as fact.

MENENDEZ DE AVILES, Pedro (Spain, Feb. 15, 1519 — Spain, Sept., 17, 1574). Spanish naval officer. Having served on board ships since the age of 14, Menendez was commissioned to drive the pirates from Spain and the Canaries (1549) and was captain of the Indies fleet (1554). Imprisoned because of the intrigues of political enemies (1563), he was contracted by Phillip II to establish and govern a colony in Florida to frustrate the expansion of the French Huguenots. He founded St. Augustine, Fla. (1565), and took Fort Saint Caroline, where he hanged the captured French, "Not as Frenchmen, but as Lutherans."

MENKEN, Adah Isaacs (near New Orleans, La., June 15, 1835 — Paris, France, Aug. 10, 1868). Actress and poet. Orphaned at a young age, she grew up in poverty and began appearing on the theatrical stages of New Orleans and other cities in the 1850s. She became famous for appearing virtually naked and strapped to a horse. She married Alexander Isaacs Menken in 1856 and kept his name throughout her other marriages. While working in England and Europe, she befriended such literary men as Charles Dickens.

MERAMEC RIVER, Mo. Waterway originating in south central Missouri, just east of Salem. It flows north, northeast, and southeast for 210 miles to empty into the Mississippi River, about 20 miles south of St. Louis.

MERCER, Hugh (Aberdeen, Scotland, c. 1725 — Princeton, N.J., Jan. 3, 1777). Military officer. A trained physician and surgeon, he came to America in 1747 and was a captain in the French and Indian War. When the Revolutionary War broke out he was made a colonel of the 3rd Virginia Regiment (Jan., 1776), and later that year was promoted to brigadier general. He led the column of attack at the Battle of Trenton, and at the council of war there he suggested the daring night march on Princeton. In the battle that ensued the following morning he was mortally wounded.

MERGENTHALER, Ottmar (Hachtel, Germany, May 11, 1854 — Baltimore, Md., Oct. 28, 1899). Inventor. He emigrated to the U.S. (1872) and became a naturalized citizen (1878) while employed in a Baltimore machine shop. Working in the shop with the plans of another inventor to make type molds of papier-mache, he began a study which led to a typesetting machine that rapidly formed columns of type by bringing copper matrices into contact with quickly cooling, molten alloy. This first invention, the linotype (1884), revolutionized printing, cutting costs and speeding the process.

MERIDIAN, Miss. City (pop. 46,577), seat of Lauderdale Co. in eastern Mississippi near the Alabama border. Settled in 1854 and incorporated in 1860, the city was founded as a railroad "junction," for which "Meridian" was erroneously thought to be a synonym. Located in a timbering region, present manufactures include auto parts, lumber products, and sound systems.

MERRIMAC. See MONITOR AND MERRIMAC, Battle of.

MESQUITE, Tex. Town (pop. 67,053), Dallas Co., in northeast Texas. Mesquite was established in 1872 as a stop on the Texas and Pacific Railroad. From 1950 to 1970, the town grew rapidly. A residential suburb of Dallas with some light manufacturing, it is the home of EASTFIELD COLLEGE.

METAIRIE, La. City (pop. 135,816), Jefferson Parish, in southeastern Louisiana, on the Mississippi River. A residential suburb northwest of New Orleans, manufacturing is varied and includes concrete, car parts, carbon paper, wood products, and fabricated structural steel. Farming in the area primarily produces cotton and sugar cane.

MEXICO, Mo. City (pop. 12,276), seat of Audrain Co., in northeast central Missouri. Federal troops camped here and badly damaged the city during the Civil War. Brick manufacturing and saddle-horse breeding are the basis of the city's economy today. It is the home of Missouri Military Academy. The city was founded in 1836 and incorporated in 1857.

MIAMI, Fla. City (pop. 346,931), seat of Dade Co., on the southeast coast of Florida. Settled in 1567 and chartered as a city in 1896, it is a major transportation, business, and resort center. The city is located on Biscayne Bay, at the mouth of the Miami River, three and a half miles west of the Atlantic Ocean. Miami's metropolitan area (2,408 square miles) is the largest in Florida, encompassing all of Dade County, which includes the cities of Coral Gables, Miami Beach, Hialeah, North Miami, and a host of smaller communities. Miami's average temperature is 81 degrees in summer and 71 degrees in winter, making it a year-round mecca for tourists.

An important industrial area, Greater Miami has over 3,000 manufacturing plants. Manufactures include clothing, transportation equipment, processed foods, furniture, and printed materials. As a transportation center, the Port of Miami handles both foreign and domestic shipping, and Miami International Airport has 100 American and foreign airlines using its facilities. Miami also has 35 radio stations, ten television channels, and two daily newspapers.

The original inhabitants of the Miami area were the Tequesta Indians who may have lived here for 2,000 years prior to the arrival of the Spaniards who established a mission here in 1567. The Indian's name for the area,

"Mayaimi," is thought to refer either to Lake Okeechobee or the Indians of the Everglades. The area was acquired by the United States in 1812. In 1835 Fort Douglas was built and troops actively campaigned to expel the Seminole Indians from the nearby swamps. Settlement by non-military personnel was slow, and it wasn't until 1895 that Miami began to grow appreciably. In that year Julia D. Tuttle, the "mother of Miami," sent railroad builder Henry M. FLAGER some flowers as proof that the Miami region not only had fertile land but had also escaped a killer frost which had affected much of the South. Her action convinced Flager to extend his Florida East Coast Railroad south to Miami in exchange for some of the area's land. Flager not only brought in the railroad, he built the Royal Palm Hotel and dredged the harbor. The city grew rapidly until the land boom collapse of 1920 stagnated the economy for almost twenty years. World War II changed the character and growth of the city, as many of Miami's hotels were turned over to the armed forces to provide billets for personnel. Following the war the city grew rapidly as a tourist area.

The present population of Miami is diverse. Since 1961 when Castro took power in Cuba, the city has been a haven for Cuban refugees. Large numbers of Haitians have also arrived, and now almost 60% of the people of Miami were born outside the United States. Besides Cubans and blacks, other significant population groups include Italians, Russians, and Germans.

Attractions in Miami include the Crandon Park Zoo, the Seaquarium, the Museum of Science and Natural History, and the Fairchild Tropical Garden, along with art museums and galleries, the opera, symphony, and theatre. Miami has a professional football team, the Miami Dolphins, who play their home games in the famous Orange Bowl, which is the sight of a college football spectacular every New Year's day. An important educational center, Greater Miami is home to the University of Miami, Teachers University, Barry College, the International Fine Arts College of Fashion, Florida Memorial College, Miami-Dade Junior College, Biscayne College, and St. John Vianney Minor Seminary.

MIAMI, University of. Independent coed institution with three campuses—the 260-acre main campus at Coral Gables, Fla., the Rosenstiel School of Marine and Atmospheric Sciences for graduate study at Virginia Key, and the medical campus at Miami. Founded in 1925, the university's major divisions include the Colleges of Arts and Sciences, the Schools of Continuing Studies, Business Administration, Education and Allied Professions, Law, Engineering and Architecture, Medicine, Music, Nursing, and Marine and Atmospheric Sciences. There is also the Institute of Molecular and Cellular Evolution, centers for theoretical studies, advanced international studies, survey of aging, and other programs.

The South provides 55% of the students, 29% are from Middle Atlantic states, 9% are from North Central states, and 7% come from New England. More than 43% of the university's graduates pursue full-time graduate study; 12% enter law school, 14% medical and dental schools, and 28% business school. In national school ratings, the university is among the top 100 in developing business executives; the top 100 in producing medical school en-

The "Calle Ocho" in Miami, Fla., an avenue of Cuban shops, nightclubs, and restaurants

trants; and in the top 120 producing dental school entrants.

Library: 1,185,817 volumes. Faculty: 1,398. Enrollment: 18,871 total graduate and undergraduate: 5,336 men, 3,953 women (full-time); 794 men, 1,242 women (part-time). Degrees: Bachelor's, Master's, Doctorate.

MIAMI BEACH, Fla. City (pop. 96,298), Dade Co., on the southeast coast of Florida. Settled in 1567 when the Spanish established a mission in the area, the city was incorporated in 1917 and today it is a resort and covention center located on Biscayne Bay just opposite the city of Miami. Miami Beach is actually an island, ten miles long and one to three miles wide, and is connected to Miami by bridges and four causeways.

In 1912 the swampy section of the island was filled in with sediment and rock pumped up out of Biscayne Bay to form a solid base for the building of a city. John S. Collins is the man primarily responsible for starting Miami Beach as a resort city. The city's growth was stunted by a land boom collapse in 1920 and the subsequent arrival of the great Depression. During World War II most of the city's hotels were

Miami Beach, Fla., a 10-mile island in Biscayne Bay, opposite the city of Miami

requisitioned to provide quarters for armed services personnel. Miami Beach boomed as a tourist center after the war, and continues to grow rapidly today.

MIDDLESBOROUGH, Ky. City (pop. 12,251), Bell Co., southeast Kentucky, in the Cumberland Mountains near the spot where Kentucky, Tennessee, and Virginia meet. A coal-mining community founded in 1890, it now has varied manufacturing. Cumberland Gap National Historic Park, Pinnade Mountain, and a resort lake are nearby.

MIDDLETON, Arthur (near Charleston, S.C., June 26, 1742 — Charleston, S.C., Jan. 1, 1787). Politician. Having been elected to the provincial House of Assembly upon completing his British education, he corresponded with Americans based in London. Following a family visit to England (1768-71), he became a Whig. He was active with the South Carolina Council of Safety (1775-76), a member of the provincial committee that wrote the state constitution, and a representative to the Continental Congress (1776-78), where he signed the Declaration of Independence. From 1778 to 1780 he was a member of the state legislature. An officer at the siege of Charleston (1780), he was taken prisoner and transported to St. Augustine, Fla., by the British. After his exchange in 1781, he served again in the Continental Congress (1781-83), again in the state legislature (1785-86), and later was a member of the founding board of trustees of the College of Charleston. He was the son of Henry MIDDLETON.

MIDDLETON, Henry (near Charleston, S.C., 1717 — Charleston, S.C., June 13, 1784). Politician. He held several ranking posts in the British colonial government until 1770, when he left in protest of their trade policies. He was a delegate to the Continental Congress (1774-76), and was president (1774-75), but his opposition to independence led to his resignation. He was later a member of the South Carolina senate (1778-80). He was the father of Arthur MIDDLETON.

MIDDLETOWN, Battle of. See CEDAR CREEK, Battle of.

MIDLAND, Tex. City (pop. 69,844), seat of Midland Co., located midway between Dallas and El Paso in the western part of the state. Midland is a center of Permian Basin oil administration, agriculture (livestock, cotton), and industry (aircraft, steel, dairy processing, plastics, chemicals, and clothing). The city developed in 1881 as a cattle-shipping center, and its greatest growth began with the discovery of oil in 1923. Now known as "Tall City" for the office buildings which tower over the surrounding flatlands, Midland administers one-fourth of U.S. crude oil, liquid gas, and natural gas production.

MIKASUKI INDIANS. Tribe of Muskogean linguistic stock that lived in Florida around Miccosukee Lake. One of the Seminole tribes, they played a prominent part in the SEMINOLE WARS. At the close of the wars the tribe split, some remaining in Florida, others going on to INDIAN TERRITORY in Oklahoma.

MILL SPRINGS, Ky. Unincorporated town in Wayne Co., on the Cumberland River. Mill Springs was the scene of the opening battle of the Kentucky-Tennessee campaign and the first western victory for the Union during the Civil War (January, 1862). It is now a small farming and manufacturing community.

MILLEDGE, John (Savannah, Ga. 1757 — near Augusta, Ga., Feb. 9, 1818). Politician and military officer. He served in the Revolutionary War and was attorney general of Georgia (1780), before becoming a U.S. congressman (1795-99). He was governor of Georgia (1802-06), and a U.S. senator (1806-09). Milledge donated the land that became the campus of the University of Georgia.

MILLEDGEVILLE, Ga. City (pop. 12,176), seat of Baldwin Co., in central Georgia, on the Oconee River. Milledgeville was laid out as the state capital (1807-68), and the old state capitol is now part of Georgia Military College. Pharmaceuticals, prefabricated buildings, and food products are manufactured today and it is a rich agricultural area. Named for John MILLEDGE, it is the home of Georgia College.

MILLER, Alfred Jacob (Baltimore, Md., Jan. 2, 1810 — Baltimore, Md., June 26, 1874). Artist. After studying under Thomas Sully, Miller joined an expedition West in 1837. While there, he made the detailed paintings of the Indians and the landscape for which he is best known.

MILLINGTON, Tenn. City (pop. 20,236), Shelby Co., in southwestern Tennessee. Incorporated in 1903, it is a rural community situated in a cotton, livestock, and poultry region. Memphis Naval Air Station is nearby.

MILLS, Robert (Charleston, S.C., Aug. 12, 1781 — Washington, D.C., Mar. 3, 1855). Architect. Considered the first American professional in the field in the U.S., he was most famous for Independence Hall in Philadelphia (1807), the U.S. Patent Office (1839), the U.S. Treasury (1836), and the Washington Monument in Washington, D.C. (1848-84). Mills followed the general Jeffersonian principle that classical edifices best suited the buildings of the new U.S. republic. He applied this principle to over 50 churches, colleges, hospitals, prisons, homes, canals, and bridges.

MINDEN, La. City (pop. 15,074), seat of Webster Parish, in northwestern Louisiana. The town, which was incorporated in 1850, is a trading and shipping center for a farm region that produces primarily cotton. Other products include natural gas, petroleum, gravel, and sand. Caney Lakes Recreational Area and Kisatchie National Forest are nearby.

MINE RUN CAMPAIGN. Civil War engagement in late November of 1863, in which Gen. Robert E. LEE managed to strengthen his positions in northeast Virginia after the defeat of the Confederate army at GETTYSBURG. The Mine Run campaign occurred from November 26 to December 1 near Culpeper, Va., just east of the Blue Ridge Mountains. The principal test took place along the Rapidan River, which Union Gen. George Meade crossed in an attempted offensive. He advanced south of the river to Mine Run with five corps, but there he found himself anticipated by the entrenchment of a far larger Confederate force. Meade withdrew to winter quarters in Culpeper, and when action resumed the following spring his position had been taken by Gen. Ulysses S. GRANT.

MINERAL WELLS, Tex. Town (pop. 14,468), Palo Pinto Co., in north central Texas. In 1885 the Crazy Well was discovered here, and its waters were claimed to have medicinal powers. By 1920 Mineral Wells had 400 mineral wells and was a flourishing health resort. Other industries include clay pipes, plastic products, and aircraft equipment.

MINING. The Southern states provide more than half the total U.S. mineral output measured in value of production. In 1980 the South had a total mineral production of approximately $60 billion, 87% of which was derived from fuels.

Texas leads both the country and the region in value of mineral fuels per year because of its combination of petroleum and natural gas reserves. Louisiana is second in both the country and the region in mineral fuels, chiefly because of its natural gas reserves. Kentucky and West Virginia are the third and fourth most productive states in the region in mineral fuels because of their coal reserves. As a group, the Southern states account for 60% of the total U.S. production of mineral fuels per year, measured by value.

The Southern states also account for one-third of the U.S. non-fuel mineral production. Texas leads the region in total value of non-fuel minerals, and it leads the country in production of sulfur and asphalt. Florida ranks second in the region in non-fuel minerals, and it leads the country in phosphate rock and in titanium. Missouri ranks third in the region in non-mineral fuels, and it leads the country in mining of lead.

Of the other states in the region, Arkansas leads the nation in bauxite and bromine, Tennessee leads the nation in zinc and pyrites, North Carolina leads the nation in mica and feldspar, and Georgia leads the nation in clay.

MINT JULEPS. A sweet alcoholic mixed drink which became popular in the Southern United States. The drink consists of bourbon whiskey, shaved ice, sugar, and crushed mint leaves, and is served in a tall, frosted glass. The drink is believed to have originated in Kentucky, where bourbon was distilled. Connoisseurs allege that a proper mint julep must still be made from only Kentucky bourbon.

MIRAMAR, Fla. City (pop. 32,813), Broward Co., in southeastern Florida. Situated in a rapidly growing area between Miami and Fort Lauderdale, Miramar is developing as a combination resort and retirement community. In the period between the 1970 and 1980 census, the population grew by 8,830, representing more than a 30% increase. It is also a residential suburb of Hollywood.

MISSION, Tex. Town (pop. 22,589), Hidalgo Co., in southern Texas. Founded in 1908, it was named for a mission three miles south of the town. Mission was the winter home of William Jennings Bryan for two years. By 1930 the town had become the center for the citrus industry in the area. Today, agribusiness and tourism are the two main industries.

MISSIONARY RIDGE, Battle of. Civil War engagement fought November 25, 1863, near Chattanooga in southeast Tennessee. Along with the Battle of LOOKOUT MOUNTAIN, fought the previous day, it was a successful defense by the Union army of its hold on Chattanooga.

The Confederate troops under Gen. Braxton BRAGG had occupied Missionary Ridge, east of Chattanooga, as they surrounded the city. They were positioned in two lines, one at the foot of the ridge and the other at the top of it. The Union troops, commanded by Gen. Ulysses S. Grant, attacked at noon and broke the first Confederate line by 4:00 P.M. Although under orders to halt at that first line, they found themselves under such heavy fire from the Confederate second line that they advanced further for their own protection and crested the ridge. Gen. William Tecumseh Sherman was the only Union officer with enough control of his men to pursue the Confederates, who retreated back into Georgia. The victory at Missionary Ridge and successful defense of Chattanooga opened the route for Sherman's march through Georgia.

MISSISSIPPI. State at the center of the Southern region located on the east bank of the river that provides its name and on the coast of the Gulf of Mexico. To the east, Mississippi has a 330-mile land border with Alabama that approximates its greatest north-south extent. To the north, it has a 120-mile land border with Tennessee that is more than 50 miles shorter than its greatest east-west extent. Most of the western border of the state is irregular, formed by the serpentine course of the Mississippi River, which separates it from Arkansas and Louisiana, but in the extreme south Mississippi has a western border with Louisiana that is formed by the Pearl River. Half of the southern border of the state is a land boundary with the eastern panhandle of Louisiana, and the other half is a 100-mile coastline on the Gulf of Mexico.

It is in Mississippi, more than any other state, that the character of the old South remains apparent today. Once the very heartland of plantation society, the state remains the leading cotton producer of the states that once re-

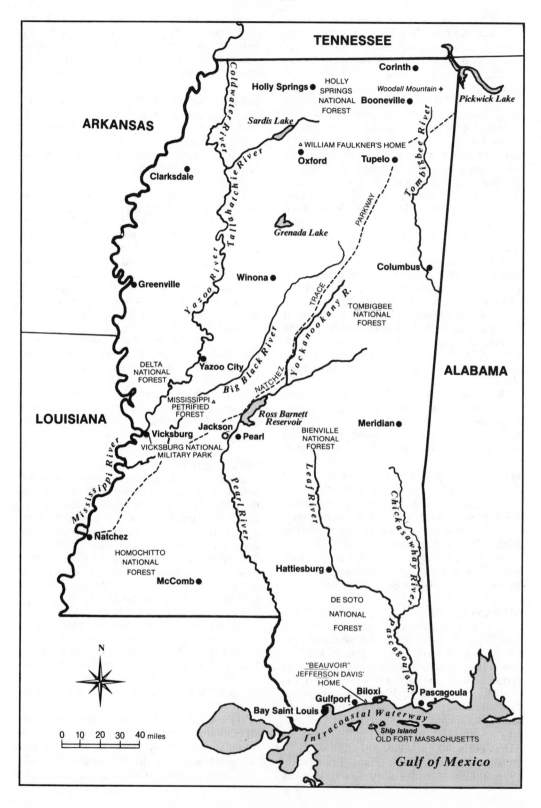

TENNESSEE

ARKANSAS

Corinth ●

Holly Springs ●   HOLLY
SPRINGS
NATIONAL
FOREST

Woodall Mountain +

Booneville ●

Pickwick Lake

Sardis Lake

△ WILLIAM FAULKNER'S HOME

Oxford ●

Tupelo ●

Clarksdale ●

Coldwater River

Tallahatchie River

Tombigbee River

Grenada Lake

PARKWAY

Columbus ●

Yazoo River

Winona ●

Greenville ●

TRACE

TOMBIGBEE
NATIONAL
FOREST

Yockanookany R.

ALABAMA

DELTA
NATIONAL
FOREST

Yazoo City ●

Big Black River

LOUISIANA

NATCHEZ

MISSISSIPPI
PETRIFIED
FOREST △

Ross Barnett
Reservoir

Meridian ●

Vicksburg ●   Jackson ⊕   ● Pearl

VICKSBURG NATIONAL
MILITARY PARK

BIENVILLE
NATIONAL
FOREST

Mississippi River

Pearl River

Leaf River

Chickasawhay River

Natchez ●

HOMOCHITTO
NATIONAL
FOREST

McComb ●

Hattiesburg ●

DE SOTO

NATIONAL

FOREST

Pascagoula R.

N

"BEAUVOIR"
JEFFERSON DAVIS'
HOME

Biloxi

Gulfport ●

Pascagoula ●

Bay Saint Louis ●

Intracoastal Waterway

Ship Island

OLD FORT MASSACHUSETTS

0 10 20 30 40 miles

Gulf of Mexico

STATE OF MISSISSIPPI

Name: *Mississippi* means "great water" in several Indian languages. The state was named for the river.

Nickname: Magnolia State, Bayou State, Mudcat State, Mudwaddler State, Eagle State, Border-Eagle State, Ground Hog State.

Motto: *Virtute et Armis* (By Valor and Arms).

Capital: Jackson.

Counties: 82. **Places over 10,000 population (1980)**: 30.

Symbols & Emblems: *Flower*: Magnolia. *Bird*: Mockingbird. *Tree*: Magnolia. *Song*: "Go, Mississippi."

Population (1980): 2,520,638. **Rank**: 31st.

Population Density (1980): 53.4 people per sq. mi. **Rank**: 31st.

Racial Make-up (1980): *White*: 1,615,190 (64.1%). *Black*: 887,206 (35.2%). *American Indian*: 6,180 (0.3%). *Asian & Pacific Islander*: 7,412 (0.3%). *Other*: 4,650 (0.2%). *Spanish Origin*: 24,731 (1.0%).

Largest City (pop. 1980): Jackson (202,895). *Others*: Biloxi (49,311), Meridian (46,577), Hattiesburg (40,829), Greenville (40,613), Gulfport (39,676), Pascagoula (29,318), Columbus (27,383), Vicksburg (25,434).

Area: 47,233 sq. mi. **Rank**: 32nd.

Highest Point: Woodall Mountain (806 ft.), Tishomingo Co.

Lowest Point: sea level, Gulf of Mexico.

State Government:

ELECTED OFFICIALS (4-year terms expiring Jan. 1988, etc.): *Governor* ($63,000); *Lt. Governor* ($34,000); *Sec. of State* ($45,000); *Attorney General* ($51,000); *Treasurer* ($45,000).

GENERAL ASSEMBLY (Salary: $8,100 plus $44 per diem living expense allowance.): *Senate* (52 members), *House of Representatives* (122 members).

CONGRESSIONAL REPRESENTATIVES: *Senate* (terms expire 1985, 1989, etc.). *House of Representatives* (5 members).

Admitted to the Union: Dec. 10, 1817 (20th state).

lied on such a one-crop economy. The state agriculture has been diversified in the 20th century, but the contemporary shift to modern manufactures that has altered the economy of neighboring states has yet to take full effect in Mississippi. As a result, Mississippi has yet to show the effects of urbanization which have changed the character of the neighboring states. There are only two standard metropolitan statistical areas in Mississippi: Jackson in the center of the state and Gulfport-Biloxi on the Gulf coast. These factors have caused Mississippi to rank lowest in the U.S. per capita income for a number of decades.

For these same reasons, however, Mississippi has been able to preserve the visible presence of the agrarian South to an unusual degree. Natchez on the lower Mississippi River maintains many old plantation homes and gardens, as does Vicksburg, 60 miles upriver, where a national military park also preserves a Civil War battleground. The great delta region further upriver also preserves the character and lifestyle of an older agricultural era of struggle against floodwaters and reclamation of alluvial lands. One great testimony to Mississippi's great consciousness of the past is the fact that it produced the novelist William Faulkner, whose most important works are all explorations of the links between past and present in Mississippi.

Most of the land area of Mississippi lies within the Gulf Coastal Plain, a region surrounding the Mississippi River that tapers to the north and ends at the confluence of the Mississippi and Ohio Rivers. In the state of Mississippi this plain is characterized by sandy terraces along the Gulf itself, including several offshore islands, and by rolling hills over most of the state land. These hills rise slightly in elevation toward the northeast corner of the state, where the state high point is located at Woodall Mountain (806 feet). The most characteristic landscape in Mississippi, however, is the alluvial bottomland along the Mississippi River called the delta. These delta lands extend along the entire western border of Mississippi, but near the center of the state's Mississippi River border they broaden into an oval region that is 60 miles wide from west to east. This principal delta region of the state, which supported its cotton crop, is isolated by the Yazoo and Tallahatchie Rivers. The division between delta and coastal plain in Mississippi is marked by an arc of loess bluffs that stretch from Memphis, Tenn., southward around the delta toward Vicksburg and Natchez.

The earliest residents of what is now Mississippi were Indians of the Chickasaw, Choctaw, and Natchez tribes. The first European explorers of these lands were the Spanish. A party led by Hernando de Soto traveled into Mississippi in 1540 and spent the winter in the north of the state. More than a century passed, however, before the next significant exploration of the region. This was accomplished by the French led by Jacques Marquette and Louis Jolliet, who came down the Mississippi River into the current borders of the state in 1673. They were followed in 1682 by Sieur de La Salle (Rene Robert Cavelier), who claimed the entire Mississippi River basin for France and called it Louisiana after King Louis XIV.

The capital of the French Louisiana territory was located first in Mobile, Ala., then in Biloxi, Miss., and finally moved to New Orleans, La., in 1722. Biloxi had become the first permanent settlement in what is now Mississippi in 1699, and Natchez, originally called Fort Rosalie, became the second in 1716. The land speculation schemes of the Mississippi Company, engineered by a Scottish businessman named John Law, failed in 1720, and the French never established more than a foothold in Mississippi. Consequently there were few residents affected when the region was ceded to England in the Treaty of Paris of 1763. The English did succeed in settling the region, but their control of it ended with the victory of the American colonies in the Revolutionary War. Then, in 1783, England ceded this "West Florida" territory to the Spanish, who disputed its borders with the new American government for a number of years. Spain relinquished most of its claim in the Pickney Treaty in 1795, but it retained control over Mississippi until surveying of the region was completed by Andrew Ellicott in 1797. Finally, on April 7, 1798, the present lands of Mississippi and Alabama were organized as the U.S. territory of Mississippi with Natchez as the capital. In this era Mississippi's history was a chaotic one of encroachments of the French and Spanish, unscrupulous land speculation such as the Yazoo Fraud, and the reluctance of Georgia to relinquish its own claims to the region. Andrew Jackson was instrumental in ending the international disputes with his victory at New Orleans in 1815, and ended the Indian conflicts with his victory at Horsehoe Bend in Alabama in 1814. These events paved the way for the division of the Mississippi Territory and its reorganization. The western portion entered the Union as the state of Mississippi in 1817, and the eastern portion entered as the state of Alabama in 1819.

In 1820 the capital of Mississippi was still Natchez and the population of the state was slightly more than 75,000. The capital was moved to Jackson in 1822, and the population was soon swollen by an influx of settlers from the east who soon displaced the state's large Indian population. The settlers came to grow cotton, which had emerged as the cash crop of the southern states after the invention of the cotton gin in 1793, and their squabbles for fertile Mississippi delta land created a local land boom. The lure of sudden wealth also brought the famous road bandits of the Natchez Trace, the main thoroughfare to Nashville, Tenn. By the 1850s, however, wealthy plantation owners had displaced the small farmers, and the expansion of their land holdings required importation of a slave population to work the lands. By 1860 the population had reached 790,000, and more than half were slaves owned by a tiny handful of aristocratic plantation owners.

At this time the economic interests in Mississippi relied so much on slavery that the state had seriously proposed secession as early at 1850, which it enacted on January 9, 1861. The prominence of Mississippi in the Confederate alliance was indicated by the election of its own U.S. Senator, Jefferson Davis, as President of the Confederate States of America. Emancipated slaves, who represented an especially large proportion of a population reduced by military enlistments, abandoned Mississippi and so undermined its economic stability. The state was then further devastated during the war by the Union Army destruction of Corinth, Vicksburg, Meridian, and Jackson. The state surrendered to the Union on July 4, 1865. It remained under a military government and subject to the counterproductive policies of northern politicians until an integrated legislature was formed in 1869 and it was readmitted to the Union on February 23, 1870.

The Reconstruction mismanagement of Mississippi's already war-ravaged economy caused an animosity toward federal legislation that created a "siege mentality" of entrenched conservatism among white Mississippians that lasted well into the 20th century. As a result, the state resisted implementation of civil rights protection, limited voting rights by poll taxes, legally instituted JIM CROW laws against black citizens, and passively tolerated the illegal actions of vigilante groups such as the KU KLUX KLAN. The state remained fiercely segregationist despite the fact that more than half the population was black until 1940, and this undermined the general quality of life, spawned a factionalism that limited the effectiveness of local government, and discouraged outside investment in the state's archaic cotton crop economy. It was not until the 1960s that significant reform occurred, and then it took place in the midst of violent murders and property destruction that gave the state an unsavory national image. The most important symbol of change was the admission of James Meredith, a black man, to the University of Mississippi in 1962 with federal protection provided by President John F. Kennedy. Since then full integration has proceeded at a steady pace, and this stabilization has altered the state's population and economic patterns.

Although Mississippi dropped from 29th to 31st among U.S. states in population in the 1970s, its population growth rate of 13.7% in that decade was above the national average. Even more important to the state's future was the fact that in that decade it recorded a net population gain from interstate migration. This net increase from migration was wholly of white persons, but a long tradition of sizable emigration from Mississippi by black residents was also brought to a virtual end in the 1960s. The total population in 1980 was 36% black, which is the highest proportion in the country.

Mississippi is a state without large population centers, although it faces them to the north in Memphis, Tenn., and to the east in Mobile, Ala. The largest metropolitan area in the state is the capital city of Jackson, the heart of a residential area of more than 300,000 that had a growth rate of 22% in the 1970s. The port cities of Gulfport and Biloxi on the Gulf coast form the only other metropolitan area in the state, one of slightly less than 200,000 residents. The south central cities of Meridian and Hattiesburg and the delta city of Greenville are the only other municipalities in the state with populations of 40,000.

Manufacturing now accounts for twice the income of farming in Mississippi. The principal manufactures are transportation equipment, wood products, electrical machinery, processed foods, and apparel. The farm income derives more from crops than livestock, although the greatest number of farms are devoted to beef cattle, dairy cows, and poultry. Mississippi leads all of the old "cotton belt" states in harvest of this traditional crop, but in modern times cotton farming has moved to new areas such as Texas, California, and Arizona. The other crops important to the state economy are soybeans, the modern substitute for cotton, and rice. Mining is the third most important sector of the state economy, with virtually all of the $866 million-per-year state mine yield petroleum and natural gas. Tourism is almost as important as mining to the state economy, with visitors to the Civil War monuments and recreational areas of Mississippi spending $850 million per year.

MISSISSIPPI, University of. State-supported coed institution located on two campuses in Oxford and Jackson, Miss. Founded in 1844, the university maintains schools of Dentistry, Medicine, Nursing, Health Related Professions, Pharmacy, Business Administration, Education, and Engineering. The College of Liberal Arts offers majors in anthropology, communicative disorders, home economics, journalism, medical technology, and theater. The university also has ROTC Army, Navy, Air Force, and Marine programs. The South provides 85% of the students; 35% of graduates pursue further study.

Library: 634,233 volumes, 4,696 journal subscriptions, 400 records/tapes. Faculty: 574. Enrollment: 9,607 total graduate and undergraduate; 3,918 men, 3,452 women (full-time). Degrees: Bachelor's, Master's, Doctorate.

MISSISSIPPI RIVER. Named "Great Water" or "Father of Waters" by the Ojibwa Indians (*mis*, "great"; *sipi*, "river"), the approximately 2,348-mile river is deserving of its name considering its role in the development of this country. It was first discovered by De Soto in the spring of 1541, not far from the site of Helena, Ark., but its source was not known until discovered by Henry Rowe Schoolcraft in 1832. Its origin, along with that of the Red River and the St. Lawrence, is Lake Itasca in the lake district of northern Minnesota.

Emptying into the Gulf of Mexico, the Mississippi, along with its two largest tributaries, the Missouri and the Ohio Rivers, drains an area of 1,243,700 square miles (an area equal to one-eighth of the entire country). The Mississippi empties approximately 600,000 cubic feet of water per second into the gulf—water from 31 states and 2 Canadian provinces.

During the early years of American colonization the river posed a barrier to westward expansion which actually benefitted the early colonies by unifying them. Settlement of the Mississippi River area was also impeded by the contest between France and Great Britain for sovereignty over the region from the mouth of

the St. Lawrence to the Gulf of Mexico. The Mississippi Territory was created by an act of Congress in 1798 and this, followed by the Louisiana Purchase in 1803, opened the river and Western lands for settlement.

The geographical importance and advantages of the river were first recognized by the early French trappers who had long used the river to transport their furs. With the territory fast becoming a corn, cotton, and wheat belt, the river became essential to American life as transportation to market from remote areas. It is estimated that in 1840 nearly half of all commercial vessels in the country were employed on the river system. With the development of the steamboat, river travel took on an air of opulence during the middle years of the 19th century. (See MISSISSIPPI RIVER STEAMBOATS.)

With the outbreak of the Civil War came the railroads and for a time they took control of transportation and river traffic dwindled. After the fall of VICKSBURG, July 4, 1863, Union forces took control of the river and the economic hardships inflicted on the South because of Union control made the battle one of the deciding victories of the War.

The increased need for transportation facilities during World War I put a burden on the railroads and river traffic once again increased, although it never again reached its earlier magnitude of importance. The memories of early river life have been preserved by Mark Twain in his *Life on the Mississippi* (1883).

The great, willful river was never easily navigable. In fact it is not navigable from its source to the Falls of St. Anthony at Minneapolis, Minn. Upstream from Minneapolis-St. Paul, for a distance of 500 miles, the river has a drop of 700 feet. In its lower region the river flows over land of its own making for nearly 1,000 miles and is subject to disastrous flooding. In 1879 the Federal government established the Mississippi River Commission, a seven-member group of engineers concerned with flood control construction and navigational improvements. The first Federal flood control acts were passed in 1917, and after the crippling flood of 1927 new legislation was passed which poured hundreds of millions of dollars annually into widespread projects. Floodways, cutoffs, and channels were constructed, and there are now 27 Federal dams and locks between Minneapolis and the Gulf of Mexico. Despite the improvements unexpected flooding continues today as the river suddenly changes its course and carves out new channels. The valuable topsoil along its banks is carried away and deposited in other areas.

The Mississippi, along with the Missouri and Red Rock Rivers, forms the world's third-largest waterway with 3,860 miles (the Nile is first with 4,132, and the Amazon is second with 3,900). It is the Mississippi that has enabled New Orleans to become the United States' second-largest port. The river's delta in the Gulf of Mexico is the recipient each year of approximately 1,000 acres of silt deposited by the river. The rich, alluvial soil deposited there has also been responsible for the delta area becoming one of the world's greatest upland cotton producers. An extensive system of levees, however, was needed to protect this rich soil from the ravaging waters at floodtime.

On the river's east bank are the states of Minnesota, Wisconsin, Illinois, Kentucky, Tennessee, Mississippi, and Louisiana. On the west bank are Minnesota, Iowa, Missouri, Arkansas, and Louisiana. Major cities on the river include Minneapolis-St. Paul, Minn.; St. Louis, Mo.; Memphis, Tenn.; Natchez, Miss.; and Baton Rouge and New Orleans, La.

Major tributaries from the west include the Missouri, White, Arkansas, Iowa, and Red Rivers. From the east it is joined by the St. Croix, Ohio, Yazoo, and Big Black Rivers, among others.

MISSISSIPPI RIVER DELTA. A large, crescent-shaped territory which covers the entire western part of Mississippi (about 13,000 square miles or roughly one-quarter of the state) surrounding the Mississippi River and its tributaries. It is also referred to as the Mississippi Alluvial Plain. Floodwaters of the region's rivers have dumped centuries of silt deposits, making it into highly fertile lowlands. Soybeans and cotton are the chief crops here. Levees have been contructed along the delta to protect farmlands from floods.

MISSISSIPPI RIVER STEAMBOATS. The paddle-wheel steamboat dominated the commerical and social life of the Mississippi River region from the 1820s to 1870s. The first steamboat was built by John Fitch of Connecticut in 1787. By 1790 he had improved the model and built a vessel which operated at eight miles an hour. Robert Fulton, often referred to as "the father of the steamboat," launched the *Clermont* in 1807 which made a run from New York City to Albany, N.Y. In 1811 the *New Or-*

Opulent lounge of the Mississippi River steamboat *Grand Republic,* c. 1880

leans was built under the direction of Nicholas J. Roosevelt, and it completed a journey from the Ohio River to New Orleans, La., that took eight months. The following year a service began between New Orleans and Natchez, Miss. Henry Miller Shreve of Louisiana made radical changes in the design of early steamboats to adapt them to the shallow water in parts of the treacherous Mississippi, and in 1816, made a record run from New Orleans to Louisville in 25 days. Cotton and slaves were the principal cargo on the steamboats and as banking capital grew so did the city of New Orleans. New prosperity was brought to communities all along the Mississippi, along with an extravagant means of travel. These floating palaces had ornate staterooms, served opulent meals, and were home to waist-coated, diamond-ringed gamblers. Few inventions had as much impact on growing America during that 50-year period. At the onset of the Civil War the steamboats gave way to gunboats which, coupled with the coming of the railroad, changed life on the Mississippi. Though there was a brief revival during the postwar period, the steamboats gradually disappeared and were replaced by barges and towboats.

A famous steamboat race with high betting stakes in which fortunes were made and broken, occurred on June 30, 1870. Capt. T. P. Leathers of the *Natchez* faced Capt. John W. Cannon of the *Robert E. Lee*. Thousands lined the shores from New Orleans to St. Louis, the course of the race. The *Robert E. Lee* won in a record time of 3 days, 18 hours, and 14 minutes.

MISSISSIPPI STATE UNIVERSITY.

State-supported coed university and land grant college located on a 4,000-acre campus in Mississippi State, Miss., a small town 130 miles northeast of Jackson. Founded in 1878, the university offers undergraduate studies in the Colleges of Agriculture, Architecture, Arts and Sciences, Business and Industry, Education, Engineering, and the Schools of Forest Resources, and Veterinary Medicine. Most undergraduate degrees are conferred in education, business and management, agriculture and natural resources, and engineering. Mississippi provides 95% of the students.

Library: 712,247 volumes, 8,656 journal subscriptions. Faculty: 821. Enrollment: 11,409 total graduate and undergraduate: 5,520 men, 3,583 women (full-time); 357 men, 271 women (part-time). Degrees: Bachelor's, Master's, Doctorate.

MISSISSIPPI UNIVERSITY FOR WOMEN.

State-supported women's institution, located on a 104-acre campus 150 miles northeast of Jackson, Miss., in the city of Columbus. The university was founded in 1884 and offers academic programs and training in education, the liberal arts, and nursing. Mississippi provides 80% of the students, and 38% go on to further studies.

Library: 35,884 volumes, 494 microfilm titles, 2,055 journal subscriptions. Faculty: 184. Enrollment: 2,070 total graduate and undergraduate; 1,464 women (full-time; 467 women (part-time). Degrees: Certificate or Diploma, Associate's, Bachelor's, Master's.

MISSOURI.

State in the north central region of the South, including points farther north than any other place in the South except the northern panhandle of West Virginia. Missouri is on the west bank of the Mississippi River, which separates it from Illinois over most of its eastern border and from Kentucky and Tennessee in the southeast. Missouri borders Iowa to the north and Arkansas to the south across a border that is broken in the southeast by the southern "bootheel" projection of Missouri. Its longest western border is with Kansas, across a land boundary and the Missouri River, but there are short borders with Nebraska in the northwest and Oklahoma in the southwest.

Located at the center of the Mississippi River division of the U.S., and bisected by its largest western tributary, the Missouri River, Missouri has a special historical status as the gateway to the American West. In the 19th century, particularly after the California gold rush in 1849, Missouri's western cities of St. Joseph and Independence were the departure points for pioneers who arrived by steamboat and departed to the northwest over the Oregon Trail and to the southwest over the Santa Fe trail. This is the heritage that is commemorated by the 630-foot Gateway Arch, properly called the Jefferson National Expansion Memorial, which now towers over the St. Louis waterfront along the Mississippi River.

In the past century Missouri's growth was most remarkable in regard to population: with fewer than 20,000 residents in 1810, it had more than 3 million by 1900. In the present century population growth has slowed, but Missouri has emerged as an economic power. Among the Southern states, it ranks behind only Texas and North Carolina in value added by manufacture, and second only to Texas in the total value of farm products. Manufacturing encourages urbanization, and Missouri includes two important U.S. metropolitan areas: St. Louis on the Mississippi River and Kansas City located 230 miles across the state on the western Kansas border. The visible character of the state, however, is a product of its agricultural economy, for fully 70% of Missouri's lands remain devoted to agriculture.

Most of Missouri's lands lie within two large topographical areas of roughly equal size, the Central Lowland plains in the north and the Ozark Plateau in the south. The plains north of the Missouri River, which crosses the state from west to east and isolates an upper third of its land area, are part of the Dissected Till Plains that extend south from Iowa. Between the Missouri and the Osage River, which meet near the central capital of Jefferson City, western Missouri includes a portion of Osage Plains that are related to the topography of Kansas. The Ozark region includes nearly all of the state area south of the Osage and Missouri Rivers. This rugged and scenic plateau is characterized by ridges cut by steep canyons and deep creek beds. It is also notable for springs, caves, and sinkholes created by groundwater dissolving underground limestone. The high point in the state lies in the southeast of the Ozark region at Taum Sauk Mountain (1,772 feet). The extreme southeast of the state, including the "bootheel," is a portion of Mississippi alluvial land isolated by the Ozark Escarpment. Originally swampy, it has been drained to create some of the most valuable farmland in Missouri.

The original inhabitants of the state were the Missouri and Osage Indians, tribes based along the banks of the Mississippi and Missouri Rivers. The early exploration of the region was conducted by the French moving south from Canada along the Mississippi River. Louis Jolliet and Jacques Marquette sailed down the river past present-day Missouri in 1673, and they were followed in 1682 by Sieur de La Salle, who claimed the region for the French and named it Louisiana after King Louis XIV. The French began to establish trapping outposts and missionary settlements within the current state boundaries by 1699, but these were abandoned after a few years. The first permanent settlement in Missouri was established by the French in 1735 at Ste. Genevieve on the Mississippi about 45 miles downstream from St. Louis. St. Louis itself was founded in 1764 by Pierre Laclede and Rene Auguste Chouteau as a headquarters for fur trading. In that same year, however, the French ceded their claims

east of the Mississippi to England and their Louisiana claim, including Missouri, to Spain.

Despite the Spanish title to the lands of Missouri, most of the effective settlement at the end of the 18th century was accomplished by Americans moving west from Kentucky and Tennessee and by French Canadians moving west from Illinois. By 1800 the American influence had become predominant, and its origin in southern states and terriories led to the importation of slavery into Missouri. In 1800 the Spanish agreed to cede Louisiana to the French as part of the complicated negotiations that resulted in the purchase of Louisiana by the U.S. from France in 1803. The Missouri Territory was set off from Louisiana in 1804, initiating an era of pioneer immigration to the Missouri and Mississippi River settlements that more than tripled the population between 1810 and 1820 to bring it past the 66,000 mark.

Population growth brought with it plans for statehood, with the territory first applying for admission to the Union in 1818. This became a national issue because of the delicate balance in federal politics between Northern and Southern interests. The ensuing debate resulted in the Missouri Compromise of 1820, by which the territory would be admitted without a ban on slavery but slavery would be prohibited in the rest of the Louisiana Territory north of 36 degrees 30 minutes latitude, which marks the southern border of Missouri. After a protracted controversy concerning the status of free black persons, who were ultimately permitted to immigrate to the state, Missouri was admittted to the Union as the 24th state on August 10, 1821.

In the early years of statehood settlement activity extended past the river settlements into the northern plains of Missouri. This was largely accomplished by emigrants from Kentucky, and it included the Platte Purchase of 1836 that extended the western border to the Missouri River. This new population was agricultural in occupation, and it strengthened the links between Missouri and the Southern, slave-holding states. For a time, however, this political affiliation was obscured by the boom of westward economic activities and pioneer settlement throughout the state. The Rocky Mountain Fur Company expanded traffic on the Missouri River and established St. Louis as a warehouse and shipping center. In 1821 William Becknell initiated the overland route to Santa Fe via mule and ox teams. Steamboat traffic along the Missouri also expanded in this era, and the commercial routes soon became highways for daily expeditions bound for the

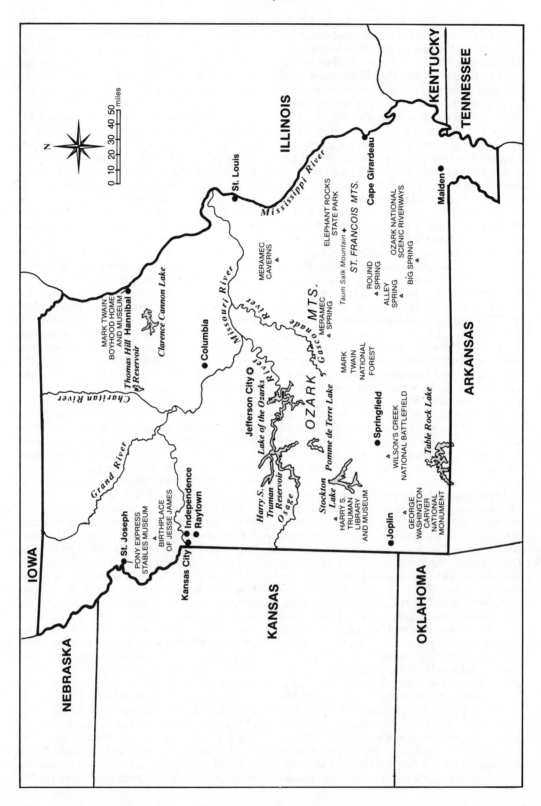

STATE OF MISSOURI

Name: For a tribe near the mouth of the Missouri River. The state is named for the river. The origin of the word is unknown.

Nickname: Show Me State, Bullion State, Lead State, Iron Mountain State, Ozark State, Puke State, Pennsylvania of the West.

Motto: *Salus Populi Suprema Lex Esto* (The Welfare of the People Shall Be the Supreme Law).

Capital: Jefferson City.

Counties: 114. **Places over 10,000 population (1980):** 57.

Symbols & Emblems: *Flower:* Hawthorn. *Bird:* Bluebird. *Tree:* Dogwood. *Song:* "Missouri Waltz."

Population (1980): 4,917,444. **Rank:** 15th.

Population Density (1980): 71.3 people per sq. mi. **Rank:** 27th.

Racial Make-up (1980): *White:* 4,346,267 (88.4%). *Black:* 514,274 (10.4%). *American Indian:* 12,319 (0.3%). *Asian & Pacific Islander:* 23,108 (0.5%). *Other:* 21,476 (0.4%). *Spanish Origin:* 51,667 (1.1%).

Largest City (pop. 1980): St. Louis (453,085). *Others:* Kansas City (448,159), Springfield (133,118), Independence (111,806), St. Joseph (76,691), Columbia (62,061), Florissant (55,372), University City (42,738).

Area: 68,945 sq. mi. **Rank:** 19th.

Highest Point: Taum Sauk Mountain (1,772 ft.), Iron Co.

Lowest Point: St. Francis River (230 ft.), Dunklin Co.

State Government:
ELECTED OFFICIALS (4-year terms expiring Jan. 1985, etc.): *Governor* ($55,000); *Lt. Governor* ($30,000); *Sec. of State* ($42,500); *Attorney General* ($45,000); *Treasurer* ($42,500).

GENERAL ASSEMBLY (Salary: $15,000 plus $35 per diem living expense allowance.): *Senate* (34 members). *House of Representatives* (163 members).

CONGRESSIONAL REPRESENTATIVES: Senate (terms expire 1985, 1987, etc.). *House of Representatives* (6 members).

Admitted to the Union: Aug. 10, 1821 (24th state).

Southwest, for California, and for the Northwest.

Political controversies returned to the foreground in the decade before the Civil War. In 1851, Senator Thomas Hart Benton, a moderate on the slavery issue, was defeated by Henry Sheffie Dyer, a Whig. In 1854 the Missouri Compromise was repealed by the Kansas-Nebraska Act, which empowered local legislatures to decide the legality of slavery within their borders, and groups of Missourians crossed the western border into "bleeding" Kansas to sway it toward slavery. In 1869 the moderate Stephen A. Douglas carried Missouri's presidential vote, but Abraham Lincoln's call for troops for the Union Army in 1861 forced Missouri to choose between North and South. Governor Claiborne F. Jackson chose the South and engineered the passage of an ordinance of secession in November of 1861. Gen. Nathaniel Lyon, however, chose the North, and he occupied Jefferson City with volunteers and expelled the Jackson legislature from the capital. In 1862 the Union Army defeated the Confederates at Pea Ridge in Arkansas, thus preserving northern control of Missouri for the duration of the war. This permitted the rise of the Radical Unionists to control the state legislature before the Confederate surrender in 1865, and the Unionist control through the Reconstruction era was preserved by enforcement of "ironclad oaths" that prevented Southern sympathizers from holding political office or voting in elections. The Democratic Party nevertheless regained its traditional control of the state in 1870, and the new constitution it passed in 1875 eliminated many of the evils of Reconstruction while preserving segregation in public schools.

By the end of the 19th century the foundations for Missouri's modern economic stature had been laid. Although supplanted by Chicago as the railroad link between East and West for passengers, St. Louis established itself as a commercial rail center after it was linked to the younger town of Kansas City across the state. The state's farmers organized groups such as the Farmer's Alliance and the Grange to protect their own interests and involve commercial banks in the state transition from small subsistence farms to large cash-crop ones. By 1900 Missouri was the fifth most populous state in the U.S. as well as an agricultural and industrial leader.

The most recent change in the character of the state came in the years following World War II, when its own Senator Harry S. Truman became President of the United States. The wartime economy had expanded the state's heavy industries, and these successfully shifted to peacetime production. Urbanization accompanied heavy industry, and the proportion of the state population living in metropolitan areas rose from 51% in 1930 to 70% in 1970. Air travel and highways supplanted railroads, but both Kansas City and St. Louis managed to increase their importance as transportation centers in this new era. Finally, moderate interests prevailed in the transition to integrated schools following the Supreme Court ruling in 1954, and Missouri was spared the racial trauma common to many other Southern states in that decade and into the 1960s.

Today St. Louis and Kansas City remain the population and manufacturing centers in the state. The St. Louis metropolitan area extends from Missouri into Illinois and included 2.3 million residents in 1980; the Kansas City metropolitan area extends from Missouri into Kansas and included 1.3 million residents in that year. The statewide population recorded only an insignificant increase in urbanization in the 1970s, a decade during which it grew at a rate lower than the national average and recorded a slight population decrease from net migration movements. In composition the state population is 10% black and 1% Hispanic, with most of these residents living in metropolitan areas. The largest urban areas other than St. Louis and Kansas City are Springfield in the southern Ozark region and St. Joseph in the northwest plains region.

Manufacturing now generates five times the income of agriculture in Missouri. St. Louis, an automobile, aircraft, and brewery center, and Kansas City, a meat packing and grain processing center, are the principal manufacturing cities in the Great Plains region to the north and west. The state farmlands lie between the corn belt to the north and the cotton belt to the south, and soybeans now exceed both of these crops in value to the Missouri economy. Livestock, however, generates slightly more farm income than crops, with cattle and hog production based in the area north of the Missouri River. Missouri also mines large amounts of lead, cement, and stone, and it has a relatively high mineral value for a state without fuel reserves. Tourists to the state spent $3.9 billion in 1980, most of it in the scenic Ozark region of southern Missouri and in urban attractions such as St. Louis and Independence.

MISSOURI-COLUMBIA, University of.

Land-grant coed institution, part of the University of Missouri system. The first state university founded west of the Mississippi River, the University of Missouri began in 1839 at Columbia, a community 125 miles west of St. Louis. In addition to its original Columbia location, the university has three other campuses at Rolla, Kansas City, and St. Louis. The Rolla branch offers programs in mines and metallurgy, engineering, and science. The Kansas City branch was once an independent institution before becoming part of the university in 1963. St. Louis is the newest campus, founded in 1963. The four branches together offer almost 500 major programs. Columbia alone has 14 colleges and schools and 290 programs.

The university is comprised of the colleges of Arts and Sciences, Agriculture, Education, Engineering, Home Economics, and Public and Community Services. There are also schools of Forestry, Fisheries and Wildlife, Nursing, Journalism, Health-Related Professions, and Business and Public Administration. A major selection of graduate schools and programs is also offered. Missouri provides 84% of the students.

Library: 1,930,000 volumes, 20,000 journal subscriptions. Faculty: 1,610. Enrollment: 23,545 total graduate and undergraduate. Degrees: Certificate or Diploma, Bachelor's, Master's, Doctorate.

MISSOURI COMPROMISE.

Acts of Congress passed in 1820-21, which temporarily settled the question of extension of slavery west of the Mississippi River. The acts allowed Missouri to be admitted to the Union as a slave state, but also stated that slavery could not be established in the remaining Louisiana Territory north of latitude 36°30'.

When Missouri requested admission to the Union in December, 1818, the balance of slave and free states was 11 each. The Missouri statehood bill reached the House of Representatives on February 13, 1819, and James Tallmadge, a New York congressman, introduced an amendment that prohibited slavery in the new state. Although the amendment was passed by the House, there was strong opposition to it by Southerners, and it was not passed by the Senate.

The issue was put off until Congress reconvened in December, 1819. On January 3, 1820, the House voted to admit Maine (which had separated from Massachusetts) as a free state. The Senate amended the bill to include Missouri (without the Tallmadge amendment restricting slavery), thus maintaining equality between free and slave states. The bill was further amended by the Senate to exclude slavery forever in the remaining Louisiana Territory north of latitude 36°30'. This compromise bill was rejected by the House, but the bills were separated and Maine was accepted as a free state in March, 1820. Missouri was instructed to draw up a new constitution that permitted slavery. The new constitution, however, included a provision that prohibited the immigration of mulattoes and free Negroes into Missouri. This provision necessitated what is sometimes referred to as the "second Missouri Compromise." Missouri was forced to delete this restriction and to pledge not to impair the rights of citizens. Only then was Missouri admitted to the Union in August, 1821. Speaker of the House Henry CLAY (a representative from Kentucky) was so instrumental in the passage of the Missouri Compromise bills that he is often regarded as their author.

Although the compromise temporarily settled the slavery controversy, it also brought up the question of whether or not Congress could impose restrictions on new states when it didn't impose restrictions on existing states. Because of the proviso which prohibited slavery only north of 36°30', the Union was committed to admitting Texas as a slave state, which it did in 1845. In 1854 the Missouri Compromise was repealed by the Kansas-Nebraska Act, which added fuel to the impending Civil War.

MISSOURI INDIANS

(people having "dugout canoes" or people having "wooden canoes"). Tribe of Siouan linguistic stock that lived on the south bank of the Missouri River near the mouth of the Grand River. They gave their name to the river and to the state itself. They were nearly destroyed in 1798 in attacks by the Fox and Sauk Indians and later suffered another tragic defeat by the Osage.

MISSOURI RIVER.

The longest tributary of the Mississippi (2,465 miles), it rises in southwest Montana and flows southeast to St. Louis, Mo. Once an important source of transportation to the Indians, the Lewis and Clark Expedition (1803) was instrumental in opening the route to settlers. Because its drainage area is nearly three times that of the Mississippi River, opinions have been expressed that perhaps the Mississippi should be considered the tributary and the entire course from Montana to the Gulf of Mexico should be considered the Missouri (if this were so, it would become the longest river in the world).

MISSOURI RIVER BASIN PROJECT.

A hydroelectric project developed in 1944 in response to the federal Flood Control Act. This plan, set forth by the U.S. Army Corps of Engineers and the Bureau of Reclamation, provided for the coordinated development and flood control of the Missouri River and its surrounding region. Besides the state of Missouri, the plan also incorporated lands in the states of Colorado, Iowa, Kansas, Minnesota, Montana, Nebraska, North Dakota, South Dakota, and Wyoming, for a total project irrigation area of nearly four million acres. The project is under control of seven federal agencies as well as the governors of the ten states involved. The purpose is to control flooding, improve navigation, and develop hydroelectric power sources along the river.

MITCHELL, Margaret (Atlanta, Ga., Nov. 8, 1900 — Atlanta, Ga., Aug. 16, 1949). Journalist and novelist. The daughter of a president of the Atlanta Historical Society, Mitchell was steeped in local history from an early age. Educated at Washington Seminary and Smith College, she began to write for the Atlanta *Journal* in 1922 under the name Peggy Mitchell. She resigned in 1926, and devoted herself to a work of fiction based on stories told by family and friends. The result was *Gone with the Wind* (1936), the romantic story about Scarlet O'Hara and Rhett Butler set against the background of a South torn by the Civil War. The novel was a great popular success and was awarded the Pulitzer Prize in 1937. It has since become one of the best-selling novels of all time and the basis for the immensely popular movie of the same name released in 1939.

MITCHELL, Mount, N.C. Yancey Co. Not only the highest peak in the state (6,684 feet), but the highest one east of the Mississippi River. It is part of the Black Mountains in the APPALACHIAN MOUNTAIN system. The peak is the central feature of Mitchell State Park, within the Pisgah National Forest.

MITCHELL DAM, Ala. The middle of three consecutive dams, in Chilton Co., located along the Coosa River in central Alabama. Constructed for hydroelectric power generation, it creates Lake Mitchell.

MOBERLY, Mo. City (pop. 13,418), Randolph Co., in the north central part of the state. The city was laid out in 1866 in the watershed between the Missouri and Mississippi Rivers, north of Columbia. Along with coal mining, there is diversified farming and poultry-raising as well as the manufacture of dairy products, hosiery, shoes, and tools.

MOBILE, Ala. City (pop. 200,452), seat of Mobile Co., in southwest Alabama. Settled in 1711 Mobile is a seaport at the mouth of Mobile Bay on the Gulf of Mexico. The second-largest city in the state, and one of the most important transportation centers in the South, Mobile not only has ready access to waterways but has many bus and truck lines. The steamship and barge lines located in Mobile ship goods out to all parts of the world. Mobile's early economy was based on lumber and cotton exporting, and the banana trade was important in the late 1800s. The opening of the Panama Canal in 1914, and the subsequent completion of several important barge lines, bridges, and the Bankhead Tunnel under the Mobile River, propelled Mobile to its present commercial status. Modern day manfactures include aircraft engines, pumps, chemicals, cement, clothing, paint, alumimum, and wood pulp and paper products. Major employers, besides manufacturing, are government services and a large shipbuilding industry.

Mobile has belonged to several countries in its nearly three hundred year history. It was first settled in 1702 as a French trading post called Fort Louis de la Mobile. The name Mobile is a French adaptation of the name of a local Indian tribe, the Maubilian, which means "canoe peddler." In 1711 the settlement relocated to the present site, and it was the capital of the Louisiana Territory until 1719. In 1763 Mobile was ceded to Britain as part of Florida, only to fall under Spanish control seventeen years later. It wasn't until 1813 that the city passed into American hands and became part of Alabama. It was incorporated as a town in 1814 and as a city in 1819. Mobile was Andrew Jackson's headquarters during several Indian campaigns, and was an important Confederate port during the Civil War and site of the Battle of Mobile Bay.

The world renowned Azalia Trail is in Mobile, and a yearly Mardi Gras festival is held here that rivals New Orlean's in importance and magnitude. Many historic homes, including the antebellum mansion Oakleigh, are open to the public. The U.S. Junior Miss Pageant and the Senior Bowl football game are held here each year. Institutions of higher learning include Spring Hill College and S. D. Bishop State Junior College. Mobile has its own symphony orchestra and opera.

MOBILE BAY, Ala. Inlet of the Gulf of Mexico in southwestern Alabama. It is approximately 36 miles long and between eight and 18 miles wide, giving the city of Mobile access to the Gulf. Its ship channel passes between Mobile Point and Dauphin Island. The Alabama State Docks here do a major import-export trade. It was here that Union Admiral David FARRAGUT won the Civil War naval battle fought on August 5, 1864. One of the state's best beach areas is on the bay.

MOBILE INDIANS. Tribes of unknown linguistic stock that were closely associated with the CHOCTAW INDIANS. Comprised of a great number of tribes, their domain extended along the shores of the Gulf of Mexico from the Atlantic to the Mississippi and northward along the coast to Georgia. They gave their name to Mobile, Ala. Under the leadership of Chief TUSCALOOSA there were early violent battles with the Spanish. About the time the English obtained possession of the country they seem to have disappeared and it is believed that they were absorbed into the Choctaw tribes.

MOBILE RIVER, Ala. River formed by the Alamaba and Tombigee Rivers. It flows 45 miles south and enters Mobile Bay. The Mobile is one of Alabama's five major rivers.

MOCOCO INDIANS. Tribe of Muskogean linguistic stock that lived in the area of Hillsboro Bay, Fla. They are noted for befriending a Spaniard, Juan Ortiz, who arrived with the NARVAEZ expedition in 1528. When De Soto arrived in Florida in 1539 the Mococos sent Ortiz, along with a group of warriors, to greet him, and Ortiz acted as De Soto's interpreter. After these early encounters, the Mococos disappear from historical records.

MONACAN INDIANS. Tribe of Siouan linguistic stock that lived near Richmond, Va., on the upper course of the James River. First encountered by Capt. Newport in 1608 their numbers declined rapidly and little is known of them after the mid-1700s.

MONCK'S CORNER, Battle of. Revolutionary War engagement near Charleston, S.C., fought April 14, 1780. In it the British routed a force of Continental cavalry as part of their effort to disperse revolutionaries inland of Charleston during their siege of that city.

The Revolutionary force was commanded by Maj. Isaac Huger. The British force was commanded by Lt. Col. Banastre Tarleton. Provided with information about the Revolutionary force's position by a slave, Tarleton attacked at 3:00 A.M., routed the American cavalry, and captured valuable horses. Losses on both sides numbered approximately 20 killed, but the Americans lost an additional 60 to capture.

The Battle of Monck's Corner caused Huger to lose contact with Charleston, which fell on May 12, and Tarleton continued to secure his control of the area at the battles of Lenud's Ferry and Waxhaw Creek.

MONITOR and MERRIMAC, Battle of. The first encounter between ironclad warships, which occurred during the Civil War on March 9, 1862, at Hampton Roads, Va. The Union *Monitor* was a true ironclad designed by John Ericsson, the inventor of that type of vessel, and launched on January 30, 1862. The *Merrimac* was a converted wooden vessel launched on March 5, 1862, and renamed the *Virginia*, a name that never entered common usage.

The box-like *Merrimac* entered the Hampton Roads channels on March 8, ramming and sinking the Union *Cumberland* and forcing the Union *Congress* to surrender. At dawn on March 9 the Union *Monitor* entered the channels, riding low in the water with only a revolving turret visible above the water line. In several hours of fighting neither vessel managed to significantly damage the other, although the *Monitor* was forced to retire at noon because of a blocked sight aperture.

Encounter between the Confederate *Merrimac* and the Union *Monitor*, March 9, 1862

The *Merrimac* was destroyed by its own crew on May 9 because, being deep draft and unseaworthy, she could not leave the harbor in which she was constructed. The *Monitor* was lost in a gale on December 31, 1862, off Cape Hatteras.

MONOCACY, Battle of. Civil War engagement fought July 9, 1864, on the Monocacy River near Frederick, Md. Although the Confederate attack was disorganized, its superior numbers, twice that of the Union forces, enabled it to win the battle.

On the morning of July 9, Confederate Gen. Jubal EARLY discovered Union forces under Gen. Lew Wallace on the Monocacy River. While Early studied the field Gen. John McCausland charged the enemy with his Confederate cavalry. He was joined in this advance across open fields by the infantry of Confederate Gen. John Gordon. When Gordon paused, his men saw Union forces on their flank, attacked without orders, and routed the enemy. Early chose not to pursue the Union troops because his ranks were in disarray and because he was already holding numerous Union prisoners.

MONOCACY RIVER, Md. Rising in southern Pennsylvania, the river flows into central Maryland to empty into the Potomac River near Frederick, for a distance of approximately 70 miles. The Civil War battle of MONOCACY was fought on the river's banks on July 9, 1864. Union troops were unsuccessful in their bid against Confederate oncomers, but their manuevers were credited with providing Gen. Ulysses S. Grant sufficient time to round up forces to protect Washington, D.C.

MONONGAHELA RIVER, Md. Formed in West Virginia by the confluence of the West Fork and Tygart Rivers, it flows approximately 130 miles northwest through Pennsylvania, to become a tributary of the Ohio River at Pittsburgh. The Monongahela and its branches form the main drainage system of the north central portion of Maryland, and are a major freight transportation route.

MONROE, James. (Westmoreland Co., Va., Apr. 28, 1758 — New York, N.Y., July 4, 1831). U.S. Representative and Senator from Virginia, Minister to France, Secretary of State to James Madison, and 5th President of the United States.

Monroe's father Spence was of Scottish descent and his mother, Eliza Jones, was Welsh. During the Revolutionary War he served in the 3rd Virginia regiment, seeing action at White Plains, N.Y., and being wounded at Trenton, N.J. Following the war he attended William and Mary College in Williamsburg, where he studied law under Thomas Jefferson and became an adherent to his philosophy of government. As U.S. Representative from Virginia from 1783 to 1786, Monroe took a position in opposition to the proposed U.S. Constitution because it lacked a bill of rights, a supplement not introduced and ratified until 1791. In 1786 Monroe took a hiatus from public service and married Elizabeth Kortwright of New York City; they had two daughters and a son who died in infancy.

Monroe returned to public life as U.S. Senator from Virginia between 1790 and 1794, and as Minister to France from 1794 to 1796. He then served as Governor of Virginia from 1799 to 1802 before going to Europe on diplomatic missions and helping to negotiate the Louisiana Purchase from France in 1803. Although he made a token run for the presidency against James Madison in 1808, he remained on congenial terms with that president and became his Secretary of State in 1811.

Monroe was elected president in a landslide in 1816 and re-elected in 1820 with all but one of the electoral college votes, the other being cast in favor of his eventual successor, John Qunicy Adams. His success in office was such that his administration was known as the "Era of Good Feeling." Under Monroe the U.S. obtained Florida from Spain and both regularized its borders and improved its relations with Canada. He also oversaw the Missouri Compromise between the congressional factions of North and South on the slavery issue. Monroe's greatest achievement, however, was the Monroe Doctrine, a cornerstone of American foreign policy still in effect that commits the U.S. to defense of North and South American countries against advances by European countries into their hemisphere.

After retirement Monroe unsuccessfully attempted to salvage his long-neglected personal finances, and he had fallen into a state of virtual bankruptcy by the time of his death.

MONROE, Lake, Fla. Lake on the Seminole-Volusia county line in the east central part of the state. It is a shallow expansion of the St. Johns River, about five miles long and three miles wide.

MONROE, La. City (pop. 57,597), seat of Quachita parish, on the Quachita River 100 miles east of Shreveport. Traders and trappers first settled the area in the early 1700s, calling it Prairie de Canots. In 1791, Fort Miro was constructed as protection against Indians. The town was named in 1819 in honor of the *James Monroe*, the first steamboat to come up the river. Incorporated in 1900, the city is the principal trade center of northeastern Louisiana, dealing in cotton, soybeans, and lumber. Manufactures include paper, furniture, and agricultural chemicals. Monroe is located above one of the largest natural gas fields in the United States, discovered in 1916.

MONTGOMERY, Ala. City (pop. 133,386), state capital and seat of Montgomery Co., on the Alabama River, in the southern part of the state. The area was originally inhabited by prehistoric Indian mound builders. Jean-Baptiste Le Moyne built Fort Toulouse on the river north of the present city in 1715. The present site was founded and incorporated in 1819 through a consolidation of two existing settlements, East Alabama and Philadelphia, and was named for Gen. Richard Montgomery, who was killed in action in the American Revolution.

During the Civil War, the city served as the first capital of the Confederacy but Union troops captured it in the spring of 1865. In the years that followed, Montgomery grew into a major market center for livestock, cotton, yellow pine, and hardwoods, and manufactures today include commercial fertilizer and textiles. The city's growth was encouraged by the establishment of the adjacent Maxwell and Gunther Air Force Bases. Maxwell serves as the headquarters for the Air University system. The capitol, where the state of Alabama voted to secede from the Union on January 11, 1861 and the Confederate State of America was established, has been preserved. Montgomery was nicknamed the "Cradle of the Confederacy" and the first White House of the Confederacy still stands. Alabama's department of archives and history is located here and claims one of the largest collections of Southern historical material.

Montgomery was the scene of considerable civil rights activity in the 1950s and 1960s, largely under the direction of Martin Luther KING, Jr., then a city minister. He led the blacks on an organized boycott of the city bus system in December, 1955, to protest segregation, resulting one year later in a court order prohibiting segregation on buses. King also led a protest march in the city following the slaying of the Rev. James Reels, a Boston minister.

MONTICELLO. Home of President Thomas JEFFERSON in Albermarle Co., Va. Designed and constructed by Jefferson, actual work on the plantation began in 1768 but was not formally completed until 1809 because of extensive remodelings. Jefferson is said to have drawn many of his architectural ideas from classical European structures, such as the Temple of Vesta in Rome and the Hotel Salm in Paris. Preserved by the Thomas Jefferson Memorial Foundation, the house features many of its builder's inventions, including his revolving desk and calendar clock.

MONTPELIER. Home of President James MADISON in Port Conway, Va. Madison spent his boyhood years on the plantation which was operated with a large slave population. After he retired from office, Madison and his wife, Dolly, returned to the plantation where he died on June 28, 1836. Both Madisons are buried there. Madison's father constructed the mansion in the 1760s.

MOONSHINE. The name given to corn whiskey that is not aged to any extent. Also referred to as "white lightning," a name well-merited, it has the clear color and raw taste of pure alcohol. Moonshine dates back to the days when the government first began imposing taxes on whiskey (1791). Distillers and private individuals, seeking to avoid the payment of taxes, set up stills in out of the way places. They usually worked at night to avoid detection; hence the name moonshine. The process, referred to as moonshining, is still common in Tennessee, Kentucky, North Carolina, and other parts of the rural South, and is said to be the preferred drink of some people.

MOORE, Marianne (St. Louis, Mo., Nov. 15, 1887 — New York, N.Y., Feb. 5, 1972). Poet and editor. When her father abandoned the family, Moore moved with her mother to Pennsylvania in 1894. There she graduated from Bryn Mawr College in 1909, studied at Carlisle Commercial College, and taught at the Carlisle Indian School (1911-15). Her first verses were published in 1915 and 1916 in innovative literary journals such as *The Egoist* and *Poetry*. In all of her work she experimented with language that was essentially prose but

Monticello, home of Thomas Jefferson, in Albemarle County, Virginia

broken into complexly patterned verse stanzas. Awarded the Bollingen Prize, the National Book Award, and the Pulitzer prizes for *Collected Poems* (1951), she devoted herself later in life to whimsical projects such as the "Hometown Piece for Messrs. Alston and Reese" of the Brooklyn Dodgers.

MOORE'S CREEK BRIDGE, Battle of. Revolutionary War engagement fought near Wilmington, N.C., on February 27, 1776. A victory for the patriots, it was the first battle of the war in North Carolina. The Revolutionary militia was commanded by Col. James Moore, who chose to tempt the Tories out of the town and upstream on the Cape Fear River. At Moore's Creek Bridge, 18 miles upstream, he built and apparently abandoned earthworks. When the Tories approached the earthworks, thinking Moore still in retreat, they found themselves bombarded by artillery placed just behind the fortification. Tory casualties were approximately 30 killed and wounded, while the patriots lost only two men.

MORE, Paul Elmer (St. Louis, Mo., Dec. 12, 1864 — Princeton, N.J., Mar. 9, 1937). Scholar and literary critic. Educated at Washington University and Harvard, where he became an expert in Sanskrit, he met and befriended Irving Babbitt, and became one of the leading exponents of the conservative New Humanist movement in literary criticism. He served as literary editor for *The Independent* (1901-03), the New York *Evening Post* (1903-09), and as editor of *The Nation* (1909-14). His best known work is *Shelburne Essays* (11 vols., 1904-21).

MOREAU CREEK, Mo. Narrow stream in Central Missouri. Traveling a distance of less than 50 miles, it drains into the Osage River, south of Jefferson City.

MOREHOUSE COLLEGE. Independent men's college located on a 25-acre campus in Atlanta, Ga. Established in 1867, the college is administered by the Baptist Church and is affiliated with the Atlanta University Center. The college was founded as a school for blacks, and its student population remains 100% black today. Morehouse is perhaps most famous for a notable alumnus, the Rev. Martin Luther KING, Jr.

Morehouse offers a liberal arts education and the majority of students concentrate their studies in the areas of business administration/commerce/management, economics, or biology/biological sciences. The college has a national student body: 50% of students are from the South, 16% are from North Central states, and 22% are from the Middle Atlantic region; 50% of graduates go on to further study.

Library: 300,000 volumes, 350 journal subscriptions, 800 records/tapes. Faculty: 141. Enrollment: 1,951 men (full-time). Degrees: Bachelor's.

MORGAN, Daniel (Hunterdon Co,, N.J., 1736 — Winchester, Va., July 6, 1802). Military officer and politician. He served with colonial forces during the French and Indian War, and at the outbreak of the Revolution was commissioned captain of a group of Virginia riflemen (1775). He accompanied Benedict Arnold on his attack on Quebec but was captured with his command after entering the well-fortified city. Released in 1776, he fought in the two Battles of Saratoga, and resigned from the army in 1779. He was recalled in 1780, was a commissioned brigadier general, and was victorious at the battle of Cowpens (January 17, 1781). From 1797 to 1799 he represented Virginia in the U.S. Congress.

MORGAN, George (Philadelphia, Pa., Feb. 14, 1743 — near Washington, Pa., Mar. 10, 1810). Indian agent and land speculator. A founder of the Indiana Company (1776) which claimed an area of nearly 3,000 square miles in what is now West Virginia, the land claim was later granted to the state of Virginia. An Indian agent during the Revolutionary War, Morgan was later instrumental in the founding (1789) of New Madrid (now in Missouri) as a result of controversial negotiations with the Spanish minister to the United States.

MORGAN, John Hunt (Huntsville, Ala., June 1, 1825 — Greeneville, Tenn., Sept. 4, 1864). Military officer. Having served as an officer in the Mexican War, when Kentucky left the Union Morgan took charge of a Confederate cavalry squadron and developed techniques of swift movement, disruption of enemy supply lines and communications, and flexible methods of attack, which were unique in his era. As a brigadier general he made an unauthorized raid into Indiana and Ohio, the most northerly penetration by the South during the Civil War.

During the raid (1863), most of his 2,000 men surrendered, and he was captured. Considered a dangerous prisoner, he was placed in a state rather than a military penitentiary. However, Morgan escaped and, in command of the Department of Southwestern Virginia (1864), resumed his raids. While under investigation for his famous unauthorized raid and loss of troops, Morgan led a last forage into Tennessee and was killed.

MORGAN CITY, La. City (pop. 16,114), St. Mary's Parish, southern Louisiana, 70 miles west of New Orleans. Called the "Gateway to the Tidelands," Morgan City was settled in 1850 and is one of the state's principal fishing ports and serves as a center for shrimp, gas, and oil industries. A Shrimp Festival is celebrated each September with the blessing of the shrimp fleet. There is also extensive truck farming and timbering.

MORGANTON, N.C. City (pop. 13,763), seat of Burke Co., in western North Carolina, on the Catawba River. Founded in 1784, today it is a lake resort and heavy industrial area. Manfactures include electrodes, furniture, hosiery, lingeries, shoes, and textiles.

MORGANTOWN, W.Va. City (pop. 27,605), seat of Monongalia Co., in north central West Virginia, on the Monongahela River approximately sixty miles south of Pittsburgh, Pa. The first settlement here was destroyed by Indians in 1758. The town was resettled in 1767 and incorporated in 1785. Present industries include coal and limestone mining, and the manufacture of textiles, glass, and chemicals. The city is the home of West Virginia University.

MORPHY, Paul Charles (New Orleans, La., June 22, 1837 — New Orleans, La., July 10, 1884). Master chess player. Learning the game at age 10, he was considered the world's greatest player by age 21. His memory was such that he could play simultaneous games blindfolded and he was a master of the open game. After a tour of Europe where he claimed the unofficial world chess championship, he returned to New Orleans in 1859 and his mental instability ended his career.

MORRISTOWN, Tenn. City (pop. 19,683), seat of Hamblen Co., in northeast Tennessee. Settled in 1783 and incorporated in 1855, the town was once a major tobacco producer. Today there is diversified farming and manufactures include furniture, textiles, and beverages. Morristown College, a two-year Methodist affiliated school, was established here in 1887.

MORTON, Jelly Roll [Ferdinand Joseph La Menthe] (New Orleans, La., Sept. 20, 1885 — Los Angeles, Cal., July 11, 1941). Jelly Roll Morton is regarded by many as the greatest modern jazz pianist. His compositions and arrangements, many of which reflect his Creole background, include "Dead Man Blues," "Moi pas l'aimez ca," "Jelly Roll Blues," and "Mama Nita." Most of his career was centered in New Orleans, La.

MOSBY, John Singleton (Edgemont, Va., Dec. 6, 1833 — Washington, D.C., May 30, 1916). Lawyer and military officer. Mosby practiced law after his graduation from the University of Virginia. When the Civil War broke out he enlisted in the cavalry and in 1863 began his famous ranger activities in Virginia. As the war progressed, Mosby received numerous promotions and eventually built his force of Mosby's Rangers into eight companies of highly trained, well-equipped men. Mosby's raids were so successful that northern Virginia became known as Mosby's Confederacy, and he continued to operate successfully until the war's end. Mosby returned to his law practice, and in later years, he was appointed consul to Hong Kong (1878-85) by President Ulysses S. Grant. From 1904 to 1910 he served the Department of Justice as assistant attorney.

MOSQUITO LAGOON, Fla. Lagoon along the coast of Volusia and Brevard Counties, off Florida's eastern seaboard. About two miles wide and 17 miles long, it is separated from the Atlantic Ocean by a narrow barrier island. To the north it connects with the Hillsborough River Lagoon; to the south, with the Indian River.

MOSS POINT, Miss. City (pop. 18,998), Jackson Co., in southern Mississippi on the Gulf of Mexico coast. It was settled in the early 1800s and quickly became a lumber empire. By 1900 it was recognized as the largest pine lumber export center in the U.S. Today the predominant source of employment is the International Paper Company. Moss Point was incorporated in 1901, and was the first and only community in Mississippi to be incorporated as

a city before first being incorporated as a town. At the time of its incorporation the population was 3,000.

MOULTRIE, Ga. City (pop. 15,708), seat of Colquitt Co., in southern Georgia, on the Ochlockonee River. Incorporated in 1890, it developed as a lumbering and naval stores market. Later, when lumber supplies began to dwindle, the community turned to livestock and diversified farming. Present manufactures include mobile homes, fertilizer, and aircraft.

MOULTRIE, Lake, S.C. Large man-made reservoir in Berkeley Co., in the south central part of the state, near Lake Marion. It was formed by the constuction of the Pinapolis Dam in 1941.

MOULTRIE, William (Charleston, S.C., Dec. 4, 1730 — Charleston, S.C., Sept. 27, 1805). Military officer and politician. He was a member of the South Carolina Assembly (1752-71) before joining the Continental Army at the outbreak of the Revolution. He held a makeshift fort of sand and palmetto on Sullivan's Island outside of Charleston against heavy British attack (1776), pushed the English out of Beaufort, S.C., and was captured at the fall of Charleston (1780). He was released in 1782 and served in a limited capacity until the end of the war as a major general. He was governor of South Carolina (1785-87, 1794-96), and the author of *Memoirs of the American Revolution* (2 vols., 1802).

MOUNDSVILLE, W.Va. City (pop. 12,419), seat of Marshall Co., on the Ohio River in the northern panhandle. The city was so named because one of the largest prehistoric Indian burial mounds was discovered here. Located in a resort area, oil, gas, and coal are the major industries.

MOUNT PLEASANT, S.C. City (pop. 13,338), Charleston Co., central South Carolina, on the Atlantic Ocean. The city has developed as a residential suburb of Charleston. Fort Sumter is nearby. The town was incorporated in 1837.

MOUNT STERLING, Ky. City (pop. 5,820), seat of Montgomery Co., in east central Kentucky. An agricultural trade center in the bluegrass region, settled about 1793. Present manufactures include electric motors, clothing, and concrete products. There are dairy cattle, poultry, and tobacco farms in the area. During the Civil War, it was captured by Confederate Gen. John H. Morgan.

MOUNT VERNON. Home of President George Washington, located a few miles south of Alexandria, Va. It was built in 1743 by Lawrence Washington, half-brother of George Washington, and named for Admiral Edward Vernon, a British naval officer and friend of Lawrence. George Washington came into possession of the plantation in 1752. In 1858 the estate was purchased by the Mount Vernon Ladies Association to preserve the home and tomb of Washington. A two-story Georgian colonial, it is copiously furnished with Washington's belongings and is one of the state's major tourist attractions. It was Washington's home from 1747 until his death in 1799.

MUDD, Samuel (Charles Co., Md., 1833 — Maryland, 1883). Physician. He set the leg of John Wilkes BOOTH after the actor shot President Abraham Lincoln (April 15, 1865). He was imprisoned for life for conspiracy despite his protestation of innocence. President Andrew Johnson pardoned Mudd in 1869 after he saved the lives of many guards and prisoners during a yellow fever epidemic in the prison.

MUHAMMAD, Elijah (Elijah Poole) (Sandersville, Ga., Oct. 10, 1897 — Chicago, Ill., Feb. 25, 1975). Black Muslim leader. One of 13 children of an itinerant Baptist minister, his education was stopped at the fifth grade. Moving to Detroit with his family to find work (1923), he experienced unemployment and welfare (1929-31) at first hand and developed a bitter hostility to public assistance that was later reflected in Muslim policies. In 1931 Poole met Wali Farad, founder of the Nation of Islam, who named him Muhammad. Upon Farad's disappearance in 1934, Muhammad was named "Messenger of Allah," and, under his leadership, the Muslims began a period of slow growth which accelerated enormously after World War II and, since his death, has been continued by his son, Wallace.

MULBERRY RIVER, Ark. River originating in north central Arkansas. It flows east and south for approximately 50 miles though the sparsely populated areas of Franklin County.

MULLAN, John (Norfolk, Va., July 31, 1830 — Washington, D.C., Dec. 28, 1909). Military officer and explorer. A graduate of both Annapolis and West Point, Mullan was instrumental in laying out a railroad route from St. Paul, Minn., to the Pacific, and a military road from Missouri to Washington.

MURFREE, Mary Noilles (Murfreesboro, Tenn., Jan. 24, 1850 — Murfreesboro, Tenn., July 31, 1922). Author. Her work appeared under the male pseudonym Charles Egbert Craddock. The *Atlantic Monthly* first published her stories in 1878, and *In the Tennessee Mountains*, a collection of short stories, was published in 1884. Her style utilized vivid scenic description, and her plots revolved around simple mountain people. Her many works include *Where the Battle was Fought* (1884).

MURFREESBORO, Ark. Town (pop. 1,883), seat of Pike Co., southwestern Arkansas, near the Little Missouri River. A residential community, it is located in a farming belt. Minerals such as mercury and cinnabar are found in the area and a defunct diamond mine where tourists may search for diamonds is nearby.

MURFREESBORO, Battle of. See STONES RIVER, Battle of.

MURFREESBORO, Tenn. City (pop. 32,845), seat of Rutherford Co., in central Tennessee. Located on the Stones River. It was settled in 1766, and it served as the state capital from 1819 to 1825. The area is noted for purebred Jersey cattle, and its factories produce silk and rayon goods, cheese, flour, and lumber. Diversified farming includes corn, cotton, and wheat. Middle Tennessee State University was established here in 1911, and Stones National Battlefield is nearby.

MURFREESBORO DIAMOND FIELD, Ark. Actually a crater within the city, precious gems have been found here in the past. A small diamond plant operated here from 1908 to 1925 but few of the stones found were of significant value. Today tourists are allowed to search within the crater for diamonds.

MURPHEY, Archibald De Bow (Caswell Co., N.C., c. 1777 — North Carolina, Feb. 1, 1832). Jurist. After graduating from the University of North Carolina (1799), he was admitted to the bar (1802). He served as state senator (1812-18) before his appointment to the North Carolina Superior Court (1818-20). He was noted as an advocate of public schools and of the abolishment of debtors' prisons.

MURRAY, Lake, S.C. Hydroelectric power source and recreation area that is located in several counties in central South Carolina. The building of the Saluda Dam on the Saluda River created this 41-mile-long lake that has a 520-mile shoreline.

MURROW, Edward Roscoe (Greensboro, N.C., Apr. 25, 1908 — Pawling, N.Y., Apr. 27, 1965). Newscaster. As European news director for CBS (1937-39) he trained and organized their European staff in preparation for World War II. As a war correspondent himself, Murrow developed a reputation for his powerful reportage from London of the Battle of Britain. He was director of the U.S. Information Agency (1961-64), and originated and produced the television shows *See It Now* and *Person to Person* (1947-61).

MUSCLE SHOALS, Ala. Town (pop. 8,911), Colbert Co., in northwestern Alabama. Located on the Tennessee River where the river descended into a series of rapids more than 35 miles long, with a 130-foot drop, the river was unnavigable until a canal was completed in 1890. The construction of the Wilson Dam (1925) and the Wheeler Dam (1936) caused the shoals to submerge. The Tennessee Valley Authority purchased land here in 1933 and made the town the center of its experimental development of phosphate and nitrate fertilizers and animal foods.

MUSKOGEE INDIANS. A main tribe of the CREEK Confederacy, they were of Muskogean linguistic stock (to which they gave their name), and originally lived in an area extending from the Atlantic coast of Georgia into central Alabama. An aggressive people, they played a greater part in the colonial history of the Gulf region than any other Indian tribe. First encountered by De Soto (1540), their numbers rapidly increased as they took in tribes that had been displaced by the settlers. Allied to the English for a time, they assisted them in destroying tribes in Florida, only to find the area so desirable that they established themselves there. They were involved in both the CREEK WAR and the SEMINOLE WARS before finally moving to the INDIAN TERRITORY in Oklahoma between 1836 and 1840.

MYAKKA RIVER, Fla. River originating in Manatee County. It flows southwest draining swamp waters through Sarasota County, where it shifts to a southeasterly course to enter Charlotte County. It then becomes an estuary for ten miles emptying into Charlotte Harbor about seven miles west of Punta Gorda.

MYRTLE BEACH, S.C. Town (pop 18,758) Horry Co., on the state's northern Atlantic coastline. Lush with the shrub growth for which it is named, the town is notable for the beaches and climate that have made it a year-round resort. There are commercial fisheries and factories that produce electronic components. Myrtle Beach State Park and a major U.S. Air Force installation are located here.

N

NACOGDOCHES, Tex. Town (pop. 27,149), seat of Nacogdoches Co., in east central Texas. Settled in 1716, and named for the Indians who originally inhabited the area, Nacogdoches was the location of the first Texas newspaper, the *Gaceta de Tejas*, started in May, 1813. Manufactures today include valves, feed, fertilizers, and aluminum furniture. Stephen F. Austin State University is located here.

NAHYSSAN INDIANS. Tribe of Siouan linguistic stock that lived in Nelson Co., Virginia, on the James River. First encountered in 1650, they suffered defeat at the hands of the SUSQUEHANNA INDIANS but rallied in turn to defeat a group of colonists who had been joined by the POWHATTAN INDIANS. At the beginning of the 18th century they joined the SAPONI and TUTELO tribes and moved into North Carolina.

NAMOZINE CREEK, Va. Tributary of the Appomattox River. It is the boundary of Amelia, Nottoway, and Dinwiddie Counties. The river was named for the Numisdsiem Indians.

NANTICOKE INDIANS ("tidewater people"). Tribe of Algonquin linguistic stock that lived on the peninsula between the Chesapeake and Delaware Bays. At war with the Maryland colonists for many years, in the early 1700s they left their domain and under the protection of the IROQUOIS INDIANS they moved north.

NANTICOKE RIVER, Md. Waterway originating in southwestern Delaware. It flows southwest approximately 45 miles, through anthracite coal mining territory, to join the Wicomico River. From there the river travels to Tangier Sound and then on to the CHESAPEAKE BAY. Nanticoke River is one of the seven primary rivers crossing the Eastern Shore area of Maryland and Virginia.

NAPLES, Fla. Town (pop. 17,581), seat of Gollier Co., in southwestern Florida. This popular resort community, noted for its beach along the Gulf Coast, was one of the first established winter resorts in the state. It is also a banking and finance center with some agriculture.

NAPOCHI INDIANS ("those who see" or "those who look out"). Tribe of Muskogean linguistic stock that lived in Alabama along Black Warrior River. First encountered by Don Triston de LUNA in 1559, their fate is unknown but

295

they are thought to have joined with the CHICK-
ASAW INDIANS.

NARROWS DAM, Ark. Hydroelectric
power dam constructed in the Ouachita National Forest, which created Lake Greeson,
near Glenwood. The dam measures 941 feet
long by 190 feet high and was built by the U.S.
Army Corps of Engineers.

NARVAEZ, Panfilo de (Valladolid, Spain, c.
1470 — Gulf of Mexico, Nov., 1528). Spanish
explorer. One of the first conquistadores, he
was sent to Florida by Charles V to establish a
settlement and search for gold. Narvaez landed
near Tampa Bay (April, 1528) with 400 men.
They marched north, harassed by Indians,
reaching the village of Apalachee, near present-
day Tallahassee. Unsuccessful in their quest for
gold, short of food, and driven back by the Indians, they fought their way to Apalachee Bay.
Their ranks now reduced to 250 men, they built
five crude boats and set out for Mexico (September, 1528). Navaez and most of his men
were lost in a severe storm off the Texas coast.

NASHOBA, Tenn. Experimental community in southwestern Tennessee, on the Wolf
River, near Memphis. Frances Wright, a Scottish reformer and abolitionist, established the
plantation with a group of her followers in
1825. They purchased slaves and brought them
here to be educated and prepared for freedom.
The venture failed when area residents called
the community degenerate and a center for free
love. By 1829, Wright abandoned the project
and arranged for the slaves, which never numbered more than 15, to be shipped to Haiti.

NASHVILLE, Battle of. Civil War engagement fought December 15-16, 1864, on the
southern outskirts of the capital of Tennessee.
A decisive victory for the Union under Gen.
George H. Thomas, it ended Confederate Gen.
John Bell Hood's attempt to invade Tennessee,
and delivered the Confederacy a second blow as
Gen. William Sherman was crossing Georgia in
his "MARCH TO THE SEA.
　　Hood had pursued the Union force of Gen.
John M. Schofield north through Tennessee,
but at the battle of Franklin he had failed to
prevent its retreat toward reinforcement in
Nashville. Both sides hoped for supplies and
reinforcements at Nashville, and the battle for
the city was delayed two weeks. The Union
benefitted from the pause, chiefly in the form of

horses for its cavalry, while the Confederate
side did not. The battle commenced on December 15 in cold weather, and on the first day the
Confederates were driven south from their position near the city. On the second day the
Confederate line, withdrawing in upon itself,
gallantly defended Shy's Hill and Overton Hill
until 4:00 PM, when it succumbed to a combination of artillery fire and cavalry charges.
　　Hood started his retreat from Tennessee on
the night of December 16, and he thwarted
Union pursuit by destroying bridges behind
him. When he reached Tupelo, Miss., on January 10, 1865, Hood voluntarily resigned his
command.

NASHVILLE, Tenn. City (pop. 448,003),
state capital and seat of Davidson Co., in north
central Tennessee on the Cumberland River.
Founded in 1779 and incorporated in 1806, it is
the center of a metropolitan area that includes
Davidson, Sumner, and Wilson Counties. The
present economy is a mix of commerce, industry, and entertainment businesses. The city
serves as headquarters for many large finanace
and insurance companies. Manufactured products include auto glass, clothing, heating and
cooking equipment, shoes, and tires. The city is
best known, however, as the country-western
music capital of the world, with a large music
recording industry, the famous GRAND OLE
OPRY and the Country Music Hall of Fame and
Museum. Several religious denominations have
educational publishing houses in the city including the largest of its kind, the United Methodist Publishing House. The city is the home of
of six religious educational institutions, along
with the Tennessee Agricultural and Industrial
State University, Vanderbilt University, Fisk
University, Meharry Medical College, and the
George Peabody College for Teachers.
　　Nashville was founded in 1779 as Fort Nashborough, and renamed in 1784 for the Revolutionary War hero Francis Nash who was killed
in the Battle of Germantown. A replica of the
original fort now stands on a bluff above the
river. Richard Henderson was one of the city's
leading settlers. A North Carolina jurist, he acquired most of middle Tennessee and Kentucky
in the Transylvania Purchase of 1775 from the
Cherokee Indians. The city developed as a river
trade depot and as the state's political center. It
was made the permanent state capital in 1843.
The arrival of rail transportation in the 1850s
hastened the city's development. Nashville was
taken by Union troops in February, 1862, and
occupied for the remainder of the Civil War.

The last major battle of the war was fought just outside the city in December, 1864, when Union Gen. George H. Thomas and his troops defeated the Confederate forces led by Gen. John Hood.

In the 1930s the city's industries flourished with the availability of cheap electrical power from the TENNESSEE VALLEY AUTHORITY dams along the Cumberland River. A full-scale replica of the Parthenon, built in 1897 to commemmorate Tennessee's statehood still stands in Centennial Park on the state's centennial exposition grounds. The state capitol was designed by architect William Strickland, and President James Polk is buried on the grounds. The Hermitage, President Andrew Jackson's home, is located 12 miles east of Nashville.

NATCHEZ, Miss. City (pop. 23,791), seat of Adams Co. on the Mississippi River, in the southwest part of the state. Settled in 1716, the city was named for the Natchez Indians, whose massacre of the French in 1729 is considered one of the bloodiest in American history. Natchez was taken by the British in 1763 and became a haven for Loyalists during the Revolution. Taken by Spain in 1779, it did not come into U.S. possession until 1798. This southern terminus of the NATCHEZ TRACE was the largest and richest city in the state prior to the Civil War. Natchez still possesses a rich legacy of antebellum culture, and has been the setting for many films and novels about the South. Today Natchez is one of Mississippi's leading cities, with large oil, natural gas, and textile industries.

NATCHEZ INDIANS. Tribe thought to have been of Muskogean linguistic stock that lived in the area of Natchez, Miss. (to which they gave their name). They were known to De Soto as early as 1541, and later encountered by de LUNA (1560) when he aided other Gulf tribes in a war against them. Their sun-worship, mound-building, and language seem to indicate a relationship with Indians of the Yucatan. A brave, wild and desolute tribe, their chief, whose power was despotic, was called the Great Sun. They kept a perpetual fire in a temple built on a mound, and when a member of the tribe died, it was their custom to destroy his relatives so that he would have company on his way to the spirit world. In 1729, after a period of general friendliness with the settlers, they destroyed the French Fort Rosalie. The following year the French and a group of CHOCTAW INDIAN allies nearly annihilated the Natchez. The survivors split into two groups, one merging with the Upper CREEK INDIANS, the other joining the CHEROKEE INDIANS.

NATCHEZ TRACE, Miss. Route extending from Natchez, Miss., to Nashville, Tenn. Indians first developed the road, but it did not grow into commercial and military importance until the late 18th century. Boatmen once floated their goods down the Mississippi River to markets in Natchez and New Orleans, La., then traveled home along the Trace on foot. In 1800 the Trace was made into a post road. During the War of 1812, Andrew Jackson marched the Trace to New Orleans and traversed it again during his Indian campaigns. The Trace was largely abandoned after the 1840s with the advent of the steamboat. In 1934 a 26,803-acre parkway was established to memorialize the Trace's former importance. Today a 447-mile long road is planned by the National Park Service to follow the Trace. About 350 miles of it have been completed.

NATCHITOCHES, La. City (pop, 16,664), seat of Natchitoches Parish, in northwest Louisiana. The oldest permanent settlement in the state, it was founded as a French military and trading post in 1715. Today it is an industrial community which offers educational and cultural centers, including Northwestern State University and the Grand Ecore Amphitheatre. Manufactures include lumber, cottonseed oil, mobile homes, and bricks. It is also the home of the Louisiana Sports Hall of Fame. Fort St. Jean Baptiste State Commemorative Area has a replica of the 1732 fort from which the French battled back Spanish invaders.

NATCHITOCHES CONFEDERACY. Group of Indian tribes of Caddoan linguistic stock that lived in northwest Louisiana. They gave their name to the oldest permanent settlement in the state. First encountered by BIENVILLE in 1700, two years later, as the result of a crop failure, they moved to a French fort commanded by Juchereau DE ST. DENIS. St. Denis befriended them and they in turn helped him to win victory over the NATCHEZ Indians. In later years they ceded their lands to French Creoles.

NATION, Carry Amelia (Garrard Co., Ky., Nov. 25, 1846 — Leavenworth, Kan., June 9, 1911). Temperance advocate. After earning a teaching certificate, she married Charles Gloyd, an alcoholic physician, in 1867. Following his death she married David Nation, a lawyer, journalist, and minister. Nation became involved in the temperance movement in 1890, after a U.S. Supreme Court decision weakened the alcohol prohibition laws in Kansas. She became well known for dressing primarily in black and white clothing, and carrying a hatchet. Nation would march into a saloon, first singing and praying, and then smashing the stock and fixtures with her hatchet. Her reform concerns also extended to art, clothing, fraternal orders, and tobacco, and her actions led to her frequent arrest but her earnings from her lectures paid her fines. Her husband disapproved of her extreme reform views, and divorced her in 1901 on charges of desertion.

NATURAL BRIDGE, Va. Village in western Virginia in the Shenandoah valley. It is famous for Natural Bridge, a 215-foot-high limestone arch, that spans a 90-foot gorge cut by Cedar Creek. It was once owned by Thomas Jefferson who sold the bridge and 157 acres of land in 1775 for 20 shillings.

NATURAL GAS. Fuel resource found in large quantities in the Southern states. A naturally inflammable mixture of gases, chiefly methane, it differs in composition from artificially produced fuel gases.

Texas and Louisiana produce 70% of the U.S. supply of natural gas. In 1980 Texas produced 7,169 billion cubic feet and Louisiana produced 6,937 billion cubic feet; by contrast, Wyoming, the third-ranking state, produced only 382 billion cubic feet.

The other important producers of natural gas in the south, ranked by yield, are: Mississippi (165 bil. cu. ft.), West Virginia (152 billion cubic feet), Arkansas (112 billion cubic feet), and Alabama (106 billion cubic feet).

NAVASOTA RIVER, Tex. River rising north of Grossbeck in central Texas. It flows approximately 90 miles to drain into the Brazos River at Navasota.

NEBO, Mount, Ark. Peak in Logan Co., in north central Arkansas. Part of a 3,403-acre state park, Mount Nebo (1,800 feet) was named for the peak from which Moses saw the Promised Land. In the 1870s apple orchards were planted on the flat top of the mountain.

NEGRO MOUNTAIN, Md. Peak (2,908 feet), in Garrett Co., in extreme northwest

Maryland and extending into southern Pennsylvania. The Allegheny range is just to the south.

NELSON, Thomas (Yorktown, Va., Dec. 26, 1738 — Hanover Co., Va., Jan. 4, 1789). Politician. As a member of the Continental Congress from Virginia (1775-77), Nelson was a signer of the Declaration of Independence. He was governor of Virginia from 1781 to 1782 and was a commander of the Virginia militia during the Revolutionary War. Nelson used his personal wealth to acquire equipment and supplies for Virginia troops and he put up the security for a state loan. Because of his patriotic generosity, he died a pauper.

NEW BERN, N.C. City (pop. 15,717), seat of Craven Co., on the eastern coast of the state at the point where the Neuse and Trent Rivers join and empty into Pamlico Sound. Settled in 1710, New Bern was the state capital until 1794, and the site of the first provincial convention in 1774. The old governor's house (1767), recently opened to visitors, was restored in 1959. North Carolina's first printing press was started here in 1749, and its first public school opened in 1764. New Bern maintains several old buildings: the Stanly House (1780), now a library; Attmore House (1790); the Presbyterian Church (1822); and Christ Church (1752). The present economy is based on tourism, tobacco, and wood products, and the manufacture of textiles and chemical products.

NEW BRAUNFELS, Tex. Town (pop. 22,402), seat of Comal Co, located on the Comal and Guadalupe Rivers in southeast Texas. Settled in 1845 by Prince Carl of Solms-Braunfels from Germany, the town's industries today include textiles, furniture, metal products, and tourism. There is also diversified farming and cattle-raising.

NEW IBERIA, La. City (pop. 32,766), seat of Iberia Parish, on the banks of the Bayou Teche, in southern Louisiana. The city was settled in the 1770s, incorporated as Iberia in 1839, and as New Iberia in 1868. It is known for the famous tabasco sauce which is distilled here. Situated in a rice, sugar cane, and oil-producing region, industries include saw mills, fur trapping, and commercial fisheries. The Dulcity Plantation served as a hospital during the Civil War. Nearby Iberia Experimental Station specializes in the breeding of foreign cattle.

NEW MARKET, Battle of. Civil War engagement fought May 15, 1864, in the Shenandoah Valley of northern Virginia. The Union and Confederate forces were virtually equal in strength, and the South emerged victorious.

The Union cavalry in the region was under the command of Gen. Franz Sigel. The Confederate forces attempting to delay his advance through the valley were under the command of Gen. J. C. BRECKINRIDGE, and included about 250 Virginia Military Institute cadets. Breckinridge attacked first, early on the morning of May 15. By noon the Union troops were falling back, and by 4:00 P.M. they were in a general retreat, hampered by rain, toward Strasburg. Sigel was relieved of his Union command on May 19 because of the defeat.

NEW ORLEANS, Battle of. Victory for the American side at the end of the War of 1812, fought January 8, 1815. The battle occurred two weeks after the official end of the war with the Treaty of Ghent, but it nevertheless boosted American morale and insured the fame of Andrew Jackson, the victorious commander.

Late in the War of 1812, the British launched a campaign to take New Orleans in hopes of controlling the Mississippi basin and isolating the southwest United States. A veteran British force under Gen. Edward Pakenham was dispatched to New Orleans for this purpose late in 1815. It encountered a breastworks fortification just downstream from the city at Chalmette manned by Jackson, and a disorganized force of Louisiana Creoles and militiamen from Kentucky and Tennessee. The Americans repelled a direct assault by the British on January 8, 1815. The British withdrew, but the American populace, not knowing of the Treaty of Ghent, exaggerated accounts of the battle to suggest a decisive, war-ending victory for Jackson against considerable odds.

NEW ORLEANS, La. City (pop. 557,482), seat of Orleans Parish, in southern Louisiana, about 110 miles north of the mouth of the Mississippi River. One of the world's most important cultural, industrial, trade, and tourist cities, New Orleans is located on a crescent-shaped bend of the Mississippi River, and has been called the Crescent City. It borders Lake Pontchartrain on the north. The second-largest port in the nation and the third-largest in the world, New Orleans' geographical location has made it a world trade center. Most of the city's economic life is connected in one way or another to the Port of New Orleans that has over 50 miles of water frontage and handles over 100 steamship lines. Manufacturing is also important to the city, including the production of processed food, space rocket boosters, lumber, paper boxes, oilfield supplies and equipment, coffee, medicines, chemicals, and paint. There are extensive commercial fisheries that handle the seafood caught in the nearby Gulf of Mexico. Neighboring farm communities produce strawberries, dairy products, cotton, pecans, and many vegetables. In the vicinity of New Orleans are such natural resources as petroleum, lime shell, natural gas, sulfur, salt, and timber. The city is a communications center with over 25 radio stations, five television stations, and a daily newspaper, the *Times-Picayune*, which was established in 1880. In addition to ship and barge lines, transportation facilities include major highways, seven rail lines, and three airports, including the New Orleans International Airport.

The history of New Orleans is long and colorful. Jean Baptiste le Moyne founded the city in 1718 and named it after Philippe II, Duke of Orleans. The city remained in French hands until the Treaty of Fontainbleau in 1762 when the Spanish took over. Control passed back to the French briefly in 1803 but that same year saw the city sold to the United States, along with the rest of the Louisiana Territory. The ways of the incoming Americans clashed noticeably with the native CREOLES who resented being placed under American rule. The British invaded the city in 1814, during the waning hours of the War of 1812, but they were defeated by the army of Gen. Andrew Jackson (January, 1815). After the war the city grew steadily, becoming a world famous trade center as well as a popular lure to tourists who poured into the city from all over the world. Steamboats, river gamblers, and horse racing were an integral part of the city's social life. But the gaiety of the city was dampened during the Civil War when it was occupied by the Union army. Commercial growth returned at the turn of the century when the waters of the port were dredged and levees were constructed to drain away the water that constantly seeped into New Orleans from the river and Lake Pontchartrain. The city is only one foot above the mean level of the Gulf of Mexico and actually below the highwater levels of both Lake Pontchartrain and the Mississippi River.

Points of interest in New Orleans include the French Quarter, the oldest section of the city, which features examples of French and Spanish architecture as well as a wealth of jazz clubs.

The city is known for its Dixieland jazz, and New Orleans is the birthplace of such jazz greats as Jelly Roll MORTON and Louis ARMSTRONG, among others. The Garden District contains houses constructed in the neoclassic style of the antebellum South, and feature exquisite gardens which are world famous. The city has many museums, including the Confederate Museum, the New Orleans Jazz Museum, and the New Orleans Museum of Art.

New Orleans is home to the New Orleans Saints professional football team, and the New Orleans Jazz professional basketball team. The New Orleans Golf Open is held here, and the New Orleans Yacht Club is the second-oldest in the country.

Tulane University, Dillard University, Our Lady of Holy Cross College, Loyola University, St. Mary's Dominican College, Louisiana State University in New Orleans, and New Orleans Baptist Theological Seminary are located in the city.

NEW ORLEANS, Surrender of. Civil War capture of the strategically important but poorly defended city at the mouth of the Mississippi by Union gunboats under Admiral David G. Farragut on April 25, 1862. The sole river defenses of the city were Forts Jackson and St. Philip, both approximately 90 miles downstream, and the Confederate troops in the city were prepared only for land attack. After bombarding the forts for a week, Farragut moved upriver past them on April 24 without losing a vessel. The Confederate troops had withdrawn from the city by that time, and Farragut took the undefended city on April 25 and accepted the surrender of its civil authorities on April 29. Once they were cut off from escape upriver, the Confederate forces in Forts Jackson and St. Philip mutinied, resulting in the surrender of the forts on April 28. The events in New Orleans were the subject of a Confederate court of inquiry in 1863. It placed blame for the surrender on the defense facilities rather than on the troops involved.

NEW RIVER, N.C. River rising in western North Carolina. It flows northward through southwestern Virginia before it joins the Gauley River in West Virginia and becomes the Kanawha. A flood control dam (Bluestone) was constructed on New River in 1952 near Hinton, W.Va. Originally called Wood's River for an early explorer, the name was changed to New River in 1750 after a man by the name of New who kept a ferry on the river.

NEW RIVER, S.C. Waterway formed by the tides of the Calibogue Sound and Tygee Rivers running together. The Walls Cut connects the New River with the Wright River. Traveling approximately 50 miles south, it drains into the Atlantic Ocean at a point on the Intracoastal Waterway.

NEW SMYRNA BEACH, Fla. City (pop. 13,557), Volusia Co., in northeast Florida, at the south end of the Halifax River. First settled by the Spanish in 1696, it was the scene of the murders of a priest and two Indian converts by the Jororo Indians when they were denied the right to practice certain tribal customs. Scottish physician Andrew Turnbull brought 1,500 Spanish, Greek, and Italian colonists here in 1767. The community did not prosper until after the coming of the Florida Eastcoast Railroad when it developed into a resort, supplemented by fishing and citrus fruit packing industries. The city was incorporated in 1903.

NEWPORT, Ky. City (pop. 30,070), seat of Campbell Co., located in the northern corner of the state across the Ohio River from Cincinnati, Ohio. Settled in 1790 and incorporated in 1795, it was named for Christopher Newport, commander of the first ship to reach Jamestown. The city's greatest growth was in the 1880s and 1890s, when it attracted a large number of German immigrants. The construction of several bridges to Cincinnati opened Newport as a suburb of that city. In the 1850s William Bailey edited the only anti-slavery newspaper in the state, but by 1859 he was forced to move to Cincinnati.

NEWPORT NEWS, Va. Independent city (pop. 144,903), located at the mouth of the James River in southeastern Virginia. The city was settled in 1621 and incorporated as a city in 1896. The excellent natural harbor, numerous dry docks, railroads, and shipbuilding facilities, have made Newport News a major Southern port and manufacturing center. Local industries include shipbuilding, textiles, electronics, paper, metal fixtures, mattresses, and building accessories. Settled in 1621 by Daniel Gookin and fifty Irish colonists, the origin of the city's name has long been in dispute. During the Civil War, Union forces established prisons and army camps here. It was the site of the famous battle between the ironclads MONITOR AND MERRIMAC in 1862. After the war, trade, manufacturing, and shipbuilding began in earnest, and Newport News was a major debarkation point

Launching of the carrier *John F. Kennedy* at Newport News Shipbuilding and Dry Dock Company

for troops and supplies during both World Wars. In 1958 the city merged with the city of Warwick and increased in size from four to 64 square miles. Points of interest include the Mariner's Museum and the James River Golf Museum.

NEWSPAPERS. The development of newspapers in the South lagged behind that of New York City and New England for two reasons. The first was the stern censorship exercised by the colonial authorities of the Atlantic states in the region. "Thank God" wrote Virginia Governor Sir William Berkeley in 1671, "we have neither free school nor printing press, and I hope we may not have for a hundred years to come." As it happened Berkeley's hope was fulfilled for fifty rather than a hundred years. The second discouragement to newspapers in the South was the slow settlement of the interior of the region and even slower development of metropolitan areas that could support newspapers.

The first newspaper in the South was the seventh in North America: the *Maryland Gazette* launched in Annapolis in 1727 by William Parks. Although not published for three years in the 1730s, it survived under various titles until 1839, two years after the establishment of the *Baltimore Sun*. The second paper was the *South Carolina Gazette*, first published in 1732, and followed by the *Virginia Gazette* first published in Williamsburg in 1736. Another paper of the same name was launched in 1766 with the backing of Thomas Jefferson; it was later published as the *American Advertiser* and the *Commerical Advertiser* before it ceased operations in 1822. Once plans were made for a national capital in Washington, D.C., hopes rose for a national newspaper. The first attempt was the *National Intelligencer* founded in 1800, but for three-quarters of a century Washington newspapers lived and died with partisan politics. Today's *Washington Post* established itself as the

leading paper of the District of Columbia soon after it was started in 1877.

In the early era of settlement of the South newspapers found their toeholds along the Mississippi-Ohio River route, the principal transportation route though the interior. Missouri's first newspaper and the first newspaper west of the Mississippi published in English, was the St. Louis *Missouri Gazette*, later called the *Republic*, founded as a weekly in 1808. The same city became a focus of newspaper activity when Joseph Pulitzer, a former reporter on the local *Westliche Post*, consolidated the *Post* and *Dispatch* in 1878 to launch his newspaper empire. River traffic on the Ohio produced the Louisville *Journal* in 1830 and Courier in 1843; they were merged into the *Courier-Journal* in 1868. Further South, the industrial activity on the Mississippi encouraged publishers to launch the first Louisiana paper, *Le Moniteur de la Louisiane* in 1794. The Louisiana *Picayune* began publication in New Orleans in 1837.

The Charleston *News and Courier* began publication in South Carolina in 1803. In North Carolina the first paper was the *North Carolina Gazette*, published in 1755, and the *Observer* began publication in Fayetteville in 1817 and became a daily in 1896. In Alabama, two papers, the *News* and the *Age-Herald* were launched in 1887 to capture a market previously left to smaller organs such as the *Mobile Centinel* (1811), the Huntsville *Mercury* (1816) and the Selma *Morning Times* (1825). The first newspaper in Kentucky was the *Kentucky Gazette* which began publication in 1787. In Georgia the first paper was the *Georgia Gazette and Weekly Mercury* begun in 1763. The *Constitution* was launched as an Atlanta daily in 1868, and by the end of the century it had become famous for the *Uncle Remus* sketches by Joel Chandler Harris. The first Florida paper was the *East Florida Gazette*, first published in 1783.

Although the *Arkansas Gazette* had begun publication in 1819, there were no papers far west of the Mississippi for some time. The first newspaper in Texas was the *Telegraph and Texas Register*, begun in San Felipe in 1835, and the important paper in Texas was the *Galveston News* established in 1842. It was followed by the Austin *Statesman* in 1871, the *Houston Post* in 1880, the Dallas *Morning News* in 1885, and the Houston *Chronicle and Herald* in 1901.

Today the South is home to several of the major newspapers in the nation, as gauged by

1982 average circulation (daily/Sunday). The largest are the *Washington Post* (790,950/986,024) and the *Miami Herald* (435,071/521,091). The principal Houston papers are the *Chronicle* (393,730/481,319) and the *Post* (376,879/440,135), and those of Dallas are the *News* (308,649)/380,981) and the *Times-Herald* (267,579/352,372). Other important papers are the Baltimore *News-American* (344,832/382,953), the St. Louis *Globe* (261,329/248,953) and the St. Louis *Post-Dispatch* (238,099/443,422).

NEWTON, John (Norfolk, Va., Aug. 24, 1823 — New York, N.Y., May 1, 1895). Military engineer. A graduate of, and later professor at, the U.S. Military Academy, he was instrumental in the building of fortifications along the Atlantic and Gulf coasts. During the Civil War he attained the rank of brigadier general and distinguished himself at Gettysburg. He is best known as the engineer who removed the dangerous rocks at Hell Gate, New York Harbor, an achievement that required the invention of new machinery and the solution of new engineering problems.

NIANGUA RIVER, Mo. River originating at the Lake of the Ozarks and flowing generally south approximately 50 miles through central Missouri. At its source are several mineral springs that were developed into a health spa. It was once called the Yungar River.

NICHOLAS, George (Williamsburg, Va., c. 1754 — Kentucky, June, 1799). Politician. Following an active career in Virginia politics, Nicholas moved to Kentucky (1790), where he was a member of the convention which drafted the first state constitution (1792). He also served as Kentucky's first attorney general.

NICHOLLS, Francis Redding Tillou (Donaldsonville, La., Aug. 20, 1834 — near Thibodeaux, La., Jan. 4, 1912). Military officer and politician. Nicolls rose to the rank of brigadier general during the Civil War, and was twice governor of Louisiana (1877-80, 1888-92). He was responsible in his second term for destroying the notorious Louisiana Lottery. From 1892 to 1904 he was chief justice of the state supreme court, and was an associate justice until 1911.

NICHOLSON, Francis (Yorkshire, England, Nov. 12, 1655 — England, Mar. 5, 1728).

Colonial governor. His first appointment was as a captain of infantry in New York. He then became lieutenant governor in Virginia (1690-92) where he supported the establishment of postal services and the founding of the College of William and Mary. In 1694 he was appointed governor of Maryland and served there until 1698 when he returned to Virginia to assume that colony's governorship. Known for his dictatorial behavior, he was recalled in 1705. He was later governor of South Carolina from 1720 to 1725.

NICHOLSON, James (Chestertown, Md., c. 1736 — New York, N.Y., Sept. 2, 1804). Naval officer. A captain in the Continental Navy during the American Revolution, Nicholson fought several battles as commander of the *Virginia*, and in 1781, while commanding the *Trumbill*, he was captured by the British vessels. He was the brother of Samuel NICHOLSON.

NICHOLSON, Samuel (Maryland, 1743 — Charlestown, Mass., Dec., 29, 1811). Naval officer. The brother of James NICHOLSON, he served as a captain in the Continental Navy during the American Revolution. He commanded the *Constitution* after its construction in 1798. In 1801 he became the first superintendent of the Charlestown (Mass.) Naval Yard.

NIMITZ, Chester William (Fredericksburg, Tex., Feb 24, 1885 — San Francisco, Cal., Feb. 20, 1966). Naval commander. A 1905 graduate of the U.S. Naval Academy at Annapolis, Md., he served as chief of staff to the commander of the U.S. Atlantic submarine force during World War I. After the Japanese attack on Pearl Harbor in December, 1941, he was promoted to the rank of commander-in-chief of the Pacific Fleet. He planned the battles of Midway and the Coral Sea, with enemy casualties numbering ten times that of the American loss at Pearl Harbor. The Japanese surrender was signed on his flagship, the *USS Missouri*, in Tokyo Bay on September 2, 1945, after his promotion to fleet admiral.

NOLICHUCKY RIVER, Tenn. River rising in western North Carolina. It flows northwest and west through the Blue Ridge Mountains for approximately 150 miles to meet the French Broad River near Greenville, Tenn. The first settlement on its banks was made in

1772. The birthplace of Davy CROCKETT is also found on the river.

NORFOLK, Burning of. Revolutionary War action by the British against the Virginia city on January 1, 1776. In the first Revolutionary War action in the South, the patriots had defeated the Tories at Great Bridge on December 9, 1775. Norfolk was occupied by the patriots on December 13, causing Royal Governor John Murray Dunmore to take refuge on ships in the harbor. After Dunmore's demands were refused and his men had been insulted for two weeks, he ordered a general bombardment of his own city by the ships on January 1. Patriots added to the conflagration by burning Tory homes. The entire city was destroyed and rendered useless to both sides. It had been the largest city in Virginia, and its destruction contributed to the general erosion of loyalist sentiment in the region.

NORFOLK, Va. City (pop. 266,979), Norfolk Co., located 90 miles southeast of Richmond, at the mouth of Chesapeake Bay in southeastern Virginia. Virginia's largest city, it was settled in 1682 on a site strategic for shipping, a trade that has helped Norfolk prosper throughout its existence. It became a world port when related industries such as ship building and ship repairing developed. Norfolk's strategic location became a disadvantage, however, during America's wars. During the American Revolution, the city was occupied by Lord John Dunmore in 1775, but was recaptured by the Virginia Militia shortly thereafter. The city was almost completely destroyed by the Virginians to prevent later British occupancy, although St. Paul's Church (1738) was spared and still remains today. The British repeatedly attacked Norfolk during the War of 1812 and, during the Civil War, Union troops under Gen. John Wool captured the city in 1862 and held it for the war's duration. As war took its toll upon the city, so did pestilence. In 1855 an estimated ten percent of Norfolk's population succumbed to yellow fever. Today Norfolk maintains its military heritage as the home of a major U.S. naval base. The prosperity brought about by Norfolk's shipping trade was further enhanced by the arrival of the railroads. Industry increased accordingly in Norfolk and the surrounding cities of Chesapeake, Hampton, Portsmouth, and Virginia Beach. Today's economy is based on shipping, shipbuilding, meat packing, breweries, the resort trade, and the manufacture of cement, chemicals, cooking oil, lumber, and machinery. Norfolk is the home of Norfolk State College (1968), Old Dominion University (1930), Virginia Polytechnic Institute, and Virginia Wesleyan College (1966). The city was incorporated as a borough in 1736 and as a city in 1845.

NORFOLK NAVAL BASE. The largest U.S. naval base, located in Norfolk, Va. It serves as the headquarters for the North Atlantic Treaty Organization (NATO) Allied Command Atlantic, the Atlantic Fleet, and the Fifth Naval District. The base houses the Armed Forces Staff College as well as the U.S. Navy's oldest supply center. The base was commissioned in 1917.

NORMAN, Lake, N.C. Lake extending over several counties in eastern North Carolina. It is the state's biggest artificial lake (32,510 acres). The Duke Power Company designed the lake, which was formed by the Conans Ford Dam on the Catawba River.

NORRIS DAM, Tenn. The first major construction completed by the Tennessee Valley Authority (1936). It impounded the Clinch River and created Norris Lake. Built at a cost of $36 million, the dam is largely solid concrete, and is 1,860 feet long and 265 feet high.

NORRIS LAKE, Tenn. Man-made reservoir created by impounding the Clinch River with the Norris Dam. Constructed by the Tennessee Valley Authority in 1936, the lake has a 705-mile shoreline and adjoining park, and serves as a major recreation spot. The lake has a storage capacity of 836 billion gallons. It was named for U.S. Senator George Norris of Nebraska.

NORTH ANNA RIVER, Battle of. Civil War engagement fought May 23-27, 1864, on the North Anna River about 25 miles southwest of Fredericksburg, Va. The battle was one in a series, begun at WILDERNESS and continued at COLD HARBOR, in which Union Gen. Ulysses S. Grant unsuccessfully chased Gen. Robert E. LEE south toward Richmond. In these actions against superior Union forces, Lee displayed his genius in defensive tactics.

Lee had fallen back from SPOTSYLVANIA to the North Anna River by May 22. Grant followed, sending an advance cavalry under Gen. Winfield Hancock toward Hanover Junction, one of the numerous other names by which the battle is known. Grant's hope was that Lee would attack Hancock, and so be prevented from entrenching his troops. Lee correctly interpreted the maneuver, and so had his troops firmly entrenched south of the North Anna River at Jericho Mills, where several Union attacks across the river were repelled.

Again denied a victory, Grant began to move toward Hanover to the southeast on May 26. Although Lee had won at North Anna, the war thus moved inexorably south toward Richmond.

NORTH AUGUSTA, S.C. City (pop. 13,593), Aiken Co., in western South Carolina, on the Georgia border. A residential suburb adjoining Augusta, Ga., it became famous in 1833 when a rail line was laid from here to Charleston, S.C., making it the longest rail line in the world at that time. Fifty years later, the first electric rail line was laid here. Along with diversified farming, varied industries produce metal awnings, plastic containers, and pottery.

NORTH CAROLINA. State in the north central part of the Atlantic seaboard of the American South. Its northern border with Virginia is a straight east-west one. Its western border with Tennessee runs southwest-northeast along the ridge line of the Great Smoky Mountains. To the south North Carolina has a 60-mile border with Georgia at its inland extremity and a 250-mile irregular land border with South Carolina that reaches from its inland area to the Atlantic. North Carolina's 300-mile Atlantic coastline is broken along its northern reach by the large Pamlico and Albemarle Sounds, which are sheltered from the sea by a long network of barrier reef islands that include Cape Hatteras.

North Carolina is perhaps the most inconspicuous of the major American states. Although it lacks such stature in the popular mind, it is the tenth-most populous state in the country. Although it is often forgotten in discussions of colonial history, North Carolina was the site of the first English colony in America, the birthplace of the first English child born in America, and the first colony to declare its readiness for independence from England. Among many other such "firsts," North Carolina lays claim to the first state university in the country, the University of North Carolina at Chapel Hill founded in 1795.

Economically, North Carolina is the leading manufacturing power in the South after Texas and the leading producer in farm profits in the South after Texas and Florida. Since 1920 the state has enjoyed a steady population growth of more than 400,000 persons per decade, and in the 1970s this level of population growth nearly doubled. However, in the midst of industrial and population growth North Carolina has retained a distinctly rural ambience. It is the least urban state in the south after West Virginia and Mississippi, and its population centers are groups of towns rather than large cities. Once considered the "Rip Van Winkle State" because it was so backward, North Carolina is now so prosperous and attractive that half of its 1970s population growth was caused by migration to it of residents from other states.

Like its neighbors, Virginia to the north and South Carolina to the south, North Carolina has a topography of high inland mountains, a central plateau, and a low coastal plain. The principle mountain ranges in North Carolina parallel its Tennessee border; they are the Great Smoky Mountains in the south and the Blue Ridge Mountains in the north. These southern Appalachian ranges include near the center of the Tennessee border Mount Mitchell (6,684 feet), which is the highest peak in the eastern U.S. The central Piedmont Plateau region of North Carolina comprises two-fifths of the state area. This rolling and forested country is crossed by numerous streams and rivers flowing to the southwest. The end of the plateau is marked by the fall line where these streams turn to rapids. At this line, running southwest-northeast through the capital city of Raleigh, the plateau lands drop off to the Atlantic Coastal Plain. This sandy and lowland plain also occupies two-fifths of the state area. Inland it is a fertile agricultural region, and along the coast it is partially submerged by the tidewater estuaries of river mouths. North Carolina generally lacks deep water harbors because of the shifting banks of dunes along its coast that have built up just offshore to form the Cape Hatteras and Cape Lookout series of barrier islands. Due to both elevation and distance from the sea, inland North Carolina has a distinctly cooler climate than the coastal areas of the state.

The European discovery of North Carolina was made by Giovanni da Verrazano, sailing under the French flag, in 1524. In 1526 a Spanish expedition led by Lucas Vazquez also sailed its coast and landed along the south Atlantic region of the state, probably at Cape Fear. The first inland exploration was made by Hernando De Soto in 1540. However, Spanish settlement activity was concentrated in Florida, and

French attention was centered on the Ohio and Mississippi valleys, leaving North Carolina free from settlement for some time after discovery.

It was the English who first took advantage of this delay in settlement. In 1584 Sir Walter Raleigh was given plantation rights to the area by Queen Elizabeth I, and later in that year his expedition under the command of Philip Amadas and Arthur Barlow landed on an island they called Roanoke after the Indian name for the place. They returned with optimistic reports of the area's potential, and in 1585 a fleet under Sir Richard Grenville returned to Roanoke to prepare the way for settlement, but facing too many hardships they returned to England with Sir Francis Drake in 1586. The following year 121 colonists under Governor John White landed on Roanoke and established the first English settlement in North America in April of 1587. John White's daughter, Ananias Dare, gave birth on August 18 of that year, and her daughter Virginia Dare was the first English child born in North America. White was subsequently forced to return to England, and he found his return to Roanoke delayed by London's predominant concern with the threat of the Spanish Armada. When he did return in August, 1590 he found that the Roanoke Colony had completely vanished, presumably destroyed by Indian attack in the early winter of 1590. This launched the mythology of the "Lost Colony" that is an essential part of North Carolina folklore today.

Soon after this, Virginia was settled primarily by colonists from Jamestown, Va., and in 1629 Charles I gave rights to areas further south to Sir Robert Heath, who was unable to finance settlement of it. Virginians continued to move into the area without royal charters, and so in 1663 Charles II gave a patent to the territory to the "Eight Lords Proprietors." A second charter of 1665 settled the Virginia border at 36 degrees 30 minutes, but the southern limit still ran far into Spanish claims on Florida. The Lords Proprietors ineffectually attempted to establish a rather feudal society on their lands, notably with the Fundamental Constitution of Carolina adopted in 1669 and abandoned in 1693. They also quarrelled with themselves, resulting in a separate colony called Albemarle along that sound in the north Atlantic portion of the state. A reorganization in 1691 installed a single governor, but his authority over Albemarle was limited. Settlements at Charleston had already resulted in a common distinction between north and south in Carolina, and in 1729, after years of effectual separation, North Carolina and South Carolina became separate royal colonies.

Amidst this governmental organization, the first towns in North Carolina had been incorporated at Bath in 1706 and New Bern in 1710. Such isolated outposts suffered from Indian attack until the conclusion of the Tuscarora War (1711-13), and also from pirate activity along the coast until the capture of Stede Bonnet and Edward Teach in 1718. Subsequent colonial growth was caused by movements of large groups of Scottish and Irish farmers from Virginia into the plateau and mountain areas of North Carolina. As it had in Virginia, this population growth polarized the small farmer society of inland North Carolina and the plantation society of its coastal regions. One product of this division was the "Regulator Movement," which sought to "regulate" unfair taxation on small farmers by resisting the agents of the eastern seats of government. The subsequent "War of Regulation" was ended by Governor William Tryon's victory over vigilante groups and the execution of six "regulators" on May 16, 1771.

Resistance to taxation was also central in North Carolina's independence movement, which met in New Bern (1774) to elect delegates to the First Continental Congress and then drove Governor Josiah Martin from the colony in 1775. On May 31, 1775, the North Carolina "Sons of Liberty" and other patriots met in Mecklenburg County and signed the disputed MECKLENBURG DECLARATION of Independence, an oath of rebellion that preceded the one signed by all colonies. This was reaffirmed at another congress in Halifax on April 12, 1776, and North Carolina was the first state to declare its independence from England. The state was also instrumental in the Revolutionary War effort, for it was the Battle of Guilford Courthouse on March 15, 1781 that checked British Gen. Cornwallis' advance and began his retreat toward Yorktown and eventual surrender there. After the war North Carolina was a champion of states rights over union, and it did not ratify the federal constitution until November of 1789. In 1792 Wake County was selected as the seat of government, and the capitol building in Raleigh as completed in 1794. The following year the University of North Carolina, which had been chartered in 1789, opened in Chapel Hill.

In the years preceding the Civil War, North Carolina was sympathetic to the South but reluctant to secede; this ambivalence was largely the product of state constitutional

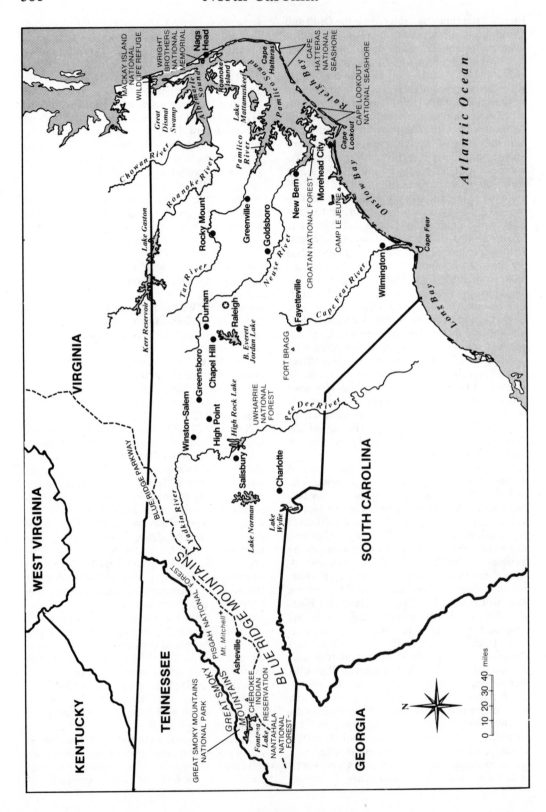

STATE OF NORTH CAROLINA

Name: For Charles I (1600-1649), King of England (1625-1649).

Nickname: Tar Heel State, Old North State, Turpentine State, Land of the Sky.

Motto: *Esse Quam Videri* (To Be Rather Than to Seem).

Capital: Raleigh.

Counties: 100. **Places over 10,000 population (1980)**: 47.

Symbols & Emblems: *Flower*: Dogwood. *Bird*: Cardinal. *Tree*: Pine. *Song*: "The Old North State."

Population (1980): 5,874,429. **Rank**: 10th.

Population Density (1980): 120.4 people per sq. mi. **Rank**: 17th.

Racial Make-up (1980): *White*: 4,453,010 (75.8%). *Black*: 1,316,050 (22.4%). *American Indian*: 64,635 (1.1%). *Asian & Pacific Islander*: 21,168 (0.4%). *Other*: 19,566 (0.3%). *Spanish Origin*: 56,607 (1.0%).

Largest City (pop. 1980): Charlotte (314,447). *Others*: Greensboro (155,642), Raleigh (149,770), Winston-Salem (131,885), Durham (100,831), High Point (64,107), Fayetteville (59,507), Asheville (53,281), Gastonia (47,333), Wilmington (44,000), Rocky Mount (41,283).

Area: 48,843 sq. mi. **Rank**: 28th.

Highest Point: Mt. Mitchell (6,684 ft.), Yancey Co.

Lowest Point: sea level, Atlantic Ocean.

State Government:
ELECTED OFFICIALS (4-year terms expiring Jan. 1985, etc.): *Governor* ($60,768); *Lt. Governor* ($50,328); *Sec. of State* ($50,328); *Attorney General* ($53,976); *Treasurer* ($50,328).

GENERAL ASSEMBLY (Salary: $6,936 plus $2,064 per year living expense allowance and $50 per diem per calendar day.): *Senate* (50 members), *House of Representatives* (120 members).

CONGRESSIONAL REPRESENTATIVES: *Senate* (terms expire 1985, 1987, etc.). *House of Representatives* (11 members).

Admitted to the Union: Nov. 21, 1789 (12th state to ratify the Constitution). One of the original 13 colonies.

amendments in 1835 that gave greater representation to the small farmers inland to correct past domination by coastal plantation owners. Only after President Abraham Lincoln's call for troops made compromise impossible did North Carolina vote for secession on May 20, 1861, thus becoming the final member of the Confederacy. In the war, however, North Carolina is thought to have lost more men in battle than any other Confederate state.

The state suffered in the Reconstruction era, during which its new born Republican Party secured readmission to the Union in 1868, but also became nationally notorious for corruption. This enabled the Democratic Party to gain control of the legislature in 1870, to impeach Republican Governor William Holden in 1871, to amend the state constitution in 1875, and to elect Democratic Governor Zebulon Vance in 1876. In the century since then North Carolina has enjoyed steady growth in population, industry, and agriculture.

The state population today is very evenly distributed over North Carolina's land area. Most of the population is rural, and 70 percent of it consists of life-long residents of North Carolina. In composition the population is 22% black, 1% Hispanic, and less than 1% American Indian, chiefly Cherokees. The large cities are dispersed across the Piedmont Plateau area of the state. Charlotte, a chemical and textile center in the south central region of the state, is the largest city, with a population of more than 300,000. The tobacco and diversified manufacturing centers of Greensboro, Winston-Salem, and High Point in the north central region, however, are collectively the largest metropolitan area in the state, with a population of more than 800,000. Raleigh-Durham, also in the north central region, is a metropolitan retail and finance center with a population of more than 500,000.

Manufacturing is the most important business in North Carolina; between 1972 and 1977 the value added by manufacture in the state economy grew by more than 60% to reach $18.2 billion per year. The most important manufactures are textiles and tobacco products, both traditional in the state, and chemicals, which is a new and growing business. North Carolina's agricultural sector is based on tobacco; the state tobacco crop is worth some $1.1 billion per year, which is more than all other U.S. states combined. The state ranks 13th in the U.S. in overall farm produce, and it is a leading producer of poultry, hogs, and soybean grain. It is also a leading producer of timber and naval stores such as turpentine and resins. Like tobacco, the timber crop supports manufacturing businesses, and North Carolina is the leading producer of furniture in the U.S. Mining of non-fuel ores is also an important business, especially of feldspar, lithium, and the greatest yield of mica. Visitors to the state spend $2 billion per year, with the principal tourist resorts being the beaches of far eastern North Carolina and the mountains of the far western region of the state.

NORTH CAROLINA, University of. State-supported coed university located in the town of Chapel Hill, N.C. The oldest state university in the nation, this institution was chartered in 1789, opened in 1795, and since 1931 has also had administrative jurisdiction over the North Carolina College for Women at Greensboro (founded 1891) and the North Carolina College of Agriculture and Engineering at Raleigh (founded 1887). Four other university campuses, at Asheville, Charlotte, Greensboro, and Wilmington have been added in the last 60 years. The other 10 state-supported North Carolina institutions, all a part of the university system, are Appalachian State University, East Carolina University, Elizabeth City State University, Fayetteville State University, North Carolina Central University, North Carolina School of the Arts, Pembroke State University, Western Carolina University, Winston-Salem State University, and North Carolina Agricultural and Technical State University. All these schools, including the 5 major university campuses, the North Carolina College for Women, and the North Carolina College of Agriculture and Engineering, have their own local boards of trustees.

The university's 14 schools and colleges give students a wide choice of academic programs and individual courses. Undergraduate studies are offered in the schools of Business Administration, Pharmacy, Nursing, Education, and the College of Arts and Sciences, which has many majors, including Afro-American studies, international studies, medical technology, dramatic arts, industrial relations, Latin American studies, African studies, and criminal justice. The students are primarily from the South, 6% are from Middle Atlantic states, 8% are black and 56% are women; 60% of graduates go on to graduate study. The university was recently ranked among the nation's top 100 producers of medical school entrants, as one of the top 35 producers of successful dental school applicants, and in the top 200 of those institutions producing future business executives.

Library: 2,000,000 volumes. Faculty: 1,745. Enrollment: 21,465 total graduate and undergraduate. Degrees: Bachelor's, Master's, Doctorate.

NORTH CAROLINA AGRICULTURAL AND TECHNICAL STATE UNIVERSITY. Comprehensive coed institution, part of the University of North Carolina system, located 78 miles west of Raleigh in the city of Greensboro, N.C. The university was founded in 1891 as a college for Negroes, and it still has a predominantly black student population. Along with the 140-acre campus, the school also owns and maintains a 593-acre experimental farm.

Most undergraduate degrees are conferred in either education, business and management, engineering, health professions, or public affairs and services. The South provides 80% of students, and 76% are from North Carolina; 20% pursue graduate or professional study after graduating.

Library: 288,694 volumes. Faculty: 347. Enrollment: 2,454 men, 1,966 women (full-time). Degrees: Bachelor's, Master's.

NORTH LITTLE ROCK, Ark. City (pop. 64,419), Pulaski Co., in central Arkansas, on the Arkansas River opposite Little Rock. Settled c. 1856, and incorporated in 1903, the city is a focal point for commerce and industry with stockyards, pulp mills, and poultry processing plants, as well as factories that produce chemicals, concrete products, coke, fertilizer and excelsior.

NORTH MIAMI, Fla. Town (pop. 42,566), Dade Co., in southeastern Florida. The town is a residential-resort suburb north of Miami, and is a popular retirement spot. Boats, furniture, and aluminum goods are produced here. A cultural, educational, and recreational complex called Interama was constructed here for the celebration of the U.S. Bicentennial (1976). North Miami is the home of Miami-Dade Junior College.

NORTH MIAMI BEACH, Fla. City (pop. 36,481), Dade Co., in southeastern Florida. Located north of Miami Beach, it is a resort area, formerly called Fulford. Manufactures include dog food, concrete, joists, and candy, along with fruit packing and shipping.

NORTH NEW RIVER CANAL, Fla. Canal in Palm Beach and Broward Counties, which originates at Belle Glade at the southern extremity of Lake Okeechobee. It extends south then southwest through the Everglades for about 60 miles where it links with the South New River Canal. From there it flows east to empty into the Atlantic near Port Everglades south of Fort Lauderdale.

NORTH RICHLAND HILLS, Tex. City (pop. 30,592), Tarrant Co., in northeast central Texas. A suburban community situated between Fort Worth and Grapevine, North Richland Hills' population was 8,662 in 1960. By 1970, it had nearly doubled to 16,514. Although its growth rate has slowed down, the city continues to grow.

NORTHERN NECK, Va. The northernmost peninsula in the state, it includes King George, Lancaster, Northumberland, Richmond, and Westmoreland Counties. The peninsula lies between the Potomac and Rappahannock Rivers.

NORTHERN PANHANDLE, W.Va. Term that refers to the narrow strip of the state which juts northwesterly between Ohio and Pennsylvania. The Ohio River flows through it. The state's primary metal industries are centered here.

NOTTELEY LAKE, Ga. Artificial lake in Union Co., in northern Georgia. The lake was created by a 184-foot dam built by the Tennessee Valley Authority in 1942. Situated at the base of Notteley Falls, it covers 4,180 acres. The lake is part of the Vogel State Park near the Appalachian Trail.

NOTTOWAY INDIANS ("adders"). Tribe of Iroquoian linguistic stock that lived in southeast Virginia. Aloof and hostile to their Algonquian Indian neighbors, they maintained their tribal identity into the 19th century.

NOTTOWAY RIVER, Va. River rising in Nottoway Co. It flows into the Chowan River. The river, named for the Nottoway Indians, was first explored in 1663.

NOXUBEE RIVER, Miss. River in east central Mississippi which flows 80 miles southeast to enter Alabama, where it joins the Sipsey River.

NUECES RIVER, Tex. River in south central Texas. It flows approximately 315 miles south and southeast to the Gulf of Mexico, near Corpus Christi.

NULLIFICATION. A doctrine asserting a state's right to declare null and void federal laws not specifically authorized by the U.S. Constitution as interpreted by that state's legislature. The doctrine was an outgrowth of the controversy over STATES' RIGHTS which arose with the adoption of the U.S. Constituion. It was expressed by factions believing strongly in state sovereignty as opposed to the power of the federal government and was based on the premise that the Union was a voluntary confederation of states; that although these states delegated some powers to the federal government, these powers would be strictly limited by the Constitution; and, in any dispute, the power of the state would prevail. Conflicts between the interests of the states and the federal government led to a number of declarations and finally implementations of this doctrine.

Its first formal manifestations were presented in the VIRGINIA AND KENTUCKY RESOLUTIONS of 1798 and 1799 written by Thomas JEFFERSON and James MADISON. Angered by the Alien and Sedition Acts of 1798, the Virginia and Kentucky legislatures passed resolutions declaring nullification a rightful remedy. The theory was tested in New England after the passage of the Embargo Act of 1807. The restrictions on foreign trade were much opposed by these states whose wealth largely derived from foreign commerce. In 1814 The Hartford Convention was called in protest to the War of 1812 and resulted in a formal condemnation of federal policies. In Georgia in the 1820s controversy arose over the jurisdiction of Indian tribes within the state's borders and the state openly defied federal claims.

Although most states practiced some form of states' rights and nullification at one time or another, its principal manifestations ultimately occurred in the South. Unlike the North which was principally a mercantile and increasingly industrial society, the South was an agrarian economy relying principally on cotton and the use of slaves to plant and harvest it. The Southern states felt that a number of tariffs and other measures passed by the federal government unfairly favored the North. As the United States expanded westward and as Northern sentiment against slavery increased, the Southern states became increasingly concerned as new states were admitted to the Union, that the number of free states remain equal to the number of slave states. This balance of power was maintained by a number of compromise measures legislated during the early part of the 19th century, such as the MISSOURI COMPROMISE OF 1820. Nevertheless, in spite of the number of stopgap measures passed to retain the status quo, there had long been growing sectionalism as well as a feeling of isolation in the South, which perceived a threat to its social and economic existence and led to increasing hostility toward the central government in Washington.

In 1832 the most extreme form of the nullification doctrine up to that time was passed by the South Carolina legislature. A state convention, under the leadership of John C. CALHOUN, passed the Ordinance of Nullification, declaring the tariff acts of 1828 and 1832 unconstitutional and therefore null and void. The state prepared to resist by force any attempt by the federal geovernment to enforce the acts. President Andrew JACKSON vehemently denounced the South Carolina ordinance and the Force Bill was quickly passed by Congress giving the president the power to use armed force to compel states to comply with federal laws. At the same time, Jackson sought to appease South Carolina and encouraged the drafting of a compromise tariff bill. This bill was hurriedly prepared by a group headed by Henry CLAY and passed by Congress in 1833. After passage of the compromise tariff bill, South Carolina rescinded its nullification of the tariff acts but passed another ordinance nullifying the Force Bill. The matter lay dormant until 1860 when the debate over nullification and states' rights versus the power of the federal government climaxed with the SECESSION of the South from the Union.

Although the theory of nullification was almost entirely suppressed by the defeat of the Confederacy in the Civil War, it resurfaced and was discussed again in 1954 by Southern defenders of segregation when racial segregation in the public schools was declared unconstitutional.

NUNES, Pedro (Petrus Nonius) (Alacar do Sal, Portugal, 1492 — Coimbra, Portugal, 1577). Cartographer and mathematician. He was a leading expert on Spanish and Portugese discoveries of the Spice Islands, Florida, and Mexico. Mapping the Spanish territories of his era, he produced the first maps of Florida. Nunes became royal cosmographer for Spain (1529) when the location of the Spice Islands was in dispute, and his studies of the globe and oceans made him the prime expert in nautical science in the 1500s.

NUNEZ CABEZA DE VACA, Alvar (Jerez de la Frontera, Spain, c. 1490 — Spain, c. 1557). Spanish explorer. He was treasurer of the abortive expedition to Florida led by Pánfilo de Narvaez (1527-28), and of 300 Spaniards who began the journey he was one of four who survived. He wandered for eight years around the Gulf Coast region and through northern Mexico, Texas, New Mexico and Arizona before returning to Spain. Reports of his explorations are said to have provoked the DE SOTO (1538) and Coronado (1540) expeditions.

O

OAK GROVE, Battle of. See SEVEN DAYS'
BATTLE.

OAK RIDGE, Tenn. City (pop. 27,662),
Anderson Co., in the east central part of the
state. Located on a 59,000-acre tract of federal
land, it was built to accommodate the World
War II Atomic Energy Program (The Manhattan Project) and its personnel, which reached a
wartime high of 70,000. The site was chosen for
its seclusion and also because it provided the
necessary resources and transportation via the
Louisville & Nashville, and Southern Railroads. Government engineers started construction of Oak Ridge (originally named Clinton
Engineer Works) in 1942 and completed it in
two and a half years under tight security. In
1944 plants here began to process uranium. By
the early 1950s, although wartime activity had
been greatly reduced, Oak Ridge still had processing plants, an atomic energy field office, and
an atomic laboratory where training and research was carried on. The government began
offering its land and homes for private purchase
in 1956 and it was incorporated as a city in
1959. Present manufactures include tools, dies,
metal fabrication, and electroplating. The city
is the home of the American Museum of
Science and Energy and the Oak Ridge Associated Universities.

OBED RIVER, Tenn. Stream rising in Cumberland Co., and flowing northeast approximately 40 miles to meet the Emory River,
southwest of Wartburg, in north central
Tennessee.

OBEY RIVER, Tenn. River rising east of
Cookeville in two forks, in north central
Tennessee. It flows north and northwest to
drain into the Cumberland River. Dale Hollow
Reservoir was created by impounding the
Obey.

OBION RIVER, Tenn. River formed by the
confluence of several forks in the northwest section of the state. The river runs southwest,
through fertile cotton-growing valleys, to
empty into the Forked Deer River and thus
into the Mississippi. The annual floodwaters of
the Mississippi often back up into the Obion.
The city of Obion is the major shipping point
along the river.

OCALA, Fla. City (pop. 37,170), seat of Marion Co., in north central Florida. The city is a
trading and shipping center, as well as a trans-

portation hub, for a major citrus-raising area. The region is also noted for its thoroughbred horses, cattle, lumber, and mineral products. Manufacturing here includes clothing, concrete goods, and metalware. It is located near the site of an Indian village that was visited by De Soto in 1539. SILVER SPRINGS, a popular tourist attraction, is nearby.

OCCANEECHI INDIANS. Tribe of Siouan linguistic stock that lived in Mecklenburg Co., Va., on an island in the Roanoke River. They gave their name to the Occaneechi Trail that extended in a southwest direction through North and South Carolina. They were a tribe noted for their trading. Harassment by the IROQUOIS and the English finally drove them into North Carolina and they eventually united with the SAPONI and TUTELO.

O'CONNOR, [Mary] Flannery (Savannah, Ga., Mar. 25, 1925 — Milledgeville, Ga., Aug. 3, 1964). Author. After graduating from Georgia College (B.A., 1945), she went on to the University of Iowa's Writer's Workshop (M.F.A., 1947). She published her first story, "The Geranium" (1946), and first novel, *Wise Blood* (1953). Despite constant illness, there followed *A Good Man Is Hard to Find and Other Short Stories* (1955), her acclaimed *The Violent Bear It Away* (1959), and other stories, including "Judgment Day" and "Parker's Back." O'Connor's highly polished fiction, often comic and misunderstood, presented characters tortured over the meaning of their lives.

OCHLOCKONEE RIVER, Fla. River originating near Sylvester in southwest Georgia. It flows primarily south through northwest Florida for a total of about 200 miles to empty into the western arm of Apalachee Bay. Near Tallahassee a dam forms Lake Talquin, which ranges from one to four miles in width and is about 14 miles long.

OCMULGEE RIVER, Ga. River rising in northwestern Georgia at the confluence of the Alcovy, South, and Yellow Rivers. It flows south-southeast to Lumber City where it joins the Oconee to form the Altamaha. Approximately 260 miles long, the river is an important trade route for its valley, and it has added to the growth of Macon.

OCONEE RIVER, Ga. River originating in northern Georgia. It flows for approximately 280 miles south-southeast to meet the Ocmulgee River, and together they form the Altamaha River. The Oconee River was the site of several Creek Indian uprisings in the 19th century. Macon and Athens are among the cities on its banks. Hydroelectric projects include the Sinclair Dam and the Furman Shoals Dam.

O'DANIEL, Wilbert Lee "Pappy" (Malta, Ohio, March 11, 1890 — Dallas, Tex., May 11, 1969). Politician. He was involved in the flour milling and merchandising business in Fort Worth, Tex., before he was elected governor of Texas (1939-41). He was a U.S. senator from 1941 to 1949.

ODESSA, Tex. City (pop. 90,027), seat of Ector Co., in west central Texas. This livestock, shipping, and oil equipment manufacturing center is located 56 miles west-southwest of Big Spring at an altitude of 2,890 feet. Named (1886) by Russian-German immigrants for the Russian seaport in the the hope that this, too, would become a center for grain growing, Odessa became a hangout for many famous and infamous early Texans. With the discovery of oil in Ector County (1928), Odessa began its rapid growth to its present industrial status. It is the home of Odessa Collee and a branch of the University of Texas.

ODUM, Howard Washington (Bethlehem, Ga., May 24, 1884 — Chapel Hill, N.C., Nov. 8, 1954). Sociologist and author. He developed regional analysis to reflect the social life of the Southern Negro. At the University of North Carolina (1920) he began pioneer work in social science, founding the departments of public welfare and sociology, establishing the journal *Social Forces*, and developing the university's Research Institute. Under President Herbert Hoover he prepared the influential report *Recent Social Trends* (1933). Author of many books, including *Rainbow Round My Shoulder* (1928), and *Southern Regions of the United States* (1936), Odum also earned a Master Breeders Award for work with cattle.

OGLETHORPE, James Edward (London, England, Dec. 22, 1696 — Essex, England, June 30, 1785). Colonist. A member of the House of Commons for 32 years, he founded the colony of Georgia as a buffer between Carolina and Florida, and as an asylum for

James Oglethorpe, founder of the Georgia Colony

debtors (chartered June, 1732). Oglethorpe led 120 colonists to settle Savannah, which he established (1733) on land ceded by the Yamacraw Creek Indians. He later brought John and Charles Wesley, Methodist missionaries, to the colony. During the war between Britain and Spain, Oglethorpe defeated Spanish troops in the Battle of Bloody March (1742), protecting Georgia from Spanish invasion from the south. As a public official, he was against slavery and the sale of rum, and personally helped finance the communities he established.

OGLETHORPE, Mount, Ga. Peak in Walker Co., in northern Georgia. A terminus for the Appalachian Trail and the southernmost peak (3,290 feet) of the main mass of the Appalachian Highland, it was named for Gen. James OGLETHORPE, founder of Georgia. A marble memorial to him stands on the summit.

O. HENRY [William Sydney Porter] (Greensboro, N.C., Sept. 11, 1862 — New York, N.Y., June 5, 1910). Author. He wrote some 300 short stories noted for carefully worked out plots, irony, and unique endings. Porter began writing while serving a three-year sentence in prison for an unexplained shortage in an Austin, Tex., bank where he worked as teller. Writing under the name O. Henry, his works include *Cabbages and Kings* (1904), *The Voice of the City* (1908), and *Roads of Destiny* (1909).

OHIO RIVER. The major eastern tributary of the Mississippi River, it is 981 miles long and rises in Pittsburgh, Pa., at the confluence of the Monongahela and Allegheny Rivers. Along its course it forms the boundaries between Ohio-West Virginia, Ohio-Kentucky, Ohio-Indiana, Indiana-Illinois, and Indiana-Kentucky. At Cairo, Ill., it enters the Mississippi. The river,

whose course flows through numerous industrial areas, has long been noted for its flooding problems that government projects are still trying to control. Freight traffic began with early settlers shipping produce to market in New Orleans by raft and riverboat, and continues today with towboats and barges carrying coal, coke, and petroleum products.

OKEECHOBEE, Lake, Fla. Lake in south central Florida at the northern end of the Everglades. The second-largest freshwater lake in the U.S., it is about 35 miles long and 30 miles wide, yet it is only 15 feet deep. Reclamation projects have led to diking the south shore of the lake in order to reduce destructive overflow during periods of heavy rain. This and the creation of drainage canals through the Everglades has furthered farming in the region. A fishing and resort area, Lake Okeechobee is dotted with several small islands.

OKEFENOKEE SWAMP, Ga./Fla. Primitive swamp in southeast Georgia and northeast Florida, about 45 miles long and 20 miles wide. This saucer-like depression is interrupted by ridges of low earth, and is covered with vines, brush, cypress woods, wet savannas, and open stretches of water containing hammocks and marshes. The Okefenokee National Wildlife Refuge (1937) is based in Waycross, Ga., and covers nearly 500,000 acres.

OKLAWAHA RIVER, Fla. River originating in Lake Apopka in Lake and Orange Counties in the north central part of Florida. It flows north gathering water from Silver Springs and Orange Lake, then turns east to join the St. John's River near Welaka. Flowing about 120 miles, the Oklawaha is dredged for navigation to Leesburg.

OKMULGEE INDIANS ("where water boils up," probably refers to the springs in Butts Co., Ga., called Indian Springs.) Tribe of Muskhogean linguistic stock that lived in the area of Macon, Ga., near the bend of the Chattahoochie River. A generally peaceful tribe, they eventually joined the CREEK INDIANS in the move to INDIAN TERRITORY.

OOSTANAULA RIVER, Ga. An extension of the Coosawattee River, it rises in northwestern Georgia and flows approximately 30 miles southwest to Rome. There it joins the

Etowah River to form the Coosa. It is one of two rivers which drain the Appalachian Valley.

ORANGE LAKE, Fla. Body of water in Alachua and Marion Counties, in the north central part of the state. Orange Lake is about 16 miles long and is part of the lake system which empties into the Oklawaha River.

ORD, Edward Otho Cresap (Cumberland, Md., Oct. 18, 1818 — Havana, Cuba, July 22, 1883). Military officer. During the Civil War he was a member of the Union Army and was promoted to major general of Volunteers (1862). He led troops in the battles of Corinth and Vicksburg in Mississippi and was in the Shenandoah Campaign. In 1866 he was commissioned a brigadier general of regulars, and he retired in 1880 as a major general by an act of Congress.

OREGON INLET, N.C. Arm of the Atlantic Ocean, that connects it with Pamlico Sound. It cuts through the Cape Hatteras National Seashore.

ORLANDO, Fla. City (pop. 128,394), seat of Orange Co., in east central Florida. Incorporated in 1875, it is a resort, agricultural, and manufacturing center, and is the largest inland city in Florida. The city has long been a center for the marketing, packing, and canning of semi-tropical products, particularly citrus fruits. It is also a banking and insurance center. The establishment of nearby WALT DISNEY WORLD (1972), and the growth of the aerospace industry, led to enormous growth in the last two decades.

ORMOND BEACH, Fla. City (pop. 21,378), Volusia Co., northeastern Florida, on the Halifax River. Founded c. 1875 and incorporated in 1929, Ormond Beach is a winter resort with many large estates. John D. Rockefeller kept his winter home, The Casements, here. Located across the river is Daytona Beach Speedway. Present manufactures include electric appliances and plastic products.

ORR, James Lawrence (Craytonville, S.C., May 12, 1822 — St. Petersburg, Russia, May 5, 1873). Politician. Orr became a practicing lawyer in Anderson, S.C. He was a state legislator (1844-48), and a Democratic member of the U.S. House of Representatives (1848-59). An advocate of secession, he was elected to the Confederate senate and served in the Confederate Army. He was governor of South Carolina in 1866. He was appointed minister to Russia by President Ulysses S. Grant in 1872.

OSAGE INDIANS. Tribe of Siouan linguistic stock that lived on the Osage River in Missouri. In addition to giving their name to the river, they also gave it to numerous cities and counties in Missouri and neighboring states, and to the osage orange, a wood favored for making Indian bows. Frequently at war with neighboring tribes, they finally ceded their lands to Missouri and Arkansas (1808), eventually moving to INDIAN TERRITORY in Oklahoma.

OSAGE RIVER, Mo. One of the state's major rivers, formed by the confluence of the Marais des Cygnes and Little Osage Rivers in western Missouri. Flowing generally northeast for approximately 250 miles, its course is impounded by Bagnell Dam in central Missouri, creating the LAKE OF THE OZARKS. It empties into the Missouri River near Jefferson city.

OSCEOLA (Somewhere along the Tallapoosa River, Ga., c. 1800 — Charleston, S.C., Jan. 30, 1838). Seminole Indian chief. He was the son of an Englishman named William Powell and a Creek Indian squaw. Osceola, whose name is a corruption of the Seminole word for "black drink," was raised by his mother in northern Florida. When U.S. commissioners negotiated treaties for the transportation of the Seminoles to Arkansas in 1832 and 1833, Osceola became famous as a leader of militant Indians, and as the chief who signed the treaties. Arrested for the first time in 1835, he was released when he feigned penitence and then immediately killed a chief who had agreed to the terms of the treaty. This precipitated the Second SEMINOLE WAR of 1836, during which Osceola succeeded in uniting militant Indians and escaped slaves in a guerilla war against U.S. troops. Osceola was successful in evading the military, inflicting sporadic casualties, and keeping reluctant Indian chiefs from undermining his campaign. His position was strong enough that in October, 1837, he requested a meeting with Gen. Thomas Sidney Jesup. Jesup granted the interview, but then had Osceola arrested on a prearranged signal. Sent in chains to Fort Moultrie at Charleston, S.C., Osceola died after less than four months in captivity. His Indian allies vented their anger at this betrayal on non-military settlers until their unity diminished and the Second Seminole War ended in 1842.

OSOCHI INDIANS. Tribe of undetermined linguistic stock but thought to have been Muskogean. They lived in Russell Co., Ala., and later migrated to INDIAN TERRITORY with the Lower CREEKS.

OSWALD, Lee Harvey (New Orleans, La., Oct. 18, 1939 — Dallas, Tex., Nov. 24, 1963). Presumed assassin of John F. Kennedy (Nov. 22, 1963). While in police custody in Dallas, Tex., Oswald was murdered by nightclub proprietor Jack Ruby [Rubinstein]. President Lyndon Johnson ordered a full report from the FBI and an investigation by a special commission headed by Chief Justice Earl Warren because the evidence against Oswald could not be presented in court.

OTO INDIANS. Tribe of Siouan linguistic stock that originally lived in Nebraska. They lived briefly in Missouri before moving on to Kansas.

OTTER, Peaks of, Va. Two peaks in the Blue Ridge Mountains west of Lynchburg. Flat Top is 4,004 feet, and Sharp Top is 3,870 feet.

OUACHITA, Lake, Ark. Lake on the OUACHITA RIVER. The longest lake in the state, 52 miles, it was impounded by Blakeley Mountain Dam (231 feet).

OUACHITA MOUNTAINS, Ark. Forested mountain range in western Arkansas, running to the Little Rock area, south of the Arkansas River. The Ouachita River runs through the range. Subdivided into the Fourche Mountains and the Athens Piedmont Plateau, much of the land is preserved in public parks and forest reservations.

OUACHITA RIVER, Ark. River rising in southwest Arkansas. It flows 600 miles east-southeast to meet the Red River in Louisiana. It branches into the Little Missouri and the Saline Rivers and is one of the state's six chief rivers. Navigable below Arkadelphia, it was once a major steamboat route.

OUTER BANKS, N.C. Chain of islands, reefs, sand bars, and sand dunes, covering approximately 175 miles from Cape Lookout to Back Bay, Va., along North Carolina's shore-line. Major features include Capes Fear, Hatteras, and Lookout, and Nag's Head. The islands are accessible either by ferry or by bridges from Point Harbor and Manteo. The Outer Banks separate Pamlico and Albemarle Sounds from the Atlantic Ocean.

OVERTON, John (Louisa Co., Va., Apr. 9, 1766 — Nashville, Tenn., Apr. 12, 1833). Jurist. After studying law, he set up his practice in Nashville, Tenn., where he roomed with Andrew JACKSON. In 1790 he was made supervisor of federal revenue for the district of Tennessee. With Jackson, he became involved in many large land deals. He was a member of the Superior Court of Tennessee (1804-10) and the state supreme court (1811-16). In 1824 he was Jackson's presidential campaign manager.

OWENS, James Cleveland "Jesse" (Danielle, Alabama, Sept. 12, 1913 — Tucson, Ariz., Mar. 31, 1980). Negro athlete. While a student at Ohio State University (A.B. 1937) performing with the school track team, he set three world records: 20.3 seconds in the 220-yard dash, 22.6 seconds in the 220-low hurdles, and 26 feet 8 1/4 inches in the broad jump; and equalled the record for the 100-yard dash of 9.4 seconds—all on the same day, May 25, 1935. At the Berlin Olympics (1936), Owens won the 100 and 200-meter runs and the broad jump. A national hero during the 1940s, in 1950 he was named by sports writers as the best track performer of the 20th century. Disturbed by trends in racial relations, Owens published *Blackthink: My Life as Black Man and White Man* (1970), in which he condemned "pro-Negro, anti-white bigotry."

OWENSBORO, Ky. City (pop. 54,450), seat of Davies Co., in western Kentucky, on the Ohio River. The state's fourth-largest city, it was settled c. 1800 and incorporated in 1866. The city is a major tobacco producer and market, as well as the trade center for a farm and oil, gas, and coal region. Diversified industries produce cigars, furniture, radio tubes, meat packing, whiskey, and steel. It is the home of Kentucky Wesleyan College (1858) and Brescia College (1874).

OXBOW LAKES, La. General name given to several half-moon-shaped fresh water lakes that are found on the west side of the Mississippi River, throughout the Alluvial Plain.

They were once actually curves along the Mississippi, but were cut off from the main stream.

OXFORD, Miss.
City (pop. 9,882), seat of Lafayette Co., in north central Mississippi. Settled in 1835, the city still offers many antebellum homes and buildings. Electric motors and appliances are manufactured here. The University of Mississippi was the site of the 1962 riot when the first black student was enrolled here.

OYSTER.
Marine mollusk, genus *Ostrea*, plentiful in the warm coastal waters of the South and an important resource for its commercial fishing industry. Oysters spawn, and the popular adage to eat oysters only in months with an "r" in their names derives more from the need to protect the spawning oysters than from any likelihood of digestive disorder after consumption.

The Southern states exceed all other regions of the country in oyster production, which is usually facilitated by use of artificial beds. Fisheries in the CHESAPEAKE BAY produce 20 million pounds of oyster meat per year, and those along the Gulf of Mexico produce more than 15 million pounds of oyster meat per year.

OZARK MOUNTAINS.
Area of rugged highlands also referred to as the Ozark Plateau stretching from St. Louis, Mo., to the Arkansas River. Covering nearly 50,000 square miles, they are mainly in Missouri and Arkansas but portions extend into Illinois, Oklahoma, and Kansas. Primarily limestone, the highest peak in Missouri is Taum Sauk in Iron County (1,772 feet). In the southern regions near the White and Arkansas Rivers, elevations occasionally reach 2,000 feet in the Boston Mountains area. They are noted commercially for lead and zinc mines. Though sparsely populated and with numerous areas of extreme poverty in rural regions, the mountains have a summer tourist trade, particularly at two state parks in Missouri: Big Spring and Lake of the Ozarks. The largest lakes in the Ozarks include Lake of the Ozarks, Table Rock Reservoir, Bull Shoals, and Beaver.

OZARKS, College of the.
Independent coed liberal arts college affiliated with the Presbyterian Church, located on a 36-acre campus in Clarksville, Ark., 100 miles northwest of Little Rock. Founded in 1834 the college offers a relatively small number of majors. Students are required to take 3 hours of religion courses. Of the undergraduate degrees conferred in a recent year, 34% were in business and management, 28% in education, 11% in health professions, and 9% in social services. Arkansas provides 57% of the college's students, and 20% of students pursue fulltime graduate or professional study immediately after graduation.

Library: 75,000 volumes, 550 journal subscriptions, 2,000 tapes/records. Faculty: 40. Enrollment: 303 men, 253 women (full-time); 45 men, 119 women (part-time). Degrees: Associate's Bachelor's.

OZARKS, Lake of the.
Located in central Missouri, it is the largest lake in the state and is one of the largest artificial lakes in the U.S. Spanning several counties, this 16,529-acre reservoir was designed by the U.S. Army Corps of Engineers, and was created by impounding the Osage River with the Bagnell Dam. The lake is 130 miles long and has a shoreline of almost 1,400 miles.

P

PACA, William (Talbot Co., Md., Oct. 31, 1740 — Abingdon, Md., Oct. 13, 1799). Politician. After graduating from the College of Philadelphia (now the University of Pennsylvania) in 1759, he was a member of the Maryland legislature. Paca was a delegate to the Continental Congress from 1774 to 1779 and was a signer of the Declaration of Independence. After serving as governor of Maryland (1782-85), he was appointed a district judge.

PADRE ISLAND, Tex. Sandbar approximately 180 miles long that parallels the southeastern Texas coast, separating the Laguna Madre from the Gulf of Mexico. Noted as the longest barrier beach off U.S. shores, its causeways give access to Corpus Christi and Brownsville. The terrain consists of tall, windswept sand dunes with some quicksand and no vegetation. The Padre Island National Seashore is located along the island. Tales of buried treasure have long been associated with the island, including a story that pirate Jean Laffite reportedly buried his wealth here in about 1820. The island was named for Padre Nicolas Balli, a Catholic priest, who settled there in 1800. Today it serves as a recreation center and the U.S. Air Force and Navy have bases here.

PADUCAH, Ky. City (pop. 34,479), seat of McCracken Co., in the southwestern corner of the state, where the Ohio and Tennessee Rivers join. The site was granted to George Rogers Clark but was settled in 1827 by his brother the explorer William Clark, and was named for a Chickasaw Indian Chief, Paduke. Its strategic position on the rivers led Gen. Ulysses S. Grant to occupy Paducah during the Civil War, causing counter raids by the Confederates under Gen. Nathan Forrest. It is an industrial and agricultural center producing tobacco, strawberries, corn, and livestock. There are coal mines in the area, and manufactures include metallurgical coke, chemicals, and apparel. It is the home of an atomic energy plant and Paducah Junior College, Kentucky Lake, and Kentucky Dam Village State Park.

PAGE, John (Gloucester Co., Va., Apr. 17, 1743 — Richmond, Va., Oct. 11, 1808). Politician. Educated at the College of William and Mary—where he met his life-long friend, Thomas JEFFERSON—his political career started with his appointment to the Virginia House of Burgesses. He became a member of the Committee of Public Safety and was lieutenant governor under Patrick HENRY. He helped draft the state constitution and was a U.S. congressman

318

(1789-1797). In 1802, he became governor of Virginia and served until 1805.

PAGE, Thomas Nelson (Hanover Co., Va., Apr. 23, 1853 — Hanover Co., Va., Nov. 1, 1922). Author and statesman. After studying law at the University of Virginia and nearly twenty years of practice, he moved to Washington, D.C. (1893), and began full-time writing and lecturing. He produced romantic verse and prose about Southern plantations and developed public interest with "Marse-Chan" (1884), a dialect poem published in the *Century Magazine* and later anthologized in his *In Ole Virginia* (1887). He was ambassador to Italy from 1913 to 1919.

PAGE, Walter Hines (Cary, N.C., Aug. 15, 1855 — Pinehurst, N.C., Dec. 21, 1918). Author, publisher, and ambassador. After attending Duke University, Randolph-Macon College and Johns Hopkins University, Page began his literary career in 1880 as a reporter for the *Gazette* in St. Louis, Mo. In later years he either reported for or edited the New York *World*, the Raleigh *State Chronicle*, the New York *Evening Post*, the *Forum*, the *Atlantic Monthly*, and *World's Work*. In 1900 Page joined Frank N. Doubleday in establishing a publishing company that later became Doubleday and Company, Inc. Page became an early and active supporter in Woodrow Wilson's presidential campaign, and when Wilson was elected, he appointed Page ambassador to Great Britain. Throughout most of his tenure as ambassador (1913-18), Page strongly advocated that the United States abandon its neutrality in World War I and join the side of Great Britain. On this issue Page was at constant odds with President Wilson. His published works include: *The Rebuilding of Old Commonwealths* (1902), and *The Southerner* (1909).

PAIGE, Leroy "Satchel" (Mobile, Ala., July 7, c. 1906 — Kansas City, Mo., June 8, 1982). Baseball player. A pitcher, he was noted for his fastball and his variety of curveball pitches, as well as his longevity in the sport. Starting in baseball's Negro Leagues in the 1920s, Paige spent his prime playing years there, prior to entering the major leagues as a 42-year-old "Rookie" with the Cleveland Indians (1948). Paige was brought to Cleveland a year after the Brooklyn Dodgers broke the color barrier with second baseman, Jackie Robinson. Despite his late beginning, the 6'3" pitcher was a deceptive, powerful addition to the major leagues and completed a relatively long career, retiring after 17 years (1965) while in his late 50s. The first black pitcher in major league baseball, Paige's records of birth were so obscure that even he was able only to estimate his date of birth. Some authorities have added as much as a decade to his age. Paige was inducted into the Baseball Hall of Fame in 1971.

PALM. Large family, *Palmae*, of monocotyledonous trees and shrubs native to tropical regions around the world and to areas of the South. The palms native to the South are members of the genus *Sabal*. Two common varieties are the Sabal palm, state tree of Florida, and the palmetto, sometimes known as the cabbage palm, state tree of South Carolina. The family of palms has a worldwide agricultural importance second only to that of the grasses, but the plants have never had any major commercial value in the South.

PALM BEACH, Fla. Town (pop. 10,415), Palm Beach Co., in southeastern Florida, on a barrier beach between the Atlantic Ocean and Lake Worth. Settled in 1871, this well-known winter resort has many large estates and luxury hotels. It did not begin rapid development until the arrival of financier Henry M. FLAGLER in 1893.

PALO ALTO, Tex. Site of the first battle of the Mexican War, Cameron Co., 12 miles northeast of Brownsville, near the Rio Grande River in the southern corner of the state. In the engagement Brigadier General Zachary Taylor led 2,300 men from the newly constructed Fort Texas on an exploratory incursion across the Rio Grande. On his return, Taylor was met at Palo Alto (May 8, 1846) by Gen. Mariano Arista and 6,000 Mexican troops. Better armed, the Americans defeated the larger Mexican force force.

PALO DURO CANYON, Tex. Rocky pass in northwest Texas, believed discovered as early as 1541. The first ranch of the Texas Panhandle was started here at the close of the Civil War. It is part of the Llano Estacado escarpment, and a state park is located here.

PALO DURO CREEK, Tex. Stream originating in southwestern Oklahoma. It flows generally southeast for approximately 100 miles to terminate north of the Sanford National Recreation Area in northwestern Texas.

PAMLICO INDIANS. Tribe of Algonquian linguistic stock that lived on the Pamlico River (to which they gave their name) in North Carolina. The most southern Algonquian tribe, they were encoutered by Sir Walter RALEIGH'S expedition in the 1580s. Nearly destroyed by a smallpox epidemic in 1696, they were reduced to one village. As small a tribe as they had become, they still joined in the TUSCARORA war against the settlers.

PAMLICO SOUND, N.C. Body of water 80 miles long in eastern North Carolina. A series of sandbars and islands divide it from the Atlantic Ocean. The Pamlico and Neuse Rivers drain into the sound, which is the location of Cape Hatteras. A part of the Intracoastal Waterway, Pamlico is the largest sound on the East Coast.

PAMPA, Tex. Town (pop. 21,396), seat of Gray Co., in northwest Texas. Founded in 1888, the town's name comes from the Spanish *pampas*, meaning plains. Located in an oil producing region, Pampa's economy is based on its being an oil field supply center, as well as a marketing center for wheat and cattle.

PAMUNKEY RIVER, Va. River that flows between King William, Hanover, and New Kent Counties. Named for an Indian tribe of that name, its drainage area near West Point is 1,419 square miles. Wild rice growing in its marshes encourages migratory birds.

PANAMA CITY, Fla. City (pop. 33,275), seat of Bay Co., in the northwest panhandle of Florida, on St. Andrew Bay east of Pensacola. Settled by Tories during the Revolution, its salt works and fisheries were raided by the Union (1863) during the Civil War. It was a ship building center during World War II and is now the home of Tyndell Air Base and the Navy Mine Defense Laboratory. Along with fisheries and truck farms, manufactures include concrete products, cypress shingles, and textiles.

PARIS, Tex. City (pop. 23,441), seat of Lamar Co., located south of the Red River, 90 miles northeast of Dallas. Originally settled as Pinhook, it was renamed in 1844, incorporated in 1854, and charted in 1905. Today it is a transportation center with four state and federal highways, five rail lines, and trucking. It is also an agricultural center producing lumber, livestock, poultry, cotton, and grains, and an industrial center for cotton products, meatpacking, furniture, processed foods, and containers.

PARKER, Clarence "Ace" (Portsmouth, Va., May 17, 1912 —). Football player. A quarterback college All-American at Duke, he was later a star with three professional teams (1937-46). He was inducted into the Pro Football Hall of Fame in 1972.

PARKER, Isaac Charles (Belmont Co., Ohio, Oct. 15, 1838 — Fort Smith, Ark., Nov. 17, 1896). Lawyer and judge. A self-taught lawyer, he was a U.S. congressman from Missouri (1871-75), before he was appointed judge of Arkansas' western district (1875). There he became known as the hanging judge because of the number of death sentences he issued. Despite his harsh rulings, he was credited with bringing judicial order to the territory.

PARKER, Quannah (near North Texas, Tex., 1845 — near Ft. Sill, Okla., Feb. 23, 1911). Indian leader. The son of a Comanche Indian chief and Cynthia Parker, a white survivor of a massacre, Parker became Chief of the Comanches in 1867. From then until his surrender in 1875, he led raids on frontier settlements. Parker later converted to the ways of the white man and became a wealthy, successful farmer.

PARKERSBURG, W.Va. City (pop. 39,967), seat of Wood Co., in the northwest part of the state. A major industrial center on the Ohio River at the mouth of the Little Konawah River, oil well machinery is the principal product but factories also manufacture aluminum goods, fiberglass insulation, plastics, and steel pipe. The town was settled in 1785.

PARRAN, Thomas (St. Leonard, Md., Sept. 28, 1892 — Pittsburgh, Pa., Feb. 15, 1968). Physician. After earning his medical degree from Georgetown University in 1915, Parran headed the venereal disease division of the U.S. Public Health Service. Later, as surgeon general of the United States (1936-48), Parran continued his fight against venereal disease. He wrote *Plain Words About Veneral Diseases* (1941).

PASADENA, Tex. City (pop. 89,277), Harris Co., located south of the Houston Ship Channel, east of Houston, in the southeastern part of the state. Pasadena is near the site of the capture of Gen. Lopez de Santa Anna (1836), president general of Mexico, after the battle of San Jacinto. Today it is a center for shipping (agricultural products, cattle), and industry (oil refining, synthetic rubber, chemicals, and paper). Two tunnels in Pasadena run under the shipping channel, providing vehicular access.

PASCAGOULA, Miss. City (pop. 29,318), seat of Jackson Co., in southeastern Mississippi. Situated at the mouth of Pascagoula River on the Gulf of Mexico, it was settled in 1718 around a Spanish fort. Pecans are grown here and manufactures include paper bags and boxes, fertilizer, petroleum products, and chemicals. There are also fisheries, a shipyard, and a U.S. Coast Guard base.

PASCAGOULA INDIANS ("bread people.") Tribe of Muskogean linguistic stock that lived in Mississippi on the Pascagoula River (to which they gave their name). First encountered by the French in 1699, they moved on to Louisiana when French rule came to a close. Closely associated with the BILOXI INDIANS, some of them joined this tribe and moved to Texas.

PASCAGOULA RIVER, Miss. River formed by the confluence of the Chickasawhay and Leaf Rivers, it empties into the Mississippi Sound, and drains into the Gulf of Mexico. U.S. dry docks and a U.S. Coast Guard base are at Pascagoula, at the river's mouth.

PATAPSCO RIVER, Md. River originating just north of Baltimore, which drains the Western Shore. It flows approximately 80 miles southeast, past Patapsco State Park (9,655 acres), to empty into the Chesapeake Bay at Baltimore Harbor.

PATSALIGA CREEK RIVER, Ala. River originating in Ramer, in southern Alabama. It flows south for more than 50 miles to meet the Conecuh River at River Falls.

PATUXENT RIVER, Md. River rising in central Maryland. It flows approximately 100 miles south-southeast to empty into Chesapeake Bay, draining the Western Shore, near Lexington Park. A U.S. naval air test center is

located along its banks. It is one of the state's longest rivers.

PEA RIDGE, Battle of Civil War engagement fought on March 7-8, 1862, in the extreme northwest corner of Arkansas. It was a clear victory for the Union over the Confederates, who called it the Battle of Elkhorn Tavern.

The Battle of Pea Ridge was a resumption of the Confederate attempt to control Missouri that resulted in the battle of WILSON'S CREEK in 1861. It took place in extremely cold, snowy weather, and Gen. Earl Van Dorn's Confederate troops, including Indian recruits, arrived at the chain of hills known as Pea Ridge after a 50-mile march. On March 7 the Confederate army attacked the Union command of Gen. Samuel Curtis and advanced along a valley that narrowed at the site of the Elkhorn Tavern. The South was in a controlled withdrawal by the end of the first day of fighting, and its Indian recruits are reported to have taken scalps from corpses on the field. On the second day of fighting the Confederate troops were driven from Pea Ridge in disorder and forced south to the Arkansas River. They were later consolidated with troops in Mississippi, and Missouri was for a time ceded to the Union.

PEACHTREE CREEK, Battle of. Civil War engagement fought July 20, 1864, just northwest of Atlanta, Ga. It occurred one month after the battle of KENESAW MOUNTAIN and was the last battle of Sherman's march across Georgia before his assault on Atlanta.

As Sherman pressed across Georgia in 1864, Confederate Gen. Joseph E. JOHNSTON had withdrawn in a series of tactical defensive maneuvers. This exasperated the Confederate high command, and on July 17 Johnston was replaced by Gen. John Bell HOOD, a more aggressive commander. Hood immediately ordered an offensive, which took the form of the Confederate movement north across Peachtree Creek on July 20. The Confederate troops, advancing in poorly timed separate parties, suffered heavy casualties in a crossfire from Union flanks. Hood then withdrew back into Atlanta, and Sherman later described the change of Confederate command as a "most valuable service" to his own campaign.

PECANS. The nut of a tree, *Carya olivaeformis*, native to parts of the South and to Mexico. Since the Civil War, the nut has been in great demand as an additive to desserts. At one time it was the single most important U.S. nut crop, but in the 20th century it has fallen second to peanuts in annual crop harvested. Large crops are still harvested from wild trees in Louisiana and Texas, and these two states are the leaders in cultivated pecan trees. In modern times hybridization has produced a variety of commercial species of pecan trees that can be cultivated in other Southern states and in states outside the South.

PECKERWOOD LAKE, Ark. Body of water in Prairie Co., in east central Arkansas. The lake is located in the rice-growing belt of the Arkansas Prairie.

PECOS RIVER, Tex. River rising in northern New Mexico near the Truchas mountains, and flowing approximately 900 miles south-southeast across the state and into Texas to drain into the Rio Grande near Del Rio. During the frontier days of the Texas Republic, this waterway served as a boundary: law and civilization were found to its east, and the wild, lawless frontier was to the west. The Pecos is the longest branch of the Rio Grande River and drains more than 33,000 square miles. Several lakes are located along it's course including the one created by the Red Bluff Dam. The river was the center of decades-long water-use arguments between Texas and New Mexico until a federal bill written in 1949 developed a compromise on the issue.

PEDEE INDIANS ("something good"). Tribe thought to have been of Siouan linguistic stock that lived in South Carolina on the Great Pee Dee River (to which they gave their name). They joined with the CATAWABA INDIANS in the mid 1700s.

PEDERNALES RIVER, Tex. Waterway originating west of Fredericksburg. It passes through the city before it winds northeast, through central Texas, to meet the Colorado River, just east of Lake Travis.

PEE DEE RIVER, S.C. River rising in the BLUE RIDGE Mountains of western North Carolina. It flows east, then southeast approximately 435 miles to empty into Winyah Bay. The river is known as the Yadkin above Troy, N.C. Largest of the three major river systems serving the state, it drains an area of 16,320 square miles.

PEMBROKE PINES, Fla. Town (pop. 35,776), Broward Co., in southern Florida. This relatively new community just west of Hollywood is primarily residential. A branch of Broward Community College is under construction here.

PENDERGAST, Thomas Joseph (St. Joseph, Mo., July 22, 1872 — Kansas City, Mo., Jan. 26, 1945). Democratic Party leader. Pendergast rose to power as a political boss in the Missouri Democratic Party after serving in various state positions. He aided in Harry Truman's Senate victory (1934), but was imprisoned in 1939 after being convicted for income tax violations and his political machine collapsed.

PENDLETON, Edmund (Caroline Co., Va., Sept. 9, 1721 — Caroline Co., Va., Oct. 26, 1803). Politician. A leading member of the Virginia House of Burgesses (1752-74) when the Revolutionary War broke out, he was, as a conservative patriot, opposed to the more radical Patrick Henry. He was member of the first Continental Congress (1774-75), and president of the Virginia Committee of Safety (1775-76). As a result of the latter position, he was head of the colony's revolutionary government. In 1788 he presided over the convention that ratified the national Constitution.

PENINSULAR CAMPAIGN, The. Civil War effort by the Union Army to reach and to capture Richmond, Va., between March and June, 1862. It was named for the fact that the Union Army, under Gen, George B. McClellan, chose to approach Richmond from the east along the peninsula between the James and York Rivers.

McClellan began by amassing 100,000 troops at Fort Monroe near the mouths of the rivers. He proceeded slowly, stopping to besiege YORKTOWN and then cautiously following the retreating Confederate troops to Williamsburg. His slow advance, however, enabled Gen. Stonewall JACKSON'S Confederate troops to create an inland diversion and prevent Union reinforcements under Gen. Irvin McDowell from joining McClellan. The Union progress was then slowed at FAIR OAKS by the Confederate Army under Gen. Joseph E. JOHNSTON, who was injured in the battle and replaced by Gen. Robert E. LEE. Soon after this, Stonewall Jackson's forces joined those of Lee. The Confederate Army fell back to Mechanicsville, and there they ended the Union campaign during the

SEVEN DAYS' BATTLE (June 26-July 1). In this campaign the Confederate Army suffered the heaviest losses, but the Union Army nevertheless failed to capture Richmond.

PENNYROYAL PLATEAU, Ky. Region in western Kentucky that begins at the APPALACHIAN PLATEAU and runs south to the Kentucky Lake. Its name comes from the small herb of the mint family which is abundant in the area. The plateau is divided into three sections: farmland in the south, the Barrens in the middle, and ridges and bluffs in the north. Pennyrile (a name variation) Forest is in the plateau region and encompasses 15,000 acres, largely in Christian County.

PENSACOLA INDIANS ("hair people"). Tribe of Muskogean linguistic stock that lived in Florida in the area of Pensacola Bay (to which they gave their name). They were first encountered by the NARVAEZ expedition in 1528. After a war with the MOBILE Indians in 1686 they moved farther inland and are thought to have eventually merged with the CHOCTAW.

PENSACOLA, Fla. City (pop. 57,619), seat of Escambia Co., at the western tip of the state's northern panhandle. The city is situated on the western side of the Pensacola Bay indentation of the Gulf of Mexico. It was settled in 1559 by Tristan de Luna, resettled in 1696 by the Spanish, and incorporated in 1822. The site of the present city, the second oldest in Florida, was first visited by the Spanish explorer Panfilo de NARVAEZ in 1528, but settlement of the area did not commence for another 31 years. It was destroyed by hurricane in 1561 and abandoned until it became strategically important in the struggle between the French and Spanish. England used the port as a base in the War of 1812 until it was captured by Andrew Jackson in 1814. In 1821 Pensacola became the territorial capital of Florida under the governorship of Jackson. Today the city is an important deep-harbor port facility, with naval stores and food processing industries. There are also commercial fisheries and wood preserving and creosoting plants. Pensacola Naval Air Station, one of the largest in the world, is located here.

PENSACOLA BAY, Fla. Bay in Santa Rosa and Escambia Counties, in the northwestern part of the state. An inlet of the Gulf of Mexico with a sheltered entrance between the west tip of Santa Rosa Island and Fort Barrancas on the mainland, the bay is about 13 miles long and averages two and a half miles in width. It is enlarged by several significant extensions: Escambia Bay on the northwest and Blackwater Bay on the northeast are the largest of these. Pensacola Bay is linked with the GULF INTRACOASTAL WATERWAY.

PEPPER, Claude Denson (Dudleyville, Ala., Sept. 8, 1900—). Politician. A graduate of the University of Alabama and Harvard Law School, he began a law practice in Perry, Fla., and later in Tallahassee. He was a member of the state legislature before he was elected as a Democrat to the U.S. Senate (1936-51). He has served in the House of Representatives since 1963. He is also a leading proponent of rights for the elderly. A liberal, Pepper has been a strong advocate for social reform and international cooperation.

PERCY, George (Syon House, England, Sept. 4, 1580 — England, March, 1632). Colonial governor. He was a member of the 1606 Virginia expedition, and succeeded Capt. John Smith as deputy governor of Virginia (1609-10). He was criticized for his management of the colony during its early years of starvation and returned to England. He was the author of *Discourse of the Plantation of the Southerne Colonie in Virginia by the English, 1606,* a history of his voyage and the explorations during the first year of the colony's existence.

PERRYVILLE, Battle of. Civil War engagement fought October 8, 1862, in central Kentucky 40 miles southwest of Lexington. It was the end of Confederate Gen. Braxton BRAGG'S unsuccessful campaign to invade Kentucky from Tennessee.

To halt Bragg's northward advance, the Union army, 60,000 strong, under Gen. Don Carlos Buell, moved south from Louisville on October 1. Bragg's force of 22,000 retreated from their encampment at Bardstown 10 miles southwest to Perryville to await reinforcements. The battle commenced before any could arrive, but Confederate Gen. Simon Buckner nevertheless broke the Union line at Russell House. The Union forces of Gen. Philip Sheridan, however, began to push the Confederate army back through Perryville by 2:30 P.M. Buell did not learn of this until 4:00 P.M. and was thus unable to deploy his full force to advantage and was deprived of a major victory.

Bragg, his invasion repelled, retreated south into Tennessee.

PERSHING, John Joseph (Laclede, Mo., Sep. 13, 1860 — Washington, D.C. July 15, 1948) Military officer. An 1886 graduate of the U.S. Military Academy at West Point, N.Y., he served in many Indian wars, the Spanish-American War, was an adjutant general in the Philippine Islands (1906-13), and was commander of the raid against Mexican revolutionary Pancho Villa (1916). A military instructor at the University of Nebraska and at West Point, he was selected by President Woodrow Wilson to command the American troops in Europe during World War I. Two months after his appointment, he submitted the "General Organization Report" in which he recommended an army of 1 million men by 1918 and 3 million by 1919. Despite U.S. concerns for such an expenditure, his recommendations were followed. He was forced to amalgamate small units of his troops with European soldiers, despite his adamant opposition. His army was never totally self-sufficient, but he returned home with a sound reputation. Known as "Black Jack" Pershing, he became general of the armies in 1919, later becoming chief-of-staff (1921-24).

PETERSBURG, Siege of. Civil War action that lasted ten months from 1864 to 1865 and ended with the fall of the southeast Virginia city into Union hands on April 2, 1865. The fall of Petersburg led directly to the Confederate surrender at APPOMATTOX Courthouse on April 9, 1865.

After being frustrated by Confederate Gen. Robert E. LEE'S defensive maneuvers in the spring of 1864, Gen. Ulysses S. Grant shifted his target from Richmond to Petersburg, which he approached by way of the south bank of the James River. The first unsuccessful Union assault on the city was launched June 9, while Grant and Lee were still at Cold Harbor. A second and more formidable assault lasted from June 15-18, with Grant reaching the field on June 16 while Lee still assumed the Union target was Richmond. Petersburg was successfully defended against this second assault by Confederate Gen. Pierre BEAUREGARD, whose 40,000 Confederate troops withstood attack by more than 60,000 Union troops. Lee, now aware of Grant's plan, took up the command in Petersburg on the morning of June 18. Grant abandoned the assault and settled on siege tactics that evening.

Both generals displayed tactical brilliance in the course of the ten-month siege, which cost the Union 42,000 troops and the Confederacy 28,000 troops. During the siege both launched peripheral actions on the north and the south banks of the James River. Lee, thought to have been the superior strategist, was limited throughout the siege by a lack of manpower and supplies. His ability to defend the city was worsened by Union Gen. William Tecumseh Sherman's MARCH TO THE SEA in Georgia, which deprived Lee of valuable food supplies.

In the final days of the siege, Lee's attempt to secure an escape route from Petersburg was denied by the Union victory at FIVE FORKS on April 1, 1865. Grant prepared for a final assault on April 2, and on that day Lee informed Confederate President Jefferson Davis that the Confederacy would have to abandon both Petersburg and Richmond. Petersburg was then evacuated on the evening of April 2, with Confederate Generals James LONGSTREET and John B. GORDON holding the city that night while Lee withdrew to Appomattox.

PETERSBURG, Va. Independent city (pop. 41,055), at the navigable head of the Appomattox River, in southeastern Virginia. A manufacturing city that produces tobacco products, apparel, food products, luggage, pens and pencils, and optical lenses, it is also a port of entry and a center for the marketing of tobacco brought in from the surrounding area. First established as Fort Henry in 1646, during the Revolutionary War it was closely associated with the Virginia campaign, and during the Civil War it was the scene of one of the longest sieges against an American city (1864-65). Petersburg National Battlefield Site, Popular Grove National Cemetery, Virginia State University, and Richard Bland College are located here.

PETIT JEAN RIVER, Ark. River originating in west central Arkansas. It flows east-northeast for approximately 40 miles, from the Petit Jean Mountain to the Arkansas River. Both the river and mountain are named for a French girl who is said to have disguised herself as a boy to accompany her sailor lover to America.

PETROLEUM. Natural fuel oil pumped from subterranean and ocean rock strata. The first oil strike in the United States was made in 1859 at Titusville, Pa., but after the turn of the century the South, and Texas in particular, emerged as the primary oilfields of the U.S. Even in 1980, after the opening of the Alaskan oil pipeline, Texas continued to lead all states in crude petroleum, and Texas and Louisiana together accounted for almost half the total U.S. crude petroleum yield. Along the Gulf coast of the Southern states, petroleum is an especially valuable resource because of the refining and refining equipment industries it supports.

The leading Southern states in petroleum in 1982 were: Texas, with 972 million barrels; Louisiana, with 458 million barrels; Florida, with 25 million barrels; and Mississippi, with 33 million barrels. See also SPINDLETOP.

PHARR, Tex. Town (pop. 21,381), in south-central Hidalgo Co., in southern Texas. Established in 1909, it is named for Henry N. Pharr, a sugar plantation owner who promoted the town site. Pharr's growing season of 327 days makes it a leading area for agribusiness, and it is also a trading center. There are oil and gas wells in the area.

PHENIX CITY, Ala. City (pop. 27,630), seat of Russell Co., on the state's eastern border across the Chattahoochee River from Columbus, Ga. A square of land was added to the northeastern portion of the county in 1932 in order to include this municipality, which was already serving as administrative center for northern Russell County. In 1943 all records were transferred and it was given jurisdiction as county seat. Primarily a residential community, it has light manufacturing including funeral supplies and textiles.

PHILLIPS, Ulrich Bonnell (LaGrange, Ga., Nov. 4, 1877 — New Haven. Conn., Jan. 21, 1934). Historian and author. He is considered a leading authority on the post-Revolutionary South. Phillips' writings, generally favoring the slaveholders' point of view, include *American Negro Slavery* (1918) and *Life and Labor in the Old South* (1929), considered a classic work on antebellum economics and social order.

PHILPOTT RESERVOIR, Va. Body of water created in 1954 by a dam across the Smith River. This 20-mile-long lake, with a shoreline of 110 miles, is in parts of Franklin, Henry, and Patrick Counties. Constructed for flood control, wildlife preservation, and electric power, the reservoir is named for a family of early settlers.

PICKENS, Andrew (near Paxtang, Pa., Sept. 19, 1739 — Pendleton District, S.C., Aug. 11, 1817). Politician. He was involved in the campaign against the Cherokee Indians after his move to South Carolina in 1752. Pickens served in the Continental Army during the Revolution and attained the rank of brigadier general. After the war he was a member of the state legislature and was elected U.S. congressman (1793-95). He was the grandfather of Francis PICKENS.

PICKENS, Francis Wilkinson (Colleton District, S.C., Apr. 7, 1805 — Edgefield, S.C., Jan. 25, 1869). Politician. The grandson of Andrew PICKENS, he was a South Carolina attorney and member of the state house of representatives. He served as U.S. congressman from 1834 to 43. Pickens was a devoted states-rights advocate and led opposition to Andrew Jackson's NULLIFICATION PROCLAMATION. He also opposed the acceptance of Abolitionist petitions in Congress. He was a state senator (1844-46), and was U.S. minister to Russia (1858-60). He was governor of South Carolina from 1860 to 1862 and demanded the surrender of federal forts in Charleston harbor.

PICKETT, Camp, Va. U.S. military installation, located mainly in Nottoway Co. This 46,000 acre installation was constructed during World War II, and was named in honor of George Edward PICKETT, a Confederate general.

PICKETT, George Edward (Richmond. Va., Jan. 25, 1825 — Norfolk, Va., Oct. 25, 1875). Military officer. After graduating last in his class from the U.S. Military Academy at West Point, he was under Gen. Winfield Scott's command in the Mexican War, serving with distinction in several conflicts. In 1861 Pickett resigned from the army to become an officer in the Confederate army. He served under Gen. Robert E. Lee in the battles of Paine's Mill and Fredericksburg. In 1862 he was promoted to the rank of major general and given command of a division. During the battle of Gettysburg (1863), troops under Pickett's command made the bloody and, some say foolhardy attack known as "Pickett's Charge." Pickett's division was almost destroyed at Five Forks a week before the war's end.

PICKWICK LANDING DAM, Tenn. Hydroelectric facility in Hardin Co., in southern

Tennessee at the state's boundary with Mississippi and Alabama. The dam, which was constructed by the Tennessee Valley Authority, stands 113 feet high and spans 7,715 feet. It impounds the 53-mile-long Pickwick Lake and is part of the Pickwick Landing State Reservoir Park.

PIEDMONT PROVINCE, Va. One of the five physiographical provinces in the state, it stretches from the COASTAL PLAIN inward toward the foothills of the Blue Ridge Mountains and covers approximately two-thirds of the state. The name means "at the foot of the mountains." Cut by numerous streams and rivers, there are relatively few flat areas. Generally ranging from 300 feet (in the east) to 1,000 feet at the base of the Blue Ridge, some hills and ridges in the region reach altitudes of over 2,000 feet.

PIERCE, George Washington (Webberville, Tex., Jan. 11, 1872 — Franklin, N.H., Aug. 25, 1956). Physicist. Winner of many awards for his work in radio communications, Pierce wrote *Principles of Wireless Telegraphy* (1910), *Electric Oscillations and Electric Waves* (1920), and *The Songs of Insects* (1948).

PIERPONT, Francis Harrison (Morgantown, W. Va., Jan. 25, 1814 — Pittsburg, Pa., Mar. 24, 1899). Lawyer and politician. Often referred to as the "father of West Virginia," he was a Virginia Unionist during the Civil War and became the leader of Union forces in the western part of the state (1861-63) when Virginia seceded. In 1861 he organized the western counties into a rump legislature and adopted the name West Virginia. From 1863 to 1865 he was governor of the "restored state" of Virginia, those counties under Union control, and from 1865 to 1868 was governor of all Virginia. Pierpont lost the governorship during Reconstruction and was a member of the West Virginia legislature in 1870.

PIKE, Zebulon Montgomery (Lamberton, N.J., Jan 5, 1779 — York, Canada, Apr. 27, 1813). Military officer. He entered the military as a boy and became a second lieutenant by age 20. He served on an expedition to explore the source of the Mississippi River, starting from St. Louis, Mo., in 1805. He also explored the headwaters of the Arkansas River and the Red River. Pike's Peak in Colorado was named for him.

PIKESVILLE, Md. Unincorporated town (pop. 18,737), Baltimore Co., in northern Maryland. A town of agriculture and light industry, it was settled before the Revolutionary War. Much of its heritage is based on war memories, including the remains of an arsenal built in 1819. A monument in honor of Queen Victoria was erected in 1901 and is said to be the only U.S. memorial to this English queen.

PILLOW, Gideon Johnson (Williamson Co., Tenn., June 8, 1806 — Helena, Ark., Oct. 8, 1878). Military officer. During the Mexican War he was appointed brigadier general of volunteers in Tennessee by his former law partner, President James Polk. His distinguished service led to his being named brigadier general in the Confederate Army during the Civil War, but he was suspended from command for his escape from Fort Donelson before the Confederate surrender.

PILOT, Mount, N.C. Surry Co., in northwest North Carolina. The peak (2,415 feet), which is located near the town of the same name, was used as a lookout post by the Confederate Army during the Civil War.

PINCHBACK, Pinckney Benton Stewart (Macon, Ga., May 10, 1837 — Washington, D.C., Dec. 21, 1921). Politician. The son of a white father and a free black mother, he was considered a freeman. Educated in Ohio, he later made his way to New Orleans (1862) where he raised an army of black volunteers for the Civil War. After the war, he turned to politics, becoming a state senator (1868-71) and lieutenant governor of Louisiana (1871-72). Pinchback served as acting state governor in 1872 and was a member of the state constitutional convention in 1879.

PINCKNEY, Charles (Charleston, S.C., Oct. 26, 1757 — Charleston, S.C., Oct. 29, 1824). Politician. A lawyer and member of the South Carolina legislature for many years, he was involved in the overhauling of the Articles of Confederation. As a member of the Continental Congress (1784-87), he played a major role in the drafting of the U.S. Constitution, and his plan of government, "the Pinckney Draught," was largely incorporated into the final version. After the South Carolina Constitutional Convention he worked for ratification and, as governor of South Carolina (1789-92, 1796-98, 1806-08) facilitated the adjustment between the state and federal governments. He also helped with the remodeling of the state constitution. From 1798 to 1801 he was a U.S. senator, resigning to become U.S. minister to Spain (1801-04), and was instrumental in winning Spain's reluctant consent to Napoleon's sale of Louisiana to the U.S. He served as a U.S. congressman from 1819 to 1821. Pinckney was first a Federalist but later joined the Jeffersonian Republican Party, a move which alienated his two Federalist cousins, Charles Cotesworth PINCKNEY and Thomas PINCKNEY, and gained him the title of "Blackguard Charley."

PINCKNEY, Charles Cotesworth (Charleston, S.C., Feb. 25, 1746 — Charleston, S.C., Aug. 16, 1825). Military officer and statesman. Pinckney was a member of the first South Carolina Provincial Congress and both houses of the state legislature. During the Revolutionary War he was Washington's aide-de-camp at Brandywine and Germantown (1777) and then participated in the southern theater of the war until he was taken prisoner at the surrender of Charleston. In 1787 he took part in the Constitutional Convention, opposing the clause that forbids religious tests as a qualification for office. In 1796 he was one of three men commissioned by President John Adams to negotiate better relations with France. During the mission, later called the XYZ Affair, the French officials pressed for a bribe, and an outraged Pinckney rejected the demand. Pinckney was twice the unsuccessful Federalist candidate for president (1804, 1808). He was brother of Thomas PICKNEY and cousin of Charles PICKNEY.

PINCKNEY, Thomas (Charleston, S.C., Oct. 23, 1750 — Charleston, S.C., Nov. 2, 1828). Politician. Educated at Oxford, he returned to America and joined the South Carolina militia at the outbreak of the Revolution. He was governor of South Carolina (1787-89) and U.S. minister to Great Britain (1792-96). As an envoy to Spain (1795) he was instrumental in finalizing the Treaty of San Lorenzo (Pickney's Treaty) that arranged navigational rights on the Mississippi River and determined the boundary between the United States and Louisiana. In 1796 he ran unsuccessfully for the vice presidency and from 1797 to 1801 he was a Federalist U.S. congressman from South Carolina. He served in the War of 1812 and in 1813 negotiated the Treaty of Fort Jackson ending the Creek War with the Creek

Indians. He was brother of Charles Cotesworth PICKNEY and cousin of Charles PICKNEY.

PINE, Southern. Collective name given to several varieties of coniferous trees native to North American and most plentiful in the South. In addition to its value in forest lands and landscaped areas, the southern pine is one of the great commercial assets of the South as sawtimber. See also LUMBER.

PINE BLUFF, Ark. City (pop. 56,576), seat of Jefferson Co., in the southeast central part of the state. The city is located southeast of Little Rock on the south bank of a 216-foot-bluff overlooking the Arkansas River. Settled in 1819 and originally called Mount Marie, it was renamed for its giant pine trees and incorporated in 1839. It was the site of a Civil War battle where Gen. John Marmaduke's Confederate forces fought off Col. Powell Clayton's Union troops in 1863. Pine Bluff is the home of a branch of the University of Arkansas. An industrial center, its manufactures include farm equipment, steel castings, and barges. It is also a cotton and livestock market.

PINEVILLE, La. City (pop. 12,034), Rapides Parish, on the bank of the Red River, at almost the geographical center of the state. The city was settled in the early 18th century and incorporated in 1878. Bailey's Dam was constructed here by Union forces during the Civil War to allow the passage of gunboats. Pineville's economy is based on diversified farming, light manufacturing, and commercial fishing. It is the home of Louisiana College.

PINKNEY, William (Annapolis, Md., Mar. 17, 1764 — Washington, D.C., Feb. 25, 1822). Politician. A prominent Maryland politician, Pickney served as joint commissioner in England with Christopher Gore from 1796 to 1804 and with James Monroe from 1806 to 1807. He was assigned to negotiate British-American differneces first over maritime claims and then over reparation for impressment and ship seizure. From 1807 to 1811, he was minister to Great Britain. He served as attorney general of the United States from 1811 to 1814 and fought in the War of 1812. Pickney was a U.S. representative from Maryland from 1815 to 1816 and senator from 1819 to 1822. A noted constitutional lawyer, he was counsel for the Bank of the United States in the Supreme Court case of McCullough *v.* Maryland (1818-19).

PINNACLE MOUNTAIN, S.C. Pickens Co., near the North Carolina border. The mountain (over 3,000 feet) is part of the Table Rock State Park system.

PISGAH NATIONAL FOREST, N.C. Western North Carolina. This 492,579-acre federal forest reserve surrounds Mount Mitchell State Park which features the highest peak east of the Misissippi River (Mount Mitchell, 6,684 feet). The first forestry school in the United States was located here.

PLAINVIEW, Tex. City (pop. 22,187), seat of Hale Co., in northwest Texas. Founded in 1887, the townsite provides a view of the surrounding plains. By 1907, when the city was incorporated, agriculture had replaced ranching as Plainview's main industry. Today, light industries include meat packing plants and clothing factories. It is home of Wayland Baptist College.

PLANO, Tex. City (pop. 72,331), Collin Co., in northeast Texas. Plano was settled in 1845-46, and called Fillmore (for President Millard Fillmore) until 1851. A suburb of Dallas, in 1960 the town's population was only 3,695. Major industries today produce boats and metal castings.

PLANT CITY, Fla. City (pop. 19,270), Hillsborough Co., in west central Florida. A commercial center, it developed with the advent of the railroad in 1885, the year that it was incorporated. In 1887, a yellow fever outbreak killed many residents, and in 1908 a fire destroyed the southern end of the town. Today Plant City is noted for its production of strawberries, as well as vegetables, citrus fruits, and phosphates.

PLANTATION, Fla. City (pop. 48,501), Broward Co., in southern Florida. This residential community is the fourth-largest in Broward County, and lies eight miles west of Fort Lauderdale and 29 miles north of Miami. Plantation was incorporated in 1953, and its 22-square-mile area has experienced rapid growth in the last 20 years because of its convenient location.

PLAQUEMINE, La. Town (pop. 7,521), seat of Iberville Parish, in southern Louisiana. Once an outlet on the Mississippi River, a buildup of silt made the river unnavigable until the Plaquemine Locks were completed in 1909.

In 1969 Hurricane Camille severely damaged homes and businesses, particularly the local oil industry. Sugar, lumber, commercial fisheries, and oil are important to the economy.

PLAQUEMINE BAYOU, La. Waterway that flows out of the Mississippi River through the Plaquemine Locks. Although originally an outlet of the Mississippi, silt buildup made it unnavigable until the completion of the locks in 1909. The bayou derives its name from the Indian word for persimmon, a fruit which grows in its valley. Sulphur wells are found nearby.

PLATTE RIVER, Mo. Waterway originating in south central Nebraska. It is created by the confluence of the North Platte and South Platte Rivers, and flows through southern Nebraska to enter the Missouri River, neat Platte City, Mo. The total length of the river is approxiamtely 320 miles.

PLEASONTON, Alfred (Washington, D.C., June 7, 1824 — Washington, D.C., Feb. 17, 1897). Military officer. A graduate of West Point (1844), he served in the war against Mexico, and afterwards in California, New Mexico, and Texas. In the fall of 1861 he was acting colonel of the Union's 2nd cavalry, and was made brigadier general of volunteers in 1862, taking command of a division of the Army of the Potomac. Pleasonton was in the battles of Fredericksburg, Chancellorsville, and Gettysburg, and was later successful in driving Gen. Sterling Price out of Missouri in 1864. The following year he was made major general in the U.S. Army.

POCAHANTAS (Virginia, c. 1595 — Gravesend, England, March, 1617). Indian princess. She was the daughter of Chief POWHATAN, who at one time ruled the Powhatan Confederacy. Pocahantas, meaning "playful one," visited the English in Jamestown, Va., during her youth. She was instrumental in influencing her father to spare the life of Captain John SMITH (1608), and when two years later the Powhatans conspired to attack the colonists, she informed the British. In 1613 the English captured Pocahantas and held her hostage at Jamestown for English prisoners held by Powhatan. While she was a captive, a mutual love developed between her and John ROLFE, an Englishman. They were married (April, 1614) and as the first Christian convert in Virginia, she was given a Christian name, Rebecca. This union insured peace between the Powhatans and the English for eight years. In 1616 Pocahantas accompanied her husband to England and received great attention at Court. Preparing her return to America in 1617 she came down with smallpox, died, and was buried in Gravesend, England. She had one son, Thomas Rolfe, who was educated in England and came to Virginia (1640) where he became a wealthy and distinguished citizen.

POCOMOKE RIVER, Md. River originating in south Delaware. It crosses Maryland's Eastern Shore, running south-southwest to enter Pocomoke Sound at Shelltown, Md., on the Virginia border. There is a state forest and a state park along the river's course.

POE, Edgar Allan (Boston, Mass., Jan. 19, 1809 — Baltimore, Md., Oct. 7, 1849). Short story writer and poet. Poe was the son of impoverished actors. His father, Irishman David Poe, deserted the family in 1809, and his mother, Englishwoman Elizabeth Hopkins, died in 1811 in Richmond, Va. Poe was then taken into the family of Richmond merchant John Allan without formal adoption. He went to England in 1815 with the Allans and was

Edgar Allan Poe

educated in schools there and in Scotland before returning to Virginia in 1820. He attended the University of Virginia for a term in 1826, but he was withdrawn by John Allan for accumulating gambling debts. Having served a successful tour of duty in the army, Poe entered West Point in 1830 but was expelled in 1831 for missing roll calls.

After West Point, Poe lived an erratic lifestyle in Richmond and New York that culminated in his death on a Baltimore streeet from alcohol-related problems. He also entered into a marriage with 14-year-old Virginia Clemm in 1836 that many consider indicative of his morbid character: she was a lifelong invalid who died in 1847.

Poe's principal achievement was to create the literary genre which came to be known as gothic horror tales. His stories include "The Fall of the House of Usher," "The Pit and the Pendulum," and "The Masque of the Red Death." He was also the founder of the modern detective story with tales such as "The Purloined Letter" and "The Murders in the Rue Morgue." His verse, which he explained in the essay "The Philosophy of Composition," is considered of less interest but has maintained an enduring appeal with works such as "The Raven" and "Annabel Lee."

POHOY INDIANS. Tribe of Muskogean linguistic stock that lived in the region of Tampa Bay, Fla. When De Soto landed in 1539 he made his headquarters in the town of their head chief. They were virtually destroyed by an epidemic in the early 1700s. They were also referred to as Pooy and Posoy.

POINDEXTER, George (Louisa Co., Va., 1779 — Jackson, Miss., Sept. 5, 1853). Lawyer and politican. A practicing lawyer in Virginia, he was a delegate to Congress from the Mississippi Territory (1807-13), and served in the War of 1812. When Mississippi became a state he was elected as a Democratic U.S. congressman (1817-19). He was governor from 1820 to 1821, and was instrumental in framing the state constitution, and in revising the state law code. He was a U.S. senator from 1830 to 1835.

POINSETT, Joel Roberts (Charleston, S.C., Mar. 2, 1779 — Statesburg, S.C., Dec. 12, 1851). Politician and botanist. He was co-founder of the National Institute for the Promotion of Science and the Useful Arts (1840), later the Smithsonian Institution. In 1809 he was a special U.S. agent to Buenos Aires and

Chile. Poinsett was elected to the South Carolina legislature (1816-18), and was a Democratic U.S. congressman (1821-25). In 1825 he left Congress to become the first U.S. minister to Mexico (1825-29). As a Unionist in the South, he opposed NULLIFICATION and, as a result, was appointed Secretary of War by President Martin Van Buren (1837-41). As a special tribute to the work he had done in Mexico and in botany, the flower he brought back from that country is named the poinsettia.

POINTE AU FER ISLAND, La. Island in St. Mary Parish, on the Gulf of Mexico below Morgan City. It is the setting of Charles T. Jackson's *The Man Who Cursed the Lilies* (1921).

POLK, James Knox (Mecklenburg Co., N.C., Nov. 2, 1795 — Nashville, Tenn., June 15, 1849). Congressman, governor of Tennessee, and 11th President of the United States.

Born on a farm of parents of Scotch-Irish descent, Polk graduated from the University of North Carolina at Chapel Hill in 1818. After studying law, he began private practice in Nashville, Tenn., which became his permanent residence. In 1824 he married Sarah Childress in Nashville.

Polk's first elected office was in the state legislature, where he served from 1823 to 1825. In 1825 he was elected to Congress, where he would remain for seven terms and serve as the Speaker of the House from 1835 to 1839, where he was known as a spokesman for the Jackson Administration. From 1839 to 1841 he was governor of Tennessee. He was defeated in bids for reelection in 1841 and again in 1843, during a brief decline of his own Democratic party and rise to power of the Whigs led by William Henry Harrison and John Tyler in the White House.

In 1844 the Whig candidate for President was Henry Clay, an opponent of expansionist policies in general and the annexation of Texas in particular. The Democrats in turn nominated Polk as the first "dark horse" candidate, one lacking Clay's fame and oratorical powers, but clearly opposed to him on this single crucial issue. Polk won the election on the basis of his expansionist stance.

Although the action was challenged by Clay, Daniel Webster, and John Calhoun, Polk as president sent the U.S. army under Gen. Zachary Taylor to the Mexican border and provoked war with that country over territorial disputes. The war ended with the U.S. annexa-

tion of California and New Mexico in keeping with America's "manifest destiny" to expand from coast to coast. On the issue of the Canadian border of the northwest Oregon Territory, however, Polk went against the hardline demand "54' 40″ or Fight" and compromised by accepting the present border at the 49th parallel. Losing popular support as a result of his opposition to extremists on both sides of the slavery issue, he declined to be a candidate for renomination in 1848 and died three months after his term as president ended.

POLK, Leonidas (Raleigh, N.C., Apr. 10, 1806 — Pine Mountain, Ga., June 14, 1864). Clergyman and military officer. A Protestant Episcopal bishop, he was missionary bishop of the Southwest (1838-41), Bishop of Louisiana (1841-61), and was a founder of the University of the South (1857). He became a major general in the Confederate Army at the outbreak of the Civil War (1861), and commanded a corps at Shiloh (1862), and the Confederate right flank at Murfreesboro (1862-63). Relieved at Chickamauga by Gen. Braxton Bragg, Polk took over the Army of the Mississippi and died at the battle of Pine Mountain.

POLK, Leonidas Lafayette (Anson Co., N.C., Apr. 24, 1837 — June 11, 1892). Agriculturist. He was president of the National Farmers Alliance (1887) and was important in the organization of the Populist Party (1891). Polk was a leading influence in the North Carolina Grange Association and founded what became the North Carolina Agricultural and Technical State University (1887).

POLLOCK, Oliver (Coleraine, Northern Ireland, c. 1737 — Pinckneyville, Miss., Dec. 17, 1823). Merchant. Settling in New Orleans, La., (1768), Pollock became a successful land speculator and was engaged in the slave trade. He contributed financially to both the colonial cause during the American Revolution, and George Rogers Clark's expedition to the Northwest Territory.

POMME DE TERRE RESERVOIR, Mo. Body of water in Polk and Hickory Counties, in south west central Missouri. This artificial lake was created by the construction of a hydroelectric dam on the Pomme de Terre River.

POMPANO BEACH, Fla. City (pop. 52,618), Broward Co., southeast Florida, on the Atlantic coast. Located nine miles north of Fort Lauderdale, this resort city was settled c. 1900 and incorporated in 1907. Present manufactures include boats, concrete products, and insecticides.

PONCE DE LEON, Juan (Valencia, Spain, 1460 — Havana, Cuba, 1521). Spanish explorer. In 1493 he sailed to the new world with Columbus, and in 1508 explored Puerto Rico. He was appointed its governor (1509-12). There had long been a legend in Spain of a "Fountain of Youth" on the island of Bimini, and in 1513 Ponce de Leon set out to discover it. On Easter Sunday, he caught sight of Florida and landed near present-day St. Augustine, naming it after the Spanish word "Easter time." After conquering the Carib Indians in Guadeloupe, he explored Trinidad, and in 1521 he returned as governor to Florida. Near Charlotte Harbor he was attacked by Indians and critically wounded. He sailed to Cuba and died before he had a chance to discover that Florida was not an island.

PONTCHARTRAIN, Lake, La. Lake in southeastern Louisiana. Named by Iberville for a French Minister of Marine, it is the largest inland saltwater lake in the U.S. It is crossed by a causeway (29 miles), connecting New Orleans with St. Tammany Parish. About 41 miles long and 25 miles wide, this lake covers 630 square miles, making it roughly half the size of Rhode Island. Both a commerical and resort center, it is linked with Lake Maurepas to the west and with the Gulf of Mexico on the east through Lake Borgne. The lake is also connected to the Mississippi River via the Bonnet Carre Spillway.

PONY EXPRESS. Postal delivery system that served the West. Starting in April, 1860, letters were dispatched from St. Louis, Mo., to Sacramento, Cal., a distance of more than 2,000 miles, via men on horseback. They traveled through great stretches of wilderness, stopping at special posts set up along the route every ten to 15 miles. The journey took eight days in each direction but this was found to be much faster than the former transit of letters by ships, stagecoaches, and wagon trains. The service was discontinued soon after the first telegram to California was transmitted from St. Louis on Oct. 24, 1861.

POPE, John (Louisville, Ky., Mar. 16, 1822 — Sandusky, Ohio, Sept. 23, 1892). Military officer. A graduate of the U.S. Military Academy at West Point, he served with distinction in the Mexican War. He became first a Union brigadier general of volunteers and then a major general in the Civil War. While in command of the Army of Virginia, he suffered a disastrous defeat at the second battle of Bull Run (August 29-30, 1862) and was relieved of his command, although he remained on active duty and from 1870 to 1883 he commanded the Department of the Missouri.

PORT ARTHUR, Tex. City (pop. 66,676), Jefferson Co., in southeast Texas. This shipping and industrial center (oil processing, petrochemicals, shipbuilding, metals) is located on the west shore of Sabine Lake, at the junction of Taylor's Bayou and the Port Arthur Ship Canal, 17 miles north of the Gulf of Mexico. Founded as a rail and shipping terminal (1895), its growth began with the development of SPINDLETOP Gusher (1901), ten miles north of Port Arthur. It is the site of Lamar College, formerly Port Arthur College, which became part of the Texas State University system in 1975.

PORT GIBSON, Battle of. Civil War engagement fought May 1, 1863, in southwest Mississippi 25 miles south of Vicksburg. It was an important victory for the Union forces on their way to besiege VICKSBURG. After moving down the west bank of the Mississippi River, Gen. Ulysses S. Grant encountered resistance at Grand Gulf, where he intended to cross the river, and so moved further south and crossed at Bruinsburg on April 30. Confederate forces were sent south from Grand Gulf to challenge his turn northward toward Vicksburg. The two forces met at Port Gibson, and the Union was victorious after a full day of fighting. In the wake of the battle, the Confederates also abandoned Grand Gulf to consolidate their troops in Vicksburg.

PORT HUDSON, Siege of. Civil War engagement fought May 27-July 9, 1863, on the Mississippi River 20 miles above Baton Rouge, La. Port Hudson was the last Confederate stronghold on the Mississippi between Vicksburg and New Orleans. It was bombarded several times during the spring of 1863, and by May 26 it was completely surrounded by the Union Army of the Gulf under Gen. Nathaniel P. Banks. Banks settled on siege tactics soon after Gen. Ulysses S. Grant did the same at

Vicksburg, but he did order direct assaults on Port Hudson during the siege. It is said that conditions under siege were worse in Port Hudson than in Vicksburg, although the latter was of greater strategic importance. The fall of Port Hudson five days after Vicksburg, cost the Confederate Army more than 7,000 men, two military riverboats, and a large garrison of munitions.

PORT LAVACA, Tex. City (pop. 10,911), seat of Calhoun Co., in southwest Texas on Lavaca Bay. Settled in 1840, Port Lavaca's name, which is Spanish for "the cow's port," comes from its use as a shipping point for cattle and cattle by-products. Current industries in the area include fishing, shipping, and tourism.

PORT ORANGE, Fla. City (pop. 18,756), Volusia Co., in northeast Florida, on the Halifax River. Settled in 1804 and incorporated in 1867, it was the site of the battle of Dunlawton in the SEMINOLE WAR. Today it is primarily a residential city ten miles south of Daytona Beach.

PORT REPUBLIC, Battle of. Civil War engagement fought on June 9, 1862, that ended Gen. Stonewall JACKSON'S Shenandoah Valley campaign and freed him to join the Confederate Army under Gen. Robert E. LEE at Richmond.

Jackson's campaign in the valley, begun in March of 1862, was a successful harrassment of the Union Army under Gen. James Shields. By June 1, however, Shields was moving south along the south fork of the Shenandoah Valley to attempt to capture Jackson, while additional Union forces under Gen. John C. Fremont moved south along the north fork of the river for the same purpose. Fremont's troops were delayed at Cross Keys by the Confederate forces under Brig. Gen. Richard S. EWELL on June 8. Having thus split the Union army, Jackson entered Port Republic, burned its bridge, and prepared to engage Shield's forces on the east side of the river. He did so at 7:00 A.M. on June 9. The ensuing battle was undecided until 11:00 A.M. when Ewell's army, delayed by the burnt bridge, arrived to reinforce Jackson's troops. During the subsequent retreat by the Union Army, the Confederates managed to capture numerous prisoners and large amounts of munitions.

Having thus occupied the Union Army in the valley for three months and having managed to evade capture, Jackson was freed by the Battle of Port Republic to travel southeast to join Lee for the SEVEN DAYS' BATTLES.

PORT ROYAL ISLAND, S.C. One of 64 islands that make up Beaufort Co., Port Royal is 13 miles long and one to seven miles wide. The island has an active tourist trade, and commercial fishing is also important. Beaufort is the primary community and is the second-oldest town in the state. The island is situated at the head of Port Royal Sound.

PORT ROYAL SOUND, S.C. Arm of the Atlantic Ocean, on the state's southern coast. It is the deepest natural harbor south of Chesapeake Bay. St. Helena Island and Parris Island are found on its north end, and Hilton Head is at the south end. Shrimping is a major industry. In 1663 the *Adventure* became the first English ship to enter these waters, although the French tried to settle the area's islands nearly a century before. Union Army movements sent 16 ships and 12,000 men into the sound in 1861. They captured it and prevented any major Confederate stronghold in the area during the Civil War.

PORT ST. LUCIE, Fla. City (pop. 14,690), St. Lucie Co., on the southeast coast of the state, 10 miles north of Fort Pierce and 110 miles north of Miami. One of the newest and fastest-growing cities in Florida, it was created and incorporated in 1961 and covers 70 square miles. The North Fork of the St. Lucie River runs through the city, which is a residential community with no industry.

PORTER, Katherine Anne (Indian Creek, Tex., May 15, 1890 — Silver Spring, Md., Sept. 18, 1980). Short story writer and novelist. Educated at convent schools in Texas and Louisiana, Porter went to New York City in 1920 and supported her studies and European travels through journalism. Her first stories were published in 1924, and her first collection, *Flowering Judas* (1930), earned her a Guggenheim Fellowship for further travel in Europe. Her important works include the novella *Pale Horse, Pale Rider* (1939), the novel *Ship of Fools* (1962), and *The Collected Stories of Katherine Anne Porter* (1965).

PORTER, Wliiliam Sydney See O. HENRY.

PORTSMOUTH, Va. Independent city (pop. 104,577), located on southeastern Virginia's HAMPTON ROADS, across from Newport

News and Hampton. Settled in 1752 and incorporated in 1858, Portsmouth has long been a shipbuilding center and is presently the home of the Norfolk Naval Shipyard. The city is also a rail center and its manufacturing plants produce wood products, fertilizers, plastics, tools, and chemicals. Founded by Colonel William Crawford, the town early on had its own shipyard, one which was to form the beginnings, in 1801, of the Navy's Norfolk Shipyard. It was this yard that produced one of America's first wooden warships, the *Chesapeake*, as well as the Confederate ironclad *Virginia*. The Naval Shipyard Museum, Trinity Episcopal Church (1762), and numerous Georgian and Federal brick and wood structures dating from the late 18th and early 19th centuries are found here.

POST, Wiley (Grand Saline, Tex., Nov. 22, 1899 — Point Barrow, Alas., Aug. 15, 1935). Aviator. He made the first around-the-world flight (eight days, 15 hours, 51 minutes) between June 23 and July 1, 1931, with Harold Gatty as navigator. He and Gatty wrote about their experience in *Around the World in Eight Days*. On July 15, 1933, Post began his successful solo, around-the-world flight, which took seven days, 18 hours, and 49 minutes, covered a total of 15,596 miles, and was made possible by an automatic pilot. He set many records during his career. His plane went down in Alaska, while on a flight with humorist Will Rogers, and both men were killed.

POTANO INDIANS. Tribe of Muskogean linguistic stock that lived in Alachua Co., Fla. Closely associated with the Timucua, they were first encountered in 1564 while at war with the UTINA INDIANS. In the early 1600s missionary efforts were begun among them at their own request. They were almost completely destroyed by an epidemic in 1672.

POTATO. Farm staple of worldwide importance second only to rice. The potato is native to the Southern region; it was cultivated by Indians in the south of North America, in Mexico, and in South America long before the first exploration of these regions by Europeans. Its commercial importance, however, is based on hybridization that had the effect of rendering the potato unfeasible in the soil and climate of the South.

In 1982 Idaho led all U.S. states in potato production of 89.9 million hundredweight (cwt.) per year. By comparison, the leading Southern state in potato harvest is Florida with

a yearly production of 6.7 million cwt. per year. The other states in the South producing significant potato harvests are: Texas, with 3.2 million cwt. per year; North Carolina, with 2.6 million cwt. per year; and Virginia, with 2.2 million cwt. per year.

POTOMAC RIVER, Md./Va. River formed by the confluence of its North and South Forks. It begins near Cumberland, Md., and flows southeast approximately 285 miles to Chesapeake Bay. Its southern region forms the northern boundary of Virginia. The river is navigable as far as Washington, D.C., and small boats are able to continue to Cumberland through the Chesapeake and Ohio Canal. In Harper's Ferry, Va., it is joined by the Shenandoah, its largest tributary. The POWHATAN CONFEDERACY of the Algonquian Indian group frequented the area of the river's headwaters. In 1608 Captain John Smith discovered an Indian chief's lodging called "Potomek." The word means both "river of swans" and "where something is brought" (referring to a precolonial trade route); the river's name comes from this Indian term.

POULTRY AND POULTRY PRODUCTS. Southern states account for 60% of the U.S. farm income from poultry and poultry products. There are more than 40,000 farms in the South producing poultry, and they generate more than $5 billion in farm sales per year.

The top three states in sales of poultry and poultry products in 1980 were in the South. Arkansas ranked first in the country with sales of $924 million, Georgia ranked second with sales of $854 million, and North Carolina ranked third with sales of $759 million. The other important producers of poultry and poultry products in the South are Alabama, with sales of $653 million per year, and Texas, with sales of $418 per year.

Broilers were the leading farm commodity in Maryland and Alabama in 1980. In 1980 two of the Southern states led the nation in the number of chicks hatched commercially: Georgia, with 670 million, and Alabama, with 600 million. Commercial hatcheries are also important in North Carolina, which produced 452 million chicks in 1980.

North Carolina also ranks second in the U.S. to Minnesota in turkeys raised, with 23.8 million in 1980. California led the U.S. in egg production in 1980, producing 8.8 billion. In comparison, Georgia led the Southern states with 5.6 billion, followed by Arkansas with 4.1 billion, Alabama with 3.3 billion, North Carolina with 3.1 billion, and Florida and Texas both produced 3.0 billion.

POUND RIVER, Va. River rising in Wise Co., and joining the Russell Fork River. A peninsula in the river caused by a sharp bend was used by Indians and early settlers to impound their animals, hence the name.

POWELL, John (Richmond, Va., Sept. 6, 1882 — Richmond, Va., August, 1963). Pianist and composer. Educated at the University of Virginia, he also studied abroad. Using Virginia folk songs as a base, he composed numerous concertos and symphonies. Among his more noted works are *Natchez on the Hill* (1932), and *The Babe of Bethlehem* (1934).

POWHATAN (c. 1550 — Virginia, April, 1618). Indian chief. Chief of the Powhatan Indians in Virginia, his Indian name was Wa-hun-sen-a-cawh. At one time he was ruler of the POWHATAN CONFEDERACY that included more than 30 tribes and about 8,000 people. He took Captain John SMITH as a prisoner in 1608, and sentenced him to death. The sympathy of POCAHANTAS, one of Powhatan's daughters, saved Smith and through her influence, and marriage to an Englishman, friendship with the English was maintained (with some interruptions) until Powhatan's death.

POWHATAN CONFEDERACY ("falls in a current of water"). Indian tribes of Algonquian linguistic stock that lived in Virginia from the Potomac River to the James River and Albemarle Sound. A well-established tribe before the first colonists arrived, their early relationships were friendly but the steady influx of settlers disturbed the peace. This Confederacy of about 30 tribes and 8,000 memners, was led by Chief POWHATAN in the early 1600s, and it was his daughter, POCAHANTAS, who married John Rolfe, an Englishman. After the death of Chief Powhatan, his people made two attempts (1622 and 1644) to exterminate the English under Chief Opechancanough, Powhatan's successor. They were so weakend by their defeats in the wars that their Confederacy dissolved. By the 1650s the confederacy had given up much of their territory and the tribes began to scatter.

PRAIRIE GROVE, Ark. Town (pop. 1,708), Washington Co., in northwestern Ar-

kansas. The town is historically important for the Civil War battle fought here in December, 1862, when Confederate forces retreated after failing to prevent the union of two Federal troops, thus strengthening the Union position. Today Prairie Grove is a residential suburb of nearby Fayetteville.

PRATTVILLE, Ala. City (pop. 18,647), seat of Autauga Co., central Alabama, 12 miles northwest of Montgomery. Daniel Pratt founded the community in 1835. Today the town's economy is based on timber, textile mills, sawmills, and the production of cotton and cotton-gin machinery.

PRESLEY, Elvis (Tupelo, Miss., Jan. 8, 1935 — Memphis, Tenn., Aug. 16, 1977). Rock-and-roll star. Starting his singing career in 1953, he did not gain national attention until

Statue of rock-and-roll star Elvis Presley in Memphis, Tenn.

the 1956 release of his record "Heartbreak Hotel." During the next five years every one of his songs ranked in the U.S. top-ten record list. He went on to gain international fame under the management of Colonel Tom Parker, and has been credited as one of the most popular and influential American singers in the history of rock music. His other records include "All Shook Up," "Hound Dog," and "Jailhouse Rock." He also performed in 33 films, including *Love Me Tender* (1956). His death was attributed to complications from drug abuse.

PRESTON, John Smith (near Abingdon, Va., Apr. 20, 1809 — Columbia, S.C., May 1, 1881). Military officer. A practicing lawyer and sugar plantation owner in Louisiana, he supported states rights while a member of the state legislature, and served in the Civil War. From 1863 to 1865 he was superintendent of the Confederate Bureau of Conscription and was promoted to brigadier general.

PRICE, Florence Beatrice Smith (Little Rock, Ark., Apr. 9, 1888 — Chicago, Ill., June 3, 1953). Composer. Graduating from the New England Conservatory in 1906, she taught at Shorter College (1906-10) and at Clark University (910-12). After further study at Chicago Musical College and the American Conservatory, she won several competitions, including the Wannamaker Prize (1931-32), and in 1933 premiered her *Symphony in E Minor* with the Chicago Symphony, the first by a black woman with a major orchestra. Price's works drew on black spirituals and other tunes, avoided jazz, and kept in the mainstream of late European romanticism. Her songs were popularized by Marian Anderson and others.

PRICE, Leontyne (Laurel, Miss., Feb. 10, 1927 —). Concert and opera singer. She studied at Julliard School of Music and several other conservatories. One of her best-known roles was as Bess in *Porgy and Bess*. Her tours have taken her throughout the U.S. and around the world. She is the recipient of over 15 Grammy awards for classical vocal recordings and the Merit Award for her role as Tosca in the NBC-TV opera.

PRICE, Sterling (Prince Edward Co., Va., Sept. 20, 1809 — St. Louis, Mo., Sept. 29, 1867). Politician and military officer. A practicing lawyer in Missouri, he was a member of Congress from 1844 to 1846, and resigned to fight as a colonel of Missouri cavalry in the war

against Mexico. Price was governor of Missouri (1853-57), and served in the Confederate Army as a major general of the Missouri militia during the Civil War.

PRITCHARD, Ala. City (pop. 39,541), Mobile Co., in southwestern Alabama. Settled in 1900 and incorporated in 1925, the city is an industrial suburb northwest of Mobile. Present industries include lumber and paper products, and meat and seafood packaging. A brisk smuggling trade took place here after the importation of slaves was banned.

PRYOR, Roger Atkinson (Dinwiddie Co., Va., July 19, 1828 — New York, N.Y., Mar. 14, 1919). Jurist, editor, and military officer. He was the founder and editor of *The South Side Democrat* (1849) in Petersburg, Va., and *The South* (1857) in Washington, D.C. From 1859 to 1861 he was a Democratic congressman from Virginia and was an advocate of secession. Pryor joined the Confederate Army as a colonel and was on the staff of Gen. Pierre Beauregard during the attack upon Fort Sumter. He was commissioned a brigadier general in 1863 and resigned later that year. Pryor reinlisted as a private, served with Futzhugh Lee's cavalry troops, and was captured and confined in Fort Lafayette in 1864. After the war he urged loyalty to the government and moved to New York City where he set up a law practice and became a justice of the state supreme court.

PUJO, Arsene Paulin (Lake Charles, La., Dec. 16, 1861 — New Orleans, La., Dec. 31, 1939). Politician. He practiced law in Louisiana in the late 1880s before serving as a Democrat in Congress (1903-1913). His committee's disclosures of national and international banking systems were influential in the passing of the Federal Reserve Act (1913) and the Clayton Anti-Trust Act (1914).

PULASKI, Va. Town (pop. 10,106), seat of Pulaski Co., in the southwest part of the state. Located in the Allegheny Mountains, it was little more than a railroad flag stop until coal was discovered in the area in the 1870s. Along with timber and farming, Pulaski's economy is based on the manufacture of hosiery, furniture, textiles, trucks, and modular homes.

PULITZER, Joseph (Mako, Hungary, April 10, 1847 — Charleston, S.C., Oct. 29, 1911). Newspaper editor and publisher. Raised in

Budapest, he tried unsuccessfully many times to enter the military until 1864, when he was inducted as a U.S. agent in Hamburg to emigrate to America and become a Union Army soldier in the Civil War. Following the war's end, he moved to St. Louis, Mo., where he did various menial jobs until he accepted a reporter's position on a German-language daily newspaper. In 1871 he bought a share of the newspaper but soon resold it and, in 1874, bought *Staats-Zeitung* and sold its Associated Press franchise to the *St. Louis Globe*. He took control of the *St. Louis Dispatch* and *The Post* in 1878 and combined them into what was to become the major evening newspaper in the city. In 1883 Pulitzer acquired the New York newspaper, *The World*, and added an afternoon edition, *The Evening World* in 1887. Having gained major political power through his publications, he was considered responsible, along with fellow publisher William Randolph Hearst, for the promotion of the Spanish-American War (1898). He endowed the Columbia University School of Journalism, which opened in 1912. He also established the Pulitzer Prizes, awarded annually since 1917 for outstanding work in biography, drama, fiction, history, music, and various categories of newspaper work.

PURCHASE, The Common nickname of the region comprising the Jackson Purchase. The land was so named after Andrew Jackson bought the property from the Indians in 1818. The Purchase covers Kentucky's western edge, from Florida to Illinois. The Kentucky Lake, the Mississippi River, and the Ohio River are on its borders. It is also known as the East Gulf Coastal Plain.

Q

QUANTICO, Va. Town (pop. 621) Prince William Co., in the northeast part of the state on the Potomac River. A community of diversified farming, it is most noted as the site of a United States Marine base.

QUAPAW INDIANS ("downstream people"). Tribe of Siouan linguistic stock that lived in Arkansas near the mouth of the Arkansas River. Also referred to as the Arkansas Indians, they gave their name to the river and the state itself. They were first encountered by explorers traveling the Mississippi River in the late 1700s. They moved into CADDO INDIAN country in Louisiana (1824) but sickness and crop failure forced them to return to their original territory.

QUINIPISSA INDIANS ("those who see" perhaps referring to "scout"). Tribe of Muskogean linguistic stock that lived on the Mississippi River north of New Orleans, La. They were hostile toward La Salle when he arrived in 1682, and little is known of them after that date. It is thought that they may have merged with the Mugulasha Indians, another small tribe.

QUITMAN, John Anthony (Rhinebeck, N.Y., Sept. 1, 1798 — Natchez, Miss., July 17, 1858). Politician and military officer. He was a practicing lawyer in Natchez, Miss., and a member of the state legislature before becoming acting governor of Mississippi (1835-36). He served as a major general during the Mexican War and was again governor of Mississippi (1850-51). Quitman was a U.S. congressman from 1855 until his death.

R

RAGTIME. American popular musical form originating in the 19th century, characterized by a syncopated melody set against a rhythmically foursquare bass. Its greatest vogue occurred between 1890 and 1914. Ragtime began in the Midwest probably the result of improvisations by black pianists and banjo players playing in saloons and sporting houses. It was influenced by dance music, marching band music and ballads combined with African, Caribbean and American rhythms. Sedalia and St. Louis, Missouri were two important early centers of ragtime. The ragtime written in these cities came to be known as the Missouri style, characterized by lyrical melodies and easy tempos. For years the form was transmitted aurally. The first published rag—"Mississippi Rag" by William H. Krell, a white bandmaster—appeared in 1897. The great popularity of ragtime is partly due to the fact that music in printed form and on piano rolls was widely available. For example, the "Maple Leaf Rag" by Scott Joplin (1868-1917), one of the most successful ragtime composers, sold over a million copies shortly after it was published in 1899. Besides Joplin, other composers in the Missouri style were New Jersey born Joseph E. Lamb (1887-1960) and James Scott (1886-1938), who was based in Kansas City. As the popularity of the form spread, other rag-

time styles emerged in other parts of the country. While ragtime was eclipsed by jazz about 1914, it enjoyed a revival in the late 1960s and 1970s with the rediscovery of the music of Scott Joplin and other ragtime composers.

RAILROADS. Rail service was begun in England as early as 1825, and it emerged in the U.S. a few years later when the Baltimore & Ohio Railroad was chartered as the first common carrier (1827). Among the first railroads in the South were the Charleston to Hamburg run (1829) of the South Carolina Canal and Railroad Company, which later became part of the Southern Railway System; the Portsmouth & Roanoke (1832), and the Richmond & Petersburg (1836) Railroads, which were forerunners of today's Seaboard Coast Line; and the Louisa Railway (1836), later part of the Chesapeake & Ohio system.

By 1840 America's railroad track mileage had surpassed that of her canals. In 1852 the westward movement of settlers led to the founding of the first rail line west of the Mississippi River in St. Louis, Mo., later part of the Missouri Pacific Railroad.

At the outbreak of the Civil War (1861) railroads were important enough to play a significant part in a war for the first time in history,

338

although both the Union and the Confederacy were untried in use of rails as a means of military support. The South did not attempt to enforce a concerted mass-transportation effort through legislation, partly because of its insistence on states' rights and partly because of stubbornness on the part of the railroaders. However, though the Southern railroads were never a smoothly functioning unit, they played an important role in the war and very likely kept the Confederacy alive for several extra months.

Southern rail lines did not make the fullest possible contribution to the Confederate cause for a number of reasons. Despite greatly expanded trackage in the years preceding secession, there was not enough of it to accommodate the demands of a mass-transit war. In addition, existing lines were often located in strategically useless areas. Because a real rail network of trunk lines had not been developed as it had been in the North, lines of continuous track were short. Another problem was a difference in gauge between one line and another: some lines had a width of five feet between rails, others had the four feet, eight and one-half inch width that was later to become standard. Consequently both goods and passengers had to be transhipped between lines, and a lack of cooperation among the railroads often made it impossible to move men and material smoothly. Thus the possession of interior lines, one of the South's few advantages, was nearly negated.

Southern tracks and trains were in much poorer shape than those in the North at the outset of the war, and they needed more repair. The inability of the South to manufacture parts for its carriers was a disabling factor. Before the war 96% of railroad manufactures were produced in the North; therefore, replacement parts were suddenly unavailable and new track had to be made from old rails taken from somewhere else. In addition, Northern forces destroyed many rail lines, or captured trains and even whole rail lines for their own use. These difficulties were compounded by the general lack of cooperation between individual railroads and the Confederate government, which was unwilling to command cooperation.

By the end of the war, the railroads were almost devastated: much of their rolling stock was gone, and many tracks, stations, and bridges were ruined. Out of 595 pieces of rolling stock in 1861, the New Orleans, Jackson, & Great Northern had, in 1865, two damaged locomotives, one sound one, a baggage car, and 18 freight cars left. The Mississippi & Tennessee had lost 81 cars. The Mobile & Ohio lost every one of its bridges and buildings for a stretch of 184 miles, and the Alabama & Tennessee Rivers Railroad had to halt service for two months. The Virginia Central possessed $100 in gold and debts totaling $1,637,118.

Some lines were able to come back quickly after the war. The federal government began selling the property of the U.S. Military Railroad cheaply to the Southern lines in an effort to establish service. Northern money and Northern iron were poured into the South, and the Western North Carolina line reported earnings for August, 1865, that were equal to any August before the war. The Virginia Central had its whole line back in operation by July of that year and the industry was on the road to recovery.

Recovery was completed and the railroad industry entered its greatest period of growth in the 1880s and 1890s. In the 1880s 70,000 miles of track were laid in the U.S. Men like Henry Morrison FLAGLER were responsible for creating economic booms and great population growth in many Southern states. Flagler consolidated and developed Florida's railroads into one efficient system, the Florida East Coast Railroad. Towns like West Palm Beach (1894) and Miami (1896) grew rapidly due to an influx of railroad workers and the economic boost of tourism and rail trade. The railroad also contributed to the relocation of manufacturing plants to states in the South.

This boom, however, brought about abuses within the industry throughout the U.S. including rate wars between lines, financial piracy, and monopoly of domestic transportation. As a result, federal regulation in the form of the Interstate Commerce Act (1887) was enacted, which placed the railroads under federal control of the Interstate Commerce Commission (ICC), and the Federal Railroad Adminstration (FRA) was charged with overseeing safety standards for the industry.

The early 1900s were the high point of rail service. During this time equipment was standardized and procedures were introduced to make rail service infinitely more efficient and safe.

The economic depression of the 1930s, however, hurt the railroad industry, since there was little money available, and there was little demand for transporting goods or for passenger travel.

During World War II the railroads proved to be a great asset to the war effort, making possible the massive relocation of men and material. Railroads handled approximately four times the number of pre-war passenger miles and two and one-half times the amount of freight.

The railroad industry was one of the first in which workers unionized. Labor disputes brought about violent strikes in 1877 and again in 1894. There followed years of relative calm but in 1946 another crippling strike was called. During the 1960s many strikes caused disruption on a national level and contributed to the reduced use of railroads.

Between 1960 and 1980 there was a severe reduction in rail travel. The numerous strikes of the 1960s, the increasing use of improved highways and airlines for passenger travel and the moving of goods, and poor management of the railroads themselves were all factors contributing to the decline.

RALEIGH, N.C. City (pop. 149,771), state capital and seat of Wake Co., in the central part of the state. Settled in 1788 and incorporated in 1798, the city was named for Sir Walter Raleigh. The site was chosen in 1788 and developed in 1792 when North Carolina decided to move its capital away from the seaboard. The first capitol was completed in 1794 but destroyed in a fire in 1831. The present capitol was completed in 1840 and stands in the middle of a four-acre square, surrounded by various state buildings. The city serves as a major retail shipping point for the eastern side of the state, and is a wholesale distribution point for foodstuffs. During the past hundred years many industries have moved into the city and they manufacture a variety of goods, including computers, electronic equipment, and processed foods. The city also serves as a research and development center for textile and chemical firms, and the corporate headquarters of several major insurance companies are located here. Andrew Johnson, the 17th president of the U.S., was born here and his home has been preserved as a historic shrine. During the Civil War, Union forces under Gen. William Tecumseh Sherman entered the city in April, 1865, and stayed for the remainder of the war. The city is the home of North Carolina State University, Shaw University, and many colleges. Raleigh is part of the three-county Research Triangle organization, which carries on cultural, scientific, and educational activities. Research Triangle Park, near the city, is located on 4,000 acres devoted entirely to research facilities.

RALEIGH, Sir Walter (Hayes Barton, Devonshire, England, 1554 — London, England, Oct. 29, 1618). English military commander and adventurer. After his education at Oriel College, Raleigh joined the military, serving with the Huguenots during the 1570s, and later fought against the Spaniards. He came under the favor of Queen Elizabeth, largely because of his service in Ireland. In 1585 Raleigh was knighted and acquired considerable wealth through the generosity of the Queen. During the remaining 1580s, Queen Elizabeth heaped upon her favorite subject titles such as vice admiral and captain of the guard, and he became a member of Parliament. Forbidden by the Queen to sail abroad, Raleigh organized expeditions to colonize America (1585 and 1587), but they were unsuccessful and ended with the "lost colony" of ROANOKE ISLAND. Raleigh's expeditions were, however, credited with introducing tobacco and potatoes to England. Raleigh had made many enemies while in Queen Elizabeth's favor and when she died they convinced her successor, James I, that Raleigh was a traitor. James placed Raleigh in the Tower of London and, after 13 years imprisonment, Raleigh was beheaded.

RAMSEUR'S MILL, Battle of. Revolutionary War engagement fought northeast of Charlotte, N.C., on June 20, 1780. A victory for the Patriots, it set back British plans to invade North Carolina after the surrender of Charleston, S.C., in May of 1780.

Ramseur's Mill (also spelled Ramsour's) was the hometown of Col. John Moore, who had fought under the British commander Lord Charles CORNWALLIS in South Carolina. On June 10, Moore called on Loyalists in the area to assemble, and by June 20 he had gathered more than a thousand, many of them unarmed. On June 20 they were routed and driven from a hill near Ramseur's Mill by a Revolutionary force of only 400 under the command of Col. Francis Locke. Most of the Loyalists deserted, and when Moore later rejoined Cornwallis he had only 30 men. Cornwallis threatened a court martial, for Moore's actions had eroded Loyalist sentiment in North Carolina and rallied many undecided citizens behind the patriotic cause.

RANDALL, James Ryder (Baltimore, Md., Jan. 1, 1839 — Augusta, Ga., Jan. 14, 1908). Author and poet. Educated at Georgetown College, he settled in New Orleans, La. There he wrote the famous war song, "Maryland, My

Maryland" (1861), later set to music, which became the battle hymn of the Confederate Army. His health prevented him from enlisting as a soldier. He later launched a newspaper career as associate editor of the *Constitutionalist* in Augusta, Ga.

RANDOLPH, A(sa) P(hilip) (Crescent City, Fla., April 15, 1889 — New York, N.Y., May 16, 1979). Labor leader and civil rights activist. The son of a Methodist preacher, he moved to New York to study at City College. There he was strongly impressed by the socialist ideas of Eugene V. Debs. Randolph organized and published the black radical journal *The Messenger,* and through this influential vehicle he promoted black causes, including the affiliation of black workers with labor unions. In 1925 he created and administered the Brotherhood of Sleeping Car Porters which became affiliated with the American Federation of Labor in 1936, and he was president of the National Negro Congress in the 1930s. In 1941 he threatened to lead a march on Washington, D.C., to protest the exclusion of blacks from industrial war work, which led to President Franklin Roosevelt's commission on Fair Employment Practices. He was director of the 1963 March on Washington that led to increased jobs and freedom for blacks.

RANDOLPH, Edmund Jennings (Williamsburg, Va., Aug. 10, 1753 — Clarke Co., Va., Sept. 12, 1813). Politician. The son of John RANDOLPH, after graduation from William and Mary College, Edmund Randolph became a lawyer. When the Revolution began, he served briefly with George Washington. In 1776 he was elected to the Virginia Constitutional Convention, and served in the Continental Congress (1779-82). Randolph was governor of Virginia (1786-88) and attended the Annapolis Convention (1786), and the Constitutional Convention of 1787 where he presented the Virginia Plan and helped prepare the first draft of the U.S. Constitution. In 1789 President George Washington appointed him the nation's first attorney general, and in 1794 he succeeded Thomas Jefferson as Secretary of State. During the talks that led to the Jay Treaty, Randolph was falsely accused of taking bribes from the French. He returned to private law practice and kept a low profile except for his role as chief defense counsel in the 1807 treason trial of Aaron Burr.

RANDOLPH, John (Prince George Co., Va., June 2, 1773 — Philadelphia, Pa., May 24, 1833). Politician. Randolph was an outspoken proponent of states' rights, and was first elected to the House of Representatives from Virginia in 1799, his stay there continued almost uninterrupted until 1829 (1799-1813, 1815-1817, 1819-1825, 1825-1829). During his brilliant, if sometimes erratic and irrational tenure in the House, he was Chairman of the House Ways and Means Committee. He was also the leader of the Jeffersonian Republicans. During his political career he persisted in advocating strong states' rights by opposing such programs as protective tariffs, a national bank, federal interference in slavery matters (although he freed his own slaves in his will), and any kind of federal financing, such as road or canal improvements. He also spoke for Southern planters who were vehemently opposed to the Missouri Compromise of 1820. Randolph served a partial term as a U.S. Senator (1825-27) to fill a vacancy, and again served in Congress (1827-29). In 1830 he was appointed U.S. minister to Russia by President John Quincy Adams but returned home soon afterwards because of poor health. He was the father of Edmund Jennings RANDOLPH and brother of Peyton RANDOLPH.

RANDOLPH, Peyton (Williamsburg, Va., Sept., 1721 — Philadelphia, Pa., Oct. 22, 1775). Politician. He studied law in England and in 1748 was made king's attorney for Virginia. Elected to a seat in the House of Burgesses (1764-74), he was the head of a committee to revise the laws of the colony, and was the author of a House of Burgesses' address to the King in opposition to the Stamp Act. Early espousing the cause of the colonists, he was a leader in political movements in Virginia and was made chairman of the committee of correspondence in 1773. Randolph was briefly president of the First Continental Congress (1774) and was elected to the Second Continental Congress but resigned due to illness. He was the brother of John RANDOLPH.

RANDOLPH-MACON COLLEGE. Independent Methodist women's college located 110 miles west of Richmond on a 100-acre campus in the city of Lynchburg, Va. The college was founded in 1891, and is considered to be the first women's college accredited by the Southern Association of Colleges and Schools. It is also the first womans' school south of Washington, D.C., to gain a Phi Beta Kappa Chapter.

Majors offered include the usual arts and sciences in addition to Russian studies, theatre, dance, American studies, classical civilization, and urban studies. The college is a member of the Seven College Exchange Program, which includes Hollins, Sweet Briar, Hampton-Sydney, Washington and Lee, and Mary Baldwin. The South provides 59% of the students 21% are from Middle Atlantic states, and 9% are from the North Central area; after graduating, 60% of students go on to earn advanced degrees.

Library: 138,000 volumes. Faculty: 83. Enrollment: 734 women (full-time). Degrees: Bachelor's.

RANSOM, John Crowe (Pulaski, Tenn., Apr. 30, 1888 — Gambier, Ohio, July 3, 1974). Poet and critic. a teacher at Vanderbilt for 23 years, he was the eldest of the southern poets known for publication of *The Fugitive* from 1922 to 1925. Ransom was a former professor of the group's other leaders, Allen TATE and Robert Penn WARREN. It was Ransom who originated the phrase "New Criticism," a type of literary study closely associated with this group, and encouraged the polemic *I'll Take My Stand* (1930), a statement of agrarian ideals central to the thought of the new Southern writers. Later he went to Kenyon College as professor of poetry, and in 1939 was founder and editor of the *Kenyon Review*. Ransom is best remembered for the poems "Bells for John Whiteside's Daughter" and "Here Lies a Lady."

RAPPAHANNOCK RIVER, Va. River rising in the north part of the state in the Blue Ridge Mountains. This 212-mile river flows southeasterly to Chesapeake Bay. Along its course it is joined by several tributaries, the largest of which is the Rapidan. A tidal stream, its name is Indian in origin and means "quick rising waters." The river's drainage area is 1,597 square miles and it is navigable to Fredericksburg.

RAWLINGS, Marjorie Kinnan (Washington, D.C., Aug. 8, 1896 — St. Augustine, Fla., Dec. 14, 1953). Author. A graduate of the University of Wisconsin (1918), her early work was as a journalist. All her novels had a Southern background, particularly the backwoods of Florida, except for her final one, *The Sojourner* (1953), which had a northern setting. In 1938 she wrote *The Yearling* which won the Pulitzer Prize in 1939 and has become an American classic. Her other works include *South Moon Under* (1933), *Golden Apples* (1935), and *Cross Creek* (1942).

RAYBURN, Samuel Taliaferro (Roane Co., Tenn., Jan. 6, 1882 — Bonham, Tex., Nov. 16, 1961). Politician. Raised on a farm in Texas, he taught school and became a lawyer in Bonham. Developing an interest in politics, he started his career as a state legislator (1907-12) and became speaker of the Texas House of Representatives in 1911. He set a record for tenure when he was elected as a Democrat to the U.S. House of Representatives for 24 consecutive terms (1913-61). Appointed chairman of the Commission on Interest and Foreign Commerce in 1931, he helped design President Franklin Roosevelt's New Deal program and co-authored six important laws to support it. Rayburn was Speaker of the House from 1940-47, 1949-53 and 1955-61. He became one of the strongest Speakers in U.S. history, able to dominate the chamber through informal influence. Highly regarded for his integrity and lack of pretension, he was extremely successful in exercising indirect control of the legislative process and of committee assignments through personal relationships with powerful committee chairmen. He was President Harry S. Truman's chief supporter in Congress and one of his closest advisers. Except for civil rights measures, he backed much of Truman's domestic program and eventually supported his foreign policy as well. During the 1950s he worked with the Eisenhower Administration to defeat Republican isolationist measures. Although a supporter of Lyndon Johnson for president in 1960, he worked with the Kennedy Administration on much of its initial legislation.

READJUSTORS. Political party that rose in Virginia during the RECONSTRUCTION era. It was so named because its supporters called for a readjustment of the large funded debt of Virginia ($40 million) in an effort to lessen the tax burden on small farmers. Its roots began in 1878 and, two years later, the party grew strong enough to capture control of the state legislature. William Mahone, the party's leader, was elected to the U.S. Senate in 1880. The party's influence faded rapidly in the 1830s when they lost control of the general assembly and the governorship.

REAGAN, John Henninger (Sevier Co., Tenn., Oct. 8, 1818 — Palestine, Tex., Mar. 6, 1905). Politician. He was a prominent figure in

Texas politics before his election as a Democrat to the U.S. Congress (1857-61). At the outbreak of the Civil War he was a member of the Texas secession convention (1861) and served the Confederacy as postmaster general and acting secretary of the treasury. After the Civil War ended, he returned to the U.S. Congress (1875-87), where he co-authored the act that establsihed the Interstate Commerce Commission (1887). He was a U.S. senator from 1887 to 1891.

RECONSTRUCTION. A term referring to the period of time (1865-77) immediately following the Civil War, and to the process of bringing back to the Union the 11 seceded states of the Confederacy. At the close of the war the Confederate states came under the military control of the U.S. government and were regarded as conquered territories rather than members of the Union. In addition to the intense bitterness felt by Southerners and Northerners alike, the problems faced during the Reconstruction period were political, economic and social. Politically it was a matter of restoring state governments; economically it was necessary to put the financially ruined states back on their feet; socially it was a matter of firmly establishing the legal status of the 4 million newly freed slaves.

President Abraham Lincoln's policy toward the South, put into effect during the war in 1863, was one of leniency. He proclaimed that if 10% of the voting population of a Confederate state took the prescribed oath of allegiance to the Union and abolished slavery, that state government would be recognized. Virginia, Tennessee, Louisiana, and Arkansas tried Lincoln's plan but Congress refused to seat their elected representatives. Upon Lincoln's assassination, April 15, 1865, Vice President Andrew Johnson assumed the presidency and continued Lincoln's lenient, moderate program. Johnson followed Lincoln's 10% plan but excepted individuals owning more than $20,000 worth of property—an attempt to put political control in the hands of small landowners. As had happened with Lincoln's plan, Johnson's was also challenged by radical congressmen wishing to control the Reconstruction process.

Johnson appointed provisional governors and by the time Congress reconvened in December, 1865, all ex-Confederate states (with the exception of Texas) had established civil governments and elected congressional representatives. Congress, however, again refused to seat them.

Northerners became enraged over the "Black Codes" which were being established in the Southern states; laws that severely limited the status of Negroes. The Black Codes were particularly harsh in Mississippi and Louisiana and were the cause of many race riots. On April 9, 1866 the Civil Rights Act was passed, the provisions of which were incorporated into the Fourteenth Amendment.

On March 2, 1867 the Reconstruction Act was passed; a congressional attempt to undermine presidential leniency and secure control of Reconstruction. The act provided for the establishment of five military districts in the remaining ten Southern states (Tennessee had been readmitted in 1866). The purpose of the act was to effect a registration of voters, including Negroes, and these voters were to elect representatives to state conventions which would write new constitutions. The constitutions were to be ratified by the voters and submitted to Congress for approval. Thereafter, when the Fourteenth Amendment was ratified by the state's legislature, the state would be readmitted to the Union. Having secured passage of the Reconstruction Act, radicals then sought to remove Johnson from office. In February, 1868, Johnson was impeached by the House of Representatives but he narrowly escaped conviction when the Senate fell one vote short. That year Ulysses S. Grant was elected President.

Following the conditions of the Reconstruction Act, in 1868 six states were readmitted to the Union: Alabama, Arkansas, Florida, Louisiana, North Carolina, and South Carolina. By July, 1870, the remaining four had been readmitted: Virginia, Mississippi, Texas, and Georgia. The political aspects of Reconstruction ended during the administration of President Rutherford B. Hayes who withdrew the last of the federal troops from Louisiana in 1877.

The political and economic situation in the South during Reconstruction unfortunately resulted in numerous CARPETBAG governments made up of individuals from the North who went South to take advantage of the unstable conditions. Generally Republican, these governments were comprised of Carpetbaggers, Negro coalitions, and SCALAWAGS (Southerners who were also after personal gain). The resulting Southern hostility toward these governments, along with resentment of the FREEDMAN'S BUREAU, a federal agency designed to help the Negroes, led to racial riots and the formation of secret terrorist societies devoted to white supremacy. The KU KLUX KLAN was the most powerful of these organizations. One of the Klan's purposes was to intimidate Negro voters, and by 1876 the Democratic party had gained control in all the Southern states except Florida, South Carolina, and Louisiana.

Although Reconstruction did result in some sound social legislation for the Negroes, such as improved education, the newly-freed slaves found that they were not much better off economically. Sharecropping, which replaced slave life on the plantations, was little more than another form of bondage. Despite the Fifteenth Amendment, poll taxes and education requirements for voting that were established in many Southern states during the 1880s and 1890s, effectively disenfranchised the Negroes. Laws prohibiting intermarriage were adopted, beginning in Tennessee in 1870, and were followed by other "Jim Crow" laws throughout the South that separated whites and Negroes on public transportation facilities, and barred Negroes from restaurants and other public establishments. By the turn of the century a distinct color line had been established in the South.

Reconstruction helped transform the South from an agrarian society into an industrial region, and resulted in improving schooling and taxation methods, but it also intensified the racial issue. It did not bring about the social changes that had been hoped for by the radical congressmen who passed the Reconstruction Act.

RED RIVER, Ark./La./Tex. River originating from two small streams: the North Fork in the Texas Panhandle and a creek in the Llano Estacado. They meet north of Vernon to form the Red River, which then travels east-southeast creating the boundaries between Texas-Oklahoma and Texas-Arkansas. The river then winds south to enter Louisiana, through the Atchafalaya River, to the Mississippi River. Lake Texoma with its Denison Dam and Lake Texarkana are found on the river in Texas. In Louisiana it is navigable to above Shreveport. One of the most important rivers of the American Southwest, it is the southernmost of the major tributaries of the Mississippi River. It measures approximately 1,300 miles long and drains 90,000 square miles. The river's name comes from the color of the heavy sediment it carries. During the Civil War, it served as one of the major export routes. The river was fully mapped after Randolph Marcy discovered its source in 1852.

RED RIVER, Ky. Easterly offshoot of the Kentucky River, which rises in Madison Co.,

central Kentucky, and flows eastward more than 75 miles through Daniel Boone National Forest to end at the southeastern tip of Wolfe Co. The Red River Gorge National Geographical Area is on the river.

REDROCK MOUNTAIN, Va. Mountain (4,434 feet), on the boundary of Russell and Smyth Counties. It was named because of the color of the rocks on its crest.

REDSTONE ARSENAL, Ala. Military installation and rocketry and spacecraft research center, located in Huntsville. The George C. Marshall Space Flight Center is part of this facility.

REED, Stanley Forman (Maysville, Ky., Dec. 31, 1884 — Huntington, N.Y., Apr. 3, 1980). Jurist. An associate justice of the Supreme Court (1938-57) appointed by President Franklin D. Roosevelt, he was a moderate influence in decisions split between liberal and conservative factions. Reed served Roosevelt as counsel for the Reconstruction Finance Corporation (1932-35) and as Solicitor General (1935-38) under the New Deal.

REED, Walter (Gloucester, Va., Sept. 13, 1851 — Washington, D.C., Nov. 22, 1902). U.S. Army pathologist and bacteriologist. Reed obtained his medical degree from the University of Virginia (1869) before he was 18. He was commissioned in the Army Medical Corps in 1875, and began to specialize in bacteriology. In 1900 he headed the commission to investigate the causes and mode of transmission of an epidemic of yellow fever among American troops in Havana, Cuba. He and other doctors conducted a series of daring experiments using human volunteers. The results of the experiments proved the fever was caused and transmitted by a virus carried by a certain type of mosquito. Shortly before Reed's death, Harvard conferred on him an honorary degree of AM, and the University of Michigan gave him the degree of LL.D. The Army Medical Center in Washington, D.C., is named in his honor.

REESE, Lizette Woodworth (Waverly, Md., Jan. 9, 1856 — Baltimore, Md., Dec. 17, 1935). Poet and educator. Known for her lyricism, condensation of form, and sincere emotion, she based her work largely on the impressions of her simple, rural childhood near Waverly, Md. She began teaching at St. John's

Parish School in Waverly and continued in the Baltimore Public School system until her retirement (1921). Her reputation as a poet began with her first published work, *A Branch of May* (1887). She produced five additional collections of poetry and two of reminiscences. She was best known for her sonnet "Years" (1891).

REFUGIO, Tex. Town (pop. 3,898), seat of Refugio Co., in central Texas. Located on the north bank of Mission River, Refugio was settled in the 1830s by Irish and Mexican colonists. The town's economy is based on oil and gas wells, cattle raising, and grain farms.

REID, David Settle (Rockingham Co., N.C., April 19, 1813 — Reidsville, N.C., June 19, 1891). Politician. A staunch North Carolina Democrat, he was a state senator (1835-42), and U.S. congressman (1843-47), before becoming governor (1851-54). Reid was a U.S. senator (1854-59), and argued in defense of slavery. He was a member of the North Carolina secession convention, and was a delegate to the 1861 peace convention in Washington, D.C., which tried to devise a means of preventing the impending Civil War. Following the war was a member of the state constitutional covention.

REIDSVILLE, Ga. City (pop. 2,296), seat of Tattnall Co., in southeastern Georgia. This agricultural community was incorporated in 1838. Cotton and tobacco are grown here and light industries include cotton ginning and naval stores.

RENO, Jesse Lee (Wheeling, W.Va., June 20, 1823 — Maryland, Sept. 14, 1862). Military officer. A West Point graduate, he served in the Mexican War and at the outbreak of the Civil War was commissioned a brigadier general in the Confederate Army. Serving under Gen. Ambrose Burnside, he was in the North Carolina Campaign, the second battle of Bull Run, and at Chantilly. He was killed during the Battle of South Mountain. Reno, Nev., is named for him.

RESACA DE LA PALMA, Tex. Valley in a dried-up water bed of the Rio Grande River, north of Brownsville. It is of historical importance as the site of the second engagement of the Mexican War on May 9, 1846. It was here that U.S. Gen. Zachary Taylor and his troops charged and defeated the forces of Mexican Gen. Mariano Aristo as they tried to return home after the battle of Palo Alto. Those Mexicans who escaped did so by crossing the Rio Grande.

REUTHER, Walter Philip (Wheeling, W.Va., Sept 1, 1907 — Pellston, Mich., May 10, 1970). Labor leader. After becoming a tool and dye apprentice at the age of sixteen, he moved to Detroit, Mich., where he was promoted to foreman in the tool and dye trade. He finished his high school education but left college in his third year to travel. He worked for a time in a Russian auto factory, an experience which left him with a strong dislike for Communism, which he fought throughout his career. Returning to Detroit, he became president of the local chapter of the United Auto Workers (UAW) union and was instrumental in making the UAW more influential in the auto industry. In 1946 he became president of the UAW, and in 1952 he became president of the Congress of Industrial Organizations (CIO). He engineered the merger of those two unions (AFL-CIO) in 1955 and became its vice president. After years of conflicting philosophies and strained relations with George Meany (president of the AFL-CIO), he broke away with the UAW and later formed the Alliance for Labor Action.

REVELS, Hiram Rhoades (Fayetteville, N.C., c. 1822 — Aberdeen, Miss., Jan. 16, 1901). Educator and politician. The first black to serve in the U.S. Senate, Revels was trained for the ministry in Ohio and at Knox College, Ill. After ordination (1845) he developed and administered a school for free Negroes in St. Louis, Mo. Revels recruited blacks to fight with the Union Army during the Civil War and served himself as a chaplain in Vicksburg, Mississippi. After the war he was elected as a Republican from Mississippi to the Senate seat that had been held by Jefferson Davis (1870), and served in that office for one year. During his time in the Senate, Revels worked to develop a cordial relationship between North and South, seeking restoration of complete civil and political rights for the defeated parties. After his term in office Revels was appointed to the presidency of Alcorn University (1876-82).

REVOLUTION, American. The war of the thirteen American colonies for independence from Great Britain, which began in New England in 1775 and concluded with the recognition of the United States of America in 1783.

The war was initiated by battles over trade and taxation policies in New England, but the Southern colonies provided the military and constitutional leaders of the independence movement, and the second, conclusive phase of the military campaigning was fought almost entirely in the South. Almost two years before the final treaty was signed in Paris, the battle between the Revolutionary and British armies ended with the surrender of Lord Charles CORNWALLIS to Commander-in-chief George WASHINGTON et YORKTOWN, Virginia, on October 19, 1781.

The causes of the war lay in colonial trade policies. As early as 1673 the English Parliament had instituted Navigation Acts that restricted exports from the American colonies to English and Irish ports. There was no significant political conflict between the home country and its American colonies, and the two-month transatlantic voyage to and from London limited British ability and willingness to infringe on habitual and open breech of trade restrictions by Americans. It was only after the expansion of its North American empire at the close of the French and Indian War in 1763 that Great Britain felt compelled to consolidate its authority over the American colonies to protect them from foreign interference and to marshal resources for payment of war debts. Beginning in 1763 Parliament passed a series of acts to enforce exaction of revenue from the colonies. By 1765 these had brought the colonial legislatures and the royal governors into open conflict over the Quartering Act to force support of the British army, which remained in effect, and the STAMP ACT to tax legal documents, which was repealed in 1766. These parties struggled again in 1767 over the Townsend Acts, a series of tariffs that had been removed by 1770 from all commodities with the exception of tea.

On December 16, 1773, Massachusetts patriots destroyed British cargos in the Boston Tea Party, forcing London into reprisals to maintain its authority. The most notorious of these Intolerable, or Coercive Acts of 1774 was the Boston Port Act, which closed the harbor pending damages for the vandalized tea. To the surprise of the British authorities, the Southern colonies rallied to the support of their New England compatriots. Virginia, North Carolina, and South Carolina sent especially conspicuous shipments of supplies to help Boston survive the British stockade, an action that indicated for the first time the solidarity of the colonies. The Virginia legislature further

passed a resolution denouncing the Port Act as a "hostile invasion," providing the earliest political indication that the trade disputes would erupt into a war of independence. Because of this resolve, drafted by Patrick HENRY, James MASON, and Thomas JEFFERSON, the royal governor Lord DUNMORE dissolved the HOUSE OF BURGESSES. The Virginians responded by forming the earliest of the COMMITTEES OF CORRESPONDENCE, networks devoted to patriotic communications between the colonies. These communications led directly to the meeting of the First Continental Congress in September and October of 1774. It was here that Patrick Henry stirred the assembly with his "give me liberty or give me death" speech. Most of the delegates from twelve colonies, minus Georgia, were more prone to negotiation, but the most probable compromise solution, from Joseph Galloway of Pennsylvania, was rejected by a bloc headed by Richard Henry LEE of Virginia, and the Congress ended with declaration of a boycott on British imports.

The war began when the British in Boston moved to capture rebel munitions and met stiff, though unsuccessful, resistance from volunteer "minutemen" at Lexington and Concord on April 19, 1775. On the same day that the Second Continental Congress met in Philadelphia, May 10, 1775, a band of Green Mountain Boys under Ethan Allen surprised and commandeered the British garrison at Fort Ticonderoga, New York. In the South, virtually simultaneous rebellion took the form of the North Carolina MECKLENBURG Resolutions of May 31 that suspended Parliamentary laws. On June 15 the Continental Congress chose George Washington commander of the Army of the United Colonies on Thomas Jefferson's nomination. Two days later, on June 17, 1775, the Boston volunteers again demonstrated their gallantry against overwhelming odds at the Battle of Bunker Hill.

The early battles of the war were fought in the New England and Middle Atlantic colonies, with the British strengthening their control of New York City and the Americans gaining control of New Jersey and defending their domination of New England. The earliest important battle in the South was near Norfolk, Virginia, at GREAT BRIDGE, where patriots drove Governor Dunmore into naval retreat on December 11, 1775. Dunmore returned to burn NORFOLK on January 1, 1776, but was driven from Virginia again a month later. The royal governor of North Carolina, Josiah MARTIN, also rallied his Tory sympathizers for a stand against the patriots, but the Americans were decisive victors at the Battle of MOORE'S CREEK BRIDGE on February 27, 1776. The first British naval strike against the South came on June 28, 1776, when General Henry Clinton attacked Charleston, South Carolina. He encountered a resiliant palmetto fort constructed by William MOULTRIE on Sullivan's Island at the mouth of the harbor and turned back toward New York after what became known as Fort Moultrie withstood a bombardment lasting eleven hours.

The British would not mount another major attack on the South for two years. But during that time the Southern colonies made major contributions to George Washington's campaigns in the North. They also furnished the leaders of the constitutional phase of the Revolutionary movement. The Virginia Bill of Rights was the first great document of the Revolution; it was drafted by George MASON and ratified by the Virginia Convention on June 12, 1776. On June 29 the same convention adopted the constitution of the independent Commonwealth of Virginia. These were the basis for the ratification in Congress on July 4, 1776, of the Declaration of Independence. The author was another Virginian, Thomas Jefferson, who, under the influence of the English philosopher John Locke, presented the argument that the British had abrogated their social contract with the Americans by depriving the colonies of essential rights. The argument was especially persuasive to lingering loyalists, notably Georgians, disillusioned with Britain but opposed on principle to armed insurrection of any sort.

When the war in the North appeared to have reached a stalemate, British Gen. Sir Henry Clinton decided to shift his attack to the South, hoping to advance northward through traditionally loyalist territory toward Philadelphia. SAVANNAH, Georgia fell to the British, led by Col. Archibald Campbell, on December 29, 1778, and British forces moved up the Savannah River to capture Augusta, Georgia, on January 29, 1779. The patriots regained some ground with victories at Port Royal, South Carolina, on February 3 and at Kettle Creek, Georgia, on February 14, but hopes of recapturing Augusta were crushed by the defeat at Briar Creek, Georgia, on February 14. By the end of the year, American forces under Major Gen. Benjamin Lincoln were still attempting to regain Savannah. A final attempt at a siege in league with the French navy led by Admiral Comte d'Estaing collapsed on October 20, 1779.

When the French left South Carolinan waters, British Gen. Clinton launched a second, full-scale attack on CHARLESTON, which finally fell after a month of British assaults on May 12, 1780. Justifiably feeling his troops in full control of Georgia and South Carolina, Clinton sailed for New York City, leaving the command to Gen. Lord Cornwallis. Cornwallis quickly gained a convincing victory over the new American commander, Gen. Horatio GATES, in the Battle of CAMDEN on August 16, 1780. Gates fled toward North Carolina, and Cornwallis appeared ready to pursue, but an American force crushed a British flank at KING'S MOUNTAIN, South Carolina, on October 7, 1780, forcing Cornwallis into winter quarters at Winnsboro for consolidation of his troops.

During that winter respite, the American command in the Carolina campaign was passed from Gates to Major Gen. Nathanael Greene, whose command opened with a surprising victory engineered by Daniel MORGAN at COWPENS, South Carolina, on January 17, 1781. Cornwallis pressed to avenge the defeat, and so was forced into a costly victory at GUILFORD COURTHOUSE on March 15, 1781. When Cornwallis and his weakened troops moved east toward naval support at the mouth of the Chesapeake, Green moved south on an inland route to wage a war of attrition that left the British with little but Charleston by the end of the war.

Cornwallis' search for naval support brought him to Yorktown, Virginia, which he began to reinforce during the summer of 1781. This disregarded his commander Clinton's orders to remain in the Carolinas while the British fleet attacked the Delaware Bay. Learning of Cornwallis' position, Washington abandoned his own plans for an attack on New York and collaborated with the French fleet for a conclusive victory on the Chesapeake. The French Admiral François de Grasse arrived at the mouth of the bay on August 30, held his position against the British fleet sent from New York by Clinton, and so cut off Cornwallis' escape to the sea. By September 28 Washington had marched 17,000 troops to the inland side of Yorktown for a siege. Cornwallis, forced into inner fortifications and faced with Washington's progressive deployment of artillery, abandoned plans for a final desperate flight and surrendered his troops on October 19, 1781.

The Revolutionary War begun at Lexington, Massachusetts, was brought to a close by this victory of Washington in his home state of Virginia. Only minor skirmishes in the west punctuated the protracted diplomatic negotiations lasting until the signing of the preliminary peace treaty in Paris onApril 19, 1783.

RHETT, Robert Barnwell (Beaufort, S.C., Dec. 21, 1800 — St. James Parish, La., Sept. 4, 1876). Politician. A lawyer who served in the South Carolina legislature, he went on to become state attorney general (1832), a U.S. Representative (1837-49), and a U.S. Senator (1850-52). Rhett was a member of the Confederate Provincial Congress (1861) and was often at odds with Confederate President Jefferson Davis.

RIBAUT, Jean (Dieppe, France, c. 1520 — Florida, Sept. 23, 1565). French adventurer and explorer. He pioneered the early colonization of Florida and South Carolina, establishing a colony at the present Port Royal, S.C., which he called Charlesfort, in 1562. In 1565, after a skirmish with members of the Spanish colony in St. Augustine, Fla., Ribaut was put to death by the Spanish.

RICE. Cereal grass native to Asia and cultivated in the American South since the 17th century. Rice thrives naturally in low-lying, subtropical areas such as those found in portions of Louisiana and Mississippi; however, irrigation has assisted cultivation in higher elevations with sufficient heat, such as those found in portions of Arkansas and Texas. In 1980 rice was the second most valuable crop harvested in Louisiana and Arkansas; it ranked third among crops harvested in Mississippi in that year. Crops are also harvested in Texas and South Carolina.

RICE, Grantland (Murfreesboro, Tenn., Nov. 1, 1880 — New York, N.Y., July 13, 1954). Journalist and author. After working for a Nashville newspaper, he joined the staff of the New York *Tribune* (1914-30). In 1930 he founded his own syndicated column, specializing in sports, "The Spotlight." His books include *Only the Brave* (1941).

RICE UNIVERSITY. Independent coed university located on a 300-acre campus in Houston, Tex. The university was founded in 1891 by a fund set up by William Marsh Rice who was a philanthropist and cotton merchant. Originally named William Marsh Rice Institute, the school began as a tuition-free institution "dedicated to the advancement of literature, science and art." In 1924 a policy of admitting only 450 undergraduates annually, and unlimited graduate students, was put into practice. This plan was not modified until 1964 when total enrollment admissions were expanded. Tuition was charged beginning in 1965.

Rice offers five college divisions: Humanities and Social Sciences, Sciences, Music, Architecture, and Engineering. Majors include chemical physics, linguistics, legal studies, managerial studies, and biochemistry. Of all recent Rice graduates, 28% immediately pursue full-time graduate study; 15% attend medical school; 2% dental school; 15% law school. Rice is rated among the nation's top 100 producers of medical school entrants and has the distinction of being one of the few institutions to have over half its medical school applicants accepted. The school is also numbered among the top 100 producers of future business executives.

Library: 1,000,000 volumes, 5,000 journal subscriptions. Faculty: 476. Enrollment: 3,484 total graduate and undergraduate. Degrees: Bachelor's, Master's, Doctorate.

RICHARDSON, Henry Hobson (St. James Parish, La., Sept. 29, 1838 — Boston, Mass., April 28, 1886). Architect. After studying at Harvard and in Paris, he returned to the U.S., and was first commissioned to design the First Unitarian Church in Springfield, Mass., in 1866. He is noted as the initiator of the return of Romanesque architecture. Richardson also built St. Asylum Church in Buffalo, N.Y., and New Brattle Square and Trinity Churches in Boston. In later years his work turned to commercial architecture, such as the design of the Marshall Field Wholesale Store in Chicago, Ill.

RICHARDSON, Tex. Town (pop. 72,496) in Dallas and Collin Counties, in northeast Texas. Richardson is primarily a residential area located ten miles north of Dallas. Its industries include electronics equipment, industrial machinery, clothing, and feed mills. Richardson's population increased 189% between 1960 and 1970.

RICHBERG, Donald Randall (Knoxville, Tenn., July 10, 1881 — Charlottesville, Va., Nov. 27, 1960). Public official. Richberg was a Chicago attorney who specialized in railroad and labor legislation. In 1933 he helped draft the National Industrial Recovery Act, for which he served as adviser and chief administrator. He was the author of numerous books including *Government and Business Tomorrow* (1943) and *Labor Union Monopoly* (1957).

RICHMOND, Ky. City (pop. 21,705), seat of Madison Co., central Kentucky, in the bluegrass region. Incorporated in 1800, it is a major tobacco and livestock market, and is noted for its thoroughbred horses. The Civil War battle of Richmond was fought here on August 30, 1862, giving a victory to the Confederacy. Eastern Kentucky University and a U.S. Army depot are located here.

RICHMOND, University of. Independent coed Baptist institution located on a 350-acre campus in Richmond, Va., The University was founded in 1830 by Virginia Baptists and called Richmond College until the name was changed in 1920. The school has several major divisions: two undergraduate liberal arts colleges— Richmond and Westhampton; the Graduate School; University College; T. C. Williams School of Law; and the School of Business Administration. The South provides 55% of the students, and 38% are from Middle Atlantic states; 23% of graduates go on to further study.

Library: 350,000 volumes, 2,400 journal subscriptions, 5,000 records/tapes. Faculty: 329. Enrollment: 4,189 total. Degrees: Bachelor's, Master's.

RICHMOND, Va. Independent city (pop. 219,214), and state capital, located on the north bank of the James River 90 miles inland from the Atlantic Ocean. Richmond is the commercial center of central Virginia and the heart of a metropolitan area of more than 630,000 residents. Located at the navigable head of the James River, the city has been a manufacturing center for most of its modern history. It is the headquarters for the Southern tobacco industry and the site of a Philip Morris plant that is one of the world's largest and most modern tobacco processing facilities. Other important manufactures are chemicals and paper goods.

Richmond is one of the most historic cities in the Southern states. The site was first visited by English settlers in 1607, when Captains John Smith and Christopher Newport sailed up the James to the Richmond falls and erected a cross on one of the river islands. Two years later the lands of the present site of the city were purchased from the local Indian chief Powhatan, and a settlement was established at a point in the city traditionally called Rockett's district. Smith, meanwhile, had settled three miles downstream on the opposite bank of the river at

City of Richmond, Va. before the Civil War bombardment

a camp called Nonesuch. When the first settlers of Richmond were ravaged by Indian attacks, they sought refuge with Smith. He treated them as competitors for the fur and tobacco resources of the region, refused to return them to their homes, and so caused the abandonment of the original settlement of Richmond.

In 1618 a series of land grants to settlers in Virginia began to encourage growth of homesteads along the James River inland to the falls at Richmond, which then became the outermost frontier trading post of the Virginia colonists. Truces had been negotiated with the Indians, but the pioneers were uneasy enough to erect Fort Charles near the falls in Richmond in 1645. The fort was supplied by William Byrd, thus beginning an era of control over the region by the Byrd family, who had inherited rights to the lands by intermarriage with the Stegg family who came to Virginia from England in 1637. It was William Byrd I who defended Richmond against Indian attack in Bacon's Rebellion of 1676.

The frontier settlement at Richmond only began its evolution into an important city in 1733, when William Byrd II visited his family tract and laid out the earliest town plan. Formal surveying of the original plot just downstream from the falls was completed in 1737. In 1742 the settlement was incorporated as a town and named after Richmond on the Thames in England because its planners envisaged a similarly civilized city. At that time the population of the settlement was 250.

Early Richmond prospered as a depot for shipping goods from the frontier inland to ports downstream and from there to England. Construction of the existing St. John's Episcopal Church began in 1741, and by 1759 Richmond had grown enough to have the Henrico County courthouse relocated within its town limits. In 1769 William Byrd III expanded his father's plans by parceling off additional lands to the west of the original city. The Virginia convention to elect representatives to the Continental Congress of 1775 met in St. John's Church in Richmond. It was on that occasion and in that place that Patrick Henry delivered his famous "give me liberty or give me death" speech. The success of the convention insured Richmond's future growth. In 1777 the public records of Virginia were moved from Williamsburg to Richmond, and in 1779 Richmond was declared the capital of the Commonwealth of Virginia. In 1780 it was the site of the first convention of the Virginia assembly. For this the city paid dearly in 1781, when British troops commanded by Benedict Arnold, the defector from the American cause, burned part of Richmond in an attempt to destroy the munitions stored in the city.

Richmond recovered quickly, however, and it was incorporated as a city in 1782. Between the Revolution and the Civil War the city enjoyed steady population growth and a building boom related to its role as state capital. The central part of the state capitol was designed by Thomas Jefferson and completed in 1792. The governor's mansion, designed in federal style, was completed in 1813. These investments by the state encouraged local business, notably the Tredegar Ironworks which was completed in 1836. In that year a railroad link joined Richmond with Fredericksburg, and by 1851 canal works had linked the city with towns upriver on the James.

All of this prosperity made Richmond the logical choice for capital of the Confederacy in 1861. In this role the city suffered from the military concentration on it by Union forces. At the outbreak of the Civil War its population was fewer than 40,000, but this was soon swollen by army officers, wounded soliders, and prisoners of war. The city was under siege for most of the war, and from 1862 on it was ruled by martial law declared by Confederate President Jefferson Davis. Richmond survived attack by land from McClellan's Union army and attack by water from the gunboat *Monitor*. Finally, On April 2, 1865, it was evacuated and burned by retreating Confederate troops.

Ironically, after the war Richmond's recovery derived from Northern businessmen's interest in its prime commercial location. The capital they provided restored the damaged railroad links and insured the city's growth to its present status as the headquarters of the tobacco industry. Richmond is now also an important center for the U.S. defense industry, and the headquarters of the fifth district of the

City of Richmond, Va. after the siege, showing the ruins of the state arsenal

Federal Reserve Bank. The city is also a media center for both broadcast and printed communications. Virginia Commonwealth University, which has the largest college enrollment in the state, is located here.

RIDGWAY, Matthew Bunker (Fort Monroe, Va., March 3, 1895 —). Military officer. A West Point graduate (1917), Ridgway was the general who executed the first airborne invasion in U.S. history with the assault on Sicily (1943), and was commanding general of the 18th Airborne when they parachuted into Normandy (1944) and of the action which followed in the Netherlands and Germany. He succeeded Dwight D. Eisenhower as Supreme Commander of Allied Forces in Europe (1952) and was appointed Army Chief of Staff (1953). Ridgway was responsible for the counteroffensive which drove the Communists out of South Korea in 1950. His memoirs were published under the title *Soldier* (1956).

RINEHART, William Henry (near Union Bridge, Md., Sept. 13, 1825 — Rome, Italy, Oct. 28, 1874). Sculptor. Rinehart rose to prominence from modest beginnings in Baltimore, and spent many years working in Italy. Along with his marble sculptures, Rhinehart executed the bronze doors for the capitol in Washington, D.C. The work for which he is best known is "Clytie," now in the Peabody Institute.

RIO GRANDE RIVER, Tex. River originating in the San Juan Mountains of southwest Colorado. The river flows through the midline of New Mexico and goes on to form the border between Texas and Mexico, and creating Big Bend National Park. Its total length is 1,885 miles. The ninth longest river in the Western Hemisphere, and the largest river in the state, its flow is erratic, ranging from a tiny stream to flood rates in excess of 600,000 cubic feet per second. Because of the flood damage potential, as well as the great need for irrigation in the state, several water projects have been developed along its course. The river drains almost 50,000 square miles, and waters most of the Lower Valley of Texas before it empties into the Gulf of Mexico near Brownsville. By an agreement with Mexico the Rio Grande is closed to navigation.

RITA BLANCA CREEK, Tex. Stream rising in New Mexico and flowing east into the northwest corner of Texas to join the Canadian River at Boys Ranch, for a total distance of approximately 75 miles.

RIVERS, Thomas Milton (Jonesboro, Ga., Sept. 3, 1888 — New York, N.Y., May 12, 1962). Virologist. A graduate of Emory College, Georgia (1909) and Johns Hopkins (1915), he began research (1918) on a form of pneumonia that accompanied measles. Working with the Rockefeller Institute for Medical Research (1937-55), he performed pioneer viral research on flu, chicken pox, and polio, and managed the research projects leading to the Salk antipolio vaccines.

RIVES, William Cabell (Nelson Co., Va., May 4, 1793 — near Charlottesville, Va., Apr. 25, 1868). Politician. An advocate of Jeffersonian politics, he was elected congressman from Virginia 1823 to 1829, and from 1829-32, he was U.S. minister to France. Elected a U.S. senator (1832), he resigned in 1834 when the Virginia Assembly asked him to oppose President Andrew Jackson's banking program. He returned to the Senate (1836-39, 1841-45) and served as minister to France (1849-53). He originally opposed secession but became a member of the Second Confederate Congress.

RIVIERA BEACH, Fla. Town (pop. 26,596), Palm Beach Co., in southeastern Florida. A resort village incorporated in 1922, it is located north of West Palm Beach on Lake Worth. A major factor in its development has been the influx of research and developmental companies as well as aerospace industries.

ROANOKE, Va. Independent city (pop. 100,427), in the southwest of the state, at the southern end of the Shenandoah Valley and between the Blue Ridge Mountains to the east

and the Allegheny Mountains to the west. It was settled in 1825 and incorporated in 1874. Called Big Lick when it was linked with Lynchburg by the Tennessee Railroad in 1852, it is now the industrial hub of a metropolitan area of 225,000 persons. The principal products manufactured are electrical and mechanical equipment, and textile goods.

ROANOKE COLONY. The first English attempt to settle the American South in 1587, which ended when the isolated homesteaders were thought to have been massacred by Indians. Given a land grant in the New World by Queen Elizabeth, Sir Walter Raleigh sent three expeditions to Roanoke. The first (1584) returned with glowing reports of the New World and was followed by a second expedition in 1585, but they suffered such hardships that they returned to England with Sir Francis Drake the following year. A third expedition consisting of seven ships and 108 colonists sailed from England on April 9, 1587, under the leadership of John White, and settled on the island, now part of North Carolina but then part of the Virginia Colony. Just after the birth of Virginia Dare, the first English child born in North America, John White returned to England for supplies. He was delayed there by the English war with Spain, and when a relief party finally reached Roanoke in 1591 there was no remaining trace of the settlers. According to legend this rescue party found the word "Croatan" carved on a tree, but this story of a final message from the "lost colony" has never been substantiated or explained.

ROANOKE ISLAND, N.C. Dare Co., in the Choatan Sound, off the Atlantic coast, in northeastern North Carolina. The island is 12 miles long and averages three miles in width. Fishing is a primary industry, and Manteo is the major community. The island's historical importance is largely tied to ROANOKE COLONY, often referred to as the "Lost Colony".

ROANOKE RAPIDS, N.C. City (pop. 14,102), Halifax Co., in northern North Carolina. This vacation spot was founded in 1893 and named for the rapids on the Roanoke River. Textiles, electronic transformers, paper, and plastics are manufactured here, and corn, cotton, peanuts, and tobacco are raised.

ROANOKE RAPIDS LAKE, Va. Lake formed by the constuction of the Roanoke Rapids Dam on the Roanoke River. Completed in 1955, the dam is 72 feet high and 3,050 feet long.

ROANOKE RIVER, Va. River rising in the southwest part of the state in Roanoke Co. It flows 380 miles and forms the boundary of seven counties before reaching Albemarle Sound, N.C. Three of the largest dams along its course are the John H. Kerr, Roanoke Rapids, and Gaston. The Indian work *roanoke* means "white shells" or "money" (Indian wampum).

ROBBINS, Fredrick Chapman (Auburn, Ala., Aug. 25, 1916 —). Pediatrician. Having earned his M.D. at Harvard, he practiced at Children's Hospital, Boston, Mass., for two years prior to joining the army. Robbins served in the Mediterranean Theatre where he was chief of the viral and rickettsial section of the 15th medical general laboratory. Joining J. F. Enders and T. H. Weller (1948) in research at Children's Hospital, he helped produce polio cultures which led to new vaccines, diagnostic techniques, and identification of other viruses. In 1954 he shared the Nobel Prize in Physiology and Medicine with Enders and Weller for breeding the poliomyelitis virus in tissue culture.

ROBERT, Henry Martyn (Robertville, S.C., May 2, 1837 — Hornell, N.Y., May 11, 1923). Military officer. A graduate of the U.S. Military Academy (1857), he was an army engineer involved in the defenses of Washington, D.C. (1861), and Philadelphia, Pa. (1861-62). Robert attained the rank of brigadier general and was chief of Army Engineers in 1901. He was also the author of *Pocket Manual Rules of Order* (1876), the result of a controversial church meeting in New Bedford, Mass., at which there was no accepted procedure and little was accomplished. He began a lengthy study of parliamentary order to formulate practical rules of conduct in public assembly. Assuming that an officer in the army corps of engineers had little expertise in such procedures, he was intitially denied publication; his first distribution of 1,000 copies to lawyers, politicians, and educators was at his own expense. Later editions, beginning with *Robert's Rules of Order*, sold over 2 million copies in his lifetime.

ROBERTS, Elizabeth Madox (Perryville, Ky., 1886 — Orlando, Fla., Mar. 13, 1941). Novelist and poet. Best known for her dialect tales of Kentucky people, her prose is regarded chiefly for its rhythmic beauty. Her works include the novels *The Time of Man* (1926), *Black is My True Love's Hair* (1938); short story collections including *The Haunted Mirror* (1932) and *Not by Strange Gods* (1941); and the poetry collections *Under the Tree* (1922) and *Song in the Meadow* (1940).

ROBERTSON, James (Brunswick Co., Va., June 28, 1742 — Chickasaw Bluffs, Tenn., Sept. 1, 1814). Pioneer. In 1771 he led a group of settlers from North Carolina to Tennessee, where he became a leader of the Watauga Association. He was one of the founders of Nashborough (1780), later called Nashville. He was instrumental in establishing peace with the Chickasaw Indians, and was a member of the Tennessee Constitutional Convention (1796).

ROBINS, Elizabeth (Louisville, Ky., c. 1862 — Brighton, England, May 8, 1952). Actress and author. An advocate of women's suffrage, she was the wife of George Richmond Parks. As an actress she was noted for her interpretations of Ibsen. Under the pseudonym C. E. Raimond she wrote, among other works, *The Magnetic North* (1904), *The Convert* (1907), and *My Little Sister* (1913), a novel about the suffrage movement in England.

ROBINSON, Joseph Taylor (near Lonoke, Ark., Aug. 26, 1872 — Washington, D.C., July 14, 1937). Politician. A lawyer, Robinson's political career began as a U.S. congressman from Arkansas (1903-13). He served two months as governor of Arkansas before he was elected to fill a vacancy in the U.S. Senate (1913-37). He was Democratic minority leader of the Senate (1923-33), and was majority leader from 1933 to 1937. In 1928 he was the unsuccessful candidate for vice president on the ticket with Alfred E. Smith. Robinson played a leading role in the passage of many New Deal measures and was the cosponsor of the Robinson-Patman Act in 1936, which legislated against price discrimination. He led the unsuccessful fight for Franklin D. Roosevelt's Supreme Court reorganization.

ROBINSON, Rubye Doris Smith (Atlanta, Ga., Apr. 25, 1942 — Atlanta, Ga., Oct. 7, 1967). Civil Rights Activist. A sophomore at Spelman College in 1960, she joined the sit-in campaign and helped found the Student Non-Violent Coordinating Committee (SNCC). In

1963 she became administrative assistant to SNCC executive secretary JAMES FORMAN and until 1967 served as SNCC's main administrative and logistical planner. By 1964 she had begun advocating Black African nationalism and a greater say by women within SNCC. In 1966 she became SNCC's executive secretary, supporting the Black Power movement launched in 1966 with JAMES MEREDITH and STOKELY CARMICHAEL.

ROCK HILL, S.C. City (pop. 35,344), York Co., in northern South Carolina. An important textile community, it was settled c. 1855 and incorporated in 1870. Pulp and paper are produced and there is a synthetic fiber factory. Its location near the Catawba River makes it a fertile peach-growing spot with many dairy and beef cattle farms. Winthrop College (1886), Glencairn Gardens, and the Museum of York County are in Rock Hill.

ROCK MUSIC (Rock and Roll). An original American musical form which saw much of its early development in the South before being modified by influences from other parts of the country and abroad (particularly England). Rock and roll has its origins in the late 1940s as a kind of heavily accented music, with debts to JAZZ, BLUES and popular music, which was played primarily by black musicians. Known as "rhythm and blues" (its politest designation) because of its blues roots, it was also labeled "race" music, and many pop music radio stations throughout the country refused to play it. This contempt was to follow rock and roll well into the 1960s as society sought, vainly and often hysterically, to "stop this trash." Led by the increasingly popular recordings of such performers as Fats Domino (1929–) from New Orleans, Chuck Berry (1926–) from Wentzville, Mo., and "Little Richard" Penniman (1932–) from Macon, Ga., rhythm and blues built up an increasingly avid audience among both white and black teen-agers.

In 1954, about the time the term "rock and roll" began to appear, a new wave burst upon the public. Elvis PRESLEY made his first recordings in Memphis with Sun Records. A year later, Bill Haley (1925-81) and the Comets' 'Rock Around the Clock" reached the top of the pop charts, and a new era in popular music had begun. These early years, in which the raucous new music vied for popularity with the bland productions of Eddie Fisher and Doris Day, saw the spectacular rise of Presley with such hits as "Heartbreak Hotel" (1955),

"Hound Dog," and "Don't Be Cruel" (both 1956), an appearance on *The Ed Sullivan Show*, and three-picture movie deal. Rock had taken the country by storm and much of this early activity was generated in the South. As it grew, it drew upon other existing forms, such as COUNTRY AND WESTERN MUSIC, to produce a hybrid form, "rockabilly," a term derived from "rock" and "hillbilly" to indicate a combination of elements taken from both. Among the best-known examples are "That's All Right" (1954) by Presley and "Blue Suede Shoes" by Carl Perkins (1932–), another Sun Records singer. Other performers, such as Jerry Lee Lewis (1935–) and Charlie Rich (1934–), shared a similar background.

Rock and roll music, played over British and West European radio stations, became equally popular in Europe, aided by the success of the film *Rock Around the Clock*, with Bill Haley and Alan Freed (1922-65), who is generally credited with first applying the term "rock and roll" to the new music. As the 1950s drew to a close the first wave of rock, which had started in the South was now firmly entrenched throughout the Western world.

In the 1960s American-influenced British groups, particularly the Beatles and the Rolling Stones, were to return the favor with the "British invasion," beginning in 1964. Thereafter, rock was truly an international affair.

ROCKVILLE, Md. City (pop. 43,811), seat of Montgomery Co., located 12 miles northwest of Washington, D.C. The city occupies 11.5 square miles of the Washington metropolitan area. The town was first laid out in 1784, and its population declined in the 1800s. During the Civil War the town resolved to make every sacrifice before consenting to separation. It suffered during the war because both Union and Confederate troops continuously passed through. Rockville remained a small town until the 1930s and then expanded along with the growth of Washington, and became heavily oriented toward the federal establishment which is the largest employer of Rockville residents.

ROCKY FACE RIDGE, Battle of. Civil War engagement fought May 7-9, 1864, near Dalton in northwest Georgia. The battle was the opening of the Union march across Georgia in 1864 that ended at Savannah, having split the Confederacy along a crucial rail link, devastated much of Georgia, and deprived Gen. Robert E. LEE in Virginia of needed food supplies.

The Confederate command of Gen. Joseph E. JOHNSTON occupied the north-south elevation of Rocky Face Ridge, south of the site of the 1863 battle of Chickamauga, in early May of 1864. In two days of tactical maneuvering, Sherman managed to pressure the Confederates into abandoning this strategic high ground. The crucial charges by the Union in this effort occurred at places known as Buzzard Roost, Poplar Place, and Snake Creek Gap. The Union failed to pursue Johnston's retreat from this area, but it did force him to abandon Dalton and withdraw further southeast into Georgia. This set the pattern of pressure by Sherman and slow retreat by Johnston, which was characteristic of the entire march across Georgia.

ROCKY MOUNT, Battle of. Revolutionary War engagement fought 25 miles north of Camden, S.C., on August 1, 1781. An unsuccessful assault on a Tory position by Revolutionary Gen. Thomas Sumter, it was one of a series of engagements in advance of the major battle of Camden. At Rocky Mount, Sumter completely surrounded a British force of 150 with his own militia of some 400. However, the British took refuge within fortified cabins and Sumter, lacking artillery, was left no alternative but to burn the cabins. He was forced to withdraw when heavy rain made this impossible.

ROCKY MOUNT, N.C. City (pop. 41,283), Edgecombe Co., in east central North Carolina. Settled in 1818 and incorporated in 1867, the city became the commercial center of a rich agricultrual area. Today it is a leaf tobacco market which also produces air pollution control equipment, cottonseed oil, cotton and rayon fabrics, fertilizer, and furniture. There are also bottling works and food and meat packing plants. Farms grow corn, cotton, peanuts, and tobacco.

RODGERS, John (near Havre de Grace, Md., 1773 — Philadelphia, Pa., Aug. 1, 1838). Naval officer. Rodgers distinguished himself as commander of the *President* in victories over several British vessels including the *Little Belt*, (1811). In 1823 Rodgers served briefly as acting Secretary of the Navy.

ROGERS, James Harvey (Society Hill, South Carolina, Sept. 25, 1886 — Rio de Janeiro, Brazil, Aug. 13, 1939). Economist and educator. He was professor of economics at several universities including the University of Missouri (1923-30), before he taught political economy at Yale. In 1931 he was made monetary advisor to President Franklin Roosevelt.

ROGERS, Mount, Va. Peak (5,729 feet) located south of Marion near the Tennessee-North Carolina line in the Blue Ridge Mountains. The highest point in the state, it was named for geologist William Barton Rogers.

ROLLA, Mo. City (pop. 13,303), seat of Phelps Co., in southeast central Missouri. Founded in 1856, it is an industrial center that produces pet food, bakery goods, and plastic pipes. Beef cattle, dairy cows, and poultry are raised, and there are numerous fruit farms. Branches of the University of Missouri and the Missouri School of Mines and Metallurgy are here.

ROLLING FORK RIVER, Ky. River rising in north central Kentucky at the Knox Reservation. The river winds approximately 40 miles southeast to the Abraham Lincoln Birthplace National Historical Site in Larue County.

ROLLINS COLLEGE. Independent coed liberal arts college located on a 65-acre campus in Winter Park, Fla., just outside the city of Orlando. Founded in 1885, Rollins was Florida's first institution of higher learning. Established by the Congregational Church, the college is now wholly independent and nonsectarian. The school offers a variety of majors in such areas as arts and sciences, pre-medicine, pre-engineering, Latin American Studies, business administration, pre-forestry, theatre arts, elementary education, behavioral sciences, international relations, and environmental studies. Graduate study is offered through the Roy E. Crummer School of Finance and Business Administration, and the Graduate School of Education and Human Development. the South provides 40% of the students, 30% are from Middle Atlantic states, 10% from the North Central area, and 20% from New England; 12% go on to graduate school.

Library: 200,000 volumes, 950 journal subscriptions. Faculty: 97. Enrollment: 662 men, 699 women (full-time). Degrees: Bachelor's, Master's.

ROME, Ga. City (pop. 29,654), seat of Floyd Co., northwestern Georgia, on the Coosa River. Founded in 1834, the town is located in a region of farms, woodland, and stone quarries.

Industries include textile and lumber mills, and clothing factories. During the Civil War, the city was the site of a Confederate victory in 1861, but the city's industrial facilities were burned by Union Gen. W.T. Sherman in 1864. It is the home of Shorter College, Berry College, and Floyd Junior College.

ROOT, John Wellborn (Lumpkin, Ga., Jan. 10, 1850 — Chicago, Ill., Jan. 15, 1891). Architect. Educated in England, he earned a degree in civil engineering at New York University (1869). Root was a leader of the "Chicago School" that promoted contemporary architecture. He broke with traditional design and evolved approaches based more on function and geometric form. Among his designs is the Monadnock Building in Chicago (1891). He was one of the planners of the World's Columbian Exposition in Chicago in 1893.

ROSENBERG, Tex. Town (pop. 17,995), Fort Bend Co., in southeast Texas on the Brazos River. The area was first settled by colonists brought in by Stephen F. AUSTIN. In 1920, the discovery of oil in the county made Rosen-

berg a boom town. Today many residents commute to nearby Houston for work.

ROSS, John (near Lookout Mountain, Tenn., Oct. 3, 1790 — Washington, D.C., Aug. 1, 1866). Cherokee Indian chief. Of Scottish-Cherokee blood, he was educated among the whites in Tennessee and fought the Creek Indians in the War of 1812. In 1828 he was made chief of the eastern Cherokee (the western division had already migrated to Oklahoma) and tried in vain to hold onto Cherokee land. He refused to acknowledge a treaty (1835) calling for the removal of his tribe from Georgia. His resistance was futile and in 1838 he led his remaining people to the Indian Territory, many of them dying on the long journey, which is often referred to as "The Trail of Tears." Upon reaching Oklahoma and uniting with the western Cherokee, he was elected leader of the entire Cherokee nation, a position he held until his death.

ROSWELL, Ga. Town (pop. 23,337), Fulton Co., in northwest Georgia. Both its proximity to Atlanta and its location on the Chattahoochee River have contributed to a major boom in population (the population in 1970 was 5,430).

"Trail of Tears." Painting by Robert Lindeux. Cherokee Indians on their way to Indian Territory

Tourism and the tobacco industry have also been important factors in its growth. Union Gen. William Tecumseh Sherman's forces camped here before their march on Atlanta during the Civil War.

RUFFIN, Edmund (Prince George Co., Va., Jan. 5, 1794 — Amelia Co., Va., June 18, 1865). Agriculturist. A farmer, Ruffin believed that worn-out soil could be returned to previous fertility by methods of crop rotation and the addition of fertilizer. He founded and edited the *Farmer's Register* (1833-42) and wrote, among other works, *An Essay on Calcareous Manures* (1832). An avid secessionist, he joined the South Carolina militia, and upon the fall of the Confederacy, committed suicide.

RUSK, David Dean (Cherokee Country, Ga., Feb. 9, 1909 —). Educator and statesman. He graduated from Davidson College and, after serving in World War II, he entered the Department of State (1946-51) where he became the Assistant Secretary of State for Far Eastern Affairs (1950), and played a major role in the U.S. decision on military action in Korea. He headed the Rockefeller Foundation from 1952 to 1960 and, as Secretary of State (1961-69), stressed the need for the U.S. and its Western allies to help underdeveloped nations. He is the author of *The Winds of Freedom* (1963).

RUSK, Thomas Jefferson (Pendleton District, S.C., Dec. 5, 1803 — Nacogdoches, Tex., July 29, 1857). Politican. After moving to Texas in 1835, Rusk became active in Texas politics, and was the first Secretary of War in the new republic's provisional government. Rusk served as chief justice of the Texas Supreme Court (1838-40), and was president of the convention that confirmed the annexation of Texas in 1845. He was a Democratic U.S. Senator from 1846 to 1857.

RUST, John Daniel (Stephens Co., Tex., Sept. 6, 1892 — Pine Bluff, Ark., Jan. 20, 1954). Inventor. Working in his sister's garage, Rust filed his first patent on a mechanical cotton picking machine in 1928. He later collaborated with his brother on many other inventions, including a cotton cleaner.

RUSTON, La. City (pop. 20,585), seat of Lincoln Parish, in north central Louisiana. It was established in 1884 as a railroad community, and today is the cultural and educational focus of the parish. The Louisiana Polytechnic Institute and Grambling State University are here. The town's economy is presently based on light industry and dairy and truck farms.

RUTH, George Herman "Babe" (Baltimore, Md., Feb. 6, 1895 — New York, N.Y., Aug. 16, 1948). Baseball player. The greatest home-run hitter in the game, Ruth discovered baseball while at St. Mary's Industrial School in Baltimore. After minor league experience with a local team, he signed with the Baltimore Orioles and was later sold to the Boston Red Sox as a pitcher. He pitched 29 2/3 scoreless World Series innings for them, and had a 94-46 overall record, but by 1918 he had been shifted to outfield so that he could hit every day. Sold to the New York Yankees in 1920 for $125,000, Ruth began the 14 seasons of home run hitting that established him as the "Sultan of Swat." He broke the home run record in three consecutive seasons (1919-21), hit 60 home runs in 154 games in 1927, led the American League in home runs for 12 seasons, and hit 50 or more home runs in four seasons, all records. His career total of 714 home runs was the record until broken by Hank Aaron in 1974. Less well-known is the fact that Ruth set a lifetime record of 2,056 bases on balls. Somewhat notorious for his rowdy nightlife, Ruth was fined for misconduct several times, and after his retirement in 1935 he failed to attract the job of team manager that he desired. He became the second player to be elected to the Baseball Hall of Fame (1936).

RUTHERFORD, Joseph Franklin (Morgan Co., Mo., Nov. 8, 1869 — San Diego, Calif., Jan. 8, 1942). Religious leader. He was the second president of the Jehovah's Witnesses (1916), having become a member of the sect in 1894 while a lawyer in Booneville, Ky. He remained president until his death, and under his leadership the group grew from 3,000 to 50,000 members.

RUTLEDGE, Edward (Charleston, S.C., Nov. 23, 1749 — Charleston, S.C., Jan. 23, 1800). Politician. In 1773 he opened a Charleston law practice and became a prominent provincial assembly member, state attorney general, and delegate to the Stamp Act Congress (1765). He was a member of the Continental Congress (1774-77), was a signer of the Declaration of Independence, and was a major figure in drawing up the U.S. Constitution. Rutledge was governor of South Carolina from 1798 to 1800. He was the brother of John RUTLEDGE.

RUTLEDGE, John (Charleston, S.C., Sept., 1739 — Charleston, S.C., July 23, 1800). Politician and jurist. After studying law in England, he established a practice in Charleston, South Carolina and began a long career in public service. He was a delegate to the Stamp Act Congress (1765), and to the Continental Congress (1774-76, 1782-83). He was chairman of the committee that framed the South Carolina Constitution in 1776, and served as the state's first president from 1776 to 1778 and then as its governor from 1779 to 1782. He was an associate justice of the U.S. Supreme Court from 1789 to 1791, and was chief justice of the Supreme Court of South Carolina from 1791 to 1795. In 1795 President George Washington nominated him for chief justice of the U.S. Supreme Court, but the Senate refused to confirm the appointment because of Rutledge's opposition to Jay's Treaty. He was the brother of Edward RUTLEDGE.

S

SABINE, Tex. Unincorporated village in Jefferson Co., in the eastern part of the state near the Louisiana border. Founded in 1878 on the west bank of Sabine Pass, Sabine was the scene of a tragic hurricane in 1886 in which 150 people were drowned. Today the area is a fishing resort. Sabine National Forest is nearby.

SABINE CROSSROADS, Battle of. Civil War engagement fought April 8, 1864, in northwest Louisiana. It marked the end of the Union advance in its Red River campaign to capture part of Texas, an express wish of President Abraham Lincoln.

At the battle of Sabine Crossroads the Union force of Gen. Nathaniel P. Banks was in pursuit of the Confederate force of Gen. Richard Taylor. Although outnumbered, Taylor ordered a defense at a crossroads three miles from Mansfield, La. He ordered a defensive charge from the Confederate position at 4:00 P.M. that caught the Union advance lines unprepared. The Confederate troops pushed forward until they encountered the main body of Union troops at a place known as Pleasant Grove. Taylor had stopped Banks at the Sabine Crossroads, but he was denied a complete rout of the Union army during the battle of PLEASANT HILL on the next day.

SABINE RIVER, Tex. River rising in Hunt Co., northeast of Dallas. This 575-mile river flows southeast and south, entering the Gulf of Mexico. It forms the Texas-Louisiana boundary from Panola Co., Tex., to the Gulf. Petroleum products are shipped through the Sabine-Neches Waterway which is part of the Gulf Intracoastal Waterway. Near the river's mouth is Sabine Lake. The river's name comes from the Spanish word *sabinas* meaning "red cedars."

SABLE, Cape, Fla. Monroe Co., in the southern extremity of Florida. The cape is a swampy peninsula about 20 miles long and between five and ten miles wide, and is connected on the east to the Everglades. On the north of the cape is Whitewater Bay; on the south, Florida Bay; and to the west, the Gulf of Mexico. East Cape, below Lake Ingraham, is its southernmost point.

SAINT ALBANS, W.Va. City (pop. 12,402), Charleston Co., in the western part of the state, at the junction of the Coal and Kanawha Rivers. Settled around 1790, it is a residential city that serves as a commercial trade center for this farm region of poultry, dairy and truck farms. There are machine shops and a

358

lamp chimney factory. In 1861 the Battle of Scary Creek was fought here.

SAINT AUGUSTINE, Fla. City (pop. 11,985), seat of St. John's Co., in northeast Florida. The city is located on a peninsula between Matanzas and San Sebastion Rivers. Anastasia Island separates Saint Augustine from the Atlantic Ocean. The oldest city in the U.S., it was founded in 1565 when a Spanish fort was built on the site of an Indian village. Ponce de Leon landed at Saint Augustine in 1513 in search of the Fountain of Youth. It was the scene of much violence, first by English buccaneers and then in the fight for possession between the Spanish, English, and Americans. Incorporated in 1824, it was held by Union troops during the Civil War. Today it is a port of entry and a major shrimping and shipping center as well as a year-round resort. A house constructed here in the late 16th century is said to be the oldest in the country. Castillo de San Marcos the oldest masonry fort in the U.S. (built 1672) is still standing. Saint Augustine is the home of Flagler College.

SAINT CHARLES, Mo. City (pop. 37,379), seat of St. Charles Co., on the Missouri River north of St. Louis. Settled by French traders in 1769 and incorporated as a town in 1809, it is the earliest permanent settlement on the river. It served as the state capital in 1826. There is diversified farming, producing corn, oats, and wheat, as well as coal, gravel, and sand deposits. Manufactures include railroad cars, steel dies, and soda water. Lindenwood College (1827) and Scared Heart Convent (1838) are found here.

SAINT DENIS, Louis Juchereau de (Beauport, Quebec, Canada, Sept. 17, 1676 — Natchitoches, Tex., June 11, 1744). French explorer. He was one of the first explorers of the Red River valley in Louisiana. He gained a wide reputation for his influence among the Indians of Louisiana and Texas.

SAINT FRANCOIS MOUNTAINS, Mo. Mountain range found on the east side of the Salem Plateau, between the Big and St. Francis Rivers. It is not a continuous chain but clusters of peaks, consisting mostly of granite. The mountains cover roughly 70 square miles and are the highest and most rugged hilltop region in Missouri. Taum Sauk Mountain, the highest in the state, is in the range and Lake Wappapello is nearby.

SAINT GEORGE ISLAND, Fla. Island in the southern extremity of the western part of the state, which shelters Apalachicola Bay from the Gulf of Mexico. Originally about 30 miles long, it was separated by a storm into two parts about 20 and 10 miles in length.

SAINT HELENA ISLAND, S.C. Island in Beaufort Co., between Saint Helena and Port Royal Sounds. The island is 18 miles long and averages four to six miles wide. Early in the 18th century, plantation owners on the island became wealthy producing indigo and cotton. After the Civil War, the island became the home of freed black slaves whose descendants still farm there.

SAINT JOHN'S COLLEGE. Independent liberal arts coed institution, located on a 36-acre campus in the Maryland capital of Annapolis. Founded in 1696 as the King William School, the college was chartered under its present name in 1784 and opened in 1786. It is the third-oldest college in the United States. St. John's maintains an additional campus, founded 1964, in Santa Fe, N.M.

The academic emphasis and structure at St. John's are unique. Classes are organized into tutorials, seminars, or laboratories. A common course of study is pursued by all students and because of this structure, the school requires all transfer students to begin as freshmen. Language, mathematics, sciences, music, and humanities requirements are stringent. Grades are given out infrequently, and there are no majors.

Most students are from the Middle Atlantic states, and 36% of students immediately pursue full-time graduate study; 8% enter medical school, 12% law school, 4% business school.

Library: 75,000 volumes, 60 journal subscriptions. Faculty: 56. Enrollment: 196 men, 160 women. Degrees: Bachelor's.

SAINT JOHNS RIVER, Fla. River originating in Brevard Co., in east central Florida near Melbourne. It flows north through eight lakes for about 285 miles to Jacksonville where it turns east and empties into the Atlantic Ocean in Duval County, in the northeast corner of the state. The river was discovered by Jean Ribault in 1562.

SAINT JOSEPH, Mo. City (pop. 76,691), seat of Buchanan Co., in the northwest part of the state, 55 miles northwest of Kansas City on the Missouri River. It was settled in 1826 by Joseph Ribidoux, who established a trading post here. In 1836 the town was part of the Platte Purchase in which several Indian tribes sold land to Missouri. The town was named by Ribidoux after his patron saint. Incorporated as a city in 1845, St. Joseph prospered by equipping prospectors during the gold rush years, and the arrival of the railroad in the mid-1800s opened the city to expanded trade. Located in a rich agricultural area, the city produces bluegrass, corn, fruit, and grains. Industries include the manufacture of textiles, candy, dairy products, and machine goods, and there are extensive meat-packing facilitites. One of the largest stationery plants in the world is located here.

SAINT LOUIS, Mo. Independent city (pop. 453,085), in the east part of the state, on the Mississippi River 20 miles downstream from its confluence with the Missouri River. One of the great economic centers of the Mississippi basin, St. Louis is the heart of a metropolitan area of 2.3 million Missouri and Illinois residents. St. Louis developed as the principal point of departure for Western settlers, and its role as "gateway to the West" is now commemorated by a 630-foot stainless steel Gateway Arch that towers over the downtown riverfront in Jefferson Expansion Memorial Park.

The city's origins are French, and they can be traced to a grant in 1764 of exclusive trading rights with the local Indians issued to the New Orleans merchant Pierre LACLEDE. Laclede immediately traveled upriver to take possession of his grant, and on February 14, 1764, he landed on the present site of the city with a party of 30 men that included his stepson Auguste CHOUTEAU. It was Laclede who named the new settlement after the patron saint of Louis XV of France.

The early history of the settlement is one of shifting colonial allegiances. By the time Laclede arrived, the French had already ceded lands on the east bank of the Mississippi to the British. This brought a migration of French settlers from that region to St. Louis on the river's west bank. In 1770 the Spanish took control of St. Louis under the terms of the earlier Treaty of Fountainebleau (1762) and made the settlement the governmental center of the "Upper Louisiana" territory. St. Louis was thus a Spanish possession during the American Revolution and so remained virtually untouched by the

Gateway Arch in St. Louis, Mo., commemorating the city's role as "gateway to the West"

war. St. Louis came under French possession again in 1800 by the terms of the San Ildefonso Treaty, but the French were by that time already negotioating the Louisiana Purchase with the U.S. The U.S. took formal possession of the Louisiana Territory on March 9, 1804, with St. Louis again serving as the seat of government for the entire territory. Incorporated in 1808, St. Louis was also the capital of the Missouri Territory (1812-21) until it became a state.

U.S. possession of the area brought a great influx of pioneers from eastern states to St. Louis, which jumped in population from 1,000 in 1800 to 5,600 in 1821. Until that time fur trading was the basis of the economy, but the first river steamboat reached St. Louis in 1817 and from that point on its economy was based on shipping and transportation. Steamboat traffic operated on both the Mississippi and Missouri Rivers, bringing settlers to the beginning of the Oregon and Santa Fe Trails. Another leap in transportation came in 1851, when the Pacific Railroad Company began construction both east and west from St. Louis. The route east to the Atlantic coast was completed in 1863, opening the city to German and Irish immigrants, who by 1870 represented more than one-third of the total population. The growth of the city was unaffected by the Civil War, which had a devastating impact on other parts of Missouri.

By the end of the 19th century St. Louis' economic prosperity brought about a cultural renaissance. Its primary intellectual body was the St. Louis Philosophical Society, which was founded in 1866 by William T. Harris and Henry C. Brockmeyer and published *The Journal of Speculative Philosophy* (1867-93). In 1878 Joseph PULITZER began publication of the St. Louis *Post-Dispatch*. Another indication of the city's cultural atmosphere at the time was the flourishing there of the poets T. S. ELIOT, Sara TEASDALE, and Eugene FIELD. By the 20th century St. Louis was prominent enough to host the Louisiana Purchase Exhibition of 1904, a centennial celebration that was at the time the largest world's fair in history.

Following World War II, however, the city underwent a period of urban decline exacerbated by the flight of its population to the suburbs. The city's population in 1950 was 856,796, but by 1980 it had fallen 47% to 453,085. Black Americans represent 43.5% of the 1980 figure. For a time the St. Louis metropolitan area expanded by this shift, growing

11% in the 1960s, but a further exurban migration brought about a 2.7% decline in metropolitan population during the 1970s. To counteract the effects of this population shift, the city began a series of bond issues for physical improvements in 1955 and an effort to attract federal funding that has produced significant interstate highway projects.

The city nevertheless remains the principal industrial hub of the Mississippi basin. It is second only to Detroit in automobile manufacture, is the headquarters of aerospace industries, home of the world's largest beer brewer, Anheuser-Busch, and the location of numerous food processing plants and textile manufacturers of national importance. It is also the largest inland freight port in the U.S., and the second-largest rail center in the country.

St. Louis is the home of Washington University, a branch of the University of Missouri, and St. Louis University. Its principal cultural facilities include the St. Louis Art Museum, the Museum of Science and Natural History, and the St. Louis Opera Theatre.

SAINT LOUIS UNIVERSITY. Independent coed Roman Catholic institution, located

West Cascade view of the falls at the 1904 World's Fair in St. Louis, Mo.

on a 225-acre campus in St. Louis. Founded in 1818, the university is one of the largest Catholic universities, and was the first university to be founded west of the Mississippi River.

The university has two other campuses, the medical campus, one mile away, and Parks College of Aeronautic Technology, in Cahokia, Ill. Undergraduate colleges include Arts and Sciences, Schools of Nursing and Allied Health Professions, Social Services, and Business Administration. Undergraduate majors include meteorology, geophysics, anthropology, communicative disorders, and geography. A church-related institution, the university requires all students to take a total of nine hours of theology during their undergraduate tenure. The North Central states provide 74% of the institution's students, 15% are from Middle Atlantic states, and 75% of students go on to further study.

Library: 1,200,000 volumes, 35,000 microform titles, 7,270 journal subscriptions, 2,588 records/tapes. Faculty: 2,237. Enrollment: 10,712 total graduate and undergraduate: 2,837 men, 2,116 women (full-time). Degrees: Certificate or Diploma, Associate's Bachelor's, Master's, Doctorate.

SAINT MARTINSVILLE, La. Town (pop. 7,965), seat of St. Martin Parish, in southern Louisiana. A rich farming region on Bayou Teche, it produces sugar cane, rice, and cotton. Salt, timber, and oil are also produced. Acadians exiled from Nova Scotia settled here about 1770, leaving the town with an old-style French atmosphere and a large CAJUN population. The Longfellow-Evangeline Commemorative Area commemorates the spot where Henry Wadsworth Longfellow wrote his poem *Evangeline.*

SAINT MARYS CITY, Md. Unincorporated town in St. Marys Co., in the southern part of the state. Founded c. 1634, it is the old-

Saint Marys City, Md., showing early fortifications built in the 1630s

est settlement in the state and was the capital of the colony until 1694. The first state assembly met here in 1635. It is the site of St. Mary's College of Maryland. In 1934 a replica of the first capitol building was constructed here.

SAINT MARYS RIVER, Ga./Fla. River originating in Okefenokee Swamp, in the northeast corner of Georgia. It forms part of the Georgia-Florida boundary. It flows in a southerly direction, then east, then bends to the north, then east again, to enter the Atlantic Ocean between Cumberland Island, Ga., and Amelia Island, Fla., north of Fernandia. Dredged for the lower 80 miles of its 180-mile course, its mouth crosses the Intracoastal Waterway.

SAINT PETERSBURG, Fla. City (pop. 236,893), Pinellas Co., on the west coast of Florida at the tip of the Pinellas peninsula in Tampa Bay. It was permanently settled in 1876 by John Williams and Peter Demens, and named after Demens' home in Russia. The railroad reached the settlement in 1888, and it was incorporated in 1892. Today's manufactures include canned foods and building materials, and there is an active trade in fish, fruit, and vegetables. Most important to the economy is its resort and recreation industry. Known as the "Sunshine City," St. Petersburg attracts large numbers of tourists and retirees. The city has many lakes and over 30 miles of ocean frontage. The Admiral Farragut Naval Academy, the U.S. Maritime Training School, and a U.S. Veterans Hospital are located here. Other attractions are the Memorial Historical Museum, the Alligator Farm, and the major-league baseball teams that hold their spring training here.

SAINT SIMONS ISLAND, Ga. Island in Glynn Co., off the coast of southeast Georgia. Timber cut on this island was used in the construction of the first U.S naval vessels, including the frigate *Constitution.* The Battle of Bloody Marsh took place here on July 7, 1742. It is now a resort area, and the site of Fort Frederick, a national monument.

SAINT STEPHENS, Ala. Former town, Washington Co., in southwestern Alabama on the Tombigbee River. The first territorial legislature of the state met here in 1818. The original settlement, a Spanish fort (1789), became part of the U.S. in 1798.

SALEM, Va. City (pop. 23,958), seat of Roanoke Co., in southwestern Virginia on the Roanoke River. Settled in 1802, it was a popular stopping point for travelers and had numerous inns and taverns. Today it is a summer resort and manufacturing city producing cigarette machinery, medicine, bricks, and elevators. It also has a tannery and meat packing plant. Roanoke College was founded here in 1842.

SALISBURY, Md. City (pop. 16,439), seat of Wicomico Co., in southeastern Maryland on the Wicomico River. Settled in 1732, today it is the state's second-largest port, and serves as the center for the region's varied industries including food packing and the manufacture of bricks and lumber. Maryland State Teachers College and Salisbury State College are here.

SALISBURY, N.C. City (pop. 21,297), seat of Rowan Co., in the midwestern part of the state between Winston-Salem and Charlotte in the Piedmont region. Settled in 1751 and incorporated in 1753, it was named for Salisbury, England. It was the home of Daniel Boone and his parents from 1755 to 1767, and in 1767 Andrew Jackson was licensed for a law practice here. During the Civil War a Confederate prison in an old cotton mill held 10,000 prisoners, 6,000 of whom died. It is the home of Catawba and Livingstone Colleges. The town's economy is based on textile manufacturing and diversified farming.

SALUDA RIVER, S.C. River rising in western South Carolina in the Blue Ridge Mountains. It flows southeast for 200 miles, crossing the Piedmont region, to meet the Broad River near Columbia to form the Congaree River. Saluda and Buzzards Roost Dams are on the river, which is a major hydroelectric power source.

SAM RAYBURN RESERVOIR, Tex. Body of water that lies at the center of several counties in eastern Texas. Approximately 60 miles long, it is an important water supply area that was formed by damming the Angelina River.

SAMAROFF, Olga (San Antonio, Tex., Aug. 8, 1882 — New York, N.Y., May 17, 1948). Concert pianist and teacher. Samaroff (a name she "adopted" because it sounded more European than her own maiden name of Hickenlooper), made her concert debut in 1905, appearing with the New York Symphony at Carnegie Hall. She appeared with all the major American orchestras, and was once married to conductor Leopold Stokowski. Samaroff taught piano at the Juilliard Graduate School of Music from 1925 until her death.

SAN ANGELO, Tex. City (pop. 73,240), seat of Tom Green Co., in the central part of the state. San Angelo, the "Sheep and Wool Capital" of the country, is also a trading center for the livestock, oil, and farming region around it. Texas A&M Research and Extension Center and San Angelo State University are here. The town was settled in 1869 and incorporated in 1889.

SAN ANTONIO, Tex. City (pop. 785,410), seat of Bexar Co., in south central Texas. It is the state's third-largest city and is a military, agricultural, industrial, and educational center. A city rich in history, it was here in 1836 that the famous battle of the ALAMO took place, an event which marked the turning point in Texas' struggle for independence from Mexico.

The military has always had a prominent place in the economy of San Antonio. Today there are five air force bases and an army post nearby by; 30,000 civilians are employed by the military. San Antonio is also a major cattle distribution point. It has been a cattle center since the late 1800s due to its location at the beginning of the famous CHISHOLM TRAIL. Once a city of few industries, today San Antonio's factories produce petroleum products, clothing, airplane parts, and oil field equipment.

The city was founded as a Spanish mission in 1718 and named by its Spanish settlers after their patron saint, St. Anthony of Padua. The city grew rapidly, was incorporated in 1809, and in two decades had become the capital of the Spanish Empire's northern territories in the New World. When the Mexican revolt against Spain broke out in 1821, the city was the scene of numerous battles. Fifteen years later San Antonio was again a battlefield, this time between Mexico and Americans fighting for their independence. Mexican forces under Gen. Santa Anna confronted Texas troops at the ALAMO, an ancient Spanish mission, and killed all the 181 Americans who were defending it. Texas forces took up the rallying cry "Remember the Alamo!" and in six short weeks soundly defeated the Mexican forces, and declared Texas a Republic. In later years San Antonio grew to become the largest city in the state, losing this status in 1930 when Houston and Dallas experienced dramatic increases in population. With the arrival of additional military installations just before World War II, San Antonio had a population growth of its own.

One of three large Spanish settlements prior to the Mexican Revolution of 1821, the city retains a great deal of its Mexican character and language. There is also a significant black population, as well as representation from other minority groups.

Along with the Alamo, the city has many famous landmarks, including several other Franciscan missions. The most famous of these is San Jose, a National Historic Landmark. La Villitia is a restored stretch of old shops located along the river. San Antonio has its own symphony orchestra and opera company, and there are many museums, including the Marian Koogler McNay Art Museum and the White Museum. The city is also the home of the San Antonio Spurs, a professional basketball team. The city has 30 radio stations, several of which broadcast in Spanish, and there are four television stations and three newspapers.

San Antonio is the home of five institutions of higher learning: Our Lady of the Lake College, Trinity University, St. Mary's University, Incarnate Word College, and the University of Texas at San Antonio.

SAN ANTONIO RIVER, Tex. River rising east of San Antonio, Tex., and passing through the city before continuing through a rich farm and oil region. It flows southeast for 200 miles to empty into San Antonio Bay.

SAN ELIZARIO, Tex. Unincorporated town in El Paso Co., on the Rio Grande River in southern Texas. Founded in 1772, it was the site of the Salt War in 1777, a confrontation between the town and a private citizen over ownership of nearby salt lakes. From 1850 to 1876, San Elizario was the seat of El Paso County. Once the seat was moved to Ysleta, San Elizario's importance declined considerably.

SAN JACINTO, Battle of. War of Texas Independence engagement, which was a victory for Texan Sam Houston over Mexican Gen. Santa Anna, on April 21, 1836, near the present site of Houston, Tex.

After the fall of the ALAMO on March 6, 1836, Sam HOUSTON commanded a controlled retreat from the Mexican force of Gen. Antonio Lopez de SANTA ANNA. Houston's primary concern was gathering volunteers, and by the time he reached San Jacinto Creek his force had

grown to 800 men. The original force of Mexican pursuers, however, numbered 900, and this was soon swollen by the arrival of 500 reinforcements. Nevertheless, on the morning of April 21 Sam Houston launched a surprise attack against the superior Mexican force at San Jacinto Creek. In only twenty minutes of fighting, the Texans killed, wounded, or captured the entire Mexican army. Santa Anna, captured in the fighting, was forced to sign an armistice that ended the war and granted Texas its independence.

SAN JACINTO RIVER, Tex. River rising in east central Texas, and running south into Galveston Bay. It is joined by Buffalo Bayou and it is at their confluence that the final battle of the Texas Revolution was fought in 1836. The river forms part of the Houston Ship Channel.

SAN MARCOS, Tex. City (pop. 23,420), seat of Hays Co., in southeast central Texas. San Marcos' economy is primarily dependent on education and tourism, although there is some light manufacturing and cattle ranching. Southwest Texas State University, Aquarena Springs, and Wonder Cave are located here.

SAND MOUNTAIN, Ga. Mountain in Dade Co., in northwest Georgia, to the south of Lookout Mountain near the Tennessee border. Farmland is found on its flat top (1,630 feet).

SANDYS, George (Bishopsthorpe, York, England, Mar. 2, 1578 — near Boxley Abbey, Kent, England, Mar. 4, 1644). Poet and colonial administrator. Known for his translation of the first ten books of Ovid's *Metamorphoses* (1626), Sandys succeeded his brother, Sir Edwin Sandys, as treasurer of the Virginia colony and director of agriculture (1621-25). He was a member of the state council several times until 1628. In 1631 he returned to England after allegedly interfering with the rights of several Virginia settlers.

SANFORD, N.C. Town (pop. 14,773), seat of Lee Co., in central North Carolina. Sanford was settled in the early 18th century as the home of Staffordshire potters, and that work is still carried on. Today it is a winter resort that manufactures cotton goods, electrical equipment, and mobile homes. Corn, cotton, tobacco, and soybeans are grown in the area. It is also one of the major producers of bricks in the country.

SANIBEL ISLAND, Fla. Island in Lee Co., on the southwest coast of Florida. A narrow barrier island about 12 miles long, it is the southern shelter of Pine Island Sound and partial shelter to San Carlos Bay. A lighthouse and Sanibel Village are at the southeast tip. The island is well known for the variety of sea shells that wash up on its shores.

SANTA ANNA, Antonio Lopez de (1794 — Mexico, 1876). Mexican statesman and military leader. He became president and dictator of Mexico four times and was exiled three times. He is best known for his command of the troops that massacred Texas patriots at the ALAMO on March 6, 1836, and for his defeat one month later by Gen. Sam HOUSTON at the battle of SAN JACINTO. He was defeated again in 1847 by the U.S. army under the command of Generals Winfield Scott and Zachary Taylor.

SANTA FE RIVER, Fla. Waterway rising in Santa Fe Lake in northeast Florida. It flows principally west for approximately 65 miles to the Suwanee River six miles southeast of Branford.

SANTA HELENA CANYON, Tex. Canyon in southern Texas, near Marathon in the Mesa de Anguila. Considered one of the most beautiful and hazardous gorges of the Grand Canyon of Santa Helena, the Rio Grande River flows between limestone walls 1,500 to 1,800 feet high for a distance of approximately 15 miles. The area is rich in metals including silver and copper.

SANTA ROSA ISLAND, Fla. Narrow barrier island in the Gulf of Mexico, running parallel with the southern shore of northwest Florida. Fifty miles long, it shelters both Pensacola Bay and Choctowachee Bay. The arm of water to the north, Santa Rosa Sound, is part of the Gulf Intracoastal Waterway. Fort Pickens (1834), on the western tip, was a Union fortress during the Civil War.

SANTEE INDIANS ("the river"). Tribe of Siouan linguistic stock that lived in South Carolina on the Santee River, to which they gave their name. They assisted the colonists in the TUSCARORA War (1711) but later (1715) entered the Yamasee War against them. The fol-lowing year they were attacked by tribes allied to the colonists and were virtually destroyed.

SAPONI INDIANS. Tribe of Siouan linguistic stock that originally lived in Albemarle Co., Va. During the 1600s and early 1700s they were constantly on the move trying to escape attacks by the Iroquois. When the attacks subsided as a result of the Treaty of Albany (1722), they moved northward into Pennsylvania with the TUTELO INDIANS.

SARASOTA, Fla. City (pop. 48,868), seat of Sarasota Co., in southwest Florida on Sarasota Bay. Settled in 1884, today Sarasota is best known as a year-round resort, and depends on tourism as its major industry. Other industries include shipping and packing of vegetables and citrus fruit, commercial fishing, and the production of metal products, mobile homes, and electronic equipment. Ringling Brothers, Barnum and Bailey Circus has its winter headquarters here. One of the largest art galleries in the state, the John and Mable Ringling Museum of Art is located here.

SASSAFRAS, Mount, S.C. Pickens Co., near the Georgia-North Carolina border. The highest peak in North Carolina (3,560 feet), it is part of the Blue Ridge Mountain system.

SATURIWA INDIANS. Tribe thought to have been of Muskogean linguistic stock that lived in Florida near the mouth of the St. John's River. They had a close relationship with the early French settlers and Fort Caroline was built in their territory. There were initial hostilities when the Spanish took control of the area but they soon submitted to Spanish rule and there were early missionary efforts among them. Little is known of them after the pestilence of 1672.

Ca'd'zan, home of John and Mabel Ringling in Sarasota, Fla.

SAVAGE, Mount, Md. Mountain (2,850 feet), Allegheny Co., in northwest Maryland near Grantsville. It is part of Savage River State Forest near the Savage River.

SAVAGE'S STATION, Battle of. See SEVEN DAYS' BATTLE.

SAVANNA, Battle of. See MARCH TO THE SEA.

SAVANNAH, Ga. City (pop. 141,634), seat of Chatham Co., in southeast Georgia, 18 miles inland on the Savannah River and the South Carolina border. A deep channel connects Savannah with the Atlantic Ocean, making it accessible to Atlantic shipping. A major industrial center and commercial seaport, Savannah has some of the world's most modern docking and warehousing facilities. Besides being an important distribution point for surrounding farm communities, Savannah is a major dispenser of goods between New Orleans, La., and Baltimore, Md. An important industry is the production of wood-related products, particularly kraft, a stong paper used primarily in the construction of heavy-duty bags. Other manufactured products include wood pulp, transportation equipment, packaged tea, chemicals, fertilizer, roofing materials, ships, cement, and refined sugar. Tourism is also an important industry.

Founded in 1733 by James OGELTHORPE, Savannah was Georgia's first settlement. Ogelthorpe, regarded as the state's chief developer, named the city either for the Spanish sabana, meaning "flat country," or for the resident Sawana Indians. Savannah was a carefully-planned city by colonial standards, built around a series of small squares. Each square contains a semitropical flora-dominated park enclosed by Greek Revival and Georgian edifices, many of which survive to this day. By 1736 John and Charles Wesley had come to Savannah to preach Methodism to the Indians. During the Revolutionary War the city was occupied by the British (1778-82).

Incorporated in 1789, Savannah grew rapidly and became in time the capital of the Commonwealth of Georgia and, briefly, the state capital (1782-85). Eli Whitney invented the cotton gin near Savannah, and the first steamboat to make a trans-Atlantic crossing, *The Savannah*, did so from this city in 1819. During the Civil War Savannah was limited as an important Confederate port due to a Union blockade, but the city was not captured until December,

1864, when Union Gen. William T. Sherman arrived here near the end of his famous MARCH TO THE SEA. Unlike Atlanta, however, Sherman spared Savannah from being burned, presenting the city to President Abraham Lincoln as a token Christmas present. This accounts for the survival of so much pre-Civil War architecture in Savannah.

The city prospered in the years following the war. In the 1950s many of the city's citizens began a massive restoration program in the old section of the town, and, to date, well over a thousand homes and other buildings have been restored. Besides the restored original section, other points of interest include the Bethesda Home for Boys, established in 1740 and regarded as the nation's oldest orphanage. One of the South's best known art galleries, the Telfair Academy of Arts and Sciences, is in Savannah. The home of Juliette Gordon Low, founder of the American Girl Scout movement in 1789, is open to the public. Savannah is also the home of Armstrong State College and Savannah State College. Nearby are Hunter Army Airfield, Fort Stewart, and the marine installation of Parris Island.

SAVANNAH, Occupation of. British action in the Revolutionary War that held the coastal Georgia city for the duration of conflicts in the Southern theater of the war. Savannah fell to the British on December 29, 1778. It was unsuccessfully attacked and beseiged by the Continental Army in alliance with the French navy in October, 1779. The British held the city until July 11, 1782, more than eight months after the British surrender at Yorktown.

The fall of Savannah was the first successful British encroachment on the Southern colonies in the Revolutionary War. British commander-in-chief Henry Clinton decided to move the theater of war to the South in November, 1778, in hope of attracting support from American Loyalists. The British force under Lt. Col. Archibald Campbell sailed from New York Bay and reached Savannah on December 23, 1778. The city was defended by a far smaller force of patriots commanded by Gen. Robert Howe. On December 19 Campbell was able to decimate the patriots by approaching the city along an obscure and undefended swamp route. The patriots had more than 80 killed and 450 captured, while the British force suffered virtually no casualties. Soon after the battle, Campbell was reinforced by the force of Gen. Augustine Prevost, sent north from Florida, and he used his position in Savannah to gain control of all of Georgia by the end of January, 1779.

On October 9, 1779, the British in Savannah were attacked by the Continental militia of Gen. Benjamin Lincoln and the French fleet of Adm. Jean d'Estaing. The British force of 2,500 repelled this frontal assault by a combined Revolutionary force of some 4,000. The attackers remained to besiege the city until October 20, when Lincoln retreated to Charleston, S.C., and d'Estaing sailed for France.

SAVANNAH, Tenn. Town (pop. 6,992), seat of Hardin Co., in southern Tennessee on the Tennessee River. Settled in 1823, it was an isolated rural community prior to the Tennessee Valley Authority's decison to install the Pickwick Landing Dam (1935) nearby. Clothing, toy guns, and molded plastics are manufactured here, and farms produce corn, cotton, hay, and soybeans. Shiloh National Military Park is nearby.

SAVANNAH RIVER, Ga. River created by the confluence of the Tugaloo and Seneca Rivers, which serves as a natural boundary between Georgia and South Carolina. From its source to the point where it empties into Tybee Sound, it covers approximately 314 miles flowing generally southeast. Augusta and Savannah are on its banks. Several dams were built along the river for hydroelectric power. The 12,900-acre Savannah Wildlife Refuge lies on both sides of the river in Georgia and South Carolina.

SAWOKLI INDIANS ("raccoon people").Tribe of Muskogean linguistic stock that lived on the Chattahoochee River in Barbour Co., Ala. Early missionary efforts by the Spanish began in 1675. Displaced by hostile tribes, they are thought to have been absorbed by the Lower CREEK Confederacy in the 1700s.

SCALAWAG. Term of contempt applied to a white Southerner who sided with the federal RECONSTRUCTION forces in the South after the Civil War, and exploited them for his own gain. A scalawag was considered meaner and even more despicable than the CARPETBAGGER because he preyed on his own kind. Originally the term had been applied to any low-down scoundrel or a critter, usually a dog or worn-out cow, that was too old or useless or both.

SCARLETT O'HARA. The South's most famous fictional heroine depicted in Margaret MITCHELL'S epic Civil War novel *Gone with the Wind* (1936).

SCHLEY, Winfield Scott (Frederick Co., Md., Oct. 9, 1839 — New York, N.Y., Oct 2, 1909). Naval officer. Schley was promoted to commodore after his rescue of Adolphus Greely from the arctic (1884). During the Spanish American War, Schley was in command at the victory of the battle of Santiago. He attained the rank of rear admiral before his retirement in 1901. He wrote *Forty-five Years Under the Flag.* (1904).

SCHOFIELD, John McAllister (Chatauqua Co., N.Y., Sept 29, 1831 — St. Augustine, Fla., Mar. 4, 1906). Military officer. An 1853 graduate of the U.S Military Academy at West Point, Schofield returned to West Point as an assistant professor of philosophy and later taught physics at Washington University in St. Louis, Mo. A Union general during the Civil War, he fought with distinction in several battles, including Sherman's Atlanta campaign, and was made mustering officer for the state of Missouri. Appointed Secretary of War in 1868 by President Andrew Johnson, he resigned after the inauguration of President Ulysses S. Grant. Promoted to major general in 1869, he made the recommendation that the U.S. acquire Pearl Harbor as a naval base. From 1876 to 1881 he was superintendent of West Point. He was made commanding general of the Army in 1888 and retired seven years later.

SCHURZ, Carl (Cologne, Germany, Mar. 2, 1829 — New York, N.Y., May 14, 1906). Politician. Involved in the German uprisings of 1848, he came to the U.S. in 1852. He practiced law in Wisconsin where he became interested in the Republican party and supported the abolitionist cause. Schurz was a devout supporter of Abraham Lincoln, who appointed him minister to Spain (1861-62). After the war he became a political journalist in St. Louis, Mo., and was elected a U.S. Senator from that state (1869-75). President Rutherford B. Hays appointed him Secretary of the Interior (1877-81).

SCOPES TRIAL. Infamous landmark judicial case which took place in 1925. In March of that year, the Tennessee legislature passed a statute that prohibited public schools from teaching theories of evolution that differed from accepted Biblical accounts. In July, John Scopes, a Dayton physics teacher, was put on trial for defying the statute by presenting Darwin's Theory of Evolution in his classroom. The American Civil Liberties Union came out in Scopes' defense, and obtained the services of a distinguished lawyer, Clarence Darrow, to argue Scopes' case. William Jennings Bryan argued for the prosecution. The trial was dramatic, drawing international attention. Although Darrow insisted the statute was a violation of the separation of church and state, Scopes was convicted. He was later released by the state supreme court on a technicality. It has been suggested that the trial was a scheme devised by a group of Dayton businessmen to draw attention to the town.

SCOTT, Hugh Lenox (Danville, Ky., Sept. 22, 1853 — Apr. 30, 1934). Military officer. A graduate of West Point (1876), Scott's initial military experience was gained in Indian campaigns. He became a specialist in Indian affairs and an expert on Indian sign language. From 1898 to 1902 he was adjutant general of Cuba and he was briefly superintendent of West Point (1906-10). He was chief of staff of the U.S. Army from 1914 to 1917, and served on the Board of Indian Commissioners after his retirement in 1919.

SCOTT, Walter (Moffat, Dumfrieshire, Scotland, Oct. 31, 1796 — Mason Co., Ky., Apr. 23, 1861). Clergyman. First a Presbyterian, he converted to Halandeanism and later became a leader in the religious movement known as The Disciples of Christ. Preacher Scott became an evangelist, stressing faith, repentance, and baptism, and preached throughout the Southern states.

SCOTT, Winfield (Petersburg, Va., June 13, 1786 — West Point, N.Y., May 29, 1866). Military officer. Scott began his military career in 1808 after two years of practicing law. He fought valiantly in the War of 1812, and was involved in the Black Hawk War (1832), and the Seminole and Creek Indian Campaigns (1835-36). In 1841 he became general-in-chief of the army and he remained in that post until 1861. During the 1847 campaign of the Mexican War he won a series of important victories that brought the conflict to an end. For his victories he received the thanks and admiration of the nation. Scott's nickname was "Old Fuss and Feathers" because of the the high standards of discipline and training he demanded

from his troops. He was an excellent soldier both in fighting and averting crises, as he did along the Canadian border in 1837 and 1839, as well as in Charleston, S.C., during the NULLIFICATION crisis. In 1852 Scott was an unsuccessful Whig candidate for the presidency. When the Civil War broke out Scott remained loyal to the Union, and planned the defenses of Washington, D.C. and then resigned from the army, citing old age and health reasons. Shortly after, President Abraham Lincoln remarked of Scott, "I cannot but think we are all his debtors."

SCOTTSBORO, Ala. City (pop. 14,758), seat of Jackson Co., in northeast Alabama near the Tennessee river. Located in an area of light farming and industry, Scottsboro is best known for lending its name to the sensational 1931 trial, the SCOTTSBORO CASE, in which nine blacks were indicted for the rape of two white women. The city was incorporated in 1870.

SCOTTSBORO CASE. Controversial criminal case in which nine young black men (the youngest aged 13) were arrested in SCOTTSBORO, Ala., on March 31, 1931, on charges of raping two white women on a freight train. Eight were convicted and sentenced to death creating a mass uprising in the liberal community, which claimed the men had been "railroaded." The U.S. Supreme Court granted a new trial in 1932 on the grounds that the defendants had been denied adequate counsel. At a new trial in 1933 one of the rape victims reversed her testimony but the jury nonetheless sentenced one of the defendants to death. Two other defendants were also sentenced to death in separate trials. The Supreme Court again revised the decisions and after several more trials and almost two decades of controversy, the men were released between 1943 and 1950.

SEA ISLANDS, S.C./Ga. Chain of islands off the coasts of South Carolina, Northern Florida, and Georgia in the Atlantic Ocean. They extend from the mouth of the Santee River to the mouth of the St. Johns River. Large plantations were developed on the islands in the 19th century but they were devastated by Union invasion during the Civil War. After the war, much of the land was parceled out to freed slaves for farming. Today the islands are largely resort spots, and noted for their subtropical climate. A marine recruit training center is found on Parris Island. Cumberland Island, Ga., is the largest of the chain.

SEBRING, Fla. City (pop. 8,736), seat of Highlands Co., in south central Florida. Planned and built by pottery manufacturer George Sebring in 1912, it was incorporated in 1913. An annual sports car race is held here each March and a state park is located nearby.

SEDALIA, Mo. City (pop. 22,847), seat of Pettis Co., in west central Missouri. The city was founded by George R. Smith in 1857, who named it after his daughter. Situated on the Missouri Pacific Railroad, it was used as a federal military post during the Civil War. Sedalia was incorporated in 1864, and was an important railhead for the Texas cattle drives of 1866. Today the city is a distribution and shipping point for agricultural products, and a diversified manufacturer of glass, textiles, shoes, and housewares. It is the site of the Missouri State fair.

SELMA, Ala. City (pop. 27,379), seat of Dallas Co., in central Alabama on the Alabama River. The area was originally settled as Moore's Bluff (or Moore's Landing) in 1816, but was renamed from "The Song of Selma" at its incorporation in 1820. During the Civil War it served as a Confederate supply post until it was burned by Union troops in April, 1865. The city was the center of a Black voter registration movement in 1965, led by the Rev. Martin Luther KING, Jr. The economy is based on light manufacturing and the region's agricultural production, including dairy, grain, livestock, and cotton. Selma is the site of Selma University and the Alabama Lutheran Academy and Junior College. Craig Air Force Base is nearby.

SEMINOLE INDIANS ("one who has camped out from the regular towns" or "wild," "undomesticated"). Tribes of predominantly Muskogean linguistic stock formed from the CREEK Confederacy. They first lived in and around Apalachee Co., Fla., some extending southward as far as Miami. They moved into the Everglades region toward the close of the SEMINOLE WAR. The Seminole migration into the state began in the mid 1700s but the greatest number came at the end of the CREEK WAR (1814). Their numbers were greatly increased by runaway Negro slaves, whom they absorbed into their tribes. Hostilities between the Seminoles and the Americans began building (some of the animosity being inspired by the British), and in 1817 and 1835 Chief OSCEOLA led the tribes in the two major Seminole wars. After

their surrender in 1842, a great number of the Seminoles were sent to the INDIAN TERRITORY in Oklahoma, and a small number remained in Florida to be absorbed into the general population.

SEMINOLE WARS. Military engagements to secure control of Florida from the Spanish, and to control the Seminole Indians. On December 26, 1817, Gen. Andrew JACKSON received orders from the United States government to end the Indian problems in Florida, which in effect meant to rid the area of the Spanish, and the Indian problem was the government's excuse for entering Spanish domain. After minor skirmishes, Gen. Jackson attacked and captured Pensacola (May 18, 1818), ran up the American flag, and appointed one of his men as governor. The Spanish were irate and demanded the return of the fort at Pensacola and other smaller forts to the north that Jackson had captured. President James Monroe refused and eventually the cession of Florida from Spain to the U.S. occurred in 1821. Though called the First Seminole War, the Seminoles played only a small part in it, and at the war's close they still remained.

In 1832 Andrew Jackson was president and he was determined to rid the eastern portion of the United States of any remaining Indians, who at the time were the Seminoles (the Creek nation and other dominant tribes having been removed to INDIAN TERRITORY in Oklahoma). In the Treaty of Payne's Landing (May 9, 1832), the Seminoles were offered $15,400 (and a blanket and one homespun frock for each Indian) if they would give up their Florida land and move to Oklahoma. The government also added a verbal clause, saying that anyone of Negro descent must remain in Florida and be sold into slavery. The Seminoles had for years absorbed runaway Negro slaves into their tribes, and this last order would have disintegrated the tribe due to the number of intermarriages that had taken place over the years. Many Seminole chiefs refused to sign, and in April, 1835, the government tried again for unanimous approval of the treaty. Chief OSCEOLA still refused to sign and returned to his home near Fort King to incite resistance against the government. Having already opposed the Americans in the First Seminole War, he was aware of their fighting strategies. He organized his people, sending women and children into safety in the swamps, and gathered warriors into small parties, using a guerilla warfare plan of attack. So began the Second Seminole War.

Skirmishes continued into 1837 when Gen. Thomas Sidney JESUP was given command of the U.S. troops and also given over 1,000 reluctant Western and Southern Indians to aid him. Osceola was captured when he and 75 warriors were meeting with the whites under a flag of truce (an ineffaceable blot upon the American army). Jesup's capture of Osceola (who died three months later in captivity), did not end the war and the Seminoles moved deeper into the Everglades.

Jesup was removed from his command and the war continued under the leadership of various generals, none of them able to subdue the Seminoles. In 1841 Gen. William J. Worth was given the command. He penetrated deep into the swamps to which the Indians had retreated, destroyed crops and villages, and finally captured the Seminole leader, threatening to hang him if the Indians did not surrender. Having reached the limit of their resistance, the Indians surrendered. Their wretched condition when they emerged from the swamps made it hard to understand why it had taken six years and $20 million to bring about their defeat. A treaty was signed in 1842 and the Seminoles were removed to the INDIAN TERRITORY in Oklahoma.

SEMMES, Raphael (Charles Co., Md., Sept. 27, 1809 — Mobile, Ala., Aug. 30, 1877). Naval officer, lawyer, and author. Appointed midshipman (1826), Semmes supervised the landing of Gen. Winfield Scott's army at Veracruz (1847) during the Mexican War and fought in the Valley of Mexico. When the Civil War began, he accepted an appointment as a commander with the Confederacy. Serving on the *Sumter*, which captured 18 vessels, and the *Alabama*, which captured 66 vessels, he had a successful career until the *Alabama* was taken by the *Kearsage* off the English coast. At Richmond, Adm. Semmes blew up his ships and with his men fought under Gen. Joseph Johnston. Following the defeat of Johnston he returned to Mobile where he took up the practice of law and wrote several books detailing his martial experiences in the Mexican and Civil Wars.

SEPULGA RIVER, Ala. River rising north of Owassa and flowing southeast for 40 miles to the Conecuh River. It is almost entirely contained in Conecuh County in southern Alabama.

SEVEN DAYS' BATTLES. Collective name given to a week of heavy fighting in the Civil War on the outskirts of Richmond, Va. The battles took place between June 25 and July 1, 1862. They ended the Union army's PENINSULAR CAMPAIGN to capture Richmond. Although the Confederate army suffered the heaviest losses, the Union army failed to take the city.

On June 25 the Seven Days' Battles opened with an indecisive skirmish at Oak Grove, a site also known as Henrico or King's School House. Major fighting began the next day at Mechanicsville, when Confederate Gen. Ambrose P. HILL attacked the Union emplacement. When expected reinforcements under Gen. Stonewall JACKSON did not arrive, Hill fell back. Under cover of darkness, the Union army also retreated from the battle site.

On June 27 Jackson and the reunited Confederate forces attacked the Union army's new position in the Battle of Gaines' Mill, a victory for the South. At the same time, however, the Confederate side launched a flank attack in the Battle of Garnett's and Goulding's Farms that was far less successful. Nevertheless, the Union army went into a retreat defended by rear guard actions at Savage's Station on June 29 and White Oak Swamp on June 30. The final battle took place on July 1 at Malvern Hill on the north bank of the James River. There the Union army repelled several Confederate attacks before falling back to Harrison's Landing on July 2.

As a consequence of the Seven Days's Battles, Union Gen. George B. McClellan came under severe criticism for the failure of the Peninsular Campaign. At the same time Gen. Robert E. Lee gave new life to the Confederacy with his tactical victory over larger forces and his successful defense of Richmond.

SEVEN MILE CREEK, Battle of. See CORINTH, Battles of.

SEVEN PINES, Battle of. See FAIR OAKS, Battle of.

SEVERN RIVER, Md. River, actually a 25-mile inlet of Chesapeake Bay, in Anne Arundel Co., in central Maryland. The capitol city of Annapolis is on its southern bank.

SEVIER, John (near New Market, Va., Sept. 23, 1745 — Fort Decatur, Ala. Territory, Sept. 24, 1815). Military officer and politician. After moving with his family to settle on the Holston River, N.C. (now Tennessee), Sevier became an Indian fighter and served in the Revolutionary War. In 1784 he and fellow settlers broke away from North Carolina and formed the separate state of Franklin with Sevier as its governor. He was imprisoned briefly by North Carolina officials in 1787 when they declared the state of Franklin illegal. He was a U.S. congressman from North Carolina from 1789 to 1791, and with the formation of the new state of Tennessee in 1796, Sevier was named its first governor (1796-1801, 1803-1809). In 1811 he was elected to the U.S. House of Representatives from Tennessee and served until his death.

SEWEE INDIANS. Tribe thought to have been of Siouan linguistic stock that lived in South Carolina on the lower Santee River. Friendly to the English colonists when they arrived in 1670, the Sewee supplied them with corn and aided them against Spanish attack. A smallpox epidemic in the 1700s nearly destroyed the tribe and the survivors probably merged with the CATAWBA INDIANS.

SHAPIRO, Karl Jay (Baltimore, Md., Nov. 10, 1913 —). Critic and poet. Shapiro studied at both the University of Virginia and Johns Hopkins. His works of poetry include: *Person, Place and Thing* (1942) and *Poems of a Jew* (1958). His critical works include *Beyond Criticism* (1953) and *In Defense of Ignorance* (1960).

SHARPSBURG, Battle of. See ANTIETAM, Battle of.

SHAWN, Edwin Myers "Ted" (Kansas City, Mo., Oct. 21, 1891 — Orlando, Fla., Jan. 9, 1972). Modern dancer. He was a former divinity student who was introduced to the study of dance as a therapy after an illness. In 1914, he met and married Ruth St. Denis, also a dancer, and together they founded the Denishawn School in Los Angeles, Cal. (1915), which was later moved to New York City. The couple ended their personal and professional association in 1930. In 1941 he founded Jacob's Pillow Dance Festival near Lee, Mass., as a summer residence/theater for his dancers and developed it into an internationally important dance center.

SHAWNEE INDIANS ("southerners"). Tribe of Algonquian linguistic stock. One of their earliest locations was in Tennessee on the Cumberland River, though they were known for their constant migration and at one time or another lived in nearly every state in the South. Constantly at war with the settlers, they joined in the Creek and Cherokee wars. In the early 1800s, Chief TECUMSEH, and his brother, Tenskwatawa, tried to form an alliance of the Shawnee tribes and bring about an uprising. Tenskwatawa was defeated at the Battle of Tippecanoe and Tecumseh acted as leader of the hostile tribes during the War of 1812. After years of defeats, the Shawnee migrated to INDIAN TERRITORY in Oklahoma.

SHEEP. The Southern states account for approximately one-fifth of all sheep and lambs raised in the U.S. Almost 90% of the sheep and lambs in the South are grazed in Texas, which produced 2.3 million head of sheep and lambs in 1980.

The other important sheep states in the South (ranked by 1980 production) are: Virginia (160,000 head), Missouri (138,000 head), Kentucky (22,000 head), Louisiana (11,000 head), Tennessee (11,000 head), and North Carolina (8,000 head).

SHELBY, Issac (Washington Co., Md., Dec. 11, 1750 — Lincoln Co., Kentucky, July 18, 1826). Frontiersman. After leading volunteers to a victory at Kings Mountain during the American Revolution, he played an important role in bringing about Kentucky's statehood, and was elected that state's first governor (1792-96). He later served with distinction during the War of 1812, and was again governor of Kentucky (1812-16).

SHELBY, Joseph Orville (Lexington, Ky., Dec. 12, 1830 — Adrian, Mo., Feb. 13, 1897). Military officer. During the Civil War he organized a Confederate cavalry brigade in Missouri that took part in many raids, including Helena, Ark. (1863), where he was wounded. He joined Gen. Sterling Price in the invasion of Missouri (1864), and at the war's end he and his men did not surrender but went to Mexico to serve Emperor Maximilian. He was a U.S. marshall in Missouri from 1893 to 1897.

SHELBYVILLE, Tenn. Town (pop. 13,530), seat of Bedford Co., in south central Tennessee on the Duck River. Incorporated in 1819, today the town's economy is based on light manufacturing including truck transmissions, furniture, and apparel. Cattle, corn, sheep, and wheat are raised in the area. Each August the Tennessee Walking Horse Celebration is held here.

SHENANDOAH NATIONAL PARK, Va.
Federal park, approved by Congress in 1926, which covers nearly 200,000 acres in the northern part of the state along the crest of the Blue Ridge Mountains. The park is 77 miles long and extends from Front Royal to Waynesboro. Established to preserve the area and offer recreational facilities, it offers unparalleled scenery. Skyline Drive, 105 miles long, is in the park and overlooks the Shenandoah Valley.

SHENANDOAH RIVER, Va.
River rising in the western part of the state in two forks, the North and the South, which unite near Front Royal and eventually join the Potomac River near Harper's Ferry, W.Va. For nearly 40 miles the forks are separated by Massanutten Mountain. This 170-mile-river flows through the fertile Shenandoah Valley, and it's name is thought to be of Algonquin Indian origin meaning "daughter of the stars," or "spruce stream."

SHENANDOAH VALLEY, Va.
Region 150 miles long and 10 to 20 miles wide, between the Blue Ridge Mountains on the east and the Allegheny Mountains on the west. Known for its fertile soil and scenic natural beauty, the valley was the site of numerous Civil War battles. Gen. Robert E. Lee used the area as one of his principal storehouses, and it was thought to be one of the best access routes for the invasion of the North.

SHEPHERD COLLEGE.
State-supported, coed liberal arts and teachers' college located 65 miles northwest of Washington, D.C., in Shepherdstown, W.Va. Founded in 1872, the 156-acre school has two adjoining campuses. In recent years 37% of the students received a degree in education, 19% in business and management, 13% in public affairs. The North Central states provide 7% of the students, 35% are from Middle Atlantic states, and 55% are from the South; 30% of students pursue full-time graduate study.

Library: 220,000 volumes, 680 journal subscriptions, 3,500 records/tapes. Faculty: 136. Enrollment: 757 men, 1,066 women (full-time). Degrees: Associate's, Bachelor's.

SHEPHERDSTOWN, W.Va.
Town (pop. 1,791), seat of Jefferson Co., in northeast West Virginia, 65 miles northwest of Washington, D.C. An agricultural community on the Potomac River, it is historically important as the site of the first successful steamboat launching in 1787 and because the first newspaper in the state was published here in 1790. Shepherdstown was once under consideration as the location of the nation's capital. It is the home of Shepherd College.

SHEPPARD, Morris
(Wheatville, Tex., May 28, 1875 — Washington, D.C., Apr. 9, 1941). Politician. Educated at the University of Texas and Yale, Sheppard was a lawyer before becoming a Democratic U.S. congressman from Texas (1902-13). He was elected to the U.S. Senate in 1913 and served until his death. Sheppard introduced the law that later became the 18th Amendment.

SHERIDAN, Philip Henry
(Albany, N.Y., Mar. 6, 1831 — Nonquitt, Mass., Aug. 5, 1888). Union general in the Civil War. Sheridan graduated from West Point in 1853, after a suspension for attacking a fellow cadet, but at the outbreak of the Civil War he was still a captain fulfilling quartermaster duties. He earned a reputation in the early battles of the war, and after being one of the last Union leaders to retreat from Missionary Ridge in Chattanooga in 1863, he was given the cavalry command of the Union Army of the Potomac. After defeating Gen. J.E.B. Stuart, who died in the battle at Richmond in 1864, Sheridan was given command of the Union army in the Shenandoah Valley. There he defeated the South at Winchester and Fisher's Hill, and in an action unwarranted by his orders he systematically devastated the entire valley. This streak of calculated cruelty resurfaced after the war in Texas, where he was relieved of his command as military governor in 1867, and in Louisiana, where he was sent to quell riots in 1875 and did so with tyrannical severity.

SHERMAN, William Tecumseh
(Lancaster, Ohio, Feb. 8, 1820 — New York, N.Y., Feb. 14, 1891). Union general in the Civil War. A 1840 graduate of West Point, Sherman, given his middle name in honor of the famous Shawnee Indian chief, served in Florida and South Carolina before resigning from the army in 1853. He was involved in the banking profession, and when this failed he became superintendent of a military academy in Alexandria,

La. He resigned from the academy when Louisiana seceded in 1861, and it was only after long thought that his dislike of secession prevailed over his Southern friendships and he accepted a commission in the Union army that was desperate for trained officers.

Although nervous enough to be called "Crazy" Sherman by some, he served with distinction under Gen. Ulysses S. Grant at Shiloh in 1862, and Vicksburg in 1863. When Grant became the Union's supreme commander in 1864, Sherman succeeded him as the chief commander of Union forces on the western front of the war. He then conducted his famous campaign to split the South. Leaving Chattanooga in May of 1864, he advanced to Atlanta and captured the city in September. After burning Atlanta, he began his "march to the sea," devastating all lands in his path and capturing Savannah in December. "I can hear Georgia howl," he is supposed to have said during the march, and his complete destruction of crops caused a shortage in supplies to the Confederate army that contributed to Gen. Robert E. Lee's decision to surrender at Appomattox on April 9, 1865. Sherman remained a soldier after the war, and it is to him that the statement "war is hell" is usually attributed.

SHILOH, Battle of. The second major battle of the Civil War, fought with heavy casualties on April 6 and 7, 1862, in southwestern Tennessee at Pittsburg Landing on the Tennessee River. In outcome a modest victory for the Union side, it was most significant for proving that the war would be a prolonged and bloody one.

Confederate forces 40,000 strong had assembled in Corinth, Miss., in March under the command of Gen. Albert S. Johnston, who would die in the battle. Union forces totaling 37,000 under Gen. Ulysses S. Grant were by April encamped at Pittsburg Landing and awaiting reinforcements under the command of Gen. Don Carlos Buell. The Confederate army moved north on April 3, hoping for a victory before Buell could arrive. The battle was delayed by rain, however, and when it commenced on the morning of April 6 the majority of Buell's forces were only seven miles away.

Grant's army was taken by surprise, and it retreated before forming a battle line near the river. Both flanks of this line were forced into further retreats by the Confederate army, but the center, at a place known now as "The Hornets' Nest," held the Union position until Buell's forces arrived in the evening of April 6.

On April 7 Grant was able to advance from this position with his reinforcements to meet the weakened Confederate army. The ensuing battle was especially bloody near Shiloh Church, for which the engagement is named, but after hours of resistance the outnumbered Confederate forces were forced into a controlled retreat. Casualties numbered about 10,700 for the South and about 13,000 for the North. The site is now memorialized by the Shiloh National Military Park.

SHREVEPORT, La. City (pop. 205,815), seat of Caddo parish, on the Red River in northwest Louisiana. The area was settled in 1834 after Henry Miller Shreve cleared the Red River of a driftwood jam and opened the river to navigation, eventually making the city a flourishing port. In 1863 Shreveport became the Confederate capital of Louisiana and was the last stronghold of the Confederacy during the Civil War. It was incorporated as a town in 1839 and chartered as a city in 1871. The city is located in a leading cotton region, which is also rich in natural gas and oil. Oil was discovered at Caddo Lake on the Texas border in 1906. The city is an important manufacturing, distributing, and trading center. Manufactures include metal products, machinery, lumber, petroleum, chemicals, printed material, and stone, clay and glass products. It is the home of Centenary College, Louisiana State University, Baptist Christian College, and a branch of Southern University. The city has its own symphony and opera company, and the Louisiana State Fair is held here each autumn.

SHRIMP. Several species of decapod (ten-legged) marine crustaceans prized as food and an important economic resource of the Gulf states of the South. Shrimp live near the shore on muddy or sandy bottoms and can be netted in large numbers.

The Southern states along the Gulf harvest more than 200 million pounds of shrimp per year, more than twice the amount harvested on the Pacific coast. There is a smaller shrimp catch in the Atlantic waters of the South, where commercial fisheries harvest approximately 30 million pounds per year. See also FISHING, Commercial.

SHRIVER, Robert Sargent (Westminster, Md., Nov. 9, 1915 —). Public official and businessman. After earning his law degree from Yale in 1941, Shriver served in World War II as a naval officer. He was employed in the business empire of Joseph P. Kennedy, married Eunice Kennedy, and became the first director of the Peace Corps (1961) after the election of his brother-in-law John F. Kennedy as President.

SHUMAN INDIANS. Tribe of undetermined linguistic stock that lived along the Rio Grande River near El Paso, Tex. A western division of the Shuman are referred to as the Suma. Missionary efforts among them began in the 1620s, but because of their constant migration and their raiding of other Indian tribes, their numbers declined and they are thought to have been finally destroyed by the APACHE.

SIKESTON, Mo. City (pop. 17,341), New Madrid and Scott Counties, in southeastern Missouri. Settled in 1860 and incorporated in 1874, the city is located in an industrial-farming area. Sikeston has cotton gins as well as flour and feed mills, and manufactures include shoes, toys, sporting goods, and building supplies. Farms produce corn, cotton, soybeans, and wheat. The Bootheel Rodeo is held each August and the Cotton Carnival is held in Septembers.

SILVER SPRING, Md. Unincorporated city (pop. 84,300), Montgomery Co., in west central Maryland. It is primarily a suburban community north of Washington, D.C., which developed after World War II, and most of its residents are federal workers. Several important research laboratories including a large naval ordnance laboratory are found here. Manufactures include precision instruments and computers. It is the site of Washington Theological Union and Tacoma Park.

SIMMS, William Gilmore (Charleston, S.C., Apr. 17, 1806 — Charleston, S.C., June 11, 1870). Author. A popular author of some 82 books, he is best known for his romantic novels set in the antebellum South. In such books as *Guy Rivers* (1834) and *The Yemassee* (1835) he glorified the Southern way of life and defended slavery. This won him a large audience in the South where he became a central literary figure of the day. He knew personally most of the Southern writers of the time and did much to stimulate them to write and publish. He was also a friend of many in the literary world of the North where his writings were as well received as they were in the South. Simms' career started at 16 when he began publishing poetry in the Charleston, S.C., papers. He

became editor of the *City Gazette* but lost his job for taking a stand against the NULLIFICATION doctrine. This, plus the death of his first wife, prompted him to move to New York where he began writing novels. He returned to the South in 1835 and later became editor of the *Southern Quarterly Review* (1849-56) while continuing to write. Besides novels, Simms wrote poetry and biographies, including one of Francis Marion.

SINCLAIR, Upton Beall (Baltimore, Md., Sept. 20, 1878 — Bound Brook, N.J., Nov. 25, 1968). Author. An ardent socialist with unfulfilled political ambitions, Sinclair gained fame when he turned from the dime novels he wrote to support himself to the composition of a Chicago stockyard expose, *The Jungle* (1906). The book was an enormous popular success, brought about reform of the labor conditions Sinclair abhorred, and enabled him to establish and support the socialist commune Helicon Home Colony in Englewood, N.J. Never concerned with the aesthetic matters of the literary craft, Sinclair wrote journalistic novels intended to expose and correct particular social inequities. His other works include *The Moneychangers* (1908), *King Coal* (1917), *Boston* (1928), which was about the Sacco-Vanzetti case, and *Plays of Protest* (1912). His *Dragon's Teeth* (1942) won the Pulitzer Prize in 1943.

SINGER ISLAND, Fla. Island (pop. estimate 8,000), Palm Beach Co., in southeastern Florida. It is part of the city of Palm Beach, and extends northward from the inlet at the city's northern limits. An exclusive residential resort community is on the island, which is noted for its beaches. The island was named for the sewing machine heir, Paris Singer.

SISSIPAHAW INDIANS. Tribe thought to have been of Siouan linguistic stock. They lived on the Haw River (to which they gave their name) in Alamance Co., N.C. A small tribe, they allied against the English in the Yamasee War (1715) and later probably merged with the CATAWBA INDIANS.

SKYLINE DRIVE, Va. Highway on the crest of the Blue Ridge Mountains that continues for 105 miles through the Shenandoah National Park, from Front Royal to Waynesboro. Known for its scenic beauty, it is the site of an old Indian trail.

SLAVERY. Institutionalized and legalized bonded servitude, usually of a labor force for economic gain. Slavery has existed in various forms since the earliest recorded histories, and it persistently reappears as an illicit trade in underdeveloped areas. The single most historically important appearance of institutionalized slavery occured in the American South, where it became the principal motivation behind the secession movement and cause of the American Civil War.

The origins of slavery are prehistoric, but the institution is known to have been accepted by the Sumerian people of Mesopotamia by 2000 B.C. In addition, the earliest known legal system, the Code of Hammurabi, included regulations on organized slavery when it was inscribed in Babylonia by 1800 B.C. The great European Classical societies also owed a considerable degree of their economic stability to slavery. Homer's *Illiad* and *Odyssey*, which date from the 800s B.C., both include references to slavery, and the population of Athens before the time of Christ is thought by some to have been half slave. Just as captures made during the Peloponnesian War fueled Grecian slave trades, so the Roman conquest of Gaul provided slave labor for that empire. By 60 B.C. Caesar's campaigns in Gaul had sent as many as 500,000 captives back to Rome as slaves. The legal status and social circumstances of slaves differs with historical time and place, but as in these formative examples, the institution is always closely allied with colonial conquest and the need for indentured labor to support further national expansion.

The first known pact to abolish a slave trade was signed by England and Tripoli in 1667, but it was only after the French Revolution in 1792 that widespread democratic reform and ethical formulations by writers such as Montesquieu and Rousseau created a climate conducive to the abolition of slavery. Colonial Argentina emancipated the children of its slaves in 1813, and this was followed by a similarly qualified emancipation in Colombia in 1821. Great Britain proclaimed an emancipation of slaves and compensation for owners in 1833; while this proved unworkable it did lead to freedom for slaves in the West Indies and South Africa in 1838 and in India in 1843. France unconditionally freed its slaves in 1848, and in 1858 Portugal freed its slaves effective twenty years later.

In North America economic, legal, and political complexities surrounding the issue of slavery were especially acute. The first purchase of slaves in the English colonies in America occurred at Jamestown, Va., in 1619, when a Dutch ship in difficulty was forced to exchange its cargo of slaves for supplies. Most British economic projections for the New World assumed that American Indians would be a ready source of labor, and when the Indians refused to be domesticated in this manner the need for slave labor became apparent, especially in the Southern colonies where agriculture was based on field crops such as tobacco. By 1650 "chattel" slavery, that which defines slaves as property, was legally recognized in the colonies. In the ensuing years, however, the mainland English colonies in America actually absorbed a very small percentage of the slave trade. It is estimated that by 1800 more than 9 million slaves from West Africa were shipped in bondage to the Americas, and of these the 13 original colonies purchased less than 5%, with much of the remainder being sent to the West Indies. In 1776 the slave population of the 13 colonies was approximately 500,000, with the overwhelming majority found south of Maryland.

The slave issue had emerged as a dominant consideration of America's politicians while they presided over the birth of the nation. The dilemma they confronted was a general ethical revulsion of slavery and economic dependence on it. National leaders from the Southern states tended to condemn slavery, but it is likely that only their relative wealth allowed them to ignore economic necessity. George Washington freed his slaves in his will, and Thomas Jefferson proposed the abolition of slavery in American territories effective in 1800. Northern politicians such as John Adams and Benjamin Franklin were freer to propose abolition because the industrial economy of their home states did not rely on field labor. Nevertheless, agricultural interests in the South remained adamant about their need for slave labor, and the resulting conflict of interest could have ended in violence long before the Civil War. Delay of the confrontation was effected by Virginian James Madison at the Constitutional Convention in 1787 when he succeeded in having ratified a document that nowhere uses the words "slave" or "slavery."

It remained inevitable, however, that the ethical interests of the North and the economic ones of the South would clash. In 1808 Northern interests succeeded in outlawing importation of slaves, but the Southern states nevertheless illegally imported an additional 250,000 slaves between that year and 1860. The Northern states began to abolish slavery within their own boundaries, beginning with Vermont in 1777, but often it was the shippers and traders from these same states who provided the illegal imports of slaves for the South. The issue was then exacerbated by the slave rebellions led by Denmark Vesey in South Carolina in 1822 and Nat TURNER in Virginia in 1831, rebellions that forced Southern plantation owners to institute harsher codes on slave behavior. Henry CLAY of Kentucky had by that time emerged as the negotiator of congressional compromises on the issue: his 1820 MISSOURI COMPROMISE admitted that territory to the Union as a slave state but banned slavery in the territories to the northwest of it.

The decade before the Civil War was marked by a series of political confrontations over the slavery issue and violent forays into the South by Northern abolitionists. Clay's Compromise of 1850 attempted to placate the abolitionist followers of Daniel Webster of Massachusetts and slave-owning followers of John Calhoun of South Carolina by simultaneously admitting California as a non-slave state and toughening the Fugitive Slave Law. 1852 saw the publication of Harriet Beecher Stowe's novel *Uncle Tom's Cabin*, a polemic in fiction against this same Fugitive Slave Law. In 1854 the Kansas-Nebraska Act decreed that the slavery issue was to be decided by the new state legislatures themselves rather than by the Federal government. The Republican Party was born in Ripon, Wisc., in the same year for the primary purpose of counteracting such legislation. 1856 brought riots over the issue in Lawrence, Kan., and the initial raids by abolitionist John Brown in Missouri. The South momentarily gained the upper hand with the Supreme Court's DRED SCOTT DECISION in 1857: it found that a slave did not become free by flight to a non-slave state, that Congress could not ban slavery from U.S. territories, and that Blacks were not granted citizenship by the Constitution. Whatever legal legitimacy this granted the slave system, however, was quickly offset by the entrenched abolitionism it provoked in the North. The extremist fringe of that movement gained national attention in 1859 when abolitionist John BROWN seized the U.S. Armory at HARPER'S FERRY, then in Virginia, and was executed later in the year for treason.

The outbreak of violence over the slavery issue became unavoidable when Abraham LINCOLN of the new Republican Party was elected Président in 1860. By the time he was inaugurated on March 4, 1861, six Southern states had already formed the Confederacy to protect the right of individual states to permit or to abolish slavery. These states fired on Union forces at Fort Sumter on April 12, 1861, and within a week Lincoln had called for military volunteers and ordered a blockade of Southern ports. By May the number of Confederate states had grown to eleven, and their victory over Union forces at Bull Run in Virginia on July 21, 1861, commenced the military conflict that would last four years.

Opinions differ over whether or not the Civil War was avoidable, but it is generally accepted that the war was fought over the specific issue of slavery rather than any more diffuse economic concerns. By the time Robert E. Lee's army surrendered at Appomattox Courthouse in Virginia on April 9, 1865, the Union had already proceeded with the legal abolition of slavery in the United States. In 1862 Congress outlawed slavery in all U.S. territories, and a preliminary EMANCIPATION PROCLAMATION was formalized on January 1, 1863, to free "all slaves in areas still in rebellion." Lincoln was assassinated in Washington, D.C., on April 14, 1865, five days after Lee's surrender, but his administration had already set in motion the political mechanism for complete abolition of slavery. This was ratified on December 18,

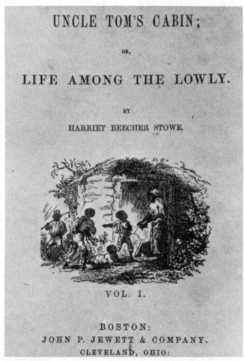

UNCLE TOM'S CABIN;

OR,

LIFE AMONG THE LOWLY.

BY

HARRIET BEECHER STOWE.

VOL. I.

BOSTON:
JOHN P. JEWETT & COMPANY.
CLEVELAND, OHIO:

Title page of *Uncle Tom's Cabin*, which helped solidify Northern sentiment against slavery

1865, as the 13th Amendment to the Constitution: "Neither slavery nor involuntary servitude, except as a punishment for crime whereof the party shall have been duly convicted, shall exist within the United States or any place subject to their jurisdiction."

SLIDELL, John (New York, N.Y., 1793 — Cowes, England, July 29, 1871). Politician. He was a prominent New Orleans lawyer and member of the Louisiana legislature before becoming a U.S. congressman from 1843 to 1845. While U.S. Senator from Louisiana (1853-61), he was influential in the election of President James Buchanan in 1856. Slidell became a Confederate commissioner to France in 1861 and was involved in the Trent Affair with James M. Mason.

SMALLS, Robert (Beaufort, S.C., Apr. 5, 1839 — Beaufort, S.C., Feb. 22, 1915). Politician. Smalls was a Negro slave and Union war hero who rose to political prominence in South Carolina during the Reconstruction era. In 1861 Smalls was impressed into the Confederate navy and assigned to *The Planter*, an armed frigate doing service in the Charleston Harbor. Smalls and 12 other slaves commandeered the vessel and sailed it into Union territory. For this daring exploit, Smalls gained national fame and a position in the Union navy. After the war, he was given a hero's welcome by his people, won the respect of the whites, and began a career of public service. He was a delegate to the National Union Convention (1864) and to the South Carolina constitutional conventions in 1868 and 1895. He served in both houses of the South Carolina legislature and was elected to Congress (1875-79, 1882-83, 1884-87). During his term as a state senator (1871-73), he was convicted of taking a bribe but pardoned by the governor. In 1897 he was appointed collector of the port of Beaufort, S.C.

SMITH, Ashbel (Hartford, Conn., Aug. 13, 1805 — Austin, Tex., Jan. 21, 1886). Poltician. After receiving his medical degree from Yale, Smith practiced in North Carolina before moving to Texas in 1837. He served as surgeon-general in the new republic, was minister to France and England, and was later appointed secretary of state in Texas. In the latter position he was instrumental in negotiating the controversial Smith-Cuevas Treaty with Mexico. Smith served briefly in the Mexican War and was elected to the Texas legislature three times

(1855, 1866, 1878). He was instrumental in the organization of the University of Texas.

SMITH, Bessie (Chattanooga, Tenn., Apr. 15, 1898 — Clarksdale, Miss., Sept. 26, 1937). Singer. Called the "Empress of the Blues," Bessie Smith was a famous black singer who made 150 recordings during her career. A student of sorts of the first great female blues singer, "Ma" Rainey, Smith rapidly developed a style of her own and came to be regarded as one of the greatest blues singer of her time. She sang with such famous instrumentalists as Benny Goodman, Fletcher Henderson, and Louis Armstrong. Some of her most famous recordings include *Jailhouse Blues* and *Cold in Hand Blues*. Smith was seriously injured in an automobile accident in 1937, and it is said that she died of her injuries because a nearby hospital refused to care for her because of her race.

SMITH, Ellison DuRant (near Lynchburg, S.C., Aug. 1, 1864 — Lynchburg, S.C., Nov. 17, 1944). Politician. He was an important organizer of the Southern Cotton Association in New Orleans, La., in 1905. Smith's political career began with his election to the state House of Representatives (1896-1900). In 1908 he was elected as a Democrat to the U.S. Senate, where he remained until his death. A Southern agrarian, Smith opposed high tariffs, hard currency and big business. He played little role in passage of the New Deal farm programs despite his position as Chairman of the Senate Agriculture Committee and opposed wages and hours laws as well as President Franklin D. Roosevelt's war policies.

SMITH, Green Clay (Richmond, Ky., July 2, 1826 — Washington, D.C., June 29, 1895). Politician. After serving in the Mexican War, he was a brigadier general in the Kentucky Volunteers during the Civil War. Smith served in the Kentucky legislature before his election as a Union candidate to the U.S. Congress (1863-66). In 1866 he was appointed governor of the Montana Territory and served until 1869. In 1869 he became an evangelist Baptist minister, and was the Prohibition Party candidate for the presidency in 1876.

SMITH, Hoke (Newton Co., N.C., Sept. 2, 1855 – Atlanta, Ga., Nov. 27, 1931). Publisher and politician. Smith was a practicing lawyer before he became publisher of the Atlanta *Journal* (1887-1900). He was Secretary of the Interior under President Grover Cleveland (1893-96), and was governor of Georgia (1907-09; 1911). In 1911 he became a Democratic U.S. Senator and served until 1921. Smith was a proponent of railroad regulation and improved public education, and gained popularity in the South due to his strong anti-Black policies.

SMITH, Holland McTyeire (Seale, Ala., Apr. 20, 1882 — San Diego, Cal., Jan. 12, 1967). Marine officer. He earned the nickname "Howlin' Mad" as a general in the Marines. He pioneered methods of amphibious warfare, and commanded forces in the Gilbert, Marshall, and Marianas Islands campaigns during World War II. Smith was commander of the Fleet Marine Force in the Pacific from 1944 to 1945.

SMITH, John (Willoughby, Lincolnshire, England, Jan., 1580 – London, England, June, 1631). Soldier of fortune, explorer, cartographer and writer. Known as Captain John Smith, he joined the French army in 1596, and later joined the insurrection against Spanish rule in the Low Countries. After a series of adventures, including being sold into slavery by the Turks, he began to feel the lure of the New World. In December, 1606, he was one of 105 stalwarts to set out in three ships bound for America. They landed in Virginia on May 13, 1607, and established the first permanent English colony in America, JAMESTOWN. Smith was named a council member of the colony (after a confrontation with his ship captain was resolved) and he soon became a leader, particularly in developing trade with the Indians. In December of that year, while foraging the countryside for food, he was taken captive by the Indians and sentenced to death. As legend has it, the Indian chief's daughter, POCAHONTAS, took Smith's head in her arms and laid her own upon it as protection against the clubs of the executioners. Chief POWHATAN gave in to this display of his daughter's courage and Smith was released. On September 10, 1608, Smith took over as president of Jamestown and his courage and resourcefulness were decisive in keeping the colony going during the first two years. He also embarked on two exploratory voyages along the Chesapeake Bay and surrounding region. In September, 1609, his term of office expired and he returned to England where he concerned himself with the colonization of New England, which he visited in 1614 and mapped a portion of the coast line. After three additional trips attempting to reach

New England, all of which ended in failure, he settled in London, England, and encouraged colonization by precept alone, producing numerous maps, pamphlets, and books.

SMITH, Lillian (Jasper, Fla., Dec. 12, 1897 — Atlanta, Ga., Sept. 28, 1966). Author, civil-rights activist. She co-founded *The North Georgia Review* in 1936. As *South Today* it became the first white-run Southern journal to publish the work of blacks. Her novels include *Strange Fruit* (1944) and *Killers of the Dream* (1949), which condemned racism. Her *One Hour* exposed the McCarthy hysteria of the 1950s, while *Our Faces, Our Words* (1964) celebrated the civil rights movement. A friend of Dr. MARTIN LUTHER KING, Jr., Smith was also on the executive board of Congress of Racial Equality (CORE).

SMITH, William Henry (Evergreen, Ala., June 18, 1859 — Birmingham, Ala., June 4, 1937). Clergyman. Smith was ordained a Baptist minister in 1887 and took his first position at Huntsville, Ala. He served as editorial secretary of the foreign mission board of the Southern Baptist Convention (1906-16), educational secretary of the State Board of the Alabama Baptist Convention (1916-20), and was president of the educational board of the Southern Baptist Convention (1923-33).

SNOW HILL, Md. Town (pop. 2,192), seat of Worcester Co., in southeastern Maryland on Chincoteague Bay. It was founded in an agricultural region of the Eastern Shore in 1642. Today it is a processing, shipping, and trade center for the area. The village proper was almost completely destroyed by fire in 1834 and 1893. All Hallows Church (1748) possesses a Bible given by Queen Anne in 1701.

SNYDER, John Wesley (Jonesboro, Ark., June 21, 1895 —). Businessman and statesman. Snyder left the banking profession to assist the Reconstruction Finance Corporation in Washington, D.C, (1937), and became executive vice president of the Defense Plant Corporation. He was federal loan administrator in 1945, and served as Secretary of the Treasury from 1946 to 1953.

SOFTWOODS. See LUMBER.

SOMERVILLE, Nellie Nugent (Greenville, Miss., Sept. 25, 1863 — Ruleville, Miss.,

July 28, 1952). Suffragist, politician. A graduate of Martha Washington College (B.A., 1880), she had early contact with CARRIE CHAPMAN CATT and FRANCES WILLARD and became corresponding secretary of the Mississippi Woman's Christian Temperance Union (1894), chairwoman of the state Woman Suffrage Association (1897), and vice-president of the National Woman Suffrage Association (1915). She was the first woman elected to Mississippi's legislature (1923-27) and there pressed a wide variety of social welfare issues. In the 1930s and 1940s, however, Somerville opposed child-labor laws and much of the New Deal.

SORGHUM. Grain-bearing grass, genus *Sorghum*, cultivated in the South for animal feed. Sorghum is native to Africa, where grass sorghums are still grown for hay. In the U.S., grain sorghums predominate, including kafir, durra, and milo. Sorghums thrive in dry areas, and the largest U.S. crops are harvested in the plains states such as Kansas and Nebraska. The largest sorghum crop in the South is harvested in Texas, where it exceeds all field crops except cotton lint in annual farm value.

SOTHERN, Edward Hugh (New Orleans, La., Dec. 6, 1859 — New York, N.Y., Oct. 28, 1933). Actor. The son of English actor Edward Askew Sothern, he made his first stage appearance in 1879 with his father's company at the Park Theatre, New York City. In 1904 he joined Julia Marlowe in a production of *Romeo and Juliet* and thereafter appeared almost continually with her and married her in 1911. He became best known for his roles in romantic comedy as well as Shakespearean productions. In 1916 he published his autobiography, *The Melancholy Tale of Me.*

SOUL FOOD. A term used to describe the food that slaves could grow, hunt or catch, along with what they could pilfer from the plantation house kitchen. Pork and corn were staples, but for slaves the amount of meat was scant, and the ration of cornmeal was usually supplemented by the addition of hominy and sweet potatoes. Because slave workers could only take time to hunt after their work in the fields was over, rabbit and opposums were the usual catch. Sesame seed, introduced by early African slaves, was widely used both as a seasoning (called benne seed), and as a token of good luck and health for the slaves.

SOUSA, John Philip (Washington, D.C., Nov. 6, 1854 — Redding, Pa., Mar. 6, 1932). Conductor and composer. He is called the "March King" for the more than 100 military marches he composed, including "The Stars and Stripes Forever" (1897), "Semper Fidelis" (1888), and "The Washington Post March" (1889). The son of a Portuguese father and a German mother, he initially followed in his father's footsteps as a trombonist, later working as a violinist and as a conductor. As leader of the Marine Corps Band (1880-92), he won such recognition that he organized his own band with which he toured the United States and Europe (1892-1911). He composed 10 operettas, including *El Capitan* (1896), which is still performed. During World War I he was director of all Navy bands. Sousa also authored three novels including *The Fifth String* (1902).

SOUTH, University of the. Independent Episcopal 4-year and professional coed school located on a 10,000-acre campus in Sewanee, Tenn. Founded in 1857, the university has been known for over a century as "Sewanee." It was an all male institution until women were admitted in 1969. Operated and owned by the Episcopal Church since its founding, the University has a College of Liberal Arts and a graduate School of Theology. The University's Department of Natural Resources is the only vocational program on campus. While most students do come from the South, only 20% are Tennessee natives. Fully 60% of graduating students go on for further study.

Library: 435,000 volumes, 1,850 journal subscriptions, 2,200 records/tapes. Faculty: 116. Enrollment: 615 men, 448 women (full-time). Degrees: Bachelor's, Master's, Doctorate.

SOUTH CAROLINA. State near the center of the South's Atlantic seaboard. Triangular in shape, it has a land border to the north with North Carolina, a southwestern border with Georgia formed by the Savannah River, and a 190-mile Atlantic Ocean coastline to the southeast.

South Carolina in many ways epitomizes the American South. Historically, it was central in the events that preceded the Civil War. South Carolina's senior statesman John C. Calhoun was the formulator of the "NULLIFICATION doctrine" on states' rights, South Carolina was the first state to secede from the Union, and Fort Sumter in Charleston, S.C., was the site of the first battle of the Civil War. In this era South Carolina was also the social epitome of antebel-

South Carolina

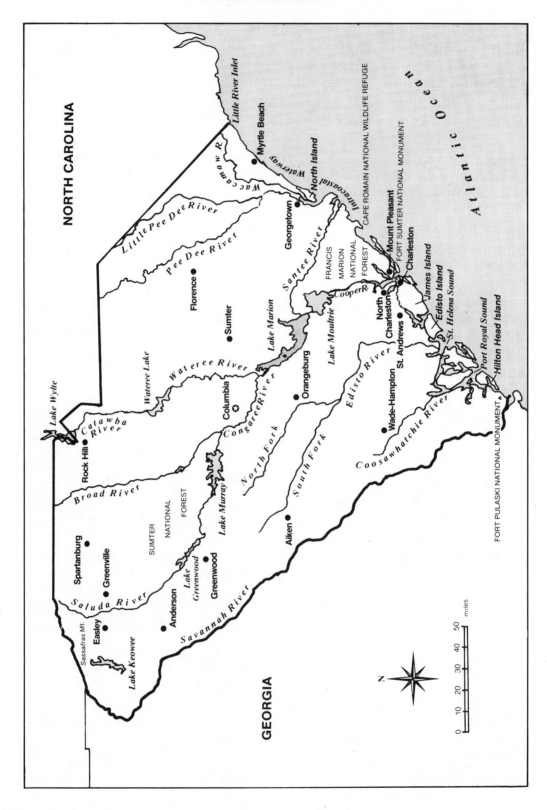

STATE OF SOUTH CAROLINA

Name: for Charles I (1600-1649), King of England (1625-1649).

Nickname: Palmetto State, Rice State, Iodine State, Sandlapper State, Swamp State, Keystone of the South Atlantic Seaboard.

Motto: *Dum Spiro Spero* (While I Breathe, I Hope).

Capital: Columbia.

Counties: 46. **Places over 10,000 population (1980):** 37.

Symbols & Emblems: *Flower:* Carolina Jessamine. *Bird:* Carolina Wren. *Tree:* Palmetto. *Song:* "Carolina."

Population (1980): 3,119,208. **Rank:** 24th.

Population Density (1980): 103.4 people per sq. mi. **Rank:** 19th.

Racial Make-up (1980): *White:* 2,145,122 (68.8%). *Black:* 948,146 (30.4%). *American Indian:* 5,758 (0.2%). *Asian & Pacific Islander:* 11,807 (0.4%). *Other:* 8,375 (0.3%). *Spanish Origin:* 33,414 (1.0%).

Largest City (pop. 1980): Columbia (99,296). *Others:* Charleston (69,510), North Charleston (65,630), Greenville (58,242), Spartanburg (43,968), Rock Hill (35,344), Florence (30,062), Anderson (27,313).

Area: 30,203 sq. mi. **Rank:** 40th.

Highest Point: Sassafras Mountain (3,560 ft.), Pickens Co.

Lowest Point: sea level, Atlantic Ocean.

State Government:
ELECTED OFFICIALS (4-year terms expiring Jan. 1987, etc.): *Governor* ($60,000); *Lt. Governor* ($30,000); *Sec. of State* ($55,000); *Attorney General* ($55,000); *Treasurer* ($55,000).

GENERAL ASSEMBLY (Salary: $10,000 plus $50 per legislative day living expense allowance.): *Senate* (46 members), *House of Representatives* (124 members).

CONGRESSIONAL REPRESENTATIVES: Senate (terms expire 1985, 1987, etc.). *House of Representatives* (6 members).

Admitted to the Union: May 23, 1788 (8th state to ratify the Constitution). One of the original 13 colonies.

lum South, with a social life and financial center in Charleston that represented the fruits of the plantation system.

Since the Civil War, South Carolina has endured some of the worst effects of the reconstruction era and subsequently negotiated the economic shift from agriculture to industry that has been crucial to the development of other states in the deep South. Manufacturing now generates nine times the income of agriculure in the state economy, and this development has encouraged recent population growth. The 1970s saw the largest proportionate and numerical population increase in the state's history, and in that decade the total state population passed the 3 million mark for the first time. In the midst of this recent growth, South Carolina has managed to preserve to an unusual extent its traditional ambience. The state's urban population is a relatively low 54%, and the traditional distinction in character between the small farms of the interior "upcountry" and larger farms of the coastal "lowcountry" remains intact today. Its successful preservation of the monuments to the antebellum South brings visitors to South Carolina and makes tourism one of its principal industries.

Topographically, South Carolina consists of two large regions divided by the fall line of waterfalls and river rapids that lies on a southwest-northeast line through the central capital city of COLUMBIA. Inland from this line, to the northwest, the state land is part of the PIEDMONT PLATEAU. This is the "up-country" of rolling hills and low ranges such as the Sand Hills. At its extreme inland corner, South Carolina approaches the Blue Ridge Mountains, and the state high point of SASSAFRAS MOUNTAIN (3,560 feet) is located near the meeting point of its Georgia and North Carolina borders. To the southeast of the fall line, the state lands drop off to the Atlantic COASTAL PLAIN, the "low-country." This was the region of plantation society, and it remains the seat of agriculture in the state. The coast itself consists of very low-lying sandy lands, with portions flooded by the ocean to isolate numerous islands, such as HILTON HEAD, PORT ROYAL, and SAINT HELENA Islands along the southern Atlantic coast. Because of the decline from inland to coastal elevations, South Carolina is drained to the southeast, toward the ocean. The central river network in the state are the numerous tributaries of the CONGAREE and WATEREE Rivers, which converge at Lake Marion to form the SANTEE RIVER. The climate of the state is a fairly consistent one of warm, humid summers, and

brief, mild winters, with only slightly cooler conditions prevailing far inland near the Blue Ridge Mountains.

The initial explorations of what is now South Carolina were carried out by the Spanish and French. In 1526 Vasquez de AYLLON of Spain attempted to establish a colony near the present site of GEORGETOWN on the INTRACOASTAL WATERWAY of the northern Atlantic coastline. In 1562 the French also attempted to establish a colony, one near Paris Island along the southern reach of the coast. Both attempts failed, largely because of greater interest in the Spanish possessions in Florida and the French ones in the Mississippi and Ohio River basins.

The English exploration of the region that was to lead to permanent settlement, began with the grant of a patent to "Carolana" to Sir Robert Heath by Charles I in 1629. In this early era the history of North and South Carolina is intertwined. In 1663, following the initial English settlement of North Carolina from Virginia, Charles II reorganized his country's interests in the region by granting a Carolana patent to the "Eight Lords Proprietors" because Heath had been financially unable to devlop his original holdings. The Lords Proprietors attempted to form a rather feudal society on the basis of the Fundamental Constitution of Carolina, but this was abandoned by 1679 because of their own disagreements with each other. Given the isolation of the colony, however, it was inevitable that early settlements would be established in the absence of organized government. The first permanent settlement in what is now South Carolina was made by William Sayle in 1670 at Albemarle Point at the mouth of the ASHLEY RIVER. In the next ten years it was relocated slightly and given the name Charles Town, which became CHARLESTON in 1783. The early financial interests in the region came from the English in the West Indies rather than from Virginia. Henry Woodward, a colonist of Barbados, helped organize the earliest plantations, and by 1700 the first slaves had arrived in Charleston to farm the lands.

The other early settlements in South Carolina were made at BEAUFORT in 1710 and Georgetown in 1729. At this time the primary concern of the colonists was defense against Indian attack from the interior and pirate raids along the coast. The Lords Proprietors proved unable to provide this defense, and in 1721 George I repurchased their patents to the region. The entire area was then reorganized by Parliament, and in 1729 North and South

Carolina were declared individual royal colonies.

The following decades saw the settlement of interior South Carolina by small farmers of Welsh, German, Scottish, and Irish descent. As it did in North Carolina and Virginia, this influx of small farmers to interior regions led to dissatisfaction with the colonial government, which was based along the coast and dominated by wealthy plantation owners. In South Carolina these two factions joined to send representatives to the Continental Congress of 1774, to drive the English governor from Charleston in 1775, and to declare independence from England in 1776. In the Revolutionary War Charleston was the site of battles in 1776 and 1780, and South Carolina contributed leaders to the patriotic cause such as the legendary "Swamp Fox" Francis MARION. Following the war, the division between "up-country" small farmers and "low-country" plantation owners was resolved by relocation of the capital city to Columbia in the central part of the state in 1786, and adoption of a new constitution that provided equal representation in 1790. The reform of the franchise to guarantee fair representation continued through constitutional amendments in 1808 and 1810.

Unlike neighboring states, South Carolina was at this time controlled in both coastal and inland areas by cotton interests. Among other effects, this united the state in support of institutionalized slavery. John C. CALHOUN of South Carolina became vice president to John Quincy Adams in 1825, and in this role he became the principal spokesman for the "nullification doctrine" in favor of a state's right to nullify federal legislation that infringed on its own sovereign rights. South Carolina was the first state to ratify a nullification ordinance in its state legislature in 1832, and secessionist agitation became widespread in the state soon after. The election of abolitionist Abraham Lincoln as President in 1860 brought an immediate response from South Carolina: on December 20, 1860, it became the first state to insist on its right to secede from a union it had voluntarily joined.

The first barrages of the Civil War were fired by Confederate troops on FORT SUMTER in Charleston harbor on April 12, 1861. Charleston remained under siege throughout the war, but it resisted until the very end. It was evacuated after the Union Army under Gen. William Tecumseh Sherman burned Columbia on February 18, 1865, but Sherman chose to head further south on his devastating "MARCH TO THE SEA," and Charleston was spared similar destruction. The state contributed more than 60,000 soldiers to the Confederate army, and one in five had died in battle by the war's end. After the Union victory, 400,000 slaves in South Carolina suddenly became voting citizens. This abrupt change in state politics and the corruption of the Reconstruction politicians who replaced the state's experienced leaders, left South Carolina an economic and social shambles. The state remained in a state of economic depression until the relocation of textile industries from New England to the cotton states began to spur a recovery in the late 19th century.

Today South Carolina is the home of diverse modern industries that have encouraged urbanization. The central capital city of Columbia is the largest in the state and also the heart of its second-largest metropolitan area. In addition to being the seat of state government, Columbia is also the educational and financial capital of the state. Charleston is the largest city in coastal South Carolina and the heart of its largest metropolitan area. In addition to its historical importance, Charleston is South Carolina's principal port, an industrial center, and the location of the U.S. military installations that are an important part of the state economy. The largest metropolitan area in "up-country" South Carolina is GREENVILLE-SPARTANBURG, the retail hub of the entire piedmont region and the center of the state's textile industries. Despite the recent growth of these cities, including the 56% population growth rate of the Columbia metropolitan area since 1960, almost half the total state population lives in rural areas. South Carolina has an extremely high proportion of life-long residents, more than 70%, and an extremely low one of persons of foreign stock or birth, less than 1%. In compostition the state population is 30% black and 1% Hispanic.

The manufacturing industries in South Carolina generate more than $9 billion per year and employ more than one-third of the work force. The principal manufactures of the state are textiles, chemicals, plastics, and paper goods. The agricultural economy of the state is divided between livestock, including poultry in the "up-country" piedmont region, and crops, notably tobacco, soybeans, and cotton, in the "low-country" coastal region. While not of great importance to the total state economy, South Carolina's mining industry is notable for the second-highest yield of the specialized ores vermiculite and kaolin. The state also has small but significant timber and commercial fishing industries. Tourism is an increasingly important contributor to the state economy, particularly in historic areas such as Charleston, and in summer resorts along the coast from northern MYRTLE BEACH to southern Hilton Head.

SOUTH CAROLINA, University of.
State-supported coed university located on a 222-acre campus in the South Carolina capital of Columbia. Founded in 1801, the university is one of the country's oldest state universities and was the first such institution to receive annual operations monies from the state. The university also maintains four 2-year branch campuses, and 4-year campuses in Spartanburg, Aiken, and Conway.

Academic courses are offered to students through the colleges of Humanities and Social Sciences, Business Administration, Education, Engineering, General Studies, Journalism, Nursing, Science and Mathematics, Social and Behavioral Sciences, Schools of Health and Physical Education, and for upperclassmen, the College of Pharmacy. Only graduate students may take degrees at the Schools of Law and Medicine and the Colleges of Librarianship and Social Work. Master's degrees are offered in 82 areas; the doctorate in 31. The South provides 90% of students and 28% of students go on for further study.

Library: 1,819,230 volumes, 1,699,611 microform titles, 16,727 journal subscriptions, 5,383 records, tapes. Faculty: 1,559. Enrollment: 26,135 total graduate and undergraduate: 8,018 men, 7,234 women (full-time). Degrees: Associate's, Bachelor's, Master's, Doctorate.

SOUTH CAROLINA STATE COLLEGE.
State-supported comprehensive coed institution located in Orangeburg, S.C., 50 miles east of Columbia. Originally founded in 1895 as a school for Negroes, South Carolina State is still predominantly black. Some 92% of all its students are state residents, and 57% are women.

Undergraduate studies are offered in the schools of arts and sciences, agriculture, education, home economics, industrial education, and engineering technology. Most undergraduate degrees are conferred in education, followed by business and management.

Library: 217,212 volumes, 929 journal subscriptions. Faculty: 250. Enrollment: 1,460 men, 1,748 women (full-time). Degrees: Bachelor's, Master's.

SOUTH FLORIDA NEW COLLEGE, University of.
Coed liberal arts college, part of the State University system of Florida, located in the Gulf coast city of Sarasota, Fla. Founded in 1960, the college became affiliated with the State University system, via the University of South Florida in 1975.

The South provides 52% of the students, and the rest come from the Middle Atlantic and New England states; 19% pursue full-time graduate study immediately after graduation, and 6% enter law school. Because New College is the honor college of the University of South Florida, students are eligible to graduate in three or three and a half years.

Library: 145,000 volumes, 212 microform titles, 956 journal subscriptions, 1,890 records/tapes. Faculty: 45. Enrollment: 253 men, 216 women (full-time). Degrees: Bachelor's.

SOUTH FORK RIVER, Ky./Tenn.
River originating in McCreary Co., in southernmost Kentucky. It is an extension of the Cumberland River and flows for 30 miles southwest into northern Tennessee.

SOUTHERN METHODIST UNIVERSITY.
Independent coed institution located in east central Texas city of Dallas. Founded by the United Methodist Church in 1911, the school is a nonsectarian institution, and no religious demands are imposed upon students.

The university includes the Schools of Humanities and Sciences, Business Administration, Engineering and Applied Science, and the Meadows School of the Arts. Majors are available in Ibero-American civilization, criminal justice, urban studies, anthropology, and geophysics. The South provides 50% of the students, 25% are from North Central states, and 25% of students pursue additional study immediately after graduating; 8% enter medical school, 7% law school, 18% business school. SMU is among the nation's top 120 producers of successful dental school applicants.

Library: 950,951 volumes, 53,000 journal subscriptions, 16,779 records/tapes. Faculty: 589. Enrollment: 8,923 total graduate and undergraduate. Degrees: Bachelor's, Master's, Doctorate.

SOUTHSIDE, Va.
Local name given to the area east of the Blue Ridge Mountains and south of the James River. Once an important tobacco growing area, much of the region is now devoted to the raising of livestock.

SOYBEANS. Leguminous plant native to Asia and in recent years an increasingly important field crop in the South. The plant yields a crop of up to 40 bushels per acre, produces hay for fodder, and resists both drought and heavy rain. It lends itself to a variety of food uses, including animal feed, and soybean oil has numerous industrial uses in the production of paints, soaps, rubbers, and other products. In the 1970s U.S. soybean production nearly doubled to reach 1.8 billion bushels per year. Much of this new planting occurred in Southern states such as Louisiana and Mississippi, where soybeans replaced cotton as a leading field crop.

In 1982 the Southern states accounted for nearly one-third of the U.S. soybean harvest. The leader in the region was Missouri, which harvested 184 million bushels worth more than $1 billion. The other leading producers of soybeans in the South in 1982 were: Arkansas, with 109 million bushels; Louisiana, with 77 million bushels; and Mississippi, with 93 million bushels; Georgia, with 68 million bushels; Tennessee, with 63 million bushels; Kentucky and Alabama, both with 53 million bushels; North Carolina, with 52 million bushels; and South Carolina with 40 million bushels. Maryland, Texas, and West Virginia harvest small crops of soybeans.

SPANISH MOSS (*Tillandsia usneoides*). Not a true moss, this grayish-color plant hangs in long tufts from trees in the tropical and subtropical climates of the South. Actually a member of the pineapple family, it has an air of mysterious beauty. Commercially it has been used, after processing, for stuffing, packaging material, and insulation.

SPARTANBURG, S.C. City (pop. 43,502), seat of Spartanburg Co., in northwestern South Carolina. Located in the foothills of the Blue Ridge Mountains, it is an agricultural region where cotton and peaches are the primary crops. Spartanburg was settled in 1780, selected as the county seat in 1785, and incorporated in 1831. Known for its textiles, its cotton industry dates back to 1816. Today it is one of the largest private textile research and development centers. Other manufactures include chemicals, plumbing supplies, along with metal, rubber, and paper products. The nearby U.S. military parks of COWPENS and KINGS MOUNTAIN mark the sites of two important Revolutionary War engagements. During the Civil War Spartanburg supplied arms and clothing to the Confederacy. Its name derives from the Spartan Rifles,

a militia group that distinguished itself in the Revolution. It is the home of Converse College (1889), and Wofford College (1851).

SPENCER'S TAVERN, Battle of. Revolutionary War engagement fought near Williamsburg, Va., on June 26, 1781. In this late phase of the war, British commander Lord Charles Cornwallis was in a controlled retreat from Richmond to Williamsburg, pursued by the Revolutionary forces under Marquis de Lafayette. In the indecisive battle at Spencer's Tavern on June 26, small detachments of both forces met in hand-to-hand combat, with both sides suffering approximately equal casualties of 30 killed or wounded. The campaign continued at Green Spring on July 6, and it eventually led to the siege of Yorktown.

SPINDLETOP. The first major oil well drilled in Texas in the 20th century. Traces of crude oil were discovered in Texas in the Corsicana area in the early 1890s by men drilling water wells. By 1899 there were some 300 oil wells in the area but they were primarily short-lived and produced only small quantites. On January 10, 1901, an exploratory well being

Oil field at Burkburnett, Texas, c. 1919

drilled near Beaumont, Tex., under the direction of Anthony Lucas, gushered in spewing oil more than 100 feet into the air. It took six days to cap the well, named Spindletop, and in that time nearly half a million barrels were discharged. A new economic base was established for the previously agricultural state, and thousands of promoters hurried to the new oil field. In the first year of its existence the Spindletop field produced four times as much petroleum as had been produced in the entire state in the previous year. Pipelines and refineries were constructed, and huge companies were organized to produce and refine the oil. Although the Spindletop oil flow slackened within a few years, almost overnight oil became the heart of the industrial economy of Texas.

SPOTSWOOD, Alexander (Tangier, Morocco, 1676 — Annapolis, Md., June 7, 1740). Colonial governor. Officially a lieutenant governor, he actually ran the Virginia colony during his term (1710-22). An advocate of frontier expansion, Spotswood led several exploratory expeditions, and through his efforts a treaty of peace was negotiated with the Iroquois Indians. After his governorship ended, he remained in the colony as a vast land owner with iron mining interests. Spotswood was responsible for the construction of stone iron furnaces at Germanna, Massaponax, and Fredericksville, which were the foundation of the iron industry in the South. He was appointed deputy postmaster general of the colonies in 1730.

SPOTSYLVANIA, Battle of. Civil War struggle, from May 9-19, 1864, around Spotsylvania Courthouse just southwest of Fredericksburg, Va. It was a second phase in the fighting begun at the Battle of the WILDERNESS and continued at the Battle of NORTH ANNA. At Spotsylvania Gen. Robert E. LEE beat Gen. Ulysses S. GRANT to the field, built entrenchments, and successfully defended them against days of Union attack.

The Union advance to Spotsylvania, a crossroads to both Fredericksburg and Richmond, was disorganized by movements at Wilderness. The Confederate army, meanwhile, formed a line north of the courthouse with the troops of Gen. Richard Anderson, Richard S. Ewell, and Jubal Early. The heaviest fighting occurred between May 10 and May 12, but it failed to significantly alter the original lines of battle. By May 18 the Confederate line was moved back to the North Anna River, a movement protected by Ewell's final raids against the Union line. Denied a clear victory, Grant vowed after Spotsylvania to continue his "relentless hammering" of Lee at North Anna.

SPOTSYLVANIA, Va. County located between Richmond, Va., and Washington, D.C. It was the site of four major battles of the Civil War: FREDERICKSBURG, CHANCELORSVILLE, WILDERNESS, and SPOTSYLVANIA Courthouse. Formed in 1720, this farming and lumbering county was named after Alexander SPOTSWOOD.

SPRINGDALE, Ark. City (pop. 23,458), Washington Co., in northwest Arkansas in the Ozark Mountains. Incorporated in 1878, today it is a shipping center for grapes and other agricultural products. There are also fruit juice and vegetable canning factories and feed mills.

SPRINGFIELD, Mo. City (pop. 133,166), seat of Greene Co., in southwest Missouri. Settled in 1829 and incorporated in 1855, the city's first growth was due to its location along land routes important during the great migration of pioneers to the Western territories. It was held for a few months in 1861 by Confederate troops, which were driven out by Federal forces in 1862. North Springfield was founded with the extension of the Atlantic and Pacific Railroad in 1870, but it merged with the older city in 1887. The economy is based on agriculture (poultry, livestock, and dairy products), and supplemented by manufacturing (steel, lumber, and clothing). Drury College, Southwest Missouri State University, Baptist College, Central Bible Institute, and Evangel College are located here, along with the international headquarters of the Assemblies of God Church.

SPRINGFIELD PLATEAU, Ark. High region of the OZARK PLATEAU. Its top ranges are fairly level, and it is considered some of the best farmland in the state.

SPRUANCE, Raymond Ames (Baltimore, Md., July 3, 1886 — Pebble Beach, Cal., Dec. 13, 1969). Naval officer. He earned his commission at Annapolis in 1906. After meritorious service at the battle of Midway during World War II, he commanded the invasion of the Marshall Islands. He retired from the navy as an admiral and commander-in-chief of the Pacific fleet.

SPRUCE KNOB, W.Va. Peak in Pendelton Co., in the eastern panhandle of West Virginia. The highest mountain in the state (4,482 feet), it is part of the Allegheny Mountain range.

STAMP ACT. Act passed by the British Parliament (1765), which required all paper, parchment, and vellum used in the Colonies to be stamped. It further declared that legal documents written on unstamped paper were null and void. The measure, intended to raise revenue for the British, was met with violent opposition in the colonies and was one of the causes leading to the Revolution. A Stamp Act congress, with delegates from all the colonies except North Carolina, Virginia, Georgia, and New Hampshire, met in New York in October, 1765, and sent a protest to the king. The colonists declared that they could be taxed only by their own assemblies, and their opposition led to a repeal of the act in 1766.

STATES' RIGHTS. A doctrine whereby the states claimed all powers not reserved by the U.S. Constitution for the federal government. The assertion of this doctrine caused many clashes between the states and the federal government up to 1860. The states based their claim on the Tenth Amendment which stated, "The powers not delegated to the United States by the Constitution, nor prohibited by it to the States, are reserved to the States respectively, or to the people." Upon the adoption of the constitution, a controversy arose between the Federalist Party headed by Alexander Hamilton and the "strict constructionists" led by Thomas JEFFERSON. Hamilton and his party preferred a broad interpretation of the Constitution, giving the federal government implied as well as expressed powers. Jefferson believed that the powers of the federal government should be limited to only those expressed in the constitution and that all other powers be reserved for the states. The first manifestation of states' rights took the form of the VIRGINIA AND KENTUCKY RESOLUTIONS of 1798 and 1799 written by Jefferson and James MADISON in opposition to the Alien and Sedition Acts of 1798. These resolutions expressed the concept of NULLIFICATION, the right to declare null and void any federal law the state decided was unconstitutional. The doctrine was asserted again in New England to protest the Embargo Act of 1807 and again during the War of 1812 when the HARTFORD CONVENTION formally condemned federal policies. In 1819 a controversy over the constitutionality of the Second Bank of the United States led to a Supreme Court decision which upheld the concept of implied powers thereby helping to consolidate the power of the central government. In the 1820s the state of Georgia defied federal claims to jurisdiction over Indian tribes in that state. A more extreme case of states' rights occurred in 1832 when the South Carolina legislature, led by John C. CALHOUN, passed the Ordinance of Nullification, declaring the tariff acts of 1828 and 1832 null and void. Both President Andrew JACKSON and the state were prepared to defend their positions with force of arms but Congress quickly passed a compromise tariff act and open conflict was avoided. Ultimately, it was the states' rights doctrine that was used by the Southern states to justify their SECESSION from the Union in 1860 thereby precipitating the Civil War.

The defeat of the Confederacy effectively crushed the doctrine of states' rights although it resurfaced in the 20th century during the period of desegregation in the 1950s and 1960s. State governors such as Orval E. FAUBUS of Arkansas and George C. WALLACE of Alabama made states' rights statements and Southern state legislatures passed a number of laws to try to circumvent federal desegregation policies. During this period federal troops were called out several times to assist the desegregation process. Although over the years the U.S. government has effectively consolidated its power, it is likely that the concept of states' rights will never completely disappear.

STAUNTON, Va. City (pop. 21,857), seat of Augusta Co., in northwestern Virginia. Settled in 1736 and named after the wife of a colonial governor, Staunton was the capital of the Northwest Territory of Virginia prior to 1784, and was a key depot during the Civil War. It was incorporated as a city in 1871 and in 1908 became the first U.S. community to choose the council city-manager plan of municipal government. Staunton serves as a shipping center for livestock, fruits, grains, and vegetables from the surrounding area. Manufactures include metal products, air-conditioners, machinery, furniture, and textiles. It was the birthplace of President Woodrow WILSON, and is the home of Mary Baldwin College, the Virginia School for the Deaf and Blind, and the Staunton Military Academy.

STEELE, Wilbur Daniel (Greensboro, N.C., 1886 — Essex, Conn., May 26, 1970). Author. Noted for his dramatic short stories set in American locales. Steele's short story collections include *The Man Who Saw Through Heaven* (1927), and *Full Cargo* (1951); his novels include *Taboo* (1925) and *Their Town* (1952). He won the O. Henry Prize four times.

STEPHENS, Alexander Hamilton (Taliaferro Co., Ga., Feb. 11, 1812 — Atlanta, Ga., Mar. 4, 1883). Vice president of the Confederate States of America. After practicing law and serving in the Georgia legislature, he served in the U.S. Congress (1843-59). Stephens voted against secession as a member of the secession convention of Georgia in 1861, but accepted his state's decision. He served as vice-president of the Confederacy from 1861 to 1865, and was an early advocate of peace, serving as a Confederate commissioner to the Hampton Roads Conference in 1865. Elected to the U.S. Senate in 1866 by the first legislature convened under the new state constitution, he was denied his seat because he was from a "rebel" state. He later served again in Congress (1873-82), and was elected governor of Georgia (1882-83).

STEVENSON, Adlai Ewing (Christian Co., Ky., Oct. 23, 1835 — Chicago, Ill, June 14, 1914). Lawyer, politician, and Vice President of the United States (1893-97). Admitted to the bar in 1858, he was elected Illinois state's attorney in 1865. He was elected twice to the U.S. Congress (1875-77, 1879-81) before being appointed first assistant postmaster general under President Grover Cleveland (1885-89). After serving with Cleveland as vice president (1893-97), he was appointed by President William McKinley to serve as chairman of a commission sent to Europe to secure international bimetallism. He was an unsuccessful candidate for vice president (1900) and for the Illinois governorship (1908).

STEWARD, Julian Haynes (Washington, D.C., 1902 — 1972). Anthropologist. He received his Ph.D at the University of California (1929) and went on to teach at numerous universities around the country. Steward was a noted expert on cultural evolution in the United States and worked at the Smithsonian Institution. While there in the Bureau of American Ethnology he edited the seven-volume *Handbook of South American Indians* (1946-59). Some of his other works include *Area Research, Theory and Practice* (1950) and *Theory of Culture Change* (1955).

STILL, Andrew Taylor (Jonesville, Va., Aug. 6, 1828 — Kirksville, Mo., Dec. 12, 1917). Physician and antislavery leader. Beginning his medical practice (1853) in Kansas and Missouri, he became involved in antislavery work and was elected to the Kansas legislature (1857). He fought for the North in the Civil War and was promoted to major. After the death of three of his children due to cerebrospinal meningitis, Still began exploring manipulatory means of treating such diseases rather than traditional methods. For 25 years he traveled around the country teaching and preaching. He founded the American School of Osteopathy (1892) in Kirksville, Mo.

STILL, William Grant (Woodville, Miss., May 11, 1895 —). Composer and conductor. Considered the foremost black composer in America, he was the first Negro to lead a symphony orchestra. Thoroughly schooled in classical music, he determined in the mid-1920s to devote his work to development of music in the Negro idiom and to subjects dealing with circumstances common to the black experience in America. His compositions on Afro-American themes include "Darker America," "From the Black Belt," "Africa," and "Song of a New Race," his second symphony. His most famous work was "And They Lynched Him on a Tree," for contralto, chorus, orchestra, and narrator, based on a Katharin Garrison Chapin poem. In the era surrounding World War II he composed "Plain Song for Americans," with words by Miss Chapin, and "In Memorium: the Colored Soldiers Who Died for Democracy."

STILLWELL, Joseph Warren (Palatka, Fla., Mar. 19, 1883 — San Francisco, Cal., Oct. 12, 1946). Military officer. Having learned Chinese, Stillwell accepted duty in China (1926-29; 32-39). He returned to China during World War II (1942) as chief of staff to Chiang Kai-sheck, and in command of American troops in continental Asia. Promoted to full general (1944) after his successful Burma offensive, Stillwell was recalled to Washington due to personal differences with Chiang Kai-sheck.

STONE, Barton Warren (near Port Tobacco, Md., Dec. 24, 1772 — Hannibal, Mo., Nov. 9, 1844). Religious leader. He was ordained a Presbyterian minister in 1789 and was an itinerant preacher throughout Tennessee and Kentucky. After disagreements within the Presbyterian Church, Stone left the Synod of Kentucky in 1803, and devoted most of his life to evangelical work. In 1824 he met Alexander Campbell and his Disciples of Christ, and he joined the group in 1842. He was publisher of the *Christian Messenger* (1826-45).

STONE, John Marshall (Milan, Tenn., Apr. 30, 1830 — Iuka, Miss., Mar. 26, 1900). Military officer and politician. Moving to Mississippi in 1855, he became a captain in the Confederate army. He was a state senator (1870-76), and was acting governor (1876-77). He served again as governor from 1876 to 1882 and 1890 to 1896. During his tenure he consolidated control of state government in the hands of whites.

STONE MOUNTAIN, Ga. DeKalb Co., in northwest Georgia, 16 miles east of Atlanta. It is considered the largest exposed granite dome (850 feet) in North America and is a memorial to the Confederacy. Robert E. Lee, Stonewall Jackson, and Jefferson Davis, all on horseback, are carved on the mountain, a project begun in 1923. The memorial encompasses 3,200 acres. In the past it had been used as an Indian signal tower and a major Ku Klux Klan meeting spot.

STONES RIVER, Battle of. Civil War engagement fought December 31, 1862, and January 3, 1863, in central Tennessee near Murfreesboro, the town for which the battle is sometimes named. The tactical victor in the battle is a matter of dispute, but the Confederate army sustained heavier losses and was forced ultimately to retreat.

The battle of Stones River was an outgrowth of Confederate Gen. Braxton Bragg's defeat at PERRYVILLE and retreat south into Tennessee. The Union army had been reorganized under the command of Gen. William Starke Rosecrans after Perryville, and on December 31 it was poised on the west back of the Stones River, opposite Murfreesboro, to confront Bragg's newly-organized Army of Tennessee. Bragg, however, struck first on that day, attacking the Union right flank and forcing it to withdraw slowly throughout the day. The heaviest losses for both sides occurred at a site called Round Forest, nicknamed "Hell's Half Acre," which the Union managed to hold until nightfall.

After a lull on January 1, the fighting moved to the east bank of the river on January 2, when Bragg attacked the Union left flank. The Union troops there were routed by Confederate Gen. John C. BRECKENRIDGE, but his advance was halted by the sudden arrival of Union reinforce-

ments. The Union regained its original position on this left flank while holding their position on the right, and Bragg withdrew through Murfreesboro on January 3. Bragg had in fact outmaneuvered Rosecrans, but with fewer troops at his disposal he could not capitalize on his tactical achievements. The fighting to a virtual stalemate had cost a quarter of the Union force of 40,000 and a third of the Confederate force of 35,000.

STONO FERRY, Battle of. Revolutionary War engagement just south of Charleston, S.C., fought June 20, 1779. The patriots in the area were led by Gen. Benjamin Lincoln, who would eventually surrender Charleston in 1780. In the battle of Stono Ferry, Lincoln made an ill-advised attack on British emplacements on a ferry between Johns and James Islands. The patriots had approximately 150 men killed in the attack on June 20, and Lincoln lost approximately the same number to desertion. The British, who suffered only light casualties, had already decided to abandon the ferry, and they did so on June 23.

STRACHEY, William (England, 1572 — 1621). Colonial official and author. He sailed for Virginia in 1609 only to be shipwrecked near Bermuda where he was stranded for a year. His experiences during this time are thought to have been a basis for Shakespeare's *Tempest*. He eventually arrived in Jamestown (1610) and was made secretary of the colony. His most noted work, one of the few sources of early Virginia history, was *The Historie of Travaile into Virginia Britannia* (1613).

STRAITS OF FLORIDA. Body of water between the southern tip of Florida and the Florida Keys on the north, and Cuba and the Bahamas on the south. Up to 90 miles in width, it connects the Atlantic Ocean with the Gulf of Mexico. The current passing through the straits from the Gulf initiates the Gulf Stream.

STRAUSS, Lewis Lichtenstein (Charleston, W.Va., Jan. 31, 1896 — Brandy Station, Va., Jan. 21, 1974). Statesman. An advocate of the development of the hydrogen bomb, he served on the Atomic Energy Commission from 1946 to 1950 and later was its chairman (1953-58). Strauss was appointed Secretary of Commerce by President Dwight Eisenhower in November, 1958, but the Senate refused to confirm the position in June, 1959.

STRIBLING, Thomas Sigismund (Clifton, Tenn., Mar. 4, 1881 — Florence, Ala., July 8, 1965). Author. He started his career writing for magazines before authoring several novels of realistic Southern life. In 1933 he won the Pulitzer Prize for his book *The Store* (1932). His other works include *Birthright* (1921) and *These Bars of Flesh* (1938), a satire.

STRITCH, Samuel Alphonsus (Nashville, Tenn., Aug. 17, 1887 — Rome, Italy, May 27, 1958). Catholic cardinal. Ordained a Roman Catholic priest in 1910, he served in many official positions in Nashville, Tenn., and in Ohio before being made cardinal in 1946. He was the first American to be appointed to the Roman Curia, the principal governing body of the Roman Catholic Church. Shortly before his death, he was appointed head of all Catholic mission work.

STUART, Alexander Hugh Holmes (Staunton, Va., Apr. 2, 1807 — Staunton, Va., Feb. 13, 1891). Politician. He was a lawyer in Staunton before being elected to the Virginia House of Delegates (1836-39). Stuart served in the U.S. House of Representatives (1841-43) and was U.S. Secretary of the Interior (1850-53). In 1857 he was elected to the state senate where he served until the outbreak of the Civil War. He condemned the secessionist movement as inexpedient, and is credited with helping to restore order to the state after the war. He was again a member of the state House of Delegates (1874-77), and supported education for blacks.

STUART, James Ewell Brown "Jeb" (Patrick Co., Va., Feb. 6, 1833 — Richmond, Va., May 12, 1864). Military officer. A 1854 graduate of West Point, Stuart served with the U. S. Cavalry in Kansas before resigning to join the Confederate Army at the outbreak of the Civil War. He was a veteran of the two Confederate victories at Bull Run (Manassas) in 1861 and 1862, but his early fame was based on a 1862 cavalry surveillance ride that in three days completely circumscribed Gen. George McClellan's Union army near Richmond. This provided precise information on the Union army's strength and emplacements, an accomplishment for which Stuart was called by Gen. Robert E. Lee "the eyes of the army" of the South. At Chancellorsville in 1863 Stuart further distinguished himself by leading a crucial flanking maneuver and then taking command of the Confederate Army after Gen. Stonewall

Jackson was wounded. Such success bred conceit, however, and when Stuart insisted on leading a flamboyant diversionary tactic at Gettysburg in 1863 he effectively rode himself out of the battle, a defeat for the South and the great turning point of the war. Stuart died of wounds received while gallantly defending Richmond in 1864 against the far stronger forces of Union Gen. Philip H. Sheridan.

STURGIS, Russell (Baltimore Co., Md., Oct. 16, 1836 — New York, N.Y., Feb. 11, 1909). Architect, critic, and author. One of the first to recognize and promote the work of architect Frank Lloyd Wright, Sturgis was a graduate of the Free Academy (now City College), of New York. He designed many buildings, including the Mechanics Bank of Albany, N.Y., Flower Hospital in New York City, and a Yale University chapel. In the early 1900s he wrote and edited books about architecture, art history, and art appreciation.

SUBLETTE, William Lewis (Lincoln Co., Ky., c. 1799 — Pittsburgh, Pa., July 23, 1845). Fur trader. His wagons were the first to cross the Rockies in 1823. Sublette amassed a fortune in fur trading and later became an important figure in the state politics of Missouri.

SUFFOLK, Va. Independent city (pop. 47,621), in southeast Virginia on the Nansemond River near Dismal Swamp. First settled by English Puritans in 1618 who were forced out in the 1640s, the town's early economy was based on tobacco cultivation. The town suffered from military encounters when it was burned by the British during the Revolution (1779) and occupied by Union troops (1862) during the Civil War. The town has long been a peanut market center and has been called the peanut capital of the world. Along with peanut products, Suffolk's industrial manufactures include confectionery, bricks, fertilizers, containers, and TV sets. Timber and agricultural produce are also an important part of its economy.

SUITLAND/SILVER HILL, Md. Unincorporated town (pop. 10,300), Prince George's Co., in west central Maryland. It is a residential suburb of Washington, D.C. The U.S. Navy Oceanographic Center and the U.S. Bureau of Census are located here, along with Washington National, Cedar Hill, and Lincoln Memorial Cemeteries.

SUMA INDIANS. See SHUMAN INDIANS.

SUMMERSVILLE, W.Va. Town (pop. 2,972), seat of Nicholas Co., in central West Virginia. Summerville is a residential village located near the Carnifex Ferry Battlefield State Park. It is famed for the story of a 20-year-old woman named Nancy Hart who led a surprise Confederate attack on Union forces here in July, 1861. The Federal troops were captured and part of the town was burned. Hart herself was ambushed and put in jail. There she worked her charm on a jailkeeper whom she fatally wounded with his gun before escaping.

SUMTER, Fort, Battle of. The opening engagement of the Civil War, a bombardment by secessionists of the Union fort in the harbor of Charleston, S.C., on April 12-14, 1861.

Fort Sumter was commanded by Maj. Robert Anderson, who consolidated Union forces from other forts in the harbor within Sumter on December 26, 1860. On January 9, 1861, the secessionists turned back a support vessel *Star of the West*, and in March they organized a volunteer assault force commanded by Confederate Gen. Pierre BEAUREGARD. The bombardment opened on April 12 and lasted until Anderson and his men evacuated the fort because of lack of supplies. An accidental explosion during the final salute ceremonies on April 14 killed U.S. Artillery Private Daniel Huff, the first man to die in the Civil War.

Sumter was attacked by the Union navy on April 7 and on September 8, 1863, but the Confederate garrison under Beauregard repelled both attacks.

The Union army raised the U.S. flag over Fort Sumter on April 14, 1865, five days after Robert E. Lee's surrender at Appomattox and a few hours before the assassination of President Abraham Lincoln.

SUMTER, S.C. City (pop. 24,890), seat of Sumter Co., in east central South Carolina. Settled in 1785 and incorporated in 1845, today it is the site of a U.S. tree nursery in a heavily forested and rich agricultural area. Sumter is the trade, processing, and shipping center for lumber, livestock, and farm products, which include cotton and soybeans. Manufactures include textile products, furniture, electric storage batteries, frozen foods, medical sup-

A Currier & Ives print of the bombardment of Fort Sumter

plies, fabricated steel, paints, and varnishes. Buried here are Gen. Thomas SUMTER, the Revolutionary War hero for whom the city was named, and Joel POINSETT, for whom the poinsettia is named. Poinsett State Park is nearby. It is the home of Shaw Air Force Base and Morris College.

SUMTER, Thomas (near Charlottesville, Va., Aug. 14, 1734 — Statesburg, S.C., June 1, 1832). Military officer and politician. After serving in the French and Indian War he settled in South Carolina. At the outbreak of the Revolution he led partisan troops and earned the title "Gamecock of the Revolution." He was a U.S. Representative (1789-93, 1797-1801) and Senator (1801-10). He was appointed ambassador to Brazil in 1810. Fort SUMTER in Charleston Harbor is named for him.

SUNRISE, Fla. City (pop. 39,681), Broward Co., in southern Florida. The sixth-largest city in the county, its development began in the 1960s. A rapidly growing area, its population has increased 600% since its incorporation in 1961. Sunrise is noted for its cultural activities, particularly Sunrise Center which is a replica of a Greek amphitheater.

SURRAT, Mary Eugenia (Waterloo, Md., May 20, 1820 — Washington, D.C., July 7, 1865). Confederate conspirator. She was alleged to have been involved in President Abraham Lincoln's assassination, probably because her son, a dispatch rider for the Confederacy, was a friend of John Wilkes BOOTH. In an irregular trial employing illegal procedure, Mary Surrat was convicted. She was hanged with seven others after a six-week trial. After her death, suppressed evidence favorable to her case, along with judicial irregularities, were exposed to show that she was probably innocent.

SUSQUEHANNA INDIANS. Tribe of Iroquoian linguistic stock that lived in New York, Pennsylvania and Maryland on the Susquehanna River (to which they gave their name). Constantly at war with the Iroquois, they were conquered by them in 1676 and forced to move into central New York. Many years later, after their numbers had significantly declined, they were allowed to return to their old territory.

SUSQUEHANNA RIVER, Md. Swift, shallow river rising in central New York and

traveling 444 miles south through eastern Pennsylvania and northeast Maryland where it empties into the northern part of Chesapeake Bay. A section of the river flows through the Allegheny Mountains. Several flood control projects are found along the river.

SUWANEE RIVER, Ga./Fla. River rising in the Okefenokee Swamp in southeast Georgia. It flows for approximately 250 miles through Florida to empty into the Gulf of Mexico near Cross City. The Timucua and Apalachee Indians referred to it as the "river of reeds," and its present name is thought to be from the Seminole Indian word *sawni* meaning "echo" or the Spanish *San Juan.* Stephen Foster brought the river to national attention when he wrote the song "Old Folks at Home" or "Swanee River" (1851).

SWANSON, Claude Augustus (Swansonville, Va., March 31, 1862 — Criglersville, Va., July 7, 1939). Politician. A practicing lawyer, he was elected a Democratic Congressman from Virginia (1893-1906). From 1906 to 1910 he was governor of the state, and in 1910 appointed to fill an unexpired term in the Senate

The Suwanee River

where he remained until 1933. President Franklin D. Roosevelt appointed him, a noted authority on naval affairs, Secretary of the Navy in 1933 and he served until his death.

SWEET BRIAR COLLEGE. Independent liberal arts women's college located on a 3,300-acre campus in Sweet Briar, Va. The college was chartered in 1901 and opened in 1906 on the site of the former Sweet Briar Plantation.

Majors offered include drama, mathematical physics, political economy, environmental studies, and international affairs. The South provides 40% of the students, and 33% come from the Northeast; 11% of students pursue graduate studies. Some 5% enter law school, others attend medical school, and 68% of students choose careers in business and industry.

Library: 175,918 volumes, 817 journal subscriptions, 2,693 records/tapes. Faculty: 84. Enrollment: 666 women (full-time). Degrees: Bachelor's.

SWOPE, Herbert Bayard (St. Louis, Mo., Jan. 5, 1882 — Sands Point, N.Y., June 20, 1958). Journalist. Swope was awarded the Pulitzer Prize in 1917 for his coverage of the war in Germany for the New York *World*, a paper he later became executive editor of. During the 1940s he served in governmental positions, and was an alternate member of the U.S. Atomic Energy Commission.

SZOLD, Henrietta (Baltimore, Md., Dec. 21, 1860 — Jerusalem, Feb. 13, 1945). Zionist and educator. She pioneered the landmark Baltimore School for Immigrant Workers (1891) and was editor of the Jewish Publication Society of America (1892-1916). In 1912 she was the founder of Hadassah, the world's largest Zionist movement. The first woman elected a World Zionist executive, she directed Youth Aliyah Bureau (1933-45), the world movement to rescue young European Jewish children from the Nazis, and strove for Arab-Jewish cooperation through common social programs.

T

TABLE ROCK RESERVOIR, Mo. Artificial lake entending over three counties in southwestern Missouri at the Arkansas border. The reservoir was formed when a dam was built in 1963 impounding the White River near Branson. There is a state park and numerous recreation areas along its 800-mile shoreline.

TACATACURU INDIANS (thought to refer to "fire"). Tribe of Muskogean linguistic stock and a subdivision of the UTINA INDIANS. They lived in Florida on Cumberland Island. First encountered by Jean RIBAULT (1562) they were friendly with the early French settlers. When the Spanish took control of the region good relations continued and they assisted them in fighting the GUALE INDIANS. In the late 1600s they left Cumberland Island (then called Tacatacuru Island) and merged with the Utina tribes.

TAENSA INDIANS. Tribe of Muskogean linguistic stock that lived in Tensas Parish, La., near Lake St. Joseph. They gave their name to the parish and also to the river and bayou of that name in Louisiana, and to a river and village in Alabama. First encountered by LaSalle in 1682 (and possibly earlier by De Soto), the Taensa were always friendly with the French.

Human sacrifice was one of their customs and when a temple caught fire during a visit from Iberville in 1700 they threw five infants into the flames thinking that they had offended a deity. Threats from the Yazoo and Chickasaw Indians forced them to move and they made new settlements in Louisiana and Alabama, eventually being absorbed into other tribes.

TALLADEGA, Ala. City (pop. 19,128), seat of Talladega Co., in northeastern Alabama near the Coosa River. Named for the Creek Indian word for "border town," Talladega was the site of Andrew Jackson's defeat of a large Indian war party in 1813. It was incorporated in 1901. Today it is the home of Talladega College and the Alabama School for the Deaf and Blind, and its principal industries include the manufacture of textiles and lumber products.

TALLAHASSEE, Fla. City (pop. 81,548), state capital and seat of Leon Co., in northwest Florida 160 miles northwest of Jacksonville. Tallahassee derived its name from the Creek Indian words *talwa* (meaning "town") and *hasi* (meaning "old" or "abandoned"). When De Soto visited the area in 1539-40, the area was inhabited by Apalachee Indians. Spanish missions were established in the area around 1675, including the Mission San Luis de Talmali in what is now Tallahassee. The mission was later destroyed and the Apalachee scattered. The city became the permanent capital of the Florida Territory in 1824, was incorporated in 1825, and was made the state capital when Florida joined the union in 1845. Tallahassee was a trade center for the cotton plantation society of middle Florida and joined the Confederacy at the outbreak of the Civil War. It was the site of the adoption of the ordinance of secession in 1861. Although it was far from significant battle areas, the Union attempted to seize the city in the battle of Natural Bridge in March, 1865.

The development of south Florida in the 1890s and early 1900s caused a relocation of commercial and business interests and Tallahassee went into a decline that lasted until the 1940s, when the increasing business of the state government caused new growth.

Located in an area of rolling hills, forests, and lakes, Tallahassee today is the heart of an agricultural region which produces livestock, cotton, sweet potatoes, and diversified farm products. Its major manufactures are paper and wood products, insecticides, feed, and boats. The state government continues to be a major employer. Florida State University and Florida Agricultural and Mechanical University are here. Nearby are Appalachicola National Forest, Wakulla Springs, and Bear Creek State Park.

TALLAHATCHIE RIVER, Miss. Waterway rising in northwestern Mississippi. It flows generally south for approximately 230 miles to join the Yalobusha River and create the Yazoo River.

TALLAPOOSA RIVER, Ga./Ala. Navigable river originating in northwestern Georgia. It flows south for approximately 270 miles through Alabama to meet the Coosa River and form the Alabama River. Martin Dam, a major hydroelectric power project, is located on the river.

TALLASSEE, Ala. Town (pop. 4,763), Elmore and Tallapoosa Counties, in east central Alabama on the Tallapoosa River. Creek Indians once lived in the region and many Indians remain today. Settled in 1820 and incorporated in 1908, its name comes from an Indian word *talise* meaning "beautiful water." Today Tallassee's manufactures include textiles and lumber. Cotton, corn, and oats are raised in the area.

TALMADGE, Eugene (Forsyth, Ga., Sept. 23, 1884 — Atlanta, Ga., Dec. 21, 1946). Politician. The governor of Georgia from 1933 to 1937 and 1941 to 1943, Talmadge became violently opposed to the New Deal after federal relief funds to the state were denied. He lost the gubernatorial nomination in 1942 but was elected again to the governorship in 1946. He died before taking office and was succeeded by his son, Herman Eugene TALMADGE.

TALMADGE, Herman Eugene (MacRae, Ga., Aug. 9, 1913 —). Politician. A Southern Democrat, Talmadge was chosen governor in a special election when his father, Eugene TALMADGE, died before taking office. After serving as governor (1947-54), he was elected to the U. S. Senate (1956-80). Talmadge was a member of the Senate subcommittee which investigated the Watergate scandal (1973-74), and was "denounced" by the Senate for financial improprieties (1979).

TAMPA, Fla. City (pop. 271,523), seat of Hillsborough Co., in western Florida. Located on Tampa Bay in the middle of Florida's Gulf coast and at the mouth of the Hillsborough River, Tampa is a well-known shipping and tourist center. It was settled in 1823 when Col. George Brooke built Fort Brooke, a military post, here after routing the Seminole Indian village of Tampa from that site. Fort Brooke gained historical notoriety in the war against the Indians, during the American Civil War (when Union gunships held the port), and during the Spanish American War (when troops were stationed here before leaving for Cuba). It was incorporated as a city in 1885.

The early economy of the city was enhanced by Henry PLANT, who was responsible for bringing the railroad to Tampa, building the Tampa Bay Hotel, for a time one of the most popular hotels in the world, and establishing a strong shipping and tourist trade. Tampa's importance as a port of entry was increased in 1914 by the opening of the Panama Canal.

The present-day economy of the city includes the manufacture of Havana cigars, an industry introduced in the 1800s, and the distribution of grapefruit. The city exports canned fruit and lumber, and has the largest concentration of phosphate in the country. There are over 700 manufacturing establishments in Tampa. Because of its warm climate and geographical location, the tourist trade is also an important part of Tampa's economy, and Busch Gardens is a main attraction. The University of Tampa

(1930), the University of South Florida (1955), and Florida College are located here.

TAMPA BAY, Fla. Bay on the west central coast of Florida. This large, well-sheltered harbor includes the ports of St. Petersburg and Tampa. About 25 miles long and 7 to 12 miles wide, it is sheltered by the Pinellas Peninsula to the west and small barrier keys to the southwest. It is separated into two arms: Hillsborough Bay and Old Tampa Bay.

TANEY, Roger Brooke (Calvert Co., Md., Mar. 17, 1777 — Washington, D.C., Oct. 12, 1864). Jurist. Appointed attorney general by President Andrew Jackson (1831), he became a national force in the "bank wars" of the 1830s, persuading Jackson not to recharter the refractory Bank of the United States (1832). Jackson appointed him the fifth chief justice of the U.S. Supreme Court (1836-64), where he asserted public rights over corporations, increased federal supremacy, expanded judicial power, and limited foreign relations exlusively to the federal government. He wrote the majority decision in the DRED SCOTT case (1857), which made the statement that moving a slave to "free" territory did not result in freedom for that slave, that Congress had no power to exclude slaves from territories, and that Negroes could not be citizens. This statement became one of the great "self-inflicted wounds" of the Supreme Court, and caused Taney, who had held the court together through difficult times, to end his years in disrepute.

TANEYCOMO, Lake, Mo. Lake in Taney Co., in southwestern Missouri near the Arkansas line. Bull Shoals Lake is just to the south and Springfield is to the north. It was created by the construction of Forsyth Dam (1,720 feet), which impounded the White River. This 25-mile lake is a resort area in the Ozark region.

TANGIER, Va. Town (pop. 771), Accomack Co., on Tangier Island in the Chesapeake Bay about 12 miles from the mainland. The island was discovered by Capt. John SMITH (1608) and was settled in 1620. The island's economy has always been based on fishing, and because of its distance from the mainland the villagers have their own culture, retaining many old customs from the past.

TANGIPAHOA INDIANS ("corncob gatherers" or "corncob people"). Tribe of Mus-

kogean linguistic stock that lived on the Tangipahoa River in Tangipahoa Parishes in both Mississippi and Louisiana. Closely associated with the ACOLAPISSA they are thought to have been absorbed by them.

TAPPAHANNOCK, Va. Town (pop. 1,821), seat of Essex Co., in eastern Virginia on the Rappahannock River. First constituted a town in 1680, it was an important port in its early years, but its trade declined with the arrival of the railroad. Though its port connections are still important, other manufactures include fish and vegetable packing, and agricultural produce.

TAR HEELS. Military nickname for North Carolina that originated during the Civil War. It came into use during a battle in which North Carolina forces, joined with Confederate Army troops, were battling against the Union. When the conflict became fierce, the Confederates retreated leaving the state militia to fight alone. Reportedly the North Carolinians vowed that when they next encountered the Confederates they would put tar on the heels of their boots so that they would "stick better in the next fight." This led to the nickname of North Carolina as the "Tar Heel State."

TARBORO, N.C. Town (pop. 8,634), seat of Edgecombe Co., in northeast North Carolina on the Tar River. Laid out in 1760, it once was the site of the state's early legislature. Manufactures include formica, plastic toys and communication cables. Agricultural products include corn, cotton, livestock, peanuts, and tobacco.

TARKIO RIVER, Mo. River rising in south Iowa. It crosses into northwest Missouri and flows approximately 50 miles to drain into the Missouri River. The Blacksnake Hills are at its mouth. The river passes through a grain production valley and has a migratory waterfowl refuge on its banks.

TARPON SPRINGS, Fla. City (pop. 13,251), Pinellas Co., in western Florida on the Gulf coast. Founded in 1876 near the mouth of the Anclote River, today it is a resort town with a large population of Greek fishermen, who go out in sponge fleets. Manufactures include apparel and chemicals. There are commercial fisheries, a tannery, and bottling works.

TATE, (John Orley) Allen (Clark Co., Ky., Nov. 19, 1899 — Nashville, Tenn., Feb. 9, 1979). Poet, critic, and teacher. Tate began writing poetry while studying at Vanderbilt University, and became a member of The Fugitives, a literary society that included Robert Penn Warren, John Crow Ransom, and Merrill Moore. Collectively they published a journal, *Fugitive,* for three years beginning in 1922. Although its life was short, *Fugitive* had great influence on Southern Agrarian writers, and inspired the "New Criticism" in literary studies. Tate was a leader in both movements, and is best known for his poem "Ode to the Confederate Dead" (1926), and his critical work *Reactionary Essays on Poetry and Ideas* (1936). He was a professor at several universities, including the University of North Carolina Women's College and Southwestern University in Tennessee.

TATTNALL, Josiah (Savannah, Ga., Nov. 9, 1795 — Savannah, Ga., June 14, 1871). Naval officer. A midshipman during the War of 1812, he attained the rank of captain (1850) during the Mexican War. Tattnall was a member of the Asiatic squadron and aided the British in attacks on Chinese forts. When he was accused of violating American neutrality he made the famous statement, "Blood is thicker than water." During the Civil War he was a captain in the Confederate Navy (1861) and was instrumental in the defense of Georgia and South Carolina. He was the commander of the *Merrimack* (also called the *Virginia*) during its famous fight with the Union *Monitor.* To avoid capture, Tatnall later ordered the destruction of the *Merrimack.*

TAWASA INDIANS. Tribe of Muskogean linguistic stock. De Soto encountered them in 1540 living near present Montgomery, Ala. Attacks by the Creeks drove them into West Florida in the early 1700s but they soon returned to their original territory. After the Treaty of Fort Jackson (1814) they were forced into Creek territory and they eventually joined the migration to Indian Territory in Oklahoma. Much was learned of Tawasa vocabulary from a captured Indian, Lamhatty, in 1708.

TAYLOR, David Watson (Louisa Co., Va., Mar. 4, 1864 — Washington, D.C, July 28, 1940). Naval officer and marine architect. A graduate of Annapolis, with the highest grades attained to that date, and at the Royal Naval College, England, Taylor soon began studies (1899) of specific ship-hull characteristics in producing water resistance. He developed significant principles of ship design based on research in his ship-model test site, the first of its kind in the U.S., built at the Washington, D.C, Navy Yard. He published *The Speed and Power of Ships* (1910), still a standard text. As rear admiral (1916-21), Taylor was in charge of the design of all naval sea and air ships, including the first plane to fly over the Atlantic.

TAYLOR, John (Caroline Co., Va., Dec., 1753 — Caroline Co., Va., Aug. 21, 1824). Politician and author. A graduate of William and Mary College, he was a member of the Virginia legislature (1779-85, 1796-1800) and a U.S. senator (1792-94, 1803, 1822-24). A Jeffersonian Democrat, he sponsored the Virginia Resolutions of 1798 and wrote several works on the Constitution and the policy of the United States, particularly on the subject of states' rights. He is most noted for *An Inquiry into the Principles and Policy of the Government of the United States* (1814).

TAYLOR, Maxwell Davenport (Keytesville, Mo., Aug. 26, 1901 —). Military officer. A 1922 graduate of the U.S. Military Academy at West Point, N.Y., he helped organize the first army airborne division, the 82nd, in the early years of World War II. He was cited for bravery when he chose to cross enemy lines at great personal risk just 24 hours before the Allied invasion of Italy (1943) to discuss the possible seizure of Roman airfields with Italian leaders. He also led the 101st Airborne Division in assaults on Normandy and the Netherlands. In 1953 he served as commander general of the 8th Army, directed the United Nations forces in Korea, was appointed army chief of staff then chairman of the Joint Chiefs of Staff in 1962, as well as serving as U.S. ambassador to South Vietnam.

TAYLOR, Richard (New Orleans, La., Jan. 27, 1826 — New York, N.Y., April 12, 1879). Military officer. After studying abroad, Taylor graduated from Yale (1845). He established a large sugar plantation in St. Charles Parish, La., and was elected to the state senate (1856-61). Taylor was appointed a brigadier general by Confederate President Jefferson Davis in 1861, and was later promoted to the rank of major general. As commander of the Confederare armies of the East, he surrendered May 8, 1865. He was the son of Zachary TAYLOR.

TAYLOR, Zachary (Montebello, Va., Nov. 24, 1784 — Washington, D.C., July 9, 1850). Soldier and 12th President of the United States. Taylor was the son of an army colonel who later became a customs official in Louisville, Ky. He had virtually no formal education, choosing an army career early in life and being commissioned as a first lieutenant in 1810 before embarking on the series of military campaigns that would gain him national fame.

After serving in the War of 1812 and being recommissioned in 1816, Taylor was sent to end Indian wars in both the West and South. In 1832 he was victorious in the Black Hawk War, and then in the Seminole War in Florida in 1837. He then settled in Louisiana with the intention of becoming a plantation owner, but in 1845 President James Polk sent him to Texas for the Mexican War of 1846. There he engineered victories at Palo Alto, Resaca de la Palma, and Monterey, but it was the victory of his outnumbered forces over those of Santa Anna at Buena Vista in 1847 that made Taylor famous throughout the country as "Old Rough and Ready." It was solely on the basis of this fame that he was nominated for the presidency by the Whig party and subsequently elected. Taylor served sixteen months in office (Mar. 5, 1849-July 9, 1850). He shocked some of his contemporaries and has intrigued historians because he was himself a former slave-holder who opposed extension of slavery into territories and new states. It was largely because of Taylor's efforts that California was admitted as a free state in 1850. His policies were never implemented, however, because he died suddenly after attending a Fourth of July celebration.

TEASDALE, Sara (St. Louis, Mo., Aug. 8, 1884 — New York, N.Y., Jan. 28, 1933). Poet. Excessively sheltered early in life by her parents, Teasdale published, while traveling with a chaperone, *Sonnets to Duse and Other Poems* (1907) and *Helen of Troy and Other Poems* (1911). These brought her some critical attention, and following her marriage in 1914 she broke away from her family to lead a more daring, although never entirely happy, life as a poet. She received the 1918 Pulitzer Prize for *Love Songs* (1917), and she published several other collections before taking her own life.

TECUMSEH (near Oldtown, Ohio, March, 1768 — Ontario, Canada, Oct. 5, 1813). A Shawnee chief, Tecumseh attempted to form an Indian confederation to halt American settlement in the Ohio Valley. He maintained that under the 1795 Treaty of Grenville all unceded lands belonged to the Indians and that the Indian tribes would have to vote collectively on further cessions because Indians did not have a concept of exclusive ownership of particular areas. He received support in his efforts from the British, who wanted a buffer state between Canada and the expansionist United States. Tecumseh's plans were never fulfilled because of the Indian defeat, under Tecumseh's brother the Prophet, at the battle of Tippecanoe (1811). Tecumseh allied himself with the British during the War of 1812 and died at the battle of the Thames.

TEKESTA INDIANS. Tribe thought to have been of Muskogean linguistic stock. They were probably the first people to inhabit the area of Miami, Fla., and they aided the early Spanish in attacks from the Calusa Indians. Early attempts to Christianize them failed as any converts quickly returned to their primitive beliefs. Along with other coastal tribes, they moved to Cuba in 1763.

TEN THOUSAND ISLANDS, Fla. Islands in Collier and Monroe Counties, off the southwest corner of the Florida peninsula east of Cape Romano. This group of small mangrove islands in the Gulf of Mexico is the site of an important clam bed.

TENNESSEE. State in the north central region of the South. It is the only state in the South that is landlocked by surrounding states. Tennessee borders North Carolina in the east, across the Great Smoky and the Bald Mountains. It extends 430 miles from that border to a western one with Arkansas and Missouri, across the Mississippi River. There is a 110 mile distance between Tennessee's long, parallel northern and southern borders. The northern border is principally with Kentucky and, toward the east, with Virginia. The southern border, from west to east, is with Mississippi, Alabama, and Georgia.

Tennessee was one of the last regions of the South to be settled, and its frontier history was epitomized by the explorations of Daniel BOONE and Davy CROCKETT. Its nickname the "Volunteer State" comes from its role in the Mexican War, but Tennessee was also a crucial battlefield in the Civil War and one of the pivotal states in the Reconstruction era that followed. The great transformation in the character of the state came with the formation of the TENNESSEE VALLEY AUTHORITY, created by an

Tennessee

act of Congress, in 1933. One of the most extensive public works projects ever launched in the U.S., the TVA built dams along the course of the TENNESSEE RIVER to control flooding, to improve navigation, and to provide hydroelectric power as a necessary resource for industrial diversification.

Since the inception of the TVA, the previously agricultural economy of Tennessee has successfully shifted to manufacturing and the population of the state has become predominantly urban rather than rural. In the 1970s the state enjoyed the greatest proportional and numerical population growth in its history. This growth was apparent in the expansion during that decade of the state's principal metropolitan area: MEMPHIS in the west, NASHVILLE in the central region, and KNOXVILLE in the east. These three cities also include landmarks that reflect the character of Tennessee. Its history as a music capital is reflected in Memphis' "home of the blues" Beale Street and Nashville's country music industry and GRAND OLE OPRY House. Its present potential as a manufacturing capital was reflected in Knoxville's 1982 World's Fair, which centered on the theme of power, especially solar power, for industry.

Tennessee is roughly divided into three topographical regions by the course of the Tennessee River through the state. From its headwaters in northeastern Tennessee, the river flows southwest into northern Alabama, and then turns north to cross the state again from Mississippi to Kentucky. The eastern region of the state isolated by the course of the river consists of Appalachian highlands. Along the North Carolina border this region includes the GREAT SMOKY MOUNTAINS, where the state's highest point is located at CLINGMANS DOME (6,643 feet), and other ranges such as the BALD MOUNTAINS that are related to the Appalachians farther north. Closer to the river this eastern highland region also includes the Great Appalachian Valley and the CUMBERLAND PLATEAU, both of which are rugged areas of eroded limestone hills and large man-made lakes. Central Tennessee, between the two crossings of the state by the river, is topographically part of the Interior Lowland Plateau that runs north from Alabama into Kentucky. In Tennessee the most agriculturally valuable part of this region is the Nashville Basin, which surrounds that city and is isolated from the rest of the plateau by the HIGHLAND RIM of distinctive rounded "knobs." Western Tennessee, the part of the state isolated by the northward course of the river, consists principally of GULF COASTAL PLAIN lands

that are moderately hilly and crossed by small serpentine streams. In the extreme west this plain drops off in a line of bluffs to a narrow fringe of the alluvial bottom lands that line the course of the Mississippi River.

The first European to view what is now Tennessee was probably the Spanish explorer Hernando DE SOTO, who sailed up the Mississippi River and seems to have landed near the present site of Memphis in 1541. The territory remained undisturbed for more than a century after this visit, however. In 1682, the French explorer LA SALLE built Fort Prud'homme on the bluffs near the same site. The fort was soon abandoned, although attempts were made to recover it, and the territory was unexplored for another long period that saw conflicting claims for rights to it by the Spanish, the French, and the English.

The English claim to what is now Tennessee dated back to the 1584 patent to Sir Walter Raleigh of the Virginia region and the unknown areas further inland. In 1663 the Tennessee region passed into the hands of the Eight Lords Proprietors who were given rights to "Carolana." They abandoned Tennessee, however, to the hostile Indians of the region until the French and Indian War made control of it strategically important. Then Virginians and Carolinians together began to cross the mountains of eastern Tennessee, and in 1756 they founded Fort Loudon on the Little Tennessee River near the present site of Knoxville. This fort, too, was abandoned after the massacre of its inhabitants by CHEROKEE Indians in 1760. Following the end of the French and Indian War these Indians ceded rights to the lands to the English in the Treaty of Fort Stanwix in 1768. This enabled the English to establish the first permanent settlements in Tennessee along the HOLSTON and WATAUGA Rivers in the extreme northeast of the state in 1769.

The first population influx in the area was insurrectionary "Regulators" who left North Carolina after the failure of their efforts to "regulate" taxation there by vigilante force. John SEVIER and James ROBERTSON soon emerged as their leaders, and in 1772 they persuaded the rest of the colonists to sign the Articles of the Watauga Association, the earliest constitutional agreement in what is now Tennessee. The onset of the Revolutionary War discouraged their efforts to secure recognition as an independent royal colony, and so in 1776 the Watauga Association was annexed by choice to North Carolina as its Washington District. In the subsequent War of Indepen-

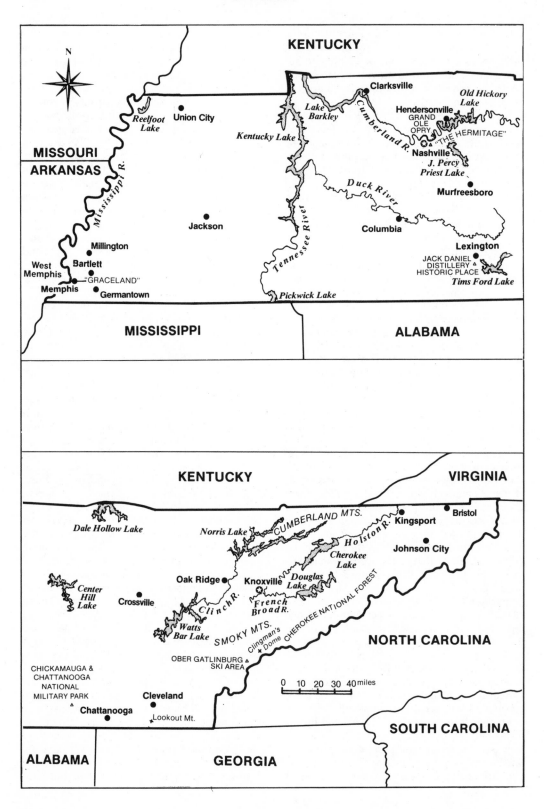

STATE OF TENNESSEE

Name: For the Cherokee village, *Tanasi.* The original meaning of the word is unknown.

Nickname: Volunteer State, Big Bend State, Lion's Den State, Hog and Hominy State, Mother of Southwestern Statesmen.

Motto: Agriculture and Commerce.

Capital: Nashville.

Counties: 95. **Places over 10,000 population (1980):** 36.

Symbols & Emblems: *Flower:* Iris. *Bird:* Mockingbird. *Tree:* Tulip Poplar. *Song:* "Tennessee Waltz."

Population (1980): 4,590,750. **Rank:** 17th.

Population Density (1980): 111.6 people per sq. mi. **Rank:** 18th.

Racial Make-up (1980): *White:* 3,835,078 (83.6%). *Black:* 725,949 (15.8%). *American Indian:* 5,103 (0.2%). *Asian & Pacific Islander:* 13,963 (0.3%). *Other:* 10,657 (0.2%). *Spanish Origin:* 34,081 (0.7%).

Largest City (pop. 1980): Memphis (646,356). *Others:* Nashville-Davidson (455,651), Knoxville (183,139), Chattanooga (169,565), Clarksville (54,777), Jackson (49,131), Johnson City (39,753), Murfreesboro (32,845), Kingsport (32,027).

Area: 41,155 sq. mi. **Rank:** 17th.

Highest Point: Clingmans Dome (6,643 ft.), Sevier Co.

Lowest Point: Mississippi River (182 ft.), Shelby Co.

State Government:
ELECTED OFFICIALS (4-year terms expiring Jan. 1987, etc.): *Governor* ($68,220); *Lt. Governor* (Speaker of the House holds this title); *Sec. of State* ($51,510); *Attorney General* ($65,650); *Treasurer* ($51,510).

GENERAL ASSEMBLY (Salary: $8,308.08 plus $66.47 per diem living expense allowance.): *Senate* (33 members), *House of Representatives* (99 members).

CONGRESSIONAL REPRESENTATIVES: *Senate* (terms expire 1985, 1989, etc.). *House of Representatives* (9 members).

Admitted to the Union: June 1, 1796 (16th state).

dence the residents of the Washington District battled British troops and loyalists in South Carolina. Their greatest contribution to the war effort was their victory, engineered by John Sevier, over the South Carolina loyalists at the Battle of KING'S MOUNTAIN in 1780.

After the Revolution North Carolina declared its intention to cede its western lands to the federal government. The federal government was slow to act, and North Carolina rescinded its declaration. This alienated the residents of the Washington District, who had not been consulted by either body, and for that reason they held a convention at Jonesborough in 1784 that declared itself the legislation of the independent state of FRANKLIN and elected John Sevier its governor. Congress, however, refused their application for admission to the Union, and the district was returned to North Carolina in 1788. In 1790 North Carolina ceded the area to the federal government, which declared it the "U.S. Territory South of the Ohio River." By 1795 the resident population had passed the 60,000 mark required for statehood, and on June 1, 1796, Tennessee entered the Union as the 16th state with Sevier as its first governor.

In the early 19th century the fortunes of the state were improved by the activities of future Presidents Andrew JACKSON, James POLK, and Andrew JOHNSON. The rapid expansion of the western region, beginning with the foundation of Memphis in 1819, improved the economy of the state but polarized its populations of western plantation owners and eastern small farmers on the issue of states' rights. After President Abraham Lincoln made his call for volunteers for the Union Army in 1861, Tennessee seceded on June 8, 1861. Senator Andrew Johnson refused to resign his seat, however, and the eastern counties remained Unionist for the course of the war. SHILOH, MEMPHIS, CHATTANOOGA, and MURFREESBORO were all sites of crucial battles in the Civil War, during which Andrew Johnson served as the Union's military governor of Tennessee. In 1865 the eastern politicians who had remained loyal to the Union were returned to power in the state. In that same year Andrew Johnson, elected vice president in an attempt to mollify the defeated South, became president on the assassination of Lincoln. In 1866 suffrage was granted to the freed slaves of the state, and in that year Tennessee, largely because of the efforts of President Johnson, became the first Confederate state to be readmitted to the Union. RECONSTRUCTION was especially difficult in Tennessee

because of animosities aroused by the impeachment trial of Johnson, the devastation brought by the major battles of the war, and the emergence of the KU KLUX KLAN as a powerful factor in state politics. Nine Tennessee counties were placed under martial law in 1869 because of Klan activities, and recovery efforts were further undermined by a damaging yellow fever epidemic in the 1870s. These developments left Tennessee an overly agriculture-dependent state until the advent of the period of federal public works projects that led to the TVA in 1933.

Since then the expansion of industrial activity in the state has brought Tennessee into a period of population and urban growth. Until the 1960s population growth was limited to natural increase and a steady migration of black residents to the centers of industry in the Great Lakes and northeastern states. In the 1970s, however, Tennessee attracted approximately 200,000 residents of other states to supplement its natural increase and the migration of black residents was brought to a near-halt. In 1980 the population passed the four million mark for the first time; in composition it was 16% black. More than 60% of the population of the state lives in urban areas. The largest metropolitan area in the state is the western one surrounding Memphis, which includes some residents of Arkansas and Mississippi within its total population of more than 909,000. The largest population center in central Tennessee is Nashville, which includes more than 828,000 residents in its metropolitan area. In eastern Tennessee both Knoxville and Chattanooga are rapidly growing metropolitan areas of well over 400,000.

The most important component of Tennessee's economy is manufacturing, and the hydroelectric plants of the TVA and subsequent highway construction have given Tennessee an extremely decentralized manufacturing sector. Its principal products are refined metals, electrical equipment, and chemicals. Almost half of the state land remains farms, however, and agriculture continues to generate more than half the income of manufacturing. The principal crops are tobacco, cotton, and soybeans harvested in the western portion of the state. Production of cattle and dairy products is based in central Tennessee, especially in the Nashville basin region that is also known for the distinctive Tennessee walking horses. Eastern Tennessee is the base of the third-largest industry in the state, mining. Tennessee mines a large volume of bituminous coal, and it also ranks first in the U.S. in zinc yield and third in phosphate rock. Tourism, to both the urban landmarks and natural preserves, generated more than $1.7 billion in 1979. Much of the tourism activity is related to the state's role as a music capital, and music performance, recording, and publishing is one of Tennessee's most visible industries.

TENNESSEE RIVER.

River formed near Knoxville, Tenn., by the confluence of the French Broad and Holston Rivers. The river flows 652 miles before becoming the largest tributary of the Ohio at Paducah, Ky. On its winding course it flows through Tennessee, Alabama, and Kentucky, and along the Alabama-Mississippi border, draining an area of nearly 41,000 square miles. Its name is thought to come from "Tanase," the name of a Cherokee Indian village. Early settlers inhabited the river's shores in the late 1700s but only the lower course of the river in western Tennessee was easily navigated for transportation. The river had a strategic military importance during the Civil War because it offered an invasion route to the South. The Confederacy constructed Fort Henry at a bend in the river where it approaches the Cumberland.

The river's development as an inland waterway did not begin until the 20th century when nine mainstream dams were constructed, creating a series of reservoirs. (See TENNESSEE VALLEY AUTHORITY.) The fifth-longest river in the U.S., major cities on the Tennessee are Knoxville and Chattanooga. Tributaries of the Tennessee are the Clinch, Little Tennessee, Hiwassee, Elk and Duck Rivers.

TENNESSEE, University of.

State supported coed university system. The administrative and main campus is located in the central Tennessee city of Knoxville. Founded in 1794 as Blount College, the school was one of the first two colleges established west of the Blue Ridge Mountains and was the first to admit women as students. In 1807 Blount became a public institution and was reorganized as the University of Tennessee in 1879. In addition to the main campus at Knoxville—with its 19 schools and colleges—other campuses and programs are found at Chattanooga, Nashville, Tullahome, Oak Ridge, Martin, Memphis, and Kingsport. The Chattanooga, Martin, and Nashville branches are the major undergraduate centers after Knoxville. In all, the university system offers a doctorate in 50 fields, bachelor's degrees in 120, and master's degrees in 141. The total land mass for all branches and programs is 35,000 acres.

The main Knoxville campus offers undergraduate studies through the Colleges of Liberal Arts, Agriculture, Business Administration, Communications, Education, Engineering, Home Economics, and Nursing, and the schools of Architecture, Health, Physical Education, and Recreation. The majority of students are state residents, and 60% of graduates go on to earn advanced degrees.

Library: 1,436,193 volumes, 10,752 journal subscriptions, 26,306 records/tapes. Faculty: 1,650. Enrollment: 30,391 total graduate and undergraduate: 12,753 men, 10,028 women (full-time). Degrees: Bachelor's, Master's, Doctorate.

TENNESSEE VALLEY AUTHORITY (TVA).

Independent federal agency established to control flooding, develop and promote navigation, and produce electrical power along the course of the Tennessee River and its tributaries. First proposed in the 1920s as a solution to the problem of what to do with the wartime MUSCLE SHOALS project in Alabama, it was redrafted and set up by President Franklin D. Roosevelt in 1933. Construction of the first project, Norris Dam on the Clinch River near Knoxville, was begun in the fall of that year. Unique among federal agencies because its headquarters are in the region instead of Washington, D.C., it has jurisdiction over a drainage area of nearly 41,000 sq. mi., including parts of Tennessee, Kentucky, Virginia, North Carolina, Georgia, Alabama, and Mississippi. An early model for other river development plans, the TVA system operates 32 major dams; 21 of them constructed by the TVA and the remainder purchased from, or operated for, private companies. The production and sale of electric power was highly criticized by privately-owned power companies who charged that the TVA was exempt from taxation and not obligated to make a profit. In 1960 the TVA was allowed to issue up to $750 million in bonds for its proposed power capacity increase in lieu of having to apply to Congress for appropriations. Along with dominating the economic life of the Tennessee Valley as far as power production (109.8 billion kilowatts were generated in 1974), and river traffic, the system has also been responsible for the establishment of recreational facilities, the control of malaria in the region, and has been involved in numerous land and wildlife conservation programs (1.5 million acres of land reforested by 1975).

Fontana Dam, N.C., a flood control project of the Tennessee Valley Authority

TENSAS RIVER, La. River rising in northeastern Louisiana. It parallels the Macon Bayou for a time before following a winding course for approximately 100 miles south to join the Red River near Acme. It is one of the state's major rivers.

TEXARKANA, Ark. City (pop. 21,459), seat of Miller Co., Ark., connected to Bowie Co., Tex., on the Arkansas-Texas border. This twin city is located 150 miles southwest of Little Rock, Ark., and 185 miles northwest of Dallas, Tex. Settled in 1873, today it is an important railroad shipping point for cotton, dairy goods, and livestock. Manufactures include cotton oil, fertilizer, feed, refined sulphur, clay goods and wood products. The U.S. Army keeps a large arsenal within the city. Nearby Lake Texarkana is a resort area. See also TEXARKANA, Tex.

TEXARKANA, Lake, Tex. Lake in Bowie and Cass Counties, in northeastern Texas. It is a large reservoir that was created by damming the Sulphur River. It is a water supply area for Texarkana and a resort area.

TEXARKANA, Tex. City (pop. 31,271), Bowie Co., Tex., connected to the seat of Miller Co., Ark., on the Arkansas-Texas state line. This twin city is located 150 miles southwest of Little Rock, Ark., and 185 miles northeast of Dallas, Tex. It is a trade center that manufactures creosote, sand and gravel, lumber, tank cars, rockwood, and mobile homes. It is the home of a federal prison, an army depot, and an arsenal. The resort area of Lake Texarkana is nearby.

TEXAS. State at the southwest limit of the South. Its only borders with other states within the South are eastern ones with Arkansas and Louisiana. To the southeast Texas has a 370 mile coastline on the Gulf of Mexico, and to the southwest it has a long boundary with Mexico formed by the Rio Grande River. To the west Texas faces New Mexico and projects the large Trans-Pecos panhandle between that state and Mexico. To the north it faces Oklahoma across a land boundary at the top of the northern Texas panhandle, which follows the Red River for most of the border.

The largest of the "lower 48" U.S. states, Texas has a special national reputation for wide-open spaces, "urban cowboy" lifestyles, and dynasties of self-made family fortunes. The special symbols of state pride are the Texas Rangers of the past who patrolled the Texas High Plains, and the gushing oil wells that have dominated the state economy since the early 1900s. These popular images of Texas all have some basis in fact, even in the modern face of the state. The state is so large, with a land area in excess of that of France, that vast expanses of it remain so undeveloped that the principal means of transportation is the private airplane. The range lifestyle also remains intact in some areas, and Texas grazing lands support twice the number of cattle of any other state. The oil rig economy is also a fact of life in modern Texas, which continues to lead all states in oil and natural gas production despite the completion of the Alaskan oil pipeline.

Beneath the stereotypes, however, there remains a remarkable diversity in the character of the state. Its topography is various enough to support rice paddies as well as mesquite and cattle. Its population is significantly ethnic, with the proportionately largest group of Spanish-speaking people the U.S. and a new and growing sector of Vietnamese people who arrived in the 1970s. Texas also contains two of the ten-largest metropolitan areas in the country, surrounding DALLAS and HOUSTON, and its population is the most urban one in the South after Maryland. The economy is rich in diversified manufactures including aerospace equipment in addition to the expected petrochemicals. Oil wealth has brought the state cultural riches such as the eminent research facilities at the University of Texas in Austin, the opera company in Houston, and the posh shopping district in Dallas. It is still possible to roam across barren unpopulated plains in Texas, but visitors to the state are more likely to encounter a very cosmopolitan state of glass and steel skyscrapers.

Topographically, Texas consists of regions of Coastal Plain in the southeast, plains in the center of the state, and basin and range in the far west. The belt of coastal plain along the Gulf of Mexico extends inland far enough to cover two-fifths of Texas. Averaging about 800 feet above sea level, the plain extends to the Balcones Escarpment in the west and the central lowland of the U.S. in the north. Along the coast itself, where elevations fall to sea level, Texas includes a network of barrier islands separated from the mainland by tidal lagoons. The largest of these, PADRE ISLAND, is the center of the National Seashore. The plains region of central Texas includes distinct regions of High Plains, Great Plains, and central Texas hills. The High Plains cover the northern panhandle, the Great Plains reach into the western panhandle, and the central Texas hills of rolling prairie reach northward toward Oklahoma. Together these plains regions represent another two-fifths of the state area. The basin and range region covers the remaining one-fifth of the state area in the far west. This Trans-Pecos region includes the state's highest point, Guadalupe Peak (8,749 feet). The special features of this region are the gorges of the Rio Grande Valley and the "lost mountains" of isolated peaks that are remote spurs of the Rocky Mountains. Across these regions from the coastal plain inland, the rainfall in Texas becomes sparser and the climate becomes less moderate: winter temperatures in Houston average above 50 degrees, for example, while winter snows are common on the High Plains.

The earliest known inhabitants of Texas were the CADDO Indians in the east, the APACHES in the west, and the COMANCHES in the north. European exploration of the territory began in 1519, when Alvarez de PINEDA sailed and mapped the Gulf coast. This Spanish exploration was followed by another under Panfilo de NARVAEZ in 1528. The second expedition was shipwrecked on the coast, leaving survivors under Alvar Nunez CABEZA de Vaca to wander inland in the company of Indians for eight years. They returned to Spanish outposts in Mexico in 1536 with fabulous stories of the Seven Cities of Cibola. As they had in Florida, these legends of immense Indian wealth encouraged further Spanish exploration in Texas, beginning with the expedition across the state by Francisco Vasques de CORONADO in 1541. The stories proved false and Spanish exploration of Texas ceased for another century.

Spain's interest in Texas was renewed by French expeditions into the region beginning with that of Sieur de LA SALLE (Robert Cavelier) in 1685. He founded the French outpost of Fort Saint Louis on Matagorda Bay southwest of Houston in that year, but it was abandoned two years later. The Spanish attempted to maintain their local supremacy by extending the system of missions that they had begun at Ysleta, c. 1681, and EL PASO in 1682. Over the next fifty years they sent nearly 100 missionary expeditions into Texas and managed to establish a permanent mission at SAN ANTONIO in 1718. The San Antonio mission became the seat of local Spanish government in 1722, but the missionary system that enabled the Spanish to con-

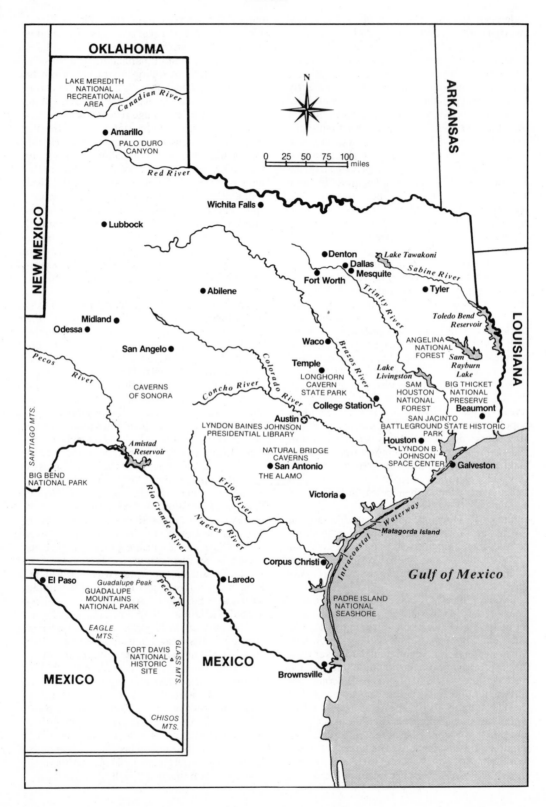

OKLAHOMA

ARKANSAS

NEW MEXICO

LOUISIANA

MEXICO

MEXICO

Gulf of Mexico

LAKE MEREDITH
NATIONAL
RECREATIONAL
AREA

Canadian River

● Amarillo

PALO DURO
CANYON

Red River

Wichita Falls ●

● Lubbock

● Denton

Lake Tawakoni

● Dallas

● Mesquite

Fort Worth ●

● Tyler

Sabine River

Trinity River

● Abilene

*Toledo Bend
Reservoir*

Midland ●
●

Odessa ●

San Angelo ●

Waco ●

ANGELINA
NATIONAL
FOREST

*Pecos
River*

*Sam
Rayburn
Lake*

CAVERNS
OF SONORA

Concho River

Colorado River

Brazos River

Temple ●

*Lake
Livingston*

LONGHORN
CAVERN
STATE PARK

SAM
HOUSTON
NATIONAL
FOREST

BIG THICKET
NATIONAL
PRESERVE

College Station ●

Beaumont ●

SANTIAGO MTS.

Austin ✪

SAN JACINTO
BATTLEGROUND STATE HISTORIC
PARK

LYNDON BAINES JOHNSON
PRESIDENTIAL LIBRARY

*Amistad
Reservoir*

Houston ●

NATURAL BRIDGE
CAVERNS

LYNDON B.
JOHNSON
SPACE CENTER

BIG BEND
NATIONAL PARK

● San Antonio

● Galveston

Frio River

THE ALAMO

Rio Grande River

Victoria ●

Intracoastal Waterway

Nueces River

Matagorda Island

Corpus Christi ●

El Paso ●

Guadalupe Peak +

Pecos R.

GUADALUPE
MOUNTAINS
NATIONAL PARK

Laredo ●

PADRE ISLAND
NATIONAL
SEASHORE

*EAGLE
MTS.*

FORT DAVIS
NATIONAL
HISTORIC
SITE

GLASS MTS.

MEXICO

Brownsville ●

*CHISOS
MTS.*

N

0 25 50 75 100
miles

STATE OF TEXAS

Name: From the Indian *texia* which derives from the Spanish *tejas* ("allies").

Nickname: Lone Star State, Banner State, Beef State, Blizzard State, Jumbo State.

Motto: Friendship.

Capital: Austin.

Counties: 254. **Places over 10,000 population (1980):** 159.

Symbols & Emblems: *Flower:* Bluebonnet. *Bird:* Mockingbird. *Tree:* Pecan. *Song:* "Texas, Our Texas."

Population (1980): 14,228,383. **Rank:** 3rd.

Population Density (1980): 54.3 people per sq. mi. **Rank:** 34th.

Racial Make-up (1980): *White:* 11,197,663 (79.4%). *Black:* 1,710,250 (12.0%). *American Indian:* 40,074 (0.6%). *Asian & Pacific Islander:* 120,306 (0.9%). *Other:* 1,160,090 (8.2%). *Spanish Origin:* 2,985,643 (21.0%).

Largest City (pop. 1980): Houston (1,594,086). *Others:* Dallas (904,076), San Antonio (785,410), El Paso (425,259), Fort Worth (385,141), Austin (345,496), Corpus Christi (231,999), Lubbock (173,979), Arlington (160,123), Amarillo (149,230), Garland (138,857), Beaumont (118,102), Pasadena (112,560), Irving (109,943), Waco (101,261).

Area: 262,017 sq. mi. **Rank:** 2nd.

Highest Point: Guadalupe Peak (8,749 ft.), Culberson Co.

Lowest Point: sea level, Gulf of Mexico.

State Government:

ELECTED OFFICIALS (4-year terms expiring Jan. 1987, etc.): *Governor* ($88,900); *Lt. Governor* ($72,000); *Sec. of State* ($61,200); *Attorney General* ($69,000); *Treasurer* ($69,000).

GENERAL ASSEMBLY (Salary: $7,200 plus $30 per diem living expense allowance for legislative session.): *Senate* (31 members), *House of Representatives* (150 members).

CONGRESSIONAL REPRESENTATIVES: *Senate* (terms expire 1985, 1989, etc.). *House of Representatives* (27 members).

Admitted to the Union: Dec. 29, 1845 (28th state).

quer and control California failed in Texas due to the hostility of the Apache and Comanche tribes.

Texas was still virtually unpopulated by Europeans when the U.S. made the Louisiana Purchase from France in 1803. A 1819 treaty fixed the boundaries of the Louisiana Territory at the present Oklahoma and Louisiana borders of Texas. In 1820 the Missouri banker Moses AUSTIN received rights for a Texas settlement from Spain, but in 1821 Mexico revolted from Spain and reorganized itself as an independent republic including Texas in 1824. By that time Moses Austin's son Stephen F. AUSTIN had renegotiated his father's rights with the new Mexican government and established the colony of Washington-on-the-Brazos near the present site of Houston. Under Austin's guidance a wave of American settlers moved into Texas, where they were called *empresarios.*

Wary of an American-inspired revolution, Mexican authorities attempted to halt immigration from the east in 1830, but the English-speaking population continued to expand to reach about 25,000 by the early 1830s. Stephen F. Austin was the leader of the Americans who hoped to establish a state within the Mexican

republic, but the coup of Antonio Lopez de SANTA ANNA in 1834 and Mexican arrest of Austin ended hope for reconciliation between the Spanish and English speakers of Mexico. On Mar. 2, 1836, the Texans of Austin's colony on the Brazos declared their independence from Mexico. The Texans had already captured San Antonio from the Mexicans, and Santa Anna then led his troops north to recapture the city. The Texas rebels occupied an old Spanish mission in the city called the ALAMO. It fell to Santa Anna on March 6, 1836. Texan heroes such as William B. TRAVIS, Jim BOWIE, and Davy CROCKETT died in defense of the Alamo, and more than 300 Texan survivors of the battle were massacred by Santa Anna at Goliad on March 27, 1836. Texas then chose Sam HOUSTON as its new military leader, and he surprised Santa Anna's troops at SAN JACINTO on April 21, 1836, to end the war and free an independent republic of Texas.

As a separate country with the Lone Star flag, Texas elected Houston its president and also voted to join the United States. Immediate statehood, however, was frustrated by European hostility to American expansion into the Southwest and the U.S. federal government's reluctance to anger its European allies. Texas

A river baptism at Fort Pena Colorad, Texas during the 1800s

nevertheless flourished as a republic. Austin was established as its capital in 1839, Houston was established in 1836, and Dallas was laid out in 1844. Mexican encroachments into southern Texas, however, started a border war that lasted until 1844. Texas was assisted in the war by the U.S. Army, and this brought it into closer contact with the federal government in Washington. President James Polk was elected in 1844 on a campaign promise to annex Texas to the Union, despite Northern states' resistance to admission of another slave state. In the next year both the U.S. Congress and the Texas Congress voted for annexation, and Texas became the 28th state in the Union on December 29, 1845. The Mexican War with the U.S. followed in 1846, but it was ended by the Treaty of Guadalupe-Hidalgo in 1848 that fixed the Texas border at the Rio Grande and ceded additional Mexican lands in the southwest to the U.S.

With the coming of the Civil War, Texas was polarized between Unionist sentiment in the ranch lands of the west and Southern sentiment in the plantation areas of the Gulf coast. Sam Houston, now governor, opposed secession and lost his office on the issue. A popular vote on February 23, 1861, ratified secession by a margin of three-to-one, a reflection of the state's population concentration in the cotton-growing areas of the Gulf coast. Texas was remote from the important Civil War theaters of action, although GALVESTON was captured by the Union in 1862 and subsequently recaptured by the Confederacy in 1863. The most notable battle within the state was at Palmito Hill on the Rio Grande on May 13, 1865, which occurred a month after Lee's surrender and was the final battle of the war. Texas was readmitted to the Union in March, 1870.

Post-Civil War Texas remained a frontier long after other Southern states had begun the transition to a manufacturing economy. Government interest focused on the Mexican border, and so the Texas Rangers became the sole protectors of the law in inland Texas. Railroads reached Kansas in the late 1860s, and this instituted an era of mass cattle drives across desolate stretches of Texas plains along the CHISHOLM TRAIL to sell beef in Kansas for the Chicago market. Railroad extension into Texas brought an influx of farmers and an era of range wars between them and the cattlemen. At the same time Indian wars continued to disrupt the state until the settlement with the Apaches in 1880.

The key to the evolution of modern Texas was the discovery of oil at SPINDLETOP near Beaumont in 1901. This brought a rapid expansion of cities such as Houston and Dallas, which were built on oil wealth in the twentieth century. The need for oil export facilities led to the dredging of Gulf ports and expansion of cities such as CORPUS CHRISTI and Galveston. World War I brought government investment to Texas in the form of military installations, a boon to the economy that continued through World War II. By that time Texas was in the midst of a process of industrialization to refine its own mineral wealth that further encouraged urbanization. In the years after World War II this industrial expansion diversified into aerospace equipment and electronics. By the 1960s Texas had completed its expansion into national economic leadership. In that decade its importance to the country was symbolized by the presidency of Texan Lyndon B. JOHNSON and the location of NASA's Manned Spacecraft Center in Houston.

These cities created by modern industrialization remain the principal population centers of Texas. Houston is the largest city in the state, although its metropolitan area population is equaled by that of Dallas-Fort Worth. These areas alone represent more than 40% of the state population, and the only other metropolitan area with a population of one million is San Antonio. The 1970s brought a remarkable immigration to Texas from the northern industrial belt along the Great Lakes, a further gain in population from natural increase, and a rise from 4th to 3rd rank among U.S. states in total population. In composition the population of the state is more than 20% Hispanic and 12% black.

Since the era between the World Wars, manufacturing has surpassed mining as the leading industry of Texas. The state manufacturers remain heavily dependent on petrochemicals produced from mining yield, but transportation equipment, electronic products, and machinery are also important manufactures. Texas continues to lead all states, including Alaska, in crude petroleum, and in the 1970s it surpassed its competitor Louisiana in production of natural gas. In agriculture Texas leads all states in value of farm property and number of farms. The principal farm products are beef cattle and cotton lint, and the Texas farm receipts exceed those of all states except California and Iowa. There are a number of other traditional industries such as timber and commercial fishing that are important to the

Cowboys on a cattle drive in 1916

state, but the Texas economy is especially notable within the South for the value of its banking and finance industries. Tourism to Texas' historical sights, park lands, urban cultural centers, and other attractions accounted for $4.8 billion in 1979.

TEXAS, University of. State-supported coed university in Austin, Tex. Chartered in 1881 and opened in 1883 the University of Texas is a vast educational system with professional and liberal arts universities located in Arlington, Austin, Dallas, El Paso, Odessa, and San Antonio. Houston, Tyler, Galveston, San Antonio and Dallas also have university Health Science Centers. There is an observatory at Mount Locke and a marine sciences facility at Port Aransas.

The largest and oldest division of the university is the University of Texas at Austin, which opened in 1883.

Undergraduate studies are offered through the Colleges of Arts and Sciences, Engineering, Business Administration, Humanities, Education, Fine Arts, Pharmacy, Natural Sciences, Social and Behavioral Sciences, the schools of Architecture and Communication, and the Lyndon B. Johnson School of Public Affairs.

Library: 4,000,000 volumes, 665,000 microform reels, 6,000 journal subscriptions, 5,000 records/tapes. Faculty: 2,000. Enrollment: 46,148 total graduate and undergraduate; 17,655 men, 14,947 women (full-time). Degrees: Bachelor's, Master's, Doctorate.

TEXAS AGRICULTURAL AND MECHANICAL UNIVERSITY. State-supported coed institution, part of the Texas A&M University System, located in College Station, Tex., a town 90 miles northwest of Houston. Chartered in 1871 and opened in 1876, A&M was once primarily a technological and agricultural college, and is the state's oldest public institution of higher education. Over the years it has grown to offer a wide variety of programs and majors. Other schools in its system are Tarleton State, Prairie View A&M, and Texas A&M at Galveston. The School of Military Sciences, located on the College Station campus, is one of the world's largest military colleges.

Undergraduate studies are offered in the colleges of Liberal Arts and Science, Agriculture, Architecture and Environmental Design, Business Administration, Education, Engineering,

Geosciences, Sciences, Veterinary Medicine, and Human Medicine. The most popular majors on campus are accounting, mechanical engineering, business administration/commerce/management. The South provides 93% of the students; about 25% of male students are enrolled in the Corps of Cadets and many of them obtain commissions in the Army or Air Force.

Library: 1,200,000 volumes, 145,000 microform titles, 16,000 journal subscriptions. Faculty: 2,764. Enrollment: 33,499 total graduate and undergraduate: 16,499 men, 9,798 women (full-time). Degrees: Bachelor's, Master's, Doctorate.

TEXAS CHRISTIAN UNIVERSITY. Independent church-related coed institution located on a 243-acre campus in the central Texas city of Fort Worth. Founded in 1873, the university is administered by the Christian Church (Disciples of Christ). The school accepts students of all faiths, however, and the only mandatory religious requirement is one religion course.

Undergraduate studies are offered by the Addran College of Arts and Sciences, Harris College of Nursing, schools of Education and Fine Arts, and the M. J. Neeley School of Business. In addition to the usual arts and sciences, majors are offered in such areas as liberal studies, criminal justice, journalism, interdepartmental programs in international affairs, Latin American studies, and geophysics. The South provides 75% of the students and 13% are from the North Central states. Some 19% of graduates pursue full-time graduate study: 1% enter medical school, 2% law school, 1% dental school. Texas Christian is among the nation's top 120 producers of dental school entrants and 25% of all University graduates choose careers in business and industry.

Library: 1,000,000 volumes, 9,000 journal subscriptions. Faculty: 420. Enrollment: 6,283 total graduate and undergraduate; 1,801 men, 2,401 women (full-time). Degrees: Bachelor's, Master's, Doctorate.

TEXAS TECH UNIVERSITY. State-supported coed institution located 300 miles west of Dallas in Lubbock, Tex. Founded in 1923, Texas Tech, with its 1,839-acre campus, is one of the largest schools in the country.

This multipurpose institution offers studies through the Colleges of Arts and Sciences, Agricultural Sciences, Business Administration, Education, Engineering, and Home Economics. Majors include advertising art, bilin-

gual secretarial, geochemistry, interior design, journalism, microbiology, group communication, and speech pathology and audiology. Of the undergraduate degrees conferred each year, most are in Education, Business and Management, Engineering, Home Economics, Agriculture, and Natural Resources. Some 90% of the students are from the South, and the majority of these are from Texas; 10% of students pursue advanced study soon after graduation.

Library: 1,500,000 volumes, 6,600 journal subscriptions. Faculty: 864. Enrollment: 23,129 total graduate and undergraduate; 10,906 men, 8,157 women (full-time). Degrees: Bachelor's, Master's, Doctorate.

TEXAS WOMAN'S UNIVERSITY. State-supported institution located on a 270-acre campus 35 miles northwest of Dallas in the community of Denton, Tex. The university also maintains campuses in Dallas and Houston. Founded in 1901 by the Texas legislature, TWU remained a women's school until recently when small numbers of men were permitted to enroll in its Institute of Health Sciences. It is one of the largest universities for women in the United States.

Undergraduate studies are offered through the colleges of Arts and Sciences, Education, Fine Arts, Health, Nutrition, Textiles, Human Development, Physical Education, Recreation, and the schools of Library Science, Occupational Therapy, Physical Therapy, and the Institute of Health Sciences. The majority of undergraduate degrees are conferred in health professions. Some 84% of students are state residents, and 35% of all students go on to graduate study.

Library: 649,496 volumes, 197,566 microform titles, 3,559 journal subscriptions, 2,672 records/tapes. Faculty: 554. Enrollment: 225 men, 4,218 women (full-time). Degrees: Bachelor's, Master's, Doctorate.

TEXOMA, Lake, Tex. Artificial lake located primarily in Sherman Co., in northern Texas. It is the largest man-made lake in the state, and was created by the construction of the Denison Dam on the Red River. Lake Texoma extends northward into Oklahoma and is a recreational area covering 225 square miles.

TEXTILE INDUSTRY. The United States is one of the leading producers of textiles in the world, producing $21 billion in sales annually. The textile industry is dominated by the South, where North Carolina is the leading producer

($4.605 billion in sales), followed by South Carolina ($2.699 billion), Georgia ($2.579 billion), Virginia ($922 million), and Alabama ($745.5 million).

Until the Civil War, the South was the agricultural center of the textile industry and New England was the manufacturing center. Sheep, which had first been introduced to the New World by the Spanish conquistadores in the 16th century, were brought to Virginia and Massachusetts by the English in 1620. The English also established the first cotton plantations in Virginia in 1650. But the growing of cotton did not become significantly important to the South's economy until the end of the 18th century, with the invention of the cotton gin. The cotton gin was developed and built (1792-94) by Massachusetts-born Eli WHITNEY, who had come to the South as a tutor. Working at Strawberry Plantation, near Savannah, Ga., Whitney perfected his machine by April, 1793. The following year it was in use throughout the South. Before his invention, cottonseeds had to be separated from the fiber by hand, a laborious and time-consuming process. This limited the amount of cotton that could be delivered to the mills, which in turn limited the amount of cotton cloth that could be manufactured or exported. The cotton gin mechanically separated the seeds from the fibers and required only one worker to operate it. In 1795, six million pounds of cotton were grown in the U.S.—increasing to 125 million pounds over the next 25 years—and cotton exports were more than 40 times greater than the year before. Cotton was on its way to becoming "King," and it held that title until the Civil War. Emerging from the devastation of the war, its plantations in ruins and its supply of free labor gone, the South began to turn toward industrialization. Alabama, for example, began to industrialize during the 1870s, although textile production did not come until later. Textile manufacturing developed in Georgia after the war and is that state's oldest and most important industry. It developed in South Carolina in the 1880s and is that state's major employer. In North Carolina it is the most important source of jobs and income.

By the 1920s, New England was losing its factories to the South, and today the South is the capital of the textile industry. This is attributable to its accessibility to markets, lower wages, improved living conditions, area development programs, fewer labor-management problems, availability of workers, lower taxes than in New England, and large investments of capital. The South accounts for 93% of the broad woven cotton goods manufactured in the U.S.; South Carolina alone produces 43% of the total. New England is still the major producer (47%) of woolens and worsted but the lead is a slim one.

Nylon was developed by chemist Wallace H. Carothers (1935), working for E. I. duPont de Nemours & Co. in Wilmington, Del., and led to the development of a wide range of man-made fibers. The South currently produces 75% of all rayon and acetate materials, and 85% of all other man-made fabrics.

THOMAS, George Henry (Southampton Co., Va., July 31, 1816 — San Francisco, Calif., Mar. 28, 1870). Military offier. He was a Union Civil War general known as the "Rock of Chickamauga" because his line of troops withstood assault after assault by Confederate troops during the battle of CHICKAMAUGA (1863). A graduate of West Point, Thomas served in the Mexican War (1846-48), and at the outbreak of the Civil War he remained loyal to the Union despite his Virginia birth. During the war he distinguished himself in numerous engagements. His victories include the battle of Mill Springs (1862), an important role in the Union victory at CHATTANOOGA (1863), and his NASHVILLE victory (1864), when his troops inflicted a major defeat on the forces of Confederate Gen. John B. Hood whose troops suffered the worst open field casualties to be experienced during the whole war by either side. Thomas died after the war while commanding the army's Division of the Pacific.

THOMAS, Martha Carey (Baltimore, Md., Jan. 2, 1857 — Philadelphia, Pa., Dec. 2, 1935). Educator and women's suffrage advocate. After earning her Ph.D. in Europe, she established Bryn Mawr College where she taught (1884-94) and served as its president (1894-1922). She also served as president of the National Collegiate Equal Suffrage League (1900-13).

THOMAS, William (Russell Co., Va., Aug. 13, 1863 — Berkeley, Calif., Dec. 5, 1947). Sociologist. After graduating from the University of Tennessee in 1884, he taught English there and at Oberlin College. From 1894 to 1918 he taught sociology at the University of Chicago. He spent the rest of his life researching and writing, and produced important theories dealing with man's relationship with his environment. He divided man's behavior into four areas that became his well-known "four wishes" theory. His published works include *Source Book of Social Origins* (1909), and *The Unadjusted Girl* (1923), and *The Polish Peasant in Europe and America* (1918-19).

THOMASVILLE, Ga. City (pop. 18,463), seat of Thomas Co., in southwestern Georgia near the border of Florida. The city is an industrial center with diversified farming that includes tobacco and soybeans. Industries include baking, lumbering, and meat packing. It is a winter resort and is famous for its roses and its annual rose festival.

THOMASVILLE, N.C. City (pop. 14,144), Davidson Co., in west central North Carolina. The first chair factory here opened around 1870, utilizing the abundant hickory and oak in the area. An industrial center today, its products include mirrors, underwear, concrete pipes, tobacco, corn, and wheat.

THOMPSON, Jacob (Casewell Co., N.C., May 15, 1810 — Memphis, Tenn., Mar. 24, 1885). Politician. He was a practicing lawyer in Pontotoc, Miss., before becoming a U.S. congressman (1839-51). Thompson was later Secretary of the Interior under President James Buchanan (1857-61). Thompson served the Confederacy as special agent to Canada (1864-65). Falsely accused of complicity in the Lincoln assassination, he stayed in Europe for several years before returning to the U.S.

THOMPSON, William Tappan (Ravenna, Ohio, Aug. 31, 1812 — Savannah, Ga., Mar. 24, 1882). Editor and humorist. While assisting James Westcott, secretary of Florida (1830), he studied law under Westcott. He returned to journalism and published the *States Rights Sentinel* (1835) in Augusta, Ga. Thompson served with the Augusta Militia in the Florida Seminole campaign (1836) and organized the literary magazine *Mirror* (1838), in which he began his humorous "Major Jones" articles. He was founder and editor of the influential *Savannah Morning News* (1850-82).

THURMOND, James Strom (Edgeville, S.C., Dec. 5, 1902 —). Politician. He studied law while teaching in the South Carolina school system, and was admitted to the bar in 1930. He won a seat in the state senate (1933-38) and was appointed circuit court judge in 1938. After returning from service in World War II, he was governor of South Carolina from 1947 to 1951, and entered the U.S. Senate in 1954 as a write-in candidate. Still in the Senate today, Thurmond is president pro tempore of the Senate and is chairman of the Judiciary Committee. In 1948 Thurmond was an unsuccessful States Rights candidate for the presidency, and in 1964 he changed his party affiliation from Democratic to Republican.

TIMOTHY. Perennial grass, *Phleum pratense*, grown throughout the South and elsewhere in the U.S. as hay for fodder. It is named for Timothy Hanson, a New Yorker who brought the seed south to Virginia in 1720. See also HAY.

TIMROD, Henry (Charleston, S.C., Dec. 8, 1828 — Columbia, S.C., Oct. 6, 1867). Poet. When Timrod became too frail to serve in the Civil War, he memorialized the turmoil in words, becoming one of the leading Southern war poets. He died of tuberculosis, and most of his work, including *Ode to the Confederate Dead at Magnolia Cemetery*, was published posthumously.

TIMUCUA INDIANS. Tribe of Muskogean linguistic stock that lived in central and northern Florida. See also UTINA.

TIOU INDIANS. Tribe of Tunican linguistic stock that lived in Mississippi on the upper course of the Yazoo River. Driven from their territory by the Chickasaw, they merged with the NATCHEZ.

TITUSVILLE, Fla. City (pop. 31,910), seat of Brevard Co., in eastern Florida, on the Indian River at the head of navigation. The city was incorporated in 1886, and was a flourishing port in the late 19th century. Today citrus fruit is shipped from here, and fishing and aerospace industries are important to the economy. The Kennedy Space Center is nearby.

TOBACCO. Plant of the *Nicotiana* species, an annual of the nightshade family, the leaves of which are cultivated for smoking in cigarettes, cigars, and pipes, and for snuff. The name is a Spanish corruption of the word for the implement used by North American Indians for smoking the leaves of the plant.

Tobacco is indigenous to North America and was discovered there by the first European explorers of the New World. A party sent by Christopher Columbus to Cuba during his first expedition is credited with the discovery of tobacco in November, 1492. His men reported the Indian practice of carrying smouldering tobacco leaves for easy kindling of fires, and also of using the smouldering leaves as a kind of incense. During Columbus' second expedition from 1494 to 1496, the Indian practice of using tobacco as snuff was discovered and reported. In 1502 Spanish explorers of South America also reported tobacco-chewing. Further explorations into the North American continent revealed that smoking tobacco leaves in pipes of various design was nearly universal among the Indians, and was often rooted in religious and ritualistic practices.

The introduction of tobacco to Europe is generally credited to Francisco Fernandes, a physician on an expedition chartered by Philip II of Spain, that returned to its homeland in 1558. Fernandes and others believed the plant to be of great medicinal value, and for this reason they sent seeds to Catherine de Medici in 1560 via the French Ambassador to Portugal Jean Nicot, whose name provides the root for the species label and also for nicotine, the drug found in the plant. Tobacco came directly to England in 1586, when the first governor of Virginia, Ralph Lane, returned home with a shipment for the owner of the colonial charter, Sir Walter Raleigh. Sometimes called *herba santa* for its supposed beneficial qualities, tobacco smoking first became popular in Europe in the English court of Elizabeth I. Smoking quickly spread throughout the continent and beyond, and its popularity has never diminished since that time.

Commercial cultivation of the tobacco plant began in Virginia in the early 17th century, and it immediately became the basis of the economy there, bringing successful growers the sudden wealth that permitted an aristocratic class to establish itself in the American South.

The economy of the Spanish holdings in Cuba and Mexico was at that time also based almost entirely on tobacco crops. Today cultivation of tobacco, assisted by the great adaptability of the many varieties of the plant, is conducted in temperate and tropical climates around the world. Large crops are harvested in countries as diverse otherwise as France, Turkey, China, and the Philippines. The greatest harvests, however, continue to be reaped where the plant was discovered, the American South and Cuba.

Although there are some fifty varieties of *Nicotiana*, the most important commercial variey is *N. tabacum*, known as Virginian

tobacco. The plant may reach a height of six feet, with central leaves as long as two feet and, if allowed to flower, has a reddish blossom at its top. The stem and leaves of the plant, which lightens in greenish color as it matures, are covered with a fuzz. One of its great agricultural assets is the fact that any single tobacco plant will produce thousands of seeds. These characteristics are all shared by the other principal commercial tobaccos: *N. macrophylla*, or Maryland tobacco; *N. persica*, or Persian tobacco, and *N. rustica*, or Mexican tobacco which was the type first grown in Virginia but is now grown mainly in Turkey.

Tobacco is generally sown in beds and then transplanted to fields after about fifty days of growth, when the plants show signs of flowering they are "topped," or trimmed to stunt the blossom and encourage leaf growth. After approximately thirty-five days of further growth, the plants are ready for harvest, which is accomplished by leveling them rather than by picking leaves. Within this basic growth pattern there are many variations contingent on the variety of plant grown, the general climate, and length of the growing season. It is for this reason that the growing of fine tobaccos is considered a delicate art.

Preparation of harvested tobacco for commercial use begins with curing, a drying process usually accomplished directly over fire or through flues that circulate heat. After this the dried plants are heaped for three to five weeks of fermentation, which occurs naturally because of the presence of enzymes. Finally, tobaccos are aged anywhere from one to five years, depending on the quality of the crop and of the product desired.

Cut tobaccos, the source of most smoking products, are produced by damping the leaves, pressing them into sheets, shredding the sheets, and then roasting the material in a rotating drum. In twist or plug tobacco for smoking or chewing, pressing is accomplished in molds and shredding eliminated. Cigars are made from a "binder," or core of cut tobacco, and a "wrapper," or whole leaf covering of especially high quality. For cigarettes, a paper wrapper replaces the tobacco one. Snuff is produced by soaking cured tobacco or cut tobacco scraps in a flavoring to make it aromatic.

One modern variation on cultivation of the product is shade tobacco, grown under cheesecloth coverings. When it was discovered that the shade of trees encouraged the growth of some tobacco varieties, the U.S. Department of Agriculture launched a program to encourage shade growth in areas where the tobacco crop was only marginally successful. Shade tobacco is now a valuable crop in Florida and Connecticut, with the product usually being reserved for cigar wrappers. The first machinery for producing cigarettes was developed in 1884 in Durham, N.C. By the 1920s cigarettes had replaced cigars in popularity, and now more than four-fifths of cultivated tobacco is used for cigarettes.

Leading U.S. Tobacco States

State	Harvest in pounds
North Carolina	693,314,000
Kentucky	510,226,000
Tennessee	172,475,000
South Carolina	124,195,000
Virginia	123,851,000
Georgia	122,050,000

Source: U.S. Dept. Agriculture (1982 harvest).

TOHOME INDIANS. Tribe of Muskogean linguistic stock that lived in Alabama near the junction of the Tombigbee and Alabama Rivers. Their history is the same as that of the MOBILE INDIANS with whom they were closely allied.

TOHOPEKALIGA LAKE, Fla. Lake located in Osceola Co., in east central Florida. It is about 11 miles long, and two to five miles wide. It is the source of the Kissimmee River that links it to Lake Hatchineha and Lake Kissimmee to the south.

TOLERATION ACT. General name given to a law calling for the freedom of an individual to practice the religion of his choice. The most famous U.S. toleration act was passed by the Maryland Colony in 1649 giving religious freedom to all Christians. The Maryland decision was considered radical by some religious establishments of the time.

TOMATOES. See VEGETABLES.

TOMBIGBEE RIVER, Ala./Miss. River formed by the confluence of Old Town Creek and East Fork River in northeast Mississippi. It follows a southeast course and joins the Alabama River near Mobile, where it is then called the Mobile River. The Tombigbee is 450 miles long and drains an area of approximately 20,000 square miles. The Black Warrior River, which joins it at Demopolis, Ala., is its chief tributary. Major cities on the Tombigbee are Columbus and Aberdeen.

TOMPKINS, Sally Louisa (Mathews Co., Va., Nov. 9, 1833 — Richmond, Va., July 25, 1916). Humanitarian. A wealthy philanthropist prior to the Civil War, she gained the use of a private home in Richmond, Va., to be used as a hospital (1861), in response to a request from Confederate President Jefferson Davis. She equipped the hospital and ran it with her own funds until 1865. In order to circumvent an order that nonmilitary hospitals be discontinued, in 1861 Davis commissioned Miss Tompkins a cavalry captain, a rank she kept without pay until her death. She was the only woman awarded a commission in the Confederate Army. "Captain Sally" supervised 1,333 patients; 1,260 of these survived.

TONKAWAN INDIANS ("they all stay together"). Tribe of Tonkawan linguistic stock that lived from Cibolo Creek to the Trinity River in central Texas. First encountered by the Spanish in the 16th century, the Tonkawan were said to have indulged in cannibalism, but it has never been determined whether this was fact or legend. A roaming, hostile tribe, they were finally gathered onto two reservations, along with other tribes, in 1855. Continued threats to settlers in the area resulted in their removal to Oklahoma, where most of them were massacred by the Delaware, Shawnee, and Caddo.

TOOMBS, Robert Augustus (Wilkes, Co., Ga., July 2, 1810 — Washington, Ga., Dec. 15, 1885). Politician. A brilliant orator, he served as U.S. Representative from Georgia (1845-53) and U.S. Senator (1853-61). After the election of President Abraham Lincoln, he advocated the secession of Georgia and was instrumental in the organization of the Confederacy. Serving for a time as a general for the South, Toombs, who wished the Confederate presidency for himself, opposed the policies of Jefferson Davis. After the war he refused to take the oath of allegiance to the federal government.

TORIES. A political group, also referred to as Loyalists, which adhered to the crown and Parliament during the time of the American Revolution, defending or condoning the oppressive measures of the British. They were a conservative group as opposed to the radical Whigs, the other popular party of the time, who denounced British measures as tyrannical and not to be endured. The Tories were of two kinds: some were honorable and conscientious men who were friends of the British government by principle and conviction; others, however, were selfish men who sided with England because they felt it to be the strongest side and wanted nothing more than economic gain. When the war ended the Tories were disbanded; some were transferred to the Royal Army and others went into exile. Many Northern Tories moved to Nova Scotia and Canada, and many Southern ones went to the Bahamas, West Indies, and Florida. Still others went to England and petitioned the English government for relief. It was estimated that over $15 million in relief was distributed by the crown to the American Tories.

TOURISM. The South—traditionally thought of as a land of cotton, tobacco, plantation houses, hot weather, ocean cities, mint juleps, and mountain hollows—is a region that has turned recently to heavy industry, oil and gas production, manufacturing, and high technology industries. It has also embraced another form of industry: tourism.

Of the estimated $150 billion spent on tourism in 1981 in the United States $69 billion was spent in the fifteen Southern states of Alabama, Arkansas, Florida, Georgia, Kentucky, Louisiana, Maryland, Mississippi, Missouri, North Carolina, South Carolina, Tennessee, Texas, Virginia, and West Virginia. The leading tourism states for out-of-state visitors were Florida and Maryland, followed by Texas, Missouri, and Louisiana.

There are many reasons for the surge in the popularity of the South as a tourist region, and climate is probably the most important factor. While some Southern states are warmer than others, none are afflicted with particularly long or harsh winters. In addition, the Carolinas, Georgia, Florida, Mississippi, Alabama, Louisiana, Texas, Virginia, and Maryland have Atlantic Ocean or Gulf of Mexico shorelines. Other states, including Missouri, Arkansas, Tennessee, and Kentucky are noteworthy for their superior inland parks, natural scenic wonders, and outdoor recreation possibilities.

Many of the nation's favorite vacation areas and events are in the South, from Walt Disney World in Florida to Hilton Head Island in South Carolina, and each year millions of Americans are discovering that the South is a serious new rival to the traditional vacation lands of New England, California, and the American West.

Alabama gains significant income from out-of-state and in-state tourists. In 1981 the state had 60 million travelers who spent $2.5 billon, or $630 for every state resident. Tourism supplies jobs in Alabama for more than 63,000 people, or one job for every $39,700 dollars spent.

The state offers mountains, forests, restored plantations, lakes, rivers, and Gulf Coast frontage. There are 22 state parks, many of which offer hiking, camping, swimming, and fishing. Anglers are attracted by both freshwater and Gulf fishing. Hunters find deer, ducks, geese and other wildlife.

Cities offering museums, art galleries, historic buildings, and various forms of recreation include Mobile, with its Mardi Gras festival and Azalea Trail, and Birmingham, which is home to the Junior Miss Pageant. Other Alabama events include the Festival of Arts (Birmingham), and the Deep-Sea Fishing Rodeo, and Rogation Days (Bayou La Batre). Historic sites and battlefields are numerous and other famous attractions include Cathedral Caverns, Natural Bridge, Crystal Caverns, the White House of the Confederacy (Montgomery), Forts Morgan and Gaines on the coast, the Booker T. Washington home and George Washington Carver Museum (both located at the Tuskegee Institute National Historic Site), and the battleship *Alabama*. Annual sporting events include the Senior Bowl (Mobile), Hall of Fame Bowl (Birmingham), dog racing, sports car racing, and the Charley Boswell Celebrity Golf Classic.

Arkansas, where the slogan is the "Land of Opportunity," is a popular destination for tourists interested in sightseeing and recreation. Although not nearly as popular as neighbor Louisiana, Arkansas still has a large number of tourists: in 1981 travelers spent $1.6 billion in the state, or $115 for every Arkansas resident. State tax revenue amounted to $68 million and federal revenues totaled $58 million. Tourism results directly in 45,962 jobs in the state.

Arkansas is a state of great natural beauty, dominated by rivers and fertile farmland in the east and south, and by mountain ranges in the north and west. The state has 36 state parks, three National Forests (Ouachita, Ozark, and St. Francis), and the National Park Service units of Hot Springs National Park, Arkansas Post National Memorial, Fort Smith National Historic Site, Pea Ridge National Military

Park, and the Buffalo National River. The state also offers excellent fishing for perch, catfish, bass, crappie, sturgeon, carp, and bream, and hunting for pheasant, woodcock, quail, rabbit, turkey, and squirrel.

Additional points of interest include the state capital of Little Rock with its museums, symphony orchestra, art galleries, and three state capitol buildings—the present one styled after the nation's capitol. Pea Ridge National Military Park (site of the famous Civil War battle), the Old Fort Museum at Fort Smith, and Arkansas Post are other highlights. Annual events in the state are the World's Championship Duck-Calling Contest (Stuggart), the Arkansas-Oklahoma Rodeo (Fort Smith), Arkansas Folk Festival (Mountain View), and the Oaklawn Horse Racing Season (Hot Springs).

Florida, the "Sunshine State," has a new slogan of late—"When you need it bad, we've got it good." It's a slogan that appeals to tens of millions of tourists each year, people who come from all over the United States and the world, particularly during the winter. So many people come to Florida that it has beome one of the nation's top three tourist attractions, along with Hawaii and Nevada. In 1981 out-of-state visitors spent over $18 billion in the Sunshine State.

As many tourists have discovered, Florida is far more than just a state lined with beautiful white beaches, with Miami as the focal point of attention. The state has a large inland region that is one of the nation's most popular recreation areas. The Florida Keys, off the southern tip of the state, offer visitors an entirely new, thoroughly tropical view of Florida. And the Gulf Coast shoreline is very different from its Atlantic counterpart.

Florida has 115 state parks and historic sites and four state forests. National parks and forests include the Everglades National Park, a 1.4-million-acre expanse of swampland in the state's southern interior which supports a variety of wildlife; Big Cypress National Preserve; Canaveral National Seashore; Gulf Island National Seashore; Appalachicola National Forest; Ocala National Forest; and Osceola National Forest. In many of these parks and forests, toursts find wildlife, museums, hiking, swimming, camping, and boating. Other outdoor recreations are hunting and fishing. Freshwater fishing in the numerous rivers, ponds, and 30,000 lakes offer anglers bass, crappie, bluegill, catfish, perch, and pan fish. The 8,000 miles of coastline is known for its on-shore and off-shore saltwater fishing: flounder, bluefish, mackerel, black mullet, pompano, redfish, sailfish, snook, sea trout, and tarpon.

Miami is Florida's most famous city, with luxury resorts, miles of beaches, nightclubs, shops, famous restaurants, historic mansions, gardens, theatre, music, and museums. Gulf Coast cities include Sarasota, Tampa, St. Petersburg, and Pensacola. The large inland cities of Orlando, Jacksonville, and Tallahassee also provide ample cultural offerings.

Other Florida attractions include the Castillo de San Marcos National Monument near St. Augustine, an old Spanish city (the oldest in Florida) known for its historic old buildings and fortifications; the antebellum Gamble Mansion in Ellentown; the Greek sponge fleets in Tarpon Springs; Olustee Battlefield; and De Soto National Memorial in Bradenton. There are also elegant summer homes on the coast; the Parrot Jungle in South Miami; Sarasota Jungle Gardens; Singing Town near Lake Wales, a carillon with 71 bells; and famous Walt Disney World in Orlando, with its new and futuristic Epcot Center. Other popular attractions are the Kennedy Space Center in Cape Canaveral, the Everglades Wonder Gardens in Bonita Springs, and the St. Augustine Alligator Farm. Annual events include the Orange Festival in Winter Haven, Azalea Festival in Palatka, and the Gasparilla Festival in Tampa. New Year's Day sports favorites are the Orange Bowl, the Gator Bowl, and the Tangerine Bowl. Other yearly highlights are the spring exhibition games put on by the many professional baseball teams who hold spring training in Florida. The state is also home to two pro football teams—the Tampa Bay Buccaneers and the Miami Dolphins. Other Florida sports include dog racing, jai alai, and auto racing (the Daytona International Speedway).

Georgia has one of the most varying geographies and climates in the South. A land of mountains, flatlands, seashore, and major cities, in 1981 50.6 million in-state and out-of-state tourists spent $7.5 billion here. Tourism directly employs 199,610 people.

The opportunities for outdoor recreation in Georgia are numerous. The coastline offers resorts, islands, and picturesque fishing communities, that offer swimming, boating, and sport fishing. The northern reaches of the state offer mountains, lakes, and winter skiing. The southern and central portions of the state are known for their farms and plantations. Fishing and hunting are found statewide. There are over 40 state parks, along with the Chattahoo-chee and Oconee National Forests. There is also a wildlife refuge in the Okefenokee Swamp.

Urban attractions—museums, sports, art, and music—are found in the cities of Macon, Albany, Columbus, Augusta, restored Savannah, and metropolitan Atlanta. Annual state events include flower shows, mountain music festivals, and statewide fairs. Perhaps the state's most famous event is the annual Augusta Masters Golf Tournament.

Historic sites include Andersonville Prison Park, Chickamauga and Chattanooga National Military Parks, Warm Springs, the Old Executive Mansion at Milledgeville, and the Confederate Naval Museum at Columbus. Sports enthusiasts come to Georgia because of the Atlanta Falcons football team, the Atlanta Braves baseball team, the Chiefs soccer team, the Flames hockey team, and many auto racing tracks.

Kentucky, the "Bluegrass State," calls to mind country music, Fort Knox, horse racing, ragged mountains, and spectacular natural scenery, which brings thousands of tourists to Kentucky where they spent $1.8 billion in 1981.

Geographically, Kentucky consists of mountains, rolling hills and flat land, lakes, rivers, and frontage on the Mississippi River. Kentucky has 40 state parks and three areas controlled by the National Park Service— Mammoth Cave National Park, Abraham Lincoln Birthplace National Historic Site, and the Cumberland Gap National Historic Park. Hunters come to Kentucky for rabbits, deer, grouse, turkey, doves, ducks, and geese. Fishermen angle for rough-fish muskie, walleye bass, crappie, and bluegills.

Louisville is the major tourist city, a metropolis with landmarks that include the *Belle of Louisville* sternwheeler, Churchill Downs (home of the Kentucky Derby), the Colonel Harland Sanders Museum, and numerous historic homes, museums, and theaters. Historic sites and points of interest outside Louisville include the buried city of Wickliffe, Frankfort with its state government buildings, the restored fort at Harrodsburg, the homes of U.S. Senator Henry Clay and Confederate cavalry commander John Hunt Morgan in Lexington, and Sinking Spring Farm, the birthplace of Abraham Lincoln.

Louisiana is one of the major tourist destinations in the South, primarily because of New Orleans. Its popularity is due also to the wealth of historical and cultural places and events in its Deep South northern section, and its central CAJUN section. The impact of tourism on Louisiana's economy is significant. In 1981 travelers spent $3.1 billion: the state earned $96.6 million in various fees, and local government received $47.9 million. Tourism results directly in 71,000 jobs which equals one job for every $29,580 spent. Of the total work force (including agricultural workers) 4.5% is employed by tourist-related business.

Geographically, the state is relatively flat, dominated equally by land and water. There are 16 state parks, 39 wildlife management areas, Alexander State Forest and Kiscatchie National Forest. Popular water-dominated recreation areas include the Gulf of Mexico, Toledo Bend Reservoir, and the Mississippi River. Fishermen come to Louisiana for striped bass, perch, carp, catfish, and crappie in the rivers, ponds, lakes, and swamps. Saltwater fishermen come for tarpon, pompano, snapper, and mackerel, and popular game are deer, bear, wild turkey, quail, ducks, and doves.

New Orleans, located on the banks of the Mississippi, is world famous for its Creole cooking, jazz, riverboats, French Quarter, cemeteries, and Mardi Gras, which is an extravaganza of costumes, parties, and ancient traditions. Annual Louisiana events include the Shrimp Festival (Morgan City), the Sugar Cane Festival (New Iberia), the Christmas Festival (Natchitoches), and Yambilee, a yam festival (Opelousas).

Famous state gardens include the American Rose Society Gardens, Zemurray Gardens, Louisiana State Arboretum, and Hodges Gardens. There is a professional basketball team, the New Orleans Jazz, and a professional football team, the New Orleans Saints. Other sporting events include horse racing, the annual Sugar Bowl college football classic and the New Orleans Open golf classic.

Maryland is a state of scenic natural beauty— —from its western Allegheny Mountains to the central hills and flatlands, from the Chesapeake Bay coastline to the rough, wave-pounded beaches of its Atlantic shore. Tourism has become the state's second-largest industry, and out-of-state visitors spent $13 billion in Maryland in 1981.

Maryland has 35 state parks, 5 state forests, and the Assateague Island National Seashore that is found along a barrier island between Chincoteaque Bay and the Atlantic Ocean. In addition to the many recreational facilities in the state, many people come to Maryland just to sample the famous Chesapeake Bay crabs, others come to visit the horse fairs of the central region.

The major city of Baltimore has historic sites as well as art galleries, a symphony orchestra, and an opera company. Baltimore sights include Fort McHenry, the U.S. frigate *Constellation*, the National Aquarium, and the Star-Spangled Banner Flag House. Another city that draws tourists is Annapolis, the capital. This small historic city has numerous restored colonial buildings, and is the home of the U.S. Naval Academy. Additional points of interest are the Antietam National Battlefield Site and the Clara Barton National Historic Site in Glen Echo. Scattered throughout the state are colonial villages and outstanding examples of antebellum architecture. Annual events include many Chesapeake Bay fishing-related festivals, the Preakness thoroughbred horse racing classic, the Delmarva Chicken Festival, the Chesapeake Bay Oyster Fleet Races, the Jousting Tournament in Cardova, and the International Race in Laurel.

Mississippi Forests, plantations, historical cities, an extensive park system, and a stretch of the Gulf of Mexico coastline are all attractions in Mississippi, and in 1980 tourists spent $1.02 billion in the state.

There are five National Forests covering a total of 1.1 million acres: Bienville Delta, De Sota, Holly Springs, Homochitto, and Tombigbee. There are 20 state parks offering numerous recreational facilities, including hunting for quail, rabbit, squirrel, deer, and turkey and freshwater fishing for catfish, bass, bluegill, bream, and crappie. The Gulf of Mexico offers red fish, mackerel, red snapper, and bonito. Supplementing the parks and forests are an unusually large number of National Park Service units, the best known being the Natchez Trace Parkway, a modern road that follows the scenic track of the old pioneer route; Vicksburg National Military Park; Brices Cross Roads National Battlefield; Tupelo National Battlefield; and the Mississippi section of the Gulf Islands National Seashore. The Old Capitol and the Governor's Mansion (1842) are in Jackson, and Natchez has restored antebellum mansions that are open to the public. The Old Light House (1848) is in Biloxi, and Pascagoula has the oldest structure still standing in Mississippi—a Spanish Fort built in 1718. Annual events include the Biloxi Shrimp Festival, the Garden Pilgrimage at Natchez, the Mississippi Arts Festival in Jackson, Mardi Gras in Biloxi, the Delta Staple Cotton Festival in Clarksdale, Mississippi State Fair in Jackson, and the U.S. Field Trials for Hunting Dogs in Holly Springs.

Missouri In the "Show Me" state, tourism, which had been the third-largest industry, moved into second place in 1982, following manufacturing. Tourist spending exceeded $4.7 billion in 1981, reflecting a 22% increase in state sales tax collection over 1980. More than 100,000 Missourians are employed in tourist-related jobs.

A state of mountains and plains, hot humid summers and brisk, sometimes bracing winters, Missouri attracts tourists year round. There are more than 40 state parks, Clark National Forest, and the Mark Twain National Forest. The state also has several national sites and the nation's first national riverway, the Ozark National Scenic Riverway. The Mississippi river offers riverboat cruises. Deer, quail, fox and raccoon are popular game for hunters who come to Missouri and the lakes and rivers provide excellent freshwater fishing.

Two Missouri highlights are Kansas City and St. Louis, sophisticated cities offering symphonies, museums, theatres, art galleries, professional sports teams and parks. Historic sites include the Jesse James home (St. Joseph), Samuel Clemen's boyhood home (Hannibal), President Harry Truman's birthplace (Lamar) and home (Independence), and the state capitol in Jefferson City, which has a famous Thomas Hart Benton mural. Annual events are the Pony Express Commemoration in St. Joseph, the State Fair at Sedalia, Maifest in Hermann, and the Ozark Jubilee in Poplar Bluff.

North Carolina Popular with tourists, the "Tarheel State" is a land of geographic extremes, mild climate, and natural scenic beauty. In 1981 the state's recreational offerings attracted $2.7 billion of in-state and out-of-state tourist money, an 11% increase from 1980. In 1981 145,000 people, or 7.5% of the entire work force, were employed in tourist-travel related jobs.

North Carolina is divided into seven sections, each with numerous natural and man-made attractions. The Land of the Sky is the state's western-most region, a land of mountains, and National forests. To the east is the High Country, a mountainous area of Scottish clansmen and dotted with state parks. The Foothills and Land of the New are areas of rolling hills, historic sites and recreational opportunities. The Heartland is the home of some of the nation's finest golf courses, schools, and museums. The Land of Cape Fear, a coastal region, contains many beaches, lighthouses, islands, fishing villages, resorts, and a rich colonial heritage.

The state's natural beauty is preserved by 14 state parks, four National Forests (Pisgah, Nantahala, Croatan, and Uwharrie), the Great Smoky Mountains National Park, the scenic Blue Ridge Parkway, and numerous National Historic sites which include the Wright Brothers National Memorial near Kitty Hawk, and the Cape Hatteras and Capelook National Seashores.

Primary cities are Charlotte, Winston-Salem, Greensboro, Durham and Raleigh, all rich in historical buildings, museums, and annual art and music festivals. Points of interest––urban and rural––include Civil War and Revolutionary War battlefields, the Carl Sandburg Home in Connemara, the Cherokee Indian Reservation, Tryon Palace (former colonial capitol) in New Bern, Nantahala Gorge in Forsyth County, and Morehead Planetarium at the University of North Carolina in Chapel Hill. Annual events include the staging at Fort Raleigh of the *Lost Colony*, a historical drama about the early English colonists on Roanoke Island; the Wright Flight Anniversary Observance at Kill Devil Hills; the Horse and Hound Show in Tryon; and the United North and South Open Golf Championship at Pinehurst.

South Carolina The "Palmetto State" has witnessed a steady yearly increase in the number of tourists who come to the state's abundant parks, resorts, and lengthy Atlantic coastline. Tourism has become a major state industry, second only to textile production. In 1981 out-of-state visitors spent almost $2.4 billion, which netted the federal, state and local governments revenues of $204 million.

The success of the tourism trade lies primarily in the lure of the state's northern mountains, extensive coastal region (resorts, beaches, and villlages) and the lake-dominated central section. South Carolina has 34 state parks, two National Forests (Sumter and Francis Marion) and five National Park Service sites (Congaree Swamp National Monument, Ninety-Six National Historic Site, Cowpens National Battlefield, King's Mountain Military Park, and Fort Sumter National Monument). Hiking, camping, and canoeing are available in the northern Blue Ridge Mountains and the Atlantic shoreline features beautiful Charleston and the resort communities of Myrtle Beach and Hilton Head Island. There is hunting for quail, duck, deer, rabbit, and turkey, and there is freshwater fishing for bass, trout, crappie, and rockfish. Saltwater fishermen angle for sailfish, bonito, mackerel, and bluefish.

The state capital of Charleston and the city of Columbia contain many of the state's most impressive historical sites and colonial-style buildings. Important annual events include sailboat regattas, the State Fair at Columbia, the Columbia Music Festival, polo games, the Tobacco Festival in Mullins, and the Cotton Festival in Camden.

Tennessee In 1981 tourists spent $2.6 billion in the "Volunteer State," an increase of 11.4% over 1980. Tourism-related jobs provide work for 4.2% of the work force, or 73,000 people.

One of the many reasons for Tennessee's popularity is protected lands. There are 28 state parks, along with the Cherokee National Forest, Great Smoky Mountain National Park, and the Cumberland Gap National Historic Park. There are also national park system areas, all Civil War related, at Chickamauga and Chattanooga, Shiloh, Fort Donelson, and Stones River. The parks and national areas offer varieties of outdoor recreation, and there is statewide hunting and fishing. Game includes wild boar, deer, black bear, rabbit, quail, dove, and squirrel, while fishing includes trout, pike, catfish, crappie, and bass.

Cities that attract a considerable number of tourists are Memphis, Knoxville, and Nashville. Knoxville was the site of the 1982 World's Fair, while Nashville draws a large number of tourists who come to see the GRAND OLE OPRY, the homes of famous country western singing stars, and the Country Music Hall of Fame and Museum. State monuments and historical sites include colonial Fort Loudoun in Vonore; The Hermitage, home of President Andrew Jackson, in Nashville; President James K. Polk's home in Knoxville; and the home of President Andrew Johnson in Andrew Johnson National Historic Site at Greenville. Annual events include the Liberty Bowl football game (Memphis), the Cotton Carnival (Memphis), the Strawberry Festival (Humboldt) and the Dogwood Arts Festival (Knoxville).

Texas With 267,339 square miles of territory, the "Lone Star State" is the nation's second-largest state. While it is not the most popular tourist state, its popularity is on the rise. In 1981 visitors spent $4.8 billion in Texas, more than was spent in the other Southern states except for Florida and Maryland.

The size of Texas provides the visitor with almost unlimited touring and recreational choices. Texas is a land of deserts, colorful Mexican border towns, rugged mountains, fertile farmland, endless plains, lush forests, the Gulf shoreline, sophisticated cities, professional sports, and ranches. It is a land where the New West and the Old West co-exist.

Texas has 90 state parks, and they are located in every part of the state. There are also many state monuments, along with Big Bend National Park, Guadalupe Mountains National Park, and four national forests: Sabine, Davy Crockett, Sam Houston, and Angeline. National grassland areas include Padre Island National Seashore, Amistad National Recreation Area, and Lake Meredith National Recreation Area. Texas is particularly noted for its hunting and fishing areas, both in coastal and inland regions.

Texas is linked to both the past and the future—from 16th century Spanish missions to the NASA Space Center. Historic sites include the ALAMO (where a group of Texas defenders died in the quest for Texas liberty); the old city of San Antonio; the San Jacinto Battle Monument (site of Sam Houston's victory over Mexican Gen. Santa Anna in 1836); La Villita, preserved arts and crafts center in San Antonio; Washington-on-Brazos, home of the Texas Declaration of Independence; the E. M. Pease Mansion in Austin; the birthplace and boyhood home of President Lyndon B. Johnson; and the Texas Memorial Museum in Austin.

Resort villages are numerous along the Gulf of Mexico, and the border towns provide easy access to Mexico. The major tourist cities in Texas are Armarillo, Lubbock, El Paso, San Angelo, Abilene, San Antonio, Laredo, Houston, Corpus Christi, Port Arthur, Waco, Austin, Beaumont, Galveston, Tyler, Wichita Falls, Ft. Worth, Dallas, Texarkana, and Longview. Texas' best known cities—Houston and Dallas—are home to professional football, basketball and baseball teams, along with symphonies, opera, museums, galleries, and sophisticated lifestyles.

Yearly events in Texas include the State Fair in Dallas; Charro Days, a four-day fiesta in Brownsville; Fiesta San Jacinto in San Antonio, the Rose Festival in Tyler; the Citrus Festival in Mission; and the Rice Festival in Bay City. Popular annual football events are the Cotton Bowl in Dallas and the Bluebonnet Bowl in Houston.

Virginia "Virginia is for Lovers" is a popular bumpersticker in Virginia. While this may be true, it is also a state for tourists; out-of-state travelers spent $2.4 billion in the "Old Dominion" state in 1981, and that amount is expected to grow dramatically in the coming years.

Virginia offers tourists both historical sites and a mild climate. Tourists are attracted to the state's Atlantic shore, particularly the Chesapeake Bay area, which is easily accessible to Washington, D.C., along with the old plantations, battlefield sites, and the homes of former presidents throughout the state. Some of the most popular tourist attractions include Williamsburg, Jamestown, Virginia Beach, Arlington National Cemetery, Richmond, Appomattox, the Shenandoah Valley, the Blue Ridge Mountains, Skyline Drive, Luray Caverns and the Cumberland Gap. Virginia has eight state forests, 19 state parks, many national forests and parks including Shenandoah National Park, Assateague Island National Seashore, George Washington National Forest, and national monuments including the Tomb of the Unknown Soldier and the Booker T. Washington National Monument.

Virginia ia a center of colonial and Civil War history. Points of interest include the famous restored colonial town of Williamsburg, the birthplaces and homes of Robert E. Lee, George Washington (Mount Vernon), Thomas Jefferson (Monticello), Benjamin Harrison and William Henry Harrison. Other popular attractions are the State Capitol in Richmond, Appomattox Court House (site of Lee's surrender and the unofficial end to the Civil War), Hot Springs resort and medicinal springs, Natural Bridge, the University of Virginia, and the Yorktown Battlefield and National Cemetery. Annual events in Virginia include Richmond's State Fair, the National Tobacco Festival, the Wild Pony Penning on Chincoteague Island, the Apple Blossom Festival in Winchester, and the Azalea Festival in Norfolk.

West Virginia One of the least populated states in the United States, West Virginia has a disproportionate share of the nation's natural beauty, and out-of-state travelers spent $1.2 billion in the "Mountain State" in 1981.

A land of mountains, valleys, wild rivers, lakes, farms, coal mines, and historic sites, West Virginia is popular with tourists who enjoy outdoor recreations. The state has 34 state parks, the Monongahela National Forest, parts of the George Washington and Jefferson National Forests, and the Harper's Ferry National Historic Park (site of John Brown's 1859 raid, and a Civil War battlefield). Hunting throughout much of the state includes game birds, deer, and rabbits in abundance, and fishermen come to West Virginia for bass and trout fishing.

The major cities of Charleston and Wheeling offer symphony, museums, and theater. Historical sites include many Civil War battlefields, the Chief Cornstalk Monument in Tu-Endie-Wei Park (Point Pleasant), Old Stone Church (Lewisburg), Covered Bridge (Philippi), Old Rehoboth Church (Union), Beckley Exhibition Mine, Cass Scenic Railroad, and the Indian burial mounds at Moundsville and South Charleston. Annual events include the State Fair in Lewisburg, the West Virginia Folk Festival in Glenville, the Tobacco Festival in Huntington, the Art and Craft Fair in Cedar Lakes, and the Preston County Buckwheat Festival in Kingswood.

TOWNES, Charles Hard (Greenville, S.C., July 28, 1915 —). Physicist. A graduate of Furman University (1935) and California Institute of Technology (1939), he worked during World War II with radar and microwave spectroscopy. He taught physics at Columbia University (1948-59), where he wrote a paper on maser and laser power in 1958. He was vice president and director of research of the Institute of Defense Analysis (1959) and joined the University of California staff in 1967. He shared the Nobel Prize (1964) with Russians Nikolai Busov and Aleksander Prochorov for work in quantum electronics with oscillators and amplifiers leading to maser and laser technology.

TOY, Crawford Howell (Norfolk, Va., Mar. 23, 1836 — Massachusetts, May 12, 1919). Biblical scholar. He was a student and later a professor at the Southern Baptist Theological Seminary until resigning in 1879 because of a theological controversy. He taught Hebrew at Harvard (1880-1909) and was the author of several volumes including *Introduction to the History of Religions* (1913).

TRANSPORTATION EQUIPMENT. Major class of manufactures in the Southern states. As defined by the U.S. Government, transportation equipment includes motor vehicles, aircraft, ships, railroad vehicles, and equipment for all of these classes of manufacture. Transportation equipment is the most important manufacture of Missouri and Mississippi. It is the second-most important manufacture of Florida. A major industry in Georgia, Louisiana, Texas, Tennessee, and Virginie.

TRANSYLVANIA UNIVERSITY. Independent coed liberal arts institution located in the central Kentucky city of Lexington. It was chartered in 1780, opened as a seminary in Danville in 1873, and moved to its present site in 1788. It was the first college west of the Allegheny Mountains (hence its name, which means "across the woods" in Latin). It was here that the first schools of law and medicine, as well as a library, were established in the west. The first college literary magazine, *The Transylvanian*, was started here and continues to be published today.

The Bachelor of Arts degree is awarded in 35 majors, all offered through the divisions of business administration, economics, education, social sciences, natural sciences and mathematics, fine arts, physical education, and humanities. The South provides 87% of the students, 40% pursue full-time graduate school, and 20% of all students choose careers in business and industry.

Library: 112,000 volumes, 435 journal subscriptions, 250 records/tapes. Faculty: 84. Enrollment: 356 men, 379 women (full-time). Degrees: Bachelor's.

TRAVIS, Col. William Barrett (near Red Banks, S.C., Aug. 9, 1809 – The Alamo, Tex., Mar. 6, 1836). Military officer. His early career included teaching and the practice of law. In 1831 he moved to Texas, where he became involved in the fight for independence. Travis led troops at Anahuac and San Antonio before he was appointed commander of the Texas patriots. His forces were charged with defending the ALAMO against SANTA ANNA's Mexican troops in March, 1836. He was one of many Texas soldiers who died there.

TRINITY RIVER, Tex. River rising in three forks in northern Texas, that eventually come together at Dallas. From there it courses approximately 500 miles generally south-southeast to Trinity Bay, an extension of Galveston Bay. One of the principal rivers in the state, it is particularly important for its irrigation projects that water the rice fields along its lower valley. Reservoirs located along the river supply water to several communities, including Dallas and Fort Worth.

TRINITY UNIVERSITY. Independent coed liberal arts institution located on a 107-acre campus in the south Texas city of San Antonio. The school is related by covenant, not legal ties, to the United Presbyterian Church. Founded in 1869, Trinity has had three homes : Tehaucana (1869-1902), Waxahachie (1902-42), and San Antonio.

Degrees are offered in a multitude of graduate and undergraduate fields, and academic emphasis is on pre-professional and professional programs, natural sciences, humanities, and social sciences. Undergraduate studies are offered in business and management studies, communications and the arts, education, humanities, sciences, mathematics and engineering, and social and behavioral sciences. The South provides 77% of the students. Almost 30% of all students pursue advanced studies soon after graduating; 10% enter business school, 3% medical school, 3% dental school, 2% law school. Trinity is among the nation's top 65 producers of sucessful dental school applicants.

Library: 499,381 volumes, 58,615 microform titles, 2,808 journal subscriptions, 4,377 records/tapes. Faculty: 300. Enrollment: 3,255 total graduate and undergraduate; 1,139 men, 1,274 women (full-time). Degrees: Bachelor's, Master's.

TRIST, Nicholas Philip (Charlottesville, Va., June 2, 1800 — Alexandria, Va., Feb. 11, 1874). Diplomat. A graduate of West Point, he was an acting professor there from 1819 to 1820. He was later United States consul at Havana (1833-41) and in 1845 was chief clerk of the State Department. In this position he was U.S. commissioner with the Army under Gen. Winfield Scott in Mexico, authorized to negotiate for peace, which he accomplished at Guadalupe-Hidalgo in Feb. 2, 1848. Trist was also a personal friend and private secretary to President Andrew Jackson.

TROTT, Nicholas (England, Jan. 30, 1663 — England, Feb. 1, 1740). Jurist. Trott was attorney general of Bermuda before he was appointed attorney general and naval officer for the southern part of the Province of Carolina, now South Carolina. He was named speaker of the Carolina Commons House of Assembly and served as chief justice of the province (1703-29).

TROUP, George Michael (McIntosh Bluff, Ga.(later Ala.), Sept. 8, 1780 — Laurens, Ga., May 3, 1856). Politician. He was a practicing attorney and member of the Georgia legislature before his election to Congress (1807-15) and the Senate (1816-18, 1829-33). As governor of Georgia (1823-27), he promoted education, roads, rail lines, and the repeal of the right to sell freed blacks. Troup defied President John Adams on the subject of Georgia's take-over of Creek Indian lands. He served again in the U.S. Senate from 1829 to 1833.

TRUMAN, Harry S. (Lamar, Mo., May 8, 1884 — Independence, Mo., Dec. 26, 1972). Senator from Missouri and 33rd President of the United States.

Following graduation from public high school in Independence, Mo., Harry Truman, whose middle initial was a relic of an unresolved family debate over whether it should stand for Shippe or Solomon, went to work on his father's farm and pursued a series of odd-job occupations. During World War I he served in the Meuse-Argonne theatre, and after armistice he returned to Missouri to open a haberdashery business that proved unsuccessful. Truman never received a formal college education, and used this fact to garner the support of the "common man," but he did attend Kansas City School of Law from 1923 to 1925.

Truman began his political career as an adherent of the Democratic party machine of Kansas City's Thomas J. Prendergast. After serving in local offices and judgeships, he was elected to the U.S. Senate in 1934 and reelected in 1940. As senator, he established a national reputation heading a committee formed to investigate defense department contracts awarded to private industry.

Picked by President Franklin Roosevelt to be his running mate in the 1944 election, Truman became president when Roosevelt died on April 12, 1945. His immediate concern was to end World War II combat in the Pacific, which he did by authorizing the world's first atomic bomb drops (1945) on the Japanese cities of Hiroshima and Nagasaki. Despite most predictions, he was reelected to a full term by defeating Thomas E. Dewey in 1948.

Truman continued the New Deal domestic policies of Roosevelt, but his most important achievements were in foreign policy. At first an advocate of cooperation with Russia, he then formulated the "Truman Doctrine" to protect countries from Russian intervention. With United Nations approval he sent U.S. military forces to protect South Korea from invasion by communist North Korea. He also established the Marshall Plan to assist European recovery from World War II, and the North Atlantic Treaty Organization (NATO) for the defense of North Atlantic countries. Although eligible for a second full term, he chose to retire in 1952 to his home in Independence, Mo.

TRYON, William (Ireland, 1729 — London, England, Jan. 27, 1788). Colonial governor. Appointed lieutenant governor of the North Carolina colony in 1764, he became governor a year later. Noted for his break up of the Regulator Movement, he was transferred to New York in 1771. He served from 1771 to 1779. During the Revolutionary War he led Loyalist raids in New England.

TUBMAN, Harriet Ross (Dorchester Co., Md., c. 1820 — Auburn, N.Y., Mar. 10, 1913). Abolition leader. Born a slave Tubman fled the South via the UNDERGROUND RAILROAD (1849) and became a frequent "conductor" herself, making 19 successful trips, and taking over 300 slaves to freedom. After the FUGITIVE SLAVE LAW (1850), she continued guiding slaves to Canada despite huge rewards offered for her. Called "General Tubman" by John BROWN, she exercised "military discipline" using a loaded revolver to encourage cooperation. Tubman served the Union Army as laundress, nurse, and spy, but was later denied a government pension.

TUCKER, John Randolph (Alexandria, Va., Jan. 31, 1812 — Petersburg, Va., June 12, 1883). Naval officer. He joined the U.S. Navy (1826) but at the outbreak of the Civil War joined the Confederate Navy as a commander (1861). He was involved in the battles of Hampton Roads and Drewry's Bluff, and from 1863 to 1865 was in charge of naval forces at Charleston, S.C. After the war he was the head of an expedition which explored the upper Amazon River in South America.

TUG FORK RIVER, Va./W.Va./Ky. Waterway rising in southwestern Virginia and running northwest for 155 miles, forming a section of the West Virginia-Kentucky border. Near Louisa, Ky., it joins the Levisa Fork River to form the Big Sandy River.

TULANE UNIVERSITY. Private coed institution in New Orleans, La. Founded in 1834, the university consists of a College of Arts and Sciences for men, Newcomb College of Arts and Sciences for women, a School of Architecture, a School of Engineering, University College for Physical Education, and a full range of graduate programs. The university also includes a School of Medicine located off-campus but within New Orleans. Students come from all regions of the United States, with only a small percentage coming from within the state.

Library: 1,200,000 volumes, 10,000 periodicals, 750,000 microfilms. Faculty: 900. Enrollment: 10,000 (66% male; 40% graduate). Degrees; Bachelor's, Master's, Doctorate.

TULLAHOMA, Tenn. Town (pop. 15,800), Coffee Co., in south central Tennessee. During the Civil War it was occupied by both Confederate and Union forces. Noted as a testing center for space vehicles and research instruments, it is the home of the University of Tennessee Space Institute. Other manufactures include apparel, boats, and concrete products. Tullahoma was settled in 1850 and incorporated in 1903.

TUNICA INDIANS ("the people" or "those who are the people"). Tribe of Tunican linguistic stock (to which they gave their name), they lived in Mississippi near the mouth of the Yazoo River. Though they had been heard of in earlier years, they were first encountered by three Canadian missionaries in 1699, one of whom stayed on with them until about 1720. They assisted the French against hostile Indians (particularly the Natchez). In 1731 the Tunica were attacked by the Natchez and both tribes suffered severe losses. Around 1800 they moved to Marksville, La., living in Avoyel Indian territory. After this time little was heard of them and it is thought that they were absorbed into other tribes.

TUPELO, Miss. City (pop. 23,905), seat of Lee Co., in eastern Mississippi north of Columbus. Settled in the late 1850s, this industrial city produces milk and dairy products as well as beverages, garments, and power tools. It is also a poultry processing and cotton ginning center. Tupelo was the site of a Civil War battle in 1864, when Union troops were attacked by Gen. Nathan Forrest.

TURNBULL, Andrew (Scotland, c. 1718 — Charleston, S.C., Mar. 13, 1792). Colonizer. A physician, he brought his family to settle in St.

Augustine, Fla., in 1766 and began colonizing the region with 1,400 Minorcan, Greek, and Italian settlers (1769). These settlers, brought to farm the huge plantations, revolted and the project went bankrupt causing Turnbull to flee to Charleston, S.C.

TURNER, Nat (Southampton Co., Va., Oct. 2, 1800 — Jerusalem, Va., Nov. 11, 1831). Slave and preacher. Encouraged by his mother to hate slavery, Turner also came to believe he was destined to lead his people out of slavery. After years of planning, he and 60 or 70 blacks began their "rebellion" on the night of August 13, 1831. The bloodiest slave rebellion in Southern history, they marched towards Jerusalem, Va., where Turner planned to capture the armory. In two days the slaves killed over 50 whites before being stopped by a large force of Virginians. Many of Turner's followers were shot or hanged and Turner himself was hanged six weeks later, shortly after his capture. Fearful for their lives, slaveholders then tightened their control over their slaves through restrictive legislation that limited the assembly, education, and movement rights of slaves. Black preachers were particularly restricted. The revolt also helped stiffen pro-slavery sentiment. Much has been written about Nat Turner but perhaps the most famous treatment is a fictionalized account of the man and his rebellion *The Confessions of Nat Turner* (1967) by William Styron.

TUSCALOOSA. (fl. 1540). Indian leader. He was chief of the MOBILE INDIANS in Alabama, and led them in the battle of Mabilia (Oct. 18, 1540) against the Spanish. They were defeated and lost over 2,500 warriors.

TUSCALOOSA, Ala. City (pop. 75,143), seat of Tuscaloosa Co., in western Alabama on the south bank of the Black Warrior River. The town was named for the great Mobile Indian chief who is memorialized by a granite monument on the courthouse lawn. Settled in 1813 and incorporated in 1819, it was once the state capital (1826-46). It is the home of the University of Alabama and Stillman College (1876), as well as Bryce Hospital, Parties State School (hospital), Veterans' Hospital and Hale Memorial Tuberculosis Hospital. Its manufactures include chemicals, paper, and tires.

TUSCARORA INDIANS ("hemp gatherers"). Tribe of Iroquoian linguistic stock that lived in North Carolina. An attack on the Indians in 1711, led by the Surveyor General of North Carolina, John LAWSON, precipitated the first Tuscarora war. They enlisted the aid of other hostile tribes but were defeated when the colonists received help from South Carolina. A treaty of peace was signed, only to be quickly broken by the North Carolinians. A second Tuscarora war broke out in 1713 but they were again subdued when Col. James Moore arrived from South Carolina with a few troops and over 900 Indian allies. After this second defeat the Tuscarora fled northward and joined their kindred in the Iroquois Confederacy.

TUSKEGEE INDIANS. Tribe thought to have been of Muskogean linguistic stock that originally lived in Tennessee on the Tennessee River, and later moved to Alabama near the Coosa and Tallapoosa Rivers. They gave their name to various places in Tennessee, North Carolina, and Oklahoma, as well as the city and seat of Macon Co., Ala. In 1717 a French fort was built near their Alabama settlement and they remained in this area under French influence until they followed the CREEK INDIANS to Indian Territory in Oklahoma.

TUSKEGEE INSTITUTE. Independent coed college located on a 5,000-acre campus in Tuskegee, Ala., 40 miles from Montgomery. Founded in 1881 by Booker T. WASHINGTON, Tuskegee began with the help of a $2,000 loan from the State of Alabama. It was established as a college for blacks and today the student population is 98% black and 1% Hispanic. Undergraduate studies are offered in the College of Arts and Sciences; and the schools of Veterinary Medicine, Education, Nursing, Applied Sciences, and Engineering.

The South provides 62% of the students, 10% are from Middle Atlantic states; 25% of Tuskegee graduates go on to further studies.

Library: 242,702 volumes, 1,064 journal subscriptions, 721 records/tapes. Faculty: 289. Enrollment: 3,763 total graduate and undergraduate; 1,646 men, 1,765 women (full-time). Degrees: Bachelor's, Master's.

TUTELO INDIANS. Tribe of Siouan linguistic stock. First encountered near Salem, Va., they moved to an island in the Roanoke River and again moved further southwest to the headwaters of the Yadkin River. They were at first closely associated with the SAPONI, and later the CAYUGA. Though living with these other tribes, they retained their own language long enough for a study to have been made of it in the late 1800s.

TWAIN, Mark See CLEMENS, Samuel.

TWIGGS, David Emanuel (Richmond Co., Ga., 1790 — Augusta, Ga., July 15, 1862). Military officer. He served as a captain during the War of 1812 and during the Mexican War was a colonel under Gen. Zachary Taylor when he distinguished himself and was promoted to brigadier general (1847). At the outbreak of the Civil War he became a commander of the Department of Texas and surrendered to the Confederacy. This action resulted in his dismissal from the U.S. Army and he became a major general in the Confederate Army (1861).

TYDINGS, Millard Evelyn (Havre de Grace, Md., Apr. 6, 1890 — Havre de Grace, Md., Feb. 9, 1961). Politician. After earning his law degree, he was elected to the Maryland legislature (1916-21). Tydings attained the rank of lieutenant colonel during World War I and received citations for meritorious service. He served in the U.S. House of Representatives from 1923 to 1927 and was elected to the U.S. Senate (1927-51). He was an active opponent of Sen. Joseph McCarthy.

TYLER, John (Greenway, Va., Mar. 29, 1790 — Richmond, Va., Jan. 18, 1862). Governor of Virginia, U.S. Senator, and 10th President of the United States. The son of Virginia Governor John Tyler, the future president graduated from the College of William and Mary in 1807 and was admitted to the bar soon after. He was elected to the Virginia House of Delegates in 1811 at the age of only twenty-one and then to the U.S. House of Representatives in 1816. Returning to state politics when his Congressional term ended in 1821, he served an additional two years in the Virginia legislature before becoming governor of the state (1825-27).

Tyler was elected to the U.S. Senate (1827) but left that office for an unsuccessful campaign for the vice presidency in 1836. In 1840, however, he ran successfully for the same office on the Whig ticket with William Henry Harrison using the slogan "Tippicanoe and Tyler, too." He became president when Harrison died on April 4, 1841, only one month after his inauguration.

Tyler's presidency was a troubled one because of his own past shifts of party loyalty and attempts to abandon the spoils system instituted by President Andrew Jackson. He did, however, oversee the annexation of Texas, the reorganization of the navy, and trade treaties with China. His opposition to a national bank eroded his support within the Whig party, and so in 1844 he chose retirement over a reelection campaign.

He followed his retirement from politics with private legal practice in Richmond. An opponent of secession during his presidency, he changed his views as the Civil War approached and was an elected member of the Confederate Congress at the time of his death.

TYLER, Tex. City (pop. 70,508), seat of Smith Co., in northeast Texas. Named for President John Tyler and settled in 1846 during the early days of the Texas Republic, Tyler's present economy is based primarily on agriculture, oil, gas, and manufacturing. It is noted for its municipal rose gardens and its annual Texas Rose Festival. It is the home of Texas College, Butler College, and Tyler Junior College.

U

UNAKA MOUNTAINS, Tenn. Range of mountains in the Appalachian Mountain range that forms part of the north central Tennessee border with North Carolina. The name is believed to be a Cherokee Indian variation of the word "white," probably so called because of the white haze which encircles the summits. The highest peak is View Point (5,259 feet).

UNCLE TOM'S CABIN. Novel by Harriet Beecher Stowe that was first published as a serial in the Washington, D.C. *National Era* (1851-52). It was published in Boston (1852) in a 2-volume set with a woodcut of a slave cabin on the cover, and in less than a year had sold 300,000 copies. The novel depicted various types of slaveowners in the South and immediately evoked the wrath of Southerners who questioned the accuracy of Stowe's facts. It was the first American novel with a black as the hero.

UNDERGROUND RAILROAD. Popular name for the various secret means used to help fleeing slaves before and during the Civil War. The system operated during the time of the FUGITIVE SLAVE LAW, and brought large numbers of slaves safely out of the South, through New England, and into Canada. The slaves were guided over generally fixed routes, primarily at night, with rest points at the homes of abolitionists. One of the first established underground stations was begun by Vestal Coffin in Guilford, N.C., in 1819, which was followed by a station in Wilmington, Del., run by Thomas Garrett. Garrett is credited with having helped over 2,700 escaped slaves. However, the Underground Railroad was far less organized and structured in the South than in the North. The most famous "conductor" of slaves was Harriet TUBMAN, an escaped slave who led 19 expeditions and is credited with guiding over 300 slaves to freedom.

UNDERWOOD, Oscar Wilder (Louisville, Ky., May 6, 1862 — Fairfax Co., Va., Jan. 25, 1929). Politician. A member of the U.S. House of Representatives from Alabama (1897-1915), and the Senate (1915-27), Underwood was a strong supporter of President Woodrow Wilson's foreign policies. He was a contender for the presidential nomination in 1912, and wrote the Underwood Tariff Act (1913) which severely reduced tariff rates until it was nullified by World War I.

UPSHUR, Abel Parker (Northhampton Co., Va., June 17, 1791 — aboard battleship

427

Princeton on the Potomac River, Feb. 28, 1844). Statesman. A practicing lawyer and later judge of the Supreme Court of Virginia (1826-41), he was appointed Secretary of the Navy (1841) by President John Tyler. In 1843 he succeeded Daniel Webster as Secretary of State and was an advocate of the annexation of Texas. He was killed with several other political figures, on the Potomac River, by the explosion of a gun aboard the U.S. steamer *Princeton.*

UTINA INDIANS. Tribe of Muskogean linguistic stock that lived in central and northern Florida. Also called the Timucua, they were encountered first by Ponce De Leon in 1513. The tribe was conquered by the Spanish and missionized by the French. During the 1600s they suffered from pestilence and attacks by the CREEK INDIANS. Their numbers declined and they are thought to have been absorbed by the SEMINOLES who moved into Florida in the mid 1700s.

V

VALLEY OF EAST TENNESSEE. An upland region of the state stretching across more than 9,000 square miles. It begins in the northeast as a continuation of the Shenandoah Valley, then moves southwest into Alabama and Georgia. Its peaks rise between 300 and 800 feet, and are overlooked by the Cumberland Plateau. The flora and fauna found here are similar to that of New England. The valley is drained by the Tennessee River.

VAN DORN, Earl (near Port Gibson, Miss., Sept. 17, 1820 — Spring Hill, Tenn., May 8, 1863). Military officer. A West Point graduate (1842), he was commissioned in the infantry and served in the Mexican War. He resigned from the army in 1861 to join the Confederate Army. He served in Texas, was promoted major general, and then commanded Mississippi troops. He was criticized for a severe loss at Corinth, and was later assassinated by a personal enemy.

VANCE, Zebulon Baird (Buncombe Co., N.C., May 13, 1830 — Washington, D.C., Apr. 14, 1894). Politician. Vance was elected to the North Carolina legislature (1854) and then to the U.S. Congress (1858-61). Vance joined the Confederate Army at the beginning of the Civil War and attained the rank of colonel. He served twice as North Carolina's governor (1862-66, 1876-78) and spent his last 15 years in the U.S. Senate (1879-94).

VANDEGRIFT, Alexander Archer (Charlottesville, Va., Mar. 13, 1887 — Bethesda, Md., May 8, 1973). Marine Corps officer. He commanded the First Marine Division in the capture of Guadalcanal (1942), which was the first full-scale U.S. offensive against the Japanese. Promoted that year to major general, he held the island against repeated attempts to retake it. Vandegrift also commanded the First Marine Amphibious Corps at the Bougainville Invasion (1943). He was appointed the 18th Commandant of the Marine Corps in 1944.

VANDERBILT UNIVERSITY. Independent coed institution located on a 320-acre campus in Tennessee's capital city of Nashville. Chartered in 1872, the university began as The Central University of the Methodist Episcopal Church, South. It was renamed in 1873 in honor of Cornelius Vanderbilt, the shipping and railroad magnate who had donated $1 million to the school. The university's religious affiliation was dropped in 1914.

429

Courses are offered through the College of Arts and Sciences, School of Engineering, School of Nursing, Divinity School, School of Law, Graduate School, Medical School, and the Owen Graduate School of Management. Majors include drama, Portuguese, molecular biology, and many interdepartmental majors. Students can also take courses at those area schools that, along with Vanderbilt, make up the Nashville University Center.

The Southeast provides 60% of the students, and 16% pursue full-time graduate study immediately after graduation; 8% enter medical school; 7% business school; and 18% law school. Vanderbilt ranks among the nation's top 100 producers of medical school entrants and in the training of future business executives.

Library: 1,400,000 volumes, 5,000 journal subscriptions. Faculty: 2,021. Enrollment: 9,125 total graduate and undergraduate; 2,767 men, 2,777 women (full-time). Degrees: Bachelor's, Master's, Doctorate.

VEGETABLES. Major agricultural resource of the South. Florida and Texas are the leading producers of vegetables in the South, and for these and other Southern states vegetable crops are an important support of canning, freezing, and other food processing industries.

Florida produces the largest crops in the nation of cucumbers, eggplants, escarole, lettuce, green peppers, and watermelons. Florida also ranks second only to California in the harvest of tomatoes, strawberries, and celery. Texas ranks second only to Florida in watermelons, second only to New York in cabbage, and second only to California in broccoli, cantalopes, carrots, honeydew melons, onions, and spinach.

VERMILION RIVER, La. Waterway rising north of Lafayette, La., and running south for more than 40 miles to empty into Vermilion Bay. When white settlers first arrived here, they discovered a tribe of Indians thought to be practicing cannibalism. The river connects with the Intracoastal Waterway and the Gulf of Mexico.

VERRAZANO, Giovanni da (Greve, Italy, c. 1480 — c. 1528). Italian navigator. While in the service of Francis I of France, he was the first European to explore and chart the North American coastline. On a voyage to find a route to the Indies in 1524, Verrazano explored the coast of North America from Cape Fear, N.C.,

north probably to Cape Breton, Nova Scotia. During this expedition he is thought to have discovered both Narragansett and New York Bays. In 1528 he embarked upon another expedition to explore Central America and reportedly was murdered by Caribbean Indians.

VICKSBURG, Miss. City (pop. 25,434), seat of Warren Co., located in west central Mississippi on the Mississippi River halfway between New Orleans, La., and Memphis, Tenn. Vicksburg is a historic and industrial center founded in 1718. The Vicksburg National Military Park and the Vicksburg National Cemetery, where 16,653 Union soldiers are buried, commemorate the siege of Vicksburg from May to July, 1863 by Union forces under Gen. Ulysses S. Grant.

Standing on a 230-foot-high peninsula over a sharp bend in the Mississippi, it was first called Fort St. Pierre by the French, and Fort Nogales (1791) by the Spanish. It was incorporated as Vicksburg in 1825 and named for Newitt Vick, who planned the city. The city's early economy was based on the production of cotton and trade on the Mississippi. During the mid 1800s Vicksburg was a violent frontier river town. The first five editors of the Vicksburg *Tri-Weekly Sentinel* (established in 1837) were murdered in the first 22 years of the paper's production. After the devastating Civil War, the city was faced with a new problem. The erratic Mississippi suddenly changed its course in 1876 and the city was left without a port. The problem was rectified at the turn of the century when the mouth of the Yazoo River was closed off and the water diverted to the old Mississippi River bed. Harbor improvements and the only rail bridge between Memphis, Tenn., and Baton Rouge, La., brought major businesses back to the city. Cotton is still grown in the area along with soybeans and corn. Today's manufactures include lumber, boats, fertilizers, and feed.

VICKSBURG, Siege of. Civil War engagement fought May 22-July 4, 1863, at Vicksburg, Miss., at the confluence of the Yazoo and Mississippi Rivers. One of the most important events in the war, the Union victory at Vicksburg split the Confederacy along the Mississippi River.

The siege was the end of the long Vicksburg campaign engineered by Union Gen. Ulysses S. Grant. He was appointed commander of Union forces in Tennessee on October 25, 1862, and persisted in the campaign for Vicksburg despite defeats at HOLLY SPRINGS and CHICKASAW

Siege of Vicksburg, May 22–July 4, 1863

BLUFFS late in 1862. From February to May, 1863, he experimented with numerous unsuccessful approaches to the city. In May, 1863, he moved south on the west bank of the Mississippi, opposite Vicksburg, and on April 30 he crossed the river at Bruinsburg, 40 miles to the south. The Union gained a foothold on the east bank of the river with a victory at Port Gibson on May 1. In his movement north, Grant first took Jackson, Miss., on May 14, thus preventing the Confederate forces there from assisting Vicksburg.

Vicksburg was defended by 20,000 Confederate troops under the command of Gen. John C. PEMBERTON. He ordered an attack east of Vicksburg at CHAMPION'S HILL on May 16, but otherwise concentrated his forces in Vicksburg for a defense of the city against Grant's inland attack. The Union launched direct attacks on Vicksburg on May 19 and May 22, but they were unable, despite superior numbers, to take the city by assault. Grant then ordered the siege that lasted until July 4, 1863.

Vicksburg was subjected to constant bombardment during the siege, and half the Confederate force was killed, wounded, or sick by its end. Pemberton chose Independence Day for surrender to give the Union a symbolic plum in exchange for more favorable terms.

Vicksburg surrendered one day after the Confederate defeat at GETTYSBURG; together these defeats are considered the effective end of the Confederate cause. In addition to opening the Mississippi to Union troop movement, the fall of Vicksburg left Pemberton with no army and Grant with a large force free for campaigns elsewhere in the South.

VINSON, Frederick Moore (Louisa, Ky., Jan. 22, 1890 — Washington, D.C., Sept. 8, 1953). Politician and jurist. Following his graduation from Centre College, Ky. (1911), Vinson began a law practice in Louisa. A prominent Democrat, he served in Congress (1924-29; 1931-38), interrupting his terms to campaign for Al Smith for president in 1930. As a prominent supporter of President Franklin Roosevelt's New Deal programs, Vinson engineered the U.S. economic mobilization for World War II. He was appointed Secretary of the Treasury by President Harry S. Truman in 1945, and was appointed chief justice of the U.S. Supreme Court in 1946. He served until his death and acquired a reputation for decisions that were at least as political as legalistic in foundation and thus open to continuing criticism.

VIRGINIA. State on the Atlantic Ocean in the northeast corner of the Southern region. It is triangular in shape, with a maximum east-west extent of 440 miles along the southern border and a maximum north-south extent of 200 miles from the southern border to the northern peak of the triangle. To the south Virginia borders North Carolina. In the far west is has a 120-mile border with Kentucky, and in the east it fronts on the Atlantic Ocean, with two Virginia counties on the southern tip of the Delmarva Peninsula forming the mouth of the Chesapeake Bay. Along the top of its triangluar shape Virginia is bordered by West Virginia to the northwest and Maryland to the northeast.

Virginia, called the "Old Dominion State," is especially rich in history. It was the location of the first permanent English settlement in America, the Jamestown colony established in 1607. It was in Virginia that the British surrendered to end the Revolutionary War in 1781, and four of the first five American presidents were residents of the state. The first slaves brought to America arrived in Virginia in 1619, Richmond was the capital of the Confederacy in the Civil War, and Appomattox was the site of the final surrender of the Confederate Army in 1865. In the course of these historical developments, the original lands of Virginia had been subdivided to form eight American states.

Modern Virginia is a state of diversified industry, population growth, and a range of striking natural scenery. The state's historical prosperity was based on tobacco farming, but today Virginia has an extremely modern industrial sector because of its excellent rail and water shipping routes. In the 1970s Virginia had a population growth rate well above the national average and attracted many new residents from other states. The natural preserves of the state run the full gamut from mountainous inland parks to sandy ocean beaches.

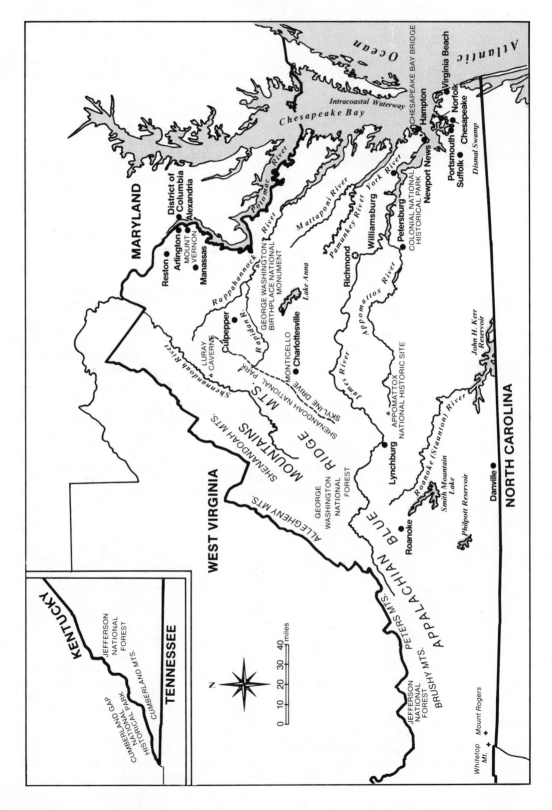

COMMONWEALTH OF VIRGINIA

Name: For Elizabeth I (1533-1603), Queen of England (1558-1603), "the Virgin Queen."

Nickname: Old Dominion, Cavalier State, Mother of Presidents, Mother of States, Mother of Statesmen, Down Where the South Begins.

Motto: *Sic Semper Tyrannis* (Thus Always to Tyrants).

Capital: Richmond.

Counties: 95. **Places over 10,000 population (1980):** 66.

Symbols & Emblems: *Flower*: Dogwood. *Bird*: Cardinal. *Tree*: Dogwood. *Song*: "Carry Me Back to Old Virginia."

Population (1980): 5,346,279. **Rank:** 13th.

Population Density (1980): 134.7 people per sq. mi. **Rank:** 16th.

Racial Make-up (1980): *White*: 4,229,734 (79.2%). *Black*: 1,008,311 (18.9%). *American Indian*: 9,336 (0.2%). *Asian & Pacific Islander*: 66,209 (1.3%). *Other*: 32,689 (0.6%). *Spanish Origin*: 79,873 (1.5%).

Largest City (pop. 1980): Norfolk (266,979). *Others*: Virginia Beach (262,199), Richmond (219,214), Arlington (152,599), Newport News (144,903), Hampton (122,617), Chesapeake (114,226), Portsmouth (104,577), Alexandria (103,217), Roanoke (100,427).

Area: 39,704 sq. mi. **Rank:** 36th.

Highest Point: Mt. Rogers (5,729 ft.), Grayson/Smyth Cos.

Lowest Point: sea level, Atlantic Ocean.

State Government:
ELECTED OFFICIALS (4-year terms expiring Jan. 1986, etc.): *Governor* ($75,000); *Lt. Governor* ($20,000); *Sec. of State* ($30,368); *Attorney General* ($56,000); *Treasurer* ($55,120).

GENERAL ASSEMBLY (Salary: $11,000 plus $75 per calendar day living expense allowance.): *Senate* (40 members), *House of Representatives* (100 members).

CONGRESSIONAL REPRESENTATIVES: *Senate* (terms expire 1985, 1989, etc.). *House of Representatives* (10 members).

Admitted to the Union: June 26, 1788 (10th state to ratify the Constitution). One of the original 13 colonies.

Virginia includes portions of three distinct topographical areas. The most western region is a mountain and valley province of the Appalachians. Many individual ranges parallel the West Virginia border, including the BLUE RIDGE and the SHENANDOAH MOUNTAINS. The highest point in the state is Mount Rogers (5,720 feet) in the Blue Ridge Mountains. Between these ranges lies the fertile Shenandoah Valley, sometimes called the Valley of Virginia. The center of the state is an expanse of PIEDMONT PLATEAU, a region of rolling uplands narrowing in breadth from 160 miles at the North Carolina border to 40 miles at the POTOMAC RIVER on the Maryland border. The eastern area of the state lies within the Atlantic Coastal Plain. Portions of the plain have been flooded by the sea, creating large tidewater estuaries at the mouth of the JAMES, RAPPAHANNOCK, and numerous other rivers flowing into CHESAPEAKE BAY. The southern reach of the coastline is extremely low in elevation and marshy, especially within the GREAT DISMAL SWAMP on the North Carolina border.

The colonization of Virginia dates from 1583, when an expedition sent by Sir Walter RALEIGH first attempted to establish a trading post for the export of TOBACCO cultivated by local Indians. His attempts, including ROANOKE COLONY in 1587, failed, but it was Raleigh who named the region Virginia after Elizabeth I, the "Virgin Queen." Early visitors returned to England with glowing accounts of the region, and the London Company was formed to organize chartered rights to Virginia just as the Massachusetts Bay Company did in New England. It was this company that sent the expedition that landed at JAMESTOWN on May 14, 1607. This party of pioneers survived, although they suffered from Indian attacks and unexpectedly harsh winters. Capt. John SMITH became their leader in September of 1608, and it was his discipline that enabled them to survive the great "starving time" in the winter of 1609-10. Hardship destroyed the settlement at Jamestown, but colonists resigned to defeat met a support party led by Lord DE LA WARR in June, 1610, and they started a new trading post at Hampton at the mouth of the James River. Their numbers were increased by the arrival of 650 new settlers in 1611, and soon plantations were laid out along the James. The first tobacco was cultivated in 1612. The growth of the settlements proceeded so quickly that in 1619 the residents formed the Virginia HOUSE OF BURGESSES, the first legislative assembly in America.

It was in that same year that the first slaves were sold in Virginia to increase a labor force dependent on indentured servants. The farm labor provided by SLAVERY led to a great boom in economic activity and expansion inland led by the developer of the tobacco industry John ROLFE, who married the Indian princess POCAHONTAS. That marriage failed to cement good relations with the Indians, however, and a century of Indian strife was epitomized by massacres in 1622 and 1644 that left hundreds of settlers dead. The farthest-inland settlers were the most vulnerable to Indian attack, and this led them to instigate the outlawed vigilante reprisals known as BACON'S REBELLION of 1676.

In 1700 Virginia had a population of about 70,000, a figure that would increase fourfold by 1750. In this era there was a great influx of small farmers from the northern colonies and from Europe, particularly Scotland, Ireland, and Germany. There farmers moved past the large and aristocratic plantations along the coast to the hilly and unclaimed interior region of Virginia, which became the first western frontier of America. Their numbers upset the uniformly Anglican demography of the colony, and Patrick HENRY became famous in 1763 for his legal victory over institutionalized church taxes.

It was on the same issue of taxation that the principles of the American Revolution were formulated by Virginia men such as George WASHINGTON, Thomas JEFFERSON, James MADISON, and James MONROE. A convention in Williamsburg, Va., framed a constitution and declaration of rights in May, 1776, in advance of the Declaration of Independence. Virginia suffered in the war by the burning of NORFOLK in 1776, the capture of Portsmouth and Suffolk in 1779, and the fall of its capital city RICHMOND to Benedict Arnold in 1781. The war was ended by the successful siege of British forces under Lord Cornwallis in YORKTOWN and his surrender there on October 19, 1781.

After the war Virginia politicians, especially James Madison, were instrumental in securing ratification of the U.S. Constitution in 1788. The key to the ratification of that document was the conspicuous absence of the word "slavery," but in 1798 Virginia directly addressed the ultimate cause of the Civil War with its opposition to the ALIEN AND SEDITION ACTS that protected Federal authority over states. For 25 years beginning with the election of Thomas Jefferson to the presidency in 1800, Virginia leaders dominated national politics and successfully negotiated compromises on the slavery issue. However, after the slave rebellion led by Nat TURNER in 1831 the state was torn by fierce debate over the slavery issue and unsuccessful legislative efforts to abolish the institution. John BROWN'S raid on HARPER'S FERRY in 1859 left the state divided over slavery, with the plantation owners of the east in favor of the institution and the small farmers of the inland regions opposed to it.

Because there was no majority opinion on slavery, the Virginia legislature was reluctant to secede at the outbreak of the Civil War. It did refuse to honor President Abraham Lincoln's call for troops for the Union Army, however, and this led to an allegiance with the Confederacy without any popular vote. It was not until April 17, 1861, that the decision to secede was mandated by a vote carried by the eastern counties. Richmond was declared the capital of the Confederacy in July of that year. This led to the creation of West Virginia and its admission to the Union in 1863.

Since it bordered on the Northern states and on Washington, D.C., Virginia was the key battleground in the Civil War. Both battles at BULL RUN, the siege at RICHMOND, the PENINSULAR CAMPAIGN, and the battles of FREDERICKSBURG and CHANCELORSVILLE were all crucial in the military struggle between North and South. The South was outmanned and outsupplied throughout these years of war, and the Confederacy lasted as long as it did only because of the genius of Virginia leaders such as Robert E. LEE and Stonewall JACKSON. When Richmond finally fell to Gen. Ulysses S. Grant's army, Lee was forced to surrender at APPOMATTOX COURTHOUSE on April 9, 1865.

In the era of RECONSTRUCTION, Virginia was designated the first military district. After years of debate the state's secessionists and unionists succeeded in unifying to regain political control in 1869, and Virginia was readmitted to the Union on January 26, 1870. It remained saddled by war debts that were not settled until 1892. By that time the extension of rail links across the center of the state and the growth of NEWPORT NEWS as a major port had begun the slow process of economic recovery. Virginia began to benefit from federal programs in the 20th century, when military camps, munitions factories, and naval installations were established in its eastern cities.

Today these eastern cities, once the heart of the old plantation lifestyle, are still the major population centers in the state. The largest metropolitan area in the state is NORFOLK-VIRGINIA BEACH on the south side of the mouth of the James River, which faces another population center, Newport News-HAMPTON, on the north side of the river. Richmond, 60 miles upriver on the James, is the second-largest metropolitan area in the state. North of these cities, on the Potomac River and the Maryland border, ARLINGTON and ALEXANDRIA are large suburban population centers within the metropolitan area of Washington, D.C. Half of Virginia's population lived in rural areas in 1960, but the growth of these cities had reduced that figure to 44% in 1980.

Between 1970 and 1980 Virginia's population increased by nearly 700,000 persons to pass the 5 million mark for the first time. Almost half of this numerical population growth was caused by a net migration gain in new residents, many of them coming from the Great Lakes and northeast regions. The total population is 18% black, a proportion that is now holding steady after decades of black migration to northern industrialized states.

These population patterns are related to the growth of a modern manufacturing sector in Virginia that now annually generates $12 billion. Among the leading manufactures are tobacco products in Richmond, shipbuilding in Newport News, and chemicals in Norfolk. The second leading industry in the state is tourism, which generates approximately $2.4 billion per year. Tourists are attracted to the areas in Virginia near Washington, D.C., but the industry also benefits from the numerous historical sites in the eastern counties and the mountain resorts in western counties. Agriculture is third in importance to the state economy, primarily because the fifth-largest tobacco crop in the U.S. is harvested in southern Virginia. The Shenandoah Valley region is rich in poultry and cattle farms, while dairy farming predominates in the Piedmont region and truck farming of fruits and vegetables is common in the coastal region. Virginia's other important industries are timber and wood products in the western mountains, coal mining in the same region, and commercial fishing out of the coastal ports.

VIRGINIA, University of. State-supported coed university located on a 1,500-acre campus in the town of Charlottesville, Va., 110 miles south of Washington, D.C., The University of Virginia was designed and founded in 1819 by Thomas JEFFERSON. Jefferson planned the curriculum as well. The school began instruction in 1825 with Jefferson elected as the first rector of the University and chairman of the Board of Visitors. James Madison and James Monroe were two of the Board's original members. Until 1904 the university was administered by a faculty chairman. Since then a president has been given these powers.

The school also maintains a branch campus at Wise, Va., called Clinch Valley College.

Undergraduate studies are offered in the colleges of Arts and Sciences, the schools of Engineering, Architecture, Nursing, Commerce, and Education. Graduate programs include the School of Law, School of Medicine, Graduate School of Arts and Sciences, and the Graduate School of Business Administration. In a recent year, 68% of students were from the South, 4% from the North Central states, 25% from the Middle Atlantic states. Some 65% of students pursue advanced studies immediately after graduation. The school is among the nation's top 100 producers of medical school entrants, one of the top 35 producers of successful dental school applicants, and in the top 100 schools for developing business executives.

Library: 2,351,842 volumes, 21,459 journal subscriptions, 10,362 records/tapes. Faculty: 1,600. Enrollment: 16,000 total graduate and undergraduate; 5,784 men, 5,280 women (full-time). Degrees: Bachelor's, Master's, Doctorate.

VIRGINIA AND KENTUCKY RESOLUTIONS. Set of resolutions denouncing the ALIEN AND SEDITION ACTS OF 1798, which were enacted by the Federalists. The resolutions stated that while the Constitution called for a pact between the states and the Federal government, the latter had no power to dictate the behavior and policies of every individual state. In addition, if the Constitution gave that power to the federal government, the resolutions said, then the states should declare the Constitution null and void. Kentucky was the first to produce such resolutions (approved November 13, 1798), written by Thomas JEFFERSON. Virginia followed by adopting its resolutions, authored by James MADISON, on December 21, 1798. These resolutions were considered the first written statement of the states' rights doctrine, a theory which gained in importance in later years with the NULLIFICATION and secession movements.

VIRGINIA BEACH, Va. City (pop. 262,199) located on both the Atlantic Ocean and Chesapeake Bay, in southeastern Virginia. Although it has many places of historical interest, including the Thoroughgood House

(1636), the present Virginia Beach is a new city. It was formed and incorporated in 1963 when Princess Anne County combined with the old Virginia Beach. With its many miles of coastline and inland waters, the resort and recreation trade make up a large part of its economy. Several military bases are also located there.

VIRGINIA MILITARY INSTITUTE. State-supported men's military college located on a 133-acre campus in Lexington, Va., a town 54 miles northeast of Roanoke. VMI is the nation's oldest state-supported military college. Founded in 1839, it is also the fourth oldest technological school and the only American "classic" military college in existence. Students (cadets) are given their education in a wholly military atmosphere, receiving Army or Air Force commissions upon graduation.

Academic emphasis is on engineering, liberal arts, and the sciences. Majors include civil and electrical engineering, physics, mathematics, and modern languages. Students come from all over the United States and some foreign countries; 65% of students are from the South. Some 89% of graduates eventually pursue careers in business, making the Institute one of the nation's top 25 schools in developing executives.

Library: 258,000 volumes, 923 journal subscriptions, 3,500 records/tapes. Faculty: 98. Enrollment: 1,271 men (full-time). Degrees: Bachelor's.

VIRGINIA POLYTECHNIC INSTITUTE AND STATE UNIVERSITY. State-supported land-grant university located on a 2,300-acre campus in Blacksburg, Va., 38 miles west of Roanoke. Founded in 1872 as a military school for men, the school has undergone many academic and name changes since its establishment. The institute is comprised of seven undergraduate colleges: Agriculture and Life Sciences, Architecture, Arts and Sciences, Business, Education, Engineering, and Home Economics.

The South provides 85% of the students and 10% are from the Middle Atlantic states; 15% of students pursue advanced studies soon after graduating. The institute ranks among the nation's top 120 producers of dental school entrants, and 60% of graduates choose careers in business and industry.

Library: 1,000,000 volumes. Faculty: 1,825. Enrollment: 21,069 total graduate and undergraduate; 10,760 men, 6,597 women (full-time). Degrees: Bachelor's, Master's, Doctorate.

W

WACCAMAW INDIANS. Tribe thought to have been of Siouan linguistic stock though none of their language was preserved. They lived in South Carolina on the Waccamaw River (to which they gave their name), and their territory at times extended into North Carolina. An attack on the colonists in 1715 resulted in a quick peace treaty and a trading post was established in their territory the following year. They made another attack on white settlements in 1720, and in 1755 they in turn were attacked by the Cherokee and Natchez Indians. They are thought to have been absorbed into the CATAWBA tribe.

WACO, Tex. City (pop. 101,261), seat of McLennan Co., in central Texas on the south bank of Lake Waco and the Brazos River, 94 miles south of Dallas on the site of what was a Hueco Indian village. Settled in 1849 and incorporated in 1856, Waco is the center of an agricultural region whose manufactures include tires and glass. It is the location of the 12th Air Force headquarters, James Connally Air Force Base, and a veterans' hospital. It is also home to Baylor University (1886), Paul Quinn College (1872), the first black college in Texas, and Cameron Park (680 acres), one of the largest city parks in Texas. In 1953 a devastating tornado killed 114, injured 597, and caused $40,000,000 in property damage.

WADDELL, James Iredell (Pittsboro, N.C., July 13, 1824 — Annapolis, Md., Mar. 15, 1886). Naval officer. Waddell was commander of the Confederate cruiser *Shenandoah* in 1864, and because he was not told of the defeat of the South, he continued in action after the end of the Civil War. Considered an outstanding commander, Waddell later sailed for private shipping companies, particularly on Asia runs.

WAKE FOREST UNIVERSITY. Independent coed liberal arts institution located on a 320-acre campus in Winston-Salem, N.C. Founded in 1834, Wake Forest is affiliated with the Baptist State Convention of North Carolina. A major sponsor of the university is the Reynolds Foundation. Primarily an undergraduate institution, Wake Forest includes the Bowman Gray School of Medicine (located four miles from the main campus), the Graduate School, the Babcock Graduate School of Management, and the School of Law.

Some 69% of students are from the South, 20% are from Middle Atlantic states, and 7% are from North Central states. Approximately

437

10% of graduates enter graduate school; 4% go to dental school, 5% medical school, 10% law school and 4% business school.

Library: 745,992 volumes, 257,233 microform titles, 9,312 journal subscriptions, 1,630 records/tapes. Faculty: 239. Enrollment: 4,787 total graduate and undergraduate; 1,843 men, 1,194 women (full-time). Degrees: Bachelor's, Master's, Doctorate.

WALKE, Henry (Princess Anne Co., Va., Dec. 24, 1808 — Brooklyn, N.Y., Mar. 8, 1896). Naval officer. He entered the Navy in 1827, served in the war against Mexico, and was considered a bold efficient Union commander in the naval warfare of the Mississippi River during the Civil war. He distinguished himself in the attacks on Fort Donelson, Island Number Ten, and in operations against Vicksburg. He was promoted to commodore in 1866, rear admiral in 1870, and retired in 1871.

WALKER, David (Wilmington, N.C., Sept. 28, 1785 — Boston, Mass., June 28, 1830). Black abolitionist and journalist. Born a freeman, Walker moved to Boston (1827) where he became involved in Boston's Colored Association. He contributed to *Freedom's Journal*, the first newspaper written for American blacks. He wrote the radical antislavery pamphlet *An Appeal to the Colored Citizens of the World* (1829), which helped begin the drive to end slavery in the United States and advised slaves to revolt against their owners. Nat TURNER'S REBELLION is said to have been a result of Walker's pamphlet. The pamphlet's distribution was banned in some Southern states and a price put on his head. Walker died in suspicious circumstances shortly after it was published.

WALLACE, George Corley (Clio, Ala., Aug. 25, 1919 —). Politician. As governor of Alabama (1963-67, 1971-), he is the first to serve the state for more than three terms. A Democrat, he was denied by law a chance to run for a consecutive term in 1967 and his wife, Lurleen, was elected with the understanding that he would continue to make the decisions. He became a controversial figure because of his opposition to the desegregation of schools, and in 1965 tried to prevent Martin Luther KING's march from Selma to Montgomery. Wallace campaigned for the U.S. presidency in 1968, 1972, and 1976. During the 1972 campaign, he was shot and has remained partially paralyzed. During the late 1970s and 1980s, Wallace modified his positions and sought to position

George C. Wallace, Alabama's governor for three terms

himself as a populist champion of both blacks and whites.

WALLACE, Lurleen Burns (Tuscaloosa, Ala., Sept. 19, 1926 — Montgomery, Ala., May 7, 1968). Albama governor. The wife of George WALLACE, she rose to national attention when she was elected to the state governorship (1966) when the law prohibited her husband from serving a second term. She died in office.

WALLOPS ISLAND, Va., Island off Virginia's northern Atlantic coast, in Accomack Co. It is named for John Wallop who received a patent for it in 1672. A National Aeronautics and Space Administration launching area was constructed here in 1959 and in 1960 a bridge and causeway were built to connect the island with the mainland.

WAR BETWEEN THE STATES. Traditional Southern name for the conflict between the Northern states of the Union and those which seceded to establish the CONFEDERACY. The phrase reflects the Southern position that sovereign states that freely joined the Union could as freely withdraw from it. Since mid-century, Southerners have increasingly accepted the term CIVIL WAR, once anathema in the South.

WARM SPRINGS, Ga. Town (pop. 425), Meriwether Co., in western Georgia near the Pine Mountains. Brought to prominence by the visits of Franklin D. Roosevelt after his attack of polio, the springs, which bring 800 gallons of 88 degree water to the surface every minute, were thought therapeutic even by the Indians who came to the area. Roosevelt often resided at the springs and supported their development. He died there in 1945.

WARMOTH, Henry Clay (MacLeansboro, Ill., May 9, 1842 — Louisiana, Sept. 30, 1932). Politician. A lawyer, he served as a Union officer in the Civil War. He was dishonorably discharged because of his exaggerated accounts of Union losses, but was later reinstated by Pres. Abraham Lincoln. Following the war, Warmouth opened a law practice in New Orleans, La., was elected governor (1868-72). Serving during a time of bitter strife over black suffrage, he tried to better relations between the races.

WARREN, Robert Penn (Guthrie, Ky., Apr. 24, 1905 —). Poet, critic, and novelist. Educated at Vanderbilt University where he met Allen TATE and studied under John Crow RANSOM, Warren became a member of the literary group, the Fugitives. He was a contributor to the influential literary journal, *Fugitive,* and the statement of Southern agrarian ideals called *I'll Take My Stand* (1930). When Ransom and Tate gravitated toward criticism, Warren emerged as the preeminent poet of this movement of modern Southern writers. In a long literary career he has produced many volumes of poetry since 1936, the novel *All the King's Men* (1947) and other prose fiction, and the influential textbook *Understanding Poetry* (1938), co-authored with Ransom.

WASHA INDIANS. Tribe of Tunican linguistic stock that lived near Bayou La Fourche, La. They gave their name to Washa Lake in Terrebone Parish. The Washa had a generally friendly relationship with the early French, and in the 1730s joined with the Chawasha. By the early 1800s they were virtually extinct.

WASHINGTON, Booker Taliaferro (Franklin Co., Va., Apr. 5, 1856 — Tuskegee, Ala., Nov. 14, 1915). Black educator and social

Booker T. Washington, first president of the Tuskegee Institute

reformer. Born a slave, he and his family moved to West Virginia after Emancipation. Washington had little formal schooling as a child and he worked as a janitor to get through the Hampton Normal and Agricultural Institute in Virginia. In 1879 he joined the teaching staff at Hampton, and in 1881 was selected to organize and build up a normal school for blacks in Alabama called TUSKEGEE INSTITUTE. Three decades later, the school had grown from a handful of students, one teacher, and a few worn-out buildings, to a vibrant campus with 1,500 students, over 100 buildings, a multitude of education programs, and a sizable endowment.

Washington was a major spokesman for blacks during the final years of the 19th century and the first decade of the 20th. Often opposed by other black leaders, Washington preached that the blacks in America should concentrate on gaining an education and building social acceptance before attempting to gain equality.

WASHINGTON, Bushrod (Westmoreland Co., Va., June 5, 1762 — Philadelphia, Pa., Nov. 26, 1829). Military officer and jurist. The nephew of George WASHINGTON, he became

Washington's literary executor and supervised preparation of John Marshall's five-volume *Life of Washington* (1804-07). After graduating from The College of William and Mary (1778), he joined the colonial army for the duration of the Revolution. After the war he studied law in Philadelphia and began a practice in Virginia. A member of the Virginia Constitutional ratification convention (1788), he was appointed to the Supreme Court by President John Adams (1798). On the death of Martha Washington (1802), Bushrod inherited Mount Vernon.

WASHINGTON, D.C. The capital of the United States (pop. 638,333), co-extensive with the District of Columbia, on the northeast bank of the Potomac River. Covering an area of 67 square miles, the city is 226 miles from New York City, 135 miles from Philadelphia, and 40 miles from Baltimore. Its metropolitan area has spread to include numerous counties and independent cities in Virginia and Maryland.

Before 1790 the Congress of the newly-born United States had met in eight different cities and there had been heated debates as to the choice of a permanent site for the nation's capital. Although there was uniform agreement that it would be wise to locate it on a navigable river and in an area easily accessible to both the Northern and Southern states, there was opposition from the North to suggestions that the new capital be in territory where slave-holding was allowed. On July 12, 1790, however, Congress approved an act locating the capital on the Potomac River in a district not to exceed ten square miles. At President George Washington's suggestion, a site was chosen below Alexandria, Va., at the mouth of Hunting Creek. The land was originally ceded by both Virginia and Maryland, but in 1846 the area containing Alexandria was given back to the state of Virginia, at their request.

A design for the city was entrusted to Maj. Pierre Charles L'Enfant, a French engineer who had served in the Continental Army. L'Enfant planned the city with broad avenues radiating from the Capitol, each bearing the name of a state. Pennsylvania Avenue was to be the main thoroughfare and streets south of it were named for Southern states; likewise, streets north of the avenue received the names of Northern states. However, in 1792 L'Enfant was dismissed and his plan largely forgotten.

In order to secure the land from the original proprietors, the government promised that once the land had been surveyed the proprietors would retain half the land and the other half would go to the public. For land taken for public use, the proprietors were paid $75 an acre, but no compensation was paid for land to be used for streets and walkways.

Although plagued by a shortage of funds, the President's House, the Capitol building, and the halls of Congress were ready for occupancy by 1800, and in the fall of that year Congress convened in the new capital for the first time.

The city was incorporated May 3, 1802. Early development was slow and the city remained a dreary place with a lack of conveniences—there was only a patch through an elder swamp from the President's house to the Capitol, a distance of one mile. Both of these buildings were burned when British troops entered the city in 1814.

Rebuilding and new construction were again hampered by lack of federal appropriations and although some work was begun on wings and a dome for the capitol building, it wasn't until the Civil War that the city began to take shape. Washington became a strategic supply depot for federal troops and, along with economic recovery, the city's population had increased ninefold (from 8,000 in 1800 to 75,000 in 1865).

In the 1870s modernization began in the form of paved streets, sewers, lighting, and landscaping. New government buildings were authorized and an abundance of monuments to national heroes sprang up throughout the city. Construction was rapid but ill-planned, and L'Enfant's original plan was not only ignored but was in fact lost; it did not resurface until 1887 by which time much damage had been done. The great influx of newly-freed slaves after the Civil War and rampant unemployment led to large areas of slums, many of which lay nearly next door to magnificent government buildings and to the capitol itself.

Washington was then developed according to what could be salvaged from the rediscovered L'Enfant plans. Most of the city's improvements during the early 1900s were due to Senator James McMillan who presented a report to the Senate in 1902 recommending a plan of development for Washington. The McMillan Report, although at times highly criticized, was the basis for city planning well into the 1950s. Government buildings were relocated, the Union Railroad Station was erected, tidal swamps of the Potomac River were drained, and a park system was designed. The first Commission of Fine Arts was appointed in 1910 and, along with a zoning board established in 1920, was instrumental in implementing a uniform style of architecture. In 1926 a permanent planning commission was finally set up which developed street plans, the park system, and transportation facilities.

Hampered by both world wars, it wasn't until the 1950s and 1960s that extensive improvement of slum areas was accomplished. Unlike some urban areas where white populations gradually move out of a section as it becomes run-down, the opposite happened in Washington in the 1950s when the Georgetown area was transformed into a highly-fashionable village and impoverished blacks were forced out. An anti-poverty program was instituted in 1965 to investigate future plans and developments, halt racial segregation, and oversee relocation and rehabilitation.

The government of Washington, D.C. is under federal supervision and, until 1970, was directed by a three-person board of commissioners. At that time a 12-member Commission on the Organization of the Government of the District of Columbia was established by an act of Congress, and the district was allowed to have a delegate to the U.S. House of Representatives. The delegate, however, does not have a right to vote. Although citizens of Washington at one time had no vote in national affairs, in 1961 the Twenty-third Amendment gave residents the right to vote in elections for the President and Vice President, and the District of Columbia was allotted three electoral votes.

The economy of Washington is based mostly on federal government employment, followed by real estate and tourism. The city attracts millions of American and foreign visitors annually, and is also a convention headquarters for numerous organizations and businesses. Although served by several rail lines, Dulles International Airport at nearby Chantilly, Va., and Washington National Airport service the greatest number of visitors. The once-important steamship business on the Potomac River is non-existant except for scenic cruises. To accommodate north and southbound travelers, the Capital Beltway around Washington was completed in the 1960s.

The nation's capital offers a wealth of cultural and educational facilities. The city's public school system was founded in 1800 by an act of Congress, and was headed by Thomas Jefferson. The system was racially integrated in 1954. Institutions of higher learning in Washington include Georgetown University (1789), the oldest Catholic university in the U.S., American University (1893), Catholic University (1877), George Washington University (1821), and Howard University, the largest Black institution in the U.S., chartered in 1867.

There are both public and private scientific and research institutions, including the National Archives, Brookings Institution, National Gallery of Art, Library of Congress, and Smithsonian Institution, founded in 1846. There are over 250 libraries in Washington, and the city is the headquarters of numerous national organizations including the Daughters of the American Revolution and the National Geographic Society.

The extensive park system in Washington includes the Mall, located between the Capitol and the Washington Monument, which covers 135 acres and includes many government and public buildings. West Potomac Park includes 900 flowering cherry trees, which were given to the city in 1912 by the people of Tokyo. The trees are a major tourist attraction every spring.

Other highlights of the capital city include the Washington Monument, 555 feet high, built between 1848 and 1885 at a cost of $1.1 million; the Lincoln Memorial, a classic Grecian structure designed by Henry Bacon and dedicated in 1922; Jefferson Memorial, dedicated in 1943; and other memorials to Daniel Webster, Benjamin Franklin, James A. Garfield, Andrew Jackson, John Marshall, and Martin Luther. The Pentagon, a 34-acre complex that houses the Department of Defense, was completed in 1943 and is the world's largest office building. One of the major cultural attractions is the John F. Kennedy Center for the Performing Arts, built in the late 1960s. Cemeteries are not allowed within the city limits. The famous Arlington National Cenetary, which contains the Tomb of the Unknown Soldier, is in nearby Arlington, Va.

The Washington metropolitan area, the seventh largest metropolitan area in the United States, includes Montgomery and Prince Georges Counties in Maryland, the counties of Arlington, Fairfax, Loudoun, and Prince William in Virginia, and the independent Virginia cities of Alexandria, Fairfax, and Falls Church. The 1980 population of the metropolitan area was 3,060,922, an increase over the 1970 population of 2,910,111. The city of Washington, however, had a 15.6% decrease in population during that time—from 756,668 in 1970 to 638,333 in 1980. The city's black population in 1980 was 448,229, over 70% of the total, and the Hispanic population was 17,652.

WASHINGTON, Ga. City (pop. 4,662), seat of Wilkes Co., in northeast Georgia. First settled in 1773, it was the state's temporary capital during the Revolutionary War. Washington was also the site of the Confederacy's last cabinet meeting in May, 1865. Several antebellum homes remain today as tourist attractions. There is some light manufacturing (fertilizer, soft drinks), and cotton is grown in the area.

WASHINGTON, George (Westmoreland Co., Va., Feb. 22, 1732 — Mt. Vernon, Va., Dec. 14, 1799). Plantation owner, Commander-in-Chief during the Revolutionary War and first President of the United States. The son of Augustine Washington and May Ball, George Washington spent most of his early childhood on a farm near Fredericksburg, Va. His father died when he was eleven, leaving George under the guidance of his half-brother Lawrence, who was the owner and developer of the plantation at Mount Vernon. Although schooled only at home, Washington quickly revealed a talent for mathematics, and in his first occupation as surveyor he plotted land in the Shenandoah Valley owned by William Fairfax. He then traveled with his half-brother to Barbados, where he caught the smallpox that left him facially scarred for the rest of his life. Lawrence died in 1752, leaving Mount Vernon to George. By the time of his death George Washington had increased the area of the plantation to some 70,000 acres, many of them within what is now West Virginia.

Washington's military career began in 1753 when he was sent into the Ohio territory during the French and Indian War. He was forced to surrender his command to the French at Fort Necessity in 1754, but he subsequently became an aide to Gen. Edward Braddock, under whom he increased his military knowledge and demonstrated the ability to resist difficulty with a discipline that would prove of great value in the Revolution. Washington was with Braddock's army when it was defeated on the way to Fort Duquesne in 1755 and also when it returned to capture that fort in 1758.

Following the war Washington returned to Virginia to oversee the operation of Mount Vernon. In 1759 he married Martha Dandridge Custis, a widow and mother of two children. He had become a member of the Virginia House of Burgesses in 1759, and served a series of successive terms there. Washington was not in any way a proponent of independence for the colonies at this time. As a plantation owner, however, he gradually developed a hostility to British control of Virginia based on a monopoly on plantation exports. Washington wanted to trade with the highest bidder, from whatever country, and in the 1770s his dissatisfaction was increased by a series of British taxation measures. The colonial governor of Virginia dissolved the House of Burgesses in 1774, and by that time Washington's shift to the revolutionary cause was complete enough for him to attend the Continental Congresses of 1774 and 1775 and to accept an appointment as commander-in-chief of the Continental Army in 1775.

In leading his army through all the major conflicts of the Revolutionary War, Washington distinguished himself as a dependable, rather than charismatic, leader and a disciplined, rather than flamboyant, tactician who quietly persevered in the face of supply and munitions shortages. It was his special ability to encourage unity among his military forces that brought him to the forefront of the new government once the war had been concluded. A strong supporter of a central government in the debates that followed the war, he was elected president of the Constitutional Convention when it met in Philadelphia in 1787. He helped get the Constitution ratified despite attacks on the document by a variety of factions, and he was then unanimously elected president in

Statue of George Washington by French sculptor Jean Antoine Houdon, in the capitol at Richmond, Va.

1789. Washington was inaugurated as the country's first president on April 30, 1789, on the balcony of the Federal Hall in New York City. He was reelected in 1792 but declined a third term, thus setting a precedent that would survive until the time of President Franklin D. Roosevelt.

The demands on Washington's two administrations were enormous, and he responded to them with the quiet determination that distinguished his military career. He established a reliable currency, founded the National Bank, and provided for payment of war debts. He also founded the military academy at West Point and successfully ended the disruption of the Whiskey Rebellion. Perhaps most important, Washington managed to establish taxation policies that encouraged industrial development and decreased American reliance on foreign imports.

WASHINGTON, Martha Dandridge Custis

(New Kent, Va., June 21, 1731 — Mount Vernon, Va., May 22, 1802). The daughter of John and Frances Jones Dandridge, she was first married to Daniel Parke Custis. Upon his death she was left a wealthy widow, and, after a short courtship, married George WASHINGTON on January 6, 1759. They had no children of their own but Washington adopted the two living children (two had died) of Martha's first marriage. During the Revolutionary War Martha usually spent the winter months away from Mount Vernon, at the headquarters of her husband. Known for her graciousness and charm, she was shown great respect and affection as the wife of the first president.

WASHINGTON AND LEE UNIVERSITY.

Independent four-year and professional men's college located on a 176-acre campus in Lexington, Va., 50 miles northeast of Roanoke. Founded in 1749, Washington and Lee is the nation's sixth-oldest institution of higher learning. Originally named Augustus Academy, the school was renamed Liberty Hall in 1776 and moved from Augusta County to Lexington in 1780. George Washington gave the school an impressive monetary gift in 1796, and in 1798 the college was renamed in his honor. Robert E. LEE became president of the school following the Civil War (1865-70), and established many academic and social traditions that survive to this day. The chapel he built is named after him and contains his tomb. The school was re-named one final time (1871) to honor Lee's memory.

Undergraduate majors include economics, history, and business administration/commerce/management. The university has an undergraduate school of commerce and a law school that is coeducational. The South provides 45% of the students, 38% are from Middle Atlantic states, 11% are from New England, 5% are from North Central states. Some 13% of all students pursue graduate study; 7% enter medical school, 14% law school, 4% business school.

Library: 350,000, 1,354 journal subscriptions, 1,000 records/tapes. Faculty: 165. Enrollment: 1,530 total graduate and undergraduate; 1,272 men (full-time). Degrees: Bachelor's.

WASHINGTON UNIVERSITY.

Independent coed university located on a 200-acre campus in St. Louis, Mo. The institution was founded in 1853.

Washington University has ten schools, five of which are for undergraduates: the School of Engineering and Applied Science, College of Arts and Sciences, School of Architecture, School of Business, and School of Fine Arts. Majors include arts and sciences, linguistics, urban studies, women's studies, anthropology, Jewish studies, Latin American studies, black studies, Chinese, dance, drama, and Japanese. The university has a national student body: 27% North Central, 21% Middle Atlantic, 17% South, 23% West. Some 60% of all students pursue full-time graduate study. Washington University ranks among the nation's top 100 producers of medical school entrants, and in the top 50 for developing business executives.

Library: 1,800,000 volumes, 15,000 journal subscriptions. 23,500 records/tapes. Faculty: 2,309. Enrollment: 8,000 total graduate and undergraduate; 2,400 men, 1,600 women (full-time). Degrees: Bachelor's, Master's, Doctorate.

WASHITA RIVER, Tex.

Waterway originating in northwest Texas. It flows east into Oklahoma, through Foss Reservoir, and then turns southwest to drain into the north end of Lake Texoma. It is approximately 450 miles long.

WATAUGA ASSOCIATION.

A pioneer settlement group that founded a community on the banks of the Watauga River, on land leased from the Cherokee Indians, in what they thought to be Virginia (1769). Two years later they discovered their settlement actually fell within the jurisdiction of North Carolina, which refused to provide them with legal protection. In 1772 the association created its own government, drafting the first known written constitution in North America called the *Articles of the Watauga Association.* Led by John BEAN and James ROBERTSON, they established an independent democracy, calling for an executive council, attorney, legislature, and sheriff. In 1776 they were able to send representatives to the North Carolina assembly. The territory was later incorporated as a part of eastern Tennessee. In the 1790s, before Tennessee became a state, this same group of pioneers established the short-lived state of FRANKLIN.

WATAUGA RIVER, Tenn. River originating in northwest North Carolina in the Blue Ridge Mountains. It flows generally northwest to meet the south fork of the Holston River near Kingsport. Settlement along the 60-mile river began in 1768. A 318 foot Tennessee Valley Authority dam (1949) near Elizabethton impounds the river creating the 6,430-acre Lake Watauga.

WATEREE INDIANS ("to float on the water"). Tribe of Siouan linguistic stock that lived on the Wateree River (to which they gave their name) near Camden, S.C. First encountered when they lived further inland, they destroyed an early fort established by the Spanish. A powerful tribe, they aided the colonists against the TUSCARORA INDIANS in 1711. They suffered great losses in the Yamasee War and are thought to have joined the CATAWBA INDIANS in the mid-1700s.

WATEREE RIVER, S.C. River rising in the western North Carolina mountains. It flows south-southeast about 400 miles to meet the Congaree River near Columbia, S.C., to form the Santee River. Its northern end is often referred to as the CATAWBA RIVER. The Catawba and Wateree Dams are on the river.

WATSON, John Broadus (Greenville, S.C., Jan. 9, 1878 — New York, N.Y., Sept. 25, 1958). Psychologist and advertising agent. A graduate of Furman University (1900), he promoted a comprehensive understanding of behaviorist theory, thus altering the course of U.S. psychological thinking by focusing on observed responses to external stimuli rather than introspective analysis. Watson was president of the American Psychological Association (1915). He was a noted educator and author of several influential works, including *Behaviorism* (1925).

WATSON, Thomas Edward (near Thomson, Ga., Sept. 5, 1856 — Washington, D.C., Sept. 26, 1922). Politician and publisher. After serving in the U.S. Congress from Georgia (1891-93), Watson was nominated as the Populist Party candidate for vice president (1896), and was nominated by the Populist Party for president (1904). He published a magazine for many years and authored several books. He was indicted and prosecuted for his attack on Catholicism in *The Roman Catholic Hierarchy* (1910), but was not convicted. He was a U.S. Democratic senator from 1921 until his death.

WATTERSON, Henry (Washington, D.C., Feb. 16, 1840 — Jacksonville, Fla., Dec. 22, 1921). Journalist and editor. He was editor of the *Republican Banner* in Nashville, Tenn., in 1861, and during the Civil War he served under Confederate Generals Nathan Forrest, Leonidas Polk and John Hood, and was chief scout during the Johnston-Sherman Atlanta campaign. After the war, he purchased the Louisivilee, Ky., *Journal,* consolidated it with the *Courier* and served for 50 years as the editor of *Louisville Courier-Journal.* The paper was widely respected in the South for its policies of public service and integrity, but unpopular for its support of conciliation between the states and of currency measures during Reconstruction. He was chiefly responsible for the nomination of Democrat Samuel J. Tilden for the presidency in 1876 and was Tilden's floor leader as Kentucky's representative to Congress (1876-77) during the Tilden-Hayes electoral conflict. Watterson was awarded the Pulitzer Prize in 1918 for a World War I editorial. In 1918 he sold his newspaper holdings, becoming "Editor emeritus," but in 1919 he resigned because of the paper's support of the League of Nations.

WAXHAW INDIANS. Tribe thought to have been of Siouan linguistic stock that lived in North and South Carolina. They joined the Yamasee war and, after their refusal to make peace with the British, were attacked by the CATAWBA INDIANS. Most of the survivors moved to Florida with the Yamasee.

WAYNESBORO, Va. Independent city (pop. 15,329), in the Shenandoah Valley in central Virginia. The city was settled in 1700 and incorporated in 1797. It was the site of a Civil War battle when Gen. Philip Sheridan in command of Union troops defeated Jubal EARLY and 1,000 Confederates on March 2, 1865. An industrial community, its manufactures include electronic equipment, textiles, furniture, and ship fittings. It is the home of Fishburne Military School (1879) and Fairfax Hall, a preparatory school.

WEAPEMEOC INDIANS. Tribe of Algonquian linguistic stock that lived in various areas of North Carolina. They were encountered by the Raleigh colonists in the late 1500s when they are said to have had about 700 warriors. After parting with most of their lands (1662) little is known of them.

WEATHERFORD, William (probably Elmore Co., Ala., c. 1780 — Monroe Co., Ala., Mar. 9, 1824). Indian chief. Known as Red Eagle, he was a leader in the Creek Indian Wars (1813-14) opposing Gen. Andrew Jackson. Weatherford conducted the slaughter of hundreds in an attack on Fort Mims (1813), and was one of the chiefs at the defeat of the Creeks at Horseshoe Bend (1814) that ended the war.

WEAVER, Robert Clifton (Washington, D.C., Dec. 29, 1907 —). Statesman. The great-grandson of a slave, Weaver put himself through Harvard, working as an electrician. He received a B.S. in economics (1929), an M.A. two years later, and a Ph.D in 1934, after which he took a position with the Department of Interior. Under President Franklin Roosevelt he was an advisor on housing and unemployment, moving into war mobilization in the 1940s. Weaver was president of the National Association for the Advancement of Colored People, and in 1961 he was appointed by President John Kennedy to run the Housing and Home Finance Agency. In 1966 President Lyndon Johnson recommended him to head the newly-formed Department of Housing and Urban Development.

WEBB, Walter Prescott (Panola Co., Tex., Apr. 3, 1888 — Austin, Tex., Mar. 8, 1963). Historian. A year after earning his Ph.D. at the University of Texas (1932), Webb became a full professor there. A distinguished scholar and speaker, Webb wrote more than 20 books about the history of America's West, including *The Great Plains* (1931) and *The Handbook of Texas* (1937).

WEEMS, Mason Locke (Anne Arundel Co., Md., Oct. 11, 1759 — Beaufort, S.C., May 23, 1825). Clergyman and author. Weems was ordained an Episcopal minister in 1784 after a European education. He became a traveling book agent in 1794 and was also the author of several books. Best known among his works is *The Life and Memorable Actions of George Washington* (1800).

WELTY, Eudora (Jackson, Miss., Apr. 13, 1909 —). Short story writer. Educated at Mississippi State College for Women and the University of Wisconsin, Welty studied advertising at Columbia University in New York City and originally planned to become a commercial artist. She began writing short stories and her first collection, *A Curtain of Green* (1941), was such a popular success that it enabled her to write full time in her hometown. A regional writer, she is noted for the colloquial accuracy of her dialogue and for her comically understated presentation of absurd rural events. She is the author of the novels *Delta Wedding* (1946) and *The Optimist's Daughter* (1972), as well as collections of short stories including *The Wide Net* (1943), *The Golden Apples* (1949), and *Thirteen Stories* (1965).

WERTENBAKER, Thomas Jefferson (Charlottesville, Va., Feb. 6, 1879 — Princeton, N.J., Apr. 22, 1966). Historian. A history professor, he taught at the Agricultural & Mechanical College of Texas, the University of Virginia, and Princeton University. Wertenbaker was a noted Virginia historian, particularly of the colonial period, and wrote numerous volumes on the subject. His most noted work was *The Shaping of Colonial Virginia* (1958).

WESLEYAN COLLEGE. Church-related women's liberal arts college located on a 240-acre campus in Macon, Ga., 85 miles south of Atlanta. Affiliated with the United Methodist Church, Wesleyan was founded in 1836. It is the world's oldest college chartered to grant degrees to women.

Majors include the arts and sciences, theater, teacher education, and business administration. The South provided 92% of the students and

50% are state residents; 25% of students pursue full-time graduate school.

Library: 113,000 volumes, 3,202 microform titles, 471 journal subscriptions, 4,811 records/tapes. Faculty: 60. Enrollment: 354 women (full-time). Degrees: Bachelor's.

WEST, Sir Thomas See DE LA WARR, Thomas West, Baron.

WEST PALM BEACH, Fla. City (pop. 62,530), seat of Palm Beach Co., in southeastern Florida on Lake Worth. A deep-water port of entry, it is opposite Palm Beach and is connected to it by bridges. Its canal extends to Lake Okechobee. The city was developed by financier Henry M. FLAGLER in 1893 and was incorporated in 1894. Today it is a center for research and production in electronic components, and manufactures include concrete and aluminum products, data processing systems, and aircraft engines. Norton Gallery and School of Art as well as an agricultural college are found here.

WEST VIRGINIA. The northernmost state in the Southern region, it is extremely irregular in shape because it is defined almost entirely by river and mountain ridge boundaries. Its longest border is with Virginia to the southeast across the ridge line of the Allegheny and Shenandoah Mountains. West Virginia also has a 100-mile panhandle on the south bank of the Potomac River that extends eastward between Virginia and Maryland. The central northern border is with Pennsylvania, and West Virginia also has a northern panhandle on the east bank of the Ohio River that extends 75 miles between Pennsylvania and Ohio. To the northwest the state borders Ohio across the Ohio River, and to the southwest it borders Kentucky across the Tug Fork and Big Sandy Rivers.

In many ways West Virginia is an anomaly among the Southern states. Geographically, it includes lands in its upper panhandle that lie further north than Pittsburgh, Pa. Topographically, it faces the Great Lakes region because it is effectively isolated from the South by the mountains of its Virginia border. Economically, too, West Virginia has more in common with the Great Lakes states than with the South because its principal industries have always been mining and manufacturing rather than agriculture.

However, the settlement and history of West Virginia are inseparable from those of the South. This was the great trans-Allegheny region of Virginia, settled when farmers landed on its eastern plantation lands and moved inland in search of arable plots of their own. In the years before and after the American Revolution these farmers, many of them of Welsh and Scottish descent, moved across the mountains to the state's central river valleys. They thus isolated themselves from Virginia's plantation society, and with the advent of the Civil War they found themselves in opposition to the secessionist sympathies of the plantation owners. During the war these western counties of Virginia voted to separate themselves from the mother state, and West Virginia was admitted to the Union as the 35th state on June 20, 1863.

The lands of West Virginia lie on the western slope of the Appalachian Mountains. West Virginia has the highest average elevation of any state east of the Mississippi River, and its topography is so rugged that the state has no large natural lakes. Its eastern half is highest in elevation, with numerous mountain ranges running southwest to northeast and separated by steep river valleys. These Allegheny and Shenandoah ranges include the high point in the state at Spruce Knob (4,862 feet) near the midpoint of the Virginia border. From these mountains the state's principal rivers flow west and north across a region of the Great Appalachian Plateau. This eastern half of the state is equally rugged if lower in elevation, with numerous rocky gorges turning rivers into rapids and waterfalls. These rivers all follow meandering courses toward the Ohio River, with the largest being the Kanawha flowing across the southern portion of West Virginia and the Monongahela flowing northward from the center of the state toward Pittsburgh. Because these lands are isolated from the ocean by the eastern mountains and subject to Canadian winds from across the Great Lakes, West Virginia has a harsher climate than any other Southern state. It has recorded temperatures of −12 degrees F. and has an average annual rainfall of 31 inches.

West Virginia was never populated by large groups of Indians, serving instead as a battleground and hunting ground for tribes on neighboring lands. The Adena and Hopewell tribes, in particular, have left evidence of their visits in the form of burial mounds located in the northern panhandle and in the Kanawha valley. The earliest exploration by Europeans was launched from what is now Petersburg, Va., by Abraham WOOD in 1671. He funded an expedition inland led by Thomas Batts and Robert Fallam in search of a river route to the "South Seas" presumed to be somewhat nearer than the Pacific

Ocean proved to be. Other expeditions followed, and in 1716 the governor of Virginia Alexander SPOTSWOOD crossed the Blue Ridge Mountains in Virginia, camped at the base of the Alleghenies on what is now the West Virginia border, and claimed what lay further west as part of Virginia. Further explorations to what is now West Virginia were made by the French from Canada along the Ohio River, and other English traders inland along the Potomac. The first documented permanent settlement, however, was not made until 1726, when the Welshman Morgan MORGAN established a homestead on Berkeley Creek in what is now SHEPARDSTOWN in the eastern panhandle.

The legal rights to West Virginia's lands were at that time a matter of some confusion. The eastern panhandle fell under a grant to English Lord FAIRFAX as the "Northern Neck" of his plantation, but there was little agreement about the inland limit of this grant. In 1746 a marker was placed at the head of the north fork of the Potomac River as the limit of Fairfax's grant, which was then surveyed by George Washington. Meanwhile, the French had laid claim to the entire Ohio River Valley, and in response to this George II of England deeded the lands between the Ohio and Monongahela Rivers to his own Ohio Company in 1649. After the English prevailed in the French and Indian War, Virginia successfully negotiated a treaty with the Indians for the territory west of the Alleghenies in 1768. Relations with the Indians were never peaceful, and they were only resolved by combat when the English defeated the Indians at Point Pleasant in Lord Dunsmore's War of 1774. In the meantime, Charles Washington, half-brother of George, had laid out Charles Town in the eastern panhandle in 1768.

During the American Revolution, by which time small farmers had settled on river valley lands across West Virginia's Appalachian Plateau, Virginia's western and eastern counties provided volunteers for the Continental Army. But in 1776 the western counties petitioned the Continental Congress to establish a separate state west of the Alleghenies to be called Westsylvania. The issue at that time was not slavery but unequal representation in the state legislature and state links with the Anglican church that were unpopular with the Welsh and Scottish farmers of the western counties. This petition was ignored, but the western counties continued to press their claims in the Virginia constitutional conventions of 1829 and 1850. Political power still resided in the east and dis-

satisfactions of the western counties became more vocal with the development of their abolitionist movements. John Brown's raid on HARPERS FERRY in the eastern panhandle in 1859 and subsequent execution in Charles Town had great local as well as national political repercussions. In 1861 delegates from the western counties gathered at WHEELING in the northern panhandle, voided the Virginia act of secession, and declared their own independence from that state. The Union, eager for such an ally in the Civil War, conditionally admitted West Virginia to the union in 1862, and formalized the admission the following year after amendments for the abolition of slavery had been introduced into the state constitution. The state was thus "war-born" in the political sense, but its hardships during the Civil War were for the most part limited to sporadic raids and minor, if strategic, battles.

At the end of the Civil War, West Virginia was an undeveloped and rural state with a population of only about 400,000, or about one-third that of contemporary Virginia. After the war, urban centers began to develop with the growth of the state's mining industry and spread of its rail links. It was at this time that ties with the Great Lakes states began to prevail over those with the South. Wheeling, on the Ohio border, was the first state capital, and in 1870 the capital was moved to CHARLESTON, which was a center of trade with Ohio 45 miles downstream on the Kanawha River. The capital was moved back to Wheeling in 1877, and then finally fixed in Charleston in 1885. Today Charleston is the largest city in the state and the center of its chemicals industry as well as state government. The other large cities in the state are located along the Ohio River and have metropolitan areas that cross state borders. HUNTINGTON is a river port and coal town along the southern part of the Ohio border; its metropolitan area of some 311,350 residents includes the cities of Ashland, Ky., and Ironton, Ohio. Wheeling is now the third-largest city in the state; it is a steel center known as the commercial hub of the Ohio Valley, and its metropolitan area includes many residents of Ohio. There are no major cities in the eastern half of the state, and this expanse of small mountain towns makes West Virginia the most rural state in the country with the exception of Vermont.

The population of West Virginia has changed with the fortunes of its coal industry. The total population figure stood at 2 million in 1950, but over the next two decades market preferences for oil and natural gas over coal led

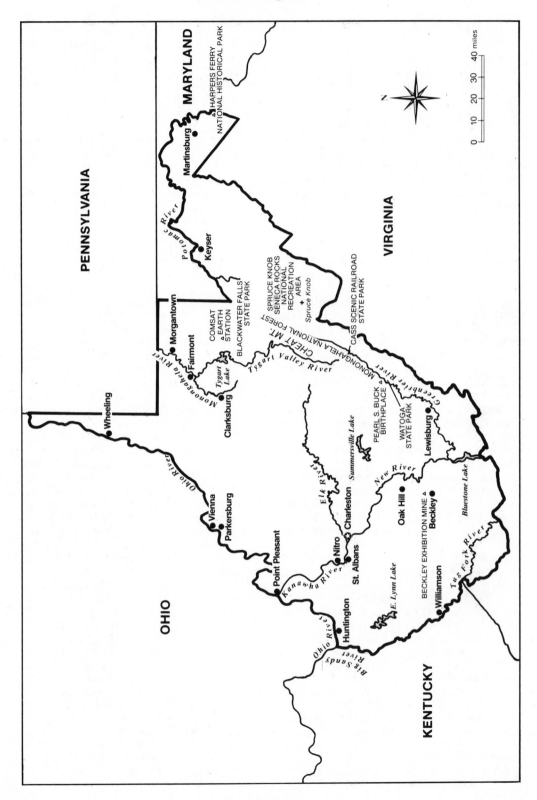

STATE OF WEST VIRGINIA

Name: For Elizabeth I (1533-1603), Queen of England (1558-1603), "the Virgin Queen." Took the designation "West" when it separated from Virginia in 1863.

Nickname: Mountain State, Panhandle State, Switzerland of America.

Motto: *Montani Semper Liberi* (Mountaineers Are Always Free).

Capital: Charleston.

Counties: 55. **Places over 10,000 population (1980):** 15.

Symbols & Emblems: *Flower:* Big Rhododendron. *Bird:* Cardinal. *Tree:* Sugar Maple. *Song:* "The West Virginia Hills," "This Is My West Virginia," "West Virginia, My Home, Sweet Home."

Population (1980): 1,949,644. **Rank:** 34th.

Population Density (1980): 80.8 people per sq. mi. **Rank:** 25th.

Racial Make-up (1980): *White:* 1,874,751 (96.2%). *Black:* 65,051 (3.3%). *American Indian:* 1,610 (0.1%). *Asian & Pacific Islander:* 5,194 (0.3%). *Other:* 3,038 (0.2%). *Spanish Origin:* 12,707 (0.7%).

Largest City (pop. 1980): Charleston (63,968). *Others:* Huntington (63,684), Wheeling (43,070), Parkersburg (39,967), Morgantown (2?,605), Weirton (24,736), Fairmont (23,863), Clarksburg (22,371), Beckley (20,492).

Area: 24,119 sq. mi. **Rank:** 41st.

Highest Point: Spruce Knob (4,863 ft.), Pendleton Co.

Lowest Point: Potomac River (240 ft.), Jefferson Co.

State Government:

ELECTED OFFICIALS (4-year terms expiring Jan. 1985, etc.): *Governor* ($72,000); No *Lt. Governor; Sec. of State* ($43,200); *Attorney General* ($50,400); *Treasurer* ($50,400).

GENERAL ASSEMBLY (Salary: $5,136 plus $50 per diem living expense allowance and $35 per diem for special sessions.): *Senate* (34 members), *House of Representatives* (100 members).

CONGRESSIONAL REPRESENTATIVES: *Senate* (terms expire 1985, 1989, etc.). *House of Representatives* (4 members).

Admitted to the Union: June 20, 1863 (35th state).

to one of the great population declines in modern U.S. history. In the 1950s and the 1960s West Virginia endured a net population loss of more than 250,000 persons, and by 1980 the total population had not yet returned to the 1950 level. The current population pattern, however, is one of limited growth, with a percentage increase that equaled the national average and even had a slight gain of residents from net migration changes. The state population is a very stable one, with 70% of the population being life-long residents of West Virginia and minority proportions of 3% black and 1% Hispanic that have changed little in recent years. The state's economic recovery from the decline of coal mining in the 1950s and 1960s has also been steady, if slow. West Virginia now ranks 45th among U.S. states in per capita income.

In the early 20th century, when West Virginia developed its mineral industry and saw its population gravitate to mining company towns, the state ranked first in the U.S. in bituminous coal production and high in yield of crude oil and natural gas. These mineral industries have suffered from competition from other states and bitter internal labor battles in the years since, but mining is still the leading industry in West Virginia. The state now ranks 7th in the

Coal barges approaching the capitol in Charleston, W. Va.

country in total mineral output, second only to Kentucky in bituminous coal, and high in oil and natural gas production and stone quarrying. The state's manufacturing sector is heavily dependent on this local mineral production and on raw materials shipped in from the Great Lakes region. Steel and fabricated metals are the principal heavy industries, and a great deal of manufacturing activity is also based on glass, chemical, textile, and plastic products. Timber and wood products are also an important industry in the eastern Appalachian regions of the state, and dairy farming is important to the areas on the western plateau. West Virginia's tourism industry generated $1.2 billion in 1981, with most visitors to the state being attracted to the parks and forests of the eastern mountains.

WEST VIRGINIA UNIVERSITY. State-supported coed university located in the city of Morgantown, W.Va., 70 miles south of Pittsburgh, Pa. Chartered as the Agricultural College of West Virginia in 1867, the present-day university has three closely linked campuses totaling 475 acres, plus 11,000 additional acres in six West Virginia counties. Also under its control is the two-year Potomac State College at Keyser and the Kanawha Valley Graduate Center.

The university offers the Colleges of Engineering, Mineral and Energy Resources, Arts and Sciences, Agriculture, and Forestry. Other schools and colleges open to undergraduates are the Creative Arts Center, College of Business and Economics, School of Journalism, and the upper division College of Human Resources and Education. There are numerous graduate programs. The North Central states provide 61% of the students and 35% are from Middle Atlantic states.

Library: 961,828 volumes, 774,334 microform titles, 9,425 journal subscriptions, 13,532 records/tapes. Faculty: 2,043. Enrollment: 21,220 total graduate and undergraduate; 7,802 men, 5,677 women (full-time). Degrees: Bachelor's, Master's, Doctorate.

WHEAT. Cereal grass cultivated since prehistoric times and brought to North America by European settlers. It is grown throughout the South, but for reasons of soil and climate the leading wheat states, "the breadbasket of America," are those to the northwest on the Great Plains.

In 1980 Kansas harvested 420 million bushels of wheat, three times more than any other state. By comparison, the leading wheat-growing state in the South is Texas, with a 1980 harvest of 130 million bushels worth $487 million. The second most important wheat producer in the South is Missouri, which harvested 89 million bushels in 1980. Most of the other Southern states harvest wheat, but none of them has an annual yield in excess of 50 million bushels.

WHEELER, Joseph (Augusta, Ga., Sept. 10, 1836 — Brooklyn, N.Y., Jan. 25, 1906). Military officer and politician. he was a lieutenant general in the Confederate Army during the Chattanooga campaign, and opposed Gen. William T. Sherman in the Atlanta campaign. Wheeler was a delegate to Congress from Alabama (1881-83, 1885-1900), and later led a brigade in the Philippine insurrection.

WHEELING, W.Va. City (pop. 43,070), seat of Ohio Co., on the Ohio River in West Virginia's northern panhandle. An industrial city, Wheeling manufactures iron, steel, sheet metal, glass, and tobacco products. It was originally settled by the Zane family (1769), ancestors of the novelist of the west, Zane Grey, and called Zanesburg. Among Grey's novels was *Betty Zane*, about his family's involvement in the Revolutionary War battle at Fort Henry. Incorporated in 1806 as Wheeling, the name Wheeling is believed to have evolved from an Indian word meaning "place of the head," which referred to scalping incidents here.

Wheeling's expansion was due, in part, to its transportation assets. It served as a port of entry; it was the western terminus of the Cumberland Road; and the Baltimore and Ohio Railroad reached the city in 1852. It also became an educational center with nearby West Liberty State College, (1837), Bethany College (1840) and Wheeling College (1954). In 1861, Wheeling served as the seat of government of the state of Virginia, and in 1861-62, it hosted the Wheeling Conventions, which led to the creation of the state of West Virginia in 1863. Wheeling was the state capital for two periods (1863-70; 1875-85).

WHISKEY REBELLION. Rebellion against a federal excise tax on domestic spirits. Also referred to as the Whiskey Insurrection, the tax was enacted by Congress (1791) as a means of raising revenue, and it was particularly unpopular in the whiskey producing states of Pennsylvania, Virginia, and North Carolina. The insurrection culminated in western Pennsylvania (1794) but was suppressed by 15,000 federal troops sent by President George Washington. Although the rebellion cost the government $1.5 million, it was instrumental in proving that the new government could enforce its laws.

WHITE, Clarence Cameron (Clarksville, Tenn., Aug. 10, 1880 — New York, N.Y., June 30, 1960). Black composer and violinist. After studying at the Oberlin Conservatory and in Europe, White taught in Boston and New York before becoming the director of music at West Virginia State College and Hampton Institute. His 1932 opera *Ouanga* won the David Bispham award.

WHITE, Eartha Mary Magdalene (Jacksonville, Fla., Nov. 8, 1876 — Jacksonville, Fla., Jan. 18, 1974). Social and community activist. After schooling in New York City, she returned south and started several successful businesses (1905-30). In 1900 she joined BOOKER T. WASHINGTON to found the National Negro Business League. In 1928 she founded the Clara White Mission, a community house that became the focus of black relief work and a WPA headquarters during the Great Depression. Her work in organizing the proposed 1941 march on Washington led to Presidential Order 8802 banning discrimination in federal hiring for defense and government. In 1967 White founded the Eartha M. White Nursing Home.

WHITE, Edward Douglass (nr. Lafourche Parish, La., Nov. 3, 1845 — Washington, D.C., May 19, 1921). Politician and jurist. White received a Roman Catholic Jesuit education before fighting briefly with the Confederate Army during the Civil War. He was then trained in a New Orleans law office, elected Democratic state senator (1874-78), was appointed to the state supreme court (1879-80), and was elected to the U.S. Senate (1891-94). President Grover Cleveland appointed him to the U.S. Supreme Court in 1894 and President William Howard Taft appointed him the ninth chief justice in 1910, and he served until his death. His major contribution to U.S. jurisprudence was his establishment of the idea that restraint of trade by a monopolistic business must be "unreasonable" to be illegal under the Sherman Anti-Trust Act of 1890 (1911). His failure to adequately define "reasonable" restraint laid many anti-trust decisions open to wide interpretation.

WHITE, Hugh Lawson (Iredell Co., N.C., Oct. 30, 1773 — Knoxville, Tenn., Apr. 10, 1840). Politician and jurist. A practicing Knoxville attorney, White was appointed judge of the Superior Court of Tennessee (1801-07), elected to the state senate (1807-09), and became U.S attorney for the Eastern District of Tennessee (1808). In 1812 White was president of the Bank of the State of Tennessee and was again a state senator (1817-25). He was elected to the U.S. Senate (1825-40) to fill the vacancy left by Andrew Jackson. A supporter of Jacksonian policies, he split with Jackson when the president backed Martin Van Buren for the presidency rather than White himself. He resigned from the Senate in a dispute with Van Buren over the Independent Treasury System.

WHITE, John (England, fl. 1585-93). Artist and colonial governor. In 1585 he was commissioned by Sir Walter Raleigh to explore Roanoke Island, now part of North Carolina, and provide illustrations of the topography along with paintings to stimulate exploration. Two years later Raleigh appointed him governor of his second colony of the island and upon his return, which was delayed until 1591, he found that the first colony had disappeared. Virginia Dare, the first child of English parents born in the new world, was his granddaughter.

WHITE, Walter Francis (Atlanta, Ga., July 1, 1893 — New York, N.Y., Mar. 21, 1955). Black leader and author. White was a strong force in the promotion of racial justice in the U.S. as described in his autobiography *A Man Called White* (1948). His other books include *Fire in the Flint* (1924), *Flight* (1926), *A Rising Wind* (1945), and *How Far the Promised Land* (1955). He was secretary of the National Association for the Advancement of Colored People (1931-55).

WHITING, William Henry Chase (Biloxi, Miss., Mar. 22, 1824 — Governor's Island, N.Y., Mar. 10, 1865). Military officer. Whiting joined the army after graduating from West Point in 1845. He resigned at the outbreak of the Civil War to join the Confederate army and served with distinction at the first battle of Bull Run in the peninsular campaign, and at Fort Fisher where he was wounded and captured. He died a prisoner of war.

WHITNEY, Eli (Westborough, Mass., Dec. 8, 1765 — New Haven, Conn., Jan. 8, 1825).

Slaves operating Eli Whitney's cotton gin that was invented in 1793

Inventor. A graduate of Yale (1792), Whitney moved to Georgia and became a tutor on a cotton plantation. He observed the slow, expensive process of hand-removing seeds from short-staple cotton (long-staple cotton had smooth seeds, which were easily removed by existing cotton gins). In 1793 Whitney was encouraged to develop a gin that would work equally well on both types of cotton. Within two weeks he had completed his machine, which was based on a cylinder with wire teeth, but it was stolen from his workshop, allowing others to copy it before he had patented it. The gin revolutionized the cotton industry, but Whitney spent much time and money in lawsuits defending himself against others who claimed the invention. Although his claim to the patent was finally awarded in 1807, he profited little. Because of his gin, cotton production rose from 138,000 pounds in 1792 to 35,000,000 pounds in 1800. In 1798 Whitney established a factory near New Haven (now called Whitneyville), Conn., to manufacture firearms. He employed the use of interchangeable parts and division of labor that was an early step toward mass production.

WICHITA FALLS, Tex. City (pop. 101,724), seat of Wichita Co., on the Wichita River in northern Texas, 100 miles northwest of Fort Worth. The city was named for a small falls in the midst of Wichita Indian territory. It was founded in the 1870s and became a cattle shipping center with the introduction of rail lines, a petroleum center with the discovery of oil (1900), and an agricultural center with the introduction of irrigation. Its products include cattle, wheat, cotton, and fruit. Wichita Falls is the home of Midwestern University (1922), a city owned and administered school.

WILDERNESS, Battle of. Civil War engagement fought May 5-6, 1864, in north central Virginia south of the Rapidan River. Considered one of the bloodiest battles of the war, it was won at great cost by the North. In this battle the Union army, recently placed under the command of Gen. Ulysses S. GRANT, finally broke the control over central Virginia held by Gen. Robert E. LEE since the opening of the war.

Grant's command was led in the field by Gen. George Meade, who crossed the Rapidan River on May 3. Lee, who was defensively entrenched in the rugged, forested "wilderness" south of the river, was expected to retreat rather than engage more than 100,000 men in the Army of the Potomac with his own force of 60,000. Due to the terrain, neither side was sure of the other's position until an accidental encounter opened the battle on May 5. The South was driven back on the first day of the battle, but it regained some ground on May 6 by counterattacks led by Gen. James LONGSTREET and Gen. Richard EWELL. Brushfires, lighted to cover these attacks, later went out of control and burned or suffocated soldiers on both sides.

The Union army lost 18,000 men in the battle, more than twice the loss of the South, but the Union had gained an edge in the maneuvering toward SPOTSYLVANIA and COLD HARBOR, where fighting was immediately renewed.

WILDERNESS ROAD. An early 18th-century route used by pioneers, which ran from the Shenandoah Valley in Virginia to Fort Watauga in eastern Tennessee. This route of westward migration was furthered by Daniel BOONE in 1775 when he took it through the Cumberland Gap into Kentucky. As travel on the Wilderness Road increased, tolls were instituted in 1797. Today it is a part of U.S. Route 25.

WILKINSON, James (Calvert Co., Maryland, 1757 — Mexico City, Dec. 28, 1825). Military officer and adventurer. After serving under Gen. Horatio Gates in the Revolutionary War, Wilkinson moved to Kentucky (1784) becoming an agent for Spain attempting to bring the western settlements under the Louisiana authority. At the same time, he worked for the American government against Spain gaining a lieutenant colonel's commission in 1791. In 1803 Wilkinson was one of the commissioners who received control of Louisiana from France, and he became governor of the territory above the 33rd parallel in 1805. In his double

capacity, he worked to conquer the Mexican provinces of Spain, and, with Aaron Burr, sent Zebulon Pike to explore the most favorable route for the conquest (1806). He then betrayed Burr's plan to President Thomas Jefferson, reached an agreement with Spain to neutralize Texas, placed New Orleans under martial law, and arrested Burr. Burr was tried for treason but released due to lack of evidence, and Wilkinson was the subject of several investigations. His career ended dishonorably after he made a fiasco of the campaign against Montreal during the War of 1812. He wrote *Memoirs of My Own Times* (1816).

WILLIAM AND MARY, College of. State-supported coed institution of graduate and undergraduate study located on a 1,200-acre campus in Williamsburg, Va.

The College of William and Mary is second only to Harvard as the oldest place of higher education in America. It was chartered in 1693 and named after the British monarchs, William III and Mary II, who shared the throne. Originally tied to the Church of England, William and Mary became nonsectarian in 1799. It is noted for having the first academic honor codes and the first Phi Beta Kappa Society.

In addition to the traditional liberal arts curriculum, there are graduate courses in business, education, and law, and a number of pre-professional programs. There is one branch campus at Petersburg. Students are primarily state residents.

Library: 660,000 volumes, 3,000 periodicals, 360,000 microfilms. Faculty: 475. Enrollment: 6,500 (50% male; 20% graduate). Degrees: Bachelor's, Master's.

WILLIAMS, John Bell (Raymond, Miss., Dec. 4, 1918 —). Politician. Admitted to the bar in 1940, Williams postponed his law career to enter the U.S. Army as an aviation cadet during World War II. He was commissioned a pilot and was the sole survivor of a five-man crew that went down in South America in 1943. He was appointed a county prosecuting attorney in Mississippi (1944-46), elected as a Democrat to Congress (1947-68), and was governor of Mississippi (1968-73).

WILLIAMS, Tennessee [Thomas Lanier Williams] (Columbus, Miss., Mar. 26, 1911 — New York, N.Y., Feb. 25, 1983). Playwright. Considered one of the greatest American playwrights, Williams twice won the Pulitzer Prize for *A Streetcar Named Desire* (1947) and *Cat on* *a Hot Tin Roof* (1955). His tense, highly dramatic plays were largely based on Southern life. Other successful plays include *The Glass Menagerie* (1944) and *Night of the Iguana* (1961). Williams also wrote one novel *The Roman Spring of Mrs. Stone* (1950), along with short stories, poetry, and one-act plays.

WILLIAMS, William Sherley (Rutherford Co., N.C., 1787 — Santa Fe Trail, Mar., 1849). Preacher, trapper, and explorer. Called "Old Bill" Williams, he was the guide for John Charles Fremont's fourth expedition West (1848). Against Williams' advice, Fremont led the party toward the headwaters of the Rio Grande River where most of them died of exposure and starvation. Falsely blamed for the error by Fremont, Williams was killed by Ute Indians while reexploring the route.

WILLIAMSBURG, Va. City (pop. 9,870), seat of James City Co., located between the York and James Rivers on a tidewater peninsula in southeastern Virginia. Williamsburg is world famous as a living museum of 18th-century Virginia life and architecture, due largely to the financial help and efforts of phi-

Reconstructed colonial capitol in Williamsburg, Va., where the House of Burgesses first met

lanthropist John D. Rockefeller. At the request of the Rev. William A. R. Goodwin, Rockefeller employed teams of archeologists, craftsmen, and artists, in the 1920s and 1930s, to restore or reconstruct sections of Williamsburg to its pre-Revolutionary days. After a great deal of research and restoration, Colonial Williamsburg was opened to the public in the early 1930s.

Originally settled as Middle Plantation (1632), the community was renamed Williamsburg in 1699 in honor of William II and made the capital of the Virginia colony. George Washington, George Mason, Patrick Henry, and Thomas Jefferson, among others, spent a great deal of time here in state government. Williamsburg was the site of Virginia's first theatre, printing press, newspaper, and paper mill. Incorporated as a city in 1722, the state capital was moved to Richmond in 1780 and Williamsburg became a quiet town until restoration began in the 1920s. Although the city's economy is primarily based on tourism, there is also some light manufacturing. The College of William and Mary was established here in 1693.

WILLIAMSON'S PLANTATION, Battle of. Revolutionary War engagement fought along the Catawba River north of Camden, S.C., on July 12, 1780. A victory for the gathering patriotic militia, it was most important for encouraging enlistment in the Revolutionary army by South Carolinians.

The battle was provoked by looting condoned by Loyalist Capt. Christian Huck in the plantations of what is now Brattonville, S.C. Huck's troops camped for the night at Williamson's Plantation, and they were surprised at reveille on July 12 by the fire of 500 patriotic troops. Huck had camped between rail fences, thus trapping them, and he was himself mortally wounded in the battle.

WILMINGTON, N.C. City (pop. 46,169), seat of New Hanover Co., in southeast North Carolina near the Atlantic coast. Located on the Cape Fear River about 30 miles from its mouth, Wilmington is a port of entry and the major seaport of North Carolina. Settled in 1730, it was the site of the first armed resistance to the Stamp Act of 1765, and was also the site of the Battle of Moore's Creek Bridge, a British effort to divide and conquer the colonies, in February, 1776. It was a blockade-running port in the Civil War and was the last Confederate port to close, remaining open until the fall of Fort Fisher on January 15, 1865. Incorporated in 1866, the city suffered severe hurricane damage in the early 1900s, recovering financially through its shipping, truck farming, and textile manufacturing. The U.S. *North Carolina* Battleship Memorial of World War II is moored on the river. Today it is a commercial center with a large export trade. Manufactures include heavy machinery, lumber products, electronics, and nuclear fuel.

WILSON, Harold Albert (York, England, Dec. 1, 1874 — Houston, Tex., Oct. 13, 1964). Physicist and educator. Educated in England, he taught in London, Montreal, and Glasgow before taking a professorship at the Rice Institute in Houston (1912-47). He achieved fame for his verification of the electromagnetic equations of such forebearers as Albert Einstein. His books include *The Mysteries of the Atom: Electricity* (1934).

WILSON, William Lyne (West Virginia, May 3, 1843 — Lexington, Va., Oct. 17, 1900). Politician and educator. He served in the Civil War as a private in the 12th Virginia Cavalry, studied law and was admitted to the bar in 1869, later practicing in Charleston, W.Va. From 1882 to 1883 he was president of the University of West Virginia. A Democratic congressman from W.Va. (1883-95), he became chairman of the Ways and Means committee (1893) and in this capacity introduced the tariff bill that bears his name, which was adopted in 1894. As Postmaster General (1895-97) he was instrumental in the establishment of rural free delivery service. He was later president of Washington and Lee University (1897-1900).

WILSON, Woodrow (Staunton, Va., Dec. 28, 1856 — Washington, D.C., Feb. 3, 1924). Educator, governor of New Jersey, and 28th President of the United States. The son of a Presbyterian minister, the future president was named Thomas Woodrow Wilson at birth. He moved with his family from Virginia to Georgia, South Carolina, and North Carolina in his youth, and first attended college at Davidson in North Carolina in 1873. The bulk of his undergraduate education, however, took place at Princeton, where he was granted the A.B. degree in 1879. Wilson then returned to the South to study law at the University of Virginia, to practice law in Atlanta, Ga., and finally to study history and political science at Johns Hopkins University in Baltimore, Md., where he was awarded the Ph.D. in 1886. After brief teaching appointments at Bryn Mawr College

in Pennsylvania and Wesleyan University in Connecticut, he accepted a full professorship of jurisprudence and political science at Princeton, where he remained until 1910.

An influential writer in his field and on educational subjects, Wilson became president of Princeton in 1902. His knowledge of political theory naturally led to ambitions for practical political influence, and in 1910 he resigned from the university and successfully ran for the governorship of New Jersey as a Democrat. Only two years later, in 1912, he became the Democratic nominee for president on the basis of support from William Jennings Bryan and won the general election when dissention between supporters of Theodore Roosevelt and William Howard Taft split the Republican party.

Reelected by a slight margin in 1916, Wilson oversaw the American involvement in World War I. He reluctantly asked Congress to declare war on Germany on April 2, 1917, which it did on April 6. In 1918 Wilson formulated the famous "Fourteen Points" he thought would make the world "safe for democracy." Peace came with the Treaty of Versailles on January 18, 1919, and because this was negotiated according to Wilson's formulations he was awarded the Nobel Peace Prize in that year. The treaty included establishment of a League of Nations, but this was not ratified in the U.S. Senate because it lacked a clause to guarantee U.S. supremacy on war votes. Wilson launched a concentrated campaign to secure ratification of the League of Nations idea, but it failed to sway the Senate.

WINCHESTER, Battle of. Three important Civil War battles occurred at Winchester, Frederick Co., in the northernmost tip of Virginia. The first and most important was Confederate Gen. Stonewall JACKSON'S defeat of Union Gen. Nathaniel P. Banks on May 25, 1862. The second occurred during the Confederate advance toward GETTYSBURG on June 13-15, 1863. The third was a Union victory under Gen. Philip Sheridan on Sept. 19, 1864.

The first battle of Winchester was part of Stonewall Jackson's effective harrassment of Union forces in the Shenandoah Valley. Union Gen. Banks was in retreat from Strasburg to Winchester after Jackson's victory at Front Royal on May 23. Jackson, whose troops were close to exhaustion from the chase, attacked the fleeing Union army at Winchester at dawn on May 25. By 7:30 A.M. they were in complete control of the field. A final attack then drove

the Union line into disorderly retreat. However, because of the condition of his troops,
Jackson was unable to capitalize immediately
on the victory.

The second battle of Winchester occurred
during the Confederate advance north to Gettysburg in 1863. On June 13 the Confederate
Army, under Gen. Richard S. EWELL, isolated
the central Union defense of the town, bombarded it with artillery, and then advanced with
both cavalry and infantry. Union losses in dead,
wounded, and captured amounted to nearly
4,500, while Ewell lost a mere 250 men.

The third battle of Winchester was a Union
victory at the outset of Sheridan's Shenandoah
campaign in response to Gen. Jubal EARLY'S
Washington raid. Early assumed that Sheridan's orders were to maintain a defensive posture, but Sheridan had persuaded Union Commander Gen. Ulysses S. GRANT to launch an
outright offensive. On September 19, 1864,
Sheridan attacked Early, who fought valiantly
in Winchester before ordering a retreat toward
Strasburg that brought him to the Battle of
FISHERS HILL on September 22.

WINSLOW, John Ancrum (Wilmington,
N.C., Nov. 19, 1811 — Boston, Mass., Sept. 29,
1873). Naval officer. He commanded the Union
Kearsage in the combat against Confederate
cruisers off the European coast (1863-64) and
sank the raider *Alabama* near Cherbourg in one
of the outstanding naval contests of the Civil
War. Winslow was promoted to commodore
and later commanded the Gulf Squadron
(1866-67) and the Pacific Squadron (1870-72).

WINSTON-SALEM, N.C. City (pop.
131,885), seat of Forsyth Co., in central North
Carolina on the Piedmont Plateau. The city
was created in 1913 from two adjacent cities,
Winston and Salem. Winston was founded in
1849 and named for John Winston, a Revolutionary soldier. Salem was laid out in 1766 by
Moravian colonists in the center of their Wa-
chovia land tract. With WEST HIGH POINT and
GREENSBORO, Winston-Salem forms a tri-city
industrial area. Along with being a major
bright leaf tobacco market, diversified industries produce textiles, beer, furniture, tobacco
products, and electrical equipment. Wake Forest University, Salem College, Bowman Gray
School of Medicine, Winston-Salem State College, and the Piedmont Bible College are
located in the city. Old Salem, a replica of the
original settlement, is the site of an annual
Moravian Easter Sunrise Service.

WINYAW INDIANS. Tribe of Siouan linguistic stock that lived in South Carolina on the
Pee Dee River on Winyaw Bay (to which they
gave their name). Hostile relations with the
early colonists, which came about after a number of the tribe were taken as slaves, did not de-
ter them from aiding the settlers in the first TUS-
CARORA War. They are thought to have
eventually united with the WACCAMAW INDIANS.

WIRT, William (Bladensburg, Md., Nov. 8,
1772 — Washington, D.C., Feb. 18, 1834).
Author and public official. With little formal
education, Wirt became a lawyer and was admitted to the Virginia bar in 1792. He argued
his first case before the Supreme Court in 1806
and was the prosecutor in the case against
Aaron BURR. He was appointed U.S. Attorney
General (1817-29) and established a precedent
of preserving all official records. In 1832 he was
the unsuccessful Anti-Masonic candidate for
President. His works include: *The Rainbow*
(1804) and *The Old Bachelor* (1810).

WISE, Henry Alexander (Drummondtown,
Va., Dec. 3, 1806 — Richmond, Va., Sept. 12,
1876). Politician. After practicing law in
Tennessee, he returned to Accomack, Va., and
was elected to the U.S. House of Representatives, where he was an outspoken defender of
slavery (1833-44). He was appointed minister
to Brazil and served from 1844 to 1847. Wise
was governor of Virginia (1856-60), and played
a role in the adoption of suffrage and taxation
reforms. The last important act of his administration was ordering the execution of John
Brown for the raid on Harper's Ferry. Although opposed to secession, when the Civil
War broke out he became a brigadier general in
the Confederate Army.

WITHLACOOCHEE RIVER, Fla. Waterway rising in Polk Co., in a swampy area in
central Florida near Polk City. It flows about
160 miles north then west, passes through Tsala
Apopka Lake, and empties into the Gulf of
Mexico south of Yankeetown.

WOCCON INDIANS. Tribe of Siouan linguistic stock that lived in Wayne Co., N.C.
They are one of the few Southern Siouan tribes
that have had a portion of their language preserved. Closely associated with the CATAWBA IN-
DIANS, they were absorbed by them after joining
the TUSCARORA war against the colonists.

WOLFE, Thomas Clayton (Asheville, N.C., Oct. 3, 1900 — Baltimore, Md., Sept. 15, 1938). Author. One of the most important of modern American novelists, Wolfe described his hometown at length in his fiction under the name Altamont (Asheville). His father was a stonecutter and his mother the proprietor of a boarding house, as are the Gants in *Look Homeward, Angel* (1929). Like Eugene Gant in that novel, young Thomas Wolfe worked at odd jobs, absorbed his father's love of poetry, and was attentive to the stories told by his mother's boarders.

In 1916 Wolfe enrolled at the University of North Carolina, where his creative energies were devoted to the theatre until his graduation in 1920. Wolfe benefited from the presence there of the Carolina Playmakers and the lectures of the group's founder, Frederick Koch. After graduation he completed an M.A. program at Harvard before heading to New York City with a play under his arm in 1922. During the late 1920s, he was deeply influenced by Aline Bernstein, the Esther Jack of his novels.

Wolfe's plays were never professionally produced, a fact that he rued for the rest of his life. While subsisting on a teaching job at New York University, he began to spin out the expansive novels on which his reputation now rests. *Look Homeward, Angel* appeared in 1929 after substantial editorial trimming by Maxwell Perkins. Presented with a long and chaotic manuscript, Perkins helped Wolfe set aside independent episodes and sometimes revise them into short stories. The novel that resulted was a great success, and it was followed by an important second novel *Of Time and the River* (1935), *The Web and the Rock* (1939), *You Can't Go Home Again* (1940), and distinguished collections of short stories. Wolfe never indulged in the experiments with style common in the work of his contemporaries, such as William Faulkner. His fame rests instead on a panoramic vision of the South, an enthusiasm for travel and appetite for life, and a continuing interest in relations between different social classes and the members of extended families.

WOLFE RIVER, Miss./Tenn. River rising in northern Mississippi. This waterway flows generally northwest through Memphis, Tenn., to empty into the Mississippi River at the western edge of Tennessee. Its 70-mile length takes it through fertile agricultural land and past the site of NASHOBA, a controversial experimental plantation of the 19th century.

WOOD, Abraham (fl. 1638-1680). Explorer and landowner. It is believed that he came to Virginia in the 1620s as an indentured servant and worked on a Jamestown plantation, later becoming one of the major landowners of the colony. Wood served in the Virginia House of Burgesses (1644-46) and in the colonial militia. In 1671 he sent the first recorded expedition to cross the Appalachian Mountains into what is now Tennessee.

WOOD, Clement (Tuscaloosa, Ala., Sept. 1, 1888 — Schenectady, N.Y., Oct. 26, 1950). Author. Wood was a lawyer and teacher before he began writing fiction, poetry, essays, and operettas. He is best known for his lyrics that were set to music, such as "The Glory Road" and "Short'nin Bread."

WOODALL MOUNTAIN, Miss. Peak (806 feet) in Tishomingo Co., rising at the north end of the Tontotoc Ridge in northeast Mississippi near the Alabama border. It is the highest point in the state.

WOODRUFF, William E. (Suffolk County, Long Island, N.Y., Dec. 24, 1795 — Little Rock, Ark., June 19, 1885). Newspaper editor and publisher. After working as an apprentice printer in New York, Woodruff founded the Arkansas *Gazette* in 1819, the first newspaper in the territory. He moved the operation from Arkansas Post to Little Rock in 1821 and remained editor until 1853. Woodruff was also the editor of the *Arkansas Democrat* from 1846 to 1853.

WOODSON, Carter Godwin (New Canton, Va., Dec. 19, 1875 — Washington, D.C., Apr. 4, 1950). Black historian, editor, and educator. Soon after receiving his Ph.D. from Harvard in 1912, he founded the Association for the Study of Afro-American Life and History. One of the association's primary goals was to train black historians. The association's *The Journal of Negro History* flourished for thirty years under Woodson's direction. His educational posts included dean of the College of Liberal Arts at Howard University in Washington, D.C., and dean of West Virginia State College. He also founded a black-oriented publishing concern, Associated Publishers. Woodson was the author of *The Negro in Our History* (1922) and *A Century of Negro Migration* (1918).

WOODWARD, Comer Vann (Vanndale, Ark., Nov. 13, 1908 —). Historian, author, and educator. His is a major historian of the South and of American race relations. Woodward has taught at the University of Florida (1937-39), the University of Virginia (1939-40), Johns Hopkins (1946-61), and at Yale (1961-77). His books include *The Strange Career of Jim Crow* (1955).

WORTH, Jonathan (Guilford Co., N.C., Nov. 18, 1802 — Raleigh, N.C., Sept. 5, 1869). Politician. A lawyer, he was elected to the North Carolina House of Commons (1830) where he led a protest against nullification. An unsuccessful congressional candidate in 1841 and 1845, he returned to the state legislature (1858) where he opposed the secession movement. He was elected state treasurer (1862-65) and elected governor, serving from 1865 to 1868 when he was removed from office.

WRIGHT BROTHERS See KITTY HAWK.

WRIGHT, Richard (Natchez, Miss., Sept. 4, 1908 — Paris, France, Nov. 28, 1960). Novelist and social critic. The son of black sharecroppers, Wright was an errand boy in Memphis when he borrowed his white employer's library card and steeped himself in the work of such socially-concious writers as Theodore Dreiser and Sinclair Lewis. During the Depression of the 1930s he joined the Federal Writer's Project and directed the Federal Negro Theater. His collection of stories, *Uncle Tom's Children* (1938) won a prize as best book submitted by anyone in the Project. As Harlem editor of the *Daily Worker* (1940), he displeased fellow communists, which led to a troubled disaffiliation from the party and eventually to expatriation from America. Considered by many the most important black writer of his time, he also wrote his autobiography *Black Boy* (1945) and several books about the lives of blacks around the world.

WYTHE, George (Elizabeth City Co., Va., 1726 — Richmond, Va., June 8, 1806). Lawyer, judge, and politician. Before the outbreak of the Revolutionary War, Wythe was a successful lawyer. One of his most famous clerks was Thomas Jefferson, whom he influenced substantially. Wythe was also a member of the Virginia House of Burgesses (1758-68), and the colony's attorney general. He was an opponent of the Stamp Act, and an advocate of independence from Britain. Wythe was a delegate to the Continental Congress (1775-77) and signed the Declaration of Independence. In 1778 he was appointed sole chancellor of Virginia and in 1787 he participated in the Constitutional Convention. Highly regarded as a lawyer and judge, Wythe was selected to chair the first professorship of law in the United States, at the College of William and Mary. (1779-91)

WYTHEVILLE, Va. Town (pop. 7,135), seat of Wythe Co., in southwest Virginia. Founded in 1792, the town is located on a plateau in the bluegrass region. Its proximity to the only salt mines in the South led to frequent military encounters during the Civil War. The town has diversified manufactures including textiles, clothing, and construction equipment, along with livestock and agricultural produce. Wytheville is the birthplace of two Virginia governors, Henry Carter Stuart and Elbert Lee Trinkle.

Y

YADKIN INDIANS. Tribe of Siouan linguistic stock that lived in South Carolina on the Yadkin River (to which they gave their name).

YADKIN RIVER, N.C./S.C. River originating in western North Carolina in the Blue Ridge Mountains. It flows east-southeast approximately 435 miles to South Carolina's Winyah Bay. Also known as the Pee Dee River, the name Yadkin is used for that part of the river north of Troy, N.C., where it joins with the Uharie. The Narrows and Tillery Dams are found along the river in North Carolina.

YALOBUSHA RIVER, Miss. River rising in Chickasaw Co., in east central Mississippi. It flows west-southwest for more than 70 miles to Greenwood. There it joins the Tallahatchie River to create the Yazoo River.

YAMASEE INDIANS. Tribe of Muskogean linguistic stock that originally lived in Georgia on the Ocmulgee River, and extended at times into Florida, Alabama, and South Carolina. They were first encountered by the Spanish and were allied with them until the 1680s when they moved into South Carolina. Though initially friendly with the English they revolted in 1715 and massacred over 200 colonists in a confrontation referred to as the Yamasee War. They were defeated by the colonists and fled into Florida. Here they again became allies of the Spanish but in 1727 they were attacked and nearly destroyed by the English. Those of the tribe that remained scattered, some joining the SEMINOLE INDIANS and others uniting with the CREEK INDIANS.

YANCEY, William Lowndes (Warren Co., Ga., Aug. 10, 1814 — Montgomery, Ala., July 27, 1863). Politician. Yancey was elected by Alabama to the U.S. House of Representatives in 1844 and reelected in 1845, but resigned in 1846 to devote his time to opposing antislavery forces. He wrote and promoted the unsuccessful "Alabama Platform" at the Democratic Convention, arguing that territories could not exclude slavery. Opposing the Compromise of 1850 and openly advocating secession and Southern independence, he promoted the Confederate presidency of John C. Breckenridge, but delivered the speech welcoming President Jefferson Davis. Yancey declined a position in the Davis cabinet but continued to work as an active supporter of the Confederate cause.

YAZOO BASIN, Miss. Large basin of the Yazoo River paralleling the Mississippi River and covering the western edge of the state. A rich cotton and oil region, it is laced with the several large tributaries of the Yazoo. Several man-made reservoirs have been constructed in the basin.

YAZOO INDIANS. Tribe thought to have been of Tunican linguistic stock. They lived in Mississippi near the mouth of the Yazoo River (to which they gave their name). They were first encountered by La Salle (1682), and a French post was established near them in 1718. Although missionary efforts were begun among them shortly thereafter, they allied with the Natchez Indians (1729), attacked the post, and disappeared soon after. They are thought to have been absorbed by the CHOCTAW or CHICKASAW.

YAZOO RIVER, Miss. River rising in the west central part of the state at the confluence of the Tallahatchie and Yalobusha Rivers. It flows approximately 190 miles southwest to drain into the Missisipi.

YEARDLEY, Sir George (London, England, c. 1587 — Va., Nov., 1627). Colonial governor. He sailed for Virginia in 1609 and became acting governor of that colony (1616-17). Twice appointed governor (1619-21, 1626-27), he is credited with establishing the first representative assembly in an English colony (1619), over which he presided.

YELL, Archibald (North Carolina, Aug., 1797 — Buena Vista, Mex., Feb. 23, 1847). Politician. Nicknamed "Old Hickory", he was a lawyer in Tennessee before moving to Little Rock, Ark. In 1832 he was appointed territorial judge in Arkansas, and was the first representative to serve Arkansas in Congress when the territory achieved statehood (1836-39, 1845-47). Yell was governor of Arkansas (1840-44), and was the founder of the state's first Masonic Lodge.

YELLOW RIVER, Ala./Fla. River rising in Covington Co., southern Alabama. It flows about 100 miles southwest through northwestern Florida. The river is joined by the Shoal River and empties into Blackwater Bay, the northeastern arm of Pensacola Bay, south of Milton.

YERKES, Robert Mearns (Breadysville, Pa., May 26, 1876 — New Haven, Conn., Feb. 3, 1956). Psychobiologist. An expert on ape psychology, he was responsible for Army psychological testing during World War I. After earning his Ph.D. at Harvard, he developed the Department of Comparative Animal Psychology there. Following the war he joined the Yale faculty (1924-56) developing the Yale Laboratories of Primate Biology, Orange Park, Fla., (1929), renamed the Yerkes Laboratories in 1942.

YOKAHOCKANY RIVER, Miss. Offshoot of the Pearl River rising in Choctaw Co., central Mississippi. It flows southeast approximately 80 miles to enter the northeast end of Ross Barnett Reservoir.

YORK RIVER, Va. Tidal estuary formed by the confluence of the Pamunkey and Mattaponi Rivers at West Point in eastern Virginia. The river was given the name of York in 1642 when Charles River shire became York shire.

YORKTOWN, Siege of. Revolutionary War action, September 28-October 19, 1781, that brought about the surrender of the British on the Yorktown peninsula in Virginia and the effective end of the war. The British commander Lord Charles Cornwallis had moved north to Virginia after his costly victory at Guilford Courthouse in North Carolina. He took up a defensive position at Yorktown against the wishes of his commander-in-chief in New York, Henry Clinton. Clinton feared that Cornwallis would be cut off by the French fleet, in alliance with the Revolutionary army, and this became the case when Adm. Francois de Grasse appeared off Chesapeake Bay on August 30 with 24 warships.

The Revolutionary Army under commander-in-chief George Washington decided in mid-August, 1781, to attempt a clear defeat of the British at Yorktown rather than in New York. By the end of September he had amassed 9,000 American troops on the land side of Yorktown to reinforce the 7,000 American and French troops already in the area. Cornwallis was forced to defend Yorktown with only 7,000 British troops. The British also sent reinforcements from New York, but these did not arrive until after Cornwallis had surrendered.

Washington began his bombardment of the city on September 28. The major break in the siege came on October 15, when the Revolutionaries took two redoubts and so contained

Storming a redoubt during the Siege of Yorktown, April-May, 1862

Cornwallis within his inner fortifications. Cornwallis asked for terms on October 17 and surrendered formally on October 19, 1781. His surrender meant the capture of one-quarter of the British army in America. It was not clear then that this meant the end of the war, but the surrender at Yorktown was followed by only minor skirmishes.

YORKTOWN, Siege of. Civil War engagement that was the first tactical encounter in the PENINSULAR CAMPAIGN of the Union Army to capture Richmond, Va. The siege lasted from April 5 to May 4, 1862, after which the Confederate Army, having successfully delayed their opponents, fell back to the defense of Richmond.

The leader of the Peninsular Campaign, Gen. George B. McClellan, decided to besiege Yorktown on his way to Richmond because he was deprived of the last reinforcements needed to take the city outright, and because his forces were frustrated by incorrect maps of their route to Richmond up the peninsula between the James and York Rivers. The city was held for the South by Gen. John Bankhead Magruder, who withdrew on May 3 knowing that his mis-

sion had been accomplished and that McClellan was about to open artillery bombardment. Before leaving, Magruder implanted some of the first land mines used in the war. McClellan, who had a far superior army in numbers, later came under severe criticism for his delay at Yorktown and the ultimate failure of the campaign.

YOUNG, Hugh Hampton (San Antonio, Tex., Sept. 18, 1870 — Baltimore, Md., Aug. 23, 1945). Urologist. Considered an authority on urological surgery, Young became Chief of the Department and Professor of Urology at Johns Hopkins University in 1898. His greatest contribution to the field was an operation for cancer of the prostate. His autobiography, *Hugh Young, A Surgeon's Autobiography* was published in 1940.

YOUNG, Lester Willis (Woodville, Miss., Aug. 27, 1909 — New York, N.Y., Mar. 15, 1959). Musician. Young began studying the saxophone at the age of 13, after playing the drums for his father's carnival show for three years, in New Orleans. After playing for several years around the country, he started to gain attention playing with Joe "King" Oliver, the famous trumpeter. Young's controversial style centered around the innovative and untraditional sounds that he produced with the tenor saxophone and he is considered one of America's most influential musicians on the evolution of jazz. He performed with Count Basie (1935-44) and with the legendary Billie Holiday. It was during this period that he made most of his recording. Young spent his remaining years performing with various bands, including Norman Granz's Jazz.

YOUNGER, Cole [Thomas Coleman Younger] (Jackson Co., Mo., Jan. 15, 1844 — Jackson Co., Mo., Mar. 21, 1916). Outlaw. He was a Confederate guerilla during the Civil War and later joined Jesse James' gang. In 1876 he and his brothers, James and Robert, were sentenced to life imprisonment after being apprehended in a bank robbery attempt. Robert Younger died in prison, but James was paroled in 1901. Cole was pardoned in 1903 and later joined a Wild West show.

YUCHI INDIANS ("those far away" or "at a distance"). Tribe of Uchean linguistic stock, a distinct group, but one closely associated with the Muskogean and Siouan. They first lived in eastern Tennessee but they apparently roamed through portions of most of the southern states, giving their name to numerous places. A warlike tribe with many subdivisions, hostilities were encountered with settlers in all of their locations. They eventually scattered, some joining the CREEKS in their migration to Indian Territory in Oklahoma, others joining the SEMINOLES in Florida.

Z

ZANE, Ebenezer (near Moorefield, W. Va., Oct. 7, 1747 — Wheeling, W.Va., Nov. 19, 1812). Pioneer and land speculator. He established, with two of his brothers, the first permanent settlement on the Ohio River (1769) at the present site of Wheeling, W.Va. There he built Fort HENRY, which he defended during severe Indian attacks in 1777 and 1782. After receiving congressional approval, he opened a trail, Zane's Trace, from Wheeling to Maysville, Ky. He settled and was proprietor of the present town of Zanesville, Ohio (1799).

ZUBLY, John Joachim (St. Gall, Switzerland, Aug. 17, 1724 — Savannah, Ga., July 23, 1781). Clergyman. Ordained a Presbyterian minister in England, in 1760 he became pastor of a church in Savannah, Ga. Zubly was an advocate of colonial rights and wrote numerous pamphlets on colonial difficulties. In 1775 he was a delegate from Georgia to the Continental Congress. When he opposed a complete break from Britain he was labeled a Loyalist and was banished from Georgia in 1777. In 1779 he returned to Georgia to continue his pastoral work.

County	County Seat or Courthouse	County	County Seat or Courthouse

Alabama (67 counties)

Autauga . . . . Prattville

Baldwin . . . . Bay Minette
Barbour . . . . Clayton
Bibb . . . . Centreville
Blount . . . . Oneonta
Bullock . . . . Union Springs
Butler . . . . Greenville

Calhoun . . . . Anniston
Chambers . . . . Lafayette
Cherokee . . . . Centre
Chilton . . . . Clanton
Choctaw . . . . Butler
Clarke . . . . Grove Hill
Clay . . . . Ashland
Cleburne . . . . Heflin
Coffee . . . . Elba
Colbert . . . . Tuscumbia
Conecuh . . . . Evergreen
Coosa . . . . Rockford
Covington . . . . Andalusia
Crenshaw . . . . Luverne
Cullman . . . . Cullman

Dale . . . . Ozark
Dallas . . . . Selma
De Kalb . . . . Fort Payne

Elmore . . . . Wetumpka
Escambia . . . . Brewton
Etowah . . . . Gadsden

Fayette . . . . Fayette
Franklin . . . . Russellville

Geneva . . . . Geneva
Greene . . . . Eutaw

Hale . . . . Greensboro
Henry . . . . Abbeville
Houston . . . . Dothan

Jackson . . . . Scottsboro
Jefferson . . . . Birmingham

Lamar . . . . Vernon
Lauderdale . . . . Florence
Lawrence . . . . Moulton
Lee . . . . Opelika
Limestone . . . . Athens
Lowndes . . . . Hayneville

Macon . . . . Tuskegee
Madison . . . . Huntsville
Marengo . . . . Linden
Marion . . . . Hamilton
Marshall . . . . Guntersville
Mobile . . . . Mobile
Monroe . . . . Monroeville
Montgomery . . . . Montgomery
Morgan . . . . Decatur

Perry . . . . Marion
Pickens . . . . Carrollton
Pike . . . . Troy

Randolph . . . . Wedowee
Russell . . . . Phenix City

St. Clair . . . . Ashville and Pell City
Shelby . . . . Columbiana
Sumter . . . . Livingston

Talladega . . . . Talladega
Tallapoosa . . . . Dadeville
Tuscaloosa . . . . Tuscaloosa

Walker . . . . Jasper
Washington . . . . Chatom
Wilcox . . . . Camden
Winston . . . . Double Springs

Arkansas (75 counties)

Arkansas . . . . DeWitt and Stuttgart
Ashley . . . . Hamburg

Baxter . . . . Mountain Home
Benton . . . . Bentonville
Boone . . . . Harrison
Bradley . . . . Warren

Calhoun . . . . Hampton
Carroll . . . . Berryville and Eureka Springs
Chicot . . . . Lake Village
Clark . . . . Arkadelphia
Clay . . . . Corning and Piggott
Cleburne . . . . Heber Springs
Cleveland . . . . Rison
Columbia . . . . Magnolia
Conway . . . . Morrilton
Craighead . . . . Jonesboro and Lake City
Crawford . . . . Van Buren
Crittenden . . . . Marion
Cross . . . . Wynne

County	County Seat or Courthouse	County	County Seat or Courthouse
Dallas	Fordyce	Scott	Waldron
Desha	Arkansas City	Searcy	Marshall
Drew	Monticello	Sebastian	Fort Smith and Greenwood
		Sevier	De Queen
Faulkner	Conway	Sharp	Ash Flat
Franklin	Charleston and Ozark	Stone	Mountain View
Fulton	Salem		
		Union	El Dorado
Garland	Hot Springs Nat'l Park		
Grant	Sheridan	Van Buren	Clinton
Greene	Paragould		

Florida (67 counties)

County	County Seat or Courthouse	County	County Seat or Courthouse
Hempstead	Hope	Alachua	Gainesville
Hot Spring	Malvern		
Howard	Nashville	Baker	Macclenny
		Bay	Panama City
Independence	Batesville	Bradford	Starke
Izard	Melbourne	Brevard	Titusville
		Broward	Fort Lauderdale
Jackson	Newport		
Jefferson	Pine Bluff	Calhoun	Blountstown
Johnson	Clarksville	Charlotte	Punta Gorda
		Citrus	Inverness
Lafayette	Lewisville	Clay	Green Cove Springs
Lawrence	Walnut Ridge	Collier	Naples
Lee	Marianna	Columbia	Lake City
Lincoln	Star City		
Little River	Ashdown	Dade	Miami
Logan	Booneville and Paris	De Soto	Arcadia
Lonoke	Lonoke	Dixie	Cross City
		Duval	Jacksonville
Madison	Huntsville		
Marion	Yellville	Escambia	Pensacola
Miller	Texarkana		
Mississippi	Blytheville and Osceola	Flagler	Bunnell
Monroe	Clarendon	Franklin	Apalachicola
Montgomery	Mount Ida		
		Gadsden	Quincy
Nevada	Prescott	Gilchrist	Trenton
Newton	Jasper	Glades	Moore Haven
		Gulf	Port St. Joe
Ouachita	Camden		
		Hamilton	Jasper
Perry	Perryville	Hardee	Wauchula
Phillips	Helena	Hendry	La Belle
Pike	Murfreesboro	Hernando	Brooksville
Poinsett	Harrisburg	Highlands	Sebring
Polk	Mena	Hillsborough	Tampa
Pope	Russellville	Holmes	Bonifay
Prairie	Des Arc and De Valls Bluff		
Pulaski	Little Rock	Indian River	Vero Beach
Randolph	Pocahontas	Jackson	Marianna
		Jefferson	Monticello
St. Francis	Forrest City		
Saline	Benton		

County	County Seat or Courthouse	County	County Seat or Courthouse
Lafayette	Mayo	Berrien	Nashville
Lake	Tavares	Bibb	Macon
Lee	Fort Myers	Bleckley	Cochran
Leon	Tallahassee	Brantley	Nahunta
Levy	Bronson	Brooks	Quitman
Liberty	Bristol	Bryan	Pembroke
		Bulloch	Statesboro
Madison	Madison	Burke	Waynesboro
Manatee	Bradenton	Butts	Jackson
Marion	Ocala		
Martin	Stuart	Calhoun	Morgan
Monroe	Key West	Camden	Woodbine
		Candler	Metter
Nassau	Femandina Beach	Carroll	Carrollton
		Catoosa	Ringgold
Okaloosa	Crestview	Charlton	Folkston
Okeechobee	Okeechobee	Chatham	Savannah
Orange	Orlando	Chattahoochee	Cusseta
Osceola	Kissimmee	Chattooga	Summerville
		Cherokee	Canton
Palm Beach	West Palm Beach	Clarke	Athens
Pasco	Dade City	Clay	Fort Gaines
Pinellas	Clearwater	Clayton	Jonesboro
Polk	Bartow	Clinch	Homerville
Putnam	Palatka	Cobb	Marietta
		Coffee	Douglas
St. Johns	Saint Augustine	Colquitt	Moultrie
St. Lucie	Fort Pierce	Columbia	Appling
Santa Rosa	Milton	Cook	Adel
Sarasota	Sarasota	Coweta	Newnan
Seminole	Sanford	Crawford	Knoxville
Sumter	Bushnell	Crisp	Cordele
Suwannee	Live Oak		
		Dade	Trenton
Taylor	Perry	Dawson	Dawsonville
		Decatur	Bainbridge
Union	Lake Butler	De Kalb	Decatur
		Dodge	Eastman
Volusia	De Land	Dooly	Vienna
		Dougherty	Albany
Wakulla	Crawfordville	Douglas	Douglasville
Walton	De Funiak Springs		
Washington	Chipley	Early	Blakely
		Echols	Statenville
		Effingham	Springfield
Georgia (159 counties)		Elbert	Elberton
		Emanuel	Swainsboro
Appling	Baxley	Evans	Claxton
Atkinson	Pearson		
		Fannin	Blue Ridge
Bacon	Alma	Fayette	Fayetteville
Baker	Newton	Floyd	Rome
Baldwin	Milledgeville	Forsyth	Cumming
Banks	Homer	Franklin	Carnesville
Barrow	Winder	Fulton	Atlanta
Bartow	Cartersville		
Ben Hill	Fitzgerald		

County	County Seat or Courthouse	County	County Seat or Courthouse
Gilmer	Ellijay	Oconee	Watkinsville
Glascock	Gibson	Oglethorpe	Lexington
Glynn	Brunswick		
Gordon	Calhoun	Paulding	Dallas
Grady	Cairo	Peach	Fort Valley
Greene	Greensboro	Pickens	Jasper
Gwinnett	Lawrenceville	Pierce	Blackshear
		Pike	Zebulon
Habersham	Clarkesville	Polk	Cedartown
Hall	Gainesville	Pulaski	Hawkinsville
Hancock	Sparta	Putnam	Eatonton
Haralson	Buchanan		
Harris	Hamilton	Quitman	Georgetown
Hart	Hartwell		
Heard	Franklin	Rabun	Clayton
Henry	McDonough	Randolph	Cuthbert
Houston	Perry	Richmond	Augusta
		Rockdale	Conyers
Irwin	Ocilla		
		Schley	Ellaville
Jackson	Jefferson	Screven	Sylvania
Jasper	Monticello	Seminole	Donalsonville
Jeff Davis	Hazlehurst	Spalding	Griffin
Jefferson	Louisville	Stephens	Toccoa
Jenkins	Millen	Stewart	Lumpkin
Johnson	Wrightsville	Sumter	Americus
Jones	Gray		
		Talbot	Talbotton
Lamar	Barnesville	Taliaferro	Crawfordville
Lanier	Lakeland	Tattnall	Reidsville
Laurens	Dublin	Taylor	Butler
Lee	Leesburg	Telfair	MacRae
Liberty	Hinesville	Terrell	Dawson
Lincoln	Lincolnton	Thomas	Thomasville
Long	Ludowici	Tift	Tifton
Lowndes	Valdosta	Toombs	Lyons
Lumpkin	Dahlonega	Towns	Hiawassee
		Treutlen	Soperton
McDuffie	Thomson	Troup	La Grange
McIntosh	Darien	Turner	Ashburn
Macon	Oglethorpe	Twiggs	Jeffersonville
Madison	Danielsville		
Marion	Buena Vista	Union	Blairsville
Meriwether	Greenville	Upson	Thomaston
Miller	Colquitt		
Mitchell	Camilla	Walker	La Fayette
Monroe	Forsyth	Walton	Monroe
Montgomery	Mount Vernon	Ware	Waycross
Morgan	Madison	Warren	Warrenton
Murray	Chatsworth	Washington	Sandersville
Muscogee	Columbus	Wayne	Jesup
		Webster	Preston
Newton	Covington	Wheeler	Alamo
		White	Cleveland
		Whitfield	Dalton

County	County Seat or Courthouse	County	County Seat or Courthouse
Wilcox	Abbeville	Grayson	Leitchfield
Wilkes	Washington	Green	Greensburg
Wilkinson	Irwinton	Greenup	Greenup
Worth	Sylvester		
		Hancock	Hawesville
		Hardin	Elizabeth

Kentucky (120 counties)

County	County Seat or Courthouse	County	County Seat or Courthouse
		Harlan	Harlan
Adair	Columbia	Harrison	Cynthiana
Allen	Scottsville	Hart	Munfordville
Anderson	Lawrenceburg	Henderson	Henderson
		Henry	New Castle
Ballard	Wickliffe	Hickman	Clinton
Barren	Glasgow	Hopkins	Madisonville
Bath	Owingsville		
Bell	Pineville	Jackson	McKee
Boone	Burlington	Jefferson	Louisville
Bourbon	Paris	Jessamine	Nicholasville
Boyd	Catlettsburg	Johnson	Paintsville
Boyle	Danville		
Bracken	Brooksville	Kenton	Independence
Breathitt	Jackson	Knott	Hindman
Breckinridge	Hardinsburg	Knox	Barbourville
Bullitt	Shepherdsville		
Butler	Morgantown	Larue	Hodgenville
		Laurel	London
Caldwell	Princeton	Lawrence	Louisa
Calloway	Murray	Lee	Beattyville
Campbell	Alexandria	Leslie	Hyden
Carlisle	Bardwell	Letcher	Whitesburg
Carroll	Carrollton	Lewis	Vanceburg
Carter	Grayson	Lincoln	Stanford
Casey	Liberty	Livingston	Smithland
Christian	Hopkinsville	Logan	Russellville
Clark	Winchester	Lyon	Eddyville
Clay	Manchester		
Clinton	Albany	McCracken	Paducah
Crittenden	Marion	McCreary	Whitley City
Cumberland	Burkesville	McLean	Calhoun
		Madison	Richmond
Daviess	Owensboro	Magoffin	Salyersville
		Marion	Lebanon
Edmonson	Brownsville	Marshall	Benton
Elliott	Sandy Hook	Martin	Inez
Estill	Irvine	Mason	Maysville
		Meade	Brandenburg
Fayette	Lexington	Menifee	Frenchburg
Fleming	Flemingsburg	Mercer	Harrodsburg
Floyd	Prestonsburg	Metcalfe	Edmonton
Franklin	Frankfort	Monroe	Tompkinsville
Fulton	Hickman	Montgomery	Mount Sterling
		Morgan	West Liberty
Gallatin	Warsaw	Muhlenberg	Greenville
Garrard	Lancaster		
Grant	Williamstown	Nelson	Bardstown
Graves	Mayfield	Nicholas	Carlisle

County	County Seat or Courthouse	Parish	Parish Seat
Ohio	Hartford	Claiborne	Homer
Oldham	La Grange	Concordia	Vidalia
Owen	Owenton		
Owsley	Booneville	De Soto	Mansfield
Pendleton	Falmouth	East Baton Rouge	Baton Rouge
Perry	Hazard	East Carroll	Lake Providence
Pike	Pikeville	East Feliciana	Clinton
Powell	Stanton	Evangeline	Ville Platte
Pulaski	Somerset		
		Franklin	Winnsboro
Robertson	Mount Olivet		
Rockcastle	Mount Vernon	Grant	Colfax
Rowan	Morehead		
Russell	Jamestown	Iberia	New Iberia
		Iberville	Plaquemine
Scott	Georgetown		
Shelby	Shelbyville	Jackson	Jonesboro
Simpson	Franklin	Jefferson	Gretna
Spencer	Taylorsville	Jefferson Davis	Jennings
Taylor	Campbellsville	Lafayette	Lafayette
Todd	Elkton	Lafourche	Thibodaux
Trigg	Cadiz	La Salle	Jena
Trimble	Bedford	Lincoln	Ruston
		Livingston	Livingston
Union	Morganfield		
		Madison	Tallulah
Warren	Bowling Green	Morehouse	Bastrop
Washington	Springfield		
Wayne	Monticello	Natchitoches	Natchitoches
Webster	Dixon		
Whitley	Williamsburg	Orleans	New Orleans
Wolfe	Campton	Ouachita	Monroe
Woodford	Versailles		
		Plaquemines	Pointe à la Hache
		Pointe Coupée	New Roads

Louisiana (64 parishes)

Parish	Parish Seat	Parish	Parish Seat
		Rapides	Alexandria
		Red River	Coushatta
		Richland	Rayville
Acadia	Crowley		
Allen	Oberlin	Sabine	Many
Ascension	Donaldsville	St. Bernard	Chalmette
Assumption	Napoleonville	St. Charles	Hahnville
Avoyelles	Marksville	St. Helena	Greensburg
		St. James	Convent
Beauregard	De Ridder	St. John The Baptist	Edgard
Bienville	Arcadia	St. Landry	Opelousas
Bossier	Benton	St. Martin	Saint Martinville
		St. Mary	Franklin
Caddo	Shreveport	St. Tammany	Covington
Calcasieu	Lake Charles		
Caldwell	Columbia	Tangipahoa	Amite
Cameron	Cameron	Tensas	Saint Joseph
Catahoula	Harrisonburg	Terrebonne	Houma

Parish	Parish Seat
Union	Farmerville
Vermilion	Abbeville
Vernon	Leesville
Washington	Franklinton
Webster	Minden
West Baton Rouge	Port Allen
West Carroll	Oak Grove
West Feliciana	Saint Francisville
Winn	Winnfield

Maryland (23 cos., 1 ind. city)

County	County Seat or Courthouse
Allegany	Cumberland
Anne Arundel	Annapolis
Baltimore	Towson
Calvert	Prince Frederick
Caroline	Denton
Carroll	Westminster
Cecil	Elkton
Charles	La Plata
Dorchester	Cambridge
Frederick	Frederick
Garrett	Oakland
Harford	Bel Air
Howard	Ellicott City
Kent	Chestertown
Montgomery	Rockville
Prince George's	Upper Marlboro
Queen Anne's	Centreville
St. Mary's	Leonardtown
Somerset	Princess Anne
Talbot	Easton
Washington	Hagerstown
Wicomico	Salisbury
Worcester	Snow Hill

Independent City

Baltimore

County	County Seat or Courthouse

Mississippi (82 counties)

County	County Seat or Courthouse
Adams	Natchez
Alcorn	Corinth
Amite	Liberty
Attala	Kosciusko
Benton	Ashland
Bolivar	Cleveland and Rosedale
Calhoun	Pittsboro
Carroll	Carrollton and Valden
Chickasaw	Houston and Okolona
Choctaw	Ackerman
Claiborne	Port Gibson
Clarke	Quitman
Clay	West Point
Coahoma	Clarksdale
Copiah	Hazlehurst
Covington	Collins
De Soto	Hernando
Forrest	Hattiesburg
Franklin	Meadville
George	Lucedale
Greene	Leakesville
Grenada	Grenada
Hancock	Bay Saint Louis
Harrison	Gulfport
Hinds	Jackson and Raymond
Holmes	Lexington
Humphreys	Belzoni
Issaquena	Mayersville
Itawamba	Fulton
Jackson	Pascagoula
Jasper	Bat Springs and Paulding
Jefferson	Fayette
Jefferson Davis	Prentiss
Jones	Ellisville and Laurel
Kemper	De Kalb
Lafayette	Oxford
Lamar	Purvis
Lauderdale	Meridian
Lawrence	Monticello
Leake	Carthage
Lee	Tupelo
Leflore	Greenwood
Lincoln	Brookhaven
Lowndes	Columbus

County	County Seat or Courthouse
Madison	Canton
Marion	Columbia
Marshall	Holly Springs
Monroe	Aberdeen
Montgomery	Winona
Neshoba	Philadelphia
Newton	Decatur
Noxubee	Macon
Oktibbeha	Starkville
Panola	Batesville and Sardis
Pearl River	Poplarville
Perry	New Augusta
Pike	Magnolia
Pontotoc	Pontotoc
Prentiss	Booneville
Quitman	Marks
Rankin	Brandon
Scott	Forest
Sharkey	Rolling Fork
Simpson	Mendenhall
Smith	Raleigh
Stone	Wiggins
Sunflower	Indianola
Tallahatchie	Charleston and Sumner
Tate	Senatobia
Tippah	Ripley
Tishomingo	Iuka
Tunica	Tunica
Union	New Albany
Walthall	Tylertown
Warren	Vicksburg
Washington	Greenville
Wayne	Waynesboro
Webster	Walthall
Wilkinson	Woodville
Winston	Louisville
Yalobusha	Coffeeville and Water Valley
Yazoo	Yazoo City

Missouri (114 cos., 1 ind. city)

County	County Seat or Courthouse
Adair	Kirksville
Andrew	Savannah
Atchison	Rockport
Audrain	Mexico

County	County Seat or Courthouse
Barry	Cassville
Barton	Lamar
Bates	Butler
Benton	Warsaw
Bollinger	Marble Hill
Boone	Columbia
Buchanan	Saint Joseph
Butler	Poplar Buff
Caldwell	Kingston
Callaway	Fulton
Camden	Camdenton
Cape Girardeau	Jackson
Carroll	Carrollton
Carter	Van Buren
Cass	Harrisonville
Cedar	Stockton
Chariton	Keytesville
Christian	Ozark
Clark	Kahoka
Clay	Liberty
Clinton	Plattsburg
Cole	Jefferson City
Cooper	Boonville
Crawford	Steelville
Dade	Greenfield
Dallas	Buffalo
Daviess	Gallatin
De Kalb	Maysville
Dent	Salem
Douglas	Ava
Dunklin	Kennett
Franklin	Union
Gasconade	Hermann
Gentry	Albany
Greene	Springfield
Grundy	Trenton
Harrison	Bethany
Henry	Clinton
Hickory	Hermitage
Holt	Oregon
Howard	Fayette
Howell	West Plains
Iron	Ironton
Jackson	Independence
Jasper	Carthage
Jefferson	Hillsboro
Johnson	Warrensburg

County	County Seat or Courthouse	County	County Seat or Courthouse
Knox	Edina	Scott	Benton
		Shannon	Eminence
Laclede	Lebanon	Shelby	Shelbyville
Lafayette	Lexington	Stoddard	Bloomfield
Lawrence	Mount Vernon	Stone	Galena
Lewis	Monticello	Sullivan	Milan
Lincoln	Troy		
Linn	Linneus	Taney	Forsyth
Livingston	Chillicothe	Texas	Houston
McDonald	Pineville	Vernon	Nevada
Macon	Macon		
Madison	Fredericktown	Warren	Warrenton
Maries	Vienna	Washington	Potosi
Marion	Palmyra	Wayne	Greenville
Mercer	Princeton	Webster	Marshfield
Miller	Tuscumbia	Worth	Grant City
Mississippi	Charleston	Wright	Hartville
Moniteau	California		
Monroe	Paris		
Montgomery	Montgomery City		
Morgan	Versailles		

Independent City

St. Louis

County	County Seat or Courthouse
New Madrid	New Madrid
Newton	Neosho
Nodaway	Maryville

North Carolina (100 Counties)

County	County Seat or Courthouse
Oregon	Alton
Osage	Linn
Ozark	Gainesville
Pemiscot	Caruthersville
Perry	Perryville
Pettis	Sedalia
Phelps	Rolla
Pike	Bowling Green
Platte	Platte City
Polk	Bolivar
Pulaski	Waynesville
Putnam	Unionville
Ralls	New London
Randolph	Huntsville
Ray	Richmond
Reynolds	Centerville
Ripley	Doniphan
St. Charles	St. Charles
St. Clair	Osceola
St. Francois	Farmington
St. Louis	Clayton
Ste. Geneviève	Ste. Geneviève
Saline	Marshall
Schuyler	Lancaster
Scotland	Memphis

County	County Seat or Courthouse
Alamance	Graham
Alexander	Taylorsville
Alleghany	Sparta
Anson	Wadesboro
Ashe	Jefferson
Avery	Newland
Beaufort	Washington
Bertie	Windsor
Bladen	Elizabethtown
Brunswick	Southport
Buncombe	Asheville
Burke	Morganton
Cabarrus	Concord
Caldwell	Lenoir
Camden	Camden
Carteret	Beaufort
Caswell	Yanceyville
Catawba	Newton
Chatham	Pittsboro
Cherokee	Murphy
Chowan	Edenton
Clay	Hayesville
Cleveland	Shelby
Columbus	Whiteville
Craven	New Bern
Cumberland	Fayetteville
Currituck	Currituck

County	County Seat or Courthouse
Dare	Manteo
Davidson	Lexington
Davie	Mocksville
Duplin	Kenansville
Durham	Durham
Edgecombe	Tarboro
Forsyth	Winston-Salem
Franklin	Louisburg
Gaston	Gastonia
Gates	Gatesville
Graham	Robbinsville
Granville	Oxford
Greene	Snow Hill
Guilford	Greensboro
Halifax	Halifax
Harnett	Lillington
Haywood	Waynesville
Henderson	Hendersonville
Hertford	Winton
Hoke	Raeford
Hyde	Swanquarter
Iredell	Statesville
Jackson	Sylva
Johnston	Smithfield
Jones	Trenton
Lee	Sanford
Lenoir	Kinston
Lincoln	Lincolnton
McDowell	Marion
Macon	Franklin
Madison	Marshall
Martin	Williamston
Mecklenburg	Charlotte
Mitchell	Bakersville
Montgomery	Troy
Moore	Carthage
Nash	Nashville
New Hanover	Wilmington
Northampton	Jackson
Onslow	Jacksonville
Orange	Hillsboro
Pamlico	Bayboro
Pasquotank	Elizabeth City
Pender	Burgaw
Perquimans	Hertford

County	County Seat or Courthouse
Person	Roxboro
Pitt	Greenville
Polk	Columbus
Randolph	Asheboro
Richmond	Rockingham
Robeson	Lumberton
Rockingham	Wentworth
Rowan	Salisbury
Rutherford	Rutherfordton
Sampson	Clinton
Scotland	Laurinburg
Stanly	Albemarle
Stokes	Danbury
Surry	Dobson
Swain	Bryson City
Transylvania	Brevard
Tyrrell	Columbia
Union	Monroe
Vance	Henderson
Wake	Raleigh
Warren	Warrenton
Washington	Plymouth
Watauga	Boone
Wayne	Goldsboro
Wilkes	Wilkesboro
Wilson	Wilson
Yadkin	Yadkinville
Yancey	Bumsville

South Carolina (46 counties)

County	County Seat or Courthouse
Abbeville	Abbeville
Aiken	Aiken
Allendale	Allendale
Anderson	Anderson
Bamberg	Bamberg
Barnwell	Barnwell
Beaufort	Beaufort
Berkeley	Moncks Corner
Calhoun	Saint Matthews
Charleston	Charleston
Cherokee	Gaffney
Chester	Chester
Chesterfield	Chesterfield
Clarendon	Manning
Colleton	Walterboro

County	County Seat or Courthouse	County	County Seat or Courthouse
Darlington	Darlington	Campbell	Jacksboro
Dillon	Dillon	Cannon	Woodbury
Dorchester	Saint George	Carroll	Huntingdon
		Carter	Elizabethton
Edgefield	Edgefield	Cheatham	Ashland City
		Chester	Henderson
Fairfield	Winnsboro	Claiborne	Tazewell
Florence	Florence	Clay	Celina
		Cocke	Newport
Georgetown	Georgetown	Coffee	Manchester
Greenville	Greenville	Crockett	Alamo
Greenwood	Greenwood	Cumberland	Crossville
Hampton	Hampton	Davidson	Nashville
Horry	Conway	Decatur	Decaturville
		De Kalb	Smithville
Jasper	Ridgeland	Dickson	Charlotte
		Dyer	Dyersburg
Kershaw	Camden		
		Fayette	Somerville
Lancaster	Lancaster	Fentress	Jamestown
Laurens	Laurens	Franklin	Winchester
Lee	Bishopville		
Lexington	Lexington	Gibson	Trenton
		Giles	Pulaski
McCormick	McCormick	Grainger	Rutledge
Marion	Marion	Greene	Greeneville
Marlboro	Bennettsville	Grundy	Altamont
Newberry	Newberry	Hamblen	Morristown
		Hamilton	Chattanooga
Oconee	Walhalla	Hancock	Sneedville
Orangeburg	Orangeburg	Hardeman	Bolivar
		Hardin	Savannah
Pickens	Pickens	Hawkins	Rogersville
		Haywood	Brownsville
Richland	Columbia	Henderson	Lexington
		Henry	Paris
Saluda	Saluda	Hickman	Centerville
Spartanburg	Spartanburg	Houston	Erin
Sumter	Sumter	Humphreys	Waverly
Union	Union	Jackson	Gainesboro
		Jefferson	Dandridge
Williamsburg	Kingstree	Johnson	Mountain City
York	York	Knox	Knoxville
		Lake	Tiptonville

Tennessee (95 counties)

County	County Seat or Courthouse
Anderson	Clinton
Bedford	Shelbyville
Benton	Camden
Bledsoe	Pikeville
Blount	Maryville
Bradley	Cleveland

County	County Seat or Courthouse
Lauderdale	Ripley
Lawrence	Lawrenceburg
Lewis	Hohenwald
Lincoln	Fayetteville
Loudon	Loudon

County	County Seat or Courthouse	County	County Seat or Courthouse
McMinn	Athens	Aransas	Rockport
McNairy	Selmer	Archer	Archer City
Macon	Lafayette	Armstrong	Claude
Madison	Jackson	Atascosa	Jourdanton
Marion	Jasper	Austin	Bellville
Marshall	Lewisburg		
Maury	Columbia	Bailey	Muleshoe
Meigs	Decatur	Bandera	Bandera
Monroe	Madisonville	Bastrop	Bastrop
Montgomery	Clarksville	Baylor	Seymour
Moore	Lynchburg	Bee	Beeville
Morgan	Wartburg	Bell	Belton
		Bexar	San Antonio
Obion	Union City	Blanco	Johnson City
Overton	Livingston	Borden	Gail
		Bosque	Meridian
Perry	Linden	Bowie	Boston
Pickett	Byrdstown	Brazoria	Angleton
Polk	Benton	Brazos	Bryan
Putnam	Cookeville	Brewster	Alpine
		Briscoe	Silverton
Rhea	Dayton	Brooks	Falfurrias
Roane	Kingston	Brown	Brownwood
Robertson	Springfield	Burleson	Caldwell
Rutherford	Murfreesboro	Burnet	Burnet
Scott	Huntsville	Caldwell	Lockhart
Sequatchie	Dunlap	Calhoun	Port Lavanca
Sevier	Sevierville	Callahan	Baird
Shelby	Memphis	Cameron	Brownsville
Smith	Carthage	Camp	Pittsburg
Stewart	Dover	Carson	Panhandle
Sullivan	Blountville	Cass	Linden
Sumner	Gallatin	Castro	Dimmitt
		Chambers	Anahuac
Tipton	Covington	Cherokee	Rusk
Trousdale	Hartsville	Childress	Childress
		Clay	Henrietta
Unicoi	Erwin	Cochran	Morton
Union	Maynardville	Coke	Robert Lee
		Coleman	Coleman
Van Buren	Spencer	Collin	McKinney
Warren	McMinnville	Collingsworth	Wellington
Washington	Jonesboro	Colorado	Columbus
Wayne	Waynesboro	Comal	New Braunfels
Weakley	Dresden	Comanche	Comanche
White	Sparta	Concho	Paint Rock
Williamson	Franklin	Cooke	Gainesville
Wilson	Lebanon	Coryell	Gatesville
		Cottle	Paducah
Texas (254 counties)		Crane	Crane
		Crockett	Ozona
Anderson	Palestine	Crosby	Crosbyton
Andrews	Andrews	Culberson	Van Horn
Angelina	Lufkin		

County	County Seat or Courthouse	County	County Seat or Courthouse
Dallam	Dalhart	Henderson	Athens
Dallas	Dallas	Hidalgo	Edinburg
Dawson	Lamesa	Hill	Hillsboro
Deaf Smith	Hereford	Hockley	Levelland
Delta	Cooper	Hood	Granbury
Denton	Denton	Hopkins	Sulphur Springs
Dewitt	Cuero	Houston	Crockett
Dickens	Dickens	Howard	Big Spring
Dimmit	Carrizo Springs	Hudspeth	Sierra Blanca
Donley	Clarendon	Hunt	Greenville
Duval	San Diego	Hutchinson	Stinnett
Eastland	Eastland	Irion	Mertzon
Ector	Odessa		
Edwards	Rocksprings	Jack	Jacksboro
Ellis	Waxahachie	Jackson	Edna
El Paso	El Paso	Jasper	Jasper
Erath	Stephenville	Jeff Davis	Fort Davis
		Jefferson	Beaumont
Falls	Marlin	Jim Hogg	Hebbronville
Fannin	Bonham	Jim Wells	Alice
Fayette	La Grange	Johnson	Cleburne
Fisher	Roby	Jones	Anson
Floyd	Floydada		
Foard	Crowell	Karnes	Karnes City
Fort Bend	Richmond	Kaufman	Kaufman
Franklin	Mount Vernon	Kendall	Boeme
Freestone	Fairfield	Kenedy	Sarita
Frio	Pearsall	Kent	Jayton
		Kerr	Kerrville
Gaines	Seminole	Kimble	Junction
Galveston	Galveston	King	Guthrie
Garza	Post	Kinney	Brackettville
Gillespie	Fredericksburg	Kleberg	Kingsville
Glasscock	Garden City	Knox	Benjamin
Goliad	Goliad		
Gonzales	Gonzales	Lamar	Paris
Gray	Pampa	Lamb	Littlefield
Grayson	Sherman	Lampasas	Lampasas
Gregg	Longview	La Salle	Cotulla
Grimes	Anderson	Lavaca	Hallettsville
Guadalupe	Seguin	Lee	Giddings
		Leon	Centerville
Hale	Plainview	Liberty	Liberty
Hall	Memphis	Limestone	Groesbeck
Hamilton	Hamilton	Lipscomb	Lipscomb
Hansford	Spearman	Live Oak	George West
Hardeman	Quanah	Llano	Llano
Hardin	Kountze	Loving	Mentone
Harris	Houston	Lubbock	Lubbock
Harrison	Marshall	Lynn	Tahoka
Hartley	Channing		
Haskell	Haskell	McCulloch	Brady
Hays	San Marcos	McLennan	Waco
Hemphill	Canadian	McMullen	Tilden

Appendix I

County	County Seat or Courthouse	County	County Seat or Courthouse
Madison	Madisonville	Schleicher	Eldorado
Marion	Jefferson	Scurry	Snyder
Martin	Staton	Shackelford	Albany
Mason	Mason	Shelby	Center
Matagorda	Bay City	Sherman	Stratford
Maverick	Eagle Pass	Smith	Tyler
Medina	Hondo	Somervell	Glen Rose
Menard	Menard	Starr	Rio Grande City
Midland	Midland	Stephens	Breckenridge
Milam	Cameron	Sterling	Sterling City
Mills	Goldthwaite	Stonewall	Aspermont
Mitchell	Colorado City	Sutton	Sonora
Montague	Montague	Swisher	Tulia
Montgomery	Conroe		
Moore	Dumas	Tarrant	Fort Worth
Morris	Daingerfield	Taylor	Abilene
Motley	Matador	Terrell	Sanderson
		Terry	Brownfield
Nacogdoches	Nacogdoches	Throckmorton	Throckmorton
Navarro	Corsicana	Titus	Mount Pleasant
Newton	Newton	Tom Green	San Angelo
Nolan	Sweetwater	Travis	Austin
Nueces	Corpus Christi	Trinity	Groveton
		Tyler	Woodville
Ochiltree	Perryton		
Oldham	Vega	Upshur	Gilmer
Orange	Orange	Upton	Rankin
		Uvalde	Uvalde
Palo Pinto	Palo Pinto		
Panola	Carthage	Val Verde	Del Rio
Parker	Weatherford	Van Zandt	Canton
Parmer	Farwell	Victoria	Victoria
Pecos	Fort Stockton		
Polk	Livingston	Walker	Huntsville
Potter	Amarillo	Waller	Hempstead
Presidio	Marfa	Ward	Monahans
		Washington	Brenham
Rains	Emory	Webb	Laredo
Randall	Canyon	Wharton	Wharton
Reagan	Big Lake	Wheeler	Wheeler
Real	Leakey	Wichita	Wichita Falls
Red River	Clarksville	Wilbarger	Vernon
Reeves	Pecos	Willacy	Raymondville
Refugio	Refugio	Williamson	Georgetown
Roberts	Miami	Wilson	Floresville
Robertson	Franklin	Winkler	Kermit
Rockwall	Rockwall	Wise	Decatur
Runnels	Ballinger	Wood	Quitman
Rusk	Henderson		
		Yoakum	Plains
Sabine	Hemphill	Young	Graham
San Augustine	San Augustine		
San Jacinto	Coldspring	Zapata	Zapata
San Patricio	Sinton	Zavala	Crystal City
San Saba	San Saba		

County	County Seat or Courthouse	County	County Seat or Courthouse
Virginia (95 cos., 41 ind. cities)		Isle of Wight	Isle of Wight
		James City	Williamsburg
Accomack	Accomac		
Albemarle	Charlottesville	King and Queen	King and Queen
Alleghany	Covington	King George	King George
Amelia	Amelia, C.H.	King William	King William
Amherst	Amherst		
Appomattox	Appomattox	Lancaster	Lancaster
Arlington	Arlington	Lee	Jonesville
Augusta	Staunton	Loudoun	Leesburg
		Louisa	Louisa
Bath	Warm Springs	Lunenburg	Lunenburg
Bedford	Bedford		
Bland	Bland	Madison	Madison
Botetourt	Fincastle	Mathews	Mathews
Brunswick	Lawrenceville	Mecklenburg	Boydton
Buchanan	Grundy	Middlesex	Saluda
Buckingham	Buckingham	Montgomery	Christiansburg
Campbell	Rustburg	Nelson	Lovingston
Caroline	Bowling Green	New Kent	New Kent
Carroll	Hillsville	Northampton	Eastville
Charles City	Charles City	Northumberland	Heathsville
Charlotte	Charlotte Courthouse	Nottoway	Nottoway
Chesterfield	Chesterfield		
Clarke	Berryville	Orange	Orange
Craig	New Castle		
Culpeper	Culpeper	Page	Luray
Cumberland	Cumberland	Patrick	Stuart
		Pittsylvania	Chatham
Dickenson	Clintwood	Powhatan	Powhatan
Dinwiddie	Dinwiddie	Prince Edward	Farmville
		Prince George	Prince George
Essex	Tappahannock	Prince William	Manassas
		Pulaski	Pulaski
Fairfax	Fairfax		
Fauquier	Warrenton	Rappahannock	Washington
Floyd	Floyd	Richmond	Warsaw
Fluvanna	Palmyra	Roanoke	Salem
Franklin	Rocky Mount	Rockbridge	Lexington
Frederick	Winchester	Rockingham	Harrisonburg
		Russell	Lebanon
Giles	Pearisburg		
Gloucester	Gloucester	Scott	Gate City
Goochland	Goochland	Shenandoah	Woodstock
Grayson	Independence	Smyth	Marion
Greene	Stanardsville	Southampton	Courtland
Greensville	Emporia	Spotsylvania	Spotsylvania
		Stafford	Stafford
Halifax	Halifax	Surry	Surry
Hanover	Hanover	Sussex	Sussex
Henrico	Richmond		
Henry	Martinsville	Tazewell	Tazewell
Highland	Monterey		

County	County Seat or Courthouse
Warren	Front Royal
Washington	Abingdon
Westmoreland	Montross
Wise	Wise
Wythe	Wytheville
York	Yorktown

Independent Cities

Alexandria

Bedford
Bristol
Buena Vista

Charlottesville
Chesapeake
Clifton Forge
Colonial Heights
Covington

Danville

Emporia

Fairfax
Falls Church
Franklin
Fredericksburg

Galax

Hampton
Harrisonburg
Hopewell

Lexington
Lynchburg

Manassas
Manassas Park
Martinsville

Newport News
Norfolk
Norton

Petersburg
Poquoson
Portsmouth

Radford
Richmond
Roanoke

Independent Cities

Salem
South Boston
Staunton
Suffolk

Virginia Beach

Waynesboro
Williamsburg
Winchester

County	County Seat or Courthouse

West Virginia (55 counties)

County	County Seat or Courthouse
Barbour	Philippi
Berkeley	Martinsburg
Boone	Madison
Braxton	Sutton
Brooke	Wellsburg
Cabell	Huntington
Calhoun	Grantsville
Clay	Clay
Doddridge	West Union
Fayette	Fayetteville
Gilmer	Glenville
Grant	Petersburg
Greenbrier	Lewisburg
Hampshire	Romney
Hancock	New Cumberland
Hardy	Moorefield
Harrison	Clarksburg
Jackson	Ripley
Jefferson	Charles Town
Kanawha	Charleston
Lewis	Weston
Lincoln	Hamlin
Logan	Logan
McDowell	Welch
Marion	Fairmont
Marshall	Moundsville
Mason	Point Pleasant
Mercer	Princeton
Mineral	Keyser
Mingo	Williamson

County	County Seat or Courthouse	County	County Seat or Courthouse
Monongalia	Morgantown	Roane	Spencer
Monroe	Union	Summers	Hinton
Morgan	Berkeley Springs		
Nicholas	Summersville	Taylor	Grafton
		Tucker	Parsons
Ohio	Wheeling	Tyler	Middlebourne
Pendleton	Franklin	Upshur	Buckhannon
Pleasants	St. Marys		
Pocahontas	Marlinton	Wayne	Wayne
Preston	Kingwood	Webster	Webster Springs
Putnam	Winfield	Wetzel	New Martinsville
		Wirt	Elizabeth
Raleigh	Beckley	Wood	Parkersburg
Randolph	Elkins	Wyoming	Pineville
Ritchie	Harrisville		

County	Land area, 1980 (Sq. mi.)	Total persons	Percent change 1970-1980	Density per square mile
ALABAMA ..	50 767	3 893 888	13.1	76.7
Autauga	597	32 259	31.9	54.0
Baldwin	1 589	78 556	32.3	49.4
Barbour	884	24 756	9.8	28.0
Bibb	625	15 723	13.8	25.2
Blount	643	36 459	35.8	56.7
Bullock	625	10 596	-10.4	17.0
Butler	779	21 680	-1.5	27.8
Calhoun	611	119 761	16.2	196.0
Chambers	596	39 191	7.8	65.8
Cherokee	553	18 760	20.2	33.9
Chilton	695	30 612	21.6	44.1
Choctaw	909	16 839	1.5	18.5
Clarke	1 230	27 702	3.7	22.5
Clay	605	13 703	8.4	22.6
Cleburne	561	12 595	14.5	22.5
Coffee	680	38 533	10.5	56.6
Colbert	589	54 519	9.8	92.5
Conecuh	854	15 884	1.5	18.6
Coosa	657	11 377	6.7	17.3
Covington	1 038	36 850	8.1	35.5
Crenshaw	611	14 110	7.0	23.1
Cullman	738	61 642	17.5	83.5
Dale	561	47 821	-9.8	85.2
Dallas	975	53 981	-2.4	55.4
De Kalb	778	53 658	27.8	69.0
Elmore	622	43 390	28.9	69.7
Escambia	951	38 440	10.1	40.4
Etowah	542	103 057	9.5	190.0
Fayette	630	18 809	15.7	29.9
Franklin	643	28 350	18.5	44.1
Geneva	578	24 253	10.6	42.0
Greene	631	11 021	3.5	17.5
Hale	661	15 604	-1.8	23.6
Henry	557	15 302	15.5	27.5
Houston	577	74 632	31.9	129.3
Jackson	1 070	51 407	31.1	48.1
Jefferson	1 119	671 324	4.1	599.9
Lamar	605	16 453	14.8	27.2
Lauderdale	661	80 546	18.3	121.8
Lawrence	693	30 170	10.6	43.5
Lee	609	76 283	24.5	125.2
Limestone	559	46 005	10.3	82.3
Lowndes	714	13 253	2.8	18.6
Macon	614	26 829	8.0	43.7
Madison	806	196 966	5.6	244.5
Marengo	982	25 047	5.2	25.5
Marion	743	30 041	26.3	40.4
Marshall	567	65 622	21.0	115.7
Mobile	1 238	364 980	15.0	294.8
Monroe	1 019	22 651	8.5	22.2
Montgomery	793	197 038	17.4	248.4
Morgan	575	90 231	16.7	156.9
Perry	718	15 012	-2.4	20.9
Pickens	890	21 481	5.7	24.1
Pike	672	28 050	12.0	41.7
Randolph	584	20 075	9.5	34.3
Russell	634	47 356	4.3	74.7
St. Clair	646	41 205	47.4	63.8
Shelby	800	66 298	74.3	82.8
Sumter	907	16 908	-.4	18.6

County	Land area, 1980 (Sq. mi.)	Total persons	Percent change 1970-1980	Density per square mile
Talladega	753	73 826	13.1	98.0
Tallapoosa	701	38 676	14.3	55.2
Tuscaloosa	1 336	137 541	18.5	102.9
Walker	804	68 660	22.1	85.4
Washington	1 081	16 821	3.6	15.6
Wilcox	883	14 755	-9.5	16.7
Winston	613	21 953	31.8	35.8
ARKANSAS .	52 078	2 286 435	18.9	43.9
Arkansas	1 006	24 175	3.5	24.0
Ashley	934	26 538	6.3	28.4
Baxter	546	27 409	78.9	50.2
Benton	843	78 115	54.8	92.6
Boone	584	26 067	36.7	44.6
Bradley	654	13 803	8.0	21.1
Calhoun	628	6 079	9.1	9.7
Carroll	634	16 203	31.7	25.6
Chicot	649	17 793	-2.0	27.4
Clark	867	23 326	8.3	26.9
Clay	641	20 616	9.8	32.2
Cleburne	551	16 909	63.4	30.7
Cleveland	599	7 868	19.1	13.1
Columbia	767	26 644	2.7	34.7
Conway	558	19 505	16.1	34.9
Craighead	713	63 239	21.5	88.7
Crawford	594	36 892	43.7	62.1
Crittenden	599	49 499	2.9	82.6
Cross	622	20 434	3.3	32.8
Dallas	668	10 515	4.9	15.7
Desha	746	19 760	5.3	26.5
Drew	831	17 910	18.2	21.5
Faulkner	645	46 192	46.3	71.6
Franklin	609	14 705	30.1	24.2
Fulton	616	9 975	29.6	16.2
Garland	657	70 531	30.3	107.4
Grant	633	13 008	34.0	20.6
Greene	579	30 744	24.1	53.1
Hempstead	725	23 635	22.4	32.6
Hot Springs	615	26 819	22.1	43.6
Howard	574	13 459	17.9	23.5
Independence	763	30 147	32.7	39.5
Izard	581	10 768	45.9	18.5
Jackson	633	21 646	5.8	34.2
Jefferson	882	90 718	6.3	102.9
Johnson	676	17 423	27.8	25.8
Lafayette	518	10 213	1.9	19.7
Lawrence	589	18 447	13.0	31.3
Lee	602	15 539	-17.7	25.8
Lincoln	562	13 369	3.5	23.8
Little River	516	13 952	24.6	27.0
Logan	717	20 144	20.0	28.1
Lonoke	783	34 518	31.5	44.1
Madison	837	11 373	20.3	13.6
Marion	587	11 334	61.9	19.3
Miller	619	37 766	13.1	61.0
Mississippi	896	59 517	-4.1	66.4
Monroe	609	14 052	-10.3	23.1
Montgomery	774	7 771	33.5	10.0
Nevada	620	11 097	9.8	17.9
Newton	823	7 756	32.7	9.4
Ouachita	737	30 541	-1.1	41.4

County	Land area, 1980 (Sq. mi.)	Total persons	Percent change 1970-1980	Density per square mile
Perry	550	7 266	29.0	13.2
Phillips	685	34 772	-13.2	50.7
Pike	598	10 373	19.1	17.3
Poinsett	762	27 032	.7	35.5
Polk	860	17 007	27.9	19.8
Pope	820	39 021	36.4	47.6
Prairie	656	10 140	-1.1	15.5
Pulaski	767	340 613	18.6	444.2
Randolph	656	16 834	33.1	25.7
St. Francis	638	30 858	.2	48.3
Saline	725	53 161	47.2	73.3
Scott	896	9 685	18.0	10.8
Searcy	668	8 847	14.4	13.2
Sebastian	535	95 172	20.1	177.9
Sevier	560	14 060	24.7	25.1
Sharp	606	14 607	77.4	24.1
Stone	606	9 022	31.9	14.9
Union	1 053	48 573	6.9	46.1
Van Buren	709	13 357	61.4	18.8
Washington	951	100 494	29.9	105.7
White	1 040	50 835	29.5	48.9
Woodruff	592	11 222	-3.0	19.0
Yell	930	17 026	19.8	18.3
FLORIDA	54 153	9 746 324	43.5	180.0
Alachua	901	151 348	44.5	167.9
Baker	585	15 289	65.4	26.1
Bay	758	97 740	29.8	129.0
Bradford	293	20 023	36.9	68.4
Brevard	995	272 959	18.7	274.2
Broward	1 211	1 018 200	64.2	840.6
Calhoun	568	9 294	21.9	16.4
Charlotte	690	58 460	112.1	84.7
Citrus	629	54 703	185.0	87.0
Clay	592	67 052	109.2	113.2
Collier	1 994	85 971	126.0	43.1
Columbia	796	35 399	40.2	44.4
Dade	1 955	1 625 781	28.2	831.5
De Soto	636	19 039	45.8	29.9
Dixie	701	7 751	41.4	11.1
Duval	776	571 003	8.0	735.4
Escambia	660	233 794	13.9	354.0
Flagler	491	10 913	145.0	22.2
Franklin	545	7 661	8.4	14.1
Gadsden	518	41 565	6.1	80.3
Gilchrist	354	5 767	62.4	16.3
Glades	763	5 992	63.3	7.9
Gulf	559	10 658	5.6	19.1
Hamilton	517	8 761	12.5	16.9
Hardee	637	19 379	30.2	30.4
Hendry	1 163	18 599	56.8	16.0
Hernando	477	44 469	161.5	93.2
Highlands	1 029	47 526	61.1	46.2
Hillsborough	1 053	646 960	32.0	614.5
Holmes	488	14 723	37.3	30.2
Indian River	497	59 896	66.4	120.5
Jackson	942	39 154	13.7	41.6
Jefferson	609	10 703	21.9	17.6

County	Land area, 1980 (Sq. mi.)	Total persons	Percent change 1970-1980	Density per square mile
Lafayette	545	4 035	39.5	7.4
Lake	954	104 870	51.3	109.9
Lee	803	205 266	95.1	255.6
Leon	676	148 655	44.3	219.9
Levy	1 100	19 870	55.8	18.1
Liberty	837	4 260	26.1	5.1
Madison	710	14 894	10.5	21.0
Manatee	747	148 442	52.9	198.7
Marion	1 610	122 488	77.4	76.1
Martin	555	64 014	128.3	115.4
Monroe	1 034	63 188	20.2	61.1
Nassau	649	32 894	59.5	50.7
Okaloosa	936	109 920	24.6	117.5
Okeechobee	770	20 264	80.4	26.3
Orange	910	471 016	36.8	517.3
Osceola	1 350	49 287	95.1	36.5
Palm Beach	1 993	576 863	65.3	289.4
Pasco	738	193 643	154.9	262.4
Pinellas	280	728 531	39.5	2 600.2
Polk	1 823	321 652	40.8	176.4
Putnam	733	50 549	38.8	69.0
St. Johns	617	51 303	65.3	83.1
St. Lucie	581	87 182	71.5	150.1
Santa Rosa	1 024	55 988	48.3	54.7
Sarasota	573	202 251	68.0	352.9
Seminole	298	179 752	114.8	603.1
Sumter	561	24 272	63.6	43.2
Suwannee	690	22 287	43.2	32.3
Taylor	1 058	16 532	21.2	15.6
Union	246	10 166	25.3	41.4
Volusia	1 113	258 762	52.7	232.5
Wakulla	601	10 887	72.6	18.1
Walton	1 066	21 300	32.4	20.0
Washington	590	14 509	26.7	24.6
GEORGIA	58 056	5 463 105	19.1	94.1
Appling	510	15 565	22.3	30.5
Atkinson	344	6 141	4.5	17.9
Bacon	286	9 379	13.9	32.8
Baker	347	3 808	-1.7	11.0
Baldwin	257	34 686	1.3	134.7
Banks	234	8 702	27.4	37.2
Barrow	163	21 354	26.7	131.3
Bartow	456	40 760	23.8	89.4
Ben Hill	254	16 000	21.5	63.1
Berrien	456	13 525	17.0	29.7
Bibb	253	150 256	4.8	593.9
Bleckley	219	10 767	4.6	49.2
Brantley	445	8 701	46.5	19.6
Brooks	491	15 255	11.0	31.1
Bryan	441	10 175	55.6	23.1
Bulloch	678	35 785	13.3	52.8
Burke	833	19 349	6.0	23.2
Butts	187	13 665	29.4	73.1
Calhoun	284	5 717	-13.5	20.1
Camden	649	13 371	18.0	20.6
Candler	248	7 518	17.2	30.3
Carroll	501	56 346	24.1	112.4
Catoosa	162	36 991	30.8	227.8
Charlton	780	7 343	29.3	9.4
Chatham	443	202 226	7.7	456.0
Chattahoochee	250	21 732	-15.8	86.9
Chattooga	313	21 856	6.4	69.7

County	Land area, 1980 (Sq. mi.)	Total persons	Percent change 1970-1980	Density per square mile
Cherokee	424	51 699	66.5	121.9
Clarke	122	74 498	14.3	610.9
Clay	196	3 553	-2.3	18.1
Clayton	148	150 357	53.2	1 016.7
Clinch	821	6 660	4.0	8.1
Cobb	343	297 718	51.3	867.2
Coffee	602	26 894	17.8	44.7
Colquitt	557	35 376	9.5	63.6
Columbia	290	40 118	79.7	138.3
Cook	233	13 490	11.2	58.0
Coweta	444	39 268	21.5	88.4
Crawford	328	7 684	33.7	23.4
Crisp	275	19 489	7.8	70.9
Dade	176	12 318	24.3	70.1
Dawson	210	4 774	31.2	22.7
Decatur	586	25 495	14.3	43.5
De Kalb	270	483 024	16.3	1 789.2
Dodge	504	16 955	8.3	33.6
Dooly	397	10 826	4.1	27.3
Dougherty	330	100 718	12.4	305.6
Douglas	203	54 573	90.4	269.2
Early	516	13 158	3.8	25.5
Echols	421	2 297	19.4	5.5
Effingham	482	18 327	34.4	38.0
Elbert	367	18 758	8.7	51.1
Emanuel	688	20 795	13.3	30.2
Evans	186	8 428	15.6	45.2
Fannin	384	14 748	10.4	38.4
Fayette	199	29 043	155.6	145.9
Floyd	519	79 800	8.2	153.9
Forsyth	226	27 958	65.2	123.6
Franklin	264	15 185	18.8	57.6
Fulton	534	589 904	-2.5	1 104.8
Gilmer	427	11 110	24.1	26.0
Glascock	144	2 382	4.5	16.5
Glynn	412	54 981	8.8	133.3
Gordon	355	30 070	27.6	84.7
Grady	459	19 845	11.3	43.2
Greene	389	11 391	11.5	29.2
Gwinnett	435	166 903	130.7	383.6
Habersham	278	25 020	20.9	89.9
Hall	379	75 649	27.3	199.5
Hancock	470	9 466	5.0	20.2
Haralson	283	18 422	15.7	65.2
Harris	464	15 464	34.2	33.3
Hart	230	18 585	17.5	80.8
Heard	292	6 520	21.8	22.3
Henry	321	36 309	53.0	113.2
Houston	380	77 605	23.3	204.4
Irwin	362	8 988	11.8	24.8
Jackson	342	25 343	20.1	74.1
Jasper	371	7 553	31.1	20.3
Jeff Davis	335	11 473	21.7	34.2
Jefferson	529	18 403	7.2	34.8
Jenkins	353	8 841	6.1	25.1
Johnson	306	8 660	12.1	28.3
Jones	394	16 579	35.1	42.0
Lamar	186	12 215	14.3	65.8
Lanier	194	5 654	12.4	29.2
Laurens	816	36 990	13.0	45.3
Lee	358	11 684	65.9	32.6
Liberty	517	37 583	113.9	72.7
Lincoln	196	6 716	13.9	34.3
Long	402	4 524	20.8	11.3
Lowndes	507	67 972	23.3	134.1
Lumpkin	287	10 762	23.3	37.5
McDuffie	256	18 546	21.4	72.5

County	Land area, 1980 (Sq. mi.)	Total persons	Percent change 1970-1980	Density per square mile
McIntosh	425	8 046	9.2	18.9
Macon	404	14 003	8.3	34.7
Madison	285	17 747	31.3	62.2
Marion	366	5 297	3.9	14.5
Meriwether	506	21 229	9.1	42.0
Miller	284	7 038	9.6	24.8
Mitchell	512	21 114	11.4	41.2
Monroe	397	14 610	32.9	36.8
Montgomery	244	7 011	15.0	28.7
Morgan	349	11 572	16.8	33.2
Murray	345	19 685	51.6	57.1
Muscogee	218	170 108	1.6	780.9
Newton	277	34 489	31.2	124.4
Oconee	186	12 427	57.0	66.7
Oglethorpe	442	8 929	17.5	20.2
Paulding	312	26 110	49.0	83.6
Peach	152	19 151	19.8	126.4
Pickens	232	11 652	21.1	50.2
Pierce	344	11 897	28.2	34.6
Pike	219	8 937	22.2	40.8
Polk	311	32 386	9.2	104.0
Pulaski	249	8 950	11.0	35.9
Putnam	344	10 295	22.6	30.0
Quitman	146	2 357	8.1	16.1
Rabun	370	10 466	25.7	28.3
Randolph	431	9 599	9.9	22.3
Richmond	326	181 629	11.8	557.3
Rockdale	132	36 747	102.4	278.5
Schley	169	3 433	10.8	20.3
Screven	655	14 043	11.5	21.4
Seminole	225	9 057	28.3	40.2
Spalding	199	47 899	21.2	240.4
Stephens	177	21 763	7.0	122.9
Stewart	452	5 896	-9.4	13.0
Sumter	489	29 360	9.0	60.1
Talbot	395	6 536	-1.3	16.6
Taliaferro	196	2 032	-16.1	10.4
Tattnall	484	18 134	9.5	37.5
Taylor	382	7 902	.5	20.7
Telfair	444	11 445	.4	25.8
Terrell	337	12 017	5.3	35.7
Thomas	551	38 098	10.2	69.2
Tift	268	32 862	20.4	122.4
Toombs	371	22 592	18.0	60.9
Towns	165	5 638	23.5	34.2
Treutlen	202	6 087	7.8	30.1
Troup	414	50 003	12.5	120.6
Turner	289	9 510	8.2	32.9
Twiggs	362	9 354	13.8	25.9
Union	320	9 390	37.9	29.4
Upson	326	25 998	10.6	79.8
Walker	446	56 470	11.4	126.6
Walton	330	31 211	33.4	94.5
Ware	907	37 180	10.9	41.0
Warren	286	6 583	-1.3	23.1
Washington	684	18 842	7.8	27.6
Wayne	647	20 750	16.2	32.1
Webster	210	2 341	-.9	11.2
Wheeler	299	5 155	12.2	17.2
White	242	10 120	30.7	41.8
Whitfield	291	65 789	19.4	226.2
Wilcox	382	7 682	9.8	20.1
Wilkes	470	10 951	7.5	23.3
Wilkinson	451	10 368	10.4	23.0
Worth	575	18 064	22.3	31.4

County	Land area, 1980 (Sq. mi.)	Total persons	Percent change 1970-1980	Density per square mile
KENTUCKY .	39 669	3 660 777	13.7	92.3
Adair	407	15 233	16.8	37.4
Allen	338	14 128	12.1	41.8
Anderson	204	12 567	34.3	61.6
Ballard	254	8 798	6.3	34.6
Barren	482	34 009	18.6	70.6
Bath	277	10 025	8.6	36.1
Bell	361	34 330	10.3	95.1
Boone	246	45 842	39.7	186.5
Bourbon	292	19 405	5.0	66.6
Boyd	160	55 513	6.0	346.1
Boyle	182	25 066	14.7	137.7
Bracken	203	7 738	7.1	38.1
Breathitt	495	17 004	19.6	34.3
Breckinridge	565	16 861	14.0	29.9
Bullitt	300	43 346	66.1	144.3
Butler	431	11 064	13.8	25.7
Caldwell	347	13 473	2.2	38.8
Calloway	386	30 031	8.4	77.8
Campbell	152	83 317	-6.1	549.7
Carlisle	191	5 487	2.5	28.8
Carroll	130	9 270	8.8	71.5
Carter	407	25 060	26.2	61.6
Casey	445	14 818	14.6	33.3
Christian	722	66 878	18.9	92.6
Clark	255	28 322	17.6	111.0
Clay	471	22 752	23.1	48.3
Clinton	196	9 321	14.0	47.5
Crittenden	360	9 207	8.4	25.6
Cumberland	304	7 289	6.4	23.9
Daviess	463	85 949	8.1	185.8
Edmonson	302	9 962	13.8	33.0
Elliott	234	6 908	16.4	29.5
Estill	256	14 495	13.7	56.7
Fayette	285	204 165	17.1	717.0
Fleming	351	12 323	8.4	35.1
Floyd	393	48 764	35.9	124.1
Franklin	212	41 830	21.3	197.2
Fulton	211	8 971	-11.9	42.4
Gallatin	99	4 842	17.1	48.8
Garrard	232	10 853	14.8	46.7
Grant	259	13 308	33.1	51.3
Graves	557	34 049	10.1	61.2
Grayson	493	20 854	26.8	42.3
Green	289	11 043	6.7	38.3
Greenup	347	39 132	17.9	112.8
Hancock	189	7 742	9.4	41.0
Hardin	629	88 917	13.4	141.3
Harlan	468	41 889	12.1	89.5
Harrison	310	15 166	7.1	49.0
Hart	412	15 402	10.2	37.3
Henderson	438	40 849	13.4	93.3
Henry	291	12 740	16.8	43.8
Hickman	245	6 065	-3.2	24.7
Hopkins	552	46 174	21.0	83.6
Jackson	346	11 996	19.9	34.7
Jefferson	386	685 004	-1.4	1 775.5
Jessamine	174	26 146	50.0	150.0
Johnson	264	24 432	39.3	92.6
Kenton	163	137 058	5.9	840.1
Knott	352	17 940	22.1	51.0
Knox	388	30 239	27.6	78.0
Larue	263	11 922	11.7	45.2
Laurel	434	38 982	42.3	89.8
Lawrence	420	14 121	31.7	33.6
Lee	211	7 754	17.7	36.7
Leslie	402	14 882	28.0	37.1
Letcher	339	30 687	32.5	90.5
Lewis	484	14 545	17.7	30.1
Lincoln	337	19 053	14.3	56.6
Livingston	312	9 219	21.4	29.6
Logan	556	24 138	10.8	43.4
Lyon	209	6 490	16.7	31.0
McCracken	251	61 310	5.2	244.5
McCreary	427	15 634	24.6	36.6
McLean	256	10 090	11.3	39.4
Madison	443	53 352	24.9	120.5
Magoffin	310	13 515	29.4	43.7
Marion	347	17 910	7.2	51.6
Marshall	304	25 637	25.8	84.3
Martin	230	13 925	48.5	60.4
Mason	241	17 765	2.8	73.7
Meade	306	22 854	21.6	74.6
Menifee	203	5 117	26.3	25.2
Mercer	250	19 011	19.1	76.1
Metcalfe	291	9 484	16.0	32.6
Monroe	331	12 353	6.1	37.3
Montgomery	199	20 046	30.5	100.9
Morgan	382	12 103	20.8	31.7
Muhlenberg	478	32 238	17.1	67.4
Nelson	424	27 584	17.5	65.1
Nicholas	197	7 157	10.0	36.4
Ohio	596	21 765	15.8	36.5
Oldham	190	27 795	89.2	146.2
Owen	354	8 924	19.5	25.2
Owsley	198	5 709	13.7	28.8
Pendleton	281	10 989	10.5	39.2
Perry	341	33 763	28.6	99.1
Pike	785	81 123	32.9	103.4
Powell	180	11 101	44.1	61.6
Pulaski	660	45 803	30.0	69.4
Robertson	100	2 265	4.7	22.6
Rockcastle	318	13 973	13.6	44.0
Rowan	282	19 049	12.0	67.5
Russell	250	13 708	30.0	54.9
Scott	286	21 813	21.5	76.4
Shelby	385	23 328	22.8	60.6
Simpson	236	14 673	12.4	62.1
Spencer	192	5 929	8.0	30.9
Taylor	270	21 178	23.6	78.4
Todd	377	11 874	9.7	31.5
Trigg	421	9 384	8.9	22.3
Trimble	148	6 253	16.9	42.1
Union	341	17 821	12.2	52.2
Warren	548	71 828	24.1	131.2
Washington	301	10 764	.3	35.8
Wayne	446	17 022	19.3	38.2
Webster	336	14 832	11.7	44.1
Whitley	443	33 396	38.3	75.3
Wolfe	223	6 698	18.2	30.0
Woodford	192	17 778	23.2	92.6
LOUISIANA	44 521	4 205 900	15.4	94.5
Acadia	657	56 427	8.3	85.9
Allen	765	21 390	2.9	27.9
Ascension	296	50 068	35.0	169.2
Assumption	342	22 084	12.4	64.5
Avoyelles	846	41 393	9.6	48.9

County	Land area, 1980 (Sq. mi.)	Total persons	Percent change 1970-1980	Density per square mile
Beauregard	1 163	29 692	29.7	25.5
Bienville	816	16 387	2.3	20.1
Bossier	845	80 721	22.5	95.5
Caddo	894	252 358	9.6	282.3
Calcasieu	1 082	167 223	15.0	154.6
Caldwell	541	10 761	15.0	19.9
Cameron	1 417	9 336	13.9	6.6
Catahoula	732	12 287	4.4	16.8
Claiborne	765	17 095	.4	22.4
Concordia	717	22 981	1.8	32.0
De Soto	880	25 727	13.0	29.2
East Baton Rouge	458	366 191	28.4	798.7
East Carroll	426	11 772	-8.6	27.7
East Feliciana	455	19 015	7.7	41.8
Evangeline	667	33 343	4.4	50.0
Franklin	635	24 141	.8	38.0
Grant	653	16 703	22.2	25.6
Iberia	589	63 752	11.1	108.2
Iberville	638	32 159	4.6	50.4
Jackson	579	17 321	8.5	29.9
Jefferson	348	454 592	34.4	1 308.0
Jefferson Davis	655	32 168	8.8	49.1
Lafayette	270	150 017	34.4	556.3
Lafourche	1 141	82 483	19.6	72.3
La Salle	638	17 004	27.9	26.7
Lincoln	472	39 763	17.6	84.2
Livingston	661	58 806	61.1	89.0
Madison	631	15 975	6.0	25.3
Morehouse	807	34 803	7.2	43.1
Natchitoches	1 264	39 863	13.2	31.5
Orleans	199	557 515	-6.1	2 796.0
Ouachita	627	139 241	20.7	222.1
Plaquemines	1 035	26 049	3.3	25.2
Pointe Coupee	566	24 045	9.3	42.5
Rapides	1 341	135 282	14.6	100.9
Red River	394	10 433	13.1	26.5
Richland	563	22 187	1.9	39.4
Sabine	855	25 280	35.6	29.6
St. Bernard	486	64 097	25.2	131.8
St. Charles	286	37 259	26.1	130.1
St. Helena	409	9 827	-1.1	24.0
St. James	248	21 495	8.9	86.6
St. John the Baptist	213	31 924	34.1	149.9
St. Landry	936	84 128	4.7	89.9
St. Martin	749	40 214	23.9	53.7
St. Mary	613	64 253	5.8	104.9
St. Tammany	873	110 869	74.4	126.9
Tangipahoa	783	80 698	22.5	103.0
Tensas	623	8 525	-12.4	13.7
Terrebonne	1 367	94 393	24.1	69.0
Union	884	21 167	14.7	23.9
Vermilion	1 205	48 458	12.5	40.2
Vernon	1 332	53 475	-.6	40.2
Washington	676	44 207	5.3	65.4
Webster	602	43 631	9.2	72.4
West Baton Rouge	194	19 086	13.2	98.6
West Carroll	360	12 922	-.8	35.9
West Feliciana	406	12 186	13.2	30.0

County	Land area, 1980 (Sq. mi.)	Total persons	Percent change 1970-1980	Density per square mile
Winn	953	17 253	5.4	18.1
MARYLAND	9 837	4 216 975	7.5	428.7
Allegany	421	80 548	-4.2	191.4
Anne Arundel	418	370 775	24.4	886.2
Baltimore	598	655 615	5.7	1 097.1
Calvert	213	34 638	67.5	162.4
Caroline	321	23 143	17.0	72.1
Carroll	452	96 356	39.6	213.2
Cecil	360	60 430	13.4	168.1
Charles	452	72 751	52.6	161.1
Dorchester	593	30 623	4.1	51.6
Frederick	663	114 792	35.2	173.2
Garrett	657	26 498	23.4	40.3
Harford	448	145 930	26.5	326.0
Howard	251	118 572	90.0	472.4
Kent	278	16 695	3.4	60.0
Montgomery	495	579 053	10.8	1 168.8
Prince George's	487	665 071	.5	1 365.6
Queen Anne's	372	25 508	38.5	68.6
St. Mary's	373	59 895	26.4	160.8
Somerset	338	19 188	1.4	56.7
Talbot	259	25 604	8.1	99.0
Washington	455	113 086	8.9	248.6
Wicomico	379	64 540	19.0	170.2
Worcester	475	30 889	26.4	65.0
Independent City				
Baltimore city	80	786 775	-13.1	9 793.1
MISSISSIPPI	47 233	2 520 638	13.7	53.4
Adams	456	38 035	2.0	83.4
Alcorn	401	33 036	21.5	82.4
Amite	732	13 369	-2.9	18.3
Attala	737	19 865	1.5	27.0
Benton	407	8 153	8.6	20.0
Bolivar	892	45 965	-7.0	51.5
Calhoun	573	15 664	7.1	27.3
Carroll	634	9 776	4.0	15.4
Chickasaw	503	17 853	6.2	35.5
Choctaw	420	8 996	6.6	21.4
Claiborne	494	12 279	21.7	24.9
Clarke	692	16 945	12.6	24.5
Clay	415	21 082	11.9	50.7
Coahoma	559	36 918	-8.7	66.0
Copiah	779	26 503	7.0	34.0
Covington	416	15 927	13.7	38.3
De Soto	483	53 930	50.3	111.7
Forrest	469	66 018	14.1	140.8
Franklin	566	8 208	2.5	14.5
George	483	15 297	22.8	31.7
Greene	718	9 827	15.0	13.7
Grenada	421	21 043	6.0	50.0
Hancock	478	24 537	41.1	51.3

County	Land area, 1980 (Sq. mi.)	Total persons	Percent change 1970- 1980	Density per square mile
Harrison	581	157 665	17.2	271.5
Hinds	875	250 998	16.8	287.0
Holmes	759	22 970	-.6	30.3
Humphreys	430	13 931	-4.6	32.4
Issaquena	406	2 513	-8.2	6.2
Itawamba	540	20 518	21.8	38.0
Jackson	731	118 015	34.1	161.4
Jasper	678	17 265	7.9	25.5
Jefferson	523	9 181	-1.2	17.5
Jefferson Davis	409	13 846	7.0	33.9
Jones	696	61 912	9.9	89.0
Kemper	766	10 148	-.8	13.2
Lafayette	669	31 030	28.3	46.4
Lamar	499	23 821	56.6	47.7
Lauderdale	705	77 285	15.2	109.7
Lawrence	435	12 518	12.4	28.8
Leake	584	18 790	10.0	32.2
Lee	451	57 061	23.6	126.6
Leflore	605	41 525	-1.4	68.7
Lincoln	587	30 174	15.2	51.4
Lowndes	517	57 304	15.3	110.8
Madison	718	41 613	39.9	58.0
Marion	548	25 708	12.4	46.9
Marshall	709	29 296	21.9	41.3
Monroe	772	36 404	6.9	47.2
Montgomery	408	13 366	3.5	32.8
Neshoba	572	23 789	14.4	41.6
Newton	580	19 944	5.1	34.4
Noxubee	698	13 212	-7.5	18.9
Oktibbeha	459	36 018	25.3	78.4
Panola	694	28 164	5.0	40.6
Pearl River	818	33 795	21.6	41.3
Perry	651	9 864	8.8	15.2
Pike	410	36 173	13.7	88.2
Pontotoc	499	20 918	20.5	41.9
Prentiss	418	24 025	19.3	57.5
Quitman	406	12 636	-20.5	31.1
Rankin	782	69 427	58.0	88.8
Scott	610	24 556	14.9	40.3
Sharkey	435	7 964	-10.9	18.3
Simpson	591	23 441	17.5	39.7
Smith	635	15 077	11.2	23.7
Stone	446	9 716	19.9	21.8
Sunflower	706	34 844	-5.9	49.3
Tallahatchie	651	17 157	-11.3	26.4
Tate	406	20 119	8.5	49.6
Tippah	458	18 739	18.2	40.9
Tishomingo	434	18 434	23.4	42.5
Tunica	460	9 652	-18.6	21.0
Union	416	21 741	13.9	52.2
Walthall	404	13 761	10.1	34.0
Warren	596	51 627	14.8	86.6
Washington	733	72 344	2.5	98.7
Wayne	813	19 135	14.9	23.5
Webster	424	10 300	2.5	24.3
Wilkinson	678	10 021	-9.7	14.8
Winston	610	19 474	5.8	31.9
Yalobusha	478	13 139	10.3	27.5
Yazoo	933	27 349	.1	29.3

County	Land area, 1980 (Sq. mi.)	Total persons	Percent change 1970- 1980	Density per square mile
MISSOURI	68 945	4 916 686	5.1	71.3
Adair	567	24 870	10.7	43.9
Andrew	435	13 980	17.4	32.1
Atchison	542	8 605	-6.9	15.9
Audrain	697	26 458	4.3	37.9
Barry	773	24 408	24.5	31.6
Barton	596	11 292	8.3	18.9
Bates	849	15 873	2.6	18.7
Benton	729	12 183	25.7	16.7
Bollinger	621	10 301	16.8	16.6
Boone	687	100 376	24.0	146.2
Buchanan	409	87 888	1.1	214.8
Butler	698	37 693	12.4	54.0
Caldwell	430	8 660	3.7	20.1
Callaway	842	32 252	24.1	38.3
Camden	641	20 017	50.3	31.2
Cape Girardeau	577	58 837	19.2	102.0
Carroll	695	12 131	-3.5	17.4
Carter	509	5 428	40.0	10.7
Cass	701	51 029	29.4	72.8
Cedar	470	11 894	26.2	25.3
Chariton	758	10 489	-5.4	13.8
Christian	564	22 402	48.1	39.7
Clark	507	8 493	2.8	16.7
Clay	403	136 488	10.3	338.3
Clinton	423	15 916	27.7	37.6
Cole	392	56 663	22.6	144.7
Cooper	567	14 643	-.6	25.8
Crawford	744	18 300	23.4	24.6
Dade	491	7 383	7.8	15.1
Dallas	543	12 096	20.3	22.3
Daviess	568	8 905	5.8	15.7
De Kalb	425	8 222	12.6	19.4
Dent	755	14 517	26.7	19.2
Douglas	814	11 594	25.1	14.2
Dunklin	547	36 324	7.7	66.4
Franklin	922	71 233	29.2	77.3
Gasconade	521	13 181	11.0	25.3
Gentry	493	7 887	-2.1	16.0
Greene	677	185 302	21.2	273.5
Grundy	437	11 959	1.2	27.3
Harrison	725	9 890	-3.6	13.6
Henry	729	19 672	6.6	27.0
Hickory	379	6 367	42.1	16.8
Holt	457	6 882	3.4	15.1
Howard	465	10 008	-5.2	21.5
Howell	928	28 807	22.5	31.1
Iron	552	11 084	16.3	20.1
Jackson	611	629 266	-3.8	1 030.1
Jasper	641	86 958	8.9	135.6
Jefferson	661	146 183	38.9	221.1
Johnson	834	39 059	14.3	46.9
Knox	507	5 508	-3.2	10.9
Laclede	768	24 323	22.0	31.7
Lafayette	632	29 925	12.4	47.3
Lawrence	613	28 973	17.8	47.2
Lewis	509	10 901	-.8	21.4
Lincoln	627	22 193	23.0	35.4
Linn	620	15 495	2.4	25.0
Livingston	537	15 739	2.4	29.3
McDonald	540	14 917	20.7	27.6
Macon	797	16 313	5.7	20.5
Madison	497	10 725	24.1	21.6

County	Land area, 1980 (Sq. mi.)	Total persons	Percent change 1970-1980	Density per square mile
Maries	528	7 551	10.2	14.3
Marion	438	28 638	1.8	65.4
Mercer	454	4 685	-4.6	10.3
Miller	593	18 532	23.3	31.3
Mississippi	410	15 726	-5.5	38.4
Moniteau	417	12 068	12.3	29.0
Monroe	670	9 716	1.8	14.5
Montgomery	540	11 537	4.9	21.4
Morgan	594	13 807	36.9	23.2
New Madrid	658	22 945	-2.0	34.9
Newton	627	40 555	23.0	64.7
Nodaway	875	21 996	-2.1	25.1
Oregon	792	10 238	11.5	12.9
Osage	606	12 014	9.3	19.8
Ozark	731	7 961	27.9	10.9
Pemiscot	517	24 987	-5.3	48.3
Perry	473	16 784	16.6	35.4
Pettis	686	36 378	6.6	53.0
Phelps	674	33 633	13.8	49.9
Pike	673	17 568	3.8	26.1
Platte	421	46 341	44.4	110.0
Polk	636	18 822	22.1	29.6
Pulaski	550	42 011	-22.2	76.4
Putnam	520	6 092	3.0	11.7
Ralls	482	8 911	14.8	18.5
Randolph	477	25 460	13.5	53.4
Ray	568	21 378	21.5	37.6
Reynolds	809	7 230	18.4	8.9
Ripley	631	12 458	27.1	19.7
St. Charles	558	144 107	55.0	258.3
St. Clair	699	8 622	12.5	12.3
Ste. Genevieve	504	15 180	18.0	30.1
St. Francois	451	42 600	15.5	94.4
St. Louis	506	973 896	2.3	1 926.4
Saline	755	24 919	.3	33.0
Schuyler	309	4 979	6.7	16.1
Scotland	438	5 415	-1.5	12.4
Scott	423	39 647	19.2	93.7
Shannon	1 004	7 885	9.6	7.9
Shelby	501	7 826	-1.0	15.6
Stoddard	815	29 009	12.6	35.6
Stone	451	15 587	57.1	34.6
Sullivan	651	7 434	-1.8	11.4
Taney	608	20 467	57.2	33.7
Texas	1 180	21 070	15.0	17.8
Vernon	837	19 806	3.9	23.7
Warren	429	14 900	53.6	34.7
Washington	762	17 983	19.2	23.6
Wayne	762	11 277	32.0	14.8
Webster	594	20 414	31.2	34.4
Worth	266	3 008	-10.4	11.3
Wright	682	16 188	18.4	23.7
Independent City				
St. Louis city	61	453 085	-27.2	7 379.2
NORTH CAROLINA	48 843	5 881 766	15.7	120.4
Alamance	433	99 319	2.9	229.3
Alexander	259	24 999	28.4	96.7
Alleghany	235	9 587	17.9	40.9
Anson	533	25 649	9.2	48.1
Ashe	426	22 325	14.1	52.4
Avery	247	14 409	13.9	58.3
Beaufort	826	40 355	12.2	48.9

County	Land area, 1980 (Sq. mi.)	Total persons	Percent change 1970-1980	Density per square mile
Bertie	701	21 024	2.4	30.0
Bladen	879	30 491	15.2	34.7
Brunswick	860	35 777	47.7	41.6
Buncombe	659	160 934	10.9	244.1
Burke	504	72 504	20.1	143.7
Cabarrus	364	85 895	15.1	235.9
Caldwell	471	67 746	19.5	143.8
Camden	240	5 829	6.9	24.2
Carteret	526	41 092	30.0	78.2
Caswell	428	20 705	8.7	48.4
Catawba	396	105 208	15.8	265.9
Chatham	708	33 415	13.1	47.2
Cherokee	452	18 933	15.9	41.9
Chowan	182	12 558	16.7	69.2
Clay	214	6 619	27.8	30.9
Cleveland	468	83 435	15.0	178.2
Columbus	938	51 037	8.7	54.4
Craven	701	71 043	13.6	101.3
Cumberland	657	247 160	16.6	376.0
Currituck	256	11 089	59.0	43.4
Dare	391	13 377	91.2	34.2
Davidson	548	113 162	18.3	206.4
Davie	267	24 599	30.5	92.3
Duplin	819	40 952	7.7	50.0
Durham	298	152 785	15.2	513.1
Edgecombe	506	55 988	7.0	110.7
Forsyth	412	243 683	13.3	590.8
Franklin	494	30 055	12.1	60.8
Gaston	357	162 568	9.5	455.0
Gates	338	8 875	4.1	26.2
Graham	289	7 217	10.0	25.0
Granville	534	34 043	3.9	63.8
Greene	266	16 117	7.7	60.5
Guilford	651	317 154	9.9	487.4
Halifax	724	55 286	1.7	76.4
Harnett	601	59 570	19.9	99.1
Haywood	555	46 495	11.5	83.8
Henderson	374	58 580	36.9	156.5
Hertford	356	23 368	-4.4	65.6
Hoke	391	20 383	24.0	52.1
Hyde	624	5 873	5.4	9.4
Iredell	574	82 538	14.3	143.8
Jackson	491	25 811	19.5	52.6
Johnston	795	70 599	14.4	88.8
Jones	470	9 705	-.8	20.6
Lee	259	36 718	20.5	141.6
Lenoir	402	59 819	8.4	148.7
Lincoln	298	42 372	29.6	142.1
McDowell	437	35 135	14.6	80.3
Macon	517	20 178	27.8	39.1
Madison	451	16 827	5.1	37.3
Martin	461	25 948	4.9	56.3
Mecklenburg	528	404 270	14.0	766.0
Mitchell	222	14 428	7.3	65.0
Montgomery	490	22 469	16.6	45.9
Moore	701	50 505	29.3	72.0
Nash	540	67 153	13.6	124.4
New Hanover	185	103 471	24.7	560.7
Northampton	538	22 584	-2.2	42.0
Onslow	763	112 784	9.4	147.9
Orange	400	77 055	33.9	192.5
Pamlico	341	10 398	9.8	30.5
Pasquotank	228	28 462	6.1	124.8

County	Land area, 1980 (Sq. mi.)	Total persons	Percent change 1970-1980	Density per square mile
Pender	875	22 215	22.4	25.4
Perquimans	246	9 486	13.6	38.5
Person	398	29 164	12.5	73.3
Pitt	657	90 146	22.0	137.3
Polk	238	12 984	10.6	54.5
Randolph	789	91 728	20.1	116.3
Richmond	477	45 481	14.0	95.3
Robeson	949	101 610	19.8	107.0
Rockingham	569	83 426	15.2	146.7
Rowan	519	99 186	10.2	191.1
Rutherford	568	53 787	13.6	94.8
Sampson	947	49 687	10.5	52.5
Scotland	319	32 273	19.8	101.1
Stanly	396	48 517	13.3	122.6
Stokes	452	33 086	39.1	73.2
Surry	539	59 449	15.6	110.2
Swain	526	10 283	16.4	19.6
Transylvania	378	23 417	18.8	61.9
Tyrrell	407	3 975	4.4	9.8
Union	639	70 380	28.6	110.1
Vance	249	36 748	12.4	147.7
Wake	854	301 327	31.6	352.7
Warren	427	16 232	5.8	38.0
Washington	332	14 801	5.4	44.6
Watauga	314	31 666	35.3	100.8
Wayne	554	97 054	13.6	175.3
Wilkes	752	58 657	18.4	78.0
Wilson	374	63 132	9.8	168.7
Yadkin	336	28 439	15.6	84.7
Yancey	314	14 934	18.3	47.6
SOUTH CAROLINA	30 203	3 121 820	20.5	103.4
Abbeville	508	22 627	7.2	44.5
Aiken	1 092	105 625	16.0	96.7
Allendale	413	10 700	9.4	25.9
Anderson	718	133 235	26.3	185.5
Bamberg	395	18 118	13.6	45.8
Barnwell	558	19 868	15.7	35.6
Beaufort	579	65 364	27.8	113.0
Berkeley	1 108	94 727	68.6	85.5
Calhoun	380	12 206	13.2	32.1
Charleston	938	276 974	11.9	295.4
Cherokee	396	40 983	11.8	103.6
Chester	580	30 148	1.1	52.0
Chesterfield	802	38 161	13.3	47.6
Clarendon	602	27 464	7.3	45.6
Colleton	1 052	31 776	14.7	30.2
Darlington	563	62 717	17.4	111.4
Dillon	406	31 083	7.8	76.6
Dorchester	575	58 761	82.1	102.2
Edgefield	490	17 528	11.7	35.8
Fairfield	685	20 700	3.5	30.2
Florence	804	110 163	22.9	137.0
Georgetown	822	42 461	26.7	51.7
Greenville	795	287 913	19.6	362.2
Greenwood	451	57 847	16.4	128.4
Hampton	561	18 159	14.4	32.4
Horry	1 143	101 419	44.9	88.7

County	Land area, 1980 (Sq. mi.)	Total persons	Percent change 1970-1980	Density per square mile
Jasper	655	14 504	22.0	22.1
Kershaw	723	39 015	12.3	53.9
Lancaster	552	53 361	23.2	96.7
Laurens	712	52 214	5.0	73.3
Lee	411	18 929	3.3	46.1
Lexington	707	140 353	57.7	198.5
McCormick	350	7 797	-2.0	22.3
Marion	493	34 179	12.9	69.4
Marlboro	483	31 634	16.5	65.6
Newberry	634	31 242	6.7	49.3
Oconee	629	48 611	19.4	77.2
Orangeburg	1 111	82 276	17.9	74.0
Pickens	499	79 292	34.5	158.9
Richland	762	269 735	15.3	354.2
Saluda	456	16 150	11.2	35.4
Spartanburg	814	201 861	16.2	248.0
Sumter	665	88 243	11.1	132.7
Union	515	30 751	5.2	59.7
Williamsburg	934	38 226	11.6	40.9
York	685	106 720	25.2	155.8
TENNESSEE	41 155	4 591 120	16.9	111.6
Anderson	339	67 346	11.7	198.8
Bedford	475	27 916	11.5	58.8
Benton	392	14 901	22.9	38.0
Bledsoe	407	9 478	24.0	23.3
Blount	558	77 770	22.0	139.3
Bradley	327	67 547	33.3	206.3
Campbell	479	34 923	34.1	72.9
Cannon	266	10 234	20.9	38.5
Carroll	600	28 285	9.9	47.2
Carter	341	50 205	16.1	147.4
Cheatham	304	21 616	63.8	71.2
Chester	289	12 727	28.2	44.1
Claiborne	432	24 595	26.6	56.9
Clay	227	7 676	15.9	33.8
Cocke	432	28 792	13.9	66.6
Coffee	428	38 311	17.6	89.4
Crockett	266	14 941	3.7	56.2
Cumberland	682	28 676	38.3	42.0
Davidson	501	477 811	6.7	954.0
Decatur	330	10 857	14.8	32.9
De Kalb	291	13 589	21.9	46.8
Dickson	491	30 037	36.7	61.2
Dyer	520	34 663	13.9	66.7
Fayette	705	25 305	11.5	35.9
Fentress	498	14 826	17.7	29.8
Franklin	543	31 983	17.2	58.9
Gibson	602	49 467	3.3	82.1
Giles	610	24 625	11.2	40.3
Grainger	273	16 751	20.1	61.4
Greene	619	54 422	14.3	88.0
Grundy	361	13 787	29.7	38.2
Hamblen	156	49 300	27.4	315.1
Hamilton	539	287 740	12.8	533.8
Hancock	223	6 887	2.5	30.8
Hardeman	670	23 873	6.4	35.6

County	Land area, 1980 (Sq. mi.)	Total persons	Percent change 1970-1980	Density per square mile
Hardin	578	22 280	22.3	38.5
Hawkins	486	43 751	29.6	90.1
Haywood	534	20 318	3.7	38.1
Henderson	520	21 390	23.2	41.1
Henry	560	28 656	20.7	51.2
Hickman	610	15 151	25.3	24.9
Houston	200	6 871	17.4	34.3
Humphreys	528	15 957	17.7	30.2
Jackson	308	9 398	15.4	30.5
Jefferson	265	31 284	25.4	117.9
Johnson	297	13 745	18.8	46.3
Knox	506	319 694	15.7	631.9
Lake	169	7 455	-7.7	44.2
Lauderdale	474	24 555	21.1	51.8
Lawrence	617	34 110	17.2	55.3
Lewis	282	9 700	43.5	34.4
Lincoln	571	26 483	8.9	46.4
Loudon	235	28 553	17.7	121.5
McMinn	429	41 878	18.1	97.6
McNairy	562	22 525	22.6	40.1
Macon	307	15 700	27.5	51.1
Madison	558	74 546	13.3	133.5
Marion	512	24 416	18.7	47.6
Marshall	376	19 698	13.7	52.3
Maury	616	51 095	16.1	82.9
Meigs	189	7 431	42.4	39.3
Monroe	648	28 700	22.3	44.3
Montgomery	539	83 342	32.9	154.7
Moore	129	4 510	26.4	35.0
Morgan	523	16 604	21.9	31.8
Obion	550	32 781	8.4	59.6
Overton	433	17 575	18.2	40.6
Perry	412	6 111	16.7	14.8
Pickett	159	4 358	15.5	27.3
Polk	438	13 602	16.6	31.1
Putnam	399	47 690	34.4	119.5
Rhea	309	24 235	40.9	78.4
Roane	357	48 425	24.5	135.8
Robertson	476	37 021	27.2	77.8
Rutherford	606	84 058	41.4	138.8
Scott	528	19 259	30.5	36.5
Sequatchie	266	8 605	35.9	32.4
Sevier	590	41 418	46.7	70.2
Shelby	772	777 113	7.6	1 007.1
Smith	313	14 935	19.4	47.7
Stewart	454	8 665	18.4	19.1
Sullivan	415	143 968	13.1	346.7
Sumner	529	85 790	52.5	162.2
Tipton	454	32 930	17.6	72.5
Trousdale	114	6 137	19.0	53.7
Unicoi	186	16 362	7.3	87.8
Union	218	11 707	29.0	53.6
Van Buren	273	4 728	25.8	17.3
Warren	431	32 653	21.1	75.8
Washington	326	88 755	20.1	272.0
Wayne	734	13 946	12.8	19.0
Weakley	581	32 896	14.1	56.6
White	373	19 567	19.8	52.5
Williamson	584	58 108	68.8	99.5
Wilson	570	56 064	51.5	98.3

County	Land area, 1980 (Sq. mi.)	Total persons	Percent change 1970-1980	Density per square mile
TEXAS	262 017	14 229 191	27.1	54.3
Anderson	1 077	38 381	38.1	35.6
Andrews	1 501	13 323	28.5	8.9
Angelina	807	64 172	30.0	79.6
Aransas	280	14 260	60.2	50.8
Archer	907	7 266	26.2	8.0
Armstrong	909	1 994	5.2	2.2
Atascosa	1 218	25 055	34.0	20.6
Austin	656	17 726	28.2	27.0
Bailey	826	8 168	-3.8	9.9
Bandera	793	7 084	49.2	8.9
Bastrop	895	24 726	42.9	27.6
Baylor	862	4 919	-5.8	5.7
Bee	880	26 030	14.5	29.6
Bell	1 055	157 889	26.8	149.7
Bexar	1 248	988 800	19.1	792.5
Blanco	714	4 681	31.2	6.6
Borden	900	859	-3.3	1.0
Bosque	989	13 401	22.2	13.6
Bowie	891	75 301	9.3	84.5
Brazoria	1 407	169 587	56.6	120.5
Brazos	589	93 588	61.4.	159.0
Brewster	6 169	7 573	-2.7	1.2
Briscoe	887	2 579	-7.7	2.9
Brooks	942	8 428	5.3	8.9
Brown	936	33 057	27.7	35.3
Burleson	669	12 313	23.1	18.4
Burnet	994	17 803	55.9	17.9
Caldwell	546	23 637	11.6	43.3
Calhoun	540	19 574	9.8	36.2
Callahan	899	10 992	34.0	12.2
Cameron	906	209 727	49.4	231.6
Camp	203	9 275	15.9	45.8
Carson	924	6 672	4.9	7.2
Cass	937	29 430	21.9	31.4
Castro	899	10 556	1.6	11.7
Chambers	616	18 538	52.1	30.1
Cherokee	1 052	38 127	19.1	36.2
Childress	707	6 950	5.2	9.8
Clay	1 086	9 582	18.6	8.8
Cochran	775	4 825	-9.4	6.2
Coke	908	3 196	3.5	3.5
Coleman	1 277	10 439	1.5	8.2
Collin	851	144 576	116.0	169.8
Collingsworth	909	4 648	-2.3	5.1
Colorado	965	18 823	6.7	19.5
Comal	555	36 446	50.8	65.7
Comanche	930	12 617	6.0	13.6
Concho	992	2 915	-.7	2.9
Cooke	893	27 656	17.8	31.0
Coryell	1 057	56 767	60.8	53.7
Cottle	895	2 947	-8.0	3.3
Crane	782	4 600	10.3	5.9
Crockett	2 806	4 608	18.6	1.6
Crosby	899	8 859	-2.5	9.9
Culberson	3 815	3 315	-3.3	.9
Dallam	1 505	6 531	8.6	4.3
Dallas	880	1 556 390	17.2	1 768.7
Dawson	903	16 184	-2.5	17.9
Deaf Smith	1 497	21 165	11.4	14.1
Delta	278	4 839	-1.8	17.4
Denton	911	143 126	89.2	157.2
De Witt	910	18 903	1.3	20.8
Dickens	907	3 539	-5.3	3.9
Dimmit	1 307	11 367	25.8	8.7
Donley	929	4 075	11.9	4.4
Duval	1 795	12 517	6.8	7.0
Eastland	924	19 480	7.7	21.1
Ector	903	115 374	24.5	127.7
Edwards	2 121	2 033	-3.5	1.0

County	Land area, 1980 (Sq. mi.)	Total persons	Percent change 1970-1980	Density per square mile
Ellis	939	59 743	28.1	63.6
El Paso	1 014	479 899	33.6	473.3
Erath	1 080	22 560	24.4	20.9
Falls	770	17 946	3.7	23.3
Fannin	895	24 285	7.0	27.1
Fayette	950	18 832	6.7	19.8
Fisher	897	5 891	-7.1	6.6
Floyd	992	9 834	-11.0	9.9
Foard	703	2 158	-2.4	3.1
Fort Bend	876	130 846	150.1	149.4
Franklin	294	6 893	30.3	23.4
Freestone	888	14 830	33.4	16.7
Frio	1 133	13 785	23.5	12.2
Gaines	1 504	13 150	13.4	8.7
Galveston	399	195 940	15.4	491.1
Garza	895	5 336	.9	6.0
Gillespie	1 061	13 532	28.2	12.7
Glasscock	900	1 304	12.9	1.4
Goliad	859	5 193	6.7	6.0
Gonzales	1 068	16 883	3.1	15.8
Gray	921	26 386	-2.1	28.7
Grayson	934	89 796	7.9	96.1
Gregg	273	99 487	31.0	364.6
Grimes	799	13 580	14.6	17.0
Guadalupe	713	46 708	39.2	65.5
Hale	1 005	37 592	10.1	37.4
Hall	877	5 594	-7.0	6.4
Hamilton	836	8 297	15.3	9.9
Hansford	921	6 209	-2.2	6.7
Hardeman	688	6 368	-6.3	9.3
Hardin	898	40 721	35.8	45.3
Harris	1 734	2 409 547	38.3	1 389.3
Harrison	908	52 265	16.6	57.5
Hartley	1 462	3 987	43.3	2.7
Haskell	901	7 725	-9.2	8.6
Hays	678	40 594	46.9	59.9
Hemphill	903	5 304	72.0	5.9
Henderson	888	42 606	61.0	48.0
Hidalgo	1 569	283 229	56.0	180.5
Hill	968	25 024	10.7	25.8
Hockley	908	23 230	13.9	25.6
Hood	425	17 714	178.2	41.7
Hopkins	789	25 247	21.9	32.0
Houston	1 234	22 299	24.9	18.1
Howard	901	33 142	-12.3	36.8
Hudspeth	4 567	2 728	14.0	.6
Hunt	840	55 248	15.2	65.8
Hutchinson	872	26 304	7.6	30.2
Irion	1 052	1 386	29.5	1.3
Jack	920	7 408	10.4	8.1
Jackson	844	13 352	2.9	15.8
Jasper	921	30 781	24.7	33.4
Jeff Davis	2 257	1 647	7.9	.7
Jefferson	937	250 938	1.8	267.7
Jim Hogg	1 136	5 168	11.0	4.5
Jim Wells	867	36 498	10.5	42.1
Johnson	730	67 649	47.8	92.6
Jones	931	17 268	7.2	18.6
Karnes	753	13 593	1.0	18.0
Kaufman	788	39 015	20.4	49.5
Kendall	663	10 635	52.7	16.0
Kenedy	1 389	543	-19.9	.4
Kent	878	1 145	-20.2	1.3
Kerr	1 107	28 780	47.9	26.0
Kimble	1 250	4 063	4.1	3.3
King	914	425	-8.4	.5
Kinney	1 359	2 279	13.6	1.7
Kleberg	853	33 358	.6	39.1
Knox	845	5 329	-10.8	6.3

County	Land area, 1980 (Sq. mi.)	Total persons	Percent change 1970-1980	Density per square mile
Lamar	919	42 156	16.9	45.9
Lamb	1 013	18 669	5.1	18.4
Lampasas	714	12 005	28.8	16.8
La Salle	1 517	5 514	10.0	3.6
Lavaca	971	19 004	6.1	19.6
Lee	631	10 952	36.1	17.4
Leon	1 079	9 594	9.8	8.9
Liberty	1 174	47 088	42.6	40.1
Limestone	930	20 224	11.7	21.7
Lipscomb	933	3 766	8.0	4.0
Live Oak	1 057	9 606	43.4	9.1
Llano	939	10 144	45.4	10.8
Loving	670	91	-44.5	.1
Lubbock	900	211 651	18.0	235.1
Lynn	888	8 605	-5.5	9.7
McCulloch	1 071	8 735	1.9	8.2
McLennan	1 031	170 755	15.7	165.7
McMullen	1 163	789	-27.9	.7
Madison	472	10 649	38.4	22.5
Marion	385	10 360	21.6	26.9
Martin	914	4 684	-1.9	5.1
Mason	934	3 683	9.7	3.9
Matagorda	1 127	37 828	35.5	33.6
Maverick	1 287	31 398	73.5	24.4
Medina	1 331	23 164	14.4	17.4
Menard	902	2 346	-11.3	2.6
Midland.......	902	82 636	26.3	91.7
Milam	1 019	22 732	13.5	22.3
Mills	748	4 477	6.3	6.0
Mitchell	912	9 088	.2	10.0
Montague	928	17 410	13.6	18.8
Montgomery ...	1 047	128 487	159.7	122.7
Moore	905	16 575	17.9	18.3
Morris	256	14 629	18.8	57.2
Motley	959	1 950	-10.5	2.0
Nacogdoches ...	939	46 786	28.7	49.8
Navarro	1 068	35 323	13.4	33.1
Newton	935	13 254	13.7	14.2
Nolan	915	17 359	7.0	19.0
Nueces	847	268 215	12.9	316.5
Ochiltree	919	9 588	-1.2	10.4
Oldham	1 485	2 283	1.1	1.5
Orange	362	83 838	17.8	231.5
Palo Pinto	949	24 062	-16.9	25.4
Panola	812	20 724	30.4	25.5
Parker	902	44 609	31.6	49.4
Parmer	885	11 038	5.0	12.5
Pecos	4 777	14 618	6.3	3.1
Polk	1 061	24 407	68.8	23.0
Potter	902	98 637	9.0	109.4
Presidio	3 857	5 188	7.1	1.3
Rains	243	4 839	29.0	19.9
Randall	917	75 062	39.3	81.8
Reagan	1 173	4 135	27.7	3.5
Real	697	2 469	22.7	3.5
Red River	1 054	16 101	12.6	15.3
Reeves	2 626	15 801	-4.4	6.0
Refugio	771	9 289	-2.2	12.1
Roberts	915	1 187	22.8	1.3
Robertson	864	14 653	1.8	17.0
Rockwall	128	14 528	106.2	113.3
Runnels	1 056	11 872	-1.9	11.2
Rusk	932	41 382	21.3	44.4
Sabine	486	8 702	21.1	17.9
San Augustine ...	524	8 785	11.8	16.8
San Jacinto ...	572	11 434	70.6	20.0
San Patricio	693	58 013	22.7	83.7
San Saba	1 136	6 204	12.0	5.5
Schleicher	1 309	2 820	23.8	2.2
Scurry	900	18 192	15.4	20.2

Appendix II

County	Land area, 1980 (Sq. mi.)	Total persons	Percent change 1970-1980	Density per square mile
Shackelford	915	3 915	17.8	4.3
Shelby	791	23 084	17.3	29.2
Sherman	923	3 174	-13.2	3.4
Smith	932	128 366	32.2	137.7
Somervell	188	4 154	48.7	22.1
Starr	1 226	27 266	54.0	22.2
Stephens	894	9 926	18.0	11.1
Sterling	923	1 206	14.2	1.3
Stonewall	925	2 406	.4	2.6
Sutton	1 455	5 130	61.6	3.5
Swisher	902	9 723	-6.3	10.8
Tarrant	868	860 880	20.3	991.7
Taylor	917	110 932	13.4	121.0
Terrell	2 357	1 595	-17.8	.7
Terry	887	14 581	3.3	16.4
Throckmorton	912	2 053	-6.9	2.3
Titus	412	21 442	28.4	52.0
Tom Green	1 515	84 784	19.3	56.0
Travis	989	419 573	42.0	424.2
Trinity	692	9 450	23.9	13.7
Tyler	922	16 223	30.7	17.6
Upshur	587	28 595	36.3	48.7
Upton	1 243	4 619	-1.7	3.7
Uvalde	1 564	22 441	29.4	14.3
Val Verde	3 150	35 910	30.7	11.4
Van Zandt	855	31 426	41.8	36.8
Victoria	887	68 807	28.0	77.6
Walker	786	41 789	51.0	53.2
Waller	514	19 798	38.6	38.5
Ward	836	13 976	7.4	16.7
Washington	610	21 998	16.7	36.1
Webb	3 362	99 258	36.2	29.5
Wharton	1 086	40 242	9.6	37.0
Wheeler	904	7 137	10.9	7.9
Wichita	606	121 082	.4	199.7
Wilbarger	947	15 931	3.8	16.8
Willacy	589	17 495	12.4	29.7
Williamson	1 137	76 521	105.1	67.3
Wilson	807	16 756	28.5	20.8
Winkler	840	9 944	3.2	11.8
Wise	902	26 575	35.0	29.4
Wood	689	24 697	32.9	35.9
Yoakum	800	8 299	13.0	10.4
Young	919	19 083	23.9	20.8
Zapata	999	6 628	52.3	6.6
Zavala	1 298	11 666	2.6	9.0
VIRGINIA	39 704	5 346 818	14.9	134.7
Accomack	476	31 268	7.8	65.7
Albemarle	725	55 783	47.7	76.9
Alleghany	446	14 333	15.0	32.1
Amelia	357	8 405	10.7	23.6
Amherst	479	29 122	11.7	60.9
Appomattox	336	11 971	22.4	35.6
Arlington	26	152 599	-12.4	5 878.2
Augusta	989	53 732	21.5	54.3
Bath	538	5 860	12.9	10.9
Bedford	747	34 927	30.7	46.7
Bland	359	6 349	17.1	17.7
Botetourt	545	23 270	27.9	42.7
Brunswick	563	15 632	-3.3	27.8
Buchanan	504	37 989	18.5	75.4
Buckingham	583	11 751	10.9	20.1
Campbell	505	45 424	4.9	89.9
Caroline	535	17 904	28.6	33.4
Carroll	478	27 270	18.1	57.1

County	Land area, 1980 (Sq. mi.)	Total persons	Percent change 1970-1980	Density per square mile
Charles City	181	6 692	8.7	36.9
Charlotte	477	12 266	-.8	25.7
Chesterfield	434	141 372	83.5	325.6
Clarke	178	9 965	23.0	55.9
Craig	330	3 948	12.0	12.0
Culpeper	382	22 620	24.2	59.2
Cumberland	300	7 881	27.5	26.3
Dickenson	331	19 806	23.2	59.8
Dinwiddie	507	22 602	-9.8	44.6
Essex	263	8 864	24.9	33.8
Fairfax	394	596 901	31.4	1 516.6
Fauquier	651	35 889	36.1	55.1
Floyd	381	11 563	18.3	30.3
Fluvanna	290	10 244	34.4	35.3
Franklin	683	35 740	26.9	52.3
Frederick	415	34 150	18.2	82.3
Giles	362	17 810	6.4	49.2
Gloucester	225	20 107	43.0	89.3
Goochland	281	11 761	16.8	41.8
Grayson	446	16 579	7.4	37.2
Greene	157	7 625	45.3	48.6
Greensville	300	10 903	13.5	36.3
Halifax	816	30 599	1.7	37.5
Hanover	467	50 398	34.5	107.8
Henrico	238	180 735	17.0	759.0
Henry	382	57 654	13.3	150.8
Highland	416	2 937	16.1	7.1
Isle of Wight	319	21 603	18.1	67.6
James City	153	22 763	27.5	148.7
King and Queen	317	5 968	8.7	18.8
King George	180	10 543	31.1	58.5
King William	278	9 334	24.5	33.6
Lancaster	133	10 129	11.0	76.2
Lee	437	25 956	27.7	59.3
Loudoun	521	57 427	54.6	110.2
Louisa	497	17 825	27.3	35.9
Lunenburg	432	12 124	3.7	28.0
Madison	322	10 232	18.5	31.8
Mathews	87	7 995	11.5	91.7
Mecklenburg	616	29 444	.1	47.8
Middlesex	134	7 719	22.6	57.6
Montgomery	390	63 516	34.7	163.0
Nelson	474	12 204	4.3	25.7
New Kent	213	8 781	65.7	41.2
Northampton	226	14 625	1.3	64.7
Northumberland	185	9 828	6.4	53.3
Nottoway	316	14 666	2.8	46.4
Orange	342	18 063	31.0	52.8
Page	313	19 401	17.0	62.0
Patrick	481	17 647	15.5	36.7
Pittsylvania	995	66 147	12.5	66.5
Powhatan	261	13 062	69.7	50.0
Prince Edward	354	16 456	14.4	46.5
Prince George	266	25 733	-11.5	96.9
Prince William	339	144 703	52.2	426.6
Pulaski	318	35 229	19.2	110.7
Rappahannock	267	6 093	17.2	22.8
Richmond	193	6 952	6.9	36.1
Roanoke	251	72 945	8.3	290.5
Rockbridge	603	17 911	7.7	29.7
Rockingham	865	57 038	19.1	66.0
Russell	479	31 761	29.5	66.3

County	Land area, 1980 (Sq. mi.)	Total persons	Percent change 1970-1980	Density per square mile
Scott	535	25 068	2.8	46.8
Shenandoah	512	27 559	20.6	53.8
Smyth	452	33 366	6.4	73.8
Southampton	603	18 731	.8	31.1
Spotsylvania	404	34 435	109.7	85.2
Stafford	271	40 470	64.6	149.3
Surry	281	6 046	2.8	21.5
Sussex	491	10 874	-5.1	22.1
Tazewell	520	50 511	26.9	97.1
Warren	217	21 200	38.6	97.6
Washington	562	46 487	13.8	82.7
Westmoreland . . .	227	14 041	15.6	62.0
Wise	405	43 863	22.0	108.4
Wythe	465	25 522	15.3	54.9
York	113	35 463	27.7	313.2
Independent Cities				
Alexandria	15	103 217	-7.0	6 867.4
Bedford	7	5 991	-.3	886.2
Bristol	12	19 042	28.2	1 644.4
Buena Vista	3	6 717	4.5	2 292.5
Charlottesville . . .	10	39 916	2.7	3 827.0
Chesapeake	340	114 486	27.8	336.7
Clifton Forge	3	5 046	-8.3	1 643.6
Colonial Heights .	8	16 509	9.4	2 149.6
Covington	4	9 063	-9.9	2 055.1
Danville	17	45 642	-1.6	2 661.3
Emporia	2	4 840	-8.7	2 000.0
Fairfax	6	19 390	-14.7	3 242.5
Falls Church	2	9 515	-11.7	4 829.9
Franklin	4	7 308	6.2	1 908.1
Fredericksburg . . .	6	15 322	6.0	2 507.7
Galax	8	6 524	3.9	788.9
Hampton	51	122 617	1.5	2 390.2
Harrisonburg	6	19 671	34.7	3 246.0
Hopewell	10	23 397	-.3	2 271.6
Lexington	2	7 292	-4.0	3 170.4
Lynchburg	50	66 743	23.4	1 347.0
Manassas	8	15 438	68.5	1 889.6
Manassas Park . .	2	6 524	-4.7	3 294.9
Martinsville	11	18 149	-7.7	1 654.4
Newport News . . .	65	144 903	4.9	2 219.0
Norfolk	53	266 979	-13.3	5 037.3
Norton	7	4 757	14.0	699.6
Petersburg	23	41 055	13.7	1 782.7
Poquoson	17	8 726	60.4	516.3
Portsmouth	30	104 577	-5.8	3 497.6
Radford	7	13 225	14.0	1 779.9
Richmond	60	219 214	-12.1	3 649.9
Roanoke	43	100 220	8.8	2 325.8
Salem	14	23 958	9.0	1 667.2
South Boston	6	7 093	3.0	1 278.0
Staunton	9	21 857	-10.8	2 550.4
Suffolk	409	47 621	5.8	116.4
Virginia Beach . . .	256	262 199	52.3	1 024.5
Waynesboro	8	15 329	-8.2	2 035.7
Williamsburg	5	9 870	8.8	1 909.1
Winchester	9	20 217	38.1	2 171.5

County	Land area, 1980 (Sq. mi.)	Total persons	Percent change 1970-1980	Density per square mile
WEST VIRGINIA .	24 119	1 949 644	11.8	80.8
Barbour	343	16 639	18.6	48.5
Berkeley	321	46 775	28.7	145.5
Boone	503	30 447	21.2	60.5
Braxton	513	13 894	9.7	27.1
Brooke	90	31 117	2.2	345.8
Cabell	282	106 835	-.1	378.5
Calhoun	280	8 250	17.1	29.4
Clay	346	11 265	20.7	32.5
Doddridge	321	7 433	16.3	23.2
Fayette	667	57 863	17.3	86.8
Gilmer	340	8 334	7.1	24.5
Grant	480	10 210	18.6	21.3
Greenbrier	1 025	37 665	17.4	36.8
Hampshire	644	14 867	27.0	23.1
Hancock	84	40 418	1.7	479.2
Hardy	585	10 030	13.3	17.2
Harrison	417	77 710	6.4	186.5
Jackson	464	25 794	23.4	55.6
Jefferson	209	30 302	42.4	144.8
Kanawha	901	231 414	.8	256.8
Lewis	389	18 813	5.4	48.4
Lincoln	439	23 675	25.2	53.9
Logan	456	50 679	9.5	111.2
McDowell	535	49 899	-1.5	93.3
Marion	312	65 789	7.2	211.1
Marshall	305	41 608	10.7	136.3
Mason	433	27 045	11.3	62.5
Mercer	420	73 942	17.0	175.9
Mineral	329	27 234	17.9	82.7
Mingo	424	37 336	13.9	88.1
Monongalia	363	75 024	17.8	206.9
Monroe	473	12 873	14.2	27.2
Morgan	230	10 711	25.3	46.6
Nicholas	650	28 126	24.7	43.3
Ohio	106	61 389	-3.2	580.6
Pendleton	698	7 910	12.5	11.3
Pleasants	131	8 236	13.2	62.9
Pocahontas	942	9 919	11.8	10.5
Preston	651	30 460	19.7	46.8
Putnam	346	38 181	38.2	110.3
Raleigh	608	86 821	23.9	142.8
Randolph	1 040	28 734	16.8	27.6
Ritchie	454	11 442	12.8	25.2
Roane	484	15 952	13.0	33.0
Summers	353	15 875	20.1	44.9
Taylor	174	16 584	19.5	95.5
Tucker	421	8 675	16.5	20.6
Tyler	258	11 320	14.0	44.0
Upshur	355	23 427	22.7	66.1
Wayne	508	46 021	22.5	90.7
Webster	556	12 245	24.8	22.0
Wetzel	359	21 874	7.7	61.0
Wirt	235	4 922	18.5	20.9
Wood	367	93 648	7.9	254.9
Wyoming	502	35 993	19.6	71.7

Appendix II

STATE INDIVIDUAL INCOME TAXES
(As of January 1, 1984)

STATE	Rate range (percent)	Income brackets ($) Lowest	Income brackets ($) Highest (over)	Personal exemptions ($) single	Personal exemptions ($) married	Personal exemptions ($) dependents
Alabama	2.0-5.0	500	3,000	1,500	3,000	300
Arkansas	1.0-7.0	3,000	25,000	17.50	35	6
Georgia	1.0-6.0	750	7,000	1,500	3,000	700
Kentucky	2.0-6.0	3,000	8,000	20	40	20
Louisiana	2.0-6.0	10,000	50,000	4,500	9,000	1,000
Maryland	2.0-5.0	1,000	3,000	800	1,600	800
Mississippi	3.0-5.0	5,000	10,000	6,000	9,500	1,500
Missouri	1.5-6.0	1,000	9,000	1,200	2,400	400
North Carolina	3.0-7.0	2,000	10,000	1,100	3,300	800
South Carolina	2.0-7.0	2,000	10,000	800	1,600	800
Virginia	2.0-5.75	3,000	12,000	600	1,200	600
West Virginia	2.1-13.0	2,000	60,000	800	1,600	800

Note: Florida and Texas have no individual income tax. Tennessee taxes interest at 6 percent, and dividends at 4 to 6 percent.

RANGE OF STATE CORPORATE INCOME TAX RATES
(As of January 1, 1984)

State	Tax (percent) minimum	Tax (percent) maximum
Alabama	5	6
Arkansas	1	6
Florida	5	5
Georgia	6	6
Kentucky	3	6
Louisiana	4	8
Maryland	7	7
Mississippi	3	5
Missouri	5	7
North Carolina	6	6
South Carolina	4.5	8
Tennessee	6	6
Virginia	6	6
West Virginia	6.9	8.05

Note: Texas has no corporate income tax.

LAND USE AND OWNERSHIP BY STATE

STATE	Urban	LAND USE (%) Crop- land	Range and Pasture	Forest	Other	LAND OWNERSHIP (%) State	Federal	Other
Alabama	5	14	13	61	7	*	3	97
Arkansas	3	24	18	42	13	*	10	90
Florida	12	9	25	35	19	1	12	87
Georgia	5	17	9	58	11	*	6	94
Kentucky	5	21	23	42	9	*	6	94
Louisiana	3	21	11	44	21	*	4	96
Maryland	19	27	8	34	12	1	3	96
Mississippi	5	24	13	48	10	*	6	94
Missouri	3	33	29	25	10	*	5	95
North Carolina	7	20	7	54	12	*	7	93
South Carolina	8	17	6	56	13	*	6	94
Tennessee	6	19	21	44	10	*	7	93
Texas	3	18	68	6	5	*	2	98
Virginia	8	13	13	52	14	*	9	91
West Virginia	5	6	13	64	12	1	7	92

* Less than 1%

THE LABOR FORCE, INCOME AND REVENUE BY STATE

STATE	CIVILIAN LABOR FORCE (excluding agriculture) Employment by Occupation (%) Total Labor Force (000)	Employ- ment Rate (%)	Govern- ment	Non- govern- ment	White Collar	Blue Collar	Other	PERSONAL INCOME (dollars) Per Capita	Per Family	STATE GOVERNMENT REVENUE (mil. of dollars) From State Taxes	From Federal Govt.	From Other
Alabama	1,642	91.2	22	78	43	41	16	7,488	16,602	1,857	1,232	1,065
Arkansas	972	92.4	19	81	43	37	20	7,268	14,356	1,161	715	419
Florida	3,925	94.0	17	83	52	30	18	8,996	17,558	4,804	1,742	1,677
Georgia	2,385	93.6	20	80	51	34	15	8,073	17,403	2,729	1,417	1,048
Kentucky	1,620	91.9	19	81	44	35	21	7,613	16,399	2,145	1,089	934
Louisiana	1,723	93.3	19	81	50	34	16	8,458	17,822	2,397	1,302	1,713
Maryland	2,133	93.6	24	76	61	26	13	10,460	22,850	2,761	1,154	1,649
Mississippi	1,024	92.5	23	77	44	39	17	6,580	14,922	1,257	913	715
Missouri	2,295	93.0	17	83	51	31	18	8,982	18,746	2,095	1,155	1,008
North Carolina ..	2,741	93.5	17	83	43	41	16	7,819	17,042	3,215	1,483	1,504
South Carolina ..	1,306	93.1	20	80	45	39	16	7,266	17,340	1,678	817	989
Tennessee	2,015	92.8	18	82	45	39	16	7,720	16,245	1,887	1,208	933
Texas	6,412	94.8	17	83	52	33	15	9,545	19,372	6,759	2,898	3,267
Virginia	2,530	94.9	24	76	55	31	14	9,392	20,423	2,743	1,333	1,580
West Virginia ...	768	90.6	21	79	41	45	14	7,800	17,621	1,219	711	710

Appendix II

EDUCATION BY STATE

	Public Schools		Higher		
	Elementary/Secondary		Education	High-School	College
STATE	Students	Teachers	Students	Graduates (%)	Graduates (%)
Alabama	759,000	41,200	145,000	56	10
Arkansas	448,000	24,100	65,000	56	9
Florida	1,510,000	78,300	346,000	65	14
Georgia	1,069,000	56,500	146,000	59	12
Kentucky	670,000	33,400	116,000	53	10
Louisiana	778,000	42,700	151,000	58	12
Maryland	751,000	41,100	197,000	69	19
Mississippi	477,000	26,300	95,000	52	11
Missouri	845,000	48,800	173,000	64	12
North Carolina	1,129,000	55,300	236,000	55	12
South Carolina	619,000	31,800	109,000	57	10
Tennessee	854,000	41,300	153,000	55	11
Texas	2,900,000	163,100	626,000	65	14
Virginia	1,010,000	58,200	251,000	64	16
West Virginia	384,000	22,200	71,000	53	9

TRANSPORTATION BY STATE

	Highways		Interstates		Railroads		Public
	1,000	1,000					Airports
STATE	mi	km	mi	km	mi	km	
Alabama	87.1	140.2	889	1,431	4,497	7,237	97
Arkansas	74.7	120.2	531	855	2,749	4,424	81
Florida	96.3	155.0	1,506	2,424	3,698	5,951	132
Georgia	104.0	167.4	1,279	2,058	5,471	8,805	125
Kentucky	69.0	111.0	741	1,193	3,572	5,749	62
Louisiana	55.8	89.8	861	1,386	3,452	5,555	74
Maryland	27.2	43.8	411	661	1,054	1,696	24
Mississippi	69.6	112.0	680	1,094	3,161	5,087	82
Missouri	117.9	189.7	1,124	1,809	5,902	9,498	118
North Carolina	92.3	148.5	859	1,382	3,640	5,858	90
South Carolina	62.1	99.9	760	1,223	2,772	4,461	66
Tennessee	82.6	132.9	1,025	1,650	3,136	5,047	77
Texas	264.9	426.3	3,245	5,222	13,304	21,411	322
Virginia	65.1	104.8	1,061	1,708	3,511	5,650	58
West Virginia	37.5	60.4	477	768	3,513	5,654	28

STATE GOVERNORS

The Governors of Alabama

	PARTY	TERM
William Wyatt Bibb	Dem.-Rep.	1819-1820
Thomas Bibb	Dem.-Rep.	1820-1821
Israel Pickens	Dem.-Rep.	1821-1825
John Murphy	Dem.-Rep.	1825-1829
Gabriel Moore	Democratic	1829-1831
Samuel B. Moore	Democratic	1831
John Gayle	Democratic	1831-1835
Clement Comer Clay	Democratic	1835-1837
Hugh McVay	Democratic	1837
Arthur P. Bagby	Democratic	1837-1841
Benjamin Fitzpatrick	Democratic	1841-1845
Joshua Lanier Martin	Democratic	1845-1847
Reuben Chapman	Democratic	1847-1849
Henry Watkins Collier	Democratic	1849-1853
John Anthony Winston	Democratic	1853-1857
Andrew Barry Moore	Democratic	1857-1861
John Gill Shorter	Democratic	1861-1863
Thomas Hill Watts	Democratic	1863-1865
Lewis E. Parsons	Democratic	1865
Robert Miller Patton	Republican	1865-1867
Military Rule		1867-1868
William Hugh Smith	Republican	1868-1870
Robert Burns Lindsay	Democratic	1870-1872
David Peter Lewis	Republican	1872-1874
George Smith Houston	Democratic	1874-1878
Rufus W. Cobb	Democratic	1878-1882
Edward Asbury O'Neal	Democratic	1882-1886
Thomas Seay	Democratic	1886-1890
Thomas Goode Jones	Democratic	1890-1894
William Calvin Oates	Democratic	1894-1896
Joseph Forney Johnston	Democratic	1896-1900
William James Samford	Democratic	1900-1901
William Dorsey Jelks	Democratic	1901-1907
Braxton Bragg Comer	Democratic	1907-1911
Emmett O'Neal	Democratic	1911-1915
Charles Henderson	Democratic	1915-1919
Thomas Erby Kilby	Democratic	1919-1923
William W. Brandon	Democratic	1923-1927
Bibb Graves	Democratic	1927-1931
Benjamin Meek Miller	Democratic	1931-1935
Bibb Graves	Democratic	1935-1939
Frank M. Dixon	Democratic	1939-1943
Chauncey Sparks	Democratic	1943-1947
James E. Folsom	Democratic	1947-1951
Gordon Persons	Democratic	1951-1955
James E. Folsom	Democratic	1955-1959
John M. Patterson	Democratic	1959-1963
George C. Wallace	Democratic	1963-1967
Lurleen Wallace	Democratic	1967-1968
Albert P. Brewer	Democratic	1968-1971
George C. Wallace	Democratic	1971-1979
Forrest H. James, Jr.	Democratic	1979-1983
George C. Wallace	Democratic	1983-

The Governors of Arkansas

	PARTY	TERM
James Sevier Conway	Democratic	1836-1840
Archibald Yell	Democratic	1840-1844
Thomas S. Drew	Democratic	1844-1849
John Seldon Roane	Democratic	1849-1852
Elias Nelson Conway	Democratic	1852-1860
Henry Massey Rector	Democratic	1860-1862
Harris Flanagin (Confederate Governor)	Democratic	1862-1863
Isaac Murphy (Union Governor)	Union	1864-1868
Powell Clayton	Republican	1868-1871
Ozra A. Hadley	Republican	1871-1873
Elisha Baxter	Republican	1873-1874
Augustus Hill Garland	Democratic	1874-1877
William R. Miller	Democratic	1877-1881
Thomas J. Churchill	Democratic	1881-1883
James Henderson Berry	Democratic	1883-1885
Simon P. Hughes	Democratic	1885-1889
James Philip Eagle	Democratic	1889-1893
William Meade Fishback	Democratic	1893-1895
James P. Clarke	Democratic	1895-1897
Daniel Webster Jones	Democratic	1897-1901
Jeff Davis	Democratic	1901-1907
John Sebastian Little	Democratic	1907-1909
George Washington Donaghey	Democratic	1909-1913
Joseph Taylor Robinson	Democratic	1913
George Washington Hays	Democratic	1913-1917
Charles Hillman Brough	Democratic	1917-1921
Thomas Chipman McRae	Democratic	1921-1925
Thomas J. Terral	Democratic	1925-1927
John Ellis Martineau	Democratic	1927-1928
Harvey Parnell	Democratic	1928-1933
Junius Marion Futrell	Democratic	1933-1937
Carl E. Bailey	Democratic	1937-1941
Homer Martin Adkins	Democratic	1941-1945
Benjamin T. Laney	Democratic	1945-1949
Sidney Sanders McMath	Democratic	1949-1953
Francis Cherry	Democratic	1953-1955
Orval E. Faubus	Democratic	1955-1967
Winthrop Rockefeller	Republican	1967-1971
Dale L. Bumpers	Democratic	1971-1975
Robert C. Riley	Democratic	1975
David H. Pryor	Democratic	1975-1979
Bill Clinton	Democratic	1979-1981
Frank D. White	Republican	1981-1983
Bill Clinton	Democratic	1983-

The Governors of Florida

	PARTY	TERM
William D. Moseley	Democratic	1845-1849
Thomas Brown	Whig	1849-1853
James E. Broome	Democratic	1853-1857
Madison S. Perry	Democratic	1857-1861
John Milton	Democratic	1861-1865
Abraham K. Allison	Democratic	1865

William Marvin	None	1865-1866
David S. Walker	Conservative	1866-1868
Harrison Reed	Republican	1868-1873
Ossian B. Hart	Republican	1873-1874
Marcellus L. Stearns	Republican	1874-1877
George F. Drew	Democratic	1877-1881
William D. Bloxham	Democratic	1881-1885
Edward A. Perry	Democratic	1885-1889
Francis P. Fleming	Democratic	1889-1893
Henry L. Mitchell	Democratic	1893-1897
William D. Bloxham	Democratic	1897-1901
W. S. Jennings	Democratic	1901-1905
N. B. Broward	Democratic	1905-1909
Albert W. Gilchrist	Democratic	1909-1913
Park Trammell	Democratic	1913-1917
Sidney J. Catts	Prohibition	1917-1921
Cary A. Hardee	Democratic	1921-1925
John W. Martin	Democratic	1925-1929
Doyle E. Carlton	Democratic	1929-1933
Dave Sholtz	Democratic	1933-1937
Fred P. Cone	Democratic	1937-1941
Spessard L. Holland	Democratic	1941-1945
Millard F. Caldwell	Democratic	1945-1949
Fuller Warren	Democratic	1949-1953
Dan McCarty	Democratic	1953
Charley E. Johns	Democratic	1953-1955
LeRoy Collins	Democratic	1955-1961
Farris Bryant	Democratic	1961-1965
Haydon Burns	Democratic	1965-1967
Claude R. Kirk, Jr.	Republican	1967-1971
Reubin O'D. Askew	Democratic	1971-1979
Robert D. Graham	Democratic	1979-

The Governors of Georgia

	PARTY	TERM
John A. Treutlen	Whig	1777-1778
John Houstoun	Whig	1778-1779
John Wereat	Whig	1779-1780
George Walton	Whig	1779-1780
Richard Howley	Whig	1780
Stephen Heard	Whig	1780
Myrick Davies	Whig	1780-1781
Nathan Brownson	Whig	1781-1782
John Martin	Whig	1782-1783
Lyman Hall	None	1783-1784
John Houstoun	None	1784-1785
Samuel Elbert	None	1785-1786
Edward Telfair	None	1786-1787
George Mathews	None	1787-1788
George Handiey	None	1788-1789
George Walton	None	1789-1790
Edward Telfair	None	1790-1793
George Mathews	None	1793-1796
Jared Irwin	None	1796-1798
James Jackson	*Jeff.-Rep.	1798-1801
David Emanuel	Jeff.-Rep.	1801
Josiah Tattnall, Jr.	Jeff.-Rep.	1801-1802
John Milledge	Jeff.-Rep.	1802-1806
Jared Irwin	Jeff.-Rep.	1806-1809
David B. Mitchell	Jeff.-Rep.	1809-1813
Peter Early	Jeff.-Rep.	1813-1815
David B. Mitchell	Jeff.-Rep.	1815-1817
William Rabun	Jeff.-Rep.	1817-1819
Matthew Talbot	Jeff.-Rep.	1819
John Clark	Jeff.-Rep.	1819-1823
George M. Troup	Jeff.-Rep.	1823-1827
John Forsyth	Jeff.-Rep.	1827-1829
George R. Gilmer	Unknown	1829-1831
Wilson Lumpkin	Democratic	1831-1835
William Schley	Democratic	1835-1837
George R. Gilmer	Whig	1837-1839
Charles J. McDonald	Democratic	1839-1843
George W. Crawford	Whig	1843-1847
George W. Towns	Democratic	1847-1851
Howell Cobb	Union (Democratic)	1851-1853
Herschel V. Johnson	Union (Democratic)	1853-1857
Joseph E. Brown	Democratic	1857-1865
James Johnson	Democratic	1865
Charles J. Jenkins	Democratic	1865-1868
Brig. Gen. Thomas H. Ruger	U.S. Military Governor	1868
Rufus B. Bullock	Republican	1868-1871
Benjamin Conley	Republican	1871-1872
James M. Smith	Democratic	1872-1877
Alfred H. Colquitt	Democratic	1877-1882
Alexander H. Stephens	Democratic	1882-1883
James S. Boynton	Democratic	1883
Henry D. McDaniel	Democratic	1883-1886
John B. Gordon	Democratic	1886-1890
William J. Northen	Democratic	1890-1894
William Y. Atkinson	Democratic	1894-1898
Allen D. Candler	Democratic	1898-1902
Joseph M. Terrell	Democratic	1902-1907
Hoke Smith	Democratic	1907-1909
Joseph M. Brown	Democratic	1909-1911
Hoke Smith	Democratic	1911
John M. Slaton	Democratic	1911-1912
Joseph M. Brown	Democratic	1912-1913
John M. Slaton	Democratic	1913-1915
Nathaniel E. Harris	Democratic	1915-1917
Hugh M. Dorsey	Democratic	1917-1921
Thomas W. Hardwick	Democratic	1921-1923
Clifford Walker	Democratic	1923-1927
Lamartine G. Hardman	Democratic	1927-1931
Richard B. Russell, Jr.	Democratic	1931-1933
Eugene Talmadge	Democratic	1933-1937
Eurith D. Rivers	Democratic	1937-1941
Eugene Talmadge	Democratic	1941-1943
Ellis Arnall	Democratic	1943-1947
Melvin E. Thompson	Democratic	1947-1948
Herman E. Talmadge	Democratic	1948-1955
Marvin Griffin	Democratic	1955-1959
Ernest Vandiver	Democratic	1959-1963
Carl E. Sanders	Democratic	1963-1967
Lester G. Maddox	Democratic	1967-1971
James E. Carter, Jr.	Democratic	1971-1975
George D. Busbee	Democratic	1975-1983
Joe Frank Harris	Democratic	1983-

*Jeffersonian-Republican, sometimes called Democratic-Republican

The Governors of Kentucky

	PARTY	TERM
Isaac Shelby	Dem.-Rep.	1792-1796
James Garrard	Dem.-Rep.	1796-1804
Christopher Greenup	Dem.-Rep.	1804-1808
Charles Scott	Dem.-Rep.	1808-1812
Isaac Shelby	Dem.-Rep.	1812-1816
George Madison	Dem.-Rep.	1816-1819
Gabriel Slaughter	Dem.-Rep.	1819-1820
John Adair	Dem.-Rep.	1820-1824
Joseph Desha	Dem.-Rep.	1824-1828
Thomas Metcalfe	*Nat.-Rep.	1828-1832
John Breathitt	Democratic	1832-1834
James T. Morehead	Nat.-Rep.	1834-1836
James Clark	Whig	1836-1839
Charles A. Wickliffe	Whig	1839-1840
Robert P. Letcher	Whig	1840-1844
William Owsley	Whig	1844-1848
John J. Crittenden	Whig	1848-1850
John L. Helm	Whig	1850-1851
Lazarus W. Powell	Democratic	1851-1855
Charles S. Morehead	Know-Nothing	1855-1859
Beriah Magoffin	Democratic	1859-1862
James F. Robinson	Union	1862-1863
Thomas E. Bramlette	Union	1863-1867
John L. Helm	Democratic	1867
John W. Stevenson	Democratic	1867-1871
Preston H. Leslie	Democratic	1871-1875
James B. McCreary	Democratic	1875-1879
Luke P. Blackburn	Democratic	1879-1883
J. Proctor Knott	Democratic	1883-1887
Simon B. Buckner	Democratic	1887-1891
John Young Brown	Democratic	1891-1895
William O. Bradley	Republican	1895-1899
William S. Taylor	Republican	1899-1900
William Goebel	Democratic	1900
J. C. W. Beckham	Democratic	1900-1907
Augustus E. Willson	Republican	1907-1911
James B. McCreary	Democratic	1911-1915
Augustus O. Stanley	Democratic	1915-1919
James D. Black	Democratic	1919
Edwin P. Morrow	Republican	1919-1923
William J. Fields	Democratic	1923-1927
Flem D. Sampson	Republican	1927-1931
Ruby Laffoon	Democratic	1931-1935
Albert B. Chandler	Democratic	1935-1939
Keen Johnson	Democratic	1939-1943
Simeon S. Willis	Republican	1943-1947
Earle C. Clements	Democratic	1947-1950
Lawrence W. Wetherby	Democratic	1950-1955
Albert B. Chandler	Democratic	1955-1959
Bert T. Combs	Democratic	1959-1963
Edward T. Breathitt	Democratic	1963-1967
Louie B. Nunn	Republican	1967-1971
Wendell Ford	Democratic	1971-1974
Julian M. Carroll	Democratic	1974-1979
John Y. Brown, Jr.	Democratic	1979-

*National-Republican

The Governors of Louisiana

	PARTY	TERM
W. C. C. Claiborne	*Jeff.-Rep.	1812-1816
Jacques Villeré	Jeff.-Rep.	1816-1820
Thomas B. Robertson	Jeff.-Rep.	1820-1824
Henry S. Thibodaux	Jeff.-Rep.	1824
Henry Johnson	Jeff.-Rep.	1824-1828
Pierre Derbigny	Jeff.-Rep.	1828-1829
Armand Beauvais	Jeff.-Rep.	1829-1830
Jacques Dupré	Jeff.-Rep.	1830-1831
Andre B. Roman	Whig	1831-1835
Edward D. White	Whig	1835-1839
Andre B. Roman	Whig	1839-1843
Alexandre Mouton	Democratic	1843-1846
Isaac Johnson	Democratic	1846-1850
Joseph Walker	Democratic	1850-1853
Paul O. Hebert	Democratic	1853-1856
Robert C. Wickliffe	Democratic	1856-1860
Thomas O. Moore	Democratic	1860-1864
Federal Military Rule		1862-1864
Henry W. Allen	Democratic	1864-1865
Michael Hahn	Republican	1864-1865
James M. Wells	Republican	1865-1867
Benjamin Flanders	Republican	1867-1868
Joshua Baker	Republican	1868
Henry C. Warmoth	Republican	1868-1872
P. B. S. Pinchback	Republican	1872-1873
John McEnery	Democratic	1873
William P. Kellogg	Republican	1873-1877
Francis T. Nicholls	Democratic	1877-1880
Louis A. Wiltz	Democratic	1880-1881
Samuel D. McEnery	Democratic	1881-1888
Francis T. Nicholls	Democratic	1888-1892
Murphy J. Foster	Democratic	1892-1900
William W. Heard	Democratic	1900-1904
Newton C. Blanchard	Democratic	1904-1908
Jared Y. Sanders	Democratic	1908-1912
Luther E. Hall	Democratic	1912-1916
Ruffin G. Pleasant	Democratic	1916-1920
John M. Parker	Democratic	1920-1924
Henry L. Fuqua	Democratic	1924-1926
Oramel H. Simpson	Democratic	1926-1928
Huey P. Long	Democratic	1928-1932
Alvin O. King	Democratic	1932
Oscar K. Allen	Democratic	1932-1936
James A. Noe	Democratic	1936
Richard W. Leche	Democratic	1936-1939
Earl K. Long	Democratic	1939-1940
Sam H. Jones	Democratic	1940-1944
James H. Davis	Democratic	1944-1948
Earl K. Long	Democratic	1948-1952
Robert F. Kennon	Democratic	1952-1956
Earl K. Long	Democratic	1956-1960
James H. Davis	Democratic	1960-1964
John J. McKeithen	Democratic	1964-1972
Edwin W. Edwards	Democratic	1972-1980
David C. Treen	Republican	1980-

*Jeffersonian-Republican, sometimes called Democratic-Republican

The Governors of Maryland

	PARTY	TERM
Thomas Johnson	None	1777-1779
Thomas Sim Lee	None	1779-1782
William Paca	None	1782-1785
William Smallwood	Unknown	1785-1788
John Eager Howard	Federalist	1788-1791
George Plater	Federalist	1791-1792
James Brice	Unknown	1792
Thomas Sim Lee	Federalist	1792-1794
John H. Stone	Federalist	1794-1797
John Henry	Federalist	1797-1798
Benjamin Ogle	Federalist	1798-1801
John Francis Mercer	Dem.-Rep.	1801-1803
Robert Bowie	Dem.-Rep.	1803-1806
Robert Wright	Dem.-Rep.	1806-1809
James Butcher	Unknown	1809
Edward Lloyd	Dem.-Rep.	1809-1911
Robert Bowie	Dem.-Rep.	1811-1812
Levin Winder	Federalist	1812-1816
Charles Ridgely	Federalist	1816-1819
Charles Goldsborough	Federalist	1819
Samuel Sprigg	Dem.-Rep.	1819-1822
Samuel Stevens, Jr.	Dem.-Rep.	1822-1826
Joseph Kent	Democratic	1826-1829
Daniel Martin	Democratic	1829-1830
Thomas King Carroll	Democratic	1830-1831
Daniel Martin	Democratic	1831
George Howard	Democratic	1831-1833
James Thomas	Whig	1833-1836
Thomas W. Veazey	Whig	1836-1839
William Grason	Democratic	1839-1842
Francis Thomas	Democratic	1842-1845
Thomas G. Pratt	Democratic	1845-1848
Philip Francis Thomas	Democratic	1848-1851
Enoch Louis Lowe	Democratic	1851-1854
Thomas Watkins Ligon	Democratic	1854-1858
Thomas Holliday Hicks	Know-Nothing	1858-1862
Augustus W. Bradford	Union	1862-1866
Thomas Swann	Democratic	1866-1869
Oden Bowie	Democratic	1869-1872
William Pinkney Whyte	Democratic	1872-1874
James Black Groome	Democratic	1874-1876
John Lee Carroll	Democratic	1876-1880
William T. Hamilton	Democratic	1880-1884
Robert M. McLane	Democratic	1884-1885
Henry Lloyd	Democratic	1885-1888
Elihu E. Jackson	Democratic	1888-1892
Frank Brown	Democratic	1892-1896
Lloyd Lowndes	Republican	1896-1900
John Walter Smith	Democratic	1900-1904
Edwin Warfield	Democratic	1904-1908
Austin L. Crothers	Democratic	1908-1912
Phillips Lee Goldsborough	Republican	1912-1916
Emerson C. Harrington	Democratic	1916-1920
Albert C. Ritchie	Democratic	1920-1935
Harry W. Nice	Republican	1935-1939
Herbert R. O'Conor	Democratic	1939-1947
Wm. Preston Lane, Jr.	Democratic	1947-1951
Theodore R. McKeldin	Republican	1951-1959
J. Millard Tawes	Democratic	1959-1967
Spiro T. Agnew	Republican	1967-1969
Marvin Mandel†	Democratic	1969-1979
Harry R. Hughes	Democratic	1979-

†Lieutenant Governor Blair Lee III served as acting governor from June 4, 1977, to Jan. 15, 1979.

The Governors of Mississippi

	PARTY	TERM
David Holmes	Dem.-Rep.	1817-1820
George Poindexter	Dem.-Rep.	1820-1822
Walter Leake	Dem.-Rep.	1822-1825
Gerard C. Brandon	Dem.-Rep.	1825-1826
David Holmes	Dem.-Rep.	1826
Gerard C. Brandon	Dem.-Rep.	1826-1832
Abram M. Scott	Democratic	1832-1833
Charles Lynch	Democratic	1833
Hiram G. Runnels	Democratic	1833-1835
John A. Quitman	Whig	1835-1836
Charles Lynch	Democratic	1936-1938
Alexander G. McNutt	Democratic	1838-1842
Tilghman M. Tucker	Democratic	1842-1844
Albert G. Brown	Democratic	1844-1848
Joseph W. Matthews	Democratic	1848-1850
John A. Quitman	Democratic	1850-1851
John I. Guion	Democratic	1851
James Whitfield	Democratic	1851-1852
Henry S. Foote	*Union-Dem.	1852-1854
John J. Pettus	Democratic	1854
John J. McRae	Democratic	1854-1857
William McWillie	Democratic	1857-1859
John J. Pettus	Democratic	1859-1863
Charles Clark	Democratic	1863-1865
William L. Sharkey	†Whig-Dem.	1865
Benjamin G. Humphreys	Whig	1865-1868
Adelbert Ames	**U.S. Mil. Gov.	1868-1870
James L. Alcorn	Republican	1870-1871
Ridgley C. Powers	Republican	1871-1874
Adelbert Ames	Republican	1874-1876
John M. Stone	Democratic	1876-1882
Robert Lowry	Democratic	1882-1890
John M. Stone	Democratic	1890-1896
Anselm J. McLaurin	Democratic	1896-1900
Andrew H. Longino	Democratic	1900-1904
James K. Vardaman	Democratic	1904-1908
Edmond F. Noel	Democratic	1908-1912
Earl L. Brewer	Democratic	1912-1916
Theodore G. Bilbo	Democratic	1916-1920
Lee M. Russell	Democratic	1920-1924
Henry L. Whitfield	Domocratic	1924-1927
Dennis Murphree	Democratic	1927-1928
Theodore G. Bilbo	Democratic	1928-1932
Martin Sennett Conner	Democratic	1932-1936
Hugh L. White	Democratic	1936-1940
Paul B. Johnson	Democratic	1940-1943
Dennis Murphree	Democratic	1943-1944
Thomas L. Bailey	Democratic	1944-1946
Fielding L. Wright	Democratic	1946-1952
Hugh L. White	Democratic	1952-1956
James P. Coleman	Democratic	1956-1960
Ross R. Barnett	Democratic	1960-1964
Paul B. Johnson	Democratic	1964-1968
John Bell Williams	Democratic	1968-1972

William Waller	Democratic	1972-1976
Cliff Finch	Democratic	1976-1980
William F. Winter	Democratic	1980-

*Union-Democratic; †Whig-Democratic; **United States Military Governor

The Governors of Missouri

	PARTY	TERM
Alexander McNair	Dem.-Rep.	1820-1824
Frederick Bates	Dem.-Rep.	1824-1825
Abraham J. Williams	Dem.-Rep.	1825-1826
John Miller	Dem.-Rep.	1826-1832
Daniel Dunklin	Democratic	1832-1836
Lilburn W. Boggs	Democratic	1836-1840
Thomas Reynolds	Democratic	1840-1844
Meredith M. Marmaduke	Democratic	1844
John C. Edwards	Democratic	1844-1848
Austin A. King	Democratic	1848-1853
Sterling Price	Democratic	1853-1857
Trusten Polk	Democratic	1857
Hancock Lee Jackson	Democratic	1857
Robert M. Stewart	Democratic	1857-1861
Claiborne F. Jackson	Democratic	1861
Hamilton R. Gamble	Union	1861-1864
Willard P. Hall	Union	1864-1865
Thomas C. Fletcher	Republican	1865-1869
Joseph W. McClurg	Republican	1869-1871
B. Gratz Brown	*Lib. Rep.	1871-1873
Silas Woodson	Democratic	1873-1875
Charles H. Hardin	Democratic	1875-1877
John S. Phelps	Democratic	1877-1881
Thomas T. Crittenden	Democratic	1881-1885
John S. Marmaduke	Democratic	1885-1887
Albert P. Morehouse	Democratic	1887-1889
David R. Francis	Democratic	1889-1893
William Joel Stone	Democratic	1893-1897
Lon V. Stephens	Democratic	1897-1901
Alexander M. Dockery	Democratic	1901-1905
Joseph W. Folk	Democratic	1905-1909
Herbert S. Hadley	Republican	1909-1913
Elliott W. Major	Democratic	1913-1917
Frederick D. Gardner	Democratic	1917-1921
Arthur M. Hyde	Republican	1921-1925
Sam A. Baker	Republican	1925-1929
Henry S. Caulfield	Republican	1929-1933
Guy B. Park	Democratic	1933-1937
Lloyd C. Stark	Democratic	1937-1941
Forrest C. Donnell	Republican	1941-1945
Phil M. Donnelly	Democratic	1945-1949
Forrest Smith	Democratic	1949-1953
Phil M. Donnelly	Democratic	1953-1957
James T. Blair, Jr.	Democratic	1957-1961
John M. Dalton	Democratic	1961-1965
Warren E. Hearnes	Democratic	1965-1973
Christopher S. Bond	Republican	1973-1977
Joseph P. Teasdale	Democratic	1977-1981
Christopher S. Bond	Republican	1981-

*Liberal Republican

The Governors of North Carolina

	PARTY	TERM
Richard Caswell	None	1776-1780
Abner Nash	None	1780-1781
Thomas Burke	None	1781-1782
Alexander Martin	None	1782-1784
Richard Caswell	None	1784-1787
Samuel Johnston	Federalist	1787-1789
Alexander Martin	Unknown	1789-1792
R. D. Spaight, Sr.	Dem.-Rep.	1792-1795
Samuel Ashe	Dem.-Rep.	1795-1798
W. R. Davie	Federalist	1798-1799
Benjamin Williams	Dem.-Rep.	1799-1802
James Turner	Dem.-Rep.	1802-1805
Nathaniel Alexander	Dem.-Rep.	1805-1807
Benjamin Williams	Dem.-Rep.	1807-1808
David Stone	Dem.-Rep.	1808-1810
Benjamin Smith	Dem.-Rep.	1810-1811
William Hawkins	Dem.-Rep.	1811-1814
William Miller	Dem.-Rep.	1814-1817
John Branch	Dem.-Rep.	1817-1820
Jesse Franklin	Dem.-Rep.	1820-1821
Gabriel Holmes	Unknown	1821-1824
H. G. Burton	Federalist	1824-1827
James Iredell, Jr.	Dem.-Rep.	1827-1828
John Owen	Unknown	1828-1830
Montfort Stokes	Democratic	1830-1832
D. L. Swain	Whig	1832-1835
R. D. Spaight, Jr.	Democratic	1835-1836
E. B. Dudley	Whig	1836-1841
J. M. Morehead	Whig	1841-1845
W. A. Graham	Whig	1845-1849
Charles Manly	Whig	1849-1851
D. S. Reid	Democratic	1851-1854
Warren Winslow	Democratic	1854-1855
Thomas Bragg	Democratic	1855-1859
John W. Ellis	Democratic	1859-1861
Henry T. Clark	Democratic	1861-1862
Z. B. Vance	Democratic	1862-1865
W. W. Holden	Republican	1865
Jonathan Worth	Democratic	1865-1868
W. W. Holden	Republican	1868-1871
T. R. Caldwell	Republican	1871-1874
C. H. Brogden	Republican	1874-1877
Z. B. Vance	Democratic	1877-1879
T. J. Jarvis	Democratic	1879-1885
A. M. Scales	Democratic	1885-1889
D. G. Fowle	Democratic	1889-1891
Thomas M. Holt	Democratic	1891-1893
Elias Carr	Democratic	1893-1897
D. L. Russell	Republican	1897-1901
Charles B. Aycock	Democratic	1901-1905
R. B. Glenn	Democratic	1905-1909
W. W. Kitchin	Democratic	1909-1913
Locke Craig	Democratic	1913-1917
Thomas W. Bickett	Democratic	1917-1921
Cameron Morrison	Democratic	1921-1925
Angus Wilton McLean	Democratic	1925-1929
O. Max Gardner	Democratic	1929-1933
J. C. B. Ehringhaus	Democratic	1933-1937
Clyde R. Hoey	Democratic	1937-1941
J. Melville Broughton	Democratic	1941-1945
R. Gregg Cherry	Democratic	1945-1949

W. Kerr Scott	Democratic	1949-1953
William B. Umstead	Democratic	1953-1954
Luther H. Hodges	Democratic	1954-1961
Terry Sanford	Democratic	1961-1965
Daniel K. Moore	Democratic	1965-1969
Robert W. Scott	Democratic	1969-1973
James E. Holshouser, Jr.	Republican	1973-1977
James B. Hunt, Jr.	Democratic	1977-

The Governors of South Carolina

	PARTY	TERM
John Rutledge	None	1776-1778
Lowlins Lowndes	None	1778-1779
John Rutledge	None	1779-1782
John Mathews	None	1782-1783
Benjamin Guerard	None	1783-1785
William Moultrie	None	1785-1787
Thomas Pinckney	None	1787-1789
Charles Pinckney	None	1789-1792
William Moultrie	Federalist	1792-1794
Arnoldus Vander Horst	Federalist	1794-1796
Charles Pinckney	Dem.-Rep.	1796-1798
Edward Rutledge	Dem.-Rep.	1798-1800
John Drayton	Dem.-Rep.	1800-1802
James B. Richardson	Dem.-Rep.	1802-1804
Paul Hamilton	Dem.-Rep.	1804-1806
Charles Pinckney	Dem.-Rep.	1806-1808
John Drayton	Dem.-Rep.	1808-1810
Henry Middleton	Dem.-Rep.	1810-1812
Joseph Alston	Dem.-Rep.	1812-1814
David R. Williams	Dem.-Rep.	1814-1816
Andrew Pickens	Dem.-Rep.	1816-1818
John Geddes	Dem.-Rep.	1818-1820
Thomas Bonnett	Dem.-Rep.	1820-1822
John L. Wilson	Dem.-Rep.	1822-1824
Richard I. Manning	Dem.-Rep.	1824-1826
John Taylor	Dem.-Rep.	1826-1828
Stephen D. Miller	Democratic	1826-1828
James Hamilton, Jr.	Democratic	1830-1832
Robert Y. Hayne	Democratic	1832-1834
George McDuffie	Democratic	1834-1836
Pierce M. Butler	Democratic	1836-1838
Patrick Noble	Democratic	1838-1840
G. K. Henagan	Democratic	1840
John P. Richardson	Democratic	1840-1842
James H. Hammond	Democratic	1842-1844
William Aiken	Democratic	1844-1846
David Johnson	Democratic	1846-1848
Whitemarsh B. Seabrook	Democratic	1848-1850
John H. Means	Democratic	1850-1852
John L. Manning	Democratic	1852-1854
James H. Adams	Democratic	1854-1856
Robert F. W. Allston	Democratic	1856-1858
William H. Gist	Democratic	1858-1860
Francis W. Pickens	Democratic	1860-1862
Milledge L. Bonham	Democratic	1862-1864
Andrew G. Magrath	Democratic	1864-1865
Benjamin F. Perry	Democratic	1865
James L. Orr	Democratic	1865-1868
Robert K. Scott	Republican	1868-1872
Franklin J. Moses, Jr.	Republican	1872-1874
Daniel H. Chamberlain	Republican	1874-1876
Wade Hampton	Democratic	1876-1879
William D. Simpson	Democratic	1879-1880
Thomas B. Jeter	Democratic	1880
Johnson Hagood	Democratic	1880-1882
Hugh S. Thompson	Democratic	1882-1886
John C. Sheppard	Democratic	1886
John P. Richardson	Democratic	1886-1890
Benjamin R. Tillman	Democratic	1890-1894
John G. Evans	Democratic	1894-1897
William H. Ellerbe	Democratic	1897-1899
Miles B. McSweeney	Democratic	1899-1903
Duncan C. Heyward	Democratic	1903-1907
Martin F. Ansel	Democratic	1907-1911
Coleman L. Blease	Democratic	1911-1915
Charles A. Smith	Democratic	1915
Richard I. Manning	Democratic	1915-1919
Robert A. Cooper	Democratic	1919-1922
Wilson G. Harvey	Democratic	1922-1923
Thomas G. McLeod	Democratic	1923-1927
John G. Richards	Democratic	1927-1931
Ibra C. Blackwood	Democratic	1931-1935
Olin D. Johnston	Democratic	1935-1939
Burnet R. Maybank	Democratic	1939-1941
J. Emile Harley	Democratic	1941-1942
Richard M. Jefferies	Democratic	1942-1943
Olin D. Johnston	Democratic	1943-1945
Ransome J. Williams	Democratic	1945-1947
Strom Thurmond	Democratic	1947-1951
James F. Byrnes	Democratic	1951-1955
George B. Timmerman, Jr.	Democratic	1955-1959
Ernest F. Hollings	Democratic	1959-1963
Donald S. Russell	Democratic	1963-1965
Robert E. McNair	Democratic	1965-1971
John C. West	Democratic	1971-1975
James B. Edwards	Republican	1975-1979
Richard W. Riley	Democratic	1979-

The Governors of Tennessee

	PARTY	TERM
John Sevier	Dem.-Rep.	1796-1801
Archibald Roane	Dem.-Rep.	1801-1803
John Sevier	Dem.-Rep.	1803-1809
Willie Blount	Dem.-Rep.	1809-1815
Joseph McMinn	Dem.-Rep.	1815-1821
William Carroll	Dem.-Rep.	1821-1827
Sam Houston	Dem.-Rep.	1827-1829
William Hall	Democratic	1829
William Carroll	Democratic	1829-1835
Newton Cannon	Whig	1835-1839
James K. Polk	Democratic	1839-1841
James C. Jones	Whig	1841-1845
Aaron V. Brown	Democratic	1845-1847
Neill S. Brown	Whig	1847-1849
William Trousdale	Democratic	1849-1851
William B. Campbell	Whig	1851-1853
Andrew Johnson	Democratic	1853-1857
Isham G. Harris	Democratic	1857-1862
Andrew Johnson (Military Governor)	Democratic	1862-1865
William G. Brownlow	*Whig-Rep.	1865-1869

DeWitt Clinton Senter	Whig-Rep.	1869-1871
John C. Brown	†Whig-Dem.	1871-1875
James D. Porter	Democratic	1875-1879
Albert S. Marks	Democratic	1879-1881
Alvin Hawkins	Republican	1881-1883
William B. Bate	Democratic	1883-1887
Robert Love Taylor	Democratic	1887-1891
John P. Buchanan	Democratic	1891-1893
Peter Turney	Democratic	1893-1897
Robert Love Taylor	Democratic	1897-1899
Benton McMillin	Democratic	1899-1903
James B. Frazier	Democratic	1903-1905
John I. Cox	Democratic	1905-1907
Malcolm R. Patterson	Democratic	1907-1911
Ben W. Hooper	Republican	1911-1915
Tom C. Rye	Democratic	1915-1919
A. H. Roberts	Democratic	1919-1921
Alfred A. Taylor	Republican	1921-1923
Austin Peay	Democratic	1923-1927
Henry H. Horton	Democratic	1927-1933
Hill McAlister	Democratic	1933-1937
Gordon Browning	Democratic	1937-1939
Prentice Cooper	Democratic	1939-1945
Jim McCord	Democratic	1945-1949
Gordon Browning	Democratic	1949-1953
Frank G. Clement	Democratic	1953-1959
Buford Ellington	Democratic	1959-1963
Frank G. Clement	Democratic	1963-1967
Buford Ellington	Democratic	1967-1971
Winfield Dunn	Republican	1971-1975
Leonard Ray Blanton	Democratic	1975-1979
Lamar Alexander	Republican	1979-

*Whig-Republican †Whig-Democratic

The Govenors of Texas

	PARTY	TERM
J. Pinckney Henderson	Democratic	1846-1847
George T. Wood	Democratic	1847-1849
P. Hansborough Bell	Democratic	1849-1853
Elisha M. Pease	Democratic	1853-1857
Hardin R. Runnels	Democratic	1857-1859
Sam Houston	Independent	1859-1861
Francis R. Lubbock	Democratic	1861-1863
Pendleton Murrah	Democratic	1863-1865
Under Federal Military Rule		1865
Andrew J. Hamilton	Conservative	1865-1866
James W. Throckmorton	Conservative	1866-1867
Elisha M. Pease	Republican	1867-1869
Under Federal Military Rule		1869-1870
Edmund J. Davis	Republican	1870-1874
Richard Coke	Democratic	1874-1876
Richard B. Hubbard	Democratic	1876-1879
Oran M. Roberts	Democratic	1879-1883
John Ireland	Democratic	1883-1887
Lawrence S. Ross	Democratic	1887-1891
James S. Hogg	Democratic	1891-1895
Charles A. Culberson	Democratic	1895-1899
Joseph D. Sayers	Democratic	1899-1903
S. W. T. Lanham	Democratic	1903-1907
Thomas M. Campbell	Democratic	1907-1911
Oscar B. Colquitt	Democratic	1911-1915
James E. Ferguson	Democratic	1915-1917

William P. Hobby	Democratic	1917-1921
Pat M. Neff	Democratic	1921-1925
Miriam A. Ferguson	Democratic	1925-1927
Dan Moody	Democratic	1927-1931
Ross Sterling	Democratic	1931-1933
Miriam A. Ferguson	Democratic	1933-1935
James V. Allred	Democratic	1935-1939
W. Lee O'Daniel	Democratic	1939-1941
Coke R. Stevenson	Democratic	1941-1947
Beauford H. Jester	Democratic	1947-1949
Allan Shivers	Democratic	1949-1957
Price Daniel	Democratic	1957-1963
John B. Connally	Democratic	1963-1969
Preston Smith	Democratic	1969-1973
Dolph Briscoe	Democratic	1973-1979
William P. Clements	Republican	1979-1983
Mark White	Democratic	1983-

The Governors of Virginia

	PARTY	TERM
Patrick Henry	None	1776-1779
Thomas Jefferson	None	1779-1781
William Fleming	None	1781
Thomas Nelson, Jr.	None	1781
Benjamin Harrison	None	1781-1784
Patrick Henry	None	1784-1786
Edmund Randolph	None	1786-1788
Beverley Randolph	None	1788-1791
Henry Lee	Federalist	1791-1794
Robert Brooke	Dem.-Rep.	1794-1796
James Wood	Dem.-Rep.	1796-1799
James Monroe	Dem.-Rep.	1799-1802
John Page	Dem.-Rep.	1802-1805
William H. Cabell	Dem.-Rep.	1805-1808
John Tyler, Sr.	Dem.-Rep.	1808-1811
James Monroe	Dem.-Rep.	1811
George William Smith	Dem.-Rep.	1811
Peyton Randolph	Dem.-Rep.	1811-1812
James Barbour	Dem.-Rep.	1812-1814
Wilson Cary Nicholas	Dem.-Rep.	1814-1816
James Patton Preston	Dem.-Rep.	1816-1819
Thomas Mann Randolph	Dem.-Rep.	1819-1822
James Pleasants	Dem.-Rep.	1822-1825
John Tyler, Jr.	Dem.-Rep.	1825-1827
William Branch Giles	Democratic	1827-1830
John Floyd	Democratic	1830-1834
Littleton Waller Tazewell	Whig	1834-1836
Wyndham Robertson	Whig	1836-1837
David Campbell	Democratic	1837-1840
Thomas Walker Gilmer	Whig	1840-1841
John Mercer Patton	Whig	1841
John Rutherfoord	Whig	1841-1842
John Munford Gregory	Whig	1842-1843
James McDowell	Democratic	1843-1846
William Smith	Democratic	1846-1849
John Buchanan Floyd	Democratic	1849-1852
Joseph Johnson	Democratic	1852-1856
Henry A. Wise	Democratic	1856-1860
John Letcher	Democratic	1860-1864
William Smith	Democratic	1864-1865
Francis H. Pierpont	Republican	1965-1868

Henry H. Wells	Republican	1868-1869
Gilbert C. Walker	Republican	1869-1874
James L. Kemper	Democratic	1874-1878
Frederick W. M. Holliday	Democratic	1878-1882
William E. Cameron	R.-Rep.*	1882-1886
Fitzhugh Lee	Democratic	1886-1890
Philip W. McKinney	Democratic	1890-1894
Charles T. O'Ferrall	Democratic	1894-1898
James Hoge Tyler	Democratic	1898-1902
Andrew Jackson Montague	Democratic	1902-1906
Claude A. Swanson	Democratic	1906-1910
William Hodges Mann	Democratic	1910-1914
Henry Carter Stuart	Democratic	1914-1918
Westmoreland Davis	Democratic	1918-1922
Elbert Lee Trinkle	Democratic	1922-1926
Harry Flood Byrd	Democratic	1926-1930
John Garland Pollard	Democratic	1930-1934
George C. Peery	Democratic	1934-1938
James H. Price	Democratic	1938-1942
Colgate W. Darden, Jr.	Democratic	1942-1946
William M. Tuck	Democratic	1946-1950
John S. Battle	Democratic	1950-1954
Thomas B. Stanley	Democratic	1954-1958
J. Lindsay Almond, Jr.	Democratic	1958-1962
Albertis S. Harrison, Jr.	Democratic	1962-1966
Mills E. Godwin, Jr.	Democratic	1966-1970
A. Linwood Holton, Jr.	Republican	1970-1974
Mills E. Godwin, Jr.	Republican	1974-1978
John N. Dalton	Republican	1978-1982
Charles S. Robb	Democratic	1982-

*Readjuster-Republican

The Governors of West Virginia

	PARTY	TERM
Arthur I. Boreman	Republican	1863-1869
Daniel D. T. Farnsworth	Republican	1869
William E. Stevenson	Republican	1869-1871
John J. Jacob	Democratic	1871-1877
Henry M. Mathews	Democratic	1877-1881
Jacob B. Jackson	Democratic	1881-1885
Emanuel W. Wilson	Democratic	1885-1890
Aretas B. Fleming	Democratic	1890-1893
William A. MacCorkle	Democratic	1893-1897
George W. Atkinson	Republican	1897-1901
Albert B. White	Republican	1901-1905
William M. O. Dawson	Republican	1905-1909
William E. Glasscock	Republican	1909-1913
Henry D. Hatfield	Republican	1913-1917
John J. Cornwell	Democratic	1917-1921
Ephraim F. Morgan	Republican	1921-1925
Howard M. Gore	Republican	1925-1929
William G. Conley	Republican	1929-1933
Herman G. Kump	Democratic	1933-1937
Homer A. Holt	Democratic	1937-1941
Matthew M. Neely	Democratic	1941-1945
Clarence W. Meadows	Democratic	1945-1949
Okey L. Patteson	Democratic	1949-1953
William C. Marland	Democratic	1953-1957
Cecil H. Underwood	Republican	1957-1961
William Wallace Barron	Democratic	1961-1965
Hulett C. Smith	Democratic	1965-1969
Arch A. Moore	Republican	1969-1977
John D. Rockefeller IV	Democratic	1977-

THE KENTUCKY AND VIRGINIA RESOLUTIONS OF 1798

KENTUCKY RESOLUTIONS
November 16, 1798

I. *Resolved,* that the several States composing the United States of America, are not united on the principle of unlimited submission to their general government; but that by compact under the style and title of a Constitution for the United States and of amendments thereto, they constituted a general government for special purposes, delegated to that government certain definite powers, reserving each State to itself, the residuary mass of right to their own self-government; and that whensoever the general government assumes undelegated powers, its acts are unauthoritative, void, and of no force: That to this compact each State acceded as a State, and is an integral party, its co-States forming, as to itself, the other party: That the government created by this compact was not made the exclusive or final judge of the extent of the powers delegated to itself; since that would have made its discretion, and not the Constitution, the measure of its powers; but that as in all other cases of compact among parties having no common Judge, *each party has an equal right to judge for itself, as well of infractions as of the mode and measure of redress.*

II. *Resolved,* that the Constitution of the United States having delegated to Congress a power to punish treason, counterfeiting the securities and current coin of the United States, piracies and felonies committed on the high seas, and offenses against the laws of nations, and no other crimes whatever, and it being true as a general principle, and one of the amendments to the Constitution having also declared "that the powers not delegated to the United States by the Constitution, nor prohibited by it to the States, are reserved to the States respectively, or to the people," therefore also [the Sedition Act of July 14, 1798]; as also the act passed by them on the 27th day of June, 1798, entitled "An act to punish frauds committed on the Bank of the United States" (and all other their acts which assume to create, define, or punish crimes other than those enumerated in the Constitution), are altogether void and of no force, and that the power to create, define, and punish such other crimes is reserved, and of right appertains solely and exclusively to the respective States, each within its own Territory.

III. *Resolved,* that it is true as a general principle, and is also expressly declared by one of the amendments to the Constitution that "the powers not delegated to the United States by the Constitution, nor prohibited by it to the States, are reserved to the States respectively or to the people;" and that no power over the freedom of religion, freedom of speech, or freedom of the press being delegated to the United States by the Constitution, nor prohibited by it to the States, all lawful powers respecting the same did of right remain, and were reserved to the States, or to the people: That thus was manifested their determination to retain to themselves the right of judging how far the licentiousness of speech and of the press may be abridged without lessening their useful freedom, and how far those abuses which cannot be separated from their use should be tolerated rather than the use be destroyed; and thus also they guarded against all abridgment by the United States of the freedom of religious opinions and exercises, and retained to themselves the right of protecting the same, as this State, by a law passed on the general demand of its citizens, had already protected them from all human restraint or interference: And that in addition to this general principle and express declaration, another and more special provision has been made by one of the amendments to the Constitution which expressly declares, that "Congress shall make no law respecting an establishment of religion, or prohibiting the free exercise thereof, or abridging the freedom of speech, or of the press," thereby guarding in the same sentence, and under the same words, the freedom of religion, of speech, and of the press, insomuch, that whatever violates either, throws down the sanctuary which covers the others, and that libels, falsehoods, defamation equally with heresy and false religion, are withheld from the cognizance of Federal tribunals. That therefore [the Sedition Act], which does abridge freedom of the press, is not law, but is altogether void and of no effect.

IV. *Resolved,* that alien friends are under the jurisdiction and protection of the laws of the State wherein they are; that no power over them has been delegated to the United States, nor prohibited to the individual States distinct from their power over citizens; and it being true as a general principle, and one of the amendments to the Constitution having also declared that "the powers not delegated to the United States by the Constitution, nor prohibited by it to the States, are reserved to the States respectively, or to the people," the [Alien Act of June 22, 1798], which assumes power over alien friends not delegated by the Constitution, is not law, but is altogether void and of no force.

V. *Resolved*, that in addition to the general principle as well as the express declaration, that powers not delegated are reserved, another and more special provision inserted in the Constitution from abundant caution has declared, "that the migration or importation of such persons as any of the States now existing shall think proper to admit, shall not be prohibited by the Congress prior to the year 1808." That this Commonwealth does admit the migration of alien friends described as the subject of the said act concerning aliens; that a provision against prohibiting their migration is a provision against all acts equivalent thereto, or it would be nugatory; that to remove them when migrated is equivalent to a prohibition of their migration, and is therefore contrary to the said provision of the Constitution, and void.

VI. *Resolved*, that the imprisonment of a person under the protection of the laws of this Commonwealth on his failure to obey the simple order of the President to depart out of the United States, as is undertaken by the said act entitled "An act concerning aliens," is contrary to the Constitution, one amendment to which has provided, that "no person shall be deprived of liberty without due process of law," and that another having provided "that in all criminal prosecutions, the accused shall enjoy the right to a public trial by an impartial jury, to be informed of the nature and cause of the accusation, to be confronted with the witnesses against him, to have compulsory process for obtaining witnesses in his favour, and to have the assistance of counsel for his defense," the same act undertaking to authorize the President to remove a person out of the United States who is under the protection of the law, on his own suspicion, without accusation, without jury, without public trial, without confrontation of the witnesses against him, without having witnesses in his favour, without defense, without counsel, is contrary to these provisions also of the Constitution, is therefore not law, but utterly void and of no force. That transferring the power of judging any person who is under the protection of the laws, from the courts to the President of the United States, as is undertaken by the same act concerning aliens, is against the article of the Constitution which provides, that "the judicial power of the United States shall be vested in courts, the judges of which shall hold their offices during good behavior," and that the said act is void for that reason also; and it is further to be noted, that this transfer of judiciary power is to that magistrate of the general government who already possesses all the executive, and a qualified negative in all the legislative powers.

VII. *Resolved*, that the construction applied by the general government (as is evinced by sundry of their proceedings) to those parts of the Constitution of the United States which delegate to Congress a power to lay and collect taxes, duties, imposts, and excises; to pay the debts, and provide for the common defense, and general welfare of the United States, and to make all laws which shall be necessary and proper for carrying into execution the powers vested by the Constitution in the government of the United States, or any department thereof, goes to the destruction of all the limits prescribed to their power by the Constitution: That words meant by that instrument to be subsidiary only to the execution of the limited powers ought not to be so construed as themselves to give unlimited powers, nor a part so to be taken as to destroy the whole residue of the instrument: That the proceedings of the general government under color of these articles will be a fit and necessary subject for revisal and correction at a time of greater tranquillity, while those specified in the preceding resolutions call for immediate redress.

VIII. *Resolved*, that the preceding Resolutions be transmitted to the Senators and Representatives in Congress from this Commonwealth, who are hereby enjoined to present the same to their respective Houses, and to use their best endeavors to procure, at the next session of Congress, a repeal of the aforesaid unconstitutional and obnoxious acts.

IX. *Resolved*, lastly, that the Governor of this Commonwealth be, and is hereby authorized and requested to communicate the preceding Resolutions to the Legislatures of the several States, to assure them that this Commonwealth considers Union for specified National purposes, and particularly for those specified in their late Federal Compact, to be friendly to the peace, happiness, and prosperity of all the States: that faithful to that compact according to the plain intent and meaning in which it was understood and acceded to by the several parties, it is sincerely anxious for its preservation: that it does also believe, that to take from the States all the powers of self-government, and transfer them to a general and consolidated government, without regard to the special delegations and reservations solemnly agreed to in that compact, is not for the peace, happiness, or prosperity of these States: And that, therefore, this Commonwealth is determined, as it doubts not its co-States are, tamely to submit to undelegated and consequently unlimited powers in no man or body of men on earth: that if the acts before specified should stand, these conclusions would flow from them; that the general government may place any act they think proper on the list of crimes and punish it themselves, whether enumerated or not enumerated by the Constitution as cognizable by them: that they may transfer its cognizance to the President or any other person, who may himself be the accuser, counsel, judge, and jury, whose suspicions may be the evidence, his order the sentence, his officer the executioner, and his breast the sole record of the transaction: that a very numerous and valuable description of the inhabitants of these States being by this precedent reduced as outlaws to the absolute dominion of one man, and the barrier of the Constitution thus swept away from us all, no rampart now remains against the passions and the powers of a majority of Congress, to protect from a like exportation or other more grievous punishment the minority of the same body, the legislatures, judges, governors, and counselors of the States, nor their other peaceable inhabitants who may venture to reclaim the constitutional rights and liberties of the State and people, or who for other causes, good or bad, may be obnoxious to the views or marked by the suspicions of the President, or be thought dangerous to his or their elections or other interests, public or personal: that the friendless alien has indeed been selected as the safest subject of a first experiment, but the citizen will soon follow, or rather has already followed: for, already has a sedition act marked him as its prey: that these and successive acts of the same character, unless arrested on the threshold, may tend to drive these States into revolution and blood, and will furnish new calumnies against Republican governments, and new pretexts for those who wish it to be believed, that man cannot be governed but by a rod of iron: that it would be a dangerous delusion were a confidence in the men of our choice to silence our fears for the safety of our rights: that confidence is everywhere the parent of despotism: free government is founded in jealousy and not in confidence; it is jealousy and not confidence which prescribes limited Constitutions to bind down those whom we are obliged to trust with power: that our Constitution has accordingly fixed the limits to which and no further our confidence may go; and let the honest advocate of confidence read the alien and sedition acts, and say if the Constitution has not been wise in fixing limits to the government it created, and whether we should be wise in destroying those limits; let him say what the government is if it be not a tyranny, which the men of our choice have conferred on the President, and the President of our choice has assented to and accepted over the friendly strangers, to whom the mild spirit of our

country and its laws had pledged hospitality and protection: that the men of our choice have more respected the bare suspicions of the President than the solid rights of innocence, the claims of justification, the sacred force of truth, and the forms and substance of law and justice. In questions of power then let no more be heard of confidence in man, but bind him down from mischief by the claims of the Constitution. That this Commonwealth does therefore call on its co-States for an expression of their sentiments on the acts concerning aliens, and for the punishment of certain crimes herein before specified, plainly declaring whether these acts are or are not authorized by the Federal Compact. And it doubts not that their sense will be so announced as to prove their attachment unaltered to limited government, whether general or particular, and that the rights and liberties of their co-States will be exposed to no dangers by remaining embarked on a common bottom with their own: That they will concur with this Commonwealth in considering the said acts so palpably against the Constitution as to amount to an undisguised declaration, that the compact is not meant to be the measure of the powers of the general government, but that it will proceed in the exercise over these States of all powers whatsoever: That they will view this as seizing the rights of the States and consolidating them in the hands of the general government with a power assumed to bind the States (not merely in cases made Federal) but in all cases whatsoever, by laws made, not with their consent, but by others against their consent: That this would be to surrender the form of government we have chosen, and to live under one deriving its powers from its own will, and not from our authority; and that the co-States, recurring to their natural right in cases not made Federal, will concur in declaring these acts void and of no force, and will each unite with this Commonwealth in requesting their repeal at the next session of Congress.

VIRGINIA RESOLUTIONS
December 24, 1798

Resolved, That the General Assembly of Virginia doth unequivocally express a firm resolution to maintain and defend the Constitution of the United States, and the Constitution of this state, against every aggression either foreign or domestic; and that they will support the Government of the United States in all measures warranted by the former.

That this Assembly most solemnly declares a warm attachment to the union of the states, to maintain which it pledges all its powers; and that, for this end, it is their duty to watch over and oppose every infraction of those principles which constitute the only basis of that Union, because a faithful observance of them can alone secure its existence and the public happiness.

That this Assembly doth explicitly and peremptorily declare that it views the powers of the Federal Government as resulting from the compact to which the states are parties, as limited by the plain sense and intention of the instrument constituting that compact; as no further valid than they are authorized by the grants enumerated in that compact; and that, in case of a deliberate, palpable, and dangerous exercise of other powers not granted by the said compact, the states, who are parties thereto, have the right and are in duty bound to interpose for arresting the progress of the evil, and for maintaining within their respective limits the authorities, rights, and liberties appertaining to them.

That the General Assembly doth also express its deep regret, that a spirit has in sundry instances been manifested by the Federal Government to enlarge its powers by forced constructions of the constitutional charter which defines them; and that indications have appeared of a design to expound certain general phrases (which, having been copied from the very limited grant of powers in the former Articles of Confederation, were the less liable to be misconstrued) so as to destroy the meaning and effect of the particular enumeration which necessarily explains and limits the general phrases; and so as to consolidate the states, by degrees, into one sovereignty, the obvious tendency and inevitable consequence of which would be to transform the present republican system of the United States into an absolute, or, at best, a mixed monarchy.

That the General Assembly doth particularly PROTEST against the palpable and alarming infractions of the Constitution in the two late cases of the "Alien and Sedition Acts," passed at the last session of Congress; the first of which exercises a power nowhere delegated to the Federal Government, and which, by uniting legislative and judicial powers to those of [the] executive, subverts the gen-eral principles of free government, as well as the particular organization and positive provisions of the Federal Constitution: and the other of which acts exercises, in like manner, a power not delegated by the Constitution, but, on the contrary, expressly and positively forbidden by one of the amendments thereto,—a power which, more than any other, ought to produce universal alarm, because it is levelled against the right of freely examining public characters and measures, and of free communication among the people thereon, which has ever been justly deemed the only effectual guardian of every other right.

That this state having, by its Convention which ratified the Federal Constitution, expressly declared that, among other essential rights, "the liberty of conscience and of the press cannot be cancelled, abridged, restrained or modified by any authority of the United States," and from its extreme anxiety to guard these rights from every possible attack of sophistry or ambition, having, with other states, recommended an amendment for that purpose, which amendment was in due time annexed to the Constitution,—it would mark a reproachful inconsistency and criminal degeneracy, if an indifference were now shown to the palpable violation of one of the rights thus declared and secured, and to the establishment of a precedent which may be fatal to the other.

That the good people of this commonwealth, having ever felt and continuing to feel the most sincere affection for their brethren of the other states, the truest anxiety for establishing and perpetuating the union of all and the most scrupulous fidelity to that Constitution, which is the pledge of mutual friendship, and the instrument of mutual happiness, the General Assembly doth solemnly appeal to the like dispositions of the other states, in confidence that they will concur with this Commonwealth in declaring, as it does hereby declare, that the acts aforesaid are unconstitutional; and that the necessary and proper measures will be taken by each for co-operating with this state, in maintaining unimpaired the authorities, rights, and liberties reserved to the states respectively, or to the people....

THE KENTUCKY RESOLUTIONS OF 1799
February 22, 1799

The representatives of the good people of this commonwealth, in General Assembly convened, having maturely considered the answers of sundry states in the Union, to their resolutions passed the last session, respecting certain unconstitutional laws of Congress, commonly called the Alien and Sedition Laws, would be faithless, indeed, to themselves and to those they represent, were they silently to acquiesce in the principles and doctrines attempted to be maintained in all those answers, that of Virginia only excepted. To again enter the field of argument, and attempt more fully or forcibly to expose the unconstitutionality of those obnoxious laws, would, it is apprehended, be as unnecessary as unavailing. We cannot, however, but lament, that, in the discussion of those interesting subjects, by sundry of the legislatures of our sister states, unfounded suggestions, and uncandid insinuations, derogatory to the true character and principles of this commonwealth have been substituted in place of fair reasoning and sound argument. Our opinions of these alarming measures of the general government, together with our reasons for those opinions, were detailed with decency, and with temper, and submitted to the discussion and judgment of our fellow-citizens throughout the Union. Whether the like decency and temper have been observed in the answers of most of those States, who have denied or attempted to obviate the great truths contained in those resolutions, we have now only to submit to a candid world. Faithful to the true principles of the federal Union, unconscious of any designs to disturb the harmony of that Union, and anxious only to escape the fangs of despotism, the good people of this commonwealth are regardless of censure or calumniation. Lest, however, the silence of this commonwealth should be construed into an acquiescence in the doctrines and principles advanced and attempted to be maintained by the said answers, or at least those of our fellow-citizens throughout the Union who so widely differ from us on those important subjects, should be deluded by the expectation, that we shall be deterred from what we conceive our duty, or shrink from the principles contained in those resolutions—therefore,

Resolved, That this commonwealth considers the federal Union, upon the terms and for the purposes specified in the late compact, conducive to the liberty and happiness of the several states: That it does now unequivocally declare its attachment to the Union, and to that compact, agreeably to its obvious and real intention, and will be among the last to seek its dissolution: That if those who administer the general government be permitted to transgress the limits fixed by that compact, by a total disregard to the special delegations of power therein contained, an annihilation of the state governments, and the creation upon their ruins of a general consolidated government, will be the inevitable consequence: That the principle and construction contended for by sundry of the state legislatures, that the general government is the exclusive judge of the extent of the powers delegated to it, stop not short of *despotism*—since the discretion of those who administer the government, and not the *Constitution*, would be the measure of their powers: That the several states who formed that instrument being sovereign and independent, have the unquestionable right to judge of the infraction; and, *That a nullification of those sovereignties, of all unauthorized acts done under color of that instrument is the rightful remedy:* That this commonwealth does, under the most deliberate reconsideration, declare, that the said Alien and Sedition Laws are, in their opinion, palpable violations of the said Constitution; and, however cheerfully it may be disposed to surrender its opinion to a majority of its sister states, in matters of ordinary or doubtful policy, yet, in momentous regulations like the present, which so vitally wound the best rights of the citizen, it would consider a silent acquiescence as highly criminal: That although this commonwealth, as a party to the federal compact, will bow to the laws of the Union, yet, it does, at the same time declare, that it will not now, or ever hereafter, cease to oppose in a constitutional manner, every attempt at what quarter soever offered, to violate that compact. And, finally, in order that no pretext or arguments may be drawn from a supposed acquiescence, on the part of this commonwealth in the constitutionality of those laws, and be thereby used as precedents for similar future violations of the federal compact—this commonwealth does now enter against them its solemn PROTEST.

SOUTH CAROLINA ORDINANCE OF NULLIFICATION
November 24, 1832

An Ordinance to Nullify certain acts of the Congress of the United States, purporting to be laws laying duties and imposts on the importation of foreign commodities.

Whereas the Congress of the United States, by various acts, purporting to be acts laying duties and imposts on foreign imports, but in reality intended for the protection of domestic manufactures, and the giving of bounties to classes and individuals engaged in particular employments, at the expense and to the injury and oppression of other classes and individuals, and by wholly exempting from taxation certain foreign commodities, such as are not produced or manufactured in the United States, to afford a pretext for imposing higher and excessive duties on articles similar to those intended to be protected, hath exceeded its just powers under the Constitution, which confers on it no authority to afford such protection, and hath violated the true meaning and intent of the

Constitution, which provides for equality in imposing the burthens of taxation upon the several States and portions of the Confederacy: *And whereas* the said Congress, exceeding its just power to impose taxes and collect revenue for the purpose of effecting and accomplishing the specific objects and purposes which the Constitution of the United States authorizes it to effect and accomplish, hath raised and collected unnecessary revenue for objects unauthorized by the Constitution:—

We, therefore, the people of the State of South Carolina in Convention assembled, do declare and ordain,... That the several acts and parts of acts of the Congress of the United States, purporting to be laws for the imposing of duties and imposts on the importation of foreign commodities,... and, more especially,... [the tariff acts of 1828 and 1832]..., are unauthorized by the Constitution of the United States, and violate the true meaning and intent thereof, and are null, void, and no law, nor binding upon this State, its officers or citizens; and all promises, contracts, and obligations, made or entered into, or to be made or entered into, with purpose to secure the duties imposed by the said acts, and all judicial proceedings which shall be hereafter had in affirmance thereof, are and shall be held utterly null and void.

And it is further Ordained, That it shall not be lawful for any of the constituted authorities, whether of this State or of the United States, to enforce the payment of duties imposed by the said acts within the limits of this State; but it shall be the duty of the Legislature to adopt such measures and pass such acts as may be necessary to give full effect to this Ordinance, and to prevent the enforcement and arrest the operation of the said acts and parts of acts of the Congress of the United States within the limits of this State, from and after the 1st day of February next,...

And it is further Ordained, That in no case of law or equity, decided in the courts of this State, wherein shall be drawn in question the authority of this ordinance, or the validity of such act or acts of the Legislature as may be passed for the purpose of giving effect thereto, or the validity of the aforesaid acts of Congress, imposing duties, shall any appeal be taken or allowed to the Supreme Court of the United States, nor shall any copy of the record be printed or allowed for that purpose; and if any such appeal shall be attempted to be taken, the courts of this State shall proceed to execute and enforce their judgments, according to the laws and usages of the State, without reference to such attempted appeal, and the person or persons attempting to take such appeal may be dealt with as for a contempt of the court.

And it is further Ordained, That all persons now holding any office of honor, profit, or trust, civil or military, under this State, (members of the Legislature excepted), shall, within such time, and in such manner as the Legislature shall prescribe, take an oath well and truly to obey, execute, and enforce, this Ordinance, and such act or acts of the Legislature as may be passed in pursuance thereof, according to the true intent and meaning of the same; and on the neglect or omission of any such person or persons so to do, his or their office or offices shall be forthwith vacated,... and no person hereafter elected to any office of honor, profit, or trust, civil or military, (members of the Legislature excepted), shall, until the Legislature shall otherwise provide and direct, enter on the execution of his office,... until he shall, in like manner, have taken a similar oath; and no juror shall be empannelled in any of the courts of this State, in any cause in which shall be in question this Ordinance, or any act of the Legislature passed in pursuance thereof, unless he shall first, in addition to the usual oath, have taken an oath that he will well and truly obey, execute, and enforce this Ordinance, and such act or acts of the Legislature as may be passed to carry the same into operation and effect, according to the true intent and meaning thereof.

And we, the People of South Carolina, to the end that it may be fully understood by the Government of the United States, and the people of the co-States, that we are determined to maintain this, our Ordinance and Declaration, at every hazard, *Do further Declare* that we will not submit to the application of force, on the part of the Federal Government, to reduce this State to obedience; but that we will consider the passage, by Congress, of any act... to coerce the State, shut up her ports, destroy or harass her commerce, or to enforce the acts hereby declared to be null and void, otherwise than through the civil tribunals of the country, as inconsistent with the longer continuance of South Carolina in the Union: and that the people of this State will thenceforth hold themselves absolved from all further obligation to maintain or preserve their political connexion with the people of the other States, and will forthwith proceed to organize a separate Government, and do all other acts and things which sovereign and independent States may of right to do.

THE CONSTITUTION OF THE CONFEDERATE STATES OF AMERICA
March 11, 1861

WE, the people of the Confederate States, each State acting in its sovereign and independent character, in order to form a permanent federal government, establish justice, insure domestic tranquillity, and secure the blessings of liberty to ourselves and our posterity—invoking the favor and guidance of Almighty God—do ordain and establish this Constitution for the Confederate States of America.

ART. I.

SEC. 1.—All legislative powers herein delegated shall be vested in a Congress of the Confederate States, which shall consist of a Senate and House of Representatives.

SEC. 2. (1) The House of Representatives shall be chosen every second year by the people of the several States; and the electors in each State shall be citizens of the Confederate States, and have the qualifications requisite for electors of the most numerous branch of the State Legislature; but no person of foreign birth, not a citizen of the Confederate States, shall be allowed to vote for any officer, civil or political, State or Federal.

(2) No person shall be a Representative who shall not have attained the age of twenty-five years, and be a citizen of the Confederate States, and who shall not, when elected, be an inhabitant of that State in which he shall be chosen.

(3) Representatives and direct taxes shall be apportioned among the several States which may be included within this Confederacy, according to their respective numbers, which shall be determined by adding to the whole number of free persons, including those bound to service for a term of years, and excluding Indians not taxed, three-fifths of all slaves. The actual enumeration shall be made within three years after the first meeting of the Congress of the Confederate States, and within every subsequent term of ten years, in such manner as they shall by law direct. The number of Representatives shall not exceed one for every fifty thousand, but each State shall have at least one Representative; and until such enumeration shall be made, the State of South Carolina shall be entitled to choose six; the State of Georgia ten; the State of Alabama nine; the State of Florida two; the State of Mississippi seven; the State of Louisiana six; and the State of Texas six.

(4) When vacancies happen in the representation of any State, the Executive authority thereof shall issue writs of election to fill such vacancies.

(5) The House of Representatives shall choose their Speaker and other officers; and shall have the sole power of impeachment; except that any judicial or other federal officer resident and acting solely within the limits of any State, may be impeached by a vote of two-thirds of both branches of the Legislature thereof.

SEC. 3. (1) The Senate of the Confederate States shall be composed of two Senators from each State, chosen for six years by the Legislature thereof, at the regular session next immediately preceding the commencement of the term of service; and each Senator shall have one vote.

(2) Immediately after they shall be assembled, in consequence of the first election, they shall be divided as equally as may be into three classes. The seats of the Senators of the first class shall be vacated at the expiration of the second year; of the second class at the expiration of the fourth year; and of the third class at the expiration of the sixth year; so that one-third may be chosen every second year; and if vacancies happen by resignation or otherwise during the recess of the Legislature of any State, the Executive thereof may make temporary appointments until the next meeting of the Legislature, which shall then fill such vacancies.

(3) No person shall be a Senator, who shall not have attained the age of thirty years, and be a citizen of the Confederate States; and who shall not, when elected, be an inhabitant of the State for which he shall be chosen.

(4) The Vice-President of the Confederate States shall be President of the Senate, but shall have no vote, unless they be equally divided.

(5) The Senate shall choose their other officers, and also a President *pro tempore*, in the absence of the Vice-President, or when he shall exercise the office of President of the Confederate States.

(6) The Senate shall have sole power to try all impeachments. When sitting for that purpose they shall be on oath or affirmation. When the President of the Confederate States is tried, the Chief-Justice shall preside; and no person shall be convicted without the concurrence of two-thirds of the members present.

(7) Judgment in cases of impeachment shall not extend further than removal from office, and disqualification to hold and enjoy any office of honor, trust, or profit, under the Confederate States; but the party convicted shall, nevertheless, be liable to and subject to indictment, trial, judgment, and punishment according to law.

SEC. 4. (1) The times, places, and manner of holding elections for Senators and Representatives, shall be prescribed in each State by the Legislature thereof, subject to the provisions of this Constitution; but the Congress may, at any time, by law, make or alter such regulations, except as to the times and places of choosing Senators.

(2) The Congress shall assemble at least once in every year; and such meeting shall be on the first Monday in December, unless they shall, by law, appoint a different day.

SEC. 5. (1) Each House shall be the judge of the elections, returns, and qualifications of its own members, and a majority of each shall constitute a quorum to do business; but a smaller number may adjourn from day to day, and may be authorized to compel the attendance of absent members, in such manner and under such penalties as each House may provide.

(2) Each House may determine the rules of its proceedings, punish its members for disorderly behavior, and, with the concurrence of two-thirds of the whole number, expel a member.

(3) Each House shall keep a journal of its proceedings, and from time to time publish the same, excepting such part as may in its judgment require secrecy, and the ayes and nays of the members of either House, on any question, shall, at the desire of one-fifth of those present, be entered on the journal.

(4) Neither House, during the session of Congress, shall, without the consent of the other, adjourn for more than three days, nor to any other place than that in which the two Houses shall be sitting.

SEC. 6. (1) The Senators and Representatives shall receive a compensation for their services, to be ascertained by law, and paid out of the Treasury of the Confederate States. They shall, in all cases except treason and breach of the peace, be privileged from arrest during their attendance at the session of their respective Houses, and in going to and returning from the same; and for any speech or debate in either House, they shall not be questioned in any other place.

(2) No Senator or Representative shall, during the time for which he was elected, be appointed to any civil office under the authority of the Confederate States, which shall have been created, or the emoluments whereof shall have been increased during such time; and no person holding any office under the Confederate States shall be a member of either House during his continuance in office. But Congress may, by law, grant to the principal officer in each of the Executive Departments a seat upon the floor of either House, with the privilege of discussing any measure appertaining to his department.

SEC. 7. (1) All bills for raising revenue shall originate in the House of Representatives; but the Senate may propose or concur with amendments as on other bills.

(2) Every bill which shall have passed both Houses shall, before it becomes a law, be presented to the President of the Confederate States; if he approve he shall sign it; but if not, he shall return it with his objections to that House in which it shall have originated, who shall enter the objections at large on their journal, and proceed to reconsider it. If, after such reconsideration, two-thirds of that House shall agree to pass the bill, it shall be sent, together with the objections, to the other House, by which it shall likewise be reconsidered, and if approved by two-thirds of that House, it shall become a law. But in all such cases, the votes of both Houses shall be determined by yeas and nays, and the names of the persons voting for and against the bill shall be entered on the journal of each House respectively. If any bill shall not be returned by the President within ten days (Sundays excepted) after it shall have been presented to him, the same shall be a law, in like manner as if he had signed it, unless the Congress, by their adjournment, prevent its return; in which case it shall not be a law. The President may approve any appropriation and disapprove any other appropriation in the same bill. In such case he shall, in signing the bill, designate the appropriations disapproved; and shall return a copy of such appropriations, with his objections, to the House in which the bill shall have originated; and the same proceedings shall then be had as in case of other bills disapproved by the President.

(3) Every order, resolution, or vote, to which the concurrence of both Houses may be necessary (except on questions of adjournment) shall be presented to the President of the Confederate States; and before the same shall take effect shall be approved by him; or being disapproved by him, may be repassed by two-thirds of both Houses, according to the rules and limitations prescribed in case of a bill.

SEC. 8.—The Congress shall have power—

(1) To lay and collect taxes, duties, imposts, and excises, for revenue necessary to pay the debts, provide for the common defence, and carry on the Government of the Confederate States; but no bounties shall be granted from the treasury; nor shall any duties or taxes on importations from foreign nations be laid to promote or foster any branch of industry; and all duties, imposts, and excises shall be uniform throughout the Confederate States.

(2) To borrow money on the credit of the Confederate States.

(3) To regulate commerce with foreign nations, and among the several States, and with the Indian tribes; but neither this, nor any other clause contained in the Constitution shall be construed to delegate the power to Congress to appropriate money for any internal improvement intended to facilitate commerce; except for the purpose of furnishing lights, beacons, and buoys, and other aids to navigation upon the coasts, and the improvement of harbors, and the removing of obstructions in river navigation, in all which cases, such duties shall be laid on the navigation facilitated thereby, as may be necessary to pay the costs and expenses thereof.

(4) To establish uniform laws of naturalization, and uniform laws on the subject of bankruptcies throughout the Confederate States, but no law of Congress shall discharge any debt contracted before the passage of the same.

(5) To coin money, regulate the value thereof, and of foreign coin, and fix the standard of weights and measures.

(6) To provide for the punishment of counterfeiting the securities and current coin of the Confederate States.

(7) To establish post-offices and post-routes; but the expenses of the Post-office Department, after the first day of March, in the year of our Lord eighteen hundred and sixty-three, shall be paid out of its own revenues.

(8) To promote the progress of science and useful arts, by securing for limited times to authors and inventors the exclusive right to their respective writings and discoveries.

(9) To constitute tribunals inferior to the Supreme Court.

(10) To define and punish piracies and felonies committed on the high seas, and offences against the law of nations.

(11) To declare war, grant letters of marque and reprisal, and make rules concerning captures on land and water.

(12) To raise and support armies; but no appropriation of money to that use shall be for a longer term than two years.

(13) To provide and maintain a navy.

(14) To make rules for government and regulation of the land and naval forces.

(15) To provide for calling forth the militia to execute the laws of the Confederate States; suppress insurrections, and repel invasions.

(16) To provide for organizing, arming, and disciplining the militia, and for governing such part of them as may be employed in the service of the Confederate States; reserving to the States, respectively, the appointment of the officers, and the authority of training the militia according to the discipline prescribed by Congress.

(17) To exercise exclusive legislation, in all cases whatsoever, over such district (not exceeding ten miles square) as may, by cession of one or more States, and the acceptance of Congress, become the seat of the Government of the Confederate States; and to exercise a like authority over all places purchased by the consent of the Legislature of the State in which the same shall be, for the erection of forts, magazines, arsenals, dock-yards, and other needful buildings, and

(18) To make all laws which shall be necessary and proper for carrying into execution the foregoing powers, and all other powers vested by this Constitution in the Government of the Confederate States, or in any department or officer thereof.

SEC. 9. (1) The importation of negroes of the African race, from any foreign country, other than the slaveholding States or Territories of the United States of America, is hereby forbidden; and Congress is required to pass such laws as shall effectually prevent the same.

(2) Congress shall also have power to prohibit the introduction of slaves from any State not a member of, or Territory not belonging to, this Confederacy.

(3) The privilege of the writ of *habeas corpus* shall not be suspended, unless when in cases of rebellion or invasion the public safety may require it.

(4) No bill of attainder, or *ex post facto* law, or law denying or impairing the right of property in negro slaves shall be passed.

(5) No capitation or other direct tax shall be laid unless in proportion to the census or enumeration hereinbefore directed to be taken.

(6) No tax or duty shall be laid on articles exported from any State, except by a vote of two-thirds of both Houses.

(7) No preference shall be given by any regulation of commerce or revenue to the ports of one State over those of another.

(8) No money shall be drawn from the treasury but in consequence of appropriations made by law; and a regular statement and account of the receipts and expenditures of all public money shall be published from time to time.

(9) Congress shall appropriate no money from the treasury except by a vote of two-thirds of both Houses, taken by yeas and nays, unless it be asked and estimated for by some one of the heads of departments, and submitted to Congress by the President; or for the purpose of paying its own expenses and contingencies; or for the payment of claims against the Confederate States, the justice

of which shall have been judicially declared by a tribunal for the investigation of claims against the Government, which it is hereby made the duty of Congress to establish.

(10) All bills appropriating money shall specify in federal currency the exact amount of each appropriation and the purposes for which it is made; and Congress shall grant no extra compensation to any public contractor, officer, agent, or servant, after such contract shall have been made or such service rendered.

(11) No title of nobility shall be granted by the Confederate States; and no person holding any office of profit or trust under them shall, without the consent of the Congress, accept of any present, emoluments, office, or title of any kind whatever, from any king, prince, or foreign state.

(12) Congress shall make no law respecting an establishment of religion, or prohibiting the free exercise thereof; or abridging the freedom of speech or of the press; or the right of the people peaceably to assemble and petition the Government for a redress of grievances.

(13) A well-regulated militia being necessary to the security of a free State, the right of the people to keep and bear arms shall not be infringed.

(14) No soldier shall, in time of peace, be quartered in any house without the consent of the owner; nor in time of war, but in a manner prescribed by law.

(15) The right of the people to be secure in their persons, houses, papers, and against unreasonable searches and seizures, shall not be violated; and no warrant shall issue but upon probable cause, supported by oath or affirmation, and particularly describing the place to be searched, and the person or things to be seized.

(16) No person shall be held to answer for a capital or otherwise infamous crime, unless on a presentment or indictment of a grand jury, except in cases arising in the land or naval forces, or in the militia, when in actual service, in time of war, or public danger; nor shall any person be subject for the same offence to be twice put in jeopardy of life or limb; nor be compelled in any criminal case to be a witness against himself; nor be deprived of life, liberty, or property, without due process of law; nor shall any private property be taken for public use without just compensation.

(17) In all criminal prosecutions the accused shall enjoy the right to a speedy and public trial, by an impartial jury of the State and district wherein the crime shall have been committed, which district shall have been previously ascertained by law, and to be informed of the nature and cause of the accusation; to be confronted with the witnesses against him; to have compulsory

process for obtaining witnesses in his favor; and to have the assistance of counsel for his defence.

(18) In suits at common law, where the value in controversy shall exceed twenty dollars, the right of trial by jury shall be preserved; and no fact so tried by a jury shall be otherwise reëxamined in any court of the Confederacy, than according to the rules of the common law.

(19) Excessive bail shall not be required, nor excessive fines imposed, nor cruel or unusual punishment inflicted.

(20) Every law, or resolution having the force of law, shall relate to but one subject, and that shall be expressed in the title.

SEC. 10. (1) No State shall enter into any treaty, alliance, or confederation; grant letters of marque and reprisals; coin money; make any thing but gold and silver coin a tender in payment of debts; pass any bill of attainder, or *ex post facto* law, or law impairing the obligation of contracts; or grant any title of nobility.

(2) No State shall, without the consent of Congress, lay any imposts or duties on imports or exports, except what may be absolutely necessary for executing its inspection laws; and the net produce of all duties and imposts, laid by any State on imports or exports, shall be for the use of the Treasury of the Confederate States; and all such laws shall be subject to the revision and control of Congress.

(3) No State shall, without the consent of Congress, lay any duty of tonnage, except on sea-going vessels, for the improvement of its rivers and harbors navigated by the said vessels; but such duties shall not conflict with any treaties of the Confederate States with foreign nations; and any surplus of revenue, thus derived, shall, after making such improvement, be paid into the common treasury; nor shall any State keep troops or ships of war in time of peace, enter into any agreement or compact with another State, or with a foreign power, or engage in war, unless actually invaded, or in such imminent danger as will not admit of delay. But when any river divides or flows through two or more States, they may enter into compacts with each other to improve the navigation thereof.

ART. II.

SEC. 1. (1) The Executive power shall be vested in a President of the Confederate States of America. He and the Vice-President shall hold their offices for the term of six years; but the President shall not be reëligible. The President and Vice-President shall be elected as follows:

(2) Each State shall appoint, in such manner as the legislature thereof may direct, a number of electors equal to the whole number of Senators

and Representatives to which the State may be entitled in Congress; but no Senator or Representative, or person holding an office of trust or profit under the Confederate States, shall be appointed an elector.

(3) The electors shall meet in their respective States and vote by ballot for President and Vice-President, one of whom, at least, shall not be an inhabitant of the same State with themselves; they shall name in their ballots the person voted for as President, and in distinct ballots the person voted for as Vice-President, and they shall make distinct lists of all persons voted for as President, and of all persons voted for as Vice-President, and of the number of votes for each; which list they shall sign, and certify, and transmit, sealed, to the Government of the Confederate States, directed to the President of the Senate. The President of the Senate shall, in the presence of the Senate and House of Representatives, open all the certificates, and the votes shall then be counted; the person having the greatest number of votes for President shall be the President, if such number be a majority of the whole number of electors appointed; and if no person shall have such a majority, then, from the persons having the highest numbers, not exceeding three, on the list of those voted for as President, the House of Representatives shall choose immediately, by ballot, the President. But, in choosing the President, the votes shall be taken by States, the Representative from each State having one vote; a quorum for this purpose shall consist of a member or members from two-thirds of the States, and a majority of all the States shall be necessary to a choice. And if the House of Representatives shall not choose a President, whenever the right of choice shall devolve upon them, before the fourth day of March next following, then the Vice-President shall act as President, as in case of the death, or other constitutional disability of the President.

(4) The person having the greatest number of votes as Vice-President shall be the Vice-President, if such number be a majority of the whole number of electors appointed; and if no person have a majority, then from the two highest numbers on the list, the Senate shall choose the Vice-President; a quorum for the purpose shall consist of two-thirds of the whole number of Senators, and a majority of the whole number shall be necessary for a choice.

(5) But no person constitutionally ineligible to the office of President shall be eligible to that of Vice-President of the Confederate States.

(6) The Congress may determine the time of choosing the electors, and the day on which they shall give their votes; which day shall be the same throughout the Confederate States.

(7) No person except a natural born citizen of the Confederate States, or a citizen thereof, at the time of the adoption of this Constitution, or a citizen thereof born in the United States prior to the 20th December, 1860, shall be eligible to the office of President; neither shall any person be eligible to that office who shall not have attained the age of thirty-five years, and been fourteen years a resident within the limits of the Confederate States, as they may exist at the time of his election.

(8) In case of the removal of the President from office, or of his death, resignation, or inability to discharge the powers and duties of the said office, the same shall devolve on the Vice-President; and the Congress may, by law, provide for the case of the removal, death, resignation, or inability both of the President and the Vice-President, declaring what officer shall then act as President, and such officer shall then act accordingly until the disability be removed or a President shall be elected.

(9) The President shall, at stated times, receive for his services a compensation, which shall neither be increased nor diminished during the period for which he shall have been elected; and he shall not receive within that period any other emolument from the Confederate States, or any of them.

(10) Before he enters on the execution of the duties of his office, he shall take the following oath or affirmation:

"I do solemnly swear (or affirm) that I will faithfully execute the office of President of the Confederate States, and will, to the best of my ability, preserve, protect, and defend the Constitution thereof."

SEC. 2. (1) The President shall be commander-in-chief of the army and navy of the Confederate States, and of the militia of the several States, when called into the actual service of the Confederate States; he may require the opinion, in writing, of the principal officer in each of the Executive Departments, upon any subject relating to the duties of their respective offices; and he shall have power to grant reprieves and pardons for offences against the Confederate States, except in cases of impeachment.

(2) He shall have power, by and with the advice and consent of the Senate, to make treaties, provided two-thirds of the Senators present concur; and he shall nominate, and, by and with the advice and consent of the Senate, shall appoint ambassadors, other public ministers, and consuls, Judges of the Supreme Court, and all other officers of the Confederate States, whose appointments are not

herein otherwise provided for, and which shall be established by law; but the Congress may by law vest the appointment of such inferior officers, as they think proper, in the President alone, in the courts of law, or in the heads of departments.

(3) The principal officer in each of the Executive Departments, and all persons connected with the diplomatic service, may be removed from office at the pleasure of the President. All other civil officers of the Executive Department may be removed at any time by the President, or other appointing power, when their services are unnecessary, or for dishonesty, incapacity, inefficiency, misconduct, or neglect of duty; and when so removed, the removal shall be reported to the Senate, together with the reasons therefor.

(4) The President shall have power to fill all vacancies that may happen during the recess of the Senate, by granting commissions which shall expire at the end of the next session; but no person rejected by the Senate shall be reappointed to the same office during their ensuing recess.

SEC. 3. (1) The President shall, from time to time, give to the Congress information of the state of the Confederacy, and recommend to their consideration such measures as he shall judge necessary and expedient; he may, on extraordinary occasions, convene both Houses, or either of them; and, in case of disagreement between them, with respect to the time of adjournment he may adjourn them to such time as he shall think proper; he shall receive ambassadors and other public ministers; he shall take care that the laws be faithfully executed, and shall commission all the officers of the Confederate States.

SEC. 4. (1) The President and Vice-President, and all civil officers of the Confederate States, shall be removed from office on impeachment for, or conviction of, treason, bribery, or other high crimes and misdemeanors.

ART. III.

SEC. 1. (1) The judicial power of the Confederate States shall be vested in one Superior Court, and in such inferior courts as the Congress may from time to time ordain and establish. The judges, both of the Supreme and inferior courts, shall hold their offices during good behavior, and shall, at stated times, receive for their services a compensation, which shall not be diminished during their continuance in office.

SEC. 2. (1) The judicial power shall extend to all cases arising under the Constitution, the laws of the Confederate States, or treaties made or which shall be made under their authority; to all cases affecting ambassadors, other public ministers, and consuls; to all cases of admiralty or maritime jurisdiction; to controversies to which the Confeder-

ate States shall be a party; to controversies between two or more States; between a State and citizens of another State, where the State is plaintiff; between citizens claiming lands under grants of different States, and between a State or the citizens thereof, and foreign States, citizens, or subjects; but no State shall be sued by a citizen or subject of any foreign State.

(2) In all cases affecting ambassadors, other public ministers, and consuls, and those in which a State shall be a party, the Supreme Court shall have original jurisdiction. In all the other cases before mentioned, the Supreme Court shall have appellate jurisdiction, both as to law and fact, with such exceptions, and under such regulations as the Congress shall make.

(3) The trial of all crimes, except in cases of impeachment, shall be by jury, and such trial shall be held in the State where the said crimes shall have been committed; but when not committed within any State, the trial shall be at such place or places as the Congress may by law have directed.

SEC. 3. (1) Treason against the Confederate States shall consist only in levying war against them, or in adhering to their enemies, giving them aid and comfort. No person shall be convicted of treason unless on the testimony of two witnesses to the same overt act, or on confession in open court.

(2) The Congress shall have power to declare the punishment of treason, but no attainder of treason shall work corruption of blood, or forfeiture, except during the life of the person attainted.

ART. IV.

SEC. 1. (1) Full faith and credit shall be given in each State of the public acts, records, and judicial proceedings of every other State. And the Congress may, by general laws, prescribe the manner in which such acts, records, and proceedings shall be proved, and the effect thereof.

SEC. 2. (1) The citizens of each State shall be entitled to all the privileges and immunities of citizens of the several States, and shall have the right of transit and sojourn in any State of this Confederacy, with their slaves and other property; and the right of property in said slaves shall not be thereby impaired.

(2) A person charged in any State with treason, felony, or other crime against the laws of such State, who shall flee from justice, and be found in another State, shall, on demand of the executive authority of the State from which he fled, be delivered up to be removed to the State having jurisdiction of the crime.

(3) No slave or other person held to service or labor in any State of Territory of the Confederate

States, under the laws thereof, escaping or unlawfully carried into another, shall, in consequence of any law or regulation therein, be discharged from such service or labor; but shall be delivered up on claim of the party to whom such slave belongs, or to whom such service or labor may be due.

SEC. 3. (1) Other States may be admitted into this Confederacy by a vote of two-thirds of the whole House of Representatives, and two-thirds of the Senate, the Senate voting by States; but no new State shall be formed or erected within the jurisdiction of any other State; nor any State be formed by the junction of two or more States, or parts of States, without the consent of the Legislatures of the States concerned as well as of the Congress.

(2) The Congress shall have power to dispose of and make all needful rules and regulations concerning the property of the Confederate States, including the lands thereof.

(3) The Confederate States may acquire new territory; and Congress shall have power to legislate and provide governments for the inhabitants of all territory belonging to the Confederate States, lying without the limits of the several States, and may permit them, at such times, and in such manner as it may by law provide, to form States to be admitted into the Confederacy. In all such territory, the institution of negro slavery, as it now exists in the Confederate States, shall be recognized and protected by Congress and by the territorial government; and the inhabitants of the several Confederate States and Territories shall have the right to take to such territory any slaves lawfully held by them in any of the States or Territories of the Confederate States.

(4) The Confederate States shall guarantee to every State that now is or hereafter may become a member of this Confederacy, a Republican form of Government, and shall protect each of them against invasion; and on application of the Legislature, (or of the Executive when the Legislature is not in session,) against domestic violence.

ART. V.

SEC. 1. (1) Upon the demand of any three States, legally assembled in their several Conventions, the Congress shall summon a Convention of all the States, to take into consideration such amendments to the Constitution as the said States shall concur in suggesting at the time when the said demand is made; and should any of the proposed amendments to the Constitution be agreed on by the said Convention—voting by States—and the same be ratified by the Legislatures of two-thirds of the several States, or by conventions in two-thirds thereof—as the one or the other mode of ratification may be proposed by the general convention—they shall thenceforward form a part of this Constitution. But no State shall, without its consent, be deprived of its equal representation in the Senate.

ART. VI.

1.—The Government established by this Constitution is the successor of the Provisional Government of the Confederate States of America, and all the laws passed by the latter shall continue in force until the same shall be repealed or modified; and all the officers appointed by the same shall remain in office until their successors are appointed and qualified, or the offices abolished.

2. All debts contracted and engagements entered into before the adoption of this Constitution, shall be as valid against the Confederate States under this Constitution as under the Provisional Government.

3. This Constitution, and the laws of the Confederate States, made in pursuance thereof, and all treaties made, or which shall be made, under the authority of the Confederate States, shall be the supreme law of the land; and the judges in every State shall be bound thereby, any thing in the Constitution or laws of any State to the contrary notwithstanding.

4. The Senators and Representatives before mentioned, and the members of the several State Legislatures, and all executive and judicial offices, both of the Confederate States and of the several States, shall be bound, by oath or affirmation, to support this Constitution; but no religious test shall ever be required as a qualification to any office or public trust under the Confederate States.

5. The enumeration, in the Constitution, of certain rights, shall not be construed to deny or disparage others retained by the people of the several States.

6. The powers not delegated to the Confederate States by the Constitution, nor prohibited by it to the States, are reserved to the States, respectively, or to the people thereof.

ART. VII.

1.—The ratification of the conventions of five States shall be sufficient for the establishment of this Constitution between the States so ratifying the same.

2. When five States shall have ratified this Constitution in the manner before specified, the Congress, under the provisional Constitution, shall prescribe the time for holding the election of President and Vice-President, and for the meeting of the electoral college, and for counting the votes

and inaugurating the President. They shall also prescribe the time for holding the first election of members of Congress under this Constitution, and the time for assembling the same. Until the assembling of such Congress, the Congress under the provisional Constitution shall continue to exercise the legislative powers granted them; not extending beyond the time limited by the Constitution of the Provisional Government.

Adopted unanimously by the Congress of the Confederate States of South Carolina, Georgia, Florida, Alabama, Mississippi, Louisiana, and Texas, sitting in convention at the capitol, in the city of Montgomery, Ala., on the eleventh day of March, in the year eighteen hundred and sixty-one.
                                        Howell Cobb
                              President of the Congress.
[Signatures]

LEE'S FAREWELL TO HIS ARMY
April 10, 1865

Headquarters, Army of Northern Virginia,
                              April 10, 1865.
  After four years of arduous service, marked by unsurpassed courage and fortitude, the Army of Northern Virginia has been compelled to yield to overwhelming numbers and resources. I need not tell the survivors of so many hard-fought battles, who have remained steadfast to the last, that I have consented to this result from no distrust of them; but, feeling that valour and devotion could accomplish nothing that could compensate for the loss that would have attended the continuation of the contest, I have determined to avoid the useless sacrifice of those whose past services have en-deared them to their countrymen. By the terms of the agreement, officers and men can return to their homes and remain there until exchanged. You will take with you the satisfaction that proceeds from the consciousness of duty faithfully performed; and I earnestly pray that a merciful God will extend to you His blessing and protection. With an increasing admiration of your constancy and devotion to your country, and a grateful remembrance of your kind and generous consideration of myself, I bid you an affectionate farewell.
                                        R. E. Lee, General

BIBLIOGRAPHY

Abernethy, Thomas P. *The South in the New Nation: A History of the South.* Baton Rouge, La.: Louisiana State University Press, 1961.

Adair, James. *History of the American Indians.* London: E. & C. Dilly, 1775.

Adams, Henry. *History of the United States,* 9 vols. New York: Charles Scribner's Sons, 1891.

Agee, James, and Evans, Walker. *Let Us Now Praise Famous Men.* New York: Ballantine Books, 1966.

Albion, Robert G. *Forests and Sea Power.* Cambridge, Mass.: Harvard University Press, 1926.

Alden, John R. *The American Revolution.* New York: Harper & Row, 1954.

———. *The South in the Revolution, 1763–1789.* Baton Rouge, La.: Louisiana State University Press, 1957.

———. *The First South.* Baton Rouge, La.: Louisiana State University Press, 1961.

Alexander, William. *Lanterns on the Levee.* Boston and New York: Houghton Mifflin Company, 1912, 1927.

Ambler, Charles Henry. *A History of West Virginia.* New York: Prentice-Hall, 1933.

American Heritage (eds.). *The American Heritage Book of the Revolution.* New York: American Heritage, 1958.

Andrews, Charles M. *The Colonial Period of American History,* 4 vols. New Haven: Yale University Press, 1934–1938.

Andrews, Matthew Page. *History of Maryland: Province and State.* Garden City, N.Y.: Doubleday, Doran & Company, 1929.

———. *Virginia, the Old Dominion.* Garden City, N.Y.: Doubleday, Doran & Company, 1937.

Ashe, Samuel A'Court. *History of North Carolina.* Greensboro, N.C.: C. L. Van Noppen, 1908.

Bakeless, John. *Turncoats, Traitors and Heroes.* Philadelphia: Lippincott, 1959.

Baldwin, Joseph. *The Flush Times of Alabama and Mississippi.* New York: Hill & Wang, 1957.

Bennett, Lerone, Jr. *Before the Mayflower.* Baltimore: Penguin Books, 1964.

Blanche, Henry Clark. *The Tennessee Yeomen, 1840–1860.* Nashville: Vanderbilt University Press, 1942.

Boatner, Mark Mayo, III. *Encyclopedia of the American Revolution.* New York: Van Rees Press, 1969.

———. *The Civil War Dictionary.* New York: David McKay Company, 1967.

Brock, Leslie V. *A Study in Colonial Finance and Imperial Relations.* New York: Arno Press, 1975.

Bruchey, Stuart. *The Roots of American Economic Growth, 1607–1861.* New York: Harper & Row, 1965.

Burgess, John W. *The Civil War and the Constitution,* 2 vols. New York: Charles Scribner's Sons, 1901.

519

———. *Reconstruction and the Constitution.* New York: Charles Scribner's Sons, 1902.

Carrington, Henry B. *Battles of the American Revolution.* New York: Barnes & Noble, 1876.

Chapin, George M. *Florida, 1513–1913, Past, Present and Future.* Chicago: S. J. Clarke Publishing Company, 1914.

Chesnut, Mary Boykin. *A Diary from Dixie.* New York: D. Appleton & Company, 1906.

Clark, T.D. *History of Kentucky.* New York: Prentice-Hall, 1937.

Clayton, Victoria Virginia. *Black and White Under the Old Regime.* Freeport, N.Y.: Books for Libraries Press, 1970.

Coleman, Kenneth. *Georgia History in Outline.* Athens, Ga.: University of Georgia Press, 1960.

Commanger, Henry Steele, and Morris, Richard B., eds. *The Spirit of 'Seventy Six.'* New York: Harper & Row, 1967.

Couch, W. T., ed. *Culture in the South.* Chapel Hill, N.C.: University of North Carolina Press, 1935.

Coulter, E. Merton. *Georgia, A Short History.* Chapel Hill, N.C.: University of North Carolina Press, 1947.

Crane, Verner W. *The Southern Frontier, 1670–1732.* Durham, N.C.: Duke University Press, 1928.

Cremin, Lawrence A. *American Education: The Colonial Experience, 1607–1783.* New York: Harper & Row, 1970.

Dabbs, James McBride. *Who Speaks for the South?* New York: Funk & Wagnalls, 1964.

Daniell, Jere. *Experiment in Republicanism.* Cambridge, Mass.: Harvard University Press, 1970.

Douglas-Lithgow, R. A. *Dictionary of American-Indian Place and Proper Names.* Salem, Mass.: Salem Press Co., 1909.

Doyle, John A. *The English in America.* London: Longmans, Green, 1883.

Dupuy, R. Ernest, and Dupuy, Trevor N. *The Compact History of the Civil War.* New York: Hawthorn Books, 1968.

———. *The Compact History of the Revolutionary War.* New York: Hawthorn Books, 1968.

———. *Military Heritage of America.* New York: McGraw-Hill, 1956.

Eaton, Clement. *The Growth of Southern Civilization: 1790–1860.* New York: Harper & Row, 1961.

Ernst, Joseph Albert. *Money and Politics in America, 1755–1775.* Chapel Hill, N.C.: University of North Carolina Press, 1973.

Fant, Mabel, and Fant, John C. *History of Mississippi.* Jackson, Miss.: Mississippi Publishing Co., 1928.

Federal Writers' Project, Works Progress Administration. *Alabama.* New York: Richard R. Smith, 1941.

———*Arkansas.* New York: Hastings House, 1941.

———*Florida.* New York: Oxford University Press, 1939.

———*Georgia.* Athens, Ga.: University of Georgia Press, 1940.

———*Kentucky.* New York: Hastings House, 1939.

———*Louisiana.* New York: Hastings House, 1941.

———*Maryland.* New York: Oxford University Press, 1940.

———*Mississippi.* New York: Viking Press, 1938.

———*Missouri.* New York: Duell, Sloan and Pearce, 1941.

———*North Carolina.* Chapel Hill, N.C.: University of North Carolina Press, 1939.

———*South Carolina.* New York: Oxford University Press, 1941.

———*Tennessee.* New York: Viking Press, 1939.

———*Texas.* New York: Hastings House, 1940.

———*Virginia.* New York: Oxford University Press, 1940.

———*Virginia.* New York: Oxford University Press, 1941.

Fisher, Sydney G. *Story of the American Revolution.* Philadelphia: Lippincott, 1908.

Fiske, John. *Old Virginia and Her Neighbors.* Boston: Houghton Mifflin, 1900.

Force, Peter, ed. *American Archives,* Fourth Series, 6 vols. Washington, D.C.: Clarke & Force, 1837–1846.

Fuller, J. F. C. *Decisive Battles of the USA.* New York: Beechurst, 1953.

Gildersleeve, Basil L. *The Creed of the Old South.* Baltimore: Johns Hopkins Press, 1915.

Gipson, Lawrence H. *The British Empire Before the American Revolution,* 15 vols. Caldwell, Idaho: Caxton; New York: Alfred A. Knopf, 1936–1970.

Greene, Francis Vinton. *The Revolutionary War and the Military Policy of the United States.* New York: Charles Scribner's Sons, 1911.

Hamilton, Virginia Van der Veer. *Alabama, A History.* New York: W. W. Norton, 1977.

Hanson, Raus McDill. *Virginia Place Names.* Verona, Va.: McClure Printing Company, 1969.

Hollis, Christopher. *The American Heresy.* New York: Minton, Balch & Company, 1930.

Jabavu, Noni. *Drawn in Color: African Contrasts.* New York: St. Martin's Press, 1960.

Jennings, Francis. *The Invasion of America: Indians, Colonialism, and the Cant of Conquest.*

Chapel Hill, N.C.: University of North Carolina Press, 1975.

Jones, Lewis P. *South Carolina: A Synoptic History for Laymen.* Columbia, S.C.: University of South Carolina Press, 1971.

La Motte, Louise C. *Colored Light.* Richmond, Va.: Presbyterian Committee of Publication, 1937.

Labaree, Leonard W. *Royal Government in America.* New Haven: Yale University Press, 1930.

LaFarge, Oliver. *Pictorial History of the American Indian.* New York: Crown Publishers, 1956.

Lane, Mills, ed. *War is Hell.* Savannah: Beehive Press, 1974.

Liddell, Viola Goode. *With a Southern Accent.* Norman, Okla.: University of Oklahoma Press, 1948.

Lovejoy, David S. *The Glorious Revolution in America.* New York: Harper & Row, 1972.

Maier, Pauline. *From Resistance to Revolution.* New York: Alfred A. Knopf, 1972.

Main, Jackson Turner. *The Social Structure of Revolutionary America.* Princeton, N.J.: Princeton University Press, 1965.

Malone, Henry. *Cherokees of the Old South.* Athens, Ga.: University of Georgia Press, 1956.

Martin, Harold. *Georgia, A History.* New York: W. W. Norton, 1977.

McGill, Ralph. *The South and the Southerner.* Boston: Little, Brown & Company, 1963.

McKinley, Albert E. *The Suffrage Franchise in the Thirteen English Colonies in America.* Philadelphia: University of Pennsylvania, 1905.

Miller, Perry. *Errands into the Wilderness.* Cambridge, Mass.: Harvard University Press, 1956.

Miller, Perry, and Johnson, Thomas H. *The Puritans.* New York: American Book Company, 1938.

Mitchell, Broadus. *The Rise of the Cotton Mills in the South.* Baltimore: Johns Hopkins Press, 1921.

Moore, Albert B. *History of Alabama and her People.* New York: American Historical Society, 1927.

Moore, Frank. *Diary of the American Revolution,* 2 vols. New York: Charles Scribner's Sons, 1860.

Morgan, Edmund S., and Morgan, Helen M. *The Stamp Act Crisis: Prologue to Revolution.* Chapel Hill, N.C.: University of North Carolina Press, 1953.

Morison, Samuel Eliot, Commager, Henry Steele, and Leuchtenburg, William E. *A Concise History of the American Republic.* New York: Oxford University Press, 1977.

Moultie, William. *Memoirs of the American Revolution,* 2 vols. New York: Longworth, 1802.

Nickerson, Hoffman. *The Turning Point of the Revolution.* Boston: Houghton Mifflin Company, 1928.

North, Douglas C. *Growth and Welfare in the American Past.* Englewood Cliffs, N.J.: Prentice-Hall, 1966.

Odum, Howard. *The Way of the South.* New York: Macmillan Company, 1947.

Olmsted, Frederick Law. *The Cotton Kingdom.* Indianapolis: Bobbs-Merrill, 1971.

Osterweis, Rollin G. *Romanticism and Nationalism in the Old South.* New Haven: Yale University Press, 1949.

Paullin, Charles O. *The Navy of the American Revolution.* Cleveland: Burroughs, 1908.

Peckham, Howard H. *The Colonial Wars, 1689–1762.* Chicago: University of Chicago Press, 1964.

Phelan, James. *History of Tennessee: the Making of a State.* Boston: Houghton Mifflin, 1888.

Phillips, U. B. *Life and Labor in the Old South.* Boston: Little, Brown & Company, 1929.

Ramsay, David. *History of South Carolina from the First Settlement in 1670 to the Year 1808.* Newberry, S.C.: W. J. Duffie, 1858.

Randall, James G., and Donald, David. *Civil War and Reconstruction,* 2nd ed. Boston: Heath, 1961.

Reese, Trevor, ed. *The Clamorous Malcontents.* Savannah: Beehive Press, 1973.

Robertson, Ben. *Red Hills and Cotton.* New York: Alfred A. Knopf, 1942.

Roland, Charles P. *The Improbable Era, the South Since World War II.* Lexington, Ky.: University of Kentucky Press, 1975.

Roller, David C., and Twyman, Robert W. *The Encyclopedia of Southern History.* Baton Rouge, La.: Louisiana State University Press, 1979.

Rudin, Louis B., and Jacobs, Robert D. *Southern Renascence.* Baltimore: Johns Hopkins Press, 1953.

Sewell, Richard H. *John P. Hale and the Politics of Abolition.* Cambridge, Mass.: Harvard University Press, 1971.

Shepard, James F., and Walton, Gary M. *Shipping, Maritime Trade, and the Economic Development of Colonial North America.* Cambridge, Mass.: Cambridge University Press, 1972.

Silverman, Kenneth. *A Cultural History of the American Revolution.* New York: Thomas Y. Crowell Co., 1976.

Simkins, Francis B., and Roland, Charles P. *A History of the South*. New York: Alfred A. Knopf, 1972.

Sirmans, M. Eugene. *Colonial South Carolina: A Political History, 1663–1763*. Chapel Hill, N.C.: University of North Carolina Press, 1966.

Smelser, Marshall. *American History at a Glance*. New York: Barnes & Noble, 1961.

Smith, Abbot. *Colonists in Bondage: White Servitude and Convict Labor in America, 1607–1776*. Chapel Hill, N.C.: University of North Carolina Press, 1947.

Smith, Henry Nash. *Virgin Land: The American West as Symbol and Myth*. New York: Vintage Books, 1956.

Tate, Allen, ed. *A Southern Vanguard*. New York: Prentice-Hall, 1947.

Taylor, Rosser H. *Ante-Bellum South Carolina: A Social and Cultural History*. Chapel Hill, N.C.: University of North Carolina Press, 1942.

Taylor, William R. *Cavalier and Yankee: The Old South and American National Character*. New York: George Braziller, 1961.

Tebbel, John, and Jennison, Keith. *The American Indian Wars*. New York: Bonanza Books, 1960.

Thomas, David Y., ed. *Arkansas and Its People*. New York: American Historical Society, 1930.

Tindall, George B. *South Carolina Negroes, 1877–1900*. Columbia, S.C.: University of South Carolina Press, 1952.

Violette, Eugene. *A History of Missouri*. New York: Heath, 1918.

Walker, Williston. *The Creeds and Platforms of Congregationalism*. 1893. Reprint. Boston: Pilgrim Press, 1960.

Wallace, David Duncan. *History of South Carolina*, 4 vols. New York: American Historical Society, 1934.

Ward, Christopher. *The War of the Revolution*, 2 vols. New York: Macmillan, 1952.

Watters, Pat. *The South and the Nation*. New York: Pantheon Books, 1969.

Weber, Max. *The Protestant Ethic and the Spirit of Capitalism*. New York: Charles Scribner's Sons, 1958.

Wertenbaker, Thomas J. *The Old South*. New York: Charles Scribner's Sons, 1942.

Wiley, Bell Irvin. *The Life of Johnny Reb: The Common Soldier of the Confederacy*. New York: Bobbs-Merrill, 1934.

————. *The Plain People of the Confederacy*. Baton Rouge, La.: Louisiana State University Press, 1943.

————. *The Road to Appomattox*. Memphis: Memphis State College Press, 1956.

Williams, T. Harry. *Romance and Realism in Southern Politics*. Athens, Ga.: University of Georgia, 1961.

Woodward, C. Vann. *Origins of the New South, 1877–1913*. Baton Rouge, La.: Louisiana State University Press, 1954.

Wright, Louis B. *Barefoot in Arcadia: Memories of a More Innocent Era*. Columbia, S.C.: University of South Carolina Press, 1974.

————. *South Carolina, A Bicentennial History*. New York: W. W. Norton, 1976.

A

Aaron, Henry Louis (Hank), 1
Aberdeen Proving Grounds (Md.), 1
Abilene (Kan.), 79
Abilene (Tex.), 1
Abilene Christian University (Tex.), 1
Abolition movement, 1-2, 40, 44, 55-56, 77, 81,
86, 91, 96, 157 *See Also;* Harper's Ferry;
Underground railroad
— explained, 1-2
— Grimke, Angelina and Sarah, 174-175
— Kentucky, 218
— leaders, 101, 119, 134, 174-175, 424, 438
— newspapers, 300
— Tennessee, 296
Absalom, Absalom! (Faulkner), 133
Acadians, 2, 103, 197, 228, 242, 243
Acolapissa Indians, 2
Act of Tolerance (1649), 31
Actors and actresses, *See Also;* Theaters and
playwrights
— Bankhead, Tallulah, 33
— Booth, Edwin, 49
— Booth, John Wilkes, 49
— Boyd, Belle, 50
— Menken, Adah I., 268-269
— Robins, Elizabeth, 352
— Sothern, Edward H., 379
Acuera Idians, 2
Acuff, Roy, 101
Adai Indians, 2, 62
Adair, James, 2-3
Adair, John, 3, 167
Adams, Charles Francis, 152
Adams, John, 86, 112, 205, 256, 327
Adams, John Quincy, 63, 102, 201, 288, 341
Adler, Cyrus, 3
Adventure (ship), 332
Adventure parks, 59-60, 315
Adventures of Huckleberry Finn, The
(Clemens), 88
Adventures of Tom Sawyer, The (Clemens), 88
Age-Herald (Ala. newspaper), 301
Agnes Scott College (Ga.), 27, 115
Agnew, Spiro Theodore, 3
Agramonte, Aristides, 232
Agricultural and Technical College (N.C.),
172-173
Agricultural Wheel Party, 3

Agriculture and agriculturists, *See Also;* crop
names
— Alabama, 3, 6, 7, 8
— Carver, George Washington, 68
— economists, 130
— equipment, 9
— experts, 11, 356
— Farmers Alliance, 132
— Florida, 143
— Georgia, 164
— Kentucky, 218
— North Carolina, 330
— Ruffin, Edmund, 356
— South Carolina, 11, 92, 383
— Texas, 12
Ahsley River, 9, 25, 97
Aiken (S.C.), 3
Aiken, Conrad, 3
Aiken State Park, (S.C.), 3
Ais Indians, 3
Akokisa Indians, *See;* Atakapa Indians
— cities, 7-8,
— Civil War, 7, 289
— colleges and universities, 8, 27-28, 43-44,
138
— names 13-14, 41, 43, 115, 116, 119, 191,
196, 286-287, 289, 325, 334, 335
Alabama
— agriculture, 8
— arts and culture, 43
— boundaries, 4-6
— cities, 7-8, 13-14, 41, 43, 115, 116, 119,
191, 196, 286-287, 289, 325, 334, 335
— civil rights, 7, 43, 289
— coal, 89
— Confederacy, 94, 95
— cotton, 100, 128
— description, 5
— economy, 8
— exploration, 6-7
— fish and fishing, 136
— history, 6, 7
— industrialization, 6, 7-8, 43
— lumber, 249
— military posts, 14
— politics and government, 33, 44, 86, 87,
137, 171, 185, 188, 193, 238
— population, 6-8
— Reconstruction, 7
— secession, 7
— settlements, 7
— slavery, 44

H

K

L

M

O

Oak, Grove, Battle of, *See;* Seven Days' Battle
Oakleigh (Ala. mansion), 286
Oak Ridge (Tenn.), 226, 312
Obed River, 312
Obey River, 109, 312
Obion River, 312
Observer (N.C. newspaper), 301
Ocala (Fla.), 312-313
Occaneechi Indians, 30, 313
Oceanography, 264
Ochlockonee River, 313
Ochlokonee River, 14, 292
Ocmulgee National Monument (Ga.), 162
Ocmulgee River, 11, 313
Oconastro (Indian Chief), 148
Oconee River, 11, 313
O'Connor, Flannery, 313
O'Daniel, Wilbert Lee ("Pappy"), 313
Odessa (Tex.), 313
Odum, Howard W., 313
Oglethorpe College (Ga.), 27
Oglethorpe, James, 7, 28, 139, 163, 313-314
Oglethorpe, Mount (Ga.), 314
O'Hara, Scarlett (fictional character), *See;*
  Scarlett O'Hara
O'Henry (William Sydney Porter), 314
Ohio, 135
Ohio Company, 166, 215, 263
Ohio River, 47, 76, 248, 314
Oil, *See;* Petroleum
OKeechobee, Lake, 39, 64, 129, 130, 224, 309,
  314
Okefenokee Swamp (Fla.), 139, 162, 314
Okinawa Campaign, 57
Oklahoma, 75, 80, 93, 98, 102
Oklawaha River, 314, 315
Okmulgee Indians, 314
Old Biloxi (La.), 41
Oliver, Joe "King", 24, 118
Olivier, Joseph ("King"), 205
Ol' Man Adam an His Chillun (Bradford), 51
Olmstead, Frederick Law, 25
Omaha Tribe, The (Fletcher), 138
Oostanaula River, 63, 97, 128, 314-315
Orange Lake (Fla.), 315
Ordeal by Slander (Lattimore), 231
Ord, Edward O., 315
Order of the American Knights, 224

Oregon Inlet (N.C.), 315
Oregon Trail, 53
Original Journals of The Lewis and Clark
  Expedition, 1804-1806, 85
Origins of the World War, The (Fay), 134
Orlando (Fla.), 315
Ormond Beach (Fla.), 315
Ornithology, 35
Orr, James L., 315
Ortiz, Juan, 287
Osage Indians, 18, 80, 281, 285
Osage River, 31, 206, 238, 290, 317
Osceola (Indian chief), 142, 315-316, 369
Osochi Indians, 316
Oswald, Lee Harvey, 316
Oto Indians, 316
Otter, Peaks of, (Va.), 316
Ouachita, Lake (Ark.), 316
Ouachita Mountains, 316
Ouachita River, 316
Outer Banks (N.C.), 316
Outlaws, 180, 203, 462
Overton, John, 316
Owensboro (Ky.), 316
Owens, James C. ("Jessie"), 316
Oxbow Lakes (La.), 316
Oxford (Miss.), 133
Oysters, 317
Ozark Mountains, 317
Ozark Plateau, 18, 23, 50, 281
Ozarks, College of the, 317
Ozarks, Lake of the, 315, 317

P

Paca, William, 318
Padre Island (Tex.), 318
Paducah (Ky.), 318
Paduke (Indian chief), 318
Page, John, 318-319
Page, Thomas N., 319
Page, Walter Hines, 68, 319
Paige, Leroy ("Satchel"), 319
Paine College (Ga.), 28
Paine, Thomas, 96
Painters, *See;* Artists
Pakenham, Edward, 299
Palm Beach (Fla.), 144, 319
Palmer, A. Mitchell, 191

Q

T

X

Y

Z